CRITICAL COMPANION TO

Arthur Miller

A Literary Reference to His Life and Work

SUSAN C. W. ABBOTSON

Facts On File

An imprint of Infobase Publishing

Critical Companion to Arthur Miller

Copyright © 2007 by Susan Abbotson

Facts On File, Inc.
An imprint of Infobase Publishing
132 West 31st Street
New York NY 10001

ISBN-10: 0-8160-6194-7
ISBN-13: 978-0-8160-6194-5

Library of Congress Cataloging-in-Publication Data

Abbotson, Susan C. W., 1961–
Critical companion to Arthur Miller: a literary reference to his life and work /
Susan Abbotson.
p. cm.
Includes bibliographical references and index.
ISBN 0-8160-6194-7 (alk. paper)
1. Miller, Arthur, 1915–2005—Criticism and interpretation. 2. Miller, Arthur,
1915–2005—Handbooks, manuals, etc. I. Title.
PS3525.I5156Z5114 2006
812′.52—dc22   2006022902

Facts On File books are available at special discounts when purchased in bulk quantities for businesses, associations, institutions, or sales promotions. Please call our Special Sales Department in New York at (212) 967-8800 or (800) 322-8755.

You can find Facts On File on the World Wide Web at http://www.factsonfile.com

Text design adapted by James Scotto-Lavino
Cover design by Cathy Rincon/Joo Young An

Printed in the United States of America

VB Hermitage 10 9 8 7 6 5 4 3 2 1

This book is printed on acid-free paper.

CONTENTS

Acknowledgments   vii

Introduction   ix

Part I: Biography   1

Part II: Works A–Z   23

Part III: Related People, Places, and Topics   355

Part IV: Appendices   481

    Selected Primary Bibliography of Arthur Miller's Works   483
    Interviews with Arthur Miller   486
    Bibliography of Secondary Sources   488
    Arthur Miller Chronology   490

Index   501

ACKNOWLEDGMENTS

This encyclopedic volume on Miller has been an endeavor of love and discovery. It has long taxed the patience of my husband and my beautiful children, who have nonetheless supported me throughout, and a huge thanks must go to them—Dave, Rachel, Harry, and Brenda. I promise to leave my computer alone . . . at least for the summer. The pioneering work of such vigorous Miller scholars as Christopher Bigsby, Steven Centola, Stefani Koorey, and Brenda Murphy has been invaluable, and without it this volume could not have been completed. I am indebted to their prior studies, insights, and research, and I am proud to know all four. The research of George Crandell and Albert Wertheim has also greatly helped to provide details for some of Miller's lesser-known work. I must also include thanks to my friends Joseph Kane and Steve Marino for their assistance on a number of points and their great commitment to advancing the work of Arthur Miller.

INTRODUCTION

Arthur Miller, despite the stature of Eugene O'Neill and Tennessee Williams, is quite possibly the most important American dramatist to date. Since his death, there have been several new books that try to assess his legacy and to offer critical and personal responses to the man and his work. All indicate the tremendous importance of his contribution to U.S., if not world, literature. His career spanned almost 70 years, during which time he not only gave us two of the world's best-known and most-performed dramas, *Death of a Salesman* and *The Crucible*, but also dozens more plays, fictional pieces, and essays. In many ways Miller has come to define U.S. drama, and all who came after him are measured against his high standard. Given the large number of students and teachers at schools and colleges around the globe who study the work of this master dramatist, this volume has been written as a much-needed reference guide to Miller's life and works for both classroom and individual use.

Critical Companion to Arthur Miller has been designed to provide a reliable, up-to-date, encyclopedic source of information on Miller for high-school- and college-level students and for teachers, libraries, and the general public. A central concern has been to make this an accessible, readable, and dependable source of information on Miller's life, career, and writing. The book covers his entire canon, including plays, screenplays, fiction, short stories, and poetry, as well as a number of the important essays and critical pieces. There are also detailed entries on literary, theatrical, and personal

figures who are related to Miller's life and career, key terms and topics connected to his work, and various theatrical companies and places with which he has been associated. Entries are cross-referenced and are easy to access.

The book begins with a lengthy biographical essay covering Miller's life and career from birth to death. Part II of the book contains entries on all of Miller's dramatic and fictional works, as well as on key essays and longer pieces of nonfiction. For each work, there is an explanation of its origins as well as a plot synopsis and a commentary discussing key critical points. For the plays, additional sections discuss first performance, initial reviews, relevant scholarship, and movie and television adaptations, and a Further Reading section gives a bibliography of important critical works. For the fiction and nonfiction entries, additional sections discuss the work's initial reception, as well as relevant scholarship and Further Reading where appropriate. For both plays and fiction, characters in the work are discussed in subentries to the larger entry on the work.

Part III of the book contains entries on people, topics, terms, theater companies, and more, all of them important to understanding Miller's life and work. Part IV contains appendices, including a bibliography of works by Miller, a list of useful interviews with Miller, an up-to-date bibliography of the most useful secondary sources, mainly book-length, and a detailed chronology of key events in Miller's life.

To indicate a cross-reference, any name or term that appears as an entry in Part III is printed on first appearance in SMALL CAPITAL LETTERS, for example, LEE J. COBB.

Many past volumes on Miller have fallen out of date, having been compiled prior to his tremendous output in his final two decades, or they are less complete, tending to concentrate overwhelmingly on *Death of a Salesman* and *The Crucible* to the exclusion of his other work. This volume devotes plenty of space to these often-taught plays but also provides a good deal of information on Miller's other notable works, covering his entire oeuvre, and offers a full picture of this seminal U.S. writer. Miller's essays can be said to represent some of the most important statements of theatrical principles since George Bernard Shaw. They rarely have been considered outside of this volume but are here outlined to help inspire many rewarding teaching and learning opportunities to complement readings of Miller's other writing.

PART I

Biography

Arthur Miller

(1915–2005)

Arthur Asher Miller was born October 17, 1915, in New York City, the second child of AUGUSTA MILLER and ISIDORE MILLER. Augusta was a first-generation American whose father had emigrated from Poland, and Isidore himself had emigrated from Poland at the age of six. His mother was age 22 and his father age 30 at the time of Miller's birth. A brother, KERMIT MILLER, three years the elder, and a younger sister, JOAN COPELAND who was born in 1922, made up the Miller family. Arthur Miller developed many of his characters from his extended family of aunts, uncles, and cousins when he became a playwright.

In his 1987 autobiography, *Timebends: A Life*, Miller describes the feeling he had while growing up that he was the opposite of his brother. Kermit was a well-behaved, good boy who took after their father, and Miller saw himself, with his ambitions and darker side, as being more like their mother. Miller always felt love and respect for his elder brother, but he viewed himself and his brother as being in competition well into adulthood. It is unsurprising that two brothers at odds became frequently occurring characters in many of his plays, from *No Villain* to *The Price*.

Despite internal family differences, Miller's social background gave him a secure sense of self. He grew up within a circle of classmates, neighbors, and friends who were predominantly Jewish. His parents may not have regularly attended services, but Miller recalls going with his family to the 114th Street synagogue as a child, and the family home was dominated by Jewish style, taste, humor, and values. JUDAISM and its beliefs heavily influenced Miller's upbringing and provided him with a strong moral and ethical center that was evident in his works and life, even while he saw himself as an atheist. His mother's father, LOUIS BARNETT, always wore a yarmulke and spoke mostly Yiddish; his great-grandfather was an observant Jew with a long beard. Miller attended Hebrew school after his regular school to learn the prayers and readings that were expected of him at his bar mitzvah, which took place when he was 13, shortly before the family moved to BROOKLYN.

From an early age, Miller admired his mother's artistry and the inquiring mind that had filled their house with books and music. It was the music that he liked best, taking piano lessons and developing a taste for classical works. He felt close to his mother and saw her as having had a great influence on the way that he viewed life. The portrait of Rose Baum in *The American Clock* is based on Augusta Miller, just as Moe Baum is ostensibly his father, and Lee Baum is young Miller himself. Less-flattering versions of Miller's parents appeared in the earlier play *After the Fall*, and aspects of his father certainly inform the father figures in *The Man Who Had All the Luck* and *The Price;* men who clearly privilege one son over the other—Willy Loman also does this, but Miller insisted that his father was nothing like his famous salesman. Miller viewed himself as the less-favored but the more-successful brother of the two.

Though unschooled, having been forced to leave school at an early age to go to work, Isidore Miller had an innate authority and a strong sense of what he felt was right or wrong. He was also a quiet man who loved and depended on his wife. Before being financially ruined by the GREAT DEPRESSION, he owned and ran a successful clothing business; the MILTEX COAT AND SUIT COMPANY. It boasted a factory, a showroom, and a front office and employed more than 800 people. Miller simultaneously hated and admired his father; he was annoyed at his father's incapacity to recuperate fully, both economically and emotionally, from the Depression, yet he was able to recognize the man's inner goodness. In hindsight, Miller realized that it was the system that failed rather than his father, but at the time, it was difficult to lay the blame elsewhere as he watched his father become increasingly useless as a provider.

At the age of eight, Miller recalled, he attended his first play with his mother at the Shubert Theater in New York City—a melodrama in which a stereotyped cannibal tried to blow up a passenger ship—and he felt impressed by the "realness" of the experience, as opposed to the few films he had seen. But he did not consider writing his own plays at this time, being far more interested in sports. Miller attended the same school to which his mother had gone, P.S. 24, on West 111th Street, only one block away from home. One of Miller's favorite pastimes was to go out alone on his bicycle, exploring. Other than that, he played the usual stickball and punchball in the streets of Manhattan, was not much on reading, and was best friends with SIDNEY FRANKS, the son of a banker who lived in the same building.

The Millers were a very contented family in the 1920s, wealthy enough to have their own chauffeur and an attractive apartment in Manhattan on the top floor of a six-story building at 45 West 110th Street, overlooking Central Park, just off 5th Avenue. Each summer, they would rent a place at Rockaway Beach to escape the heat of the city. But even before the WALL STREET CRASH, business had begun to slow, not helped by the numbers of relatives whom Isidore felt duty bound to employ, including Miller's uncles MANNY NEWMAN and Lee Balsam. In 1928, the family relocated, first to one-half of a roomy Brooklyn duplex, then to a small six-room house, where Miller unhappily shared a bedroom with his dour Grandfather Barnett, at 1350 East 3rd Street in the Midwood section of Brooklyn. With the crash, finances tightened even further, for his father had invested heavily in stocks, as had most other businessmen of that era.

The family's formerly idyllic life turned sour, and such change was depicted in detail with the Baum family in *The American Clock*. Miller, like Lee Baum, drew his savings from the bank to buy a bicycle just before a run on the banks in 1933, but as he celebrated his good fortune, the bicycle was stolen from outside the house. As the Depression deepened and business dropped, the Millers were forced to give up more of their former comforts. Just like Rose Baum, Augusta Miller had to sell or pawn all of her jewelry, lose her piano, and begin to resent her husband's incapacity to win out over the general collapse of the country. Still, they did their best to create a comfortable home and to survive.

At their new Brooklyn house, Miller planted a pear tree in the backyard that still exists today. In 1931, he used money saved from his preschool bread-delivery rounds to buy lumber to build a back stoop on the house; these were early signs of Mill-

er's lifelong interest in trees and carpentry. Both of these activities are echoed in *All My Sons* and *Death of a Salesman*, albeit with different impact, offering early examples of how Miller would use his private experience to facilitate his writing but also illustrating how such incidents would be artistically adapted; the Keller tree is used as a symbol for the missing son, and the Loman boys steal the lumber for the stoop that their father builds.

The Miller's Brooklyn home was on a dead-end street that led to a baseball field and a cemetery beyond and was close to the elevated train tracks that ran between Manhattan and Coney Island. Instead of punchball and stickball, the youths now had room for football and baseball; Miller took second base while Kermit pitched. The neighborhood still evokes the setting of the Loman house in *Death of a Salesman*, with close-set homes and nearby apartments that overshadow the area. But the Millers were not isolated here, for across the street were the homes of their relatives, the Newmans and the Balsams, who had moved to Brooklyn after World War I almost 10 years earlier. Miller would grow up close to his Uncle Manny, whose whole family would later provide models for the Lomans. He would go on fishing trips with his cousins Abby and Buddy Newman.

On first moving to the area, Miller attended James Madison High School, which was a lengthy walk from the house. It was from there that his brother graduated before heading to New York University, but in 1930, the city built Abraham Lincoln High, which was closer to home, and Miller was reassigned there.

At Abraham Lincoln, Miller had a better reputation for sports than for academics, doing poorly in his classes, especially math, just like Biff Loman from *Death of a Salesman*. He had passed six feet tall even before turning 16 and played both basketball and football. It was while playing football for the school team that Miller ripped the ligament that would later prevent him from being called up in World War II.

During their summer vacations, Miller and his brother helped out at their father's business as the family tried to keep it afloat. In 1932, Kermit quit university to work in the business full time. With his junior driver's license, Miller gave up his bakery job to drive a delivery truck for a school friend's father, Sam Shapse, an auto-parts retailer in Long Island City. However, this business went under in 1932. He graduated from high school that following summer, although he had failed algebra several times, with an ambition to pursue a college degree, despite what had happened to his brother. His grades were unremarkable and the more prestigious colleges were clearly out of grasp both academically and financially, but he spoke to a neighbor who was enrolled at the UNIVERSITY OF MICHIGAN and discovered this university could be within reach. He applied straight away. His grades proved to be too poor, and he was rejected on both this and a follow-up application.

Not wishing to give up his ambitions, Miller enrolled in night school at New York City College, which was free to local students who had no funds, while he helped out at his father's business, which was still limping along. He soon realized that he should either work or attend school full time—trying to do both at the same time was impossible and he withdrew after a few weeks of classes. Despite having been twice rejected, Miller wrote a plaintive letter that finally persuaded the dean at Michigan to allow him to enter on probation, with the understanding that he would first need to show them a bank account that contained $500 to prove that he could cover himself financially. Having quit New York City College, he looked for paid work, even offering his services as a singer on a local radio station to try to save up the money that he would need to attend university as a full-time student.

Shapse put in a good word to get Miller a job clerking at CHADICK–DELAMATER AUTO PARTS WAREHOUSE on 10th Avenue in Manhattan, an area that would later become the site for the Lincoln Center for the Performing Arts and the home of the REPERTORY THEATER OF LINCOLN CENTER. Chadick–Delamater did not usually employ Jews—giving Miller his first real experience of American ANTI-SEMITISM. Earning $15 a week, he began to save for college. It was on the subway to and from this job that he began to read serious literature—most notably, the Russian novelist, FYODOR DOSTOYEVSKY's, *The Brothers Karamazov*—and to realize that writers have the amazing power to affect how people see the world around them. Previous to this he had read little more than popular boys' adventure stories, such as *Tom Swift*. Dabbling with writing, he tried short stories, such as "In Memoriam," based on one of his father's aging salesmen. Miller views the time he spent in the auto-parts warehouse as his "entry into the big world beyond home and school." It was this time of his life that he later recalled in *A Memory of Two Mondays* (1955). By the fall of 1934, he had saved enough to head to Michigan, leaving Kermit behind to look after his parents.

Miller elected to major in journalism and by May had joined the staff of the MICHIGAN DAILY, the college newspaper, as a reporter. He reported on activities taking place both on and off campus, from interviews with on-campus speakers and reports on campus studies to pieces on union activity and Senate bills. He washed dishes at a co-op cafeteria in exchange for free meals and existed on the $15 monthly pay he received for tending the rats at a local genetics laboratory. In his sophomore year, he met his future wife MARY GRACE SLATTERY at a party, and she would become his first non-Jewish girlfriend. Although not members of the Communist Party, Miller and Slattery had strong sympathies with the Communist cause, and they spent much of their time together. Miller joined the peace movement and signed the Oxford Pledge that declared that its signatories would not take part in any future war.

Funds were running low, and his father's business had finally gone under, so there was no chance of any financial support from home. Miller needed to find extra income to stay enrolled. He saw the Avery Hopwood Awards—competitive writing awards administered each year by the university—as his main chance, and these had been another reason why he had chosen Michigan. Miller spent his 1935 spring vacation week writing a play, for that had seemed to him the most tangible of the genres. In 1936, he entered this play for a Hopwood Award and won a prize of $250 for *No Villain*, a drama largely based on his own family, about a coat manufacturer facing a strike and potential bankruptcy and how his two sons react toward their father's dilemma. He spent $22 of his prize money on a 1927 Model T Ford, and feeling confident as a playwright, he switched his major to English and continued writing plays.

The following year, a rewrite of *No Villain,* now titled *They Too Arise,* with far more complex characters and themes, won a $1,250 scholarship award from the THEATRE GUILD's Bureau of New Plays to study playwrighting with KENNETH ROWE, a professor at Michigan. Rowe would have a huge influence on Miller's early development as a dramatist during his remaining two years of college. Miller credits Rowe with teaching him about the dynamics of constructing a play. *They Too Arise* would receive brief productions at both Ann Arbor, by a Jewish student-theater group, and in Detroit through the FEDERAL THEATER PROJECT. Miller, in 1937, won a Hopwood Award in Drama again, this time for *Honors at Dawn,* another play about strikers and two brothers at odds that pointed out corruption in both the industrial and academic worlds.

At the close of the academic year, he returned to New York with fellow student RALPH NEAPHUS, with whom he had washed dishes at the cafeteria. They drove Miller's Ford, and Neaphus shared the gas costs. Neaphus planned to join the Abraham Lincoln Brigade that was heading to Spain to assist communist troops who were fighting the fascists in the Spanish civil war. Although tempted by a sense of adventure and natural sympathy for a socialist cause, Miller decided not to go with him. However, he did write a letter to the president of the United States, Franklin D. Roosevelt, protesting his country's attitude toward the civil war. Returning to Michigan, he met and became friendly with NORMAN ROSTEN who had come to study under Rowe. Rosten had been working with the Federal Theater for the previous year and had won the same Theatre Guild competition as Miller.

Miller's 1938 entry to the Hopwood competition, *The Great Disobedience,* written for one of Rowe's playwrighting classes, was less successful, failing to captivate the judges. They still awarded it second place but found it "muddled" and "turgid." Based on information gathered during visits to Jackson Penitentiary where a college friend, Sid Moscowitz, had been given the job of prison psy-

chiatrist, the play was more an attack on CAPITALISM than a call for prison reform. In this story of industrial and penal corruption, Dr. Victor Matthews is railroaded into a prison sentence and is forced to rely on the conscience of the prison psychiatrist to survive the attentions of a sadistic deputy warden. A development was suggested in Miller's work in that he was beginning to research his topics rather than to write purely from his own experience. Rowe allowed it a laboratory production at the university to help Miller develop a sense of how it could be improved.

Miller was also busy revising *They Too Arise* into *The Grass Still Grows,* which nearly doubled the play's length and turned it into a comedy, for an anticipated New York production that never came to fruition. It was rejected by the Jewish producers on BROADWAY as being "too Jewish."

Graduating from Michigan in 1938, Miller returned to New York and moved in with his parents again. He regularly corresponded with his former professor Kenneth Rowe, using him as a sounding board and a sympathetic ear. Rowe had given him a letter of recommendation to join the Federal Theater Project, a government-run, national agency that had been formed to provide salaries for artists during the lean Depression years. Slattery had dropped out of college to follow him and had taken up residence with a roommate on Pierrepont Street, where Miller could occasionally spend the night (the same street on which he and Slattery would later share an apartment). Rosten encouraged Miller to join him in working for the Federal Theater. In his autobiography, Miller says that he turned down an offer of $250 a week from Twentieth Century-Fox to work as a script writer at this time, taking instead the weekly salary of $22.77 from the Federal Theater, because he felt that films were too controlled and that theater offered him a greater freedom. To obtain the position, he had to pretend that he was not living with relatives, and so his old friend Sid Franks allowed him to put up a cot in the small apartment where he now lived with his father until Miller was approved. Once accepted into the program, Miller was able to rent a studio apartment on East 74th Street. Rosten was also able to set Miller up with his agent, Paul Streger, who worked with Leland Hayward and Company.

For the Federal Theater, Miller worked with Rosten. They collaborated on the short play *Listen My Children,* a comedy with music that satirized committee work. It was never produced. Miller also wrote several short stories, one about a salesman on a train, another about a student hitchhiking home, and another featuring a group of black characters. He sent these off to many of the leading magazines of the period, including *Harpers,* but none of them were accepted. Copies of these early attempts at short fiction can be found in the archives at the HARRY RANSOM RESEARCH CENTER in Texas. The first radio piece Miller managed to sell, for the sum of $100, was *Joe, the Motorman,* which was performed on the *Rudy Vallee Variety Show* with Everett Horton playing Joe; in Miller's own opinion, it was "junk." In 1939, *Columbia Workshop* (CBS) broadcast *William Ireland's Confession,* a short drama about a forgery case in Ireland that involved Shakespearean papers; it was based on a true story. In June 1939, the Federal Theater was shut down on the suspicion that communists had infiltrated it. Miller was forced to go back on relief and to return to his parents' house.

Miller continued work on a solo piece, a historical verse drama for the radio that depicted the ravaging of Mexico during its conquest by Cortés. Having begun life as *The Children of the Sun,* this slowly evolved into *The Golden Years.* However, it would be 47 years before it would be aired, and then it would only be so in Britain. In 1940, he took a paid job to go to North Carolina to collect dialect speech for the folk division of the Library of Congress. Here, he gained a new appreciation of the black experience in the South. Interviewing black women strikers in a local bar in Wilmington, he learned about their difficulties with the unions and developed an interest in their struggles with racism. He also faced racism in a personal sense, one man threatening him with a shotgun and shouting, "Get out, you Jew!"

Returning to New York he decided, despite the uncertainty of his future career and the fact that she was a Catholic, to marry his college sweetheart, Mary Slattery. They went to Slattery's family in Lakewood, Ohio, to marry. Her relatives had initial suspicions of this Jew marrying into their family, but Miller won their respect by his forcefulness in clearing up a problem that they faced with the dispensation that they needed from the Catholic Church to carry out the ceremony on which they had planned. Miller and his new wife moved into an apartment in Brooklyn Heights at 62 Montague Street. Hardly more than a week later, he went off alone, being only able to afford a single ticket, on the merchant freighter SS *Copa Copa* to South America to research a play on which he was working, *The Half-Bridge.* This was indicative of how his youthful marriage would proceed, with Slattery (and later their children) often being left behind as Miller put his work first; it would place an inevitable strain on their marriage.

During the next few years, Slattery worked as a waitress and then as an editor for Harper and Brothers to help support them; Miller tried to earn his share by writing scripts and radio plays, mostly for the popular radio shows *Columbia Workshop* (CBS) and the *Cavalcade of America* (NBC). Miller recalls introducing himself to one of his heroes, playwright CLIFFORD ODETS, in a local store in 1940 but making a poor impression. Miller began a novel attacking U.S. racism, partly inspired by the recently published *Native Son* by Richard Wright; set on a freighter that was manned by a deeply racist crew, the novel featured two black characters trying to survive, but the book was never completed. In 1941, he applied for a Rockefeller Fellowship and was turned down. He also worked as a shipfitter's helper on the night shift at the BROOKLYN NAVY YARD; this was his his contribution to the war effort. Remaining politically involved, Miller showed his social conscience in 1941 by writing an article, "Hitler's Quarry," for the inaugural issue of *Jewish Survey;* centering on the evident persecution of Jews around the world, the article included a stern condemnation of the U.S. State Department for its failure to assist Jews in Europe who were trying to escape the Nazi threat.

Although not every radio play from this period on which he worked was produced, such as *The Four Freedoms,* Miller used this opportunity to develop and refine his radio-writing skills, trying to keep the script down to the usually required 30 minutes. It also helped him to stay in contact with an artistic community. One play, *Thunder from the Hills,* about Benito Juárez's fight for liberty, was recorded for *Cavalcade of America* in 1942 and gave him the opportunity to work with Orson Welles. Probably the most striking among these radio plays was his 1940 political satire for *Columbia Workshop, The Pussycat and the Expert Plumber Who Was a Man,* subtitled, "A Fantasy," in which a talking cat is elected mayor. The biographical *Joel Chandler Harris* and *Captain Paul,* the latter about John Paul Jones to help celebrate Navy Day, were produced in 1941. The following year, *Toward a Farther Star* about Amelia Earhart was aired, as were several other pieces with patriotic themes, including, *Battle of the Ovens* about Revolutionary War bakers, *I Was Married in Bataan* about the trials of army nurses, and *The Eagle's Nest* that related Giuseppe Garibaldi's fight for a unified Italy to the contemporary conflict against fascism. In 1943, radio listeners heard *Listen for the Sound of Wings,* about the trials and resistance of the anti-Nazi German Pastor Martin Niemoeller; in 1944, *The Story of Canine Joe,* about the role that dogs played in helping to win the war, was broadcast.

However, Miller was not content with writing for the commercial radio, feeling restricted and confined by the demands of the networks and their advertisers. He had worked on a novel version of *The Man Who Had All the Luck* for which he had been given a small advance. However, on reading an early draft, the publisher decided to reject it. Miller also continued to write stage plays and search for a producer. *Boro Hall Nocturne* was completed in about 1942. A wartime piece about Nazi saboteurs and those willing to aid them, the play was notable mainly for Miller's obvious turnaround from his earlier pacifism. Never produced, it soon lay forgotten. By 1943, he had completed *The Half-Bridge,* a tale of a merchant marine whom a Nazi agent unsuccessfully tries to seduce into using his ship for piracy and insurance fraud. He could not find a producer for this play either on stage or in radio; however, a shorter piece of his, *That They May Win,* was produced by the Stage for Action theater group in New York, and it became one of their most popular plays. Essentially propaganda, it urged women to inform on profiteers and to show their men who were fighting abroad that they were fighting on the home front to keep prices under control to support the families of these armed-services members.

Toward the end of 1943, on the basis of his growing reputation as a radio dramatist, Miller was given the lucrative opportunity to work on the screenplay *The Story of G.I. Joe* for $750 a week. It was to be based on the wartime correspondence of Ernie Pyle. Miller toured several army camps to collect background information, but the studio disliked what he produced, finding that it painted too harsh a picture for Hollywood, and he was dropped from the project. Through her publishing connections, Slattery was able to help him publish a book in 1944 based on his experiences in the camps, *Situation Normal. . . .* An account of army life in diary form, it notes both the racism and the surprising lack of idealism that he discovered among the troops whom he interviewed. He dedicated it to his brother Kermit, who was serving abroad. Miller and Slattery had moved into a duplex at 102 Pierrepont Street to gain a little more space. Novelist Norman Mailer lived upstairs when he was not away for the war. It was here that Mailer wrote *The Naked and the Dead* while Miller worked below. On September 7, 1944, the Millers had a daughter, JANE MILLER; in October, his first short story, "Ditchy," was published in *Mayfair Magazine,* and in November, Miller had his first Broadway play produced.

In his search for a producer, Miller attracted the attention of Joseph Fields, a writer of musical comedies, who wanted to be involved with something more serious. Fields had read Miller's latest play, *The Man Who Had All the Luck,* which Miller had adapted from his novel that had been rejected. Liking the play immensely, Fields acquired the backing from Herbert Harris to direct it on Broadway. At this point, Miller's luck ran out; the play closed after only six performances (which included two previews), despite winning the Theatre Guild National Award. The play tracks the rise of prosperous businessman David Beeves, who simply cannot accept his good life and is led to consider suicide (in the novel, he actually committed suicide). The play had been poorly produced and was summarily dismissed by critics. Discouraged by the way *The Man Who Had All the Luck* had been received, Miller considered abandoning playwriting for good although he was continuing to find success as a radio dramatist. Turning back to fiction, he spent six weeks writing *Focus* (1945), a controversial novel that explored issues of U.S. anti-Semitism. It sold more than 900,000 copies in hardback alone and was widely exported and translated. It was the first substantial income that Miller earned from his writing and included money for the film rights, although it was not filmed until 1962. It was also an early example of American literature openly tackling such a topic.

Miller had been writing episodes for the CBS radio series *The Doctor Fights* since June 1944 and would continue to do so for a year. One, starring Robert Montgomery, included a scene in which an American pilot's legs are amputated by a Japanese pilot as he floats down on a parachute. The play's focus is on the plight of the amputee as he later recovers in hospital, and Miller had to argue to keep his bleakly realistic depiction intact. Other radio work included his 1945 adaptation of Jane Austen's *Pride and Prejudice* to fit a one-hour format for *Theatre Guild of the Air*. Miller's version incorporates several jokes and owes more to Miller than to Austen. An adaptation of Ferenc Molnár's *The Guardsman* was also aired, and there were more wartime sagas, including *The Philippines Never Surrendered,* about a brave school superintendent on the island of Mindanao, and *Bernadine, I Love You,* that relates how a lonely soldier is helped by the Red Cross to contact his wife. *Grandpa and the Statue* was broadcast on *Cavalcade of America* and explored the symbolism of the Statue of Liberty, with Charles Laughton playing the grandpa.

In 1946, Miller successfully adapted George Abbott and John C. Holm's *Three Men on a Horse* for radio and published a short story about the impact of battle injuries on war veterans, "The Plaster Masks" in *Encore: A Continuing Anthology.* He further showed his political involvement at about this time with the short agitprop *You're Next* and an article in *New Masses* magazine that debated the significance of the poet EZRA POUND's

Arthur Miller as a young aspiring playwright. *Courtesy Billy Rose Theatre Collection, The New York Public Library for the Performing Arts, Astor, Lenox and Tilden Foundations.*

pro-fascist stance. He also returned to work on a full-length play about success, as well as GUILT AND RESPONSIBILITY, a play that revolved around another controversial issue: war profiteering. It was a topic upon which he had brushed in his radio work, but it would now take center stage.

Miller spent a number of years developing *All My Sons*, honing it to perfection. The story about a father who gets away with selling faulty aircraft parts to the air force but ultimately pays the price as his sons turn against him was presented in a realistic style as a purposeful crowd pleaser. By 1947, it was ready. Miller's agency had been bought out by MCA, and KATHERINE BROWN was assigned to represent Miller; it was a good match, and they worked together for the next 40 years. She offered his new script to several producers, and the Theatre Guild was interested but noncommittal. Attracted by two men who had been the leading lights of the GROUP THEATER and were still gaining in reputation, on Miller's suggestion Brown sent the play to

HAROLD CLURMAN and ELIA KAZAN. They accepted the play immediately, bringing Walter Fried on board to help produce, and it was decided that Kazan would direct. This time, there would be no early closure; indeed, the play ran for 328 performances. Championed by the New York Times theater critic BROOKS ATKINSON, who welcomed such a serious work in a theater that he saw as growing too socially trivial, All My Sons won solid reviews, some major AWARDS, and professional recognition for Miller as a playwright. He was interviewed for the first time for a New York Times article by John K. Hutchens, a sure indication that the public now knew his name.

Shortly after this success, Miller worked for a week at a Queens beer-box factory assembling boxes for minimum wage, as both an act of contrition and to keep in touch with real people. The play had provided Miller with sufficient funds to purchase an old farmhouse in ROXBURY, CONNECTICUT, to use as a vacation home, as well as 31 Grace Court, an elegant terrace in Brooklyn Heights, for the family's main residence. He was even able to afford a maid to help out around the new home. Grace Court was a duplex and came with sitting tenants in the lower section, the Davenports. After a time, Miller tired of being a compulsory landlord, and so he and his family looked for a single-family dwelling. They moved into a picturesque former coach house at 151 Willow Street, where they would live together until Miller left them for MARILYN MONROE.

Still at Grace Court, however, the couple increased their family with ROBERT MILLER, born on May 31, 1947. Although Miller's main focus was on becoming a known playwright, he continued to be politically active and aware during this period, being involved in several antifascist and pro-communist activities. His name appeared in an advertisement in the Daily Worker protesting the treatment of German antifascist refugees, and he auctioned off his manuscript of All My Sons to raise funds for the progressive Citizens of America. He also continued to write other material, including the radio play The Story of Gus for the OWI Domestic Radio Bureau as part of an unproduced series that depicted the lives of merchant marines;

a short story about a couple who have their house burgled, "It Takes a Thief," that was published in Collier's; an article for The New York Times on "Subsidized Theatre;" and a piece for Jewish Life titled "Concerning Jews Who Write."

After All My Sons, Miller felt that the RED HOOK shipping area of Brooklyn might offer him something new on which to write, but trying to gain the confidence of the longshoremen who worked there was next to impossible. Miller became intrigued by the story of Pete Panto, who had tried to lead a rank-and-file revolt against bosses who were possibly Mafia and certainly corrupt. Panto had vanished, was presumed dead, and seemed a heroic figure to Miller—someone who defied evil and was destroyed in the attempt—the very stuff of TRAGEDY. Befriended by a local lawyer, VINCENT LONGHI, Miller gained a knowledgeable guide to the area, and the two traveled to Europe together where Miller could get a better sense of the Italian background from which many of the Red Hook inhabitants came. He would later try to tell Panto's story in The Hook, a film that he never had the chance to make, but his inquiries also gave him the material to create A View from the Bridge in 1955. All My Sons remained in the public eye with a Universal film production, starring Edward G. Robinson and Burt Lancaster released in 1948, but Chester Erskine's screenplay had changed the mood of the play, turning it into a film noir with an upbeat ending in which Kate urges Chris and Ann to live. Miller would often find his plays intrinsically transformed by such adaptations, making it no wonder that he was so wary of Hollywood.

After the success of All My Sons, Miller felt free to create something more adventurous, hopefully, something never before seen on stage. He wanted to do something that would convey to his audience a sense of the simultaneity that he felt existed in people's lives, to give audiences a sense of what went on in a person's head as his life played out around him. Seeing tension as the very stuff of drama, Miller tried to recreate in a play what he saw as the contradictory forces that operate on people—past against present, society against individual, greed against ethics. Though as yet unsure of his topic, he had the idea of a form that would help to convey these contradictions by being "both infinitely compressed and expansive and leisurely, the story itself both strange and homely." Finding himself unable to get the play started in his Brooklyn home, he went to the Connecticut countryside and, on the property he had bought there, built himself a small studio in which to work. He recalls writing the first act in two days and then taking a more leisurely six weeks to complete the play.

KERMIT BLOOMGARDEN was keen to be involved with the new Miller play, and it was agreed to bring him on board to coproduce with Walter Fried; Kazan would again direct, and JO MIELZINER would create the challenging set and lighting design. After a brief, highly successful tryout in Philadelphia, *Death of a Salesman,* a play about the life and death of salesman Willy Loman, premiered on February 10, 1949, at the Morosco Theater in New York. It starred LEE J. COBB and MILDRED DUNNOCK, and the enthusiastic reviews by such eminent critics as the *New York Times's* Brooks Atkinson swiftly made *Death of a Salesman* the "must-see" play of the season. The response was tremendous: Miller won a string of major awards, including the Pulitzer Prize, the New York Drama Critics Circle Award, the Theater Club Award, and a Tony. The play was soon performed throughout the United States and Europe, the published script became a best seller, and it is the only play ever to be a Book-of-the Month Club selection. At times comic, yet also poetic, tragic, and with a realistic veneer that made it easy to involve any audience, *Death of a Salesman* was a new type of serious play that merged the forms of REALISM and EXPRESSIONISM to suggest new directions and possibilities for all of American drama. The play's tremendous success also put Miller on a firm financial basis for life.

Trying to defend his controversial designation of the play as a tragedy, Miller published "Tragedy and the Common Man," and "Arthur Miller on the Nature of Tragedy" in the *New York Times.* Miller produced many such essays during his career that expounded his views on theater, politics, history, and social theory and that indicated his desire to be more than a playwright, someone who might shape the direction of U.S. drama, if not the United States itself. Many of these essays would be collected into

two volumes: *Theater Essays of Arthur Miller* (1978; expanded in 1996) and *Echoes Down the Corridor* (2000). Miller also attended the controversial pro-Soviet Cultural and Scientific Conference for World Peace at the Waldorf–Astoria Hotel to chair an arts panel with fellow playwright Clifford Odets and composer Dmitri Shostakovich, just one of such actions that would encourage the HOUSE UN-AMERICAN ACTIVITIES COMMITTEE (HUAC) to investigate both him and Odets.

After *Death of a Salesman,* Miller worked on his screenplay for *The Hook,* his story about waterfront corruption. He planned for Kazan to direct, the two having become close while working together. Knowing from the start that it would be difficult to get backing for such a controversial film, especially given the growing paranoia of the times, Miller refused to compromise. His screenplay did what he saw as the socially responsible thing—trying to expose the corruption that he had discovered on the waterfront two years earlier. Unfortunately, he was entering an era when social responsibility was being conflated with COMMUNISM and when studios felt it too dangerous to back such projects.

HUAC, set up in 1938, had been behind the closing of the Federal Theater Project, which Miller had joined for a short time. However, there was not the right political and cultural climate in the United States to allow HUAC to become really powerful until the 1950s. A number of people in the theater, such as Miller's friend Elia Kazan and fellow playwright Clifford Odets, during the next few years would admit to having had socialist sympathies to HUAC in acts of public contrition, and would name others of similar sympathies, thus putting those others under intense scrutiny. This act of naming was seen as an act of betrayal by those to whom the finger was now pointed, especially when it led to those people becoming blacklisted and no longer able to work; Kazan's and Miller's friendship fell apart for several years after Kazan took the stand in 1952.

Meanwhile, in 1950, actors FREDRIC MARCH and his wife Florence Eldridge saw themselves losing work because they were suspected of being communists. In response, they decided to stage Ibsen's play *An Enemy of the People,* in which they saw the lead characters' situation as resembling their own: All are accused by a mob hysteria that views them as a threat to the well-being of the larger society. March and the prospective director Robert Lewis asked Miller if he would write a new adaptation, which he willingly did, working from a literal translation of the Norwegian. He condensed the five-act play into three and cut many of the more ponderous speeches. Given the climate of the times, the production was not a great success, closing after only 36 performances, and the press accused Miller of creating anti-U.S. propaganda.

Miller was never actually blacklisted and was able to work in the theater during this time, but he did lose two potential film contracts, and there was some active campaigning by patriotic groups, such as the American Legion and the Catholic War Veterans, against his plays. Miller responded by speaking out publicly against HUAC's influence and for artistic freedom, although he found it impossible to convince newspapers to print anything written directly against Senator Joseph McCarthy, chief perpetrator of this "witch hunt." Meanwhile, Miller was strongly suspected of holding communist sympathies and was being daily observed by the Federal Bureau of Investigation (FBI). Although never at the center of the situation, Miller was affected, and more importantly, he realized just how far the United States as a nation was being affected by this growing atmosphere of distrust. When Miller was finally subpoenaed, he refused to cooperate, seeing the whole thing as an unnecessary and cruel exercise. He was cited for contempt.

In 1951, Miller first met Marilyn Monroe, while in Hollywood with Kazan to check out the film production of *Death of a Salesman* and to promote his screenplay, *The Hook*. The film starred Fredric March, who had turned down the original stage role. In his autobiography, Miller relates his first impression of Monroe as being pretty much what the world saw—the "quintessential dumb blonde" who was "ludicrously provocative." However, after a few brief, casual meetings, he began to see her differently. Drawn not only by what he saw as her great physical beauty but also by her surprising freshness and idealism, he could not get Monroe out of his mind, although he was still married to Slattery and a father of two. His mounting

celebrity and the pressures of a writing career had been putting an immense strain on his marriage for some time, and meeting Monroe was, perhaps, the final straw. Miller was attracted to both Monroe's intense sexuality and her vulnerability, and she to his strength and sense of certainty. Monroe seemed to hope that Miller would be able to protect her from the hostile world that she saw around her. This was, ultimately, a task at which he failed and about which he writes compassionately in his autobiography. But for the time being, Miller resisted Monroe's charms and returned to his wife. His confession of temptation to Slattery put a further strain on their relationship.

The year 1951 saw another short story published. "Monte Sant' Angelo" tells a tale of cultural recognition and connection, as an American Jew explores an Italian township in the hope of finding some relatives, despite his family having been decimated by the HOLOCAUST. This was no doubt partly inspired by his 1948 trip with Longhi, but it was also evidence of Miller's continuing fascination with the concepts of identity and community. Meanwhile, under the influence of HUAC, Hollywood was unhappy with Miller's disturbing depictions of the United States. Plans to produce *The Hook* were shelved, and the American Legion threatened to picket the film of *Death of a Salesman*. To soothe opposition, the production company, Columbia, offered to show *Death of a Salesman* accompanied by a film short that supported U.S. businessmen and explained how Loman was not a typical salesman. Miller objected and threatened to sue Columbia if they did this. The film was released in December 1951 on its own but was not a great success. This is possibly due to the fact that people were wary at this time of accepting anything critical of U.S. values. Setting these problems aside, Miller turned his attention to an idea that had been forming in his mind for his next play, *The Crucible*. The play would draw a clear parallel between the U.S. anticommunist paranoia of the 1950s and the 1692 SALEM WITCH TRAILS, exposing both to be maliciously motivated with ritualistic, public denunciations of innocent people.

Miller spent much of 1952 researching witch trials at the Historical Society in Salem, Massachusetts. Thus he ensured that the play would have an accurate historical basis that could also guard him against accusations of creating a flimsy social satire. The play premiered in 1953 in New York City in a production by JED HARRIS that Miller saw as too cold and stylized, and it was greeted by a mixture of praise, suspicion, and contempt for its evident parallels to HUAC's witch hunts. It was not until two years later, when a better production appeared, performed Off-Broadway at the Martinique Hotel that critics proclaimed it a "great" play. This time it ran for nearly two years. *The Crucible*, with its clear message of resistance against tyranny, has since grown to be Miller's most widely produced work. Miller had tried to fix up the premiere of *The Crucible* after Jed Harris had left the production, but got his first chance to direct one of his own plays from the start in 1953, when he was asked to work on a production of *All My Sons* for the Arden, Delaware, summer theatre.

Invited in 1954 to attend the Belgian premiere of *The Crucible*, Miller was unable to attend as the United States refused to renew his passport, seeing him as a dangerous dissident. That same year, both the Canadian CBC and the U.S.'s NBC produced toned-down radio versions of *Death of a Salesman*. The adaptations by Alan Savage and Robert Cenedella, respectively, severely cut the play to eradicate most of its social themes, quite likely a reaction to an uneasy social atmosphere as much as obeisance to the demands of entertainment. The CBC version focused on the drama as a family play, while the NBC version stripped away all of the characters' complexity and introduced it as a simplistic melodrama. It was clear that Miller's social themes had become suspect after his evident anti-McCarthy stance in *The Crucible*.

Meanwhile, in 1954, Monroe divorced her husband, baseball star Joe DiMaggio, to become once again free. She and Miller had been corresponding since their initial meeting, but in 1955, she moved to New York, not just to see him but also to obtain some distance from Hollywood, the scene of her recent divorce, and try to break into stage work. Making friends with Miller's friend Rosten gave her a useful cover for seeing Miller. Kazan had introduced her to the ACTORS STUDIO and its leading

lights LEE STRASBERG and PAULA STRASBERG, and through the Strasbergs, the couple finally met up again. Miller gave up resisting, and he and Monroe embarked upon an affair. That same year, city officials were pressured to withdraw permission for Miller, on suspicion that he might be a Communist, to make a documentary that he had been putting together about juvenile delinquency in New York. Three years later, when HUAC's influence was on the wane, *Esquire* magazine published Miller's "Bridge to a Savage World," which was the film treatment of this unproduced documentary.

The year 1955 also saw two new plays, the one-act version of *A View from the Bridge*, about a man who reports on two illegal immigrants to keep one away from his niece, and *A Memory of Two Mondays*, a nostalgic piece about a group of people working in an auto-parts warehouse. These were played together at the Coronet Theatre in a double bill, using the same cast for each play. It only ran for a disappointing 149 performances. Kermit Bloomgarden had brought in ROBERT WHITEHEAD to help him produce. To try to explain the relevance of the type of theater he was attempting, Miller wrote the essay "On Social Plays," to be published alongside the plays. He also published the essays "The American Theater," in which he speaks strongly against the restrictiveness of Broadway, and "A Boy Grew in Brooklyn," an account of his childhood; both appeared in *Holiday* magazine. By October, Slattery had heard enough in the media about her husband's ongoing affair with Monroe, and Miller moved out to live at the Chelsea Hotel.

In 1956, Miller spent six weeks in Reno establishing the residency requirement for a Nevada divorce from Slattery. There he wrote the short story "The Misfits," that would appear in *Esquire* magazine the following year. While in Reno, he was also subpoenaed to appear before HUAC. In *Timebends: A Life*, Miller relates how Francis E. Walter, the chairman of the HUAC before which he had been summoned, reportedly offered to waive Miller's appearance before the committee if Miller would allow Walter to be photographed shaking hands with Monroe. Miller rejected the offer. At his hearing, he stood on principle, refusing to name names, and was given a period to change his mind before being cited for contempt. Meantime, he was awarded an uncontested divorce and married Monroe on June 28; she even converted to Judaism for her new husband. The media were fascinated by what they deemed an unlikely match between intellect and beauty. Slattery took Willow Street, and Miller kept the Roxbury house; there was also a sizable settlement based on a percentage of his income until she remarried, which she never did.

Although the University of Michigan awarded him an honorary doctorate in 1956, Miller did not receive the same approbation from HUAC which, on his subsequent refusal to change his mind, cited him for contempt, a charge he would now have to defend in court. He was nevertheless allowed a temporary passport to travel to GREAT BRITAIN with his new wife, who was to film *The Prince and the Showgirl* there with the British actor Laurence Olivier. The decision was also made to sell the Roxbury house and to look for another property in the same area that he and his new wife could make their own. While in England, Miller revised *A View from the Bridge* into two acts for Peter Brook to produce in London, and the resulting production fared better than its earlier counterpart. He was also working on a lengthy introduction for a collected edition of his works that would become a striking theatrical commentary. In the *Tulane Drama Review,* scholar Tom Driver would call this "one of the major documents of American theater," and Miller would dedicate the 1957 volume "To Marilyn." On his return to the United States, Miller was scheduled to defend the charge of contempt and to face a possible prison sentence if found guilty.

After a 10-day trial, during which Miller's lawyer insisted that HUAC was after Miller only to recover the limelight because of his connection to Monroe and during which he attacked the relevancy of the questions that Miller had been asked to answer, Miller was found guilty and given a $500 fine and a suspended jail sentence. If he had been subpoenaed in HUAC's earlier years, the sentence might have been harsher, but by 1957 the public was beginning to grow bored with the repetition of the committee's proceedings. Rather than accept this conviction, Miller appealed. In 1958, the conviction was overturned by the U.S. Court of Appeals

on the grounds that the questions that he had been asked to answer served no legislative purpose, but Miller still had to pay the $40,000 in costs. That same year, Miller was elected to the National Institute of Arts and Letters and the following year was awarded their Gold Medal for Drama.

After bouncing around between several city apartments and a rented retreat in Amagansett, Long Island, in 1958, the couple found a suitable property at 323 Tophet Road, not too far from the old Roxbury place. Monroe had wanted to rebuild and hired famed architect Frank Lloyd Wright to draw up plans, but Miller preferred simply to renovate the old farmhouse. He did, however, at Monroe's insistence, buy up much of the surrounding land to create a nicely secluded estate of 340 acres. Here, they set up home, with Monroe cooking and cleaning in between film work. However, this period was to prove difficult for Miller. Apart from the troubles with HUAC that had made producers a little wary of Miller, his second marriage was not going well. They had moments of marital bliss, but Monroe's drinking and dependency on drugs, problematic before their marriage, were not improving. Miller felt impelled to help his wife face her work commitments but discovered that this was to be a full-time task. Also, Monroe, eager for a child, suffered a series of miscarriages.

Distracted by personal problems Miller lost touch with his audience and faced a creative slump. Although he continued to publish the occasional short story, including "I Don't Need You Anymore," "Please Don't Kill Anything," and "The Prophecy," as well as some important essays, including "The Family in Modern Drama" and "The Playwright and the Atomic World" (which was later retitled "1956 and All This"), he produced no new drama for several years. The public was forced to be content with several film productions of past plays, and these were all produced abroad. They included two British television productions, *Death of a Salesman,* and *The Crucible;* two French films, *The Crucible,* retitled *The Witches of Salem,* with a screenplay by JEAN-PAUL SARTRE, and *A View from a Bridge* with a screenplay by Norman Rosten; and a Canadian production of *The Crucible.* The United States was only host to an operatic adaptation, *The Crucible:*

An Opera in Four Acts by Robert Ward and Bernard Stambler, produced, presented, and recorded with New York City Opera performers.

Unable to understand the self-involved and self-indulgent mood of the country, Miller felt uninspired and unwilling to write drama. He disliked the trendy ABSURDISM of such writers as SAMUEL BECKETT, seeing it as too nihilistic. The central work that emerged from this period was the result of an attempt to help his wife. Marilyn was growing frustrated by the insipid roles that she was being given, so Miller adapted his short story about a struggling group of cowboys, "The Misfits," into a screenplay, vastly expanding what had been the minor role of Roslyn to give his wife a serious role. John Huston agreed to direct, and an all-star cast with CLARK GABLE, Montgomery Clift, and ELI WALLACH backed up Monroe. However, due to her growing insecurities, the filming in Nevada during 1960 was close to a disaster, and the finished movie opened in 1961 to tepid reviews. Miller revisited this experience in his 2004 play, *Finishing the Picture*. Prior to *The Misfits*, Monroe had been contracted to appear in the romantic comedy *Let's Make Love* and had persuaded her husband to rework its screenplay to improve her role. Her costar was Yves Montand, and there were increasing rumors of an affair between him and Monroe. Miller's marriage was on the rocks even before they headed to Nevada.

In 1961, Miller and Monroe agreed to divorce after a short separation. Miller had grown increasingly weary of his wife's insecurity, mood swings, and dependency on drugs and alcohol. Feeling shut out by her personal assistant, Paula Strasberg, Miller saw that his wife was in trouble, but he felt powerless to help her and could no longer watch her destroy herself. That same year, his mother died at age 70. Monroe attended the funeral, just as she would stay friendly with Miller's father in his remaining years, even taking him with her to meet the president. During the filming of *The Misfits*, Miller and Monroe had both met INGEBORG MORATH, a professional photographer, when she was taking rehearsal photographs. Monroe had liked her for her sensitivity and kindness, but Miller also recognized her evident strength and independence; meeting again months later, after his separation from Monroe, Miller and Morath became friends.

On February 17, 1962, Miller married Morath, whose stable nature he found far preferable to the roller-coaster relationship he had had with Monroe. On hearing of Monroe's death six months later, Miller was stunned. Monroe still seemed so vivid to him that he could not, at first, believe that she was dead. He did not attend her funeral, not wanting to become part of the publicity circus that would surround such an event, but privately mourned the premature death of a woman whom he still partly loved. In the fall, he and his new wife had their first child, Daniel Miller. It became evident shortly after that Daniel suffered from a severe case of Down syndrome, and like so many couples in that position in the 1960s, it was decided that Daniel would be best cared for in a facility. They enrolled him at Southbury Training School, which would be close enough to visit. Miller always kept this personal catastrophe very private, and Daniel lived into his early forties.

The publication in 1962 of an essay about New York street gangs, "The Bored and the Violent"; a short story "Glimpse at a Jockey," about problems in the life of a New York jockey; as well as a television presentation of *Focus* with James Whitemore were Miller's output for that year, but America still awaited a new play. Miller had been working on one piece for several years, referred to in notes as *The Third Play*, and parts of this had now evolved into *After the Fall*, which Miller had close to final shape in 1961. Whitehead and Kazan were heading up the Repertory Theater of Lincoln Center and had asked Miller in 1960 for a new play to inaugurate the expected 1963 opening; while delays pushed back that opening date to the following year, Miller would keep his play on hold. A 1962 visit with Morath to the Mauthausen concentration camp had provided further ideas for the drama. Morath often traveled as part of her job as photographer, and Miller who, previous to marrying her, had only left America on rare occasions now began to travel abroad quite frequently.

By 1963, Miller and Morath had made the Roxbury house their main residence, although they also permanently rented suite 614 at the Chelsea Hotel so that Miller could more easily visit his older children. This also gave them both a place from which they could work when in town. That year, the couple also was relieved to have a healthy baby girl, REBECCA MILLER, born on August 7. Miller published his one and only children's book, *Jane's Blanket,* which was dedicated to his first daughter Jane who was nearing age 20. It was possibly an attempt by Miller to let his firstborn know that she was still dear to him as he gained a new daughter; Jane had been affected the most by his first divorce. The book itself can also be read as a metaphoric lesson for how Miller desires his first daughter to view their relationship—with the central blanket representing the father, whose importance in his daughter's life naturally slackens over time as she takes on other interests and grows beyond her need for parental support. Jane would marry the sculptor Tom Doyle three years later.

After the Fall finally opened at the Repertory Theater in January 1964. Conveying the psychological drama taking place in the head of Quentin as he tries to place his life, loves, and fears into perspective, many critics chose to read Quentin as a surrogate for Miller himself, especially given the presentation of Quentin's three wives who seemed remarkably close to those of Miller. It was the similarity between Maggie and Monroe that raised the most response. Although Maggie is a singer rather than an actress, she has many of Monroe's well-known mannerisms and traits and the same personal background. She was also portrayed as promiscuous, temperamental, and self-deceiving. The play drew fierce disapproval from many critics for what they felt was a vindictive portrayal of Monroe. Miller, throughout, refused to accept that Maggie's character in *After the Fall* was strictly based on Monroe, and in a article that was typical of his stance, "With Respect to Her Agony—But with Love," he asked critics to judge the play by its artistic merits rather than as a piece of autobiography.

In February 1964, partly as an escape from the media backlash, the couple traveled to Europe for Morath to visit family, and while there, Miller covered the war-crimes trial of a group of former Aus-

chwitz guards in Frankfurt, Germany, for the *New York Herald Tribune.* When the producer Robert Whitehead asked Miller for another play for later that year, he swiftly wrote *Incident at Vichy,* inspired by his recent trip. The play depicted the roundup of Jews in Vichy France during World War II. Less controversial than *After the Fall,* which ran for 208 performances given its reputation, *Vichy* managed 99 performances but met mixed reviews. The veracity of events in this play was also questioned, and again Miller pleaded dramatic license but to deaf ears. Miller began to spend more time in Roxbury building an extension, planting trees, and tending to his property.

In 1965, while visiting Paris, Miller was asked by David Carver, the secretary general of PEN, an international organization of playwrights, poets, essayists, and novelists that had formed after World War I to combat censorship and nationalistic pressures on writers, to become the organization's presidency. He had been chosen as a writer who had admirers and followers in both the East and the West. It was hoped that he could act as a potential connecting force. He was also selected because of his known commitment to liberal politics. Miller accepted, partly out of interest in being given an official excuse to make contact with eastern European writers whose plight he found to be particularly interesting. Miller attended his first PEN conference in Blad, Yugoslavia, in 1965. In 1966, Miller lost his father on the same day that he made his opening speech at the New York PEN Congress.

In 1966, CBS aired the first American television production of *Death of a Salesman,* starring Lee J. Cobb and Mildred Dunnock from the original production, and 17 million viewers saw the play. However, his two-act *A View From the Bridge* could not get a Broadway opening; it was directed by ULU GROSBARD in an Off-Broadway theater.

Two short stories, published later on in 1966, seem highly reflective of his life at this point. The first, "Recognitions" (later revised as "Fame"), apppeared in *Esquire* and tells about a rich and famous Jewish playwright who is sick of insincere adulation and wants people to see the real him over the media image and to treat him more naturally.

In the second, "A Search for a Future," published in *The Saturday Evening Post,* a son learns from his elderly father how to better appreciate life. Miller also published the essay "Our Guilt For the World's Evil" in which he both defended *Incident at Vichy* and propounded the theories of innocence, guilt, and responsibility that are so central to his work.

In 1967, he produced a collection of short stories titled *I Don't Need You Anymore.* Although most of these had been published before and were written during a 16-year period, in a brief introduction Miller explained how he saw them as interrelating to create a unified vision. Miller also visited Moscow to persuade Soviet writers to join PEN and the following year petitioned the Russian government to lift their ban on the works of Aleksandr Solzhenitsyn. A 1967 television production of *The Crucible* on CBS with GEORGE C. SCOTT brought that play a much wider audience and reaffirmed Miller as a political playwright. In 1968, elected by his Roxbury neighbors, he attended the Democratic National Convention in Chicago as the Eugene McCarthy delegate. In sympathy with McCarthy's antiwar platform, he had made speeches on his behalf and written articles for the press. He related his experience at the convention, including his reactions to the violence over the VIETNAM WAR that he witnessed both inside and outside the amphitheater, in "The Battle of Chicago" for the *New York Times.* He would also attend the 1972 Democratic convention in Miami, again as an elected delegate.

The Price premiered in New York in 1968, and, with it, a return to more familiar Miller territory: the division and connection between family members. Miller had been working on this play since the early 1950s. We watch as two brothers attempt to sell off their deceased father's furniture and come to terms with each other. The production was a troubled one, with Miller having to take over the direction after the actors had fallen out with the original director, Ulu Grosbard. Also, David Burns, who was playing the role of the furniture dealer, Solomon, was rushed to hospital with a serious illness and was replaced by his understudy, Harold Gary, during the previews. But *The Price* had the longest run of a Miller play for some time, lasting for 429 performances. His publisher also sent him a plaque to mark the one-millionth copy sold of *Death of a Salesman.* Still, Miller would see his plays largely misunderstood for some time to come as he remained out of critical favor. There was even a humiliating exchange that year in the columns of the *New York Times,* debating his merits as a playwright.

In 1969, he visited Czechoslovakia to show support for writers there and briefly met VÁCLAV HAVEL, then a famous dissident writer but who later became the democratically elected president of Czechoslovakia. Havel would be the inspiration for Sigmund in Miller's 1977 play *The Archbishop's Ceiling* produced by the John F. Kennedy Center for the Performing Arts in Washington, D.C., which depicts a group of writers trying to survive against various threats of suppression. That same year, Miller's term as president of PEN ended, but he continued to work with the organization, becoming vice-president of the U.S. section. He refused to allow his works to be published in Greece in protest of the government's oppression of writers at that time. He also published *In Russia,* an account of his 1967 trip to Russia and an exploration of the Russian cultural consciousness, for which Morath provided the photographs. As a result of this book, coupled with Miller's work to free dissident writers, his works would be banned in the Soviet Union the following year. Meanwhile, expanding to the poetic genre, *Harper's* published Miller's "Lines from California: Poem," which mocked the facile lives of Californians.

Although he has been accused of paying little attention to events of this period, Miller was highly vocal against the Vietnam War, as evidenced by a 1969 op-ed piece in the *New York Times,* "Are We Interested in Stopping the Killing?" that questioned United States's involvement in Vietnam. He had attended a 1965 "teach-in" at the University of Michigan to protest the war and had spoken out at various antiwar demonstrations, even flying to Paris in an attempt to negotiate with the Viet Cong. He also wrote a short play in the late 1960s, *The Reason Why,* which was performed in 1970 alongside a one-act version of *Fame* (based on the story that had appeared in *I Don't Need You Anymore*) at the New Theater Workshop in New

York. That same year, *The Reason Why* was filmed on Miller's own estate in Roxbury with Eli Wallach and Robert Ryan. While symbolically referencing the Vietnam War, it also explored the ways people became inured to killing. Miller was involved in politics on the local level too, offering his support to a Roxbury high-school teacher who refused to say the Pledge of Allegiance in her classroom.

In 1971, Miller was elected to the American Academy of Arts and Letters and television productions of both *A Memory of Two Mondays* and *The Price* were aired. Throughout the 1970s, we would see his continuing commitment to fellow writers as he helped free the Brazilian playwright Augusto Boal from prison, appeared on a panel before the Senate Permanent Subcommittee on Investigations to support the freedom of writers throughout the world, and petitioned the Czech government to halt arrests of dissident writers. His essay "What's Wrong with This Picture?" that was published in *Esquire* in 1974 was an urgent call to recognize the conditions for artists in Czechoslovakia. His involvement also continued on the home front with the PETER REILLY murder case that would later fuel his short play *Some Kind of Love Story.* Connecticut resident, Reilly, had been falsely convicted of murdering his mother and in 1976 Miller hired a private detective to help uncover evidence that would prove Reilly's innocence. He also put together a collection of anecdotes that he published in 1977, titled *In the Country.* It depicts the daily politics and life of rural Connecticut and is illustrated with photographs by Morath.

Miller continued to experiment with new dramatic forms while U.S. critics remained unhappy with his work. In 1974, he tried his hand at a full-blown musical called *Up From Paradise* that was presented by The University of Michigan Theatre Program in Ann Arbor, Michigan. It was a revised version of his 1972 rewrite of the Cain and Abel story as a comic folk tale with serious undertones, *The Creation of the World and Other Business* that had briefly appeared at the Shubert Theatre in New York. Neither met much success and both closed after very brief runs. *The Archbishop's Ceiling* that premiered in Washington, D.C., for a limited run in 1977 fared little better. Nothing seemed to

suit. Even the 1978 television production of the comic *Fame* developed from his short story about the tenuousness of reputation met a lukewarm reception. Several short stories, a play sketch, and a poem also saw publication, but Miller's career seemed to be on hold. After a trip to China in fall 1978, Miller produced *Chinese Encounters* the following year, his third book of reportage done in collaboration with his wife.

Miller's dramatic output in 1980 saw two full-length works produced. The first, *The American Clock,* was performed at the Spoleto Festival in North Carolina then transferred to the Biltmore Theatre in New York City, but it closed after a mere 12 performances. With music and more than a 50-character cast, it was envisaged as a moving collage of U.S. life in the 1930s and an encomium to the concept of U.S. DEMOCRACY. The premiere production failed to catch the spirit of the play, and it was not until PETER WOOD's 1986 NATIONAL THEATRE production in Great Britain that it really came together and caught the audience's imagination and approval. The second work was the Holocaust film *Playing For Time,* based on the memoirs of FANIA FÉNELON, a French singer held at Auschwitz. This was aired on CBS. The controversial choice of VANESSA REDGRAVE, an outspoken supporter of the Palestine Liberation Organization (PLO), to play the Jewish Fénelon caused a greater stir than the film itself, but Miller defended her right to appear in the movie. He would later adapt his screenplay for a theatrical production that was performed briefly at the Studio Theatre in Washington D.C. in 1985 to little notice or acclaim. The play would win better accolades the following year when it was presented at the Edinburgh Festival in Scotland.

Unperturbed, Miller traveled and continued to work on a variety of projects. In 1981, he visited Paris where productions of *A View from the Bridge* and *Incident at Vichy* were running. He also traveled to Venezuela, which, coupled with a trip the following year to Colombia, would give him much of his material for *Resurrection Blues* (2002). He participated in a 1982 antinuclear march. The 1980s would see him produce two sets of intriguing one-act plays, virtually ignored in the United States but well-received in Britain. In 1982, *Elegy for a Lady* and *Some Kind of Love Story* were directed by Miller and performed at the Long Wharf Theater in New Haven, Connecticut, under the collective title of *2 by A.M.*—changed to *Two-Way Mirror* for the London premiere in 1989. In *Elegy for a Lady,* a man is given advice and enlightenment from the proprietress of a boutique. In *Some Kind of Love Story* a private detective interviews a possible witness in a criminal case. This latter story would evolve into the screenplay *Everybody Wins* at the end of the decade. Produced in 1987, *Danger: Memory!* was composed of the one-acts *Clara* and *I Can't Remember Anything. Clara* shows a man's reactions to the vicious murder of his daughter; *I Can't Remember Anything* depicts the squabbling relationship of two elderly friends. All four plays used minimalistic or highly representational sets and made great use of lighting, sound, and image to get their points across, showing firm evidence of Miller's constant exploration of theatrical limits. In 1982, he also wrote a short satirical play in support of Havel, called *The Havel Deal,* in which a Communist proposes the arrest of Western writers, as was occurring to writers in Czechoslovakia at that time.

In 1983, Miller accepted an invitation to go to the China to direct *Death of a Salesman* at the BEIJING PEOPLE'S ART THEATER. On his return, Miller published a journal of this landmark production, *Salesman in Beijing.* While he was over there, the Roxbury house was gutted by fire, and Miller lost many of his books, although luckily most of his manuscripts had been stored in a nearby barn and were unharmed. Rather than rebuild, Miller decided to restore the ruined building.

Despite receiving the Kennedy Center Honors for distinguished lifetime achievement in 1984 and honorary degrees for him and his wife from the University of Hartford, during the 1980s Miller's reputation at home remained limited. However, abroad, it was soaring, especially in Britain. The 1986 British production of *The Archbishop's Ceiling,* with a revised script, was received very differently from its U.S. counterpart. Successful London productions of both *The American Clock* and *A View from the Bridge* were mounted in 1986. Numerous other productions of Miller's work appeared in Britain throughout the decade, including well-received premieres of his one-acts, *Danger: Memory!* in 1988 and *Two-Way Mirror* in 1989. To prove their appreciation of his stature, in 1987, the UNIVERSITY OF EAST ANGLIA named its center for American studies the Arthur Miller Centre, under the direction of scholar CHRISTOPHER BIGSBY. Arrangements were also made for his early radio play *The Golden Years* to at last be produced; it was aired on BBC Radio. In honor of Miller's 75th birthday in 1990, British director DAVID THACKER mounted a celebration that included London revivals of *The Price* and *The Crucible.*

On the political and social side, Miller continued writing letters of support for political causes across the globe and spoke out against what he saw as unnecessary restrictions or intolerance at home, from mandated school prayer to immigration LAW. In 1985, he traveled to Turkey for International PEN with British playwright HAROLD PINTER, with whom he had become friendly. The pair argued with officials at the U.S. Embassy concerning U.S. complicity in torture and were effectively asked to leave. Miller also went as a delegate to a meeting of Soviet and U.S. writers in Vilnius, Lithuania, where he tried to persuade the Soviets to stop persecuting writers. Miller was one of 15 writers and scientists invited to the Soviet Union in 1987 to a conference with Mikhail Gorbachev on Soviet policies. The 1986 monologue, *I Think About You a Great Deal,* and a short untitled play (not produced until 2001) in honor of Václav Havel's receipt of the Erasmus Prize while still in jail showed his continued support for this political figure. As part of a 1988 musical revue that commented on U.S. society called *Urban Blight,* he wrote another monologue, *Speech to the Neighborhood Watch Committee,* about the destructive effects of material possessions. The 1989 essays "Conditions of Freedom," published to accompany a new edition of *The Archbishop's Ceiling* and *The American Clock,* and "Again They Drink from the Cup of Suspicion" in the *New York Times* were both keen social analyses that gave insight into the plays they covered.

Although the people of the United States did not appreciate Miller's new works, they still revered his old, as evidenced by both the amazing success of DUSTIN HOFFMAN's 1984 stage production of *Death of a Salesman,* which made more than $3 million in ticket receipts within three days of opening, and the subsequent televised version that aired on CBS in 1985 to an audience of 25 million. There was also a television production of *All My Sons* on PBS *American Playhouse* in 1987. Still, Miller's 1987 autobiography, *Timebends: A Life* seemed better received in Great Britain than in the United States, one British critic calling it "autobiography as art." However, it was still chosen as a Book-of-the-Month Club popular selection. Trying to explain why he felt that Miller was better received on British shores in Bigsby's *Arthur Miller and Company,* critic Michael Billington suggested that it was because Miller displayed a European dramatists' tendency "to ask daunting questions rather than provide [the] comforting answers" that American audiences and critics seemed to prefer. Miller became more vocal than ever against the dominance of Broadway and the difficulties of producing serious drama in the United States.

Although well past retirement age, in the 1990s Miller did not slacken. His next full-length play, *The Ride down Mt. Morgan,* would premiere in London in 1991. The choice of London was partly a reflection of Miller's growing despair about being given unfair press in the United States but also because he was particularly keen to have MICHAEL BLAKEMORE direct. *The Ride down Mt. Morgan,* about one man's ego and the troubles that he causes in his desire for complete autonomy, was later revised and presented in 1996 to full houses at the WILLIAMSTOWN THEATRE FESTIVAL, Massachusetts, although its planned transfer to New York did not take place until 1998 at the Public Theatre. It was not played on Broadway until 2000. Still, the United States was not neglected, and Miller continued to be engaged at home in theatrical, social, and political arenas.

In 1990, *Everybody Wins,* the film based on *Some Kind of Love Story,* was released, with Nick Nolte and Debra Winger, and a television production of Miller's version of *An Enemy of the People* appeared on PBS's *American Playhouse.* In 1991, a single-scene version of *The Last Yankee* was produced off-Broadway, with the expanded two-scene version coming two years later. *The Last Yankee,* set in a mental hospital, depicts the

pressures that face married couples in a postmodern age of chaos and insecurity. The interchanges between the play's four characters create a masterly quartet, which again was better received in Britain when produced there in 1993. In 1992, a novella *Homely Girl, A Life*—an account of a Jewish woman's self-discovery—was published, and a film based on the book would be made in 2001, titled *Plain Jane* (the title of the British version of the book). It was partly filmed at Miller's Roxbury house, and the playwright acted in a small role. Another important essay, "About Theater Language," accompanied the 1994 edition of *The Last Yankee.* A tongue-in-cheek op-ed piece he wrote for the *New York Times* in 1992 called for the privatization of executions that could then be held in sporting arenas to a paying audience and prefigures the concept behind his 2002 play, *Resurrection Blues.*

By the 1990s, Miller's academic reputation began to rekindle in his home country. In 1992, the First International Arthur Miller Conference was held at Millersville University in Pennsylvania, and at the Second International Arthur Miller Conference in 1995, the ARTHUR MILLER SOCIETY was founded. This organization would go on to hold a series of major conferences dedicated to his works at various locations across the United States from California to New York, soon becoming a regular event. They would produce a biannual society newsletter that in 2006 graduated into the *Arthur Miller Journal.* There was also an Arthur Miller Symposium that was held at University of Evansville, Indiana, in 1998 and a Symposium on Miller and the Holocaust held at Kean University, New Jersey, in 1999. In 1993, Miller was awarded the National Medal of the Arts by President Clinton.

Miller's interest in 1994 returned to both the Holocaust and the 1930s with another new play, *Broken Glass,* that had moderately successful runs on both Broadway and London stages. Many saw this realistically rendered tale of a woman's paralysis and her husband's inability to face his complicity in this as a return to the earlier style of Miller, albeit somewhat stripped. The productivity continued. In 1995, Miller's screenplay for *The Crucible* was filmed with Daniel Day-Lewis. Making it a family get-together, Robert Miller was coproducer, and

Rebecca Miller was on set as the production's still photographer. There, she grew friendly with Day-Lewis who would become her husband. *The Ryan Interview* was performed at the Ensemble Studio One-Act Play Marathon in 1995. A television version of *Broken Glass* broadcast in 1997 allowed that play to reach a greater audience, and another film version of *Focus,* starring William H. Macy, was released in 2001.

The ethereal *Mr. Peter's Connections,* a 1998 play that was firmly experimental, with multiple time-lines and blurring of reality, was somewhat reminiscent of *After the Fall* as a man's past life is examined and found wanting. This was part of a whole season of Miller's work presented by the SIGNATURE THEATER. A series of successful high-profile revivals, initiated by the Signature theater season, included *A View From the Bridge* with Anthony LaPaglia, the 50th anniversary production of *Death of a Salesman,* with BRIAN DENNEHY and ELIZABETH FRANZ, *The Price, The Crucible* with Liam Neeson, *The Ride down Mt. Morgan,* with Patrick Stewart, and *The Man Who Had All the Luck* with Chris O'Donnell, all produced in New York between 1998 and 2002. An operatic version of *A View from the Bridge* by William Bolcom, for which Miller wrote the aria *An Immigrant's Lament,* was also seen in 1999.

Toward the close of the century, various award-giving foundations increasingly acknowledged Miller. Although he was sadly overlooked for a Nobel Prize, in the final decade of his life, Miller's tremendous body of work was recognized by the William Inge Festival Award for distinguished achievement in American theater, the Edward Albee Last Frontier Playwright Award, the PEN/Laura Pels Foundation Award to a master American dramatist, the Lucille Lortel Award for Lifetime Achievement, an NEH Fellowship, the John H. Finley Award for Exemplary Service to New York City, and the Jerusalem Prize (for which he wrote the speech, "Why Israel Must Choose Justice"); he was also named as the Distinguished Inaugural Senior Fellow of the American Academy in Berlin and awarded an honorary doctorate from Oxford University. There were also extensive tributes to Miller on his 80th and 85th birthdays in both Great Britain and the United States. Many fellow playwrights, such as EDWARD ALBEE, David Rabe, and Harold Pinter, voiced their deep admiration of Miller.

The revised and expanded collection of *Theater Essays,* edited by STEVEN CENTOLA and published in 1996, is evidence of Miller's extensive contribution to criticism of American drama; the 2000 essay collection *Echoes Down the Corridor* emphasized his thoughts on more social and political topics; so did his monograph *On Politics and the Art of Acting,* that was based on his Thomas Jefferson Lecture for the NEA, which was published in 2001. On the local level, Miller became involved in another legal case; the appeal of a brain-damaged plaintiff, Richard Lapointe, who had been convicted of rape and murder but against whom the evidence was suspect. Still traveling, even in his eighties, he went to Cuba in 2001 with William Styron and others on a visit that aimed to strengthen U.S. cultural links with the island nation; he was able to meet with FIDEL CASTRO, an encounter about which he wrote two years later in "A Visit with Castro."

Moving into the 21st century, Miller's dramatic work remained strikingly original and with an evident bias towards the comic. First was the satirical *Resurrection Blues* (2002) that depicted a fictitious Latin American country in which the local dictator is planning to televise a crucifixion. This premiered at the Guthrie Theater, Minneapolis, and then saw productions at other regional theaters. Two short stories "The Performance" and "The Bare Manuscript" appeared in the *New Yorker* in 2002; the first relates a 1936 meeting between a Jewish performer and Hitler, and the second depicts a writer scribing his latest work on a naked woman while reminiscing about a past that rekindles his spousal passion. In 2003, *Esquire* published the brief but evocative "Presence," in which the central figure has an epiphany after seeing a couple making love on the beach. Miller also published a novella in *Southwest Review* in 2004, which was titled *The Turpentine Still.* Set in Haiti, the piece attracted little notice. The year 2004 also saw a Broadway revival of *After the Fall* that still could only gain mixed reviews and the premiere of his final play, ironically titled *Finishing the Picture,* at the Goodman Theater, Chicago. This was another comedy and was largely based on Miller's experiences filming *The Misfits,* in which he satirizes the various characters involved, from director to acting coach to starlet.

After Morath had undergone chemotherapy for lymphoma, the couple hoped she had it under control, but at the start of 2002, it came back aggressively, and on January 30, his wife died. Kermit Miller would also die on Miller's own birthday the following year. Miller's health was beginning to fail; in 1997, he had undergone retinal eye surgery to correct his vision, and after Morath's death, reports circulated of hospitalization for ailments including pneumonia, cancer, and a heart condition. The 2005 short story "Beavers" in *Harper's* magazine would be his final publication while alive. Before impending nuptials to his new companion, painter AGNES BARLEY, could occur, Miller died at age 89 of heart failure at his home in Roxbury on February 10, 56 years to the day that *Death of a Salesman* had opened on Broadway. Barley, his sister Joan, and daughter Rebecca and her family were at his bedside. Having been diagnosed as incurable earlier in the week, he insisted on being taken to Roxbury to die. At his death, at least three major film versions of his works—*A Ride Down Mt. Morgan*, *A View from the Bridge*, and *The Man Who Had All the Luck*—were being planned, as well as the London and New York premieres of *Resurrection Blues*. Not all of these came to fruition, but there has since been an upsurge in productions of Miller's plays, several new collections of essays and tributes, and another, long-awaited collection of his short fiction, *Presence: Stories by Arthur Miller*, published in 2007.

Roxbury, Connecticut, announced May 7, 2005, to be the town's first official Arthur Miller Day. Family and neighbors attended a gathering at the local Town Hall, where a bust of Miller created by Washington sculptor Philip Grausman was on display. At the New York memorial service several days later, family and friends read passages from his work and spoke about his legacy. Playwrights Tony Kushner and Edward Albee were particularly outspoken, with Albee concluding, "Some writers matter and some do not. Some of our most clever writers don't matter. They teach us nothing, and they do not render ourselves coherent. Arthur Miller was a writer who mattered. A lot." Miller's legacy continues in the works that he left behind.

PART II

Works A–Z

"About Theater Language" (1994)

This essay originally appeared as an introduction to a 1994 edition of *The Last Yankee* but has been reprinted since in *Arthur Miller Plays: Five* (1995) and in the revised edition of *The Theater Essays of Arthur Miller* (1996). It provides the bedrock for Miller's "Notes on Realism" which covers much of the same territory, describing the impact of EUGENE O'NEILL, CLIFFORD ODETS, and TENNESSEE WILLIAMS on U.S. theater and their connection to REALISM. Both also discuss the language of Sean O'Casey, J. M. Synge, and SAMUEL BECKETT. Where this essay differs is that after Beckett's influence has been covered, Miller goes on to describe in some detail his intentions behind *The Last Yankee* as "a comedy about a TRAGEDY." He discusses the play as an attempt to capture a sense of the modern despair with life and to expose "the moral and social myths feeding the disease."

Miller explains how, in *The Last Yankee*, he wanted to present authentic characters in a universal situation. Patricia Hamilton is trapped by a "success mythology," and Leroy's transcending love suggests a way forward that offers hope. Miller set the play in a mental institution rather than in someone's home, as he felt that it gave his characters a wider social implication suggesting that insanity has become the last refuge of too many American citizens, and we are all, in a sense, facing the possible restrictions of institutionalization in our insane quest for constant satisfaction. His aim was to try "to make things seen in their social context and simultaneously felt as intimate testimony," wanting his work to be "absorbed rather than merely observed." The play's ambivalent ending is intentional as its "theme is hope rather than completion of achievement, and hope is tentative always." Miller wanted the play to extend a plea for people to stop needless competition. Widening his focus at the close of the essay, he concludes in the same way that he does in "Notes on Realism"—with a call for a better balance in future plays between feeling and thought.

After the Fall (1964)

Rather than the usual BROADWAY opening, the new REPERTORY THEATER OF LINCOLN CENTER produced Miller's first play of the 1960s. ROBERT WHITEHEAD and ELIA KAZAN, who were heading the project, had asked him as far back as 1960 to provide the inaugural play. He decided to give them *After the Fall*, a play on which he had been working for some time but had not yet completed to his satisfaction. After his divorce from MARILYN MONROE, Miller was able to find time to complete it and reportedly had done so even before Monroe had died. The play, however, would not be produced until 1964. The opening date had been 1963, but the Vivian Beaumont Theatre that was being built for the Repertory Theater was way behind schedule, so they ended up building a temporary theater in Washington Square Park to stage Miller's first play in eight years. The resulting production satisfied audiences more than the critics, who mostly reacted with shock and scorn. It ran within a rotating repertory for 208 performances.

The issue of survivor guilt is central to *After the Fall*, and the play's direct connection to the HOLOCAUST is inescapable. While working on the play, Miller and INGE MORATH had visited Mauthausen concentration camp together. Miller felt that he had witnessed at first hand people's dangerous and irresponsible drive to forget or pretend innocence to deny GUILT AND RESPONSIBILITY. He objected to such a reaction, believing instead that we should each accept some responsibility for evil in the world. In *Timebends: A Life,* Miller explains that *After the Fall* "was about how we—nations and individuals—destroy ourselves by denying that this is precisely what we are doing."

In the late 1950s Walter Wanger had suggested to Miller that he write a screenplay for the French novel *The Fall* by ALBERT CAMUS. Miller felt drawn to Camus's story in which the main character is forced to question his own ability to judge, given the knowledge that he himself had erred, but Miller wanted to take this idea further and address questions that Camus does not face. In Camus's novel, the hero fails to help a suicidal girl and feels guilty.

Miller wondered what would happen if the hero actually tried to help but then realized that this could achieve no good as such people could only help themselves. Miller also wished to explore reasons for which the hero might offer help, to assess whether or not there could be selfish motives. The play that he produced explores these issues, but some critics felt that he did this on too personal a level.

It seems impossible not to connect Quentin and his two failed marriages, including one to a superstar, with Miller. In *Timebends: A Life,* Miller repeats his continued claim that the play was "neither more or less autobiographical than anything else I had written for the stage," but he saw most critics refusing to look beyond the autobiographical elements on its initial showing. Centering on the portrayal of Maggie as Monroe, critics were scathing about Miller's depiction of their icon as a flawed human being. As theater scholar, Terry Otten, insists, "No work of [Miller's] has been more maligned and disregarded by U.S. drama critics," and he concludes by suggesting that this was "the drama that essentially drove Miller from the American stage." Throughout most of the following two decades, Miller had little success on U.S. shores, although his respect and popularity continued to grow in Europe and in other parts of the world.

It is easy to compare the details of a play like *After the Fall* with what we know of Miller's own biography (three wives from very similar backgrounds, similar dealings with the House Un-American Activities Committee [HUAC], and almost identical family backgrounds and histories), but it limits Quentin to only see him as Miller's alter ego. There is undeniably something of Marilyn Monroe in Maggie as a type, but it is not strictly a biographical portrait. When Miller began to write the part of Maggie, Monroe was still alive, but she died at about the time the play was being finished, and she was still very much a public icon at the time of its production. Miller is convinced that this timing is what ruined the play's reception—and it certainly did not help that the director Elia Kazan had the actress playing Maggie, Barbara Loden, wear a blonde wig.

The following is a synopsis of the original play, but *After the Fall* has enjoyed several revivals, for which Miller rewrote the script. His revisions mostly condense the second act—some critics felt that it overwhelmed the first act—but the play has continued to provoke cautious reception even into the 21st century. Monroe's specter seems still to haunt the play, and both the 1984 Playhouse 91 production with Frank Langella and the 2004 Broadway revival with Peter Krause met mixed reviews, as did the National Theatre's 1990 version in Great Britain, despite the director Michael Blakemore's decision to cast black actress, Josette Simon, as Maggie to help reduce the distraction of the Monroe connection.

SYNOPSIS

Act One

The play begins in darkness, but as the light rises, we see characters enter to take their places at various levels on the stage. All of the play's characters are connected to Quentin, the protagonist, whose memory creates them and who enters last. His creations seem to be communicating to him in whispers ranging from anger to appeal, but as he begins to speak, they fall still and silent. Quentin addresses an unknown "Listener," who appears to exist just beyond the front of the stage.

Quentin insists that he has stopped by wherever he is on a social visit to ask for advice on an important decision that he faces. He tells the Listener how he quit his job as a lawyer the previous year, shortly after his second wife Maggie died, and that his mother died soon after. He speaks about a woman, Holga, whom he recently met on a trip to Germany and of whom has become fond. As he mentions various characters and events in his life, we see the relevant characters, some of whom are already present in the background, stir on stage, or appear in view.

Holga is about to arrive in America for a conference and will see him again. It is largely to assess the possibilities of his future relationship with Holga that Quentin now analyzes his past. After two divorces and a series of unsatisfactory relationships with other people, Quentin is unsure if he should be considering a third marriage, even

Scene from the 1984 Playhouse 91 production of *After the Fall,* with Frank Langella as Quentin and Dianne Wiest as Maggie. *Photo by Peter Cunningham, courtesy Billy Rose Theatre Collection, The New York Public Library for the Performing Arts, Astor, Lenox and Tilden Foundations.*

though he feels close to Holga. He remains hopeful but uncertain if he should trust such a feeling when his life has been filled with the despairing events that he proceeds to reenact. His greatest fear is that no one is actually present to help him judge his life, and because of this, he is on his own. Quentin relives scenes from his past, trying through these to come to terms with who he is and to avoid what he suspects may be an inevitable despair.

The first of his creations is Felice, a woman for whom he acted as divorce lawyer and with whom he subsequently had a brief affair, even though he admits that he had no real affection for her. Felice confesses how she went to bed with her husband the night before her divorce, having felt a renewed attraction from the dignified way that Quentin had forced him to behave. We also briefly see Quentin's first two wives, Louise and Maggie, as well

as Holga, to emphasize his obsession with female relationships in his life. Felice claims that he helped liberate her by making her realize that blame is not always necessary, and she blesses him for that knowledge.

Quentin begins to recall his mother's funeral as a precursor to assessing her influence on him and how, shortly before this, he and his older brother, Dan, had announced her death to their father. Their father had been very dependent on their mother and is recovering from an operation in hospital, so Dan wants to delay telling him. Dan idolizes his father, but Quentin feels otherwise and rather bluntly announces that she is dead. Their father is devastated and instantly claims blame for all the trouble that he put her through in caring for him. Quentin recalls having spread himself against his hotel room wall in a crucifixion pose between two light fittings, but Maggie interrupts, calling him a liar, and he stops.

While in Germany prior to his mother's death, Holga had shown Quentin a concentration camp that deeply affected him, largely because he was unsure how to react. Holga reads about the horrors that went on in a Nazi torture chamber, but Quentin asks her to come outside and sit. Although not Jewish, Holga spent two years during WORLD WAR II in a forced-labor camp. She even had trouble entering the United States because of this experience, as they felt that she must have been either Jewish or a communist. She tries to embrace Quentin, but he pushes her away, making her feel embarrassed. She offers to go, unsure of how he feels about her. She does not care about marriage but would like a commitment of some kind. He can neither commit himself nor leave her, which leads him to consider the survivor guilt that affects them both—she from her wartime experiences, he from his life experiences. Holga had worked against Hitler, felt shame at her country's involvement, and has learned to live with uncertainty; it is this quality that Quentin most admires about her. He apologizes, and she goes to pick flowers.

Quentin struggles to understand what the Holocaust means to him, seeing only despair in its presence. He recalls the way that his mother talked to him as a boy, with a mixture of compliment and criticism. He worries that he has been unable to mourn his mother, Rose. She was a vibrant character who simultaneously admired and denigrated her husband, resenting her lost opportunities in life both before and after she met him. Although initially wealthy, Quentin's father lost his money after the WALL STREET CRASH, and although there was little that he could have done, Rose bitterly blames her husband. Trying to keep his business going, he used up all of their financial reserves, and Rose vindictively calls him a moron. Quentin returns to Holga, trying to hide from this past by loving her, but he feels guilty. She explains that since World War II, no one is innocent and that people should learn to live with this.

Holga explains how, toward the end of the war, she had nearly despaired and committed suicide, but a recurring dream saved her. She dreamed of an idiot child who she now feels must have represented her life and from whom she initially ran away but found that it always followed her. She finally realized that she had to embrace it and did so, despite her disgust, having come to the understanding that to get on with life, one must learn to take the bad with the good and just keep going. Hope is not innate but is something one creates. Quentin is not yet ready to believe. He thinks of his first wife, Louise, and their close friends, Elsie and her husband Lou.

Quentin recalls how ridiculously idealistic he felt when he first married. He remembers when Elsie showed him her naked body while his friend Lou was going over a legal brief for him outside. Lou, a college teacher, was subpoenaed to appear before HUAC and refused to testify, an experience that threatens to destroy his life and career. He admires Quentin as a lawyer and asks him to let Elsie read the brief, too. Elsie has persuaded her husband not to publish a textbook on which he has been working in case it further riles the college against him. The college is already wary of Lou's involvement with HUAC. Their friend, Mickey, spoke up for him in the past and saved his job, but Lou feels very insecure. He confesses that an earlier book that he had published deliberately whitewashed the Russians (again at the insistence of his wife) rather than having told the truth and made the communists look bad. He now regrets this decision, as it makes him feel vulnerable before the HUAC committee, but Elsie is angry with him for telling Quentin about this and contemptuously derides his delicacy.

Wrapped up in his own worries about HUAC, his career, and other concerns, Quentin has neglected Louise, who is fed up being ignored and plans to see a psychoanalyst to change her life. They have scarcely talked in the past seven years, and she questions the point of their continued marriage. She offers him a chance to talk, but he does not know how to respond and angers her further. He returns to his mother, recalling her disgust at his father's illiteracy and supposed hopes for Quentin, and he realizes that she had tried to use him as an accomplice against his father. He wonders how much she is to blame for how he has turned out.

Mickey arrives to speak to Quentin and offers some advice about marriage, suggesting that he pay Louise more attention. To Quentin's horror, HUAC has also subpoenaed Mickey. But unlike Lou, Mickey wants to give them the names that they demand, partly to keep his job secure and partly because he feels that he had been fooled by COMMUNISM and should speak against it. Mickey has already testified once and plans to go back; he asks Lou to join him, but he really wants permission to name him. Lou demands that Mickey not name him as it would mean instant dismissal from his teaching post, and he accuses Mickey of having sold out. Mickey, in turn, accuses Lou of being a hypocrite because of his earlier book and then leaves as Elsie comforts Lou. Mickey senses that Quentin, too, no longer wants to be his friend.

Louise wonders why Quentin became angry with her at a party the previous night, and he implies that it was because she was too talkative. He is reluctantly defending Lou and is nervous about how this will be taken. Louise's psychoanalyst has improved her confidence, and she is now more assertive, which Quentin finds unsettling. He also carries the guilt of an affair that his wife discovered and holds against him. Despite their supposed efforts to change, the marriage is falling apart, and Louise has already threatened divorce. He asks her to take some of the blame, and she calls him an idiot.

He finds refuge in the comparatively naive Maggie, an attractive receptionist at his LAW offices. He meets her at a bus stop, and she relates how one man gave her a dog then another one took it away, and they chat. A stranger tries to drag her off on the pretense of helping her buy some records, and Quentin feels drawn to protect her. Maggie explains how most men treat her as a joke. She has recently been having a reluctant affair with a married judge, but he died. Talking about her days as a hairdresser, she has Quentin feel her hair. Quentin is charmed and warns her to be more careful. As men begin to surround her, Quentin offers her a taxi fare to get her safely away.

Feeling rejuvenated, Quentin makes advances to Louise, who rebuffs him, mystified. He has missed another parents' meeting at his daughter's school and also an important meeting at work, and they have been calling for him. The head of the law firm, Max, is pressuring Quentin not to defend Lou because it will make Quentin look as if he supports Communism. Quentin is unsure what to do. Not knowing where he has been and suspecting the worst, Louise is belligerent. He tells her about meeting Maggie. This makes her angrier, and she demands he sleep on the sofa. He worries about what his daughter, Betty, will think.

Max telephones to announce that Lou has jumped in front of a train and is dead. Quentin feels bad because he had not wanted to defend Lou and suspects that Lou knew that. Recognizing his own betrayal, Quintin begins to see how people allowed the Holocaust to happen—from relief that someone else was being killed and not they. The sound of Maggie dying follows this. Louise tries to compliment Quentin on sticking by Lou, and they try to find a meeting ground, but they fail. Quentin tries to understand how and why people hurt one another and the nature of truth as he prepares to face Holga, who has arrived. As Quentin's Listener has to leave for a moment, Quentin hears Maggie call as he lights a cigarette.

Act Two

Act two begins with Quentin lighting a cigarette to indicate no passage of time. He watches Holga arrive, but when his invisible Listener returns, momentarily recalls Maggie in her wedding dress. It is his relationship to Maggie with which he must now deal before he can commit himself to Holga. Felice and Mother appear as Quentin tries to understand what has drawn women to him. Maggie calls him on the phone; it has been four years since they first met. Holga loves him but has had moments of unhappiness and self-doubt, one of which he recalls and likens to a time when Louise also voiced disappointment with him. Yet, he remains attracted to Holga's insistence that he is not beholden to her.

Quentin's mother recounts the promise that she felt when she was pregnant with him. She insisted that he go to college, which provoked an estrangement between him and his father, who had wanted him to stay home and help run the business. It is left to Dan to help out, and Quentin happily leaves to pursue his own dreams with Dan's encouragement. The books that Dan promises to send him lead Quentin to recall Maggie asking him what to read. She has become a famous singer and has invited Quentin to her home to offer him credit for inspiring her. Although still married, he goes. She is nervous but is pleased to see him and is eager to keep him there, as she is desperate for a friend. He is flattered and tries to uncover the motives behind his responses to her.

Maggie is drinking. She unsuccessfully has tried to speak to the man whom she thinks is her father but who left when she was a baby. She gives snippets of her life as a star and recounts how she publicly stuck up for communists in Quentin's honor. She admires him for not laughing at her or trying to sleep with her, but he admits to his Listener that he has laughed behind her back and was only too timid to try. She is scared to be alone, having nightmares about her mother who once tried to smother her. She blesses him as Felice once did, and he compares his compassion toward Maggie to the way his brother treated him. He again strikes his crucifixion pose but gives it up in self-disgust.

Quentin recalls a time as a young child when he felt betrayed by his mother because she went on a vacation to Atlantic City without him. He cannot mourn his mother or Maggie. He meets Maggie again; she is in disguise so that fans will not recognize her. They try to plan future meetings. Both have busy schedules, but she offers herself to him completely. He worries that others are taking advantage of her, such as her agent to whom she is leaving everything in her will. Maggie confesses to having slept with a lot of men, which she has done as an act of charity. Fans spot her and demand autographs, asking her to dance and take off her sweater, at which Quentin whisks her away. She takes him to her apartment and seduces him.

As she takes off his shoes, he thinks about his family and grows angry as he struggles to uncover who he really is beneath the layers of deception. He warns Maggie against people who use her, telling her that she is better than that, which makes her admire him the more. She starts to undress, and Quentin shifts to his defense of Reverend Har-

ley Barnes, who is being questioned before HUAC. He is realizing that just saying no to evils like the committee was not enough and that they should have done more. Maggie rises, and it is implied that Quentin stayed the night. He tries to decide whether he really loved her or he just used her as did the others. Soon after this, they marry, and Quentin begins to help her with her career. He seems in awe of her beauty at this point, though she still seems insecure.

Maggie becomes jealous and more demanding. Quentin, meanwhile, worries about finances but tries to keep up with and accommodate her whims, both personally and professionally. She wants to develop as an artist but feels held back and is becoming vindictive, complaining about musicians, and directors with whom she works. She also wants more and more attention from her husband, and he is finding it onerous. She is drinking more heavily and missing engagements. She threatens to replace Quentin with another lawyer, feeling that he is not doing enough, and she complains about his mother. She grows nasty, but recalling how betrayed his father felt when he left, Quentin insists that he will stay by her.

Quentin wants to walk to clear his head but takes away Maggie's pills before he goes, worried that she might overdose as she has done before. She insults him, suggesting that he is a closet homosexual to drive him away. She is very drunk, and he is angry, feeling that his love is being tested to its limits. Figures from his past again intrude, and he sees Lou committing suicide. He has saved Maggie from suicide twice, but his patience is wearing thin, and he wants her to take responsibility for her own life. She appears drunk again, alone at their beach cottage. He returns from work and says that he will sleep in the living room. He has called a doctor to help her. She drinks more and takes some pills. He plans to leave but instructs the maid to call an ambulance if Maggie goes too far. Maggie pleads with him to stay, offering him the pill bottle, but he will not take it; he cannot play her games anymore. He explains that he does not have the limitless love of God and is leaving so that she can no longer play the part of his victim but must fend for herself.

Quentin declares that they are equally to blame for this and that both used the other, but Maggie will not accept this and accuses him of lying. She recalls finding a hurtful note that she had found in which he wrote that the only one whom he would ever love was his daughter. He says that he only wrote this after she had turned on him, reminding him of Louise, and he felt uncertain of her love. She persuades him to lie beside her, asking him to not argue, but he no longer trusts her. He demands the pills; she swallows some more before he knocks them away. Feeling that her action is threatening him by trying to make him the cause, he starts to throttle her in desperation.

Quentin recalls again locking himself in the bathroom to worry his mother when she had gone away without him. He begins to throttle his mother and falls back in horror. Maggie accuses him of trying to kill her, as he tries to help her up; then she falls unconscious. He calls for an ambulance and explains how she was saved on that occasion and lived a while longer, although he confesses that a part of him had wanted her to die to free him. Knowing that love has limits and that there is some evil in us all that makes us capable of murder, he is fearful of committing to Holga, but he decides to take the chance. Holga's understanding that no one is innocent and her continued hope despite people's flawed nature inspires him. He acknowledges all of the people from his past; then he moves to greet Holga and exits, taking his demons with him.

CRITICAL COMMENTARY

After the Fall is not a realistic play that tries to emulate real life on stage but an expressionistic piece that attempts to create the fluid memories of its protagonist, Quentin, as he tries to evaluate his life for an unseen Listener. The figure whom Quentin addresses remains unknown throughout the play as Miller leaves it to his audience to decide whom it might be: Psychiatrist, priest, judge, old friend, God, or even the audience itself. The break between the acts comes when the Listener momentarily has to leave, implying that without a witness, Quentin is unable to proceed. His biggest fears are that he is alone, that God is no longer listening, and that with no one to hear his confession, he can

never be free of his guilt. Holga leads him to understand that freeing yourself of guilt is unnecessary and that it is better to embrace it and move on.

Because of its very visual structure, *After the Fall* is easier to watch than to read, but if one considers it more as a poetic libretto than a chronological narrative, a libretto in which mood is a key factor and in which various characters will interrupt to speak key phrases that resonate at various points in the action, *After the Fall* is easier to follow. One central conceit is that of the idiot—a description used by Quentin's mother toward his father and by both Louise and Maggie toward Quentin. It encapsulates an attitude of selfish dismissal, a refusal to recognize a common humanity, and it is Holga who teaches him to claim the idiot child, embracing it just as she embraces Quentin and thereby accepting its humanity, however flawed.

Miller was at this point more experienced as a playwright than when he tried to depict the inside of Willy Loman's head in *Death of a Salesman*. In one sense, this play shows the culmination of Miller's desire to find a form that could aptly convey the mind of a single protagonist to the audience. Throughout the play, to allow for a fluid movement of the characters as they flit in and out of Quentin's memory, the open stage is kept predominantly bare of furnishings, although Miller suggests that the setting include three rising levels that are made to look like sculptured lava, with ledges and contours to accommodate the cast. These levels curve back and forth across the stage in no fixed pattern but with the dominating symbol of the "blasted stone tower of a German concentration camp" at the top. By this threatening tower, Miller wishes to convey the continuing dark presence of the Holocaust in the minds of the cast and the audience. It symbolizes the awful truth that Quentin seeks: that all people are capable of evil either by committing it or by passively allowing it to happen.

Throughout the play, Quentin relates various events of his life to the beliefs and attitudes that allowed the Holocaust to happen. He casts himself in the role of a survivor but one whose guilt is evident as he accepts partial responsibility for all of the failures of family, marriage, and friendship in his past. The title evokes the biblical Fall when humanity lost its innocence and was forced to live with the knowledge of good and evil; the play considers how blame, responsibility, guilt, and betrayal affect how we live our lives in such a world. The "death of love" that Quentin ultimately faces is not a denial of the possibility of love but a recognition of the false idealization of love in which he had believed and an acceptance of love's limits, given the limitations of a flawed humanity. Miller is less interested in assigning blame, which he sees as ultimately reductive, than in discovering a means of forgiveness that can allow life to continue.

Quentin's concern, especially in the first act of the play, seems to be to locate his own identity, feeling that it has become lost in the pressures that are placed on him by others. He discovers that there is a tension between how people see themselves and how others see them and that division can come between people and create destructive pressures in any relationship—be it a friend, spouse, or parent. Quentin traces the gradual breakdown of his first marriage against the background of his relationships with his family and his friends. He tries to see himself as victim, even attempting to compare himself to Christ, although Maggie refuses to allow him that vanity. Quentin's vision of himself as a sacrificial figure is sheer escapism—a means of avoiding responsibility rather than accepting it—that must be broken if he is to uncover the truth of who he is.

People from his past, mostly women, frequently make brief appearances as Quentin decides which life episode he should next analyze. This scattershot approach also allows him to draw connections between them, likening Maggie to Felice in their joie de vive, Holga to Louise in their fear that he has become uninterested, or Maggie to his mother and Louise in their reactions to their husbands (each being drawn to a declaration that their husband is an idiot). By making connections, he begins to uncover his place and influence in the web of their lives and to gain a better sense of his own identity. In act two, he finally focuses on what we now realize is the most important event in his history—how he came to leave Maggie. All the other relationships were being explored to prepare him to confront this one and understand its nature.

Maggie is attracted to Quentin because she thinks that he takes her seriously, which few men have done. He feels guilty, as he does not think he was ever as noble as she believed. Yet, he did try to save her from being taken advantage of by others, even as he felt himself taking advantage of her. The excitement of their initial affair and marriage soon palls, and their relationship becomes tense and strained. Quentin is ashamed of Maggie's sexually free past and she becomes possessive and demanding. Looking after her has become a full-time job, and as her demands grow, he becomes more uncomfortable with their relationship. As a result, they grow further apart. Turning to excessive alcohol and drugs, Maggie becomes increasingly difficult, to a point where Quentin no longer feels that he can stay with her. He sees leaving Maggie as a betrayal of the same kind as his weak support of his friend Lou or as when his mother tricked him as a child to go on holiday without him. He tries to get Maggie to take responsibility for her own life, but she refuses. She will end by killing herself, the ultimate act of irresponsibility. Quentin remains unsure of how much blame he should shoulder for this, but he accepts that he was partly at fault.

Quentin's final discovery is that no one can be totally innocent, as we are all willing to betray others to save ourselves when placed in such a position. In this way, Quentin sees that blame for an event like the Holocaust needs to be accepted by everyone, however distant the event, for we are all capable of acting as the Nazis did. While Quentin recognizes that his brothers died in the camps, it was also his brothers who built and operated them, and he cannot acknowledge one connection without the other. In the face of such knowledge, the only remedy is not to give up hope; it is this aspect of Holga's personality that draws Quentin to her. She has faced and accepted the war with its countless deaths and cruelties; Quentin's challenge is to accept the "death of love" that allowed him to abandon Maggie to her inevitable fate while recognizing that his reaction was less monstrous than it was human. People are all capable of being victims and victimizers, sometimes almost simultaneously, and the only way to move forward in life is to accept the truth that we live in a fallen world in which some cruelty may be unavoidable. Taking a chance and allowing himself to love again, as Quentin does to the accompaniment of all of his demons, is his only recourse. Just as Holga embraced her idiot child, at the play's close so, too, does Quentin embrace his demons.

FIRST PERFORMANCE

After the Fall was first performed at the ANTA–Washington Square Theatre, New York City, on January 23, 1964, with the following cast:

> *Quentin:* Jason Robards, Jr.
> *Felice:* Zohra Lampert
> *Holga:* Salome Jens
> *Dan:* Michael Strong
> *Father:* Paul Mann
> *Mother:* Virginia Kaye
> *Nurses:* Faye Dunaway, Diane Shalet
> *Maggie:* Barbara Loden
> *Elsie:* Patricia Roe
> *Lou:* David J. Stewart
> *Louise:* Mariclare Costello
> *Mickey:* Ralph Meeker
> *Man in Park:* Stanley Beck
> *Carrie:* Ruth Attaway
> *Lucas:* Harold Scott
> *Chairman:* David Wayne
> *Harley Barnes:* Hal Holbrook
> *Porter:* Jack Waltzer
> *Maggie's Secretary:* Crystal Field
> *Pianist:* Scott Cunningham
> *Others:* Clint Kimbrough, John Philip Law, Barry Primus, James Greene

Directed by Elia Kazan
Set and lighting designed by JO MIELZINER
Music by David Amram
Produced by Robert Whitehead for the Repertory Theater of Lincoln Center
It ran for 208 performances.

INITIAL REVIEWS

Early audiences responded well and attendance had been so good that Miller wrote another play to add to the company's repertoire, *Incident at Vichy*. But an unduly harsh response from critics, coupled with the Repertory Theater project clearly com-

ing apart, eventually brought closure to *After the Fall.* Most reviews, such as those by John McCarten and Walter Kerr, refused to go beyond the figure of Maggie as representing Marilyn Monroe and condemned the play as discomforting and needlessly confessional. Theater scholar John Gassner was also uneasy with the play's private revelations but at least commended Miller's attempt to go beyond realism and "restore to playwriting some of the elbow-room it lost with the advent of realism." Others reviewers, including Tom Prideaux, praised Miller's courage in so openly exposing his private life and felt that it was justified by the universal relevance he gives to his experience. As Jonathan Price suggested, "honesty impelled him to deal with materials from his private life, but he has managed to see them as public issues."

Miller repeatedly insisted that the play was not strict autobiography, as in his 1964 *Life* article, "With Respect to Her Agony—But with Love," in which he unequivocally states that Maggie is not Marilyn Monroe and asks audiences and critics to view the play as a "dramatic statement of a hidden process which underlies the destructiveness hanging over this age." LILLIAN HELLMAN's mocking parody, "Lillian Hellman Asks a Little Respect for Her Agony: An Eminent Playwright Hallucinates after a Fall Brought on by a Current Dramatic Hit," was a typical response to this claim. Most not only insisted that Maggie had to be Monroe but also that the portrait was an insult. Miller's reputation seemed to be ruined in U.S. theater for several decades to follow. Monroe had become an icon within the U.S. mindset, and while critics could appreciate Miller's revelation of the truths behind other U.S. myths, they did not want their vision of Monroe tarnished.

Norman Nadel had praised the play as "a powerful drama—one to arouse an audience and enrich a season," but much of that arousal turned out to be negative. Robert Brustein wrote a lengthy scathing review, calling the play "a spiritual striptease while the band plays mea culpa" in "a three-and-one-half hour breach of taste, a confessional of embarrassing explicitness," John Simon described it as "megalomania combined with hypocrisy," and Lee Baxandell declared it "defective in its aesthetic and moral structure." While Nathan Cohen saw the autobiographical elements as irrelevant, he disliked the play because he found its central protagonist too "shallow and illogical." But while critics like Henry Popkin saw Miller as trying to absolve Quentin (and also himself) of guilt—"The others are guilty; only Quentin is innocent"—others, including Howard Taubman, saw the opposite, viewing Quentin as a character who bravely accepts responsibility for his actions. Many, including John Chapman and Richard Watts Jr., judged Jason Robards, Jr.'s, performance of Quentin, as "monumental," and "one of his finest performances" and deserving of "high praise," even while they had reservations about the play itself. While productions of *After the Fall* have continued to meet mixed receptions, with the distance of passing time and as reactions to Monroe have calmed, scholars are beginning to reevaluate it as one of Miller's better works and certainly a major theatrical experiment.

SCHOLARSHIP

The initial scholarly response to *After the Fall* was generally as dismissive as that of the critics, but early champions of the play were Robert A. Martin, Dennis Welland, and William R. Brashear, who all wrote defenses that asked for the piece to be given greater respect, pointing out its universal aspects over the specific and underlining its social message regarding the nature of love and humanity's quest for understanding. Opinions have continued to be strongly divided on several of the play's aspects, including whether or not it should be read autobiographically, whether the characters are negative or positive representations, whether or not the play's structure and technique are successful, and what Miller's aim was in writing the play. Most acknowledge that whether they liked it or not, the play marked a decided shift in Miller's focus, as Otten describes, "from the devastating forces of society to the dark passages of the human psyche."

In discussing the play's structure and technique, Edward Murray views it as defective in its construction and annoyingly repetitive, while Arthur Ganz feels the structure is "striking and unconventional" but weakened by inconsistency. Other scholars have responded with similar ambivalence, including Allan Lewis, who describes it as "sensitive, and compelling, and incomplete," and Welland, who insists that the play, "for all its faults, merits respect greater than is sometimes accorded it" but feels that it lacks a convincing theatricality. However, Welland does praise the concept and thoughtful insights of the piece, declaring it to be the "most humane of all of Miller's plays up to this point."

Several scholars have chosen to sidestep the autobiographical arguments and explore the literary ones instead, such as the connection between Miller and Camus, with the most recent being Derek Parker Royal. Others, including Susan Sontag, C. J. Gianakaris, Baldev Rathod, Peter Buitenhuis, Alan Casty, and Paul T. Nolan, have variously considered the play's connections to John Osbourne's *Inadmissible Evidence,* Shakespeare's *King Lear* and *Measure for Measure,* TENNESSEE WILLIAMS's *The Glass Menagerie,* SAUL BELLOW's *Herzog* and Peter Shaffer's *Equus.* All of these studies contain useful insights. Irving Jacobson also has compared Quentin to figures as diverse as Hitler and Christ, and John S. Stinson views both Quentin and Maggie as Christlike redeemers. In a detailed analysis of the play in his 2005 study of Miller, Christopher Bigsby considers both the play's relationship to Camus and the unproduced screenplay that Miller wrote which lies in archives at the HARRY RANSOM RESEARCH CENTER.

Those scholars who find the autobiographical elements inescapable are torn between viewing Miller's insistence that all are guilty as a trick to excuse himself for his past mistakes and the death of Monroe or as a brave self-examination in which Quentin is found guilty and faces that burden squarely. David Savran condemns the play as "a self-serving construction designed by Miller to quell the gossip surrounding one of the most public marriages of the 1950s and to clear his name of responsibility for Monroe's suicide," while Martin Gottfried suggests that the play was Miller's attempt to stay honest and to expose his own "moral inadequacy." Welland's insightful insistence that the play is less about blame than about forgiveness points to the latter response as being the more productive, and Brenda Murphy extends this reasoning. Otten's study of the play describes *After the*

Fall as "one of [Miller's] most powerful works" and points out that "Miller centers less on exposing the source of guilt than on its ongoing consequences," asking us to view the play ironically as he feels Miller intended.

CHARACTERS

Dan   Unlike Quentin, and very like Miller's own brother, KERMIT MILLER, Dan always idolized their father and was prepared to give up any chance of an education or career for the good of the family. A scholar at heart, he generously sacrifices his own dreams, even sending his books to Quentin whom he encourages to go to college and not to worry about the family. Quentin takes a more selfish route and so despises his brother for seeming the better man.

Elsie   Elsie plays the role of a sexual temptress. She contrasts to a woman like Felice by allowing us to see that Quentin does not always respond to feminine wiles and can say no. Quentin recalls her attempted seduction when she showed herself naked to him; this to him was proof that all women are untrustworthy, for he is a friend of her husband Lou and to sleep with her would be a betrayal of Lou by them both. Elsie could be the tempting Eve to his innocent Adam, but his innocence is a pose, even though he refuses this temptation. Quentin also sees in Elsie's dominance over Lou, whom she calls a "moral idiot," a reflection of the way his mother treated and internally despised his father. Yet, like the marriage of his parents, there are moments of tenderness and affection between Elsie and Lou. Lou, like Quentin's father, is portrayed as a well-meaning but weak man whose sense of wholeness is dependent on his wife's good feeling.

Father (Ike)   Very like Miller's father ISIDORE MILLER, although virtually illiterate, Ike has built up a prosperous business and generously shares his wealth with the extended family. However, he loses his capital when the stocks crash, and he uses up what little they have left by trying to keep his business afloat. He cannot forgive Quentin for leaving the family to go to college and pursue a career of his own; he expected Quentin to stay home and help as his brother Dan did. Though his father's dependency on his wife despite her, at times, caustic treatment of him is often suggested, and although he appears devastated at the news of her death, Quentin points out that his father nevertheless continues his life without her. He, too, is a survivor, but at the time, Quentin saw this as yet another betrayal.

Felice   Felice idolizes Quentin, having had a brief affair with him after he had been her divorce lawyer. Although Quentin admits that he never loved her, he did help Felice rebuild confidence in herself after a messy divorce and to see herself as a desirable woman again. Quentin describes himself as a mirror in which Felice "saw herself as . . . glorious." However, he decides that he probably took more than he gave and feels guilt over their affair. What he taught her about there being no one to blame is a fairly shallow philosophy and one that she uses to justify a nose job and to begin a hedonistic existence. Quentin will come to see the vacuity of such a philosophy with its misleading suggestion of perfect innocence.

Holga   Holga is the complete opposite of Maggie, which is a major part of her attraction for Quentin. Similar to Miller's third wife, Inge Morath, also a European with unpleasant memories of the war, Holga's greatest strength—one that Quentin strives to emulate—is that of self-knowledge: She is undemanding and independent even while she offers to make a serious commitment to their relationship if he accepts. She was horrified to recognize what the Nazis were doing in their death camps, especially as many in her own family were German officers, and she joined a vain conspiracy to try and assassinate Hitler. Her fellow conspirators kept her involvement a secret; still she spent two years in a forced-labor camp, no doubt because of her lack of support for the Nazis. However, Holga does not see herself as any better than those who stayed free, and she accepts partial blame for what the German nation did to the Jews.

Despite knowledge that many of her compatriots allowed the Holocaust to happen and even facilitated the deaths, Holga cannot entirely condemn them, recognizing the harsh reality behind the passivity or involvement of most. Like Maggie, she also considered suicide but thought too much of herself to go through with it; she realized that suicide is only an admission of hopelessness and that she is a figure who refuses to give up hope. It is her steadfastness that allows Quentin to recognize the possibilities of future commitment, despite one's past betrayals. Under her tutelage, he embraces his "idiot child," accepting the negative side of his nature as a part of a human whole for which he will be responsible, even as he may strive to lessen its influence.

Lou and Mickey Quentin's friends, Lou and Mickey, are used to show the two extremes of response to HUAC. Each has his counterpart among Miller's friends. While Lou refuses to comply and offer any names, Mickey tells all to expose communist dogma and keep his job. Lou is partially based on LOUIS UNTERMEYER, who lost his position on a television show when suspected of being a communist and went into seclusion. Mickey is reminiscent of Kazan, who testified before HUAC, which action led to his estrangement from Miller for a number of years until they began to work together again on this play.

Unlike Untermeyer, Lou loses everything and is ultimately destroyed as he gives up hope and throws himself in front of a train. To assuage his own guilt, Mickey tries to justify what he has done but loses many friends in the process. Each is given a chance to explain his decisions, and Quentin refuses to take sides for each has good reasons for following the course of action he takes. Quentin continues to help others, such as Reverend Harley Barnes, to refuse to name names but is never himself called to testify as Miller was. Quentin also comes to the realization that just refusing to name names had not been enough, just like those who refused to be involved with the Holocaust, as they still allowed the evil to happen.

Even Lou, who can be admired for not naming names before HUAC, is also capable of a betrayal, for which he feels guilt. In the past, he had written a book about Russia and whitewashed several details so as not to show the Russians in a bad light. He now wants to correct these lies but has not the courage to put this into print, especially given the pressure that his wife exerts to keep him silent so that he might keep his job the longer. Although Quentin egotistically views his friend's suicide as a brave gesture to save Quentin from having to ruin his reputation by defending Lou in court, it more likely indicates Lou's loss of faith in himself, given that neither wife nor friends truly support him any longer.

Louise Louise was Quentin's first wife and in some ways was like Miller's first wife, MARY SLATTERY. While Miller had two children by Slattery, Louise and Quentin just have the single daughter, Betty. The play depicts the lengthy breakdown of their relationship as Quentin first begins to take Louise for granted and then, when she becomes more independent, realizes how little they have left in common. All that remains to their marriage are suspicions, accusations, and guilt. A year after they married, Quentin had confessed to meeting a woman with whom he had wanted to sleep, meaning it as a compliment because he had resisted, but Louise was angry. Their marriage is filled with such miscommunications.

Although depicted as cold and self-centered through Quentin's eyes, Louise is also shown to be an intelligent woman who comes to realize that she no longer has any place in her husband's list of priorities. She reaches a stage when she sensibly decides to take charge of her life, no longer waiting for Quentin to fix everything. Since he believes in the sanctity of marriage and because they have a daughter together, he tries to resuscitate their marriage, but his efforts are neither consistent nor totally sincere. Their eventual divorce seems inevitable to both sides.

Maggie As life with Louise begins to pall, Quentin finds excitement in the arms of Maggie, a former receptionist at his law firm who becomes a famous singer after being inspired to try a new career by Quentin's caring behavior. She seems a magnet for both men and abuse, but he is seduced by her initial warm-hearted innocence. She mistakes Quentin's reticence to sleep with her as respect, and just as with Felice, he becomes a mirror in which she can see a more positive vision of herself. But it is a vision based on a lie because Quentin saw her no differently than the other men; he was just too timid to act on his attraction. Maggie offers Quentin the chance to be needed that Louise has long since refused him and an active sex life in which Louise has no interest (even making him sleep on the sofa). Ironically, with Maggie, it will come to be Quentin who decides to sleep in the living room as their relationship inevitably falls apart.

Maggie exudes what Miller has called a tyranny of innocence; her dependency on others and their opinions is so extreme that she has no real concept of self, becoming whatever plaything men demand to make them happy. When the boys ask her to strip and dance, she willingly obliges without a thought. She seems to be the ultimate victim and places herself firmly in that role. Quentin tries to teach her self-respect, but it is a lesson that she seems incapable of learning, having learned rejection from an early age from an abandoning father and abusive mother. Utterly naive about her own attraction and the way men use her, she draws Quentin into an embrace that ultimately threatens to stifle. Her depiction can be seen as a compassionate rendering of an emotionally insecure woman whose needs outweigh her demands. To counter critics who see Maggie as a negative depiction of Monroe, playwright David Rabe insists that the portrait "treats her with more dignity than anybody else has ever treated her in her career or life."

Promiscuous and self-destructive, Maggie's increasing use of alcohol and drugs alienates her even from those who want to help. She has made a number of suicide attempts to gain attention, but finally Quentin refuses to help her, insisting that she take responsibility for her own life. He also begs for her to admit that she is partly responsible for the breakdown of their relationship. She refuses on both counts and kills herself, leaving Quentin with the burden of guilt that this is something that he might have prevented had he been a stronger man, yet with also the understanding that his relief at being free is all too human a reaction. Although a famous singer rather than a movie star, it is hard not to see

Monroe behind this portrait, even though some of the details are not exact.

Mother (Rose) Quentin's mother, Rose, (partly based on Miller's own mother AUGUSTA MILLER), like Felice and for a time Maggie, idolized and blessed Quentin, although she was also not above manipulating him for her own ends. Rose is convinced that her younger son is destined for greatness and simultaneously corrects him as she constantly holds him above his brother, who generously bears no resentment. Feeling that she has a special bond with Quentin, she "seduces" him to act as an accomplice in her battles against her husband, continuously forcing him to take her side and subtly to denigrate his father whom she cannot forgive for losing the family fortune. Quentin's realization of this manipulation sours his memories of her and leaves him unable to mourn.

Despite her professed love for him, Quentin sees Rose's capacity for betrayal, as when she went away on holiday without him to be free of a demanding child, which made him feel tricked and abandoned. She is similarly ambivalent about her husband: She suggests that she could have done much better, and so she denigrates him; in the next sentence, she asserts that he is a great man. For all her antagonism, their marriage lasts up to her heart attack on the way home from the hospital where her husband is having an operation. It is a death that upsets her husband but concerns Quentin mainly because he cannot mourn.

Quentin In some ways, Quentin is the only character whom we can assess as he creates the play, and each of the other characters only exist in the way that they relate to him. Felice, Elsie, Louise, Maggie, Holga, and Mother (Rose) are the main women in Quentin's life. Each one is different in terms of herself, how Quentin views her, and how she treats Quentin. Each represents a subtly different type of relationship even while all relate to one another. Quentin uses past experiences to analyze his own character by trying to understand what lay behind the things that he said and did and how he responded to events. Just as he felt caught between his parent's arguments,

Quentin feels caught between friends and opts out of becoming deeply involved with either, protecting himself by staying apart—but in doing this, he has lost the sense of who he really is.

Working up to his third marriage, Quentin's life appears to have been a series of betrayals and letdowns. Initially, he enjoys casting himself as victim in his relationships, claiming that women have injured him and seeing himself as having suffered for others in a Christlike fashion—a pose that he quite literally tries to adopt at times to the anger of his victims. It is a pose that he too will come to see is false. His growing honesty about his past betrayals allows him to become more sympathetic as he attempts to face the truth and accept responsibility for past actions. Quentin tends to detach himself from people when things become too problematic, which has led to a series of failed relationships. For his relationship with Holga to work, he must now find strength to commit and to fight his tendency to hang back from responsibility. Miller allows Quentin to be very human with the same kind of flaws, doubts, and uncertainties that many of us face. In this way, if Quentin can find hope, as he finally does, then Miller is letting us know that there is hope for us all.

Quentin is a lawyer and treats his life as if it were a law case that he is investigating. In many ways, he is his own "Listener," as the play could be seen as an interior monologue in which Quentin judges himself, acting as prosecution and defense. He sees his relationship with his mother as being at the heart of his trouble with other women, as he still resents her betrayals—going on holiday without him and using him in her battle against his father—and, therefore, expects all women ultimately to act in the same hurtful way. But Quentin must learn to accept his own share of the blame, which he does by the play's close, and ironically having found himself guilty rather than innocent, he leaves the stage with the hope of a brighter future with Holga.

MOVIE AND TELEVISION ADAPTATIONS

In 1967, Paramount Pictures bought the film rights to *After the Fall* although Miller stipulated that they were not to refer to Monroe in any of their publicity. Miller wrote a screenplay in which he took out the character of Holga, reduced the role of the parents, and centralized attention on Maggie, who was now a film star. However, this project never materialized. Directed by Gilbert Cates, *After the Fall* was eventually made for television and aired on NBC on December 10, 1974, starring Christopher Plummer and Faye Dunaway (who had played the minor role of one of the nurses in the original production). Miller reworked some of the scenes for this version, emphases were changed, and the overall structure of the play was tightened, but John O'Connor of the *New York Times* still reviewed it as "an egotistical abomination" (91), despite feeling that it was an improvement upon the original stage production.

FURTHER READING

Baxandell, Lee. "Arthur Miller: Still the Innocent." *Encore* (May–June 1964), 16–19.

Bigsby, Christopher. *"After the Fall." Arthur Miller: A Critical Study.* Cambridge: Cambridge University Press, 2005, 228–247.

———. "The Fall and After: Arthur Miller's Confession." *Modern Drama* 10 (September 1967): 124–136.

Brashear, William R. "The Empty Bench: Morality, Tragedy, and Arthur Miller." *Michigan Quarterly Review* 5 (1966): 270–278.

Brustein, Robert. "Arthur Miller's Mea Culpa." *New Republic*, February 8, 1964, 26–30.

Buitenhuis, Peter. "Arthur Miller: The Fall from the Bridge." *Canadian Association for American Studies Bulletin* 3 (Spring–Summer 1967): 55–71.

Burhans, Clinton S., Jr. "Eden and the Idiot Child: Arthur Miller's *After the Fall.*" *Ball State University Forum* 20, no. 2 (Spring 1979): 3–16.

Casty, Alan. "Post–Loverly Love: A Comparative Report." *Antioch Review* 26 (Fall 1966): 399–411.

Centola, Steven R. "The Monomyth and Arthur Miller's *After the Fall.*" *Studies in American Drama 1945 to the Present* 1 (1986): 49–60.

———. "Unblessed Rage for Order: Arthur Miller's *After the Fall.*" *Arizona Quarterly* 39, no. 1 (Spring 1983): 62–70.

Chapman, John. "*After the Fall* Overpowering." *New York Daily News*, January 24, 1964, n.p.

Cismaru, Alfred. "Before and *After the Fall.*" *Forum* 11, no. 2 (1973): 67–71.

Cohen, Nathan. "Hollow Heart of a Hollow Drama." *National Review,* April 7, 1964, 289–290.

Engle, John D. "The Metaphor of Law in *After the Fall.*" *Notes on Contemporary Literature* (1979): 11–12.

Fallaci, Oriana. "A Propos of After the Fall." *World Theatre* 14 (1965): 79, 81, 83–84, 87.

Ganz, Arthur. "Arthur Miller: After the Silence." *Drama Survey* 3, no. 4 (Spring–Fall 1964): 520–553.

Gassner, John. "Broadway in Review." *Educational Theatre Journal* 16 (May 1964): 177–179.

Gianakaris, C. J. "Theatre of the Mind in Miller, Osbourne and Shaffer." *Renascence* 30 (1977): 33–42.

Gottfried, Martin. *Arthur Miller: His Life and Work.* New York: Da Capo, 2003.

Hellman, Lillian. "Lillian Hellman Asks a Little Respect for Her Agony: An Eminent Playwright Hallucinates after a Fall Brought on by a Current Dramatic Hit." *Show* (May 1964), n.p.

Jacobson, Irving. "Christ, Pygmalion, and Hitler in *After the Fall.*" *Essays in Literature* 2 (August 1974): 12–27.

Kerr, Walter. "Miller's *After the Fall*—As Walter Kerr Sees It." *New York Herald Tribune,* January 24, 1964, sec. 1, p. 11.

Koppenhaver, Allen J. "*The Fall* and After: Albert Camus and Arthur Miller." *Modern Drama* 9 (September 1966): 206–209.

Lewis, Allan. "Arthur Miller—Return to the Self." *American Plays and Playwrights of the Contemporary Theatre.* Rev. ed. New York: Crown, 1970, 35–52.

Martin, Robert A. "Arthur Miller's *After the Fall:* The Critical Context." In *The Achievement of Arthur Miller: New Essays,* edited by Steven Centola, 119–126. (Dallas, Tex.: Contemporary Research, 1995).

McCarten, John. "Miller on Miller." *New Yorker,* February 1, 1964, 59.

Meyer, Nancy, and Richard Meyer. "*After the Fall:* A View from the Director's Notebook." In *Theater: An Annual of the Repertory Theater of Lincoln Center, Volume Two,* edited by Barry Hyams, 43–73. (New York: Hill and Wang, 1965).

Miller, Arthur. "With Respect to Her Agony—But with Love." *Life,* February 7, 1964, 66.

Moss, Leonard. "Biographical and Literary Allusion in *After the Fall.*" *Education Theatre Journal* 18 (March 1966): 34–40.

Murphy, Brenda. "Arendt, Kristeva, and Arthur Miller: Forgiveness and Promise in *After the Fall.*" *PMLA* 117, no. 2 (March 2002): 314–316.

Murray, Edward. "Point of View in *After the Fall.*" *CLA Journal* 10 (1966): 135–142.

Nadel, Norman. "Miller Play One of Inward Vision." *New York World-Telegram,* January 24, 1964, n.p.

Nolan, Paul T. "Two Memory Plays: *The Glass Menagerie* and *After the Fall.*" *McNeese Review* 17 (1966): 27–38.

O'Connor, John J. "TV: Miller's *After the Fall* on NBC." *New York Times,* December 10, 1974, 91.

Otten, Terry. *The Temptation of Innocence in the Dramas of Arthur Miller.* Columbia: University of Missouri Press, 2002.

Popkin, Henry. "*After the Fall,* 'The Real Shocker.'" *Vogue,* March 15, 1964, 66.

Price, Jonathan. "Arthur Miller: Fall or Rise?" *Drama* 73 (Summer 1964): 39–40.

Prideaux, Tom. "A Desperate Seach by a Troubled Hero." *Life,* February 7, 1964, 64B–65.

Rathod, Baldev C. "A Natural Guiltiness: A Comparative Study of *After the Fall* and *Measure for Measure.*" In *Arthur Miller: Twentieth Century Legend,* edited by Syed Mashkoor Ali, 230–238. (Jaipur, India: Surabhi, 2006).

Royal, Derek Parker. "Camusian Existentialism in Arthur Miller's *After the Fall.*" *Modern Drama* 43 (2000): 192–203.

Savran, David. *Communists, Cowboys, and Queers: The Politics of Masculinity in the Work of Arthur Miller and Tennessee Williams.* Minneapolis: University of Minnesota Press, 1992.

Simon, John. "Theatre Chronicle." *Hudson Review* 17 (Summer 1964): 234–236.

Sontag, Susan. "Theater." *Vogue,* August 15, 1965, 51–52.

Stanton, Stephen S. "Pessimism in *After the Fall.*" In *Arthur Miller: New Perspectives,* edited by Robert A. Martin, 159–172. (Engelwood Cliffs, N.J.: Prentice–Hall, 1982).

Stinson, John J. "Structure in *After the Fall:* The Relevance of the Maggie Episodes to the Main Themes and Christian Symbolism." *Modern Drama* 10 (1967): 233–240.

Taubman, Howard. "A Cheer for Controversy." *New York Times,* February 2, 1964, sec. 2: 1.

Watts, Richard, Jr. "The New Drama by Arthur Miller." *New York Post*, January 24, 1964, 38.

Welland, Dennis. *"After the Fall." Arthur Miller: A Study of His Plays.* London: Methuen, 1979, 90–104.

Wertheim, Albert. "Arthur Miller: *After the Fall* and After." In *Essays on Contemporary American Drama,* edited by Hedwig Block and Albert Wertheim, 19–32. (Munich: M. Hueber, 1981).

All My Sons (1947)

Miller wrote the play *All My Sons* over several years, wanting to perfect it prior to performance rather than suffer the ignominy of another BROADWAY failure as *The Man Who Had All the Luck* had been. Miller had recently been assigned a new agent KATHERINE BROWN, who offered the play to Herman Shumlin, producer and director of LILLIAN HELLMAN's plays, who was looking for a good social drama. Shumlin claimed he could not understand it, and turned it down. She tried the THEATRE GUILD who were interested, but reluctant to commit. Miller suggested they offer it to HAROLD CLURMAN and ELIA KAZAN who had come to fame with the GROUP THEATER; Clurman accepted immediately and Kazan was chosen to direct.

The play has often been viewed as a work heavily influenced by the social plays of HENRIK IBSEN in terms of its classic structure, the way it allows the past to encroach on the present, and its adherence to REALISM. Miller admits this influence. He had experimented with form and style in most of his previous plays and had little success; this time he was determined to write a realistic play that would be widely accepted in a theatrical climate almost exclusively devoted to realism.

Miller's mother-in law, Julia Slattery, had told him about a young girl in Ohio who turned her father into the FBI for having manufactured faulty aircraft parts during the war. The timely idea of a play about a war-profiteer grew from that piece of gossip, but the characters and complex relationships we see are pure Miller. Although some complained that the play's subject was unpatriotic and that U.S. manufacturers would not have acted like Joe Keller, reports of the dealings of the Wright Corporation with the army at that time, with their falsified tests and reports, their refusal to destroy defective material, and the court sending several of the company's officers to jail, suggested otherwise. But the play's focus on a particular family and the relationship between a father with his two sons—a dynamic that Miller continued to explore throughout his career—makes it more than political commentary. *All My Sons* opened at the Coronet Theatre in New York City at the beginning of 1947 while the experience of the recently fought WORLD WAR II was still fresh in people's minds.

The play's working title had been *The Sign of The Archer*, directing us to the date of the son Larry's death under the sign of Sagittarius and the horoscope on which the Keller's neighbor, Frank Lubey, is working. This emphasizes the key role that Miller sees Larry playing despite Larry's having died two years before the play even begins; this also underscores Miller's perception of how the past continually influences the present; it finally highlights Miller's interest in fate and how that applies to the action of the play. Keller may have avoided legal punishment, but there are moral laws that he has broken with his criminal act, laws that appear to be judged by a higher court. Another working title had been *Morning, Noon, and Night*, which reflects the play's close adherence to the Greek conception of the three unities, which insist that a drama should take place at a single location within a 24 hour period. The play had a lengthy run, won both the Donaldson and the New York Drama Critics Circle Awards, and put Miller on the map of American theater.

SYNOPSIS

Act One

The Kellers' backyard is hedged in, offering no escape for its inhabitants. To one side is the stump of a broken apple tree that becomes increasingly significant as the play progresses. It is a fairly opulent yard, and whoever owns it is a financial success; that man is Joe Keller. Keller is a businessman whose business has taken over his life—even on a Sunday morning, he cannot separate himself from commerce as he reads the want ads in the paper while sitting in his yard. A neighbor, Dr. Jim Bayliss, sits with him, and they make small talk. Another neighbor, Frank Lubey, joins them, and Keller offers him a section of the paper. Frank comments on the tree that was blown down the previous night during high winds. He points out the tree's connection to Keller's son Larry for whom it was planted as a memorial. Larry, we learn, has been missing in action for three years and Frank, at Keller's wife's request, is preparing a horoscope to see if the day Larry went missing was a favorable day on which nothing truly bad could have happened to him. Kate Keller wants to believe that her son is still alive, even while everyone else has accepted that he is dead.

Jim Bayliss asks Frank if he has seen his young son, Tommy, who has run off with his thermometer.

When Frank suggests that Tommy might have the makings of a doctor, Jim strenuously objects, suggesting that the life of a doctor holds no rewards. Jim asks where Ann is, and Keller tells them that she is asleep in the house because she arrived late the night before. Ann, we will learn, is the daughter of Keller's old neighbor and business partner, Steve Deever, in whose house Jim and his family now live. Jim's wife, Sue, comes to tell her husband that he is needed by a patient. It is clear that Jim is unhappy with his job as a doctor and that Sue is unhappy with her husband; she is jealous of his female patients and disappointed by the modest amount of money that he makes.

Frank's wife, Lydia, calls to Frank to come home and fix the toaster. These people happily come and go, showing how Keller is popular and accepted

Scene from the 1990 L.A. Center Theatre production of *All My Sons*, with Gregory Wagrowski, Julie Fulton, and Bill Pullman. *Courtesy Billy Rose Theatre Collection, The New York Public Library for the Performing Arts, Astor, Lenox and Tilden Foundations.*

by his neighbors. Lydia also asks after Ann, and we learn that Ann used to be Larry's girlfriend. Lydia is one of Ann's contemporaries and points out how, while she is married with three children, Ann remains single and alone. Chris Keller comes out, and Frank calls Lydia home. Chris looks like his father, but it is clear that he is more educated—he reads the book section of the paper. Keller tries to talk to him about the tree and is worried how his wife will react. A neighbor's son, Bert, arrives to play. Keller plays an imaginary game with the local children, in which he makes them his deputy police officers and pretends to have a jail in his cellar—highly ironic for a man who we will learn has broken the LAW but avoided punishment. Bert reports on what the local children have been doing and asks to see the jail. Keller tells him that this is not allowed but reminds him that he has a gun, so he really must be a lawman. Bert tells Keller about a dirty word that Tommy has said but is too embarrassed to repeat it, so Keller sends him off to look for more suspicious happenings.

Chris and Keller discuss the broken tree. Chris saw his mother Kate outside late last night and heard her cry when the tree broke. They are both worried about how the broken tree will affect Kate. She is the only person who still acts as if she believes that Larry is alive, and they have never contradicted her belief, although Chris is uncertain that this has been the right thing to do. Chris now needs her to accept Larry's death because he wants to marry Ann, something he could not do if Larry were still alive. Keller refuses to help Chris deal with his mother. He would prefer it if Chris would forget about Ann and not shake things up, but Chris refuses. He has not asked Ann yet, but he is determined that she is the girl for him. He provokes his father into agreeing to help by threatening to move away and leave the family business. Unlike his father, Chris hates the business; this scares Keller, who feels that he has sacrificed much to keep the business going for his sons.

Kate enters to tease Keller about throwing out a sack of potatoes, thinking that they were garbage. She complains of a headache and talks about Larry, recounting a dream that she had in which Larry was falling and she could not save him. The

tree breaking has clearly upset her, and she sees its breaking as a bad omen. Chris finds it impossible to turn the conversation toward his plans for Ann because Kate insists that Larry is alive and that Ann is keeping herself free because she is waiting for Larry. When Chris tries to make her face the truth of Larry's death, she refuses to listen and sends him away to get aspirin. But Kate knows the score; as soon as Chris leaves she tells her husband that they must stop Ann from marrying Chris and start acting as if they all believe Larry is alive. Keller refuses to take sides, despite Kate's mounting anger. In revenge, when Bert returns, Kate sends him packing, ordering Keller to stop playing the jail game as it is tempting fate. These two obviously share a guilty secret despite Keller's assumed innocence.

Chris brings Ann with him, and when he compliments her appearance, his mother suggests that she has put on weight. Ann looks to see how the place has changed in the three years that she has been gone. Jim Bayliss comes over to say hello but must soon return home because another patient has called. Ann is shocked to see Kate acting as though Larry will return for she has accepted Larry's death and moved on. Chris and Keller joke around to break the tension. Ann tells them that when her father has served his sentence, her mother plans to take him back. Since Kate keeps asking Ann about Larry, Ann bluntly tells her that she is no longer waiting. Kate, however, is not ready to give up.

When Frank comes to say hello and ask after her family, it is clear that Ann is uncomfortable talking about her father. Her brother George is now a lawyer. Ann asks if the neighborhood still talks about her father's case, and Keller says not. He explains how his jail game with the local children grew out of their confusion over what had actually happened. The group recalls the case that got Steve sent to jail, a case for which Keller was also indicted but was later exonerated. Keller bluffed it out, and the neighbors soon forgave him, but Steve was found guilty and is seen as a murderer for selling cracked cylinder heads to the air force, causing 21 planes to crash. Keller is proud of the way in which he beat the charges and rebuilt his business. He insists that Steve should come back to this town to live rather than hide away when he gets out. Ann cannot understand why Keller holds no grudge against Steve, as she, George, and even Chris hate and utterly reject him.

Ann suggests that Larry could have flown a plane with one of those faulty parts. Kate tries to shut them all up, but they ignore her; she leaves in exasperation. Keller insists on explaining that the parts had gone to a model of plane that Larry never flew. Keller defends Steve (and, surreptitiously, also himself) by explaining how the parts came to be shipped in the first place. Their company was under pressure to produce and could not afford to lose a day's production, so the hairline cracks were covered up. Keller insists that if he could have gone into work that day, he would have junked the parts, but Steve had not been able to make that call because he was too fearful of the consequences. Keller's explanation of Steve's behavior seems so convincing that it can almost be believed to be true, partly because Keller himself seems to believe it. He wants Ann to forgive her father so that he might find absolution for himself. He insists that there was no evil intent, but this does not matter to Ann or Chris: They both see the end effect as overriding intent and refuse to excuse or forgive the man whom they see as guilty. Keller suggests that they go out to eat and leaves to make the reservation.

Ann and Chris are left alone to discuss their relationship. Chris admits his love, and Ann is relieved to hear him finally say it because she loves him too. Chris, however, feels awkward, largely because of his war experiences. He saw many men die, but he survived and now feels guilty of taking advantage of his survival. Ann tries to persuade him that he has earned what he has and that he should accept it. They kiss but are interrupted as Keller comes to tell Ann that she has a phone call from her brother George. They decide to wait until after dinner to tell Kate that they plan to marry. Keller is nervous about why George might be calling and why he should be visiting his father after having ignored him for so long. He even suspects that Ann might only be there to find out some information on him. He insists that Chris take his company without shame, and Chris agrees, although he feels a little unnerved as to why his father is saying all of this

now. Ann's conversation with George is audible; George is clearly upset and is planning to come to see them. While Chris takes Ann for a drive, Kate and Keller worry about what George has learned from his father.

Act Two

Act two begins later that evening as the family waits for George and prepares to go to dinner. Chris clears away the tree, and his mother tries to win him to her side, suggesting that he needs to protect his parents. Chris is unconcerned and unsuspicious. Ann chats with Sue Bayliss, who comes looking for her husband. Jim has gone to fetch George from the station. More is told about the Baylisses' unhappy marriage as Sue complains about Jim's relationship with the Kellers. Inspired by Chris's idealism, Jim wants to do medical research, but Sue insists that he remain as a higher-paid doctor. Because of his family responsibilities, he capitulates, but he resents both his work and his wife. Sue sees Chris as a hypocrite who lives off his father's business and lets Ann know that although the community has forgiven Keller, they believe that he was guilty. He is only admired for being smart enough to beat the charges. This raises the issue of whether or not Chris knows the truth or whether he really believes his father to be innocent. Chris returns to ask Sue, who is a nurse, to help calm his mother down because she seems agitated. Ann is shocked at what Sue has told her and shares this with Chris, wanting to know if he is keeping any secrets. Chris insists that he could not accept his father if he suspected anything, which satisfies Ann and prepares the audience for Chris's eventual rejection of his father when he uncovers the truth.

Keller plans to bribe George into complicity by offering to set him up in town as a lawyer; he even tells Ann that he is prepared to offer Steve a job, which horrifies Ann and Chris. Keller is nervous about his future relationship with Chris and wants the children to forgive Steve so that they will go easier on him if they learn the truth. Lydia comes over to fix Kate's hair for their outing, and Keller takes her in with him. Jim arrives looking worried; he has kept George in his car and suggests that Ann and Chris take him somewhere else to sort things out. Ann nearly accedes, but Chris refuses to avoid a confrontation as it implies guilt. He insists that George join them.

George enters in a belligerent state and seems unsure of how to behave to either his sister or Chris. They introduce him to Sue, and he is fairly blunt with her when she invites him over to her house, saying that he prefers her house the way it was when he lived there. Jim takes her home, and Chris tries to be friendly as they catch up on what each has done since the war. George is wearing his father's hat and seems troubled by his recent meeting with his father. His father has told him that when the faulty parts were coming off the line, he had called for Keller, but he been told Keller had the flu and could not come in. When he spoke to him later on the phone, Keller had said to cover up the cracks and that he would take responsibility, but in court, Keller denied the phone call and let Steve take full blame. George tells all this to Chris, but Chris refuses to believe it, and the two argue the feasibility of the case.

George had believed Keller's story of what happened because Chris had and because he admired Chris. This is the first time that he has talked to his father about it, and now he can no longer believe in Keller's innocence. George wants to take Ann away as he does not want her marrying into such a family. He insists that Chris must have known the truth all along, and he will prove it by talking to Keller, but Chris asks George not to make a fuss as his mother is not well. Ann supports this. However, Kate joins them before they can get George to leave. She begins to mother George, deflating his anger and breaking the tension. Lydia runs on to greet George, obviously an old girlfriend, but when he left to fight in the war, she went with Frank instead. Kate tells George that they want him to move back and that she will find him a nice girl. As the mood lightens, Keller enters.

George greets Keller politely, and Keller asks after his father, telling George that he would welcome Steve back. George points out that his father hates Keller. Keller reminds George of previous times when Steve has not accepted fault after a mistake and tried to blame others, in an effort to convince George not to trust anything that his

father might have told him. George is convinced by his argument, and the atmosphere lightens as he decides to join them for dinner, until Kate lets slip that Keller has not been out sick for 15 years. George picks up on this as Keller's whole defense had been that he was not at work the day that the parts were shipped because he was laid up with flu—it becomes clear that he had purposely stayed home to avoid blame. Tempers are held in check while Frank comes by to report on Larry's horoscope. He has discovered that the day Larry died was a favorable day on which only good things could have happened to him. Chris is irritated by this as he feels that it gives his mother false hope about his brother. George suggests that he and his sister both leave at once. Kate is delighted at the idea that Ann might leave and has already packed her bags, but Ann refuses to leave unless Chris tells her to go. She escorts George to his taxi.

To Kate's horror, Chris insists that he plans to marry Ann and that Larry is dead. As Keller tries to support his son, Kate turns on him, physically striking him in her frustration. Kate declares that they have to believe that Larry is alive because if he was dead, then his own father killed him. Chris sees the implication of Keller's guilt in this and finally accepts the truth: His father knew about the faulty parts. Chris turns on his father who breaks down and confesses, trying to justify what he did—but his excuses seem feeble next to the moral implications of the act. Trying to convince Chris that he did it for him, thinking that this will make it all right, just angers Chris further. Chris attacks his father calling him worse than an animal before he stumbles away in distress with his father calling after him.

Act Three

The final act is brief, taking place in the early hours of the morning as Kate sits up waiting for Chris's return and Ann waits inside her room. Jim keeps Kate company and asks her what has happened. He confesses that he had realized a long time ago that Keller was guilty but is sure Chris had not known. Kate thinks that Chris must have known on some level, so she is surprised that he has taken it so badly. Jim believes that this discovery will change Chris, forcing him to lose his idealism. He wishes that it could be otherwise because Jim finds that the belief that some ideals cannot be compromised is uplifting, but he cannot believe that Chris will turn in his own father. He recalls a time when he had rebelled and run off to pursue medical research, but when Sue came and cried, he returned and became a general practitioner to support her. When Keller enters, Jim offers to go and look for Chris.

Keller is on edge and does not know what to do. They wonder how much Ann has worked out and why she is still there. Keller asks his wife for advice, and Kate suggests that he offer to turn himself in to gain Chris's forgiveness, assuring him that Chris would never allow him to go to jail. Keller dislikes this idea, as he still does not feel he has done anything wrong—he did what he did for his family and believes that this justifies it. Even Kate knows that there are some things bigger than the family, but Keller insists that if there really are, then he will put a bullet in his head. They wonder what Chris is thinking and if his war experiences have changed him. Keller insists that Larry would not have acted this way, and Kate tries to calm him.

Ann enters and tells the Kellers that she will not try to reopen the case. They must, however, admit in front of Chris that Larry is dead so that he will stay with her because she cannot stand to be alone any longer. Kate refuses, despite Ann telling them that she has firm proof. Protectively sending Keller into the house, Ann reluctantly shows Kate a letter that she received from Larry; the letter's contents cause Kate to break down. Chris returns. He has decided to leave and start a new life alone; having lived off his father's money and blinded himself to the truth, he feels compromised. He will not allow Ann to go with him. Ann will not accept this, insisting that he needs to sacrifice his father so that he and she can be together. Chris refuses, excusing his father as having simply followed the "dog eat dog" law of the land and, therefore, not being responsible. Ann calls to Kate to help her get Chris to turn in his father, but Kate refuses. At this point, Keller returns, and he and Chris have their final confrontation.

Keller tries to persuade Chris to stay—offering to give their money away and even to go to jail, despite his lack of guilt. Chris cannot turn him in but feels the loss of the idealized picture that he has held for so long of his father. Ann forces the situation by giving Chris Larry's letter before Kate can stop her. This rekindles Chris's idealistic fury against Keller as he reads how Larry committed suicide out of shame for his father's actions. The letter also drives Keller to accept his guilt and to recognize the responsibility to others that he has up until now ignored: "Sure, [Larry] was my son. But I think to him they were all my sons. And I guess they were." Chris is determined to take him to jail. Keller seems ready to go, entering the house to get his jacket. But while Kate tries to dissuade Chris, they hear a gunshot. Keller has taken his own life, and Kate and Chris are left distraught, holding one another in their grief.

CRITICAL COMMENTARY

Miller utilizes a Greek tragic format in *All My Sons* that hinges upon issues of fate. Keller is fated to die, partly because of who he is and partly because of the world in which he lives. The Greeks believed in a world controlled by fates that were directed by the gods, but Miller prefers to believe that people's characters have the biggest influence in determining their fate. Failure, in Miller's eyes, should not be blamed on an indefinable hostile fate or social system but on individuals who refuse to accept their responsibilities and connection to fellow human beings. It is the flaws that exist in Keller's character that ensure his defeat rather than any divine authority. Keller knowingly shipped out faulty aircraft parts that may have caused numerous deaths. To try to save his business, he has knowingly put others at risk. Because he refuses to accept responsibility for his actions, his guilt drives him toward the destruction of his relationship with both the sons whom he so wanted to have follow in his footsteps, and finally, of himself.

Once Keller committed the crime, his fate was sealed, and it would only be a matter of time before the "birds come home to roost," as Miller likes to put it. Ann's arrival is the catalyst for the truth to come out, especially as she carries with her the ultimate proof of Keller's moral guilt: Larry's letter. From the moment of Ann's arrival, tension starts to mount in the Keller household. The reading of the letter is no less a climax for Keller than Oedipus's discovery that he too has killed one of his own blood and becomes as equally self-destructive.

Keller chose to ignore his responsibilities to anyone outside of his immediate family, including his friend and partner Steve Deever and the pilots flying the planes to which his faulty parts were supplied. For Keller, his belief in family first and the power of bluff have been instilled in him by the approval of his society, but that does not make him right. He stubbornly refuses to see the bigger picture until the very end when he is confronted with evidence of his son's suicide. Larry had killed himself because he had seen the wider implications of his father's actions from the start and felt too ashamed to live. Keller finally sees this when he admits to Chris that all the pilots killed by his faulty parts were in a sense his sons and that he should have treated them with the same regard.

Keller is exonerated by the flawed U.S. legal system for the crime that he committed and allows his partner to take full blame. Deever was not wholly innocent as he agreed to cover up the cracks, so we never perceive his punishment as unfair or feel any real sympathy for him; yet, Keller must also pay for his actions, if not not in a legal sense then certainly in a moral one. Miller's image of the Keller house as a prison—Keller jokes with the local children that he has a jail in his basement—only serves to suggest where Keller should rightfully be. Yet, in another sense, he truly *is* in a prison, a restrictive prison of denial in which he has to constantly conceal the truth. The timeless quality of the Keller house, which is observed by those who have not seen it since the trial, indicates that this is a family for which time has essentially stopped.

Even knowing Keller's guilt as all of his neighbors do, his community accepts and forgives him—but his sons cannot. Keller's defense is that he did it for his sons so that he would have a thriving business to hand to them. However, when we consider the murderous indifference of his actions, we realize that he is morally lax and deserves punishment. George, a lawyer and therefore a representative of legal justice, manages to uncover the truth but seems unable to pursue this realization toward any legal action. He leaves it instead to Keller's

own son, Chris. The moral punishment that Chris forces home to Keller is the loss of his sons. Chris finds his father guilty of social irresponsibility and demands that he be sent to jail to pay legally for his crime. Keller's suicide can be read as either the desperate response of a man who is left with no way out or as a just act of self-immolation in recognition of personal guilt.

Miller wrote this play with the intention to shock and promote discussion. Its small-town U.S. location, found to be fraught with corruption, is indicative of the extent to which Miller felt that the moral turpitude of America had spread. Although it contains many universal lessons, the play is also a very timely one. Written and set in 1947, *All My Sons*, with its tale of a family torn apart by secrets and lies, portrays many discordances that arose within U.S. families during the 1940s. The decade began amid the throes of a destructive international conflict and saw the development of even more destructive, domestic conflicts within the family itself.

The GREAT DEPRESSION of the 1930s had seriously undermined the prestige of many fathers in taking away from them the role of provider. Following on the heels of the Depression, World War II accentuated these familial difficulties. Fathers and sons were dislocated from their homes by the draft, some never returning. Those who returned either found that the world had changed in their absence or felt a need to change it in the light of their experiences. Their efforts met great resistance, but the mood of change was in the air, however hard that some chose to ignore it. Both change and resistance would serve to deepen the gulf between father and child; this is tellingly portrayed in Miller's tale of the Kellers.

World War II helped to drive an ideological wedge between those who fought and those who stayed home. Men like Chris and Larry Keller who had gone to fight were changed by their experience; affected by the sacrifices that they saw their comrades make, they developed a heightened sense of social responsibility. This leads Larry to kill himself for shame at what his father has done and leads Chris to set himself almost impossible idealistic standards by which to live. Shaken by the horrors of World War II, society recognized the need for change, but the soldiers who fought often held different views from those who stayed at home as to how to initiate that change.

For those at home, such as the older generation of Kellers, a return to the prosperous twenties, with its emphasis on work and individual family units, offered greater security. But men like Chris, who by their service had experienced a new community-based society of mutual help where one's "family" was society itself, found themselves at odds with such an introverted concept. This socialist spirit, which had been growing in the United States since the Depression, was at odds with the selfish capitalistic spirit that had captured the country in its postwar economic boom. But Chris, despite his newfound socialism, is still a product of the more traditional generation and is reluctant to throw away his old values. While he dislikes his father's CAPITALISM, he still loves and admires his father, and he is confused as to what he should do.

Like so many young men of the time, Chris finds that he needs a strong father figure to allow him to make sense of the changing world, a figure who would remain unchanging and inviolate, from whom he could derive stability for himself. Joe Keller, like many fathers of his time, cannot possibly live up to such an ideal given that those same social pressures affecting Chris are also affecting him. Keller tries to offer Chris the only stability that he knows in the form of his business, but Chris is looking for a moral stability rather than this material one. Keller, for all his faults, tries to be the best father that he can be, given the constraints of the time and his own nature and beliefs (themselves products of that time). But having successfully tapped into the ever-flowing stream of U.S. materialism and competitiveness that was so prevalent in the 1940s, he is faced with offspring who have formed value systems that are totally alien to him.

Many of the play's dominating symbols are physically present on the stage. Most important is Larry's tree. Planted at the news that he was missing in action and broken down at the start of the play, the tree shows how the Kellers' false vision of

Larry will be broken down during the play as they learn the truth about his death. The remainder of the play's setting is designed to emphasize the restrictions under which this family lives: *"The stage is hedged on right and left by tall, closely planted poplars which lend the yard a secluded atmosphere."* The house *"looks tight"* as it exudes an aura of restriction and privacy. We are in a time where as long as you keep your dirty washing private, the neighbors are unconcerned. This is shown by the neighbors' evident knowledge of Keller's guilt, yet continued friendship with the man.

The names of Miller's central characters are also significant. It is not by chance that the name *Keller* sounds like *killer* or the *cellar* in which Keller metaphorically hides his guilt. Meanwhile, Chris can be seen as a martyr, or even a christ as his name suggests, but he is a christ who has lost faith in his father and so is unable to raise his Lazarus (Larry) from the dead. Chris's character, in conflict as much within himself as against his father, is summed up in his military epithet, "Mother McKeller." He is both mother and killer; he has a desire to protect and destroy almost simultaneously, and this conflict finally burns him out.

FIRST PERFORMANCE

All My Sons previewed at the Colonial Theatre in Boston and then opened at the Coronet Theatre in New York City on January 29, 1947, with the following cast:

Joe Keller: Ed Begley
Kate Keller: Beth Merrill
Chris Keller: ARTHUR KENNEDY
Ann Deever: Lois Wheeler
George Deever: Karl Malden
Dr. Jim Bayliss: John McGovern
Sue Bayliss: Peggy Meredith
Frank Lubey: Dudley Sadler
Lydia Lubey: Hope Cameron
Bert: Eugene Steiner

Directed by Elia Kazan
Set and lighting designed by MORDECAI GORELIK
Produced by Elia Kazan, Harold Clurman, and Walter Fried
It ran for 328 performances.

INITIAL REVIEWS

Reviews of the premiere of *All My Sons* were fairly mixed, despite the standing ovation given the author on opening night. But most of those who criticized certain aspects of the play praised Elia Kazan's direction and felt that Miller was a playwright of talent who was worth watching. As Ward Morehouse exclaimed, "the Broadway theater has a new playwright of enormous promise." Critics, including John Gassner, observed the social and political ramifications of the play and considered its moral implications of personal and social responsibility, some even accusing Miller of being a communist.

A number of critics, including John Lardner and Joseph Wood Krutch, felt that the play was too contrived and predictable. In a thoroughly negative review, John Simon charged it with having "more plot and circumstance than the theme requires." While Howard Barnes admitted that Miller displayed a sense of form and an obvious "acute feeling for the theater," he condemned the play for what he saw as Miller's failure "to superimpose a classical tragic outline on subject matter which is, at best, confused." John Mason Brown reported that the play fails due to a "false and unresolved central theme." Such critics were no doubt put off by the play's ambiguous ending and uncomfortable with the darkness of Miller's vision.

However, BROOKS ATKINSON, whose opinion as the *New York Times* critic carried much weight, saw the play as "fresh," "exciting," "honest," "forceful," and "a piece of expert dramatic construction." He enjoyed the realistic dialogue and the vivid characters whom he felt had been plucked from "the run of American society" but presented "as individuals with hearts and minds of their own." He was not alone in such an assessment. Louis Kronenberger may have found aspects of the play a little melodramatic, but on the whole, he found it to be a "compelling play" by a playwright with strong dramatic, humanistic, and moral sensibilities. William Beyer described *All My Sons* as the "most moving and provocative new play of the season." Such praise no doubt assisted in the decision to award the play both the Donaldson Award and the New York Drama Critics Circle Award that year, beating out EUGENE O'NEILL's *The Iceman Cometh*.

Miller felt that most people at the play's premiere had not really understood what he was trying to do. Countering the complaints that the play was overly plotted and contained implausible coincidences, Miller suggested, especially in the shadow of Greek masterpieces such as Sophocles' *Oedipus* plays, that coincidence is the very stuff of drama, if not of life. He had purposefully modeled *All My Sons* on such notions of TRAGEDY.

SCHOLARSHIP

In the *Cambridge Companion to Arthur Miller*, STEVEN CENTOLA suggests that *All My Sons* has a "resonance that transcends its contemporary society and immediate situation," in its depiction of the effects of the human "impulse to betray and to deny responsibility to others." The play's exploration of guilt, responsibility, and the father–son relationship, all staples within many of Miller's subsequent plays, is the most commonly critiqued. James Robinson views the father–son conflict as having a particularly Jewish nature, Terry Otten offers a nicely detailed reading of Kate Keller, and Susan Abbotson places the play in a sociohistorical context.

Other critics have considered the play's tragic possibilities. Qun Wang views *All My Sons* as a tragedy in the same way that *Death of a Salesman* and *The Price* are tragic—because of the confusion that the characters face in trying to choose the right way to live and the wrongheaded choices that they make. Arthur Boggs, on the other hand, feels that the play fails as a tragedy because none of the characters arrive at a true recognition in the way, for example, that Oedipus does.

Brenda Murphy summarizes the Ibsenesque influence on *All My Sons* as the way Miller depicts the past coming into the present, his representation of the principle of causation, and the play's insistence on the "individual's responsibility to society even when that means the sacrifice of the claims of family." Albert Wertheim offers an interesting analysis and comparison of the play to Edward Mabley and Leonard Min's *Temper the Wind* (1946), and Syed Mashkoor Ali compares it to Miller's favorite Shakespeare play, *King Lear*. Amar Nath Prasad explores the play's symbolism, while Stephen Marino examines the play's poetic language, especially in terms of its religious allusions, to try to resolve the debate concerning whether *All My Sons* is a social drama or a family play, finally asserting that it deliberately portrays a conflict between the two. Paul Rosenfelt also includes this play in his discussion of absent figures in drama.

Aside from production reviews and the general volumes on Miller, there has not been a great deal of specific scholarship printed on this play, and the majority appears in Harold Bloom's 1988 collection of essays on *All My Sons* in his series *Modern Critical Interpretations*. This volume offers a good sampling of how the play has fared critically. Of the 12 critical essays contained therein, those by Sheila Huftel and CHRISTOPHER BIGSBY concentrate on the play's Ibsenian connection, while those by Edward Murray, Barry Gross, Orm Överland, and Leonard Moss each find various faults with its structure and language. For example, Murray finds the play unconvincing and suggests that it fails to comprehend the complexity of human experience, while Orm Överland argues that the play fails as realism. Leonard Moss finds the play's structure and language unconvincing. Arvin R. Wells, Dennis Welland, June Schlueter, and Centola meanwhile defend both. Schlueter describes the play's structure as organic, Welland views it as a well-crafted, universal picture of the difficulties that people have facing moral responsibilities, and Wells describes it as a classic conflict between moral responsibility and rigid idealism. Most are interested in the play's real or imagined universal impact and its author's apparent beliefs as reflected in the characters and situations that he presents.

General consensus is that *All My Sons* is not Miller's best or most important play but that it deserves recognition, as Centola explains in the *Cambridge Companion*, for its display of an "extraordinary skill in handling dramatic form" and because it is Miller's "first major theatrical achievement."

CHARACTERS

Bayliss, Jim and Sue The neighbors offer interesting contrasts to the Kellers and the Deevers, just as their obvious regard for Keller, despite all of them knowing what he did, gives us a taste of this whole community's sense of moral values. Dr. Jim Bayliss has none of the solidity of Keller or sense of satisfaction. Both he and his wife, Sue, feel that they could have done better with their own lives as well as with each other. The main problem is Jim's desire to become a medical researcher, a desire that he has had to sacrifice for the needs of his family. He tried once to pursue this dream, but when Sue came and cried for him to return, his sense of guilt brought him back to an existence that he despises and that he sees as worthless, being at the beck and call of rich patients who have little wrong with them. Jim has compromised, but it is his sense of responsibility that made him do so. Responsibility, however morally right, can be confining and destructive, which is a lesson that both Keller and Chris will ultimately learn.

Sue financed Jim through medical school and now expects him to make a high salary as payback; though jealous of any attention that Jim receives from his female patients, she continually pressures him to make more money. This echoes how Keller says that he felt pressured to make money for his family's sake as much as for his own. Their son Tommy Bayliss, an apparently wild child who steals his father's equipment and terrorizes the neighborhood girls, shows how little control parents often have over their children. This underlines the hopelessness of Keller's desire that his children might follow him.

Although Jim and Sue are relatively recent neighbors, having moved into the Deevers's old house after they left, Jim has become close friends with Chris, whom he admires deeply as a man of principle. Seeing himself as too weak not to compromise, Jim lives vicariously through his friend's idealistic outlook. He sadly expects that Chris will not be able to send his father to jail and will end up compromising his idealism. But Chris stays true to his principles, willing to sacrifice his own father for moral justice, to show just how hard it has become to be a man of principle in this society. We are left to wonder which path is better: compromise or idealism.

Bert A young child from the neighborhood, Bert looks up to Keller, and his admiration may soften our condemnation. After Keller returned from the penitentiary after his trial, the local children associated Keller with the legal system, and Keller builds on their belief that he was a kind of detective. He plays a game in which he deputizes them, has them look for suspicious activities in the neighborhood, and then report back to him. Given Bert's enthusiasm for this, one wonders how prescient Miller was in regard to the mindset of the informer, which would become a major aspect of many lives during the period of HUAC and the political witch hunts of the 1950s.

Deever, Ann   Ann, like Chris, is more cautious than George or Larry, which may be why she and Chris seem so suited. Also, like Chris, in her firm rejection of her father (and her later request that Chris too reject his father), she seems a fierce idealist. However, because of Larry's letter, she knew from the start of Keller's guilt and yet kept quiet until she saw no other alternative to getting what she wanted, which compromises her idealism. This is a compromise Chris, too, will have to make if he is ever to be happy. He refuses, and by his reaction to his father's death, one supposes that he will live a life of guilt thereafter.

Ann plans to marry into the family that destroyed her father because that unpleasantness is overshadowed by her desperate desire not to be alone. She plans to hold onto Chris whatever happens. Indicating her decision, she has told George her design to marry Chris even before he has proposed. Despite the suspicions of all three Kellers, she is not interested in justice, but has come for only one thing: a husband. To this end, she is prepared to sacrifice her relationship with her entire family, including her brother George. It is uncertain by the end of the play whether she will succeed in holding on to Chris or not, as Kate, who has been trying to keep them apart throughout the play, seems to have reclaimed her son and holds him tightly in her arms. Ann, however, as suggested by her actions throughout the play, will not give in without a fight.

Deever, George   Like Chris, George has had his outlook on the world changed by his war experiences and seems to have that same rash streak that

no doubt led Larry to commit suicide. But George has not the same ability to follow through with what he starts, possibly a weakness inherited from his father. Trying to gain Keller's admission of guilt, he frequently backs down and allows himself to be calmed by the motherly attentions of Kate and to be placated by Keller's reasoning. Even when his lawyer's sharpness finally catches the Kellers in the lie that determines their guilt, George does little with his discovery, weakly declaring an intention to leave and vainly trying to persuade his sister to accompany him. He came to town as his father's avenger, even wearing Steve's hat, but he effectively leaves it to Chris to punish the man who put his father into jail.

Deever, Steve   Joe Keller's old neighbor and business partner, Steve Deever, is a shadowy figure about whom we hear a lot but never see. Steve has been estranged from his children since his incarceration for allowing faulty parts to be sold to the air force. He has not the stomach for suicide but has almost vanished into his jail cell through the total alienation that his children have displayed. Steve has a weaker personality than Keller, and it is hard to feel sympathy for him; he was complicit in the crime for which he was jailed and had simply hoped that he could escape blame, as Keller did, by making someone else responsible.

Keller, Chris   To some degree, Miller modeled Chris on his brother Kermit. In his autobiography, Miller tells of Kermit's war experiences as an infantry captain who cared deeply for his men, carrying one on his back for hours in freezing weather to a first-aid station while his own feet were frozen and gangrenous. In *Timebends: A Life*, Miller relates what he saw as evidence of his brother's "pathological honesty." This sounds very much like Chris, who had been known as Mother McKeller to his battalion.

We can infer from Chris's attitude to Steve how he will view his own father once he discovers his guilt. His innocence toward his father's crime is strongly suspected, even by those who most admire him, but his burning outrage when he is presented proof suggests that it was a knowledge of which he may have been truly unaware. As a socialist, Chris will condemn his own father for his callous refusal to take responsibility for the deaths of numerous pilots and will insist that "there's a universe of people outside and you're responsible to it." His father thought that the family group took precedence, but Chris honestly believes otherwise.

His friends and neighbors view Chris as a moral idealist, which is a hard role to fulfill. There are those, like Sue, who despise him for this, but others look to him to determine how they should behave—he inspires Jim to want to become a medical researcher, and the Deever children to believe in Keller's innocence and their own father's guilt. But Chris is unsure as to what he wants to do for himself. The road of the idealist is never easy. He feels torn between keeping his father happy by staying in the family business and refusing to be caught up in the morally suspect world of commerce.

For all his idealism, Chris is not perfect. His insistence that Kate face the truth of Larry's death is a purely selfish one, for he sees that as the only way that she will accept his marriage to Ann. It is also equally possible that he has known about his father's guilt and has suppressed that knowledge deliberately to back away from any confrontation because he has so much invested in his father's supposed infallibility. To accept his father as flawed is to face his own potential failings. He survived a war in which many died, and that is something that troubles his moral sensibility. Chris tries to take on a responsibility for his fellow man against his father but, ironically, without the support of his father, he finally crumbles and returns to the safe inertia of his mother's arms. His brother Larry's rebellion was better sustained in that he died for something that he believed.

Keller, Joe Miller carefully gains our sympathy for Keller before he reveals his crime. This is a man who takes the time to play games with the neighborhood children, an affable and simple man, admired by his surviving idealistic son as well as the neighbors who know exactly what he has done. His human side is fully engaging. Yet, he is also a hard businessman, one who may have indirectly murdered 21 pilots and tricked someone else into taking full responsibility, but there seem to be extenuating circumstances. Even Chris admits that they live in a "dog eat dog" world and that Keller did what he did to keep his business afloat and provide for his family. So in one sense, Keller is as much a victim as a victimizer.

Joe Keller is a "man among men" because he has made it in this society and that, to many, is cause for respect and admiration. His desire to pass his business on to his sons is rooted in love. Keller's regard for his sons is undeniable, and his belief in the sanctity of fatherhood is clear as he cries, "A father is a father." This affirms his belief that blood should always be put before outside concerns. He tells Chris: "What the hell did I work for? That's only for you, Chris, the whole shooting match is for you!" and he is eager to include Chris in his business. This desire to bond with his son is, in a sense, what frees him from moral responsibility and allows him to ship those faulty parts with a clear conscience.

Keller also shows pride in the ability that he has to pass on such a thriving business firm, and it worries him deeply that Chris may not accept his gift. Despite a lack of education, Keller has gained ascendancy over many others: "I got so many lieutenants, majors, and colonels that I'm ashamed to ask someone to sweep the floor." He revels in his financial, and therefore, social superiority. Having faced the accusations against him boldly, his boldness won him the case. But he has been morally misled by the mores of an unsavory society, a society that Chris comes to describe as "the land of the great big dogs." Keller has been taught that it is the winner who continues to play the game and that society can turn a blind eye to moral concerns so long as the production line keeps rolling—this is the essence of capitalism. It is what he tries to teach his son, but it is something that his son does not want to hear. It is not until the end of the play that Keller sees what his sons saw all along: We have social responsibilities beyond the immediate family. Keller cannot survive the rejection of his sons, and he literally ceases to exist once this occurs—he commits suicide.

Keller, Kate (Mother) Kate is the real kingpin of the Keller family. It is Kate whom everyone, including the neighbors, must serve to please, and it is Kate to whom everyone turns for advice and comfort. Yet, Kate is a woman who ignores realities of which she disapproves, such as the likelihood of Larry's death and also Chris and Ann's relationship. She focuses instead on anything that she can adapt toward her version of reality. Kate feels the guilt of what her husband has done, and throughout the play, she threatens to burst with the pressure of keeping his dark secrets. Her insistence that Larry is alive is intrinsic to her ability to continue supporting Keller.

Miller's opening description of Kate speaks volumes: "A woman of uncontrolled inspirations and an overwhelming capacity for love." *Uncontrolled* and *overwhelming* are the keys to her character—there is something about her that refuses to be dominated, and it will be she alone who stands firm against the cataclysmic events of the play. She insists on her son Larry's continued existence because "if he's dead, your father killed him." Even though the faulty plane parts that Keller allowed to be shipped could not have been used in Larry's plane, Keller did kill his son: Larry committed suicide because of his father's actions. Kate represses the very idea of Larry's death, for to acknowledge it would be to reject her husband. Yet, she displays an underlying antagonism toward her husband throughout the play that is unsurprising in the light of her evident adoration of Larry.

Kate has a dream in which she sees her son falling and in which she unsuccessfully tries to save him. This tells us that she knows subconsciously that Larry is dead, and because she envisions him falling through the sky, she blames her husband and his faulty aircraft parts for that death. Kate's anger with Keller shows most clearly when she actually smashes her husband across the face, but her behavior toward him is cold for much of the play, as she orders him about and tells him to be quiet. Kate finally acts on her contempt for her husband, though her disclosure may not be conscious, for it is she who betrays Keller to both George and Chris and brings the truth into the open.

It is reasonable to ask why Kate has kept quiet for so long and has not acted sooner. Is it that, unconsciously, she wants control? We see this desire in her frequent attempts to dominate and insist on everyone doing what she wants. Her power is strong: She has everyone on edge, wondering what her reactions will be and trying to please her. "What's Mother going to say?" Keller declares, worrying about her reaction to the broken tree. We should note the way in which she is *mother* even to him, especially as his control gradually slips. Keller has relinquished his power to Kate, for in keeping his secret, his wife has control over him. As Keller becomes more and more unable to control events, he turns to Kate for advice, and she suggests a course of action that will once more cover up the truth. It is a deceit to pacify their son, for Keller to pretend to offer to go to prison—an offer that Chris, a man of principle, contrary to his mother's expectations, takes at face value and accepts with devastating results.

Kate keeps control by refusing to face the truth and by forcing others to do the same. Her refusal to face Larry's death has the others running in circles. She also refuses to accept the rift between Chris and his father and suggests that they use subterfuge to cover it up. The knowledge of Larry's suicide totally destroys Keller's ability to maintain any illusion, and so he kills himself. But though she may have lost her husband, Kate regains control of her errant son as Chris turns to her, not to Ann, for comfort. Chris had rebelled against his mother in his decision to marry Ann and in his desire to face the truth, but Kate now quiets him and suggests that it would be better to forget. Chris turns himself over to her, and she takes charge, which does not bode well for the future.

Keller, Larry   Larry has a palpable presence on stage even though he has been dead for two years. This palpability is partly achieved through the broken tree that is placed in Keller's yard to symbolize this presence but also through the memories of his family and friends. Though he never flew the type of plane for which Keller had sent the faulty parts, his death symbolizes those of the 21 pilots who did. Keller ironically tries to convince himself that Larry would not have been as judgmental of his actions as Chris, but of the two sons, Larry's response was eventually and in many ways the harsher. While

Chris wants to hold his father legally accountable and send him to jail, Larry insists on moral accountability by performing an action that will lead Keller to kill himself. If we view Larry's suicide as an act of responsibility and atonement for the family guilt, then so too might we view Keller's.

Lubey, Frank and Lydia   Frank and Lydia Lubey are happy, partly because Frank has no idealistic desires but is content to conform. Frank was just old enough to avoid being drafted and unlike Chris, Larry and George, whose lives were all deeply affected by their war experiences, was able to stay home and raise a family. In a sense, this has allowed him to maintain a certain innocence. Frank Lubey has the life that George might have had if he had not gone to fight in the war, even down to being married to George's old girlfriend, Lydia. Sweet though she seems, Lydia has clearly compromised her own feelings in her desperation to get a husband and have children. Rather than wait for George to return from the war, she married the first man who asked. We see in Ann's actions an echo of that desperation, reminding us of something else brought about by World War II; a shortage of husbands, given the number of men who never returned.

MOVIE AND TELEVISION ADAPTATIONS

So far, there have been two film versions of this play. The first, in 1948, was produced by Universal Pictures and directed by Irving Reis. It was designed as a star vehicle for Edward G. Robinson as Joe Keller and Burt Lancaster as Chris, both of whom were praised for their performances. Indeed, acknowledgement of Miller's authorship was minimal, and the screenplay was written by Chester Erskine, who wrote it as a film noir with political overtones. Emphasis is firmly placed on both the relationship between Chris and his father and Chris's desire to leave the nest; to this end, the neighbors' characterizations are simplified rather than used as foils to the main characters. The film closes with Kate urging both Chris and Ann to live, which offers a more upbeat ending. Critics reacted to the film as they had to the play; some negatively critiqued it as too fabricated or simply unengaging, while others lauded its serious social and moral commentary.

Iris Merlis produced the 1987 version for the PBS *American Playhouse* series that was closer to the original play but met with a similar mixed reaction. John J. O'Connor called it "a good solid revival" but felt that the final moments were too melodramatic, while Ed Siegel suggested that it "isn't the best play you'll ever see, but its power and force make it a welcome return." It was directed by Jack O'Brien and starred James Whitemore as Keller, Aidan Quinn as Chris, Michael Learned as Kate, and Joan Allen as Ann. The film was released on MCA Home Video that same year.

FURTHER READING

Abbotson, Susan C. W. "A Contextual Study of the Causes of Paternal Conflict in Arthur Miller's *All My Sons*." *Hungarian Journal of English and American Studies* 11, no. 2 (Fall 2005). 29–44.

———. "Materialism, Socialism and Paternal Conflict in Arthur Miller's *All My Son*." In *Arthur Miller: Twentieth Century Legend*, edited by Syed Mashkoor Ali, 40–58. (Jaipur, India: Surabhi, 2006).

Ali, Syed Mashkoor. "*King Lear* and *All My Sons:* Some Parallels." In *Arthur Miller: Twentieth Century Legend,* edited by Syed Mashkoor Ali, 77–87. (Jaipur, India: Surabhi, 2006).

Atkinson, Brooks. "Arthur Miller: *All My Sons*." In *The Lively Years: 1940–1950.* New York: Associated Press, 1973, 188–191.

———. "Arthur Miller's *All My Sons* Brings Genuine New Talent into the Coronet Theatre with Expert Cast of Actors." *New York Times* January 30, 1947, 21.

Barnes, Howard. "Too Many Duds." *New York Herald Tribune,* January 30, 1947, 15.

Beyer, William. "The State of the Theatre: Midseason Highlights." *School and Society,* April 5, 1947, 250–251.

Bloom, Harold, ed. *Modern Critical Interpretations of Arthur Miller's* All My Sons. New York: Chelsea House, 1988.

Boggs, W. Arthur. "*Oedipus* and *All My Sons*." *Personalist* 42 (Autumn 1961): 555–560.

Brown, John Mason. "New Talents and Arthur Miller." *Saturday Review of Literature,* March 1, 1947, 22–24.

Centola, Steven R. "*All My Sons*." In *Cambridge Companion to Arthur Miller*, edited by Christopher

Bigsby, 48–59. (Cambridge, London: Cambridge University Press, 1997).

Gassner, John. "The Theatre Arts." *Forum* 107 (March 1947): 271–275.

Gorelik, Mordecai. "The Factor of Design." *Tulane Drama Review* 5 (March 1961): 85–94.

Hutchens, John K. "Mr. Miller Has a Change of Luck." *New York Times*, February 23, 1947, sec. 2, pp. 1, 3.

Kronenberger, Louis. "A Serious Theme Makes for Compelling Theater." *New York PM Exclusive* 31, January 1947. In *New York Theatre Critics' Reviews* 8 (1947): 477.

Krutch, Joseph Wood. "Drama." *Nation*, February 15, 1947, 191, 193.

Lardner, John. "B for Effort." *New Yorker*, February 8, 1947, 50.

Lerner, Max. "Sons and Brothers." *Actions and Passions: Notes on the Multiple Revolution of Our Time.* New York: Simon and Schuster, 1949, 22–24.

Loughlin, Richard L. "Tradition and Tragedy in *All My Sons.*" *English Record* 14 (February 1964): 23–27.

Marino, Stephen A. "Religious Language in Arthur Miller's *All My Sons.*" *Journal of Imagism* 3 (Fall 1998): 9–28.

Morehouse, Ward. "*All My Sons*, Intelligent and Thoughtful Drama Superbly Played at Coronet." *New York Sun*, January 30, 1947. In *New York Theatre Critics' Reviews* 8 (1947): 477.

Murphy, Brenda. "The Tradition of Social Drama: Miller and His Forbears." In *Cambridge Companion to Arthur Miller*, edited by Christopher Bigsby, 10–20. (Cambridge, London: Cambridge University Press, 1997).

O'Connor, John J. "Arthur Miller's *All My Sons* on 13." *New York Times*, January 19, 1987, C16.

Otten, Terry. *The Temptation of Innocence in the Dramas of Arthur Miller.* Columbia: University of Missouri Press, 2002.

Prasad, Amar Nath. "Symbolism in Miller's *All My Sons.*" In *Arthur Miller: Twentieth Century Legend*, edited by Syed Mashkoor Ali, 59–66. (Jaipur, India: Surabhi, 2006).

Robinson, James A. "*All My Sons* and Paternal Authority." *Journal of American Drama and Theater* 2, no. 1 (Winter 1990): 38–54.

Rosefeldt, Paul. "From *Strange Interlude* to *Strange Snow*: A Study of the Absent Character in Drama." *Journal of Evolutionary Psychology* 23, nos. 2–3 (2002 August): 117–130.

Siegel, Ed. "*All My Sons* a Sign of Hope." *Boston Globe*, January 19, 1987, 23.

Simon, John. "*All My Sons.*" *Newsweek*, February 10, 1947, 85.

Srivastava, Ramesh K. "The Manifest and the Hidden in Arthur Miller's *All My Sons.*" In *Perspectives on Arthur Miller*, edited by Atma Ram, 120–129. (New Delhi, India: Abhinav, 1988).

Wang Qun. "The Tragedy of Ethical Bewilderment." In *The Achievement of Arthur Miller: New Essays*, edited by Steven Centola, 95–100. (Dallas, Tex.: Contemporary Research, 1995).

Wertheim, Albert. *Staging the War.* Bloomington: Indiana University Press, 2004.

The American Clock (1980)

With its 21 songs and tunes and more than 50 characters, *The American Clock* is, in many ways, one of Miller's most ambitious plays. As with other plays of this period, it went through several forms before coalescing into what Miller felt was a satisfactory production, most notably the one mounted in GREAT BRITAIN in 1986 at the NATIONAL THEATRE, directed by Peter Wood. It was first produced under the direction of Dan Sullivan who previewed it in New York and then ran it at the Spoleto Festival in South Carolina. But it officially opened six months later at New York's Biltmore Theatre with a new director, Vivian Matalon. Swiftly closing, Miller made substantial changes, adding important new characters, including Arthur Robertson, Theodore K. Quinn, and Banks; many of the songs; and new scenes such as the Taylor farm auction, the marathon dance, and the collage of soldiers at war. It is this version, published in 1989, on which the synopsis, the critical commentary, and the characters sections are based.

Miller describes the play as a mural in which he tries to balance epic elements with intimate psychological portraits to give a picture of both a society and the individuals who make up that society. The final version is an amalgam of Miller's own memories of the period, with the Baum family being based on his own, and episodes described by reporter Studs Terkel in his oral history *Hard Times* (1970).

For Miller, the GREAT DEPRESSION marks a point in U.S. history when the United States realized that it would need to recognize both society and the individual to survive. Whereas many of Miller's earlier plays depicted the individual's responsibility within society, *American Clock* offers the obverse as it explores society's responsibility toward the individual. Miller insists that although the Depression is often depicted as an era of futility and slight hope, he allows his play to end on an optimistic note. He points out that optimism was not entirely killed in the 1930s, being evidenced in the upbeat songs, musicals, and comedies of the period. The vaudevillian form of the final script conveys an authentic sense of the Depression era, as vaudeville was an up-and-coming genre of the period, reflecting people's comic response to the pressures around them. It was, perhaps, rooted in the sense that things could not possibly get worse, so they had to get better. "Underneath it all, you see," Miller tells CHRISTOPHER BIGSBY, "you were stripped of all your illusions, and there's a certain perverse healthiness in that . . . And I suppose that way in the back of your brain, you knew you were in America and that somehow it was going to work out."

SYNOPSIS

Act One

The play begins with a band playing "Million-Dollar Baby" as a baseball pitcher tosses a ball, and everyone joins in the song while Theodore Quinn tap-dances with evident joy. The cast members sit on stage and move easily in and out of scenes to try and maintain a continuous flow of action, only broken by the interval. Rose, Lee, and Moe Baum take turns speaking to introduce the country's firm belief in never-ending prosperity in summer 1929. Robertson offers the image of the country bowing to a golden calf that is wrapped in the U.S. flag. A bootblack, Clarence, tries to buy more stocks, but Robertson warns him to sell. We are told that Clarence does not take this advice and will lose everything, just as the big financiers did.

Rose is playing her piano while her son Lee sings "I Can't Give You Anything But Love," before explaining how upset he was when she cut her hair. Ignoring his distress, she insists that they sing "On the Sunny Side of the Street." While Moe buys more stock on the phone, Rose gives their chauffeur Frank instructions and argues with her sister Fanny concerning with whom their father should live. Neither one really wants the burden and the responsibility. Rose is also jealous of her mother-in-law, upset that Moe bought them both the same diamond bracelet. Moe seems so busy that he has little time for his son, uncertain even how old he is or when he last had a haircut.

Robertson advises a friend, Dr. Rosman, to sell his stock and explains why learning that people have stopped buying everyday items makes him think that a crash is coming. He is worried how a crash will affect the little people but uncertain how he can help. Financiers Jesse Livermore and William Durant sit in a speakeasy, listening to the owner Tony tell them how Randolph Morgan jumped off a building when he lost everyone's money. Livermore sees this action as noble, but Durant disagrees. Morgan's sister Diana joins them, looking for her brother. She is anxious about events. Livermore is confident that Rockefeller can turns things around, but when he hears that Durant has just lost control of General Motors, he despairs. Durant faces it bravely, but Livermore borrows money from Robertson and then kills himself. Not trusting banks, Robertson keeps his money in his shoe. It is he who tells Diana that her brother is dead.

Lee withdrew his savings to buy a new bicycle. His mother sends him to the pawnshop with her jewelry as his friend Joe stops by with a signed photograph that he has received from Herbert Hoover. Moe lets Frank know that he has been taking advantage of Moe's good nature and fires him. The Baums have moved to BROOKLYN, and Grandpa complains about the smallness of the house. Grandpa mocks Moe's insistence on trying to pay back debts after going bankrupt. He comments that Hitler will not last six months and that the Germans are decent people. Lee returns with news that the banks have closed, delighted that he got his money out, but then his bicycle is stolen.

Lee still thinks that the family has money to send him to college.

In Iowa, a drought has punished farmers like Henry Taylor, whose crops have failed. His farm is up for compulsory auction because he could not make payments, and his fellow farmers have come to help. Judge Bradley insists that the auction proceed, but the farmers take over and force the auctioneer to sell the farm for a single dollar so that Taylor can have it back, even though he has no money to run it. Banks, a black ex-soldier, tells how the Depression hit farming communities and forced many to take to the road just in search of food. Banks relates how one fellow hobo, Callahan, helped him, but most people whom he met were out for themselves. He sings "How Long," but that changes into "The Joint is Jumpin'" with marathon dancers crossing the stage. Taylor begs for work and food at the Baums' house. As he faints, they give him water and a meal. Rose is even prepared to let him stay in their basement, but Moe gives him $1 and sends him along.

Quinn enters, dancing, and talks to Robertson. He has recently become president of General Electric but is unhappy; he has begun to see how unfairly such conglomerates operate, with secret monopolies that crowd out the small businesses. He wants more honest competition, seeing that as the American way. Robertson thinks that he would be foolish to resign because it will change nothing. Interviewed by a reporter, Quinn relates his tale of rags to riches, paying attention to the details—calculating the optimum number of lamps for the best profit, knowing his business down to the number of bricks in the wall—and announces his intent to resign and to begin a small business advisory. He continues to dance, content in his renunciation of the corporate world.

Lee has realized that there is no money for college and gets a job. His cousin, Sidney Margolies, is trying to write a hit song. Sidney's mother, Fanny, tells him that he should court the landlady's daughter, Doris Gross, so that they can live rent free. However, Sid and Doris discover that they like each other. Moe walks Lee to work and asks for a quarter to get downtown, which makes Lee feel of use.

Act Two

Rose refuses to sell her piano and is feeling the pressure. Lee has saved enough to go to university, where his friends Joe, Ralph, and Rudy are graduating and are worried about their future: Joe advises Lee to read Marx and plans to be a dentist; Ralph is trained in aircraft design but will go into the ministry (until a war comes along and reinvigorates the aircraft industry); and Rudy plans to sign on for further courses rather than be unemployed. Lee wants to go into journalism. After graduation, he travels South to gain some experience. In Mississippi, he sees a different world, even more destitute than the North, despite tobacco companies and others making money by exploiting workers.

Joe sells flowers on the subway for a living and visits a prostitute, Isabel. He is worried about the sense of intolerance in the air—it reminds him of the German depression and how they began using the Jews as scapegoats. He realizes that in the United States, the poor are the scapegoats. Joe reads communist literature while envisioning a purer socialism that is based on love, but he is utterly alone. Banks is still wandering, searching for work. Rose loses her piano. Lee meets Isaac, a black café owner down South, who is surviving the Depression well; he trades for a $30 radio from the local sheriff. On the radio, they hear Roosevelt trying to buoy up the nation.

Doris and Sid argue and consider dating other people but end closer than ever as they have fallen in love. Unable to find work as a journalist, Lee applies for a WPA job for which he first needs to be on Relief. He can only be placed on Relief by having his father pretend that he hates his son and has thrown him out of the house. Robertson suggests that the American spirit has not been broken because they built the Empire State Building during this time. There is a mix of ethnicities at the Welfare office, and they squabble and bemoan the state of things. Irene persuades Grace to give the remains of her baby's bottle to feed the starving Matthew Bush who has collapsed. She lectures them to consider the collective power of COMMUNISM, but Moe gives his dime to buy the man some more milk rather than as dues to the Workers Alliance. Still, Irene rallies them with a call to solidarity. Talking to the Welfare official, Moe bursts out in anger at his son's lack of belief in anything.

Joe commits suicide out of despair. Lee visits Edie, a committed communist, who helps write Superman comic strips, and they argue politics. He does not see communism as the answer and has become very cynical; annoyed, Edie asks him to leave. Rose plays cards with her relatives as she lays low to avoid the rent collector. They are in danger of eviction but have still taken in a penniless sailor, Stanislaus, who helps with chores. Rose keeps control in front of everyone but confesses that at times, she locks herself in the bathroom and screams. She struggles to maintain her sanity. Moe arrives home to calm her, insisting that they will be all right. Worried about Lee, they pray for the country as someone pounds on the door.

With the advent of WORLD WAR II, jobs became available. Banks reenlisted; Sidney went into security. Many were killed in the fighting. Time telescopes to include the Korean War and the VIETNAM WAR, suggesting that war has become a constant— a part of the capitalistic cycle. Sidney and Lee meet by chance and reminisce about the 1930s. Sidney still writes songs and is happy with Doris, but Moe and Rose are dead. Lee tries to come to terms with his mother's contradictions and decides that she had a life spirit that still inspires him. Rose goads him and the cast into singing "Life Is Just a Bowl of Cherries" as Quinn breaks into a soft-shoe dance. While Robertson suggests that the war saved America, Quinn counters that it was really Roosevelt and the return of belief.

CRITICAL COMMENTARY

Miller sees the Depression as a major landmark in the U.S. sensibility as the time when Americans were first forced to face up to the uncertainty of their existence and were made to consider the true meaning of DEMOCRACY. In *Timebends: A Life*, Miller states his intention to make the play an encomium to U.S. democracy, "At the play's end . . . we should feel, along with the textures of a massive social and human TRAGEDY, a renewed awareness of the American's improvisational strength, his almost subliminal faith that things can and must be made to work out. In a word, the feel of the energy of democracy. But," he adds, "the question of ultimate survival must remain hanging in the air."

Miller allows no scene breaks and presents us with a fluid montage of constant action. The characters often address the audience directly as if to include them as part of the throng. The effect that he wishes—and with the right direction and cast achieves—is a collage of the American people, past and present. They present an extended community that is constantly shifting, changing, evolving, and ultimately surviving before our eyes. They represent the United States of America. To affirm this, Miller begins by presenting onstage two quintessentially U.S. pastimes—jazz and baseball—with the band playing "Million Dollar Baby" to emphasize the U.S. obsession with wealth. Since the play begins in the 1920s, when wealth abounded, everyone willingly sings the song.

There are, importantly, aspects within the play, despite its fluidity and constant shifts of mood, time, and place, that remain fixed throughout. Such aspects allow us to perceive the possibility of constants that offer a sense of continuity and comforting permanence. The band remains on stage from start to finish, the Baums are a central focus of the play, and a key voice in both this opening chorus and the closing one is Theodore Quinn, a perfect representation of U.S. zeal and spirit.

Its joint narrators Arthur Robertson and Lee Baum also unify the play. Lee, youthful and initially naive, attempts to make sense of events as they unfold. Robertson, older and wiser, is a man who has an intuitive understanding of events even before they occur. Together, they analyze and offer an interpretation of how the United States survived the calamitous Depression and what lessons we can take from their survival for the future. Both are importantly involved in the action as well. They are not outside commentators so much as involved participants, which gives their words a greater credibility. As narrators, Lee and Robertson will, on occasion, offer different interpretations of past events. Miller wishes to ensure that we do not uncritically accept either of their views but recognize that each reads the past, as do we all, through their own individual experiences and perspective.

Through these narrators, Miller wonders why it was that the Depression did not destroy the United States for good. The answer he ends up with is that the American capacity for belief saved the day.

Robertson's opening biblical image of the country kneeling to a golden calf evokes a prophecy of doom. We all know what happened to those original, misguided idolaters: They paid a harsh price for their faith in little but wealth. These people too, are soon to suffer, as the WALL STREET CRASH is imminent. The great flag of the United States, in her red, white, and blue, once an emblem of liberty and equality, is now denigrated as a wrap for the golden calf, showing people who are obsessed with notions of success and wealth above and beyond any notion of democracy. Even the lowly shoeblack Clarence has put all his savings into the almighty stock market, refusing to accept that he could possibly lose despite Robertson's timely advice for him to sell. When the market crashes, Clarence will be left with less than $50. By showing Clarence as an investor, Miller shows how the crash had repercussions at every social level.

It is, of course, not just the city people who suffer. Due to weather conditions as punishing as the stock market, we see the more tangible products of farmers failing as much as the intangible dealings of city financiers. Miller shows the Taylors' farm being put up for compulsory auction by its bank creditors. In this way, both nature and city finance have a destructive impact on a family. The neighbors, threatened by similar treatment, rally around their fellow farmer. By a show of physical force, the only power that they retain without having any money themselves is that they enforce a sale of Taylor's property for $1 and return it to him. It will be a momentary victory for he has no money to run a farm whether he owns it or not, and he will soon be forced out onto the road to find a living.

Judge Bradley, who initiated the sale, declares that the return of the farm to Taylor for $1 is sheer theft and "a crime against every LAW of God and man," but Miller wants his audience to recognize the unfairness of this. The judge insists that they all must obey the legal system to ensure order. But where is the order in having your livelihood sold off to the highest bidder and your family home stripped away?

Henry Taylor is a decent family man who has had an unavoidably fallow season. Judge Bradley may have the law on his side, but every moral instinct and law says that Taylor should be allowed to keep his farm. To survive, these people are going to have to rely on the support of their community, not the law and not God. The initial reaction of many people to the crash and the events that followed was, unfortunately, to withdraw into their own private little worlds, either through shame, guilt, or despair. Miller has Irene sing "Tain't Nobody's Bizness" to evoke this isolationist mood, a song that portrays a miserable existence in which the singer insists on complete privacy and detachment. However, such isolation is unproductive.

In contrast to this, Miller shows the powerful antidote of random acts of kindness, often given by people who do not even know the recipient: Brewster helping Taylor, Callaghan helping Banks, the Baums helping Taylor. Such acts of kindness are positive signs of connections being forged, even though the majority seems to remain out only for themselves. As a recipient of such kindness, Taylor, for his part, is not lazy or expectant. Taylor is prepared to work for his food and does not expect a handout; he is uncomfortable asking the Baums for even that much. His lack of greed is evident when he only drinks half of the glass of water that they give him.

Taylor is quite literally starving to death. It is a level of poverty that can still shock the Baums, who survive in comparative comfort. They feed him, and Moe gives him $1, an ironic echo of the amount for which Taylor's farm was fruitlessly rebought, but Moe refuses to allow him to sleep in their basement. The dollar will do little lasting good and is as much a sop for the conscience as a gesture of compassion. As Moe tells his son: "Life is tough, what're you going to do?" However, Lee, in his idealism, does not accept this as a valid response and is unhappy with what he sees as his father's refusal of responsibility. But Moe's philosophy may be a necessary balance—he helps a little but not to a point where he damages his own prospects.

With his mix of characters at the Welfare office, Miller allows us to see the idea of the United

States's "melting pot" philosophy, while pointing out how little "melting" has taken place. Times of trouble tend to set these various groups against each other rather than to allow them to bond together. A potential common ideology, such as Communism, allows for some bonding, but it is a solution that we know in hindsight will not hold. It is also, as Lee knows from his close scrutiny of the hatred between the strikers at the various car plants, only offering a surface solution that does not reach down very far.

The real antidote to the calamities of the Depression, and Miller's suggestion of the only possible thing in this world that can be inviolable, is love. The Baums introduce it with Rose and Lee playing and singing "I Can't Give You Anything But Love." The song's sentiments contrast well with the opening scene of acquisitiveness, and it evokes the possibility of people who are not obsessed with things. And yet the Baums, too, have to learn this lesson in the course of the play because, initially, the whole family is distracted by acquisition. Their Grandpa has also become a nuisance who has to be shunted back and forth between the sisters rather than embraced as an emblem of the families' connection. They waste their time in petty jealousies and quarrels. Rose is jealous of her mother-in-law, Moe enjoys nastily teasing his sister-in-law, and he is so busy that he scarcely has time for his own son (unaware of how old he is or when he had his last haircut). They will learn, through the trials of the Depression, how to become a closer and, in certain ways, more fulfilled family unit.

Robertson introduces the clock image of the play's title: "There's never been a society that hasn't had a clock running on it, and you can't help wondering—how long? How long will they stand for this?" This recalls an earlier fragment that had Banks hitting the road in an unsuccessful search for work. He sings a couple of verses of the song "How Long" to indicate his discontent; the song then changes to "The Joint is Jumpin'" with a group of weary marathon dancers dancing across the stage. The implication is of a certain indomitableness of spirit, despite wearing odds; these people are exhausted but keep going against all reasonable expectations. Robertson's image sees time as ticking away for everyone, to indicate that nothing lasts forever and that all things must change. In this constant change, hope can always be found if sought, for despite the fact that change can be for the worse, it is just as possible that it may be for the better; indeed, change often holds both options simultaneously. For example, although Moe feels humiliated at being reduced to having to borrow a quarter from his son, Lee is able to feel great pride in being able to help his father. Though we see the conditions for the play's characters continue to worsen, as long as they maintain the idea of an American clock that will keep on ticking, regardless, they can retain hope.

Miller uses the three main Baums to illustrate his perception of the major and different reactions people had to the Depression: Moe responds practically, Lee ideologically, and Rose emotionally. In combination, the three offer a comprehensive picture of the overwhelming impact of the Depression on the American psyche and disposition; apart, they allow us to explore personalized aspects of the larger social changes that occurred during this period. The country is saved, not just by the onset of war as Robertson suggests, but also, as Quinn adds, by a reaffirmation of belief in themselves, partly engendered by President Roosevelt. Quinn leads the final chorus with his soft-shoe dance, as everybody sings together, including hopefully the audience as well—providing a prime picture of an America that is prepared to face, without despair, every disaster.

FIRST PERFORMANCE

Initially directed by Dan Sullivan, *The American Clock* first previewed at the Harold Clurman Theatre in New York and then played on May 24, 1980, at Spoleto's Dockside Theater, Charleston, South Carolina. Slightly altered and with a new director, it opened at the Biltmore Theatre in New York, on November 20, 1980, with the following cast:

Lee Baum: William Atherton
Moe Baum: John Randolph
Clarence, Waiter, Isaac
Jerome, and Piano Mover: Donny Burks
Rose Baum: JOAN COPELAND

Frank, Livermore, Stanislaus and Man in Welfare
Office: Ralph Drischell
Grandpa, and Kapush: Salem Ludwig
Fanny Margolies, and Myrna: Francine Beers
Clayton, Sidney Margolies, and Ralph: Robert
Harper
Durant, Sheriff, Toland, and Piano Mover: Alan
North
Tony, Henry Taylor, and Dugan: Edward Seamon
Waiter, Bicycle Thief, Rudy, Piano Mover, and
Ryan: Bill Smitrovich
Joe, and Matthew Bush: David Chandler
Doris Gross, Isabel, and Grace: Marilyn Caskey
Irene: Rosanna Carter
Jeanette Ramsey, Edie, Lucille, and Attendant:
Susan Sharkey

Directed by Vivian Matalon
Set by Karl Eigsti
Produced by Jack Garfein and Herbert Wasserman
Music by Robert Dennis
It ran for 12 performances (and 11 previews).

INITIAL REVIEWS

Critics were positive about the previews at the Clurman Theater and the subsequent Spoleto production. Frank Rich had declared Miller "back on top
of his talent," and the play "an endlessly mysterious personification of American fortitude," but he
felt that the rewritten version directed by Vivian
Matalon was "smashed almost beyond recognition."
Leo Sauvage agreed, saying that the Spoleto version "had warmth, understanding and meaning"
but that the Biltmore one was ruined by "shoddy
sentimentality" and poor production. Reviewing the
Matalon version, Clive Barnes felt that it had great
potential but that "the scatter-shot image of the
play . . . is almost impossible to handle on stage."
Walter Kerr concluded "The feeling of the evening
is both impersonal and incomplete," and Jack Kroll
felt that the play "never finds an effective dramatic
shape." However, John Beaufort and Howard Kissel remained impressed; Beaufort described actors
filling the stage "with a pulsing, occasionally furious
energy that makes their shared ordeal seem immediate and relevant," and Kissel called the play "a
collection of vignettes, simply, sharply etched, but

with the impact of monumental figures frozen in
time." The play also drew some attention by having
Miller's sister Joan play the part of Rose, based on
her own mother.

Miller had changed his original concept under
pressure from director and backers and was unhappy
with the Biltmore production, feeling that the staging was misguided and the overall production too
dour. He much preferred the later version, closer
to his original script, that tried out at the Mark
Taper Forum in 1984 and finally coalesced under
the guidance of Peter Wood in 1986. Reviewing
Wood's production, David Nathan declared that
the director "handles the complexities as if they did
not exist, moving fluently between public and private worlds . . . exacting performances of simplicity and truth and sometimes extraordinary grace
and musicality." Christopher Edwards described it
as "brilliantly staged . . . a touching, amusing and
cleverly wrought piece of theatre," and after praising the play, Michael Coveney suggested that "we
may have to look at all [Miller's] plays of the last
decade or so much more carefully." The American
Clock was also one of the plays revived as part of
the Signature Theater's Miller season in 1998.

SCHOLARSHIP

As with most of Miller's work from the 1980s, The
American Clock has garnered little critical attention
thus far. Gerard Weales's article is predominantly
an assessment of the changes between the initial
production and the later revisions, explaining why
the revised version works so much better. Based on
his own direction of the play, Peter W. Ferran discusses his interpretations of character and format,
suggesting that it is unique among Miller's work
in terms of its theatricality, especially in its use of
shifting narrators and vaudevillian aspects.

Critical books published since the 1990s tend
to include just summaries of the play and fairly
peremptory commentary, with little in-depth discussion. Notable exceptions are Dennis Welland,
Christopher Bigsby, and Terry Otten who each
tackle the play in greater depth. Both Welland and
Bigsby explore its structure, its autobiographical
elements, and its social commentary, while Otten
shows the ways in which the play "is both experi-

mental and a reiteration of seminal Miller themes." However, Otten reads the play's ending as more pessimistic than is suggested in this commentary.

CHARACTERS

Banks Banks is one of the black characters in the play. A World War I veteran, he has been forced to become a hobo during the Depression years after his family farm was ruined financially and he describes such a life. A fellow hobo named Callahan helped him once, but most of the people he meets are out for themselves. When World War II comes along, he is able to reenlist and begin life anew but only by facing imminent death in war. His characterization is deliberately vague to allow him, in one sense, to represent all overlooked minority American groups.

Baum, Lee Although Lee is factually autobiographical, he does not operate as a mouthpiece for Miller and is shown as a figure who is searching for meaning. Lee is a young boy when the Depression hits, and it is in the wake of the eradication of previously thought inviolable beliefs that he must decide by what values he will live. Throughout the play, he displays a keen awareness of his responsibility to others. He knows, almost instinctively, that the way in which Taylor is treated is "all *wrong*." Despite the fact that since the crash, even college graduates cannot get jobs, Lee shows an unrestrained ambition by still wanting to go to college, even when he realizes that his parents cannot afford it. He proves his spirit by finding a job and saving the necessary funds.

Growing up in a nation that has had the rug pulled from under its feet and will remain unsure of its footing for some time, Lee searches for an ideology that will satisfy his sense of community. It is not surprising that for a long time he finds it hard have faith in anything. He explores the pros and cons of the various ideologies that he sees vying for control. He is made to realize, by his university friends, that CAPITALISM will lead to war, as his friends Ralph and Joe point out the relationship between war and the country's economics. Joe also points him in the direction of Karl Marx, but Lee is wary of Communism's dogmatic side. He trav-els south to broaden his knowledge but finds few answers there among the anger and violence that he witnesses. All social systems seem corrupt, and so he hides in a cynicism that he finds to be safer than believing and being disappointed. For this, the idealistic Edie throws him out in disgust.

The charade that Lee plays at the Welfare office with Moe begins humorously but brings out his father's distress at his son's evident lack of faith in anything. However, the sacrifice turns out to be worthwhile as, through this work, Lee discovers something in which he can believe. Lee's WPA project, to write a detailed U.S. history, is an important one—it will remind Americans of their more glorious past and place them in a time line that can make it easier for them to hold on for a better future. The United States becomes an ongoing process rather than a dead end. It is through this that Lee begins to have a sense of the thing in which he should believe: the United States itself. It is a concept that he finally understands through his vision of his own mother and the "headful of life" that he gains from thinking of all the contradictions for which she stood.

Baum, Moe Based on Miller's father, ISIDORE MILLER, Moe Baum begins a wealthy and prosperous business and has his own chauffeur, but like so many others, he has overinvested in stocks. Moe is an ordinary man who displays extraordinary courage in the way that that he deals with his fall in fortune. He recognizes the importance of maintaining a strong sense of self in the face of all that befalls him and his family. He does this by struggling to retain his dignity and honor—despite bankruptcy, he continues to try to pay off his debts. His dismissal of the chauffeur, whom he has been allowing to cheat him for years, is done firmly but without malice. He offers some aid to the suffering community that he sees around him—feeding the homeless, handing over small sums of money to people like Henry Taylor and Matthew Bush—without allowing it to grow out of proportion to the family's means.

Miller describes Moe Baum in an interview with Matthew Roudané as the opposite of Willy Loman: "He does not have illusions. He is a realistic man and does not surrender to his own defeat." Moe remains a strong figure to the end as Miller explains because he is able to "separate himself from his condition" and "avoid self-destructive guilt." What is most important about Moe is his continual refusal to buckle. He strives to provide for his family as practically as possible—moving to a smaller apartment, cutting back on everything but the necessities—and he does not hide behind feelings of guilt or shame when things grow tough. Moe acknowledges the real state in which society finds itself and remains strong, even as he sees everything around him collapsing and men like Joe killing themselves. "We are going to be alright. . . . It can't go on forever," he assures his wife. His final words in the play display this refusal to give in: "I'm trying! God Almighty, I am trying!"

Baum, Rose   Based on the playwright's mother, AUGUSTA MILLER, Rose Baum finds it harder than her husband to face the truth. She keeps pretending that things will pick up. Throughout the various calamities that the Baums must face, Rose responds less practically but far more imaginatively, and events take a graver emotional toll on her. Rose frequently tries to look on the bright side, pointing out how the crash has at least brought families, such as theirs, closer together through sheer necessity. Her efforts to keep happy, however, are motivated by a refusal to admit their real poverty and position, holding onto dreams of a past gentility to survive. For Rose, her piano symbolizes her more glorious past when she was a wealthy woman; it is a past that she finds hard to let go. Through her books and songs, she avoids truths and pretends that everything is fine and "S'Wonderful," pushing money troubles aside with a carefully chosen lyric. But eventually, the piano must be sold, which, for a time, plunges her into despair.

An impending eviction, during which Rose feels that she will be totally disconnected from any tangible possessions, threatens to destroy Rose's struggling faith. She declares: "The next time I start believing in anybody or anything I hope my tongue is cut out!" Yet, despite her words, we must look at her actions—she still helps other people, such as Stanislaus, who is staying with them and work-

ing for his keep. Rose is not a fool; she can keep track of a deck of cards just as she can keep track of what is really happening to her and her family. It is just that she ultimately insists on viewing these events through the lens of her own optimism. Rose survives by treading a very fine line between hope and despair and managing to just about keep her balance through her ability to live in contradictions, as her son finally recognizes. Though she may occasionally lock herself in the bathroom to vent her despair and frustration, in front of others she tries to preserve an attitude of control and hope. It is Rose's essential optimism and belief in life that allow her, and the rest of America, to survive and to continue to function. Rose sings out at the close of the play, refusing to give in, and the rest of the cast join her.

Edie   Edie works as a cartoonist, drawing Superman, and in the same way her whole world is built upon well-meaning fantasy. She may be right when she declares in Communism's defense that "Everything's connected," but she is shown to be, essentially, too idealistic to be entirely credible.

Financiers   (William Durant, Jesse Livermore, and Randolph Morgan)   At the news of the crash, many financiers, such as Randolph Morgan, instantly committed suicide. Others, such as Jesse Livermore, comfort themselves with empty optimism over the possibility of men like John D. Rockefeller saving the day. Livermore's contrived idealism can even transform Morgan's cowardly suicide into "gallantry," and it is not surprising when we later learn that he ends up taking the same path. He had believed in the country's economic prosperity so completely that when he does finally face up to the fact of his own ruin, he loses all faith and is unable to continue living. William Durant has a clearer vision than Livermore; he knows that he is about to lose everything and faces up to that fact straight away. He knows that suicide is no answer and recognizes the illusion of the wealth with which they have been living. He will not fall prey to it again. When it is suggested that he borrow money to stave off his inevitable fall, he declines. His advice to young Diana Morgan, Randolph's sister, is to be strong and face the truth. Durant may have lost General Motors, but he does, at least, survive, unlike Livermore. He ends his days running a bowling alley in Ohio.

Grandpa (Charley) Grandpa is Rose Baum's father who lives with the family both before and after the crash. He is based on Miller's own grandfather, LOUIS BARNETT, with whom he reluctantly had to share a bedroom when he was Lee's age. Refusing at first to even acknowledge the family's loss of fortune, Grandpa selfishly insists that they get a larger house. Grandpa's reaction to the Depression is the worst possible: He insists that people are not connected and should only worry about themselves, as he does. Miller makes it clear that we are not to allow Grandpa any credibility. Early in the play, we are shown how wrong his views are when he insists that Hitler can only stay in power for six months at most. We also witness his unrealistic response to Taylor's plight, suggesting the man should simply borrow money to buy his farm back. Grandpa is living in fierce denial of the changing times, and what he says should not be believed.

Irene Irene is a black woman who appears at certain points in the play. Her main performance is not until the scene at the Relief office where she espouses Communism as a sane response to the times. Suggesting that Communism encourages a much-needed solidarity in an era that is marked by chaos and loss, she sees it as the best hope for true equality in the United States. She is right that solidarity is the answer, but Miller makes us realize that these people need not embrace communist dogma to find this, as we see them come together to help Matthew Bush out of human compassion. Though a communist, it is really Irene's knowledge and experience as a black woman that will help these people. Irene offers her experience in survival, as someone who has faced hardship all of her life, to her fellow white Americans. She informs them that the way to survival is to be part of a community in which everyone willingly helps everyone else. In the resulting unity, each individual will find strength.

Isaac Isaac represents one aspect of the black experience in the South and runs a small café. For him, poverty is nothing new, and he needs little readjustment to cope with the Depression; indeed, the Depression has become a leveling force that may allow him to get ahead of those who formerly dominated. The town sheriff gives a $30 radio to Isaac in return for a $10 chicken meal that he needs to impress his relatives in the hopes of getting a paying job.

Joe (Joey) Growing up alongside Lee, Joe shows the more negative possibility of Lee's future. Just as Lee struggled to become a journalist, Joe struggled to become a dentist. Once qualified, he does not have the cash to begin to practice and is reduced to selling flowers for his meager living. In frustration, he turns to Marxism for answers—and this is the same Joe who, as a boy, had written to Herbert Hoover, the staunchly Republican president, to wish him success. But communism is a system that ultimately fails to sustain Joe, who later throws himself under a train in despair. It is probable that Miller based this character on Joe Feldman, an avid Marxist student whom Miller had known at the UNIVERSITY OF MICHIGAN.

Margolies Sidney, and Doris Gross While Lee seems to have more gumption than his cousin Sidney, who just sits around playing the piano and dreaming of writing a hit song, appearances can be deceptive. Sidney may stay at home, but he pursues his dreams no less forcefully. It is through him that we witness firsthand the dynamics of love. His mother suggests that he date their landlady's daughter, Doris Gross, in the hopes of getting a free apartment. Poverty changes the way relationships work as people look for different things as a solution. The relationship between Sidney and Doris begins out of necessity but swiftly blossoms into true love as the couple becomes one of the few who survive. Sidney prospers as a security guard and even has some songs published. Although he never composes the great hit for which he had hoped, he is satisfied.

Quinn, Theodore K. Based on a friend and neighbor of Miller's from the 1950s, a one-time vice president of General Electric who had been in charge of the Small Business Administration during World War II, Theodore K. Quinn (Ted) has lived the American dream. Miller's character has risen to the top as president of General Electric from lowly origins, largely by being aware of the individual elements that make up the company as a whole—as in his analysis of the bulbs and his knowing the number of bricks in the wall. However, he now sees that the perceived pinnacle of the American dream is an empty goal; the massive conglomerate that is GE is utterly soulless. A popular and carefree figure, shown by Robertson's introduction and Quinn's own song and dance, Quinn is able to find enjoyment in these times, buoyed by his own faith in humanity. He represents Miller's concept of responsibility in the play by his insistence that the higher place a person has in society, the bigger should be the person's responsibility to others. He decides to go back to basics to assist the "little people" to survive intact in a faceless corporate world. His desire to help others is rooted in his belief in the importance of U.S. individualism; it is these individuals whom he wants to assist. Despite a lingering uncertainty as to whether it is really so wise to be renouncing the corporate world, he seems to be ultimately happier once the decision has been made, as evidenced by his final song and dance.

Robertson, Arthur A. Alongside Lee Baum, Arthur A. Robertson acts as a narrator, who is both a part of the events and able to comment on them to the audience. Robertson is another financier but one who is able to face reality and to act to save his fortune. At the start of the play, he warns people whom he knows of an impending market crash, even though he has no firm proof and only a hunch that it will occur. He is always connected to the truth—it is noticeably he who tells Diana that her brother has killed himself. He has recognized, as so many have failed to, that "the market represents nothing but a state of mind" and can be changed as swiftly as a person's mind; it is not the reliable fortress that men like Livermore had convinced themselves that it must be. Robertson is also an optimist, reading the erection of the Empire State building during this period as a sign that Americans refused to give in to the Depression.

Robertson is a good model of behavior as he is aware of the consequences of his actions on others and tries to make responsible choices. He is reluctant to cash in the rest of his securities in case it starts a slide in market prices that could harm "widows and old people." He, like his friend Quinn, displays a concern for the "little people," even though he is unsure how to help. To make a public announcement regarding his views, as he considers doing, may warn the "little people," but it could also make matters worse by ensuring a crash that he is not sure is certain to occur (even though it turns out that he was right); therefore, he decides to sell out quietly so as not to rock the boat.

MOVIE AND TELEVISION ADAPTATIONS

Michael Brandman produced a film version of this play for TNT cable network in 1993. Directed by Bob Clark, it starred Mary McDonell, Darren McGavin, David Strathairn, Jim Dale, Loren Dean, and REBECCA MILLER as Edie. It was adapted by Frank Galati who made a number of changes, even down to altering characters' names; thus the Baums are now the Baumlers, Arthur Robertson becomes Arthur Huntington, Henry Taylor is Wynn Taylor, and Diana Morgan—in a vastly expanded role in which she becomes a prostitute and has a brief affair with Huntington to add a love interest—is renamed Diana Mosely. This last change was presumably to distance her from the real life counterpart on which Miller had originally based the character. While Miller intended the play to have an immediate resonance with the 1980s in which it was produced, Galati treats it as a piece of nostalgia, underlined by his decision to conflate several characters with older versions of themselves, including Arthur Huntington, Lee Baumler, Wynn Taylor and Doris Gross, each looking back.

Galati effectively eviscerates the play. While he includes many of Miller's longer episodes, he leaves out most of the songs, linking episodes and several characters. This version has no Banks, Joe, Ralph, Stanislaus, or Matthew Bush, all of whom add nuances to the original design. It also omits all references to the impending war or any other armed conflict, and reduces Quinn's important role to an opening dance. The form of Miller's play is lost in what becomes more of a straighforward history lesson about the Depression, backed by numerous still photographs from that period. The central Baumler family also have less nuance as many of their scenes have been severely cut and their characterizations simplified.

The use of newsreel stills and snippets of popular music from the time created a sense of period, but television critic Walter Goodman reported that it never made "a stimulating connection . . . between viewers and anyone on screen," and he found its scattered approach too bewildering to follow. In trying to simplify its form, Galati had ironically made it less focused. Matt Roush viewed it in this fashion and accused the film of "meandering on a broad social canvas," even while Ray Loynd felt this was a "rare example of a major playwright's work finding its more natural form on the TV screen." Clearly Loynd had never seen the original play.

FURTHER READING

Barnes, Clive. "This *Clock* is a Bit Off." *New York Post,* November 21, 1980. In *New York Theater Critics Review* 41 (1980): 81–82.

Beaufort, John. *"American Clock." Christian Science Monitor,* November 24, 1980. In *New York Theater Critics Review* 41 (1980): 83.

Bennetts, Leslie. "Miller Revives *American Clock* Amid Resonances of 30s" *New York Times,* July 14, 1988, C23.

Bigsby, Christopher. *"The American Clock." Arthur Miller: A Critical Study.* Cambridge: Cambridge University Press, 2005: 337–351.

Coveney, Michael. *Financial Times,* August 7, 1986. *London Theatre Record* 6, no. 16 (1986): 838.

Dreifus, Claudia. "Arthur Miller on TV." *TV Guide* 41. (August 21, 1993): 24–27.

Edwards, Christopher. *"The American Clock." Spectator* August 16, 1986. In *London Theatre Record* 6, no. 16 (1986): 837.

Goodman, Walter. "Brooklyn Then and Now, In Arthur Miller's Eyes." *New York Times* August 23, 1993, C14.

Ferran, Peter W. *"The American Clock:* 'Epic Vaudeville.'" In *Arthur Miller's America: Theater and Culture in a Time of Change,* edited by Enoch Brater, 153–163. (Ann Arbor: University of Michigan Press, 2005).

Kerr, Walter. "A History Lesson From Miller, A Social Lesson from Fugard." *New York Times,* November 30, 1980, sec. 2, pp. 5, 14.

Kissel, Howard. *"The American Clock." Women's Wear Daily,* November 21, 1980. In *New York Theater Critics Review* 41 (1980): 82.

Kroll, Jack. "After the Fall." *Newsweek,* December 1, 1980. In *New York Theater Critics Review* 41 (1980): 88–84.

Loynd, Ray. "Miller's *American Clock* Ticks on Screen." *Los Angeles Times,* August 23, 1993, F3.

Miller, Arthur. "Conditions of Freedom." *The American Clock and The Archbishop's Ceiling.* New York: Grove, 1989: vii–xix.

———. *Timebends: A Life.* New York: Grove, 1987.

Nathan, David. Review of *The American Clock. Plays and Players* 397 (October 1986): 22.

Otten, Terry. "Other Plays of the 1970s and 1980s." *The Temptation of Innocence in the Dramas of Arthur Miller.* Columbia: University of Missouri Press, 2002: 178–184.

Rich, Frank. "Play: Miller's *Clock* at Spoleto USA: The Hoover Years." *New York Times,* May 27, 1980, C7.

———. "Play: Miller's *American Clock:* Collapse of a Dream." *New York Times,* November 21, 1980. In *New York Theater Critics Review* 41 (1980): 80–81.

Roush, Matt. "A Slow *Clock." USA Today,* August 23, 1993, D3.

Sauvage, Leo. "Dramatizing Despair." *New Leader* 63, December 29, 1980, 15–16.

Schonberg, Harold C. "Joan Copeland Remembers Mama—And So Does Her Brother Arthur." *New York Times,* November 16, 1980, Sec. 2, 1, 5.

Terkel, Studs. *Hard Times: An Oral History of the Great Depression.* New York: Pantheon, 1970.

———. "Studs Terkel Talks with Arthur Miller." *Saturday Review,* September 1980, 24–27.

Weales, Gerald. "Watching the *Clock."* In *The Achievement of Arthur Miller,* edited by Steven Centola, 127–134. (Dallas: Contemporary Research, 1995).

Welland, Dennis. "The Passage of Time." *Miller: The Playwright,* 2d. ed. New York: Methuen, 1983, 148–157.

"The American Theater" (1955)

Written in 1954, this essay was originally published in *Holiday* magazine in 1955, and later reprinted in *The Theater Essays of Arthur Miller* (1978) and several other anthologies. "The American Theater" is one of Miller's earliest assertions of the attraction and limitations of the BROADWAY system. Told in a fairly jocular tone, it describes what he sees as the state of the U.S. theater in the 1950s and concludes with some reminiscences of the production of *Death of a Salesman*. With "practically no exceptions," he begins, "the new American plays originate on Broadway. . . . I wish they didn't, but they do." Acknowledging the breadth of theatrical interest, aware that serious drama is not for everyone, he does not undervalue the lighter fare of musicals and light comedy but speaks of the glamour of the theatrical profession at every level. However, he insists that the difference between "Show Business" and the "Theater" needs consideration. Theater, in his opinion "happens at the moment to be in a bad way," and he bemoans what he suspects may be a "vanishing institute." In part, this essay is Miller's argument against allowing this to happen.

Mocking the media impression of theater that he sees as unnecessarily trivializing and distracting in its tabloid emphasis on glamour and gossip, Miller asserts that there is a "real theater" that is being overlooked. Real theater, Miller wants his reader to realize, is something far more important than the "carnival image" most media coverage suggests because of its ability to inspire and uplift. Miller goes on to describe the way in which a person might respond to a theatrical experience as opposed to movies or television. The most important difference is the way in which a good play allows a viewer to feel as though he or she is a part of the occasion rather than an onlooker, making for a more visceral experience that Miller equates to attending a church service.

After commenting on the numerical decline of theaters at that time, Miller goes on to describe the difficulties and attraction of the acting profession and the changes he sees that took place in the theater since the days of flamboyant producers such as David Belasco and John Golden. While objecting to a self-preoccupation, which he sees as endemic to both actors and Broadway in general, Miller seems nostalgic for the era of stars that at least had the merit of emphasizing the importance of the theatrical institution. He recognizes how the decline of the theatrical impresario to the rise of the businessman producer has helped undercut the place of theater in people's lives. Bemoaning how the onset of movies has caused theater to lose its place in the heart of the common people, Miller clearly objects to the view of theater as catering only to a small elite. But while television and the movies can replace the population's need for entertaining melodramatic fare, theater, he insists, still has sufficient vitality to attract ordinary people and can offer them deeper rewards.

Miller light-heartedly describes the current process of putting on a play in the United States, with its ups and downs, from finding backing though auditions and rehearsals to final production. He includes accounts of how both MILDRED DUNNOCK and LEE J. COBB, initially seen as unsuitable for their roles, came to play Linda Loman and Willy Loman. Being involved with the creative production of a new play, Miller concludes, is for him one of the most fulfilling and exciting experiences that he has known. He recalls moments during the production of *Death of a Salesman* that speak to the true glamour of the theater—its ability to speak to the ages and attain a kind of immortality in that. Theater, for Miller, can do something that he feels movies cannot, "move us one step closer to a better understanding of ourselves," and so is fully worth preserving.

The Archbishop's Ceiling (1977)

Miller has said that although he now sees *The Archbishop's Ceiling* as a 1980s play in the way that it responds to such events as Glasnost and the ways in which individuals and society are disconnecting, its roots lie in the transitional mood of the 1970s during which it was written. This was the period when the idealism of the 1960s disintegrated to be replaced by a society in which market economy values and the concept of power as separate from humankind took over from the idea of a humanity that was both connected and empowered.

Fraught by setbacks, *The Archbishop's Ceiling* was initially scheduled for a New Haven opening, but being unready, it was held back until an April 1977 production at the Kennedy Center in Washington for a four-week run. It met with overwhelmingly negative criticism, so plans were scrapped for a New York production, and Miller did extensive rewrites during the next few years. The play reopened in GREAT BRITAIN, directed by Paul Unwin, at the Bristol Old Vic in 1985, followed by a Royal Shakespeare Company production directed by Nick Hamm the following year.

The lapse in time between the disastrous premiere and these later, more successful British productions allowed Miller to return to an earlier script that he had preferred and to rewrite scenes that had not been working. He eradicated the character of Maya's former husband Martin, simplified Maya's character, took out some confusing stage business, and centered all scenes within the single claustrophobic set (where previously he had used the kind of scene changes that he had used in *Death of a Salesman* to indicate characters meeting elsewhere). Audiences now got the sense that the play was about something more than Eastern dissidents; it was also a reflection of life in the West, as well as a treatise on the nature of art, power, and how reality could be perceived. The following synopsis is based on the revised stage version that Miller published in 1989.

SYNOPSIS

Act One

The time and place of the play is purposefully indistinct, taking place "some time ago" at the "former residence of the archbishop" in an unnamed European capital. We can only suppose that we are dealing with events that may have taken place in politically torn Prague in the 1970s. The ceiling of the room is ornately decorated, though grimed, and the furnishings are a mix of old and new to show the place as the product of more than one period and influence.

U.S. writer Adrian is visiting old friends, escaping from a boring symposium in Paris. While waiting, he casually examines the room, lifting up lamps and cushions, alerting the audience that all is not as it appears. Maya enters with coffee, and the two make small talk. We learn that Maya admires *Vogue* magazine and has had a drinking problem that she is trying to control. This is Marcus's place, although Maya and he broke up some months back. Marcus is in London promoting the last of his books, which has just been translated into English. Adrian lives with Ruth back in the United States, has recently abandoned a book that he had been working on for two years, and dined the previous evening with Sigmund and Otto and their wives, whom Maya also knows.

Adrian and Maya had an affair in the past, and he seems interested in renewing this, pointing out that he and Ruth are not married. Ruth had become suicidally depressed but is now on drugs and is feeling better. However, she now seems somewhat soulless and is working for a magazine a little like *Vogue*. Adrian wonders if the lives of Hamlet or Socrates would have been the same if they had had recourse to curative medicines. Adrian is concerned with people's relationship to power, especially in countries with oppressive governments, and how that affects the art which they produce. They discuss writers, and Adrian confesses his desire to write about Maya and her country. Maya is skeptical as to how Adrian would be able to understand enough to do this truthfully. He questions her about Marcus, whom he has been told is collaborating with the government even though they jailed him in the past. Maya is upset at his suspicion that she and Marcus deliberately compromise writers to betray them, and Adrian apologizes.

Adrian was shocked that police officers were watching him in the restaurant with Sigmund, but Maya points out Sigmund would be used to this and was being deliberately provocative by dining in public. She is worried that Sigmund may get himself arrested, and Adrian blurts out where Sigmund has hidden his latest manuscript. Maya follows him into the corridor, where presumably there are no microphones, and criticizes him for giving such information and insists that he announce that he has taken the manuscript and sent it abroad. He obeys, stunned by the possibility that microphones could be hidden in the main room. Adrian is arranging a rendezvous with Maya when Marcus enters with a young lady. He tells them that Sigmund is downstairs and suggests that they throw a party.

Marcus gives Maya new shoes which he has brought back and sends her to fetch some food, making sure that Adrian does not go with her. He introduces Irina, a pretty Danish girl who speaks broken English. Sigmund arrives, and Marcus goes into the bedroom to phone and invite more people. Sigmund tells Adrian that the authorities have taken his manuscript, but it was before Adrian had said anything. Adrian warns Sigmund about microphones, but he says he does not care. With gestures and roundabout speech because of the possibility they may be overheard, Adrian offers to smuggle the book out. It turns out that this was the only copy. Sigmund plans to ask Marcus for help, but Adrian suggests that he should just leave the country. Sigmund refuses. Marcus asks to talk to Sigmund and seems reticent when they insist that he talk to them both in this room. Adrian threatens to go public if the manuscript is not returned and to his surprise, Marcus encourages him to emphasize this.

While drinking, they discuss the deteriorated state of England and the United States. As Maya returns, we hear men shouting; thugs have been sent to call Sigmund a traitor. Upset to learn that Sigmund has lost his manuscript, Maya berates Adrian for thinking naively that these kinds of things only happen here. Marcus insists that the rumors of his being an agent are false, and Adrian details his own lackluster resistance to the VIETNAM WAR. As Adrian tries to convince everyone to go elsewhere to talk more freely, Marcus explains that they are waiting for Alexandra, daughter of the minister of the interior, whom he hopes will help Sigmund. Sigmund beckons Adrian outside.

Sigmund believes that Alexandra will arrest him, and Maya joins them to tell Sigmund to leave the country. Sigmund asks Adrian to help him get Marcus's gun as he thinks that they will not arrest

an armed man. Adrian refuses, suggesting that they ask Marcus for help. Sigmund, suspecting that Marcus is jealous of his popularity, cannot ask but tells Adrian that he may. Adrian calls Marcus out, who confirms that the government wants Sigmund to leave the country and may even return his manuscript if he does. Adrian says that he has already sent a manuscript out, but Marcus knows that this is a lie. Maya implores Marcus to help, insisting that the manuscript is worth it. They begin to return inside as Maya and Marcus insist there is no proof that microphones are there, but Sigmund gets the gun, and Adrian demands that Marcus repeat what he has said in the main room.

Act Two

Back in the main room, Marcus admits that the government is planning a trial for Sigmund, and a threatening secret policeman warned him to tell Sigmund to leave. Learning that Adrian is thinking of writing a book about them, Marcus tries to explain the differences between himself and Sigmund. He is more willing to compromise, sees himself as a practical realist, and believes that the government is an improvement on what it once was. He sees Sigmund's idealistic writing as needlessly forcing the government to behave more ruthlessly than necessary, and it may ruin things for everyone.

They wait for Alexandra and talk about mundane everyday concerns for a moment to show how lives go on. Adrian is amazed to learn that Marcus was once in the U.S. Army and had edited an underground literary magazine, having been the first to publish Sigmund's work. Maya, becoming drunk, recalls the beauty of Sigmund's early writing, and Irina goes to play the piano. Adrian confesses his lack of understanding and his feelings of having missed out on history's big events, which have made him seem rootless. Marcus tells about how he went to the United States to lecture and was arrested as a communist spy; then when he was deported back to his own country, he was arrested there as a U.S. spy.

Adrian suggests that they stand up and fight, but Sigmund explains that different people fight in different ways. Americans, he believes, keep hope alive through a gambling spirit, while his people do it through telling lies and constantly acting as if in a play. He then challenges Marcus about making the whole trial scenario up, pointing out that to arrest him could cause a stir the government would rather avoid. Marcus, in turn, accuses Adrian of being a reporter who is looking for an exposé. Marcus tries to justify his actions further, pointing out that their choices are limited. Maya grows angry with Adrian for daring to judge them and their country. The phone rings, and it is Alexandra for Sigmund; the government has decided to return his manuscript. They try to think of why, but Maya insists that to seek a reason is pointless and that Sigmund would be foolish to stay in the country. He remains adamant; he cannot leave and so tries to work out the government's plan.

Sigmund once read a novel in which someone fired a gun using the piano. He tries this out, and it works, which proves to him that writing contains some element of truth. He gives the gun to Marcus, who is furious with what he sees as Sigmund's self-aggrandizing behavior. Adrian takes Marcus's side and pleads with Sigmund to go, but Sigmund worries because he believes that he would not be able to write if separated from his homeland. Maya admits that her belief government-planted microphones are there and that she and Marcus will suffer if Sigmund does not leave, but Sigmund will not weaken. As Marcus goes to answer the door to Alexandra, Maya forgives Sigmund and thanks him for his strength, as Irina offers to play more music.

CRITICAL COMMENTARY

In *The Archbishop's Ceiling,* Miller presents us with a play in which reality is ever in question, partly to explore what place morality might have in such a world. Miller may set his play in eastern Europe, but he uses this setting as a symbol for conditions that he feels are universal. The basic premise of this room being bugged is not paranoia but a reasonable possibility, even within the United States after the 1983 Watergate scandal. The play's setting represents a worldwide problem of surveillance and censorship and one that goes beyond mere politics, for Miller uses the political metaphor to address

deeper concerns regarding the function and nature of reality, truth, compromise, and art.

Miller details a highly complex interior set, intended not to be realistic but offered as a complex, multilayered symbol. The thick walls and the solidity of the room convey the idea of a trap of the type in which many postmodern people feel themselves caught. The room is a reflection of the mood of an age in its "weight and power, its contents chaotic and sensuous." The baroque decor has the natural complexity that is necessary to mirror the complexities of the contemporary people who now inhabit it. Filled with items from the past, the way that they are stacked implies that these things, like the past, have ceased to have real meaning in such a world. Yet, they remain a continuous and haunting presence and possibility. The title ceiling is given prominence by being first to be lit. Its cherubim and the four winds that are blowing are "darkened unevenly by soot and age." Being from an age when belief in the divine was easier and less complex, they are now neglected, as religion has been. This is, after all, a disused religious dwelling. The sense of disrepair and neglect, despite the former opulence of the place, depicts a society that has been reduced from its former glory.

Who can one trust in such dark times? The difficulty of trust between these characters is conveyed effectively by more than their consistently cautious speech. Frequently, Miller describes how one character will separate from the others to stare out to the front to emphasize their feelings of isolation even within this small group. He also emphasizes the number of times that they speak without looking at each other, indicating both a lack of connection and the possibility of continued evasion. A clear example of this behavior occurs when Adrian "evades" Marcus's eyes, being unable to answer his question; Sigmund, unsure of them both, stares out front. But without trust, how will people connect?

The characters in this play are doubly actors. They play the parts that Miller has written, but these characters themselves are all actors of another kind, playing parts that they are constantly devising for themselves or being coerced to play by outside forces. The varied roles that the characters play, Maya indicates, spring from either a desire to protect themselves or others, or from a desire for political or personal gain. They are all aware that everyone plays a part; Marcus even describes the secret police officer who tells him to warn Sigmund to leave as though he were "putting on an act." It is understandable that Sigmund begins to doubt the police officer's existence. The ideal seems to be to be able to control your own role as Sigmund strives to do, despite the damage that might cause.

Throughout the plot's twists and turns, the audience is consistently kept uncertain regarding the actuality of the ceiling microphones, Marcus's allegiances and aims, what the government has planned for Sigmund, and more. What we observe is how people react when they have the feeling that they might be under constant observation and when they are faced with unending uncertainty. It becomes more comforting to believe that the microphones exist, for that allows them a role to play. Disbelief would strip their lives of significance, while belief offers them a sense of importance. Thus, the microphones simultaneously become a violation and confirmation of their existence. Ultimately, it matters little if the bugs are in the ceiling or not; it is sufficient that the characters believe that they are, as it is that belief that directs their behavior.

The play consistently provokes questions rather than answer them, showing the indeterminacy of life. One question is whether or not Marcus admires Sigmund and is trying to help or Marcus is jealous of Sigmund's popularity and is ensuring his downfall. Sigmund suspects jealousy, but that may just reflect his own feelings of self-importance. Both Maya and Adrian insist that Marcus admires Sigmund and is willing to sacrifice himself to save him; as Maya explains more than once, Marcus did not have to return from London and could have stayed there. We never learn for sure the literal truth about Marcus, and Miller's point may be that both views are simultaneously valid. Marcus is a complex human being and cannot be reduced to a single interpretation.

In some ways, Sigmund's persecution is partly necessary to create his stature as a writer; as Adrian suggests, his opposition provides him with a distinct identity: "If they ignored him, he would

simply be another novelist." We never learn what the topic of Sigmund's novel is, which emphasizes that it is not the content that is important but the existence of the work itself. Maya describes it as telling "All we ever lived," and later, it becomes clear that it contains a central female character based on Maya. In this light, Maya becomes a symbol of the nation itself, with all of its insecurities, fears, evasions, and hopes.

Sigmund sees the central difference between the United States and his own country in the way they each engender the hope that he feels is essential to the survival of all. Americans find hope in taking a gamble, as with a slot machine. Sigmund and his countrymen are not gamblers, but they find hope in telling lies, lies that are not really meant to deceive but are part of an act: "We must lie, it is our only freedom. To lie is our slot-machine—we know we cannot win but it gives us the feeling of hope. . . . Our country is now a theater, where no one is permitted to walk out, and everyone is obliged to applaud." Now Sigmund is being asked to walk out, but he refuses. He is as confused as the others about what to believe, but he holds onto one truth that he feels is certain—his patriotism. It is this that grounds him and gives him the stability and the stature the others seek.

Each character has created a world from his or her personal perspective, formed by the lies that each decides to accept and the realities that each chooses to recognize. Thus, Sigmund sees tanks; Maya and Marcus do not. Adrian sees society as made up of isolated individuals, but Marcus can only see a collective community in which individuality is impossible. While each maintains his or her own separate reality, each remains isolated. What they need—and what Sigmund finally provides—is a fiction on which they can agree. His popularity is based on his ability to create memories for them all: He is a kind of head liar whose art offers a vision to provide them all with hope and belief. We see this when Maya talks of his writing, recalling, "A story full of colors, like a painting. . . . It was a miracle—such prose from a field of beets. That morning—for half an hour—I believed Socialism." Sigmund uses the piano to fire the gun to assert the potential truth of fiction and by this act takes control. He hands the gun to Marcus as he realizes that he does not need it to exert his power; his strength lies in his integrity as a writer. In his refusal to leave the country, he becomes a fixed entity in a chaotic and constantly changing world and becomes a beacon by which the others can be guided and made to feel secure.

Sigmund needs his roots to be effective in the world at large. He may be trapped in the nation in which he lives, but it is also his home; he draws strength from that, as much as the strength that he draws from honest contact with other people. Maya, finally, gives Sigmund what he wants—an honest human response, uncluttered by lies and deception—as she reaches out and touches his face and accepts him with gratitude and understanding. The music that Irina requests at the close seems to mark the celebration of a triumph.

FIRST PERFORMANCE

The Archbishop's Ceiling premiered at the Eisenhower Theater, Kennedy Center, in Washington, D.C., on April 30, 1977, with the following cast:

Adrian: Tony Musante
Maya: Bibi Andersson
Marcus: Douglas Watson
Martin: Josef Sommer
Irina: Bara-Cristen Hansen
Sigmund: John Cullum

Directed by Arvin Brown
Set by David Jenkins
Produced by ROBERT WHITEHEAD, Roger L. Stevens, and Konrad Matthaei
It ran for 30 performances.

INITIAL REVIEWS

Dennis Welland admires Miller's commitment to experimentation but suggests that the play's "lack of success in the [American] theatre may be attributable largely to his demanding too much of his audience or perhaps expecting an audience more sensitive in its response to tone, nuance, hint and inference than is altogether reasonable." Miller himself felt that the play failed in the United States, partly because so many Americans refused to see its relevance to their own lives. Dissatisfied with

the casting and the theater space he was given, Miller also felt the premiere production had been botched.

The 1977 production met fierce disapproval from William Glover and David Richardson. Richard Coe, wondering if Miller had been pressured into putting it on before it was ready, suggested that the play was in need of more work, being long-winded and lacking in pace. R. H. Gardner described it as "less a play than a polemic, though what its argument is remains unclear," and Gerald Weales found the characters complex but ultimately limited and the whole lacking in humanity.

The revised production offered in Great Britain nearly a decade later was better received, although many critics remained dismayed by the play's deliberate indeterminacy and sense of repetition. However, Michael Billington described the Old Vic production as "a complex, gritty, intellectually teasing play," and John Peter declared that "there's nothing self-righteous or complacent about this work: It is full of a gaunt and warm humanity." Meanwhile, Jane Edwardes reviewed the Royal Shakespeare production as "a powerful exploration of a world in which morality no longer appears to provide easy answers."

SCHOLARSHIP

There has been very little scholarship on this play, probably due to its poor reception and infrequent performance. Although based on the premiere production that included the character of Martin, Gerald Weales's review, though guarded, offers useful commentary on the other characterizations, and while Dennis Welland bemoans the play's apparent inaccessibility, he also offers some insight into its presentation. Among the few early critical pieces that address *The Archbishop's Ceiling*, CHRISTOPHER BIGSBY's "Afterword" directs us to consider Miller's concerns in the play beyond politics, with "life as theatre, with the coercive power of private and public fictions, with the nature of the real and with the necessity to reconstruct a moral world in the ethical void left by the death of God," and his chapter on the play in his 2005 study of Miller offers a detailed analysis of the play's background and themes. June Schlueter also recognizes its complexity in her exploration of the play's commentary on truth and art.

More recent studies covering Miller's works have necessarily contained at least partial chapters that have begun to consider the depths of the play. These include Alice Griffin's insightful, though brief, consideration of its symbolism and Stephen Marino's longer analysis that explains how Miller expresses the power of the state "and the way citizens handle this power—in metaphors of angels and alcohol." There is also a timely reading of the play from William Demastes as an exploration of "cultural divisiveness . . . in a world that has lost moral control of its own destiny," while George Castellitto reads the play through a Bakhtinian lens, pointing out the dialogic nature of the verbal interactions between the characters, which is caused by their suspicions of being bugged. Terry Otten recognizes that *Archbishop's Ceiling* marks "a major shift in Miller's evolving dramatic vision," being the first play that "confronts the full force of postmodern cynicism," while Andrew Sofer explores it as an exploration of dramatic form, that "undermines the 'I' and turns resistance into performance," and Susan Abbotson reads the play as a lesson in responsibility and connection. STEVEN CENTOLA wrote the only published journal article thus far on this play, with his exploration of the significance of Maya.

CHARACTERS

Irina   Irina is a young Danish girl who is married to the head of Danish programming at the BBC. She may or may not be sleeping with Marcus or being used by him to compromise other writers. She seems an archetypal dumb blonde who only speaks in broken English. In many ways, she represents the *Vogue* image of women that Maya admires in her evident distance from the rest of them, her inability to express any clear sentiment or belief, and her constant search for pleasure. She seems there as little more than eye candy to boost Marcus's image. She is never involved in their discussion but is only a pretty distraction.

Marcus   Marcus is a writer with a checkered past. During WORLD WAR II, he had gone to London to escape the Nazis and signed up to serve for three years in British military intelligence, returning to his homeland after the war. Before COMMUNISM took over his country, he had published a few books to some acclaim and had been invited to the United States to lecture at a university. While traveling, a communist regime overran his country and on arrival in the states, he was arrested as a communist spy. Deported back home, he was arrested by the communists as a U.S. spy and sent to a labor camp for six years. He also had edited a literary magazine that published poems of Auden and the first writings of Sigmund until it had been closed down by the government. He attends writer conferences as a representative of his country, but Maya and Sigmund insist that his writer's spark has left him. He makes his living by selling the rare books that his father left him, for which business, the government allows him a passport to travel.

Marcus may or not be a government collaborator. There are rumors that he brings writers to his dwelling and seduces them with pretty women to compromise them and force them to obey the government. He has lived with Maya for some time, but they have recently parted, although she still stays at his home when he is away. He has government connections as he calls the daughter of the minister of the interior to come to see Sigmund, and it is to him that Sigmund goes for help, but whether he has true influence or is just another pawn is hard to judge. He was in London, where his last novel was finally being released; there, he says, he was accosted by a secret policeman who told him that they would arrest and detain Sigmund if he did not emigrate. He has come back to both warn and help Sigmund or to ensure that he leaves, as the government wants.

On Marcus's entry, he immediately takes control and seems a figure of power, sending Maya on an errand and stopping Adrian from going with her. His accusations that Adrian is playing a double game could be to keep everyone off guard and himself at the helm. But his attitude and friendship toward Sigmund are kept ambiguous throughout; is he jealous of Sigmund's popularity as a writer or a devoted fan? Has he returned to save Sigmund or to condemn him? Whether he puts self, art, or country first changes with whoever is making the speech, and each possibility is credible. He certainly seems to be living a privileged life in a restrictive regime, which makes him suspicious, but it could just be to create a good impression for foreigners, as Sigmund suggests.

Marcus sees himself as a profound realist and optimist who can find the good even in an oppressive regime. He simply ignores the bad. The Marcus of the past was a vital and vibrant figure, deserving of great respect, but what remains is a pale and impotent shadow of his former self. Once a promising writer, he now leads an increasingly trivial life filled with wine, women, and song. He sees this as a compromise and the only effective way to live in a nation where even the political leaders have little true freedom, but it is really an avoidance of responsibility. By distancing himself from his struggles and beliefs, he has distanced himself from that which formerly gave his life meaning. He sees Sigmund, with his insistence on their nation's corruption and his insistence for change, as an unrealistic and naive idealist striving toward an unreachable goal.

Although Marcus seems to be in the driver's seat directing everybody else and checking his watch to keep to some prescribed timetable, he is ultimately unable to control them in the way that he wants. Marcus began as idealistic a writer as Sigmund is now, but during the years, he has turned into a man more like Adrian, who allowed himself to become disconnected from his beliefs and his country. Now, it seems most likely that Marcus only looks out for himself and does not care whom he hurts. Yet, Miller allows us to feel compassion for him—given his past experiences, it is scant wonder that Marcus has lost his sense of idealism. Sigmund has yet to face such trials.

Martin   In the 1977 script, Martin was Maya's former husband who is almost certainly a government agent and plays the role of a listener. He has access to Sigmund's phone conversations and may, if they do exist, control the ceiling microphones. He manipulates the action through a series of well-timed phone calls that suggest that someone is listening and keeping tabs. In rewrites, Miller erased this character from the script, realizing that his inclusion made the existence of listening devices too certain.

Maya   In the original script, Maya was a more political figure, but here, she has shied away from politics for some time and is content to write comic anecdotes for her radio show and keep her head down. She has lived with Marcus for some time and has in the past also slept with Adrian (maybe even at Marcus's request). In the earlier version, it was clear that she had also slept with Sigmund, but in the finished script, this is less obvious—he certainly admires her and has based the central character in his latest book on her (as has Adrian), but he seems more devoted to his wife, Elizabeth. Maya has a deep admiration for Sigmund as a writer.

Her declaration that "everything in *Vogue* magazine is true" while being clearly aware of the artistry and artifice behind it says something regarding the relationship between art and reality in the play. In many ways, *Vogue* is a clear picture of the reality of Western civilization in all of its gaudy sensuality and opulence, at least in terms of how it is viewed by many in the Eastern bloc. But it is a sensuality and opulence without feeling that can never be very satisfying. This reflects how Maya's life has become. She is possibly one of Marcus's whores and is quick to flirt with Adrian, even though she seems to despise him once she gains the free speech of the drunk. Maya claims that she is drawn to the *Vogue* models' "vacancy" because she feels that it must make life far easier when one knows and feels nothing. She tries to achieve that same vacancy in her own life by drinking heavily. However, her humanity will insist on breaking through with thoughts and feelings that she cannot effectively suppress.

Maya begins to drink as soon as Adrian asks about conditions in her country, clearly a defensive action to avoid thought on the matter. A large part of that from which she is hiding is the hypocrisy of the men in her life. Each seems to her, despite their denunciation of success and power, to be longing for both. Although Maya has switched off her idealism in a way that Sigmund refuses to do, there remains a strong bond between Maya and Sigmund, which may be why he has chosen her as his muse. Each takes great pleasure in the smaller things in life: a new haircut, good food and drink. Sigmund, however, seems to be the stronger of the two, the one more willing to stand by his beliefs. By the close, despite her efforts to get him to leave and his decision to stay, she thanks Sigmund for offering a ray of hope.

Ruth   Ruth lives with Adrian in the United States and is a troubling figure. She has been suicidal but is now taking pills to hide from her depression. She survives, but her life contains no self-awareness—her own security rests on a refusal to face the terrors of life. She refuses to even think of herself anymore. She has "sold out" so far to the business world she has no other life. It is most likely this that most upsets Adrian as he no longer holds a central position in her life. Instead of resisting "power" or even recognizing it enough to fear it, she becomes a part of it by embracing commercialism totally; she has become the assistant to the managing editor of a magazine—no doubt one like *Vogue*—now a part of that vacant, commercial world that only knows how to sell empty dreams to people who cannot face reality. Full of renewed energy, it is expended in swimming 50 laps a day rather than in doing anything useful for the community.

Sigmund   Sigmund is a "heavy man" who commands a "unique respect" from Maya, which gives us a comforting sense of his solidity and character as soon as he enters the room. He has little of the confusing ambiguity that we find in Marcus. Sigmund knows that one must keep human bonds alive to stay connected to others in this political chaos. It is because of this that he suggests to Marcus at the height of one of their heated political arguments that, instead, they talk to each other about themselves. He does not just give Maya a peck on the cheek as Marcus does but kisses her palm—a gesture of intimacy and respect that shows how connected to people Sigmund is. He and Maya are constantly touching one another throughout the play—not in a sexual way but in an evident need for comfort and for a physical connection to support the spiritual one. Sigmund likes people—he warmly embraces Adrian on seeing him. Though he has an ego, he does not allow it to blind him to the feelings of others. In an essay on the play, Miller

suggests that out of all the characters, Sigmund is "most alive" and the best writer because he has the greatest sense of life.

When Adrian tells Sigmund that the room is bugged, it is clear that Sigmund is neither surprised nor does he particularly care. He openly declares that his manuscript has been taken, found by the government before Adrian had blurted its whereabouts. The simple precariousness of art is underlined by the fact that this was the only copy of his novel. Sigmund has come to try to get help from Marcus in retrieving it, and one must wonder what kind of compromise he may have to make to facilitate this. We discover that it is to leave his homeland and that it is a compromise he stoutly refuses.

Sigmund has a clearer view than Adrian of people's humanity. He seems to understand Maya, and he recognizes the complexity in Marcus that Adrian keeps missing. He exudes a certain honesty, unlike Adrian and Marcus whose motives are frequently kept hidden. Sigmund lets his feelings be known—it is this that led to his manuscript being confiscated, as they knew it was finished because he was openly so happy. He plays the microphone game, guarding his speech when necessary, but his reactions and feelings are honest ones. The comical gestures between himself and Adrian as they covertly discuss Sigmund's options draw us to like Sigmund despite his bluntness and evident stubbornness; these gestures come across as more honest than the evasions of the rest. Miller admits that he based Sigmund on Václav Havel, the dissident writer who later became president of the Czech Republic, a man whom he deeply admired and whom he wished the audience also to respect. Havel was noted for his humanistic administration that became a model of democracy in the Eastern bloc. But there are also elements of Miller himself in Sigmund, as the playwright who felt he was being silenced in his native land though lionized abroad, but who refused to leave.

Adrian bemoans the modern emphasis on commercialism and entertainment over significant art. However, he fails to realize that the artist's job, if he has something worth conveying, is neither to embrace the commercialism and entertainment nor to withdraw into a sterile artistic isolation. The artist needs to connect with his audience—albeit a more difficult task in contemporary times—and through this connection, he will have the necessary impact, even though his message may take time to reach larger numbers. Sigmund recognizes that art must be grounded in something beyond the artist himself and cannot exist in isolation. He grounds his art in his feelings for his homeland, which is why he feels unable to leave, even if staying endangers his ability to continue writing. To leave would silence Sigmund forever.

Wallach, Adrian   Adrian represents the type of uncommitted U.S. writer whom Miller most despises. His liberalism is hypocritical, discredited by his inability to understand the political situation or connect to other people, and his own self-serving agenda. Adrian has hit a writer's block and has come for inspiration, mostly from Maya, a past lover. He acts as though he would like to rekindle this relationship—talking of his sexual tension and visions of her inner thigh—but it soon becomes evident that Adrian is a figure who has difficulty committing. Throughout the play, he switches his allegiance from character to character, never certain whom to support. He is largely here to stay away from Ruth, a woman with whom he lives but to whom he is unable to commit and with whom he no longer feels comfortable, even as he declares that he may still marry her. He is an irresponsible figure who needs to learn how to connect properly with others on a level of mutual understanding. Only then will he gain any satisfaction from his relationships—although it will be at an inevitable sacrifice of some of the freedom that he is so loathe to lose.

Adrian's inability to make connections applies to more than people. What is happening to Sigmund as a politically engaged artist is not unusual; artists everywhere suffer from constrictions, whether they are overtly government imposed or clouded in economics and social taboos. Adrian is able to recognize the nightmare of living as Sigmund does but refuses to see the similarities to his own country. Because he had protested Vietnam and not suffered for his actions, he feels that his country allowed the freedom of speech Sigmund is denied. But the Vietnam War lasted for more than eight years, and

his protests had little impact. Sigmund's recent letters to the European press and the United Nations have had a far greater impact. Adrian's stances have less to do with personal belief than with what good public relations are for an ambitious writer. Sigmund's actions and writing are both more personally motivated and less controlled—he is far less able to compromise than a man like Adrian, who has so few convictions.

Adrian is unable to see the humanity in the figures before him, as he is obsessed with their relationship to power. This blinds him to any honest vision of them as individuals; therefore, anything he might attempt to write about them could only be a work of fiction. As he becomes drawn into Sigmund's dilemma, he begins to learn and see more clearly the doubleness of lives that are lived under constant surveillance and uncertainty. But what he still fails to recognize is that his own life holds the same kind of doubleness, deception, and duplicity. Adrian is obsessed with power and is excited by the glimpse of power that he has been given in this room. It thrills him that Maya may be a government agent and, therefore, a figure of power, as well as justifying his characterization of her in his abandoned novel. He prefers his fictional Maya to the actual one and is anxious to make Maya conform to the way that he has written her—it is the way he exerts control over people. He does not for a moment, however, stop to consider the human possibilities of Maya or the people he may be hurting by his irresponsible comments and his arrogant attempts to play games with the people who are looking on.

Adrian has always felt somewhat dislocated from his society: "History came at us like a rumor. We were never really there." Though having served in the U.S. Army, he was too young to be in Korea and too old for Vietnam and consequently feels separated from the big political events of his era. Lacking real social experience, largely because of his own disengagement, he feels insubstantial and rootless. It is partly this European country's sense of history that has drawn him to both write about it and now visit. He is on a search for the roots that he needs to give him a sense of security. Adrian rejects the ambiguities that he encounters as too discomfiting and insists on answers that he is unable to uncover; consequently, he is never able to feel sure of his ground.

Adrian is momentarily coaxed from his personal closed world when he connects with Sigmund and offers to take his manuscript out of the country. This is an act that would irrevocably involve him in these people's lives and burden him with great responsibility. However, he is not forced to follow through and remains in ignorance as he continues to encourage Sigmund to leave his country. He cannot understand Sigmund's need to stay because Adrian has separated art from life, and that is what is essentially wrong with his writing.

FURTHER READING

Abbotson, Susan. "*The Archbishop's Ceiling*: A Lesson in Responsibility." In *Arthur Miller: Twentieth Century Legend,* edited by Syed Mashkoor Ali, 259–286. (Jaipur, India: Surabhi, 2006).

Bigsby, Christopher. "*The Archbishop's Ceiling.*" *Arthur Miller: A Critical Study.* Cambridge: Cambridge University Press, 2005, 295–311.

———. Afterword. *Archbishop's Ceiling.* Methuen, 1984, 91–95.

Billington, Michael. "*The Archbishop's Ceiling.*" *Guardian,* April 19, 1985. In *London Theatre Record* 5, no. 8 (1985): 375.

Castellitto, George P. "Bakhtinian Heteroglossia in Miller's *The Archbishop's Ceiling.*" In *Arthur Miller: Twentieth Century Legend,* edited by Syed Mashkoor Ali, 287–295. (Jaipur, India: Surabhi, 2006).

Centola, Steven R. "The Search for an Unalienated Existence: Lifting the Veil of Maya in Arthur Miller's *The Archbishop's Ceiling.*" *Journal of Evolutionary Psychology* 21, nos. 3–4 (August 2000): 230–237.

Coe, Richard L. "Miller's *Archbishop's Ceiling*" *Washington Post,* May 2, 1977, B1, B7.

———. "What Happened to Miller's Play?" *Washington Post* May 15, 1977, H1.

Demastes, William. "Miller's 1970s 'Power' Plays." In *Cambridge Companion to Arthur Miller,* edited by Christopher Bigsby, 139–151. (New York: Cambridge University Press, 1997).

Edwardes, Jane. "*The Archbishop's Ceiling.*" *Time Out,* November 5, 1986. In *London Theatre Record* 6, no. 22 (1986): 1,194.

Gardner, R. H. Revision of *Archbishop's Ceiling* by Arthur Miller. *Baltimore Sun,* 1977, n.p.

Griffin, Alice. "Plays of the 1980s." *Understanding Arthur Miller.* Columbia: University of South Carolina Press, 1996, 158–172.

Marino, Stephen A. "Metaphors of Survival: *Incident at Vichy* and *The Archbishop's Ceiling.*" *A Language Study of Arthur Miller's Plays: The Poetic in the Colloquial.* New York: Mellen, 2002, 107–134.

Miller, Arthur. "Conditions of Freedom." *American Clock* and *The Archbishop's Ceiling.* New York: Grove, 1989, vii–xix.

———. *Timebends: A Life.* New York: Grove, 1987.

"New Play by Miller is Faulted in Washington." *New York Times,* May 3, 1977, 50.

Otten, Terry. "*The Archbishop's Ceiling.*" *The Temptation of Innocence in the Dramas of Arthur Miller.* Columbia: University of Missouri Press, 2002, 166–177.

Peter, John. "Looking Up to Big Brother." *Sunday Times,* April 21, 1985, 41.

Schlueter, June. "Power Play: Arthur Miller's *Archbishop's Ceiling.*" *CEA Critic* 48–49 (1985–87): 134–138.

Sofer, Andrew. "From Technology to Trope: *The Archbishop's Ceiling* and Miller's Prismatic Drama." In *Arthur Miller's America: Theater and Culture in a Time of Change,* edited by Enoch Brater, 94–108. (Ann Arbor: University of Michigan Press, 2005).

Wandor, Michelene. Review of *Archbishop's Ceiling* by Arthur Miller. *Plays and Players* 400 (January 1987): 25–26.

Weales, Gerald. "Come Home to Maya." *Commonweal* 104 (July 8, 1977), 431–432.

Welland, Dennis. "Meditations on Life and Letters." *Miller: The Playwright,* 2d. ed. New York: Methuen, 1983, 133–143.

"Arthur Miller on *The Crucible*" (1972)

This essay first appeared in 1972 in the magazine *Audience* and was reprinted in the revised edition of *The Theater Essays of Arthur Miller* (1996). It contains Miller's response to JEAN PAUL SARTRE's 1957 film version of *The Crucible, Les Sorcières de Salem (The Witches of Salem)*. While Miller asserts that it is preferable to change things in a film version and wise not to try to copy a play precisely, he felt that some of the changes were unnecessary and that the work was "weakened and made less actual, rather than more pointed, by Sartre's overly Marxist screenplay." Sartre's overemphasis of class issues simplified the play's conflict, even making it less real as in the depiction that Salem's respectable people suffered as much as the poor. For Miller, Sartre changed the play's theme. "The original play," Miller insists, "stresses individual conscience as the ultimate defense against a tyrannical authority, but conscience in the screenplay is more an expression of rebellion against a class oppressor than a transcendence of man over himself." To this end, Sartre's version becomes despiritualized as it becomes too pointedly politicized in its desire to present us with heroic representatives of COMMUNISM. The film's different agenda makes it less universally human than Miller's original play. Despite such complaints, Miller enjoyed the film's setting; applauded the acting, especially the complexity of the Proctors' marital relationship and the threatening sexuality of Abigail; and found Sartre's version "a stimulating and even gripping picture" and "a strong film in its own right." Pointing out that U.S. movie companies had been too fearful of the "righteous Right" to produce a film of his play themselves, he is grateful that at least this "version" of his play exists in celluloid.

"The Bare Manuscript" (2002)

Published in *New Yorker* in 2002, the short story "The Bare Manuscript" is a redemptive tale of a writer's discovery that the power that breathes life into his work is love, as he rediscovers the love that first drew him to his wife, Lena. Clement Zorn rides on his early successes, having lost his original passion about writing. His marriage of more

than 20 years never found its feet, and he has sought solace in numerous sexual affairs. Were it not for the charity of those who believe in his ability, who give him a house in which to live, or who loan him holiday homes and cars, his life would be impoverished.

The vision of a girl walking along the beach inspires him to believe that if he could write on the naked flesh of a woman, it would help him surmount his writer's block and restore something elemental to his writing. His plan actually works as he pens the story of how he first met his wife at the beach up until his first betrayal; this memory, so keenly recalled, rekindles both his passion for his writing and for his wife.

The story begins as he is writing on the naked back of Carol Mundt and moves back and forth from that point. Mixing the exotic with the mundane, Clement pauses while she goes to the bathroom. His excitement as he writes is redolent of having sex, and Miller forges a link between pen and penis, although Clement views the woman as unattractive: too tall, too assertive, and too unfeminine. Carol passively accepts her role, proud to be used as his canvas, believing him to be a well-known writer despite the shabbiness of his living space. The situation inspires and liberates Clement who has not written so effortlessly since his first and most-acclaimed novel. As he writes, he recalls scenes from his past.

More than 10 years ago, he began to have affairs, finding that sex freed him to write a little. At about the same time, Lena, having studied social psychology at college, encouraged him to see a psychiatrist. They talked about his father, an abusive disciplinarian whose treatment gave him psychoses but about whom he could never write. His first novel had been a thinly disguised portrait of his mother. He and Lena have lived a pleasant bohemian life and survive through the national crises of their era from blacklisting to the new conservatism, feeling morally and intellectually superior, but with no real direction or commitment, even to each other. Understandably, their marriage has gradually become a sham, and Clement reflects on how that occurred. Despite being lucky, his life has had no real focus other than Lena, and she has become indistinct over the years. Lena is as frustrated as he but unable to decide what to do.

Returning to their courting days, Clement recalls vainly trying to persuade Lena to sleep with him. He loves her, but she is uncertain and noncommittal. Soon after, the couple visit Lena's mother, Mrs. Vanetzki. A widow whose her husband went crazy by his change of circumstance after emigrating to America, she has three children, of whom college-educated Lena was her biggest hope, but Lena has no greater direction than her siblings. Her sister Patsy is easygoing but content and quite willing to flaunt herself in front of Clement. Brother Steve sleepwalks, but he has a promising career as a technician. They joke about Steve needing sexual release and tease Clement about a sexual innocence that they assume, which makes him feel inadequate. Declaring his love for Lena, the mother warns him against marriage, as her daughter is too mixed-up and his career as a writer is less than likely to sustain them. They agree that she is probably right.

Clement recounts his indirect advertisement for a human canvas and discovery of Carol. As he first begins to write on Carol, he ironically chooses to write about the love that he felt on first meeting Lena and how they were attracted. Once done, he and Carol awkwardly transcribe the text to a laptop. Feeling an intimacy, they shower together and have sex. He offers her money, and when she realizes that this will be the only time that they do this, she accepts. As he reads through his manuscript, Lena returns, and the anger that he initially feels on seeing her turns to love in the glow of his text.

Though one may wonder how much of Lena's courtship is based on Miller's first wife MARY SLATTERY, the central metaphor of the story—that every effective manuscript is an act of love—is what most strikes the reader. Clement uses his too-long-buried love of Lena to revitalize his art, and although he ends uncertain if he can continue, he has made the first step toward allowing Lena a purpose and place in his life. The production of this new work allows him to bare his soul, reexamine his past, and rediscover direction in his own life as well.

"The Battle of Chicago: From the Delegates' Side" (1968)

This essay first appeared in *New York Times Magazine* in 1968 and was Miller's report on serving as a Eugene McCarthy delegate at the 1968 Democratic convention in Chicago. It was reprinted in a pair of essay collections about the Chicago riots in the 1960s but most recently in *Echoes Down the Corridor* (2000). The essay details Miller's experiences as a delegate and his thoughts on the violence and lack of communication that occurred both inside and outside the International Amphitheater that hosted the event, a violence that he sees as the "result of the suppression, planned and executed, of any person or viewpoint which conflicted with the president's."

Miller describes what he felt was a split between professional politicians for whom any position is expendable and those like McCarthy who took a more moral stance. However, given the docility of so many of the delegates, the former were allowed to carry the day with slogans rather than anything of substance. Although 80 percent of Democrats were against the VIETNAM WAR, the delegates were largely restricted from any real debate for fear of fracturing the party, and majority views were allowed no voice. Those like Miller who supported McCarthy and refused to compromise on Vietnam were frowned upon as foolishly trying to rock the boat. Miller relates the inflammatory speech of one Congressman who mocked the concern of the nation's youth and turned the issue into a generational conflict. Upset that despite an egalitarian political system, the United States cannot do a better job of debating real issues, Miller complains about the way in which so many of the older generation simply refuse to listen to the young because they are young. It is this narrow-minded propensity that Miller feels broke the social compact of U.S. liberty that led to the protestors outside being so viciously attacked.

Asked by a young reporter how he can continue to have faith in democratic policies, Miller argues, what are the alternatives? Neither has a clear answer, but Miller suggests that the problem is a lack of strong leadership rather than that the party or process is worthless. Miller describes venturing outside with several other delegates to show support for the youths who have been beaten by the police. The next day, he is part of a television discussion and bemoans the fact that everyone erroneously believed that it was being censored by the government because of the suspicious political climate that had been created by the way the party and the media had restricted debate during the convention and ignored the voices of the youths outside. Such suppression, Miller concludes, is only a degree away from the Soviet Union's jailing their dissenters.

Battle of the Ovens (1942)

Broadcast by Du Pont as part of the *Cavalcade of America* series on June 22, 1942, with Jean Hersholt in the lead role, the radio drama *Battle of the Ovens* offers itself as an exemplar of the worth of American pluck and spirit and would seem a fairly typical patriotic war play of the period. However, it is interesting for both its Revolutionary War setting, already considered in the earlier radio drama *Captain Paul,* and its depiction of the informer as a positive figure. Although based on factual evidence, Miller adapts details of the story to highlight the issues that he sees as most important. The play has never been published, but a typescript can be found at the University of Colorado at Boulder.

Christopher Ludwick is a staunch American who is frustrated at being too old to fight in the war against the British. He contributes by sharing his skills as a master baker of 40 years by baking for the people to keep their spirits up and sending his apprentice, Jerry to bake for the army. Commodities are in short supply, and Christopher is surprised when Jerry, for whom he feels a paternal responsibility, tries to sell him flour. Jerry explains that this flour comes from the army whose policy is to give its bakers a pound of flour for every pound of bread they produce. With the other ingredients combined, it only takes a half-pound of flour for a pound of bread, and the army bakers are keeping the extra flour for their own benefit. Christopher views Jerry's flour as having been stolen and views

the practice as an insult to his trade. Jerry sees it as a reasonable opportunity to make a profit, but Christopher attacks his old apprentice, refuses his flour, and threatens to have him arrested.

Unable to write himself, Christopher dictates a letter to his wife to inform the army of this practice and is subsequently nominated to oversee the army bakers and make them honest. As baker in general for George Washington's army, he puts an end to the abuse and allows the army to become more efficient. In this way, informing is shown as a tactic by which the American way can be improved and strengthened, a point that Miller will reinforce in his 1943 agitprop *That They May Win.* By the next decade, Miller would be taking a very different view of the informer.

"Beavers" (2005)

This was the final short story that Miller sent for publication during his lifetime, and it appeared in *Harper's* in February 2005 shortly after his death. Full of naturalistic detail, it seems reminiscent of his earlier piece, "Bees," being similarly about unwanted wildlife on a man's property that is reluctantly destroyed. But while the bees return, it is only the memory of the beavers and the uncertainty of what they were doing that lingers, and this ambiguous aspect is the keynote of the tale. While "Bees" was openly autobiographical, this story has an unnamed protagonist. Although his wife is named Louisa, like one of Miller's friends and neighbors (the Calders), the story's emphasis on his having planted trees decades previously on a property very like Miller's ROXBURY, CONNECTICUT, estate makes it seem closer to home.

The man approaches his pond and watches for signs of beavers. Noticing gnawed tree stumps, he is angry at the beavers for destroying his trees and worries that they will decimate the entire area. He sees a beaver swimming into its lodge and is amazed at how quickly this has been built; nothing had been there the day before. Worried also that the beavers' excrement will make his pond toxic so that he and his wife will not be able to swim, he runs to the house to get a gun. He fires into the water to scare it away, but the beaver confidently swims across the pond, and with apparent defiance, breaks a bush and starts to try to plug the overflow pipe, which will raise the level of the water. Since the pond is already deep enough for its lodge, the protagonist cannot understand why. The unnecessary aspect of this further destruction upsets his view of nature as "an ultimate source of steady logic and order" as opposed to the greed and stupidity of humans. It bothers him to see a beaver acting both greedily and stupidly, even as he is impressed by its "absolute dedication," the very opposite of his own uncertainties and insecurities. He decides to ask for advice.

The druggist's son Carl, who works with cement and rocks and likes to hunt, comes by. Inspecting the pond, he declares that he will have to kill the beavers. Though reluctant to condone death, the protagonist loves his trees and bows to Carl's authority, once he ascertains that it is legal to kill them. Feeling the "joy of the kill" move into him as he watches Carl stalk and kill two beavers, the first beaver's apparently pointless actions still bother him. Trying to come up with solutions which he cannot convince himself are true, he finally wonders if the beaver could have been showing off to his wife, blocking the pipe as an act of love. This he tentatively accepts, as love has no reason, but remains haunted by their deaths, even while he is pleased to have his property back unspoiled. A simple story about ridding a pond of beavers becomes an exploration of human rapacity and agression, balanced against more uplifting possibilities of motivation reflected in the natural world. Miller had depicted this incomprehensible but erstwhile possibility of love in the characters of Douglas and Denise in *The Turpentine Still* the year before, and it was clearly a matter that concerned him in his final years, as he prepared to embark upon what would have been his fourth marriage.

"Bees" (1990)

The short story "Bees" was written especially for *Michigan Quarterly Review* and appeared in the

Spring edition of 1990. Subtitled "A Story to Be Spoken," it is a self-mocking monologue from Miller that recounts how he discovered a large colony of bees living in the wall of his first ROXBURY, CONNECTICUT, farmhouse soon after he moved in with his young son, ROBERT MILLER, and wife MARY SLATTERY. His wife and child are not named in the story, as if to distance himself, or perhaps his audience, from the people involved—after all, his subject and focus are the bees of the title, and he offers a testament to their ability to survive and an inspiring study of bee behavior.

His son is stung by a bee in the living room, but for a time, Miller cannot discover how they are entering the house. While fixing a fence, he spots a swarm that settles in a nearby oak and assumes that the bees have left, but this turns out to be the hive of a newly hatched queen. The next evening, bees are again inside, and he spots a gap in the wallboards. There is a hive inside the wall. Although this area had been full of farmers, it is now suburban, and his neighbors can offer little advice, so he buys a can of DDT and sprays it through the crack. He assumes that they are exterminated, but the next evening sees more bees. He ups the dose to the same affect and wonders at their amazing resistance, lightheartedly worrying if they may come after him in revenge. He tries plastering up their outside entrance, but they keep breaking away the plaster. In desperation, he tries a sulfur candle that appears to work and, upset to see them so easily defeated, clears away the dead bees and paints the cavity with asphalt tar to take away the scent.

Miller bluntly states, "Then we divorced and I sold the house," but he buys another up the road and several years later, the man who currently owned the old place dropped by to ask if he had ever had any trouble with bees. It seems they have returned in full force, and Miller is elated at this evidence of their determination and refusal to be chased away. The story becomes a tale of continuation despite the obstacles and the odds. After explaining all he had previously done, he advises the man to sell the house, although, Miller jokes, he declined to advise him about whether or not he should divorce his wife.

Bernadine, I Love You (1945)

Broadcast on March 5, 1945, the radio drama *Bernadine, I Love You* was a fairly standard script and less engaging than Miller's usual radio work. Working with an uncommonly romantic topic for Miller, it tells the story of a lonely American parachutist, played by William Bendix, who is helped by the Red Cross to make contact with his wife. It is a patriotic celebration of the usefulness of the Red Cross and the suffering that the average American soldier often faced so far from home. Never published, a typescript for this can be found at the New York Public Library's Center for the Performing Arts.

Boro Hall Nocturne (ca. 1942)

A WORLD WAR II play written at about the same time as *The Half Bridge*, *Boro Hall Nocturne* also takes as its subject Nazi saboteurs and U.S. collaborators. As a pacifist, Miller had initially been against the war, but by this point, he was clearly a supporter. The play was neither produced nor published and is most notable for its consideration of the existence of U.S. ANTI-SEMITISM at that time. A manuscript rests at the HARRY RANSOM RESEARCH CENTER.

Set in the sector headquarters of the Air Raid Protection Service in downtown BROOKLYN, it begins at three in the morning. The building is dilapidated and mostly empty, with the striking exception of a piano. The air-raid warden on duty, Mr. Goldberg, a piano tuner by trade, is asleep. Transports are leaving the nearby dockyard to join the Atlantic convoys. Alexander Kelley, a musician who has just been drafted and is meant to report for duty that morning, relieves Goldberg. Uncertain that the war is right and determined to selfishly pursue his music, Kelley destroys his draft card. During the lean years of the GREAT DEPRESSION, Goldberg had generously helped Kelley, and they have since become firm friends. This is one reason why Kelley has refused to join an anti-Semitic group that has been beating up local Jews.

A Nazi professor of music, who is acting as a saboteur with the help of an American ally, and several Italian workers, one of whose homes is destroyed in an attack now being unleashed down the Eastern coast, join these two. As the men hear news of the attack over the radio, the professor's involvement is realized. He stabs his collaborationist ally but is arrested. Having witnessed this inhuman display, Kelley decides to report for duty after all, realizing that the battle for American survival will need the help of every loyal citizen. The play was clearly meant as wartime propaganda and serves its purpose well: to rally people to support the war effort, whatever their initial reluctance about U.S. involvement.

"A Boy Grew in Brooklyn" (1955)

An essay that first appeared in *Holiday* magazine in 1955, this was part of a series of "nostalgic hometown stories by America's greatest writers." Describing facets of his childhood in BROOKLYN, Miller recounts how much the borough has changed and offers the piece as an elegy to the close-knit community that he fondly recalls but is now vanished. The piece was later reprinted in *Echoes Down the Corridor* (2000). Much of this material is repeated in *Timebends: A Life* (1987), such as his exploits on his bakery-delivery route, reactions to the WALL STREET CRASH, and his grandfather, LOUIS BARNETT's fake deathbed scene, but the essay also contains some unique details. These include additional material on his father, ISIDORE MILLER, which interestingly relates him to Joe Keller, friendly with the neighborhood children and fond of a prank. We also learn about locals like Ike Samuels who ran the hardware store and talks himself out of faulty repairs, the "village idiot" Danny (called Sammy in *Timebends: A Life*) who refers to everyone by their phone number, and Nick, an itinerant man who was hired by his aunt and who would become the model for Stanislaus in *The American Clock*, all offering proof of Miller's instinct for comic characterization.

"Bridge to a Savage World" (1958)

In 1955, Miller had been working on a documentary about juvenile delinquency and youth gangs in New York City in the hope of being able to discover an effective solution to what he saw as a tremendous waste. He spent two months virtually living with various gangs, witnessing episodes of violence and secret mediation sessions. Fearing a socialist agenda at a time when such beliefs were considered unpatriotic, the city council's permission to make the film was withdrawn. Three years later, in 1958, when the influence of the HOUSE UN-AMERICAN ACTIVITIES COMMITTEES was on the wane, Miller was able to publish "Bridge to a Savage World" in *Esquire* magazine. This essay was an intentionally rough description of the film treatment that had never been produced, outlining his general intent and illustrating the arc of his plotline with some actual incidents that he recalled. The supposed thugs whom he describes turn out to be mostly "scared kids underneath it all" who "have never known life excepting as a worthless thing; they have been told from birth that they are nothing, that their parents are nothing, that their hopes are nothing." Miller insists that it will take more than love and compassion to lead these youngsters to better lives; it will take hard work such as that done by the courageous employees of the New York City Youth Board, who pioneer a new form of social work that moves away from the office and meets the youths on their own terms on the streets.

Miller's film was to focus on Jerry Bone, an amalgam of the Youth Board workers whom he had met and some of the worst cases in the South Bay Rangers gang whom he tried to help, including Jouncey, Rabbit, Joe Meister, and Paul Martense. He describes Jerry in detail and his efforts in trying to raise up the "seemingly incorrigible young men to decency." Having once been a gang member, Jerry better understands them and is even prepared to overlook the occasional crime to gain their confidence, though this makes him suspect by the police. It is he who represents the bridge of the title. Despite their occasional betrayals, he

sticks by the boys to a degree that scares his wife and perseveres for several years, until he has to quit to tend to his own family: His work has led him to neglect his own children who are now becoming delinquents. Although he cannot save every youth whom he touches and although several sadly fail to surmount the awful conditions that they face, ending as drug addicts or in prison, Jerry has his victories, including Paul who plans to carry on his work once Jerry leaves.

Miller does not want to sugarcoat the lives of these youths and suggest that it will be easy to help, but he offer a realistic picture of the tremendous pressures that they are under. They try to use Jerry just as they feel used, but in his refusal to go along, they learn that there are other ways of dealing with situations without losing their sense of honor. Despite its violent subject matter—and these youths' lives are filled with violence as they casually battle rival gangs, beat up their girlfriends, organize gang rapes, and become hooked on drugs—the film treatment contains several comedic episodes, such as an organized camping trip and the dances and debates that Jerry encourages as he tries to transform the gang into a social club. Under Jerry's care, once he convinces them to trust him by standing up for them against the police and setting a consistently good example, many of these youths learn that they have choices. Even if they cannot surmount the difficulties, Miller depicts them as struggling to try for the sake of a man who has become a substitute father figure for most and has shown them they have personal worth.

Broken Glass (1994)

Fifty years previously, Miller had heard of a woman in his neighborhood who became mysteriously paralyzed in her legs, befuddling her doctors. The image intrigued him, but for a long time, he could not decide how to use it. He also recalled that the husband had always dressed in black. He finally brought these two memories together to form a play that he first called *The Man in Black*, which evolved into *The Gellburgs* and ended up as *Broken*

Glass. The changing titles trace the development of a story that initially centered on an individual, then became a tale about a couple, and ended up as a reflection on the broader society, crystallized in its reaction to news of *Kristallnacht* (the night on which the Nazi government sent people out to attack Jewish buildings and people in an explosion of violence that would indicate what was to come but of which few around the world took note).

On the surface, the play tells the story of Sylvia and Phillip Gellburg, who after years of marriage come to realize that they hardly know each other at all. Phillip is the only Jew working at a very traditional Wall Street bank where he mainly works on foreclosings. Obsessed with work and his own desire to assimilate, Phillip has little time for his wife until she demands his attention by suddenly falling prey to a mysterious paralysis after seeing the events of *Kristallnacht* in the newspaper. Up until now, Sylvia has been a quiet little housewife, but she needs to express her buried fears and longings. Dr. Harry Hyman is called in to help, and though no specialist, he decides that the case is a psychiatric one and proceeds to try to treat Sylvia. Hyman, however, has problems of his own that become apparent during his interaction with the Gellburgs.

Though set in 1938 in the wake of *Kristallnacht, Broken Glass* responds to problems that have not evaporated for audiences in the 1990s but become more urgent. As Miller told Charlie Rose: "In each of us, whether recognized or not, is that same bloody ethnic nationalism. This is not coming from the moon. This is coming from us. And we have not come close to even confronting this thing." The notion of difference, when pursued too stringently and unalloyed with the acceptance of universal humanity, can lead to unnecessary fragmentation, harmful restrictions of the individual, and the destruction of society as a whole. Written in the shadow of atrocities in Rwanda and Bosnia, the play conveys the necessity of a humanistic response to a violent contemporary world.

Each production of the play, from its tryout in Long Wharf through its premieres in New York and London to a subsequent filmed version, had slightly different endings as Miller struggled to find the right balance. The final conversation between Hyman and Gellburg varied, and there was indecision about whether to depict Gellburg as dying or living or to leave his fate ambiguous—but Sylvia rises to her feet at the close of every version. Miller ultimately fine-tuned the dialogue and decided to leave the possibility of Gellburg living, as the character has another heart attack but falls unconscious rather than dead. The London premiere also had one additional scene added at the suggestion of the director, DAVID THACKER: It comes before the final climax and features the play's three women, offering their different outlooks on the issues. The synopsis is based on what Miller called his "final acting version," published by Penguin in 1994.

SYNOPSIS

Act One

The mournful sound of a lone cellist, music that begins each subsequent scene, is heard as Phillip Gellburg waits to see Dr. Harry Hyman. Hyman's wife, Margaret, keeps Gellburg company and tries, unsuccessfully, to put him at ease. She relates how she met her husband, and after she calls him Goldberg by mistake, Gellburg explains his last name. Gellburg is proud of the uniqueness of his name, declaring that it is of Finnish origin. When she hopes that he will feel better soon, he tells her that he has come about his wife, Sylvia, whose legs have suddenly become paralyzed. He is here to get the results of tests given by a specialist. Margaret leaves as her husband enters.

Hyman jokes about his wife and compliments Sylvia to put Gellburg at ease, but it only embarrasses him. He admits that doctors are often defective, and in this case, they cannot uncover what is causing Sylvia's paralysis. He asks Gellburg what he thinks of the news from Germany about *Kristallnacht,* as this is something that has recently upset Sylvia. However, Gellburg offers little response, other than coldly suggesting that German Jews can be pushy. Hyman, too, ends up rationalizing the event as an aberration, given the decent Germans whom he has met in the past. Gellburg is worried what Sylvia may be telling Hyman, but Hyman implies that it is only good, and Gellburg seems proud of Sylvia's intelligence and knowledge of current affairs. Hyman suggests that her problem is psychological and tries to coax Gellburg to open up about their marital relationship; Gellburg is reticent but insists that they have sex regularly.

Gellburg explains how Sylvia's paralysis came on shortly after seeing pictures of *Kristallnacht;* then he becomes emotional as he recalls the details of her collapse. He loves her and feels powerless. Hyman asks Gellburg about his work in the mortgage business; Gellburg tells him about his boss, Stanton Case, who spends most of his time on his yacht. Gellburg is the only Jew employed by Case and the only Jew to have ever set foot on his yacht. They discuss why Gellburg wears black and whether or not Sylvia could just be pretending; Gellburg raises the possibility of her being possessed by a dybbuk. Before he leaves, Hyman suggests that Gellburg try to be more loving to Sylvia. Once he is gone, Margaret criticizes Gellburg as too controlling, and she and her husband discuss the case. Margaret is suspicious of Hyman's interest as Sylvia is an attractive woman. He offers to drop the case and then seductively reaffirms his attraction to his wife to keep her happy and distract her from her suspicions.

The next scene takes place in the Gellburg's bedroom where Sylvia's sister Harriet is helping out. Harriet asks Sylvia about her illness; they discuss Harriet's family and consider Sylvia's interest in Germany, which Harriet feels is too far away to care about. Gellburg arrives home early, having brought his wife some of her favorite pickles. Sylvia keeps apologizing for her illness, and there is clearly tension between them, but Gellburg tries to be pleasant. They have a letter from their son, Jerome, away in the army. Sylvia is unhappy with this career choice that she feels her husband pushed on her son. Gellburg tells her that he plans to make some changes, such as teaching her to drive. He tells her something of what the doctor told him about her case being psychological. He shows deep concern and awkwardly admits that he loves her, but she laughs in bewilderment. We learn that he has been impotent as they discuss their past problems, but she is not very sympathetic, tired of putting other people before herself. He tries to force her to stand, but she collapses.

Back in Hyman's office, Hyman is interviewing Harriet to find out more about the family. She talks about her cousin, Roslyn Fein, whom he once dated and who thought that he was great. He is flattered. Harriet criticizes Gellburg, explaining how unpopular he is and how she hates his attitude towards being Jewish, a strange mix of self-hatred and misplaced pride. She cannot imagine the couple splitting up, partly because this was less of an option for couples in the 1930s, but she relates past times when Gellburg has been overly aggressive toward Sylvia, even while she admits that he definitely adores her.

Gellburg's boss, Stanton Case, is looking for a property on which to build an annex for the Harvard Club and asks Gellburg for his opinion. Gellburg talks about his son—Case pulled strings for him to enter West Point—but it is evident that Case is not interested. Gellburg advises him against the property, based on some circumstantial evidence that he has uncovered, and Case thanks him, telling him to take a drink; however, he does not stay to share one with him.

Hyman visits Sylvia after he has been horseback riding. While examining her, he tries to encourage her to move, and she responds in delight at his flirtatious manner. He threatens to give up the case, but she persuades him to bear with her and asks him to talk. She talks about how she loved the job that Gellburg had forced her to give up. Hyman tries to convince her to move, but she wants to talk about Germany. She confesses that she feels that there is something dark inside her, but Hyman distracts her by suggesting that she imagine that they have just made love, and he kisses her, hoping to shock her into some confidence. She waits until he has left before responding, but as her legs fall open, it is clear she is attracted to the idea.

Back in Hyman's office, Gellburg is short with Margaret and resentfully rejects the cocoa that she offers him. He has come to ask Hyman for help with his impotency, but he then tells him that he made love to Sylvia the night before, though is upset that she now refuses to acknowledge that it happened. He voices his suspicions that Sylvia is making everything up to somehow hurt him. Hyman is unsure whom to believe, and sensing this, Gellburg angers. Hyman is worried that Sylvia may have mentioned his flirting but even though

Scene from the 1994 Long Wharf Theatre production of *Broken Glass,* with Amy Irving and Ron Rifkin. *Copyright Charles Erickson.*

she has not, Gellburg tells him that he no longer wants him on the case and storms out. This makes Margaret suspicious of what her husband has been doing with Sylvia, and she urges him to give up the case, but he refuses.

Act Two

Gellburg comes to apologize to Case for giving him what turned out to be bad advice on the property that he had wanted. Gellburg had misread the evidence, and a rival beat Case on the low offer that Gellburg had advised him to make. Case is angry and snidely suggests that Gellburg sold him out to a fellow Jew, an accusation that horrifies Gellburg.

Hyman visits Sylvia, who has prettied herself up in preparation, and they begin reminiscing about their carefree childhoods. When Sylvia realizes that Hyman has come to drop her case, she offers to tell him her dream. She is being chased, and a man pushes her down, begins kissing her, and then starts to cut off her breasts; she thinks it was Gellburg, but it is not the idea of Gellburg attacking her that she finds frightening, and Hyman sees this. She kisses Hyman and then begins to weep. He asks if she and Gellburg have recently made love. Deeply embarrassed that he might believe what her husband has told him, she denies this. She explains that they have not had relations for 20 years, ever since she had her father talk to him about impotence when he had not slept with her for a month. When he recovered from this embarrassment, she tried to get him to talk to the Rabbi about their poor sexual relationship, which only worsened the problem. Hyman warns Sylvia that his wife is suspicious, but she asks him to stay until Gellburg gets back.

Sylvia talks about Germany again, and Hyman insists that the Germans are too cultured to turn into such thugs. It all falls down on Sylvia, and she begins to despair for everyone, crying, "What is going to become of us?" She is especially resentful that Hyman intended to pass on her case. She almost manages to stand but again collapses just before her husband walks in. Gellburg is angry to see Hyman there, and in Hyman's reaction to stay involved, he promises to return. Sylvia tells her husband that she nearly walked and insists that he allow her to keep Hyman as her doctor. She then takes charge, insisting that he face up to Germany, demanding that he not to sleep with her again, and telling him off for pretending that he had made love to her. She bemoans the way in which she has lived her whole life and asks him what happened. He confesses that he became impotent because of the anger that she held towards him when he would not let her return to work after Jerome was born, partly manifest in her refusing to have more children. Becoming distraught at the prospect of being unable to sleep beside his wife, Gellburg breaks down, and Sylvia, while remaining firm, reaches for him in pity.

Back in Case's office, Gellburg complains about losing his boss's confidence after all his years of service. Case remains complacent until Gellburg confronts him with his obvious racism; then Case grows angry. Gellburg apologizes, but his boss stays resentful, and Gellburg has a heart attack. Case calls for a doctor but noticeably never touches Gellburg to see if he is alright.

The next scene is the one added for the British premiere between the play's three women. Harriet is amazed that Gellburg survived his attack and is surprised that he was released so soon from the hospital. Margaret has made Sylvia a cocoa that she enjoys. Sylvia believes that he has come home so he can talk to her and feels ridiculous that they have put this off so long. She asks to be taken to him, but they insist that she let the doctor decide and not to blame herself for what has happened. Sylvia still feels partly responsible. Margaret suggests that you cannot fight character—just do the best you can—as she goes to ask Hyman if Sylvia can see her husband.

Hyman feels that Gellburg should be in the hospital in case of a relapse; they are evidently friends again. Gellburg felt a moment of vision when he had his attack but cannot recall what it was. He has realized how Case used him and will no longer be in the foreclosure business. His son is coming home to visit and, if he rests, the doctor thinks that Gellburg could live a while longer. Gellburg asks about Sylvia, and Hyman admits that she is fearful of her husband. Amazed, Gellburg recalls the early happy days of their marriage when he felt comfortable in the neighborhood and proud of his wife. He and Hyman discuss what it means to them to be Jewish. When Gellburg asks Hyman why he married a non-Jew, Hyman accuses Gellburg of trying to assimilate. Gellburg now seems happy to be Jewish and understands his wife's fear of what is happening in Germany. He tries to enlist Hyman's help to reconcile him to his wife, and Hyman suggests that forgiveness of everyone is the best path forward.

Margaret brings Sylvia in and leaves. As Gellburg apologizes, Sylvia insists that it was all her own fault. Both begin talking and confessing their true feelings. Gellburg insists that he will change if he lives. To Sylvia's alarm, he begins to have another attack. He calls out to her for forgiveness, and she cries, "There's nothing to blame," thus easing his burden. As he falls back unconscious, she manages to rise to her feet and take a step towards him as the lights fade.

CRITICAL COMMENTARY

Broken Glass is strongly informed by events leading up to the HOLOCAUST. Believing strongly that something like the Holocaust involves everyone, Miller insists that there can be no turning away without cost. The denial, resignation, or ignorance that we observe in different characters in *Broken Glass* is tantamount to complicity. Nonaction, Miller informs us, whatever its rationale, becomes destructive when it allows certain other actions to occur. Thus, the issue of potency versus impotency is central to the play. Though represented mainly by its sexual connotation, Miller wishes the implication to spill into every aspect of life. What use is Doctor Harry Hyman's evident potency when he himself is incapable of true commitment or fidelity to either his culture or his wife? What value is Phillip Gellburg's commercial success when he understands so little of who he is and what he does? Of what use is even Sylvia Gellburg's compassion when she has lost touch with her own selfhood so much, that she no longer retains even the capacity to stand? The play explores the difficulties faced by those who neglect that important balance between self-awareness and connection to others, for it is through such neglect that a Holocaust can occur.

Neither Hyman, Gellburg, nor Sylvia has attained a proper balance, and each depicts a different aspect of failure. Miller wants us to recognize and learn from their mistakes. Their reactions to *Kristallnacht* are indicative of their failures and differences. Though managing to be somewhat self-aware, Hyman refuses to acknowledge the true identity of others and views Germans with nostalgic pleasure rather than as dangerous killers. His sense of connection is severed by his own selfish needs. Gellburg may accept the truth of events, but he refuses to allow them any relevance in his own life for he lacks both self-awareness and community spirit. Sylvia fully recognizes her communal identity and insists upon a connection, both personally and humanistically. However, she has lost touch with herself, which has led to a symbolic but also literal paralysis.

It is hard to resist comparing *Broken Glass* to a Greek drama. Miller has said that its relatively short length was an intentional emulation of such dramas. Also, its evident concern with people's identities and place in society are issues that lie at the heart of most Greek plays. One can even begin to see how the play's predictability, against which some critics jibed, is yet another aspect of its format that relates it to Greek dramas, whose impact largely depended upon the audience knowing what happens next.

Both Gellburg and Hyman's self-obsessed concerns may seem trivial in the face of the larger concern that Sylvia introduces, but they are concerns that need addressing. Gellburg and Hyman try to rationalize events taking place overseas in an effort to defend and preserve their own fragile beliefs. Their failure is an indication of the innate wrong-

ness of beliefs that they had each adopted and the need for them to discover something more worthwhile in which to believe. We should also note that it is not just Gellburg and Hyman who dismiss concern for the German Jews but the majority of Americans. Harriet and her husband both agree that Sylvia's worries are not real concerns.

Gellburg is Miller's central focus, and Sylvia tends to be pushed to the side, which reflects the way that she has allowed her life to run. Reservedly stiff and "proper" (until the more truthful realities of his life start to insist on recognition), Gellburg continuously offers up glimpses of his inner torments in his outbursts of anger and occasional hesitancies. Even in silence, his dark, brooding presence on stage commands attention. An earlier title for the play, *The Man in Black,* indicates the importance behind this aspect of his characterization. The blackness of his dress and the paleness of his complexion are emblems of the emptiness inside the man. He is, as Miller suggests "in mourning for his own life," and it is a life that he himself is largely responsible for stifling. Gellburg has lost the ability to connect and communicate to Sylvia how he feels about her, and Sylvia has blinded herself to her husband's inner torment.

For people who are supposedly trying to be frank with each other, these characters are poor communicators. Though Sylvia, finally, speaks openly and directly to her husband, we must remember that this is only after 20 years of self-imposed silence. Gellburg and Hyman are equally self-restricted in their attempts to communicate. At one point, Gellburg attempts to dismiss Hyman, mainly as a result of his self-consciousness regarding his impotency. Hyman's passionate response, instead of calming Gellburg, serves to make him uneasier. Failing to communicate, Hyman does not react to Gellburg's fears but his own; he feels guilty for having flirted with Sylvia and thinks that Gellburg may suspect. Each isolates himself from the other by his own self-involvement, and confusion results as each fails to recognize the other's feelings of guilt and inadequacy. It is such failures of communication that lie at the heart of the play's aura of ambiguity. There are declarations and conversations throughout the play that are filled with ambiguity as unresolved as the ending. For example, Sylvia's sudden cry: "What is going to become of us?" leaves us wondering whether she refers to humanity, Jews, her relationship with her husband, or her relationship with Hyman.

One image that is invoked by the play's title is that of the multiple reflections that one sees in a broken mirror, each related, yet unique in its own perspective: A powerful symbol to illustrate the relationship between the individual and society. The glass on stage in the original production was significantly never broken as the Gellburgs' resentments, and worries are continually bottled up, and neither initially seeks to understand the other. Their suffering stems from their inability to break the glass that surrounds them. Appearances are upheld, and personal feelings are repressed as they try to live their lives as good middle-class Americans. As the Gellburgs' lives constrict, we see a connection between them and their Jewish counterparts in Europe who were being frozen into ineffectuality in the ghettos, and the millions outside who refused to get involved. The Gellburgs need to face and overcome both the chaos of a dehumanized world as represented by the escalating Nazi horrors and their own inhuman relationship—inhuman for its lack of true communication and connection. To do this, both need to face and come to terms with their own individual identity.

The image of broken glass has further possibilities, being as multifaceted as the item invoked. It is certainly intended to bring to mind the shattered windows of *Kristallnacht*. It may also allude to the glass that the bridegroom breaks at a Jewish wedding ceremony and the various Rabbinic explanations for this action—from being a reminder of the destruction of the Temple in Jerusalem to a symbol of our imperfect world—all involve some sadness. This symbol of sadness, so prominently displayed on a joyous occasion, serves as a reminder of the duality of human existence. We may celebrate, but others are mourning; we may enjoy peace, but others are suffering war. This is why observant Jews feel commanded to work for the improvement of this world and the enrichment of the lives of all its inhabitants. This is something both the Gellburgs have forgotten.

In Miller's world, it is important that one takes responsibility even for things that one cannot control, as a refusal of responsibility is ultimately a refusal of humanity. Ignoring responsibilities, either personal or social, will interfere with an individual's ability to connect. Miller has declared that, through his plays, he tries "to make human relations felt between individuals and the larger structure of the world." Citing the sense of connection they had in Elizabethan drama, he admits that such a sense is lacking in the contemporary world but suggests that it can be reformulated: "We have to invest on the stage connections that finally make the whole. For they exist, however concealed they may be."

Both Gellburgs avoid their personal needs and fears by immersing themselves in either work or the home. Their problems fester and grow, nurtured by their mutual silence. Each secretly holds the other to blame: Gellburg sees his wife as emasculating, and Sylvia sees her husband as tyrannical. As critic John Lahr pointed out: "They're both right, and they're both wrong. What's true is the psychological dynamic, in which blame becomes a way of not dealing with unacceptable feelings." Neither has been fully honest or supportive of the other. Gellburg is too wrapped up in his own divisions to tell Sylvia how much he loves her or to allow her the freedom that she wants. Allowing her to work would have broken the control that he feels he needs to assert to give him a sense of security. Sylvia, having married a provider for the sake of her family, is full of regret but instead of speaking out, maintains a 20-year silence during which she helps drive her husband to impotency.

Much was made of the various endings of the play and Miller's difficulties in finalizing the piece. In earlier versions, Gellburg was shown clearly to die at the close; in the later his fate was more ambiguous. Whether Gellburg lives or dies is less important than what happens to Sylvia, and her reaction is the same in every version: She rises to her feet. Gellburg has dominated our attention throughout the play, but Sylvia now insists that we look at her as she faces certain truths and allows herself to take center stage. A progression has been made that may seem minor, but it is enough to suggest the possibility of hope.

Numerous reviews of the play discussed how dissatisfied critics felt on leaving the theater; for them the ending seeming unresolved and uncertain. But rather than a failing of the play, this may be an indication of its effectiveness. Miller intends to discomfort his audience: The eerie cello music, with its sense of menace, that is repeated throughout the play is an indication of this. In *Timebends: A Life,* Miller points out how audiences, in the United States particularly, have a tendency to resist plays that challenge and ask them to judge themselves. Perhaps the final dissatisfaction with *Broken Glass* stems from learning that this menace is not so much the expected Nazism as it is the common failings within each and every one of us that all too often prevent us from fully connecting with our fellow human beings. After all, as Miller is fully aware, the lesson of *Kristallnacht* was not heeded until after the elimination of six million Jews—there is a guilt attached to that neglect that everyone must continue to share. The Gellburgs may begin to uncover the roots of their problems, but they are still a long way toward solving them. Sylvia regains her feet by the close of the play; however, though she is standing, it remains unclear as to what she is standing for and where her first steps will lead. Miller suggests that it is partly the audience's responsibility to help create a world in which Sylvia can safely walk.

FIRST PERFORMANCE

Broken Glass opened for a month at the Long Wharf Theatre in New Haven, Connecticut, on March 1, 1994, and then transferred to the Booth Theater in New York starting on April 24, 1994, with the following cast:

Phillip Gellburg: Ron Rifkin
Margaret Hyman: Frances Conroy
Dr. Harry Hyman: David Dukes
Sylvia Gellburg: Amy Irving
Harriet: Lauren Klein
Stanton Case: George N. Martin

Directed by John Tillinger
Set by Santo Loquasto

Produced by ROBERT WHITEHEAD, Roger L. Stevens, Lars Schmidt, Spring Sirkin, Terri Childs, and Timothy Childs, in association with Herb Albert
Music by William Bolcom
It ran for 73 performances in New York.

INITIAL REVIEWS

Reviews of both the Long Wharf and New York productions were mixed. Jeremy Gerard saw it as "an unfinished work whose power has only been partly realized," Michael Phillips as too "reductive," "simple," and lacking in "dramatic instinct," while Frank Scheck complained: "You feel that there's a great play buried in *Broken Glass,* but like its heroine, it can't seem to rise to its feet." However, Clive Barnes looked past these complaints feeling that the play "reveals the shrewd theatricality of a master," Edwin Wilson felt that it was Miller's "best play of recent years" full of "nuance and reverberation," and Lahr called it "a brave, big-hearted attempt by one of the pathfinders of postwar drama to look at the tangle of evasions and hostilities by which the soul contrives to hide its emptiness from itself."

The British premiere directed by David Thacker at the NATIONAL THEATRE, that opened the same April as the New York production, fared better, including a transfer to the Duke of York Theater, an Olivier Award for Best New Play, and an extensive British tour. Although some critics, including Louise Doughty, felt that it was too melodramatic and undeveloped, Michael Billington viewed it as "a wise, humane and moving play," John Peter as a "grand, harrowing play, deeply compassionate and darkly humorous . . . one of the great creations of the American theatre," and Benedict Nightingale opined, "you won't see a more sympathetic yet less sentimental piece of characterization anywhere in London." David Nathan praised the play's Jewish elements, declaring it "springs from the core of Miller's unequivocal Jewishness."

SCHOLARSHIP

As a relatively recent play, *Broken Glass* has attracted little scholarship thus far. Some of the early reviewers, such as John Lahr or John Peter offer intelligent and thoughtful commentaries, while others, such as

Robert Brustein and John Simon, who both grew particularly antagonistic toward Miller in his later years, are less helpful, being more concerned with their own agendas than in addressing the issues of play. CHRISTOPHER BIGSBY's program notes for the premiere production help elucidate Miller's dual concern with both private and public worlds, and he expands on this in one section of his essay in *The Cambridge Companion to Arthur Miller.* Joyce Antler's article for *American Theatre* discusses Miller's use of the Holocaust as a metaphor, and Susan Abbotson's article draws out the play's universal relevance, offering detailed studies of the characters. In terms of comparative studies, Barbara Ozieblo holds the play up against Maria Irene Fornes's *Fefu and Her Friends,* Robert Combs makes connections to the work of HAROLD PINTER and TENNESSEE WILLIAMS, Thomas Adler compares it to Miller's novella *Homely Girl: A Life* in terms of their moral insight, and Gerald Wooster and Mona Wilson compare it to *The Man Who Had All the Luck* as a parellel study of "manic depressive envy dynamics" in "interpersonal relationships."

Among recent books that include a brief discussion of the play are those by Alice Griffin and Terry Otten. Although Griffin strangely misreads Hyman as "contented," "happily married," and "objective," she offers a good introduction to the play's themes and central relationship. Otten recognizes the culpability of all the play's characters, as "Miller implicitly condemns not only the American government for its indifferent response to the horrors of the war, but also the Jewish community for its own blind retreat into innocence." He also offers some interesting connections to Miller's earlier work and discusses the play's "insistent tragic impulse." Stephen Marino's exploration of Miller's language considers the play's network of metaphor and imagery, while Bigsby's 2005 study of Miller offers a detailed analysis of the play's characters and themes, pointing out several differences between the U.S. and British versions.

CHARACTERS

Case, Stanton As a character, Stanton Case, Gellburg's ruthless boss, seems rather stereotyped as the WASP anti-Semite with his constant references to "you people" and his refusal to share a drink with a man on whose advice he relies. When Gellburg collapses in his office, Case cannot even bring himself to touch him. A not-so-subtle inversion of the more usually stereotyped minority, such as the Jew, he passes his time at the yacht club while Gellburg does all his dirty work, and then Case discards the Jew swiftly after his usefulness is over.

Gellburg, Phillip Phillip Gellburg's problem is far more complicated than Dr. Hyman's picture of him as a self-hating Jew, for Gellburg both loves and hates his Jewishness. Declaring himself and his son to be the first or only Jews to do this and that, he seems not embarrassed but proud of his heritage. But is he proud of his achievements as a Jew or despite his Jewishness? This is kept deliberately ambiguous. Partly due to his recognition and fear of American ANTI-SEMITISM, Gellburg has tried to sever his connection with other Jews. Yet, his own Jewishness is unavoidable: He has a Jewish wife, he speaks Yiddish, he is prone to Jewish folk beliefs, and his achievements mean more, either way, because he is Jewish.

Like Hyman, Gellburg is so self-involved that he has no real place for a community in his life. Even though he has striven to be accepted there, he cannot feel comfortable in the anti-Semitic U.S. community, nor is he happy in the Jewish community for which he feels such antipathy. Even worse, he has no place in the larger community of humankind because he has no sense of himself anymore and has lost touch with his own humanity. He is a man doubly caught, first, between his own JUDAISM and the popular idea of the United States as a melting pot, and second, between his rejection of his Jewishness and his fear of the anti-Semitism he sees around him. Unable to voice his inner confusion, he breaks down whenever he is pushed to a point where he may have to break his self-imposed silence and speak out about his problems. To escape the confusion, he strives to emphasize his uniqueness—as in his insistence on his unusual name and Finnish origins—to avoid having to be a member of any community for which he feels such ambivalence, but it is an empty identity that he creates.

Gellburg may have problems as a Jew, but they stem from his problems as a human being. Concentrating on his work, he allows himself no personal side, ever on duty as the foreclosure man. He is acting a part in which he conceals and suppresses his own humanity. Unable to trust himself, he has lost the capacity to trust others. This inability to trust leads him to fail even at work, for it is instrumental in his losing the property that his boss had wanted. Gellburg's growing nervousness when questioned and his inability to look anyone in the eye indicates the erosion of his sense of self, as it shows him trying to conceal the fact.

Gellburg desperately desires a sense of control in his life to protect him against the chaos that he sees around him. He acts like a dictator at his grandmother's funeral and even, on occasion, plays the tyrant at home to seem in control, but it has not helped. His work had given him a sense of power and control, but he loses that as he comes to realize how empty his work actually is. By the close of the play, as he recognizes that it is impossible to separate himself from his community, he can no longer find pride in a job that is based on dispossessing others.

A conscious suppression of his uncontrollable love for Sylvia is related to Gellburg's mania for control. We are constantly told that he loves and even adores his wife, and the difficulty that he has admitting this to Sylvia is related to his fear of such uncontrollable feelings that he stifles and twists but is incapable of destroying. Capable of flashes of violence as he throws a steak at his wife or pushes her up the stairs, he is also capable of great tenderness. However, he feels ashamed at such outbreaks and tries to restrict such emotional responses, but in so doing, he suppresses his humanity. By refusing to allow his love any freedom, Gellburg has grown as distant from his wife as from their wider community.

Gellburg, Sylvia An average Jewish housewife from the 1930s, Sylvia Gellburg's tale, that of a woman who suddenly experiences a mysterious paralysis, was one that Miller had kept in his memory for 50 years. Sylvia's struggle to understand why her legs are paralyzed is tied to her struggle to

understand her own existence. Unlike her husband, Sylvia is closely in touch with her community, so much so that she has lost her sense of self. As she exclaims: "I'm here for my mother's sake, and Jerome's sake, and everybody's sake except mine." She has lived her life so long for others that she has lost all connection with her own selfhood, but she begins by blaming others for this. With Gellburg dominating every scene in which he appears, Sylvia tends to be pushed to the side, but this only reflects the way that she has allowed her life to run.

With *Kristallnacht*, Sylvia's sense of community is challenged by both the behavior of the Nazis and the apparent apathy toward this by all around her. This provokes Sylvia to a mix of rage and regret, disgusted at herself as much as at others. She has let herself become as pale and drained of vitality as her husband, and even her laugh is "dead." Having withdrawn from their marriage as much as Gellburg, she "punished" her husband when he would not let her work by restricting life in refusing to have another child. Despite her condition, she has shown no interest in healing the relationship with her husband and is derisive toward him when he feebly attempts to reconnect. She tells Hyman that she pities Gellburg, but not once in the play does she ever speak of loving him as he does of her. She has failed to consider his private nature when speaking to her father about their sex life, which instead of helping only exacerbated Gellburg's feelings of guilt and embarrassment. Caught up in her own confusions and feelings of betrayal, she has failed to recognize that he is suffering too.

Miller is not writing a case study of Sylvia's illness, as Lahr points out: "He is aiming at something much more ambitious: An anatomy of denial. . . . Her private sense of humiliation is projected onto her fury about the public humiliation of the Jews." Sylvia has settled and accommodated herself to a point that ultimately becomes untenable even for her self-effacing spirit, and this manifests itself in her objections to the Nazis' treatment of Jews in Europe. When Sylvia rises for the first time in the play, she is driven to do so by her fear that no one will do anything about the suffering in Germany. Theater scholar, Alice Griffin, reports Miller as saying that this is the first time in Sylvia's existence that she has taken her life into her own hands. It marks an important turning point in Sylvia's relationship with Phillip. She may have allowed herself to be a victim, like so many of the Jews in Europe, but, as Miller insisted, "she is also a revolutionary." Miller concluded by pointing out the fact that at the end "it is Sylvia who is giving the orders, not Phillip."

Distracted by Hyman's vitality, as are all his conquests, it is, finally, an acknowledgment of the truer connection that had been stifled between her and her husband that gives Sylvia the strength to rise, coupled with her decision to face up to her own responsibility for the way that she is. Her paralysis has been an emblem of her loss of control, related to a denial of certain responsibilities that she had to herself as much as others. She comes to realize her own complicity in this, declaring: "What I did with my life! Out of ignorance . . . Gave it away like a couple of pennies—I took better care of my shoes." She finally takes on responsibility for her condition and ceases to hide behind blaming others. Miller suggests that it is the acceptance of such responsibilities that offers a person real control in his or her life. This return to control is reflected in her ability, by the play's close, to stand once more.

Harriet Sylvia's sister, Harriet, is offered as a contrast to Sylvia and, perhaps, with her brisket and her love of gossip, is a caricature of the Jewish housewife of the 1930s. Not a great thinker, she is content with her life, her husband, and her son's decision not to pursue a college degree. She is also unconcerned about what is happening in Germany. Her function is mostly to offer further details of the couple's past.

Hyman, Harry Dr. Harry Hyman is the family doctor who is called in to tend to Sylvia when she suffers from paralysis. Initially, in contrast to the pinched, repressed Gellburg, Hyman seems full of life; a romantic hero, underlined by the fact he even rides horseback. But as Bigsby points out, his "appetite for life . . . makes him vulnerable to his own passions." Hyman may have a capacity to enjoy life (that the Gellburgs have lost a long time since), but he is dissatisfied with the quality of that

life. This leads him to flirt and possibly to play around, partly as a way to relive his youthful fame as we see him reminiscing with great pleasure about Roslyn Fein. But he also does this to boost his own slipping feelings of self-importance; as he tells Gellburg, "Some men take on a lot of women not out of confidence but because they're afraid to lose it." We might also note, that for all his life force, his marriage is evidently as barren of children as it is of commitment.

We should take early warning when Hyman himself informs us that doctors are often "defective" and that we should look for his defect; we need not look far. Miller wants us to question both Hyman's sexuality and his sense of security for both are highly suspect. Hyman has a degree of self-knowledge, and he understands his own insecurities as much as he fears them, but he does nothing with that knowledge because he is unable in the end to make any real connection. Hyman admires Sylvia's sense of connection and is drawn to it, though how she achieves it is a mystery to him. Some reviewers complained that Miller leaves Hyman hanging at the close, with no clear signal as to how we are supposed to view him. This may be true but certainly is no error; Hyman is an illustration of those individuals for whom the answers are ever out of sight because of a fundamental lack of commitment in their lives.

Hyman's central problem is his complacency. When problems loom, be it his wife's displeasure or Nazi oppression, he throws up a smoke-screen defense of illusion to protect himself and to prevent him from having actually to do anything more permanent to solve the problem. Hyman's wife is a woman who suffers as much from her husband's potency as Sylvia does from her husband's impotency. Hyman has a history of infidelity, and it becomes increasingly clear that he is little better as a doctor than as a husband, despite all of his pretension to care. He is certainly not intended to be the voice of right or a model of behavior as some critics intimated. His psychiatric treatment of Sylvia, telling her to focus her concentration on her legs to awaken their power, borders on the immature. His diagnoses tend toward inaccuracy as he simplifies issues to suit his own jaded and narrowed view of the world—hardly surprising from someone who so patently lacks a true vision of social obligation.

Hyman acts at being a part of the community by taking on a neighborhood practice, but as his wife points out: "Why, I don't know—we never invite anybody, we never go out, all our friends are in Manhattan." His capacity to create illusions may attract women, but it also leads him to hide from certain necessary truths, such as what was really going on in Germany. Hyman's simplification of opera is an indication of his facile level of response to everything; it precludes any necessity for deep commitment and leads to an easier (if somewhat shallow) life. He looks for easy answers and thereby vastly simplifies the Gellburgs' problems. He stereotypes them and reduces the fundamental importance of what they must each attempt to face. Telling Phillip Gellburg that he needs to show his wife a little more love is both facile and unhelpful. He needs to dig deeper to uncover the true extent of the disease, but such digging would necessitate getting his own hands a little too dirty, and he is rather squeamish. It is easy to question others but harder sometimes to question yourself.

Hyman, Margaret Dr. Hyman's wife acts as a foil to Sylvia. Another woman of the 1930s, Margaret tends to allow her husband to dominate. While Sylvia suffers from a husband's suppression of emotion, Margaret has the opposite problem; aware of her husband's attraction to other women, past affairs have made her ever watchful for further signs of betrayal. She becomes highly suspicious, and rightly so, of his relationship to Sylvia. Yet, she has an attitude to life that makes her feel that you cannot change people but that you just need to make the most of what you get. Although she worries about her husband and is unhappy with where they live, wanting to be more in the thick of things, she snatches what pleasure she can, and their marriage survives.

MOVIES AND TELEVISION ADAPTATIONS

BBC and PBS, as part of *Mobil Masterpiece Theatre,* joined to produce a televised version of the British production of *Broken Glass* with Henry Goodman and Margot Leicester that was aired in 1996.

Produced by Fiona Finlay and directed by David Thacker, the screenplay was created by Thacker and David Holman. Although some found it too close to soap opera and many still found the ending problematic, most agreed that it was worth watching, and Bruce McCabe called it "one of the most cathartic theatrical experiences you'll ever have in front of the TV." Matt Roush saw it as an excellent adaptation that was "elusive, mysterious, and in its final moment, breathtakingly tragic."

FURTHER READING

Abbotson, Susan C. W. "Issues of Identity in *Broken Glass:* A Humanist Response to a Postmodern World." *Journal of American Drama and Theatre* 11 (Winter 1999): 67–80.

Adler, Thomas P. "To See Feelingly: Moral (In)Sight in Arthur Miller's *Homely Girl, A Life* and *Broken Glass*." *Shofar: An Interdisciplinary Journal of Jewish Studies* 22, no. 4 (2004 Summer): 14–21.

Antler, Joyce. "The Americanization of the Holocaust." *American Theatre* (February 1995), 16–20+.

Barnes, Clive. "Fear and Self-Loathing Amid *Broken Glass*." *New York Post,* April 25, 1994. In *New York Theatre Critics' Reviews* 55 (1994): 123.

Bigsby, Christopher. "*Broken Glass*." *Arthur Miller: A Critical Study.* Cambridge: Cambridge University Press, 2005, 391–404.

———. "Miller in the Nineties." *Cambridge Companion to Arthur Miller.* New York: Cambridge University Press, 1997, 178–182.

———. "Miller's Journey to *Broken Glass*." Program for *Broken Glass,* by Arthur Miller. Long Wharf 1 March–3 April, 1994, 21–25.

Billington, Michael. "Putting the Pieces Together." *Guardian,* August 6, 1994, sec. 2, p. 26.

Brustein, Robert. "Separated by a Common Playwright." *New Republic,* May 30, 1994, 29–31.

Combs, Robert. "Internalizing Terror: Reflections of Arthur Miller's *Broken Glass* in Pinter and Williams." In *Arthur Miller: Twentieth Century Legend,* edited by Syed Mashkoor Ali, 353–361. (Jaipur, India: Surabhi, 2006).

Doughty, Louise. "Shard Time: Night and Day." *Mail on Sunday,* August 14, 1994: 30.

Forsyth, Alison. "Beyond Representation: The Drama of Traumatic Realism in Arthur Miller's *Broken*

Glass." *Hungarian Journal of English and American Studies* 11, no. 2 (Fall 2005): 89–107.

Gerard, Jeremy. Review of *Broken Glass,* by Arthur Miller. *Variety,* April 25, 1994. In *New York Theatre Critics' Review* 55 (1994): 128.

Griffin, Alice. *"Broken Glass." Understanding Arthur Miller.* Columbia: University of South Carolina Press, 1996, 182–190.

Hopkinson, Amanda. "A View from the Bridge." *New Statesman and Society,* August 5, 1994: 31–32.

Lahr, John. "Dead Souls." *New Yorker,* May 9, 1994, 94–96.

Marino, Stephen A. "Images of the 90s: *The Ride Down Mt. Morgan* and *Broken Glass.*" *A Language Study of Arthur Miller's Plays: The Poetic in the Colloquial.* New York: Mellen, 2002, 135–156.

McCabe, Bruce. "Gripping Tale of *Broken Glass.*" *Boston Globe,* October 20, 1996: 4.

Miller, Arthur. Interview with Charlie Rose. *The Charlie Rose Show.* PBS, August 31, 1994.

"Miller's Tales." *New Yorker,* April 11, 1994: 35–36.

Nathan, David. *"Broken Glass." Jewish Chronicle,* August 12, 1994. In *Theatre Record* 14.16 (1994): 977–978.

Nightingale, Benedict. "Smashed Certainties." *The Times,* August 6, 1994, E5.

Otten, Terry. *"Broken Glass." The Temptation of Innocence in the Dramas of Arthur Miller.* Columbia: University of Missouri Press, 2002, 228–239.

Ozieblo, Barbara. "The Complexities of Intertextuality: Arthur Miller's *Broken Glass* and Maria Irene Fornes' *Fefu and Her Friends.*" In *Crucible of Cultures: Anglophone Drama at the Dawn of a New Millennium,* edited by Marc Maufort and Franca Bellarsi, 101–112. (Brussels: Peter Lang, 2002).

Peter, John. "A Raw Slice of Humanity." *Sunday Times,* August 14, 1994, sec. 10, pp. 20–21.

Phillips, Michael. *"Broken Glass* Makes Things Perfectly Clear." *San Diego Union–Tribune* April 25, 1994, E1.

Roush, Matt. "'Talk is Cheap,' But *Broken Glass* Shatters." *USA Today,* October 18, 1996, D3.

Scheck, Frank. "Grains of a Good Play Exist in Arthur Miller's Strained *Broken Glass.*" *Christian Science Monitor,* April 27, 1994. In *New York Theatre Critics' Review* 55 (1994): 126–127.

Simon, John. "Whose Paralysis Is It Anyway?" *New York,* May 9, 1994, 80–81.

Simonson, Robert. "Backstage with Amy Irving." *Theatre Week,* June 13, 1994, 19–21.

Strickland, Carol. "Arthur Miller's Latest Message to Humanity." *Christian Science Monitor,* April 26, 1994, 12.

Wilson, Edwin. "Miller Resurfaces at Tony Time." *Wall Street Journal,* May 5, 1994. In *New York Theatre Critics' Reviews* 55 (1994): 132.

Wooster, Gerald, and Mona Wilson. "Envy and Enviability Reflected in the American Dream: Two Plays by Arthur Miller." *British Journal of Psychotherapy* 14, no. 2 (1997): 182–188.

"Bulldog" (2001)

Published in *New Yorker* in 2001, "Bulldog" is one of Miller's later short stories, but it seems a continuation of the 1959 tale, "I Don't Need You Any More." The protagonist this time is age 13 and unnamed but has the same autobiographical thrust as 5-year-old Martin, with the older sensible brother, close maternal bond that he seeks to escape, and same imaginative and inquiring mind. His family lives in the Midwood district of BROOKLYN in the 1930s, where the Miller's family had moved in his teenage years after his father's bankruptcy; even the pear and apple trees that Miller had planted in the backyard are referenced. Whether or not the rest is true is up to speculation—Miller was deliberately cagey when interviewers asked—but what we get is another highly symbolic tale of maturation and growing independence. Told from the naturalistic viewpoint of the growing teen, the story recalls a bygone era with humor and telling detail. A recording of ELI WALLACH reading the tale aloud in 2002 for NPR's *The Connection* can be heard in their archives, and Miller allowed the story to be reprinted in Nadine Gordimer's 2003 collection, *Telling Tales,* to raise funds for AIDS.

Despite a bankrupt father and struggling family, the protagonist decides to spend his savings on a dog. His father is napping and mother is playing bridge, and neither seems to object, so he answers an advertisement for some Black Brindle Bull puppies. His brother mocks his desire for a dog and his evident ignorance as to how to care for one. This only makes him more determined. It is an hour's ride on the train, and he observes the neighborhoods through which he passes on a hot summer day. Schermerhorn Street seems different from his own Jewish neighborhood, less friendly, and he feels uncertain, but he finds the apartment and rings the bell. A woman with long black hair in a pink robe, at whose face he is too embarrassed to look, answers the door and invites him in. Tall for his age, she is surprised to learn that he is only age 13; she shows him the puppies. He is disappointed the dogs look nothing like the bulldogs that he looked up in the *Book of Knowledge*.

Regretting his desire, the protagonist politely holds a puppy, no longer really wanting one, yet finding the experience "very soft and kind of disgusting in a thrilling way," an observation that conveys his adolescent yearning and fear. He is uncertain what to do, as the woman fetches him a glass of water. She hands him the water and lets her gown fall open to reveal her breasts, and then kisses him. The next thing he knows is that they are having sex on the carpet. It is his first time, and his experience is almost dreamlike as well as being faintly comic as he points out how his head banged against the leg of her couch. It is not until he is on the train going home with a puppy that she has given him for free that the protagonist seems to awaken.

His mother is surprised to see the puppy and uncertain what to do. They offer it cream cheese to eat, and it pees on the floor. As his mother stoops to clean this up, now awakened to the female form the protagonist is reminded of Lucille, the woman who just seduced him, and feels embarrassed. They feed the puppy various inappropriate foods, and it seems to settle in, being named Rover. As time goes by, the protagonist keeps thinking of Lucille, especially when stroking Rover, and wonders how he can see her again.

Keen on drawing, he places a chocolate cake that his mother has baked on a chair to sketch it but then becomes distracted. He goes outside to check the bulbs and trees that he has planted and then, looking at the baseball field at the bottom of their yard, is reminded of a baseball that he had,

and he goes to look for that. Suddenly, he hears strange noises and runs to find his mother in a panic and the dog acting crazy and foaming at the mouth. It has eaten most of the cake. Unsure what to do, he calls the ASPCA, and they come and take the dog away.

The protagonist feels relief at no longer being responsible for the dog, though he feels bad about how he treated it. A stocking ad reminds him of Lucille, and he wonders if he can tell her that he needs another dog to get the chance to see her again, but he does not want to lie. Deciding whether or not to risk calling her, he goes to the piano—playing calms him. As he plays, he begins to feel different, and apart from his family, from whom he now has secrets. He senses that he is developing away from his childhood and feels deliriously happy because of his new status. His playing grows discordant and wonderful, and his mother comes in amazed. Even while she basks in his genius, he senses a widening gulf between them and he begins to see himself as having a wholly separate identity.

Captain Paul (1941)

One of Miller's earlier radio dramas, the biographical *Captain Paul* about John Paul Jones as the founder of the American Navy was aired on October 27, 1941, to celebrate Navy Day on the *Cavalcade of America* series. Jones was played by Claude Rains. Set during the Revolutionary War, as would be another radio play the following year *Battle of the Ovens*, *Captain Paul* is intended as a commentary on the U.S.'s upcoming, inevitable entry into WORLD WAR II; to stay free, the United States will have to fight. Unpublished, a typescript can be found at New York Library's Center for the Performing Arts.

Chinese Encounters (1979)

First excerpted in *Atlantic Monthly* under the title "In China" and in *Reader's Digest* as "China Scenes,

China Voices," this book of reportage is based on Miller's encounters and insights during a six-week trip to China in fall 1978 as a guest of the Association for Friendship with Foreign Countries and was published in 1979 as *Chinese Encounters*. Photographs taken by INGEBORG MORATH, who went with him on the trip, accompany the text and make up well more than half of the book. The photographs are accompanied by captions and are occasionally interspersed with verses from several Chinese poets, including translations of ancient poets including Han Yu, Du Fu, and Ma Qih Yuan as well as modern ones such as Wu–chi Liu and Kiang Kang–Hu. There are also some selections from EZRA POUND's translations of *The Book of Songs* from the Chou dynasty.

Miller's essay begins with "Cautionary Words" about the difficulties of reading another culture accurately. Insisting that he has no expertise on Chinese matters, he asserts an interest in their political and cultural arenas and wonders if something positive might have evolved from the tempestuous factionalism of their recent history. Miller divides his encounter into 16 sections, which fill the first 106 pages of a 246-page book. Morath's photographs cover artists whom they meet, tourist sites that they visit, and candid shots of ordinary scenes and people; she was not restricted in what she was allowed to shoot and took advantage of this growing openness toward visitors. Miller appears in several pictures, twice sitting with their interpreter-guide, Su Guang, once in a teahouse under a portrait of Chairman Mao, once on a train, and twice with theater groups.

Miller questions everyone whom he meets, from Chinese peasant to official, British and American expatriots, old and new Chinese writers and artists, as well as his various interpreter–guides to uncover the impact of the Cultural Revolution, the national perception of Chairman Mao, the ascendancy and fall of the Gang of Four, and the current opening up to the West. What he finds are a people who have "learned to distrust their own judgment of reality" and seem uncertain of the future direction. His words and Morath's photographs join to offer a sense of "China's contradiction—her ancientness and solemnity, which ceaselessly work against and with her epic struggle to change herself at last

and become a modern nation." The couple visit various sites, travel by train and barge, and view several cultural performances, the predominance of which are found to have, despite their intrinsic differences, surprising commonalities to Western equivalents. Miller identifies a "pragmatic idealism" in the Chinese who were born of a necessity that throws off guilt and refuses to blame the past. This he equates to the U.S. worship of practicality that is most prevalent in its business philosophy.

Comparing the Chinese to the ancient Greeks, Miller sees a culture in which the needs of the people outweigh those of the individual. He sees Chinese COMMUNISM as having evolved differently from that of the Soviet Union, despite its continued adherence to Stalinist thought. Chinese Communism appears less stringent, but without any codified LAW, it remains inherently unstable. Despite China's claim to an egalitarian society, he finds much evidence of social inequity in their dismissiveness toward the peasantry and is uncomfortable with their reverential treatment of foreigners. Miller asserts that any effective system needs to allow dissent and worries that the Chinese have not implemented this because many of their writers remain silenced, the press is government owned, and there is no legal system of recourse. "Nothing is safe from man," he insists, "and everything is up for grabs when there is no law."

Miller finds the blind obedience of Chinese to those in charge troubling. Though dead, Chairman Mao remains worshipped almost as a god and is distanced from the atrocities that were committed by the Gang of Four which included his wife, Jiang Qing, even while it is obvious that he must have been complicit to some degree and when in full power had reigned as viciously as they. Miller invents a short scenario that is reminiscent of SAMUEL BECKETT in which Mao stays silent while opposing revolutionaries battle for his approbation, seeing silence as his method of rule because it keeps all uncertain and allows no one to object. Contemporary poverty and troubles are blamed on the recently discredited Gang of Four rather than on the standing government. Although Miller finds the Chinese surprisingly willing to discuss the successes and failures of their system, it shocks him more to discover that it is a system in which they still believe but apparently have little idea how to fix.

Miller is struck by China's "nearly total ignorance of the West's culture" even among the better educated. Few, to his embarrassment, have even heard of him. The only recent American literature their initial guide, poet and playwright Qiao Yu, had been able to obtain were *Jonathan Livingston Seagull* and *Love Story*. But as Miller realizes, there are five times as many Chinese as Americans, and yet "How many Chinese writers did I even know the names of, free as I was to read anything?" U.S. culture, he realizes, is no less insular and ignorant of China as they are of the United States. He partially blames the 1950s era for this as a time when Communist fears led the United States to dismiss and exile anyone close to Chinese culture or politics.

As part of his mission to "find out what I could about creative people's lives in China," Miller interviews several artists—including Cao Yu, who will invite Miller back in 1983 to direct a production of *Death of a Salesman* for the BEIJING PEOPLE'S ART THEATER that Miller will record in *Salesman in Beijing*—and attends a number of theatrical performances, from Chinese Opera to modern realism. He is surprised to witness such strong female characters in Chinese theater given the conservative gender expectations of a culture that dislikes seeing women in control and that frowns on couples even touching in public. Enjoying the humor and the spectacle that he discovers in Chinese drama, he finds the artificiality of the opera delightfully honest, but the exaggerated gesture and movement of this form seem to imbue all of Chinese theater, which makes their attempts at realism troubling. The emphasis on style over plot works effectively in the complex operatic fable *The White Snake,* in which a snake-demon marries a mortal and in which we witness the ensuing trouble that this causes the couple, but this emphasis seems unsuited to such political melodrama as *Bi An (Another Hope),* about the Russian assassination of an African revolutionary, which was intended as realism. Attending another modern play, *Loyal Hearts,* by Su Shuyang, Miller found its tale of a doctor who is under threat of dismissal and reeducation for creating a life-saving

drug that the government ridiculously decides privileges the bourgeoisie as blatant propaganda, and is surprised when told such a play would be over the heads of most Chinese. This seems indicative of a cultural naiveté and a dangerous inability to even conceive of social criticism.

Miller is repeatedly struck by the number of artists who have been imprisoned, reeducated, or killed under the auspices of what he perceives as the surreal force of the Cultural Revolution, and yet, he finds little evidence of any resentment over this. This attempt to narrow public thought and to equalize the national intellect smashed both educational and cultural systems in China; although efforts are being made to rebuild, progress is slow. Due to restricted training schools, there are few young practitioners in the theater, and the older artists tend to be fairly conservative. Writers in China, Miller learns, earn no royalties as they are salaried by the state and are "paid regularly whether or not they produce any work." Left under the jealous ministrations of Jiang Qing, an ex-actress and one of the Gang of Four, all art has been long stifled and drama become formulaic, based on her declaration of Eight Model Works and her insistence that China "needed no more than eight plays." Yet, even the uniformity of thought that such rules have tried to instigate is not complete, and Miller discovers evidence of some dissident writers, even if little known in the West, which restores his faith in a Chinese future.

There is much that Miller finds attractive in China, despite his reservations. He cites the countryside's "pervasive beauty," the people's innate sense of "aesthetic harmony," the wonderful food, and the dignity of the elderly. He also realizes that conditions have greatly improved on what they were at the height of the Cultural Revolution. He admires a positive spirit in the Chinese that seems to resist demoralization, despite an endemic poverty that allows few running water, a generation missing due to the destructive force of the Cultural Revolution, and a chaotic system of production that is patently inefficient and bogged down by outmoded technology. People design and build tractors who have never driven one or know for what they are used. Their resulting designs are flawed and wasteful. Miller looks in on a clothing factory and is appalled by the conditions, although he admits the workers seem less driven than those he recalls from his father's factory, MILTEX COAT AND SUIT COMPANY. Miller finally decides that China's biggest problems are overpopulation, an insufficient social structure to handle this, and China's lack of a vital culture. Giving us insight into his own view of an artist's role, as the catalyst that provokes a nation to "confront herself" and orient reality so as to "toughen a nation's spirit against self-pity and self-delusion and may, as has happened, cry up warnings of calamity in good time," Miller concludes that China can only benefit from allowing its artists greater freedom.

Clara (1987)

Miller wrote this one-act play as part of the double bill *Danger: Memory!* to accompany *I Can't Remember Anything*, which deals with similar themes from a different angle. Although the play's title is *Clara*, it is less about her than about her father, Kroll. There is an intentional echo of "clarity" in the name *Clara* that points us to what it is that Kroll needs—greater clarity in his life.

SYNOPSIS

The play begins with Kroll prostrate on the floor in his daughter's apartment; he has collapsed from shock at the sight of his daughter's murder. Detective Lew Fine enters to question him and uncover the information that he needs to catch the murderer, while other detectives search for clues and take photographs. Kroll rouses but seems disoriented, imagining that Clara has gone skiing rather than accept the reality of her death. Fine keeps reminding him that she is dead but Kroll finds it hard to focus. He sidetracks, telling Fine how he reminds him of Bert Fine, an old friend who once betrayed him, and uncovers various similarities, including that both had a son who committed suicide.

Fine makes us realize that Clara knew her murderer. Kroll explains how her social work has always led her to dangerous places, but he points out that she never seemed fearful. She has been working on rehabilitating male prisoners and recently brought one home for dinner. After a struggle, Kroll recalls the name: Luis. Fine continually prods Kroll with questions, even asking him if he killed Clara to shake him up; Kroll behaves so cagily that it almost seems credible. Having once run his own landscaping business, Kroll now works for the disreputable Ruggieri family. At various points in the play, the ghost of Clara walks past, reacting to her father.

Fine begins to badger Kroll, who is reticent and is torn between pride of his daughter's liberalism and guilt that this liberalism has led to her death. Clara speaks, reenacting a conversation that she had with her father concerning Luis. Kroll confesses he allowed her to go with Luis, as he had been fearful she might have been a lesbian. Kroll has been fighting his own prejudices on this and other matters for some time. He is fearful that naming a Hispanic for the crime will make him seem prejudiced. However, Fine keeps reminding him that they live in a racist, biased world and that you may as well accept that and hate right back. When an old recording of "Shenandoah" plays, Kroll recalls his experiences at Biloxi, where he saved some black men from being lynched. This was the story that had inspired his daughter to help others. It reminds him of that for which he once stood. He can now name his daughter's killer with a clear conscience.

CRITICAL COMMENTARY

Clara is not a realistic work; the name that Detective Fine needs could easily be gained by a phone call to Kroll's wife, but Kroll must recall this name from his own resources, symbolically, for his own salvation, and Fine allows him the time to do so. Images are flashed in the air in counterpoint to the dialogue—from the bloodied corpse of Clara to the name of the murderer—to indicate the harsh realities that Kroll struggles to face. Kroll's progression toward the truth of his own life is symbolically marked by the encouraging presence of Clara, initially appearing physically and then speaking; when she vanishes at the close, it indicates that Kroll has finally accepted her death and his own part in it. His reward is to recall Luis's last name and where he works; but more than that, he has fought an internal battle over what values to believe and has come to realize that his liberal values are the right impulse, whatever happens as a result. At this point, he stands "erect and calm"—a direct contrast to the inert figure slumped on the floor at the start of the play.

Kroll is not a bad man, nor is he perfect. In the past 20 years, he has lost much of the idealism that allowed him to lead a black company, save a group of soldiers from being lynched, and inspire his daughter to help others. He has become embroiled in racist housing policies and now works for a shady building contractor, Charley Ruggieri, with whom he has attended sex parties. He has lost his commitment to aiding others and has concentrated too much on himself. He feels guilty for allowing Clara to be with a man who murdered a former girlfriend, especially as he did so not out of liberal conscience but out of fear that she may be a lesbian. Kroll's own confession is balanced against his incrimination of another because the two are linked—as he ascertains Luis's guilt so that he will simultaneously ascertain his own.

The danger in accepting his guilt is that it might also lead to the invalidation of the liberal values that he inculcated in his daughter, values that were partly responsible for her getting murdered. Her demise was unfortunate, but the values of social commitment and open-mindedness by which Clara lived remain worthwhile. Kroll needs to reaffirm these values in his own life, having long left them behind as he had been drawn into the sad, corrupt world of Charley Ruggieri. To reaffirm his older beliefs will not only validate his daughter's life but also allow her death to have meaning.

Even while Fine allows Kroll the space to rediscover himself, he also tempts him toward taking a less liberal position. With the horrors of his job, Fine is certainly closer to the dark side of humanity, which may give him a clearer understanding of evil. The trouble with Fine's understanding is that it is too cold—it has no heart or compassion. His unemotional reaction to his son's suicide, describing it as a mere statistic, seems at clear odds with Kroll's emotional response to his daughter's death. Fine seems to prefer to see everyone "one step away from a statistic," but in this, he loses his humanity. Fine himself admits that he has "limitations" and,

on close inspection, that they are important ones. Fine lacks a capacity for love and pity.

What Fine does is catch criminals, but we still need to address the reasons why they became criminals in the first place and try to prevent this at the source, as Clara has been doing. If Kroll had been unable to transcend his personal guilt and hatred in the way that he does, he would have ended up like Fine, who can only see unavoidable greed, racial tension, and continual discrimination in the world. Fine points to a recognition of the world's undeniable evil in his evocation of the HOLOCAUST, what Miller sees as the prime 20th-century proof that evil does exist, but Fine is unable to take the next step—he has allowed hate to take over. His bitter outlook may have been formed by experience—as a Jew, a homicide detective, and a father whose son committed suicide—but these reflect a world that he should fight to change rather than accept.

FIRST PERFORMANCE

Clara premiered at Lincoln Center in New York on February 8, 1987, with the following cast:

> *Albert Kroll:* Kenneth McMillan
> *Detective Lieutenant Fine:* James Tolkan
> *Tierney:* Victor Argo
> *Clara:* Karron Graves

> Directed by Gregory Mosher
> Set by Michael Merritt
> Produced by Bernard Gersten
> It ran for a limited engagement of four weeks.

INITIAL REVIEWS

Critical response was mixed, but both *Clara* and its companion piece *I Can't Remember Anything* fared better in their 1988 London premiere than in the United States. In the United States, Robert Brustein berated *Clara* as "crude," and David Lida complained about the overtly didactic nature of both plays, although William A. Henry III felt that "their contemplative voice is well worth hearing." In London, Christopher Edwards insisted that *Clara* "bears the touch of the master in both construction and tone," while Kenneth Hurren saw it and its companion play as "illuminated by an implacable liberalism underpinned with innate compassion," and Sheridan Morley saw them as having "the fascination of late sketches by a master painter of the human condition."

MOVIE AND TELEVISION ADAPTATIONS

Burt Brinckerhoff directed William Daniels and Darren McGavin in a television film of the play made for A&E Cable Network for *Playwrights Theater* that was aired on February 5, 1991. Although Kevin Kelly called the film a "muddled mess," Ray Loynd reviewed it as "spare and unwavering" and a "wrenching work."

FURTHER READING

Brustein, Robert. "Danger: Manipulation." *New Republic* March 9, 1987, 26.

Centola, Steven R. "Temporality, Consciousness, and Transcendence in *Danger: Memory!" The Achievement of Arthur Miller: New Essays.* Dallas, Tex.: Contemporary Research, 1995, 135–142.

Edwards, Christopher. "*Danger: Memory!" Spectator,* April 16, 1988. In *London Theatre Record* 8, no. 7 (1988): 429–430.

Henry, William A., III. "Cry from the Heart." *Time,* March 9, 1987, 88.

Hurren, Kenneth. *"Danger: Memory!" Mail on Sunday,* April 10, 1988. In *London Theatre Record* 8, no. 7 (1988): 431.

Kelly, Kevin. "'Clara': A Muddled Mess from Miller." *Boston Globe,* February 5, 1991, 54.

Lida, David. "*Danger: Memory!*—A Review." *Women's Wear Daily,* February 9, 1987. In *New York Theatre Critics' Reviews* 48 (1987): 346.

Loynd, Ray. "'Clara' a Wrenching Work by Arthur Miller." *Los Angeles Times,* February 5, 1991, F9.

Morley, Sheridan. *"Danger: Memory!" Punch* April 22, 1988. In *London Theatre Record* 8, no. 7 (1988): 427.

Tuttle, Jon. "Strange Faces, Other Minds: Sartre, Miller and 'Clara.'" *Journal of American Drama and Theatre,* 15, no. 3 (Fall 2003): 38–45.

"Clinton in Salem" (1998)

Originally published as an op-ed piece in the *New York Times,* this comparison of the hoopla surrounding Clinton's sexual disgrace and the SALEM WITCH TRIALS was reprinted in *Echoes Down the Corridor* (2000). The main similarity rests in the hatred and holier-than-thou tone of the accusers along with a more general desire to uproot crime and cleanse a society. The main difference is the current public's refusal—unlike in Salem—to join in the condemning, having recognized the political manipulation behind the accusation. While sexual prudery motivated both witch-hunters of old and those pillorying Clinton, changing sexual mores allow the public to be less condemnatory.

Miller suggests that Clinton's unpopularity with some, and continued popularity with others, may rest on a sexual desire that makes him human and on Toni Morrison's suggestion that he was America's "first black president" in many respects. Summing up, Miller points out that the worst historical scapegoating in Western society has been connected to either female sexuality or blackness—and Clinton combined the two—but to accept such prejudice can only ever be destructive. He concludes that the greatest change since Salem days is the Bill of Rights and the Fifth Amendment in particular, which allows U.S. citizens to now transcend theocratic judgments that threaten their individual liberty.

"Conditions of Freedom" (1989)

"Conditions of Freedom: Two Plays of the Seventies," was an essay first published as the introduction to a 1989 Grove Press edition of *The American Clock* and *The Archbishop's Ceiling* and later was collected in *The Theater Essays of Arthur Miller* (1995). The essay discusses what Miller felt was the general mood of the 1970s. Although the anti-VIETNAM WAR movement was still active, he saw that and other political movements as being less forceful and idealized than they had been in the 1960s. Lost were the laudable desires for nonaggression and human connection, as people (not only in the United States but also in Eastern Europe, the Soviet Union and France) seemed to have given up hope that these might be won in the face of an unassailable power structure that silenced all opposition. For Miller, the 1970s was "the era of the listening device" in which governments and businesses abroad and at home bugged anything and anyone to obtain information and maintain their power. Such surveillance, Miller claims, must surely affect everyone, whatever their hope of appeal, and make them less likely to resist those in power. Miller shares some of his experiences with so-called dissident writers from other countries with whom he was able to meet through his association with PEN, such as the Czech playwright VÁCLAV HAVEL.

Miller allows that on the surface *The Archbishop's Ceiling* is a study of how people might live with (and be affected by) such constant bugging, but it is also an exploration of something more universal about the essence of people, their capacity for adaptability, and the human temptation to play specific roles for those in charge. In this way, aside from the degree of mercy and love involved, Miller suggests that earthly power differs little from spiritual power in its ability to affect the way people live. Miller explains that the character of Sigmund in the play is the "most alive" in his refusal to accept the power structure and its demands and that he gains the strength to do this through his art. This clearly reflects, for Miller, the importance of art and the necessity that it not be restricted.

Miller goes on to relate how he worked on *The American Clock* for about 10 years before he was happy with its form and style, which ultimately found its true expression in the "epic and declarative" 1986 NATIONAL THEATRE production that was directed by Peter Wood. For Miller, the GREAT DEPRESSION, which forms the background for this play, was a surprisingly positive period of U.S. history, despite the obvious devastation, because it taught Americans lessons about interdependency and personal vulnerability which he sees as necessary to revisit in the self-serving, hedonistic 1970s. *The American Clock* was written partly to remind Americans of the true nature of DEMOCRACY by bringing to life a more humanitarian era during which people cared about each other on a societal level as much as on a personal one. Miller explains the rationale behind the vaudeville aspects of the play and the real-life

model on which he based Theodore K. Quinn: "[A] successful businessman interested in money and production" whose "vision transcended the market to embrace the nature of the democratic system." He concludes with a discussion of some of the staging aspects of Wood's production to show how this achieved his initial ambition—to fuse "emotion and conscious awareness, overt intention and subjective feelings."

Given its content, the title of the essay would indicate that the best society allows individuals certain freedoms while insisting that they maintain a level of social responsibility: Such are the "conditions" of freedom.

The Creation of the World and Other Business (1972)

Although *The Creation of the World and Other Business* takes as its text the book of Genesis, this play does not retell the biblical story verbatim but explores resonances in the story of the creation of humanity as applied to concerns of the moment. Early typescripts carried the description "a Catastrophic Comedy." Miller has spoken of the occasion for the play as having two influences: first, the revolts of the 1960s that made him wonder what would happen to the idealists of that time when faced with their inevitable disillusionment, and second, the VIETNAM WAR where once again humankind had been drawn into murderous violence to resolve its differences. It remains the most neglected of his full-length plays alongside its musical version, *Up From Paradise*, written two years later.

The production was a rocky one, with director HAROLD CLURMAN and some cast members being replaced before the final opening. Miller reputedly found it difficult to write an ending with which he was happy and so he kept rewriting, but he felt it was a good play. Clurman described it as a "philosophical comedy" but quit the show before its New York opening because of differences of opinion as to its interpretation.

SYNOPSIS

Act One

As night becomes day, we see God, deep in thought, seated above and Adam below in an impressionistic Paradise beside a tree with a prominent apple. God visits Adam, and they joke together as God encourages Adam to name some things. Realizing that Adam needs a female, God offers to provide one, but Adam is uncertain. However, once Eve is created, he is delighted by his new partner, and they seem to be almost totally united in thought. God's only rule is that they not eat the apple from the Tree of Knowledge or they will lose their immortality.

The angels Chemuel and Raphael congratulate God on creating Eve and begin a celebratory chorus, but God is evidently tired of their easy praise and prefers to talk to Lucifer. God is concerned because Adam and Eve are not multiplying; indeed, they seem utterly uninterested in sex. God asks Lucifer for help, and Lucifer suggests that the answer is to reduce their complete innocence and allow for difference, which has the capacity to make sex seem more attractive. If sex were more wonderful than other everyday activities, then people would be more likely to indulge. God refutes Lucifer's claims that He planted the Tree expecting Adam to eat from it and gain more knowledge, pointing out that giving Lucifer more knowledge only created a rival. He insists that the Tree remain untouched.

Lucifer rationalizes himself into believing that God is just testing him and wants humankind to have knowledge, so he tries to coax Adam to eat an apple. Refusing, Adam goes for a swim, but Eve is curious and takes a bite. Thrilled by her new self-awareness, Eve forces Adam to eat, too. When God discovers that they have broken His rule, He curses Eve and sends them both out of Paradise, telling Adam that he is in charge; He also condemns Lucifer's involvement. The angels try to cheer God up, Azrael even offering to kill Adam and Eve, but God points out that He still loves them. He decides to talk to Lucifer, who tries to justify his actions, insisting that without evil, good has no true meaning. God sends him to hell, insisting that He no longer loves him. Lucifer vows revenge and leaves, while God comments that He will miss him.

Act Two

Eve is very pregnant. However, she is unaware of what is occurring and assumes that she has been overeating until Lucifer informs her otherwise. He approaches her in a dream and argues his case, implying that he helped her become pregnant. He tries to persuade her to kill the child to upset God. The intensity of labor almost leads her to agree, but Eve resists and wakens, shaken. Adam and Eve have been having a hard time surviving, unused to fending for themselves.

Eve feels that she is really the one whom God blames, and she suggests that Adam try to go back to Paradise without her. He complains about Eve's size and is antagonistic to whatever is inside her. She explains that it is a child and tells him about Lucifer's visit. Learning of Lucifer's desire to kill the child makes Adam recant his former insensitivity, and the couple comes together as before. They notice an immediate improvement in their surroundings, as if God approves. Eve goes into labor and calls for help in her pain. Before Lucifer can answer her call, God, with the assistance of His angels, arrives to aid her through the delivery. He names the baby whom she produces, Cain. Delighted with the new child, God, Eve, and Adam dance off stage, while Lucifer kisses the baby and begins to plot anew.

Act Three

God becomes annoyed that humanity has become so involved in daily life that they seem to have forgotten about Him. He decides to remind them of their mortality and sends down Azrael to give them a dream of Death. Witnessing this, Lucifer assumes that God means for someone to die. To thwart Him, Lucifer decides to try to stop any killing. Just before this, he had been planning to create unrest between Cain and Abel after failing to goad Eve into dissatisfaction over her earthly life. Adam, Eve, Abel, and Cain recall their dreams of death and decide that it was a vision of Abel's demise.

Cain questions his parents about their relationship to God and the inequities of their lives. He and Abel argue over work, and Eve defends Abel. Cain feels put upon but resists his anger by hugging his brother. Then a snake drops from Heaven, and they hear coyotes howl. Lucifer flings the snake away as Adam and Eve decide to confess to their sons how they came to leave Paradise. Cain takes the news harder than Abel, admonishing his parents for not asking for God's forgiveness and continuing to act as if still innocent. He makes them all pray.

Lucifer persuades Abel to agree to build a fence that Cain had demanded by telling him that his brother is dangerous. Cain suggests that he build it across the other side of the mountain, and out of fear, Abel agrees. Cain begins to build an altar to God on which he places an offering of his vegetables. To Cain's disapproval, Eve suggests that Abel make an offering too, and he slaughters a lamb. Lucifer appears with the head of a bull announcing that he is "God on earth" and that they can do whatever they want. While Adam attacks him, Eve goes to his defense, accepting his offer. They begin a dance into which she draws her two sons, and then to Lucifer's delight, Cain begins to have sex with his mother while Abel waits his turn. God arrives to break the mood.

Lucifer suggests a truce, offering to take charge of humanity in all its imperfection, leaving God to try to work on their improvement. Swallowing His anger, God inspects the offerings. He is satisfied but praises Abel's lamb the most. While He goes off walking with the others, Cain stays behind, sulking, and kicks down the altar. He decides to send his family away and keep the farm for himself. Lucifer warns him that God is tricking him into killing his brother and tries to get him to hide. Cain insists on seeing Abel first and, finding fault in all Abel says, attacks and kills him with a flail. The others return looking for Abel and find the corpse. Cain blames God for showing Abel favoritism, but God points out that He simply prefers lamb to onions. Cain asks if this is God's justice, and God points out that He has never used that word and that everyone is different. Eve demands that God kill Cain as a murderer, especially as Cain is so unrepentant.

Lucifer insists that God is to blame because He sent down Azrael, but God explains that He was testing Cain, hoping that his love would outweigh his envy; and that Cain simply failed the test. Dissatisfied by their responses to events—Eve blames

God, Adam holds no one to blame, and Cain refuses responsibility—God gives up on humanity. He leaves them to Lucifer, to live lives without any rules. Lucifer is uncertain that he wants the job, and Eve remains unhappy, wanting something done about Cain. She rejects Lucifer as she and Adam praise God, realizing that unlike Lucifer, God actually loves them. Lucifer pleads with Cain to reject God, but he feels too empty to care.

God sentences Cain to live with his guilt and sets the mark of a smile on him, which he cannot relax. Then God leaves, telling them that they will not see Him again but must look for Him in their hearts. They are distraught and confused as Lucifer leaves them too. Eve and Cain argue as each tries to understand what has happened. Cain continues to refuse responsibility, and since his parents ask for repentance, he leaves. Adam turns to Eve asking her to forgive Cain, but she cannot. The play ends with Adam's desperate pleas for "Mercy!"

CRITICAL COMMENTARY

Closely following the Genesis story with a few gags thrown in, Miller is trying something new in *The Creation of the World and Other Business.* Despite its almost farcical humor at times, we should not be distracted from the deeper commentary on the nature of humanity, mostly illustrated through the debates between God and Lucifer. This is after all about how humankind was created, not just the world, and this, in large part, is the "Other Business."

It is noticeable in the opening description that even as night becomes day, some shadows remain, and the costume of the "naked" man is covered in a pattern of light *and* dark. Thus, from the start, we are reminded that good and evil as commonly symbolized in terms of light and dark are both eternally present. In one sense, they each define the other as Lucifer suggests, for without evil, good loses its intensity of meaning. Similarly, guilt helps define innocence, and sin the possibility of virtue. To be totally innocent and perfectly good as Adam and Eve are in Paradise is to condemn the human race to a bland nonexistence. Humanity becomes defined by its mix of good and evil, the real question becoming, which takes precedence? The ambivalent answer is that either one is possible; it is all a matter of personal choice. Humankind, made in the image of God, is willfully capable of both creation and destruction. The play's title might also be interpreted as an indication of this concern with opposites, with "Other Business" indicating the potential destruction of the world, as the opposite of its creation.

The play focuses on the nature of free will, centering on Miller's belief that what this intrinsically comes down to is each person's choice between good and evil. Diametrically opposed alternatives, be it life and death, love and hate, or creation and destruction, are exhibited throughout the play. What Miller suggests is that it is part of human nature to sometimes choose the more negative of the two, and he illustrates this propensity by exploring the time when humankind was first given the capacity to choose, a period that culminated in fratricide. In this regard, the play is very much a companion piece to Miller's earlier existential play *After the Fall,* as both explore the conditions and difficulties of living in a postlapsarian world.

Prefall Adam and Eve seem united in thought, each completing the other, but this unity is also possible in the postlapsarian world. Even in Paradise, there were signs that their unity was not complete as Eve suggests renaming Adam's "prndn" a "louse" and pretty much forces him to eat the apple. Just by creating woman, God created sufficient difference to allow for more than one response to events. The onset of knowledge destroys the possibility of absolutes for humankind as it introduces the concept of ambiguity. Nothing can be absolute in the postlapsarian world. In a world in which good is no longer the only option, humanity has a choice between good and evil.

The fact that God has Adam doing the naming implies an element of free will from the start with humankind in charge of their own destiny. Eve makes a conscious choice to eat the apple, however much goaded by Lucifer, just as she later chooses to keep her child rather than to destroy it. When the couple is sent out of Paradise, they may lose their security, but they gain independence. This move also benefits God, making God happier when they choose to praise Him. Outside

Paradise, the couple find life more of a struggle, but they also find it more rewarding. The world of humankind is varied and potentially preferable to that of God, who finds His own angels something of a bore and can even miss Lucifer for his more lively rebellion. For Miller, innocence is a deadening force that is best avoided. In Paradise, there was no conflict, and everyone lived in an inescapable stasis, but on Earth, people face the ups and downs of life in all of its messy pain and joy. Therefore, the Fall is not bad; it is simply the price for being human.

Eve's speech demanding why God allowed her son to be killed reflects the cry of anyone bereaved. She insists that the murderer be recognized and forced to pay, but it is suggested that the better way is for the murderer to seek forgiveness rather than face a forced punishment. Eve and Cain are unable to compromise, resulting in a stalemate, with Adam caught, ineffectually, in the center. Such in some sense is the condition of life in all its contradictions. The irony of the smile with which God marks the first murderer reflects the true ambivalence of humankind's existence.

The central difference between God and Lucifer is that God is love and cares for everything around Him (including Lucifer), but Lucifer only cares about himself. He wants to teach God a lesson by destroying, but Eve instinctively knows that one cannot teach God. The choice is to attempt to emulate God through creation, despite any attendant pains, or to become evil. God asks for humankind to choose "the way of life, not death," but it can only ever be a request, not an order. Cain is faced with this choice, and he makes the wrong one this time; he chooses death and destruction over life, creation, and love. Yet, his right to choose is what makes him human, and on a different occasion, he might choose otherwise. Cain loves Abel but allows his jealousy and anger to overcome this. Love, apparently, is not enough to keep people from evil, but it remains something to which they can return. A hope is suggested in the idea that humankind, having been made out of God's love, may be drawn more powerfully toward good than evil. This may allow hope, but since perfection has become impossible in a postlapsarian world, the possibility of choosing evil must always exist as well.

FIRST PERFORMANCE

The Creation of the World and Other Business previewed under the direction of Harold Clurman, but it moved from the Eisenhower Theatre, Kennedy Center, Washington, D.C., to the Shubert Theatre, New York, on November 30, 1972, with a new director and the following cast:

Adam: Bob Dishy
God: Stephen Elliott
Eve: Zoe Caldwell
Chemuel, The Angel of Mercy: Lou Gilbert
Raphael, An Angel: Dennis Cooley
Azrael, The Angel of Death: Lou Polan
Lucifer: George Grizzard
Cain: Barry Primus
Abel: Mark Lamos

Directed by Gerald Freedman
Set by BORIS ARONSON
Produced by ROBERT WHITEHEAD
Music by Stanley Silverman
It ran for 20 performances.

INITIAL REVIEWS

Reviews of this production were almost completely negative. Clive Barnes, Brendan Gill, and T. E. Kalem were pretty typical of the overall response. Barnes viewed the play as a "victory of craft over artistry" and disliked what he described as a "comic strip version of Genesis." Gill saw it as an "incoherent assortment of debates," and Kalem as "feeble, pointless play." Only Leonard Harris, reviewer for CBS, seemed to find anything of value, calling it "amusing" though "minor" and concluding that it was "played by all the cast with wit and clarity." That it was meant to be comic is without a doubt, and despite flashes of humor throughout his work, critics have always been suspicious of Miller as a comic writer. It is possible that such poor reviews were less a reflection of the quality of the production than of the reviewers expectations, illustrated by Martin Gottfried's complaints that Miller should waste his "tremendous talent" on such a "foolish project."

SCHOLARSHIP

This is possibly the most overlooked of Miller's plays, and STEVEN CENTOLA's 1985 essay seems to go against the critical grain with its insistence that it was worthy of reconsideration if only because "it represents Miller's first experiment with comedy" and contributes further information on Miller's "vision of the human condition." Dennis Welland questions both Miller's taste and tone but spends time comparing the play to Marc Connelly's *The Green Pastures* (1930) and the later *Up From Paradise* (1974), as well as discussing the characterizations of God and Lucifer, which is more than many other books on Miller have done. Even CHRISTOPHER BIGSBY, in his comprehensive study of Miller's works, only spends four pages discussing the play. Describing it as an ironic exploration of metaphysical concerns provoked by world events, Bigsby views the play as a response to contemporary times rather than a retreat to the past, but he is not enamored.

Of those who offer longer discussions of the play, Manish Vyas discusses the play's social paradigms, and although Terry Otten views it as "a slight work," he spends time detailing its origination and form, and he recognizes, as do June Schleuter and James Flanagan, that the play typifies many of Miller's most essential concerns. In a refreshingly positive essay, William Demastes sees the play as an interesting attempt to "demythologize" the biblical story and make it contemporary, and he offers detailed analyses of Lucifer and God. Like Centola, Demastes claims that the play is "worthy of close attention since it crystallizes persistent concerns Miller has had and suggests future directions he would take."

CHARACTERS

Abel More favored by their mother, Eve, than his brother Cain and seemingly also more favored by God who congratulates him heartily on his offering of lamb, Abel is a dreamer rather than a doer. Ironically, less "able" than his brother, he haphazardly tends the sheep, often allowing them to feed on his brother's crops. The whole family laughs at the idea that Abel could possibly exchange places with his brother. He loves Cain and does not flaunt his easier life but also refuses to allow his brother to chase him off. This results in his death at Cain's hand, despite Lucifer's warnings to Abel not to goad his more dangerous brother.

Adam   Adam is presented as a follower rather than a leader, something of a good-hearted, rather naive innocent and as such is fairly ineffective. When God is not present to order him, he tends to let his wife influence his decisions, despite having been told that he is in charge. Not so intelligent, he seems easily manipulated by his wilier wife, yet staunchly rejects Lucifer whenever Lucifer tries to influence him. Delighted with the orderly life of Paradise, he spends much of the play hoping to return, and his final cry for "Mercy" might as easily be directed to God as to Eve or Cain.

Angels (Chemuel, Raphael, and Azrael)   These three angels are barely distinguishable from one another—each functions as a yes-man to God, illustrating the lack of choice inherent within Paradise. Chemuel, the Angel of Mercy, and Raphael fawn and praise and do whatever they are told. As the Angel of Death, Azrael is somewhat darker but just as obedient. God prefers the more challenging company of Lucifer.

Cain   More practical than his dreamer brother Abel, Cain is a hard worker on whom the family depends for all of their crops and much of the upkeep of their home. He loves his brother but harbors a grudge, jealous that Abel is more favored by their mother and is allowed to live an easier life. His desire for his mother's favor is even played out in Oedipal terms as he mounts her during the dance in act three. This colors how he views everything that his brother says and does in terms of a rivalry of which only he is aware and finds insult where often none was intended.

Ironically, given that he turns out to be the biggest sinner in murdering his brother, initially Cain is the most devout of the family. He worries that they do not seek God's guidance more than they do and creates the first Sabbath to praise God, building the altar on which to make an offering. His devotion swiftly turns to anger as he hears God

praise his brother's lamb more than his offerings, and he violently breaks the altar that he had built, just as he breaks God's hopes by allowing his envy to override his love. The smile that God places on his face is at odds with the agony in his eyes and is yet another sign of the ambiguity of life.

Eve   Created from Adam's rib, Eve shows elements of independent thought at very start, asking "why" and renaming Adam's "prndn" a "louse." Her curiosity is the catalyst for getting them both thrown out of Paradise, but it is also what helps humankind to multiply. Although at times she sides with Lucifer, her independence also allows her to be free of Lucifer's persuasion when she wants. She accedes to eating the apple but stands firmer against the killing of her own child and, in the end, chooses God over Lucifer, recognizing that God's demanding love has greater importance than Lucifer's casual offer of freedom. In her unforgiving demand for Cain's death, she proves herself to be as capable of evil as her son and as fully human.

God   At the start, God often comes across as indecisive and even a little foolish. His experiments seemed to be based on guesswork and at times go awry; Miller's God is omnipotent but hardly omniscient. Humankind, to a degree, is just another of God's experiments, as yet unfinished. It is not until God banishes Adam and Eve from Paradise and sends them to Earth that humanity is truly created. God explains that He does not love evil, as in the form of Lucifer; yet God cannot feel wholly content without its presence, knowing that good only becomes so in its opposition to evil. His Paradise with its strict rules and unchanging existence bores even God. He is quick to find more pleasure in humankind's occasional praise than in all the songs of the angels, whose mindless admiration annoys for they have no choice to do otherwise. It is for this reason that God allows humankind choice in whether or not to please Him.

Though powerful and well intentioned, Miller's God seems less than infallible. This could stem from the difficulty any omnipotent figure might face in allowing his creation true freedom. He is petulantly unhappy when humankind chooses to ignore God for a time, sending down His Angel of Death to provoke them into action and angrily threatening to abandon them to Lucifer after their confused response to Abel's death. He does in the end leave, despite Adam and Eve's declaration of love, announcing that He will never physically return, but says that people can look for God in their hearts. This leaves us with the sense that humankind truly has been left in charge. Although God may be ever watching and even caring, He will not interfere again. This places the burden for the future on humankind rather than on God, and is meant as a call for action rather than despair.

Lucifer   In the first act, particularly, Miller ensures that we find Lucifer to be in many respects more attractive and sympathetic than God. He seems to advocate choice and the efficacy of difference and has many of the reactions and arguments that we might have expected from God. It is hard to view him as the villain because he seems genuinely to want to help both God and humankind. Yet, we should be suspicious; on a number of occasions, God implies that Lucifer's ambitions are more self-involved and are concerned with his own promotion. Lucifer argues that evil has a justified place in the world in that it helps to define good and to give it its potency. He sees God's force as unreasonable and denigrates Him as "a spirit to whom nothing is sacred." But as the source of all sacredness, God cannot feasibly worship a higher force than Himself, and this becomes typical of the false logic that Lucifer employs to his own ends. Lucifer's world in which no rules apply is as bad as the world of total rules from which he had helped Adam and Eve escape and is equally as mindless.

Yet, Lucifer is necessary. Without his input (possibly physical as well as philosophical), Adam and Eve would have remained barren, and so in one sense, humanity has been created by the devil as much as by God. In God's perfect world, Adam and Eve were unable to procreate; it was only through the introduction of knowledge, via Lucifer's seduction of Eve, that the couple became interested in sex—thus we have original sin tied directly to the devil. Perfection, Lucifer suggests, is uncreative and unproductive and progress depends on variety and curiosity—neither of which Adam and Eve enjoy while they remain in Paradise without any cares. To this degree, he is right, but his contribution is ultimately negative. What Lucifer offers is mindless pleasure, which works against the choice God allows because when one can do anything without restriction, the concept of choice becomes eradicated.

FURTHER READING

Barnes, Clive. "Arthur Miller's *Creation of the World*." *New York Times*, December 1, 1972, 28.

Bigsby, Christopher. "*Creation of the World and Other Business*." *Arthur Miller: A Critical Study*. Cambridge: Cambridge University Press, 2005, 289–293.

Buckley, Tom. "In the Beginning Miller's Creation. . . ." *New York Times*, December 5, 1972, 49, 67.

Centola, Steven R. "What Price Freedom? The Fall Revisited: Arthur Miller's *The Creation of the World and Other Business*." *Studies in the Humanities* 12 (June 1985): 3–10.

Clurman, Harold. "Letter to Boris Aronson Apropos of *The Creation of the World and Other Business*." *On Directing*. New York: Macmillan, 1972, 292–299.

Deedy, John. "Critics and the Bible." *Commonweal*, January 5, 1973, 290.

Demastes, William. "Miller's 1970s 'Power' Plays." In *Cambridge Companion to Arthur Miller*, edited by Christopher Bigsby, 139–151. (New York: Cambridge University Press, 1997).

Gill, Brendan. "Here Come the Clowns." *New Yorker*, December 9, 1972, 109.

Gottfried, Martin. "*Creation of the World and Other Business*." *Women's Wear Daily*, December 4, 1972. In *New York Theatre Critics' Reviews* 33 (1972): 153.

Harris, Leonard. "*The Creation of the World and Other Business*." CBS. WCBS. New York. In *New York Theatre Critics' Reviews* 33 (1972): 154.

Kalem, T. E. "Adam and Evil." *Time*, December 11, 1972, 122.

Otten, Terry. "*The Creation of the World and Other Business*." *The Temptation of Innocence in the Dramas of Arthur Miller*. Columbia: University of Missouri Press, 2002: 158–164.

Schlueter, June, and James K. Flanagan, editors *Arthur Miller*. New York: Ungar, 1987.

Vyas, Manish A. "*The Creation of the World and other Business:* Miller's Journey from Social to Familial." In *Arthur Miller: Twentieth Century Legend,* edited by Syed Mashkoor Ali, 246–258. (Jaipur, India: Surabhi, 2006).

Welland, Dennis. "Versions of Genesis." *Miller: The Playwright,* 2d ed. New York: Methuen, 1983, 125–132.

The Crucible (1953)

Miller's interest in the SALEM WITCH TRIALS was partly prompted by reading Marion Starkey's *The Devil in Massachusetts.* While researching witch trials at the Historical Society in Salem, Massachusetts, Miller found the core of his plot in Charles W. Upton's 19th-century book, *Salem Witchcraft.* Here, he found references to most of the main characters who appear in his play. In terms of the play's historical accuracy in portraying the Salem witch trials of 1692, in a note at the start of the play script, Miller declares that his play is predominantly accurate as regard to facts but that he has made some changes for "dramatic purposes." The major changes are the fusing of various original characters into a single representative, reducing the number of girls "crying out" and the number of judges, and increasing Abigail's age. While he based characters on what he learned through letters, records, and reports, he asks them to be considered properly as "creations of my own, drawn to the best of my ability in conformity with their known behavior."

The printed play contains extensive notes detailing the historical background of Salem society in the 1690s and numerous facts regarding the actual lives of the main characters who are involved. Miller wanted his critics to know that he had not made up these events but that people really allowed such things to occur. These notes illustrate the extensive research that Miller undertook to write *The Crucible.* And yet there have been criticisms of the play's historical inaccuracies, despite Miller's opening disclaimer.

There are many details in the play that are firmly supported by trial transcripts and other records of the time, such as Tituba's confession, Sarah Good's condemnation on being unable to cite the Ten Commandments, Rebecca's steadfastly claimed innocence, Giles Corey's complaints against his wife's preventing him from saying his prayers, and Mary Warren's poppet being given to Elizabeth. The notable details that appear to have arisen more from Miller's imagination are the presentation of Abigail and her lust for Proctor; the development of both the Proctors, with John especially depicted as a liberated thinker; and Proctor's confession and recantation. Miller also makes the judges much more accommodating than the originals, who would never have listened to counterarguments. It was the moral absolutism of many Puritans of that era which allowed no dissent that Miller wished to capture and expose. The actual prosecution was truly as blind to facts and relentless as they appear in the play, and there were many, like the Putnams, who took full, mercenary advantage of the situation.

The HOUSE UN-AMERICAN ACTIVITIES COMMITTEE (HUAC) hearings of the 1950s, at which any U.S. citizens suspected of having communist sympathies were challenged to publicly confess, had become, for Miller, a target ripe for ridicule. He had also been seeking a way in which he could convey his anger at such proceedings within a dramatic form. He initially resisted the idea of depicting these hearings in the form of an old-fashioned witch trial as too obvious. However, as the HUAC hearings grew more ritualistic and cruelly pointless, he could no longer resist, despite the obvious risks, for the parallels were far too apt to ignore. By showing the connection of McCarthyism to the way people acted in Salem, Miller suggests that the 1950s U.S. vision of COMMUNISM was a moral issue that viewed communists as being in league with the devil. This was what made people hate communists so thoroughly and allow them to drop all of the usual civilities. Any opposition to HUAC was seen in terms of "diabolical malevolence" that allowed no sympathy, and any sign of fear or reticence would be taken as an admission of guilt.

Miller saw how both the HUAC hearings and the witch trials had a definite structure behind them, designed to make people publicly confess. In both cases, the "judges" knew in advance all the information for which they asked. The main difference was that Salem's hearings had a greater legality as it was against the LAW in 1690s America to be a witch, but it was not against the law to be a communist in the 1950s. Miller does not attempt a one-to-one analogy between his characters and those involved in HUAC because this would have made the play too contemporary. The reason that the play has remained so popular is that it offers more than a simple history lesson of either the original witch trials or of HUAC—what Miller explores are the prevailing conditions that precipitate such events. The play, however, as critic James Martine states, "struck its own effective blow at McCarthyism." The original production was still playing on the day that Ethel and Julius Rosenberg were being executed, and Miller recalls how after Proctor's execution the audience silently rose to its feet with heads bowed for several minutes. He saw it as a sign that the play was being viewed as an "act of resistance."

Although *The Crucible* first appeared on Broadway at the Martin Beck Theater in New York of January 1953, it was not until the 1960s that it became widely popular, perhaps needing some separation of time from the communist hunts of HUAC against which it so bravely spoke. On reflection, many critics who had found fault with the premiere production rethought their decisions, such as John Gassner who by 1960 came to see *The Crucible* as a powerful drama that surpassed most others of its era. In 1961, Robert Ward paid homage by writing *The Crucible: An Opera in 4 Acts, Based on the Play by Arthur Miller*, that helped underline the play's intensely dramatic nature, as well as the tragic stature of its characters. The multiplicity of subsequent productions of the play soon made this the most produced of Miller's dramas and offers testament to the timelessness of its themes.

SYNOPSIS

Act One

Set in Salem, Massachusetts, of 1692, *The Crucible* begins in the bedroom of Reverend Samuel Parris's daughter, Betty. Parris kneels in prayer, weeping at the bedside of his comatose 10-year-old daughter. He sends away the family slave, Tituba, who is concerned about the girl but allows entry to his 17-year-old niece, Abigail Williams, and her friend, Susanna Walcott. Susanna tells him that the doctor has no cure and suspects witchcraft. Although Parris insists that "unnatural causes" cannot be at fault, he has already sent for the Reverend Hale to look into such possibilities. He would like to keep this whole matter a secret, but the townspeople are already alerted.

Prior to Betty's coma, Parris caught her and Abigail dancing "like heathens" in the forest. The shock of discovery caused Betty to faint, and she has not regained consciousness. Parris is worried how it will look for the minister's daughter to be thought a witch. He presses Abigail for details, wanting to know if they had been conjuring spirits, but she insists that they were only dancing. Abigail seems penitent but is dissembling. Tituba was with them incanting spells over a fire, and one of the girls was naked. Abigail was dismissed from the Proctors' service seven months prior, and although she insists that it was maliciousness on Elizabeth Proctor's part, her uncle is suspicious. It is rumored that her reputation is suspect. Locals, Ann and Thomas Putnam, arrive with stories of Betty flying like a witch, clearly determined to believe the worst. Parris denies their gossip but dislikes disagreeing with such a wealthy couple, concerned for their support.

The Putnams' daughter, Ruth, is also behaving strangely and they are convinced that it is the work of the devil. Putnam dislikes Parris because he had beaten his brother-in-law to the post of minister and is happy to cause trouble for him, so he insists that witchcraft is afoot. Ann lost seven babies prior to Ruth and is determined to blame someone. She had sent Ruth to Tituba, whom she believes to have supernatural powers, to discover who "murdered" her babies by conjuring up their spirits. Parris realizes that Abigail has been lying, although she insists that only Tituba and Ruth were involved, and he worries as to how this will affect his reputation.

The Putnams press Parris to declare publicly that witchcraft is abroad. Mercy Lewis, the Putnams' servant girl, arrives to check on Betty and give news of Ruth. Parris leaves with the Putnams to lead the gathering villagers in prayer, and Abigail remains to talk with Mercy. She warns her to stick to her story that they were just dancing. Mary Warren, who replaced Abigail as the Proctors' servant, joins them. She is fearful and wants to confess, especially as she was only an onlooker. As Abigail tells Betty that they have told her father everything, she runs to jump from the window. Abigail pulls her back and violently threatens all of the girls to stay quiet about what they really did; Abigail had drunk blood as part of a spell to kill Elizabeth. Betty reverts to her coma as John Proctor enters to fetch Mary.

Proctor angrily sends Mary home with the threat of a beating for she had been told not to leave the house. Mercy follows, leaving him and Abigail together. Abigail is flirtatious, assuring Proctor that no witchcraft was involved and that the girls were just playing. She thinks that he has come to see her and tells him how she longs for him. He denies that there is anything between them. Abigail becomes angered by his refusal to have anything more to do with her. They have had relations in the past, and Abigail refuses to believe that Proctor does not prefer her to his wife, even though he insists otherwise. He has been sexually attracted but is trying to resist and becomes angry when she insults his wife, threatening her with a whipping. She weeps and claims that he owes her something for taking her innocence.

They are distracted by a psalm drifting in from outside and Betty screaming. Parris, the Putnams, and Mercy Lewis rush in to see what is happening, joined by two respected elders of the village, Rebecca Nurse and Giles Corey. Ann insists that it is a clear sign of witchcraft that Betty cannot bear to hear the Lord's name, and Parris agrees. Rebecca calms Betty down with her presence and suggests that the children's odd behavior is just childish mischief and that the townspeople would be foolish to search any deeper. The Putnams and Parris insist that it is something more serious. Proctor is angered by the superstitions of Parris and the Putnams, pointing out that they should have called a meeting of the town before calling for a witch-finder. Rebecca worries that they are heading toward trouble and cautions them to blame themselves for their misfortunes rather than look for scapegoats. Ann is jealous that Rebecca lost none of her children and refuses to listen.

They squabble, Putnam criticizing Proctor for not attending church and Proctor accusing Parris of being a poor minister. Parris complains that the town does not pay him enough. He accuses Proctor of leading a faction against him, and Putnam joins in the accusations. Rebecca tries to calm them down, asking Proctor to shake hands, but he refuses. Giles wonders if something bad is afoot in the town, making them all contentious; he himself has been to court six times this past year. Proctor teases him about being cranky, trying to laugh him out of it, while Putnam argues about who owns the lumber that Proctor intends to go and cut. When Giles offers to help Proctor cut the wood, Putnam threatens them with a writ, just as Reverend John Hale arrives.

Hale compliments Rebecca and the Putnams on their reputations. Proctor leaves with a warning to Hale to use his good sense. Hale instructs the group not to give in to superstition and insists that they all accept his authority. Rebecca disapproves of their malicious tone as they relate their suspicions and leaves, making the rest resentful over her attitude of moral superiority. Giles questions Hale about his wife's tendency to read books, complaining that he cannot pray when she does so. Hale examines Betty, but she is unresponsive. He then questions Abigail about the girl's exploits in the forest. As he begins to draw out the truth, to protect herself, Abigail accuses Tituba of calling the devil and making her drink blood. Tituba is brought in to defend herself. From Barbados, Tituba has been showing the children some of her native rites. She is now fearfully led into confessing complicity with the devil and to name others as witches to save her life. Putnam even suggests a few names to help her. Abigail joins in adding more names, and then Betty joins her, as the adults scurry to arrest the accused.

Act Two

Act two begins eight days later in the Proctors' house. Elizabeth is putting their sons to bed as Proctor enters and adds salt to the meal that she is cooking. There is tension between Elizabeth and Proctor; both speak and behave overcautiously.

He compliments her cooking, trying to please, and goes to kiss her, but she does not react. Proctor wishes Elizabeth to be warmer toward him, while she is suspicious that he still sees Abigail. Their servant, Mary, is an official of the court that has been set up in town. Four judges have come down from Boston to try the accused. Matters have escalated, and there are now 14 people in jail who are faced with hanging unless they confess to witchcraft. The town supports the trials as Abigail leads the girls to accuse more people.

Elizabeth asks Proctor to stop this dangerous nonsense, reminding him what Abigail told him about its having nothing to do with witchcraft. Without other witnesses, he is uncertain if anyone will believe him if he denounces Abigail. Elizabeth is shocked to realize that he had been alone with Abigail. She suspects that Proctor is reluctant because of feelings for Abigail, but he angrily denounces her jealousy as unfounded. He is tired of being suspected and judged, but Elizabeth suggests that it is only his guilt pressing him. Arriving home, Mary deflates their argument. Proctor goes to shake her, but her evident distress and weakened state make him hold back. Mary gives Elizabeth a small rag doll, called a poppet, which she made in court. She has been there all day and is shaken by what she has witnessed.

The girls have accused 25 more people, and the court has declared that Goody Osbourne must hang. If the accused confess their allegiance with the devil, as Sarah Good has done, they go to jail, but if they refuse to confess they are hanged as unrepentant witches. Mary relates how Sarah sent out her spirit to choke the girls in the courtroom. This is some kind of hysterical reaction—Mary's proof of Sarah's evilness is based on her mumbling under her breath when Mary refused a handout. When asked what she mumbled, Sarah insisted that it was the Ten Commandments. However, when asked, she could not name a single commandment, so the judges condemned her as a witch. The Proctors are horrified, telling Mary that she must not attend court again, but she insists that she is needed. When Proctor goes to whip her for disobedience, she stands firm against him. She relates how Elizabeth came under suspicion

(from accusations by Abigail), but the court apparently dismissed the idea when Mary defended her. She realizes that she has power and insists that the Proctors treat her better. She goes to bed, leaving the Proctors to worry.

Proctor feels that he must tell Ezekiel Cheever, the court's clerk, what Abigail told him about it being a game. Elizabeth feels that this may not be enough, asking Proctor to talk to Abigail, realizing that she is in mortal danger. She knows that Abigail wants her husband and is out to replace her. She makes Proctor see that Abigail may have read his embarrassment as continued favor. He needs to make it clear that she has no hope. Angry at Elizabeth's perception that he still feels attracted to Abigail, Proctor agrees to go just as Hale arrives. Although convinced that witchcraft is about, Hale is unsure about the girls, especially now that they are targeting more respectable women, such as Elizabeth and Rebecca. He is investigating further. Questioning the Proctors about their religious adherence, Hale has noted that Proctor rarely attends church and that he failed to baptize his third son.

Proctor defends himself, pointing out that his wife had been sick the past winter and that his dislike of the minister has been the real reason keeping him away from church. He has been a staunch church member in the past, nailing on the church roof and hanging the door. Hale asks Proctor to name the Ten Commandments. Proctor significantly forgets adultery until delicately reminded by his wife. Elizabeth asks Hale outright if she is under suspicion, and he evades a direct answer, so she presses Proctor to tell him about Abigail's admission that there was no witchcraft involved. Hale is shocked, pointing out that some have already confessed. Proctor insists that such confessions mean little when the alternative is to be hanged. Hale asks him if he will tell the court this, but Proctor is reluctant. He feels that if Hale can doubt Elizabeth who has never lied, then the court may not take his word against Abigail's. Both Proctor and Elizabeth shock Hale by admitting that they find it hard to believe that witches exist. Elizabeth insists that they are both godly people and that he would be better questioning Abigail about the Gospel.

Hale advises them to baptize their son and to go to church. Then they are interrupted by Giles and Francis Nurse, arriving to announce that their wives have been arrested on charges of witchcraft. Ann Putnam has charged Rebecca with murdering her babies, and someone resentful has charged Martha Corey about a pig that he had bought from her that died when he neglected it. The news of their arrest shakes Hale, but he insists that they all accept the justice of the court and allow no one to be above suspicion. Cheever and Marshal Herrick arrive to arrest Elizabeth, asking for a poppet that they have been told is Elizabeth's and that proves her witchery. Abigail has stuck herself with a needle and has declared that Elizabeth sent a spirit to do this; they find a needle sticking in the poppet. Mary explains that the poppet and needle are hers; she made it in court sitting next to Abigail. Elizabeth's reaction to this evidence against her is to declare that Abigail "must be ripped out of the world," and they take that as further proof that she has tried to murder Abigail.

Proctor tears their warrant and tries to send them from his house. He turns on Hale, asking why they never question Parris's or Abigail's innocence and just believe the children and others who are seeking vengeance for old offenses. Rather than cause trouble, Elizabeth agrees to go. Proctor promises to free her shortly as she fearfully leaves. Giles and Proctor urge Hale to see the girls' accusations as fraudulent, but Hale stands firm that such confusion would not have fallen on the town if all were innocent. In the guilt of his recent adultery, Proctor falls quiet. As everyone leaves, Proctor remains with Mary, whom he insists must speak to clear Elizabeth. In fear of Abigail, Mary refuses, but Proctor says that he is prepared to confess his own adultery to destroy the court's faith in Abigail.

There is an additional scene at this point, not always included, that Miller added during the initial production. Five weeks after Elizabeth has been arrested, the day before her trial, Proctor secretly meets Abigail. She seems close to madness; her body is covered in scars that she believes were caused by spirits sent against her by townspeople, despite the implication that they are self-inflicted. She displays a continued passion for Proctor, insist-

ing that his attentions brought her to life and that she cannot wait to be his wife. He warns her to tell the truth or be exposed, both about the business with the poppet and about their past relationship. Abigail does not believe him, insisting that he still prefers her to Elizabeth and is just asking this out of guilt toward his wife.

Act Three

Act three moves to an anteroom outside the courtroom. Next door, Judge Hathorne questions Martha Corey, who proclaims her innocence. When her husband, Giles, speaks in her defense, he is brought into the anteroom for questioning. Governor Danforth, leading the panel of judges, demands that Giles be less disruptive and offer his evidence in a proper affidavit. Giles feels guilty that he complained about his wife's reading. Meanwhile, Francis Nurse, whose wife Rebecca has been condemned, insists to the shocked judges that the girls are frauds. Hathorne threatens him with contempt, but Nurse stands firm, saying that he has proof. Danforth warns Nurse that he has put 400 in jail throughout the area, has sentenced 72 to hang, and is not to be trifled with.

Proctor enters with Mary, who has agreed to tell the truth. Danforth decides to hear what they have to say. Mary admits that the girls are pretending, and Parris insists this must be a lie. Danforth is uncertain regarding Proctor's motivation for presenting Mary, fearing that Proctor is trying to undermine the court rather than just save his wife. This suspicion is increased when Cheever relates how Proctor railed against the court when he arrested Elizabeth, and Parris points out how infrequently he attends church, but Proctor stands firm. They tell him that Elizabeth has declared herself pregnant. The judges are uncertain if this is true, but Proctor insists that his wife would never lie. To test him, Danforth offers to let Elizabeth live to give birth if Proctor will drop his protest, but he refuses, realizing that too many other innocents are condemned. Danforth angrily agrees to hear the deposition.

Proctor shows a list of people that Francis has compiled who believe that Elizabeth, Rebecca, and Martha are innocent. To Francis's dismay, the judges decide to arrest all these people for examination. Proctor offers Giles's deposition that accuses Thomas Putnam of prompting his daughter to cry witchery on people to obtain their property. Danforth insists that Giles name his witness, but knowing that to name the man would send him to jail, Giles refuses and is arrested for contempt. Hale is becoming increasingly worried by the reactions of the court and asks that they allow Proctor a lawyer to guide him; he is concerned that they may have signed people's death warrants based on false evidence. Danforth dismisses his concerns and insists that they proceed.

They read Mary's deposition, and Danforth questions her to see if Proctor is forcing her to lie, but she stands firm. Susanna, Mercy, Betty, and Abigail are brought in to face their accuser and are asked to respond. Abigail insists that Mary lies. Danforth questions her about the poppet found at the Proctors' house, and she denies ever having seen it. They start to argue over whether Elizabeth could ever have had a poppet until Proctor redirects their attention to Abigail, insisting that she is trying to murder his wife. His accusations of Abigail laughing during services and leading the girls to dance naked affect Danforth. Hathorne asks Mary to show how she pretends to faint in court, but Mary cannot do this without the proper atmosphere. This restores Hathorne's and Parris's belief that she is lying, but Danforth remains uncertain.

Danforth questions Abigail, but her insistence of innocence weakens his resolve. Abigail pretends that Mary has sent a spirit against her, and the other girls join in accusing Mary. Mary becomes hysterical, losing control, so Proctor grabs Abigail announcing that she is a whore. To back his charge, he confesses his adultery. His friends and the judges are shocked. Abigail denies the charge, and Danforth calls for Elizabeth to support Proctor's accusation. Not knowing that her husband has confessed, Elizabeth cannot publicly betray him, and for the first time ever, she lies. She declares that no adultery took place and makes Proctor seem the liar. He tells her that he has confessed, and she is horrified as she is taken away. Proctor and Hale both insist that Elizabeth was lying to save her husband's good name, but everyone is distracted by the girls

again pretending that Mary's spirit is attacking them. Danforth insists that Mary stop, and in fear of her own life, Mary cries out against Proctor. Danforth turns on Proctor, who declares, "God is dead!" and accuses them all of working for Satan, which seals his fate. All the judges, except Hale, who denounces the proceedings, are convinced by the girls' performance and have Proctor arrested.

Act Four

Act four takes place three months later, inside the jail, where Sarah Good and Tituba, who confessed themselves witches, now languish. Marshal Herrick is drunk, unhappy with his role in these proceedings. The women joke that they are waiting for the devil to come and fly them to Barbados as Herrick sends them to another cell. Hathorne

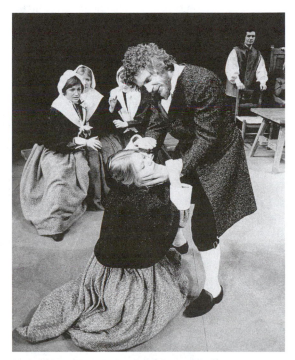

Scene from the 1964 National Repertory Theater production of *The Crucible*. Deputy Governor Danforth (Thayer David) threatens the girls (Barbara Stanton, Pamela Given, Susan Carr, and Kelly Jean Peters). *Courtesy Billy Rose Theatre Collection, The New York Public Library for the Performing Arts, Astor, Lenox and Tilden Foundations.*

and Danforth come in and seem anxious about why Hale is praying in the jail cells and about the strength of their support. Parris has called them and comes to explain that Hale is trying to persuade the condemned to confess to save their lives. Any confessions will make the other condemned seem the more guilty, which would help the judges maintain their sense of probity, so Parris has been helping him. Parris also tells them that Abigail and Mercy have stolen his savings and absconded. A nearby town, Andover, is rebelling against the witch courts, and the girls fled in case Salem follows suit. There is fear of riot, and Parris's life has been threatened; he is worried at the town's reaction to them hanging such citizens as Rebecca. He suggests that they postpone the hangings, but Danforth refuses. To pardon others would cast doubt on the guilt of the 12 already hanged.

Having had no success, Hale enters to ask Danforth to pardon the prisoners or give him more time. Danforth sees any delay as a sign of weakness and insists that the seven marked to die at sunrise must be executed. Hale has not seen Proctor, so Danforth suggests using the pregnant Elizabeth to lead Proctor toward a confession. While the Proctors are being fetched, Hale relates the sorry state of the township, with crops and livestock neglected and orphans wandering the streets because so many have been imprisoned. He is disgusted at his own part in this. Elizabeth is brought in, and Hale pleads with her to get Proctor to lie to save his life. Hale explains how he has lost his faith, given the way religion is being used to destroy so many innocents, and tells Elizabeth to choose life over truth. She is suspicious, thinking that this a trick, but when Danforth accuses her of lacking pity, she offers to speak with her husband.

Proctor is brought in, and the couple is almost overcome with emotion at the sight of one another. Hale persuades the rest to leave them alone. Proctor asks for news of their sons, and Elizabeth tells him that they are safe. Elizabeth also tells him that more than 100 have confessed, but Rebecca and Martha, like them, remain firm. He asks after Giles, and she relates how Giles died under torture. His refusal to respond to charges meant that his lands cannot be forfeited by his death and, therefore, his

sons may inherit his farm. Proctor suggests that he may as well confess and live, as he feels too dishonest to hang with such moral individuals as Rebecca and Martha. Elizabeth assures him that she does not see him as dishonest and confesses her own feelings of blame in his adultery because she has been cold. As Hathorne reenters, Proctor declares that he will confess to stay alive; the judges are elated.

They plan to write down his confession and post it on the church door after he has signed it. As they lead Proctor to admit that he has bound himself to the devil, Rebecca is brought in to witness in the hope that she will follow suit. She adamantly refuses and is shocked at Proctor. The judges ask Proctor to damn the others, saying that he saw them with the devil, but he refuses to name anyone but himself. He reluctantly signs his confession but cannot hand it over, refusing to accept that it needs to be displayed, knowing that it will badly reflect on the other condemned. Overwrought, he admits that his confession is a lie. Proctor realizes that he is not so morally bad and rips the confession apart, choosing to die beside the others rather than become a hypocrite. He kisses Elizabeth with passion, telling her to stay strong. Rebecca offers him support as Danforth orders the hanging to proceed, and they are taken outside. Parris and Hale beg Elizabeth to get Proctor to change his mind, but she honors his decision; knowing that it was the right thing to do, she refuses. The curtain falls to the sound of the drums heralding the executions.

Afterword

In an afterword titled "Echoes Down the Corridor," Miller relates subsequent events in which Parris is voted out of office, Abigail becomes a Boston prostitute, and Elizabeth remarries four years later. Twenty years after these proceedings, the government awarded compensation to the victims who were still living and to the families of the dead; although the full truth remains clouded as some beneficiaries turned out to be informers rather than victims.

CRITICAL COMMENTARY

Salem, Massachusetts, in the spring of 1692 is described as a newly founded, religiously devout township. A communal society has formed, backed by an autocratic theocracy to help it attain the discipline necessary for survival; they are naturally suspicious of individuality, seeing it as a threat to their imposed sense of order. Salemites have worked hard to survive, constantly threatened by the surrounding wilderness. Concentrating on survival has left them little opportunity to misbehave, but ironically, although their recent ancestors came to this land to avoid persecution, they have become intolerant and are constantly judging each other's behavior. Their way of life is strict and somber, all dancing and frivolity is frowned upon, and the witch trials offer them a release of pent up frustration and emotion. Under the guise of morality, they are given the opportunity to express envy and hostility toward their neighbors and take vengeance. The large cast helps convey a community in all of its diversity, and this communal reaction to events enhances the play's REALISM.

Miller insists that while McCarthyism may have been the historical occasion of *The Crucible,* it is not its theme. We never go inside the courtroom because Miller is not interested in the proceedings as much as the motivations behind them, and the fears of those involved. One issue that concerns Miller is the tension that people experience between conscience and their predilection toward selfishness as well as the inevitable moral consequences of allowing the latter an upper hand. *The Crucible* exposes the extent to which many people use troubled times, such as the trials, to pursue selfish ends. In contrast to these types, Miller elevates and celebrates people of individual conscience, such as the Nurses, the Coreys, and the Proctors, who refuse to do this.

The Crucible depicts how unscrupulous people, from the Putnams to the trial judges, declare the presence of evil to cripple whomever disagrees with them, not just religiously but politically and socially. Such people assume a moral high ground so that anyone who disagrees is deemed immoral and damned, without recourse to defense. Tituba and the children were trying to commune with dark forces, but if left alone, their exploits would have bothered no one—their actions are an indication of how people react against repression rather than against anything truly bad. But evil is undeniably at large in the world, and Miller believes that all people, even the apparently virtuous, have the potential to be evil given the right circumstances, even though most would deny this. Miller offers Proctor as proof; he is a good man but one who carries with him the guilt of adultery. However, men like Danforth, Hathorne, and Parris complicate this category because they do evil deeds under the pretense of being right.

In *The Crucible,* Miller wanted to go beyond the discovery of guilt that has motivated his plots in earlier plays to a study of the results of such guilt. He centers this study on John Proctor, a man split between the way in which others see him and the way in which he sees himself. His private sense of guilt leads him into an ironically false confession of having committed a crime, although he later recants. What allows him to recant is the release of guilt that was given to him by his wife's confession of her coldness and her refusal to blame him for his adultery. Elizabeth insists that he is a good man, and this finally convinces him that he is.

Miller sees *The Crucible* as a companion piece to *Death of a Salesman* in the way that both explore the realm of conscience. Through Willy Loman and John Proctor, Miller examines the conflict between a person's deeds and that person's conception of himself. While Loman never resolves this conflict and consequently never discovers who he is, Proctor finally comes to some understanding, evidenced in the way that he claims his identity in the form of his "name." In *The Crucible,* Miller explores what happens when people allow others to be the judge of their conscience; in *Death of a Salesman,* the central character does not get this far as Loman refuses to allow his guilt any reality. What both plays do is to explore the social forces that operate on people to show the falsity of our belief in individual human autonomy. Both Proctor's and Loman's actions are largely dictated by forces outside themselves, forces that seem to demand of them reactions and sacrifices that they have little choice but to give. Total freedom, Miller suggests, is largely a myth in any working society.

Some critics like to view *The Crucible* as a debate on the theme of marriage and what a marriage requires to make it work. Issues of trust, love, and what a partner owes the other are all discussed in the play. It is Giles Corey's idle tongue and distrust of his wife that contribute to her being hanged. But it is the marriage of John and Elizabeth Proctor that lies at the play's center and the love triangle that Miller creates between Abigail and the Proctors. When we consider that at the time of writing this play, Miller himself was considering an affair with MARILYN MONROE while still married to MARY SLATTERY, it is not surprising to find such an issue explored. It is also interesting that the play was dedicated to Mary [Slattery] Miller, as if as some kind of apologia.

Proctor and Elizabeth love each other, but seven months before the play began, Proctor had an affair with their serving girl, Abigail, while his wife was sick. We do not know how long this would have continued had not Elizabeth discovered her husband's adultery, but Proctor insists that it was nothing more than animal passion. Abigail is sent away, but the trust between the married couple has shattered, and all ease between them is gone. Insecure of her own attractiveness, Elizabeth looks for signs that her husband continues to stray. Tortured by guilt at what he sees as a moment of weakness, Proctor vacillates between apologetic attempts to make his wife happy and anger at her continued distrust. It is not until both suffer at the hands of the court that they come to an understanding of each other and their mutual love. Each is willing to sacrifice everything for the sake of the other. Proctor tries to free Elizabeth by blackening his own name with a public confession of adultery, while she lies for the first and only time in her life to save him from ignominy. Their final scene together is deeply touching, as we see Elizabeth declare her love and her willingness to sacrifice that love by allowing Proctor to die rather than to relinquish his integrity.

Miller created his own poetic language for this play, based on the archaic language that he had read in Salem documents. Indeed, the first draft of the play was written in verse and then later was broken down into prose. Wanting to make his audience feel that they were witnessing events from an earlier time, yet not wanting to make his dialogue incomprehensible, he devised a form of speech for his characters that blended into everyday speech, using an earlier vocabulary and syntax. Incorporating more familiar archaic words like *yea, nay,* or *goodly,* Miller creates the impression of a past era without overly perplexing his audience.

While Miller's mastery of language seems most evident in the way that he manages to create an apparently period, everyday speech, it rises to the level of poetry with its sophisticated metaphors. The "crucible" of the title is a place where something is subjected to great heat to purify its nature—as are the central characters of Proctor, Elizabeth, and Hale. All endure intense suffering to emerge as better, more self-aware individuals. Complex imagery is built up through the concerns and language of the play—ideas of heat and light against cold and dark are played off against our common concepts of heaven and hell, good and evil. Numerous images of cold and winter, along with the hardness of stone are used to indicate the harshness of the Puritan life, trapped in a cycle of toil, unrelieved by leisure (singing, dancing or any frivolous behavior are not allowed), by both the hard landscape that they strive to tame and their own restrictive religion. Abigail tells Proctor that he is "no wintry man," which is true in that he refuses to abide by many of the strictures of his community and determines to have a mind of his own. It is partly this independent spirit that makes him such an obvious target.

For the people of Salem, Satan is alive nearby in the dark forest. The forest acts as a representation of Hell which is to be avoided at the cost of sin; godly folk stay home at night. The main sin is sex, which has been notoriously equated with the devil by way of original sin, both then and now. The girls dance illicitly in the dark woods around a fire (another Hellish symbol). Mercy is naked, while Abigail drinks blood to cast a spell on Elizabeth to try to break up a marriage. Abigail's devilment is continually reinforced by the symbols that surround all that she says and does: She has been initiated into the joys of sex by her former employer through her "sense for heat" and still feels that Proctor "burning" for her. He is described in his adulterous lust as a "stallion," in other words, less than human.

By fixating so much on sin, the religious extremists, represented by men like Parris and Danforth, become sinful and turned from God. Early in the play, Proctor accuses Parris of preaching too much "hellfire and bloody damnation" and saying too little about God; this becomes a kind of prophesy as Parris and the judges become more devilish in their treatment of others. It is significant that where they send the supposedly "saved" Sarah Good and Tituba who have falsely confessed becomes for the women a hell from which they pray to be saved by the devil—by supposedly saving them from Satanic forces, the judges have delivered them into Satan's hands. However, the fearful possibility of a devil is undercut and mocked by these women as they equate him to a lowing cow. They are evidently far less superstitious than those who are supposedly wise enough to sit in judgment of them.

FIRST PERFORMANCE

The Crucible previewed in Wilmington, Delaware, and then opened at the Martin Beck Theatre in New York City on January 22, 1953, with the following cast:

Reverend Parris: Fred Stewart
Betty Parris: Janet Alexander
Tituba: Jacqueline Andre
Abigail Williams: Madeleine Sherwood
Susanna Walcott: Barbara Stanton
Mrs. Ann Putnam: Jane Hoffman
Thomas Putnam: Raymond Bramley
Mercy Lewis: Dorothy Joliffe
Mary Warren: Jennie Egan
John Proctor: ARTHUR KENNEDY
Rebecca Nurse: Jean Adair
Giles Corey: Joseph Sweeney
Reverend John Hale: E. G. Marshall
Elizabeth Proctor: Beatrice Straight
Francis Nurse: Graham Velsey
Ezekiel Cheever: Don McHenry
Marshal Herrick: George Mitchell
Judge Hathorne: Philip Coolidge
Danforth: Walter Hampden
Sarah Good: Adele Fortin
Hopkins: Donald Marye

Directed by JED HARRIS
Set by BORIS ARONSON
Produced by KERMIT BLOOMGARDEN
It ran for 197 performances.

INITIAL REVIEWS

Despite its later success, the play's initial reception was relatively poor, although this may have been partly a fear of the repercussions of liking a play that was critical of current politics. The drama won Tony and Donaldson Awards for Best Play, but a number of well-known critics were quick to condemn both play and playwright. After *Death of a Salesman*, some felt let down and saw *The Crucible*, in comparison, as less innovative and, therefore, a step backward. Although it had its champions, including John Chapman and Robert Coleman, who found the play "stunning" and "intensely dramatic," Walter Kerr felt that it was too mechanical and overtly polemic. Eric Bentley attacked Miller and the play, claiming that Miller's naive liberalism and depiction of innocence reduced it to melodrama. Even Miller's staunch ally Brooks Atkinson had reservations, feeling that the play was "powerful" but contained "too much excitement and not enough emotion" and so lacked the stature and universality of a masterpiece. John Mason Brown felt that it was weaker than Miller's previous work, although its "one indisputable virtue is that it is about something that matters."

There had been difficulties with this initial production. Unwilling to ask his usual director ELIA KAZAN due to Kazan's testimony to HUAC, Miller had to find someone else to direct. Despite a reputation of being difficult, Jed Harris was chosen. His working relationship with Miller was strained from the start. Harris disliked Miller's choice of Arthur Kennedy to play Proctor and demanded a series of rewrites from Miller in an unsuccessful attempt to undermine the playwright's confidence so as to gain full control of the production. His direction of the play was very static as he had characters make speeches to the audience rather than each other and often kept them frozen in tableaux while speaking their lines. This approach influenced those critics who viewed it as cold, unemotional, and lacking in heart. After the initial reviews, Harris withdrew and left Miller to try and salvage the production. Improvements were made, but not enough to save the run.

SCHOLARSHIP

As critic and scholar, Gerald Weales suggests, "Anyone with a touch of conscience, a hint of political interest, a whisper of moral concern will be drawn to *The Crucible*" (xvii). It has become the most performed of Miller's plays and, after Thornton Wilder's *Our Town*, possibly the most performed of any American drama. There has been a substantial amount of scholarship written on *The Crucible* in a variety of areas, with several essay collections and a few books devoted entirely to the play. James J. Martine's *The Crucible: Politics, Property and Pretense* covers the play's literary and historical context, as well as offering readings of character relationships and the play's central issues—including its structure, setting, props, major themes, and nature as a tragedy. Claudia Johnson's *Understanding The Crucible* reprints selected secondary material to vitalize the play's themes, the substance of a tragic hero, and Miller as a social playwright.

Many of the articles in three collections of essays on *The Crucible*—edited by Harold Bloom, John Ferres, and Gerald Weales—are reprints, but each provides a good selection of scholarship on the play, and Weales also includes some reviews and interesting documents about Salem and its witches. The books by Dukore and Partridge offer more general introductions to the play, aimed directly at students and covering such essentials as characterization, setting, use of language, and general themes.

Articles both within these various collections and beyond include several discussions of the play's historical accuracy (predominantly in terms of the 1692 witch trials rather than the HUAC trials). Margo Burns created a useful website that details the 1692 trials and how far Miller followed these in his plot and characterizations. More judgmental, Mark Graubard and Cushing Stout both analyze the play's historical account and find it to be unrealistic and to some degree, misleading. Meanwhile, Peter A. Foulkes considers the rationale behind Miller's representation of the witch hunts and suggests that the play should be "regarded not as propagandist but as attempted demystification of propaganda."

Other notable areas of concern are the character and nature of John Proctor, the play's symbolism and use of language, feminist explorations of the way women are treated in the play, and its tragic nature. Typical of these are Timothy Miller's discussion of Proctor as a Christian revolutionary in his adversarial stance toward institutionalized religion; John M. Ditsky's analysis of image patterns and Stephen A. Marino's study of the play's intricate use of figurative language; Cristina C. Caruso and Wendy Schissel's descriptions of how the play promotes patriarchal myths; and Nirmal Mukerji's outline of Proctor's stature as a tragic hero. Another interesting take is Robert Lima's consideration of the sexual aspects of the play and how this determines characters' behavior. The collected editions of essays typically cover these main areas, too. Other critics, including David M. Bergeron and Herbert Bergman, offer interesting comparisons of the play to the work of Nathaniel Hawthorne, Terry Otten views it in conjunction with British playwright Robert Bolt's *A Man for All Seasons* (1960) as being works about historical determinism and individual choice, and Jeanne–Marie Miller draws connections to CLIFFORD ODETS as a fellow allegorist of the McCarthy era. Douglas Tallack draws connections between the play's presentation of history and Miller's later autobiography, *Timebends: A Life*.

Regarding the play's reception, Joan DelFattore has written about censorship, summarizing the form and content of attacks on the play along with rationales for countering the complaints. There are also several studies of the 1984 WOOSTER GROUP attempt to adapt sections of the play as an experimental pastiche called *L.S.D. (. . . Just the High Points . . .)*. Miller caused a stir by bringing an injunction against the group to disallow them the use of any scenes from his play in this satirical piece. Arnold Aronson outlines the details and intent behind the Wooster production, and Alexis Greene documents the resulting controversy brought about by Miller's refusal to allow his writing to be so used. Patrick C. Woliver discusses Ward's operatic adaptation of the play, alongside its performance history as an opera, and Klaus–Dieter Gross discusses the difference between play and opera.

CHARACTERS

Corey, Giles and Martha   Still a "powerful" man at 83 years old, Giles Corey, like his father before him, is a contentious figure—forever taking people to court—and an independent spirit. He married Martha late in life and only then began to attend to his prayers, so it is little wonder that he often stumbles over them. Proctor good-naturedly tells us that he paid a fine for slandering Giles, even though he denies having said a word, and they remain friends, helping each other with the harder farm work. Giles may be argumentative, but it is without malice. He has a courage that reminds us of the strength of the pioneer stock from which he sprang and even offers some comic relief in a fairly dour play. At heart, he is a good man, and he dies for his beliefs no less bravely than does John Proctor. His refusal to speak as they weigh him down with rocks until he dies means that they could not confiscate his lands as they could of those they charged or condemned.

His wife, Martha Corey, whom we briefly hear offstage but never see, is similar in nature to Rebecca Nurse, an ideal Puritan. Her interest in books indicates a lively mind rather than allegiance to the devil. She is charged of witchcraft by a fellow townsperson to whom she had sold a pig that later died from neglect. The man had been unable to keep pigs since then most likely for the same reasons but took out his frustration by blaming Martha. Plenty of other townspeople vouched for her, but they too were arrested, and since she refuses to confess to being in league with the devil, she is hanged alongside Proctor.

Danforth, Deputy Governor   Deputy Governor Danforth is a formidable figure. Brought in from Boston to judge the trials, he is as intelligent and strong willed as Proctor and becomes his main antagonist. Unlike Proctor, however, he is unwilling to change. Of all the judges, Miller wants us to find him the most contemptible. He is responsible for putting 400 in jail throughout the area and sentencing 72 to hang. His proud announcement of these facts to Giles suggests that he enjoys power and views himself as superior to those he judges. Although he listens to counterarguments, it is not with an open mind.

Miller has described him as the "rule bearer" of the play, who guards boundaries strictly because he cannot cope with the potential chaos that is caused by free thought. He is loath to relinquish control to anyone and forcefully dominates even his fellow judges. It is unclear as to when he recognizes that the girls have duped him, but there is a strong likelihood that he knows this, yet hangs the condemned anyway rather than seem weak by recanting. He speciously argues that it is for a higher good. He places his own reputation above innocent lives and uses religion to justify the deceit, which makes him a truly evil force.

Girls of Salem   Mercy Lewis, Susanna Walcott, Betty Parris, Ruth Putnam, and Mary Warren are among the young girls who follow Abigail's lead. All have led limited lives up until this point, have been bullied by employers, and have been forced to be quiet and subservient. The only freedom that they have had is sneaking off to the woods for fun and games with the only person in town of a lower social standing than they—the black slave, Tituba. We see in detail with Mary how harshly even good people like the Proctors treat their servant girls, restricting what they can do and whipping them when they fail to follow every command to the letter. Abigail offers the girls a chance to be at the center of attention and treated as special. We see Mary blossom into independence at the understanding that she can no longer be treated with disdain by her employers.

Yet, Mary is also the weakest of the group and is uneasy in conflict. Mercy was worried from the start that Mary would be the one most likely to confess to their exploits in the woods. The fact that Proctor could break her decision not to testify prepares us for her folding in the final act and turning on her employer to save herself. While some, like Mary, seem to be drawn into the court activities by a kind of group hysteria and intend little harm, there are others, such as Abigail and Ruth (who may be working for her father) who are clearly attracted to the power that they see themselves holding over the townspeople as they deceitfully offer the judges any names they like.

Hale, Reverend John Reverend John Hale comes from Beverly, a nearby town, where the previous year he thought he had found a witch who was casting a spell over a young girl, though it turned out to be a simpler case of neglect. Nearing age 40, he is an intellectual and has a reputation for understanding the demonic arts, so Parris has called him to Salem to investigate the rumors of witchcraft. Hale truly believes that witches exist, and it disturbs him when the Proctors express their doubts. Beginning the play a conceited figure, Hale sees himself as a superior intellect, happily determined to uncover the villagers' evil spirits. Events conspire to make him reassess his beliefs and soon his convictions are eroded by doubt.

Hale's questioning comes too late, but it helps expose the closed logical system of the judges when one of their number turns so strongly against them. In contrast to the other judges, by honestly considering the evidence before him, Hale shows himself to be more rational and conscientious. Fairly early into the proceedings, he begins to wonder how trustworthy the girls might be as he privately interviews those they name, such as Rebecca and Elizabeth. He assures the Proctors that Rebecca's goodness is self-evident, just before her arrest is announced. This shows us how little influence Hale has on these proceedings. Recognizing the deception of the girls, he denounces the proceedings and tries to save the victims but becomes too cynical. It was a courageous act to turn against the court, but he loses direction thereafter. Urging people who he knows are innocent to confess to save their lives casts aside any possibility of their having honor or nobility. He becomes a lost figure, not knowing in what to believe and unable to understand the Proctors' noble behavior in provoking the court to hang an innocent man as he urges Elizabeth to change Proctor's mind.

Hathorne, Judge One of the judges brought in from Boston, Judge Hathorne is described as a "bitter, remorseless" man. He is certainly more concerned with his own power than he is with uncovering the truth. His refusal to even listen to others makes him contemptible. He has chosen to believe the girls and will allow nothing to shake that belief, so he sees any evidence brought to challenge this as necessarily false. He defers to Danforth, recognizing his greater power, but is insistent on finding those accused guilty, even if it means harassing inconvenient witnesses like Mary to eradicate their credibility.

Nurse, Francis and Rebecca Town elders Rebecca and Francis Nurse offer a kinder picture of Puritanism than that depicted by the Putnams. Francis Nurse is the opposite of Thomas Putnam, being a man who puts others before himself, living a genuinely moral life. He is genuinely shocked by Danforth's reaction to the document that he has had his friends sign in support of his wife, never wanting to bring trouble on anyone else. He has been the town's unofficial judge up to this point, which is evidence of his probity as it was not a position he sought. However, it has also made him and his family targets by those of a jealous nature. Many of the town's older families, such as the Putnams, resented the prosperity of the Nurses, seeing them as upstarts.

Francis's wife, Rebecca, is the ideal Puritan who lives her faith, always showing kindness and compassion to others and displaying a gentleness in her life that is rightly respected—she can calm down Betty by her mere presence. It is no wonder that so many Salem people risk themselves by vouching for her. But she has a powerful enemy in Ann Putnam, who is jealous that Rebecca had 11 healthy children and so many grandchildren while seven of her babies died. Ann accuses Rebecca of murder, and it is a sign of the times that the court even considers such a charge. Rebecca is rightly horrified that Proctor is endangering his soul by offering false testimony, and she never wavers in her refusal to cooperate with the court. She goes to her death with the same dignity with which she has always lived.

Parris, Reverend In his midforties, Reverend Parris is the current minister of Salem. Parris was previously in business in Barbados, from where he brought his slave, Tituba. He now runs his ministry like a business. He has been in Salem for three years and struggled to gain the respect of his congregation. As the third minister that they have had in seven years, he wants to ensure that he is not so easily dismissed and has been demanding the deed to his house. He translates any dissension from his views into personal persecution. A pompous man, he likes to be in charge but will bow to the authority of such men as Thomas Putnam because of their wealth or to Danforth because of his political position. He has estranged honest men such as John Proctor because of his evident materialism and concentration on negative aspects of their religion. He preaches so much "hellfire and bloody damnation" that people are reluctant to bring their children to church.

There is no one in the play, including his fellow judges, who respects Parris. As a minister of God, he strikes an ungodly figure, being petulant, selfish, conceited, unmerciful, and awkward in his relationships with others, especially children. A widower, he has little interest in children and is clearly at a loss as to how to treat his own daughter. Parris's first thought on his daughter's apparent bewitchment is how it affects him and his standing in the community. It is also clear that he would be prepared to condemn his niece, Abigail, rather than to allow her reputation to sully his by association. He is initially less active than the Putnams in bringing the trials forward and even withholds information about the girls' activities, but this is because of his own insecurities rather than any reticence toward endangering villagers' lives. It is he who brings in the witch-finders, despite his initial insistence that witchcraft cannot be involved, and he becomes a staunch advocate of condemning anyone whom the girls name without allowing any proper defense.

Parris turns against the idea of the witch trials only when his own life is threatened, and he gains no sympathy on discovering that Abigail and Mercy have stolen his money. He helps Hale pray with the condemned in the hope that he and Hale can persuade them to confess so that he will have his probity as a judge secured—Hale, at least, is trying to save lives. According to Miller's afterword,

Parris was soon after voted out of office and left the town, never to be heard from again.

Proctor, Elizabeth A local farmwife, Elizabeth Proctor, like her husband, is a sensible person. That is why she, too, finds it hard to believe in witchcraft. She begins the play angry and suspicious of her husband, having recently discovered his adultery. But her pregnancy is evidence that she and Proctor have continued relations since Abigail left. Bravely, she allows herself to be taken to jail, sure of her innocence. Although her pregnancy saves her from being hanged with the rest, she is no less firm in her refusal to confess. Her nobility is further underlined by her ability to accept her husband's decision to be hanged at the close. Hale and Parris wrongly read this as a sign of indifference, but Elizabeth's love for Proctor is never greater than when she allows him to die.

Elizabeth's love and respect for her husband was first proven when she lied for him about the adultery (her only-ever lie) in an effort to save him embarrassment; it is ironic that it is this lie that condemns him in the eyes of the judges. Her suffering in jail causes her to reflect on her former treatment of Proctor, and in their final meeting, she confesses that she has been cold toward him in the past. She takes on partial responsibility for driving him into the arms of Abigail, and she insists on her husband's essential goodness. It is this belief that strengthens Proctor to choose a dignified death rather than an ignoble betrayal by signing his name to a false document. Because of her pregnancy, Elizabeth is allowed to live until the child is delivered, and by that time, the hysteria had died down sufficiently that she was simply released. According to Miller's afterword, she was given some recompense from the government for her suffering and the loss of her husband, and she later remarried.

Proctor, John Although the original John Proctor was not a major figure in the Salem trials, Miller's Proctor is the central protagonist of *The Crucible*. In his midthirties, Proctor is a straightforward man who is impatient with any foolishness in others. He represents the voice of common sense in the play, being rightly skeptical of the whole court. A freer thinker than many of his neighbors, he insists that the whole idea of witchery is a sham. However, this is a period of time when common sense has vanished, and so his skepticism just makes him appear more suspicious to the biased judges. Proctor's honestly motivated dislike of Reverend Parris as an ungodly materialistic and Proctor's subsequent refusal to attend church or to have his third son baptized also work against him.

Proctor is not without fault. He is a man of deep passion, which makes him often impatient and prone to intense frustration and anger. His relationship with Elizabeth highlights his passion—one moment deeply solicitous, the next furiously angry. At times he seems unable to control his temper: His treatment of both Mary and Abigail becomes physically violent. One wonders how far this anger might be rooted in his awareness that these events in one sense are his entire fault: perhaps if he had left his servant girl alone, she might never have been driven to such revenge. Proctor is also an adulterer, having slept with Abigail Williams in the heat of passion while his wife was ill. Miller describes him as a sinner, not just in the general sense "but against his own vision of decent conduct"—in other words, he has become his own harshest critic. However, he is also fully repentant, and Miller expects us to forgive him his lapse, even if he cannot do so himself. He loves his wife, Elizabeth, is keen to please her, and does all he can to save her after her arrest, even to the point of endangering himself.

Proctor faces the dilemma of the innocent person who must falsely confess to a crime to save his own life. He considers telling this lie because he feels guilty about an adultery for which he has not been punished. Proctor knows that his confession to a lie is wrong, but he plans to go through with it partly to punish himself. Proctor's ultimate refusal to accede to the confession indicates his awareness that he has a responsibility to himself and his community and that he would rather hang than participate in the false judgment of either. Through Proctor and the others who die with him, Miller wishes to show the heroism of these victims to lead us to recognize and celebrate the existence in the world of such personal integrity.

Putnam, Ann and Thomas One of the richest men in the town, Thomas Putnam is a sour man who is filled with grievances against others, grievances that have been created mostly by his own imagination and sense of self-importance. One genuine grievance, however, is against certain Salemites concerning the attempted appointment of his wife's brother-in-law, James Bradley, to the post of minister. Bradley had been well qualified and had a majority of votes, but a small faction within the town, which included the Nurses, managed to block him from acquiring the post, and Putnam felt that his family honor had been belittled. Putnam had also had an earlier minister, George Burroughs, jailed for debts that he had not actually owed, so it is little wonder that Parris is so wary of him.

Greedy and argumentative, Putnam is not above manipulating truth and law to his own vindictive ends, and it is entirely credible that he persuaded his daughter Ruth to cry out against men whose lands he desires. He argues with John Proctor about who owns a tract of timberland, and he had such ongoing arguments with many other of the town's landowners, including the Nurses. A bitter man, he even tried to break his father's will because he disagreed with the amount that had been left to a stepbrother. This was another public failure to embitter him further against the town.

His wife, Ann Putnam, is no less self-absorbed and vindictive and, for a religious woman, ascribes far too much value to silly superstition. It is she who sent her daughter into the woods to persuade Tituba to conjure up a spell to explain why she has lost so many children. Infant mortality back then was high, and her loss of seven babies would not have been so unusual for the period. In their self-opinionated and self-serving rectitude, the Putnam's offer the worst face of Puritanism.

Tituba and Sarah Good Tituba and Sarah Good confess to witchery rather than hang, and they are readily believed because neither has a good reputation in the town. The first group hanged was of a similar low standing, which is why Salem went along with the judges' decisions. Sarah Good is a drunkard and a vagrant, and the town is glad to be clear of her. Tituba, on the other hand, shows more personal concern for Betty Parris than Betty's own father and seems to be a decent woman. But as a black foreigner, Tituba has already been judged by this racist township as having an allegiance to dark forces. She was a natural choice for Abigail to blame and to be instantly believed.

Though an adult, the color of Tituba's skin and subsequent low standing in the town has made her seem less of a threat to the girls. With Tituba, they have been more open than with other adults, but her knowledge of what they have done represents a danger that Abigail knows needs to be quelled. Tituba may have used her cultural knowledge to assist their requests for potions and charms, but she has done so with no sense of allegiance to the devil as the Salemites view him.

The freedom with which both Tituba and Sarah make fun of the devil while in jail strongly suggests that neither one truly believes that such a figure exists. But while Tituba and Sarah survive, there is no triumph in their survival—they lose everything by confessing to something they have not done. The scene in which a tipsy Marshal Herrick enters their jail cell seems a deliberate echo of the drunken-gatekeeper scene in another famous play about witches, *Macbeth*.

Williams, Abigail In the original Salem account, Abigail Williams was much younger, but Miller increased her age to allow for the love triangle between her and the Proctors. Abigail is the most complex of the girls of the town who cry out against their elders. Both clever and cunning, her intense cynicism toward the so-called respectability of the town is partly supported by the way in which we see them act. Her understanding of people's darker sides—she views no one as free of corruption and selfish motivation—allows her to be very manipulative; she can even stand up to a figure like Danforth. Where Danforth is an upholder of the rules, she is the exact opposite: a total anarchist who refuses to be bound by any rules.

Abigail was awakened to her sexuality a few months before the play begins after a brief affair with her former employer, Proctor, and is no longer content to play the role of meek serving girl. An orphan whose parents were brutally slain by Indians, she has been dependent on her churlish uncle, Parris. Abigail sees in Proctor someone who treated her as a woman rather than as a childish nuisance. Her desire for him seems to transcend the physical, and she has magnified the importance that he holds in her life beyond reasonable expectation. The additional scene that Miller wrote featuring Abigail and Proctor shows her to be a borderline psychotic, possibly out of her irrepressible desire for Proctor. She seems to believe truly that she is being attacked by the spirits of those whom she has had convicted. If mad, however, she quickly recovers her sensibility by the final act as she faces up to Danforth and forces the judges to overlook Proctor's charges of her corruption by leading Mary to accuse him in turn of witchcraft.

Abigail cleverly uses the town's superstitious leanings to her own advantage to claim greater respect in the community and to revenge herself upon Elizabeth whom she sees as having "blackened" her name with her dismissal and who she sees has having kept her from Proctor. The way in which she sacrifices former friends like Tituba to the court without a thought suggests amorality in her nature. She will allow Mary to turn on her beloved Proctor in an act of self-preservation, and when the possibility of rebellion arises, she quickly flees, stealing Parris's savings on the way just to prove her truly disreputable nature. In Miller's afterword, he tells us that she later became a prostitute in Boston.

MOVIES AND TELEVISION ADAPTATIONS

Miller enjoyed the 1957 French film version of the play, retitled *Les Sorcières de Salem*, or *The Witches of Salem*, for which playwright and philosopher JEAN-PAUL SARTRE wrote the screenplay, but felt that the Marxist references that Sartre had included were too heavy handed. Most of the critics agreed. The film, directed by Raymond Borderie and starring Yves Montand and Simone Signoret, met mixed reviews, with some, such as Bosley Crowther, announcing it a "persistently absorbing film" with "outstanding performances;" others, such as Stanley Kauffmann, felt that Sartre's emphasis on socialist political agitation distorted Miller's drama.

While Isabel Quigly saw it as both forbidding and insightful, it had also become an "appalling politically pointed tale" that the reviewer from *Time* felt missed the mark by identifying "the witch burners as colonial capitalists and the hero as a son of the suffering masses."

There have also been several television versions of the play, including two in 1959, one by the Canadian Broadcasting Corporation with Leslie Nielsen and Diana Maddox and one by Granada TV in GREAT BRITAIN with Sean Connery and Susannah York. Alex Segal directed a version for CBS in 1967 with George C. Scott, but reviewer Jack Gould felt that it lacked tension and seemed "cold and remote." The version of *The Crucible* with which Miller was most closely involved and for which he rewrote some scenes is the 1996 version for Twentieth Century-Fox. Directed by Nicholas Hytner, it starred Winona Ryder, Joan Allen, and Daniel Day–Lewis (who soon after married Miller's daughter REBECCA MILLER) and was filmed on Hog Island, Massachusetts. Coproduced by David Picker and Miller's son, ROBERT MILLER, this version also had a more favorable reception. Richard A. Blake saw it "as an incisive examination of the human condition," and Edward Guthmann referred to it as "at once stunningly cinematic and perfectly faithful to Miller's text." Jay Carr praised the film, announcing the drama to be "more electrifying than ever, boldly focusing as much on repressed sexuality as on political paranoia and conflagration." There was an increased emphasis on the sexual aspects of the story, and fastidious attention was paid to try to make the setting and costumes authentic.

FURTHER READING

Alter, Iska. "Betrayal and Blessedness: Explorations of Feminine Power in *The Crucible, A View from the Bridge,* and *After the Fall.*" In *Feminist Rereadings of Modern American Drama,* edited by June Schlueter, 116–145. (Rutherford, N.J.: Farleigh Dickinson University Press, 1989).

Ardolino, Frank. "Babylonian Confusion and Biblical Inversion in Miller's *The Crucible.*" *Journal of Evolutionary Psychology* 24, nos. 1–2 (March 2003): 64–72.

Aronson, Arnold. "The Wooster Group's *L.S.D. (. . . Just the High Points . . .).*" *The Drama Review* 29, no. 2 (Summer 1985): 65–77.

Atkinson, Brooks. "At the Theatre." *New York Times,* January 23, 1953. *New York Theatre Critics' Reviews* 14 (1953): 386.

Bentley, Eric. "Miller's Innocence." *New Republic* 128, February 16, 1953, 22–23.

Bergeron, David M. "Arthur Miller's *The Crucible* and Nathaniel Hawthorne: Some Parallels." *English Journal* 58 (January 1969): 47–55.

Blake, Robert A. "Convictions." *America,* February 15, 1997, 24–26.

Bloom, Harold, editor. *The Crucible: Modern Critical Interpretations.* New York: Chelsea House, 1999.

Booth, David. "Dubious American Ideal: Gender and Historical Knowledge in *The Crucible.*" *Soundings: An Interdisciplinary Journal* 84, no. 1–2 (Spring–Summer 2001): 31–49.

Bovard, Karen. "Witch-Hunting, Thwarted Desire, and Girl Power: Arthur Miller's *The Crucible.*" In *Women in Literature: Reading through the Lens of Gender,* edited by Jerilyn Fisher, Ellen S. Silber, and David Sadker, 82–84. (Westport, Conn.: Greenwood, 2003).

Bredella, Lothar. "Understanding a Foreign Culture through Assimilation and Arthur Miller's *The Crucible* and Its Dual Historical Context." In *Text, Culture, Reception: Cross–Cultural Aspects of English Studies,* edited by Rüdiger Ahrens and Heinz Antor, 475–521. (Heidelberg: Winter, 1992).

Brown, John Mason. "Seeing Things: Witch-Hunting." *Saturday Review* 36 (February 14, 1953), 41–42.

Burns, Margo. "Arthur Miller's *The Crucible:* Fact & Fiction." Available online. URL: http://www.ogram.ord/17thc/crucible.shtml. Accessed on May 22, 1998.

Carr, Jay. "*Crucible* Bewitches." *Boston Globe,* December 20, 1996, E1.

Caruso, Cristina C. "'One Finds What One Seeks': Arthur Miller's *The Crucible* as a Regeneration of the American Myth of Violence." *Journal of American Drama and Theatre* 7, no. 3 (Fall 1995): 30–42.

Chapman, John. "Miller's *The Crucible* Terrifying Tragedy about Puritan Bigotry." *New York Daily News,* January 23, 1953. In *New York Theatre Critics' Reviews* 14 (1953): 383.

Coleman, Robert. "*The Crucible* A Stirring, Well-Acted Melodrama." *New York Daily Mirror*, January 23, 1953. In *New York Theatre Critics' Reviews* 14 (1953): 385.

Crowther, Bosley. "Screen: French *Crucible*." *New York Times*, December 9, 1958: 54.

DelFattore, Joan. Fueling the Fire of Hell: A Reply to Censors of *The Crucible*." In *Censored Books: Critical Viewpoints,* edited by Nicholas Karolides, Lee Burress, and John M. Kean, 201–208. (Metuchen, N.J.: Scarecrow, 1993).

Ditsky, John M. "Stone, Fire and Light: Approaches to *The Crucible*." *North Dakota Quarterly* 46 (Spring 1978): 65–72.

Dukore, Bernard F. *Death of a Salesman and The Crucible: Text and Performance.* Atlantic Highlands, N.J.: Humanities, 1989.

Ferres, John H. *Twentieth Century Interpretations of The Crucible.* Englewood Cliffs, N.J.: Prentice–Hall, 1972.

Foulkes, Peter A. "Demystifying the Witch Hunt (Arthur Miller)." *Literature and Propaganda.* London: Methuen, 1983: 83–104.

Gassner, John. *Theatre at the Crossroads.* New York: Holt, Rinehart and Winston, 1960.

Gibbs, Wolcott. "The Devil to Pay." *New Yorker* 28, January 31, 1953: 47–48.

Gottfried, Martin. *Jed Harris: The Curse of Genius.* Boston: Little, Brown, 1984.

Gould, Jack. "Arthur Miller's High Pitched *The Crucible*." *New York Times*, May 5, 1967, 79.

Graubard, Mark. *Witchcraft and Witchhunts Past and Present: The Blame Complex in Action.* Rockville, Md.: Kabel, 1989.

Greene, Alexis. "Elizabeth LeCompte and the Wooster Group." In *Contemporary American Theatre,* edited by Bruce King, 117–134. (New York: St. Martin's, 1991).

Gross, Klaus-Dieter. "*The Crucible* as Drama and as Opera." *Zeitschrift für Anglistik und Amerikanistik: A Quarterly of Language, Literature and Culture* 49, no. 1 (2001): 44–58.

Guthmann, Edward. "A *Crucible* for All Time." *San Francisco Chronicle*, December 20, 1996, C1.

Hendrickson, Gary P. "The Last Analogy: Arthur Miller's Witches and America's Domestic Communists." *Midwest Quarterly* 33, no. 4 (1992): 447–456.

Johnson, Claudia Durst, and Vernon E. Johnson. *Understanding The Crucible.* Westport, Conn.: Greenwood, 1998.

Kauffmann, Stanley. "Torture, New and Old." *New Republic,* December 22, 1958, 21.

Kerr, Walter F. "*The Crucible* Retells Salem's Violent Story." *New York Herald Tribune*, February 1, 1953, sec. 4: p. 1.

Kirchway, Freda. "*The Crucible*." *The Nation* 176, February 7, 1953, 131–132.

Lima, Robert. "Satan in Salem: Sex as *Grimoire* in Arthur Miller's *The Crucible*." *Stages of Evil: Occultism in Western Theater and Drama.* Lexington: University Press of Kentucky, 2005, 147–158.

Marino, Stephen. "Arthur Miller's 'Weight of Truth.'" *Modern Drama* 38, no. 4 (Winter 1995): 488–495.

Marlow, Stuart. "Interrogating *The Crucible*: Revisiting the Biographical, Historical and Political Sources of Arthur Miller's Play." In *Staging a Cultural Paradigm: The Political and the Personal in American Drama,* edited by Barbara Ozieblo and Miriam López-Rodríguez, 79–100. (New York: Lang, 2000).

Martin, Robert A. "Arthur Miller's *The Crucible*: Background and Sources." *Modern Drama* 20 (1977): 279–292.

Martine, James J. *The Crucible: Politics, Property, and Pretense.* New York: Twayne, 1993.

McGill, William J., Jr. "The Crucible of History: Arthur Miller's John Proctor." *New England Quarterly* 54, no. 2 (June 1981): 258–264.

Miller, Arthur. "Again They Drink from the Cup of Suspicion." *New York Times*, November 26, 1989, sec. 2, pp. 5, 36.

———. "Why I Wrote 'The Crucible.'" *New Yorker*, October 21–28, 1996, 158–160.

Miller, Jeanne–Marie A. "Odets, Miller and Communism." *College Language Association Journal* 19 (June 1976): 484–493.

Miller, Timothy. "John Proctor: Christian Revolutionary." In *The Achievement of Arthur Miller: New Essays,* edited by Steven Centola, 87–93. (Dallas, Tex.: Contemporary Research, 1995).

Mukerji, Nirmal. "John Proctor's Tragic Predicament." *Panjab University Research Bulletin: Arts* 4, no. 2 (April 1973): 75–79.

Nanda, Bijaaya Kumar. "Communal Ideology and the Human subject in *The Crucible*." In *Arthur Miller: Twentieth Century Legend*, edited by Syed Mashkoor Ali, 141–154. (Jaipur, India: Surabhi, 2006).

Otten, Terry. "Historical Drama and the Dimensions of Tragedy: *A Man for All Seasons* and *The Crucible*." *American Drama* 6, no. 1 (Fall 1996): 42–60.

Partridge, C. J. *The Crucible* Oxford: Blackwell, 1971.

Pearson, Michelle. "John Proctor and the Crucible of Individuation in Arthur *Miller's The Crucible*." *Studies in American Drama* 6, no. 1 (1991): 15–27.

Plakkoottam, J. L. and Prashant K. Sinha, editors. *Literature and Politics in Twentieth Century America.* Hyderabad, India: American Studies Research Centre, 1993.

Quigly, Isabel. "Sabbath Witches." *Spectator* September 6, 1957, 310.

Rabkin, Gerald. "Is There a Text on this Stage?: Theatre, Authorship, Interpretation." *Performing Arts Journal* (1985), 26–27.

Schissel, Wendy. "Re(dis)covering the Witches in Arthur Miller's *The Crucible*: A Feminist Reading." *Modern Drama* 37, no. 3 (1994): 461–473.

Starkey, Marion L. *The Devil in Massachusetts.* New York: Knopf, 1949.

Strout, Cushing. "Analogical History: *The Crucible*." *The Veracious Imagination.* Middletown, Conn.: Wesleyan University Press, 1981, 139–156.

Valente, Joseph. "Rehearsing the Witch Trials: Gender Injustice in *The Crucible*." *New Formations* 32 (Autumn–Winter 1997): 120–134.

Ward, Robert. *The Crucible: An Opera in 4 Acts, Based on the Play by Arthur Miller,* libretto by Bernard Stambler. New York: Highgate, 1961.

Weales, Gerald, ed. *The Crucible: Text and Criticism.* New York: Penguin, 1996.

Westgate, Chris. "Asking 'Queer Questions,' Revealing Ugly Truths: Giles Corey's Subversive Eccentricity in *The Crucible*." *Journal of American Drama and Theatre* 15, no. 1 (Winter 2003): 44–53.

"Witches of Salem." *Time*, January 5, 1959, 84.

Woliver, C. Patrick. "Robert Ward's *The Crucible*: A Critical Commentary." *Opera Journal* 26, no. 1 (March 1993): 3–31.

The Crucible (1996)

There had been several movie versions of *The Crucible* prior to 1996, briefly described in the previous entry, but this version, directed by Nicholas Hytner in 1995 for Twentieth Century-Fox, is the one with which Miller was most closely involved and for which he added and rewrote several scenes as well as streamlining the play's rhetoric. Shot entirely on Hog Island, Massachusetts, the movie pays exquisite attention to its historical setting and period representation in terms of setting, costumes, and properties. Miller also had his family closely involved, with his son ROBERT MILLER coproducing and his daughter REBECCA MILLER shooting on-set stills. Rebecca would soon after marry the film's star, Daniel Day-Lewis.

A national controversy that was contemporary with the film's production was the sexual scandal of President Clinton. Possibly feeling that the McCarthyism connection would be less obvious to a 1990s audience, this version of *The Crucible* seems more concentrated on issues of sex and religion and that of sexual repression, which unites the two. While critics were generally favorable, Owen Gleiberman particularly praised the opening sequence for setting "a mood of eroticized fear and delirium that reverberates through the movie," and Stanley Kauffmann felt that the play seemed buoyed by its distance from the politics of the 1950s. The sexual tension between Proctor and Abigail is insistent from their first appearance together and in each subsequent encounter. Hale's visit to the Proctors and Danforth's later questioning of Elizabeth are both more pointedly focused on the issue of adultery.

It is clear from the new opening scene, in which a group of Salem girls make love charms with Tituba to catch themselves good husbands, that sex is on everyone's mind, but it is something that can only be discussed in the dark woods. Abigail is teased by her friends for wanting Proctor, but Tituba objects to making a charm to bind a married man. Abigail's wild response is to smear her face with chicken blood and incite the girls into a raucous and sensual dance. It is this that Parris witnesses as he finds his daughter clearly paralyzed by the fear of his discovery. There is no doubt that the problem in Salem is not witchcraft. Religious hypocrisy is foremost, and instead of an anteroom to the court, Danforth's interrogation of Proctor takes place in the town church. It predominantly features a pulpit toward which he has Proctor and Abigail face in a parody of marriage as Elizabeth is called in to testify. It is the same pulpit from which the sanctimonious Parris will later excommunicate 14 godly citizens.

After the new opening, the film proceeds closer to the original play, though it is interspersed with vignettes to help build character and relationships. We hear the villagers spitefully gossiping about events. We see Proctor at work with his sons in the fields as Giles and Martha Corey come to fetch him to town. Before he leaves, he suggests that Elizabeth cut some flowers for the house as it is "winter in here yet." We also see Goody Osbourne being teased and dismissed as she begs. In addition, we witness scenes that the play relates secondhand, such as Martha Corey being charged because of a goat (rather than a pig) that had died, Giles Corey being pressed to death, and several trials, including those of Sarah Good, Goody Osbourne, old Jacobs, and Martha. At Jacobs's trial, both the Nurses and Martha show evident disapproval of the court and sympathy for the defendant, which suggests further reasons why they are allowed to be charged.

The role of Abigail seems to be presented with more sympathy. When Tituba confesses, Abigail is genuinely surprised. The idea that she and the girls are young and impressionable and are just imitating Tituba's frenzied behavior, as they have in the past during their secret dances, seems closer to reality than any malevolent streak. Their reaction is presented as the gabbling of geese rather than as human speech, and it is Tituba's turn to look shocked at what she has apparently unleashed on the town. Abigail is a teenager who is passionately and fatally in love with a married man. When she and Proctor first talk together, their mutual attraction is evident. Proctor is clearly resisting temptation and trying to calm the fire between them. When Abigail kisses and gropes him, he lingers before turning away. Their second meeting alone

together takes place earlier in the time line, before Elizabeth has even been charged, with Proctor asking Abigail not to name his wife. This acts as a goad for Abigail, the thwarted lover, to do just that. Before she leaves town near the close, Abigail visits Proctor in his chains and begs him to go with her, declaring "I never dreamed any of this for you. I wanted you, that is all." He refuses, saying that they can only meet again in Hell, where he sees both heading for their past adultery.

Miller seems to want the audience to view the coupling of Proctor and Abigail more sympathetically by making it more strikingly credible. Proctor's character, too, seems softer. We see him with his sons not only in the fields but reading the Bible, significantly the Book of Daniel. He, too, will soon be thrown to the lions, and it will be his self-conviction that pulls him through, at least with his name intact. He is a man who is caught between two passions, and his dealings with Abigail seem to have been more than casual sex. His portrayal is less aggressive, especially in his dealings with Mary; yet Mary turning on him remains understandable. The film depicts 13 girls advancing threateningly toward Mary, even before she testifies. She is outnumbered and scared. As she tries to tell the truth, the camera circles to show her growing confusion as the adults question her. The group rushing outside to plunge into the water supposedly to escape the demons that are being thrust upon them seems to be an ironic inversion of a baptism, and the symbolism seems inescapable. Mary makes a covenant with the devil by accusing Proctor, who stands alone in a Christlike pose, while Danforth passes judgment from the unchanging rock of his unwavering religious conviction as he raises himself above the citizenry by standing on an actual rock.

One other major change is the addition of Judge Sewell. Sewell offers a voice of reason that warns the others from the start against the possibility of madness in their witnesses and becomes a counterpoint to Danforth's stern insistence. Sewell wonders about the number of children involved, recognizes the land-grabbing truth behind Putnam's accusations, and is uncertain from the very first hanging. However, Danforth has a superior authority and dismisses his concerns, bullying him into compliance. Danforth seems less the rule-bearer than an egoist who thinks he knows best and demands full control. When Abigail, worried that Hale might be about to interfere, accuses Hale's wife, Danforth refuses to listen, insisting that she is mistaken because a reverend's wife is inviolable.

We witness the Salemites initially celebrate as the first group are hanged, but their hysteria dies down as the presence of death begins to pall. We see them start to spurn Abigail, which provokes her departure, and when time comes to hang Proctor alongside Rebecca and Martha, the townspeople are far less enthused. Several call "God bless you" as the condemned pass to the gallows, and they stand silently watching, weeping in disbelief, as the three are hanged. Rebecca begins to recite the Lord's Prayer, and Martha and Proctor join her up to the closing line "for ever and ever," but no one speaks "Amen" as the film cuts to a tight shot on the hanging rope. This ending underlines who the godless truly were during this period in American history, and it is little wonder that no one can sign off on the central prayer of their faith. Significantly, in this trinity of death, Proctor is central, thus reinforcing his connection to a beleaguered Christ.

PRODUCTION DETAILS

The Crucible was released in 1996, with the following lead actors:

John Proctor: Daniel Day-Lewis
Abigail Williams: Winona Ryder
Judge Danforth: Paul Scofield
Elizabeth Proctor: Joan Allen
Reverend Parris: Bruce Davison
Reverend Hale: Rob Campbell

Directed by Nicholas Hytner
Screenplay by Arthur Miller
Produced by Robert Miller and David V. Picker

FURTHER READING

Blake, Robert A. "Convictions." *America,* February 15, 1997, 24–26.
Carr, Jay. "*Crucible* Bewitches." *Boston Globe,* December 20, 1996, E1.

———. "Arthur Miller Revisits Salem Reshaping His Play." *Boston Globe,* December 15, 1996, N1.
Gleiberman, Owen. "Bewitching Hour." *Entertainment Weekly,* November 29, 1996, 68.
Gordinier, Jeff. "Casting a Spell." *Entertainment Weekly,* December 6, 1996, 18–27.
Guthmann, Edward. "A *Crucible* for All Time." *San Francisco Chronicle,* December 20, 1996, C1.
Kauffmann, Stanley. "Latter-Day Look." *New Republic,* December 16, 1996, 30–32.
Max, D. T. "Double Trouble." *Harper's Bazaar,* January 1997: 92–95.
Morgan, Edmund Sears. "Bewitched." *The Genuine Article.* New York: W. W. Norton, 2004, 61–69.
Morgan, Marie. "*The Crucible.*" *New England Quarterly* 70, no. 1 (March 1997): 125–129.
Navasky, Victor. "The Demons of Salem, with Us Still." *New York Times,* September 8, 1996, sec. 2, p. 37.
Rizzo, Sergio. "'Hystorical' Puritanism: Contemporary Cinematic Adaptations of Nathaniel Hawthorne's *The Scarlet Letter* and Arthur Miller's *The Crucible.*" In *Classics in Film and Fiction,* edited by Deborah Cartmell, I. Q. Hunter, Heidi Kaye, and Imelda Whelehan, 93–115. (London: Pluto, 2000).
Seiler, Andy. "Miller Recharges *Crucible.*" *USA Today,* November 27, 1996, D1.
Seymour, Gene. "Of Crucibles, Blacklists, Scoundrels, and Toads." *Newsday,* November 24, 1996, C14.

"*The Crucible* in History" (1999)

Originally presented as a lecture at Harvard University in May 1999, Miller offered this unpublished speech for inclusion in *Echoes Down the Corridor* (2000). In it, he discusses the cultural forces and historical context that affected his creation of *The Crucible.* Although he covers this material in *Timebends, A Life,* here he goes into more detail, offering further examples of the mood of the 1950s against which he had reacted. The parallel that Miller saw between the SALEM WITCH TRIALS and the Red hunts of the 1950s are clearly outlined, by which "suspicion itself" ridiculously became "evidence of disloyalty." Describing a 1950s era that was marked by fear, Miller highlights events that strike him as particularly indicative of this to show how the American far right took advantage of public concern following the 1949 Chinese revolution to try to "destroy the least credibility of any and all ideas associated with socialism and COMMUNISM." Acknowledging that the paranoia of the times was not entirely fantasy, Miller insists that it was nevertheless exaggerated for political capital. He recalls the irony by which *Death of a Salesman* was reviled by the leftist intelligentsia, and yet it led to Miller being suspected of communist sympathies in its creation.

Miller compares living in the late 1940s into the 1950s as akin to being trapped in an Escher design, in which it was impossible to get a fix on anything because viewpoints seemed to blatantly contradict one another. He created *The Crucible* partly to make sense of how U.S. support for its Soviet Union ally from WORLD WAR II became so speedily switched around and how firm patriots were branded traitors. Referencing his own dealings with the HOUSE UN-AMERICAN ACTIVITIES COMMITTEE (HUAC) and the censorship of his plays by the American Legion and the Catholic War Veterans, Miller indicates how personal experience gave him a better understanding for those writers whom he tried to help through PEN. What struck Miller most about the 1950s was the sense of impotence against forces that seemed as omnipotent and unpredictable as they were patently absurd. Talking of his own relationship to Marx and how the 1930s helped form his socialist beliefs (being a majority view back then), Miller explains how he rejected communism just as he rejected Hollywood, as being too restrictive of the artist.

Miller sees *The Crucible*'s initial importance resting on the fact that it was "the first and practically the only artistic evidence Europe had of resistance to what was considered a fascistic McCarthyism," although he also points out its resonance with any of the world's attempts at dictatorship. He wrote the play as a response to the "climate of fear" that had overtaken the United States in the 1950s to try to give what was happening a greater tangibility as "it was precisely the invisibility of ideas that was helping to frighten so many people." Noting how so few of the accused defended their principles, Miller asserts that the left was silenced not only by a restriction of debate but also by its own reluctance to speak. It was this unspoken sense of guilt that gave Miller the idea for John Proctor, whose adulterous secret threatens to undermine his moral compass. Miller relates the evolution of his play from reading Marion Starkey through Salem trial transcripts to stage production. He also refutes those critics who complain that his parallel was unfair because witches were not real and communists were—asserting that people had believed witches to be real in Salem times. For Miller, the better question was how far were communists of the 1950s a real threat? It is evident that he felt this threat to be as nebulous as the accusations leveled against himself and many other artists of that period.

Danger: Memory! (1987)

On February 8, 1987, Miller premiered two new one-act plays at New York's Lincoln Center, under the direction of Gregory Mosher. *Clara* and *I Can't Remember Anything* were given under the collective title of *Danger: Memory!* On one hand, both plays bemoan the dwindling of U.S. radicalism, but Miller has also long been interested in the way the past intrudes upon the present and the way we access that past through memory. In these short plays, Miller illustrates some of the dangers associated with memory. The plays illustrate contrasting views: While *I Can't Remember Anything*, ironically given its title, seems to show the dangers of overindulging in memories of the past, *Clara* suggests that not allowing ourselves to remember can be equally as dangerous. Miller recognizes that memories may relieve, reaffirm, and support us, but only as long as they are kept in their proper perspective; these two plays explore what that proper perspective should be.

The plays met with a predominantly negative reception in the United States where critics mostly agreed that they were poorly written, too overtly moralistic, and their characters were underdeveloped. Under Jack Gold's direction at the Hampstead Theatre in London the following year, critics were more positive. Although some found the plays confusing and insubstantial, the majority of British critics welcomed pieces evidencing a development in Miller's style toward the more abstract and austere.

Death of a Salesman (1949)

After the success of *All My Sons*, Miller felt empowered to create something more risky and began to cast about for something on which to build his next play. After meeting his uncle MANNY NEWMAN at a matinee performance of *All My Sons* and asking how he was doing, Miller got the first glimmer of a new idea. Instead of replying, Manny had gone straight into saying how well his sons were doing, as if he felt that he had to build them up in competition against their successful playwright cousin. The fact that Manny did not even pause before taking their conversation in an unexpected direction gave Miller the idea to write a play without transitions, where the dialogue would flow from one scene to the next without any apparent breaks. Instead of using a chronological order in which single events followed on from one another, he wanted to create a form that displayed the past and the present as if they were both occurring at the same time. In this way, he would be able to transmit to the audience exactly what was going on inside the mind of his protagonist; indeed, an early title for the play was *The Inside of His Head*. It would be retitled: *Death of a Salesman*.

In spring 1948, Miller spent six weeks writing *Death of a Salesman* in a small studio that he had built for himself outside the ROXBURY, CONNECTICUT, house. Miller had been interested in carpentry since he was a teenager when he bought a stack of lumber to build a porch onto the family house with his Uncle Lee Balsam. Miller gave the father of his new play, Willy Loman, the same love of craftsmanship and working with wood. His uncle Manny

became a prototype for Willy. He was someone who also worked with his hands and a salesman with a wild imagination and tendency to brag. Manny would manipulate the truth to his own advantage and saw everything as some kind of competition that he and his family had to win. He was also prone to black moods and bouts of despair and may have committed suicide. Manny's eldest child Buddy, like Willy's son Biff, was athletic and popular, and the younger son Abby, like Willy's younger son Happy, was a ladies' man.

Directed by ELIA KAZAN, who had done such a good job on Miller's previous play, *All My Sons*, and supported by an ingenious set and lighting designed by JO MIELZINER, *Death of a Salesman* premiered on February 10, 1949, at the Morosco Theater in New York City. Enthusiastic reviews swiftly made it the "must-see" play of the season, and Miller garnered nearly every award available. At times comic, yet also poetic and tragic, it also had sufficient REALISM to make it easy to involve any audience; but *Death of a Salesman* was a new type of serious play merging the forms of realism and EXPRESSIONISM to suggest new directions and possibilities for all of U.S. drama. It has become, perhaps, the best-known U.S. play worldwide.

SYNOPSIS

Act One

A faint melody is played on a flute, and the Loman house, surrounded by apartment buildings, is revealed. The action of the play begins as elderly traveling salesman Willy Loman arrives home, late and exhausted. His wife, Linda, is worried to see him as he was away on business and not expected back so soon. She worries that he has smashed the car, but he tells her that he just felt overwhelmed and had to return. When Linda suggests that he ask for a desk job, he insists that he is needed on the road and then asks about his sons. Their oldest, Biff, is visiting after a long absence, and their younger son, Happy, is staying so that they can all be together.

Linda is happy to have their sons home, but relations are strained between Biff and his father. Willy's ambivalence toward his son is evident in the way that he declares that Biff's "trouble is he's

Scene from the 1949 Morosco Theater production of *Death of a Salesman,* with Mildred Dunnock, Lee J. Cobb, Arthur Kennedy, and Cameron Mitchell. Note the original split-level set designed by Jo Mielziner. *Courtesy Billy Rose Theatre Collection, The New York Public Library for the Performing Arts, Astor, Lenox and Tilden Foundations.*

lazy" and then a few seconds later states "There's one thing about Biff—he's not lazy." Biff is 34 and has worked a series of low-paying, temporary jobs. However, his father still wants to believe that he has great promise. In frustration, Willy criticizes Linda and complains about the way that the neighborhood has become so built up while his wife tries to calm him. As Willy grows more irate, his sons wake and overhear him. Willy responds to Linda, reminding her that "You're my foundation and my support" as he settles down and promises to try to not fight with Biff. Linda suggests that they go on a picnic, leading Willy to recall an earlier car that he had owned.

Willy heads to the kitchen to get a snack, still talking to himself, and the scene switches to the boys' room where they discuss their father's con-

dition. Happy is frustrated at his father's inability to function normally. The brothers reminisce about their youth. Biff recalls arranging Happy's first sexual encounter, and Happy credits him with teaching him everything he knows about women. But times have changed, and where Biff used to lead, now he is more reserved. Happy asks why, and Biff blames his father, feeling that he is constantly being mocked. Happy voices concern about how Willy has been acting, talking to himself and losing concentration. Biff explains how he hates the business world and the grind of the lower-level jobs that were all he could command. He has discovered enjoyment in working as a ranch hand but realizes that he cannot advance too far in such a job.

Biff is uncertain what he should do and asks Happy if he is content. Happy responds, "Hell, no!"

He is in a dead-end sales position with little hope of promotion; he lives alone and seems equally discontent. Biff suggests that they buy a ranch together, and Happy finds the idea attractive but realizes that this is no way to get rich, so he backs out, saying that he has to prove a few things first in the city. Happy leads a dissolute life, sleeping with his bosses' girlfriends in a kind of petty revenge because he wishes that he had their positions. He also takes bribes from manufacturers. Although he seems penitent, underneath he is proud of his deceit and is unlikely to change. Biff plans to ask an old employer, Bill Oliver, for a loan to start his own ranch. Happy encourages him, although he thinks that it would be better to start a business in town. As Biff recalls a carton of basketballs which Oliver believed that Biff had stolen from him, doubt is cast on how valued an employee he had been. Biff and Happy are interrupted as Willy grows louder. Biff is angry, but Happy is just embarrassed, hoping that Biff will take responsibility for their father and persuading him to wait until morning rather than make a scene now.

Attention shifts to Willy who is falling into a past memory of when he was advising a teenage Biff to be careful with girls. Willy recalls his sons simonizing the same car that Linda had brought to mind, and they physically appear as youths. Biff has a new football that he has stolen from school, but Willy lets this pass, even praising his son's initiative. Both sons idolize their father and strive to please him. Willy boasts of his exploits on the road and declares that one day, he will have his own business. His neighbor, Charley, already has his own business, but Willy denigrates him as a lesser man because he is not "well-liked." Biff promises to make a touchdown in his next game for his father.

Bernard, Charley's son, comes to warn Biff that he is failing math class and may not graduate. All three Lomans tease him. Biff expects to get to college on a sports scholarship and so pays scant attention to his studies. Willy boasts that his sons will achieve more than Bernard because they are more attractive and better liked. Linda joins them with laundry to hang, and at their father's insistence, the boys scurry to help. Linda asks how much Willy has sold and although he initially lies

about the amount, Linda patiently waits for the truth, which is that he has barely earned enough to pay their bills. He worries that people do not like him, admitting that people seem to respect men like Charley who talks less, but Linda cheers him up, insisting that he will be fine. As she assures him that he is the handsomest man she knows, we hear The Woman laugh. Willy has been meeting someone on the road to cheer himself up. She is a secretary who enjoys his company and puts him through to the buyers. He gives The Woman new stockings, while back at home Linda darns her old stockings for want of new. Willy guiltily demands that she stop.

Bernard and Linda list things that Biff is doing wrong—not studying, stealing, being rough with girls, driving a car without a license, acting stuck up—and Willy becomes angry at them, insisting that it cannot be his fault that Biff is like this. The adult Happy comes to calm his father, and Willy talks about his older brother Ben who became rich at 21 having discovered a diamond mine. Willy is beginning to regret not taking Ben up on a business offer that he once made. He becomes angry at Happy because he sees his life beginning to unravel and that Happy is doing little to help. Charley comes to see what is happening and offers to play cards, while Happy returns to bed. They gently squabble as they play; Charley offers Willy a job, but Willy turns it down. Willy becomes distracted by a memory of Ben visiting him on his way to Alaska. In real time, he had recently heard that his brother had died but left all his money to his seven sons.

As Willy talks to Ben, Charley becomes confused, thinking that Willy is talking to him; the two argue, and Charley leaves. The dream takes over, and we learn of the influence that Ben has had on Willy over the years. Ben had not seen Willy since he was three, but Willy has longed to meet his brother, hoping that he can better discover from him a sense of his own identity. Although Ben abandoned him, Willy admires his brother for being rich. Willy has Ben tell his sons about their grandfather, whom Ben describes as a "wild-hearted man." A younger Charley enters to warn Willy that Biff is stealing lumber and may get caught, but Willy ignores this, teasing Charley about his attire. He asks Ben for advice and gets the mantra, "When I walked into the jungle, I was seventeen. When I walked out I was twenty-one. And, by God, I was rich!" which Willy seems to accept as an answer. As Ben leaves, Willy is drawn back to the present, with Linda asking him if he is alright. He asks her what happened to the diamond watch fob that Ben had given him, and she reminds him that he pawned it years back to pay for one of Biff's correspondence courses. Though in his slippers, Willy decides to go out for a walk.

Biff joins his mother to find out what is wrong with Willy. Linda instinctively tries to calm Biff's fears but then decides to let him know that his estrangement from his father is the root of the problem. She chastises Biff for never writing and for arguing with his father when he sees him. She asks Biff why he is so antagonistic, but he evades answering. Linda is also beginning to give up hope that Biff will ever settle down and tells him to grow up. She sticks by her husband, making it clear to Biff that he is not to come home anymore if he cannot get on with his father. Biff is angry, pointing out that Willy has always treated Linda badly, and Happy has to hold him back from going after Willy. Linda knows that Willy is not perfect, but she loves him and insists that "Attention must be paid" as Willy is going through hard times.

Her husband has not told her, but Linda knows that Willy has been taken off salary, is making no sales to earn commission, and has borrowed money from Charley to hide the fact. Happy has given little money to help, being too wrapped up in his own life to notice. Linda criticizes both sons for their wasteful and selfish lives and for not caring about their father. Linda is especially puzzled over why Biff is so antagonistic since he and his father had been so close, but Biff remains evasive. Reluctantly, he promises to stay around to help, but Linda demands more, telling him that Willy has been trying to kill himself. The insurance company is investigating his car "accidents," and Linda mentions a woman, which makes Biff nervous. However, the woman whom Linda means is one who witnessed Willy crashing on a bridge on purpose. Linda has also found rubber tubing in the basement with which she believes that Willy is planning to gas himself.

Biff agrees to try harder, and then he and Happy argue about how to advance in business. It is clear that neither are hard workers, always trying to bend the rules. Biff suggests that they would all have been better off as carpenters, but Willy, returning from his walk, disagrees, and he and Biff begin to argue. Considering what he has just learned, Biff backs down and tries to cheer his father. He tells him his plan to see Oliver to obtain a loan to start his own business. As Biff falters, Happy encourages this idea by suggesting that he and Biff are planning a sporting-goods partnership; their father is enthused by this dream. For a moment, the whole family is excited. Then Willy and Biff fall back into arguing after Biff defends his mother when Willy treats her dismissively. Linda tells Biff to make up, which he does to keep the peace, and cheers Willy back up. Happy declares his intention to get married, but no one takes any notice. Willy goes to bed recalling Biff's greatest moment—when he won the high school football championship—while Biff goes to remove the rubber tubing.

Act Two

Bright music suggests a lightened mood from the night before. It is morning, and Biff and Happy have already left, but Linda and Willy breakfast together and speak hopefully of the future. Willy imagines his sons prosperous and married, while he and Linda live out in the country where the sons can come and visit. Linda reminds him that they need extra money for the insurance, which is in the grace period, and money for various essential repair jobs. Willy complains about his "race with the junkyard" to pay off his big-ticket items before they break down, but they do almost own their house. Willy is even hopeful that he could grow something in their small garden. Linda tells Willy that his sons plan to meet him later in the day for a celebratory dinner. After he leaves, Biff telephones while he is waiting for Oliver. Linda tells him to wait patiently, reminding him to be good to his father.

Willy has finally accepted Linda's suggestion that he demand a desk job at the company and is full of hope for the prospect. It is clear on his arrival that his boss, Howard Wagner, has little time for him. Fascinated by his latest acquisition, a wire recorder, Howard hardly listens to what Willy says, making him listen to his family on the recorder. Willy finally makes his request, and Howard unsympathetically refuses, saying that he has no place for him in the office. Willy tells him about Dave Singleman, an old-time salesman who inspired Willy as a younger man to go into sales. Singleman had lived and died traveling on the railroad, and his funeral drew a crowd of friends from around the country. Willy bemoans the old days when this type of salesman was more popular and reminds Howard of all the years that he has put into the company. Howard is not interested, and as soon as he can, he fires Willy, which he has been hoping to do for some time. He suggests that Willy look to his sons for help when Willy insists he needs income, but Willy is appalled at the thought of being so dependent. The shock sends Willy to seek advice from his brother Ben.

On his way back from Alaska, Ben had stopped by again to see if Willy is interested in managing some timberland that he has bought, and Willy recalls this visit. Not liking Ben, Linda encourages Willy to turn it down, saying that he has good prospects where he is, and Ben leaves. Willy then recalls the glory of Biff's championship game, with Bernard trotting after Biff, eagerly holding his shoulder guards, and the chance of his son getting a college scholarship. Charley teasingly deflates what Willy sees as the importance of the game, putting it into a more reasonable perspective, but this is Willy's biggest moment of glory, and he is angry at Charley.

Meanwhile, Willy has arrived at Charley's office, and hearing him seemingly talking to himself, Charley's secretary Jenny asks Bernard, who is waiting to see his father, to deal with him. As an adult, Bernard is now a successful lawyer with a wife and two sons of his own, although he modestly plays this down to Willy. Willy lies about Biff's great prospects but cannot resist asking Bernard how he managed to do so well while Biff turned out so poorly. Bernard asks him why Biff ruined his chances by refusing to retake the Math class. Willy pretends to have no idea, but as Bernard keeps asking, Willy becomes argumentative until Charley interrupts. Charley sends his son off; proudly letting Willy know that Bernard is about to argue a case in front of the

Supreme Court. Bernard, good-naturedly, tries to give Willy the best advice he can, but not knowing the truth, he can only offer platitudes.

Charley gives Willy his usual $50, but Willy needs more. Charley again tries to get his friend to accept a job, but Willy responds angrily; his pride will not allow him to work for a man whom he has derided for all these years. He tells Charley that he has been fired, and Charley gives him the money he needs, pointing out that being well liked is not a good business philosophy because it is money that really talks. Charley is concerned about Willy's state of mind and worries that he may be considering suicide. He warns Willy against it. Willy admits that Charley is his only friend as he leaves to meet his sons for dinner.

Happy is already at the restaurant, acting big for Stanley, the waiter, and attracting a girl, Miss Forsythe. He pretends to be a champagne salesman to pick her up, and when Biff arrives, he tells her that Biff is a professional football player, sending her to find a friend to make a foursome. Biff has come down to earth, realizing that the dream that the family had constructed of his borrowing money from Bill Oliver and becoming a successful businessman was entirely unrealistic. He waited all day to see him, and Oliver did not even remember who he was. In revenge, Biff slipped into his office and stole his fountain pen before running out. He is a little drunk and plans to force his father to face the truth, although Happy insists that it is better that he maintain the lie.

When Willy arrives, Biff begins to tell him what happened, but his father cuts him off realizing that it is not good news. Announcing he just got fired, Willy tries to strong-arm his stunned son into creating a happier version of the meeting. As his father's refusal to hear the truth frustrates Biff, Willy hears voices from the time when he and Biff originally fell apart. As Biff tries to tell his father that Oliver would not see him, Willy bemoans Biff failing his math, and we see Bernard telling Linda that Biff has gone to Boston to see his father. Caught in his memory, Willy misses everything that Biff is currently telling him. He focuses for a moment on the fact that his son stole a pen but slips back into the memory. His behavior worries Biff so much that he begins to fall back on the lie to calm his father down, telling him that Oliver will loan the money. It begins to work, but Biff cannot maintain the pretense. Willy thinks that he is doing this out of spite, and Happy calms them both down as Miss Forsythe returns with her friend, Letta. Biff tries to get Willy to sit for a drink but hearing The Woman's voice in his head, Willy goes to the washroom.

Biff vainly appeals to Happy for help, but Happy does not want to accept any responsibility. Distraught and feeling inadequate to help his father, Biff runs out. Happy follows with the two women, callously leaving his father alone in the washroom and announcing, "That's not my father. He's just a guy." Meanwhile, in the bathroom, Willy relives the whole experience of Biff arriving at his hotel room in Boston. Willy had tried to hide his lady friend, Miss Francis, in the bathroom, but she refused to wait, coming out just as Willy is promising to fix Biff's math problem. Young Biff loses all faith in his father when he realizes that he is an adulterer. Calling him a liar and a fake, he dashes away. Stanley discovers Willy shouting to himself and explains that Biff and Happy already left. Disappointed, Willy decides to buy some seeds on his way home.

The boys arrive home late to find their mother fuming at the way that they treated their father and determined to throw them both out for good. Happy tries to pretend that they never left their father but Linda calls them both animals, accusing Happy of whoring and throwing the flowers that he had brought her to the ground. Biff wants to confront his father, but Linda insists that he leaves Willy alone. She orders Happy to pick up the flowers, and he refuses, heading upstairs while Biff picks them up. Biff accepts her criticisms but despite his mother's pleas, heads outside to see his father. Willy is planting seeds and talking to Ben about his plan to kill himself to get Linda money and to show Biff, by his massive funeral, how truly popular he was. Ben offers doubts—pointing out the insurance company may not pay out and that Biff may hate Willy or see him as a coward for doing this—then he fades away.

Biff joins Willy to tell him that he has decided to leave for good and brings him inside. Willy finds this news hard to process but decides that Biff is doing this out of spite. Willy refuses responsibility for Biff's failure, and Biff's insistence that he does not blame his father makes Willy feel more guilty and belligerent. All the shouting brings Happy down. As Willy curses him, Biff tries one final time to get his father to face the truth, confronting him with the rubber tube and declaring that the whole family are fakes. Although Linda and Happy try to stop him, Biff insists on speaking the truth as he sees it: Happy has a lowly job without prospects and is wasting his life, Biff himself is a thief and a bum who has never held down any kind of job, and his father is a "dime a dozen" like the rest of them. Willy refuses to accept any of this, continuing to accuse Biff of spite, but when Biff breaks down into tears, he understands that his son still loves him.

Exhausted, Biff heads upstairs as Ben suggests that he will be "outstanding, with twenty thousand behind him." With Ben's encouragement, Willy decides to go through with his suicide plans so that Biff will have enough money to make a success of his life. He sends Happy and a worried Linda to bed, saying that he needs to sit. Ben offers final words of advice, then vanishes, and Willy nearly panics but steels himself to do this for his son. He drives off to crash his car one last time. Linda and Biff both call out for him to stop, but it is too late. The family, along with Charley and Bernard, walk to stare at Willy's grave.

Requiem

At the close of the play, there is a short scene following the group standing at the graveside as they discuss what Willy's death means. Linda seems stunned; she cannot understand why no one else showed up for the funeral or why Willy killed himself. Biff views his father as a man who held the wrong dreams, but both Happy and Charley disagree. Charley points out that dreams are all some men have and insists that Willy was a great man. Happy seems determined to follow in his father's footsteps, forever the dreamer, but Biff refuses to be dragged back in. Linda asks them all to go and, alone for a moment, lets out her true grief. She feels utterly lost without her husband; they have paid off the house, but she has no one left to live in it. As she begins to weep, Biff leads her away, and the flute sound is heard once more as the surrounding apartment buildings are emphasized.

CRITICAL COMMENTARY

Miller's lengthy setting and character descriptions contribute much to an understanding of the play. Willy is presented as living in a claustrophobic urban setting that is indicative of the harsh life that he has chosen. His home is surrounded by apartment houses that emanate a threatening orange glow. When memory takes over, this glow gives way to a more dreamlike background with shadowy leaves and music, evoking a happier, pastoral era. At the close of the play, however, we see the looming "hard towers" of the apartment building dominating the setting once more. When Willy initially goes from the real world into his first reverie, the apartment houses in the background are faded out, and the lighting suggests that the stage is covered with leaves, as the opening pastoral music reasserts itself. With this change in atmosphere, Willy's dream world of the past is recreated for the audience as it occurs in Willy's memory.

The opening setting provides the background for Willy Loman's life and some of the rationale behind his death. The faint pastoral melody played on a flute recalls both Willy's father who played such an instrument and the pastoral dream that may have suited Willy's nature better than the harsh world of business that he chose. Miller's emphasis on the refrigerator in the kitchen and a silver athletic trophy above Willy's bed represent the only achievements in Willy's life—a few basic luxuries for the house and a fleeting, winning moment from his family's past. The refrigerator, we later learn, is on the verge of breaking down, and the trophy was won by Willy's oldest son, Biff, just before he dropped out of high school and became a virtual vagrant. Willy's activities, aside from his job as a salesman, are part of a symbolic network. He plants seeds just as he plants false hopes. Both will die and never come to fruition because the house has become enclosed by the city and because his dreams are unrealistic in the harsh, competitive society that these apartments represent. The front porch, constructed out of stolen lumber, is indica-

tive of how their lives, as well as their house, have been built on something false. Willy does not fit into the modern world of machinery; likewise, the values that he espouses, where deals are made with a smile and a handshake, are those of a bygone age. To illustrate this point, Miller frequently depicts Willy's uneasy relationship with machinery such as his car, his refrigerator, and Howard's recording machine.

Writing in a style that scholar Brenda Murphy has coined subjective realism, *Death of a Salesman* carefully blends a realistic picture of a salesman's home and life in the post-Depression years with the subjective thoughts that are going through its central protagonist's head. The play's clever use of time that allows the audience to view both past and present occurring at the same moment on the same stage set fully captured the concept of simultaneity for which Miller had been striving. The Lomans act and sound like natural, everyday people who face everyday social and domestic concerns. However, Willy's waking–dream sequences that recall past moments in time, the increasingly evident symbolism of various stage effects (lighting and sound), and the play's subtle protest against accepted social expectations also satisfy the requirements of an expressionistic work.

Although Willy Loman's situation is often described as timeless, *Death of a Salesman* can be read as an illustration of the historical economic interests and forces operating on U.S. society from the turn of the century to when the play was written. This was a period of major changes in the economic structure of the United States. Willy witnessed the pioneers' sense of hope and possibility at the beginning of the new millennium, a time when his father and brother both left home to embrace such possibilities to the full. While his father vanished from sight, his brother came out ahead. Willy lived through the wild prosperity of the 1920s and was inspired by meeting successful salesman Dave Singleman to go into sales. This was a period when he felt he could become successful in the big city, until the 1929 WALL STREET CRASH marked the start of the GREAT DEPRESSION. The Depression lasted throughout the 1930s, and Willy evidently found his products increasingly hard to sell in a period when nobody had money to buy anything but necessities.

With the economy being jump-started for the 1940s by the increased market demands and industrial advances of WORLD WAR II, Willy saw a renewed sense of vigor in the U.S. economy that probably created much of the hope that he places in the prospects of his sons. However, it is becoming a young man's world, and Willy, in his sixties, is swiftly becoming outmoded, his sales style also being out of date. It is hardly surprising that he ends up being fired as he illustrates to his own boss his incapacity to make a sale when he fails to persuade him to give him a desk job. The play was written and is set in 1948 at the time when forces of CAPITALISM and materialism came to the fore and technology made its greatest inroad into the lives of everyday people. *Death of a Salesman* depicts the impact of these forces on the lives of an ordinary family—the Lomans. It is little wonder that so many of those watching the original production felt that they were witnessing their own story or that of a family member.

The Lomans are depicted as social failures in their inability to make money and live happily and comfortably, but the deeper question asked by the play is whether this failure is because of their own inadequacies or caused by society's unrealistic standards of success? In Miller's opinion, the blame of failure should not be attached to insignificant cogs in the social machine like the Lomans but should be partially attributed to the larger social forces that operate on people's lives. Economics play an important part in the creation of such forces. By the time the play was written, Miller saw business matters at odds with conventional morality, with humanity threatened by the onset of technology and the growing pressures of ownership; all these issues are reflected in the dilemmas of the Loman family and the other characters to whom they are economically linked.

Miller's strong sense of moral and social commitment runs throughout the play. The aim of *Death of a Salesman* is twofold: First, Miller wanted to write a social drama that confronted the problems of an ordinary man in a conscienceless, capitalistic social system; second, he wanted that same play to be a modern tragedy that adapted older tragic theories to allow for a common man as tragic protagonist. Willy's apparent ordinariness should not blind us to his tragic stature; Miller insists that a common family man's situation can be as tragic as the dilemmas of royalty because he ties his definition of heroism to a notion of personal dignity that transcends social stature. Willy is heroic because he strives to be free and to make his mark in society, despite the odds against him. Though he is destroyed in the process, he is motivated by love, and his destruction allows for learning to take place. Through Willy's sacrifice, Biff is able to accept his father's love while recognizing the emptiness of the dream that Willy espoused. Willy had accepted at face value overpublicized ideas of material success and therein lays his tragedy, for he will kill himself in his pursuit of such a dream. His downfall and final defeat illustrate not only the failure of a man but also the failure of a way of life.

A central thematic issue in this play is Miller's consideration of the problematic and elusive American dream of success and how success is interpreted by society. Miller sees many people's lives being poisoned by their desire to be successful. People like the Lomans are doomed to try for success but fail, with all the resulting guilt that such failure brings. Others like Ben and Howard display an ability to make money that deems them successful but at the cost of their own moral integrity. Charley and Bernard, on the other hand, are successful, but they do not allow their desire for wealth to run their lives. This enables them to maintain their moral integrity and offer us a potential solution to this social problem that, Miller believes, lies at the heart of the U.S. democracy.

The Loman family survives intact for many years largely through their capacity to dream. Such dreams are highly ambivalent, especially when they turn out to be so patently false; they may provide a momentary respite from a harsh reality, but are they not more destructive in the long run? When Biff is led to dream that he and Happy can start a business on a loan from Bill Oliver, we see the family revitalized and Willy gain the strength to go and ask for a better job. But to feed the dream, Biff has to reinvent not only his own abilities but also his relationship with Bill Oliver. Such dreams can never be fulfilled as long as they are based on lies. While the dream is maintained, it may grant strength, but as soon as reality intrudes, the dream is shattered and lays the dreamer open to harsh disillusionment.

But the question remains in the play: Is it possible to live in dreams? Charley tells us, "A salesman is got to dream" and seems to suggest that Willy had no other option, which also leads us to wonder from where do Willy's dreams originate. It is evident that Willy's family experience has been influential in his development. Both his father and his older brother Ben are portrayed as archetypal pioneers—men who have successfully tamed the West—whom Willy is tempted to emulate, despite their evident self-absorption and lack of compassion. However, their sense of freedom and adventure clashes with Willy's more humane sense of responsibility and his caution; Willy is not only the product of his family upbringing, but he is also a product of a far wider array of cultural myths and values. It is little wonder that Willy is unable to find happiness—for he is being influenced continuously by conflicting ideologies that can never allow him to feel any satisfaction.

The play explores the changing role of capitalism in society and its impact on people's lives. Willy is living in a time when the nature of business itself is undergoing intrinsic changes, partly due to the capitalist pressure to make more money and to become more efficient. *Death of a Salesman* depicts a definite clash between capitalistic business and morality. It is clear that Miller would prefer us to follow the example of Charley rather than Howard or Ben. Ben abandons his family, Howard ruthlessly fires an old man, and Happy admits to taking bribes; none of them feels any remorse, and a capitalist system encourages such behavior. The best way to survive in such a system is to become a better and more ruthless capitalist than your fellow worker. However, a character such as Charley seems to have found a way to survive in business with his morality intact; he is able to do this largely by limiting his expectations and refusing to ignore the plight of others.

The desire to be successful and the fact that a capitalistic society encourages such a desire leads to another major theme in the play: Miller's consideration of the force of materialism in people's lives. In the search for the "good life," people like the Lomans surround themselves with many things above and beyond the necessities of life. However, these goods are only available at a price, and not everyone in society can afford all that the advertisers convince that them they must have to be considered happy. The Lomans try to keep up with a refrigerator, a vacuum, and a new car, but they find themselves in a constant state of worry that they may not be able to meet all their payments. However, they do not dare be satisfied with less, for that would make them feel like failures. They become caught in a world where they must work to live and rarely have the time to sit back and enjoy life itself.

The issue of family and the relationship that exists between members of a family are also of great interest to Miller. In the 1940s, the father was still viewed as the provider of life, both biologically and economically. Fathers were also responsible for teaching their children proper morals and values through instruction and by setting themselves up as good examples. Children should be able to view their father with the proper mix of awe, devotion, and love. A major problem occurs with fathers like Willy Loman because they prove themselves to be so fallible. They fail to exhibit the right morals and values in their own lives, thus making it hard for children to respect and follow their lead. The kinds of relationships that Willy and Charley have with their sons are very different. They teach their offspring different sets of values, and we can see by their sons' resulting success or failure as to who was in the right. While Willy teaches Biff and Happy that all they need to be successful is to be well liked, Charley makes sure that Bernard understands that he has a better chance to get ahead through thoughtfulness for others and hard work.

Central to the play is the relationship between Biff and his father. As a young man, Biff idolized his father so much that on learning that Willy was not infallible, Biff's whole world was turned upside down. His struggle to be free of his father's expectations indirectly leads to the only way this could be possible, by his father's death. Unwittingly, Biff gives his father the one spur he needs to kill himself—not that his son spites him but that he loves him. Returning this love, Willy kills himself because this is the only way he can give his son the money that he sees him needing to be successful; this is the biggest gift that he knows to give him, however wrongheaded it might be. It is unimportant whether the insurance money is paid out or not because Biff does not even want it. What both he and his father really want is a return to a simpler time when they could just love each other without all of the external pressure to be successful.

It is easy to be disturbed by the apparently passive female stereotypes that we find in *Death of a Salesman*—the good housewife, the call girl, the mousy secretary—but Miller wanted his play to be realistic, and in U.S. society of the late 1940s, this is how many women were viewed. *Death of a Salesman* is a profoundly masculine play, told from a man's point of view (Willy Loman's). The men take center stage in what is a male dominated world where men do business, play sports, go adventuring, and try carpentry. Although more than a third of its cast is women, the play centers on issues of male bonding and the relationships between fathers and sons. Women have been marginalized and appear as loyal wives, like Linda, or easy women, like The Woman, Miss Forsythe, and Letta; or they have been silenced and hardly are featured at all, such as Willy's mother, Ben's wife, or Charley's wife (the first two are given a brief mention; the latter no comment at all).

Although Willy calls Linda his "foundation and support," as indeed she is, he shows little respect or regard for her in the way that we see him treat her. He cheats on her and rudely tells her to shut up. What seems worse is that Linda accepts such treatment. She subordinates her life to Willy, shares his dreams, and appears to have none of her own. But Linda is not stupid or weak; she displays great perception and can be tough when necessary. She is the main reason why this family has managed to stay together, hence her depiction as a mender who tries to mend everything from stockings to people. She also knows what these repairs cost, and this knowledge gives her the strength to break the family apart, sending her sons away if they threaten her husband. In this light, Linda can be seen as working against the stereotype of the weak, maternal figure.

She loves her husband and is prepared to sacrifice anything to make him happy. This is the way in which she has chosen to define her life, and it is not so unusual for the 1940s when women had less independent options. As a result, it is little wonder that she seems so lost at the close without him.

FIRST PERFORMANCE

Death of a Salesman had tryouts in Philadelphia, and opened at the Morosco Theater Theatre in New York City on February 10, 1949, with the following cast:

Willy Loman: LEE J. COBB
Linda Loman: MILDRED DUNNOCK
Biff Loman: ARTHUR KENNEDY
Happy Loman: Cameron Mitchell
Bernard: Don Keefer
The Woman: Winnifred Cushing
Charley: Howard Smith
Uncle Ben: Thomas Chalmers
Howard Wagner: Alan Hewitt
Jenny: Ann Driscoll
Stanley: Tom Pedi
Miss Forsythe: Constance Ford
Letta: Hope Cameron

Directed by Elia Kazan
Set and lighting designed by Jo Mielziner
Music by Alex North
Produced by KERMIT BLOOMGARDEN and Walter Fried
It ran for 742 performances.

INITIAL REVIEWS

Response to *Death of a Salesman* was tremendous, both in its Philadelphia tryouts and its Broadway opening; audience and critics had been riveted. Miller won a string of major awards, including the Pulitzer Prize, the New York Drama Critics Circle Award, the Theater Club Award, and Tony Award. The play was soon performed throughout that United States and Europe. The published script became a best seller and was the only play ever to be a Book-of-the Month Club selection.

Kazan, who had successfully produced Miller's earlier play *All My Sons*, persuaded Miller to accept Lee J. Cobb as Willy Loman, even though he had written the part for a small man. Cobb made the part his own, although Dustin Hoffman also made a mark on the role playing it more closely to Miller's original vision in 1984. Jo Mielziner designed a set and lighting that helped convey Loman's mental state, and Alex North provided music that would add another layer of symbolism. Robert Coleman called the play "emotional dynamite" and reported that "sobs were heard throughout the auditorium, and handkerchiefs were kept busy wiping away tears." BROOKS ATKINSON declared it "superb," "deeply moving," and a "wraith-like tragedy," insisting that Miller had "looked with compassion into the hearts of some ordinary Americans and quietly

Barbara Clothe and Richard Ward in a scene from the 1972 Centerstage production in Baltimore of *Death of a Salesman,* directed by Lee D. Sankowich. The play has been produced several times with an all-black cast, as here. George C. Scott's 1975 production featured black actors only in the roles of Charley and Bernard. *Courtesy Billy Rose Theatre Collection, The New York Public Library for the Performing Arts, Astor, Lenox and Tilden Foundations.*

transferred their hopes and anguish to the theatre." Richard Watts asserted, "Under Elia Kazan's vigorous and perceptive direction, *Death of a Salesman* emerges as easily the best and most important new American play of the year."

The play's portrait of Willy Loman managed to strike an emotional chord that continues to reverberate. A man of his time and yet also, somehow, timeless, Loman has attracted international audiences and continues to interest them even to the present day. Theater scholar Brenda Murphy talks about "the ease with which audiences all over the world have understood and sympathized with the plight of Willy Loman, and have grasped the issues of the play." The 1983 production of *Death of a Salesman* that Miller himself directed in the People's Republic of China at the BEIJING PEOPLE'S ART THEATER, was a landmark in foreign diplomacy. Aside from the Chinese production and countless U.S. and European productions, the play has been successfully produced in countries as diverse as South Africa, Korea, Japan, Mexico, the Soviet Union, and Australia. There have also been at least seven film and television versions.

SCHOLARSHIP

Out of all of Miller's plays, *Death of a Salesman* has elicited the most scholarship. Among the most prominent have been collections of essays and whole books devoted to this single play. In *The Burning Jungle*, Karl Harshberger reassessed the roles of the play's leading characters, while Brenda Murphy's *Miller: Death of a Salesman* gives a well-researched and insightful overview of major stage and film productions of the play. Jo Mielziner's memoirs also offer substantial detail on how he came to design the play's set and lighting.

As teaching aids, Matthew Roudané's *Approaches to Teaching Miller's Death of a Salesman* and Brenda Murphy and Susan C. W. Abbotson's *Understanding Death of a Salesman* offer useful guidelines to approaching the play in the classroom. The former includes essays to initiate discussions on the play's place in U.S. theater, performance aspects, critical concerns, and Miller's use of U.S. myths, while the latter reprints selected secondary material to vitalize the play's themes, which include background myths, economics, business, family, sports, and U.S. life.

Death of a Salesman: Text and Criticism, edited by Gerald Weales, contains the play's full text and also five of Miller's theater essays, 21 reviews and essays, and other useful material. Bernard Dukore has edited a similar volume. Walter Meserve's *The Merrill Studies in Death of a Salesman* includes foreign reviews, essays on the usual themes; books edited by Helen Wickham Koon, Harold Bloom, Thomas Siebold, and John Hurrell all reprint a selection of essays from leading scholars on a variety of topics. Even the more general essay collections edited by Robert W. Corrigan and James J. Martine are dominated by discussions of *Death of a Salesman*. The Arthur Miller Society's 1999 conference was dedicated to the play's 50th anniversary, and Stephen Marino edited *"The Salesman Has a Birthday,"* a volume of the best papers presented.

Numerous essays appear in other collections and journals. Comparisons have been made between *Death of a Salesman* and the work of EUGENE O'NEILL (particularly *The Iceman Cometh*), TENNESSEE WILLIAMS, HENRIK IBSEN's *The Wild Duck*, DAVID MAMET's *Glengarry Glen Ross*, and even Cherríe Moraga's *Shadow of a Man*. Amrendra Narayan Singh considers the play beside *After the Fall*, and there have been at least two studies comparing the play to August Wilson's *Fences*. Willy has been compared to King Lear, and his inner psyche has been thoroughly explored. Ben, Bernard, Biff, and even Dave Singleman have received individual studies, and there are several discussions of the play's women, including those by Gayle Austin and Charlotte Canning. Common topics include debates of whether or not the play is a tragedy, the innovation and impact of its dramatic form, and various aspects of U.S. business culture. More unusual are those discussions of the play's Jewish aspects by Joel Shatzky or Dan Vogel and John S. Shockley's intriguing comparison of Willy to Ronald Reagan.

Scholars, including CHRISTOPHER BIGSBY and Terry Otten, have convincingly argued that the Willy/Biff relationship is central to the play—this father–son relationship is most popular topic of study. Bigsby's 2005 study of Miller points out that the play is "not an attack on American values" but is "an exploration of the betrayal of those values and the cost of this in human terms." While such critics as ERIC BENTLEY were early to find fault with Miller's poetic style, Lloyd Gareth Evans took a closer and more positive look at Miller's use of language in 1977, and in recent years, we find Matthew Roudané declaring Miller to be "one of the most gifted and radical sculptors of language in American drama." Stephen Marino undertakes a close textual analysis of Miller's figurative language and reveals "Metaphors of sports and trees—expressed by images and symbols of boxing, burning, diamonds, nature, fighting, air, and smells" throughout the play. The Indian commentator Jayasree considers how Miller expands the notion of realism in the play, and short pieces, including those by Terry Thompson and Frank Ardolino, explore specific references in the play to such things as Hercules, Adonis, facial hair, sports, names, and numbers.

CHARACTERS

Bernard   Not a central character, the Lomans' neighbor Bernard is offered as a foil to the Loman boys. He also shows, alongside his father Charley, that it is possible to be successful without being unpleasant as is Ben or Howard. As a child, Bernard seems to idolize the tougher, sporty Loman brothers, especially Biff, but unlike Biff and Happy, he has a strong work ethic, does not expect to get through on charm, studies hard at school, and is consequently a highly successful lawyer. By the play's close, he is on his way to argue a case in front of the supreme court and to stay with friends in the Hamptons. He also has a wife and children, something neither of the Loman brothers has achieved. For all of his success, though, Bernard is not boastful, being a polite and gentle man who talks respectfully to Willy when he meets him in his father's office.

Charley   Biff and Happy refer to their neighbor as "Uncle" Charley but it is unclear whether he is a relative or just a close family friend. Charley's son, Bernard, also calls Willy "Uncle," and although more studious than Miller, he has the same lanky awkwardness that Miller had at that age. Miller insisted that Willy was nothing like ISIDORE MILLER, but Miller had grown up across the street from two of his uncles, and the good natured Charley could be modeled on his father during his more successful years; he was not a big talker and had offered his brothers-in-law jobs when they needed them, although in *Salesman in Beijing* Miller describes his character as "gruff, ignorant, and peasantlike," which runs contrary to how he viewed his father.

In one sense, Charlie offers an ideal in the play: He runs his own business, is content with his life, and is a pleasant, good-natured man—all things that seem to be beyond Willy's grasp. Charley is satisfied with moderate success without feeling compelled to be the best, and he does not take short cuts, relying instead on steady, hard work. He does not trust the easy success of a scholarship by winning a football game; he feels that you get what you work for. Ever in the background, not forcing himself but trying to help his unfortunate neighbor through a difficult time, Charley loves and respects Willy in a way that few others do. Indeed, Willy, in a rare moment of honesty, remarks that Charley is his only friend. This turns out to be true, as outside of immediate family, Charley and his son, are the only people who show up at Willy's funeral. It is here that Charley gives a speech to explain what was so special about Willy in response to Biff denigrating the way his father lived.

Charley passes his mode of living on to his offspring, as Willy does, but his are clearly the better values by which to live—his son Bernard is a caring, compassionate adult and is nothing like the self-involved Loman brothers. Willy criticizes him for not being able to use tools as Willy can, but Charley does what is suited to his nature, unlike Willy, who refuses to accept that he would have been happier as a carpenter.

Loman, Ben Willy's older brother Ben died two weeks before the play begins and left his fortune to his seven sons but nothing to his brother. Willy recalls Ben on several occasions during the play and brings him to life for the audience, but this is a Ben of the past. Willy seems to recall him especially at those moments when he feels the most vulnerable and in need of guidance. However, Ben has

no real answers. As a self-made man, Ben tells his tale of finding a fortune in the African jungle as if it were a solution, but it is merely a boast. Ben was a selfish man and survived the jungle by plundering it, just as he makes money in Alaska by denuding the countryside. His father had left a wife and two young sons to seek success in Alaska and was never heard from again. Ben similarly ignores family responsibility as he follows the father's footsteps, leaving his mother and younger brother to fend for themselves.

Ben's uncaring attitude toward others may have helped him achieve great wealth, but he has made his fortune mostly by luck; Linda is right to be suspicious of where his offer will lead Willy. Willy's life may have been different if he had followed his brother to Alaska, but there is no guarantee that it *would* have been any better. Ben's lack of family feeling can be seen in the mean way in which he trips Biff, the brusque way that he treats Willy, and the long years of silence. Yet, it is Ben to whom Willy goes for advice before his act of suicide, and although Ben warns Willy the insurance company may not pay out, he does finally encourage him in this act. Since we never see a real Ben, given that he died before the play begins, it is possible to question the authenticity of his presentation—with his fortune in diamonds and seven sons, he sounds more the product of a fairy tale than of reality. Although Linda confirms his existence and the diamond he once gave them, aspects of his story may be colored more by Willy's need for a strong heroic figure than by a true portrait of his brother.

Loman, Biff Although Miller himself had been weak at math and a high school football player, Biff is more closely modeled on Miller's cousin Buddy Newman, another sportsman who also was popular with the boys as well as being a rather wild child. The name *Biff* seems to indicate an abrasive nature and someone who will have to fight to get what he wants, but the name is ironic for Biff's life so far has been marked by his inability to stick to anything and to quit anytime things become too difficult.

As a youth, Biff idolized his father and was led to believe that since he was "well liked" he could get away with anything. He is highly popular in the small world of high school, which only feeds this belief. He begins to steal, no doubt feeling that everything should be his by right; a football from school, lumber for the house, a crate of balls from Bill Oliver. Willy is desperate that Biff should succeed in life, so instead of punishing him, he condones the thefts and makes excuses, neglecting to instill in his son the moral values that a parent should teach a child. Biff is successful in high school as a football player but reaps no benefit from this because he never goes to college. Initially, he had planned to retake the math course he needed, but he catches his father with a mistress, and this changes everything.

Biff's self-confidence dissipates as he loses respect for his father. As a result of this, his belief in the fantasies that his father has fed him cannot be maintained, but he has nothing with which to replace them. Without direction, he leaves home after arguing with Willy. He travels from job to job, unable to maintain any position for long because he cannot take orders. He even does time in jail for stealing a suit. But out in the real world, away from the destructive influence of his father, Biff begins to recognize his own true nature and replace his father's dream with one of his own. Whether or not Biff can achieve his dream of working with the land is not as important as the fact that it is more suited to his nature than trying to be a hot-shot business man.

The older Biff may not like his father, but he still loves him, and this sucks him back into his father's dreamworld for a time. When Linda warns him that his father is considering suicide, to cheer his father up, Biff creates a fantasy in which Bill Oliver will lend him the money to start his own sporting-goods firm and he and Happy will become rich. His family is able to maintain this illusion, agreeing that Oliver had really liked Biff and planning their advertising campaign as if this plan could not fail. Biff is forced back into reality when he waits all day to see Oliver and the man does not remember who he is. As if to put that dream behind him, or perhaps to reassert his own nature, Biff steals Oliver's pen before leaving his office. He then tries to explain to his father what he sees as the truth about the Lomans, but

Willy is incapable of accepting such a vision; all he sees is that his son still loves him and so is worthy of the sacrifice he is now prepared to make.

Loman, Harold (Happy) Based on Miller's cousin Abby Newman who had had a reputation with the ladies, Miller created Harold Loman. Called Happy by his friends, Biff's younger brother invokes a happy-go-lucky personality. However, we soon learn that this is a deluded happiness. Happy is not happy at all but pushes his inner discontent to one side and lives a bitter and aggressive life, sleeping with his bosses' wives and girlfriends to get petty revenge for their being higher up on the corporate ladder. Forever seeking both parents' attention with his declarations that he is losing weight or getting married, Happy is as consistently ignored; that no doubt accounts for his own ability in return finally to ignore what is happening to his parents.

Happy does not reach the same level of awareness as Biff, for by the close of the play, he determines to live life as his father, having learned nothing of what that means. Since his childhood, Happy has admired his father and his older brother, forever fighting, largely unsuccessfully, for their attention and approval. Although Biff left home, Willy remained as a role model, and Happy has become a pale imitation of his father. Bereft of even the few decencies that Willy retains, such as a conscience and sense of responsibility, Happy presents an entirely disreputable figure. Despite his supposed love and respect for his father, Happy has no compunction about abandoning Willy in a bar when he is clearly distressed, even denying that Willy is his father to escape embarrassment. He would rather chase women than deal with his own father's evident distress, and it is little wonder that his own mother turns on him so coldly for this. His response to her is equally cold when he refuses to pick up the flowers, leaving Biff to play the role of dutiful son.

Unlike his father who must work on commission, Happy is salaried, but he has not advanced in business; he is an assistant to an assistant buyer. He resents everyone who is over him at work, seeing himself as the better man because of the false illusions that his father fed both children growing up.

He lives the rootless life of a bachelor who sleeps with a string of women, and despite his claims that he wants to marry, he also admits that he would never give up this sexual freedom by choice. Because he finds women so easy to charm, he no longer values any woman enough to sustain a relationship. He is a morally bankrupt individual, and Linda rightly calls him, "a philandering bum."

Loman, Linda Linda's central importance seems to be as a voice of protest and outrage against what is happening to her husband. She insists that "Attention must be paid" to Willy and his suffering. As Linda recognizes, Willy is a human being, and it is a terrible thing that happens to him. Dreams, illusions, and self-deceptions feed the action of this play; Linda, in contrast, seems very much planted in reality with her concerns over house payments, mending work, insurance premiums, and her husband's care. She knows exactly what her sons are, and she does not hold back on telling them, especially when they hurt her husband. Yet, despite Linda's clear sight, she allows her family's dreams to flourish; she even encourages them. It is only when they are dreaming of a brighter future that the family can operate together, and for Linda, the truth is a small sacrifice to pay for the happiness of her family.

Although Willy often derides and shouts at her, a tendency that leads Biff to try to defend her, Linda is no doormat and has chosen the life she leads. Willy loves her despite his adultery, and he harbors a deep guilt over this sexual betrayal, as evidenced in his anger at seeing her mending stockings. He tells her that she is his "foundation" and "support," and it is true, even if at times she secures him so tightly that he dare not risk uprooting the family to head to Alaska on his brother's offer. She loves him deeply and having little chance for her own self-achievement, being a fairly typical woman of the period, has dedicated her whole life to his happiness. In every scene, her central concern is Willy. She turns on her own sons to protect him and at the close is bereft without her life's companion.

Loman, Willy Willy's name is a childish version of the more adult William, indicating an intrinsic immaturity in his nature. As Willy tells his older brother, "I still feel—kind of temporary about myself." The Loman men all need to grow up and find true direction in their lives, especially Willy with his unrealistic dream of wanting everyone to like him. Loman is often read as indicating Willy to be a low-man, common and insignificant, as opposed, perhaps, to Dave Singleman, the salesman who is "singled" out. Miller, however, declares that this was unintentional, saying that he picked the name of Loman subconsciously from a movie he had once seen: *The Testament of Dr. Mabuse.* For Miller, the name *Lohmann* evokes the voice of a "terror-stricken man calling into the void for help that will never come," and this certainly applies to the character Miller created.

Willy Loman's whole life seems to have been a sellout. His sons have turned out badly, and his relationship with Biff has soured. But although a braggart and adulterer, Willy Loman is not a bad man—in fact, he is loved by all who are close to him. It is their love that allows us to see his better side and to sympathize with his plight. Willy also loves his family and tries to give them what he feels they are worth, even to sacrificing his own life. Unlike his father and brother, Willy stayed with his family and tried to be responsible. Willy's problem is that he wants to be successful but has not been given the personality, ability, or luck to achieve this goal. Overweight, overtalkative, and now overage, he has become redundant in a business world that only tolerated him in the first place. But Willy refuses to give up without a fight. He is a human being and demands the respect and dignity that most human beings deserve, and this determination makes him heroic.

Willy is the salesman of the title, but the first salesman whose death that we hear about is Dave Singleman. Willy idealizes Singleman's death, but realistically the man passed away on a train still trying to make that big deal, and despite the many people who attended his funeral, he died alone. Salesmen must always be on the move, and such a life inevitably wears people down. Singleman was a salesman of the past who could still manage to get by on being liked; Willy attempts to emulate Singleman's life in a less sentimental age. Working against greater odds, Willy runs out of steam, and it is his death with which the play ends. His funeral is not nearly so well attended, indicating a society in which people hold less importance, and this seems to be the final invalidation of Willy's insistence that personality is the key to success.

Willy recalls his idealized past both as an escape and an attempt to discover what went wrong. Convinced that his current unhappiness is due to his failure to make his mark in the business world, he searches for the answer to the question that he has asked all his life: How do you become successful? Willy has convinced himself that the answer is to be well liked, and he passed this belief onto his sons. However, Miller makes it clear that being well liked has little to do with success. Miller uses various characters in the play to exemplify that people become successful through hard work (Charley and Bernard), inheritance (Howard), or sheer luck (Ben). Neither Howard nor Ben waste any time trying to be liked, and both are depicted as selfish, impolite, and rich.

Willy would have been happier working with his hands, and his constant attempts to grow something in the garden suggest his connection to nature, but it is a connection that has become sterile within the urban restrictions his job choice has created. He derides Biff's suggestion that he would have been better off as a carpenter, for he views being a salesman as a vocation. It is, alas, a vocation to which, it seems, he has become increasingly unsuited, but having made the decision to follow this dream, he cannot change direction. His fate becomes somewhat inevitable, given the poor choices he has made.

Wagner, Howard Related by his recording device (an early version of a tape recorder) to cold technology, Howard foreshadows the hard-hearted businessmen who decimate their work forces as cheaper automation takes over. Howard has not worked for his success; he inherited it from his father. He has no time for his father's old salesman and does not listen to what Willy tries to tell him. The fact that he listens so poorly to Willy is only further testament to Willy's ineffectiveness as a salesman. Howard represents a new development in the business world—the uncaring and exploitative way of doing business in which being well liked holds no relevance and all that matters is the profit line.

Woman, The (Miss Francis) By the late 1940s, the "working girl" was becoming a social reality that some welcomed but by which many more felt threatened. To diminish such a threat, these women were often discredited and belittled wherever and however possible, largely to affirm old-fashioned opinions of what was right and proper for men and women to do. On the surface, "The Woman," as she appears in the script and not even humanized by her name, Miss Francis, is portrayed as being close to a whore, sleeping with Willy in return for stockings. She is a fleshy character but is not fleshed out, becoming the scapegoat for Willy's bad behavior. However, we know that Miss Francis chose Willy—she is in control here. Though shown as a temptress—laughing as she appears in a black slip to a background of sensuous music—being the cause of Willy's alienation from his son, she is also shown to have power that is antagonistic to that of the men: She threatens to disrupt the patriarchal dream of a cozy home life with the "little woman" and so represents the growing potential independence and strength among women of the time.

MOVIE AND TELEVISION ADAPTATIONS

There have been at least eight film and television versions of this play. The first was created in 1951 by Columbia Pictures with FREDRIC MARCH as Willy Loman. Directed by Laslo Benedek, with a screenplay by Stanley Roberts, Miller disliked the adaptation and the way that March played Willy as apparently psychotic. Reviews were mixed. While Bosley Crowther felt that it was better than the play, John McCarten found it downright boring. March's performance was received with a similar ambivalence. However, the film's failures have more to do with the difficulty in transposing the subjective realism of the stage play into film terms. Its essential focus is on the centrality of the father/son relationship between Biff and Willy, and in that aspect, at least, it is successful. The studio was meanwhile so worried about the reaction that businessmen might have to the play's criticism of capitalism that they tried to convince Miller to agree to it being screened with an accompanying short, explaining how great modern salesmen truly were. Miller threatened to sue; it was shown without the short.

Among other notable screen versions, Lee J. Cobb and Mildred Dunnock were finally captured on film in 1966 for CBS television, which was later released on DVD as part of the *Broadway Theatre Archive* series. Directed by Alex Segal, who had worked on the teleplay with Miller, this version better reflected Miller's vision. Due to time restrictions, a fair amount was cut, and the resulting film focused more on business than family aspects. Public and critical response was overwhelmingly positive, and it won a number of awards, with television critic Jack Gould praising the production as "a veritable landmark in studio drama." In 1985, DUSTIN HOFFMAN recreated his 1984 stage version in a film directed by Volker Schlöndorff and a teleplay again by Miller that this time cut very little. More expressionistic than the 1966 film, this version best captured on film the dramatic form of the play. It was shown on television to an audience of between 20 and 25 million, and reviews were again favorable, with Mark Dawidziak calling it "a splendid marriage of theater and television." In 1996, while directing Alun Armstrong in the role at the NATIONAL THEATRE, DAVID THACKER also directed a television version of the play for the BBC with Warren Mitchell reprising his 1979 stage role of Willy. The 1999 50th anniversary production with BRIAN DENNEHY as Willy and ELIZABETH FRANZ as Linda was also filmed and was aired on Showtime in January 2000. David Patrick Stearns reviewed it as "more than a play, but an inkblot with which we examine ourselves."

FURTHER READING

Adamczewski, Zygmunt. "The Tragic Loss—Loman the Salesman." *The Tragic Protest*. The Hague: Nijhoff, 1963, 172–192.

Ardolino, Frank. "'I'm Not a Dime a Dozen! I Am Willy Loman!': The Significance of Names and Numbers in *Death of a Salesman*." *Journal of Evolutionary Psychology* 23, nos. 2–3 (August 2002): 174–184.

———. "Like Father, Like Sons: Miller's Negative Use of Sports Imagery in *Death of a Salesman*." *Journal of Evolutionary Psychology* 25, nos. 1–2 (March 2004): 32–39.

Atkinson, Brooks. "At the Theatre." *New York Times*, February 11, 1949: 27.

August, Eugene. "*Death of a Salesman*: A Men's Studies Approach." *Western Ohio Journal* 7, no. 1 (1986): 53–71.

Austin, Gayle. "Arthur Miller's *Death of a Salesman*." *Feminist Theories for Dramatic Criticism*. Ann Arbor: University of Michigan Press, 1990, 47–51.

Babcock, Granger. "What's the Secret?: Willy Loman as Desiring Machine." *American Drama* 2, no. 1 (Fall 1992): 59–83.

Barat, Urbashi. "Past and Present Reading *Death of a Salesman* in the Light of *The Wild Duck*." In *Arthur Miller: Twentieth Century Legend*, edited by Syed Mashkoor Ali, 99–109. (Jaipur, India: Surabhi, 2006).

Bateman, Mary B. "*Death of a Salesman*: A Clinical Look at the Willy Loman Family." *International Journal of Family Therapy* 7 (Summer 1985): 116–121.

Becker, Benjamin J. "*Death of a Salesman*: Arthur Miller's Play in the Light of Psychoanalysis." *American Journal of Psychoanalysis* 47, no. 3 (Fall 1987): 195–209.

Bentley, Eric. "Better than Europe?" In *Search of Theatre*. New York: Knopf, 1953, 84–88.

Bigsby, C. W. E. *A Critical Introduction to Twentieth-Century American Drama, 2: Tennessee Williams, Arthur Miller, Edward Albee*. Cambridge: Cambridge University Press, 1984.

———. "*Death of a Salesman*." *Arthur Miller: A Critical Study*. Cambridge: Cambridge University Press, 2005, 100–123.

Bloom, Harold, editor. *Arthur Miller's Death of a Salesman*. New York: Chelsea House, 1988.

———. *Willy Loman*. New York: Chelsea House, 1991.

Canning, Charlotte. "Is This a Play About Women?: A Feminist Reading of *Death of a Salesman*." In *The Achievement of Arthur Miller*, edited by Steven Centola, 69–76. (Dallas, Tex.: Contemporary Research, 1995).

Centola, Steven R. "Family Values in *Death of a Salesman*." *CLA Journal* 37 (September 1993): 29–41.

Coleman, Robert. "*Death of a Salesman* is Emotional Dynamite." *Daily Mirror,* February 11, 1949. *New York Theatre Critics' Reviews* 10 (1949): 360.

Comeford, AmiJo. "Willy Loman: A Tragic Residence for Confusion and Conflict." *Journal of the Utah Academy of Sciences, Arts, and Letters* 77 (2000): 172–177.

Cook, Larry W. "The Function of Ben and Dave Singleman in *Death of a Salesman.*" *Notes on Contemporary Literature* 5 (January 1975): 7–9.

Crowther, Bosley. "*Death of a Salesman.*" *New York Times* December 21, 1951, 21.

Dawidziak, Mark. "Hoffman and *Salesman* Shine in TV Staging." *Akron Beacon Journal,* September 15, 1985: n.p.

Dukore, Bernard F. *Death of a Salesman and The Crucible: Text and Performance.* Atlantic Highlands, N.J.: Humanities, 1989.

Evans, Lloyd Gareth. "American Connections—O'Neill, Miller, Williams and Albee." *The Language of Modern Drama.* Totowa, N.J.: Rowman and Littlefield, 1977, 177–204.

Fichandler, Zelda. "Casting for a Different Truth." *American Theatre* (May 1988): 18–23.

Gould, Jack. "TV: *Death of a Salesman.*" *New York Times,* May 9, 1966: 79.

Hampton, Gregory. "Black Men Fenced in and a Plausible Black Masculinity." *CLA Journal* 46, no. 2 (December 2002): 194–206.

Harshburger, Karl. *The Burning Jungle: An Analysis of Arthur Miller's Death of a Salesman.* Washington: University Press of America, 1979.

Hays, Peter L. "Arthur Miller and Tennessee Williams." *Essays in Literature* 4 (1977): 239–249.

Jayasree, A. "Expanding the Horizon of Realism: Arthur Miller's *Death of a Salesman.*" In *Arthur Miller: Twentieth Century Legend,* edited by Syed Mashkoor Ali, 117–127. (Jaipur, India: Surabhi, 2006).

Kang, Taekyeong. "Mirror and Door: 'Will–y Lo–man' as a Desiring Subject." *Journal of Modern British and American Drama* 16, no. 2 (August 2003): 5–43.

Kataria, Gulshan Rai. "King Lear and Willy Loman as Victims of Persona Identity." *Perspectives on Arthur Miller,* edited by Atman Ram, 35–49. (New Delhi: Abhinav, 1988).

Koon, Helen Wickam, editor. *Twentieth Century Interpretations of Death of a Salesman: A Collection of Critical Essays.* Englewood Cliffs, N.J.: Prentice–Hall, 1983.

Manocchio, Tony, and William Petitt. "The Loman Family." *Families under Stress: A Psychological Interpretation.* London: Routledge, 1975, 129–168.

Marino, Stephen A. "*Death of a Salesman:* Unlocking the Rhetoric of Poetic Power." *A Language Study of Arthur Miller's Plays: The Poetic in the Colloquial.* New York: Mellen, 2002, 29–53.

———, ed. *"The Salesman Has a Birthday": Essays Celebrating the Fiftieth Anniversary of Arthur Miller's Death of a Salesman.* Lanham, Md.: University Press of America, 2000.

Martin, Robert A., editor. *Arthur Miller: New Perspectives.* Englewood Cliffs, N.J.: Prentice–Hall, 1982.

Martine, James J., editor. *Critical Essays on Arthur Miller.* Boston: Hall, 1979.

McCarten, John. "The Current Cinema." *New Yorker,* December 22, 1951, 62.

McCormick, Frank. "'Like a Diamond Shining in the Dark': Ben's Role in *Death of a Salesman.*" *Notes on Contemporary Literature* 35, no. 2 (March 2005): 11–12.

Mielziner, Jo. *Designing for the Theatre: A Memoir and a Portfolio.* New York: Bramhall House, 1965.

Miller, Arthur. "In Memoriam." *New Yorker,* December 25, 1995, and January 1, 1996, 80–81.

Murphy, Brenda. *Miller: Death of a Salesman.* Cambridge: Cambridge University Press, 1995.

———. "Willy Loman: Icon of Business Culture." *Michigan Quarterly Review* 37, no. 4 (Fall 1998): 754–766.

———, and Susan C. W. Abbotson. *Understanding Death of a Salesman.* Westport, Conn.: Greenwood Press, 1999.

Novick, Julius. "*Death of a Salesman:* Deracination and Its Discontents." *American Jewish History* 91, no. 1 (March 2003): 97–107.

Otten, Terry. "*Death of a Salesman.*" *The Temptation of Innocence in the Dramas of Arthur Miller.* Columbia: University of Missouri Press, 2002, 26–59.

Partridge, C. J. *Death of a Salesman.* Oxford: Blackwell, 1969.

Ribkoff, Fred. "Shame, Guilt, Empathy, and the Search for Identity in Arthur Miller's *Death of a Salesman.*" *Modern Drama* 43, no. 1 (Spring 2000): 48–55.

Roudané, Matthew C., editor. *Approaches to Teaching Miller's Death of a Salesman*. New York: MLA, 1995.

———. "*Death of a Salesman* and the Poetics of Arthur Miller." In *The Cambridge Companion to Arthur Miller*, edited by Christopher Bigsby, 60–85. (Cambridge, England: Cambridge University Press, 1997).

Shatsky, Joel. "Arthur Miller's 'Jewish' Salesman." *Studies in American Jewish Literature* 2 (Winter 1976): 1–9.

Shockley, John S. "*Death of a Salesman* and American Leadership: Life Imitates Art." *Journal of American Culture* 17, no. 2 (Summer 1994): 49–56.

Singh, Amrendra Narayan. "Form in Arthur Miller's Plays: A Brief Study of *Death of a Salesman* and *After the Fall*." In *Arthur Miller: Twentieth Century Legend*, edited by Syed Mashkoor Ali, 110–116. (Jaipur, India: Surabhi, 2006).

Stavney, Anne. "Reverence and Repugnance: Willy Loman's Sentiments toward His Son Biff." *Journal of American Drama and Theatre* 4, no. 2 (Spring 1992): 54–62.

Stearns, David Patrick. "*Salesman* Rings Better than Ever." *USA Today*, January 7, 2000, E13.

Thompson, Terry W. "The Ironic Hercules Reference in *Death of a Salesman*." *English Language Notes* 40, no. 4 (June 2003): 73–77.

———. "Miller's *Death of a Salesman*." *Explicator* 60, no. 3 (Spring 2002) 162–163.

———. "Miller's *Death of a Salesman*." *Explicator* 63, no. 4 (Summer 2005): 244–247.

Vogel, Dan. "From Milkman to Salesman: Glimpses of the Galut." *Studies in American Jewish Literature* 10, no. 2 (Fall 1991): 172–178.

Walton, James E. "*Death of a Salesman*'s Willy Loman and *Fences*'s Troy Maxson: Pursuers of the Elusive American Dream." *CLA Journal* 47, no. 1 (September 2003): 55–65.

Watts, Richard. "*Death of a Salesman* A Powerful Drama." *New York Post*, February 11, 1949. *New York Theatre Critics' Reviews* 10 (1949): 359.

Weales, Gerald, editor. *Death of a Salesman: Text and Criticism*. New York: Penguin, 1996.

Wiley, Catherine. "Cherríe Moraga's Radical Revision of *Death of a Salesman*." *American Drama* 11, no. 2 (Summer 2002): 32–46.

Yoon, So–young. "Willy Loman's Portrait: Trauma of the Absence of the Father." *Journal of Modern British and American Drama* 16, no. 3 (December 2003): 181–209.

"Dinner with the Ambassador" (1985)

Miller traveled a lot on behalf of the rights of other writers, and this essay account, first printed in *Nation* in 1985 and reprinted in *Echoes Down the Corridor* (2000), relates his experiences with fellow playwright HAROLD PINTER as they visited Turkey on behalf of International PEN. They went to demonstrate their "moral solidarity" with Turkey's writers, artists, and political prisoners in the hopes of influencing the country's military government to be less restrictive. Key government figures whom they had hoped to interview were unavailable, but they met with various artists who had been imprisoned and tortured without charges, as well as publishers and editors on both sides of the conflict. After giving some social and historical background on Turkey's 1980 military coup and the numbers detained and executed, the essay focuses on the week's "climax," a dinner given in honor of Miller by U.S. ambassador Robert Strausz–Hupé.

Miller describes their right-wing host and contrasts the elegance of the dinner to the plight of political prisoners being ignored for expediency's sake. Inspired by Pinter's growing righteous indignation over the attitudes of the guests with whom they were seated, after the ambassador's welcoming speech, Miller quietly thanks him for his hospitality but then publicly criticizes the complacency of the United States in the face of the injustices that he and Pinter have witnessed. He refutes his host's claim that Turkey is becoming a DEMOCRACY, speaks in support of the Turkish Peace Association that had been a particular target of the government, and asks the United States to hold itself to a higher standard of intervention. Although the ambassador is visibly shaken, Miller notes a fair amount of approval from other guests. Shortly after this, Pinter further insults the ambassador with his candor and feels it best they both leave. News of the press conference that they jointly gave before leaving the country was largely suppressed, and U.S. policy did not change by their intervention, but they felt that at least the oppressed in Turkey were given some hope that the world had not forgotten them, making their trip worthwhile.

"Ditchy" (1944)

Published in *Mayfair Magazine* in October 1944, "Ditchy" was Miller's first published short story. Long unacknowledged, it was rediscovered in the 1990s by scholar George Crandell while looking through materials at the HARRY RANSOM RESEARCH CENTER. It tells the tale of a young man in his twenties revisiting the place where he grew up near Central Park and going to the spot where he had been mugged at the age of seven. As the unnamed protagonist recalls that time when three Italian boys viciously beat him for his roller skates, a similar trio confronts him. This time, he reacts differently, with the maturity that the passing years have brought. He befriends one of the youths, called Ditchy, recognizing in an empathetic leap that Ditchy's aggression is a symptom of a harsh upbringing and the unrelenting pain that a mouth full of rotten teeth causes. Offering compassion rather than anger, the man takes the youth to a dentist, who pulls his teeth, and then the man treats the youth to an ice cream.

The recollections might be autobiographical—Miller grew up in this same area and had been mugged as a child for his roller skates—but the focus is on Miller's interest in wayward youth, especially in how thugs evolve and what motivates them, an interest that would be developed further in later projects. Through the compassion of the protagonist, Ditchy significantly loses his teeth, a symbolic suggestion that kindness wins more battles than aggression and a call to deal with troubled youths more sympathetically to ensure that they head along wiser paths.

The Eagle's Nest (1942)

The radio drama *The Eagle's Nest* was aired on December 28, 1942, as part of the *Cavalcade of America* series, starring Paul Muni as both the 19th-century revolutionary Giuseppe Garibaldi and Alberto Liguri, a contemporary Italian fighting against fascism. Showing the connection between the stories of these two Italian patriots, Miller highlights their joint commitment to freedom and DEMOCRACY which are at odds with the dictatorship of Mussolini and is an unabashed piece of U.S. propaganda. Garibaldi's 1860s fight to unify Italy is paralleled to Liguri's current fight against the Nazis, to drive home the ways in which freedom can be endangered if the wrong people are given power. Unpublished, a typescript can be found at New York Public Library's Center for the Performing Arts.

Echoes Down the Corridor (2000)

Compiled by STEVEN CENTOLA from various writings that Miller penned between 1944 and 2000, *Echoes Down the Corridor* is an excellent companion piece to the revised *Theater Essays of Arthur Miller* (1996) that Centola also edited. The 43 essays in this collection are presented in roughly chronological order and mostly have been reprinted from elsewhere, but these are generally more reflective of Miller's social and political views than his artistic ones, although there is some theatrical commentary interspersed. Centola's aim was to present the reader with a comprehensive array of Miller's skill as an essayist, and so the pieces are partially selected for their variety of style.

The collection contains short sections from several of Miller's books of reportage during these years, including *Situation Normal . . .* (1944), *In Russia* (1969), *In the Country* (1977), *Chinese Encounters* (1979), and *Salesman in Beijing* (1984), with essays that originally graced the pages of the *New York Times, Esquire, Harper's, Holiday, The Nation,*

The Saturday Evening Post, and elsewhere. In "Preface," Miller expresses surprise at how much he had written about political life but recognizes evidence of his longtime social commitment in this. Offering an overview of U.S. social criticism from the 1930s through to the century's close, Miller warns against the watering down of protest in art.

Booklist's Ray Olson enjoyed the memoir type essays but found the "political commentary and satire . . . leaden even when it isn't dated." However, *Publisher's Weekly* declared, "The distinguished playwright's personal dignity and decency resonate throughout this low-key but affecting collection . . . illuminating the fundamental beliefs that underpin his activism as well as his art," and Nora Sayre felt that "no other writer I have read has brought such life to domestic cold war" and suggests that Miller's "dramatist's gift for writing scenes enhances his recollections." She concluded, "Miller is hardly our leading optimist. But he is an adventurous student of change, an unwavering dissident, and I find that reading him makes me patriotic."

FURTHER READING

"*Echoes Down the Corridor.*" *Publisher's Weekly* 247.35, August 28, 2000, 65.

Olson, Ray. "*Echoes Down the Corridor.*" *Booklist* 97.2, September 15, 2000, 204.

Sayre, Nora. "A View from the Stage." *New York Times Book Review,* November 12, 2000, 42.

Elegy for a Lady (1982)

Although initially rejected by U.S. critics on its 1982 premiere, the brief one-act play, *Elegy for a Lady,* which accompanied *Some Kind of Love Story* on the double bill *Two-Way Mirror,* won better reviews in GREAT BRITAIN and with subsequent U.S. performances. In *Timebends: A Life,* Miller tells us that the concept of *Elegy for a Lady* intrigued him "as an attempt to write a play with multiple points of view—one for each of the characters, plus a third, that of the play." He goes on to describe *Elegy for a Lady* as, "A play of shadows under the tree of death." CHRISTOPHER BIGSBY suggests that

one should not try to decode the play in terms of single meanings, as it is "a chimerical work," offering a misleading veneer that conceals hidden depths. Despite its deceptively simple language and effects, the play encompasses a multiplicity of potential meanings.

SYNOPSIS

The Man enters a space that represents a boutique to buy a gift for his lover. He asks the Proprietress, who is a similar age to his lover, for help in choosing an appropriate gift. He tells her that his lover is dying, it is suggested, of cancer. He has considered flowers but is uncertain of what type. The Proprietress tries to find out more information to guide him wisely, but he actually knows very little about this woman. He is married, an older man, and uncertain how long they have even been together. His lover has recently become distant, and he is unsure of their relationship, including an uncertainty as to how he feels about it. Having kept their affair a secret, he is surprised that he is talking so frankly to the Proprietress.

He considers a silk kerchief and notes that the Proprietress looks very like his lover. She rather vehemently points out that death is not inevitable and holds her abdomen. They consider other gifts but nothing suits. He recalls past times with his lover as the Proprietress makes tea. She draws out the callous way that he has managed a relationship that, for him, has been about pleasure without commitment. The Proprietress seems to become the lover, explaining how she would have allowed for his behavior out of love, and now offers him absolution for his guilt over this. She suggests that they just view each other as friends, though this disturbs him. They embrace, and the Man chooses a watch for the gift and leaves.

CRITICAL COMMENTARY

Reality in *Elegy for a Lady* is as unsubstantial as the true relationship between the Man and his lover, about which he has been less than honest to himself and her. During the play, he is forced to face certain truths regarding why he needed her, what he gave her, what she gave him, what she really needed, and what their relationship has actually meant. This allows him to see himself more honestly and to affect an attitude of responsive guilt that humanizes him sufficiently to be forgiven. What he comes to see is that his relationship with this woman is ultimately meaningless because he refused all along to invest it with any meaning. He denied life to the relationship, just as he denied his lover the baby that, we learn to suspect, she had secretly wanted.

Miller asks that the scene be dreamlike but not a dream: It is "the kind of waking projection the mind often ventures into when it is stymied by life." Faced by the possibility of his lover's death, the Man has been led to consider his own mortality and to judge the worth of his existence. The vagueness regarding the woman's illness strongly suggests that the only thing dying is their relationship, largely because it has been given no real substance on which to feed. The Man has refused to open himself to the involvement, commitment, and pain that a meaningful affair would demand. We come to realize that he has not even been a friend to this woman, let alone a true "lover." The Man knows virtually nothing about her, neither her interests nor her likes nor her beliefs. It is easy to have the impression that the Man has simply used this woman as an aid to regaining his receding youth. Only his word exists to the thought that she is as uncommitted as he has been, and the tone of the Proprietress's responses seems to imply that the woman has loved him deeply; her supposed independence was just something that she faked to keep him happy. It is apparently her love that finally gives him the absolution from guilt that he ultimately seeks.

The Man explains that his reaction to what he believes is his lover's impending death is unlike his relief at seeing others pass on; this time, he feels as if he's "being pulled under . . . and suffocated." He would like to be able to leave and remember her happy rather than alone and dying. Though on one hand this may seem to be an attempt to escape the unpleasantness of a sick lover, his feelings could also imply an involvement that he is denying—he may not feel love, but he certainly feels responsible (possibly because he has used her) and consequently guilty.

From the start there exists an implicit connection between the play's two characters. The ambiguity of the play's presentation could imply that either might be the product of the other's imagination, but it is the Man whom we see first. The Proprietress variously depicts a complete stranger with whom he can confide, a representative woman whom he can try to understand, and the lover with whom he needs to define his relationship. Unable to connect with his lover in reality, he does so through the freedom of illusion, and having done so, he can now affirm their connection or its lack, in the real world. His desire, yet inability, to choose a suitable gift reflects the struggle which he undergoes to create a proper connection—the connection is finally made by the watch that signifies all that the couple really have given each other—a little time.

Defensively, the Man separates himself from his lover by insisting that she held no real feelings for him just as he held none for her; but is this a truth or another evasion? The Proprietress reproaches him for his heartlessness, but the truth seems to be that each has been equally self-protective and reluctant to bare their selves to the vagaries and uncertainties of a real relationship. The Man's indecision over whether to see them as having had love or a friendship has resulted in their having neither. For all that, the Man keeps saying that he is looking for the right gift to say the right thing—he begins by looking for a gift that will say nothing, rather than suggest any commitment. His final choice of the watch shows more feeling: It becomes an emblem of the time that they both will continue to have, albeit not together. The interplay between the Man and the Proprietress has led him to a better understanding of himself and others, giving him strength to continue into the future with a better recognition of his relationship and responsibilities to those around him.

FIRST PERFORMANCE

Elegy for a Lady previewed at the Long Wharf Theatre in Connecticut, on October 26, 1982, with *Some Kind of Love Story* with the same two actors as part of a double bill titled *2 by A. M.* The title was changed for its 1989 British premiere to

Two-Way Mirror. The following cast played it in Connecticut:

Man: Charles Cioffi
Proprietress: Christine Lahti

Directed by Arthur Miller
Set by Hugh Landwehr
Music by Stanley Silverman

INITIAL REVIEWS

The few reviewers who bothered to attend the U.S. premiere disliked it. Alain Piette felt it was "poorly developed," and Kevin Kelly an "entirely gratuitous exercise;" even Frank Rich, who was sympathetic to Miller's desire to experiment with "aesthetic simplicity," felt that the staging was badly conceived and that the attempt, though worthy, was unsuccessful. The 1989 British premiere, directed by DAVID THACKER with Helen Mirren and Bob Peck, was better received. Although some critics remained confused by the play, feeling it too sketchy and introspective (see Hiley), Michael Billington praised its "economy of language," while David Nathan enthusiastically likened it to "a Pinter conversation piece." Dan Jones saw it as "haunting" and "poetic" while praising both the acting and direction.

FURTHER READING

Bigsby, Christopher. Afterword. *Two-Way Mirror.* London: Methuen, 1984, 67–70.

Billington, Michael. "The Contours of Passion." *Guardian,* January 25, 1989, 46.

Hiley, Jim. *"Two-Way Mirror." Listener,* February 2, 1989. In *London Theatre Record* 9, nos. 1–2 (1989): 67.

Jones, Dan. *"Two-Way Mirror." Sunday Telegraph,* January 29, 1989. In *London Theatre Record* 9, no. 1–2 (1989): 66.

Kelly, Kevin. "Arthur Miller's New Work a Double Disaster." *Boston Globe,* November 18, 1982, 67.

Nathan, David. *"Two-Way Mirror." Jewish Chronicle,* January 27, 1989. In *London Theatre Record* 9, no. 1–2 (1989): 62.

Peter, John. "Reflecting Our Split Lives." *Sunday Times,* December 2, 1990, sec. 7, p. 4.

Piette, Alain. "'Elegy for a Lady' and 'Some Kind of Love Story.'" *Theatre Journal* 35, December 1983: 554.

Rich, Frank. "2 by Arthur Miller." *New York Times,* November 10, 1983, C21.

An Enemy of the People (1950)

Although Miller had always been an admirer of HENRIK IBSEN, it was the idea of director Robert Lewis and actors FREDRIC MARCH and Florence Eldridge for Miller to write a new adaptation of Ibsen's 1882 play, *An Enemy of the People.* Upset that they had apparently lost movie contracts due to their suspected COMMUNISM, March and Eldridge felt that a play in which a minority is unfairly persecuted for unpopular beliefs would send a timely message. Lars Nordenson provided Miller with a literal translation from the Norwegian, and Miller sought to tone down some of Ibsen's rhetoric to focus on what he saw as the play's polemic against fascism disguised as democratic action. He trimmed Ibsen's five act play into three acts and cut some of the more ponderous speeches, making the play's hero, Dr. Thomas Stockmann, less of an ambiguously flawed elitist and more of what Miller would call a holy fool. The basic plot remained intact, the language was made more colloquial, and the town's mayor, Stockmann's brother Peter, was given a lengthy additional speech in which he villainously defends totalitarian tactics in the interest of peace and security, essentially promoting mob rule.

Given the climate of the times in which a play advocating free speech would be viewed as critical of a government trying to contain what they saw as a communist threat, the production was not a great success, closing after only 36 performances. Although Miller had been unhappy with Robert Lewis's direction, finding it too self-indulgent, he found himself accused of creating anti-American propaganda and of making Ibsen shudder in his grave. There has been little scholarship on the play other than comparisons with Ibsen's original, most of which favor Ibsen, although Miller's version has been filmed three times and is frequently revived on stage.

SYNOPSIS

Act One

Set in a Norwegian town, Dr. Thomas Stockmann is the medical officer of a brand new health spa that has been attracting much tourism and boosting the town's economy. Family and friends gather at his house, mostly joyful at his rising importance, while he takes a walk with his sons. His brother Peter, the town mayor, joins them to try to discover what Stockmann is working on. He is jealous of Stockmann's part in discovering the curative nature of the local waters and feels that he is in competition with his brother. The liberal editor of a local paper, Hovstad, has come to ask permission to publish an article that Stockmann had written praising the waters, but Stockmann refuses, explaining that he has good reason. Peter is annoyed at his secretiveness, feeling that he is just doing it to be the center of attention, and leaves. Stockmann's daughter, Petra, arrives home from her work as a schoolteacher with a letter for her father. Suspicious after a spate of illnesses among the previous season's guests, Stockmann decided to have the water tested, for they had not taken his advice as to where to lay the pipes, and this letter contains the results. The water contains dangerous bacteria, probably coming from his father-in-law's tannery.

His friends applaud this discovery, and he expects the town to follow suit and willingly close the spa to make costly changes. Hovstad, particularly, urges him on to expose the corruption that led to this dreadful error, but Stockmann wants to first speak to his brother. Peter is a leading investor in the new spa, and rather than hurt a lucrative business on which he insists the town depends, he suggests that Stockmann's analysis could be wrong and objects to any closure. He demands that his brother take back his report, but Stockmann angrily refuses. Peter threatens to have him dismissed from his post as medical officer and leaves after calling his brother a "traitor to society." Mrs. Stockmann is worried how this will affect the family and begs her husband to back down, but he insists that he cannot live with such injustice.

Act Two
Hovstad plans to print Stockmann's report in the hope that it will topple the town's governing body that he sees as too conservative. He and his backer wonder if they may be able to coax Stockmann into underwriting the paper in the future with his father-in-law's money. However, after an intimidating visit from Peter, who calls into question the veracity of the report and threatens to tax the whole town to pay for the changes, they turn about and join in the cover-up. Stockmann is horrified that they will not even print his report if he paid them to do so.

Stockmann organizes a public meeting to tell the townspeople directly about the report, but he is trumped by his brother, who takes over the meeting. Peter plays on the people's greed by pointing out the huge loss in revenue if such a report were broadcast. When Stockmann tries to read his report, he is shouted down and is horrified at what he sees as a miscarriage of DEMOCRACY. He mocks those who had formerly supported him and refuses to accept the majority decision. He is declared an enemy of the people for not conforming to their viewpoint.

Act Three
People are throwing stones through his windows, and Stockmann plans to leave for America. He receives an eviction notice; he and his family are being shunned and threatened by everyone in town; even Petra has been fired from her teaching post. Peter comes with a letter of dismissal but offers to take it back if Stockmann will retract his report; Stockmann refuses. In a perverse effort to absolve his tannery of the pollution, Stockmann's father-in-law has spent his daughter's inheritance on shares of the spa and offers Stockmann these shares, pointing out that if the report is released, these shares will be worthless. Even Hovstad offers him a lucrative deal. Stockmann refuses all bribes and decides to stay put and fight for the truth by starting a new school that will teach its pupils to resist what he sees as mob rule. The play ends as Stockmann protects his family from stones being thrown through the windows.

CRITICAL COMMENTARY
When Miller changed Stockmann's original line "The majority is always wrong!" to "The majority is never right until it does right," he illustrates the central difference between the plays and the playwrights. Where Ibsen believed in an aristocracy of intellect but allows his Stockmann to become too egotistical to be unambiguous, Miller believes in the possibility

of social reform and a true democracy and allows his Stockmann to take an unimpeachable moral stance. As CHRISTOPHER BIGSBY explains, Miller wanted "a saner spokesman for the nonconformist, someone whose resistance to the majority has a moral base." Thus Miller purposefully removed Stockmann's more extreme language and contempt for the common man to make him more sensitive and appealing, even while still ridiculously idealistic.

Miller wanted to use Ibsen's play to highlight a contemporary fear of the tyranny of the majority to counter the rise of McCarthyism and to promote the social importance of individual freedom. The pressure to conform in U.S. society in the 1950s was high, and Miller wanted to show the wrongness of this and to applaud those who resisted. Stockmann stands by his beliefs and has his livelihood taken away, a very real threat for many Americans under investigation by the HOUSE UN-AMERICAN ACTIVITIES COMMITTEE (HUAC). Miller was aware of the risk that he was taking in such a confrontational stance, but like his hero, he felt that it was a truth that needed stating.

In Miller's hands, the play becomes an exploration of individual and community rights in the face of principle and a study of the nature of rule. Miller depicts the bureaucrats who run the town as authoritarian and narrow minded and fully prepared to sacrifice the individual for what they determine to be the good of the whole. Tolerance of other opinions only extends as far as the dissent remains unproblematic and does not actually threaten the public's material well being. Expecting a human rapacity that will reflect his own, Peter Stockmann cleverly manipulates the townspeople with an apparently reasoned speech that appeals to all of their worse instincts. Those who initially support Stockmann for all the right reasons hypocritically backpedal rather than face any personal danger. Their inability to hold true reflects a human weakness against social coercion; it is always hard to be in a minority, but that should never be conflated with being wrong.

Filled with a purer democratic spirit, Thomas Stockmann rails against such a restrictive governing body but finds himself powerless against it. An idealist and less attuned to human nature than his brother, he cannot understand why the townspeople

would keep hold of the lie rather than pay the cost of the truth and relocate the piping using tax revenue. Though at times bombastic, he is nevertheless right. He is offered various compromises, but he rejects them all, preferring to suffer with his integrity intact. Rather than see the townspeople's fears as valid, he is prepared to accept the role of the people's enemy, embracing his martyrdom with an almost perverse pleasure. Sadly, his family must also suffer alongside him, but Miller suggests acceptance of this is worth the sacrifice. His wife is initially unhappy with his course of action, urging him to be like the rest of society and "learn to live with injustice," but she comes to accept the necessity of fighting for the truth and stands with her husband at the close.

FIRST PERFORMANCE

An Enemy of the People opened at the Broadhurst Theatre in New York City on December 28, 1950, with the following cast:

Morten Kiil: Art Smith
Billing: Michael Strong
Mrs. Stockmann: Florence Eldridge
Peter Stockmann: Morris Carnovsky
Hovstad: Martin Brooks
Dr. Stockmann: Fredric March
Morten: Ralph Robertson
Ejlif: Richard Trask
Captain Horster: Ralph Dunn
Petra: Anna Minot
Aslaksen: Fred Stewart
The Drunk: Lou Gilbert
Townspeople: Lulla Adler, Barbara Ames, Paul Fitzpatrick, James Karen, Michael Lewin, Salem Ludwig, Gene Lyons, John Marley, Arnold Schulman, Robert Simon, Rod Steiger

Directed by Robert Lewis
Set and costumes by Aline Bernstein
Produced by Lars Nordenson
It ran for 36 performances.

INITIAL REVIEWS

John Chapman praised the production as "intensely alive and intensely angry," and BROOKS ATKINSON declared, "You can hardly escape the power and excitement of a bold drama audaciously let loose in the theater by actors and stage people who are not afraid of their strength," praising Miller's translation as "compact, idiomatic and eminently actable." But while Atkinson and Arthur Pollock, found Miller's translation of Ibsen's play refreshing and vivid, some, such as the reviewer for *Theatre Arts*, felt that Miller's version was too melodramatic. Others saw his revision of Stockmann as a less ambiguous hero running counter to Ibsen's original vision, and Robert Coleman declared the play "a rip-roaring, muddle-mooded melodrama" that would make Ibsen "shudder." Reviews were fairly mixed, and audiences stayed away, perhaps wary of attending anything advocating nonconformity under the shadow of McCarthyism. In his negative review of the play, Alan Thompson concluded that it was a work of "agitational propaganda," which he apparently failed to realize was largely the point.

MOVIE AND TELEVISION ADAPTATIONS

To date, there are three filmed versions of Miller's adaptation of the play. In 1966, the *Broadway Theatre Archive* series released a version directed by Paul Bogart, starring James Daly, Philip Bosco, Timothy Daly, and Kate Reid. Then in 1976, Steve McQueen put on weight and grew a beard to play Thomas Stockmann in a big picture version of the play. Some changes were made, but it is fairly faithful to Miller's text; however, Warner refused to distribute the film, uncertain of its reception, and it stayed in the vaults until 1981 when it was finally screened at the Public Theater and then released to television. McQueen had wanted to be taken more seriously as an actor, but he seemed miscast in the role, and neither Miller nor the critics were particularly pleased with the production. The most recent version was the PBS *American Playhouse* production in 1990 starring John Glover, Valerie Mahaffey, and George Grizzard, and it was relocated to Maine. Jack O'Brien directed, and Miller was happier with this version, which ran just under two hours. Some critics felt that the play had become too dated, others argued for its continued topicality, and reviews remained mixed. John O'Connor praised it as "a powerful depiction of social corruption and selfishness" and applauded its sense of outrage.

FURTHER READING

"*An Enemy of the People.*" *Theatre Arts* 35 (March 1951): 15.

Atkinson, Brooks. "First Night at the Theater." *New York Times*, December 29, 1950, 14.

———. "Ibsen in a Rage." *New York Times*, January 7, 1951, sec. 2, p. 1.

Bigsby, Christopher. "*An Enemy of the People.*" *Arthur Miller: A Critical Study*. Cambridge: Cambridge University Press, 2005, 138–146.

Bronson, David. "*An Enemy of the People*: A Key to Arthur Miller's Art and Ethics." *Comparative Drama* 2 (1968–1969): 229–247.

Chapman, John. "Arthur Miller and Fredric March Put New Anger in Ibsen's *Enemy*." *New York Daily News*, December 29, 1950. In *New York Theatre Critics' Reviews* 11 (1950): 155.

Coleman, Robert. "*Enemy of the People* Muddled in Version by Miller." *New York Daily Mirror*, December 29, 1950. In *New York Theatre Critics' Reviews* 11 (1950): 156.

Dworkin, Martin S. "Miller and Ibsen." *Humanist* 3, May/June 1951: 111–115.

Haugen, Einar. "Ibsen as Fellow Traveler: Arthur Miller's Adaptation of *Enemy of the People*." *Scandinavian Studies* 51, 1979: 343–353.

Lindholdt, Paul. "Greening the Dramatic Canon: Henrik Ibsen's *An Enemy of the People*. *Interdisciplinary Literary Studies: A Journal of Criticism and Theory*, 3, no. 1 (Fall 2001): 53–65.

Miller, Arthur. "Ibsen's Warning." *Index on Censorship* 18, nos. 6–7 (July–August 1989): 74–76.

O'Connor, John. "*Enemy of the People* set in Maine." *New York Times*, June 13, 1990: C18.

Pollock, Arthur. "There's Truth for Everybody in *An Enemy of the People*." *Daily Compass* January 10, 1951: 12.

Thompson, Alan. "Professor's Debauch." *Theatre Arts* (March 1951): 25–27.

Everybody Wins (1990)

In 1986, there was much gossip that a film titled *Almost Everybody Wins*, first with Warren Beatty starring and producing and later something produced by Linda Yellen, directed by Peter Yates, and starring Ed Harris was about to be made. The film was to be based on Miller's one-act play *Some Kind of Love Story*. It was not until 1988 when producer Jeremy Thomas convinced Miller to give him the screenplay that the retitled *Everybody Wins* was directed for Orion Pictures by Karel Reisz, to be released in 1990. This screenplay expands an intriguing two-character play into a full-length mystery movie. Miller increased the cast by 16 and added multiple locations to a far more complex plot. The resulting text is less ambiguous than the play and more of a political statement regarding the corruption of the U.S. LAW enforcement and judicial systems, alongside explorations of faith and desire. The film is fairly faithful to the published screenplay, but a few scenes were rearranged, others were cut, and Angela's multiple personality disorder was played down. The following synopsis is based on both versions, indicating points of divergence.

SYNOPSIS

A private investigator, Tom O'Toole, drives to the house of Angela Crispini for an interview, and in the movie the song "I Want To Be Seduced" plays in his car. Reluctant yet to talk, through flattery, Angela persuades him to accompany her to the penitentiary to see Felix, a convicted murderer whose release, she hopes, Tom can help affect. Discovering that the prosecutor is Charlie Haggerty, a man against whom he has pitted himself before, Tom becomes more interested. Felix looks scared and beaten as he explains how he visited his uncle, Dr. Victor Daniels, on the night of the murder, but insists he did not harm his uncle. Felix was convicted on circumstantial evidence: a tooth of his comb was discovered at the crime scene. Tom suspects that this was a plant and accompanies Felix to his appeal hearing. The appeal is denied. Haggerty is angry to see Tom involved, but Tom suspects that he knows Angela. Tom asks his friend, retired judge Harry Murdoch, to help with the case.

Tom is uncertain of Angela's involvement; especially as she warns him that the police are watching her. She says that she has evidence that Felix was framed but evades Tom's questions by seducing him. Returning home in high spirits, when Angela calls to ask him back, he agrees to take on the case. Tom's sister, Connie, a high school teacher who moved in with him soon after his wife died, warns him against Angela, not trusting her motives. Tom ignores her and goes to see Amy, the girl whom Felix said that he had gone to see on the night of the murder. She lives with a group of bikers near a cemetery and is a drug addict. While there, Angela calls to tell him not to talk to Amy until she arrives. In the movie, Angela is less assertive and just asks him to ignore Amy. Meanwhile, Amy tells Tom that Jerry killed Daniels and confessed to the police but was sent home. Jerry is in the cemetery praying at the gravesite of Civil War soldier Major McCall, around whom he has built a personal cult.

Tom finds an old mill where Jerry and his friends are creating a place of worship, but he just misses Jerry's departure. He discovers Angela there, but she behaves like a different person whom she calls Renata. No alternative names are suggested in the movie, and the conversation at this point is mostly cut. "Renata" is angry with Tom. Tom peruses Felix's case file and tells Connie that he may drop the case but goes to visit the murder site. This is overgrown and vandalized, with "Love ya Jerry!" painted on the wall. In the movie, the wall says "Jerry is God!" and this scene is swapped with one that plays later on in the screenplay when the police deliver a harmonium to Jerry's church.

Tom enters a bar to think about what he has seen but cannot settle down. Outside, he sees Angela and follows her. He watches her being propositioned by a car driver and grows jealous, so he talks to her. She is glad to see him but is fearful when a car pulls up with Bellanca, the chief of police, inside. The screenplay implies that this is the same car, but the movie shows different vehicles and simplifies this whole sequence, dropping the part where Tom tells Angela that he loves her. Angela asks Tom to take her home. She has a black eye, given to her, she says, by a policeman. They go to a diner where she persuades Tom again to stay on the case, and they return to her house.

Tom visits Haggerty to ask for the case files, which Haggerty reluctantly grants. Bellanca is also there and angrily tells him that Angela is a hooker.

Tom takes the court transcripts to Murdoch before going to Angela's. He needs to know why she is involved, but she is reticent, though she tells him that her father raped her and reminds him that Daniels was her physician. As they argue, she turns into Leontine, a crude whore, before falling asleep from exhaustion (the movie again leaves out the alternate name). Returning to Amy, she takes Tom to meet Jerry. Once an addict, Jerry is now clean and is the leader of his biker friends. When a steel tube topples, Tom pushes Jerry out of the way and wins his confidence. Jerry explains his cult and talks about Angela. Jerry admits that his conscience troubles him, but when Amy says too much, he hits her. Tom asks him to call if he wants to talk and returns to Angela's.

Angela explains that she has multiple personality disorder and has slept with Daniels because he footed her medical bills (in the movie, there is no mention of these, and their relationship seems less venal). She and Tom sleep together again. Tom mounts surveillance on Jerry's place where he sees the police carrying in a harmonium for his church (this scene is played earlier in the movie). Returning to Murdoch, Tom is warned against the case as Haggerty is trying for senator and will be reluctant to lose. Murdoch admits that the case was weak but wants to know how Angela is involved. The movie plays the scene where Tom visits Daniels's house at this point and omits the following scene in which Angela takes Tom bowling and annoys him by flirting with other men.

Tom's sister is not happy that her brother is still on the case and suggests that she should leave because she feels that she is in the way. Meanwhile, Jerry calls and asks to talk. Tom sees him, and he says that he needs to have Angela there too. Back at Angela's, she explains that Jerry ran drugs for Daniels, killing him because Daniels would not help build his church. The police were reluctant to arrest him because he knew that they were on the take, but they might kill him if he talks to Tom. Angela confesses that she was Haggerty's girlfriend and that he nearly left his wife for her, but she left him because of what he did to Felix. When Tom expresses extreme doubt, she becomes Renata in defense (a less obvious personality switch in the movie) and then shows him photographs and a ring.

Tom is called to the jail to talk to Felix, who is on hunger strike. Tom assures him that he will help, arranging to meet the prison chaplain later. At the church, he sees Angela taking communion and praying; she knows the chaplain and had asked him to persuade Tom to keep working the case. The screenplay implies that the chaplain is attracted to Angela, but that is omitted from the movie. Back home, Tom and Connie violently argue about Angela but make up. This is another scene that is omitted from the movie, a scene in which Connie is far less belligerent toward Angela. Meeting Angela, Tom sees that she has a bruised lip—she was hit by Haggerty who wanted his letters back. Tom wants these, but she is reluctant to get Haggerty into trouble. She agrees to give him one letter. They find that her house has been ransacked, but her locked filing cabinet is intact. She and Tom physically fight when Tom tries to open it. He leaves when she refuses to give him any letters and is followed by a motorcyclist who tells him that Jerry wants to talk.

Jerry has his motorcycle on the roof, seemingly contemplating something desperate (in the movie, he just stands quietly by the water). He tells Tom how Angela helped him get into Daniels's house. He agrees to tell Murdoch everything, but as they ride there, in his elation at having confessed, Jerry crashes his bike and dies. Refusing to give up, Tom persuades Murdoch and Angela to talk (in the movie, he just takes Angela straight to Murdoch). After this, Murdoch takes over, explaining that he has sent Angela out of state for protection and will sort things out. He has Felix freed on bail, and Tom is delighted until he goes to see Murdoch and discovers that the corruption aspect is being ignored. As Tom begins to leave, Angela attracts his attention. She is in Murdoch's guesthouse. Murdoch is throwing a party that Haggerty and Bellanca are both attending. Angela is happy that Felix is saved and has become Murdoch's girlfriend. Tom is angry but goes when she asks so that he will not get into trouble. Felix sees Tom leaving and thanks him; life goes on as before. The movie finishes as Tom walks off, but the screenplay has him driving out of town much as he arrived.

CRITICAL COMMENTARY

An essay "On Screenwriting and Language" accompanied the published screenplay; it explained Miller's belief that in films the language necessarily becomes "a servant to the images." A reading of the screenplay shows that Miller tried to follow this through with as much detail regarding what the audience sees as to what they hear. The resulting movie is a very visual piece, from its opening evocation of a sleepy Connecticut town, which we will learn is a hotbed of corruption, to the strange symbolism of Jerry's church. The town's supposed healer, Doctor Daniels, is at the center of a drug ring, of which the police and the district attorney are fully aware and from which they profit in kickbacks. They will frame an innocent man for the murder rather than risk the real killer facing trial in case he informs on them all. Tom's sister, Connie, points out the depth of their society's corruption, beginning even at high school as she feels pressured to inflate grades of students who participate on sports teams. Even Tom, for all his noble motives in taking the case to expose corruption, is also motivated by lust for Angela and a desire for revenge against Haggerty. His other work is equally suspect as he investigates a prospective vice president for a company to find out whether or not he is homosexual.

Very few people in this world want to take responsibility for their actions. Yet, the real murderer, Jerry, who is strongly associated with Christ in both text and image, feels an increasing need to atone for the crime. His resulting death, however, achieves little. It does not save society as the corruption remains intact, but at least Felix, as lucky as his name implies, is freed. The fact that Jerry is a murderer and that even the chaplain falls prey to sexual desire suggests a fallen world in which religion has lost its efficacy, an increasingly typical trope in Miller's work. Jerry is constructing his own church, which is based around another violent figure, a Civil War soldier, Major McCall. It is a primal one in which they make animal sacrifices but one that leads Jerry to want to pay penance for his crime, and in that, there may be hope.

Images of the Virgin Mary are prolific in both movie and screenplay and are largely associated with Angela, who may have been a whore but has an essentially innocent core. Playing down her multiple personalities in the movie makes some of her behavior harder to follow, but she remains a sympathetic character, with even Tom accepting her switch to Murdoch as a natural self-defense. In the collection *Arthur Miller Plays: Five*, published in 1995 by Methuen, Miller interestingly returned to his original title, *Almost Everybody Wins*. While the 1990 screenplay has Tom declare love for Angela and shows many others lusting after her, the movie omits these details. This makes Angela less of an object of desire and more human. She saves Felix as a kind of atonement for her life, telling Tom in the movie, "It's the one good thing I've ever done." In a morally dilapidated modern world, it has become increasingly hard to make a difference, as Tom discovers, and victories, when they come, are necessarily slight.

PRODUCTION DETAILS

Everybody Wins opened in 1990 with the following lead actors:

> *Tom O'Toole:* Nick Nolte
> *Angela Crispini:* Debra Winger
> *Jerry:* Will Patton
> *Connie:* Judith Ivey
> *Judge Harry Murdoch:* Jack Warden

> Directed by Karel Reisz
> Screenplay by Arthur Miller
> Produced by Jerry Thomas

INITIAL REVIEWS

Critical reaction to this movie was overwhelmingly negative. David Ansen declared it a "joyless fiasco," Stanley Kauffmann felt that it "fails to achieve even mediocrity," and Vincent Canby called it a "mess," pointing to its "lapses in continuity" and undeveloped themes. General opinion was that the dialogue was stilted, the characters unengaging, and the plot unappealing. Pauline Kael was a lone voice who found the screenplay "surprisingly cool, quirky" and urged her readers to see it.

FURTHER READING

Ansen, David. "Doing the Very Wrong Thing." *Newsweek,* February 5, 1990, 72.

Canby, Vincent. "A Heroine Fixated on Everything."
  New York Times, January 20, 1990, 13.
Caryn, James. "Arthur Miller Embraces the Screen."
  San Francisco Chronicle, November 24, 1988, E3.
Kael, Pauline. "*Everybody Wins*." *New Yorker*, December 17, 1990, 120–121.
Kauffmann, Stanley. "*Everybody Wins*." *New Republic*, March 5, 1990, 26.
Miller, Arthur. *Everybody Wins*. New York: Grove Weidenfeld, 1990.
———. "People." *Newsday*, March 27, 1989, 8.

"Fame" (1966)

Originally published in *Esquire* under the title "Recognitions," Miller retitled this short story "Fame" in 1967 when he included it in his *I Don't Need You Any More* collection. It has been reprinted in several other places since then, including HAROLD CLURMAN's 1971 edition of *The Portable Arthur Miller*, the 1987 collection *The Misfits and Other Stories*, and most recently, with the novella *Homely Girl* in *Homely Girl, A Life, and Other Stories* in 1995. Miller revised this story into a short play in 1970 and subsequently into a two-act comedy for NBC's *Hallmark Hall of Fame*, which aired on November 30, 1978, and was the first writing that Miller had done directly for television. The core of this original story is a commentary on the insubstantial nature of fame or reputation. The episode has some autobiographical basis and as CHRISTOPHER BIGSBY points out "captures [Miller's] own ambiguous feelings about fame."

The story begins by describing how successful Jewish playwright Meyer Berkowitz is becoming sick of what he feels is the insincere adulation of people who often just stop him in the street to have the self-gratifying pleasure of having spoken to someone famous. He avoids people on the street, uncertain of how to respond should they recognize him. He still feels a little ashamed of his good fortune and insecure in his success, even while he enjoys the popularity. He rationalizes this ambiguity by deciding that what he wants is for the public to see him, the man, rather than the media figure whose face has appeared on the cover of *Look*.

He goes into Lee Fong's restaurant to have a drink at the bar, equally worried that someone might recognize him or that he might go unnoticed. Not married, he worries about trusting any girl's reaction to him now he is famous. The restaurant owner recognizes him and offers a drink on the house. His nervousness mounts as he worries over whether or not he can write another great play and overcome his writer's block, when a small man taps him on the shoulder. Initially, the playwright assumes that he has been approached because he is famous; he has failed to recognize an old schoolmate, Bernie Gelfand. He recalls little more than the name, although Gelfand, upset at his lack of recognition, insists that they were once "best friends."

Not having connected Meyer with the famous playwright, Gelfand boastfully speaks of his own achievements within the shoulder-pad industry. Noticing the frayed clothing that Meyer habitually wears, Gelfand assumes that his friend's accomplishments must be minor. When Berkowitz teasingly lets him realize that he is actually the same Meyer Berkowitz who wrote the hit plays *I See You* and *Mostly Florence*, Gelfand, as Meyer expected, becomes profoundly embarrassed over having boasted about a success that now pales by comparison. Swiftly, Gelfand leaves with his mousy wife in tow, and Berkowitz realizes the price of fame: It makes it impossible for others to treat you naturally as a fellow human, and it creates artificial but unassailable barriers between people.

The story exposes Miller's uneasy recognition that fame distorts how others see you and can interfere with relationships. It becomes something one both welcomes and rejects, and the act of being recognized or not becomes equally ambivalent. Success offers a sense of achievement and a boost to the ego, but it can also isolate and lead to a kind of guilt when facing those less fortunate. It becomes hard to judge whether others are reacting to a person's fame or to the individual, and this provokes the likelihood of dishonest or shallow relationships. Meyer knows that his revelation will embarrass Gelfand, but he receives a perverse pleasure from doing it, nonetheless. It is not a friendship that he had valued, having forgotten all about the man, but his response allows him to see that it is he who creates the barriers as much as an adoring public. As Bigsby suggests, Miller has transformed an anecdote "into a fable."

FURTHER READING

Bigsby, Christopher. "Fiction." *Arthur Miller: A Critical Study.* New York: Cambridge University Press, 2005, 444–472.

Fame (1978)

In 1966, Miller wrote a short story "Recognitions," which he retitled "Fame" when it appeared in the 1967 short-story collection *I Don't Need You Any More.* After this, Miller developed his consideration of the rewards and detriments of fame into a one-act play that was produced in 1970 at the New Theater Workshop with ELI WALLACH and Anne Jackson, playing with a stage version of *The Reason Why.* This eventually evolved into a two-act comedy for NBC's *Hallmark Hall of Fame,* which aired on November 30, 1978. Directed by Marc Daniels, it starred Richard Benjamin as popular playwright Meyer Shine and had a running time of 53 minutes. This was Miller's first play written directly for television. It remains unpublished, but there is a manuscript at the HARRY RANSOM RESEARCH CENTER. It drew little attention, with a curt review from the *New York Times* complaining that it had too much exposition and that the film was overlong. Miller described it as "a comedy about some of the absurdities of being famous," although he admits that it also touches on deeper issues, such as concepts of mortality and the relationship between public and private lives.

In the initial short story, the playwright is called Meyer Berkowitz, and the film's tale of Meyer Shine begins in the same way by having several brief encounters, underscored by the issue of the playwright's fame and how that affects his relationships with others. Shine's meetings are more developed but are essentially the same: a series of people in New York who admire him and insist on recognizing his acclaim. Shine is uncomfortable with the fame that three (up from two in the story) successful plays have brought him, and he is uncertain how to react or relate to these eager well-wishers. He wonders what or whom they are acknowledging—Shine as a human being or writer, his plays, or his publicity image—as he asks in a mirror, "Who are you?"

In the next section of the film, Shine is about to depart for Italy, where he is to meet a famous Italian film director with whom he will adapt his play, *Mostly Florence,* for the screen. His unassuming personality initiates his uneasy relationship toward popularity. A friend warns him, with lurid detail, about all the perils of Europe, making him even more nervous about the trip. On arriving, the car promised by the film's producer is not there, and Shine is forced to deal with his own inadequate language skills in an alien environment. This again leads him to ponder who he is and what his relationship to others might be. Accepting a ride from a non-English speaking native, played by Raf Vallone, he begins to panic, thinking that he has been kidnapped. This turns to embarrassment as he realizes that the man is just a teacher who enjoys his plays and, having recognized him, was trying to help. He ruminates over the implications of being well-known.

The Italian director is expansive in his praise of Shine's work, but Shine soon realizes that the director plans to make substantial changes to his play for the film version. An Italian starlet accompanies the director, and Shine assumes, as does she, that she is to play the film's lead, Florence, who is something of a MARILYN MONROE. Very beautiful, she fittingly looks the part. Florence's beauty is key, as it is something that she cannot resist exploiting, especially in her career as a fashion model. However, it has created a public image that is at variance to her true nature, an image in which she now feels trapped. This has led her to view her beauty as fake and to destroy her self-confidence. To Shine's dismay, the director wants to make Florence a female jockey rather than a model, and rather than cast the film star in the lead, use a homely American jockey called Mona, whom he now introduces.

Mona, played by Linda Hunt, has no real interest in the role, but having studied contemporary drama for her doctoral dissertation, wanted to meet a playwright whom she has admired. Of all those who have recently praised Shine and his work, she is the most intelligent and insightful. She helps him come to a better understanding of his own play through their conversation. She equates his heroine's feeling that her beauty is not real to Shine's own attitude toward fame. With this insight, Shine is better able to understand and come to terms with the nature of his reputation. He returns to New York, and Mona, rather than the beautiful Italian film starlet, stays in his mind. This encounter has given Shine more confidence in his role both as a playwright and as a public figure. He realizes that the public image and the private man need not be one and the same and that it is possible to create art simply for enjoyment. As Shine tells the playgoer at the close who tells him how much she enjoyed his play, "Good, that's why I wrote it."

"The Family in Modern Drama" (1956)

Based on an address given at Harvard University, Miller's essay "The Family in Modern Drama" was first printed in *Atlantic Monthly* in 1956. It has since appeared in *Modern Drama: Essays in Criticism* (1965) and *The Theater Essays of Arthur Miller* (1978). In it Miller attempts to define the difference between plays that deal with the family and those that take on the wider society. For Miller, family plays are written in prose and seem to demand REALISM in their presentation, while social dramas ask for a higher language and lend themselves to EXPRESSIONISM. The chosen dramatic forms seem related to the subject of the play, but Miller also questions previous definitions of those forms, seeking to expand them to test their limits. His ultimate aim is the quest for a form that can successfully combine the best of both as a means to mend the increasing split "between the private life of man and his social life."

From the start, Miller questions the way in which we use such dramatic terms as *realism* and *expressionism,* offering his own definitions. While realism uses

prose and maintains a "fourth wall" to encourage an audience to believe that they are witnessing actual events, Miller reminds us that it is nevertheless "a style, an artful convention." HENRIK IBSEN's characters and situations may seem real, Miller insists, yet his subject matter is worked out on a symbolic level, showing that realism is capable of greater complexity than some would allow. Although Miller sees U.S. theater since the 1920s being outwardly impatient with the realistic form, he goes on to suggest that many U.S. plays are realistic in disguise and that the way to identify a realistic play is to consider its subject matter. While family relationships are best conveyed using realism, plays about social relationships tend toward symbolism or expressionism. Miller illustrates this dynamic at work in the plays of both Ibsen and EUGENE O'NEILL.

Miller breaks to ask a question that has become central to all of his work, a question that he feels should lie at the heart of all "great" plays: "How may a man make of the outside world a home?" His word choice implies the connection of family to society, supported by his belief that it is within the family that humankind learns those values and elements that are necessary to survive in the wider world. He identifies these as "safety, the surroundings of love, the soul, the sense of identity and honor." It is, however, the depiction of these values within a wider social context that gives them weight. He points out that if *Death of a Salesman* were only about family relationships, it would "diminish in importance," but "it extends itself out of the family circle into society," and its vision is expanded "out of the merely particular toward the fate of the generality of men."

Miller then tries to show the relevancy of expressionism to the "family–social complex." He describes expressionism in a technical sense as realism stripped down to metaphor and abstraction, which are shown representationally on stage, using poetic language. As such, it is a form, he suggests, that dates back to Aeschylus who chose to eliminate "psychological characterization in favor of . . . the presentation of forces" and so is nothing new. Miller describes expressionism as a form that calls to the intellect, whereas realism has emotional appeal. He adds to this that when dealing with the public and society, we appeal to intellect as opposed to the emotional response that we reserve for the privacy of the family. He also asserts that the "language of the family is the language of the private life—prose" and the "language of society, the language of the public life, is verse." Thus, he builds a case that realism and prose are used for family drama and expressionism with its higher language for social drama. T. S. Eliot's *The Cocktail Party* puzzled audiences, Miller posits, because it mixed the two, presenting a family drama too poetically, whereas his earlier *Murder in the Cathedral* coupled a poetic mode with a social vision and was better received.

Using his definitions, Miller asks that we look again at Thornton Wilder's *Our Town*. Rather than the realistic family drama as it is sometimes considered, Miller shows how *Our Town,* as its title suggests, is concerned with a wider social vision, presented expressionistically with poetic language (which does not, Miller reminds us, have to mean verse). The play's only flaw, in Miller's eyes, is a limit in the form itself—that it must ultimately sacrifice psychological characterization for symbol.

Offering more evidence of why people tend to connect the idea of family to realism, Miller points out that while we learn familial roles subjectively before we are even conscious of ourselves, social roles are learned at a time when we have already formed an identity, and so are more objective. Since what we feel seems more real, the subjective roles appear more authentic, while those that we have to intellectualize from an objective stance seem more arbitrary and mutable.

When Miller goes on to disparage the inability of realism or expressionism to "bridge the widening gap between the private life and the social life," we begin to see the true purpose behind this exploration of form. Miller himself is in search of that bridge. He disdains contemporary efforts in poetic drama as too personal and lacking in social import, describing them as "mood plays" that abjure plot and rely too much on improvisation. He worries that U.S. drama might be becoming too focused on the self and oversentimentalized. He puts forward a challenge to himself and other playwrights to "embrace the many-sidedness of man," and to "tell what ought to be." "There lies," he boldly concludes,

"within the dramatic form the ultimate possibility of raising truth-consciousness of mankind to a level of such intensity as to transform those who observe it." Miller is in quest of this very possibility.

Finishing the Picture (2004)

The title of Miller's final play to be produced during his lifetime was unintentionally ironic; it was one on which he had begun working in the late 1970s but set aside. It was not until 2002, after the death of INGE MORATH, that he returned to it. The title partly refers to Miller's effort to complete the story behind events that took place during the filming of his 1961 film *The Misfits* with MARILYN MONROE. But the play is less about Monroe than about the power that surrounded her iconic status and how different types reacted to that power. Miller told theater critic Mel Gussow that the play depicts "the metaphor of power as performance." As with *After the Fall,* Miller staunchly denied that the play was autobiographical. He insisted that although his characters were based on real people, they are simply characters and not accurate portrayals of actual people.

Director Robert Falls, who had worked with Miller on the 50th anniversary Broadway revival of *Death of a Salesman,* put his own mark on the production with the inclusion of video images before each scene and a cinematic technique in the second act that displayed a live feed of the actors speaking to Kitty. At first, Miller was nervous of their inclusion, but he saw how they helped underline those aspects of the movie industry that he was attempting to expose, which include its artifice and the self-centered nature of many of those involved. Unlike a number of his earlier plays, Miller left this script relatively untouched during rehearsals and production. The play premiered at the Goodman Theater in Chicago in 2004, but as yet, there are no plans for it to play elsewhere or to be published.

SYNOPSIS

Act One

Before each scene, a collage of raw black-and-white footage, presumably from the movie being made, is shown on scrims fronting the stage set. At the play's start, frames of an attractive woman's body parts follow an initial countdown sequence as she meanders through the desert with a man and kicks off her shoes. No faces are shown, and we can only guess that this might be the film's star, Kitty, being visually objectified for us before the dialogue even begins.

Set in Reno, Nevada, in 1960, during the election fight between Nixon and Kennedy, the stage action begins at dawn with first-time movie producer, Phillip Ochsner, on his hotel veranda noticing a distant forest fire. Ochsner, a former trucking magnate turned producer for Bedlam Pictures, arrived the previous night to find out why his film is nearly five weeks behind schedule and millions over budget. Kitty has taken to her bed while the cast and crew wait for her to emerge. Ochsner intends to assess Kitty to see whether it is possible for her to complete her contract or safer for him to abandon the picture. Having seen some rushes, Ochsner is more concerned about the "coldness" of the film than its star's behavior. If he stops production, he can collect insurance, but this would ruin Kitty's future prospects and possibly send her irretrievably over the edge. He is reluctant to do this. The night before, he began a relationship with Kitty's personal assistant, a woman in her forties, Edna Meyers.

Ochsner is a recent widower, and both he and Edna are surprised at the depth of their mutual feelings, but they plan to keep them a secret for the time being to avoid gossip. Kitty stumbles into the penthouse doorway, naked. Edna, swiftly covers her and guides her to Ochsner's bedroom where Kitty spends the rest of the play occasionally mumbling incoherent words from the bed but mostly curled up and comatose. Various characters come to discuss Kitty's behavior and offer suggestions concerning what to do about it. They also ruminate on their own lives and involvement with the movie industry. The film's director, Derek Clemson, feels sorry for Kitty: He knows that she has had a terrible upbringing and suspects that she is trying to escape this through drugs. The cinematographer, Terry Case, bluntly reduces movies to the simplest level, suggesting that they are based on "ass" and "animalism." He recommends a tough-love approach to Kitty.

Flora Fassinger, who runs a drama studio with her husband Jerome, flounces in to complain about the size of her room and the lack of a chauffeured car. Supposedly Kitty's drama coach, she is more of a stand-in for Jerome, whom Flora idolizes. Wearing five watches set to different time zones to enable her to keep track of her husband's star pupils, she indiscriminately worships financial success over true artistry. Kitty is her meal ticket, and she intends to keep her dependent, acting as an intermediary between Kitty and Clemson to keep her presence essential. Her central concern is always for her own status.

We discover that Kitty's marriage to the film's screenwriter, Paul, is in trouble and that she is approaching desperation. Although she is admired around the world, she is unhappy—as Clemson points out, just as the nation of America is. Edna compassionately sees Kitty as afraid after having lost belief in herself. The decision is made to fly in Jerome, at a considerable expense, to see if he can invigorate Kitty. The forest fire continues to rage as news comes that the power supply to the hotel may need to be cut.

Act Two

The film images at the start of Act Two depict a mountain scene slowly metamorphosing into Kitty's body; that then turns into an inferno. The action begins with the arrival of Jerome Fassinger, who has flown from New York. He appears wearing a ridiculous cowboy ensemble, including boots and hat. Full of his own importance, even lording it over Ochsner who is footing his bills, Jerome is determined not to accept any responsibility for Kitty. However, he will take full credit if he can persuade her to return to work.

All of the characters come to talk to Kitty as she veers in and out of lucidity. As they talk, their faces are projected through live video onto a transparent screen in front of the staged scene so that the audience can see what Kitty sees. We do not hear her voice, so it is as if we are listening to a series of monologues, revealing both the nature of the speakers and the kind of relationships they have with Kitty. She and Edna are friendly, but Kitty is cautious of her director and worried about her relationship with Paul. Ochsner tries to connect with his star by talking about his own problems, including his wife's recent death and his son's suicide. He explains how he rose from militant Marxist to millionaire and ponders how this good fortune occurred. He feels that he and Kitty may be equally bewildered by fate, recommending that she try accepting whatever happens rather than worrying and take responsibility for her own life.

Jerome and Flora come to talk but are initially ineffective. Jerome begins a confusing story about Eleanora Duse, and Kitty begins to cry. Rather than energize Kitty, he has reduced her to tears. Then, much to Jerome's pleasure, as he intends to take full credit, Kitty seems to improve, offering to appear for the day's shoot. However, against Edna's wishes, Paul insists on seeing her. He rips off her bedsheet and sends her into hysterics. Paul has become resigned to the idea of his marriage being over; not even this screaming fazes him. His love has turned to a kind of hatred, and he can only recommend, much like Ochsner, that Kitty take responsibility for herself because it is clear that no one else wants to. Kitty collapses and is to be hospitalized for a week, after which she may or may not complete the picture.

While Kitty sleeps, Edna tries to persuade Paul that his marriage can be saved. He denies this, knowing it to be false as he and Kitty have both failed each other. The telephone rings with news that the fire is out and that everyone is safe. Arrangements are made to take Kitty to hospital while Edna prepares for a dinner with Ochsner and sighs at her reflected image in the mirror. She feels tired and plain but, nevertheless, remains hopeful.

CRITICAL COMMENTARY

Never enthused by the Hollywood process, Miller questions the artistic pretension of the movie industry and satirizes a business which he views as determined to turn everything and everyone into product. The fact that we never can be certain if this picture will ever be finished or, given Ochsner's doubts, if it is even worth completing are essential ambiguities regarding the value of art itself. Recognizing an undeniable relationship between money and art—for the former is needed to pro-

duce the latter—Miller does not mock the film's backer but mainly the crew responsible for creating the movie. These people address Kitty for their own selfish reasons and try to manipulate her to satisfy their agendas—few display any real regard. Whether or not the picture is finished affects them all in different ways, and they each have a stake in its completion, Edna seeming to be the possible exception. The vignettes at Kitty's bedside in act 2 reveal more about the characters who speak—their desires, fears, and needs—than about Kitty. Kitty has become their mirror, the screen that projects their deepest needs and desires. She has ceased to be a person.

Flora's incapacity to acknowledge the spurious quality of the work in which her husband's ex-students are engaged shows how her self-absorption has ruined her artistic judgment. Miller is also concerned with the tenuous balance between the capacity to create art and the danger of becoming too self-absorbed. If this balance is thrown, then each can destroy the other. In a troubled culture that has made it increasingly difficult to gain a sense of self or direction and purpose, the price of creativity can be harsh. Kitty has become her performance and has lost all sense of self. She wants love, but the power that she represents destroys all chance of that happening. People can no longer respond to her on a human level but only as a product. Her fragility is part of her charm, and to negate that would make her less marketable.

Miller considers the necessary conditions for a satisfying relationship within this environment through his depiction of three couples—Kitty and Paul, the Fassingers, and Ochsner and Edna. Ironically, the most recent of the three has the potential to last the longest. Not as gifted as Paul and Kitty or even as the Fassingers (who display some artistic credibility despite their self-concern), Ochsner and Edna have a patience and an ability to compromise that is far better suited to emotional survival. Edna is perhaps the only person to care truly about Kitty, while Ochsner, despite his business background, is apparently quite sensitive. He combines his practical outlook with an open-minded idealism to make him still more attractive. Ochsner is closer to being Miller's mouthpiece than the figure of Paul, who fares little better than *After the Fall*'s Quentin in terms of sympathy as he reacts to his failing marriage in a similarly self-involved fashion.

Miller has described the play as being about power, and the power relationship between Kitty and those who are both dependent on her and in conflict with her is key. However, Miller is more interested in the consequences of Kitty's actions than in the reasons why she behaves as she does. Hence Kitty rarely speaks and never offers her point of view. She remains paradoxical as a woman who gives people joy just from looking at her but is personally too depressed to continue. Like the women in *The Last Yankee*, Kitty's condition is a reflection of a malaise that runs throughout U.S. society. As CHRISTOPHER BIGSBY points out, with the country in an election year and Nixon and Kennedy "arguing over the future of the country and the sky lit by flames, there is more than a hint of apocalypse." Yet the play is also framed by the hopeful romance of Ochsner and Edna, two people who unexpectedly find a void that is filled by the other's presence and who find potential love even on the edge of the abyss. It is hard not to see in this couple something of Miller's unexpected relationship with AGNES BARLEY at the time when he was completing this play.

The fire that had begun to rage at the beginning has burned out by the end of the play, and as one character explains, "The fire makes the seeds germinate. The fire. The heat. It opens up the seeds." So the apocalyptic fire becomes an image of growth for the future. Yet it is a mitigated hope, for although the fire is extinguished, who knows when human carelessness will set it blazing again? Like so much of Miller's work, this play ultimately is underpinned with a concern for responsibility to one another, suggesting that a failure to take responsibility will always have a severe cost. Because of this failure on the part of most everyone we see, including Kitty herself, the potential beauty of Kitty has become both silenced metaphorically and literally, and the picture is not completed within the span of the play.

FIRST PERFORMANCE

Finishing the Picture premiered at the Goodman Theatre in Chicago on September 21, 2004, with the following cast:

Jerome Fassinger: Stephen Lang
Flora Fassinger: Linda Lavin
Edna Meyers: Frances Fisher
Phillip Ochsner: Stacy Keach
Derek Clemson: Harris Yulin
Paul: Matthew Modine
Kitty: Heather Prete
Terry Case: Scott Glenn

Directed by Robert Falls
Set by Thomas Lynch
Produced by David Richenthal
It ran for a limited engagement of seven weeks.

INITIAL REVIEWS

Reactions were fairly mixed, but the previews went well enough to extend the run for an additional week. Linda Winer, for example, declared: "Deeply profound, it is not. It is, however, disarmingly entertaining," and Michael Phillips called it "a static memory play, though not without its moments of electricity." He felt that the play was disjointed, presenting too many angles, and that the production was both wordy and poorly paced. Michael Kuchwara, on the other hand, called it a "startling and deeply felt new play . . . rich in characters and ideas." His description of the play as a "vibrant rumination on, among other things, art, commerce, politics and that knottiest theme of all, relationships between men and women," indicates that he enjoyed its diversity rather than found it problematic.

Most critics perceived that here was an unusually humorous work from Miller, especially in his portrayal of the Fassingers. Damien Jaques called it Miller's "most humorous work," and described its one-liners as "Neil Simon on a pretty good day." Several, like Richard Christiansen, felt it to be a valuable addition to Miller's canon but second rank due to certain flaws in its construction and an unevenness of character. *Variety* could not pass the Monroe connection, and other dismissive reviews from such papers as the *New York Times* and the *Wall Street Journal*, whose Terry Teachout called the play "quite horrible," no doubt made it harder to raise money for a New York production. A year after his death, Miller's estate declared it had no plans to either publish or authorize further productions of this play.

SCHOLARSHIP

Outside of Christopher Bigsby's brief chapter based on Miller's manuscript and various production reviews, nothing else has been published thus far on this interesting play. As yet unpublished and with only the single Chicago run, it may be some time before this changes.

CHARACTERS

Case Terry As cinematographer, Terry Case is a no-nonsense, seen-it-all Hollywood veteran who recommends Kitty be treated with firmness. Unromantic, he reduces Kitty to her shapely posterior and sees her as a creature to be controlled rather than as a human being with feelings. He delivers much of Miller's commentary on the people and process of movie making; yet he, for all his candor, is as much a part of the dehumanizing problem as they are. More levelheaded than people like the Fassingers, essentially he is just as heartless.

Clemson, Derek While John Huston directed *The Misfits*, Derek Clemson seems less a portrait than a stereotypical representation of this famed director. Flora's insistence on being a go-between has disrupted his relationship with his star, who responds to him cautiously despite his sympathies. Burly and gruff, he is good natured and observant, but he is also as much a businessman as he is an artist—this grounds him—he will make money as readily from smuggling artifacts as from making movies, which suggests that for him money is the bottom line. He tries to complete his movie, even while realizing what that might cost its star. While he sees Kitty as doomed with "100 pound weights on her ankles" and "ghosts sitting on her chest," his movie comes first.

Fassinger, Jerome, and Flora Jerome Fassinger is the head of a prominent acting studio which Kitty has been attending; Flora Fassinger, his devoted wife, is present as Kitty's acting coach but behaves more as a chaperone by insisting on being an intermediary between Kitty and her director to ensure that she is indispensable. Based on real-life couple Lee and Paula Strasberg, pioneers of Method acting with the Actors Studio, they are comically satiric, though without being demeaning. Miller may have disliked the Strasbergs' involvement with Monroe, but he does not deny their artistic commitment, which allows them dignity through their belief in the importance and craft of acting.

The flamboyant Jerome is called in to back up his wife and to talk Kitty into returning to the set, but he seems more obsessed with his own self-image, parading around in a cowboy outfit. He is not keen on responsibility: "Suddenly, everything depends on me?" he complains. "I have never said I was responsible for her!" When faced with Kitty, he is initially ineffective, reducing her to tears, but then claims all credit when she revives. He is only interested in self-promotion and the ascendancy of his acting school; having Kitty as a pupil is merely a means to that end, and he will only allow that connection to be positive.

Flora's eccentricity is even more obnoxious; a parody of the name-dropping show-business type who is utterly focused on perks and status. She keeps Kitty psychologically dependent to boost her own sense of power by which she can demand a better hotel room and a chauffeur. She worships her egotistical husband, acting as his surrogate but bowing completely to his authority when he is present. The watches by which she keeps track of the various performances of her husband's star students reinforce this unreasoned idolatry—she is not concerned with the quality of those performances as much as the number and the salaries.

The humor of their presentation distracts from the unhealthy power that they hold over Kitty. Their pomposity hides their lack of concern for a charge who has become dependent on their approbation. They cut Kitty off from others who may be more able to help her fragile ego recuperate as they insist that only they know what to do. Kitty has lost touch with who she is, and they are only interested in the image and not the person and so cannot help her in that quest. First and foremost in both their minds are their studio and the cash flow that keeps this afloat; Kitty is just a means to this end.

Kitty   Kitty may be based on Monroe, but Miller does not want that parallel to distract, and so he gives her virtually no lines and insists that she not be played as a blond. Although a central figure, we see her face little more than we hear her, for she spends most of her onstage time curled up in bed. She wanders in and out of the action but is never in close focus. The play is less about Kitty than how others respond to her, for Miller's target includes everyone who is involved in the creative process of filmmaking, from creator to consumer. Kitty seems to be the figure on which they all feed. Through their various reactions to Kitty, we get the measure of those around her while she herself remains something of a mystery.

Kitty seems seriously disturbed, eating ice cream for breakfast, popping pills, and wandering the hotel naked. She has been to at least two well-known analysts who have apparently been unable to help. As Clemson explains, she has "ghosts sitting on her chest . . . Ghosts of things she's done." She struggles not to be objectified, but that is seemingly her fate. Those around carefully administer to her every whim but none really give her what she needs—consideration as a human being rather than as a fetishized object.

Dependent on others who are too self-concerned to really help, she is also the one on whom everyone else depends. She has come to define herself against how well she can wield her power over others. Paul points out that knowing that 40 people are waiting in the lobby for her proves that she exists. Movies have taken over her existence, but outside of movies, she has ceased to exist as a person. Her fellow artists, meanwhile, are not so narrowly defined; for example, Clemson has his artifact sideline to keep him solvent, Terry may be the recipient of an oil fortune, and the Fassingers have their acting studio. Without her movies, Kitty may just fade out of existence.

Meyers, Edna   As Kitty's faithful assistant, Edna takes the role of bright-eyed encourager, even though in her forties. A warm human being who always believes the best of others, her relationship with producer Phillip Ochsner is sweet and uncomplicated. They display a seemingly grounded and realistic romance in counterbalance to the Hollywood nonsense around them. Though mousy, she is a positive figure in her care for others, and without her, Kitty would be permanently lost.

Ochsner, Phillip   The film's producer, a former trucking-company executive, is depicted as a sane and forthright figure. He is wise to the world and its ambivalences and is ready to take responsibility for himself and others. Having started out as a militant Marxist, he had entered a union organization and ended up a millionaire through several lucrative shipping contracts. His wife recently died, and his son earlier committed suicide, so his life has had its downs as well as ups—this also makes him a more balanced figure. This is the first movie that he has produced, which may explain why he has not yet been seduced by the Hollywood rigmarole. Although he is centered on business, it is with a decency that makes him more appealing than many of the artists on display. He is not the stereotypical power-hungry philistine but a sensitive, level-headed decision maker. His connection with Edna humanizes him further for it is a serious attempt at a real relationship. It also connects him to Miller himself, with a wife recently dead, and a new hopeful relationship to a younger woman, Agnes Barley.

Paul   As screenwriting husband to Kitty, Paul is both exhausted and bemused by his wife. Marked by sorrow and regret, he sees Kitty's pain but feels unable to help. Through him, Miller may be indirectly answering the charge that was most often brought against him—that he wrote *The Misfits* to cash in on his wife's fame. Paul, however, is concerned with beauty rather than money: "Everyone wants something from her," he says. "We're no exceptions; we want a beautiful film, so we insist she wake up bright and fluffy even when she feels like dying."

While fairly reserved and philosophical in the first act, Paul explodes in the second as he tries to understand why his relationship has so evidently failed. Miller does not make him particularly likable or sympathetic. Just like Henrik Ibsen's Torvald in *A Doll House*, Paul has failed to provide the expected miracle that his wife needed to save their marriage. Paul is emotionally stiff and has been unable to give Kitty the love that she so desperately needs—"We each promised to cure the other, but we turned out exactly as we were"—but he at least acknowledges his shortcoming, as does Quentin in *After the Fall.*

FURTHER READING

Bigsby, Christopher. *"Finishing the Picture." Arthur Miller: A Critical Study.* Cambridge: Cambridge University Press, 2005: 437–443.

Christiansen, Richard. "Miller's Tale." *The Guardian,* October 30, 2004: 16.

Egerton, Kate. "Review of Arthur Miller's *Finishing the Picture* at the Goodman Theatre in Chicago, IL." *Arthur Miller Society Newsletter* 10 (December 2004): 7–8.

Gussow, Mel. "Miller Keeps Writing, Stacking Plays Like Firewood." *New York Times,* April 15, 2004: E3.

Jaques, Damien. "Arthur Miller Lets the Good Gossip Flow in *Finishing." Milwaukee Journal Sentinel,* October 9, 2004: 1.

Jones, Chris. "Miller on *Picture:* It's about Power." *Chicago Tribune,* October 7, 2004: n.p.

Kuchwara, Michael. "Chaos in *Finishing Picture." The Associated Press Online,* October 5, 2004.

Langteau, Paula. *"Finishing the Picture* at the Goodman." *Arthur Miller Society Newsletter* 10 (December 2004): 4–7.

Phillips, Michael. A Misfit *Finishing. Chicago Tribune,* October 7, 2004: n.p.

Solomon, Deborah. "Goodbye (Again), Norma Jean." *New York Times,* September 19, 2004, sec. 6: 63.

Teachout, Terry. "View: First-Rate Second City; Chicago's Thriving Theater Scene Has a Few Lessons to Teach Broadway." *Wall Street Journal,* October 8, 2004, W1.

Winer, Linda. "Painting Yet Another *Picture* of Marilyn." *Newsday,* October 7, 2004: n.p.

"Fitter's Night" (1966)

"Fitter's Night" was the only short story that Miller wrote directly for his 1967 *I Don't Need You Any More* collection, as all of the other stories there had been previously published elsewhere. "Fitter's Night" has subsequently been reprinted in HAROLD CLURMAN's 1971 edition of *The Portable Arthur Miller,* the 1987 collection *The Misfits and Other Stories,* and with the novella *Homely Girl* in *Homely Girl, A Life, and Other Stories* in 1995. It recounts one evening in the life of shipfitter first class Tony Calabrese, who, like Miller once did, works on the docks at the Brooklyn Naval Shipyard during WORLD WAR II. The characters, including Tony, are based on people whom Miller had met during the nearly two years he worked there on the night shift. Tony is called to a difficult repair job on a ship. Although he feels that he is being suckered into doing the job against his will—a little like his marriage—having completed the dangerous repair, he feels good about having completed the job, wins real respect from the ship's captain and crew, and discovers a new sense of purpose and connection in his life.

The story opens with a lengthy evocation of the BROOKLYN NAVY YARD as the night shift arrives; then it focuses in on Tony, an Italian American in his forties. He has held several jobs as a steamfitter and is good at what he does, but his work history is patchy, and he has not been the most reliable employee. In the past, he has bootlegged and has worked for the unions, but he has never managed to achieve the high life that he craves. He has skill and likes flaunting it, but he is not the kind of man to get ahead as he is generally too ready to take it easy rather than to push himself. Planning his day after he gets out from work, he thinks about seeing his children and his mistress, but his wife is left out of the picture. He is given an easy work assignment and orders his helper, Looey Baldu, to complete the job while he goes to find a coffee and take a nap.

Calling the British sailors "faggots" because they obey rules, and being openly derisive of his fellow workers, Tony's intellect seems to be as limited as his prospects. He meets a similar type, whom they call Hindu, who tells him about nearly being caught by his girlfriend's husband. Both try to go through their shifts doing the least work possible and are faintly despised by Baldu, who has quit his more lucrative meat-delivery job to do this work out of patriotic fervor, having been found unfit for service. Looking for a place to nap, Tony recalls how his traditional Italian family tricked him into marrying a woman he despises and with whom he has refused to sleep for the past 12 years. His resentment of his wife, Margaret, seems to be all that gives his life meaning.

Having been raised in the thrall of a wealthy grandfather living back in Calabria, when Grampa decided to come to America, Tony determined to win him over, get his money, and move to Buffalo with Patty Moran, a disreputable Irish girl from the local saloon with whom he had been sleeping. He met Grampa at the boat, bought him a new suit, and took him on the town. However, his mother had other plans; Tony had been seen talking to a neighborhood Italian girl, Margaret, and his mother was arranging a marriage. She persuaded her father to offer Tony all that he has if Tony will marry Margaret and settle down. The promise of that money leads Tony to get a regular job and settle down, although he still visits Patty rather than sleep with his wife. However, Margaret complains, and in fear that his grandfather will go back on their deal, Tony reluctantly has sex with his wife.

Baldu wakes Tony to say that their boss is looking for him, and he goes to find out why. In contrast to Tony, Baldu loves his wife and feels uneasy when he becomes attracted to anyone else. He is frustrated working with Tony and Hindu, seeing them as lazy and disliking the inefficiency of their workdays. He hopes that this will mean an important job for a change. As Tony, the Hindu, and Baldu are driven to the urgent repair job that they have been called to complete, Baldu sits in the back of the truck, and Tony recalls the rest of his history.

Grampa hounded Tony to stop drinking and whoring and got him to stay home with his now pregnant wife. After Margaret had twins, Tony went to claim his money, only to find out that it was all in Italian lire that had become virtually worthless. His grandfather had only discovered this two weeks previously and apologizes, but Tony feels duped and blames his whole family.

The job is to repair some bent rails that deliver the depth charges on a destroyer that must meet its convoy that morning. The exceeding cold makes the repair close to impossible, but Tony is impressed when ship Captain Stillwater shows him what is needed and talks to him as an equal. He senses that the men on this ship are depending on him, but he urges the captain to wait until the next day to do the repair properly. He is surprised at the captain's reluctance, expects him to be disappointed, and is further intrigued at the captain's continued plea. Recognizing that he is being given a choice to do the job or not, he surprises himself by offering to try. He feels as if this is the first time in his life that he has been given complete freedom to choose for himself. Hindu is stunned, and Baldu is elated.

Tony competently completes the dangerous repair with aid from Baldu, who now grows in his respect, and is given the chance to sit inside the truck on their return, while Hindu is put in the back. Tony basks in the memory of a job well done and the respect he was given by the ship's crew, and the captain in particular. It has allowed him to see himself in a new light and to lose some of the defensive cynicism that has been dragging his spirits down and fixing his existence in a meaningless spiral. As CHRISTOPHER BIGSBY explains, Tony exists as if his life is "on hold," but this experience allows him to see the "missing connections that have left him adrift and undefined." However, where he can go from here is left unsaid and makes this glimpse of his potential finally more ironic than triumphant.

FURTHER READING

Bigsby, Christopher. "Fiction." *Arthur Miller: A Critical Study.* New York: Cambridge University Press, 2005, 444–472.

Focus (1945)

Disappointed by the failure of his first BROADWAY play, *The Man Who Had All the Luck,* Miller decided to try his hand at fiction and penned his first and only full-length novel. Originally titled *Some Shall Not Sleep,* he eventually settled on the more succinct title, *Focus,* since the way in which people perceive others is so essential to his tale. His subject was a topic about which many were strangely silent—the casual racism and ANTI-SEMITISM that he saw around him in U.S. society. He depicts it as backed by mainstream religion, fueled by ignorant, disgruntled people who seek scapegoats for their own frustrations, and permitted by the moral inertia of the masses who want only a quiet life. Miller writes about the novel's intention to illuminate racism in Jane Smiley's *Writers on Writing* (2003).

Miller's novel predates by two years Laura Z. Hobson's best-selling book (made into an award-winning movie by ELIA KAZAN) *Gentleman's Agreement*, about a journalist who poses as a Jew to expose anti-Semitism. Its own sales were respectable, topping 90,000 copies in hardback and winning Miller some serious attention. It was also widely exported and translated, and author Malcolm Bradbury describes it as a pioneering and definitive, though too long undervalued, "postwar Jewish–American novel." It also marked the first substantial income that Miller received from his writing, which gave him the freedom to take time to perfect his next play, *All My Sons*.

SYNOPSIS

Lawrence Newman dreams about a strange carousel. Uneasy about the machinery that operates it, he imagines a giant factory underground but is awakened by a woman's cries of distress. A man is attacking her in front of Newman's house, but no one tries to intervene. Realizing that she is Hispanic and falling back on racist racial stereotyping, Newman convinces himself that she must be at fault and returns to sleep.

Newman owns a house on a suburban street where he lives with his paralyzed mother. As he heads to work, he buys his usual paper from Mr. Finkelstein at the corner store. Waiting for his train, he reads graffiti on the platform, much of it anti-Semitic, and on the train, he plays a game of trying to spot the Jews. His next-door neighbor Fred comes to chat, and Newman feels uncomfortable, seeing himself as superior to this common laborer. He learns that the attacker the night before was another neighbor and that the men put him to bed because he was drunk and chased the woman off. Fred expresses his disgust that Finkelstein's family is moving onto their street; he dislikes all Jews.

He and some friends are organizing a meeting to do something about this, but Newman declines his invitation to join, feeling uneasy with such open bigots.

Newman works as a personnel officer for a huge corporation, where he hires and fires office staff. Sitting in an office with glass walls, an idea that he had proposed, he observes the stenographers under his command. The problem is that his vision has become increasingly poor. His immediate superior, Mr. Gargan, asks to see him, angry that Newman hired a girl who turned out to be Jewish, which is against company policy. He blames Newman's shortsightedness and insists that he get glasses. Newman already has glasses prepared, but has been reluctant to fetch them as he knows that they make him look Jewish. He goes to the optometrist for his new spectacles and takes them home. His mother confirms his opinion, and he falls asleep haunted by the sound of the woman calling for help, the image of the carousel, and a vision of a Jewish cemetery being wrecked.

As work continues, he interviews Gertrude Hart for a position. He is immediately attracted, as she reminds him of a dream woman whom he has created, but thinking her Jewish, he refuses her the job on a fabricated excuse. He wonders if she thinks that he is Jewish and almost wishes that she does as she becomes angry and storms out. This has happened to her before. Called to see Gargan again, we learn that one of the higher management team thinks Newman looks too Jewish with his glasses and wants him moved to a less conspicuous spot. Newman resigns rather than accept the humiliation of demotion after 25 years of service, and he steals his fountain-pen desk set to take home.

At home, he reassesses his position, taking his glasses on and off, uncertain whether he should wear them or not. Going to water his grass with them on, he senses his neighbor Carlson making a connection between Newman and Finkelstein's extended family who is moving in down the street. Going to get his Sunday-morning paper, Newman is caught in a conflict between his neighbors and Finkelstein; he accedes to his neighbors and buys his paper instead from the non-Jewish street seller and is rewarded by feeling that he is one of the group. However, his guilt at snubbing Finkelstein is compounded by his neighbor Mrs. Depaw's evident disgust at his actions.

Tension on the street mounts as Carlson and Fred complain about the "invasion," and Newman tries to decide whose side he is on. Fred joins him on the porch to sound him out and possibly recruit him to the group he is forming, with the backing of local priests, to harass Jews. He is interested in Newman's war experience, but Newman is reluctant to talk about it. Fearful of what Fred will think if he declines, Newman agrees to attend his next meeting. Again he feels included, and this gives him strength and hope to find a new job.

Mr. Stevens at Akron Corporation tells him that he has no openings, and Newman has no luck the rest of the day. That evening, he goes for dinner with an old acquaintance, from whom he learns that Stevens had had an opening in personnel. His enthusiasm dwindles as he realizes that he is now being viewed as a Jew and that it will be far harder to get employed. He goes to see Fred to revive his former sense of comradeship and confide the details of shooting a German during his service in World War I. He also paints his shutters the same shade as the others on the street so as not to stand out, but Fred and Carlson seem to increasingly ignore him, and he worries about ever finding work. One morning, to his horror, he finds that his garbage has been tipped out; it seems they have decided that he is Jewish.

The viewpoint changes to that of Finkelstein. His garbage has also been kicked over, but he is less shocked, being used to such treatment. He wonders if Newman might be Jewish, and when Newman comes to ask him who did it, he tells him that it was the Christian Front and that they probably tipped Newman's garbage by mistake. Finkelstein has also had a threatening note telling him he has five days to get out.

Returning to Newman's point of view, when he asks Fred about the garbage incident, he assures him that it must have been a mistake. Newman has realized that the only way to get work is to try a Jewish company, and when he goes in for an interview, he meets Gertrude. She recalls him and accuses him of turning her down because he had

wrongly assessed her as Jewish. Looking again, he sees his mistake and apologizes. He confides his attraction, and she softens toward him and offers to help him become employed. She confesses that she had thought him Jewish too, and telling him to come back in an hour, he leaves feeling elated.

Newman dislikes his new job, but he has fallen in love with Gertrude. So desperate is he for love, he tends to downplay any potential faults that he notices as they begin to date. Worldlier than he, she tells him that she had once worked in Hollywood and had a screen test but had looked too Jewish to get anywhere. Walking in the park, a girl asks for help finding her friend who has gone off with a sailor. Gertrude eagerly offers aid, but as they seek the missing girl, Newman suddenly feels empowered to kiss Gertrude. She is surprised at his passion and beginning to see a future with him urges him to be more ambitious and also pressures him into proposing. Both Episcopalians, he plans to introduce her to his mother, feeling shaken by the speed of events.

Newman drives Gertrude to the country for their honeymoon, planning to stay at a hotel which he has frequented before. On arrival, they are denied a room because they look too Jewish—this is a restricted hotel. Newman is mortified, but Gertrude is caustically angry. She does not object to the hotel being restricted but to being taken as a Jew. They go to a restaurant and order clams to show the world that they cannot be Jewish, given that observant Jews are not supposed to eat shellfish.

On their return, they learn that Finkelstein fought with the street seller, and his storefront window was broken. Gertrude fearfully advises Newman to befriend Fred. She recognizes one of the men attending a meeting at Fred's house and knows that this means that violence against Jews is about to escalate. She confesses that she has lied to Newman about her Hollywood days. She was actually the live-in girlfriend of a dog manicurist who organized a hate group to try to rid Hollywood of Jews. Worried that they might both end up in jail, she left him and came East. She insists that Newman go to the rally and speak up to make sure that these people do not mark them as Jews. Though fearful of involvement, Newman reluctantly agrees, but again he dreams of the carousel and the Hispanic girl. He wakes to see thugs again turning over his garbage. Unable to confront them, he goes outside when they have gone but then runs back inside when he sees Finkelstein, whose garbage has also been spread, start to walk down the street toward him.

The viewpoint returns to Finkelstein, who is worried about his family. Not an observant Jew, he feels a pull to visit his father's grave. While there, he recalls a Polish story that his father used to tell him. A baron's serfs rebel against oppression and steal his money. He commands a Jewish peddler, Itzik, to go and exchange his wares with the serfs for the money. Itzik senses that the baron's plan is to then attack him and get the money, but he just goes home and waits. His home and family are destroyed, the baron walks in and takes the money, and Itzik goes insane. Finkelstein's father saw the moral as being that there is nothing else that Itzik could have done, but Finkelstein is dissatisfied. Leaving the cemetery, he sees a gravestone toppled and marked with a yellow swastika. He decides not to be like Itzik and accept the role of victim but to fight back. He goes to buy some baseball bats for his store.

As the heat continues, tensions rise. It has been nearly 40 days without rain. Newman attends the rally where the crowd seems hypnotized by the hatred that a priest is spouting. Too reticent to applaud, the mob attacks Newman as a Jew and throws him out. The police outside advise him to go home. He senses that he is being followed, but it is only Finkelstein, concerned for him, having seen what happened. As they walk together, Finkelstein tries to understand Newman, whom he suspects may be with the Christian Front. Asking Newman directly, "Why do you want I shall get out of the neighborhood," Finkelstein forces Newman to face the obvious untruthfulness of the Jewish stereotype by making Newman see him as an individual rather than as a race.

Gertrude is angry with Newman for being beaten. Frustrated, he goes to talk to Fred, telling him to get his group to leave them alone. He asks if Fred thinks he is Jewish, and Fred admits that he has suspected Newman, especially since he married a Jewish girl. Even as he denies that they are Jewish, Newman knows Fred will not believe him, but he insists that he will not move away. Recalling how little help the Hispanic girl had received from his neighbors and realizing that he would be in the same position if attacked, he goes to warn Finkelstein that things are going to get nasty.

He advises Finkelstein to go to the police, but Finkelstein points out that the police will do nothing unless other people complain and support him. Newman suggests that he move, to which Finkelstein asks him if he is a Jew. When he denies this, Finkelstein asks why Newman does not move since they think he is a Jew. He is angry at Newman's lack of support over the Sunday newspaper, pointing out that it is people like Newman who are allowing this to happen because of their passivity. As a patriot, Finkelstein demands that Newman no longer put up with such overt racism.

Newman waits for the attack, as Gertrude suggests they move or try to befriend Fred again. His sympathy for Finkelstein is growing, and he is finding Gertrude's evident racism troubling. After an argument, they head to the cinema, and enter halfway through a movie about Jews being persecuted in Europe. The audience is audibly disturbed because the actors do not fit their negative stereotypical view of Jews, and Gertrude is angry with Newman for taking her to such a movie. He explains that he does not support the Christian Front, but she is uninterested. Content in her racism, she is only out to save herself. As they argue, they sense that they are being followed. An older man and five youths attack as they reach their street, with some splitting off to go to Finkelstein's store. Newman points to send the rest that way but is ignored. He sees Finkelstein face his attackers with two baseball bats, as Gertrude runs off.

Newman joins Finkelstein, who hands over one bat, and although the two sustain some injuries, they drive the youths away. Newman finally recognizes Finkelstein's humanity, helps him into his store, and then is invited into his home. It strikes him how normal it is. Finkelstein has sent his family to relatives for safety. Newman feels a sudden calm, as if the tension he has been under has passed. No longer torn or confused, he embraces his own humanity, just as he embraced that of Finkelstein.

On leaving Finkelstein, Newman realizes that no police have been called and that Gertrude has done nothing to help. Learning that she instead went to see Fred against his express wishes, he is distraught at her abandonment. As Fred comes out with her to talk, he dismisses them both and walks away, a changed man. He feels disgust in the way that he had hoped to send the attackers toward Finkelstein and is now ready to stand up for himself. He, too, now refuses to be a victim. He goes to the police station and reports the attack, and when the desk sergeant assumes that he is Jewish, he accepts the label.

CRITICAL COMMENTARY

Miller's story of anti-Semitism on the home front must have been intentionally combative. It highlights a trenchant fascism at home, even brandishing a swastika, while U.S. troops were still fighting the fight against fascism abroad. Given that Miller has always been a pacifist, this questioning of the motives behind WORLD WAR II is unsurprising. He calls to question the spurious moral superiority of a culture that sees itself as above the enemy by revealing its own prejudice, moral inertia, and petty violence.

Newman's recurring dream of the carousel and its underground machinery becomes a metaphor for the underground way in which prejudice seems to be manufactured in America—with negative stereotyping and outright lies. A "murderous monster" is being created that Finkelstein, quite rightly, realizes will ultimately destroy the whole country if it is not stopped. "How many times must it happen," he asks Newman, "How many wars we got to fight in this world before you will understand what they are doing to you?" Finkelstein knows that it is not the Freds and Gertrudes and their like that need to change but the morally deficient bystanders who are in the majority and are being sullied by their acceptance of a bigotry that they know is morally wrong. Once they speak out against such racism, it can be brought to a stop, just as Finkelstein's harassment could be halted if just a couple of the other men from the street would go and complain to the police, as Newman does at the close.

Finkelstein's family story about Itzik the peddler is one of violence and death, in which the victim is used by the baron to reclaim his money from a peasantry he dare not push too far; the Jewish man makes an easy scapegoat. Playing by the rules of the enemy makes a person complicit in his or her own victimization, and Finkelstein refuses to be intimidated any longer. "I don't know how to fight them but I will fight them." The United States of the 1940s was uneasy, its people waiting for the end of a war into which they had not expected to be drawn and fearing another depression once the troops came home. They are ready to hit out at any scapegoat who is offered, especially when such offerings are given a sense of credibility by the priesthood. Newman is one of them, until Finkelstein forces him to recognize him as a person and question his racist beliefs.

It is Newman's moral inertia that most troubles him, indicated by his recurring worry about the Hispanic woman whom he ignored. Newman once killed a man in the war, and even the hurt he did to this faceless enemy has continued to trouble him for years; once Finkelstein becomes fully human to him, it would be impossible for Newman ever to hurt him. However, it takes a long time for this to occur as Newman's prejudices have run deep and unchallenged for many years; they become a hard habit to break. Although the story is told mostly from Newman's point of view as he agonizes over what to believe, Miller switches perspective occasionally to Finkelstein to adjust and tighten our focus on characters and events.

The concept of focusing underscores Miller's story on many levels as he focuses the reader's attention on a dark and controversial aspect of U.S. culture. Newman's vision changes focus once he puts on his new glasses, a catalyst for change in his life. It also alters at other points in the novel once they are set in motion by this initial catalyst. Gertrude constantly changes in his and our vision (which is largely dependent on his)—at first, he thinks she is Jewish, then an attractive Gentile, and finally an unpleasant and narrow-minded bigot. Her reaction at the hotel exposes the widening difference between them; she sees nothing wrong in restricting clientele but just wants them to know she is not Jewish, while he is beginning to view such restrictive treatment as wrong. Despite the violence that is directed at Finkelstein and Newman, Miller's ultimate message is one of hope. Both survive by joining forces, and Lawrence has the possibility of becoming a new man as his name has suggested all along by taking the social action that Finkelstein has recommended to save the United States from a bigoted minority.

INITIAL REVIEWS

For a first novel by a relative unknown, *Focus* garnered fairly respectable reviews. Alfred Butterfield, reviewing it for the *New York Times*, praised it as a "strong, sincere book bursting with indignation and holding the reader's attention" but felt that it ultimately lacked "substantial meaning." Although Saul Bellow found it "implausible" and the *New Yorker* complained about its predictability, Leo Kennedy applauded its "indictment of bigotry and social irresponsibility" and felt that the book was "consummately skillful." Iris Barry called it "a first-rate horror story, cleverly as well as passionately devised," and reviewers from both *Saturday Review of Literature* and *Booklist* responded positively. The general consensus was that this was an eloquent and significant work, notable for its forthright treatment of a topic that few writers had faced.

SCHOLARSHIP

There has been little study of this book in journals aside from Lob Ladislaus's comparison of it to Max Frisch's *Andorra* and David Mesher's more detailed exploration. Mesher sees the book as a landmark U.S. novel, possibly the first to address the issue of the Holocaust, as it offers an "accurate contemporary expression of the American Jew's reaction to the destruction of European Jewry." Recent studies of Miller that go beyond his dramatic oeuvre include increasingly lengthy discussions of the novel, suggesting that its importance is becoming more widely recognized. Bradbury offers an insightful overview, and CHRISTOPHER BIGSBY, describing its writing as an "act of courage" given the racially charged atmosphere in the United States at the time of its publication, offers welcome attention to the role of Finkelstein. Arvind Singh Adhikari discusses the book's message of universal brotherhood in his contribution to *Arthur Miller: Twentieth Century Legend*.

CHARACTERS

Finkelstein Miller's choice for a representative of the Jewish people in the story is the man who runs the corner store, Finkelstein. A secular figure, he is a Jew in name only, but it is an identity that he embraces. Familiar with racism, he is nonetheless not ready to give in to its pressure. When he receives a threatening notice to leave, he sends his family to relatives for safety and buys himself some baseball bats with which to defend himself. He refuses to accept his father's story of Itzik as suggesting that nothing can be done. He declares his intention to fight by initially confronting the street seller who is trying to take his business and by coming out to meet his attackers at the end rather than cowering in his house and allowing them to run roughshod over him. He recognizes in Newman a man of intelligence, and he feels betrayed when Newman acts no better than a man of ignorance like Fred. It is this disdain that pressures Newman to reassess his own position and to discover a common humanity with his Jewish neighbor.

Fred Fred lives next door to Newman and is a laborer at the same firm that employs Newman. While Newman works at a respectable firm, Fred accepts him as an equal, even while Newman secretly believes himself to be superior, but once Newman buys his new glasses and loses his job, the doubts increase to the point where Fred does not even believe Newman's point-blank denial that he is a Jew. Almost ironic, given that his own prejudices against most ethnic groups are based on false stereotypes, Fred himself is a stereotype of an ignorant, violent working-class man with guns in the house and a love of hunting. More a follower than a leader of men, he helps organize a local hate group, but it is not he who commits the violence that we witness; Fred even claims ignorance when Newman is attacked. The implication that he might be able to control what happens becomes increasingly doubtful. Once indiscriminate hatred is unleashed, it tends toward mob violence rather than an organized attack, and wheels are set in motion that will be hard to stop.

Newman, Gertrude (Hart) Gertrude initially asks for a job at Newman's old firm, and he turns her down, thinking that she is Jewish. Later, she is able to get him a job at the Jewish firm that eventually employs them both. Recognizing Newman's naivete, she recreates herself somewhat to attract him, being desperate for a husband so that she can quit working and lead an easier life. She later confesses to the lies that she has told about her time in Hollywood—she never sang or had a screen test but worked as a typist; the actor who she supposedly dated turned out to be a bigoted dog manicurist—and it is clear that she is an experienced deceiver. It is really Gertrude who proposes and pushes for marriage, leaving Newman uncertain as to how all this came about. Once wed, she continually pressures him to make more money, and there is a strong suspicion that she sees him as little more than a meal ticket. Gertrude longs for the high life, as indicated by the expensive clothes that she orders to try on and then returns. When Newman is faced with a beating, she runs away to Fred rather than help or even call the police. Her own safety takes priority over that of anyone else.

Gertrude's admiration for Father Crichton, who represents Father Coughlin, the radio evangelist and notorious anti-Semite priest, tells us early on that she is actually more racist than Newman and has no qualms about scapegoating Jews. It is ironic that everyone who meets her assumes that she is Jewish, but this perennial discrimination has apparently soured her rather than made her more sympathetic or compassionate; she actively despises every minority group. Unlike Newman, who seems scared of his own shadow, she is willing to be involved, as when she helps the girl in the park to find her friend or answers back the hotel man who refuses them a room on their honeymoon. But this willingness is extended only to her own social group, and often only to advance herself, as with her easy involvement in the Hollywood hate group and her readiness to join Fred's.

Wilier than her husband, Gertrude senses at once that they need to befriend Fred and to make it clear to their neighbors that they are equally as racist if they are to avoid a beating. She calls her husband "Lully" as if to lull the Jewish sounding "Lawrence" into something less threatening. We initially feel sympathy for her when Newman callously turns her down for the job even while objectifying her body. This continues as she rises above this to find him work rather than try for revenge, but as her small-minded racism becomes increasingly evident, she becomes little better than Fred, Newman's bigoted neighbor. It is not surprising that it is with Fred that we last see her as Newman walks off in disgust at her lack of support.

Newman, Lawrence A veteran of World War I, where he killed a German, Newman is pleased to have been able to survive the GREAT DEPRESSION in his middle-management role at the corporation. Proud to own his home, he differentiates himself from his neighbors, over whom he feels morally superior, by painting his shutters a different shade of green. However, when he senses their growing suspicions over his ethnicity, he quickly toes the line and paints them to match the neighboring houses. His efforts to fit in, however, come too late. A lifetime of staying aloof has damaged his authenticity with these men, and they turn a blind eye as his garbage is overthrown and he is beaten on the street.

Newman's potential for rebellion is indicated early on in details such as the painting of his shutters a different shade, although he is not sufficiently brave to choose another color. Newman is a man who despite his surface temerity is bored with his routine and is in search of adventure. He is reminiscent of T. S. Eliot's Prufrock, fearful of taking the plunge and trapped by his own indecision. He is overly fastidious in all he does, too fearful to be untidy; he craves excitement but can only experience it vicariously as he is too fearful to commit to any tangible action. As he realizes when Gertrude first insists that he attend Fred's rally, Newman has been perfectly comfortable hating Jews so long as he never actually had to do anything about it. His reluctance is less an awareness of his ignorant racist outlook at this point but more a product of a dislike of being involved in group endeavors. An inveterate snob, he is also cripplingly self-conscious and hates to look foolish. In a sense, he has withdrawn from life with all of its messiness, which is how he justifies his inaction at the start as the woman vainly calls for aid. His racist reactions and expectations of the Hispanic woman's lifestyle increase in irony as he falls victim to the same limited thinking in the minds of his neighbors.

Newman lives with his paralyzed mother, her physical paralysis mimicking his moral one, and longs for a woman of his own. His recurring nightmare of the factory beneath the carousel indicates his awareness of the destructiveness of prejudice, but it is an awareness deeply buried in his subconscious. He selects Gertrude because she best fits the woman of his secret dreams, but as ever, any decision based on appearance alone is bound to backfire. He loves the way Gertrude looks from the start, but even then is put off by her BROOKLYN accent that sullies his idea of the perfect woman. As their relationship develops, he realizes that there is something far more ugly about Gertrude than her accent, and that is her self-concern and open bigotry. By the end of the book their relationship seems to have little future.

Newman, like his neighbors until the book's end when his focus has been altered, tends to stereotype others by their appearance alone. It is partly his desire for order that makes him categorize everyone he meets, to keep them safely in their place. He makes a game out of it—trying to spot the Jew on the train going to work—a skill on which his livelihood depends as he is a personnel officer at a firm that will not hire Jews, and he must weed out any candidates trying to hide this detail. He judges solely on appearance, as others will begin to judge him. It is this realization that brings home to Newman the injustice with which he has treated others. He also is made to see the falseness of the stereotypes that he had unquestioningly accepted as he and Finkelstein become friends and he has the opportunity to see inside Finkelstein's home. It is far easier to believe the stereotype in the general, but it collapses when he is faced with an individual. By the close, he has found an inner calm in his recognition of the perversity of racism, and no longer feeling conflicted, he can allow himself to be seen as a Jew in solidarity with a neighbor whom he knows deserves better.

MOVIE AND TELEVISION ADAPTATIONS

Focus has twice been made into a movie, but Miller wrote neither of the screenplays. A 1962 television presentation starring James Whitemore came out to little fanfare, but the 2001 movie version, produced by Michael Bloomberg and ROBERT MILLER, directed by Neal Slavin, and starring William H. Macy and Laura Dern, was a little better received. *Vanity Fair* called it "a rare cinematic jewel" and Stephen Holden a "grim political what-if." Holden enjoyed its surreal style and admitted that "despite its didacticism" it "builds up a thunderhead of suspense," but he felt let down by the ending, which was "timid and inadequate." Jay Carr was also put off by its "didactic and placard-like" tone, and despite being "earnestly and handsomely crafted," felt that the movie seemed "embalmed in its own time" and too dated for a 21st-century audience.

Although Kendrew Lascelles's 2001 screenplay sticks fairly faithfully to the original novel, the character of Gertrude is altered to become a lot more sympathetic. She complains less than in the book, is less pushy, and is more supportive of her husband throughout. She sticks beside him when he is attacked by the Union Crusaders (as Fred's group is renamed)—only running when he orders her to go—and again at the close. When he goes to the police station to report the beating, she joins him, and they allow the policeman to believe that they are both Jewish. In an effort to emphasize Newman's paralyzing inaction, the film makes more of the Hispanic woman who is beaten at the start. Police detectives come asking if anyone saw anything, Finkelstein is involved in trying to help identify her, and we learn that she is in a coma and later dies. This gives Newman a greater hold over Fred, who helped cover up the original attack, now a homicide. Much, also, is made of a billboard across from Finkelstein's corner store that depicts a happy family in a car and reads with bitter irony, "There's no way like the American Way."

FURTHER READING

Adhikari, Arvind Singh. "Arthur Miller's *Focus* on Racial Prejudice through Mistaken Identity." In *Arthur Miller: Twentieth Century Legend*, edited by Syed Mashkoor Ali, 8–20. (Jaipur, India: Surabhi, 2006).

Barry, Iris. "Look through This Glass." *New York Herald Tribune Weekly Book Review,* November 18, 1945, 4.

Bellow, Saul. "Brothers' Keepers." *New Republic,* January 7, 1946, 29.

Bigsby, Christopher. *"Focus." Arthur Miller: A Critical Study.* New York: Cambridge University Press, 2005, 67–77.

Bradbury, Malcolm. "Arthur Miller's Fiction." In *The Cambridge Companion to Arthur Miller,* edited by Christopher Bigsby, 211–229. (Cambridge, England: Cambridge University Press, 1997).

Butterfield, Alfred. *"Focus." New York Times Book Review,* November 18, 1945, sec. 7, p. 15.

Carr, Jay. *"Focus* Not Sharp Enough for this Era." *Boston Globe,* November 9, 2001, E4.

"Focus." New Yorker, November 3, 1945, 102.

Holden, Stephen. "Surreal Fable Considers the Realities of Prejudice." *New York Times,* October 19, 2001, E16.

Kennedy, Leo. *"Focus." Chicago Sun Book Week,* November 11, 1945, 28.

Lob, Ladislaus. "'Insanity in the Darkness': Anti-Semitic Stereotypes and Jewish Identity in Max Frisch's *Andorra* and Arthur Miller's *Focus." Modern Language Review* 92, no. 3 (July 1997): 545–558.

Mesher, David R. "Arthur Miller's *Focus:* The First American Novel of the Holocaust?" *Judaism* 29, no. 4 (1980): 469–479.

Miller, Arthur. "Shattering the Silence, Illuminating the Hatred." In *Writers on Writing,* edited by Jane Smiley, 163–167. (New York: Holt, 2003).

"Get It Right. Privatize Executions" (1992)

Miller published this provocatively titled, tongue-in-cheek op-ed piece in the *New York Times* in May 1992 as a goad against those who support the death penalty. Another satire in Swiftian vein, like his 1954 "Modest Proposal," here Miller suggests that it would make sense to carry out the execution of convicted criminals in large sporting arenas, like Shea Stadium, and charge for admission. The funds raised would help pay for the prison system, and a percentage could go to the family of the condemned or a trust fund for prisoner rehabilitation.

Electric-chair executions would be presented as theatrical events, with singing, fanfares, and speeches. This concept prefigures Miller's 2002 play *Resurrection Blues,* in which an island dictator plans to televise the execution of a troublesome local rebel to raise capital for the nation. Miller's real agenda comes through at the close as he proffers a hope that in presenting executions in this fashion, people will "grow tired of the spectacle" and become "willing to consider the fact that in executing prisoners we merely add to the number of untimely dead without diminishing the number of murders committed."

"Glimpse at a Jockey" (1962)

The short story "Glimpse at a Jockey" was initially published in 1962 in *Story* and reprinted in *The Noble Savage* the following year. It was then included in Miller's 1967 collection *I Don't Need You Any More* and repeated in *The Misfits and Other Stories* (1987). On the surface, it is a three-page monologue of a New York jockey chatting to a stranger in a bar, expressing his distaste of current horse-racing with all the pressure to win and relating how he found his long lost father and bought him a lawnmower. Reminiscent of EUGENE O'NEILL's *Hughie* (1958), the one-sided conversation of the title character is the revelation of an apparently successful past but an obviously flawed present. The jockey's speech obliquely reveals the undercurrents of his life that have brought him to this "saloon," far from family and home, dissatisfied and lost.

The jockey sits in a high-class saloon in New York City, chatting to someone. Just like *After the Fall,* it is unclear who the listener might be, barman or customer, friend or foe, but from the jockey's commentary about the "loyalty of men" and how he feels more comfortable with males, we should assume that it is a man. We can also assume from this that he has had trouble with women in his past, despite his supposed 18 happy years of marriage. He has money to be drinking in such a place and has been successful in his trade, so his declarations of happiness should ring true, but there is a false note in both his repetition of the fact and in his repeated declaration "I love them all." His vocal contentment is undercut by the increasingly evident dissatisfaction with life, both personal and professional, which lies behind his stories. His voluble drunken state has loosened his tongue, and he speaks without reservation. Although he talks to another person, the other person never responds, and his solitary voice suggests the real reason for his speech: To uncover for himself who he is.

Unnamed, which suggests from the start a loss of identity that becomes more and more evident as he continues to speak, the jockey begins by relating the ups and downs of the jockey business in which he works. He admires riding skill but clearly feels that this comes second place in a field where winning has become all-important. This drive to win has destroyed much of his enjoyment of the sport. He has been treated something akin to a movie star when on top of his game, but he explains how when left in a hospital for three months after a bad fall, all the followers left, and only two of his close male friends continued to visit. From this, he asserts that men are more loyal, but the claim seems spurious given the other evidence that he furnishes. In his opening paragraph, he describes a man cheating on his wife, as indeed he plans to do by the tale's close, and his story will soon turn to relating how his father abandoned him when he was one year old. He also has not been loyal to the profession that he admires by selling out for the big wins.

Further evidence of his dissatisfaction comes when he tells how he recently went to see a psychiatrist. The therapy was a failure as the man was more interested in getting racing tips than helping, but the jockey never says why he sought psychiatric help in the first place. He says that he loves his wife and kids but then undercuts the declaration by saying "but you draw a line somewhere, someplace," implying that his love has limits. The burning question is why? Why is this man unable to fully commit? He obviously has deeper issues than those to which he admits. Declaring that he is ready to die, one wonders if this betokens a buried suicidal depression rather than the feeling of having achieved all that he needs, as he suggests on the surface.

His view of the world is very negative, and he himself not a pleasant man, with his open racism and blatant philandering. When he starts to talk about going to see the father who had walked out on his family, we begin to approach the root of the problem—like Willy Loman, not knowing his father has hurt this man's sense of who he is. The father had seen him on television and written to see if this was his son. The jockey decided to go to meet the father he had never known. He is disappointed to find a regular guy, a house painter by trade, with whom he has nothing in common; the man does not even share his racist outlook. He is desperate for a connection to center himself: "I was ready to lay down my life for him." However, he cannot find any point at which to start; his father has no real interest in his son other than a potential source of financial aid. He buys his father a large lawnmower, the motor of which drowns out any future chance of conversation between them.

He ends by suggesting to his listener that they should pick up two women who have been looking their way, further evidence of his own lack of marital loyalty. The women are not even attractive, but he does not want to be alone. As CHRISTOPHER BIGSBY surmises, "The man who tries so hard to conceal himself, in fact slowly reveals the drama of his life which has been the slow loss of meaning, the sacrifice of value to ambition, of love to obsession." Also pointing out that in his torrent of speech, the jockey never allows his speaker any response, Bigsby allows for the harsh reality that in his quest for truth, this jockey has been less than honest: "So long as he sings his tainted aria there is no opportunity for his listener to question, reproach, despise, engage." The jockey ends as he began, still fundamentally alone, the fate of all who refuse full commitment.

FURTHER READING

Bigsby, Christopher. "Fiction." *Arthur Miller: A Critical Study*. New York: Cambridge University Press, 2005: 444–472.

The Golden Years (1939–1941)

Early titles had been *Children of the Sun* and *Montezuma,* but Miller finally settled on *The Golden Years* for this historical drama about the overthrow of the Aztecs by conquistadors, written but unproduced during his time with the FEDERAL THEATER PROJECT. With a cast that includes 25 speaking parts and possible extras, it was not something that regular theaters would produce. The resources of the Federal Theater, however, had made a production seem possible, but sadly they were closed down before this was done. Miller subsequently offered it to the GROUP THEATER and the THEATRE GUILD, but neither seemed interested. Partly inspired by Archibald MacLeish's 1937 radio verse drama *The Fall of the City,* about Cortés and his conquests, which had been rebroadcast in 1939, *The Golden Years* marks an obvious swing in Miller's writing from the blatant politics and realism of his student works to an attempt to grasp something more epic. Parts of the manuscript are in verse, and much of the speech was pointedly poetic to underscore the rituals encompassing both protagonists; its 16th-century Mexican setting was one that Miller had needed to research, distanced as it was from his personal life.

While researching Miller's papers at HARRY RANSOM RESEARCH CENTER, CHRISTOPHER BIGSBY came across the manuscript and feeling the play worthy of attention took it to the BBC for production as a radio drama. Miller did a little tidying up, mostly deleting what he described to Bigsby as "some purple passages," and the play was finally broadcast in GREAT BRITAIN in 1987 to a positive response. Although less of a success, it was also produced there for television on Channel Four shortly afterward. It has never been produced onstage, for which it was originally written.

SYNOPSIS

Act One

The play begins in the palace of Montezuma in Tenochtitlán, the capital of the Aztec empire, one autumn night in 1519. Aztec emperor Montezuma sits on a large throne surrounded by his council of generals—his young warrior nephew, Guatemotzin, and two older men, Cuitlahua (Montezuma's brother) and Cagama. Montezuma is concerned that his star "seems bleeding," and they assess the implications of this. While Guatemotzin is keen for battle, the others, bowing to the wishes of their emperor, favor waiting while the signs are properly read. The astronomer's calculations indicate doom and destruction as the moon eclipses. They prepare a human sacrifice to divert harm. The Spaniards have been attacking and looting, but Montezuma is torn between two responses: to declare war or to accept the invaders as gods like himself.

A young boy is to be willingly burned alive to take a message to the gods to pacify them. A judge who has been condemned to death for taking a bribe is also eager to die, which intrigues Montezuma. On being asked, the judge explains that he sees Montezuma's fall as inevitable because he has stretched his resources too far and impoverished his people through constant war. Agreeing that his "empire is cracking" despite his councilors claiming otherwise, Montezuma seeks advice as to how to prevent this. He rejects Guatemotzin's desire for war but knows of no other way to rule than by force. The judge suggests that Montezuma kill himself and die at the height of his power rather than stay to watch the dissolution of the empire that he has created.

The Spaniards only number 400, and the Aztecs can field 80,000 once they decide to attack, but Montezuma wants to wait. He recalls the Aztec legend of the god Quetzalcoatl. Reminiscent of Jesus, Quetzalcoatl was a white god after whose disappearance, murder and war filled the world but who had promised to return and herald "golden years" of peace and prosperity. Montezuma suspects that Cortez may be Quetzalcoatl and will not strike until he knows for sure. Tecuichpo, Montezuma's daughter, is pleased that her father sends the judge to his death for she had not liked his predictions, although she agrees with her father that the Spaniards should be welcomed. She has dreamed of a white swan dying in her hands, and Montezuma looks for further meaning in this, while Guatemotzin continues to insist that the Spaniards are simply men who need to be fought.

A courier brings Cortez's helmet that has been stolen from the Spanish camp so that Montezuma may compare it against the one on the statue of Quetzalcoatl. If it differs, he will attack, but if the same he will accept Cortez as a god. As the eclipse begins, they start to burn the boy, and Montezuma calls to the heavens to return their light. A wind blows out the sacrificial fire, everyone panics, and Montezuma commands the wind to stop blowing. Before they can make the sacrifice, the light returns, offering a serious blow to their belief system, setting them further on edge and in doubt.

Meeting Cortez and his men, we swiftly learn that they are not gods but men pursuing personal wealth and glory. The Spaniards are in disarray, with Cortez injured and his men fighting among themselves. He takes charge, reorganizing them. Marina, a native who allowed Cortez to baptize her in the hope of escaping the constant fighting of her homeland, has been helping him with her knowledge of the land. Her hope is to bring the emperor and his people to Christ and to put an end to war. Cortez agrees that this is his aim also, though he seems to be focused on a more tangible conquest—goading his men into staying with promises of wealth. Marina is upset at the carnage, but when she suggests that they leave, Cortez refuses. He tricks Xicotenga, one of Montezuma's rivals, into believing him a god and supporting him against Montezuma. Cortez ends the scene declaring his love to Marina—even as she fears that he loves gold more than god—and promising her an opulent life beside him as his queen.

Montezuma's high priest addresses the statues of Quetzalcoatl, the god of peace, and Huitzilpochtli, the god of war, hoping that one or the other might spur the emperor to fight the invading Spaniards. Montezuma compares the helmets and finds them identical. He publicly decides to welcome Cortez and his men into his empire as gods, although in private he remains conflicted with doubt. Despite their evident strength as warriors, he has heard that Spaniards bleed and die, neither of which should be possible for gods.

Act Two

Montezuma dresses in splendor to welcome the Spaniards. Guatemotzin still wants to attack, especially since Xicotenga's men are with them, but Montezuma insists that he hold back. The leaders exchange gifts, and Cortez flatters the Aztec emperor. When Montezuma asks him why he has come, he claims to be bringing Christianity. Offering the Spaniards his old palace, Montezuma gives them free rein of the city, although he asks that Xicotenga's men be sent outside, to which Cortez agrees. After giving Montezuma a crucifix, Cortez moves to embrace him. A fight nearly ensues over Montezuma's startled response on being touched, and the Spaniards react violently to this. Tecuichpo is more suspicious than her father of their motives, although Cortez quickly smoothes things over.

Two weeks later, the generals are concerned by the aggressive manner of Cortez, but Montezuma remains patient, ensuring his followers that the Spaniards will leave. Tecuichpo loves Guatemotzin and talks to Cortez's second-in-command, Pedro Alvarado, to elicit information. He flirts and tries to kiss her until Cortez reins him in, reminding him that he needs to be mapping the territory. Despite Father Olmedo's advice to go slower, Cortez is impatient that Montezuma is not yet converted, feeling that this would better ensure their safety. His aggression worries Marina, who fears that he might hurt the emperor. Cortez distracts Montezuma, but Guatemotzin catches Alvarado drawing military maps. When Montezuma again asks what Cortez wants, he is assured that it is only to bring him to Christ, but when news arrives that another Spanish force has landed to arrest Cortez for treason, Montezuma warns Cortez to leave or die. However, to his generals' dismay, he orders no arms to be drawn against the Spaniards. Aware that he is behaving unreasonably, Montezuma cannot stop himself and sobs to Tecuichpo as the curtain falls.

Act Three

Marina warns Cortez that Montezuma's generals have decided to rebel and attack the Spaniards, so he must leave at once. To Marina's great concern, Cortez plans to take Montezuma captive to ensure that he can return to the city after he leaves to quell the new Spanish force. He shows his men the royal tomb full of precious artifacts which he plans to loot to ensure his soldiers' loyalty. Marina is horrified at such sacrilege and threatens to tell the emperor, but Cortez slaps her into submission.

Montezuma is angry to hear that Cuitlahua has given an order to attack the Spanish. One commander, Quauhopoca, has brought him the head of a Spaniard in a box, but unlike old times, Montezuma is reluctant to look. Trusting Cortez's word that he will leave, he insists that the Spanish soldiers entering the palace are there to "say farewell" and orders his generals arrested for treason. Tecuichpo comes to their defense, berates her father for the way that he privileges the abusive Spaniards, and runs away. Meeting Montezuma, Cortez complains that he has turned against him, and Montezuma insists that he has not, announcing his intent to arrest the rebellious generals. Cortez takes Montezuma captive, threatening to destroy his city if he does not come quietly, and leads him away in shackles.

Cortez defeats the rival Spanish force, but in his absence, Alvarado riles the Aztecs into attacking by publicly burning Quauhopoca and killing a group of nobles during a religious celebration. Under siege, the Spaniards are melting the taken gold into ingots before making their escape. Montezuma is disgusted at what they are doing to his artifacts. He knows now that they are not gods and that he has been a fool. Cortez demands that Montezuma tell the people to let them leave or he will destroy the city; the emperor agrees, hoping to stop further bloodshed. He speaks to his people, apologizing for his poor judgment, but they see him as dishonorable and fire arrows at him. One hits its mark, and he falls. Sending Tecuichpo to safety with Guatemotzin, he refuses Father Olmedo's offer of baptism and declares that the Christian god is more bloodthirsty than his own. He curses the Spanish and warns Cortez that his fate will be as his, "the destiny of all oppression." Cortez leaves to fight his way out as Marina remains, concerned for the emperor. Forgiving his people for his death, Montezuma declares that he has been destroyed by his effort to restore them to a golden age of prosperity and peace. As the prophecy of Quetzalcoatl is repeated, we hear the cannon boom, and the play ends.

CRITICAL COMMENTARY

Subtitled *A New World Tragedy*, the play is an exploration of the hearts and minds of two men: Cortez as he plunders, and Montezuma as he dithers and allows his kingdom to be decimated. Montezuma appears caught in a Hamletlike quest for meaning that stifles him into a similar inaction. Highly superstitious, a series of unusual natural occurrences have convinced him that a major upset is about to occur, but he is uncertain as to what; his uncertainty paralyzes him into doing nothing. Although set in 16th-century Mexico, the story clearly reflects Miller's concerns in the 1930s with U.S. and European inactivity in the face of Hitler. Just as Montezuma seems mesmerized by the approach of Cortez, who callously takes over and destroys everything in his wake, so Miller saw Europe apparently paralyzed in the face of Hitler and his fascist threat. Like Hitler, Cortez pursues his ambition without doubt or conscience, and Montezuma simply cannot summon the will to stop him. Miller hoped that Europe might decide otherwise.

The Aztec world is one that is full of signs and portents, and Montezuma becomes lost in his attempts to read accurately what these mean. He truly believes that he is a god, as when he commands the wind to stop blowing out the sacrificial fire, but when the eclipse ends before the sacrifice has been made, it confounds that belief and leads him into debilitating confusion. On one level, the Spaniards are just as ruthless as he, conquering as violently and confidently using fear as a weapon. Since he considers himself a god whom other mortals may not even touch, his logic makes him think that this may mark the Spaniards as equal and gods as he is. He hopes that they have come to apotheosize him into an even greater godhead and to bring his kingdom into a golden era of plenty. Such an outcome would affirm for him his own position as god and eradicate his doubt.

One might think that the opportunity of becoming a god might interest Cortez, but he is solely interested in the gold and pretends to godhead only to gain more. Cortez takes full advantage of Montezuma's hesitancy to maneuver into a position of power. Less a leader than a despot, Cortez's concern does not stretch beyond his own needs, which is why he will beat Marina when she does not comply and leave her behind without compunction. His desire to convert Montezuma comes not from devotion but from a need to create an ally to protect him against the masses whom he plans to pillage. His lack of faith in anything but wealth is indicated by the way he melts down into bare ingots the artifacts that he has looted from the royal tomb, destroying both their historical and spiritual significance. His very presence in the New World indicates his disregard of anyone else's authority—he was expressly told by the governor of Cuba not to go inland, and he has pressed his followers into treason with promises of great wealth. He has baptized Marina and used her knowledge of the territory and the people to advance, telling her that he is coming to bring Christianity to the natives, but all he has brought is death and destruction. While Cortez hides his truer motives behind masks of civility and indignant posturing, his second in command, Pedro Alvarado, is more openly the opportunist, raping native girls and massacring a host of peaceful Aztec nobles so as to strip them of their trinkets.

Next to the barbaric Spaniards who have supposedly come to civilize the heathen, Montezuma appears to be far more decent and high minded. He seriously wants to be a god and thinks that by bringing his people into an era of peace and prosperity, he can become the greatest god of all. By this blind ambition, he fools himself into losing everything by trusting in Cortez who, he had convinced himself, could help in this and thus, almost tragically, becomes the agent of his own downfall. Yet, Miller ultimately depicts Montezuma's downfall at the hands of his own people as less than tragic, and more the inevitable defeat of a tyrant, for Montezuma's hopes for the future have never been more than words, and his legacy is one of violence and inequity. His people are fearful because Montezuma wished to keep them that way, to make them easier to dominate and for them to accept his rule.

The difference between Montezuma and Cortez is emphasized by their speech—as Montezuma's poetry is in direct contrast to Montezuma's blunt prose—but this is just a surface indication of far deeper divisions that cannot allow these two men to comfortably coexist. Montezuma's world is founded on a cosmology that views him as a god, and it is an artistic society that is full of beauty, despite its underlying flaws. Cortez is a man who is full of ambition and desire, and his pragmatism leads him to view Montezuma's world purely in financial terms. He has no compunction over destroying such a world in his pursuit of his personal agenda—to become wealthy and powerful. Yet, we mourn with difficulty Montezuma's downfall, since his was a society, for all of its surface attraction, that was based on aggression and blood sacrifice. Rife with poverty and injustice, as indicated by the reports we hear of conditions outside the palace and the corrupt judge, this is a kingdom that is about to implode under the weight of its own inequalities. In the same way, we might find it difficult to regret the destruction of certain elements of the older aristocratic and anti-Semitic European nations during WORLD WAR II.

FIRST PERFORMANCE

The Golden Years first aired on BBC Radio 3 in Great Britain on November 6, 1987, and was later adapted for television. The radio broadcast featured the following lead actors:

Montezuma: Ronald Pickup
Guatemotzin: Kim Wall
Cuitlahua: John Samson
Cagama: Brian Hewlett
Tecuichpo: Victoria Carling
Quauhopoca and Judge: Norman Jones
Hernando Cortez: John Shrapnel
Donna Marina: Hannah Gordon
Pedro de Alvarado: John Hollis
Fr. Olmedo: Norman Bird

Directed by Martin Jenkins
Music by Christos Pittas

INITIAL REVIEWS

Reviews of the radio broadcast were respectful, with Peter Davalle insisting that the play contained "flashes of psychological insight (and certainly of poetry) that are worthy to stand alongside anything in later Miller." He even compared it favorably to Peter Shaffer's *The Royal Hunt of the Sun* (1964), a similar tale of Spanish conquistadors in South

America. Alan Ryan found it too "propagandistic" but "interesting on several levels," and B.A. Young described it as "a baroque piece, with proper attention given to excitement and tension." David Wade complimented Miller's ability to emphasize the dramatic over the merely historical. Of the subsequent television adaptation, with its emphasis on dialogue over action, Bigsby suggests that it translated poorly to that medium and "suffered from its literalism," seeming "somewhat static and protracted."

FURTHER READING

Bigsby, Christopher. "The Golden Years, The Half-Bridge, Boro Hall Nocturne." *Arthur Miller: A Critical Study.* Cambridge: Cambridge University Press, 2005, 27–39.

Davalle, Peter. "Radio Choice." *The Times,* November 6, 1987, 23.

Ryan, Alan. "The Golden Years." *Sunday Telegraph,* November 8, 1987, 18.

Wade, David. "Red Square vox pop." *The Times,* November 9, 1987, 20.

Young, B.A. "The Golden Years." *Financial Times,* November 7, 1987, n.p.

Grandpa and the Statue (1945)

Broadcast by Du Pont as part of the *Cavalcade of America* series on March 26, 1945, with Charles Laughton playing the Grandpa, Miller's aim in the radio drama *Grandpa and the Statue* was to offer a new approach to shows about the Statue of Liberty. Rather than simply celebrating its symbolism, he wanted to address its connection to immigrants to the United States and the importance of Emma Lazarus's plaque, "Give me your tired, your poor, your huddled masses." He hoped to combat some of the nation's growing racism by tying to rekindle in this time of war the notion that immigrants should be welcomed rather than despised. The play was published in several general volumes of radio plays, including *Radio Drama in Action* (1945), *Plays from Radio* (1948), and *Drama on the Air* (1951).

Set in an army hospital overlooking New York Harbor, young Monaghan sits in his wheelchair looking out of the window at the statue. He recalls to a fellow patient his Irish grandfather's evolving relationship with the Statue of Liberty. Notoriously stingy, when asked by his neighbor on Butler Street, BROOKLYN, to contribute 10 cents to the fund to build the statue's base, old Monaghan refuses. Only having read about it in papers, he denies that it exists, but when his neighbor takes him to see it in the warehouse he objects, first because the statue is in pieces (must be secondhand) and then because he sees the inscription of the date of Independence Day on the statue as cold and unwelcoming.

Monaghan persuades his grandson and other neighborhood children that the next big storm will bring the statue down, but they lose interest when given a chance to visit it. Even his grandson is attracted and asks Monaghan to take him. On the boat to the statue, Monaghan asks fellow passengers about it, and they seem utterly uninterested, but while in the head of the statue, they meet a veteran of the Philippine war. His view of the statue as representing American beliefs and being a memorial to his brother who had died in that war gives the grandfather a change of heart. When his grandson points out Lazarus's plaque, it brings Monaghan to tears and unaccustomed generosity (by placing a half-dollar in a crack by the plaque and giving his grandson money to get peanuts) as he realizes that the statue is actually saying the "Welcome All" that he had hoped. The message, his grandson tells his friend back in 1945, makes him feel as if he is home.

The subtle but additional layer of meaning in the play is what this statue means to young Monaghan, clearly a wounded veteran of WORLD WAR II. Despite being in a wheelchair, he can look on that statue like the veteran whom he and his father had met and see it as a symbol of the American belief system for which he had recently fought. To him, it clearly symbolizes home, and a place worthy of defense.

The Grass Still Grows (1939)

In 1939, Miller revised *They Too Arise,* the play he had developed from his first play, *No Villain,* into *The Grass Still Grows.* He nearly doubled the play's length and turned it into a comedy for an anticipated New York production, that never came to fruition. He had hoped that the FEDERAL THEATER PROJECT might stage it, but this organization had been abolished before he had completed revisions, and it was summarily rejected by the Jewish producers on BROADWAY as being "too Jewish." His mentor of the period, KENNETH ROWE, with whom Miller had studied playwriting at the UNIVERSITY OF MICHIGAN, described the play as "a happy blend of serious and hilarious, sentiment and philosophical reflection," and LEE STRASBERG praised the play but was reluctant to pick it up for production, having already done a Jewish play that year. In his analysis, CHRISTOPHER BIGSBY suggests that "CLIFFORD ODETS seems to make way for Philip Barry," as the "political earnestness has disappeared," and for him the play reflects Miller's efforts to "attune himself to a New York theatre no longer showing any interest in left-wing drama." Neither produced nor published, the manuscript lies in the archives at the HARRY RANSOM RESEARCH CENTER.

Presumably in an effort to make the play more marketable, Miller eliminated much of the ideology, taking out speeches praising the workers and deleting the strike. The sister is removed, and Arnold is reinvented as a newly qualified doctor, while his brother Ben is now the hopeful writer who constantly makes sacrifices to help the family. Ben sees his own efforts as worthless beside his brother's potential. The central conflict becomes which brother will win the hand of Helen, the daughter of Roth, a prosperous manufacturer whose business is a rival to their father's, and so gain access to wealth. Arnold comically masquerades at one point as an expert in the garment trade, and it is he who eventually is chosen by Helen as they elope together (although they decide to postpone the marriage at the last minute), leaving Ben free to marry his girlfriend Louise, the bookkeeper at his father's company. Ben shows himself to value love over money, but we never get a clear picture of where he will go from here.

Unlike the earlier versions of the play, here, the grandfather does not die but becomes a comic character who fills the small house with furniture that reminds him of a happier past. Although the

mother becomes angrier, it is for comic contrast, and the father seems more beloved by both sons. Social issues are not eradicated but are peripheralized and made less earnest. The workers want to help keep the business afloat and send the foreman, Max Schneeweiss, to offer Abe funds to keep the business going. Initially, he cannot accept, but events will make the offer seem preferable to working with Roth. Abe has a brother, Dave, who works as a scab for Roth but decides to quit after his wife leaves him. The Simons again reject Roth's offers of help on a moral basis, and Abe saves the family business by finally accepting money from his workers and turning it into a type of cooperative. The play ends happily as the family prepares for a double wedding.

This version of Miller's initial play is certainly less melodramatic than the original, although some of the speeches remain a little stilted and didactic, but Miller shows a comic flair at times which prefigures much of the humor in his later plays. Even the title suggests something less ominous than its precursors, but this is perhaps to its detraction, for although the play is witty, it also lacks the substance and dramatic conviction of its precursors. However, as the work of a fledgling playwright, it showed much promise of development.

The Great Disobedience (1938)

Miller's third and final Hopwood entry was *The Great Disobedience*. Miller claims that this play is the first he actively researched; it does take place in an environment alien to Miller's former experience. The idea for the play came out of his visits to Jackson Penitentiary to see a college friend, Sid Moscowitz, who had been given the post of prison psychologist for 8,000 inmates, and it explores what Miller perceived to be a connection between prison and CAPITALISM. The play was unpublished and unproduced, although a workshop reading was given in class under the guidance of Miller's professor, KENNETH ROWE. The manuscript can be found at the UNIVERSITY OF MICHIGAN. This time, the judges were less enthused; it was even viewed as "turgid" by one of them, and the play was only awarded second place.

Victor Matthews is an inmate. Previously employed as a compensation doctor by a rubber company, he has become an encumbrance for his refusal to deny the company's liability in medical cases. Discovering that he has performed a life-saving, but illegal, abortion, the company has him prosecuted and sent to jail. The prison becomes a metaphor for the outside society dominated by capitalism, which has caused freedom to become a mere illusion as people become trapped in a cycle of false need and hope. But Matthews has not been entirely abandoned and is to be aided by Caroline and Karl Mannheim, two old student friends, although their efforts are thwarted by the whims of a sadistic prison warden.

Mannheim happens to be the prison's psychologist, and his dilemma makes him the play's protagonist. A fierce liberal, he is eager to improve conditions in the prison, but he has not the strength of will to make the difference that he would like. He pacifies rather than cures, which ultimately helps the authorities rather than the prisoners. He fills his office with art and collects evidence of the corrupt prison system as stays against the horrors he witnesses, but he is unwilling to directly challenge the system he abhors. Victor, whose sanity under such conditions is hanging by a thread, imagines that Caroline, who loves him, is bearing a child who will one day challenge the system that has ruined all of their lives. Mannheim, too, is coming close to insanity with the pressure on him to preserve the status quo as opposed to doing what he knows to be right. He finally submits evidence of prison-guard drug trafficking, and the warden is removed, but the man who replaces him is equally corrupt, and nothing is really achieved. Mannheim quits, but the doctor who replaces him is just as idealistic and as prone to compromise. The play ends on a call from an enlightened Mannheim for a new kind of doctor with the courage to rebel rather than conform. It is this plea for social reform that marks the play most strongly as one of Miller's, but it also shows his early interest in finding subject matter that is beyond his personal experience.

The Half-Bridge (1940–1943)

Offered as both a stage play and a radio drama, *The Half-Bridge* is typical wartime patriotic propaganda in which an enthusiasm for depicting evil Nazis and U.S. resistance to them overwhelms artistic sensibilities. Melodramatic to the point of incredulity, full of unconvincing characters, and overplotted, the play was neither produced nor published. Its manuscript rests at the HARRY RANSOM RESEARCH CENTER. Based on information gathered while aboard the freighter SS *Copa Copa* in 1940, Miller relates the tale of *Bangkok Star*'s first mate, Mark Donegal, and his development from self-centered mercenary into humanitarian idealist during WORLD WAR II. With its maritime connection and moments of lyricism, an indebtedness to EUGENE O'NEILL seems apparent. The title refers to the idea that people project one-half of a bridge and seek others with whom to complete the structure, a not-so-subtle image for the importance of human connectivity to which Miller would return far more gracefully in later works.

Set in New Orleans, the play begins with the ship's crew returning after a night ashore drinking, and Donegal's meeting Anna Walden, a woman seeking passage to escape the repercussions of killing a would-be rapist. Donegal helps smuggle people from South America for Gestapo officer, Dr. Luther. Ship's Captain Shulenberg has an unspoken homosexual attraction to Donegal and shares the take. Under Luther's instigation, they plan to use the *Bangkok Star* to raid merchant ships to disrupt the war effort. Donegal sees this as his chance to raise funds to finance a lucrative project in Brazil, exploiting a hidden civilization. A darker plot emerges as Donegal learns that the ship is owned by Nazis who want it sunk so that they can claim insurance. Objecting to this and urged on by Anna, Donegal's conscience is reinvigorated, Luther is killed, and the couple escapes.

Although more crudely drawn, Donegal prefigures future Miller protagonists as the conflicted idealist searching for a satisfactory mode of life. An adventurer who has turned his back on a United States that he sees as corrupt and disengaged, he uses this to justify his own moral lapses. Donegal is caught between a sense of despair at the state of the world and hope that it can be bettered. During the play, through the onset of love for another in the form of Anna, he comes to recognize the self-limiting nature of his selfishness and embrace a more humanistic worldview.

"Ham Sandwich" (1976)

Written for *Boston University Quarterly* as one of two short works, the other being the play "fragment" *The Poosidin's Resignation,* in under 500 words, Miller conveys that moment old friends face when they realize that they no longer have a viable relationship. More an impressionistic sketch than a full-blown story, "Ham Sandwich" encapsulates in brief but keen strokes a moment in time. With the same compression that we see in Ernest Hemingway's shorter pieces, Miller describes a dinner party to which a couple, two old friends of the hosts, have come after an absence of five years. While alcohol starts the conversation flowing after a jilted start, the covert glances and repetitions of "too bad" tell the truer lack of connection that these people now feel about one another. The sentences initially seem as disconnected as the people, but even as they coalesce around the wonder of Lindbergh crossing the Atlantic with only a ham sandwich (or maybe something more) for sustenance, it becomes clear that their past will not be sufficient to carry their friendship forward any further. The mood is regretful but stoic; they cannot emulate Lindbergh's flight. Any attempt to keep the relationship aloft is doomed to failure, and the visiting wife—unnamed as are all the characters to further underscore their emotional distance—drunkenly weeps and significantly crashes.

"Hitler's Quarry" (1941)

First published in the inaugural issue of the *Jewish Survey* in 1941, this essay was Miller's first print publication following his graduation from the UNI-VERSITY OF MICHIGAN. An early call to Americans to take note of the persecution of Jews in Europe, it is an example of Miller's engagement with his fellow Jews, his awareness of world events, and of his outspoken political involvement. More than a year before the U.S. government would publicly acknowledge the Nazi agenda, Miller insists that people recognize the current persecution of Jews around the world. He offers supporting evidence for his claims that are garnered from wire service and newspaper reports and that illustrate the "immense geographic sweep" of Hitler's pursuit of Jews. He censures all who remain indifferent and excoriates both the United States and Britain for their refusal to help the thousands of Jews who are "attempting to escape Nazism." Holding everyone to account for the unchecked spread of Nazism, he sternly observes, "It is not the Jews alone who suffer by tyranny." Overlooked by critics who erroneously preferred to see Miller as disengaged from Jewish issues, the piece was brought to light again by scholar George Crandell in *ANQ* in 2000 under the title "Arthur Miller's Unheard Plea for Jewish Refugees: 'Hitler's Quarry.'"

Homely Girl, A Life, and Other Stories (1995)

Published in 1995 to celebrate Miller's 80th birthday, the title story of this collection of short fiction was the only relatively new piece, having previously been published in a signed limited edition in 1992. The "other stories" were "Fame" and "Fitter's Night," both of which had appeared in Miller's 1967 collection, *I Don't Need You Any More.* Of note is a caricature of Miller by his friend Alexander Calder that is printed opposite the title page.

Reviewers responded positively, with David Henderson complimenting the "adroitness" of Miller's writing, and *New York Times Book Review*'s David Walton describing the stories as "gracefully written," only complaining that there were not more of them. Sybil Steinberg announced that the stories were evidence of Miller's "mastery of literary realism," and Michael Harris pointed out that they were a good reminder "that the distinguished playwright is a good writer, period." Overall, there was a far stronger consensus that here was good writing than there had been for his 1967 collection, even though this contained two of the same stories.

FURTHER READING

Harris, Michael. "3 by Miller Underscore His Certain Talent." *Los Angeles Times*, November 26, 1995. Book Review, 14.

Henderson, David W. *"Homely Girl, A Life, and Other Stories." Library Journal*, October 1, 1995, 122–123.

Steinberg, Sybil S. *"Homely Girl, A Life, and Other Stories." Publisher's Weekly*, August 28, 1995, 101–102.

Walton, David. "Miller's Tales." *New York Times Book Review*, December 24, 1995, Sec. 7, p. 10.

Homely Girl, A Life　(1992)

Conceived as a novella, *Homely Girl, A Life* is one of Miller's longer fictional works. It was first printed in *Grand Street* in 1992 and later that same year in a signed limited edition by Peter Blum Books, illustrated by Louise Bourgeois with 10 drawings and eight collages. In GREAT BRITAIN, the title for its 1995 publication was changed to *Plain Girl, A Life*, as the word *homely* has a different connotation to the British, suggesting someone who is more of a homebody than simply unattractive. In 1995, it was again published in the United States with two earlier stories in the collection *Homely Girl, A Life, and Other Stories*. The story recounts the life of the daughter of Jewish immigrants, Janice Sessions, the homely girl of the title, from youth into her sixties.

SYNOPSIS

Janice Sessions wakes beside her 68-year-old blind husband, Charles, to find that he has died in the night; she feels momentarily lost. She begins to look back over her life since childhood. Although she has a nice body, she has always been obsessed with the plainness of her face. Her mother did not help in this, showing constant disappointment in her daughter's looks. Her first husband, Sam Fink, had been a plain man but politically committed, and this fire in him had attracted her, coupled by his apparent adoration of her despite her appearance. Coming from a wealthy background, the family had disapproved of her match to this working-class supporter of COMMUNISM. They had met when she was in her twenties during the 1930s when it was fashionable to be a socialist and ANTI-SEMITISM seemed to be on the rise in her New York City hometown. Her marriage is more a response to the political climate of the times than a true union.

She recalls her father, Dave Sessions, after whom she felt that she had taken and with whom she often sided against her mother. Her father had faith in her, but he died in the late 1930s. He was cremated, and after the funeral, she went to a bar for a drink with her brother, Herman and his plump wife, Edna. Herman wanted to combine their inheritances and buy real estate while it was cheap, but Janice did not want to talk business at such a time and angrily left, but inadvertently she forgot her father's ashes that were sitting on the bar. She returned to look for them, but they were gone, and the barman sympathized and bought her a drink.

She explains why she married Sam, a book dealer and a committed activist, and describes their life together. She was sexually unfulfilled but allowed Sam and his beliefs to dictate their lives. She contrasts this to the great sex life she had with her second husband and the equality of their relationship. After four years of marriage to Sam, she took to drink, and freed by the alcohol she began to resist, admitting her boredom with her husband's politics. When Stalin made a pact with Hitler, her husband's refusal to reject communism caused her to lose respect for his beliefs, about which he was less certain than she had thought. Sam signed up for the army during WORLD WAR II and while he was training she had an affair with a mutual friend, Lionel Mayer. Sexually but not emotionally fulfilled, she remained unsettled. When her husband left for Europe, she registered as a graduate student in art history. She further empowered herself by seducing an older professor, Oscar Kalkofsky, and enjoying the sense of freedom it gave her.

On Sam's return, she was uncertain how to break from him until he brazenly confessed to having raped a German farmwoman. She left him and moved into the Crosby Hotel, allowing Mayer to molest her in return for typing work. Her brother, now a ruthless property manager, visits in another effort to have her join him in his business. She again refuses, seeing it as too venal. She recalls reading books, watching movies, and living off her inheritance until she met Charles Buckman, a classical pianist who lived on an upper floor of the hotel. Blind but confident, he instantly attracted her. She escorted him to his gym, and he invited her for a drink. They enjoyed each other's company, soon married, and had 14 happy years together. The year following his death, Janice, now 61, heard that the hotel where they met was to be demolished, and she returns for one last look. She considers why she was so happy with Charles. The story ends with a sense of her renewed hope for the future, having learned to be comfortable with who she is, and to follow her heart rather than just her intellect.

CRITICAL COMMENTARY

Although the story begins as a kind of flashback after Janice wakes up beside the dead body of her second husband, it also goes beyond this event to the future, time bending in the same way that Miller achieved in his autobiography to show how the past informs the present. Interestingly, both texts are subtitled "A Life," as if to suggest that this is the fashion in which every individual's life runs. Miller's intent is to give a seamless picture of the evolution of Janice into selfhood. Janice's problem is a lack of self-confidence fueled by an obsession with appearance that she has always taken pains to deny. She refers to triviality as her nemesis and abhors the "bourgeois obsession with things," unaware that this is exactly how she lives her life. She relishes her new high heels because they make her legs look shapely, even while struggling to believe in Stalin's professed antimaterialism. She is so obsessed with how she appears to others that she has never allowed herself to live naturally and to do the things she wants. There is a disconnection between her emotional response and her intellect, or as CHRISTOPHER BIGSBY suggests, the trouble with her initial life is that it is all external.

She marries Sam because she admires his apparent certainty in contrast to the ambivalence she feels about herself. Her support for the communist cause is tied to her support for her husband, and when she begins to lose faith in the former, the latter soon follows. She begins to realize that she is profoundly unhappy in her marriage, sexually dissatisfied and feeling demeaned by her husband's arrogance. She attempts to escape through drink, feeling liberated enough by the alcohol to speak her mind, but to act on this is still beyond her. Her next escape is through sex, as she embarks on affairs with Mayer and then Kalkofsky. Although she has the satisfaction that she has initiated these encounters and enjoys the sexual union, her relief that they are uninterested in any permanent relationship indicates a lack of progression. She treats herself as a sexual object rather than as a person, highlighted by the way she later virtually prostitutes herself to Mayer in return for typing work.

Strongly reminiscent of HENRIK IBSEN's Nora Helmer from *A Doll House,* Janice feels trapped in an unhappy marriage with a husband, Sam, who tries to dictate all of her tastes and allow her no opinions of her own. Like Nora, Janice waits for a miracle, becomes disappointed as her husband's petty limitations are revealed, and leaves him to find her true self. There is ironically little real difference between Sam and Herman, despite Sam's communist sympathies and Herman's Republican ones. Their careers both seek to profit from the misfortune of others—Herman by buying up real estate during the Depression and Sam buying up books from estates in decline. Janice, in direct contrast, refuses to go along with any of her brother's lucrative housing deals and would rather become an editor and be involved with the making of books than with treating them as a commodity. When Sam tries to justify his neglect of her by his obsession with fascism, she neatly undercuts his pose with the understanding that he is really just scared of sex.

Initially, Janice survives by seeing the irony in events, such as the Irish-Catholic barman who is undoubtedly anti-Semitic sympathizing over the loss of her father's ashes, not aware that her father

In 2001, Miller's 1992 novella *Homely Girl: A Life* was made into a film titled *Eden*. Some scenes were filmed on Miller's estate in Roxbury, Connecticut, including this one with Samantha Morton playing the part of Janice Sessions, (renamed Sam in the film) who is visiting her ailing father, played by Miller himself. *Photograph by Inge Morath: Magnum Photos.*

was Jewish. She even sees the humor in having left her fastidious father's ashes in a bar, although she feels bad about being so careless. But this is living by the intellect alone, and it is stifling emotion—not allowing herself the luxury of feeling almost as if she does not hold herself worthy. She demeans herself before others can, but it is a self-negating defense. Her experience with Charles, however, changes all of this.

Charles is blind, and this changes the way she responds to him. She acts on her attraction to him, feeling freed by his inability to see her plainness. But in classical fashion, although his eyes are sightless, Charles sees Janice clearly, attracted to her intellect and her physique. Her disconnection is gradually healed by their loving relationship, revealed by her sadness on his death that he never saw her face. She felt empowered with Charles in

a way that she could not with Sam—she felt his dependence on her, which elevated her in her own eyes and allowed her to stop obsessing over her homeliness. Ironically, the blind man teaches her to see past appearances.

At the close—in a scene that is reminiscent of Jay Gatsby staring in hope at the orgiastic green light—Janice, under the green traffic light, finds beauty even in the dilapidated neighborhood where she used to live. Thankful for her 14 years with Charles, she is content to move on and is working as a volunteer for a civil-rights movement. Having found herself, she can now contribute to society in a more meaningful fashion than she was ever able to do in her years with Sam. Bigsby's discussion of the novella highlights Janice's changing and often paralyzing connections to past and future and concludes that Janice eventually comes through these with Charles to discover "the value of relationships, the virtue of passion and the true value of love."

MOVIE AND TELEVISION ADAPTATIONS

Amos Gitai directed a movie version of this novella in 2001 with Samantha Morton playing the lead role of Sam (as the female protagonist was renamed), Tom Elliot Jane, and Daniel Huston. Titled *Eden*, it was filmed in Israel, Italy, and the United States, and some scenes were even shot at Miller's home in ROXBURY, CONNECTICUT, where Miller played the role of Janice's father. It drew little approbation from critics, although Gitai was nominated for a Golden Lion award at the Venice Film Festival.

FURTHER READING

Bigsby, Christopher. "Fiction." *Arthur Miller: A Critical Study.* New York: Cambridge University Press, 2005: 444–469.

Shulman, Robert. "Arthur Miller. *Homely Girl, a Life and Other Stories:* The Popular Front Considered." *Arthur Miller Society Newsletter* 2 (December 2000): 12–15.

Honors at Dawn (1937)

Honors at Dawn was Miller's second attempt to win an Avery Hopwood award after his success the previous year with *No Villain*. Integrally, it was a fairly similar play, dealing with family issues, striking workers, and the threat of big business—all pressing concerns at the time that Miller was writing. The play was unpublished and unproduced, although a manuscript can be found at the UNIVERSITY OF MICHIGAN. It was awarded first prize by the Hopwood committee, which included Susan Glaspell, and was described by one of the judges as "superior to the other entries and compares quite favorably with other full-length proletarian plays of recognized merit." Evidently influenced by the work of CLIFFORD ODETS, the play offers rousing addresses, violent action, and authentic proletarian speech. Though not as subtle as Miller's later works, it confirms Miller's socialist concerns, along with his interest in warring brothers and the morality of informing.

The play features two brothers, Harry and Max Zibriski, sons of poor Polish immigrants. Harry believes in the American dream and is a junior-college student in engineering and aiming for an easy and rich future. His older brother Max, a mechanic, works at the giant automobile factory, Castle Parts, no doubt based on one of the General Motors plants that Miller had visited as reporter for the MICHIGAN DAILY. The workers at Castle Parts strike for more pay and union recognition, and 23-year-old Max half-heartedly supports them by handing out flyers. A manager offers him a raise and a better job in exchange for informing on his fellow workers and when he refuses, fires him and has him beaten up.

Back at the Zibriski farm, their widowed mother stirs soup and chats to a neighbor, Smygli. Originally from Poland, Smygli speaks broken English but is formerly a graduate in philosophy. Reduced to mere subsistence, running a farm in his new country after his attempt at running a hot-dog stand failed, he nonetheless loves America, not like Harry for its opportunities of material success or even Max for its socialist possibilities, but purely and simply for its sense of democratic freedom. Free of limiting ideologies, he offers an interesting contrast to the conflicted brothers, and it is his awkward speech alone that seems limiting. His easygoing nature suggests that he is a precursor to Gustav Eberson in *The Man Who Had All the Luck.* Harry is visiting from college and persuades Max to join him there. While Max is looking for somewhere free of the corruption from which he has suffered, Harry's aim is to attain an easy management job rather than the hands-on labor that Max previously enjoyed and which Harry despises.

Back at college, Harry asks the dean for a student loan to bankroll his high living. The factory owner happens to be a major donor to the university and wants to eliminate radicals there, too. He offers two new engineering buildings in return for the dismissal of a History professor who has spoken out against big business. Stating he will not hire any graduates who, in his eyes, support COMMUNISM, the industrialist pressures the university's president to accede to his demands. The president has the dean approve Harry's loan in return for informing against his colleagues, an offer that Harry zealously accepts. Max is horrified to see the corruption that he had sought to escape present itself in such censorship at the college.

After three student activists are expelled, Max realizes that it must have been Harry who informed on them and angrily denounces him. Harry's girlfriend dumps him in exchange for Max, evidently the better man. By the year's end, Max returns to his former workplace to offer support to his less-educated colleagues as they go on strike, "It's gonna be ours," he exclaims, adopting a Marxist stance. He is shot in the shoulder while giving a rousing speech articulating his graduation into a better understanding of the needs of his fellow workers. A union man agrees, telling him that he has graduated "With honors," and in the dawn light, Max envisions his future back at the plant as an activist, fighting for the working class.

The Hook (1951)

Miller and director ELIA KAZAN had vainly tried to get backing for this screenplay about corruption and racketeering on the BROOKLYN waterfront in 1951. The studios strongly suggested that Miller change it into an anticommunist statement, by recasting its gangsters as communists who were trying to take over the unions, but Miller refused and withdrew his script. It was never produced. Unpublished manuscripts are kept in the archives at the HARRY RANSOM RESEARCH CENTER and the Lilly Library at Indiana University. The initial plan had been to raise funds to produce this one locally, but Kazan felt his increasing fame as a director could secure them Hollywood financing. He was wrong—given its controversial subject matter, studios were reluctant to commit without extensive rewriting.

Subtitled *A Play for the Screen,* the idea for *The Hook* had come from Miller on learning of the disappearance of Peter Panto, a Brooklyn longshoreman who had defied the corruption of his union. Miller felt the story better suited to film than the stage. The title referred to both the RED HOOK section of Brooklyn where it would take place and the baling hook that longshoremen perennially carried. An earlier draft titled *Shape-Up* referred to the exercise whereby the hiring boss chose his workers for the day. In this version, the central character had been Danny Banta, a man whose brother Pete was killed by gangsters for his outspokenness against the union. In seeking the truth, Danny becomes embroiled in trying to help the workers and initiates a strike, although his brother's killers are never brought to justice. The later screenplay is substantially altered, but its focus remains on the corruption of the dockside.

The Hook's protagonist is Marty Ferrara, a longshoreman in his thirties, and begins during the morning "shape-up," as the workers are being selected. The boss, Rocky, callously chooses his men, even tossing two of the brass checks that the chosen are given into the air for the remainder to scrabble over for his amusement. Marty voices disapproval over the way his fellow-workers are being demeaned. The president of the union local, Louis, has gangster connections and is on the side of the bosses rather than the men. Pushing the crew to work too fast while unloading a ship, there is a fatal accident as steel bars from an overloaded crane fall onto Marty's friend, Barney. Marty is further disgusted as everyone is ordered back to work. He wants to quit but does not know what else to do. Sitting on a children's swing in a local playground, he shares his frustration with his wife, Therese.

Marty tries working as a bookie, but he feels guilty taking money from the poor and returns to the docks. On learning that some men are being cheated out of pay, he calls for a strike, but the men are too fearful and leave him to walk out alone. Reluctant to take the lead, he nevertheless decides to speak out at the next union meeting where he is discredited as a troublemaker. Those who offer vocal support are swiftly silenced, and Louis demands that Marty hand over his work credentials and be thrown from the union. Marty denounces Louis, calling his actions fascism, and after one more vain attempt to rally the workers, he leaves.

Unable to find work anywhere, Marty becomes destitute and turns to drink. But when repossessors arrive at his home, he is spurred to challenge

Louis for the presidency. He puts up a good fight and gets some men behind him, but Louis stuffs the ballot and declares himself the winner. Marty and his followers break into the safe where Louis had placed the votes and count them for themselves, only to discover that Louis really had won. The men had been too fearful to vote against him. The union tries to buy off Marty with a job as union delegate, but he exhorts the men again to rebel, turning down the job. Miller's first completed screenplay ends as the workers begin to riot in a symbolic celebration of Marty's unbreakable spirit and moral rectitude. Kazan disliked this vague ending, wanting something more decisive, and his 1954 waterfront movie, *On the Waterfront,* scripted by Budd Schulberg, would have a less ambivalent finale. However, several other scenes are strongly redolent of Miller's screenplay, and it is clear that it had a direct influence on this later piece. Brenda Murphy insightfully discusses this and the development of the screenplay in *Congressional Theatre* (1999), while Albert Wertheim's essay "*A View from the Bridge,*" in *Cambridge Companion to Arthur Miller* (1997), offers a critical discussion of the screenplay.

I Can't Remember Anything (1987)

Miller wrote this one-act play as part of the 1987 double bill *Danger: Memory!* to accompany *Clara,* which deals with similar themes from a different angle. In *Timebends: A Life,* Miller explains that he based the play's characters Leo and Leonora on his friends Alexander and Louisa Calder—both heavy drinkers who felt as if they had come from a previous era and become cut off from the present, although in some ways the dead figure of Leonora's husband Frederick seems more reminiscent of his life-loving friend "Sandy" Calder. The play deals with that perennial Miller concern, the necessity for people to acknowledge their past as an active part of their current existence. Nothing can be more important to our placing of the past in our

lives than the concept of memory, but as Miller recognizes, memory holds many dangers, some of which he attempts to illustrate in *I Can't Remember Anything* which (ironically, given its title) shows the dangers of overindulging in memories of the past.

SYNOPSIS

The play begins in Leo's New England kitchen just as his friend of many years, Leonora, arrives. She pours herself a drink, and she takes out a package that she has received from her son, Lawrence, who is at a monastery in Sri Lanka. Leo thinks that she drinks too much, complains about his arthritis, and tells her how he plans to leave his organs for medical research. Leonora is feeling useless, her memory appears to be failing, and her life has lost its sense of purpose. Leo had forgotten that he invited Leonora to dinner, and they mock each other's loss of memory. They both vainly try to remember trivia, and then Leo recalls Leonora's dead husband Frederick, who was the life of the party, and the opulent dinners that Leonora once cooked.

After three years of silence, Lawrence has sent her a record and a note to tell her that he is separating from a wife whom Leonora cannot recall. Leo is looking at a friend's bridge design but is finding it hard to concentrate. Unlike Frederick, whom he deeply admired and who, he recalls, stayed sharp to the end, Leo feels his mental facilities beginning to decline. Leonora complains about a dentist and a plumber whom Leo recommended and then tells him about a deer that she saw by the roadside. Leo declares his belief in COMMUNISM, and Leonora, who is rich, asks his advice as to which charities she should donate money. Both decry the modern decline in people's beliefs. Leo recalls how his father died in the mines, and Leonora changes the subject to a thieving raccoon about which Leo had told her.

They miss all their dead friends and only have each other left. Leonora recounts how she met Frederick and asks Leo why he does not become discouraged; his optimism apparently annoys her. But Leo senses that his life has been unaccomplished. Leonora plays Lawrence's photograph record, and they dance a samba together. Then Leo goes back to work, and Leonora goes home, later calling him to say goodnight. This is the ending in the initial 1986 Grove edition of the play. In the 1987 Dramatists Play Service version that was published after the play had been produced, Miller added a major argument between Leo and Leonora before and after she plays the record; in it, Leo asks Leonora not to come round every day, as she has been doing, as she is making his health suffer. She leaves in umbrage, and he seems elated that he has finally curtailed their friendship, declaring that he never cared for Leonora but only for Frederick. When she phones, he repeats his demands. However, the 1994 Methuen series of Miller plays reprinted the earlier version, so it remains unclear which ending Miller preferred.

CRITICAL COMMENTARY

Leo is not in the best of health, evidently suffering from arthritis and an unhealthy obsession with death and dying. He argues with Leonora over which of them will die first and surrounds himself with images of death in the line drawings of departed friends. This is what the past has become for him, an arena of death. He needs a more positive way of dealing with the past that will allow him to concentrate on life—which can then give him a future. He tries to do this by centering his remembrances on images of food and parties, but he knows in his heart that this time has passed, that he no longer has Frederick to follow, and he feels lost in the modern world. But Leo's key quality is that he is "stubborn," and he has not yet entirely given in to this death impulse. This manifests itself largely through his connection with Leonora, despite his attempts by the close of the play to sever that connection.

Leonora drinks too much, a classic symbol of avoidance; what she avoids most is her own life. Saying that she can no longer taste food, she cuts herself off from even physical sensations. When Leo reminds her of eating bread the week before— symbolically the staff of life—her self-imposed forgetfulness dissipates, and she begins to remember. But Leonora is unhappy, less from her apparent loss of memory than from her inability to forget entirely. She does remember, despite her attempts not to do so: She allows herself to recall trivial things like the

dentist, the plumber, and the raccoon but tries to suppress personal aspects of her life as if she is trying to eradicate herself by eradicating her past. For Leonora, the past is too painful because memory insists on involvement of a kind that scares her; but such involvement is necessary to fully live and should not be avoided.

The similarity between the characters' names suggests their close connection; Leonora provides both a contrast and a compliment to Leo. Where he is small and sickly, she is as large and colorful as her wrap, evoking a life that she would like to deny but cannot escape. Where Leo wants to immerse himself in his past but is beginning, reluctantly, to forget certain details, Leonora pretends to remember nothing though the memories insist upon imposing themselves. It will be a balance between these two that will offer the best way to live, and their connection to each other can help them survive; alone, each runs the evident (and ultimately selfish) danger of totally withdrawing from life—Leo into his past and Leonora into oblivion.

The picture that we are given of Frederick, Leonora's dead husband, ironically, is brimming with life, both in his connection to food (bread and salami) and his sexuality (he is described making lascivious jokes and as having slept with many women). In trying to forget him, Leonora separates herself off from a potential source of life. Of course, she is also separating herself from a potential source of pain, which is why she has buried his memory, but to live a full life necessitates some pain. Leo forces her to remember, and it is necessary that she does. Frederick had, symbolically, built bridges for a living and for the living—with his death, it has been hard for both Leo and Leonora to maintain such connections/bridges and to build further ones, but this also is necessary.

Leonora recognizes her connection to Leo, and may believe that through this, she can reconnect to others or with hope itself. She insists that Leo always sees the purpose in things because this is what she herself so desperately needs to do. She displaces her belief onto her closest friend so she can remain close to it without having to feel that it may betray her. Although a recluse, Leo resists his impulse to cut himself off entirely, evidenced by his continuation of hope despite seeing the world as intrinsically evil. His decision to leave his organs to the hospital may reaffirm his morbid fascination with his own impending death, but it is also an act of attrition, fellowship, involvement, and connection that seems to counter his current isolation—although he offers the organs for research rather than as a donor.

For Leo, the past is not enough, and for Leonora, the present fails to satisfy. While Leonora in her despair is drawn to Leo's optimism, he is drawn in his sickliness to her life force. Their connection to each other keeps them both on the side of life: He forces her to remember (even as she goads him into remembering for her); she forces him to hope (even as, or partly because, she tries to argue him out of his optimism). For a time, they sustain each other: Leonora's memories assist Leo in remembering as he begins, unwillingly, to forget; Leo's hope assists Leonora in refusing to give in finally to the despair against which she has been struggling. What each needs to learn is that the past is neither a refuge nor a curse but an aid toward ensuring a healthy present and future. Once Leonora renews her connection to the past that she has tried to eradicate, she may draw strength from it as well as warning. However, that connection needs to be honest.

Leo's life is an illusion that is based on an idealized past from which he cannot progress. He will not allow anything to tamper with his whitewashed memory of Frederick. Despite Leo's commendations of Frederick, he seems to have been a rather coarse, loud-mouthed, and unfaithful individual. When Leonora shows an unwillingness to continue talking about Frederick, Leo grows increasingly upset with her. Leo has been nice to Leonora purely out of selfish motives, to try to maintain a link through her to his dead friend and leader. Now that she is refusing to play the game by refusing to remember, he attempts to cast her off as an unnecessary burden, despite her evident need for his company to maintain her own sanity.

Lawrence, Leonora's son, never appears in the play, but he recorded and sent the samba record to which they dance. He, too, appears to have been searching for some kind of hope in a disappointing world, staying at a monastery in Sri Lanka. He may even be finding some direction as he is now reconnecting with his mother after three years of silence and ending an unsuccessful marriage. The record that he sends allows Leonora and Leo to recall something vital from their past which may help sustain them into the future—not death or betrayal but a moment of joy and the comradeship of dance. Together, they do an old-fashioned samba to the record, and are strengthened by this moment of close connection—they even flirt a little to show the sexual vibrancy (life force) that the dance has awakened. However, the revised ending of the play shows Leo breaking this by his banishment of Leonora, and we are left to wonder if either can survive alone.

FIRST PERFORMANCE

I Can't Remember Anything premiered at Lincoln Center in New York on February 8, 1987, with the following cast:

> *Leo:* Mason Adams
> *Leonora:* Geraldine Fitzgerald

> Directed by Gregory Mosher
> Set by Michael Merritt
> Produced by Bernard Gersten
> It ran for a limited engagement of four weeks.

INITIAL REVIEWS

Critical response was mixed, but both *I Can't Remember Anything* and its companion piece *Clara* fared better on their 1988 London premiere than in the United States where the critics preferred *I Can't Remember Anything*—even Robert Brustein called it an "appealing genre piece"—but others felt that its symbolism was vague and that the play was too sketchy and insubstantial. William Collins complained that Miller's "voice is muffled, his presence attenuated. And his intentions are not altogether clear." In London, Blake Morrison saw it and its companion play as "two complex realist dramas which show [Miller's] creative powers, at 73, still in full spate," and Sheridan Morley saw them as having "the fascination of late sketches by a master painter of the human condition."

FURTHER READING

Abbotson, Susan C. W. The Dangers of Memory in Arthur Miller's *I Can't Remember Anything. Journal of American Drama and Theatre* 18, no. 2 (Spring 2006): 27–40.

Brustein, Robert. "Danger: Manipulation." *New Republic* March 9, 1987, 26.

Centola, Steven R. "Temporality, Consciousness, and Transcendence in *Danger: Memory!" The Achievement of Arthur Miller: New Essays.* Dallas, Tex.: Contemporary Research, 1995, 135–142.

Collins, William B. "Arthur Miller's New Plays Explore Memory's Frailties." *Philadelphia Inquirer,* February 10, 1987, C5.

Edwards, Christopher. *"Danger: Memory!" Spectator* 16, April 1988. In *London Theatre Record* 8, no. 7 (1988): 429–430.

Morley, Sheridan. *"Danger: Memory!" Punch* 22, April 1988. In *London Theatre Record* 8, no. 7 (1988): 427.

Morrison, Blake. *"Danger: Memory!" Observer,* April 10, 1988. In *London Theatre Record* 8, no. 7 (1988): 431.

I Don't Need You Any More (1967)

All of the short stories in this collection, aside from "Fitter's Night," had been previously published in a variety of magazines including *Esquire, Atlantic Monthly,* and *The Noble Savage* within a period of 15 years. In a brief introduction, "Foreword: About Distances," Miller admits that they were not written as a series but is surprised at a "certain continuity" that he discovered in placing them together. The short story, he explains, is a form that offers him the opportunity to condense both action and character and to "see things isolated in stillness." It allows him to pay attention to detail in a way that he cannot do in drama and with his reader to embrace a directness that he feels is impossible to accomplish in a play. The collection is comprised of "I Don't Need You Any More," "Monte Sant' Angelo," "Please Don't Kill Anything," "The Misfits," "Glimpse at a Jockey," "The Prophecy," "Fame," "Fitter's Night," and "A Search

for a Future." Both "The Misfits" and "Fame" were later developed into screenplays.

Although some critics felt that Miller should better stick to plays and found general fault with these short stories as being too obviously plotted, anecdotal, or lacking in drama, many discovered that there was one story which they felt was a gem. *Times Literary Supplement* chose "A Search for a Future," BROOKS ATKINSON "The Misfits," Larry Earl Bone "Please Don't Kill Anything," and Isaiah Sheffer "Fitter's Night." Jerome Charyn declared the title story a "masterpiece." This suggests that the stories were better than might be expected from Stanley Koven's assessment of them as a "bunch of flurry dilemmas" in *Commonweal.* John Wakeman praised the collection for *New York Times Book Review* as "exact, humane, knowledgeable writing, free of affectation and self-congratulation," and Paul Zimmerman at *Newsweek* felt the stories effectively blended "insight and outlook."

FURTHER READING

"At Another Distance." *Times Literary Supplement,* November 30, 1967, 1125.

Atkinson, Brooks. "A Theatre of Life." *Saturday Review,* February 25, 1971, 53.

Bone, Larry Earl. "I Don't Need You Any More." *Library Journal,* February 1, 1967, 596.

Charyn, Jerome. "Arthur Miller Off Stage." *Book World,* February 12, 1967, 4, 17.

Koven, Stanley. "I Don't Need You Any More, Arthur Miller." *Commonweal,* March 17, 1967, 686–687.

Sheffer, Isaiah. "Storytelling Dramatists." *New Leader,* June 5, 1967, 24.

Wakeman, John. "Story Time." *New York Times Books Review,* April 2, 1967, 4.

Zimmerman, Paul. "Offstage Voices." *Newsweek,* February 27, 1967, 92.

"I Don't Need You Any More" (1959)

The short story that would provide the title for Miller's 1967 collection *I Don't Need You Any More* first saw publication in *Esquire*'s December 1959 edition. The story was also reprinted in 1987's *The Misfits and Other Stories*. Miller relates the story of a five-year-old Jewish boy who expresses a desire to see the wider world and begins his growth away from maternal cushioning to his mother's displeasure and father's approval. He writes this lengthy story from the consciousness of the boy, emulating the rhythms, wonderment, and confusing contractions of a young child's mind. Not yet fully initiated into the adult world, he is uncertain of much that is going on around him, but during the course of the story, we see his understanding grow.

There are numerous details regarding appearances and relationships that suggest that the story is heavily rooted in Miller's childhood experience. The boy's obsession with the way his ears stick out, his reaction to witnessing the Simchat Torah celebrations at temple, his father's illiteracy, his belief in the older brother's perfection, his mother's coddling, belief in his potential, and love of music and books are all evidenced in Miller's autobiography, *Timebends: A Life*. In 1921, when this tale most likely takes place, Miller's family still owned a summer home in Rockaway by the beach, which is apparently the setting for the tale. As CHRISTOPHER BIGSBY also observes, AUGUSTA MILLER was most likely pregnant at that time, which could explain some of the mother's mood swings in the story and the sense that Martin's position in the family is soon to change.

Martin, the young boy who is the story's protagonist, lives near the ocean and is a part of a strong Jewish community. Being young, the boy is uncertain which Jewish holiday they are celebrating (it is Yom Kippur, given the fact the adults and his older brother Ben are fasting). He has been watching the ocean grow stormier during the past few days and imagines it to be full of sins. Angry that he has not been allowed to fast like his father and Ben, he feels left out and overlooked. He feels himself restricted more by women than by men, but mostly by his mother because she refuses to tell him things that he wants to know. He imagines the waves threatening him and considers running home to tell his mother as he usually does to gain attention, but then he realizes that his fantasies are no longer so compelling now he is older—they are

viewed more as lies than as fascinating stories. His relationship with all of his family is changing, and he feels torn between embracing the change and wanting it to be as it was.

He returns home, reacting with disgust at his mother's offer of a glass of milk. He is determined to view her as ugly and everything she does negatively, resentful of the way that he sees their relationship as having distanced of late. Behaving violently and rudely, he provokes his mother into taking notice. When she scolds him, he hits her, and after she declares that she will tell his father, he screams at her "I don't need you any more!" Feeling the truth of his declaration, he is surprised at his mother's hurt reaction. He returns to the beach where he recalls his mother meeting a man whom she had once dated. The incident had worried him; he was unable to imagine his mother with anyone other than his father. He senses his mother is pulling away from him, for example, leaving the room when he dresses; he is confused as to why. After greater thought, he realizes that it is more that he is pulling away from her as his view of her is changing with age. He relives their recent confrontation, analyzing it for potential meaning in the way that he now looks at everything in his life.

Men from his synagogue approach the shoreline to perform the Tashlich ceremony that marks the close of the Yom Kippur service that they are following. They ceremoniously berate themselves and cast their sins upon the water, but Martin is frightened and confused by their presence, recalling his similar feelings at a Simchat Torat service when the old men danced with the Torah scrolls. Meeting his father and brother after the service concludes, they gently mock his belief that he saw something silvery fly out of the cantor's hand into the water. He sadly realizes he is not yet a part of their world. When they arrive home, his mother tells them how he acted. His father is unimpressed but threatens him with his belt to satisfy his wife. As they break their fast, Martin seethes with resentment at what he sees as Ben's perfection.

Trying to behave more independently by eating his matzah-ball soup without aid, Martin causes havoc at the family table and spills hot soup on his lap. As he changes, his brother berates him for being mean to their mother. Uncertain what to do with his wet trousers, Martin retreats to the safety of childhood and calls for his mother. She refuses to come, but his father feeds the boys, and Martin relaxes after making his brother laugh. Going to apologize to his mother and say goodnight, Martin realizes suddenly that his father approves of his growing independence. He feels torn between his parents as they argue over him. His resentment builds, he lashes out violently, and he is taken to his room, his parents worried over his health. Their concern calms him until his father again accuses his mother of spoiling him, telling her to leave him alone. Ben still feels that Martin has behaved badly so Martin is again caught, this time between his father's approval and his brother's disapproval. While the family sleeps, the boy creeps outside and returns to the beach where he has a renewed vision of his own potential and place within the family.

Miller's decision to set the story during Yom Kippur, a holiday which emphasizes personal renewal, underscores the Martin's development. Shortly after heralding the new year over Rosh Hashanah, on Yom Kippur, Jews are asked to atone for their sins of the past year and to start the new afresh; this is symbolized in the Tashlich ceremony where crumbs are cast onto flowing water to represent the sins being washed away. So the boy analyzes his own sense of guilt, moves on from his past dependencies, and begins the new year with a fresh outlook. His growth has been less than that from child to adult—he is after all only five—but from innocence to awareness. He is now ready to be responsible, not just for himself but for his whole family.

As Bigsby points out, Martin's cry of "I don't need you any more" is "less an expression of independence than a confession of bewilderment." For much of the tale, the boy is caught between conflicting emotions and desires, parents and sibling, mother and father, wanting to be a part of the family and wanting his own independence. Miller eloquently captures this sense of confusion in the almost stream of consciousness narrative that he offers. The language may be more than a five year old might be expected to achieve, but the emotional torture of growing up is accurately captured. It is as writer Malcolm Bradbury describes, "Among

Miller's finest pieces, this is a story of powerful evocation, about the way we struggle through life to some sort of respectful, obedient, half-known moral consciousness." It is also, as Christiane Desafy–Grignard suggests, an exploration of Jewish identity.

FURTHER READING

Bigsby, Christopher. "Fiction." *Arthur Miller: A Critical Study.* New York: Cambridge University Press, 2005: 444–472.

Bradbury, Malcolm. "Arthur Miller's Fiction." In *The Cambridge Companion to Arthur Miller,* edited by Christopher Bigsby, 211–229. (Cambridge, England: University Press, 1997).

Desafy–Grignard, Christiane. "Jewishness and Judaism Revisited in Two Short Stories by Arthur Miller: 'Monte Sant' Angelo' and 'I Don't Need You Anymore.'" *Journal of the Short Story in English* 43 (2004 Autumn): 87–106.

Jacobson, Irving. "The Child as Guilty Witness." *Literature and Psychology* 24, no. 1 (1974): 12–23.

I Think About You a Great Deal (1982)

In 1979, the Czechoslovakian writer VÁCLAV HAVEL was sentenced to four-and-a-half years imprisonment for "criminal subversion of the republic" in response to his outspokenness against government prosecutions. The short dramatic piece, *I Think About You a Great Deal,* was written as an expression of solidarity with Havel and was performed at the International Theatre Festival in Avignon on July 21, 1982.

Although a monologue, the piece demands two actors, as one remains silent to represent the way in which writers like Havel were being silenced by their governments. The speaker is called the Writer, and he talks aloud to the Imprisoned One, explaining what this man means to him and why he thinks about him a great deal. The Imprisoned One sits silently and listens. The Writer sorts through his mail, selecting two letters of importance and dumping the rest in his wastepaper basket. The mail that he drops includes requests from a series of liberal causes whose concerns imply that the world is in the process of self-destruction. The writer sincerely hopes that "Things just can't be this bad." Yet the incarceration of this man, clearly meant to be Havel, is a slap in the face for those who believe in socialism. Imprisoning writers, he suggests, makes "war on the imagination."

The Writer recalls a promising playwright whom he once knew who sold out in return for a comfortable life–he quit drama to write more lucrative advertising copy for General Motors. This is something Havel has refused to do, wanting to maintain artistic control over his writing, even if that lands him in jail. Miller admires such commitment, and his Writer persona offers moral support and a promise to "hold your space open for you, dear friend." He evokes the connection between all writers who accept a moral outlook, which unites them against the powers that threaten and gives them the strength to survive.

I Was Married in Bataan (1942)

Aired on October 5, 1942, as part of the *Cavalcade of America* series, this was not one of Miller's better radio dramas. It tells the true story of Lt. Dorothea Daley Engel, an army nurse, who wrote about her war experiences in an article titled "I Was Married in Battle" in *American Magazine*. Played by Madeleine Carroll, Dorothea English, as Miller renames his romantic heroine, falls in love with a soldier during the battle in Bataan, the Philippines, but loses him in a series of disastrous events. In a postperformance address, Carroll makes an urgent plea for more nurses to sign up and help the armed forces; getting to this point seems to have been the main thrust of the drama. As Albert Wertheim suggests, "The weakness of the play surely stems from Miller's being compelled to write in the service of dramatic ends other than his own," as was the case with several of his radio plays. Although unpublished, typescripts for this drama can be found at the HARRY RANSOM RESEARCH CENTER and the New York Public Library.

FURTHER READING

Wertheim, Albert. *Staging the War.* Indiana University Press: Bloomington, 2004.

"Ibsen and the Drama of Today" (1994)

First written for inclusion in *The Cambridge Companion to Ibsen* (1994), Miller's essay "Ibsen and the Drama of Today" was later reprinted in the revised edition of *The Theater Essays of Arthur Miller* (1996). Miller has written on several occasions about HENRIK IBSEN, and this particular essay tries to make a case for Ibsen's continued contemporary relevance. It begins by repeating a section from Miller's discussion of Ibsen in the 1957 "Introduction to Collected Plays" but proceeds to update his commentary to show how his earlier description of Ibsen's emphasis on "process, change, development" seems to becoming once again in vogue.

While Miller does not believe that many contemporary playwrights look to Ibsen's methods as models, he feels that "his standing as a modern has nevertheless improved" since he last wrote about him. In the 1930s, Ibsen had been a favorite of the Left for his "radical politics" but was rarely performed because his plays were perceived as dry and insufficiently entertaining. Critics wrongly thought, in Miller's eyes, that Ibsen lacked a "poetic spirit," and they did not view him as they did George Bernard Shaw—as a "visionary architect." Miller suggests that we partly miss Ibsen's lyricism because we only hear him in translation. His ideas, however, are sufficient to make his plays worthwhile and, Miller insists, not just the realistic social plays but also his mystical and metaphysical dramas. While the realistic plays seem more optimistic, given their demand for change, Miller views Ibsen's later plays as more pessimistic in their concern with aging, cowardice, and the unchanging quality of life.

Miller outlines disagreements regarding how to read *An Enemy of the People*. Where some view its message as anticapitalistic, others see potential fascism in its call for an intellectual elite; Miller feels that both interpretations are imposed and that Ibsen's real concern is in the "holiness" of truth that often demands a sacrifice from those who wish to uphold it. Praising the way Ibsen has "*everything* fit together like a natural organism," Miller makes comparisons to Greek drama in the way that Ibsen similarly displays an "obsessive fascination with past transgressions as the seeds of current catastrophe" to reveal "a secret moral order." Miller describes Ibsen's characters as being given a "spiritual CAT scan," in that he allows us to see them from within as well as from without, a conception that partly gave Miller the inspiration for *Death of a Salesman*.

It is Ibsen's sense of the past and its influence on the present that so attracted Miller, a sense that he sees as all too often missing in contemporary works and one that trivializes them in his eyes. While detective stories, currently popular, suggest the influence of the past, they lack any "visionary moral values" as they are more concerned with keeping their reader guessing, and so they only offer the skeleton of what Ibsen achieves "without soul or flesh." Miller also critiques ABSURDISM, for its dismissal of the past as irrelevant, its obsessive concern with the immediate here and now, and its preference of situation over character. Miller suspects that the horrors of the HOLOCAUST initiated people's belief in the absurd as a means of trying to deal with the untenable. Miller feels that critics have wrongly come to judge Ibsen's dramas as "well-made plays" rather than as revolts against the form as Ibsen had intended and that the contemporary age is suspicious of the sense of fate behind Ibsen's work because it seems to want to reject such a possibility.

Miller suggests that the key difference between Ibsen and that other innovator of modern drama August Strindberg is that Strindberg was more iconoclastic, unveiling hypocrisy but offering nothing with which to replace it. Ibsen seeks a better system. Miller suggests that people are more drawn to Strindberg because of his pessimism regarding humanity's potential, a pessimism that is seemingly supported by world events such as the Holocaust, the implosion and growing consumerism of the Soviet Union despite its rationalist and anticapitalism agendas, and the global advance of a heartless U.S. CAPITALISM. But while absurdism may better reflect this chaos, Miller suspects that Ibsen has regained popularity because of his contrasting sense of seriousness, structure, and causation if only as stays against such confusion. Miller suggests that the increasing productions of *All My Sons* seems to reflect this renewed interest in more tightly structured plays and concludes that a recent series of political and business scandals are further proof of the importance of a past that can resurface with a vengeance, just as he and Ibsen portray in their plays.

An Immigrant's Lament (1999)

An Immigrant's Lament is the title of a six-stanza aria that Miller wrote for William Bolcom's 1999 opera version of *A View From the Bridge*. Sung in act two, scene five, it takes place near the end of the play as Marco prepares to revenge himself on Eddie. Sung by Marco, it offers this reticent character a greater eloquence by allowing him to voice more expansively his anger and reasons for going after Eddie. He explains how he came to America on a "ship called Hunger" to escape the poverty of a homeland where his wife and children were starving. He left them behind but felt recompensed by the warm embrace of the United States where he could work, and he worked hard. But now Eddie has degraded his brother, insulted his blood, and ruined everything. He is intensely angry with Eddie for forcing him toward a vengeance that he feels honor bound to pursue and for being instrumental in his being sent back to his family with nothing. Although Eddie has the LAW on his side, Marco berates the United States for allowing such injustice. The repetition of the phrase "ship called Hunger" throughout the aria allows us to understand the precariousness of Marco's dream and the terrible fate to which Eddie's actions have consigned him.

In the Country (1977)

With little structure beyond an effort to depict an anecdotal sense of the changing structure of the Connecticut community in which they had lived for so many years, *In The Country* is the second photographic journal collaboration between Miller and INGE MORATH. His wife provided the photographs and he the text. The text is divided into 12 chapters, some of which are only a page long, and these are spread throughout the folio and total about 34 pages. Miller's image appears once, holding a sapling in conversation with neighbors, showing his connection to the land, although there are several candid shots of his children and friends at play, and the book is dedicated to the couple's daughter, REBECCA MILLER.

Miller's text offers a wryly humorous and often affectionate depiction of some of the characters and events that he has witnessed living in rural ROXBURY, CONNECTICUT. Despite having lived there for more than 25 years, Miller still feels as if he is the outsider and views the true country people as having a culture from which he is excluded. He reflects on life in the country as one who was "born and raised in city apartments." He recalls first buying property in the area and attracting a bad case of poison ivy through ignorance that, he reasons, taught him not to view nature too sentimentally. Considering the history of the area, he points out how most of the old farming families are now relatively impoverished and how the country is slowly being transformed and losing its separate identity from the city. Strangers move in who no longer work the land, as farmers sell out to developers. Miller mourns a loss even while he recognizes its inevitability and acknowledges, "the city man's illusions of rural stability, enduring values, and inner peace are just that, illusions of a continuity long since vanished."

Offering a sample of the people whom he has met, Miller shares anecdotes about several neighbors and their dogs, some named and others not. The life and situation of Bob Tracy, who sold junk and does odd jobs since the dissolution of his family's farm—and will provide the material for the character of Mr. Ryan in Miller's 1995 piece *The Ryan Interview*—is described in close detail. Shy of women and a permanent bachelor, Bob lived simply and frugally, mystified by the throwaway culture around him. We learn of Gussie and the development of her ménage à trois with her husband and a hired man; Rayburn, who "knows cement" and sacrifices the opportunity of a lucrative job offer from a millionaire by poaching a deer on the man's property; a local garage owner who finds the new influx of people harder to trust; a farmer's son turned housepainter who longs to be a creative writer but is without talent and who ends permanently crippled after a work accident to live in a limbo of dissatisfaction. We also meet Bert, the dairy farmer who in his sixties sold out and moved to Florida without regret. It is his place that Miller bought as his second Roxbury home.

Miller also relates some of his political adventures in the area: how one Roxbury native had the boldness to meet Senator Joe McCarthy's challenge to people to provide evidence that he had lied, and how Miller reluctantly was elected as the Democratic delegate to the 1968 Chicago convention and came to see this as a reminder of his civic responsibilities and warning against cynical complacency. We also hear of an attempt by the power company to put up electric pylons through the area and how this was defeated by the report of a single man who proved to the company that the scheme was inefficient and proved to Miller that one should never give in because the odds seem too great. However, he also sees this incident as evidence of the growing pressures of the encroaching city.

For Miller, the country, despite the relative isolation of its inhabitants, has a stronger sense of community than the city and is not the refuge of individualism that many believe. County communities allow for more trust and tolerance than found elsewhere, but they are being lost to progress. Now, doors are locked and burglaries commonplace. While solidarity still exists between older country residents, as these sell out and move away, the country is becoming a "workless suburb of strangers." It is perhaps this bleak outlook that colors the choice of the book's first and last photographs of snowy woodland scenes, with the final one containing in its foreground a land-locked eaglelike sculpture by their neighbor and friend Alexander Calder.

Critical reaction to the book was largely laudatory, enjoying this mellower side of an often-caustic playwright. Anatole Broyard agreed with Miller's assessment that American nostalgia for the country life was largely based on a misunderstanding that it was "the last stronghold of a vanished individualism," when in actuality country life relies on a strong sense of community. Albert Johnston found the journal a "muted, thoughtful, and sometimes witty" collection of stories about rural life in New England, while Harold Otness described the photographs as "provocative" and Miller's text a wistfully nostalgic and effective portrayal of a changing rural community.

FURTHER READING

Broyard, Anatole. "A Calder on Every Lawn." *New York Times*, February 10, 1977, 37.

Johnston, Albert. *"In The Country." Publisher's Weekly,* January 24, 1977, 321.

Otness, Harold. *"In The Country." Library Journal,* March 15, 1977, 722.

"In Memoriam" (ca. 1932)

This short story, little more than a character sketch, is one of Miller's earliest attempts at writing, composed around 1932 when Miller was only 17 years old. "In Memoriam" was found by AUGUSTA MILLER in 1949 in a box of papers and was later brought to light by critic John Lahr; he discovered it in the archives at HARRY RANSOM RESEARCH CENTER while looking for something with which the *New Yorker* could honor Miller on his 80th birthday. It was first published in that magazine at the close of 1995 and was reprinted in *Sales and Marketing Management* in August 1996. A note on the manuscript read, "The real Schoenzeit of the story threw himself in front of an El train the day following the incident;" the incident being his embarrassment at having to ask for train fare from his boss's son.

Based on personal experience when helping out at his father ISIDORE MILLER's business, Miller describes his impression of Alfred Schoenzeit, an indifferent salesman but an intriguing character whose name ironically means "beautiful time." A prototype for Willy Loman, Schoenzeit was "never complete," crippled by an uncertainty about the profession that he had chosen which did not entirely suit his nature. Miller sees beneath the jovial exterior a deeply dejected man. He relates how one day he accompanies Schoenzeit on a business call to carry his samples. They wearily trudge the five or so blocks to the el, where Schoenzeit has to ask his young helper for the fare. They travel in awkward silence. Schoenzeit's trip is a failure because he sells nothing and is treated rudely, but on their return journey, he is more talkative. He asks Miller about his plans, takes him back to the business, thanks him, and leaves. Much later, Miller hears that Schoenzeit is dead. Although he had not thought about him since, the news causes a "glowing smile within my soul," as if he is thankful for the man's release from a too painful existence.

In Russia (1969)

In Russia is the first photographic journal collaboration between Miller and INGE MORATH and is based on their 1967 trip to the Soviet Union. Extracts initially appeared in *Harper's* magazine, and the book was published in 1969. Morath provided 175 pages of captioned photographs and Miller the 57-page essay that begins the book. Although some geographical sites are depicted, the emphasis is on the artistic community, and several photographs show Miller sitting with artists whom they encountered. Quotes from writers who evoke different images of Russian life, including Andrey Voznesensky, Yevgeny Yevtushenko, Konstantin Simonov, and Boris Pasternak, are interspersed throughout photographic section, and the book is dedicated to Morath's parents, Edgar and Mathilde. The first and final images are of a sleigh ride, conveying a sense of Russia as a nation hurtling through a period of change; the images are supported by accompanying quotations from Alexander Pushkin and Nikolai (or Nikolay) Gogol's *Dead Souls*.

Miller arrives in Russia wondering whether this socialist experiment has worked on any level and curious to see if the Russians possess a better sense of community than he sees in the West. Explaining how Americans, coming from a similarly large nation, believe that they can understand the scale of life in Russia, Miller suggests that their desire to find fault through a common demonization of COMMUNISM often leads to them to judge the evident "poverty, inefficiency, or dirt" unfairly while ignoring such conditions within the United States itself. As he will point out later, poverty holds people back more than any authoritarian government and is ultimately the worse evil. Miller insists that Americans and Russians do have a lot in common, including their belief in a classless society that spreads the "benefits of progress . . . among all the people" and their "absolute faith in progress." But they are also, he observes, the two societies in the world that are "most racked in their spirit by the hypocritical class contradictions in their social lives." He later points out that much of U.S. art has been as conservative and self-censored as that in Russia, especially during the reign of the HOUSE UN-AMERICAN ACTIVITIES COMMITTEE in the 1950s. The main difference, Miller believes, is that the Russians tend to be more philosophical than Americans.

Although Miller insists that his book's aim is neither political nor sociological but is a consideration of the veracity of the images that he has witnessed in Russian literature that "underlie the Russian cultural consciousness," he cannot resist in engaging in both political and social commentary as he criticizes the nation's underlying ANTI-SEMITISM and references the years of Stalin's purges while considering their effect on the nation's artists and general psyche. He is also highly critical of Russian involvement in Czechoslovakia, whose socialism he praises in contrast to Russia's as "anti-ritualistic, practical, and humane." However, there is a strain of unshakeable idealism in Russia that Miller finds attractive.

Miller's truer aim is to discover why Russians who were able to leave did not and what it is about Russia that held them captive beyond and despite its politics. The book is partly an exploration of the sense of destiny that Miller sees supporting Russian patriotism which allows people to keep going despite blatant "official hypocrisy and bureaucratic stupidity." Miller links this to FYODOR DOSTOYEVSKY's "conception of Russia as being fated to lead mankind to salvation" that binds Russians together despite centuries of suffering. While he initially views Russia as having a stern barrenness that brings to mind the apocalypse, as he explores more deeply into the provinces, he discovers a Spartan nation living more closely to the land, with a 19th-century mentality and evoking an intent, similar to London, "of remaining forever and changing only when it must." He wonders, "Can it be that all feeling in Russia is historic?" One of their favorite side trips is to the State Horse Farm where they experience the freezing but exhilarating sleigh ride that is so often depicted in older Russian literature.

Running counter to this historical sense is what Miller views as the "astonishing theatrical work" of Vsevolod Meyerhold, Yevgeny Kakhtangov, and Alexander Tairov, "who thrust a metaphoric theater into the place of the old realistic one years before the West borrowed their methods." However, Miller sees a Russian tendency to keep modernity hidden—after all, Meyerhold was eliminated by Stalin—both as if it were a threat and from a seeming preference to keep the nation in stasis. Miller is clearly impressed by Russian theater but less by its playwrights than its practitioners—the directors, designers and actors. He praises the "vividness of so much Russian acting," amazed at how so simple a thing as a fake nose can create a whole new character, and the Russian actor's "genius for physicalizing." He describes the directing styles of Oleg Efremov and Yuri Lubimov and praises both the vitality of their productions and the passion of Russian audiences.

The Russian attitude toward artists is something that strikes Miller as key to better understanding the country as it reflects "the concomitant attitude toward community itself." Russian writers, Miller believes, are less competitive than those in the West, often keen to "extol the works of a competitor" and to "draw one's attention to others less renowned but equally talented." For Russians, literature evidently holds a special importance because "nowhere else are writers so close to being worshipped by the readers," and Miller cites the status of Leo Tolstoy as evidence of this. He proceeds to add that "nowhere does a regime go to such extremes to honor and hound them [writers]." Miller observes how the repression of a writer's work has ironically become "a mark of art's importance, otherwise why would government bother policing it?"

Miller divides writers in Russia into two schools by their conflicting attitudes toward power and describes them with several examples. Conservatives, such as Mikhail Sholokhov or Konstantin Simonov, who "desire authority and fear chaos," tend to focus on the strengths of Russian society and view injustice as a temporary mistake. They mostly use REALISM and support the existing power system. They are unsettled by an individualistic vanguard that developed in apparent opposition, who are critical of the system, and who seek to challenge or mock it. Some, such as Yevgeny Yevtushenko and Andrei Voznesensky, manage to do this without excessive government censure. Since all books in Russia are printed by the state and vetted by the Communist Party, others, including Yuli Daniel and Andrei Sinyavsky, resorted to having their works published abroad. Daniel and Sinyavsky had been tried and sentenced by the state for "anti-Soviet activity" the year before but, unprecedented in the Soviet Union, pled not guilty. Their trial would prove to be the starting point of the modern Soviet dissident movement that would help end Communist rule, and Miller insightfully recognizes the divisiveness of their case at this early stage.

During the trip, Miller meets with various writers—conservative and vanguard—and government officials, most notably Madame Ekaterina Furtseva, who vets all new work (and whose forthright portrait got Miller's work subsequently banned in Russia for a time). He discusses censorship with Furtseva and notes what he felt were disturbing changes made to his script in a recent Soviet production of *A View from the Bridge*, which he feels altered the psychological motivation of the characters. He is surprised at her promise to look into and rectify this and strongly suspects that she sees the absurdity of her position as government censor in a supposed people's state. He suggests to her as he does to others, "Let the people decide . . . what is valuable to them and what is destructive." Miller views censorship as demeaning to a nation since those works being censored are critical rather than harmful and are aimed less at overthrowing the government than in trying to bring the Soviet Union "closer to its own ideals." Miller accepts that total freedom for writers can bring much that is worthless, but he feels that this is a necessary price and that the benefits outweigh the waste. He poignantly observes, "If writers too must merely celebrate the system, where will the voices be found to correct what needs to be corrected?"

Miller enjoys the sense of old Russia that pervades the country and feels that the new Russia is trying to break free of this but remains uncertain as yet of its identity. This leads him to ponder the nature of freedom, especially as it pertains to the Russians. He senses an underlying resistance in Russians to the contradictions of the regime but is uncertain whether the nation is rallying to fight or getting ready to capitulate entirely. Looking forward to the future, he considers the possibility that there might be a better system than either socialism or private ownership that would not force people to choose between two inhumane extremes. As he moves into the final section, Miller offers a series of impressions of places and people whom they have met: Various cemeteries, a synagogue, hotel rooms and homes evidently bugged (and the ways that the Russians deal with this imposition), and a sparsely attended opera performance in the provinces as opposed to the reverent full house that they witness at the Bolshoi Ballet on their final evening. This latter is sandwiched between meeting two artists, both hounded to distraction by the government. They leave with a sense of relief, and Miller describes life going on in all of its messiness around the globe as their plane takes off, placing the artist front and center of this chaos, in the hope that this figure might be able to lead people to accept an "unadmitted commerce of a human kind" rather than fall back into a "terror of each other that will finally murder us all." In an atomic age, Miller is clearly concerned that Americans recognize the humanity of their enemies before going into a conflict that might destroy both sides.

Although F. D. Reeve attacked the book as pretentious and drab and failing to capture the character and humor of Russian people, most reviewers applauded the book of reportage as sincere and effective. J. Robotham described it as "one of the most interesting of Russian travel books," Victor Burg called it "strictly personal and concernedly honest," and *Times Literary Supplement* praised Miller's probing enquiry into Russian life and cultural politics.

FURTHER READING

Burg, Victor. "Arthur Miller *In Russia*." *Christian Science Monitor,* January 8. 1970, 17.
"The Chemistry of Travel." *Times Literary Supplement,* January 22, 1970, 76.
Reeve, F. D. "*In Russia*." *Book World,* January 4, 1970, 11.
Robotham, J. "*In Russia*." *Library Journal,* February 1, 1970, 496.

Incident at Vichy (1964)

In February 1964, partly as an escape from the media backlash following the opening of *After the Fall,* Miller and INGE MORATH traveled to Europe for his wife to visit family. While there, Miller covered the war-crimes trial of a group of former Auschwitz guards in Frankfurt, Germany, for the *New York Herald Tribune.* When ROBERT WHITEHEAD asked Miller for another play for the REPERTORY THEATER OF LINCOLN CENTER for later that year, Miller swiftly wrote *Incident at Vichy.* He based it on a true story that he had heard from his friend, Dr. Rudolph Loewenstein, a Jewish psychoanalyst who had been detained during the war with false papers and was saved by a stranger who had wordlessly handed him a pass. The character, Von Berg, was based on Prince Josef von Schwarzenberg, an Austrian aristocrat whom Miller's wife, Inge Morath, had known and who suffered because of his resistance to Nazi oppression. Miller's play depicted the roundup of Jews in Vichy France during WORLD

WAR II. HAROLD CLURMAN would direct and help create the play's stylized presentation. Some questioned the veracity of events in the play, and while Miller pleaded dramatic license, several critics condemned the play as misleading. The HOLOCAUST, still fairly fresh in people's memories, was considered by many too touchy a topic for dramatic license.

SYNOPSIS

The setting is Vichy France in 1942 in a police station. Six men and a teenage boy sit on a bench—they do not know one another—and wait anxiously. Lebeau complains that he needs coffee and asks Bayard if he knows what is going on. Each has been picked up on the streets, but Bayard assures him that it is nothing. Lebeau tries to get the attention of Marchand, who reluctantly responds, insisting that it must be a routine identity check. Suspecting something more, Lebeau asks Bayard if he is "Peruvian" (he means Jewish), and Bayard insists that he not ask such things in public. Having already had his facial features measured, Lebeau is ready to panic, angry that he had not left the country when he had the chance. Marchand asks a passing guard for a phone but is ignored.

Monceau speaks up in support of Marchand, telling Lebeau to be quiet. They ask a gypsy why he is there, hoping that it is for stealing and not just because he is a gypsy. The gypsy claims innocence, and Lebeau criticizes the way that they all judge by appearance. As the rest criticize the gypsy, Lebeau defends him, insisting that the Germans are a threat to everyone. When the Major limps in, the Waiter greets him as someone whom he knows from his restaurant, and Marchand tries to obtain his assistance. The Major tells Marchand to wait for the Chief of Police and swiftly leaves. The Waiter defends the Major, but Lebeau asks if the Major knows that the Waiter is Jewish.

Professor Hoffman and two Detectives bring in Leduc, Von Berg, and an Old Jew to join the detainees. Leduc complains, declaring he is a combat officer, but he is ignored. The Detectives go to track down more Jews with orders to take people singly so as not to start a panic. Marchand asks to be interviewed first and is escorted into an office.

Spotting the Major, Leduc points out that they have fought in the same battle, but the Major, although sympathetic, awkwardly leaves. Leduc asks the others what is happening, and Lebeau suggests that they are being rounded up for forced labor. Bayard explains that he has seen Jews from Toulouse at the railyard on a Polish train. When Monceau suggests that they are volunteers, Bayard points out that they were locked in and crying and that the railcars smelled bad. They focus again on the gypsy—if he is there for stealing it is routine, but if not, then a roundup is likely. The gypsy insists that he is innocent. Von Berg asks if they have been arrested because they are Jewish, making it obvious that he is not, and they quickly deny that they are, too.

Bayard advises them all to try to escape if they end up on a train and not to believe the rumors of resettlement. Monceau calls them hysterical, refusing to believe that the Nazis are killing Jews, "I mean Germans are still *people*," he declares. Leduc agrees, explaining that this is why it is so awful, but Bayard dehumanizes the Germans as fascists. Hearing that Leduc studied in Vienna, Von Berg reveals that he is an Austrian prince and asks if Leduc knew his cousin. As Leduc wonders why such a man has been detained, Von Berg suggests that it is Nazi resentment toward nobility. But his dismissal of Nazis as vulgar brutes who cannot appreciate refinement and artistry seems shallow, and he sees this as Monceau points out how much Germans appreciate good music. Marchand returns with a pass and is shown out, ignoring the others.

When the Gypsy is taken in, he has to leave his pot behind, and Bayard steals its handle. Complaining that since Jews are not a race, therefore they cannot have distinctive features to mark them, Leduc inspires several detainees to study their appearance in their papers. The Old Jew falls, but Von Berg catches and helps him back up. Though having a beard himself, Lebeau criticizes the Old Jew for wearing such an obvious sign of JUDAISM, and they all argue over who looks the most Jewish. Bayard is called in but is sent back as Ferand brings coffee for the police. Monceau advises Bayard to look more confident and less like a victim, suggesting that they each need to "create one's own reality in this world."

They argue politics, and Bayard voices his Communist beliefs, but Leduc is skeptical that these are productive against fascism. Bayard voices a belief in a future working-class victory until Von Berg points out that most Nazis are working class and that ordinary people adore Hitler. On his way out, Ferand whispers to the Waiter. Both weep in despair, and the Waiter announces to everyone that the Nazis plan to burn the Jews in Poland. Monceau still refuses to believe. As the Waiter also warns that they will be checking for circumcisions, Bayard is called. Trying to be assertive, he only succeeds in annoying the Police Captain.

Leduc shares his cigarettes and suggests that they try to overcome the single guard, but they are reticent. The waiter tries to run but is easily caught. He pleads to the Major to help him, but he is ignored, and the Captain drags him off, beating him into submission. The Major suggests that they just ask the men if they are Jewish. Hoffman mocks the suggestion, knowing that no one would openly admit this. Pointing out that many non-Jews are circumcised, including himself, the Major objects to checking men's penises. Hoffman regards it as part of a process and threatens to report the Major if he refuses to comply. The Major insists on leaving for a break.

The Boy offers to help Leduc break out, but Monceau still refuses, and Lebeau is too weak to be helpful. Monceau recounts how he left Paris after ditching books that the Nazis had forbidden but forgetting that his name and address were inside. He left in a panic but regrets his decision. Leduc feels that the Nazis are relying on them not to believe the truth and that Monceau subconsciously left those books on purpose to have an excuse to leave. Von Berg talks about a small orchestra that he sponsored and how he offered to protect its Jewish members but had been unable to do so. Realizing that Von Berg will be set free, the Boy asks him to return his mother's ring—he had been picked up on his way to the pawnshop. Von Berg asks Leduc how he can help him, but Leduc is starting to lose hope. He cannot get Monceau to face the truth, and Lebeau's wish to be Von Berg indicates an internalized guilt about being Jewish that can only make the Nazi agenda easier. Leduc does not know how to fight such passivity.

When Leduc complains about Nazi racism, Monceau says that everyone is racist and that all they can do is to try to obey the LAW, even when it seems wrong. Leduc sees this as blind indifference to reality, and they argue. Von Berg agrees to take the Boy's ring, and the Boy leads Leduc to break out just as the Major returns and stops them. He has been drinking and warns Leduc that there are more guards outside. Leduc suggests that the Major shoot himself and that the guards allow them to go. Asking Leduc why he feels he deserves to live better than him, the Major is angered by the reply he receives: "Because I am incapable of doing what you are doing." Leduc pleads with him to let them go and tells him that they will remember him as a decent man, but the Major is a lost soul and declares that there is no decency left. He curses them all, and when Hoffman pulls him away, he brandishes his gun, firing into the ceiling. He challenges Leduc about how he would feel if they let just him go, and Leduc cannot respond. They take Lebeau, Monceau, and the Boy into the office.

Only the Old Jew, Leduc, and Von Berg remain, and the Old Jew begins to rock in silent prayer. Leduc asks Von Berg to tell his wife everything. Von Berg tries to find hope, and Leduc is unimpressed at Von Berg's suggestion that this is also hard for him, given that he will survive. Von Berg confesses that he considered suicide in the face of the indifference that he saw in others concerning the Nazis taking his musicians. Leduc feels that Von Berg is still not facing reality and objects to the way that the Nazis make death seem preferable to fighting them. He asks Von Berg not to mention the furnaces to his family, and Von Berg insists that he will try and help them financially. He suggests offering a bribe to the Major but knows that this would be unwise. It upsets him to see Leduc in despair.

Hoffman comes for the Old Jew, grabbing the bundle that he is holding and releasing white feathers everywhere. When Von Berg offers sympathy, Leduc responds angrily, suggesting that Von Berg must subconsciously hate him and all Jews or he would not have allowed this to happen so easily, which makes Von Berg reconsider his responsibility. Von Berg is called, and it is clear that he will soon be released. Alone, Leduc nervously takes out a knife and considers fighting his way out. Von Berg returns with his pass, giving it to Leduc along with the Boy's ring. Despite feeling guilt at Von Berg's sacrifice, Leduc takes the pass and passes the guard. Hoffman comes out, sees Von Berg, and calls the alert. Von Berg sits quietly as the Major stares at him, neither understanding the other, as four new detainees are brought in.

CRITICAL COMMENTARY

Lebeau may use the code word *Peruvian,* in place of *Jewish,* but he is in less denial of his ethnicity than those like Bayard who constantly try to stop him even saying that. It is as if these Jews have become ashamed of themselves and, in this, allow the Germans an extra hold over them. When Lebeau keeps insisting that the Germans are a threat to them all, the rest answer in fierce denial. They refuse to believe even while in their hearts they know that it must be true and so make themselves complacent and willing victims. The only one whom Leduc can fire into helping him try to rush the guard is the young Boy, although Lebeau offers his weak support. Monceau advises Bayard to look more confident and less like a victim, but it takes more than a surface appearance: They also need to throw off their internalized feelings of victimization to be free. Monceau merely avoids confrontation in the hope that it will go away, while Lebeau has heard bad things about Jews for so long that he has come to believe them. Their fear has made them passive to their fate. Leduc is a fighter who refuses to see himself as lesser in worth than another just because he is Jewish, and his initial response is to try to fight his way out rather than to wait passively to be taken to the furnaces.

While finding no support in either Judaism or his nation, Bayard has his hopes in communism, but Leduc is skeptical of this offering any hope against the Nazi brand of fascism, pointing out that feeling part of a collective movement will not help an individual who is being tortured. He views Bayard's outlook as a negation of selfhood that is little better than being killed. However, Bayard at least shows some evidence of facing the reality of what the Nazis are doing and of fighting back when he steals the pot handle to use as a tool to facilitate an escape from the inevitable railcar. His political beliefs have also steeled him against the capitalistic seduction that appears to have drawn Marchand into working with the enemy. Marchand helps the ministry of supply and so is supporting the German war. It is unsurprising that he feels uncomfortable talking to his fellow detainees.

Von Berg accepts the Waiter's declaration about the Nazi agenda because it seems to him typical of the way they operate—doing the inconceivable to paralyze opposition. He imagines the Nazis truly believing that burning Jews was a noble endeavor and asserts this as another instance of his belief that vulgarity is taking over the world. But he criticizes from the sidelines, and his sympathy is useless. He loves his cousin, a notorious Nazi who is responsible for the dismissal of all the Jewish doctors from medical school, and he never tried to stop his cousin. He promised to protect the Jews in his orchestra but watched as the Nazis took away his oboe player.

When Von Berg asks Leduc if they can part friends, Leduc sees such an agreement as pointless as he has given up on humankind. Responding angrily, Von Berg insists that ideals still matter, even when little can be done. Leduc counters that beneath it all, Von Berg is simply relieved that he is not him and would not seriously lift a finger to help, thus making him complicit with the crime. "Each man has his Jew," he declares, and it seems hardwired into human nature to hate the Other—even Jews do this—and so Von Berg's friendship cannot matter while he allows such things to happen. He points out that the cousin whom Von Berg had mentioned with affection was a notorious Nazi, and until he can see what that means through Leduc's eyes, he cannot see that his complacency makes him complicit and just as monstrous. He asks not for guilt but for responsibility, and Von Berg begins to see the difference.

From his first entrance, the German Major is ill at ease. Miller tells us that there is "something ill about him," and it is not just his physical ailment; he is sick at heart from the abominable routine

into which he has been coerced. As the Waiter greets him, even defending him as a good man, and Marchand tries to get his ear, he passes them on to the Chief of Police and exits as swiftly as he can, not wanting to have to face his involvement. He later runs out for a stiff drink to avoid interrogating further prisoners, but he is forced by Hoffman to return and do his duty to the Reich. However, as Leduc will suggest, he could refuse, even if that might mean his death, and it would have been a nobler path. It is one path that the Major is too scared to take, hiding behind his duty to a German hierarchy rather than face his duty to his fellow human. Von Berg, in contrast, does the complete opposite. He rises to Leduc's challenge to be responsible rather than guilty, which leads him to sacrifice his own safety by giving up his pass and allowing Leduc to escape.

FIRST PERFORMANCE

Staged for the Repertory Theatre of Lincoln Center, *Incident at Vichy* opened at the ANTA-Washington Square Theatre in New York City on December 3, 1964, with the following cast:

> *Lebeau:* Michael Strong
> *Bayard:* Stanley Beck
> *Marchand:* Paul Mann
> *Police Guard:* C. Thomas Blackwell
> *Monceau:* David J. Stewart
> *Gypsy:* Harold Scott
> *Waiter:* Jack Waltzer
> *Boy:* Ira Lewis
> *Major:* Hal Holbrook
> *First Detective:* Alek Primose
> *Old Jew:* Will Lee
> *Second Detective:* James Dukas
> *Leduc:* Joseph Wiseman
> *Police Captain:* James Greene
> *Von Berg:* David Wayne
> *Professor Hoffman:* Clinton Kimbrough
> *Febrand:* Graham Jarvis
> *Prisoners:* Pierre Epstein, Stephen Peters, Tony
> Lo Bianco, John Vari

Directed by Harold Clurman
Set designed by Boris Aronson
It ran for 99 performances.

INITIAL REVIEWS

Although some critics praised the play, with Howard Taubman describing it as "a moving play, a searching play, one of the most important plays of our time" and Norman Nadel calling it a "pungent drama," a display of great "craftsmanship as a playwright," and an "outstanding cast," the reviews were predominantly negative. While some felt that the historical situation had been accurately reflected, others were outraged at what they felt were liberties taken with actual events. Miller's refusal to assign blame for the Holocaust to the Nazis alone discomfited many, as did his insistence that anyone who had not actively helped to prevent the Holocaust was as complicit in the evil as those who gave the orders to exterminate Jews. Some criticized the piece as too talkative with insufficient action and felt that ideas had buried the drama. Douglas Watt complained about "an indulgence in philosophical claptrap," Robert Brustein, the play's "noisy virtue and moral flatulence," and John McCarten its lack of "dramatic flair," and "stilted" dialogue. J. W. Lambert found the characterizations too stereotyped, and Henry Popkin accused Miller of presenting a "ritualized discovery of evil in a haze of facile small talk." The play has seen few revivals.

SCHOLARSHIP

Scholarship on *Incident at Vichy* is limited, and some of it is highly critical, but the play is discussed in most general books on Miller. Harold Clurman's director notes were published and include first impressions, character breakdowns, and conversations surrounding its premiere performance. In the past, scholars considered its moral arguments regarding the Holocaust, including Lawrence Langer, who applauds Miller's dissemination of blame, and Ellen Schiff, who explores what the play's characters suggest about Jewish identity. Lawrence Lowenthal and others have offered Sartrean readings considering the play's existential aspects that explore concepts of the Other, innocence, and choice. Among the play's detractors are Philip Rahv and Leslie Epstein. Rahv rejects the ending as "melodramatic contrivance" and Epstein as "gratuitous, unmotivated" and "phony." But while

Epstein accuses Miller of moral nihilism, objecting to Leduc's claim, "Each man has his Jew; it is the other," Rahv feels Miller was not specific enough in his extension of guilt and suggests that the play unnecessarily overcomplicates the relatively simple issue of German expansionism.

In more contemporary scholarship, Brenda Murphy suggests a universal relevance in the way that Miller uses "Nazism as a touchstone for all dehumanizing governmental oppression in the 20th century," while Janet Balakian highlights the "'choral,' metaphoric, and non-realistic fabric" of the play, and Stephen Marino connects it to Miller's later *The Archbishop's Ceiling*, pointing out how both use images of food and drink as "metaphors for political survival." Terry Otten offers an insightful reading that concentrates on Leduc's "capacity for evil" and Von Berg's lack of innocence, while Kinereth Meyer suggests that Von Berg is depicted as an ironic "Christian savior." Estelle Aden explores the play's contemporary relevance at the beginning of the 21st century, and CHRISTOPHER BIGSBY emphasizes the play's motif of waiting and makes comparisons to SAMUEL BECKETT, Franz Kafka, and ALBERT CAMUS. He also takes issue with three of the play's harsher critics: Rahv, Epstein, and Brustein.

CHARACTERS

Bayard One of the initial detainees, in his twenties, Bayard is an electrician and a communist supporter who feels he has been betrayed by the French bourgeoisie. Yet the Soviet communists have been of little support to France, and it is unsurprising that they are unreceptive to party politics. He believes in a future victory for the workers but has blinded himself to what workers can do, for Nazis are a working-class party. Poor but clean, he offers a contrast to the bearded and unkempt Lebeau. He is the austere worker against Lebeau the effete artist, but their fates will be the same at the hands of the Nazis. Also Jewish, he knows from working at the train yards what is going on. He realizes that Polish engineers are taking Jewish prisoners back to Poland, and at the very least, the prisoners are being put to hard labor. He does not believe the rumors of resettlement, and stealing the handle from the gypsy's pot shows that he is prepared to fight, getting a tool to help him escape from the railcar.

Lebeau Another detainee, 25-year-old Jewish painter Lebeau's family was offered U.S. visas in 1939, but his parents were reluctant to leave behind all their possessions, and so the family stayed. Knowing that the Nazis are looking for Jews, although he has false papers saying that he is not Jewish, Lebeau usually stays indoors to be safe. However, as a painter, he felt the need to get out and see something new, but he was picked up by Hoffman while walking. He had his nose, mouth, and ears measured, was brought to this detention center for further interviews, and remains in a state of panic for most of the play. He is weak from hunger, not having eaten since the day before, and he is bedraggled, not having shaved in a while and his clothing a mess. Uncertain of himself, he hopes that his papers will convince them that he is not Jewish. He has Bayard check them for authenticity, recognizing Bayard as someone who is more in the know. He has been driven to a point where he has lost touch with himself and is even beginning to believe the Nazi opinion of Jews. He would like to resist but physically and psychologically no longer has the strength.

Leduc A trained psychiatrist, Leduc has been in hiding with his wife and two young children outside of town because they are aware that Jews are being collected. He came into town to find medicine for his wife's toothache and was picked up on entry. His profession makes him question everyone's motives, and he is constantly seeking a better understanding of the mindsets of his fellow detainees. This allows him to draw them out better for the audience to see how they tick. He has studied in Germany and Austria, is an experienced and knowledgable man, but struggles to make sense of the Nazi agenda. He fights for his personal survival, but the horror of what the Germans are doing nearly cripples him until Von Berg's act of decency gives him new strength, and allows him to escape.

Major Wounded at battle in Amiens, the Major is regular army rather than SS. A cultured man, he plays the piano, speaks good French, and is usually a pleasant man. Unfit for fighting, he has been sent to oversee the rounding up of Jews in Vichy France, a task that he finds demeaning and offensive, but he is too fearful to refuse. He drinks heavily to soothe his distress, but he feels morally challenged by Leduc. His discomfort is emphasized by the way he so often ignores the detainees when they try to talk to him and by his resulting anger against Leduc. A moral coward, his response to Von Berg's act of responsibility is both anger and confusion.

Marchand One of the initial detainees, Marchand, is a well-dressed businessman who is impatient to leave. He has papers to say that he is not Jewish and is released by the officers. Whether or not he is Jewish is left unsaid, and while the others thought him Jewish like themselves, they, like the Nazis, were judging by appearances. He shows no fear facing his captures or asking for a phone to let people know that he will be late for meetings, and it may just be this bravado that effects his release, as he plays up his connections to the ministry of supply.

Monceau Another detainee is 28-year-old actor Monceau who is initially the cheerful optimist. He is elegant but has fallen on hard times. A traveling actor who plays leading roles, he used these skills when he was stopped before and managed to brazen it out. While in Paris, he tried to rid himself of books that he owned that had been banned by the Nazis by leaving them around the city. Having done this, he realized that his name and address was inside each one and quickly left town. Although Monceau now professes that this was a mistake, Leduc suggests that he did it all on purpose to give himself an excuse to leave because he knows more about what is happening than he admits. His denial of what the Nazis are doing is ridiculous, given his experience, and his attitude is something like that of an ostrich, burying his head in sand. He will be sent to the death camps, still denying that they even exist.

Old Jew

Brought in by the Detectives with Von Berg and Leduc, the Old Jew is a nonspeaking role but a clearly symbolic one with his bundle of white feathers. He prays for help but is led out like the rest and does not reappear. Miller may intend the feathers which he carries to indicate a potential lack of courage that was shown by so many Jews in their passive acceptance of the Nazi agenda, though this is a symbol over which there has been some debate. The play controversially argues that the lack of resistance by those involved on all sides—Nazis, Jews, Germans, Austrians, and anyone else with knowledge of events—was tantamount to complicity. By also including a young Boy in the lineup, Miller ensures that we realize that age offered no defense against the Nazi agenda.

Von Berg, Prince Wilhelm Johann A prince of a minor house in Austria and an amateur musician, Von Berg sponsored an orchestra, a number of whose members were Jewish. Although he tried to shelter them at his house, he recalls his oboist being taken by Nazis, who patiently listened to the end of the orchestral piece before snatching him. A Catholic with little interest in politics, he feels that he has a duty as nobility to set a cultural example and take on certain responsibilities. His cousin whom he still regards highly turns out to be a notorious Nazi. Allowing his refinement to distance him from actual events, Von Berg is well meaning but too effete. Initially, he sees the Nazi agenda as vulgar and seeks a refuge in art, but he comes to realize that these murders are more than a lack of cultivation—they are something far darker. As nobility, he feels that he has a certain responsibility to set an example of right behavior, and though he knows that the way the Nazis are treating Jews is wrong, he does little to stop them permanently until he bravely offers Leduc his pass, accepting his challenge to offer it as not guilt but as responsibility.

MOVIE AND TELEVISION ADAPTATIONS

Incident at Vichy was produced by George Turpin and directed by Stacy Keach for PBS in 1973, and later was released as part of the *Broadway Theatre Archive* series. It starred Rene Auberjonois, Ed Bakey, Lee Bergere, Tom Bower, Harry Davis, Richard Jordan, and Harris Yulin. The play was shortened from the original, but John O'Connor felt its impact "remains unchanged" and announced it a "fine production," despite having some reservations about the play itself. He especially commended the performances of Jordan, Yulin, and Auberjonois.

FURTHER READING

Aden, Estelle. "Forty Years after Vichy: A Study of Miller's *Incident at Vichy*." In *Arthur Miller: Twentieth Century Legend*, edited by Syed Mashkoor Ali, 239–245. (Jaipur, India: Surabhi, 2006).

Balakian, Janet N. "The Holocaust, the Depression, and McCarthyism: Miller in the Sixties." In *Cambridge Companion to Arthur Miller*, edited by Christopher Bigsby, 115–138. (Cambridge: Cambridge University Press, 1997).

Bigsby, Christopher. *"Incident at Vichy."* *Arthur Miller: A Critical Study.* Cambridge: Cambridge University Press, 2005, 248–270.

Brustein, Robert. "Muddy Track at Lincoln Center." *New Republic,* December 26, 1964, 26–27.

Clurman, Harold. "Director's Notes: *Incident at Vichy*." *Tulane Drama Review* 9, no. 4 (Summer 1965): 77–90.

Epstein, Leslie. "The Unhappiness of Arthur Miller." *Tri-Quarterly* (Spring 1965): 165–173.

Lambert, J.W. "Play in Performance: *Incident at Vichy*." *Drama* 80 (Spring 1966): 20–21.

Langer, Lawrence. "The Americanization of the Holocaust on Stage and Screen." In *From Hester Street to Hollywood*, edited by Sarah Blacher Cohen, 213–230. (Bloomington: Indiana University Press, 1983).

Lowenthal, Lawrence D. "Arthur Miller's *Incident at Vichy*: A Sartrean Interpretation." *Modern Drama* 18 (March 1975): 29–41.

McCarten, John. "Easy Doesn't Do It." *New Yorker,* December 12, 1964, 152.

Marino, Stephen. "Metaphors of Survival: *Incident at Vichy* and *The Archbishop's Ceiling*." *A Language Study of Arthur Miller's Plays: The Poetic in the Colloquial.* New York: Mellen, 2002, 107–134.

Meyer, Kinereth. "A Jew Can Have a Jewish Face?: Arthur Miller, Autobiography, and the Holocaust." *Prooftexts* 18, no. 3 (September 1, 1998): 239–258.

Murphy, Brenda. *Congressional Theatre.* Cambridge: Cambridge University Press, 1999, 226–240, 283–285.

Nadel, Norman. "Miller Calls World as Witness." *New York World-Telegram,* December 4, 1964, n.p.

O'Connor, John J. "TV: *Incident at Vichy.*" *New York Times,* December 7, 1973, 82.

Otten, Terry. *"Incident at Vichy." The Temptation of Innocence in the Dramas of Arthur Miller.* Columbia: University of Missouri Press, 2002, 134–145.

Popkin, Henry. *"Incident at Vichy." Vogue,* January 15, 1965, 27.

Rahv, Philip. "Arthur Miller and the Fallacy of Profundity." *The Myth and the Powerhouse.* New York: Farrar, Straus and Giroux, 1965, 225–233.

Schiff, Ellen. "The Jew as Metaphor." *From Stereotype to Metaphor: The Jew in Contemporary Drama.* Albany: State University of New York Press, 1982, 211–217.

Taubman, Henry. "Theatre: *Incident at Vichy* Opens." *New York Times,* December 4, 1964, 44.

Watt, Douglas. "'Arthur Miller's *Incident at Vichy* Joins Lincoln Center Repertory." *New York Daily News,* December 4, 1964, 64.

"Introduction" to Arthur Miller's *Collected Plays* (1957)

Miller's "Introduction" to his *Collected Plays* is divided into seven sections that begin with Miller's description of the importance of drama as "an expression of profound social needs." Pointing out how drama differs from other literary genres in its emphasis on performance, an aspect that also dictates a certain brevity, he insists that this should alter how plays are aesthetically viewed. While plays may address universal issues or specific concerns, Miller suggests, "the nature of the questions asked and answered" determine a play's level of REALISM, and most plays are a complex mix of realism and nonrealism rather than purely either one. Offering *Death of a Salesman* as an example, Miller suggests that in its psychologically developed characters and its attempt to answer "as many of the common questions as possible," it appears to be realistic but that in the way it presents time and uses symbolism,

it is nonrealistic. Miller tells us that his approach is "organic," by which he will vary his use of time, presentation of character, and other dramatic elements to better highlight whatever conflict around which he constructs each play.

In the next section of the essay, Miller asserts his belief that plays need ideas, without which they are worthless, but they need ideas that an audience can generally understand rather than concepts that are too new. Anything that is overly innovative is antagonistic in a populist literary form such as drama. Given that plays are performed in front of an audience that reacts not only to the play but also to rest of the audience, Miller believes that plays need to exhibit commonly understood social standards by which an audience can gauge its communal response. Each of his dramas, Miller declares, "was begun in the belief that it was unveiling a truth already known but unrecognized as such." For Miller, the playwright's job is to allow each audience member the opportunity to see his/her connection to others, "to make man more human, which is to say, less alone."

In the third section, Miller defines his relationship to HENRIK IBSEN and complains about the lack of seriousness that he sees in much of contemporary theater; a theater which he views as inclined toward "forms of adolescence rather than analytical adulthood." The nature of all drama, in Miller's view, is to educate, but the trick is to mask this aspect so as to attract an audience. Briefly discussing *The Man Who Had All the Luck* and his earlier "desk-drawer plays," Miller explains how the problems that he had with these led to an epiphany that he should make the father–son relationship central to his next plays, hence his focus in *All My Sons* and *Death of a Salesman.* In writing *The Man Who Had All the Luck,* Miller feels that he "had tried to grasp wonder" directly, and failed in the attempt. He embraced in its place an emphasis on cause and effect that he considered far more concrete and effective and which would allow for wonder to enter naturally rather than be forced.

Miller speaks briefly of his admiration for the pioneering work of the GROUP THEATER in the way that they forged such strong connections between actor and audience. Although he disliked some of

the plays they produced, he found every performance inspiring. In response, he strove to produce
a play that could appear to be natural, without
artifice, and so wrote *All My Sons.* He describes the
evolution of the play, the artistic decisions made in
its structuring, and how it related to his previous
play, *The Man Who Had All the Luck,* in that both
were concerned with a man's inability to "relate
himself to what he had done." Joe Keller's real
problem, Miller insists, is not that he criminally
sold faulty parts and tried to cover this up but that
he cannot see his connection to the rest of humanity. Such people, Miller feels, are a threat to society
and need to be exposed. Ibsen's influence rests in
"his ability to forge a play upon a factual bedrock,"
the way in which he brings "the past into the present," and his revelation of "the evolutionary quality
of life"—the possibility of "process, change, development." Miller shows how these concepts inform
All My Sons and his other work. For Miller, the
"real" in Ibsen's realism is his "insistence upon valid
causation," and he sees himself similarly striving as
a playwright "to make understandable what is complex without distorting and oversimplifying what
cannot be explained."

The essay's fourth section describes Miller's
development from *All My Sons* to *Death of a Salesman* and how he moved from a "revelation of process" to "a kind of moment-to-moment wildness
in addition to its organic wholeness." He relates
moving from the linearity of the earlier play to the
complex simultaneity of the latter, in which Willy
Loman becomes "his past at every moment" and
the process of his "way of mind" dictates the form
by which this is related. Miller explains how he
built the play around Willy's desire to confess his
guilty secret. Whereas the situation behind *All My
Sons* is gradually revealed and the play builds to
a climax, in *Death of a Salesman,* Willy's suicidal
desire is thrown straight at you, and the play's end
is implied from the start. Miller structures the play
around that sequence of memories that are needed
to move Willy to his inevitable end.

Considering what he saw as the failed attempt
to film *Death of a Salesman* with FREDRIC MARCH
in 1951, Miller suggests that what makes the play
difficult as a movie is that film tends to make

Willy's memories too visually tangible, which he
sees as one of the major differences between the
media. Considering scholarly and critical reactions
to the play from around the globe, Miller points
to the varying ways in which people responded to
the drama and its characters. He mocks those who
reduce it to Freudian parameters or as a critique of
American business, asserting that his intention had
been to offer a paean to a man who valiantly tries
to resist not being given the opportunity to leave
his thumbprint on the world. Although he had not
set out to write a TRAGEDY, Miller feels that the play
evolved into one, and he outlines his reasons why,
measuring Willy against Oedipus. For Miller, Willy's death should be viewed as a victory, despite the
wrongheaded values on which it is based, because
it is motivated by Willy's understanding that "he
is loved by his son and has been embraced by him
and forgiven." Recognizing that this system of love
as central to the play is crucial to understanding its
intended optimism, Miller offers it as an opposing
system to the patently destructive "law of success"
that so cripples people like the Lomans.

In the next section, Miller refutes claims that he
is a politically biased writer and points to some of
the conflicting political arguments that have been
leveled at his work. Although politically committed, he feels that to be too stringently political in
a play destroys the effectiveness of its dramatic
impact. For him, playwrighting "springs from an
inner chaos crying for order, for meaning, and that
meaning must be discovered in the process of writing" rather than predetermined. The "truth" for
Miller usually rests in contradictions that can only
be balanced rather than solved.

In the sixth section, Miller explains how he
moved from *Death of a Salesman* to *The Crucible* and
how these plays connect, both dealing with issues of
subjective reality. While *Death of a Salesman* was an
intentionally emotional piece, strongly influenced
by EXPRESSIONISM, he decided to make *The Crucible*
the precise opposite. Miller asserts that the play was
less about McCarthyism than about those conditions and mindsets that allowed the HOUSE UN-
AMERICAN ACTIVITIES COMMITTEE to thrive. Guilt
is central to *The Crucible,* not just in its revelation
but also in the way that it can manipulate lives.

Miller explains how he created the idea of an affair between John Proctor and Abigail from incongruities that he saw in the records of the SALEM WITCH TRIALS rather than on any firm evidence and that his play was not intended to be strictly historical. His one regret was his decision to mitigate the evil of the real Danforth because he had thought that people might find it too incredible. He now feels it important for people to accept that everyone is capable of evil as this is part of the human condition and helps us to define what is good.

After wondering if the theater's surface adherence to realism might actually be hiding a fear of facing what lies beneath, and after summing up his opinions on what *The Crucible* concerns, Miller outlines in the final section his development of *A View from the Bridge* from a one-act to a two-act play and comments on *A Memory of Two Mondays*. The latter he refers to as a "pathetic comedy" that explores the concepts of heroism and endurance. Miller defends complaints that are leveled at each, describing both plays as intentionally theatrical, although the revised version of *A View from the Bridge* moves closer to realism. To some degree, he feels that the differences between his two versions of *A View from the Bridge* reflect many of the contrasts between audiences in the United States and GREAT BRITAIN and their expectations of theater. He preferred the London production because the set and the extra players allowed Eddie Carbone to be placed in a social context that emphasized the wider implications of the story. Miller also admits a personal connection to the characters in *A View from the Bridge*.

Expanding notions of conventional realism has been, Miller explains, one of his theatrical aims, along with promoting a humanistic vision of life. But he also suggests that new theatrical forms are only worthwhile if they can help heighten consciousness and extend meaning: "Drama . . . ought to help us know more, and not merely spend our feelings." Asserting the central principle behind his work, "The prime business of a play," Miller insists, "is to arouse the passions of its audience so that by the route of passion may be opened up new relationships between a man and men, and between men and Man."

Although reviewer BROOKS ATKINSON described the "Introduction" as "forbidding," "humorless and a little pretentious," he nonetheless acknowledged the integrity of its author. The general reaction of critics was to critique the style of the writing but to applaud the essay's message. Alan Brien felt that the introduction was "painfully and often clumsily written," full of "polysyllabic words, untidy sentences, snippets of sociological jargon," and yet he concludes that the essay is also "one of the most important texts in the modern theatre," an opinion about which J. L. Styan concurs, describing it as "doubtless among the most important pieces of critical writing about drama in our time." In his introduction to *The Theater Essays of Arthur Miller* (1978), where the piece was reprinted, Robert Martin asserts his belief that this essay is Miller's "major contribution critically for the literature of his time" and marks a change in Miller's interest from defining terms and exploring the theoretical aspects of his craft to offering a detailed "commentary on the issues and problems of the contemporary theater."

FURTHER READING

Atkinson, Brooks. "Five by Miller." *New York Times,* June 9, 1957, sec. 2, p. 1.

Brien, Alan. "There Was a Jolly Miller." *Spectator,* August 8, 1958, 191–192.

Styan, J. L. "A View from the Crucible; or, the Compleat Playwright." *Michigan Quarterly Review* 18 (1979): 509–515.

"It Takes a Thief" (1947)

The short story "It Takes a Thief" was first published in *Collier's* magazine and was reprinted in a collection of crime stories, *Crime and Crime Again* (1986). A tale of moral over legal justice, it relates the case of the Sheltons who thought they had escaped with a tax free fortune that the husband has skimmed from his business, only to have it stolen, with them unable to reclaim it. They are left in a limbo of uncertainty, just waiting for the day on which the police can prove to whom the money belongs. Related in a lighthearted fashion by a colloquial narrator who apparently lived in their neighborhood, the waiting spoken of at the story's start becomes somewhat more sinister by the tale's close.

The Sheltons are a wealthy, upper-middle-class couple, clearly fortunate, but apparently ordinary on the surface. Shelton made his money in automobiles, initially by selling used cars to the war plants and then selling new cars in a growing economy. Their children are grown and when one evening they go out nightclubbing until the early hours, they arrive home to find their house burgled. We sympathize as they look in horror to see what has been taken, fearful that the crooks may be lingering. As Shelton is telephoning the police to report the crime, our suspicions are aroused when his wife stops him before he gives his name and address. However, the police trace the call and come to find out what has happened.

Shelton apologizes, blaming the excitement of the moment, and they tell the police about jewelry, silver and a fur coat that are missing, but they fail to mention the $91,000 in cash that had been in their home safe. Wondering what will happen if the thief is caught with the money, Shelton ironically assures his wife that "they never catch thieves." Eight days later, the police call Shelton to identify the items. Not knowing if they have the money, Shelton wonders how he can explain it away, and we realize that it is cash that he took from his business and did not declare on his taxes. The police bring in the thief with a bag that contains Shelton's jewelry, and they ask if he has lost anything else, such as money. Fearfully, Shelton says no. The thief is puzzled; thinking that they are framing him, he insists that he took cash from Shelton's safe. He is led away, and the detective puts away the cash. Reluctant to see it go but unable to claim the cash without seeming shady, Shelton asks the detective what will happen. He is told that it will be held while the police wait to find out more about it.

The Sheltons are haunted for the rest of their lives, rarely leaving the house, waiting for the police arrest them. The motto invoked by the title becomes true, as the thief who burgled their home exposes the bigger thieves: the couple evading their taxes. Although we do not see them held account-

able by the LAW, their punishment of forever waiting to be caught is far worse than the limited jail sentence that the robber will receive, and the storyteller feels that justice has been done.

Jane's Blanket (1963)

Miller published *Jane's Blanket,* his only children's book, the same year as the birth of his second daughter, REBECCA MILLER. The book was not dedicated to his new arrival but was named after and dedicated to his first child, JANE MILLER, who was now nearing 20 years old. The book can be read as a metaphoric lesson for how Miller desires his first daughter to view their relationship—the blanket represents the father, whose importance in his daughter's life naturally slackens over time as she takes on other interests and grows beyond her original childish need for parental support. Though currently out of print, the book was quite popular on publication. Released in 1963 by Crowell–Collier with illustrations by Al Parker, it was revised and reissued in 1972 by Viking Press with illustrations by Emily A. McCully.

According to Miller's papers, which are held at the HARRY RANSOM HUMANITIES RESEARCH CENTER, Miller's first title for this book was *Jane and her Blanket*; he later changed it to *Jane's Blanket*—this subtle change toward the possessive makes for a stronger connection between the child and the item, directing us to consider the nature of possession itself, and it also concentrates our attention on the blanket rather than on Jane by making the blanket the sole subject. This is further supported by the first page of the book which tells us far more about the blanket than about Jane—the blanket is small, pink, soft, and warm, while Jane is merely described as a "little baby."

Jane's Blanket relates the story of a little girl who carries a blanket with her for security. As a baby, she holds her "bata" when being fed by her mother and while in her playpen or crib. If she cannot see or feel the blanket, she cries. Miller relates the gradual expansion of the child's world as she begins to sleep in a bed, reach the table, and become tall enough to look out of the window. As a toddler, she does not carry the blanket everywhere but continues to sleep with it. Her mother buys her a new blanket, but Jane insists on the old one, even though it is now too small for her and is worn out. She begins school, learns to ride a bicycle, and becomes old enough to do chores. The blanket is forgotten for a time but then recalled and reclaimed. Jane sets it on the windowsill, uncertain if she should sleep with something so small and ragged. When she wakes, she sees a bluebird pulling out its threads, and her father explains that it is doing this to line its nest. Jane leaves the blanket for the bird to take after her father assures her that the blanket will remain hers wherever it is as long as she can remember it. This transforms the tale of a little girl and her blanket into an acceptance and embrace of the needs of others and an understanding of the power of memory.

Joel Chandler Harris (1941)

One of Miller's earliest radio dramas, the biographical *Joel Chandler Harris* was aired on June 23, 1941, as part of the *Cavalcade of America* series. Played by Karl Swenson, Miller presents Harris as a man obsessed with the United States's need to remember its roots, even if that means its association with slavery, and through this to recognize the value of ordinary people. Harris's creation of an oral history of sorts through his Brer Rabbit tales and other stories is presented as a means of uniting those who listen—worthwhile to recall given that the country would soon be at war. Unpublished, a typescript can be found at New York Public Library's Center for the Performing Arts.

The Last Yankee [single scene] (1991)

Miller wrote this brief two-character one-act play for a festival in 1991. Set in a state mental hospital, we meet two husbands, Leroy Hamilton and John Frick, whose wives are patients at the facility; that is the only thing they have in common. Leroy Hamilton is a freelance carpenter and a descendent of Alexander Hamilton, and Frick is a conservative businessman. They have come to visit, and while they sit together in the waiting room, they strike up a conversation. When Miller wrote an additional scene for this play in 1993, he retained the first one virtually intact, with just the extension of one line and a couple of stage directions. When the short version was first performed, it was ignored by the critics, although its revival in 1998 as part of the SIGNATURE THEATER's season on Miller met mixed reviews. The two-scene version fared little better in the United States.

The conversation between the two men reveals a deep rift in their outlooks, and it is this aspect, reminiscent of playwright SAMUEL BECKETT, on which this version seems to concentrate, illustrating the way in which humans are so poor at communicating their true feelings and concerns. So caught up in their own lives and problems, Leroy and Frick converse, but neither really understands the other or makes any true connection. They begin and end with Frick staring out at the empty parking lot.

FIRST PERFORMANCE

The Last Yankee played at the ensemble Studio Theater in New York City in June 1991 as part of the Marathon Annual Festival of New One-Act Plays, with the following cast:

Leroy Hamilton: John Heard
John Frick: Biff McGuire

Directed by Gordon Edelstein

The Last Yankee (1993)

Initially written and performed in 1991 as a single scene in which two husbands discuss their wives' conditions while sitting in the waiting room of a mental hospital, Miller decided to return to *The Last Yankee* two years later to write an additional scene in which we could meet the wives. The first scene was left intact with only slight additions. Leroy's line, "I'd like them to be a little more sure before I take her out again," now continues, "Although you can never *be* sure," to indicate Miller's belief that life is uncertain at best. The rewrite also includes stage directions to have Leroy carry a banjo case and Frick a valise, adds an awkward pause during their dialogue, and offers the final direction *They sit for a long moment in silence; each in his own thoughts* to indicate their continued inability to communicate properly with each other on any meaningful level. This two-scene version was premiered in both New York and GREAT BRITAIN in January 1993 with different casts, and DAVID THACKER directed the London version.

In CHRISTOPHER BIGSBY's *Arthur Miller and Company* (1990), Miller describes the United States as a nation full of crazy people, insisting, "More hospital beds in the United States are occupied by depressives than any other disease, by far." In the play, madness becomes both fact and metaphor—it offers itself as the common refuge of a general public that is unable to face up to certain truths. The play takes place in a state establishment for the insane, but its inmates represent the United States as a whole, as the character Patricia insists, "Anybody with any sense has got to be depressed in this country." But Miller cannot let it rest there, and the play becomes an attempt to find a solution to this dilemma. The advice that he finally offers is to accept responsibility for oneself and others and to renew social and personal connections as a barrier against such despair.

SYNOPSIS

In the first scene, Leroy Hamilton, a freelance carpenter and descendent of Alexander Hamilton, and John Frick, a conservative businessman, meet in the visiting room of the state mental hospital. Both have wives who are currently staying in this establishment. His first time, Frick checks with Leroy on the routine and makes small talk, commenting on the size of the parking lot and relating how he asked a patient for directions. Frick is disturbed at the number of people of color in the hospital, but he thinks it is a pleasant place. They compare their wives' conditions, when they first began and how they have been coping. Both wonder why Patricia

and Karen are so fearful and depressed, but they can come up with no clear rationale. Leroy warns Frick not to give up or to feel too sorry for himself.

Patricia's family wants her moved to a private facility, but Leroy cannot afford this, and preferring her closer, he will not let them pay. Frick could afford a private place, but he has brought Karen here to save money. He complains about how much he has to pay for a plumber, but he is taken aback when Leroy tells him that he is a carpenter, having thought him something more prestigious. Leroy used to buy wood supplies from Frick's supply company. Frick recalls an article about Leroy being descended from Alexander Hamilton and asks about his work. Leroy has been renovating churches. Frick is curious as to why he settled for carpentry, thinking that he could have done more with his family connection. Upset, Leroy chastises Frick for his snobbishness. Clueless as to why Leroy became angry, Frick returns to commenting on the parking lot, and then they sit in silence.

The second scene begins with an unnamed patient lying motionless in bed in Patricia's room. Patricia is playing ping-pong with Karen offstage but quits the game. They come into the room to talk. Karen's conversation seems filled with non sequiturs, but Patricia patiently offers her support. Patricia needs to decide if she will go home today. She has stopped taking her pills as Leroy had advised, and feels much better, but she is still uncertain about whether she can cope. Both women are building up courage to go out to their husbands. It annoys Patricia that her husband is not wealthy and will not accept help from his well-to-do relatives. Karen admits that she is rich but not happy, and she recently overdosed on pills. They discuss places to shop for groceries, and Karen tells Patricia about her tap dancing and feeling haunted by her mother, who left her family farm to a distant cousin. Patricia recalls her mother and brothers and all the wonderful things they did though, she confesses, both brothers killed themselves.

Karen goes to find her husband, and Leroy enters. He notices that Patricia is looking good, and she admits she is feeling better. They talk about their children, and Leroy tells her that he upped his price on his last job and got it. Feeling better able to live in the present, Patricia says that she is thinking of coming home, but Leroy leaves it up to her. He suggests that it was her family's unrealistic expectations that have made her so dissatisfied. She begins to see what a terrible time he has had in dealing with her illness, but he refuses to blame her. She complains that he is too isolated, and he grows angry with her view of him as a failure. Trying to lighten things, he recalls her father's response to him. As a Swede, he had hated Yankees, so Leroy declares a hope that he is the last Yankee so that people will let such hatred go, and he reminds Patricia of his belief in a noncompetitive life to which she feels drawn.

Patricia tells him that she has stopped her medication; he is delighted. She asks how has he coped with her illness, suspecting that he has seen other women, but he denies this, saying that he just played the banjo and kept hoping that she would get better. She needs to know why he has stuck by her, and what the future will hold; he explains that it is useless to look to the future but to enjoy the here and now. He tries to teach her something about spirituality, insisting that she must love life as it is, not as she wants it to be. He takes his banjo to play a tune, and the Fricks join them. To Leroy's amazement, Frick thanks Patricia for helping his wife, while Karen goes out to put on her tap-dancing attire. Frick is embarrassed about her hobby, but Patricia encourages him to lighten up and pay more attention. Karen returns and asks Frick to sing "Swanee River" for her, which he reluctantly attempts. While Patricia and Leroy are complimentary, Frick loses his patience and explodes with anger. Karen tries to defend him, and he apologizes and tries to be nice, but it is too late. He leaves, frustrated by Karen's unresponsiveness. Leroy tries to pick out the tune, and Karen begins to dance but cannot continue and leaves. Patricia reaches out to Leroy; they connect, and she is ready now to leave with him. As the two walk out together, the patient in the bed finally stirs but then falls back into stillness.

CRITICAL COMMENTARY

The "last Yankee" of the title seems to refer to Leroy, as the descendant of Hamilton who sup-

ported the Union, but its meaning remains unclear. It could mean "last" as in "no more"—despite the fact that Leroy has seven children—or "the most recent type." As a Yankee, with no other ethnic background, in one sense, Leroy becomes isolated. As Patricia points out "they've got their Italian-Americans, Irish-Americans, Hispanic-Americans—they stick together and help each other. But you ever hear of Yankee-Americans?" She goes on to insist that all a Yankee can do in American society is to "sit there all alone getting sadder and sadder."

But being a Yankee also has value, evoking traditional Protestant virtues of modesty, sacrifice, perseverance, and hard work. Leroy comments on the way that men like Frick dismiss laborers like Leroy as "dumb swamp Yankee[s]" and highlights the irony of such views since without such men, America mostly likely would never have been built. Frick refuses to get his point, however, and loops back to the start of their conversation as if to block out all that has passed between them. They end, sitting in silence, a point that Miller emphasizes in the longer version, clearly unable to communicate to each other what they believe or feel.

However, Leroy does not offer an ideal, and each of the play's four speaking parts, with their mix of negative and positive attributes, contributes to the overall solution. The husbands are only partly to blame for their wives' conditions for the wives themselves have some responsibility and must learn as many lessons as their respective husbands. A number of critics have described the precision of the play's construction in musical terms in an effort to show how each character contributes to the overall impression.

Leroy and Frick seem to be in complete opposition. One is poor with many children, the other rich with no offspring. Where the motivating force of Leroy's life is love (although their relatives have offered to finance a better home, his wife is here because it is close enough for him to visit) for Frick it is money (Frick can afford to send his wife to a nicer place but refuses to do so to save the money), and money comes first in Frick's every consideration. While Leroy, unconventionally, carries a banjo, Frick carries the more practical valise of clothing for Karen. While Leroy exhibits tolerance and patience toward others, Frick is impatient and is clearly prejudiced. Our first view of the two patently emphasizes their difference, with Leroy sitting quietly reading and Frick pacing and on edge. Yet Leroy also isolates himself, has little ambition, and keeps apart from society, while Frick, albeit materially, seems more a part of his community, as well as demonstrating that inspiring American dream of rags to riches. They each have very different priorities, and yet each has something positive to offer, and a balance between the two may be the better path to mental health.

Just as Leroy balances Frick, so too does Patricia balance Karen, or at least, complement her. Patricia's surety and sense of self, coupled with Karen's knowledge that love, open communication, and certain freedoms matter more than money, may provide an ideal. Karen is partly lost because she feels totally separated from her sense of the past, while Patricia is too tied to her past. The past and a clear memory of that past are important but only insomuch as they relate to the present, and while the present may be depressing, it is pointless to worry and become depressed over the future because such thoughts kill the optimism and hope that are necessary for survival in the present. The trick, Miller suggests, is to learn to see the wonderful in the everyday.

Patricia needs to connect, not just with her husband but also with the times. She lives too much in the past and the future but never in the present. She will learn during the course of the play to concentrate on each day as she lives it. The perfection for which she has striven is a virtual impossibility—unless you are prepared to simplify your expectations vastly. To Leroy, one can find perfection in something as ordinary as "a hot bath." He knows that Patricia needs to take responsibility for her own life, so he leaves the decision as to when she leaves the home to her. She has allowed social expectations to rule her life in a way that Leroy refuses. She needs to accept that her family's dream of everything being "wonderful" is unreal and dangerous, as its inflated expectations can kill optimism.

Patricia needs to learn to see the wonderful in the everyday as Leroy does and to look at the world with realistic expectations. By this, optimism can be reborn, and the strength to go on can be renewed. Leroy sees the spirituality in "ice skating" as it allows you to forget yourself and to "feel happy to be alive." His work building church altars and his profession as a carpenter, like Jesus, further emphasis his spiritual aspect. Patricia desperately needs to discover some spirituality in her life. True spirituality is a natural thing, not imposed dogma, and as Leroy declares: "We are in this world and you're going to have to find some way to love it!" This is, perhaps, the best advice that Miller can offer. The answer is to grasp hold of love and optimism to crowd out the fear, hate, and confusion. To do this effectively, you need the support of companionship, as it is too much to do alone.

To view the world rationally and look for logical explanations is doomed to failure, for as Leroy tells us, "you can never *be* sure," a line that Miller added to ensure that we do not miss the point. The human drive to know and to understand may be unquenchable, but we must learn to accept incomplete answers if they are the best that we can ever reach. In contrast to the continuing disconnection between Karen and Frick, Leroy and Patricia finally reconnect as "she reaches out and touches his face." She does this both in love for him and in gratitude for his attempting to help her new friend. She still engages in a "struggle against her self-doubt," but she is not allowing it to defeat her, especially as she realizes that she has her husband there to help. He carries out her bag with his banjo, and their two lives are similarly united at this point. Their difficulties are solved for the meantime, and they end the play united in vision with a shared realization that nothing is permanent but to make the best of what they have.

FIRST PERFORMANCE

The Last Yankee opened at the Manhattan Theatre Club in New York City on January 21, 1993, with the following cast:

Leroy Hamilton: John Heard
John Frick: Tom Aldredge
Unnamed Patient: Charlotte Maier
Patricia Hamilton: Frances Conroy
Karen Frick: Rose Gregorio

Directed by John Tillinger
Set by John Lee Beatty

INITIAL REVIEWS

Reviews of the New York production were fairly mixed, with those in the negative camp finding fault with the play's sketchy quality, its ambiguity, and what they felt were dated issues. Edith Oliver felt it too much a lecture of which she missed the point, and Michael Feingold, "a leftover cry from a world that has long ceased to exist." However, Melanie Kirkpatrick called it "funny and tragic, sobering and uplifting" and praises the way that the play elevates "ordinary events into poetry," Richard Corliss found it "poignant" and reminiscent of the later work of Matisse in spirit as it reveals "the contours of a soul," and David Patrick Stearns felt that it "showcases Miller's ability to present an everyday scene that effortlessly crystallizes basic human truths." Howard Kissel saw something fitting in the timing of the play's opening just after Bill Clinton's inauguration: "a young President devoted to change and hope . . . Miller's play is also about renewal, reassessment of values and belief in the future." He is also one of several critics who note the musical nature of the play, calling it a "well-wrought piece of chamber music."

SCHOLARSHIP

Susan Abbotson published a journal article that explores Miller's exposure of the "false myths of American society," and the play is briefly discussed in recent books on Miller. The most insightful of these are Terry Otten and CHRISTOPHER BIGSBY. Bigsby depicts Leroy as a man who is seeking "contentment outside the parameters of national myths" in a play about tensions that exist "in the culture at large." Otten connects Patricia to Willy Loman and discusses the play's "artistic ambiguity." Otten has also published an essay that explores the play's relationship to comedy and tragedy. Heather Neill's interview with David Thacker and Miller prior to the London production and reviews such as those by Sheridan Morley, John Peter, and Irving Wardle also offer useful interpretative details. Wardle considers the play, asking the question: "How would America's founding fathers respond if they could see what posterity has done to their earthly paradise," while Morley views it as taking "the pulse of an America no longer in the best of spiritual or emotional health." Peter explores it as a "requiem with a fugitive bass-note of hope."

CHARACTERS

Frick, John Frick is a self-important businessman, just turned age 60, who owns several operations. Having survived poverty during the GREAT DEPRESSION, he has come far financially but has no offspring, and his wife Karen has recently been admitted to the local mental hospital. He is a man who judges by appearance, and his inability to read Leroy is an early indication of just how wrongheaded he can be. He feels fooled by Leroy, whom he judges by his Ivy League dress and educated voice to be something "better" than a carpenter. We should recognize that Frick's condescension toward a perfectly valuable occupation is as ridiculous as judging Leroy by his attire in the first place. But Frick is incapable of clear vision—of himself or of others. Frick can scarcely recognize his own wife's humanity as shown in the way that he describes her condition as if she were a broken-down car. Frick shows himself to be a total hypocrite as he insists that Leroy should charge as much as he can get, although he has just been complaining that a plumber (who charges the same rate) is "destroying the country" by charging such sums.

Finance rules Frick's life and outlook, and his name calls to mind the 19th-century "Robber Baron," which sets him in decided contrast to Leroy's old Yankee background. It is easy to sympathize with Leroy and his restraint in the face of such an ignorant, pompous windbag. As Leroy suggests, it is people like Frick who are promoting the madness with their false views and expectations. He likes to sound off about things about which he knows little, enjoying the sound of his own voice more than trying to communicate. He cannot accept madness or see other people for who they really are because his vision is blinkered by his own self-concern and egotism.

Frick is both opinionated and racist, even blaming his wife's condition on "these Negroes." He has a selfish need to blame someone—but never himself—for anything bad in the world. Leroy tries to warn him that he needs to look beyond his own concerns and that such reactions are selfish: "Start feeling sorry for yourself, that's when you're in trouble. . . . After all, she can't help it either, who you going to blame?" but Frick, selfishly embarrassed, constantly interrupts his wife and prevents her from speaking. Ashamed of her tap-dancing hobby, he tries to stop her telling anyone about it and puts it down when people find out. He has neither patience nor understanding for his wife.

But Frick is not the absolute villain. Unlike Leroy, he provides his wife with all the prosperity that the United States can offer to the hard worker. While Leroy was born in the 1940s, Frick is older, having grown up in the 1930s. This age difference is reflected in their outlooks. The 1940s were a time of chaos but also of prosperity. Leroy, coming from a "good" family, has never had to face real poverty. Frick may be obsessed with prosperity, partly, from having been denied it in his youth. Frick has lived the American dream and is proud of his rags-to-riches story, but he now has to consider what he has really achieved. He has plenty of money but little happiness. One suspects that, at heart, he actually loves his wife—which makes their disconnection all the more tragic.

Frick, Karen   In her sixties, Karen is wife to John Frick, and that is her only real identity. She has just been admitted to the mental hospital and made a connection with Patricia. Karen's thinness emphasizes the emaciation of her whole life, her lack of children, and its barrenness. There is a suggestion that she may have tried the ultimate self-effacement and attempted suicide in Arkansas. She submerges herself completely, talking to Frick about his interests and never asserting her own. Now, she has broken down, Frick does not know how to help her, as he does not know who she is. But the blame is not entirely Frick's, for Karen is also personally responsible for her own destruction. She has allowed this to happen by denying herself an identity. Utterly passive, she does whatever she is told, apparently incapable

of independent thought. When no one is there to direct her, she freezes into inactivity.

Karen's world seems to have no sense of connection, as shown by the non sequiturs with which she begins to speak. Yet, she makes sense on her own terms, explaining to Patricia how she got from Chevrolet to General Motors. However, she needs someone there to listen and to understand—two things of which Frick is incapable. Rootless, her mother having given the family farm to a cousin, she has no past to put things into perspective. Life has become too confusing, which is why she has fallen back on letting others tell her what to do; it frees her of decision. Alone and frightened, she degenerates into something of a performing poodle, but there is a purposeful irony in her spirited tap routine.

Karen's tap dancing is an attempt to communicate to her self-absorbed husband, but he refuses to listen. He can only respond with embarrassment while Leroy and Patricia offer the only encouragement. Frick starts by singing too fast and ends in anger. At Karen's request, he sings "Swanee River"—ironically, a song of nostalgic longing for family—missing the fact that Karen is yearning for a proper family connection just as the lyricist describes. Her dance for a moment holds "a promise of grace" to illustrate the rightness of her impulse, but as her dancing grows more sensuous and Karen's humanity becomes emphasized, Frick loses patience and puts an end to the freeing movement, sending Karen back into debilitating despair. Leroy, kindly, attempts to bring her out of this by picking out the tune on his banjo, and Karen valiantly tries to respond, but a key element is missing—her husband—and she cannot continue. Her self-assertion dissipates as the opposition becomes too much for her to bear. As she exits, we are given the strong impression that Karen's future is not bright.

Hamilton, Leroy   At 48, Leroy is a carpenter who mostly deals in renovations but tends to undersell his product. His wife Patricia has been in and out of the mental facility while he has been left to raise their seven children, aged 5 to 19. Linked by birth to Alexander Hamilton, Leroy represents a historical concept of being "American" as outlined by the Constitution, which was probably cowritten by Hamilton and Thomas Jefferson. Yet, Hamilton is a highly ambivalent figure; although his association with the writing of the Constitution would seem to set him on the side of individual rights and freedom, he was also a keen Federalist who advocated protective tariffs and a strong central government in preference to allowing the states their own autonomy. As the key finance figure in the country—first Secretary of the Treasury—he is also associated with the partially destructive, materialistic aspects of U.S. thought. A man who evidently held the seeds of his own destruction, he died in his late forties in a duel with the vice president, Aaron Burr. Leroy is about the same age that Alexander Hamilton was when he fought his duel with Burr but is of a very different nature.

Leroy's philosophy regarding U.S. competitiveness, "We're really all on a one-person line," seems to suggest that competition is largely unnecessary and can be destructive, being divisive rather than allowing connection. Emphasizing individuality makes competition meaningless—which takes a lot of pressure off daily life. Leroy's banjo has been his therapeutic aid; many times when things became too bad with his wife, he would play his banjo. He likes the banjo for its "clean," uncluttered sound— and this is his solution for how to live life as a whole, but it is not an entirely realistic expectation, as life is often messy.

Leroy refuses to do a job that he hates, as his father did, simply to satisfy social expectations. Independent of society, he also will not allow false expectation to dictate his life, although he recognizes the necessity of remaining within social boundaries. He sticks by his wife through her years of mental problems and adequately provides for his large family. In some ways, he is the "ideal Yankee," both free and able to accept responsibility, and Miller may intend for Leroy to stand for the spirit of Yankeeism that comes to the rescue of modern America, as symbolized by Patricia.

Leroy's strong belief in the equality that lies at the heart of democracy, his evident tolerance and patience, all encourage us to see him as a perfect figure—and yet, Leroy, too, has his faults. He is too isolated from others, which is the root of his problem with his wife; she feels that they are too separate from the rest of society. It is hard for Patricia to trust him because she does not understand his value system. Leroy needs to see Patricia's insecurities and to deal with them rather than to wait calmly for her to get over them on her own—so his fault is one of omission that is not unlike Frick's.

Hamilton, Patricia Patricia is married to Leroy and has a history of depression. This time, she has been in the hospital for seven weeks; it is her third admission. From our first view, she seems "normal," a well-balanced individual, but Patricia is a muddle of positive and negative views and all of her assertions are not trustworthy. She is not the voice of truth, though she is capable of speaking truths. She is scared of the responsibilities that she knows are part of the social contract. She is wary of Leroy's work ethic, a victim of the belief in the get-rich-fast-and-easy money cult that destroyed her brothers. She needs to touch base with what really matters, that is, people, not things. For too long, she has been more concerned with things—upset, for example, that her husband does not have as good a car as other men who, she feels, have only "half his ability." Her obsession with money is shown in the way she is *quickly interested* in Karen's wealth.

Patricia is a woman on the edge, trying to find a way by which she can live with uncertainty, as she must if she is to survive. There are no guarantees in life, and she must learn to accept this. As Miller told Helen Neill, Patricia and her siblings have suffered because "they've been built up to believe something glamorous is going to happen to them, that they are going to be lifted up by a magical wave and find prosperity and fame. It is not an uncommon complaint." Patricia idealizes her "golden" family to the detriment of her husband, but their achievements have been fairly meaningless, brief bylines in the history of sport, as they themselves have finally realized. The whole family was raised with high expectations, and both Patricia's brothers commit suicide in the end out of "disappointment."

Patricia's evident concern for Karen and the way in which she tries to draw her out shows her growth away from self-concern. Patricia has blamed Leroy for her state up until now, but she has finally realized that she must take responsibility for her own condition. The first step in this was to stop taking her tablets, which only took away any necessity to feel responsible for anything. The next is to better accept Leroy's way of life. To help her, he offers a compromise and meets her part way, by beginning to charge more for his work.

Unnamed Patient This patient is present but motionless throughout scene two. Just before the final curtain, the patient "stirs, then falls back and remains motionless" as "a stillness envelops the whole stage." This image indicates that while Patricia and Leroy may have the strength to get on with their lives, there remain, unfortunately, many in society who do not. The patient symbolically acts as both warning and accusation.

FURTHER READING

Abbotson, Susan C. W. "Reconnecting and Reasserting the Self: The Art of Compromise in Arthur Miller's *The Last Yankee.*" *South Atlantic Review* 63, no. 4 (Fall 1998): 58–76.

Bigsby, Christopher. *"The Last Yankee." Arthur Miller: A Critical Study.* Cambridge: Cambridge University Press, 2005, 382–389.

Corliss, Richard. "Attention Must Be Paid." *Time*, February 8, 1993, 72.

Feingold, Michael. "Post-Miller Time." *Village Voice*, February 2, 1993. In *New York Theatre Critics' Reviews* 54 (1993): 26.

Green, Blake. "A Literary Lion Still Roars." *Newsday*, January 17, 1993, 15.

Kirkpatrick, Melanie. "Arthur Miller, Alive and Home Again." *Wall Street Journal*, January 27, 1993, A14.

Kissel, Howard. *"Yankee* Explores Rebirth of Nation." *Daily News*, January 22, 1993. In *New York Theatre Critics' Reviews* 54 (1993): 29.

Morley, Sheridan. "In *The Last Yankee* Miller Is Taking American Pulse." *International Herald Tribune*, February 3, 1993, n.p.

Neill, Heather. "Hands Across the Sea." *Sunday Times*, January 17, 1993, sec. 8, p. 20.

Oliver, Edith. "Yankee Doodling." *New Yorker*, February 1, 1993, 102.

Otten, Terry. *"The Last Yankee." The Temptation of Innocence in the Dramas of Arthur Miller.* Columbia: University of Missouri Press, 2002, 220–228.

———. "The Last Yankee: A Comedy about a Tragedy." In *Arthur Miller: Twentieth Century Legend,* edited by Syed Mashkoor Ali, 362–371. (Jaipur, India: Surabhi, 2006).

Peter, John. "America the Grave." *Sunday Times*, January 31, 1993, sec. 8, p. 21.

Simonson, Robert. "Values, Old and New: Arthur Miller and John Tillinger on *The Last Yankee.*" *Theater Week* (January 18–24, 1993), 13–18.

Stearn, David Patrick. "Off-Broadway Show on Love among the Disenchanted." *USA Today*, January 28, 1993, D8.

Wardle, Irving. "Miller Back on Form with a Loser's Tale." *Independent*, January 31, 1993, 19.

"Lines from California: Poem" (1969)

"Lines from California: Poem" is a 36-line poem about the superficiality of life in California. It reads like a series of observations, each sentence set in its own stanza, by which Miller sequences what he suspects might be the Californian redefinitions of such concepts as tragedy, brotherhood, sacrifice, progress, philosophy, and war. Every concept is belittled and reduced by its redefinition. First published in *Harper's* in 1969, it was reprinted in HAROLD CLURMAN's edition of *The Portable Arthur Miller* in 1971.

Californians, according to Miller, are obsessed with money, possessions, boundaries, and people's backgrounds. Miller describes them as living as if they are "on a perpetual cruise" during which, part of the deck "is always on fire," to depict what he sees as a frenetic insistence on appearing to be at leisure. They concentrate on minutiae and appearances, ignoring any harsh realities as inappropriate to their hermetically sealed perfection. He jokes about the Californian culture of cars, in which only those without work seem to be without wheels. Miller depicts a self-involved and shallow society, and he presciently concludes by warning that such ways of thought may be taking over the rest of the country: "They know they are the Future/They are exceedingly well armed."

Listen for the Sound of Wings (1943)

Broadcast on April 19, 1943, as part of the *Cavalcade of America* series, the radio drama *Listen for the Sound of Wings* is, according to Albert Wertheim, "one of Miller's finest radio scripts." Recounting the real-life tribulations of Pastor Martin Niemoeller, played by Paul Lukas, and his struggles against Nazi oppression, the point is made early on that while in the United States people are granted freedom of worship, this is not the case in Nazi Germany, and Miller pointedly adds to the story that Germans are not allowed freedom of speech either. While Niemoeller initially accepts Hitler's atheism as a tactical ploy, once one of his parishioners is shot for speaking against the Führer, he realizes the fight for free speech could well be to the death. He refuses to be silent and uses his pulpit to speak out against Hitler and the Gestapo who harass him. Sent to a concentration camp, he is brutally tortured but refuses to recant, becoming an inspirational martyr for the rights of free speech. Never published, a typescript for this drama can be found at the HARRY RANSOM RESEARCH CENTER, and the Museum of Radio and Television holds a recording.

FURTHER READING

Wertheim, Albert. *Staging the War.* Indiana University Press: Bloomington, 2004.

Listen My Children (1938)

Written with fellow playwright NORMAN ROSTEN while both were working for the FEDERAL THEATER PROJECT, *Listen My Children* was a one-act play that was never produced. Described as a "comedy satire with music," it provides early evidence of Miller's use of music to counterpoint drama. Miller was not particularly fond of this early work and described it as a "farcical sort of play about standing and waiting in a relief office." He wanted to write something more serious than light political satire. However, when Miller appeared before the HOUSE UN-AMERICAN ACTIVITIES COMMITTEE (HUAC) in 1956 to be questioned about his political associations, the opening scene from this play was read as potential evidence that Miller had communist sympathies.

This expressionistic and overtly satirical scene, which Miller credits mostly to Rosten, features a committee frenetically working while a secretary feeds them castor oil each time an alarm rings. The room is filled with bunting and large, ticking clocks, and at its center is a man bound and gagged with water dripping on his head and branding irons at the ready. HUAC suggested that congressional investigating committees such as their own were the targets of the play, but Miller evaded the charge. The opening sounds like a play that Miller described to critic Martin Gottfried as portraying "a mad Star Chamber where witnesses were gagged, bound and tortured," but Gottfried erroneously connects this description to another play written around the same period, *You're Next*. The manuscript was never published but can be found in the Rare Books Division of the Library of Congress.

"Lola's Lament" (1995)

Written for a collection of poems that were created by writers about their dogs to raise funds for the Company of Animals Fund, "Lola's Lament" was Miller's contribution to *Unleashed: Poems by Writers' Dogs* (1995). This lighthearted 27-line poem is split into three stanzas and appears in a section titled "Canine Nervosa." It is spoken from the perspective of Miller's dog, Lola. Lola protects her family, worries at every unfamiliar noise, and is insecure in an uncertain world where violence could come from any angle. She guards the house, sleeping lightly, and barks at anything that she finds to be unusual. With her more attuned senses that can spot the wildlife that her owners miss when out on a walk, she is amazed at their limited vision, which seems to protect them as much as she. The first stanza describes her mission to guard, and the second a walk in the woods. The final stanza comically contradicts the first, which claims a suspicion of everyone by asserting her love of visitors whom she makes a point of greeting noisily and enthusiastically. "Between the dangers/And the greetings" she concludes, "I'm simply exhausted."

The Man Who Had All the Luck (1944)

MARY SLATTERY had an Aunt Helen whose husband, Peter, had hanged himself in his barn. What interested Miller when first hearing this piece of his wife's family history was the fact that the man had been popular and always able to find a job even during the GREAT DEPRESSION. Despite his prosperity he had grown increasingly paranoid, and this psychosis led him to suicide. That this occurred in a country setting far away from the pressures of city life made it all the more intriguing. Miller had also recalled a piece of recent family history in which Moe Fishler, his cousin Jean's husband, and another evidently troubled man to whom success came easy, had suddenly died while bathing alone at the beach. He would later tell this tale in detail in the short story "The 1928 Buick."

Miller originally wrote *The Man Who Had All the Luck* as a novel in which David goes from success to suicide. However, David's initial triumph over fixing the car was not done by Gus, who did not yet exist, but because he took it to another garage and then claimed he had fixed it himself. Thus, his success is built on a lie rather than on the compassion of the later version. Various subplots told the stories of David's three friends: Shory, who lost his legs in the war and feels inadequate for the woman he loves; Amos, whose father has ruined his pitching by having him train in isolation; and J.B., who

accidentally kills his own desperately wanted child when drunk. These plots would be severely trimmed for the play, Amos would become a brother, and Miller would continue his exploration of father-son and brother-brother conflicts.

Despite having paid an advance, on reading an early draft, Miller's publisher decided to turn the novel down. Miller converted it into a play. He gave this to producer-writer Joe Fields. Fields was usually involved in musical comedy but was keen to deal with something more serious. Liking the play's cautionary tale of the rise of a fortunate businessman and his resulting fear that it might all be taken away, Fields acquired backing from Herbert Harris to direct it on Broadway. Karl Swenson, an actor who had appeared in a number of Miller's radio dramas, was cast in the lead. Sadly, the play closed after only six performances (which included two previews and one matinee), despite winning the Theatre Guild National Award. Miller felt that the play had been poorly produced—the director not understanding its fabulist nature—and summarily dismissed by critics. Discouraged by their response, he seriously considered giving up writing for the stage.

The Man Who Had All the Luck was published prior to its stage production in *Cross Section: A Collection of New American Writing* in 1944, and a few of the details were different from what appeared on stage, remaining closer to the novel. For example, in the published version, David is an orphan with the last name of Frieber, and his wife Hester ensures that her husband kills the mink and takes responsibility. In the production, however, Miller altered the protagonist's last name to Beeves, adapting to a father-and-brother subplot, and allowed the mink to survive. Another important change from the novel was the inclusion of Gus, who would help David fix the car rather than take it elsewhere and lie to get ahead. This version was later printed in GREAT BRITAIN by Methuen with *The Golden Years* in 1989 to mark revivals at the Bristol Old Vic and London's Young Vic, and in *Arthur Miller Plays: Four* in 1994, but was out of print in the United States for many years. After a successful 2001 revival starring Chris O'Donnell that began at the WILLIAMSTOWN THEATER FESTIVAL and moved to New York in 2002, Penguin finally issued an authoritative version of the play in 2004, with a foreword by CHRISTOPHER BIGSBY. *New Yorker*'s Nancy Franklin described the 2002 production as "beautifully cast," and the play with "plenty of life in it" even after 58 years, while the *New York Times* found it compelling and wondered how it had been so easily dismissed all those years ago. There is currently a movie version in the works to be directed by Scott Ellis with a screenplay by REBECCA MILLER.

SYNOPSIS

Act One

The play begins in a barn in a small Midwestern town, where David Beeves is running an auto repair shop. J. B. Feller drops by to find David busy with people and asks for alcohol top ups that are given during the unseasonably cold weather. David tells his friend that he has decided to talk today to his girlfriend's father, who does not approve of their relationship. As David leaves to tend to customers, Shory enters in a wheelchair. Shory and J.B. affably spar, and Shory insists that David will not go to see Andrew Falk, Hester's father, as it is something that he has been putting off for seven years. J.B. tells him that he has just learned from his wife that they cannot have children and that he is thinking of helping David, for whom he feels a paternal interest. His brother-in-law, Dan Dibble, has a mink ranch and needs a good mechanic.

David returns as his Aunt Belle enters with clean clothes. She has brought the wrong ones and cries, although David is not cross. Shory teases her, and she runs home; then he tries to persuade David not to go, as Falk has threatened to kill David. Pat and Amos Beeves (David's father and brother) arrive,

Scene from the Williamstown Theatre Festival's 2001 revival of *The Man Who Had All the Luck,* starring Chris O'Donnell as David Beeves, that subsequently transferred to Broadway. *Courtesy Richard Feldman/Williamstown Theatre Festival Archives.*

and although Shory appeals to Pat to intercede, Pat leaves the decision to David. David wants to marry Hester but is uncertain if he should force things. Pat is only interested in Amos, whom he is obsessively training as a baseball pitcher although he has yet to get a scout out to see him play. David suggests that he call the Detroit Tigers again and learns that Pat has never called, preferring to let things happen by chance. The others suspect that it is more because he is worried that a scout might reject Amos. As the older men go to play cards, the brothers talk. Amos asks David to take over his management as he feels that he is not getting anywhere, but David persuades him to stay with Pat because he knows even less about baseball than he does about mechanics.

Hester arrives to tell David that her father is home, and David admits his trepidation, wondering whether they should wait or marry without telling him. Hester is reluctant to wait and will not marry without telling her father, so he agrees to go. As they embrace, Dibble arrives looking for J.B., who comes in and tells David that if he can fix Dibble's car, Dibble will give David a lot more business. Uncertain of his ability, David agrees to try, and as he leaves to find Falk, Hester's father walks in. Falk orders his daughter home, and she goes even though David asks for her to stay. Putting everyone down, Falk angrily warns David from Hester before storming off. His car will not start, but rather than let David help, he pushes it off himself. Soon after, Dibble arrives in a state: He has just run over Falk by accident. Hester returns to announce that her father is dead, though she insists that it was no-one's fault, and David comforts her. He feels as if he is in a dream as now there is no barrier to marrying Hester.

In the next scene, David is vainly trying to fix Dibble's car that night. Unable to sleep, Hester comes to see how he is doing and encourage him, and she lets slip that Dibble had taken the car to other mechanics who had failed. When she leaves, Gustav Eberson wanders in to introduce himself. He plans to open another repair shop in town, and David generously wishes him luck. Gus advises him about fixing the car, and they make friends. When David falls asleep from exhaustion, Gus covers him with his coat and fixes the car. When David wakes

the next day as everyone arrives to see how he made out, he is almost as surprised as they to find the car working perfectly. To keep Dibble happy, he pretends that the problem was some minor detail rather than the crankshaft as the other mechanics had said. He is rewarded with Dibble's trust and the offer to repair all of his tractors. J.B. offers to finance him for the additional equipment that he will need. As Dibble is paying him, Hester notices Gus's coat, and David runs out to find him.

Act Two

Three years later, we move to the interior of the Falk farmhouse where David and Hester, since married, now comfortably live. They are preparing for a party. Gus arrives; he now works with David as a partner in the auto repair shop after Gus's own business failed. Gus asks David when he plans to have children, and David confesses his belief that he may be sterile. While Gus feels that this would be unfair, David thinks that it may be just because everything else has gone so well for him. Dibble arrives and tries to persuade David into mink farming, but David is unsure, as minks are hard to keep. Dibble assures him that if he works hard, they will be fine, despite the uncertainties of the trade, even though Gus views it as too much of a gamble. David is tempted as he feels that his other achievements were too easy. Amos and Pat arrive, excited about the upcoming game to which a scout is finally coming. J.B. does not want his wife to see him drinking but tells of his plan to adopt, and they all drink a toast to everyone's luck and "to our children," before heading to the game.

Later that night, after the game, they are having a barbeque outside and celebrating Amos's game, which was a shutout. David comes in to get his checkbook and buy the minks from Dibble. Amos is sleeping while Pat waits for the scout to arrive. David is pleased that things seem to be happening for his brother. J.B. brings in a new valise that they all bought for Amos, who wakes up and is delighted at the gift. Pat takes Amos to shower, even bringing his own towels to make sure that he does not pick something up. We learn that J.B.'s wife, angry at his getting drunk again, has told him that she could have children but lied as she did not want to give a drunk a child. He is distraught and warns David that his luck, too, might change.

They are worried because the scout is late and the guests are beginning to leave. Feeling that his brother deserves to make it, David plans to go to find the scout, but Shory stops him, pointing out that people do not always get what they deserve. He tells how he really lost his legs, not in the war as everyone thought, but during the armistice when he was in a brothel and the building collapsed after its boiler burst. He sees this as an example of the unfairness of life. David lets Shory know that he called to get the scout here and that he did not come just by chance. Then the scout, Augie Belfast, arrives, apologizing for his tardiness. He compliments Amos on his pitching and confesses that he has been to see him play during the past two years but could not make up his mind. On learning this time that Amos practices in the cellar, he realizes why; Amos cannot cope with crowds and other players. Although he is sympathetic, Augie tells them that Amos is worthless as a professional player. David angrily refuses to believe this and insists that Amos can make it, but the scout leaves.

Amos attacks his father, blaming him for his failure, and David pulls him off. Pat asks Amos to forgive him, and David insists that Augie is wrong and that they can fix this. Amos believes that the scout was right and refuses to touch a baseball again. When David tries to talk him out of it, Amos points out that only David gets everything that he wants. David denies this, pointing out that he has no children. Then Hester confesses that she is pregnant and had been waiting to tell him. She runs off crying, suspecting that David does not really want a child, but Amos takes this as proof that he was right about David's luck.

Act Three

Eight months later, the men are playing cards in David's living room as Hester is in labor upstairs. Belle is assisting and comes in from time to time to report; she is upset that David has not yet bought a baby carriage. David enters and seems calm. He has been mating his minks and feels confident that they took. Pat joins them. He has decided to go

back to sea to give Amos some space. Amos is working at David's new gas station, which is doing well—soon after opening, a major highway was built to go past it. David still hopes that Amos will pitch again, though Amos is adamant he will not. David asks his father not to go, but Pat feels that he must and goes to play cards while waiting for his train. David asks Gus for permission to mortgage their repair shop, as he needs more cash for the mink, having mortgaged everything else. Gus is shocked that he is in so much debt on something so risky and cannot understand why David seems so confident. J.B. tells David that he has ordered a baby carriage for him, assuming that he just forgot, but David is terse.

We learn that Hester fell some time back and was warned that it may have damaged the baby. David now believes that the baby is dead and so, as a balance, his minks must thrive. Gus refuses to sign the mortgage, seeing David's belief as horrifying. He tries to get him to see that his good fortune is deserved, but David cannot see this and feels that he will have to pay a price someday. Shory agrees with David, although Gus points out that if Shory had not been chasing whores, he would not have lost his legs. J.B. offers to loan David the money that he needs as Belle enters to tell David, to his horror, that he has a healthy baby boy. As they congratulate him, he runs out of the house.

A month later during a stormy night, Hester is pacing. She calls Gus to come, explaining that Dibble phoned to say that his minks were dying because of silkworm in the feed and that David uses the same fish. She wants Gus for support for when she tells David, whom she has not warned. He comes to check that everyone is fine, and Hester tries to get him to stay. She dislikes the attention that he is giving the minks and the way that he ignores his own son. He wants to be rich for her, but she says that she does not need this and asks him to pick up his child. He runs out again. Gus enters to calm her and suggests that she just wait and see what happens. He lets her know that he is tired of David's obsession and is leaving for Chicago, where he has another job lined up. He fears that David is going crazy and wants her to take him to a doctor, but Hester refuses. She wants the minks to die because, she thinks, this will give David the disaster he was expecting and fix everything. Gus is not convinced, feeling that David has lost direction and no longer feels "the boss of his life," and the minks dying might send him over the edge. Hester admits that she knew that the fish were tainted before David had started the feeding but said nothing. Gus tells her that David took out a large life-insurance policy, and if he loses the minks, he may try to take his own life. Horrified, Hester tries to go outside, but Gus stops her.

David reenters as Gus is holding Hester and wonders what is going on. Hester tells him about Gus's Chicago plans. The phone rings; it is the food supply man looking for Dibble, and David learns from him about the fish and what Hester has done. He asks her why, and she declares her intention to leave. Thinking that she plans to leave with Gus, he begins to blame him, but Hester sets him straight. When David goes to attack Gus, she slaps him. He breaks down weeping, saying that he loves her. Dibble arrives to help, and we learn that David had thrown out the infected fish and that his minks will be fine. He had not liked the way the fish looked, and Dibble is amazed that he was so conscientious as to check every fish. David offers Dibble some of his breeders to help him out, but Dibble is uncertain that he wants to continue. Hester insists that it was David's diligence that saved him, not fate, and goes to tend the crying baby. David seems to come to terms with his luck, albeit with some reserve, and wills himself to join her upstairs, even as the thunder rolls in the distance.

CRITICAL COMMENTARY

Questions of luck, personal agency, and fate are central to the play. David's good luck unnerves him, and he feels certain that he will eventually be forced to pay a price for his fortunate life. Early on he asks, "How do you know when to wait and when to take things in your hand and make them happen?" The answer Miller implies is that you cannot know, but you must just do the best you can. As Gus and Hester point out, David is a decent man who tries to help others and works hard, and he may just deserve all that he has. Shory and J.B. argue otherwise, but that is because they have been

let down by their own mistakes. J.B. is a drunkard, and Shory chased whores; both lose because of their flaws rather than because fate demands some kind of payback. David is so convinced that he will have to pay for all of his good fortune that he initially believes his son to be dead, and when he is born healthy, David refuses to touch him, feeling that he was not deserved. Expecting disaster to fall, he takes out an insurance policy, preparing to take his own life to avert the curse that he feels is coming and to ensure that if things should go awry with the mink, at least Hester will not be left penniless.

Where Pat leaves Amos's career largely up to fate, never calling for a scout, David, despite his qualms, actively creates his own fortune. Shory argues that people are like jellyfish in a current—unable to choose which way they go—but the play's action does not bear this out. David mostly succeeds because he makes sensible and kindly choices. He creates his own fortune to some extent: He buys the alcohol so as not to hurt the salesman's feelings; he welcomes Gus despite Gus's intention to set up a rival business; he repeatedly phones the scout until he comes to one of Amos's games; his mink are not poisoned because he checked every single fish that he fed them. David is not to blame for Andrew Falk's death—he had even offered to get his car started for him, but the old curmudgeon had refused and gone off alone, pushing an unlit car along a dark road. He cannot even be faulted for not calling Dibble about the dark speckles that he saw as it would not have been in time: Dibble was the supposed authority, and he had not thought it anything truly serious. David's diligence allows him to take Dibble's place as the foremost mink ranch of the area, but it is a position for which he has worked hard and deserves.

What happens to David's brother, Amos, is sad but no fault of David who does his best to aid his brother. It also offers the flip side, which is the element that most threatens to unhinge David—while his good actions are rewarded, Amos's dedication is all for nothing. There are no guarantees, and to accept that is to accept a world in which bad things happen to good people. Life is arbitrary, but people are free to choose what they do with such contingency. Rejected by a single scout, Amos quits and refuses to touch another baseball; one has the feeling that David could never have taken such a course or given in so easily. It is his unrelenting energy that leads David to doctor the fish and save his mink, and by the close, he begins to see that what a person does can make a difference. At this point, he can accept his son and embrace a renewed sense of hope, albeit with continued trepidation as indicated by the rolling thunder, as the future can never be certain.

FIRST PERFORMANCE

The Man Who Had All the Luck previewed in Wilmington, Delaware, and then opened at the Forrest Theatre in New York City on November 23, 1944, with the following cast:

Shory: Grover Burgess
J. B. Feller: Forrest Orr
Hester Falk: Eugenia Rawls
David Beeves: Karl Swenson
Aunt Belle: Agnes Scott Yost
Patterson Beeves: Jack Sheehan
Amos Beeves: Dudley Sadler
Dan Dibble: Sydney Grant
Gustav Eberson: Herbert Berghof
Harry Bucks: James MacDonald
August Belfast: Lawrence Fletcher

Directed by Joseph Fields
Set designed by Frederick Fox
Produced by Herbert H. Harris
It ran for 4 performances.

INITIAL REVIEWS

Critics felt that the play was too diffuse and generally panned it, so Miller's first Broadway production was swiftly closed. Howard Barnes described it as "incredibly turbid in its writing and stuttering in its execution" and concluded that the play was "unpleasant, unexciting and downright mystifying." Louis Kronenberger called it "far from satisfactory," being neither compelling nor significant, and Ward Morehouse announced that it was "an ambling piece, strangely confused at times and rather tiresome for a considerable portion of the evening." However, not all the reviews were negative: John Chapman felt that the play needed work but that

Miller displayed a "sense of theatre and a real if undeveloped way of making stage characters talk and act human," and Burton Rascoe felt that it was a "touching" and "intelligent drama." Revivals in Great Britain in 1990 and New York in 2002 fared much better.

SCHOLARSHIP

The play's poor initial reception led most scholars away from discussing *The Man Who Had All the Luck* until recent years, although Kenneth Tynan included it in his exploration of the commonalities between TENNESSEE WILLIAMS and Miller in 1954, and Robert Sharpe discussed it as one example of Miller's developing sense of dramatic irony. Dennis Welland was the play's earliest defender of sorts, pointing out its obvious relation to Miller's later work, and Brenda Murphy offers a useful comparison of the play to HENRIK IBSEN's *The Master Builder*. Gerald Wooster and Mona Wilson link it to *Broken Glass* as a similar study of "manic-depressive envy dynamics as they occur in interpersonal relationships." In both the "Introduction" to the 2002 edition of the play and his own *Arthur Miller: A Critical Study*, Bigsby offers useful insights regarding the play's development from novel to drama and readings of the play as a "debate about human agency and the capacity for change" that were directly related to Miller's concern with the apparent political and moral paralysis of Europe and America in the face of fascism from that era.

CHARACTERS

Beeves, Amos At the play's start, Amos is age 24 and has been in serious training all of his life to become a baseball pitcher. His father dogs him to practice constantly, having him throw balls in the cellar seven days a week since he was 12 and encouraging him to forget his schoolwork. Not as quick or intelligent as his younger brother, Amos looks up to David, even asking him to manage him, feeling his father is not getting him anywhere, but David encourages him to stick with Pat. When the scout finally sees Amos play, he rejects him because Amos cannot deal with crowds or other players. Amos blames Pat for his poor training and swears never to play baseball again. With no other skills, he works pumping gas at his brother's station and resenting David's apparently endless good fortune.

Beeves, David   At the play's start, David Beeves is age 22 and has been dating Hester Falk since their early teens. His mother died when he was seven, and his Aunt Belle, a kindly but fussy lady, raised him. His father has paid him little attention, only having time for David's older brother, Amos, and David reciprocates, having little time for his father. He has been working since he was 15 when he took a job in Shory's supply store, a job for which the other neighborhood children were too scared to apply as Shory is in a wheelchair. Since then, he has converted Shory's storage barn into a makeshift auto repair shop and has been doing well mending cars, despite having had no automotive training.

David is the lucky man of the title, as everything that he touches seems to come out right. Although it is April, freak cold conditions have allowed him to sell off a large drum of alcohol that he had been persuaded to buy and to turn a good profit. Refusing to allow his daughter to marry David, Andrew Falk is run over and killed to leave the way open for David and provide him with a nice farmhouse. When his future depends upon fixing Dibble's car, Gus arrives to fix it for him and then has to come and work for him after his rival repair shop goes out of business. After David opens a gas station, a highway is built to go past it, and when given tainted food, his conscientiousness causes him to throw it away rather than feed it to his minks. His good luck unnerves him, as he expects to have to pay for it someday, but that day never arrives. He ends the play a wealthy man with a loving wife and healthy son, everything he had ever wanted.

Beeves, Patterson (Pat)   After being at sea, Pat Beeves settles home and decided from the birth of his eldest son, Amos, to train him to be a star baseball pitcher, even to the point of allowing him to neglect everything else. He has left his other son, David, to his own resources. Unfortunately, his training isolates Amos so much that he is useless in a real game with other people. The fact that Pat takes his own towels even to Hester's house so that Amos will not catch anything is indicative of how

far Pat sterilizes his son's existence. But Pat's commitment is suspect; he leaves too much to fate. He never called to get a scout to come, and if it had not been for David, Augie Belfast may never have seen Amos play. Although the news is bad, at least Amos knows that baseball has no future for him. When Amos refuses to forgive Pat for misleading him, Pat cannot live with his guilt and goes back to sea.

Dibble, Dan   A wealthy farmer, Dibble has made his fortune raising mink. Taking a liking to David, largely because David undercharged him for a car repair, he allows him to buy into the business. Unlike David, he trusts no one, counts every penny, and is less diligent, the latter leading to his downfall as he feeds the tainted fish to his minks without checking it through. Although David kindly offers to provide him with breeders to begin again, Dibble, an old man, is reluctant to reengage in the gamble of raising mink. David replaces him as the wealthy and successful ranch owner, and although we know that he could fall as easily as Dibble, we also feel that his success is more deserved.

Eberson, Gustav (Gus)   An immigrant from Austria, Gus has worked for several years with Ford and Hudson Motors learning to be a good mechanic before coming to this small town in search of a red-haired wife and a better sense of community. A decent man, he only opens a repair shop because he believes that the town can sustain two and not to be a rival to David. David's kindly reaction leads him to want to help him fix Dibble's car and later to accept David's genuine offer of partnership when his own business fails. Unable to settle and unnerved by David's loss of direction and approaching insanity, he decides at the close to move on to Chicago, still in quest of a good woman. Before he leaves, he tries to get David the psychiatric help that he thinks David needs, not wanting to give up on a man whom he admires.

Falk, Hester   Hester has loved David all of her life, but her father has been a problem. Her mother died when she was young, and Andrew Falk has been very strict and always disliked David, whom he felt was worthless and without direction. While her father is alive, she cannot give herself to David, indicated by her obeying her father rather than David in the barn. His death, however, allows her the freedom to marry the man she loves. After three years, she becomes pregnant and, despite a nasty fall, gives birth to a healthy baby boy. She is distressed David will not hold their son, and when given the opportunity to kill the mink by which he seems obsessed, she takes it to try to bring her husband back to how he was. Her plan fails, but she seems content as she encourages her husband once more to come and pick up their baby. She has faith in his ability to overcome all odds, just as she was confident that he could fix Dibble's car.

Feller J. B. (John)   At age 50, J. B. Feller is a portly and wealthy manager of a large department store. Having drunk too much in the past, he is trying to live more cautiously, but he keeps slipping off the wagon. His wife tells him that she cannot have children, and he worries to whom he might leave all that he has accomplished. She later confesses that she would not give him children because he is a drunk. Since David reminds him a little of himself as a young man, he takes a paternal interest and tries to help him where he can. Despite his disappointments, J. B. is an optimist who thinks that people can make things happen if they try hard enough, which is in direct contrast to his friend Shory.

Shory   A veteran from the war, Shory lives in a wheelchair, but he owns a prosperous supply business. He likes David ever since he came to work for him as a teen, and he also takes a paternal interest. Unlike his friend J. B., Shory sees people as victims of fate, unable to change the way their lives run. Having survived all the fighting, he had lost his legs in a freak accident during the armistice when a boiler blew up in the house where he had gone with a woman. Gus, however, points out that if Shory had not been whoring, he would still have his legs.

FURTHER READING

Barnes, Howard. "P.S.—He Needed It." *New York Herald Tribune*, November 24, 1944, 22. In *New York Theatre Critics' Reviews* 5 (1944): 73.

Bigsby, Christopher. "*The Man Who Had All the Luck.*" *Arthur Miller: A Critical Study.* New York: Cambridge University Press, 2005, 54–66.

Chapman, John. "A Good Try, But Is Out of Luck." *New York Daily News*, November 24, 1944. In *New York Theatre Critics' Reviews* 5 (1944): 73.

Franklin, Nancy. "Back to the Woods." *New Yorker*, May 13, 2002, 101.

Kronenberger, Louis. "A Big Problem, A Small Play." *PM*, November 24, 1944. In *New York Theatre Critics' Reviews* 5 (1944): 73.

Morehouse, Ward. "The Man Who Had All the Luck Is Folksy, Philosophical and Tiresome." *New York Sun*, November 24, 1944. In *New York Theatre Critics' Reviews* 5 (1944): 74.

Murphy, Brenda. "*The Man Who Had All the Luck:* Miller's Answer to *The Master Builder.*" *American Drama* 6, no. 1 (Fall 1996): 29–41.

Rascoe, Burton. "Good Luck at the Forrest." *New York World-Telegram*, November 24, 1944. In *New York Theatre Critics' Reviews* 5 (1944): 74.

Sharpe, Robert B. "Modern Trends in Tragedy." *Irony in the Drama.* Chapel Hill: University of North Carolina Press, 1959, 180–203.

Tynan, Kenneth. "American Blues: The Plays of Arthur Miller and Tennessee Williams." *Encounter* 2, no. 5 (1954): 13–19.

Welland, Dennis. "Three Early Plays." *Miller: A Study of His Plays.* London: Methuen, 1979, 20–35.

Wooster, Gerald, and Mona Wilson. "Envy and Enviability Reflected in the American Dream: Two Plays by Arthur Miller." *British Journal of Psychotherapy* 14, no. 2 (1997): 182–188.

A Memory of Two Mondays (1955)

In 1955, actor/director Martin Ritt, who was appearing in CLIFFORD ODETS's *The Flowering Peach*, asked Miller if he had a one-act play that he could give him to offer as a reading with his company one Sunday evening as an added draw. Miller offered him *A Memory of Two Mondays*, a strongly nostalgic piece that recalled Miller's months of work at

CHADICK–DELAMATER AUTO-PARTS WAREHOUSE as he earned the necessary funds to get him to the UNIVERSITY OF MICHIGAN. Miller's agent, KAY BROWN, felt the play too good for a single reading and suggested that Miller write another to create a full evening that was worthy of production. Miller quickly wrote *A View from the Bridge* as a curtain raiser. In the meantime, *The Flowering Peach* had closed, so Miller's double bill was produced as a full BROADWAY production.

In an interview filmed by Albert Maysles to accompany the 1970 filmed version, Miller speaks of the romantic nostalgia that people have for the GREAT DEPRESSION of the 1930s as being ridiculous; for him, it was a period in which life was frustrating and nothing less than "gruesome." Although the people whom we see in this play are lucky enough to have jobs, their lives are mostly empty and dulled by the repetitiveness of those jobs; the only refuge being booze and sex, both of which cause damage. Miller admits a special affection for this play because it springs from personal experience, but the play's characters are based on memories over several years, and this is not a direct recreation of actual events.

SYNOPSIS

The shipping room of a large auto-parts warehouse provides the play's location. On a hot Monday morning in the summer of 1933, Bert enters with *War and Peace* and the *New York Times*. The manager, Raymond Ryan, arrives, carrying a tabloid and asks Bert questions about the whereabouts of Tommy Kelly, whether Bert is really going to college, and what he is reading. Aside from Bert's assurance that Tommy will be along soon, Raymond is mostly uninterested in Bert's responses, telling him to sweep up. Agnes joins them and speaks of a nephew who is interested in reading and world events like Bert is, but she herself is not. All of the workers gradually drift in: Patricia, a young lady with several boyfriends; Gus and Jim, still drunk from a weekend binge; and Kenneth, a gentle Irishman recently arrived in America.

Raymond is concerned because his boss, Mr. Eagle, will be visiting today and he wants everyone to look good. Patricia teases Gus, and he jokes with

Agnes until Raymond tells them to stop. Agnes asks after Gus's wife, Lilly, whom we learn has been sick, although Gus left her all weekend to go drinking and whoring with his friend Jim. Jim advises Gus to call Lilly, which he does but has little conversation as she cannot hear on the phone. Barging in on Patricia in the bathroom, Gus revenges himself on her teasing him. Kenneth wants to clean the workspace, but no one else cares. Friendly toward Bert, Kenneth recites poetry to him and asks about his book, although Gus responds grumpily to their conversation as if such thoughts are annoying.

Filling orders, they chat about their weekend, and Kenneth wonders about where the parts are heading. When Bert leaves to fetch a part, Kenneth tells Gus to be easier on Bert, wonders if he should wash the windows, and begins to sing. Patricia compliments his voice, and Gus embarrasses her again. Kenneth tells him to stop, but Gus chases Patricia. She bumps into Larry, with whom she flirts, having heard that he has bought a sports car despite having recently had triplets with his wife. He offers to drive Patricia home sometime, and she shows interest. Gus criticizes Larry's choice of car, but Larry defends himself, explaining that he was sick of "dreaming about things." Kenneth complains about the mice, shows his secondhand shoes, asks after Tommy, and wonders how Jim manages to work so hard. Jim jokes that it is because he never married, and he recalls his days out West fighting the Indians.

A driver, Frank, comes looking for orders; he intends to make his trip worthwhile by setting up a woman to visit in the location. Larry asks Raymond for a raise but is turned down, and two younger workers enter, Jerry Maxwell and Willy Hogan. Jerry has a black eye from trying to steal someone else's girlfriend. Tommy staggers in, almost comatose. They try to wake him, worried that Eagle might fire him, and they send Bert for a shot of whiskey as Agnes wipes Tommy's face with a cloth. Larry sulks because he was denied his raise and was teased about his car, the younger men discuss baseball, and Kenneth again considers washing the windows. A mechanic enters looking for an unusual part. Larry knows exactly where to find it, a compendium of knowledge that he feels is not appreciated. When Eagle enters to use the bathroom, they pose Tommy as if he were working—Bert steadies him and pretends a conversation. As Eagle comes out, Tommy wakens, answering a baseball question from before. Gus compliments Bert on helping out, as Agnes is called to her switchboard, and Raymond sends Tommy to see Eagle. Agnes returns with news that Lilly is dead. Gus feels guilty about leaving her all weekend. Tommy has been given a final warning but still has his job and, and Gus advises him to use this last chance.

Kenneth asks Bert to help him clean the windows, and as they do so, they are amazed at what they see outside. The action is not realistic, and the speech is in blank verse, offering a connecting interlude of commentary as the seasons turn. Bert has enough money to leave and is not sad about this as he recognizes, "There's something so terrible here" in the never-ending, soul-destroying routine. He wonders why Kenneth has fallen prey to the place; he has intelligence but insufficient will power. Kenneth complains about his landlady and his dissatisfaction with life. He now drinks and is forgetting his poetry. Considering the civil service, he is unsure if that will be any better. Bert has nearly completed reading *War and Peace* and has given his notice at work. Raymond turns down his offer to help train a replacement, and Bert thanks Larry for his help. When Tommy enters, he is much livelier, having given up alcohol. Kenneth asks him how he did this, and Tommy tells him will power, warning Kenneth to use a little himself. As they offer Bert advice about what to study, Gus and Jim enter.

Gus is dressed up and carrying new fenders for his car. He and Jim have been walking all over, trying to get up courage to go to the cemetery. Gus is carrying the insurance money that he received from his wife's death and gives some to Kenneth for shoes and to Bert for books or candy. Gus is angry at this place, feeling that he has wasted his life here with nothing to show for it. He rocks the scale and releases mice who scurry around; then he offers Patricia $5,000 to go with him to Atlantic City, an offer that she refuses. Looking through the newly cleaned windows, Jerry notices that a brothel has set up opposite their building; the men, to Kenneth's disgust, all look. Patricia complains to Larry that he is selling his car. She had not taken their relationship seriously and sees other men, and Larry upsets her by responding spitefully, telling her that she will end up in the brothel.

Gus openly drinks as Eagle enters to use the bathroom. The others try to take his bottle away, but he is drunk and mean. He confesses his guilt over Lilly. Kenneth complains to Eagle about the whorehouse but is summarily dismissed; then he picks a fight with Jerry that Raymond has to break up. Summing up his years at the firm, Gus leaves with Jim in tow. A short poetic interlude takes place in which Bert wonders why he can leave and they all stay in their crippling routines. He admits that he will always remember them, while suspecting that they soon will forget him. The final scene occurs the following day. Jim arrives to inform them that Gus died after spending all his money on phone calls to everyone whom he ever knew and having a crazy night of fun. Agnes cries while the rest return to work. As Bert says his goodbyes, he receives perfunctory responses. He tells Kenneth that he will visit, but Kenneth knows that he will not. He lets Bert know that he got so drunk the previous night that he plans to quit drinking and go into civil service to straighten himself. Wishing Bert luck, he sings "The Minstrel Boy" as Bert heads out and everyone continues with their work.

CRITICAL COMMENTARY

Miller wrote the play as a compacted group of memories lived during several years to establish the mood and the setting for the depiction of a young man; Bert passes through a place in which the rest are trapped, as he moves on with his life. Bert looks on these people with pity, though at least they had work and an income during those lean years. These are the people who stayed, like Miller's brother KERMIT MILLER, and quietly accepted their responsibilities, doing jobs that they hated and suffering in a shallow existence. While Bert cannot understand the choice that they have made, he also admires it; he suggests erecting a statue to such people. But much like Miller, Bert cannot accept such a narrow existence and feels compelled to go, even while he realizes that this act can be viewed as somewhat selfish.

Surrounded by dirty, unwashed windows, the play's setting appears as a messy, uncared for workspace, but it is also a refuge of sorts, a place where these people are given a safe routine to mark their time and where friends who in some way care about them come to see them. With only one bathroom for everyone, there is little privacy, and these people know each other's lives fairly intimately. We see both Raymond and Mr. Eagle as well as the men and women who work on this floor use this bathroom, that makes it a leveler of sorts. After all, Raymond, as the manager, earns little more than Larry, who finds parts. Their lives are connected. Their concern over Tommy and later Gus is genuine and supportive. Nearly every one of them reaches into his pocket for the money to buy Tommy the whiskey that they think may help him recover. Yet, those lives remain narrowly bounded by alcohol, sex, unhappy marriages, and baseball, and nothing changes as the workers pursue the same conversations at the close of the play that they do at its start.

Bert is ever the outsider as from the start they know that he does not intend to stay. He marks himself as different by the weighty novel he carries, his *New York Times* (as opposed to a tabloid), and his intention to attend university. Most of the people in this workspace have little time for Bert because he is different from them, although they warm to him when he helps Tommy. But they see no point to his reading lengthy Russian novels and taking a fancy paper like the *New York Times* to keep abreast of the world news. Hitler means nothing to them when Bert tries to discuss his fears of growing fascism, for their lives and interests are too restricted. Whenever he tries to engage his boss, Raymond, he is told to sweep up. As a recent newcomer, Kenneth understands, but he is soon sucked in to be like the rest of them, drinking to hide the disappointment. Raymond turns down Bert's offer to help train his replacement, and most of them are too busy to even notice his departure. It is as if everyone is a little sore at him for getting out, though also amazed at his will to do so. Though young, Bert exhibits a stronger willpower than Tommy, who had to give up drinking, because he addresses the root cause of dissatisfaction rather than simply curing a symptom.

FIRST PERFORMANCE

A Memory of Two Mondays previewed at Fallmouth Playhouse and then opened at the Coronet Theatre in New York in a joint bill with *A View from the Bridge* on September 29, 1955, with the following cast:

Bert: Leo Penn
Raymond: David Clarke
Agnes: Eileen Heckart
Patricia: Gloria Marlowe
Gus: J. Carrol Naish
Jim: Russell Collins
Kenneth: Biff McGuire
Larry: Van Heflin
Frank: Jack Warden
Jerry: Richard Davalos
William: Antony Vorno
Tom: Curt Conway
Mechanic: Tom Pedi
Mister Eagle: Ralph Bell

Directed by Martin Ritt
Set designed by BORIS ARONSON
Produced by KERMIT BLOOMGARDEN, ROBERT WHITEHEAD, and Roger L. Stevens
It ran for 149 performances.

INITIAL REVIEWS

Reviews were mixed; while several critics found the play overly wordy and aimless, others applauded its realistic dialogue and creation of mood. BROOKS ATKINSON dismissed it as too "pedestrian," and William Hawkins as "plotless," but Frank O'Connor called it "a beautiful play," and Shepard Trauber praised Miller as a playwright "whose thinking about human beings is always profound." In 1976, it was paired with Tennessee Williams's *27 Wagons Full of Cotton;* it met the same fate, despite a stellar cast that included Meryl Streep, John Lithgow, and Tony Musante.

SCHOLARSHIP

This is one of Miller's more overlooked plays in terms of scholarship. Although it is mentioned in most full-length studies, little beyond its autobiographical and nostalgic nature is described. Benjamin Nelson and CHRISTOPHER BIGSBY go into more detail. While Nelson's reading is fairly standard, Bigsby points to the play's sense of "regression" in the move from summer to winter and insists that the play is anything but "pedestrian" or even "warm-hearted" as some critics have suggested because it offers a negative vision of "entropy." Terry Otten's analysis emphasizes the play's repetitions, viewing Raymond's line "It's the same circus every Monday morning" as central, and summing up Miller's intent more positively than Bigsby as creating "a nostalgic panegyric to a community of oppressed workers struggling to survive the agony of the Depression." John Ditsky, picking up on the play's several Irish characters, offers a reading of the play within the terms of modern Irish drama, and Subbulakshmi Sundaram chooses to consider Miller as a dramatist through the lens of this particular play.

CHARACTERS

Agnes The opposite of Patricia, Agnes is a kindly spinster, who is likely to remain so for life, and is in her late forties. These men are her family, and she cares for them all, even while they tease her and mock her good nature. Her attitude to Bert is motherly, but once he chooses to remove himself from this environment, she loses interest.

Bert Eighteen years old at the play's start and given his high school grades, Bert is uncertain if he can get to college, but he is willing to give it a try. Determinedly saving $11–12 a week out of his $15 pay, reading *War and Peace,* and carrying the *New York Times,* he is far more abreast of both politics and arts than any of his workmates—even Kenny who, the longer he works at the warehouse, recalls less and less poetry. Concerned about Hitler and shy with women, Bert is a semiautobiographical figure, based on the young Arthur Miller. His musings about the worth of these people and why he went off to college are an attempt in part for Miller to justify his own journey to Michigan while his brother stayed at home to help out.

Gus At 68, Gus has worked here for 22 years. With a Slavic accent and full of mischief, he once fought for the United States, enjoys teasing the ladies, goes out whoring, and drinks heavily. His liveliness is dimmed when he learns of his wife Lilly's death. He feels guilty because he had left her that weekend to go drinking and whoring. Unable to face her grave, he takes her insurance money for one last binge and dies in the back of a taxi with Jim and a prostitute.

Jim Jim is the oldest of the workers, in his seventies, with memories of having in his past fought Indians out West with the cavalry, suggesting the America of old offered more excitement than the industrial world of the play's present. Jim's current life is a lot tamer as he packages and ships auto parts. A hard worker despite his drinking, he is constantly on the move. He accompanies Gus on his binges and is with him when he dies.

Kelly, Tommy Tommy has worked here for 16 years but has developed a drinking problem. Married, with a daughter soon to be confirmed, he cannot afford to lose his job but has been given several warnings. After the latest in near squeaks, as his workmates help convince the boss that he is fully conscious, he decides to turn a new leaf and amazes them all by kicking his drinking habit. He then becomes less sympathetic as he boasts of will power to Kenneth, who seems to be following in his earlier footsteps.

Kenneth In America for six months, Kenneth, an Irish immigrant, is slowly settling in. Life is harsh despite having this job. His landlady overcharges and gives him little heat and the same lunch every day. He buys secondhand shoes in which he has to cut a hole to fit, so in the winter the water infiltrates them. Gus gives him the money to buy some new ones as he settles his accounts before his last binge. Kenneth comes to America full of hope, spouting songs and poetry, but finds himself stuck in a grimy workplace that soon chills his spirit. His constant requests to clean their workspace indicates the way in which he feels it stifling him in its dust. He befriends Bert, whom he realizes has more to him than the rest despite his age, and convinces him to help clean the windows.

Delighted at being able to see the outside world once more, this benefit soon crumbles as, to Kenneth's horror, a brothel sets up business across the way. Kenneth maintains the respect for women that most of the others have lost. While the men leer at the prostitutes, Kenneth complains to the manager, who coldly suggests that, perhaps, he should not have cleaned the windows. Kenneth turns to drink and forgets his verse. Near the close, having had a bad drunken incident in which he pushed over a bar, he vows to enter the civil service, even if it means being a guard in the local insane asylum, the only job available, to earn a better wage and escape this place. Kenneth sings "The Minstrel Boy," an Irish song of a brave young boy heading to battle, at various times throughout the play, and again at the end as Bert leaves. Kenneth has given up the fight, but he sees in Bert a strength to keep going and is comforted by the possibility that someone can leave this grim workplace, even if the way might not be easy. One suspects that his might be Bert's fate if he were not so determined to go to college.

Larry   Larry has just fathered triplets with his wife, making him seem more virile than Raymond with mere twins. Larry knows where every part is located in this warehouse, and beginning to feel trapped and underappreciated, he asks for a raise but is denied as Raymond makes little more than he. He buys himself a fancy sports car and flirts with Patricia to try to revivify his life, but he is unable to hold on to either. A kindly man, Bert insists that he could not have survived without Larry's help, but Larry is left having to face the mundane and limited reality of his narrow existence.

Patricia   At 23, Patricia is a pretty girl but is dangerously close to having a bad reputation, although her refusal of Gus's offer may suggest some hope. She flirts with married-man Larry and dates him when he has his fancy sports car, but Patricia soon leaves him for another, not trusting his professions of love. She and Gus goad each other, she calling him King Kong and he walking in on her in the bathroom and offering her money to go to Atlantic City with him. To some extent, she embodies the desires of the hopeless men working in this storeroom.

Ryan, Raymond   As the manager of the floor, Raymond tries to keep everyone working. He is in his forties, has twins at home, and cannot afford to lose this job. Never having been to college and viewing Bert's efforts as pretentious and annoying because he will have to hire someone to take his place, Bert's attempted conversations with Raymond usually end with his boss telling him to go and sweep up.

MOVIE AND TELEVISION ADAPTATIONS

NET Playhouse created a film version of the play in 1970, broadcast via NBC and ITV on each side of the Atlantic in 1971 and released in 1974 as part of the *Broadway Theatre Archive* series. Directed by Paul Bogart and produced by Jacqueline Babbin, it featured Kristoffer Tabori, Jack Warden, J. D. Cannon, Dick Van Patten, George Grizzard, Estelle Parsons, and Dan Hamilton, with Harvey Keitel, Tony Lo Bianco and Jerry Stiller in minor roles, and is a very faithful adaptation. Julius Novick reviewed it as "a gentle, lyrical, Chekhovian evocation of the past with a special unpretentious charm," and Raymond Williams found it to be "memorable" and "very powerful."

FURTHER READING

Atkinson, Brooks. "Theatre: *A View from the Bridge*." *New York Times*, September 30, 1955, 21.

Bigsby, Christopher. "*A Memory of Two Mondays*." *Arthur Miller: A Critical Study*. New York: Cambridge University Press, 2005, 174–177.

Ditsky, John M. "All Irish Here: The 'Irishman' in Modern Drama." *Dalhousie Review* 54 (Spring 1974): 94–102.

Hawkins, William. "2-in-1 Bill Staged at Coronet." *New York World-Telegram*, September 30, 1955. In *New York Theatre Critics' Reviews* 16 (1955): 274.

Nelson, Benjamin. "*A Memory of Two Mondays*: Remembrance and Reflection in Arthur Miller." *Arthur Miller: Portrait of a Playwright*. New York: McKay, 1970, 199–208.

Novick, Julius. "Arthur Miller: Does He Speak to the Present?" *New York Times*, February 7, 1971, sec. 2, p. 17.

O'Connor, Frank. "The Most American Playwright." *Holiday*, February 19, 1956: 65, 68, 70.

Otten, Terry. "*A Memory of Two Mondays.*" *The Temptation of Innocence in the Dramas of Arthur Miller.* Columbia: University of Missouri Press, 2002: 88–93.

Sundaram, Subbulakshmi. "Experience as Education: *A Memory of Two Mondays.*" In *Arthur Miller: Twentieth Century Legend,* edited by Syed Mashkoor Ali, 353–361. (Jaipur, India: Surabhi, 2006).

Trauber, Shepard. "Drama." *The Nation,* October 22, 1955, 348–349.

Williams, Raymond. "Remembering the Thirties." *The Listener,* April 8, 1971, 460–461.

"Miracles" (1973)

First printed in *Esquire* in 1973, this lengthy essay analysis of the social climate of the 1930s against that of the 1950s and 1960s was reprinted in *Echoes Down the Corridor* (2000). Miller sees a connection between the 1930s and the 1960s in that both were eras of tumultuous change in the United States. Although he feels that the 1930s offered more serious lessons, the contrast went deeper than the commonly held belief that "the Thirties revolt was one of the mind while the latest is one of the gut." He describes the devastation of the GREAT DEPRESSION years and his own early understanding of socialism as a way of blaming the system rather than individuals such as his father. Blaming the population's innate conservatism and materialism, he suggests that many wrongly misinterpreted what COMMUNISM could accomplish, just as they would the rebellion of the young in the 1960s.

Radicals in both the 1930s and the 1960s wanted to change the system to benefit humankind. The thirties reacted to an impoverished culture and aimed for a better future, while the sixties, partly in response to such shattering developments as the HOLOCAUST and the bomb, was a response to overblown consumption that asked to live more fully in the here and now, but both were restricted by their own dogma and a nation that was too concerned with capitalist values. The miracles of the title are those moments of clearer sight despite the dogma—an awareness of the importance of the environment, the uselessness of war, and the corruption of such individuals as Richard Nixon—which give hope that things can be better, especially in a nation that allows for dissent, despite her misguided moments of barbarism.

"The Misfits" (1957)

As a short story, "The Misfits" was originally published in 1957 in *Esquire.* It would appear again in Miller's 1967 collection *I Don't Need You Any More* and several other publications in a slightly extended form in which several of the descriptive passages were expanded. The basic plot and characters, however, are the same. This is the original story from which the later 1961 movie evolved. Both short versions offer a simpler tale than the vastly expanded movie version that was written as an acting vehicle for Miller's wife at that time, MARILYN MONROE; indeed, in this story, Roslyn is a minor figure who is only referred to and never appears. Inspired by Miller's time spent in Nevada while waiting out his residency to be divorced from his first wife MARY SLATTERY, "The Misfits" offers a character study of some of the local cowboys whom Miller had met while living in the state.

The story opens at night outside Bowie, Arizona, with a description of the bleak natural environment. The wind sweeps across the desert at the foot of some mountains. Dwarfed by these surroundings and yet also blending in as if a part of them, "three cowboys slept under their blankets." They even dream of the wind and appear content away from the bustle of humanity that they have left behind. Gay Langland is first to rouse, and we focus on him as he rises and begins to make the morning coffee. Gay likes to be useful and feels discontent when doing nothing, but everything is done at an easy methodological pace. One suspects that he left his wife six years previously, as much because she no longer needed him as for her adultery. Feeling that they would be better off with their mother, he also left behind his two children and has not seen them in the past three years, even though he misses them and they live less than 100 miles away. Something of a fatalist, he has moved on and does not want to return to that part of his life. Now, he is seeing an educated Eastern woman, Roslyn, who makes him laugh and supports him in return for odd jobs. She is in her forties like Gay. He feels a need to be more independent before he can take their relationship any more seriously, which is why he is out here hoping to catch some mustangs to sell for pet food.

Perce Howland is next to wake. He is only in his twenties and has been making a living at the rodeos, bucking broncos. He met Gay five weeks before when buying drinks for everyone in a bar after a rodeo win; they became friendly, and he now hangs out with Gay and Roslyn. Instead of heading back up to Nevada, he has come mustanging with Gay to see what it is like. Having watched his own father die at the rodeo and having suffered serious injuries himself, Perce lives for the moment, aware that life can be brief. He plans to stay with the rodeo circuit, even while agreeing to go with Gay on another mustanging trip up north at the close.

Gay had earlier tried to wake their pilot, Guido Racanelli, who uses his plane to look for mustangs from up ahead, but he just rolled over and stayed asleep. Since losing his wife and baby during a difficult childbirth seven years previously, Guido has lost his zest for life and is worried that he may be trying to commit suicide subconsciously. He has not been able to look at another woman since his wife died. On his last mustang run, he nearly crashed the plane and he is reluctant to go up again. He feels as beaten up by life as is his flying jacket. He has kept the group waiting for three days until he has perfect conditions before going up, but they are running out of food, so Gay gently pressures him to fly once he wakens, and he agrees. Guido is an extreme contrast to Gay and Perce, being overweight, bald, and from back East. Gay and Perce are handsome Western cowboys with spare frames and natural skills, but they are cowboys in a world that has technologically advanced from traveling by horseback. They cannot even catch these mustangs without Guido's plane to spot and herd them.

While Guido flies off, Guy and Perce prepare their equipment. There is a sense of comfort between them, even though Gay is secretly worried that Roslyn may prefer Perce to himself. The older

man is surprised by how often his young protégé speaks of the very thing about which he has been thinking. Gay feels a bond with Perce that he could probably never have with a woman, not entirely trusting the gender. Both have the same outlook on life, spurning wages and wanting to rule their own lives, and in this, Guido is little different—he turned down an airline job to keep his freedom. Gay is more worried by Perce's disapproval of what they are doing to the mustangs than of losing Roslyn to him; after all, he suspects that Roslyn will soon move back East. He is glad of Perce's agreement to accompany him up north, and he contentedly drives the truck back into town with Perce sleeping beside him near the story's end.

It is Guido who devised the process by which the group catches the mustangs, which accounts for its technical nature. Chasing mustangs in a truck and roping them with old tires to stop them running holds little of the glamour of a cowboy on the range and illustrates the outmoded quality of such an image. The only horses here are the poor mustangs whose fate is to be chopped up for meat, as they are too scrawny to be used as regular mounts. This seems to illustrate the general degeneration of the Western life. The small mustang herd is "beautiful," but it is a beauty that has no real place in the modern world and will soon be destroyed. The mustangs are as much misfits as the men who catch them. The story's final image is those four mustangs standing caught in the desert, tired and thirsty, waiting for the men to return to take them to their fate. The foal with them is not even haltered but stands beside its mother, unable to leave. It is an innocuous fate against which they have no power to rail, and so they simply accept it, just like Gay, Perce, and Guido.

There may seem to be a resonance in Gay's situation, given that Miller himself was a similar age when he left his wife and two children, only in his case it was he and not his wife who had committed the adultery. Also, unlike Miller, this is a group of directionless drifters, and none of them has a secure sense of where he is heading. Each takes life as it comes and abhors the idea of salaried work that would keep him fixed. Given the materialistic society from which they are remaining apart, they are the misfits of the title, but they seem content with that role as it is one that they have purposefully chosen, even if it is viewed as wasteful and destructive.

Malcolm Bradbury rightly views the story as depicting "waste, mechanized futility, and the corruption of the natural," and the meager profit that the men make from their roundup only reinforces these negative aspects of their trip. However, it is hard also not to sympathize with these men, however brutal their plan. Their excursion into nature to find these mustangs may incorporate modern technology, but it also allows them to utilize skills that are no longer deemed relevant in a society that is fast losing touch with its past. There is a quiet bond and a caring camaraderie between these men that has value. They recognize the beauty of the mustang, but they also accept that modern society no longer has a place for it. Their appreciation, however fleeting, at least invigorates us to better acknowledge what has been lost.

FURTHER READING

Bradbury, Malcolm. "Arthur Miller's Fiction." In *The Cambridge Companion to Arthur Miller,* edited by Christopher Bigsby, 211–229. (Cambridge, England: Cambridge University Press, 1997).

Miller sitting with his second wife, Marilyn Monroe, and director John Huston during the filming of *The Misfits* in 1960. *Photograph by Inge Morath: Magnum Photos.*

The Misfits (1961)

Miller ostensibly wrote the screenplay for the movie *The Misfits* as a gift for his wife at that time, MARILYN MONROE, to both cheer her up after a recent miscarriage and to offer her a more serious acting role. The title implies that it is based on his 1957 short story, "The Misfits," but it is really very different. Set in Nevada rather than the story's Arizona location, the town of Reno becomes more central than the great outdoors, and the development of the three male characters leads them away from their earlier depictions. Most importantly, the story's off-scene girlfriend of Gay Langland now takes center stage. No longer the same age as Gay and a college graduate from back East, Roslyn has become a youthful but disillusioned "interpretive

dancer" who never finished high school and has just divorced an emotionally abusive husband. Her edgy characterization and desire for Gay not to kill the rabbits or the mustangs better recalls another Miller story, based on Monroe, "Please Don't Kill Anything." The film's ending apparently gave Miller trouble: In one version, he left the central character Gay defeated by the wild mustang, rather then taming it only to release it, and he rewrote it several times before being satisfied. In another version Miller had Gay seriously hurt, and Roslyn and Perce have to take him into town, with Roslyn declaring that she will die if Gay does not recover. Miller rewrote the final scenes several times before being satisfied. He allows Gay and Roslyn to stay together, although Monroe had felt that the couple should part, a development that would probably have been truer to the movie's design. However, their disagreement was really an indication of their outlook on their own marriage.

In his description of Roslyn, Miller had tried to present the best of Monroe and those elements of her nature that had first attracted him to her. He created a character with all of Monroe's innocence of experience and instinctive compassion but without any of her mounting vindictiveness, cruelty, and anger. He hoped that this idealization might inspire Monroe to better see these qualities in herself and find a way forward. The expert psychiatrists she had been seeing seemed unable to guide her toward any positive sense of self-esteem. Miller helped gather around her the perfect cast and crew for the film and came with her to Nevada in some hope that they might be able to salvage their marriage. However, Monroe saw the film as an insult: She had wanted a challenging acting role and felt that Miller had simply written her the same role she always played—Marilyn Monroe—which, in a sense, he had.

As the filming proceeded, Monroe grew more and more openly hostile toward her husband, leaving him stranded in the desert at the end of a shoot and moving out of their joint suite to stay with Paula Strasberg, who seemed more sympathetic to her needs. Monroe was caught in a self-destructive pattern from which she could not break free, and rumors abounded that she had been sighted traveling naked in the hotel elevator. In an unpublished memoir, *Reno, 1960,* that Miller had worked on in 1978 but dropped as he felt it was ultimately too personal, he describes hearing this news of his wife and going back to his room alone with a bottle of whiskey. On another occasion Miller entered her room to witness a doctor giving his wife an injection, and she screamed at him to get out. Near relapse, Monroe was flown out to the coast for medical treatment, and while there vainly tried to meet up with Yves Montand. On her return she stopped by to visit her previous husband, Joe DiMaggio. It was increasingly evident that she saw no future with Miller.

The movie was filmed during 1960 in black-and-white under the direction of John Huston for Seven Arts Productions and released by United Artists in New York in 1961. The publication of the cinema novel—*The Misfits*—(1961) expands on the characterizations and settings in a way the film dialogue could not convey without a voiceover, which Miller did not want to use. The screenplay was not published until 1989. The shoot was a difficult one, with disagreements between Monroe and those around her, and everyone was bothered by Monroe's consistent tardiness as they waited for her in the heat to start filming. Her evident illness delayed production and the producers grew worried over Huston's gambling habit. Miller and Monroe, although together on the set, were obviously finished as a couple and would divorce soon after. Miller himself offers his vision of all of this in his 2004 play, *Finishing the Picture.* The movie has become even more noted as the last movie appearance of Monroe and CLARK GABLE, who died of a heart attack shortly after completing the filming.

SYNOPSIS

Guido, a mechanic, arrives at the apartment of Roslyn Taber to look over her car. He meets her landlady and friend, Isabelle Stears, a voluble divorcee who is coaching Roslyn on her divorce proceedings. The brand-new car shows much damage because men have driven into it, either distracted by its beautiful driver or trying to get her attention. She just wants to sell it, and, attracted, Guido promises to get a good price before giving her a lift into town. Outside the court, Roslyn meets her husband, Raymond, who asks her to change her mind. She refuses, saying that he has never been there for her and that she is sick of being overlooked. Guido heads to the train station to find his friend, Gay Langland, who is seeing off a lady friend. Gay gives this woman the brush-off and then suggests to Guido that they get out of town for a while. He teases Guido about holding the same job for two months. Guido tells him about Roslyn, and they arrange to meet later in a bar.

As Gay leaves with his dog, Roslyn passes by with Isabelle. Roslyn is now divorced, and she and Isabelle decide to go for a drink to celebrate, although Roslyn looks sad as she removes her ring. Isabelle suggests that she stay on in Reno and tries to cheer her up. Roslyn spots a dog and calls it over; it is Gay's dog—they are drinking in the same bar. Guido introduces them, and the four drink together. As Gay and Roslyn spar, Gay tells her how great it is out in the countryside, and Guido offers her his house in which to stay. She agrees to look, and Guido goes to quit his job before the four head out beyond the town limits. Isabelle warns Roslyn about cowboys being attractive but unreliable.

The isolated house is what Guido was building for his wife when she died in childbirth. He had a flat tire and no spare, so he had been unable to get help. The house has remained half-finished since. He had known his wife since they were seven, and she never complained in all their time together, but Roslyn is appalled at her death and suggests that the wife maybe should have complained; then perhaps she would still be alive. The men persuade Roslyn to stay, and the four drink and swap stories. Isabelle mentions a cowboy whom she had liked but who left, and when Roslyn discovers that Gay knows the man, she suggests that they find him, but Isabelle declines.

Roslyn and Gay dance together, and we learn she used to be a dancer. Guido becomes jealous, cutting in and dancing impressively. Roslyn is upset when he confesses that he never danced with his wife. Beginning to panic, she cries, "We're all dying and not teaching each other what we need to know." She is looking for some kind of connection. They continue to drink and get very drunk. Roslyn runs outside, dancing around the yard and hugging a tree. Gay drives her back to town, telling her that she is beautiful but "the saddest girl I ever met." He offers her his friendship if she will stay.

The next morning, Gay cooks her breakfast. They talk about their pasts and begin to bond. Gay is divorced from a woman who cheated on him and has two children whom he sees while on the rodeo circuit. He takes Roslyn riding and swimming, and they set up house together in Guido's place, planting the yard and fixing the place up. When Gay wants to shoot a rabbit that has been eating the vegetables they planted, Roslyn pleads with him not to. Guido and Isabelle come to visit, and Roslyn tries to make Guido feel at home. He is overwhelmed at how perfect she has made his house, telling her, "You have the gift for life," see-

ing himself and the others as just hiding and watching life go by in comparison.

Guido asks Gay to go mustanging with him, and he agrees, if they can get another man. They head to a local rodeo to find one. On the way, they spot Perce Howland at a phone booth and pick him up. His conversation with his mother on the phone tells us that he is estranged from his family. He and Gay know each other, and Gay offers to pay Perce's entrance fee at the rodeo if he will join them on the mustang hunt. Down-at-heels, Perce asks for a bottle of whiskey before he rides. In a bar, the men begin to bet on how long Roslyn can keep a game with a rubber-band-connected bat and ball going, and she makes $145. The men are all watching, and when one grabs her rear end, Guido puts a stop to it. Feeling guilty, Roslyn gives a lot of her winnings to a church lady who is collecting for charity. Perce is thrown from a bronco and hurt, but only Roslyn worries, wanting to take him to a doctor. He goes on a bull from which he is also thrown, and Gay has to drag him away from the animal. Roslyn runs to the car to cry, too sensitive to accept the tough rodeo life.

They go to a bar where Gay starts to grow jealous at the attention Perce is giving Roslyn. While Perce and Roslyn dance and go outside together, he and Guido drink. Perce asks Roslyn if she belongs to Gay, and she is uncertain. Impressed by her concern for him, he does not want to hurt her. He tells of how, one time, he was badly hurt. His girlfriend and two friends just left him when he was unconscious, and he has not seen them since. Opening up further, he relates how a stray hunting bullet killed his father, and his mother married a man whom he hates and who has done him out of his inheritance. "Who do you depend on?" he asks, before Gay comes to break it up and to ask Roslyn to come and meet his children. The children leave before he returns, and he drunkenly howls his distress, feeling abandoned by them and uncertain of Roslyn.

Guido drives while Gay and Perce sleep, and he talks to Roslyn. He blames his war experience dropping bombs on why he did not love his wife enough. He is still interested in Roslyn, but he scares her by driving too fast. When they get back to his house,

Guido starts to work on the extension that he never finished as if to reclaim his home, and his hammering wakes the others. They all bunk down, but Gay is unhappy that the other two are there. He and Roslyn argue but make up. He offers to get straight and settle down for her, but as he goes to bed, she murmurs "Help!"

The next day, they go mustanging, and the four of them camp out together. Guido compliments Roslyn's sensitivity, but she becomes upset when she learns that they are catching the mustangs to sell for dog food. Gay gives her a history lesson about mustangs, explaining, "Nothing can live unless something dies." He tries to have her compare their catching mustangs to her dancing in a nightclub; both do something they enjoy, but the purity of the experience is ruined by others, as they have no control over the outcome. They must sell the horses for meat, and men will leer at her body. They go to sleep.

The next day, Guido flies the plane to flush out the horses and drives back a group of five plus a foal. Roslyn finds it hard to watch as they chase the mustangs in the truck and rope them. The men work hard, and when Roslyn tries to interfere, Gay tosses her to one side. Seeing how upset she is, he suggests to the others that they give her the horses, but when she offers to buy them, he changes his mind. Back in the truck, Guido tells Roslyn that he will quit doing this to be with her, but she rejects him. When they have checked the ropes on all the horses, Gay works out the men's cut, but Perce refuses his share. Roslyn bursts out, calling them murderers, saying that she hates them. Guido says that she is crazy, but Gay is moved by her passion, telling Guido to shut up. When Perce offers to free the horses for Roslyn, she declines, as she does not want to cause a fight.

When Guido goes to leave in his plane, Perce takes the truck and begins to cut the horses free. Gay tries to get the stallion back by grabbing a dangling rope. Worried for him, Roslyn asks Perce to help, but he knows Gay wants no assistance. Gay and the horse battle for dominance. Gay wins and ties the horse back down. After Guido compliments him, Gay sets the horse free. He caught it to prove his independence from Roslyn, but he frees it

because he knows that it is wrong to kill it—"Gotta find another way to be alive." He orders the mare cut loose too and offers to take Roslyn back to town. Saying goodbye to Perce and Guido, they drive away together with Gay declaring to Roslyn, "I bless you girl" as he puts his arm around her.

CRITICAL COMMENTARY

The movie's title sequence pictures floating jigsaw pieces as symbols for the characters whom we are about to meet. Together, they will create a picture of a group of misfits who bond together in their collective pain to form a supportive unit. The men revolve around Roslyn, all wanting her, but Gay, as the most promising and least damaged of the three, is the one who ultimately wins her. She acts as a catalyst to all three men to reevaluate their lives, find them empty, and want to change how they have been living. The men's mantra "It's better than wages" has been an excuse not to face up to a changing world that has outmoded their former lives. Despite their offers to change for Roslyn, it is Gay whom she chooses and, ultimately, only Gay who seems to have the strength to embrace the future. It is having Roslyn beside him that gives him that strength, but the other two are left standing alone in the desert. Having lost the girl and with little other option, Perce will reluctantly return to the rodeo circuit, and Guido talks of selling his house to buy a new plane and look for more mustangs. They will remain in the rut in which we first saw them.

Despite their claims of freedom, these men are as trapped in their lives as any of the wage earners whom they mock. While in the short-story version, the men had been pictured as fairly positive free spirits, in the movie this aspect of their lives has become a negative. They need to find new direction in their lives, as the old myths are no longer enough. When Isabelle mentions a cowboy whom she had liked but who left, and Roslyn suggests that they find him, Isabelle declines, telling her "You've got to stop thinking you can change things." But things need to change, or else they stagnate. They have all had unhappy lives, and this has led to them hiding away rather than being hurt further. Guido recognizes that they are all looking for a place to hide and are watching life go by, except for Roslyn. Though hurt by her past, Roslyn has not yet given up on life, and her care for others allows her to connect and to force them out of their shells for at least a time.

The film emphasizes its Reno location, a town only good for divorce and gambling, and contrasts this to the country locales. But even in the desert, we find life somewhat limited. These cowboys are no longer comfortably at one with nature as they had been in the earlier short story. Roslyn seems to be what makes the difference, and her physical presence changes how they perceive the natural world. Their life as cowboys is all in the past, and their current round of catching mustangs for dog food and making a few bucks on the rodeo circuit is a pale imitation of that past life. They are as much a part of the modern world, in all its brittle commercialism, as the rest of the saps whom they deride for collecting weekly wages. There is talk of past roundups of 1,000 horses, but Guido has only located a herd of 15, and that is reduced to five when the horses are finally flushed out, showing the reduction of this way of life. The money that they would make is ridiculously small for the effort that it entails. Roslyn has won more at the bar. Gay reenacts his cowboy ritual but comes to see its ludicrous outcome and frees the horses that he has trapped. His declaration, "Gotta find another way to be alive," illustrates his realization that the freedom that he so long touted was not a reality and that he needs to find a new way to live.

PRODUCTION DETAILS

The Misfits was released in 1961 with the following lead actors:

Guido ELI WALLACH
Roslyn Taber Marilyn Monroe
Isabelle Stears Thelma Ritter
Gay Langland Clark Gable
Raymond Taber Kevin McCarthy
Perce Howland Montgomery Clift

Directed by John Huston
Screenplay by Arthur Miller
Music by Alex North
Produced by Frank E. Taylor

INITIAL REVIEWS

Reviews of the film were predominantly scathing. While most reviewers generally complimented the acting and the direction, their ire was aimed at the screenplay. Roger Angell described the film as a "dramatic failure," disliking what he saw as Miller's obtrusive symbolism and sentimentality, while Bosley Crowther complained that the "characters and theme do not congeal." Isabel Quigley labeled it "morbid," and "pretentious triviality." Alan Dent announced that it was "a messy and disappointing film" and felt that rather than expand her acting repertoire, Monroe played her "usual character—a luscious little half-wit who trades all the time on the fact that men, everywhere, find her irresistible." Not the usual Hollywood fare, the critics' expectations were perhaps disappointed, although some reviewers found *The Misfits* a welcome change. *Variety* described the mustang sequence, especially, as a "gem of filmmaking," and William Hamilton praised Miller for adapting the Western to the serious purpose of expressing the competing myths of "freedom and conformity." While Stanley Kauffmann felt the film to be ultimately "unsuccessful," he still applauded Miller's screenplay as being "several universes above most American films."

SCHOLARSHIP

While *The Misfits* has a mention in most biographies of its various stars and while there have been plenty of photographs available from both the shoot and stills from the movie, there has been relatively little serious study of the movie and its themes. Articles such as Hollis Alpert's piece for *Saturday Review,* which was based on the differences between Miller's book and screenplay, or James Goode's *The Story of "The Misfits"* (1963), which was reprinted in 1986 as *The Making of "The Misfits,"* and Alice McIntyre's piece for *Esquire* observe the genesis of the movie and the difficulties of the filming. George Kouvaros covers similar material in the more scholarly forum of *Film Quarterly.* Even R. Barton Palmer's discussion in *The Cambridge Companion to Arthur Miller* is more centered on the difficulties of filming such a piece rather than an exploration of the film's themes, though he also considers the film a poor adaptation of the short story, much preferring the earlier fictional text. CHRISTOPHER BIGSBY recognizes the difference between screenplay and fiction, but he bases his distinction more on the lengthier cinema–novel treatment that he feels offers more nuance. He points to Roslyn in both as "a source of moral and spiritual reproach as well as of a vivifying energy." In articles, Henry Popkin has explored the theme of communication in the movie, and David Press reads it as an affirmation of "the Western as debilitated, exhausted myth which misshapes experience, cripples consciousness, and masks meaning in layer upon layer of self deception." More recently, Cheryll Glotfelty has explored how the movie depicts the changing nature of the West and the role of the cowboy, Warren French analyzes the reactions of Leonard Moss and Scott Hammen to the movie, and Ajay Gehlawat explores the film as Miller's attempt to reappropriate Monroe's Hollywood image.

CHARACTERS

Guido   Working as a garage mechanic for regular pay, his friend Gay teases Guido for selling out to wages, but he soon quits his job to join the others on their jaunt to the country. He is the first to fall under the spell of Roslyn and uses the pathos of his dead wife, who died while giving birth, to attract her. But if he had not isolated his wife in their desert home and had the spare tire to put on his truck to fetch a doctor, she might have lived. Roslyn sees the neglect behind this marital relation. Though sympathetic to his pain, he is not what Roslyn seeks. He is ultimately too selfish, a quality that she recognizes in the true picture of his relationship to his wife. Though an excellent dancer, he had never taught his wife to dance. It seems that he married her more for her uncomplaining nature than for any real attraction. He later confesses that he never really loved her, and he suspects that he may have become incapable of love after his war experiences dropping bombs on an unsuspecting enemy.

In his connection to trucks and planes and his once studying to be a doctor, Guido seems the more modern of the three men and less the cowboy, although he does help them rope the mustangs. His life though is as faulty and incomplete as

his plane, the house that he was building, and the studies that he left behind. It is Guido who sees the pictures of Roslyn from her dancing days, which perhaps accounts for his more aggressive bid for her attentions. But it is also that aggressiveness that assures he loses her. She much prefers the kindlier attention of Gay, as Guido behaves more like one of the men from the old days who used to leer at her dancing.

Howland, Perce   Perce's father was killed some years previously by a stray bullet from nearby hunters. His mother remarried, and the new husband has taken over, telling Perce that he can work for wages on the ranch that he had thought to inherit. He feels disinherited and at odds with his family, as evidenced by his taut phone call to his mother and his plaintive cry to Roslyn of "Who do you depend on?" His life has been one of extended loss, as in his tale of how his girlfriend and his buddies abandoned him while he was unconscious after a bad rodeo fall. Unlike the Perce in the short story, this man is a broken rodeo rider, no longer able to stay the course, but with little idea of where else to find the money for his drinking. He is no longer Gay's protégé but is an old friend and is equally living on a vision of a past that is no longer evident. He makes his bid for Roslyn, warmed by her sympathy for the injuries that he got at the rodeo, but he is too damaged for her to accept. He declines his portion of the profit and frees the mustangs to please her—even though she asks him not to—but is left behind when Gay leaves with the girl at the close.

Langland, Gay   Gay is lonely and makes up to women passing through while getting divorces to pass the time. He enjoys their company but does not want to commit, as evidenced by his brush-off of the woman near the start. Fearful of commitment since his wife cheated on him, Gay has built up a fake image of himself as a free soul, attuned to nature, but his only dealings with nature are now destructive as he hunts the mustangs for dog food. It is hard for him to give up his vision of the past, as indicated by his anguish at his children not staying to meet Roslyn, but they are from another period in his life, and it is now time to move on. In Roslyn's objections, he sees the truth in what he does, but he must accept this on his own terms rather than on those of the woman; this is the reason why he must decline her offer to buy the mustangs from him, even while he had been willing to free them to make her happy.

With Roslyn, Gay feels the sense of peace that he had once felt on the prairie, and she gives his life a direction that it has not had in a long time. He finds himself wanting a commitment, making her breakfast and fixing up Guido's house to make her happy. He is attracted to the way that she devours experience, illustrated by the way she eats, and through her eyes, Gay begins to see himself in a new light. Surprising himself, he admits that he would not know how to say goodbye to her, and he does not. Rather than lose her, he decides to give up his old way of life and chooses her over the mustangs.

Stears, Isabelle Coming from a conservative Virginian background, after coming to Reno for her divorce 17 years ago, Isabelle felt attracted enough by its freedom to stay. She has a house and rents rooms to women in town who are seeking a divorce; Roslyn's will be the 27th divorce that she has witnessed. Her adherence to living life as it comes and her refusal to commit makes her a female version of the cowboys whom she and Roslyn meet, and she, like they, bears the scars of her encounters, sporting a broken arm when we first see her. She warns Roslyn against cowboys, saying that they are all unreliable; yet she herself cannot avoid their attraction. At the start, she balances out the foursome with Gay and Guido, but once Perce enters the picture, she recedes, and we see no more of her as all three men vie for Roslyn.

Taber, Roslyn Roslyn is fearful—of life, of commitment, and of the violent culture of the men whom she meets. No less beaten by her encounters than the brand new Cadillac convertible that she wants to sell, her mother, it is said, often abandoned her, and her life as a dancer was more than salubrious, as evidenced by the pictures that Guido glimpses in her closet. Her marriage has been a disaster, coupled to a husband who apparently spent all his time at work and seemed never there. Raymond apparently wanted her as a trophy wife, and she no longer wants to play that role, divorcing him on grounds of cruelty, although she seems unable to relate to men other then through her sexual attraction. Her desire is to connect, and her fear is that this may be impossible on anything but the most superficial level. She cries out when drunk, "We're all dying and not teaching each other what we need to know." It is this desperation that leads Gay to call her "the saddest girl I ever met."

Though she inspires others to see anew by her honest responses, Roslyn is no less restricted and disillusioned by her own past disappointments. Her extreme empathy is both a blessing and a burden. She strives for an unrealistic ideal and must be brought to a realization that life contains pain as well as love—each gives the other fuller meaning. She is attracted to the freedom of the cowboys whom she encounters, while being fearful of the cruelty that they accept as normal. She cries out "Help!" at Gay's offer to get straight and settle down for her because she is as fearful of commitment as he, scared that it may all fall apart. But commitment must always be a leap of faith and can never be as certain as she demands. Each must make some sacrifice, and Gay is clearly ready to meet her half way in his readiness to set up house with her in Guido's home and to put down his gun against the rabbits that are eating their vegetables. Although he must do it on his own terms, he does release the mustangs that they catch at the close in an effort to try a new way of living that she can find acceptable. Their leaving together at the close may only offer a tenuous hope, given their pasts, but it is a possibility nonetheless. Each seems ready for a commitment that they had previously denied was even an option.

FURTHER READING

Alpert, Hollis. "Arthur Miller: Screenwriter." *Saturday Review*, February 4, 1961, 27, 47.

Angell, Roger. "The Current Cinema: Misfire." *New Yorker*, February 4, 1961, 86, 88.

Bigsby, Christopher. *"The Misfits." Arthur Miller: A Critical Study.* Cambridge: Cambridge University Press, 2005, 213–227.

"Conversation at St. Clerans between Arthur Miller and John Huston." *Guardian,* February 25, 1960, 6.

Crowther, Bosley. "*The Misfits.*" *New York Times,* February 2, 1961, 24.

Dent, Alan. "Alien Values." *Illustrated London News,* June 10, 1961, 992.

French, Warren. "Miller at the Movies: *The Misfits.*" In *Arthur Miller: Twentieth Century Legend,* edited by Syed Mashkoor Ali, 216–219. (Jaipur, India: Surabhi, 2006).

Gehlawat, Ajay. "*The Misfits:* Marilyn and Arthur." In *Arthur Miller: Twentieth Century Legend,* edited by Syed Mashkoor Ali, 220–229. (Jaipur, India: Surabhi, 2006).

Glotfelty, Cheryll. "Old Folks in the New West: Surviving Change and Staying Fit in *The Misfits.*" *Western American Literature* 37, no. 1 (Spring 2002): 26–49.

Goode, James. *The Story of "The Misfits."* Indianapolis: Bobbs–Merrill, 1963. Reprinted as *The Making of "The Misfits."* New York: Limelight, 1986.

Hamilton, William. "Of God and Woman: *The Misfits.*" *Christian Century,* April 5, 1961: 424–425.

Hammen, Scott. *John Huston.* New York: Twayne, 1985.

Kauffmann, Stanley. "Across the Great Divide." *New Republic,* February 20, 1961, 26–27.

Kouvaros, George. "*The Misfits:* What Happened around the Camera." *Film Quarterly* 55, no. 4 (Summer 2002): 28–33.

McIntyre, Alice T. "Making *The Misfits* or Waiting for Monroe or Notes from Olympus." *Esquire,* March 1961, 74–81.

Miller, Arthur. "The Misfits." *Esquire,* October 1957, 158, 160–166.

———. *The Misfits.* New York: Viking, 1961.

———. *The Misfits.* In *Film Scripts Three,* edited by George P. Garrett, O. B. Hardison Jr., and Jane R. Gelman, 202–382. (New York: Irvington, 1989).

———. "Please Don't Kill Anything." *Noble Savage,* March 1, (1960), 126–31.

"*The Misfits.*" *Variety,* October 18, 1961, 6.

Moss, Leonard. *Arthur Miller,* 2nd. ed. New York: Twayne, 1980.

Palmer, R. Barton. "Arthur Miller and the Cinema." In *Cambridge Companion to Arthur Miller,* edited by Christopher Bigsby, 184–210. (New York: Cambridge University Press, 1997).

Popkin, Henry. "Arthur Miller Out West." *Commentary,* May 1961, 433–436.

Press David. "Arthur Miller's *The Misfits:* The Western Gunned Down." *Studies in the Humanities* 8, no. 1 (1980): 41–44.

Quigley, Isabel. "The Light That Never Was." *Spectator,* June 9, 1961, 840–841.

Toubiana, Serge. *The Misfits: The Story of a Shoot.* London: Phaidon, 2000.

Mr. Peters' Connections (1998)

Begun in 1995 and tentatively titled *The Powder Room, Mr. Peters' Connections* is clearly the play of an older writer looking back on his life, the figure of Cathy-May is redolent of MARILYN MONROE, and other aspects of the play have autobiographical status, but this is less confession than exploration, less a glance at the past than a search for the future (to borrow the title of one of Miller's own stories). As a study of the elderly, it offers exquisite insight into the fears and concerns of those who are approaching inevitable death while holding fast to life. The hope with which we are left is that love might be the answer, and it is for love of his daughter that Peters will continue to live as long as he can.

A relatively short play, Miller offered this to the SIGNATURE THEATER to premiere as part of their Miller season in 1998, and they were able to sign Peter Falk to play the lead. It opened in London at the Almeida Theatre, directed by MICHAEL BLAKEMORE, two years later. The style is highly representational, full of imagery, and ambiguous characterization. As a play about life's troubling incoherence, it seems inevitable that Miller makes it difficult to tell what is real and what is fantasy, who is alive and who is dead. Some critics disliked this aspect of the play, while others saw it as a clear indication that Miller was continuing to experiment with form and ideas even into his eighties.

SYNOPSIS

Set in an abandoned New York nightclub, Adele, a black bag lady, sits at a table drinking wine and observing herself in a mirror. Calvin enters, followed by Harry Peters, to whom he is showing the place. Peters slips into reverie, wondering what it is these days that moves him, declaring a need to make sense of his life and find the "subject." He plays some notes on the piano, and it continues to play by itself, while Peters waits for his wife to arrive. Calvin reminds him of someone whom he cannot place. He recalls a past lover, Cathy-May, and becomes excited at the memory of her body. She materializes, naked and in high heels, although she has been long dead. He points out his continued attraction but refuses the dance that she offers.

Peters tells Calvin about being an airline pilot, and they discuss the wonderful ladies' powder room. Peters is edgy, finding Calvin too know-it-all, and their rivalry becomes patently ridiculous as they argue about who is the busier and who has the narrower feet. Peters relates a dream that he once had in which he stepped into a perfect world, but he knew it was unreal. Peters seems uncertain as to what he is doing here. He remembers going to buy new shoes and decides to leave, but then Calvin reminds him that he must wait for his wife. Cathy-May reappears in a filmy dress but seems incapable of independent movement. Peters recalls his time flying planes in the war and longs for the simplicity of that period. Life has become too complex and overwhelming; Adele advises him to drink more.

Returning to his childhood, Peters explains how as a teen he washed planes at the airport for pocket money and flying lessons. He recalls how well-respected airline pilots used to be, especially among women. He tries to nap, but Calvin keeps talking until Peters suggests that they both keep quiet. Then Adele speaks about the mahogany toilet seats in the ladies room, imagining all the ladies who have sat on them in the past. Larry Ledesco enters looking for his wife, and Peters recognizes him from the shoe store where he just bought a pair of shoes. While Larry looks in the back, Calvin asks about Cathy-May, sexually objectifying her. She reappears in middle-aged clothing, an image of what she may have looked like had she lived. This time, Peters dances with her before she moves away. Calvin explains how this building began life as a bank, and Peters recalls the period. As Calvin suggests that since women tend to outlive men,

they must have all the money, Peters briefly falls to sleep.

Peters relates being grounded as a pilot because of his age and complains about the current political scene. Calvin tells how the bank was turned into a philanthropic library and then became a liberal café in the 1930s. After this, it was a successful nightclub until the VIETNAM WAR era, when it went under. When Calvin comments that he no longer gets old, Peters realizes that he must be another dead figure from his past. Again Peters tries to leave and is reminded that he must wait for his wife. Calvin considers the culture in London and how that seems less transient than culture in America. They also discuss Russia and how the socialist hope engendered in the 1940s fell through. Peters feels like a relic from the past and is upset at modern youths' lack of interest in history. He sees the modern world as meaningless, where women can have their breasts enlarged or reduced for the same price, which is about the same amount that it cost his father to buy their family home. Nowadays, he feels that people view sex as more important than the home. They joke about various modern-day operations that people have that seem unnecessary.

Larry reenters, asking them to look out for his wife and making racist remarks about the neighborhood, for which Peters chastises him. Larry complains that he has a right—his store was robbed by "niggers," and he is "fed up," to which Adele retorts, "Us too," explaining that poverty is a root cause of black crime. Larry tells them that his wife is called Cathy-May and leaves. Peters feels guilty over his past affair with her. He asks Adele why she is here, and she explains that she lives here and pretends to be a nurse. Peters wonders if it could be possible that Cathy-May was still alive.

Leonard and Rose enter; she is pregnant and needs to sit. Leonard is not the father but is her current lover. Calvin mocks their modern immorality and goes offstage into his office. Peters talks to the couple, wondering if they are alive or dead. They discuss bananas and try to find the subject, while Adele lists all the extras on her mother's Buick. As Peters begins a disjointed diatribe against the inanity of contemporary culture from its movies to the way people do laundry, to his delight, Rose tries to follow. Rather than start a new conversation, she adds to his. He then bemoans the reduction of the image of the president from a serious moral man to a mere entertainer. Leonard tries to join the conversation, but his discussion of Romans and Teutonic tribes annoys Peters, who asks him to stop.

Leonard frets about laundry that he has left at the cleaners as Rose goes to the ladies room. He tells Peters that he is a composer and an inventor, while Peters tries to decide whether he is awake or dreaming. Peters begins to worry about where his wife might be, saying they are sick of each other but "happy" together. He confesses that Calvin is his brother who drowned 20 years ago and then asks Leonard to look outside for his wife, although he momentarily cannot remember his own wife's name. When the name returns, he wonders if his amnesia is an indication that he has had enough of life, especially since society and politics have grown so despairing. Charlotte, his wife, finally arrives, full of compliments for the nightclub and for Rose. Charlotte used to be a dancer but is now a decorator, and Rose was thinking of hiring someone to decorate her apartment. Peters suggests that his wife check out the ladies room, and Rose agrees. Charlotte tells them that she has four daughters who are all flight attendants, but when she leaves, Peters says that this is a lie.

Rose wonders what her relationship with her baby will be. When Charlotte returns, she insists that Peters also look at the ladies room; he agrees only if Leonard will go with him. Charlotte asks Rose about her baby and suggests that she tell Leonard that he is the father. She recalls how she first met Peters at the theater. When the men return, they are unimpressed. Saying that she is part gypsy, Charlotte tells Rose that she will be having a girl. Leonard asks, if she were thinking of starting a new nightclub, would she consider discussing the music with him because he plays in a band. Charlotte goes to find Calvin to make an offer and tells Peters to explain to the young couple his philosophy. He is reluctant, but as Rose lies on the floor and Leonard asks to be the father, he begins to recount his vision of an Eden from which they flung away those with avarice and greed, and it was these from whom humanity was formed.

When Calvin reenters, he calls "Harry," and Peters answers with "Charley" and reminisces about their childhood together, but Calvin refuses to admit any relationship. Cathy-May reappears in a sexy outfit and a dog collar. Peters rests his head on her breasts as she breathes and calls her name. Larry storms in. He shouts at her for losing her shopping and wearing no panties, and he humiliates her further by violently trying to show the rest her lack of underwear. Peters tries to stop him but cannot. The struggle stops as Larry begins to kiss her and calls Peters over to listen at her breast. Peters remarks about dying alone as Cathy-May becomes motionless. Adele tells a story about being a substitute teacher who fluctuates between hope and despair. Peters desperately asks them all to think of the subject, and the actors form a tableau until Rose calls "Papa," asking Peters to stay and telling him she loves him. The play ends with Peters hoping that this might be the subject he sought.

CRITICAL COMMENTARY

In a preface to the play, Miller explains that Peters is in a state where his mind "is freed to roam from real memories to conjectures" to explain that what we witness essentially takes place inside the protagonist's head, a little like *Death of a Salesman* and a lot like *After the Fall*. Miller revisits many of his most memorable topics regarding abusive relationships, sibling rivalry, existential anguish, and the degradation of modern politics and social custom. On all of these, he offers commentary and on a few newer ones such as medical advances and racism, but they do not represent the subject of his play.

Indeed, it is the subject that Peters earnestly seeks throughout, and it is the process by which he does this, rather than the answer that he tentatively discovers, that provides the theme. Miller has written a mood piece in which we observe Peters gradually making connections between people and life experiences as he tries to make sense of everything. He needs to know the subject to piece it all together. It is a quest on which many of Miller's characters have embarked in the past to try to make sense of their messy lives. The subject that we are finally led to believe is love, as Peters's daughter suggests by offering her love as sufficient reason for Peters to stay.

At the start of the play, Peters seems uncertain of everything: who these people are, why he is here, why he is even still alive. His attention and understanding seem to slip in and out of focus as he dips into the past, takes a short nap, or mentally blocks out his own wife's name. Is Peters growing forgetful with age, or is the lack of coherence more symbolic, revealing his initial lack of connection and his dreamlike disorientation as he tries to work things through. Peter's dream of the perfect world suggests a man in search of perfection but unable yet to accept the truth that nothing can be perfect and real because life is too messy. He resents losing the freedom of flight, but his purchase of shoes symbolizes an acceptance that he is grounded. The apparent simplicity of flying during the war displays a negative past of disconnection in which he unfeelingly dropped bombs on fellow human beings; it is by walking the streets that he will meet people and be able to truly connect.

Despite its abstract design, the play is given an unusually specific setting, which in the revelation of its history becomes an additional character in the play. The building's history through bank, library, liberal café and nightclub offers a metaphor for the development of a country, from blatant CAPITALISM through kindly philanthropy, earnest socialism and hedonistic self-concern. Peters's suggestion that they blow it up conveys his initial attitude toward the contemporary United States itself, just as the attractive ladies' powder room might represent a positive feminine force in the play, though a force against which the men remain wary. The fact that the building fell into decline during the VIETNAM WAR suggests the cultural impact of this event on the U.S. psyche. For Miller, Vietnam had a profound affect on people's capacity for belief in anything and killed both optimism and pessimism in the United States. Through this, the United States is presented as a country that is still in search of ideals, without having the stabilizing history of GREAT BRITAIN and having rejected the socialist path of the Soviet Union. Peters thus repre-

sents the U.S. everyman whose survival becomes imperative.

Peters is on the edge between life and death at an age where he seems equally drawn to both. Nearly everyone he knew, bar his wife, seems dead. He has outlived his usefulness as a pilot, the thing he most enjoyed, and finds modern life empty of meaning or value, so why continue? He begins to play "The September Song" on the piano at the start but is unable to continue, having lost his memory of the love that the song recalls, but the piano keeps playing, and this place may help him remember. He initially declines to dance with Cathy-May, and when Calvin offers a sexual vision of the way ladies at the bank behaved, he asks him to stop as if he does not want to be aroused because this is a reminder of life and is a less safe topic than the dead past which expects nothing more of him. But life draws him back: The hopeful vision of his pregnant daughter, the connections being forged between young and old, his acceptance of guilt over his treatment of Cathy-May, and the possibility of a future nightclub opening all combine to suggest the possibility for redemption that he had begun to think was lost in a world where greed seems innate. The family unit that seems to be forming at the play's close suggests the strongest loving community to combat such greed rather than to accept passively its inevitability.

FIRST PERFORMANCE

Mr. Peters' Connections was produced by the Signature Theatre in New York City as part of their season on Miller. It ran from April 28 to June 21, 1998, with the following cast:

Calvin: Jeff Weiss
Harry Peters: Peter Falk
Adele: Erica Bradshaw
Cathy-May: Kris Carr
Larry: Daniel Oreskes
Leonard: Alan Mozes
Rose: Tari Signor
Charlotte: Anne Jackson

Directed by Garry Hynes
Set designed by Francis O'Connor
Produced by the Signature Theatre
Limited run of 40 performances.

INITIAL REVIEWS

While the bigger-name critics were fairly scathing, though some of them more so of the production than of the play, reviewers for smaller papers tended to be more congratulatory. Clive Barnes felt that it was a "good play," but saw its production as a "travesty," while Michael Feingold asked for "a director who could approach [Miller's] discontinuous universe more daringly." Vincent Canby described it as "an anti-dramatic reverie," Ben Brantley disliked its "experimental, ruminative style," and Robert Brustein called it "windy, tiresome, self-conscious" and complained that it had no plot, form, "or even much effort at characterization." However, Robert Melton felt it was "Miller's strongest play in 30 years" and praised its technique and his ability to give existentialist questions "stunning dramatic force and shape." Clifford Ridley enjoyed the play's "cautious optimism" and eloquence, Linda Winer described it as "strange and beguiling," and Rohan Preston, although reviewing the Guthrie Theater Lab production of 1999, called it a "poetic and gusty new play" that "shimmers as it distills its jazzy poetry."

SCHOLARSHIP

Too recent to have garnered much critical attention, *Mr. Peters' Connections* has been discussed in the greatest depth by CHRISTOPHER BIGSBY, who views it as a "contemplation of life itself whose intensity and coherence slowly fade, whose paradox can never be resolved, as it is also a confrontation with death," notes its connection to the work of ANTON CHEKHOV, and concludes that the play "recalls the surviving possibility of community."

CHARACTERS

Adele   Adele, the black bag lady who sits in the nightclub throughout the play, the play's notes describe as a construct of Peters's experience of black people and as such represents a sweep of class and prejudice. Never more than a stereotype, she indicates sad limitations in the public's awareness of black roles in society, but her presence suggests that this is something with which we should begin to connect. Her drinking, her retort to Larry, and her portrayal as a despairing substitute teacher evidence her frustration with her role in society. Her

potential for good is indicated by the image of her as a nurse. The mirror she holds seems less for her eyes than for those of the audience.

Calvin   Calvin is a manifestation of Peters's brother, Charley, who drowned 20 years previously. While alive, he was prone to cruel practical jokes, and it seems that he continues to enjoy one-upping people even in death as he shows off his knowledge and spars with his brother over who has the smallest foot. Too self-concerned to think of others, he refuses to acknowledge his connection to his brother and ends the play staring into empty space, which is all that his life has left.

Cathy-May   As a woman defined more by her body than her mind, it is unsurprising that Cathy-May only has four lines. She appears throughout the play in various states of undress and prostration. One in a line of characters that are based on Marilyn Monroe, she is shown as a woman who is incapable of independent thought or movement, having been reduced to a sexual icon by the men around her. This objectification eventually stifles all life from her, and Peters and Larry equally share the guilt as neither has treated her with love. Peters at least acknowledges this and feels guilt.

Ledesco, Larry   A shoe-store salesman from next door to the nightclub, Larry comes in and out looking for his wife. Prone to racist and sexist thought and behavior, Larry is the imagined husband of Cathy-May, had she lived. Reminiscent of one of Sam Shepard's brutish males, or possibly an unflattering portrait of Monroe's one time husband, Joe DiMaggio, Larry treats his wife as an object, making her wear a dog collar in case she is lost, and he demeans the very sexuality that attracts him in a display of violence and contempt. The closing image of him standing by an inert Cathy-May holding an empty shopping bag depicts the fruitlessness of such self-concerned behavior.

Leonard   Leonard is a composer and an inventor in his twenties who seems unable to compose or invent. His indecisiveness is a factor in this as he agonizes over his laundry rather than his future.

Recently split from a girlfriend, he now dates Rose and during the play decides that he would like to be the father of her child. This decision, coupled with his offer to Charlotte to play in the new club with his band, suggest a positive development and an effort at connection.

Peters, Charlotte The wife, for whom Peters waits for much of the play, joins him near the close in a whirlwind of energy. Charlotte plans to buy and reopen the nightclub, feeding her recently embarked career as a decorator. With her four daughters and wild gypsy connection, she offers a formidable feminine force and seems to energize all around her. When she first met her husband, she was a dancer with the Rockettes, a particularly U.S. emblem of celebration, and her decision to reopen the club suggests a positive engagement, albeit one that must avoid the trap of capitalism (she is last seen holding a calculator).

Peters, Harry Harry Peters is an elderly man who realizes that a lot of his friends have died and that his own end must be close. As a teen, he had had a love affair with planes, going to the airport to wash planes for pocket money and flying lessons. He joined the air force in WORLD WAR TWO and then became an airline pilot for 28 years. Married near the end of the war to Charlotte, whom he saw dancing with the Rockettes, his marriage has survived an affair with Cathy-May, for which he feels guilty, and probably others. Though still spry, the airline pressured him to give up piloting because of age regulations. He then lectured at Princeton for several years before retiring. He is uncertain what he should do next, if anything. Prone to naps, he is wearing down, but his mind and his appetites remain vital. He just needs to find the subject to give his life enough coherence to continue, and his daughter, Ruth, finally suggests this to him as love.

Rose At the play's close, Rose becomes Peters's daughter, but for most of the play, she is a passing stranger who has come into the club to rest up, having grown tired walking. She is pregnant and plans to have the child, an obvious symbol of hope for the future, although she has no relation-

ship with the biological father. She has been seeing Leonard, who would like to help her raise the child. Her career as a dancer connects her to Charlotte and to the positive feminine life force in the play which is at odds with the desiccated life force of Cathy-May, who has allowed men to define her.

FURTHER READING

Barnes, Clive. "Not Quite Miller Time." *New York Post,* May 18, 1998: n.p.

Bigsby, Christopher. *"Mr. Peters' Connections." Arthur Miller: A Critical Study.* New York: Cambridge University Press, 2005: 405–420.

Brantley, Ben. "Peter Falk's Search for Meaning." *New York Times,* May 18, 1998: E1.

Brustein, Robert. "Still Searching for Theatre." *New Republic,* August 3, 1998: 29–30.

Canby, Vincent. "This Time, Peter Falk Is Part of the Mystery." *New York Times,* May 24, 1998, sec. 2: 4.

Feingold, Michael. "The Old Miller Stream." *Village Voice,* May 26, 1998: 147.

Melton, Robert W. "Book Reviews: Arts and Humanities." *Library Journal,* September 15, 1999: 83.

Papatola, Dominic P. "Mr. Miller's Connections." *Saint Paul Pioneer Press,* October 28, 1999: E1.

Preston, Rohan. "Miller Time." *Minneapolis Star Tribune,* October 31, 1999: F1.

———. "Mr. Peters' Poetically Questions Reality, Illusion." *Minneapolis Star Tribune,* November 5, 1999: B4.

Ridley, Clifford A. "Mr. Peters' Raises Many Questions, Enjoyably." *Philadelphia Inquirer,* May 18, 1998: D6.

Winer, Linda. "Old Coat, New Shoes, Bared Souls." *Newsday,* May 18, 1998: B2.

"A Modest Proposal for the Pacification of the Public Temper" (1954)

First published in *Nation* in July 1954 and later reprinted in *Echoes Down the Corridor* (2000), Miller's ironic essay took Jonathan Swift's satiric lead in suggesting an outlandish remedy for difficult times.

Rather than callous attitudes toward an Irish famine, Miller's target is the paranoia caused by fears of COMMUNISM in the 1950s, fed by the investigations of the HOUSE UN-AMERICAN ACTIVITIES COMMITTEE. His proposal is that from age 18, everyone is sent to jail every two years until they can prove with documents and witnesses that they are patriots.

Miller lists the duties of all those involved, from judge to citizen, and defines various classifications. A "Conceptual Traitor's" crime might range from personally speaking against the nation to not actively denouncing another's speech, and these are hereafter closely monitored; an "Action Traitor" attends meetings or is suspected of having done so by a Committee of Congress and is punished with fines and imprisonment; "Unclassified Persons" are those who are incapable of coherent English, insane, elderly, infirm, children, members of the FBI or of investigating committees, and are released immediately. Pointing out that since people go to jail willingly, it will be better than in Russia, Miller quips that licensing citizens in this way is little different from demanding driving or dog licenses to ensure public safety. Thus, Miller mocks the period's apparent willingness to trample on civil liberties and condemn people without firm proof.

"Monte Sant' Angelo" (1951)

This prize-winning short story first appeared in *Harper's* in 1951 under the title "Monte Saint Angelo" and was reprinted in *Prize Stories of 1951* (1951), *These, Your Children* (1952), *Stories of Sudden Truth* (1953), and *A Treasury of American Jewish Stories* (1958). It also has been reprinted with its corrected title, "Monte Sant' Angelo," in both of Miller's collections *I Don't Need You Any More* (1967) and *The Misfits and Other Stories* (1987) and in *The Literature of American Jews* (1973) and *A Treasury of Jewish Literature from Biblical Times to Today* (1992). Based on an idea that Miller had had when exploring Italy with his friend VINCENT LONGHI back in 1948, it tells the story of Bernstein, an uneasy American Jew, who accompanies his friend's search for relatives in an Italian village.

The friend is named Vinny, no doubt in tribute to Miller's friend. Knowing that his own relatives were wiped out during the HOLOCAUST, Bernstein is surprised by his recognition of a fellow Jew, which gives him a renewed sense of connection and self-esteem. In honor of Miller's story, in 2005, the town of Monte Sant' Angelo in Italy organized events around the tale, including an illustration competition, with plans for the winning series of illustrations to be developed into a cartoon animation of the story.

Tall, broad shouldered, and dark haired, Vinny Appello and Bernstein look very alike, but where Vinny is open, passionate about people and life, and proud of his Italian heritage, Bernstein is purposefully closed, defensively aloof, and uncertain of his own identity as an American Jew. Just the fact that we never learn Bernstein's first name is further evidence of this secrecy. Despite their very different natures, Vinny and Bernstein are close friends. They have been traveling together in Italy for four weeks. Vinny has been taking the opportunity to look up his various relatives: Bernstein grudgingly goes along, partly because he knows that he cannot undertake such an endeavor given that his relatives were wiped out by the Nazis. He is somewhat jealous of the opportunity that Vinny has to uncover a sense of the past and family history that he feels is lost to him. The story begins as their guide drives them up a steep climb toward the remote Italian mountaintop community of Mont Sant' Angelo.

Vinny explains that his relatives have inhabited this town since the 12th century when two of his ancestors had helped to build the town church. Brothers and monks, they had reportedly been buried in the church, and he hopes to find their crypt. He also has an aunt whom he plans to meet, his last surviving relative in the township. Their arrival causes a stir, and it is obvious that the secluded town has few visitors. When Vinny asks after his aunt, the townspeople are uncertain at first of who she is; an old widow lady has little impact on their community. However, they track her down and knock on her door. Her reaction is unsettled; she had not known that she had any living relatives, and she does not recognize Vinny as kin and is uncertain how to treat him. She is also worried that she may be expected to provide hospitality despite her apparent poverty. Despite such an ambivalent welcome, which confuses Bernstein, Vinny is happy just having made the connection and leaves to find the brothers' crypt. Here, however, they are less lucky, and after an abortive search, they repair to a restaurant for lunch.

While Bernstein considers his friend's endeavors and contentment regardless of success, he feels a growing need to reconnect that "broken part of himself" that he senses. It is at this point that a local man catches his eye, and he feels "an abrupt impression of familiarity." He is a seller of cloth named Mauro di Benedetto, or as Vinny translates, "Morris of the Blessed. Moses." Given this unusual name, the way he ties a bundle, and the fact he is here collecting a loaf of bread on a Friday that he professes that he needs to reach home before sundown for his evening meal, Bernstein decides that he must be Jewish. The man, however, does not even understand what a Jew is, asking if it is perhaps some kind of Catholic, and denies any Judaic connection. His Friday routine is done because that is the way that his father always behaved.

All knowledge of JUDAISM has been eradicated from the minds of these people, and yet Bernstein feels certain that this man is Jewish and is performing the Shabbat rituals even while he remains unaware of the fact. Also, because of this, he feels a cultural connection to the man as a fellow Jew, which also makes him feel less isolated in the world. It is a testament to the strength of Judaism, its emphasis on community, and a belief in tradition. Bernstein reconsiders his own relationship to the faith of his ancestors and discovers a value to the past that he has ignored up until this point. He begins to understand how the past continues to live and to impact the present, despite such obstacles as entrenched ANTI-SEMITISM, and in this he finds his own self-esteem reestablished. Rejuvenated by this, he offers to help his friend look again for his buried ancestors, and this time they find them. In Bernstein's obvious approval of the search this time, Vinny feels validated, and the two end closer friends than before.

In two rare studies of Miller's short fiction, Irving Jacobson sees the tale as unique in Miller's

canon for its depiction of "an adult [who] comes to feel himself at home in the larger world outside the family structure," and Christiane Desafy–Grignard considers the tale's treatment of Jewish identity. While the tale certainly is, as Malcolm Bradbury suggests, "a reflective story about the ambiguity of identity and ancestry," it also has a very personal angle for Miller, as CHRISTOPHER BIGSBY considers: "Bernstein's denial and Bernstein's affirmation are both part of Miller's sensibility and this tightly controlled story explores that tension." Both Bernstein and Miller discover a renewed connection to their Jewish roots in the course of the story.

FURTHER READING

Bigsby, Christopher. "Fiction." *Arthur Miller: A Critical Study.* New York: Cambridge University Press, 2005, 444–472.

Bradbury, Malcolm. "Arthur Miller's Fiction." In *The Cambridge Companion to Arthur Miller,* edited by Christopher Bigsby, 211–229. (Cambridge, England: Cambridge University Press, 1997).

Desafy–Grignard, Christiane. "Jewishness and Judaism Revisited in Two Short Stories by Arthur Miller: 'Monte Sant' Angelo' and 'I Don't Need You Anymore.'" *Journal of the Short Story in English* 43 (2004 Autumn): 87–106.

Jacobson, Irving. "The Vestal Jews on 'Mont Sant Angelo.'" *Studies in Short Fiction* 13 (1976): 507–512.

"The Nature of Tragedy" (1949)

Miller's follow-up essay to "Tragedy and the Common Man" that had caused such a furor among critics and academics was "The Nature of Tragedy." It came out one month later, this time in the *New York Herald Tribune* and is possibly one of his most quoted essays. It was reprinted in both editions of *The Theater Essays of Arthur Miller.* Having thrown down the gauntlet, Miller now sought to establish in more detail his concept of modern TRAGEDY and to offer some clarification of his earlier claims. He begins by asserting that "the idea of tragedy is constantly changing" and will in all honesty "never be finally defined," but then he proceeds to do the best that he can to define what he sees as the competing dramatic modes of his era. The essay becomes a plea for playwrights not to dilute the tragic potential of their work and settle for pathos because, he feels, the lessons of tragedy are too important to ignore.

Much of this essay is concerned with clarifying terminology, and Miller begins by trying to separate what he sees as the commonly confused ideas of the tragic and the pathetic. If a man is walking down the street, Miller explains, and a piano falls on his head, this can only be pathetic, not tragic, because accidental death carries no deeper meaning. Tragedy may elicit feelings of pathos, but it has an added dimension that brings the onlooker "knowledge or enlightenment." The knowledge that is gained is something that pertains "to the right way of living in the world." Miller sees pathos as derived from melodrama but tragedy as coming from a higher form of drama.

Recognizing that drama must have conflict, Miller asserts that if that conflict is only between individual people, then the best that can be achieved is melodrama. When the conflict is expanded to include also conflicting ideas within an individual, then a "higher" drama is achieved. As Miller explains, "When I show you why a man does what he does, I may do so melodramatically; but when I show why he almost did not do it, I am making drama." In brief, a melodrama contains a single action that is usually based on a conflict between characters that leads to individual pathos. Tragedy reveals a psychological complexity that grows from conflict within the mind of each character and that has repercussions on the wider society.

Miller complains that few real tragedies are being written in his period because most playwrights have given up trying to find the answers to life and because there is a general disagreement as to what would give people satisfaction. Miller feels that literature that ignores the tragic dimension ultimately devalues humanity because it cannot allow for the celebration of humankind's potential, which Miller sees as lying at the heart of tragedy.

Miller points to the central irony of tragedy—that in presenting its audience with a sad story, it is also showing humankind's best hope. You should come away from tragedy, he suggests "with the knowledge that man, by reason of his intense effort and desire, which you have just seen demonstrated, is capable of flowering on this earth."

Miller asserts that literary endeavors that take "the path of behaviorism" and conclude that a person is "essentially a dumb animal moving through a preconstructed maze toward his inevitable sleep" are unnecessarily despairing. "Tragedy," on the other hand, "is inseparable from a certain modest hope regarding the human animal," and it "arises when we are in the presence of a man who has missed accomplishing his joy." But to reach that hope, the dramatist must create characters with a psychological complexity that will allow an audience to believe in their reality. In tragedy, the dramatist must show not only why characters' lives "are ending in sadness, but how they might have avoided their end." The nature of tragedy, Miller concludes, is to furnish humanity with "the most perfect means we have of showing who and what we are, and what we must be—or should strive to become."

"1956 and All This" (1956)

Originally published in *Colorado Quarterly* as "The Playwright and the Atomic World," this essay was renamed "1956 and All This" for its inclusion in *The Theater Essays of Arthur Miller* (1978), as the original title was seen as too dated. It is a lengthy piece in which Miller considers world affairs based on the differences between U.S. culture and that of other countries. Suspecting that much can be learned from a nation by its art, he takes as a starting point the way that foreigners have reacted to his plays. Despite U.S. expectations that no one outside of the United States would understand *Death of a Salesman*, the play struck an international resonance that crossed all cultures, thus proving a universal humanity that could be the starting place for better relationships abroad. Miller's essay is a call for a better understanding between cultures, something that he strongly believes a nation's writers can help accomplish if they are respectfully heeded.

Miller is openly unhappy with the U.S. foreign policy since the close of WORLD WAR II, seeing the country's increasing armaments as counterproductive to its supposed aims: "A reliance on force is always a confession of moral defeat." He feels that COMMUNISM has not been stopped, just deferred, and the U.S. approach seems to him ultimately negative, an antipolicy rather than a policy. The country, Miller insists, needs a new approach if it is ever to move forward out of its current fear and stalemate. His main quarrel is that "policy has ceased to reflect the positive quality of the American people," and Miller proceeds to describe that quality. U.S. pragmatism may seem at odds to the more philosophic and aesthetic judgments of Europe and beyond and may seem to be analogous to her preference of applied science over pure science, but it need not be seen as heartless or unintelligent. U.S. antiintellectualism has its dangers, which include promoting an "inability to see the context behind an action" and laying the country open to "extremely dangerous suspicions" from those abroad who misinterpret U.S. short-sighted actions as brute territorialism rather than fear or naiveté, but it also ensures that the common man is not left out or left behind.

Miller feels that the United States needs to recognize how negatively it is perceived abroad and to reshape that perception. A president such as Abraham Lincoln knew that to dehumanize an enemy was counterproductive to future security and that the desire should always be toward peace rather than war. Communism, Miller insists, can only come to power against tyranny, not DEMOCRACY, so it is better to fight tyranny than communism. If the United States tried to eradicate poverty rather than communism, the country would probably create more freedom around the globe and make itself more popular on the international stage. Miller suggests that the United States use its technological advances to help others rather than just to raise itself and it should allow foreign policy to be motivated by love rather than fear. He concludes by suggesting that the country let go of its fear of World War III because such an outcome is untenable to all sides and because it is ridiculous to base

foreign policy on its expectation. The United States was founded on the love of freedom, and her aim abroad should be to bring those in poverty freedom from their misery rather than to waste more time gathering misguided support among tyrants against the Soviet Union.

"The 1928 Buick" (1978)

Published in *Atlantic* magazine "The 1928 Buick" is a short story that recalls defining incidents from Miller's youth. In *Timebends: A Life*, Miller relates how Moe Fishler had married Jean, Miller's cousin and the daughter of his Aunt Esther, who had lived across the street when Miller was growing up in BROOKLYN. Although based on real events, Miller changes details in his story, such as the importance of the doctor who brought the body home, and adds a layer of symbolism to give the whole a greater impact. The story begins in the summer of 1930 when Miller would have been 14, and Miller describes a neighbor's 1928 Buick coupe. Miller was a car enthusiast all of his life, owning a series of vintage cars, and his admiration for this particular model shines through the loving details that he shares. The story, however, is somewhat tragic, telling of wasted potential and loss as a picture is built of the clannish isolation of people on Miller's old street, the empty repetition of their lives, and the toll this took. It is this that Miller had sought to escape on his journey to the UNIVERSITY OF MICHIGAN, and that is the darker undercurrent of the tale.

The Buick belongs to Max Sions, a young man who, despite the GREAT DEPRESSION, is doing better than most of the neighborhood. He bought the car cheaply from a manufacturer who had gone bankrupt. He plans to marry Miller's cousin, Virginia, and offers to let Miller ride the few blocks to her apartment. Max is short but attractive and is meticulous in his appearance. Young Miller admires his style and sees a huge difference between Max and Max's father, who is an untrustworthy butcher, far less refined, and an inveterate gambler and womanizer. Max's mother has given up on her husband and lives only for her son, waiting for him daily on their porch to return from work. Virginia's father, in contrast, is a kind and gentle soul, as are the rest of her family. None too intellectual, the womenfolk spend all their days in cleaning and sewing. Max takes Virginia for a ride to Sheepshead Bay.

Seven years later, Miller is visiting from college. "I loved to return home and dreaded it," he tells us, "the threat of it, of failing to escape into my own life, and the boredom of those repeated embraces." He spots the Buick on the Sions's driveway, uncared for and sadly deteriorated. The man next door works on his 1927 Model-A Tudor, which Miller informs us only had 900 miles on it when he died. The sense of the closed-off street with the cemetery at its end is of enervation and decay. Max and Virginia evidently have become an unhappy couple, as Max goes alone to Coney Island. Max has a new car, and Miller senses that he also wants a new wife and to escape this depressing neighborhood. When he drives off, both his mother and his wife watch in silence from the porch. Wondering if he should offer to buy the Buick, Miller never gets his chance as that night Doctor Levy arrives with the corpse of Max in his car. Max had caught the doctor's eye as Max stood at the beach weeping, in a pose reminiscent of the statue of David. When he collapsed, the doctor ran to save him but was too late.

The two women are distraught, and it is left to Max's more composed father to bring his son's body inside. While Miller apologizes for his relatives, the women drive Doctor Levy away, as if partly blaming him for Max's death. They will only listen to their own doctor, who soon arrives. When Doctor Levy comes to the funeral, the women again shun him, but he walks out of the cemetery beside Max's father, and Miller senses a connection between them. Each offers the other the attention that they crave but are denied from the rest. Miller never got the courage to ask Virginia for the Buick, and he closes by describing how she spends the rest of her life in a kind of daze, sheltering in her home. It is precisely this kind of narrow existence that so appalls Miller and provoked him into leaving behind his old life.

No Villain (1935)

Never produced, this was the first play Miller wrote. It was created in 1935 during the spring break of his freshman year at the UNIVERSITY OF MICHIGAN as a possible entry for a university-administered award that Miller felt he must try to win to get sufficient funds to stay enrolled. Although Miller had little idea how to write a play, he asked a neighbor for advice as to an acceptable length, and won a $250 Hopwood Award the following year. The judges were not unanimous, but one described the play as having "an excellent modern theme, handled with a tender insight into character." Never published, the manuscript is in the archives at the University of Michigan. Future years brought requests to stage *No Villain*, but Miller always refused, knowing this to be a work of trial and error. In 1936, Miller rewrote the play as *They Too Arise*, and by 1939, he developed it further into *The Grass Still Grows*.

The play's epigraph from Frederick Engels regarding the relationship between labor and capital and those in control of both show the influence of COMMUNISM on Miller at this time. However, the drama is based on Miller's personal experience and is set in the same area of BROOKLYN in which he had lived. Like the Millers, the Simon family are Jewish, with two sons (Ben and Arnold), a daughter (Maxine), and a live-in grandfather. Ben and Arnold are the same ages as KERMIT MILLER and Miller, and Ben has given up college to help his family, while Arnold is a freshman at the University of Michigan, hoping to become a writer. The head of the family, Abe, just like ISIDORE MILLER, runs a failing coat company that had once prospered and dotes on his daughter. The mother, Esther, unhappy with her family's fall in fortune, is reminiscent of AUGUSTA MILLER.

The Simons anxiously await the arrival of Arnold, who is hitchhiking home because they could not afford to send him bus fare. Business has been bad of late, and a loan from the bank is due for repayment in two days. The men avoid talking about this, and so Esther worries more about what might be happening. The family humorously bicker and tease, and Ben reads a letter from Arnold that describes Arnold's involvement in the antiwar movement at college. The family worries that he has turned into a communist. Ben patiently tries to explain to his parents how Marxism promotes a new economic system that is built on social equality, which would help current workers, but precludes people like Abe from owning their own businesses. They are happy to see Arnold arrive safely home, as the grandfather lights candles to mark the Sabbath.

The second act opens at the Simon Coat and Suit Company and literally divides the stage between the workers and management. This symbolizes their actual separation in the world of business. Shipping clerks throughout the area have gone on strike, affecting the business, which cannot get orders delivered. Abe wants his sons to help him break the strike as he has not the funds to repay his bank loan. While Ben is sympathetic to his demands, Arnold is adamantly against them, and tension mounts in a series of scenes that depict the family's attempts to make deliveries and stay solvent. In the midst of this, the grandfather dies, and the bank forecloses the business.

In a minor subplot, a rich manufacturer, Roth, proposes that Ben marry his daughter Helen so that he might groom Ben as his heir, but Ben objects to this solution. The final act begins with family and friends sitting around the grandfather's coffin in the parlor. When Roth arrives with Helen and tries to talk about a future union, Ben grows angry, sends away the mourners, and declares his intention to begin a new kind of business that is more committed to its workers. Through this, Ben articulates the issue of responsibility beyond the individual; despite his support of his father, he has throughout the play espoused left-wing convictions. However, his final vision is vague at best, offering little in the way of a concrete solution: "I've got to build something bigger . . . Something that won't allow this to happen . . . Something that'll change this deeply . . . to the bottom."

Arnold, evidently Miller's alter ego and mouthpiece—even being called "Art" several times in the play—is overshadowed by Ben. Arnold spouts Communist principle, and his radicalism sets him at odds against parents who are resistant to any philosophy that precludes ownership. An idealist to the point of pompous self-righteousness, he rejects what he sees as his family's materialism and wants to change the world. Ben is more human, sympathizing with both his father and the workers under him and seeking a way to make all content. The Simons struggle to survive, caught between their own employees and the larger companies that forever threaten such small businesses.

There are, as the title indicates, no real villains in the play, just a 1930s middle-class family reacting to a rapidly changing world. It is the system, if anything, that is at fault, and the central conflict is between private interest and a wider public concern. The father finds change the hardest and prefigures *All My Sons'* Joe Keller in his desire always to put family first. He sees the world in terms of "dog eat dog" where every man must fight for himself. The brothers' struggle to find an acceptable way ahead that includes a greater responsibility toward others (just like Keller's sons), being at odds with their father's belief, provides the core of the play's drama.

No Villain is not great drama, but for a first play, it shows promise and points to areas of interest and techniques that would become trademarks of Miller's work. After a humorous beginning, the play evolves into an intense family drama, pitting father against sons, brother against brother. Although the play depends too much on speeches over dialogue to convey its issues, it is a more finely realized piece than much agitprop of the period. Unlike agitprop, it offers a wider social perspective, more detailed characters, and a greater display of sympathy for those beyond the working class; indeed, its working class is peripheralized, present but voiceless. The workers at Abe's business mutely work through the crisis, hardly cognizant of what is happening; the strikers are kept offstage, and we are aware that greater business powers are in control here. It is within the family that the play's true conflict lies, although that family represents a microcosm of the larger society in all of the social divisions and uncertainties of its time.

"Notes on Realism" (1999)

Originally published in *Harper's*, this essay was soon after reprinted in *Echoes Down the Corridor* (2000). In it, Miller relates what he feels to be 20th-century U.S. drama's greatest accomplishments, against a consideration of how the term REALISM might be better judged and applied. The essay begins by Miller noting changes to BROADWAY, which he no longer views as a place of U.S. theatrical innovation. A new play like *The Crucible,* he asserts, would not be produced in the current Broadway climate, although he later admits that it has always been difficult to have any serious play produced. Part of the current problem is the soaring cost of production and the domination of the *New York Times* over reviews. However, even where stylistic innovation is promoted, Miller finds much of it more trendy than fulfilling, largely because too many artists are unnecessarily antagonistic to their work being seen as realistic. Realism, Miller asserts, is more complex than many would allow and provides the bedrock for much of what can be deemed positive in U.S. theater; he then proceeds to explain what he means.

Pointing out that no play can reflect true reality because it is always a play, nevertheless realism was the dominant form of U.S. theater's development in the first half of the 20th century. The epic-populist work of the Living Newspaper theater of the 1930s however, was an exception to this rule, but this was because it had been assisted by government subsidy and so had no need to be commercial as most plays do if they want to reach an audience. Miller refers to his first play, *No Villain,* as being "purely mimetic, a realistic play about my own family." Since then, however, he has presented more stylized treatments of life, especially due to his interest in the social themes, which he feels necessitate a more elevated diction than realistic prose. He feels that the term *realism* is unnecessarily restricting and ludicrous when applied to such revolutionary artists as HENRIK IBSEN, ANTON CHEKHOV, August Strindberg, or CLIFFORD ODETS.

Miller praises Odets as a "trailblazer not just because of his declared radicalism but because of the fact that his plays were so manifestly *written.*" Referring to Odets's stylized dialogue as "personal jazz" with "slashes of imagery," Miller acknowledges its poetic influence on him as a writer. Just as he refutes any limiting description of Odets as a social realist, he makes similar claims regarding the contributions of TENNESSEE WILLIAMS. Although a play like *The Glass Menagerie* has been termed realism on psychological terms, Williams's work is filled with symbolism and a "tragic vision" beyond conventional realistic plays. EUGENE O'NEILL was a more openly "aesthetic rebel," but this made him an "isolated phenomenon" on Broadway. His refusal to worry about commercial popularity freed him to experiment with "the unfamiliar world of spirit and metaphysic" that so marks his plays. Most popular playwrights, however, Miller insists, depend upon a veneer of realism to please the audience, even while the better ones play with the form.

Looking beyond U.S. drama at the language of Irish playwrights Sean O'Casey and J. M. Synge, both realistic in one sense, Miller points out how their dialogue, too, has the "lift of poetry," just as he sees in the plays of Ibsen. Moving on to ABSURDISM and SAMUEL BECKETT, Miller asserts that these "both obscured and illuminated the traditional discussion of theater style." He describes Beckett's style as that of a "presentational thematic play," in which the language is stripped "clean as a bleached bone" to allow his theme its fullest potential. Until the 1950s, playwrights had transcended realism through elevated language, but after this, Miller sees many doing it by emulating the "most common, undecorated speech" they could—in HAROLD PINTER, to create an "atmosphere of sinister danger," and in Beckett a "threatening sense of immanence familiar from bad dreams." Yet even as these playwrights shear away every metaphor or simile from their speech to create a new language, they do not make the mistake of leaving structure behind, which is why, for Miller, their plays work better than many of their imitators.

Finally, speaking of his own work, Miller declares that he has shifted styles continuously throughout his career "according to the nature of my subject," using differing forms of language to try to "find speech that springs naturally out of the characters."

But although such speeches may "sound like real," Miller insists, they only seem that way and are "intensely composed." For Miller, the style of a play is ultimately less important that its message, that is, "the degree to which it illuminates how life works in our time." Ideal plays, Miller concludes, offer that same balance between "idea and feeling" that we find in William Shakespeare, and recent plays that have presented "indicated rather than felt emotion" seem to him misguided, with too much weight being given to the idea and not enough to feeling. For Miller, all good drama needs roots in reality to engage its audience, and plays that direct their arrows toward the "wayward air" rather than the "castle of reality" can never be as effective.

On Politics and the Art of Acting (2001)

This lengthy essay was originally delivered as the Jefferson Lecture for 2001, an honor awarded to Miller by the National Endowment for the Humanities for distinguished intellectual achievement in the humanities. These lectures are intended as a public forum to address topics of broad concern to the humanities and are given annually. The speech was subsequently published as a single volume with photographs to illustrate the personalities discussed. Given on March 26 before an overflow crowd of 2,600 at the Kennedy Center's Concert Hall, the speech was considered controversial. Many Republicans saw it as a provocative attack on their party, but Miller's criticisms and fears seem equally well directed at the Democrats. The lecture was a call to arms against what Miller saw as the U.S. public's complacency toward its own political leaders and an insistence that a nation can be only as great as the true vision of its leaders, regardless of how good they look on television.

Miller combines anecdotes of various experiences—personal, theatrical, and political—to provide a commentary on the state of the nation's leadership—past and present—and this country's increasing inability to the tell the difference between illusion and reality. Analyzing the public personas and policies of a variety of political leaders since Abraham Lincoln, but concentrating on Franklin Roosevelt, Ronald Reagan, Bill Clinton, and George W. Bush, Miller measures them in terms of appearance against achievement and considers how far the public's perception of each empowered them in the role of U.S. president.

Taking as a starting point what he saw as the fiasco of the 2000 presidential elections in which Miller saw the whole nation being tricked into acting as if a president had been fairly elected, Miller uses this as evidence of the deterioration of DEMOCRACY in the United States: "It was said that in the end the system worked, when clearly it hadn't at all." Then he makes "some observations about politicians as actors" by outlining how various political leaders have presented themselves to the public. Recognizing the need for politicians to be part actor since the days of Lincoln's stump speeches, Miller also considers the dangerous impact of television on the way the public views their political potential and draws comparisons between what he perceives as good and bad acting.

It is Franklin Roosevelt who emerges as Miller's favorite president for best balancing acting skill against substantive integrity. As he explains at another point, a president cannot possibly please everyone, but when a public begins earnestly to expect them to do so, then dishonesty is inevitable, unless there is a man of integrity holding the post. Miller recalls that many of Roosevelt's policies were unpopular when they were first introduced, but they were presented as part of a determined agenda to improve the country, rather than to win votes. Miller himself disapproved of Roosevelt's policies regarding Spain and Jewish immigration, but he concludes, "I am sure, the good he did far outweighs the evil." About other presidents, he is less certain: "Our latter-day candidates are like insurance men at a picnic," always working on image and rarely becoming human.

Miller's acerbic wit draws out what he sees as the poor acting skills of George W. Bush and Al Gore as he critiques their performances alongside those of Ronald Reagan and Bill Clinton. Reagan is called "a Stanislavskian triumph," a man in whom "the dividing line between acting and actuality was simply melted, gone," while Clinton is compared to both Br'er Rabbit and Till Eulenspiegel, the mythical archprankster of 14th-century Germany. Both Reagan and Clinton are described as becoming their performance and so being highly persuasive; Bush and Gore are seen as men who exhibit "an underlying tension between themselves and the role," which reduced their effectiveness.

Aware that human nature has always responded more to a politician's acting skill than proposals or moral character, Miller insists that it is important for the future of democracy that the public become more aware of the true character of those who have been elected to lead. "When one is surrounded by such a roiling mass of consciously contrived performances, it gets harder and harder for a lot of people to locate reality anymore." Thereby, a consummate actor like Reagan could "salute a cemetery of Nazi dead" and not appear hypocritical. The moral outrage that this should have caused was placated by Reagan's apparent sincerity, but to allow the act to outweigh the action in such cases is what Miller sees as the real danger in mixing politics with acting. Hitler and Stalin, he reminds us, in the eyes of their followers, were "profoundly moral men" and "revealers of new truths;" but allowing them power created dangerous dictatorships. He warns against being seduced by the smiling faces of the media and allowing someone else to make the hard decisions. Miller considers it the public's responsibility to see through the act and to confront the true ideology of its leaders if such dictatorships are to be avoided in the future.

Miller makes detailed comparisons between the way in which an actor presents a role and the ways in which political leaders express their supposed personality. A politician faces the same audience-management problem as an actor on the stage—both need to offer a performance that will illicit a "single unified reaction" from their audience. The way in which television magnifies personality makes the overemphatic gestures and expressions of Bush and Gore seem contrived and dishonest; this is bad acting. Miller admits, however, that since winning the election, Bush has become "more relaxed and confident" in his seat of power. He goes on to wonder if Bush's "syntactical stumbling in public" may be part of that same act that he suspects Dwight Eisenhower used to seem more "convincingly sincere," and thus indicate Bush's improvement as an actor.

The technique Miller reveals that modern-day politicians are pursuing is to appear authentic rather than to worry about actually being authentic. Gore's one truly honest reaction in the debates, "shaking his head in helpless disbelief at some inanity Bush had spoken," actually damaged his reputation, as the press charged him with "superior airs" and "disrespect." Miller, in turn, charges the U.S. press, with being "made up of disguised theater critics" for whom "substance counts for next to nothing compared with style and inventive characterization." And so he places in the sidebar another longtime complaint, that of the dumbing down of U.S. mainstream theater, for which he blames the critics.

Recalling how audiences flocked to witness Yiddish actor Jacob Ben-Ami perform what seemed like a real suicide attempt on stage, Miller highlights the audience's willing gullibility by revealing how the actor actually created the scene by imagining that he was about to step into a cold shower. Miller bemoans how a similar degree of gullibility seemed to lead the public to accept at face value Bush's false claims of support for education, child protection, and the environment, all of which he attacked shortly after taking office. Miller's concern is that the United States needs more than someone "good at characterizing a counterfeit with the help of professional coaching" to lead the nation. When real trouble comes, it would be better to have a figure of more substance and integrity at the helm.

Miller's call for the public to question the authencity of its political leaders seems a timely one given the falling presidential ratings of the beginning of the century as the United States was once more led into a foreign war for spurious reasons. Miller explains how a good actor such as politician Huey Long recognized "power's ability to create illusion in the service to his cause," but "democracy's future depends," Miller insists, "on how well we recognize and control" these illusions and question the causes to which service they are being utilized.

Miller views the 2000 election as a "demonstration of negative consent" as the public did not love either of the leading candidates, partly because neither man played the role very well. While a good actor can make you love him, such as Ronald Reagan and Bill Clinton, a true star has the ability to make you want him or her to love you and is far more powerful. Miller describes Roosevelt as having this quality, along with actor Marlon Brando. Fortunately, it was a power that Roosevelt used wisely, but Miller's point is that the public needs to be more wary as to whom they grant such power in future. If politics are like theater, then the 2000 elections show the extent to which bad theater is becoming the norm in this country. Miller wishes the substantive content of both to improve. Art, he suggests, is an important means of steering people toward the truth and may offer the best corrective to the distorted politics of our time.

"On Social Plays" (1955)

This essay was originally written as a preface for the published one-act versions of *View from a Bridge* and *A Memory of Two Mondays*. Although Miller concludes by describing his intentions in writing these two plays, much of this essay takes on a wider scope as Miller attempts to define what he feels is true "social drama" and discuss its relevance as an art form. It is this concern that makes this essay such an important piece of theatrical theory. It was reprinted in *The Theater Essays of Arthur Miller* (1978) and several other places. This is where Miller first explores his belief that the central thrust of social drama is to explore "how are we to live?" both as individuals and alongside others, which is a concept lying at the heart of Miller's own work.

Beginning with a discussion of Greek drama, Miller explains how for the civically engaged Greeks all drama was social and dealt with "the relations of man as a social animal, rather than his definition as a separated entity." Their interest lay in the fate or destiny of an entire people rather than in that of isolated individuals. Even as Greek drama changed and developed, it never lost this universal concern. Modern society, Miller complains, has perverted the term *social drama* to indicate only works that attack or arraign social evils and are predominantly the work of socialists or communists. Describing such a concept as "tired and narrow," Miller attempts to offer a broader picture of what social drama should mean: "To put it simply, even oversimply, a drama rises in stature and intensity in proportion to the weight of its application to all manner of men." In Miller's opinion, drama that does not have this social aspect is not good drama of any definition.

Miller suggests that U.S. drama deals too much with men outside of society, a concept that was impossible for the Greeks to even consider. True social drama, for Miller, "is the drama of the whole man," that is, a person as both an individual and a member of his or her society. The Greeks were able to contemplate the development of the individual alongside that of society but not apart from it. Reduced to the single theme of frustration, as individuals seek and fail to find a way to join society, U.S. drama, Miller feels, has become too focused on the "separation of man from society." Russian plays present a similar "drama of frustration" as they display "the inability of industrialized men to see themselves spiritually completed through the social organization," although in the Russian case Miller sees this frustration as remaining unacknowledged and covered up by notions of tragic sacrifice. In Miller's eyes, modern humanity has lost its connection to a social whole and needs to strive toward regaining this. Miller states his ideal as being that person who lives "most completely when he lives most socially," not from conscience or duty but from natural inclination.

Miller continues by declaring provocatively that modern theater has "exhausted" realism and become bored with the form. Suggesting that the prose of realism lends itself to a discussion of private individuals (men) while verse leads to more universal considerations (Man), then true social drama needs to find a balance between the two as it asks "how are we to live?" Declaring that the world is changing, Miller offers his hope for its future improvement by sharing a democratic, humanistic vision to counteract the contemporary trends of CAPITALISM and COMMUNISM that have each lost this balance, capitalism being too centered on the self and communism too centered on the group. He challenges his reader to strive for a world in which people are not treated as "integers" who are given no role in the larger society but as fully involved human beings.

Linking his concept of social drama to that of TRAGEDY, Miller suggests that people who are trapped in a system without freedom, be it capitalism or communism, can only be portrayed as pathetic. To be tragic, they must be both a part of a society and individuals who are capable of challenging that society. The tragic hero's quest is social, not private, as he or she tests social mores to improve the social whole. Though he or she may be destroyed in the process, this process should still convey a sense of "victory" rather than "doom," as a person's willingness to die to improve the social whole bespeaks the "absolute value of the individual human being" against the dehumanizing modern "needs of efficient production." Miller points to *Death of a Salesman* to illustrate his point, in the way that it portrays the isolation of the modern human due to the "patterns of efficiency." Willy Loman may not be a particularly good man, but what happens to him should not be allowed to happen to a human being.

Digressing from his theme momentarily, Miller asks that art remain challenging for audiences because he feels that it will become denigrated if it aims to please everyone to draw a better box office. He insists that a subsidized theater is the only way to ensure this so that theaters will not be constrained by their ticket receipts. This is a theme to which Miller will return throughout his career.

Returning to topic, Miller suggests that the aim of social drama until the 1930s was different from that of the 1950s. While earlier social drama only needed to point out certain ills in society, with the alienating effects of technology since the 1940s, there has grown a need for social plays to offer a corrective to this and to help people find their place in a changing world. Thus "the new social dramatist . . . must be an even deeper psychologist

than those of the past" but must also be careful not to isolate the psychological life of characters from the society around them. Class is no longer an issue as people have become united in a general concern for values and the future in the wake of the nuclear bomb. If those values are not furnished, then Miller fears a nuclear holocaust. "The new social drama," he concludes, "will be Greek in that it will face man as a social animal and yet without the petty partisanship of so much of past drama." Miller's vision is for a social drama that addresses humankind as well as individuals and that seeks meaning to help direct future generations.

In discussing *A Memory of Two Mondays*, Miller tells us that it is a play "about mortality," in that Bert seeks through his observations of his fellow workers a better way to live. The play's warehouse is offered as a microcosm of the world, and the different characters depict different modes of living. Miller tells us that he wrote *A View from the Bridge* as a one-act play because "I did not know how to pull a curtain down anywhere before its end," but he feels that it is close to being a full-length play. He admits to having had the ideas for both plays for some time, but they only came to fruition when he saw that he could write each as a single act. In discussing *A View from the Bridge*, he identifies themes of incest, homosexuality, and the "question of codes," and he explains why he purposefully gave little background material for the characters—so as not to distract from the "clear, clean line of [Eddie's] catastrophe." He wanted to present a story in its essence that would have a "myth-like march" in its presentation. He intends the play "to strike a particular note of astonishment at the way in which, and the reasons for which, a man will endanger and risk and lose his very life."

"Our Guilt for the World's Evil" (1965)

Published in the *New York Times Magazine* on the heels of the opening of *Incident at Vichy*, Miller begins this essay by outlining the true story of a person's sacrifice for a stranger on which he based the play. The incident had haunted him in the 10 years since a friend had related it, and it brought back to mind each time that he heard of others acting less heroically and turning a blind eye to crime rather than be involved: "Wherever I felt the seemingly implacable tide of human drift and the withering of will, in myself and in others, this faceless person came to mind." While *Incident at Vichy* is ostensibly about the Nazi horror, Miller intended its theme to be a more universal one regarding people's relationship to injustice and violence. It is a theme that he sees as having contemporary importance in many arenas including civil rights, the treatment of Vietcong prisoners, juvenile delinquency, and moral responses to the HOLOCAUST. In all, the question of human solidarity, or its lack, appears primary.

What Miller wants to bring to attention is the "relationship between those who side with justice and their implication in the evils they oppose" because if this is not faced, then more atrocities like the Holocaust can occur, and racism will never be quelled. When people turn their heads from injustice or violence, Miller insists, they become implicitly involved with it. He feels that people need to acknowledge how much of their gain is through someone else's loss and to reach a better perspective. He challenges every white reader, not just those in the South, to recognize their own racism in that sense of comfort they secretly feel that they are not black. Through the character of Von Berg, Miller wanted to show how a person might discover "his own complicity with the force he despises," and choose to take responsibility for that, not through passive guilt but through positive action. Connecting to recent events in the United States, Miller points to the deaths of three civil-rights workers in Mississippi the previous year as further evidence of people who are willing to put their lives on the line for the rights of others, against those who refused to act. Injustice, Miller asserts, profits (psychically or materially) those whom it does not diminish, and there is no middle path, so it must be fought against by all who do not wish to be a part.

Referencing the Germans who allowed the Holocaust to happen, Miller insists that contin-ued blame is unproductive, and a better lesson to be drawn is one of empathy. In similar conditions and given what Miller believes to be a natural human propensity for hostility and aggression, we all might have been sucked in as easily, and so should guard against that for the future. We do this by acknowledging our own "guilt for the world's evil" and by becoming determined to fight against it. Pointing out U.S. passivity at photographs of tortured Vietcong prisoners from the VIETNAM WAR, Miller suggests that all people of the United States are complicit in such torture as they have armed the torturers and implicitly condone their actions. Referring to the biblical Cain, Miller suggests that he is an emblem for humankind's capacity for evil that all must accept, though not passively. Von Berg offering Leduc his pass, Miller concludes, was less an act of brotherly support than a self-corrective.

"The Performance" (2002)

Published in *New Yorker* in 2002, "The Performance" is one of Miller's later short stories. Through an unnamed narrator, the experience of tap-dancer Harold May's greatest performance is told, and its implications are analyzed. In a series of memories, the narrator recalls meeting May in 1947, who recounts to him his experience from 10 years before while the narrator interjects commentary on its implications to him in the present time. May's performance in 1937 was for Hitler, who enthusiastically asked May to manage a school of tap dancing for him in Berlin, a request that May reluctantly refused.

The narrator, who confesses to being a well-known writer since the 1940s, describes meeting May at a drugstore soda fountain to hear his story. From Ohio, May is boyishly blonde with blue eyes, somewhat reminiscent of Harold Lloyd, and hoping that the narrator will be able to make something of his tale. He explains how, while scratching out a living dancing in 1930s America, he had been offered a lucrative opportunity on the European circuit where tap dancing was a great novelty. In

1936 Hungary, he puts together a small troupe and tours European cities, taking in sights and developing an appreciation for the places' history.

In Budapest, Damian Fugler, who highly praises his act, invites May to come to Berlin for a single high-paying performance. Offered a year's salary, he jumps at the chance without even asking for whom the performance is to be given, although the swastika on Fugler's calling card offers a clue. The next day, his troupe sets off by train, and we first learn that May is Jewish as he grows nervous at the German border. He recalls stories that he has suppressed in his consciousness about German ANTI-SEMITISM, but having been insulated in foreign countries where he did not speak or read the language for much of the past year, he pushes these stories to one side, especially considering how pleasant everything looks in Berlin. They are put into the best hotel and treated like stars.

As the time for the command performance approaches, May accepts that it must be for Hitler, and warns his troupe. Momentarily considering suicide as a way out, May decides that as an American he is safe and goes to the club, where they remove the regular customers as Hitler and his entourage arrive. Hitler, Goering, and the rest are transfixed by May's show and have him repeat it three times. The actors are kept nervously standing on stage as Hitler talks to Fugler. Then May is invited to meet Hitler, who through Fugler, offers a proposal to head a new school of tap dancing to invigorate the German people, after which Hitler shakes hands, smiles, and leaves. May is seduced by the sense of power emanating from Hitler and flattered by his obvious admiration of his artistry.

May goes along with the plan for a few days, even allowing himself to be tested by a eugenics professor and declared pure Aryan, but he finally realizes that he cannot go through with this, however attractive an opportunity it seems. However, he feels guilty about having misled them, being sympathetic to both Hitler and Fugler. Faking a seriously ill mother in Paris, he prepares to leave but is stopped by Fugler, pleading with him to stay. Announcing that he is Jewish, May is surprised by Fugler's reaction, which is to shake his hand

and say "How do you do?" as if meeting him for the first time. He and the narrator assume that it was from shock at having lost his big chance and realizing that he had introduced a Jew to Hitler. Returning to the drugstore, we learn that May got out safely and eventually returned to the United States but is still uncertain as to what to make of his experience. Leaping 50 years on, the narrator comments on how this story has always haunted him but that he could not write about it. He feels that it was too disturbing, and he wanted to offer a more positive outlook.

At various points during May's relation of the past, we switch to dialogue between himself and the narrator in the drugstore, which gives us a different perspective—the tale is told post-HOLO-CAUST, which necessitates a different view of Hitler and the Germans. On several occasions, May tries to justify his reactions by reminding his listener that this all happened before people really knew anything, but even by 1947, the narrator is disgusted. May remains grateful for the chance that he was given and is uncertain about how he feels toward Germans, who aside from their aberrant racial beliefs seemed so normal. It has led him to lose touch with reality, and everything has become dreamlike to him.

Similar to his depiction of Dr. Mengele and others in *Playing for Time*, Miller encourages us to feel the discomfort of recognizing elements of humanity in a person who is so reputedly monstrous. It is a humanity to which May responded and with which he cannot come to terms, and the narrator's observation regarding how the telling of this story has seemed to age May suggests the weight of that burden on him. How is the United States so different from Berlin May asks near the conclusion of the tale, and why might U.S. citizens not as easily be misled into self-destruction as the Germans? At the tale's start, Miller subtly implies a U.S. anti-Semitism not so unlike that in Germany: He mentions a writer friend, Ralph Barton, whose real name was Berkowitz but was obviously changed to appear less Jewish. Miller's message is ultimately that even Americans need to be wary of becoming like the Germans because being equally human, they are equally as prone to corruption, however innocent things might appear on the surface.

The Philippines Never Surrendered (1945)

This 1945 radio drama was based on a *Saturday Evening Post* article about U.S. school superintendent Edward Kuder who in 1942 had urged the native inhabitants of the Philippine island of Mindanao to resist a Japanese invasion and strike back. Aired on April 30, 1945, the role of Kuder was played by Edward G. Robinson. The Japanese are portrayed as cruel and tyrannical, and the Americans, embodied by Kuder, are concerned and paternal. It is little wonder that the Moros natives elect to keep the Philippines free of the former, even while they embrace the guidance of the latter. Initially, Kuder instructs the Moros in various acts of sabotage, but as the conflict with the Japanese intensifies, he encourages this to escalate into open warfare to repel the invaders. Although V–J Day was still three and a half months away when this play was aired, at its close, Miller moves into a present when victory appears inevitable. Kuder lies in a military hospital and celebrates both the spirit of the Philippine resistance and the return of General MacArthur to the islands, with a clip from his actual speech. Never published, typescripts can be found at HARRY RANSOM RESEARCH CENTER and New York Public Library.

"The Plaster Masks" (1946)

The second of Miller's published short stories, "The Plaster Masks" is based on his experiences in veterans hospitals during WORLD WAR II while researching material for his screenplay of *The Story of G. I. Joe*. It was published in *Encore: A Continuing Anthology* in 1946. In the story, Miller tries to come to an understanding of the impact of war injuries on veterans of the war, and, as a pacifist and a noncombatant, uncover his own feelings and connection to such men to gain a better understanding of how to view himself.

A writer comes to the hospital to ask if he can interview badly injured soldiers for a radio broadcast. The surgeon in charge is uncertain if this will be the right kind of publicity, but he wants people to know what is being done for these men and how wrong it is that they have been damaged like this. The writer does not want a puff piece that asks for pity but wishes to convey the reality of these soldiers' lives. He observes several consultations as the surgeon schedules patients for reconstructive surgery. The men have severe injuries that include missing limbs and sections of the head, but they are mostly spirited and comradely. The hospital has young boys helping the patients, and the writer wonders why they are not repulsed by what they see, and he cannot understand why the soldiers are not more bitter.

Spotting a young woman embracing her blinded husband, the writer feels pity but senses that this is the wrong emotion. He seeks an evasive truth. He interviews a sculptor who makes plaster masks of the men's faces before and after surgery to help the surgeon envision his work; he is overwhelmed at their sheer number. The sculptor suggests that the men are content because at least they are still alive, but the writer still wonders in what ways such injuries must change a person. As he leaves, he notices a postsurgery mask that looks like him and asks to see the initial mask. He examines the injuries and imagines that they are his own, and he at last approaches the understanding he sought— that these men do not feel damaged but whole and that they take strength in what remains rather than longing for how they were.

Miller describes patients' horrific injuries in blunt, unsentimental detail, juxtaposing describing such elements as a patient's even, white teeth against the fact that he has no left ear. "War is a crime against the body," the surgeon insists, and Miller's intent appears to be an exposure of what war does to human beings and the ways in which it destroys their bodies. Avoiding jingoistic, whitewashed images of brave soldiers, he depicts ordinary men who cope and survive but at a terrible cost. However, they are not men to be pitied but to be admired for their strength of spirit.

Playing for Time (1980)

Miller was approached by producer Linda Yellen and asked to write a screenplay based on the memoirs of Fania Fénelon for a CBS television film. Fénelon, a cabaret singer and member of the French resistance, had been arrested by the Nazis in 1943 and taken to Auschwitz, where she was enrolled in the camp orchestra and managed to survive both there and during her later transfer to Bergen–Belsen until that camp was freed by allied forces. It was not until 1977 that Fénelon had felt able to write the memoir of her HOLOCAUST experience, which Miller closely follows in his screenplay, although the timing of some events is altered to smooth the dramatic flow. Certain speeches are created for Fania to underscore Miller's message, and the name of a Fénelon friend is changed from Clara to Marianne. Five years on, Miller would also adapt this piece for the stage.

There was some controversy over the choice of the pro-Palestinian activist VANESSA REDGRAVE to play the part of a Jewish Holocaust survivor in the film, but Miller supported her selection on the grounds that her political beliefs had no bearing on her ability as an actress. In the 1990 collection of interviews and writings about Miller, *Arthur Miller and Company*, Redgrave suggests that *Playing for Time* goes beyond "films which depict the horrendous bestiality of German Fascism . . . to the essence of this problem. [Miller] showed us how Fascist ideology operates in and through human beings and just how difficult it is for human beings to struggle against being dehumanized." This was essentially Miller's aim.

Yellen told interviewer Judy Mann: "This piece as a picture was meant to bring people together. . . . The message of the film, and why this group was so special, was that the survival of one depends on the survival of all. In the way the film is a microcosm of our world, of our society. Instead of ripping apart the groups, the way the other people do in the film,

Fania . . . recognizes this human interdependence. That's what makes the picture more than a record of the most hard time in our civilization. It is a statement that transcends that and is a statement of how we should live because we're all playing for time, and we all better be in harmony a lot more than we are."

SYNOPSIS

The film opens with a black screen with some red lines that merge to form a profile of Fania's face combined with a swastika and half of a cello; we hear Fania singing a song with the lyrics "Must go on . . . We'll meet again." After this, the scene opens to reveal Fania singing at a small, French, wartime cabaret shortly before she is picked up to be taken to the camps. She presents a kindly figure, clearly not a person of any political threat, who offers only love and friendship to her audience as she sings to them, "I'll be yours." This cozy scene is then contrasted to real footage of the Nazi occupation of France and then cuts to a group of people who are crammed into a boxcar, with Fania offering Marianne a piece of sausage.

The two women share the fact that each is only "half-Jewish" and that their boyfriends were with the French resistance. Speaking to others in the boxcar, Fania tries to work out where they might be heading and asks the soldiers to do something about the dead man in their boxcar. All are concerned that they may be being taken to their deaths. Arriving at Auschwitz, they see Dr. Mengele who divides everyone up; then guards intimidate them, taking away luggage and clothing. Fania complains that she is French and not Jewish, but she is ignored; at least she is in the group that is saved for labor and not with those who are sent to immediate death. In their quarters, Fania finds a dead woman in her bunk but is forced to deal with it herself.

Time passes as the women are introduced to work; then the Blockawa asks if anyone can sing *Madame Butterfly*, and Marianne pushes Fania forward. Fania is brought to audition for the camp orchestra. Several of the other musicians know of Fania as a famous singer and pianist, and they introduce themselves. Alma Rosè, the niece of Gustav Mahler, leads the orchestra. A tough taskmaster, Alma senses a rivalry in Fania's talent but at the women's camp commander Lagerführerin Mandel's insistence accepts her into the orchestra. Fania bravely refuses unless they take Marianne too. Everyone is shocked, but Marianne thus is allowed, and Mandel even gives Fania some boots. The orchestra plays and upsets Alma by playing too loudly, but after she storms out, the women explain to Fania that they did this to cover up Liesle's poor playing to keep her safe. Alma's ego is pushing them to play complicated pieces that they cannot manage, and they feel very vulnerable. Alma coaxes Fania to orchestrate new pieces for them—they are eager to please the Nazis; Fania agrees merely to stay alive.

Fania is exasperated by Marianne's selfishness and warns her to think more of others. To cheer the women, Fania tells them stories of Parisian life and entertains them. She goes to watch the group play a march for the prisoners heading to work and, seeing her as a collaborator, one woman spits in her face, making her feel guilty about her privileged position. Alma tells her not to be so sensitive. Fania sees Marianne allowing a guard to grope her in return for food. Marianne offers her a sausage, and although Fania disapproves of how she got it, sensibly eats it. When new prisoners arrive, Fania tries to turn away from the horror, but the camp electrician, a mysterious figure named Shmuel insists that she not turn away so that she can bear witness.

When Lotte comes to ask Fania for advice, she reveals her love for a fellow prisoner Hèléne, a love Fania encourages. She is horrified by the Nazis' approval of her music because their love of music humanizes them and makes what they do more monstrous. In an act of rebellion, she insists that they call her Goldstein rather than Fénelon. In appreciation of the music, Mandel gets Fania a toothbrush, and Marianne mocks her, suggesting that what she does is no different from her own prostitution. The other women support Fania though and reject Marianne's negativity. Again, Fania suggests to Marianne that she share more, but Marianne is too self-concerned.

When Alma needs a translator to ensure that her sick cellist, Paulette, is taken to the hospital rather than the gas chambers, we meet Mala.

Multilingual, she assists the guards with her talent but works against them behind their backs. The women all admire her, even Alma. Alma continues to bully her orchestra, trying to scare them into playing better so that they will not be killed. Fania disapproves, feeling that Alma is unnecessarily harsh. Alma defends herself, explaining how she has taken refuge in her art, and to survive, she refuses to see what the Nazis are doing. She plays her violin beautifully as if to prove her point.

When Kapos come to divide the Jews from the Aryans, Marianne points out that she and Fania are only half-Jewish. They are given permission to cut their Jewish stars in half to the disgust of the other Jews. Declaring herself "a woman, not a tribe," Fania feels torn but decides to wear the whole star. Shmuel again advises her to continue watching. They learn that Mala has escaped, which gives them all hope. Mandel introduces them to a little Polish boy, Ladislaus, whom she has decided to adopt, even while sharing news that the rest of his transport, most likely including the boy's mother, will be killed. Then we learn that Mala has been captured, beaten, and executed. Alma insists that the orchestra keep practicing, as officers take away their piano and one of their poorer players, Greta. Alma meekly allows this, too scared to object. They are told that they will be needed to play at the hospital for the patients so that Doctor Mengele can observe the effects of music on the insane.

Alma is angry with Fania for going behind her back and requesting more food for the orchestra. Paulette returns from the hospital with news that the plan is to gas all the patients after the concert; though still unwell, she managed to be discharged. A fellow Jew in the orchestra, Etalina, tells of how she saw her whole family arrive on a train and be taken straight to the gas chambers. Fania comforts her, and though weak herself, Fania also helps Paulette by washing her clothing and helping her sleep. A Polish Catholic, Elzvieta confides in Fania, feeling guilty because her compatriots have done so little to help the Jews. Fania hugs her, understanding her conflict. The sound of bombers increases, and it becomes evident that the allies are getting closer, but it is uncertain if they can get there in time.

Alma tells Fania that she is to be transferred to play for the soldiers and that she is recommending that Fania take over from her as conductor. Fania does not approve of Alma's willingness to play for the enemy but thanks Alma for helping save them. One of the camp officers, Frau Schmidt, who has been trying to get a transfer invites Alma to dinner and poisons her. They make Olga, the incompetent accordionist, the new conductor because she is Aryan. Marianne disgusts them all by sleeping with the man who executed Mala, and Doctor Mengele disgusts them by his apparent grief at Alma's death. They want to separate themselves from the Nazis, but Fania insists that they are not that much better, so it is foolish to feel morally superior. Mandel asks them to sing to comfort her, upset at having had to give Ladislaus back to be killed.

The Nazis are growing uneasy because they are losing the war and trying to cover their tracks by killing prisoners. Fania asks Elzvieta to take her diary, uncertain that she will make it, but Elzvieta refuses, feeling that this would leave Fania no reason to stay alive. As troopers take the Jews off to the woods, most likely to shoot them, Marianne flirts to stay alive and is rewarded with being made Kapo and told to herd them into a barn—she turns on her fellow prisoners without compunction. Thus, when the allies arrive in the nick of time, led by Shmuel, Marianne is placed with the German prisoners. Fania leads the freed prisoners and the allied forces in the uplifting "La Marseillaise" "March on, be not afraid. . . ." The final scene shows a brief reunion of the survivors more than 30 years later.

CRITICAL COMMENTARY

The dark background with the blood-red marks in the film's titling is ominous, especially as it forms into the well-known symbol of Nazism; yet, this is balanced with the image of an orchestral instrument to show the two main forces that will be acting on Fania during the play: The evil, dehumanizing effects of the Holocaust that threaten to engulf her against the humanizing and transcendent possibilities of her music with which she is able to stay connected. Fania is a fighter who sings "La Marseillaise" and who will not capitulate readily to Nazi oppression, but Nazis and their inheri-

tors will always be with us, as evidenced by her other song, "We'll meet again." Their legacy of hatred is more than a history lesson but is also a message for contemporary times. Miller wants us to bear in mind that this is essentially a memory play, a retelling of the past to inform the present.

The people who are depicted in the boxcar, beyond their common fears, are not a unified group but are a disparate collection of individuals who stay apart from each other. Fania seems to be a notable exception who increases our sympathy for her character as she offers Marianne food and companionship. Fania is an older, sophisticated lady in comparison to the naive and youthful Marianne. While Marianne reacts emotionally, Fania is more rational; it is this that allows her to perceive more clearly the meaning behind events. She and Marianne bond partly because neither has any feeling of being Jewish but see themselves solely as French. Also, Fania adopts a motherly attitude toward this spoiled young girl, taking pity on her almost paralyzing fear. The choices that they make at the camp eventually drive them apart, but at the start, Fania's care and Marianne's fear draw them together. Against these brief human portraits, the frequently interspersed clips of the constantly turning train wheels convey the relentlessness mechanization of the Holocaust's destruction. These clips are repeated throughout the movie.

Conditions in the boxcar had been dreadful, but on arrival at the camp, these prisoners seem to have everything that makes them human taken away, from their few simple possessions to their dignity and identity. The process is cruel and heartless but orderly. They lose their luggage, their clothes, and then their hair. Hair is a very personal reflection of one's appearance, and the way that the haircutter's scissors cut through these people's self-images is a strong indication of the way that their rights are being shorn away. The final loss is their names as they are tattooed with numbers. These are the lucky ones who are not taken straight to be killed. The carelessly brutal way in which the Kapos treat the prisoners can be contrasted to the care with which they handle their belongings. In this camp, things are viewed as more valuable than people. But just because they treat these people as worthless does not mean that they are, and it is a definition against which all camp inmates must struggle to maintain their spirits and survive.

To survive is the primary aim in the camps, but Miller wants us to realize that there are different ways to survive, and some routes lead to a more profoundly disturbing spiritual death, as with Marianne, than literal death. Survival comes at a cost, but there are certain prices that a person should not pay, for to survive without retaining a basic humanity, Miller suggests, is hardly survival at all. We see Fania vacillate between assertions of independence and obsequiousness; sometimes she makes demands and at others she simply goes along, but she maintains a defiantly humanistic core throughout.

Key to survival in this camp are the notion of identity and the ability to maintain one's humanity in the face of a dehumanizing Nazism. The orchestra plays loudly as much to announce their existence as to protect Liesle, although Alma insensitively misses these emotional aspects when she criticizes them. Alma tries to keep their music separate from their camp lives, but of course the two are inextricable; the music has become both an outlet for pain and desire as well as their means of survival. They cannot play like a regular orchestra, as Alma hopes in her escapist dreams, because they are performing under extraordinary conditions that she chooses to ignore. Alma has blurred the line between pleasing the SS and trying to save her own life, a line Fania prefers to keep distinct.

Fania, in contrast to Alma, speaks out when she can, insisting that Mengele call her Goldstein rather than Fénelon. As an individual, Fania reacts against an overwhelming, external power that is trying to destroy her identity. In response, she asserts that identity in controlling her name. Fania also speaks out in front of the Nazis to gain things for others, such as food or aid for a particular friend. Alma is horrified by such outbursts, fearing they will either undercut her own power or turn the Nazis on them.

We should recognize at once an incongruity between the cultured rendition and recognition of *Madame Butterfly* and the decrepit, worn state of the woman (Fania) who performs it, along with the way that they treat her—worse than one would treat an animal. It is reflected in the neat, smart, and self-important Nazis, like Mandel, against the ragged and filthy prisoners whom they direct to produce their cultural program. The ultimate horror for Fania is the Nazis' love for her music—even Mengele is visibly stirred by her singing—because it humanizes them and so makes what they do so much worse. It would be far easier to dismiss them as unfeeling monsters. How can men like Mengele shed a tear over Alma and waste emotion over good music when they destroy so many human beings without a shred of emotion? But such apparent contradictions are essential to Miller's depiction. To imply that the Nazis are not human because of their inhumane agenda is to lessen the impact of the lesson of the Holocaust that he so keenly wishes to convey. The Nazis, he insists, were human beings, and they could at times display humane reactions. As human beings, everyone else has the same capacity for evil that the Nazis displayed, and there is a constantly need to guard against this. Miller has this central lesson of the play, emphasized by Fania in her debates with her fellow inmates.

Fania sees the danger in Marianne's selfishness. These people need to support each other to survive. Fania humanely offers to share anything that she has as opposed to Marianne's increasingly animalistic behavior. However, divisions between the people in the camp are harsh, and even among inmates there is a clear and divisive class system. The Polish women may be prisoners, but they do not face the same death sentence that hangs over the Jewish women, and so they feel superior and look down on the Jews. There is also a long history of ANTI-SEMITISM among the Polish, and even though with the Jews they share the Nazis as a common enemy, they mostly feel little compassion for Jews. But as Miller tries to show, it is wrong to judge individuals by a seemingly national trait: Elzvieta may be Polish, but she is kindly toward Jews despite Etalina's scorn, although she is wrong to excuse her countrywomen's hatred as sheer stupidity. As Fania points out, ignorance is no excuse for evil, and it is the task of those who know to ensure that the ignorant see the error of their ways. This is part of the communal responsibility.

Her friendship with Marianne becomes an increasing burden for Fania, who is horrified by Marianne's prostitution to get food. When Marianne initially shares this food, knowing how it was won, Fania does not want to accept it. For her, this would be an acceptance of Marianne's behavior, which she cannot condone, and her disapproval eventually turns Marianne against her. Unlike Fania, Marianne has given up all real hope, which is partly why she no longer cares what she does. Fania bemoans this evident loss of self-respect, but Marianne is too self-involved to listen. She will even sleep with Mala's executioner to obtain some privileges for herself, and she will beat Fania with a club when Fania is barely able to walk. Marianne is placed with the German prisoners at the close to indicate that by her selfish actions, she really has become one of the enemy.

Fania struggles to keep going under tremendous pressure, as Miller wants us to see her as human and not as a superhero. Her vitality is drained away and she feels she reaches a limit of what can be endured. However, she does keep going by continuing her mission to observe and by remaining human. She continues to do things for others, such as Paulette's laundry, and selflessly offers a sympathetic ear to other people's troubles. She is rewarded by flickers of hope that help to buoy her spirit, such as the possibility of feeling and even of love in this place, as Lotte tells her of her regard for Hélène. Shmuel is also constantly at her side to encourage her in her role as recorder of the events when she considers turning away as Alma does. Her final victory is apparent in the stirring "La Marseillaise" that she sings near the close and in the brief reappearance meeting with her campmates several decades later. This also serves as an indication that their history remains alive and has relevance to contemporary times.

FIRST PERFORMANCE

Playing for Time was first presented on CBS on September 30, 1980, and subsequently aired in GREAT BRITAIN on the Independent Television Network on January 11, 1981, with the following lead actors:

Fania Fénelon: Vanessa Redgrave
Alma Rosè: Jane Alexander
Marianne: Melanie Mayron
Lagerführerin Mandel: Shirley Knight
Elzvieta: Marisa Berenson

Directed by Daniel Mann
Music by Brad Fiedel
Produced by Linda Yellen for Syzygy Productions.

INITIAL REVIEWS

Response to the television film was fairly positive, although Fania Fénelon disliked both Miller's adaptation of her memoirs and the choice of Redgrave to play Fania. Redgrave's performance, however, won high praise from critics, and *Newsweek*'s Jack Kroll felt that it effectively conveyed "the anguish of a civilized woman who must surrender part of her humanity to survive." John O'Connor saw the production as "totally uncompromising in its depictions of hope and despair, of generosity and viciousness, of death and survival in the bizarre, nightmare world of a concentration camp," and Robert McLean viewed it as "a triumphant hymn to the human spirit." Though describing it as "grim" and "painful to watch," Dennis Welland suggests that it is redeemed by both the sheer quality of the performances and the facts of history—Fania survives, and the Nazis are defeated.

The *New York Times*'s Anthony Lewis commented on the way the film shows "how the camps turned the victims into objects" and illustrates "how the process of dehumanization worked in Nazi Germany—and worked elsewhere since." As Lewis realizes, Miller's aim is not just to educate his audience about the Holocaust but also to show us the results of such brutality whenever we allow it to occur. Miller's agenda, Lewis concludes, is to ensure that "No one can be naive anymore about human nature." While Arthur Unger described it as "among the most memorably effective literary efforts to emerge from the Holocaust" and was concerned at some people's dismissal of it for an alleged "pro-Nazi bias in its presentation of Nazis as complex human beings," he praised the film as "an honest attempt to explain the inexplicable," and describes it as raising important questions regarding the limits of decency, the price of survival, and the ethical complexity of individuals.

SCHOLARSHIP

Scholarship has been minimal, but it centers on the efficacy of the film's message regarding how human beings behave in extreme circumstances. Susan Abbotson considers the play as offering a contemporary lesson in survival; while Jeanne Johnsey, concentrating on the scene where Fania asserts that her name is Goldstein, explores how Fania manages to preserve her identity against such overwhelming odds. Robert Feldman focuses on the problem of evil in the play, and CHRISTOPHER BIGSBY offers a good analysis of the differences between Fénelon's original memoir, Miller's screenplay, and the later play version, pointing out that the immediacy of the film experience makes it a lot more shocking than the book, and the stage version allows for "a version not contaminated by the legerdemain of aesthetics." In overviews of Miller's Holocaust drama in general, Edward Isser considers the universalistic aspects of the play, and Kimberley Cook the way in which gender operates.

CHARACTERS

Elzvieta   Her ability to play the violin has brought the Polish Catholic Elzvieta to join the camp orchestra and allows her to avoid the harsh labor that is given the rest of the prisoners. Her concern for Fania is evident from when she first sees her and helps clean her with a cloth. She shows that there is hope even among the Polish who have been largely scornful and unpleasant toward the Jews. She tries to explain to Fania her feeling of an encouraging responsibility and guilt for what is happening to the Jews in the camp. She has fought with the Resistance and has led a life free of anti-Semitism, and yet she still accepts a responsibility for what is happening here, and she sees the human connection between all people, be they Gentile or Jew. Elzvieta pretends no self-protective innocence and tries to help where she can. She, as much as Fania, offers a model of right behavior.

Fénelon, Fania   Fania is based on the real-life woman from whose memoirs this play evolved,

although the character whom we see is a dramatic construct rather than a realistic portrayal. A Jewish mother is sufficient to have Fania sent to the concentration camp where her musical ability allows her to avoid the heavier work and join the orchestra that was formed from camp inmates by their Nazi overseers. Although her body and spirit become severely weakened, she keeps herself alive to tell the story of her experience.

Fania realizes early on that if she is to survive, she must hold onto both a sense of her self and have a goal for the future toward which she can strive. Initially, she denies her Jewishness and insists on her identity solely as a French woman. In this, she denies an important aspect of herself that she will need to survive; it will help provide her with pride, moral values, and a sense of companionship with the other Jews. Her eventual embrace of her mother's maiden name, Goldstein, and the Jewish star allow her to find greater strength and to assert herself in a positive, dignified fashion. The goal she selects is "to try to remember everything," and this plants the seed of her tremendous capacity to survive.

Fania has a sense of commitment to others that allows her to think beyond her self. In the boxcar, she had reached out to others and prior to imprisonment had been a member of the French Resistance. Fania does not turn away from the dead as Marianne does, but she also does not want to be associated with them, at first, and on finding both the corpse in the boxcar and another in the bunk, she calls out to have them removed by someone else. In each case, her cries are in vain, indicative of the fact that she must learn to deal with the dead herself—this is part of her responsibility as a survivor. They have been silenced, and it will be up to her to embrace them and tell their story, as well as her own, which is something that we know she achieves—this whole film evidences her accomplishment.

Fania's music is also an aid in her survival. It allows her and Marianne to join the orchestra and so gain a few privileges and less strenuous work details to maintain their physical strength. It even psychologically strengthens her sufficiently to assert her humanity riskily to the Nazi, Mandel, by insisting that she will not join the orchestra unless Marianne is also included. The rejuvenating power of music keeps her alive both through her orchestral engagement and through its ability to free her in a spiritual capacity, allowing her to keep in touch with something of beauty and meaning in her ugly, chaotic world. Fania's tales and songs of Paris allow the whole group to escape briefly the dangerous and drab camp that they inhabit. It is little wonder that Shmuel chooses her to be the storyteller of the future and ensures that she remembers everything.

Fania forces herself to look continuously out of the window and take on extra duties that she will see everything that happens. She wishes to be a faithful recorder and a firsthand witness to what went on in this place. She even keeps a diary to assist her in this task and to ensure that there is some kind of backup in case she herself does not survive. On the point of giving up toward the close, Fania tries to convince Elzvieta to take this diary to ensure the information it contains survives, but Elzvieta sensibly recognizes the importance for Fania to keep trying and so refuses to take it, leaving her with no choice but to survive.

Fania is aware enough throughout to feel ashamed of her own involvement in this destruction as a member of the orchestra that accompanies the process. One prisoner actually spits on her, which upsets her greatly, but she is also intelligent enough to realize that joining the orchestra has given her the strength to survive and tell the story that needs to be told. Her personal torture is in some ways the burden of having to live and be a witness of such horrors. It is not an easy task, and she constantly struggles to complete it, but responsibilities are rarely undemanding, Miller seems to suggest, if they are to have any meaning.

Mala We hear about the Jewish prisoner Mala rather than see her. Previously active in the Belgian resistance, she twice escapes from the camp but is always brought back. Though seeming to capitulate to the Nazis by aiding them in finding seamstresses, translating for them, and freely doing anything they ask, internally she is resisting all the way as she is

constantly planning to aid her fellow prisoners. She is eventually caught and hanged for her efforts, but she remains a beacon of hope and possibility to the others by her example of courage. Even Alma admires Mala and finds hope in her very existence. Mala's relationship with the Polish prisoner, Edek, offers another example of a Pole prepared to accept the Jews as equals.

Marianne It is clear from the start that Marianne will have trouble surviving. She has led a sheltered, protected life up until now. Though 20 years old, she acts even younger, clinging to Fania's kindness and selfishly taking full advantage of it, as might a very young child. She is naive to a dangerous degree and unwilling to give this up. Her lack of knowledge and self-awareness is going to work against her in a place where a strong sense of self may be the only defense against the surrounding brutality. Ignoring the spiritual, Marianne concentrates entirely on her physical needs and ends up losing all respect, dignity, and direction.

Marianne clings to Fania for support and becomes a succubus, drawing sustenance, both literal and spiritual from sex. Unable to face even single corpses, as in the boxcar and later in their bunk, it is not surprising that she remains protectively ignorant of the more massive slaughter that takes place, ignoring the meaning behind the constant smoke in the air. When threatened, she will sacrifice anyone else to save herself. On hearing that the orchestra, her entrance into which Fania has managed, may suffer if they can learn no new pieces, she volunteers Fania to orchestrate for them when Fania does not even know how to do this. Fania just accepts the lie and tries her best to fulfill it.

Marianne is the complete opposite of Fania, immature and selfish, incapable of helping anyone other than herself. She capitulates to the Nazis body and soul, becoming a prostitute and losing every ounce of self-respect. Her essential problem is her inability to see beyond her own needs—she becomes as much a fanatic as the Nazis as she too refuses to recognize the humanity of others in her obsession for personal survival. She will lie, cheat, steal and flatter her way through this crisis with no thought of pride or wrongdoing—like a young child who has never learned the difference between right and wrong. Marianne is a creature wholly of the senses, and she responds instinctively, like an animal might. We see early signs of this in the sensual way that she eats and the ease with which she later uses her body to gain more food. She has no conscience, and so her behavior creates in her no feelings of guilt. She refuses to recognize any responsibilities in her drive merely to continue living, not even any responsibility to her own self and to her own dignity. She becomes a mere husk of a human being.

Rosè, Alma   The German Jewish leader of the camp orchestra, selected for both her exquisite violin playing and being part of a prominent musical family, Alma Rosè is a complex and often contradictory figure. Aware of the danger of their position, she strives to save the women in her orchestra, but she also often loses her temper and lashes out at these same women. They provide her with a safety valve for her frustration with the Nazis, against whom she dare not lash out. She is both monster and victim: monstrous when her behavior fails to separate her from the Nazis, but vulnerable in her deeply disguised inability to deal with the situation. Her way of dealing with the horror is to separate herself from it by inhabiting only the world of her music. She refuses to allow the horrors of the camp to intrude. She does not have the strength of will to stand up to the Nazis directly that Fania has. Alma agrees with everything they tell her and never argues when they take away her piano or her accordionist.

Unable to assert any real control over her own life, Alma tries to assert control over the music, insisting on perfection. Her own playing is beautiful, but it is art without a sense of responsibility, and it can only achieve a momentary respite. She pointedly closes her eyes when she plays, blinding herself to the real world that she must inhabit—but it is a world that even she will eventually be forced to acknowledge. Alma might have foreseen her end—poisoned by a German jealous of her transferral—if she had been a little less blind to the realities around her, but she goes to her death igno-rantly. She had thought that she was different from and better than the other prisoners, but the sight of her dead body, with its shorn head, disproves such beliefs.

Shmuel   Shmuel is an apparently half-wit prisoner who has been employed to fix the wiring. He selects Fania to record events and passes on messages from the outside. His practical job is indicative of his more spiritual dimension. He connects with Fania and makes sure that she will continue to connect with others into the future by ensuring that she will be able to tell the tales of their past. On his various appearances, Miller associates Shmuel with images of God and of angels: He seems to represent the presence of pure faith in this hell, a faith in the possible transcendence of goodness and in an optimistic future. As an electrician, it is his job to shed light, which he efficiently does: the light of both knowledge and hope. He provides Fania with information regarding who and how many are being gassed to round out her report, as well as passing on the news of the allied landing in France and seemingly leading those allies to free Fania at the close.

FURTHER READING

Abbotson, Susan C. W. "Re-Visiting the Holocaust for 1980s Television: Arthur Miller's *Playing for Time*." *American Drama* 8, no. 2 (Spring 1999): 61–78.

Bigsby, Christopher, editor. *Arthur Miller and Company*. London: Methuen, 1990.

———. "*Playing for Time*." *Arthur Miller: A Critical Study*. Cambridge: Cambridge University Press, 2005, 312–324.

Cook, Kimberley K. "Self-Preservation in Arthur Miller's Holocaust Dramas." *Journal of Evolutionary Psychology* 14, nos. 1–2 (March 1993): 99–108.

Feldman, Robert. "The Horror of the Holocaust: Miller's *Playing for Time*." In *Arthur Miller: Twentieth Century Legend*, edited by Syed Mashkoor Ali, 335–352. (Jaipur, India: Surabhi, 2006).

Johnsey, Jeanne. "Meeting Dr. Mengele: Naming, Self (Re)presentation and the Tragic Moment in Miller." In *The Achievement of Arthur Miller*, edited by Steven Centola, 101–107. (Dallas: Contemporary Research, 1995).

Kelly, Kevin. "Miller is Proud of the Product." *Boston Globe*, September 30, 1980, n.p.

Kroll, Jack. "The Activist Actress." *Newsweek* 96 (September 29, 1980), 52–58.

Isser, Edward R. "Arthur Miller and the Holocaust." *Essays in Theatre* 10, no. 2 (May 1992): 155–164.

Lask, Thomas. "Author Decries Casting of Miss Redgrave by CBS." *New York Times*, October 23, 1979, C7.

Lewis, Anthony. "Abroad At Home; After Auschwitz." *New York Times*, October 2, 1980, A23.

Mann, Judy. "Art is Long, But Life, Politics Are Short." *Washington Post*, September 26, 1980, B1, B6.

McLean, Robert A. "Amid the Horror Emerges a Heroine." *Boston Globe,* September 30, 1980.

O'Connor, John J. "TV: Vanessa Redgrave, Inmate." *New York Times*, September 30, 1980: C9.

Unger, Arthur. "Moving—and Controversial—New Arthur Miller Drama." *Christian Science Monitor,* September 3, 1980, 19.

Welland, Dennis. "The Passage of Time." *Miller: The Playwright.* 2d. ed. New York: Methuen, 1983, 144–157.

Playing for Time (1985)

Playing for Time first appeared as a television film but was later adapted by Miller into a two-act stage play by Miller. He had been frustrated by having to rewrite some of the material for the film, but he could now replace the elements that he had been forced to leave out for the stage version. Initially performed on September 22, 1985, at the Studio Theatre in Washington, D.C., it has been rarely produced since, possibly due to its large cast and difficult subject, although it won the top prize the following year at the Edinburgh Festival in GREAT BRITAIN. A tentative BROADWAY production starring Julie Andrews never materialized.

Though essentially the same plot, the order of events was switched around, and there were some differences, partly due to the change of medium. Several additional scenes were added in which characters only describe events that were pictured in the movie. Most notable was the development of Fania Fénelon into a narrator. Fania's opening monologue connects us with her immediately as both the spokesperson (these are her memories) and the most sympathetic character (in order that we trust those memories). Miller also asserted that the stage production should not strive for verisimilitude as the film had done but use representational details to convey the camp experience, which would change the nature of the play's impact. He intentionally strives to make a connection between the theatricality yet realness of a stage production and the theatricality and realness of the Nazi agenda as an analogy to contemporary behavior.

Another changed aspect is the play's greater emphasis on the character of Shmuel and his connection to Fania. In the film, Shmuel makes slight impact on his first appearance. He makes no contact with Fania, and we are given no clue as to his job, which is fixing wires—in other words, making connections. Revising this scene for the play, Miller emphasizes the significance of this character and ensures that we see the bond between him and Fania immediately forged. The play's closing scene (with which Fénelon's memoir had actually begun) in which Fania meets up with fellow prisoners Charlotte and Liesle is shown briefly in the film version but has been extended in the play. We only learn the details of the camp's liberation as Fania here remembers it for the waiter, Paul, before her friends arrive. When her friends arrive and catch up, we realize that life has definitely won through. Fania is once again a popular singer in the clubs of Europe, and Charlotte has given birth to two children, to show the cycle of life continuing. All three women show a lasting bond of friendship that has been made all the stronger by the past that they share. We learn that Marianne died from cancer shortly after the war. This acts as a literal representation of the spiritual disease that she carried to the end in her inability to recognize the humanity of others, something from which many Nazis and HOLOCAUST onlookers had also suffered. It is a disease against which Miller wishes to warn his audience, for Miller clearly does not see the guilt of the Holocaust as resting solely on the backs of the Nazis.

"Please Don't Kill Anything" (1960)

Based on an experience that Miller had undergone while one time walking on the beach with his wife MARILYN MONROE, the much-published short story "Please Don't Kill Anything" first appeared in 1960 in *Story,* was reprinted that same year in *The Noble Savage,* and again in *Redbook* the following year. It also appeared in Miller's 1967 collection *I Don't Need You Any More,* and *The Misfits and Other Stories* (1987), as well as in *Avant Garde* magazine in 1968. It tells the story of a couple whose walk on the beach becomes a serious venture as the wife persuades her husband to help save dozens of fish discarded by the fishermen. Her identification with the suffering fish speaks volumes regarding her psychological fragility, and although her husband dutifully saves them all, there remains an undercurrent that they are fighting a losing battle.

It begins as a beach is emptying for the day. The fishermen begin to haul in their catch as a couple arrives for a walk on the sands. Intrigued, the wife suggests that they watch. Her husband, Sam, is wary, knowing that the sight of dead fish will upset her, but he allows her to observe. Impressed by her beauty, as the husband proudly realizes most men to be, an old fisherman politely answers their questions. The wife identifies with the caught fish, worrying as to their reaction at being captured, and begins to panic. Her husband spots the signs and tries to calm her, pointing out that these fish will be used to feed people and are not dying in vain. Just then, the fishermen begin to toss the unwanted fish they cannot sell onto the beach. The wife watches in horror as they "began to swell."

She asks the fisherman if he will put these back in the water. Although he says "sure," it is evident that he plans do nothing and is just saying that to make her feel better. As his wife begins to become upset again, Sam reluctantly tosses one of the fish back in the sea to please her. Not wanting to deal with the dozens of other fish lying on the beach, he tells her that it is a pointless task, especially as many of the fish must already be dead. She asks the fisherman if that is so, and he tells her that they are

more likely still alive. Though reluctant to touch the slimy fish herself, she vainly tries to flip one back in using her sandal. Taking over, her husband picks it up and throws it in the water, laughing at what a ridiculous sight this must be for the fishermen. She apologizes but insists they should try to save all the fish. To prove that this is a pointless exercise Sam picks up what he thinks is a dead fish and throws that back. To his wife's delight, the fish revives and swims away. At her elation, he now feels compelled to throw in the rest.

His embarrassment melts away as he warms to the task, until there are only two fish left. Both look fairly swollen so he decides to leave these to let his wife see that such waste is a fact of life and needs to be accepted. He also still feels self-conscious about what the fishermen think and hopes that this will make them look less crazy. However, she refuses his lesson and insists that he save these fish, too. Just as Sam tosses in the penultimate fish, a retriever dog runs onto the beach and fetches the fish back each time he throws it. As a small minnow falls out of the mouth of the fish, he tries to make her accept the chain of death that supports the chain of life and give up, but she insists that he keep trying. While the dog goes after the fish that he again throws, Sam retrieves the other fish; she distracts the dog with a stick while he throws back the final fish. He points out that the fish, if allowed to die, would not have been wasted as the tide would have taken them out to feed other fish, but she insists that what they did was worthwhile. He feels a warm glow developing from having done this and recognizes that she is right; the results may not be lasting, but for the moment, they have staved off disaster. They kiss, and he is further rewarded by a declaration of her love, and they walk home.

Though obviously proud of the way his wife looks and the way other men view her, it is evident that Sam begins by seeing himself as the superior intellect and as far more worldly than his wife. He continuously casts himself in the teaching role, reducing her to a diminutive "puss," and viewing her as "a little girl" in her responses. He feels that she needs to be taught some of the harsh realities of life to better survive, but it is ultimately she who teaches him something special about the value of life. As he finally realizes, she is also a "woman" who knows about "absurdities" and is not ignorant of the inconsequence of their act but still feels that it was worth doing. In the warm glow that he experiences at the close, he knows that she is right, and to live with optimism is the only way. Comparing the writing to that of Ernest Hemingway, CHRISTOPHER BIGSBY, one of the few scholars to even reference this interesting tale, insists that the power of the story "derives from its indirection, from what is not said." Bigsby persuasively suggests that given the time frame of Miller's own relationship with Monroe, this is a prescient story on Miller's behalf about "the end of love," and the tale's action underscores that the wife is "fighting a losing battle . . . clearly on the edge of breakdown, neuraesthenically sensitive. The husband, equally clearly, is aware of her fragility and of his own inability, finally, to save her. What we are left with as they hold hands is the space between them."

FURTHER READING

Bigsby, Christopher. "Fiction." *Arthur Miller: A Critical Study.* New York: Cambridge University Press, 2005, 444–472.

"The Poosidin's Resignation" (1976)

Written for *Boston University Quarterly* as one of two short works, the other being the brief story "Ham Sandwich," Miller describes this dramatic piece as a playfully conceived fragment in angry response to politicians of the period: "The principals were so outrageous, it was impossible to feel much more than contempt at their endless lying, self-praise, lugubrious insensitivity to the monstrousness of their deformities." At this time, the nation was still evaluating the fallout of Watergate and two decades of VIETNAM WAR. Written in doggerel, much of the opening scene in which young men are sent into the flames of a furnace to honor the god of war is nonsensical. Key buzzwords stand out, such as *freedom* and *security,* but they seem

to be contradicted by the actions that are taking place.

One man objects and asks why a nation is destroying her young in this way and is unable to get a clear answer. His pleas are superseded by two lengthy speeches: the resignation of the former "poosidin" (read *president*) and the inaugural speech of the incoming "poosidin-elect." They are hard to tell apart, and both pompously speak of their own greatness and the necessity of war to make themselves greater, "No Great Poosidin can be great without great unimies" says the outgoing, and while the incoming admits that he was elected on a promise of peace, he outlines his plans to achieve this by fighting. As the hypnotized mob applauds, we see it that it is unlikely that the flames of the furnace will be extinguished anytime soon. The speeches are full of wordplay and effectively convey Miller's interest in language and his continued desire to experiment.

"The Presence" (2003)

Published in *Esquire* in 2003, and the title of Miller's 2007 posthumous collection of tales, "The Presence" is one of Miller's later short stories. It tells of the encounter of an older, unnamed male protagonist with a young couple who are making love in the dunes, an experience that seems to revivify the protagonist's sense of life by taking him beyond himself. In his *Arthur Miller: A Critical Study*, CHRISTOPHER BIGSBY calls this a "striking work" in which "prose is pressed in the direction of poetry, as language carries the idea of fact elevated into myth."

One foggy morning, a man wakes beside his sleeping wife, with whom he has argued the night before, and rises to go for a solitary walk on the beach. His mood is dour and resentful toward his wife. Approaching the dunes, he spots a couple making love and retreats up the path, unaroused and embarrassed. After a short wait, he returns, certain that they will be finished, only to see them having sex even more ardently. Although attracted to the male's vitality and his apparent dominance of his woman, the man returns again to the road, not wishing to hear their groans, not wishing to feel even vicariously involved. Waiting longer, he once more walks down and finds the male cocooned in a sleeping bag, but the woman is standing in the water washing her hands. He silently watches her. She notices but ignores him as she returns to sit and then recline next to her lover.

The man walks along the surf, contemplating the water. His description is evocative of the sexuality and the underlying menace of the scene that he has witnessed. Becoming hungry, he starts for home but cannot tear himself away from the couple. He senses unhappiness in the woman, although he has no evidence. The woman sits up, stares at the sea, and, seeing the man, walks toward him. Asking the time, she wonders if he is a local, and he explains that he is visiting. Watching her gestures, he gets the feeling that she is in charge.

He suddenly recalls making love on this same beach himself 30 years prior to a woman who is long dead. Unlike the other couple, they did it in silence, at night, and in longer grass, but those were different times, and the memory is bittersweet. The woman knows that he was watching earlier, and though he denies it, she convinces him to admit that they looked great. Explaining that she did not directly see him but knew that he went and came back because she had felt his "presence," they remain in silence as he ponders the implication of this. She walks into the water, and he follows. Swimming together, she suddenly wraps her legs around him, and they kiss; then she returns to her lover.

Coming out of the water, the man checks his penknife, a gift from his wife, for water damage and sits on the sand to dry off. He and the woman stare at each other, feeling their connection; then he lies back and falls asleep. Awaking, the couple is gone, and he is initially upset at finding no trace except a white t-shirt that may or may not have been hers; he is unsure if he has dreamed everything. However, walking home, he is overcome with happiness from the experience, real or not. As Bigsby suggests, "The beach is now empty but a presence remains, a sense of immanent meaning." Time, people and the sea all flow together, interrelate, and life again has purpose.

FURTHER READING

Bigsby, Christopher. *Arthur Miller: A Critical Study.* New York: Cambridge University Press, 2005: 459–460.

The Price (1968)

Miller had formulated some of his ideas for the play *The Price* in the early 1950s, but it took nearly two decades and the encouragement of director ULU GROSBARD to bring it to fruition. Written mainly in 1967, his own father having died the previous year, Miller tells the tale of the effect of a dead father on his two living sons, one of whom, like Miller's childhood friend, SIDNEY FRANKS, joins the police force to earn the income to support his impoverished father. Obviously, the tale of brothers in conflict and a family that was ruined by the GREAT DEPRESSION is a familiar Miller story, but it is only tangentially autobiographical. The script was handed to ROBERT WHITEHEAD to produce, and Grosbard was hired to direct.

The production was a troubled one. Jack Warden, originally cast as Walter Franz, felt uncomfortable in the role, asked to be released four days before the tryouts in Philadelphia, and was replaced by Pat Hingle. David Burns, the actor playing Gregory Solomon, was rushed to hospital with a serious illness, and his understudy, Harold Gary, had to take over during the previews. Meanwhile, the actors were generally dissatisfied with the direction of Grosbard, and one week before the scheduled BROADWAY premiere, Miller himself had to take over as director and to postpone the opening for two weeks. Still, with a run of 425 performances, it was by far the most successful Miller play for some time. Nevertheless, contradictory reactions to the play sparked a newspaper debate between critic Albert Bermel, who argued that Miller had shown no development since his earlier work, and HAROLD CLURMAN, who despite having negatively reviewed the play, defended Miller's development as an artist. Reviews of the play were similarly divided.

Although the play's characters seem most influenced by the Great Depression and WORLD WAR II and the play's conventional structure may appear to be equally dated next to the avant-garde productions of the off- and off-off Broadway scene of the period, the play is a timely one. In some ways, it deliberately offers itself as an alternative to the negative rationale of ABSURDISM and the rise of emotionally driven performance art. It also indirectly addresses major issues of the late 1960s, such as civil rights and the VIETNAM WAR, in its deconstruction of the myth of the American dream, its depiction of the consequences of choice, and its insistence on the relevance of the past to the present.

SYNOPSIS

Act One

The play opens in the late afternoon on a stage cluttered with furniture. Victor Franz, a police sergeant who is approaching 50, enters the single floor into which his family had been sent to live. The uncles who took over and rented out his father's home as apartments after the father went bankrupt in the WALL STREET CRASH allowed them to live on in the attic space. Feeling a little awed on his initial entry, Victor plucks the harp, cranks the phonograph, and notes various items that hold particular memories, including his brother's oar and his own fencing equipment. Finding an old laughing record, he puts it on the phonograph and laughs along. His wife, Esther, arrives and annoys her husband by already having had a scotch. The house is about to be demolished, and he needs to remove the stacks of furniture that his father kept. He has arranged to meet a dealer who is shortly expected, after which he and Esther plan to go to the movies. He has been trying to get in touch with his older brother, Walter, to decide what to do, but Walter has not returned his phone calls. They reminisce about neighbors whom Victor recalls who lived in the building when he lived there during the Depression. Esther is worried that Victor will not drive a hard enough deal for the furniture.

Esther notices that her husband is still in uniform, and Victor explains how his suit was ruined by spilled coffee and is at the dry cleaners. Esther expresses dissatisfaction with her life, wanting more

cash and a sense of direction. Victor has not spoken to Walter for 16 years. Although entitled to half of the profit, Esther is hoping that Walter will not claim it because he has plenty of money. Victor had looked after his father and had freed Walter to complete medical school and become a successful surgeon. Esther wants Victor to take early retirement and to try a new (better paid) career. He is unsure what else he could do at his age without any real qualifications. Esther suggests that he should have Walter help him as he has influence, but Victor's resentment of Walter is too great. Esther wants him to take a risk, but after 28 years on the force, he is fearful giving up such security even though he dislikes the job.

Victor recalls his father, who was crushed by the Depression. Feeling the need for another drink, Esther offers to pick up his suit. He shows her an old radio that he once made and recalls living in this room. He is as dissatisfied with life as his wife and is unsure what he has achieved. She asks him to show her how he used to fence, and as he lunges at her with a foil, Gregory Solomon arrives. An elderly furniture dealer, he is coughing from his climb up the stairs but is full of life. They offer water and coax him to sit in the center armchair. Introducing each other, Solomon compliments Esther and her outfit before she leaves to fetch the suit.

Victor shows Solomon the furniture and asks for an estimate. Solomon delays, trying to make a connection so that Victor will trust him; he praises some pieces but complains about the salability of others to try to keep the price down. He also wants to check that Victor has full ownership before he makes a deal. Victor promises to get a statement from his brother. Solomon had not expected so much furniture, preferring to buy just the choice pieces, but Victor insists that it is all or nothing. As Solomon recalls his days in the theater as an acrobat and shows him his British navy discharge papers to prove his age, Victor starts to warm to him, even as he is keen to get the deal done. Solomon senses, however, that Victor does not trust him, so he threatens to leave without giving a price. Victor backs down, and they start to deal again, Solomon explaining that he is semiretired and nervous about such a huge commitment.

Solomon complains that people prefer disposable furniture these days as they are fearful of commitment and that much of this furniture is too solid to be popular. At 89, he sees Victor as a youngster in need of advice and makes up his mind to buy the furniture as a refusal to give in to old age. As if to celebrate his rebirth or perhaps just his positive feeling of connection with Victor, he takes out a hard-boiled egg to eat as he starts to list the items in the room. Victor recounts more detail about his family's swift downfall after the crash, how his mother soon after died, and how his father just would sit and listen to the radio between occasional low-paying jobs. Solomon is amazed at the father's attitude, himself having lost everything several times and always making a comeback. He reveals that he had a daughter who committed suicide in 1916 and that she has been haunting him lately; he wonders if he could have done anything to help her.

Solomon explains his philosophy that life is all about decisions and learning to live with those that you have made. Victor tells how he quit college to take a job with the police force to earn sufficient money to help his father. With a wife and a child and the worry of war, he never felt free to quit and do something else, but he knows that his wife is disappointed with their life. He resents his brother Walter whom he felt was stingy in sending only $5 a month toward their father's upkeep. What rankles more is that his father still seemed to prefer Walter. Solomon offers Victor $1,100 for the furniture, and Victor is uncertain as he plans to split it with Walter. Solomon offers to make up a fake receipt to fool the brother, but Victor refuses. As Solomon presses him to make the sale, Victor reluctantly agrees, but as Solomon begins to count bills into Victor's hand, Walter arrives. Seeing Walter's disapproval of the sale price, Victor stops taking the money.

Act Two

The second act continues straight on without a gap as Walter asks after Esther and the brothers talk about their children. Victor's son, Richard, is on a full scholarship to MIT, while Walter's daughter Jean is a fashion designer and his sons are college dropouts who see themselves as musicians.

As they make small talk, Solomon worries about Walter's intentions, fearful for his deal. Walter says that he wants nothing and only came to say hello, but Solomon keeps interrupting, especially when Walter shows interest in the harp. The harp had been a wedding present to their mother from her father, and Solomon insists that it forms the "heart and soul" of his offer, even while pointing out that its sounding board is cracked. Walter asks for one of their mother's evening gowns for his daughter. He also asks about the family piano, which Victor explains was sold along with the family silver a long time ago. Walter tells Victor that he looks like their father. Solomon tries to give Victor the rest of the payment, but Victor is too distracted.

Walter evidently wants to say something but is uncertain where to start. He admits that he is divorced, just as Esther returns. She is surprised to see Walter, but as he compliments her and they chat, she warms to him. When he expresses his belief that Solomon is offering too low a price, she sides immediately with Walter against her husband. As they urge Solomon to raise his offer, Victor comes to the dealer's defense, feeling that his judgment is being criticized. Victor tells Walter that he will get half, but Walter refuses, telling Victor that he has "earned it." Tempers mount as Victor feels mocked by Walter's attempts to obtain a higher price and as Solomon, sensing that he may be losing the deal, accuses Walter of doing this to make an impression, having called the furniture "junk" when he arrived. Victor suggests that Solomon go into the next room while they discuss what to do. When Victor tries to return the money that he had taken so far, Solomon has a dizzy spell. Asking for another snack from his bag, Walter helps him into the next room.

Esther questions Victor, who is upset that she is siding with Walter against him. She is impressed by Walter's generosity and angry at her husband's reluctance to accept. Walter reenters and suggests an alternative plan, in which they get Solomon to appraise the furniture at a high sum, donate it to the Salvation Army, and then Walter (with his higher tax bracket) will list it as a charitable contribution on his tax return and split his savings with Victor. Although legal, Victor is uncertain about this. Walter confesses that his life has been a selfish one and that he has made little time for relationships but that he is trying to live better. Noticing the fencing equipment, he recalls how their mother used to love to watch Victor fence and suggests that he look for the fancy gauntlets that she had once bought him; they find them in a drawer. Although his mother's favorite, Victor cannot recall her face, which troubles him. Solomon calls Walter away to talk.

In Walter's absence, Victor explains to Esther that he wants an apology from Walter and that he needs to clear the air before accepting anything. She is angry and threatens to leave him if he will not take the money, feeling that he is just using Walter as a scapegoat for his own inability to take charge of his life. On his brother's return, Victor explains how humiliated he felt when Walter would not answer the phone. Walter offers to let him keep the entire sum of his savings, saying that Solomon has reluctantly agreed to do the appraisal. He confesses that he had a breakdown and after three years of recovering was now simplifying his life. He has sold off many of his holdings and even offers his services to the city hospital. He realizes that he has been too focused on money, used people in the past, and lost touch with his own humanity. He is now trying to change all that. His spur was finding himself drunk with a knife, planning to kill his wife. He professes admiration for Victor who chose to quit school, stay with their father, and lead a simpler life, although he recognizes that this was not done without a price. A series of bad choices as a surgeon have made him reevaluate himself as a doctor and his life in general. He blames their father for making him so callously ambitious and for feeding his fear that he would lose everything if he stopped pushing. As he offers Victor his friendship, complimenting him and Esther on their more meaningful lives, they remain unconvinced.

Walter offers to get Victor a job as a medical liaison in the new hospital wing, and Victor seems tempted. Solomon interrupts to tell Victor that he will add $50 to his offer if Victor will stick with their deal. Victor ignores Solomon but turns down his brother; he is too angry with him to accept anything and is further riled by Walter's comment that

it was a pity that he had not pursued his science any further. He knows that he has no qualifications for the job that Walter offers, but he secretly blames Walter for this. While Walter gives up and goes to leave, Esther urges Victor to address what really bothers him. Victor complains about the measly $5 a month that Walter had sent to help look after their father, but Walter points out that their father could have worked or gone on welfare and did not need Victor to give up his career for him. Solomon again interrupts, this time to agree to do the appraisal and to tell the brothers to no longer pursue such a pointless argument. They agree and decide to sell the furniture to Solomon and be finished, but Esther angers at their avoidance of the truth and challenges them finally to face it.

What really upset Victor was Walter's refusal to give $500 that Victor had needed to complete his degree, and they relive the period when Victor had asked him for this. We learn that Walter had initially refused, telling Victor to ask their father for the money as he knew that their father had some, and then a few days later, Walter had telephoned to offer the cash. Walter spoke to their father, who had suggested that Victor needed to look after him and so did not need the money. Their father never told Victor about this conversation, but neither had Walter, and Victor sees his reasoning as faulty and geared to let himself off the hook. Why, he asks, is Walter so keen to give him things if he feels no guilt? He also defends his choice to stay with his father because to accept that his father might have managed without him would make his sacrifice appear worthless. Walter accuses him of faulty reasoning, suggesting that Victor must have known that their father had some income and that he could have pursued his studies if he had really wanted. Walter tells Victor about the $4,000 that their father had invested and how he, Walter, had offered to help his brother if the father would allow him to continue his studies. The father declined.

Walter defends their father, understanding how the crash had mentally conditioned him not to trust anyone and explaining that their father had never truly expected Victor to sacrifice so much. As Walter berates him for trying to make him seem the bad guy, Victor confesses that he knew his father had something. Esther is enraged at the sacrifices that he had forced her to make to help a man who could have supported himself. While Victor defends him, Esther rejects the father as a liar. Victor admits that he had asked him for the tuition money but received laughter in response. Not knowing how to respond, Victor had gone outside and been faced with images of people who were out of work. He saw his father as damaged by the Depression in a way that he could not help his son, and Victor felt sorry for him. He stayed because he decided that his father needed someone—Walter had left, and his mother had been no support, throwing up on her husband when he announced his bankruptcy.

Walter refuses to believe Victor's reasoning, suggesting that there had never been any love in their family, only a drive to succeed, and suggests that Victor made his sacrifice in an effort to deny this truth. While Walter had followed that drive to succeed, Victor had sought love, and though between them they could make up a whole person, individually they will always be disappointed. Esther begins to see a truth in this, which draws her to sympathize with her husband. Victor is not placated and refuses to condone or forgive Walter. Walter admits that he feels that Victor has always mocked him with his self-sacrifice to try to make him feel guilty, and he turns on the couple, violently flinging his mother's gown at Victor and storming out in his frustration. Though Victor considers going after him, Solomon says that it is no use; Esther agrees.

Esther recalls when she first came to the house at 19 and how Victor had admired his older brother, planning to be a doctor like him; the father had seemed to be a "sweet, inoffensive gentleman." The crash destroyed all of this, and things cannot go back to how they were. Solomon agrees, pointing out that even if his suicidal daughter had talked to him, he could not change the past. Solomon gives Victor the full payment and begins to take inventory. Victor suggests that he and Esther decide to see a movie, but when he goes to change into his suit, she tells him not to bother but to stay in his uniform. As they leave, Victor asks Solomon to leave him his fencing gear, and Solomon thanks him for the opportunity of a new job to keep him alive. Solomon is nervous at the size of the task, but he plays the laughing record as he sits in the armchair and begins to laugh along with it.

CRITICAL COMMENTARY

The play's setting with its layering of old furniture immediately evokes a past that hangs over the entire action of the play and suggests a subtext to the plot. The heavy wood has such a strong physical presence that it becomes an additional character in the play. We are shown 10 rooms of furniture crowded into a single room, which represents the detritus of the Franz family—moments of competitive strength with the fencing foil or the oar; the family's lost wealth with the lap rug, top hat, and fancy gowns; and the ambiguous laughing record, which somehow binds Victor and Solomon who open and close the play by laughing along with it but also recalls the father's cruel laughter at Victor when he asked him for money. All of this is filmed over with dust but will be brought out on display for this final reckoning.

The armchair in center stage substitutes for the absent father who perennially sat in it while alive, balanced by the mother's harp to one side, with its cracked sounding board to suggest the discordance in their relationship. Though deceased, these parents still haunt both their sons, and their presence remains constant in these physical objects. It is significant that, on entry, Esther seats Solomon in the father's chair, and he proceeds to take a fatherly interest in Victor's outcome, praising him, defending him against the others, and advising him against bad behavior. It is their father with whom neither sibling has come to grips, but as each begins to accept Solomon, their relationship to their father comes into better focus. As his biblical namesake before him, Solomon is a wary judge, accomplished at getting to the truth. He knows from the start that the brothers' differences are irreconcilable and that they each must simply accept the price that they must pay for the lives that they have chosen, but they do not heed his advice to stop the argument. Their revelations are painful to each, but they do not substantially change anything.

The idea of the price invoked by the play's title applies to many things: The price paid for things—be it a movie ticket, a new suit, a typing service, or a college degree—is closely accounted. There is also the elusive price of the furniture that Victor is so eager to sell—when Solomon goes to leave, insulted that Victor does not trust him, he makes the point that he has not yet given him a price. Sometimes, a price is hard to determine: When Solomon finally offers $1,100, we assume, like Victor, that this is fair, but Walter and Esther undercut this with their suggestion that it could be worth more than $3,000. Walter even suggests a tax scam whereby it would be valued at $25,000. The price is indeterminate as the furniture is valued differently by different people. But more especially, the price refers to the price that people pay for the choices that they make in their lives, and the point is that every choice has a price of some kind, even though it might be hard to determine at the time.

Victor knows the price that he paid to look after his father: He gave up the possibility of a promising career in science to work in the police force and live in relative penury for the rest of his life. What he needs to know is what he gained from this sacrifice, and it is his confusion over this that creates his dissatisfaction. Esther's desire for more money makes him view it from a financial viewpoint, but he need only look at his brother to see that money will not make the difference. Where Walter's quest for money has led to breakdown, divorce, estrangement from his brother and children, and a crisis of conscience, Victor's settling for less has allowed him to build a loving marriage, have a good relationship with his son, and live life with a clear conscience (he has arrested only 19 people in 28 years of service, indicative of the lack of real conflict in his life). He just needs to accept that this was the better path for him. Esther, with her good taste, can buy a simple suit and look great, and can buy it at far less cost than the expensive coat that is worn by Walter.

However, in Miller's production note to the play, he insists that there should be a "fine balance of sympathy" between Walter and Victor. Both have good intentions, and we need both kinds of people to operate the world. Walter and Victor perform valuable services, and society needs both its surgeons and its police officers, those who take risks and those who play it safe; those who break rules and those who maintain strict order; those who are lionized by the public and those who perform a public service. Their fault is to blame the other for how they feel about this. Walter's guilt is his own and has nothing to do with Victor, just as Victor's choice to take the more secure but less rewarding path was his alone.

While neither of the brothers can come to terms with the other's point of view, Esther is another story. Initially unhappy with her life to the point of alcoholism and even threatening to leave Victor if he will not accept his brother's handouts, she learns a new respect for her husband, the life he has chosen, and the ambivalent human reasoning that has led to his career in the police force. Although her husband may be fearful of risk, he is also a loving individual whose choices have been marked by their consideration for others. Her attraction to him is evident when she admires his fencing and when by the close she accepts him as he is, in his policeman's uniform. She ends the play content to remain as they are, happy that at least she has her husband's love. This is more than could be said about his parents or his brother, despite Walter's desire to change his ways.

Solomon's philosophy that life is all about decisions and learning to live with those you have made is key. His daughter committed suicide, but he knows that he can do nothing to change that fact and must simply live with it. His complaint, that people dislike old furniture because it is too permanent, says much for Miller's criticism of contemporary culture with its overinflated fear of commitment. His suggestion that religion or political involvement could fill that gap is interesting, given Miller's stance as an atheist, but unsurprising as each demands comparable involvement. When Solomon begins to laugh along with the record at the play's close, we can read it as a sign of his vivacity and spirit and not an absurdist reaction to the pointlessness of life. Laughter for Miller has meaning, and it can be negative as in the father's hurtful laughter, but it can also be a curative against a culture too wrapped up in itself to enjoy the life on offer.

FIRST PERFORMANCE

The Price previewed in Philadelphia and then opened at the Morosco Theatre in New York City on February 7, 1968, with the following cast:

Victor Franz: Pat Hingle
Esther Franz: Kate Reid
Gregory Solomon: Harold Gary
Walter Franz: ARTHUR KENNEDY

Directed by Ulu Grosbard
Set and costumes designed by BORIS ARONSON
Produced by Robert Whitehead
It ran for 425 performances.

INITIAL REVIEWS

Critical reaction was not just mixed but was diametrically opposed. While John Simon called the play "a bore" and complained that it was "improbable, uncompelling, old-fashioned, humorless for all its jokes, and undramatic," John Chapman called it "absorbing" and "splendidly acted" and found it "spell binding in its intensity as it moves headlong, without interruption, from a lightly amusing beginning to an emotion-stirring finish." Robert Brustein complained about poor writing which "gives us merely the appearance of significance, behind which nothing meaningful is happening," while Clive Barnes was "deeply moved" and praised it as "one of the most engrossing and entertaining plays that Miller has ever written." Indeed, several reviewers, including Richard Cooke, celebrated what they saw as Miller's return to "the full exercise of his talents." Some complained about careless writing but were also perturbed by the play's irresolution, even while others applauded this as a strength. Whether it is the "powerful compassionate play" that dissects "the frailties of man with consummate artistry" that Mary Raines praised or "a carelessly written . . . failure in logic" as Martin Gottfried declared, Penelope Gilliatt's response may help account for the confusion. She pointed out that the play, which she described as "beautifully intelligent," is "obdurately at odds with anything else in the New York theatre." After the New York production closed, the play transferred to London, with new actors in the roles of the brothers, and set

a theater record there with a 51-week run. It has had several successful revivals since on both sides of the Atlantic.

SCHOLARSHIP

Considering the relish with which many critics welcomed the play, it has received relatively little critical attention outside of a few studies outlining why this was considered a return to form and why Gregory Solomon is such a great character. Renee Winegarten's assessed Solomon as the "first positive symbol of that dignity and self-respect which [Miller's] earlier characters found only in death." Jozsef Czimer and Ann Massa offer some interesting production comparisons between the United States and Europe, and Gerald Weales explores the language of the play and ways in which Miller uses this to inhibit understanding between the brothers. James Robinson views the Franz family as illustrative of Judaic concerns regarding assimilation into "American capitalist culture," while Milton Chaikin analyzes the implications of an alternative ending with Victor quitting the police force and pursuing his dream of a scientific career. More recently, Varró Gabriella has considered the play's connections to Sam Shepard's *True West* (1980).

Books on Miller mostly have a short chapter or section in which the play's theme regarding the price paid for life choices is outlined, along with analyses of what each of the four characters represent in relation to this, although central attention is usually given to Walter and Victor. Not to be missed is CHRISTOPHER BIGSBY's lengthy analysis of the play as related to Vietnam and other events of the late 1960s when it was written, which contextualizes the play from a fresh and illuminative viewpoint.

CHARACTERS

Franz, Esther Esther expresses dissatisfaction with her life, feeling trapped by mediocrity. She looks down on her husband's job as a policeman and hates to go out with him in his work clothes. Though she loves Victor, she longs for more money. Bored, she has trouble getting out of bed and has recently taken to drink. Their son Richard has left home for college, and she feels at a loose end. When Victor lunges at her with the fencing foil, she is excited and finds him dashing, which indicates that the passion still remains in their relationship, despite her gripes. Esther is complimented by each of the men in the play as she wears a new and flattering suit, which also indicates her ability to look stunning even on a budget because she has good taste. At the close, Esther telling her husband not to change into his suit from his uniform tells us that she has finally come to terms with who he is and that she is no longer embarrassed about being seen with a policeman.

Franz, Mr. (Father)   A prosperous businessman, Victor and Walter's father, Mr. Franz, was a millionaire before the Wall Street crash bankrupted him. Within five weeks, he had lost nearly everything, but he was allowed to live on a single upper floor of his family home by relatives who were more fortunate than he. Soon after this downfall, his wife died, and he seemed to lose all will to do anything. He would mostly sit in his armchair listening to the radio, though occasionally he would take a menial job for pocket money. Victor suggests that his father had strongly believed in the system, and when that system collapsed, so did he, feeling that it must have been his own fault.

Although he retained $4,000, his father had Walter invest this money for him and kept it secret from Victor, whom the father tricked into looking after him by making Victor believe that his father would be destitute. When Victor asked him for money to complete his degree, his father just laughed. Victor quit college and took a job with the police force to sustain them both; he tended his father until his death. By all accounts, Mr. Franz had not had a very loving marriage, his wife complaining that she had lost a musical career by marrying him and literally throwing up on him when he announced his bankruptcy. Although he is long dead when the play starts, the chair at center stage represents his constant presence and influence on his sons' psyches.

Franz, Victor   Born into the home of a millionaire, Victor's memories of childhood are of the fancy French gauntlets that his mother bought him,

her fur travel rug, and the family chauffeur. This has been soured by his memory of their mother vomiting over his father at the news of his father's bankruptcy and by what he has come to see as his brother's mean neglect of him and his father. His mother died shortly thereafter, and nowadays he can scarcely remember her face, even though he was her favorite. Younger than Walter, Victor showed more promise at school and planned to become a doctor as his brother did, but with the Depression, he lost the financing to finish his degree. His father tells him to ask his brother for the $500 that he needs to complete college, but knowing that their father has $4,000 stashed away, Walter is reluctant to hand it over, even while Victor is supporting their father who is scavenging food from restaurant garbage.

About to hit 50, Victor is reassessing his life and feels uncertain of his achievements. His wife's new habit of drinking and her constant pushing him to earn more money both annoy and confuse him. His inner tension is reflected in Esther's complaint that he has been grinding his teeth in his sleep. He is uncertain as to how he came to be in the position he is in, never having envisioned himself as a policeman for 28 years. He dislikes his job, tries to get airport duty to stay out of the thick of things, and is counting the days until he can afford to retire. His early promise in science is nothing more than a dream now, which he acknowledges when he points out to Walter that high school kids know more about science than he. He knows that he has no credentials for the job that Walter has suggested, and he sees it as charity. The fact that he never really bargains with Solomon and just accepts his price indicates a key difference between him and Walter; Victor, as Alfieri in *A View from the Bridge* suggests, is prepared to "settle for half." While we might see irony in his depiction as a fencer, he does keep his fencing equipment at the close, which suggests that he is not as beaten as Walter believes. Like Solomon, with whom he is linked by the laughing record, Victor may be able to bounce back and begin life anew.

Franz, Walter   The elder of the Franz brothers, Walter has focused on himself for most of his life.

In medical school when the crash took away the family money, he refused to be held back by the rest of his family and completed his studies. Working as a surgeon, he sent home $5 a month toward his father's upkeep and refused Victor the $500 that he needed to complete his degree because he knew that their father had funds of his own. Not having spoken to his brother in 16 years, Walter has led the high life while his brother slogged the beat. He skis, regularly rides horseback, has owned a string of nursing homes, and has become very wealthy. He has also messed up his relationship with his three children, has been divorced by his wife, and has had a nervous breakdown from which it took him three years to recover. As a surgeon, he made a series of risky decisions that led to patients dying; this has led him to lose confidence in his own ability as a surgeon. He is trying to reevaluate his life and has come to try to mend bridges between himself and his brother. He offers him the only things that he understands—money and a comfortable job, which out of pride, Victor refuses.

Walter tells Victor quite bluntly that he had always planned to pursue his studies and ambitions no matter what and had advised Victor to do the same and not let his father drag him down. He feels that their father exploited Victor and points out to him that his father was not sick and could have worked or even gone on welfare and that he would have survived, as so many others had done. Victor disagrees because he views life differently from his brother and that for him, the human cost is worth more. Victor knew that their father had money, but he also knew that it meant something to have his son stand beside him in a way that the rest of the family had not. Walter, in his self-imposed solitary existence, cannot be expected to understand this perspective.

Solomon, Gregory If we are to believe his stories, the elderly Jewish furniture dealer, Gregory Solomon, who Victor calls to appraise his family inheritance, left Russia 65 years ago when he was age 24 after two failed marriages and has since worked as an acrobat in a family act alongside many vaudeville greats and served in the British navy. Past-president of the Appraisers Association

(which he declares to the amusement of Esther and Walter that he "made all ethical") and, although semiretired, he is still considering taking on a major consignment of furniture (too heavy for Victor or Walter to carry). He is age 89 and still kicking. He has lost everything several times in his life but always found the energy to begin anew. His clothing may be frayed, but he shows the lightest spirit of those in the play and clearly has the ability to move on. His constant appetite, be it for an egg, a chocolate bar, or an orange, illustrates his appetite for life itself. He has lived in six different countries and has been married four times, at age 19, 22, 51, and 75; the ease at which he apparently bounces back makes one want to play the lottery on those numbers.

On the surface, with his ethnic inflections and phraseology, Solomon provides comic relief in the play, but his role is far more layered. He also provides the possibility of a professional contentment with his job and a man at ease with his life, just as Charley was in *Death of a Salesman*. His age bespeaks a wisdom that we discern in his reactions to modern culture and the arguments between the brothers. His daughter, who committed suicide at 19, still haunts him, but he knows enough to understand that even if he could talk to her again, he could not change anything. When others make choices, just as when you make those choices yourself, you have to live with the consequences. When he makes the decision to take on the furniture, we see Solomon revivified by the future possibilities this entails. Unlike either Walter or Victor who still remain wary, he is openly willing to start anew and take a risk, not surprising because he has done this before. As he sits on the father's chair, he comes to represent a far more sage father figure than the chair's original inhabitant, and his example may hopefully inspire others to follow his lead.

MOVIE AND TELEVISION ADAPTATIONS

A television movie of the play, produced by David Susskind and directed by Fiedler Cook, was aired on NBC on February 3, 1971, as part of their *Hallmark Hall of Fame* series. It starred GEORGE C. SCOTT, Barry Sullivan, Colleen Dewhurst, and David Burns (who had recovered from the illness that prevented him from playing Solomon in the original stage production). It met with reasonable reviews, although Julius Novick of the *New York Times* was fairly scathing, finding it dated and pretentious. To date, the production has not been released on video.

FURTHER READING

Barnes, Clive. "Theater: Arthur Miller's *The Price*." *New York Times*, February 8, 1968, 37.

Bigsby, Christopher. "*The Price*." *Arthur Miller: A Critical Study*. Cambridge: Cambridge University Press, 2005, 271–288.

Brustein, Robert. "The Unseriousness of Arthur Miller." *New Republic,* February 24, 1968, 38–41.

Chaikin, Milton. "The Ending of Arthur Miller's *The Price*." *Studies in the Humanities* 8, no. 2 (1981): 40–44.

Chapman, John. "*The Price*, Miller's New Play, Absorbing, Splendidly Acted." *New York Daily News*, February 8, 1968. In *New York Theatre Critics' Reviews* 29 (1968): 353.

Clurman, Harold. "Theatre." *Nation,* February 26, 1968, 281–283.

Cooke, Richard P. "Restoration of Miller." *Wall Street Journal,* February 9, 1968. In *New York Critics' Reviews* 29 (1968): 353.

Czimer, Jozsef. "Price and Value." *Hungarian Quarterly* 10 (Winter 1969): 169–174.

Gabriella, Varró "Acts of Betrayal: Arthur Miller's *The Price* and Sam Shepard's *True West*." *Hungarian Journal of English and American Studies* 11, no. 2 (Fall 2005): 63–76.

Gilliatt, Penelope. *Observer,* February 11, 1968. In *London Theatre Record* 10, no. 3 (1990): 173.

Gottfried, Martin. "Theatre: *The Price*." *Women's Wear Daily,* February 8, 1968. In *New York Theatre Critics' Reviews* 29 (1968): 354.

Massa, Ann. "*The Price*." *Journal of Dramatic Theory and Criticism* (Spring 1990): 210–211.

Novick, Julius. "Arthur Miller: Does He Speak to the Present?" *New York Times*, February 7, 1971, sec. 2, p. 17.

Raines, Mary B. "*The Price*." *Library Journal,* April 15, 1968: 1,649–1,650.

Robinson, James A. "Both His Sons: Arthur Miller's *The Price* and Jewish Assimilation." In *Staging Difference: Cultural Pluralism in American Theatre and Drama*, edited by Marc Maufort, 121–139. (New York: Lang, 1995).

Schiff, Ellen. "Myths and Stock Types." *From Stereotype to Metaphor: The Jew in Contemporary Drama*. Albany: State University of New York Press, 1982: 68–73.

Simon, John. "Settling the Account." *Commonweal,* March 1, 1968: 655–656.

Weales, Gerald. "All about talk: Arthur Miller's *The Price*." *Ohio Review* 13, no. 2 (Winter 1972): 74–84.

Willett, Ralph W. "A Note on Arthur Miller's *The Price*." *Journal of American Studies* 5 (December 1971): 307–310.

Winegarten, Renee. "The World of Arthur Miller." *Jewish Quarterly* 17 (Summer 1969): 48–53.

"The Price—The Power of the Past" (1999)

Written as a response to a BROADWAY revival of Miller's 1968 play, *The Price*, this short essay first appeared in the *New York Times* and then was reprinted in *Echoes Down the Corridor* (2000). Miller begins by admitting to the semiautobiographical nature of the play and outlines the plot. Discussing what he feels to be the lasting significance of its themes, he asserts that he wrote *The Price* in 1967 as a reaction to the VIETNAM WAR and a disturbing surge of avant-garde plays in the tradition of ABSURDISM. "I was moved," he explains, "to write a play that might confront and confound both."

While Miller enjoys absurd humor, he states that the determination of absurdist playwrights of the 1960s to find fault with traditional theater and refusal to create character, structure, or plot in their works is, in his opinion, detrimental to good drama. He also feels that such theater, which seemed concerned only with the immediate present, could not adequately respond to the situation in Vietnam by identifying "its roots in the past." Miller blames the United States's "rigid anticommunist theology" born in the 1940s and panicked division of Vietnam to prevent Ho Chi Minh taking full control for the loss of U.S. and Vietnamese life in the 1960s and 1970s. Miller explains how he wanted to reconfirm "the power of the past" to try to make sense of such insanity by openly depicting the process of cause and effect: "If the play does not utter the word Vietnam, it speaks to a spirit of unearthing the real that seemed to have nearly gone from our lives." In *The Price,* the past that intrudes is the specter of the WALL STREET CRASH and the 1930s, but it is one that for Miller proves that life has a certain structure, with "beginnings, middles and a consequential end," just like a good play.

"The Prophecy" (1961)

This lengthy short story was originally published in *Esquire* in 1961 and seems influenced by Miller's tumultuous marriage of the time to Marilyn Monroe, being a tale of misunderstanding and evasion between several couples. Miller and Monroe divorced in 1961, and there is much in the portrait of the character Joseph Kersh to compare him to Miller. The story was reprinted in Miller's 1967 collection *I Don't Need You Any More* and again in *The Misfits and Other Stories* (1987). "The Prophecy" depicts the relationships of several couples, some adulterous, who live their lives behind masks, fearful of the truth, and unable to understand one another's needs. At times, those masks lift and allow for some progression, but mostly, despite the story's title, they struggle through in the dark, not knowing what the future will hold.

The story sets its initial mood by evoking winter as a depressing time of year when things and people can too easily be hurt or broken. The weather forces people, trapped in their homes, to turn inward and to make life-changing decisions. This apparently happens to several of the couples in the story who are separated or divorced by its end. Only Stowe and Cleota Rummel remain happily together, albeit trapped in an almost mindless routine. Married for 30 years, the pea in Cleota's bed of happiness is

Alice, Stowe's older sister, who holds an insistent claim on her brother that Cleota finds discomfiting. Alice, though, will die in the spring and leave Cleota sole access to Stowe. But when the story begins, she is very much alive, and Stowe is abandoning his wife to escape the winter's cold, heading down alone to Florida to help with an installation of his work.

Stowe is a celebrated architect in his mid-fifties. His workspace is strewn with the detritus of past experiments and careers, but he has found his groove, and he designs one successful building after another. He is apparently secure in a life of routine, although occasionally bored by its consistency. His wife Cleota, age 49, is upset at his decision to leave, but when he makes her laugh on his departure, he placates her, reminding her of the man with whom she first fell in love. Once gone, she begins to feel liberated, looking forward to being in the house alone and unsupervised. However, the thought that if Stowe died she would be like this forever unnerves her, and she is grateful that she has dinner guests coming soon.

Alice arrives first. Annoyed that she has not been invited to the dinner party, she enters on the pretense of needing to call to get her phone serviced, although being on the same line, she knows that Cleota's phone is down too. Cleota resents her sister-in-law's intrusion, feeling that she has come to assert her rights over Stowe and his house. Alice knows that Cleota resents her and feels that it is unreasonable, but she sees it as inevitable, given her assessment of Cleota as "Eternally Dissatisfied" and in need of someone to oppose. Freed by Stowe's absence, Cleota rudely sends his sister away, nastily hoping that Alice will die.

Cleota recalls her father, an unlucky anthropologist who drowned, but who was nevertheless contented in a life guided by passion. She feels that she lacks his centeredness and blames Alice for intruding in her relationship with Stowe. Cleota's dinner guests consist of an old school friend, Lucretia; her houseguest, a Jewish seer Madamme Lhevine; and a past neighbor, John Trudeau, who is visiting the area with his mistress, Eve Saint Bleu. The mix is awkward and the party drags until Lucretia suggests that Lhevine tell Cleota's fortune. Declining,

Lhevine suggests that Cleota is "there already" and needs no help. This intrigues and confuses Cleota, who goes to get coffee. She wonders why her practical friend would believe in such a woman but has the insight that Lucretia is in trouble and that her marriage is on the rocks. Her "prophecy" comes true as Lucretia joins her and confesses that she is getting divorced. Trudeau announces that he must leave—his girlfriend is upset at Lhevine's insistence that her aunt could not have been a gypsy fortune-teller—and Cleota senses that he, too, is desperately unhappy.

Left alone, the three women drink, and Cleota becomes attracted to Lhevine's philosophy about the power of people's inner voices. Lhevine does not read fortunes so much as people—she has a knack of seeing beneath the masks. She tells Cleota that the old woman "will live longer than he," correcting herself from her first statement of the "older woman." Cleota assumes that this refers to Alice and Stowe and is devastated that her dreaded sister-in-law will outlast her husband and never allow her to possess him completely.

In his late thirties, Joseph Kersh comes to the door looking for company and is welcomed. Uncertain of joining a group of drunken women, he nevertheless enters and prepares to be the person whom he believes that Cleota expects to see. He suspects that Cleota is unhappy, and he keeps secret his own unhappiness, being married to a woman he does not love. Lhevine reads him with a perspicacity that unnerves him. Joseph feels himself superior to women and dislikes being recognized so clearly by a female; he switches quickly from attraction to repulsion. He is as self-centered and conceited as most, although he works hard at conveying the opposite impression. When he, too, mentions that he had a gypsy aunt, they all fall about laughing, making him even more self-conscious.

Lhevine and Lucretia leave, but Cleota begs Joseph to stay. He thinks that she wants to seduce him, but it is more that she fears being alone. She tells him of Lhevine's prediction and, to assert herself, tries to attract Joseph. He considers sex with her and although he feels that it would be too awkward, he allows himself to be pressured into

carrying her upstairs. He cannot go through with it though and abruptly leaves. He feels Cleota's anger being aimed at him, but hers is more a general disappointment over life. When she goes to see him the next morning to apologize, sober and shorn of her fear, he views her differently and tries to kiss her, but now she turns him down, although she is flattered.

Some months on, Joseph, having divorced his wife, is in the neighborhood again to sell his country retreat and decides to visit the Rummels. He knows that Alice died in the spring and wonders if Stowe is still alive. He finds Stowe and Cleota out walking together. They are curt with him, conservatively disapproving of his divorcing a woman whom they liked. He leaves, and they walk on and begin to laugh together without the shadow of Alice between them.

When, on her brief visit before the dinner party, Alice had absent-mindedly moved a mask near the phone, Cleota screamed, "*Please* don't, Alice!" She does not want her safe veneer touched by this woman and moves the mask back to its original position as soon as Alice is encouraged to leave. The image of the mask lies behind this whole tale where the majority of characters wear masks to protect themselves from the uncertain danger of being fully known, even as they seek to see beneath the masks of others to understand them better. Beneath her calm exterior, Cleota is desperately unhappy with her life, seeing death ahead without having reached fulfillment, and Alice's view of her as "Eternally Dissatisfied" seems accurate. When Trudeau, with his young mistress, was about to leave, Cleota imagines "a slight shift in his eyes confessing to her that his life was misery," and again we see someone living a lie, cheating on his lovely wife, and not even enjoying it. Her friend Lucretia has been pretending that she has had a marriage for the past few years, but after a few drinks, she finally admits that her husband is effectively gone from her life. Alcohol, it seems, allows people to drop their masks for a time.

When Joseph arrives, we meet another deeply unhappy character beneath his jovial veneer as he sorts through his collection of masks before selecting which role to play: "With women, he usually found himself behind any one of various masks, depending on the situation." A Jewish writer whose works are fraught with easy moral lessons, his own life is far more complicated. He is caught in a marriage to a woman who loves him and whom he no longer loves. His experience with Cleota allows him finally to face this truth and to get a divorce, but he also will lose his friendship with the Rummels.

Madame Lhevine's real ability is to see beneath people's masks and to recognize their true selves, but even she can be misleading. Her prophecy that the old woman "will live longer than he" is of course vague, and it is Cleota who takes it to refer to Alice and Stowe. Cleota's understanding is wrong, unlike her premonition about Lucretia. Since it is Alice who dies first, one wonders to whom Lhevine's prophecy might have really referred, maybe even to Cleota as she has begun to view herself as old? Or does the central prophecy's inaccuracy merely underline the pointlessness of trying to foretell the future, suggesting that it is more worthwhile to live in the present, however limited that may be. The final image of Stowe and Cleota laughing together is a positive one, however long it may last.

For Malcolm Bradbury, the story captures "the sensation of life, its moments of senselessness, its challenge, and its metaphysical difficulties," while CHRISTOPHER BIGSBY sees it as "a judgement on a decade." He reads the tale as an indictment of "a society seemingly content to embrace materialism, substitute mysticism for religion and sexual and psychological game-playing for an engaged life." Several couples in the tale exemplify the impermanence of relationships, and although Cleota and Stowe survive, Bigsby questions the monotony of their routine life and their "bland withdrawal of commitment."

FURTHER READING

Bigsby, Christopher. "Fiction." *Arthur Miller: A Critical Study*. New York: Cambridge University Press, 2005, 444–472.

Bradbury, Malcolm. "Arthur Miller's Fiction." In *The Cambridge Companion to Arthur Miller*, edited by Christopher Bigsby, 211–229. (Cambridge, England: Cambridge University Press, 1997).

The Pussycat and the Expert Plumber Who Was a Man (1940)

The Pussycat and the Expert Plumber Who Was a Man, for which Miller was reportedly paid $100, was broadcast in 1940 as part of the *Columbia Workshop* series and subsequently was published in William Kozlenko's *One Hundred Non-Royalty Radio Plays* (1941). Subtitled "a fantasy," this radio play's fanciful scenario about a cat, called Tom Thomas, who runs for mayor and wins is an early example of Miller's caustic, ironic humor. With its puns, witticisms, and almost slapstick situations, this might well be viewed as Miller's first comedy, albeit not his strongest. In it, he derides public figures, especially politicians, as corrupt and self-involved and mocks the integrity of the press, as well as the gullibility and foolishness of the voting public. A modern take on "The Emperor's New Clothes," the little boy becomes Sam, an expert plumber, who has the integrity to be incorruptible and to speak the truth despite a sycophantic majority.

The play begins with George and Adele Beeker being awakened one night by their cat, Tom, who speaks aloud to them in English. Terrified, believing their cat to be possessed, the Beekers panic but are calmed as Tom explains how he taught himself human speech. He announces his plan to run for mayor and blackmails George into assisting him by threatening to tell his wife about an affair. Blackmail will be the key to his future success as he has a spy network of cats that have unearthed "enough on every big man in this town to make him do whatever I command." Those without a guilty secret he plans to smear by making one up, knowing that he can get the press to print it. He needs George to write letters and keep records.

Tom accosts the incumbent Mayor Johnson whom he blackmails with information on tax evasion and bribery into recommending Tom for office. The mayor tries to kill him but stops when Tom reveals that he has arranged for full disclosure on his death. Aware that people are unlikely to vote for a feline openly, Tom plans to offer the public a positive-sounding but faceless name for which to vote. Brief scenes at the local gas station, hairdressing parlor, and dry cleaners indicate that his strategy works as, in the absence of information, people create their own ideal image of the candidate. Tom wins, but the mayor is worried as to what will happen when they see that they have voted for a cat when people gather at City Hall to meet their new mayor. Tom brings in leading townsman Dan Billings to bribe and blackmail him into publicly announcing that the new mayor is wonderful but shy and too busy to meet anyone. Tom then announces his plan to run for governor.

He expands his spy-cat network across the state and obtains the information to blackmail all of the key people who are needed to promote his campaign. At the convention site, Sam, a plumber is working in the room next to Tom's and decides to sneak a look at this exciting new candidate. Horrified to discover a cat, he plans to tell everyone what he has seen. Tom offers him a fortune to stay quiet, insisting that there is no real difference between a man and a cat, so why not let him govern? Sam insists that, unlike a cat that is only out for itself, a man can have integrity; he proves this by exposing Tom. The crowd chases Tom off, and he returns to the Beekers. There, he reveals to George his discovery that cats and men are different, as some men are capable of ideals and are unafraid to speak the truth. George persuades him to return to acting like a cat.

Because he had no record, it was easy for voters to imagine Tom as anything that they want him to be; he became a blank slate on which they wrote their dreams. Tom represents the all-too-common politician in Miller's view, a politician who is all talk and mirrors but no substance; a man who is more concerned with gaining power than contributing to the social good. Tom believed that he could never be exposed because everyone could be either blackmailed or bribed into toeing the line. What Miller also suggests is that despite a self-interested majority, there remain sufficient people of insight and integrity in society to counter this and to ensure that justice prevails. The fact that he gives this role to a lowly plumber and pointedly

privileges a member of the proletariat with having innate goodness is suggestive of his socialist leanings of the time.

On March 16, 1998, as part of the SIGNATURE THEATER's season of Miller plays, following a discussion between Miller and Charlie Rose, *The Pussycat and the Expert Plumber Who Was a Man* was given a special stage performance at the New Victory Theater, featuring Matthew Broderick and Rebecca Schull. This was later broadcast on National Public Radio.

"Rain in a Strange City" (1974)

"Rain in a Strange City" is a short impressionistic prose poem about the positive effects of rainy days. Accompanied by a photograph of people scurrying in a London rain shower, Miller wrote this philosophical piece for *Travel and Leisure* magazine in 1974, and it was later reprinted in *Echoes Down the Corridor* (2000). It reflects in part Miller's extensive travels from Moscow to Dublin, travels that include Paris, Budapest, Stockholm, Vienna, Rome, and Mexico City, along with his vision of a united and peaceful world.

Written one chilly late morning as he sits looking out on a rainy day, Miller feels connected to all the cities where he has been, their differences leveled during a rainfall that makes all behave in the same way to reveal a common humanity. The piece illustrates Miller's sense of the universal as he describes how rain converts all cities into the same vision and leads people to join together in camaraderie against the wet. Miller offers quixotic lists of things that must be hidden from rain and things that can enjoy it, suggesting a comforting two-sided nature of life. "It is perhaps that nothing can be done," is a mantra to which he returns, suggesting the inevitability of rain, that forces people to suffer it without complaint, and allows them to relax their resistance and become friendlier and less aggressive to one another, even halting armies in their tracks.

The Reason Why (1970)

Written as a short play in the late 1960s partly as a response to the U.S. involvement in Vietnam, *The Reason Why* is a conversation between two friends, Charles and Roger, on the nature of killing and the pointlessness of war. Urged by producer Gino Giglio, Miller rewrote this into a short film, and director Paul Leaf was invited to shoot the 14-minute film on Miller's estate in ROXBURY, CONNECTICUT, in 1970. It stars ELI WALLACH and Robert Ryan as Charles and Roger and the voice of Miller's sister, JOAN COPELAND, as Charles's offstage wife.

The men have a quiet conversation about the reasons why people might shoot at something as they sit outside and watch the local wildlife. The suggestion is made that killing may be both addictive and dehumanizing as Charles explains how, two years previously, he slaughtered 42 woodchucks in an effort to save his vegetable garden and felt "all emptied out afterwards." It is a clear metaphor for the U.S. war against the Vietnamese people. In response, Roger talks about his wartime experiences of killing. Watching a woodchuck on the hill before them, Charles takes a shot and misses, but then he shoots again and kills it. Although he had momentarily begun to admire the woodchuck as a living creature, he turns against it, calling it a rat. When his friend asks him, "What the hell you do that for?" he can only reply, "I dunno." Thus, in this antiwar piece, Miller conveys the mindlessness of killing that destroys not only the victim but also something of the killer's own humanity and intellect. This, to Miller, is part of the real cost of war. The answer to the title, which refers to the reason that people kill, Miller suggests, is because the human animal has an impulse to violence and murder that is dangerous to ignore. This was staged as a one-act play at The New Theater Workshop in 1970.

FURTHER READING

Funke, Lewis. "Stars Help Arthur Miller Film TV Antiwar Allegory." *New York Times*, November 17, 1969, 58.

Resurrection Blues (2002)

In 1981, Miller traveled to Venezuela, and the following year he visited Colombia. These two trips gave him the idea for a play based on a fictitious South American banana republic that would both satirize the kind of governments that he saw operating in that area and the hypocrisy of U.S. involvement. Despite the serious nature of its targets, *Resurrection Blues*, as it came to be called, is fairly unusual for Miller in that it is presented as a full-blown comedy with one liners, stereotypical comic characters (including a stoned hippie and a rapacious advertising executive), and numerous innuendoes about erectile dysfunction (the title itself offering yet another).

Miller admitted that he also intended for the play to highlight the "vulgarity and the spiritual wasteland of the communication industry" and that he chose the ultimate bad-taste reality-show scenario to do this—the U.S. film crew's intention to film a real-life crucifixion and to intersperse it with advertisements for medical products. The idea echoes Miller's 1992 satirical op-ed "Get it Right. Privatize Executions," in which he suggests that it would make sense to carry out the execution of convicted criminals in large sporting arenas and charge for admission to help pay for the prison system. Although in neither case does he view the attempt as wise, what he recognizes is that there are too many people who would want to watch such spectacles, which says something fairly negative about the state of society. He was also writing this play around the time of the controversy over whether or not to film the execution of Timothy McVeigh (the final court decision was not to allow it).

Resurrection Blues premiered at the Guthrie Theater in Minneapolis in 2002 to fairly little acclaim, and there followed further regional productions in San Diego and Philadelphia, as well as a reading at the WILLIAMSTOWN THEATRE FESTIVAL, but Miller was unable to get the play financed for BROADWAY. Kevin Spacey, as artistic director of The Old Vic in GREAT BRITAIN offered to produce the British premiere in 2006 for which Miller had just completed the rewriting before he died. Robert Altman was invited to direct—the first time he had done so for the stage—and he gathered an all-star cast that included Matthew Modine, Maximillian Schell, Neve Campbell, Jane Adams, and James Fox. There were rumors that he would follow the production with a film version, but it received negative reviews, and they were forced to close a week early.

At the Guthrie, Miller gave the theater permission to print his script. There are some differences between this and the version published in 2006 by Penguin. In the interim, Miller made various changes, mostly minor ones that altered the nuances of certain characters (referenced in the relevant character discussions) and cuts to streamline the play. The most significant revisions were the eradication of an entire scene that he had written between Jeanine, Henri, and Emily in which Henri brings Emily to talk to his daughter. Several references to U.S. support of Felix's government that was providing him with equipment and expertise to eradicate the popular guerrilla front were also cut. Miller refines much of the information from the missing scene into a short prologue that is spoken by Jeanine as a monologue from her wheelchair, but it leaves audiences with just the guilt for encouraging such television stunts as the desire to film a crucifixion. The following synopsis is based on the later Penguin edition, on which the play's British premiere was based.

SYNOPSIS

The initial prologue depicts Jeanine, who is speaking from a wheelchair and is covered in bandages. She explains how she jumped out of a window to commit suicide. Her brigade had been captured, and everyone was shot but her because she is related to the country's dictator. As she fell from the window, she experienced a sense of release and gained a clearer view of life. She asserts a new faith in the world and is vaguely pleased that her father, Henri Schultz, has returned to the country to be with her. Jeanine mourns for a nation that she describes as a place of "death and dreams" and decimated by greed and a military government. She relates how an unnamed man joined her on the ground where she fell and how she now feels redeemed by his love. She wheels her chair into the offstage darkness as the stage brightens.

Scene one takes place in the office of General Felix Barriaux, the nation's chief of state. Henri arrives to see his cousin earlier than scheduled, and Felix tells his secretary to interrupt him after 15 minutes. He also asks her to forget about the previous evening when he had been unable to perform with her in bed. He greets Henri, and we learn that the country has been in a protracted state of civil war, although a relatively quiet one at the moment. They talk about Jeanine's fall, but Felix appears unsympathetic and more interested in a recommendation for a good dentist. Henri wants to talk about something, but Felix keeps going off at a tangent. Henri reminds Felix of when, as students, they had visited the villages and had been appalled at the living conditions. He berates Felix because nothing has apparently changed since he has been in control. Felix points to some new developments, but Henri insists that the nation is in a bad way, commenting on its air pollution, poor infrastructure, and a dead baby whom he saw lying in a gutter.

Henri is also worried that he had not sufficiently supported his daughter in the past. He asks Felix about a man named Ralph, whom the peasants are worshipping as the Messiah. Felix has him in custody as his followers have killed police officers. Henri asks about the rumor that Felix plans to crucify him and warns that this would be a terrible idea and might provoke conflict, but Felix wants to make a strong statement to scare the people. He views Henri's solicitation for the people skeptically, because Henri is one of the 2 percent who own 96 percent of the nation's land. Henri plans to sell some property, but Felix believes that this would be a pointless gesture. He shares news of an offer of $75 million from a U.S. agency to film the crucifixion (a sign of inflation as in the 2002 version this had only been $25 million). Henri is horrified at the thought, especially considering the advertising that they will include, and he tries to talk Felix out of it, but Felix is convinced that Ralph is an impostor and wants the money to restore the country.

Henri admits that he saw Ralph being arrested and that his demeanor made him think that the peasants could be right. When Felix opens the door to show him Ralph in his cell, a white light pours in, coming from Ralph. Felix still insists that he is nothing special. Henri is less certain and confesses that Ralph has made him reassess his own life. This makes Felix pause. He offers to call the United States, possibly to reconsider.

We move to the mountaintop on which they plan to film. The director Emily Shapiro and her producer Skip Cheeseboro enjoy the breathtaking view. They share memories of past advertising campaigns that they have shot together as the Captain introduces Henri and comments on the impending crucifixion. Emily does not know about her assignment, and Skip tries to break it to her. Two soldiers enter and ignore Skip's pleas to stop building the crucifix, but Emily finally understands and is horrified. Skip tries flattery and bribery to keep Emily involved, but she finds the plan "deeply offensive." Then she calls her mother to remind her to feed her cats.

Emily mentions the crucifixion to her mother, who seems unconcerned after learning that the person to be crucified is not Jewish. Emily is pregnant and just committed to a new apartment, so she cannot afford to walk out, especially as she left a shoot the previous year and could lose her job permanently if she goes again. Cameraman Phil and soundwoman Sarah enter, and Sarah grabs the telephone to find out the results of her pregnancy test. Phil is surprised but not outraged to learn about the shoot. Emily asks Skip about arrangements regarding having a doctor present or giving the man painkillers. Skip is more worried about having the scene look authentic and threatens Emily that she will not work again if she leaves.

Felix arrives and is attracted to Emily, asking her to dinner. They plan further how to do the crucifixion, but then Felix confesses that Ralph has escaped. Skip is upset, but Emily and the film crew cheer. Felix assures Skip that they will recapture him, but Skip worries about his exclusivity if there is a delay. Felix explains that his soldiers will shoot anyone who tries to get through, and Skip is relieved. Emily agrees to dine with Felix, while Henri asks how Ralph escaped. The guards say that he walked through the wall, but Felix does not believe them. After Felix leaves, Henri asks Emily to get Felix to stop this, and she agrees to try.

The next scene shows Felix interrogating a new prisoner, Stanley, one of Ralph's apostles. Felix bribes him to say where Ralph is, but Stanley does not know. When Felix asks if he thinks Ralph is the son of God, Stanley is uncertain. Stanley tries to explain Ralph's relationship to love, and Felix is intrigued to learn that when Ralph lies next to Jeanine and lights up, she has an orgasm. Ralph frequently changes his name to avoid becoming a "celebrity guru," and Stanley says that Ralph did walk through the wall. Felix now wants to meet Ralph to see if he can help his erectile dysfunction, but he suspects that Stanley has been sent. Stanley admits that he allowed himself to be arrested on purpose but only to have the chance to explain the situation. Ralph wants to be crucified as he thinks that it may help restore the people's faith. Felix loses patience, but when he takes Stanley to jail, the room lights up to indicate Ralph's return. It then goes dark as he leaves once more, and Stanley suggests that he was providing a distraction to help a friend.

The next scene shows Henri talking to Skip. Citing the Egyptian lack of images of Jewish captives and the fabrication of the Gulf of Tonkin incident that led the United States into the Vietnam War as evidence, Henri suggests to Skip that Ralph does not exist but is just a creation of their collective imagination, each seeing in him the things that they most need. He insists that people live mostly in the realm of imagination to avoid the unpleasantness of life. After insisting that they must kill Ralph before he forces everyone to face their painful realities, Henri tells Skip to leave. Skip refuses, seeing himself as not responsible in any way, even though, as Henri points out, it is his money that may force Felix to crucify a man.

That evening, Felix and Emily dine, openly flirting. Emily likes him and is sympathetic about his erectile dysfunction, suggesting that it may be having a job that demands that he suppress himself too much. She senses that he is uncertain about killing Ralph and agrees to sleep with him if he lets Ralph go. He accepts, and they exit, heading for the villages.

The final scene begins the following day with Jeanine rising from her wheelchair. Henri is amazed as her spine had been crushed, and he realizes that Ralph must have helped her. He asks Jeanine if she knows where he is, insisting that he wants to stop the crucifixion. Jeanine is unsure if she can trust him; she had followed his lead in joining the guerillas, but he had left the country, distracted by philosophy.

Felix arrives with Emily; they have been making love much of the night, and he is elated. He was also surprised at how much good the villagers' belief in Ralph has elicited and wants to offer him a government position, having sent Stanley with a message. Jeanine is skeptical Ralph will accept, thinking that he would prefer Felix to resign. Felix assures her that he is sick of the killing and wants change. Emily suggests that Felix announce that Ralph is no longer wanted, but Felix explains that he would lose face by this.

Stanley returns to tell them that Ralph (who now calls himself Charley) is undecided about the crucifixion, unsure if people will feel let down if he backs out. Stanley suggests that they forget about Charley as he is doing more good than harm, but Felix refuses, viewing Charley as dangerous. Stanley asks to speak to Jeanine alone, so Felix and Emily leave. Stanley explains how the villages are competing to be the crucifixion site for the honor, but also in hopes that it will increase their property values and create a tourism boom. He asks Jeanine to talk Charley out of letting himself be killed. He suggests that if Felix will stop his persecutions, Charley might just disappear.

A light appears above them, evidently Charley, and everyone gathers. Jeanine expresses her love, while Stanley tells him to leave. Felix offers to call off the search if he leaves quietly and agrees to Jeanine's additional requests that he empty the jails and prosecute his torturers. Skip is outraged at this breach of contract. He pleads with Charley to come and be crucified for the good of his company's investors. Wanting the money, Felix changes his mind and asks Ralph to let himself be crucified, but Emily tells him that he would do better to stay away. Henri thanks him for helping his daughter and apologizes for his past neglect. Even the cameraman admits that he would rather not have to film him being crucified. Felix decides that he will

keep the advance that he has been given, and as Skip argues with him over this, the light fades. They all weep and say "Good-bye," except for Skip who angrily storms off. Jeanine suggests that Charley might come back another time, and Stanley has the last word, as he welcomes Charley to drop by anytime, he salutes, and walks off alone.

CRITICAL COMMENTARY

Miller was fascinated by the idea of the crucifix and what it represents. As a pacifist and coming from a religious background that has few icons beyond the Bible, the idea of a faith that is represented by an icon of torture no doubt intrigued him. The uncomfortable connection between religion and violence is evident in people's reactions to the potential Messiah. The decision to repeat the crucifixion reflects a world that has learned very little in the past 2,000 years. As Stanley explains, the villagers are vying for the privilege of hosting the crucifixion for both the honor and in hope that it will raise their property prices because the pursuit of money has become the dominant faith. A sense of civilization become utterly corrupt pervades the play, while Marxist principle is reduced to a bunch of drug dealers.

However, the play is neither a critique of Christianity nor necessarily of politics (except obliquely—especially with the eradication of most of the references to U.S. involvement in their civil war and drug trade), but it is an exploration of faith in an increasingly cynical world. Even Stanley and Jeanine, Ralph's most loyal followers, remain uncertain as to his divinity. Stanley's life has been one long quest for something in which to believe, but now that he may have found it, he cannot trust his own judgment. In a world where so many are seeking faith, it has become increasingly difficult to settle for any one belief.

The return of Christ as a rebuke to contemporary values is not a new conceit, and Miller confronts it with comic blatancy. Ralph's request, "Just don't do bad things. Especially when you know they're bad. Which you mostly do," seems reasonable, but when you make your decisions based on a capitalist economy rather than from a moral basis, then bad things seem inevitable. Ralph must leave by the close because the world is not yet ready for the Second Coming, and despite his message of love, violence seems to be the inevitable result if he remains.

Miller is also targeting the crass, mercenary opportunism of the media, which is fed by the increasing materialism of people who are caught in a capitalist culture. In this unnamed country, 2 percent of the people own 96 percent of the land and have very little thought for the disenfranchised peasantry. Felix advises Henri against helping them, explaining that "You can't teach a baboon to play Chopin," showing how far he has dehumanized his fellow citizens. The improvements that he plans should he get the $75 million do not seem to address the fact that in one of the most fertile places on Earth, people are starving. Felix is, of course, just emulating the social outlook of the dominant society. The U.S.'s interest in his country is purely commercial, they have been turning a blind eye to the revolution and its atrocities for years. Only now have they come to film an event that they believe will gain them a huge bonus in advertising: the exclusive worldwide rights to a lengthy crucifixion. The fact that no one even questions people's desire to watch such an event says as much about their own lack of humanity as those who might tune in.

Miller is not shy of pointedly exposing the arrogance of the first world toward the third. For Skip, it is fine to film a crucifixion as this is the kind of barbaric thing that they do in such a country, but he insists that it is different in the United States. However, the truth is that he is just as uncivilized because he is condoning such atrocity by his desire to film and make money from it. Indeed, Miller wants us to recognize that the United States is no different from this fictitious state. Skip refuses to recognize the moral lack of difference between performing a crucifixion and filming it, but that does not make him right. He fatuously intones, "I will not superimpose American mores on a dignified foreign people," but by turning an execution into a media event, this is precisely what he is doing, and they are not the American mores of which Miller is most proud.

Emily's ability to make "real things look fake, and that makes them emotionally real" strikes at the heart of a commercial culture in which everything is airbrushed and people's emotions cannot ever be truly felt. This seems to be a more modern take on HENRIK IBSEN's concept of the "life-lie." It is further backed by Henri's suggestion that people live most of the time in the realm of imagination because there they can control their lives (and deaths) better and avoid the unpleasantness of life. Both Miller and Ibsen are concerned with the dangers that accrue when a person sets aside his or her own reality and presents a fake persona to the world.

Despite much humor in the rest of Miller's work, his evident comic intent in this play surprised and annoyed many critics. The comedy is not subtle, but nor was it meant to be. In large part, such black, satirical comedies depend on the outrageous ridiculousness of their premise and the antisocial behavior of their characters to make their point. For a mass murderer, Felix is deliberately depicted as endearing and comic to show us how complacent toward violence we have become. That he plans to crucify a man to prove that he is not the Messiah, and by so doing suggest to the world that the man must be, is another incongruity that Miller offers to undercut the authenticity of his claims. Miller mocks his characters as they inhumanely discuss the possibility of literally crucifying someone by having their discussion interrupted first by a hammer and finally by a chainsaw—an old-fashioned execution being facilitated by modern power tools. This ensures that we see both the ridiculousness of their ambition and the unpleasant implication of "the more things change, the more they stay the same." Continuing to defy expectation, Miller has the supposed Messiah's mouthpiece be not some intellectual or saintly person but a burnedout hippie, Stanley. That such a man could speak truths, such as the way to improve the world is to love one another, and speak them on such an incredibly accessible level mocks the audience's expectation rather than the idea itself.

FIRST PERFORMANCE

Resurrection Blues opened for a limited run at the Guthrie Theater in Minneapolis, Minnesota, from

August 3 to September 8, 2002, with the following cast:

General Felix Barriaux: John Bedford Lloyd
Henri Schultz: Jeff Weiss
Emily Shapiro: Laila Robins
Skip L. Cheeseboro: David Chandler
Phil: Peter Thoemke
Sarah: Laura Esping
Police Captain: Emil Herrera
Jeanine: Wendy vanden Heuvel
Stanley: Bruce Bohne

Directed by David Esbjornson
Set designed by Christine Jones
Produced by Guthrie Theater.

INITIAL REVIEWS

The play has elicited mixed reviews of every production thus far, but they have not been as resoundingly negative as some would imply. Also, given the brevity of most of the runs, especially with the British premiere, there is an implication that the problem may be as much with the production as with the play. At the play's premiere, Michael Billington called it "a funny, pertinent and sharp-toothed satire aimed at the materialist maladies of modern America," and although Elysa Gardner was initially surprised by its "darkly comic tone," she found Miller's ear "still finely tuned to the pulse of modern life." Robert King enjoyed the play's ironies and felt it to be insightful, while Rohan Preston enthusiastically declared it to be, "a play about America. It is about how values can be corrupted by a military–political–electronic–media axis. It is about religious succor and the power of the imagination and art in a time when rampant materialism crushes all things illusory."

On the more negative side, Sarah Rudolph may praise Miller as "an astute social critic" and compliment the play's "biting wit," but she felt it "too unwieldy" and "burdened by stylistic contradictions." Bruce Weber, meanwhile, gave the *New York Times* verdict that the play was an "indignant" but "disappointingly unpersuasive work. . . . Mr. Miller too often falls on the wrong side of cliché," and his "persistent sex jokes are juvenile and truly beneath a playwright of Mr. Miller's stature."

Most negative reviews seem to reflect this affectation, that the play is bad because it is not a typical Miller play.

SCHOLARSHIP

Being a recent play with few productions that was only published in 2006, critics have had little opportunity to consider *Resurrection Blues* beyond reviews. However, CHRISTOPHER BIGSBY, Kate Egerton, Joseph Kane, and Jeffrey Mason have already published fairly detailed analyses. Kane and Egerton both concentrate on the play's comic aspects. Kane explains that comedy is "nothing new" for Miller, pointing out various prior examples and relating the play to earlier Miller material. Egerton offers a view of the play as a parody of modern materialism, in which the real likelihood of a crucifixion taking place is never seriously entertained. She and Mason both view this unnamed nation as the U.S.'s doppelganger. Basing his analysis on the earlier version, Mason considers Miller's history of activism and views the play as Miller's "cynical denunciation of a post-millennial age when the values and aspirations he so long defended are, perhaps, no longer viable." This is not the first time that Miller has revised a play to allow it to become more optimistic. The lines on which Mason bases this evaluation were later cut, but his analysis of the play's exploration of power and ironic heart remain completely valid, and he makes some useful connections to Miller's earlier plays. Bigsby, also working from the earlier script, offers some interesting background history to the play's development and assesses it as the attempt to depict a world "not only with no sense of values but in which there is no sense of the real."

CHARACTERS

Barriaux, Felix As the chief of state of an unnamed nation high in the Andes, Felix appears to be humorously self-concerned and resistant to belief—a South American version to some degree of *The Ride down Mt. Morgan*'s Lyman Felt. His life philosophy is "fuck them before they can fuck you," and although he saved Jeanine, he let her 15 comrades die and shows little compassion for her suffering since then. He initially refuses to believe that Ralph could be anything more than a charlatan, like himself. Although as a student he had been motivated to initiate changes in his impoverished nation, once in power he has done little but rule with an iron fist. The new buildings, industries, and stores cater only to the upper level of society and have not altered the poor living conditions of the majority. He breaks unions by killing the organizers, executes guerrilla fighters without compunction, and has a reputation for torture. He uses his position to maintain the ruling elite, having decided that the peasants could not handle or appreciate any greater prosperity. Under his rule, girls of eight are forced to become prostitutes, the drug trade is rampant, and dead babies lie in the street. Although he says that he hopes to use the $75 million from the U.S. deal for the good of the nation, he is more interested in getting shoes for his police and dental treatment for prostitutes than in providing basic necessities for his people.

Discontented, Felix sleeps in a different place every night for fear of assassination and has been suffering from erectile dysfunction for some time, a clear symbol for the inefficacy of his rule. He and his cousin Henri are both growing old and losing their vitality. Felix's attraction to Emily appears to revive him on more than one level, as he visits the villages and has a new respect for the peasantry and for Ralph. His offer to bring Ralph into his government seems genuine as is his realization that they should be evolving toward a DEMOCRACY if they are to survive, but the lure of that money ends up overwhelming Felix and forcing his hand to try to persuade Ralph to be crucified.

Cheeseboro, Skip L. As the producer who has set up the deal to film a live crucifixion, it is clear that Skip has little sense of morality and holds human life cheap. His relief that Felix would kill any outsiders trying to access their site to ensure his exclusivity is further evidence of this. His only concern is to make money. He tries a variety of approaches from flattery to threats to get Emily's compliance and is the only character at the close who refuses to say goodbye to Ralph, instead stomping off in anger. His argument with Ralph, that if he fails to be crucified, Skip's stockholders will lose money,

shows exactly where his priorities lie. He defends his choice to film the crucifixion by asserting that Ralph is a dangerous rebel, but when Henri points out that if Felix cannot find Ralph he will crucify someone innocent to satisfy Skip, we can see that the guilt of the person crucified does not truly concern Skip. He refuses to accept any responsibility at all for the crucifixion, even while it is his money that is provoking Felix to go through with it, even against his own conscience. The more he tries to sanitize the crucifixion, insisting that there can be no screaming or assistance, even while he will not allow for drugs or tequila to calm the victim, the more we realize that it will never take place.

Jeanine Despite her initial monologue, the character of Jeanine is less developed in the rewrite of the play with the eradication of a lengthy conversation between her, Emily, and Henri. After finishing college, she was inspired by her father to join the rebels as he had done. Unfortunately, he left to study philosophy abroad, apparently abandoning her and the cause. Felix's police captured her whole guerrilla platoon and executed everyone except Jeanine. As his relative, she was allowed to live, but turned to drugs to cope with her survivor guilt. Her husband left her, and after a while, even the drugs were not helping. Feeling an utter failure, she attempted suicide.

It is as much the freeing sensation of falling as waking up beside Ralph empathizing with her pain that makes her reassess her life and decide to live. Although she has a renewed sense of purpose, she broke her spine and is trapped in a wheelchair. Jeanine sees her country as being destroyed by greed and too much killing but is at a loss how to help. As Ralph appears to mend her spine, so too might his message of love lead her to a more fruitful path than the violent cycle of old.

Phil and Sarah The cameraman and the soundwoman are minor roles but contribute to several of the play's themes. Sarah's pregnancy, announced shortly after we hear of Emily's, evokes the possibility of future growth, just as Phil's fairly calm reaction to the news of what he is to film suggests the potential receptivity of the audience. Although neither would absolutely refuse to do their job, both show a preference for not having to film Ralph's crucifixion—cheering at the news that he has escaped—that again reinforces our sense that the crucifixion will not actually happen.

Ralph (Charley)   We never meet Ralph in the play, although his presence is evoked on several occasions by a bright white light. While this could be an allusion to the light-bringing Archangel Raphael, it also allows for Miller to maintain the character's essential ambiguity. Ralph represents pure spiritual love as opposed to the earthly one that Felix pursues, which partly accounts for Felix's initial disdain; He only becomes interested in Ralph on learning that Jeanine appeared to have an orgasm when bathed in Ralph's radiance. Ralph could be a figment of their collective imagination, as Henri suggests, or a real Messiah. Either way, his message of love mostly is overlooked as these people are not yet ready to embrace his simplistic but humanistic vision of a world where people do not do bad and accept responsibility for all other humankind. Jeanine and Stanley invite him to return, and in that possibility, we are left with hope intact.

When Felix initially captures the man whom he ironically views as a dangerous revolutionary leader, Ralph impresses Henri with the way he transcends the violence of his capture, refusing to be drawn in. He escapes by walking through his prison walls and then soon after briefly returns, perhaps to create a diversion to help his follower, Stanley. Stanley acts as his mouthpiece for much of the play, explaining Ralph's indecision over the crucifixion. He is uncertain whether the people would be better served by his allowing himself to be crucified or not, but in the end chooses simply to disappear. Ralph's ambiguity is further heightened by his constant change of name—although he begins the play as Ralph he ends it as Charley—and he has been known by several others. What connects the names seems to be their ordinariness; this entity, after all, is concerned with other people rather than himself, and he displays no ego. Yet his desire not to become a "celebrity guru" or become known as a magician because he can walk through walls also creates a suspicion as to his authenticity, for given the social background from which we must view the play, we can recognize that he may be as obsessed with image as everyone else.

Schultz, Henri   The rewritten version of the play is kinder to Henri, making him seem less materialistic and more genuinely willing to change his way of life. By the close of this version, Henri accepts his responsibility toward his daughter and his country, and there is a sense that his life will change for the better; Ralph has inspired him to love. In the earlier version, it had been Henri who brought the film offer to Felix, and several instances where Jeanine critiques his belief in possessions were cut. In both versions we are told that Henri began as a Marxist who wants to help his country, even while he was one of the richest people in it. He joined the guerrilla force, but soon after, he left to study philosophy; an interest that has taken him all over the world and has led him to recognize Marxism as an outmoded concept. He currently lives in Munich where he lectures in philosophy. Reminiscent of Albert Kroll in *Clara,* who inspired his daughter to go into social work but then let those inspirational values slide in his own life, Henri similarly feels guilty at having abandoned his country and his daughter, Jeanine, soon after she had joined him with the guerrillas. He has recently remarried and returned to his homeland to see if he can help Jeanine recover. Taking his new wife to the villages, he recognizes how little has changed despite decades of revolution, aside from a burgeoning following for a man whom they call Ralph.

Henri is cousin to Felix and spends much of the play trying to advise him and others as to what to do. He is prone, as his daughter complains, to be all talk and no action, overphilosophizing himself into stasis. He is ambivalent toward Ralph, attracted by the man's obvious ability to transcend violence, but at one moment he demands that Ralph be killed to save them all from having to face reality, and the next he implores for Ralph's safety for humanitarian reasons. His reasons for trying to prevent the crucifixion are also ambiguous. Is it to prevent what he thinks may be a resulting escalation of violence, or is it to save face by not having the medical products that his company sells associated with such an event? While his idea that they are all creating Ralph out of their own needs has some credibility—we never see Ralph or hear him speak—this could also be another way in which Henri avoids the truth.

Shapiro, Emily Emily is a conundrum; although she is rightly appalled at the prospect of having to direct the filming of a live crucifixion, her sincerity is undercut by both her banal choice to call her mother to ask her to feed the cats in the middle of the discovery and her decision to go through with it rather than lose her job. She can walk off a shoot where they kill baby seals but apparently not one where they plan to kill a human being in the most gruesome fashion imaginable. She says that she hates what she does, and yet she still does it. She has traveled around the world filming advertisements, but it is only the products that she truly recalls, suggesting that her life has been trapped and reduced by the very luxury items that she sells.

Whether or not she sleeps with Felix from attraction or as a means of getting him to leave Ralph alone is also ambiguous, more so in the rewrite as in the original where she had slept with Felix even before they dined and is far less coy. That she is pregnant, even though uncertain of the identity of father, seems a positive aspect of her character, symbolically suggesting her capability for growth and potential fertility, as opposed to the sterility of Felix when we first meet him. Her constant reminders of how terrible a real crucifixion might be as they nail him, screaming, to the cross with no doctor, medication, or hat both enforce the horror of the intent and assure us that it will never occur, for what Skip wants is a sanitized version of crucifixion, and that simply will not be allowed by Miller.

Stanley As the doped-up hippie, Stanley is somewhat of a cliché, reminiscent of Leonora's son Lawrence from *I Can't Remember Anything*. Stanley has also spent time on an Indian ashram trying to find himself. In addition, he has tried alcohol, alfalfa therapy, Buddhism, and veganism. The irony is that

this social reject is the one who is most attuned to Ralph's message, and he declares it in terms that all can understand but toward which most appear completely blind.

FURTHER READING

Bigsby, Christopher. *"Resurrection Blues." Arthur Miller: A Critical Study*. New York: Cambridge University Press, 2005, 421–436.

Billington, Michael. "The Crucifixion Will Be Televised." *Guardian*, August 21, 2002, n.p.

Egerton, Kate. "A Funny Thing Happened on the Way to the Cross: Arthur Miller's *Resurrection Blues*." *Journal of American Drama and Theater* 18, no. 2 (Spring 2006): 9–26.

Gardner, Elysa. "Miller Imbues *Blues* with Darkly Comic Tone." *USA Today*, August 12, 2002, E1.

Kane, Joseph. "Arthur Miller: Comedian: Comedy that Draws Blood in *Resurrection Blues*." In *Arthur Miller: Twentieth Century Legend*, edited by Syed Mashkoor Ali, 390–408. (Jaipur, India: Surabhi Publications, 2006).

King, Robert L. "Politics, Television, and Theatre." *North American Review* 289 (September/August 2004): 37–42.

Mason, Jeffrey D. "Arthur Miller's Ironic *Resurrection*." *Theatre Journal* 55 (December 2003): 657–677.

Preston, Rohan. "Arthur Miller Lightens Up a Bit in *Resurrection Blues*." *Minneapolis–St. Paul Star Tribune*, August 11, 2002, n.p.

Rothstein, Mervyn. "So Tragic, You Have To Laugh." *New York Times*, July 28, 2002, sec. 2, p. 5.

Rudolph, Sarah J. *"Resurrection Blues/Good Boys." Theatre Journal* 55 (October 2003): 546–549.

Weber, Bruce. "It's Gloves-Off Time for an Angry Arthur Miller." *New York Times*, August 15, 2002, E1.

The Ride down Mt. Morgan (1991)

Foremost in Miller's work has always been the needs, desires and responsibilities of the U.S. family, and even more specifically the U.S. male, who is dealt with in *Death of a Salesman* in 1949 and reconsidered 40 years later through the social climate of the 1980s in the evolving story of Lyman Felt in the play *The Ride down Mt. Morgan.*

There are many similarities between Willy Loman and Lyman Felt beyond the echo in their names. Both are salesmen, selling the materialistic U.S. dream of wealth and success by denying certain aspects of reality. But there is an intrinsic difference; Lyman Felt is what Willy Loman wanted to be: handsome, well liked, and successful. Lyman possesses a self-confidence that Loman cannot attain, partly because he has never faced the ignominy of impending failure. He has been better suited to play the capitalistic game, partly by his more resistant personality and his ability to find scapegoats to deflect his own responsibilities. While Loman was a man who strove against the inherent difficulties of living during the 1940s and the 1950s, Lyman is a man for the 1980s and, unlike Loman, a successful businessman. Where Loman is powerless, Lyman is fully empowered. But we can also see, even more clearly than *Death of a Salesman* displays, just how misguided Willy's desires were as we witness the dangerous and unsatisfactory life that Lyman has created with all those skills and advantages for which Willy longed.

Miller premiered *The Ride down Mt. Morgan* in 1991 in London. Tired of the harsh realities of producing a serious play on the BROADWAY stage, he allowed it to run where he felt it would meet with a warmer and kinder reception. Although a hit in London, the play was not produced in the United States until the summer of 1996 at the WILLIAMSTOWN THEATER FESTIVAL, with slight changes, and with F. Murray Abraham in the lead role. Based on

Scene from the 1996 Williamstown Theatre Festival American premiere of *The Ride down Mt. Morgan,* with Michael Learned, F. Murray Abraham, and Patricia Clarkson. *Courtesy Richard Feldman/Williamstown Theatre Festival Archives.*

the success of this, Miller revised the play for a limited run in New York in 1998 and a subsequent Broadway opening in 2000, both with Patrick Stewart playing Lyman. First published in 1991, the play was published again in 1999 in this revised edition. Although the plot remains essentially the same in both versions, some details have been changed. Essentially, the 1999 version tries to make the transitions between scenes smoother and easier for the audience to follow, deletes the role of the father and references to a child whom Lyman may have fathered with another woman, and slightly alters the ending to make Lyman appear closer to understanding, although the play continues to refuse to give easy solutions. It also adds extra hospital staff who double up as figures in some of Lyman's dream sequences.

SYNOPSIS

Act One

The opening scene reveals Lyman in a hospital bed, his body covered in incapacitating casts, and in the original script, the silent, ghostly presence of his father stands over him. Lyman talks in his sleep, imagining that he is addressing a business conference, while Nurse Logan listens in amusement. Dreaming of his father wakes Lyman up, and he chats with the nurse who fills him in on his injuries, caused by his having skidded his car down a mountain. She worries him by announcing that his wife, Theo, and daughter, Bessie, are waiting to see him; Lyman has been doing something wrong. He tries to imagine what they must be saying as they sit in the waiting room, and we witness the possible scene in which they show a brave face, complain about Lyman's mother being too possessive, and meet Leah, who has also been notified of the accident. Lyman is a bigamist, and Leah is his second wife. The prospect of his two wives meeting both horrifies and fascinates him as he imagines the slowly dawning realization between the two that they are both currently married to the same man. As Theo finally faints from the shock, the scene switches to a subsequent discussion between Leah and Lyman's friend and lawyer, Tom Wilson, as Leah decides what to do about this situation. She is mostly concerned regarding money, wanting to

ensure that their son, Benjamin, is not disinherited. We also learn that the life Lyman has been leading with Leah is entirely different from his life with Theo. With Theo, he played the cautious family man, but with Leah, he liked to take risks.

We learn that Lyman convinced Leah that he had divorced Theo but never actually went through with it. Tom is fascinated by what Lyman has been up to, and he now recalls to Leah a past discussion that he had with Lyman about the feasibility of bigamy, in which Lyman had told him that he was in love with another woman. From Lyman's discussion with Tom, recreated for us on stage, we realize his marriage to Leah was partly a desire to change the life he was leading, in which he was suffering a midlife crisis that was filled with affairs and fears of impending death; he also was still being accosted by people who criticized him for betraying his business partner to the authorities. Leah recreates for Tom the scene telling when she became pregnant with Benjamin; she had refused to continue being the mistress, and Lyman had promised to marry her. Leah was highly attracted to Lyman's great appetite for life, but she is now thoroughly disappointed in him.

The scene returns to Lyman's bedside, and we realize that everything so far may have been purely in his imagination, but then Tom enters and tells Lyman that his two wives have indeed met and that Lyman's imagination has followed reality fairly closely. Theo and Bessie come to talk with him; both are very angry, and Lyman tries to hide by pretending to be asleep as he decides what to do. To Theo's annoyance, Leah joins them. In his imagination, Lyman creates a scene in which, after some initial wrangling, he is able to control all three women, getting Theo and Leah to lie beside him on the bed. He recreates his first liaison with Leah, and they seem close as he confides in her many details about his past and upbringing. In a phone call that he made at this time to Theo, we see that their relationship was far more conventional and less open. But this scene fragments as it switches back to when Theo and Leah first came in, and we see that Lyman's imagination has not created a realistic outcome, as the two women prepare to fight and Lyman loses control.

Act Two

Act two begins with Theo and Tom in the waiting room discussing what Theo should do; she is very confused. Leah joins them and tells them how Lyman's car accident is looking suspiciously like a purposeful act, and they wonder if he might be suicidal. The hostility between Theo and Leah is revealed in numerous petty comments that they make to each other, but both are primarily concerned about how their respective children will cope with this whole mess. Theo is astonished at the different type of person Lyman has been with Leah and is unsure how much to believe. Considering this other side of his nature, she tells Tom about a time that she imagined that Lyman tried to kill her by letting her go into shark-infested waters. She recreates the scene in a number of ways until it becomes unclear as to what really happened—it is even possible that he saved her life. Their marriage has had its ups and downs in the past, and Theo has no idea of what she should do next.

Meanwhile, Lyman is sleeping and having a strange fantasy about his wives that is played out on stage. Theo and Leah seductively compare their culinary skills and seem to be deciding how best to share their husband. At first, their advances seem provocative but turn threatening as they begin to eat him. In the original production, at this point, his father enters to add a further threat to this nightmare as he antagonizes his son over money. The nurse wakes Lyman and calms him down, sympathizing with him and telling him about her family. Tom enters to talk to his friend, telling him that he thinks Theo may take him back. Lyman tries to rationalize his behavior, admitting that he has been selfish and has betrayed people, but justifying it by saying that this is how the world works and that he has been truthful on one level. Lyman wants to find a way to keep both women, and at this point, Bessie and Theo reenter.

By Lyman's responses, we realize that Theo is acting strangely as she berates her husband for past annoyances. She recalls a time when they went skinny-dipping at the start of their relationship. It is evident that she has loved him. Their daughter Bessie becomes incensed by this talk and tries to break it up, but Theo refuses to leave and asks

Bessie to wait outside. Lyman tries to convince Theo that their marriage was stronger after he took up with Leah because he was more tolerant with both of them, knowing he had the other to turn to. Instead of placating Theo, this idea turns her against him, deciding that he is incapable of love. At this point, Lyman recreates a series of memories to explain his behavior, beginning with a safari during which he confronted a lion and on which he had gone with Theo and Bessie shortly after marrying Leah.

Lyman sees his moment with the lion as a turning point in his life, as it was here that he made the decision to never feel guilt. The lion backs off, and Lyman is exhilarated by his own sense of power and feeling of affinity with this "king of beasts." His high spirits infect both Theo and Bessie, whose evident love and respect for Lyman at this point severely contrasts with their current feelings in the hospital. Lyman next recalls how he felt blackmailed into marriage by Leah, who had threatened to abort their child. In the original version, he explains that his need to marry Leah and to keep Benjamin is partly fueled by guilt from an earlier illegitimate boy who he had fathered and for whom he had refused to divorce Theo and marry the mother. He then explains how he tried to ask Theo for a divorce but had not had the courage to go through with it. Leah has the baby even though she knows that he is not yet divorced, but then she threatens to marry someone else, which provokes Lyman to try again.

We briefly return to the present as Leah comes to visit Lyman in the hospital to discuss their son, about whom she is worried. While she tries to get Lyman to confess some guilt, he responds by trying to get her to accept some responsibility. Like Theo, his response turns her against him, and she also sees him as someone who is incapable of love. She recalls a time when he stayed with her in a hotel near his home with Theo so that he could walk by the house with Leah, as if to mock his first wife. Our sense of his audacity increases as he relates how he had sent Leah back to their hotel while he went to see Theo to make love to her. He was glorying in his own power over two separate women and feeling like a god. Leah had not known about this and is disgusted. She insists that he gives her their house and business and will not allow him to see Benjamin until he signs a quitclaim. They argue over what he should tell Benjamin about this whole thing but are interrupted by Bessie who comes with the news that Theo has had an attack.

Theo has taken off her skirt to indicate her decision to go against convention and admit her own sexuality. Deciding that she wants Lyman back, she is even willing to share him. To her daughter's horror, Theo accepts responsibility for her husband's adultery, seeing herself as having provoked and deserved it. This acquiescence excites Lyman, who sees her return to him as possible. Leah tries to make Theo see Lyman as untrustworthy, but he works on her, too, to convince her that he has really done her a favor. Bessie continues to stand firm against him, as everyone bursts into tears. Tom tries to take control, telling the women to stop loving Lyman before he destroys them all and attempting to coax Lyman to confess to having a conscience. He has better luck with the former than the latter; Lyman refuses to accept any guilt, but Theo and Leah decide to leave.

In the original version, at this point, Lyman again sees his father's ghost, which is what provokes him to confess to Leah what he was doing on the mountain—trying to surprise her by arriving unexpectedly because he was suspicious that she had a lover. Bessie tries one last time to get her father to think of others, but he seems incapable of looking beyond his own selfish needs. Leah is not impressed and leaves on the heels of the others, and Lyman is left alone with the nurse. They talk again about her family, and she kisses his forehead before she leaves. Suddenly touched by the sheer contentment and simplicity of the nurse's life, Lyman seems to reach some kind of epiphany at the close, but in his isolation, he is unsure what next to do. The play originally ended with his anguished cry, belying what he has insisted on all along—that he feels no guilt, fear, or pain, which allows the audience to join with the nurse in sympathizing with this lost soul. In the later version, the play continues to conclude more positively: Lyman declares that he has found himself at last, and his final words, "cheer up!" suggest a more hopeful outcome, despite their potential irony.

CRITICAL COMMENTARY

The Ride down Mt. Morgan takes place in troubled times and addresses the difficulties of living in an amoral, chaotic, postmodern society. The play is partly an evocation of life in the United States in the 1980s, and the importance of Reaganism to this play has been recognized. Lyman's marriage to Leah occurs in the same year that Ronald Reagan became president, and Lyman's bigamous behavior becomes a reflection of the values and type of leadership that the United States subsequently experienced. The play portrays a harsh, hostile world that is filled with conflict and betrayal. Complete fragmentation ever threatens, and this is a fact that all the characters must face: It is something with which they must learn to live. The sense of control toward which Miller has many of the characters strive is shown to be necessary, to a degree, and exhibits a healthy desire for self-determination—but too much control can be as dangerous as too little control. Characters like Leah, who insist on complete control, become limited and limiting, while a man like Tom, who has too little control, has his potential partly wasted. A balance must be sought between these two extremes to allow for both individuals and society to function within an encouraging network of possibilities and to avoid the pitfalls of living in a postmodern age.

Miller seems to suggest that to acknowledge the chaotic state of the postmodern contemporary world in which we live is the first step to be taken before we can discover the means to be content in such a world. *The Ride down Mt. Morgan* presents a picture of such a chaotic world. This play conveys the uncertainty of everyday life where a person must battle objectification and the pitfalls of an overcommercialized culture, and it conveys the effect that all of this has on the people who must live those lives. Both individualism and any sense of a supportive society are under threat. We witness the characters trying to live lives that contain dignity and a certain amount of nobility. Miller leaves the struggle unresolved, but through the calm voices of Bessie and Nurse Logan, he offers some potential directives for consideration: Think of others, and be satisfied with less.

A central issue of *The Ride down Mt. Morgan* is Miller's perennial concern with discovering the right balance between social and individual responsibilities in order to live a useful and contented life. In the play, Miller does not try to show us a single ideal American but asks us to uncover a compromise between the various characters whom we meet. While Lyman fluctuates between deception and sincerity, so do the rest of the cast. Each character is a complex mix of lies and truth—consider Theo's recollections about the shark, Leah's explanation of why she marries Lyman and her manipulations to achieve this, and the way that Tom leads a vicarious life through Lyman while on the surface condemning him.

Lyman is the play's central figure and is the most duplicitous, with his two wives, two lives, and struggling between his relationship to both Jewish and WASP lifestyles. He is a man who is simultaneously trapped by his casts (and his responsibilities), yet free in his imagination—but he is not alone. The act of finding a balance among these conflicting desires, needs, and beliefs is complicated because it inevitably involves others. Lyman dreams of an ideal situation in which his two women unite and give him everything he wants, but we are shown the unreality of such an expectation. Lyman's dream swiftly turns into a nightmare as the women begin to devour him (sucking his fingers). However, Leah and Theo are as conflicted as Lyman. Both latch on to Lyman and insist that he provide a bedrock of stability in their lives. The wives fool themselves into thinking that they have control. They too need to learn that nothing can be that certain and secure; they too need to face the uncertainties of real life.

Miller seems to suggest that vision is integral to leading a satisfactory life because it is needed to create the better fictions toward which we aim. Lyman's greatest strength is that he has vision. He has great potential, and at times, we inevitably are absorbed by his energy for life, even accepting some of his rationalizations, but by the end, we should realize that it all comes down to the fact that he has lived selfishly and only has listened to half truths (his own, ignoring those of others). He suffers for this, as he had all along needed a balance to be whole and content. He has lived his life, for all its apparent variety, too one-sidedly. When you live for yourself alone, then that is with whom you are finally left.

Miller reveals a total disconnection between the characters in *The Ride down Mt. Morgan*, but he replaces this sense of disconnection with a desire for connections that are made evident through notions of responsibility, mostly voiced through Bessie. Miller has characters in the play embody the various traps that people face during their development into useful, satisfied human beings. By so doing, he warns his audiences against some of the pitfalls that they, too, must face. Theo and Tom tend to restrict themselves by relying on conventions and by allowing others to dominate their lives. Being overly conservative turns out to be as restricting as being overly selfish like Lyman, who is ultimately restricted by false feelings of superiority. This is similar to the self-defeating trap of anarchy into which Leah falls; she damages herself and others because this trap continuously forces isolating rebellion rather than socializing compromise.

We should recognize the subtle contrast to Lyman that is provided by Nurse Logan. She talks more of her family than of herself, listening rather than telling. She is satisfied and content with no sign of angst. She does not need everything explained or understood but accepts mystery and is satisfied. In this light, it may be Lyman's ambition that ultimately reduces him. His desire for continued excitement escalates, as does his need to take greater and greater risks; a fall was inevitable, but we see him go full circle. By the end, the commonplace events and concerns that are described by Nurse Logan have become unusual and exciting to Lyman—he has gone so far from that kind of life that it now seems strange and alien to him. The Logans have the simpler response to life that was perhaps his father's, and they have that contentment that Lyman has sought.

The play suggests that modern society forces us all to live increasingly complicated lives—but, humanly, we cannot keep up and should not try. Lyman's final confession is given more to the audience than to Leah as Lyman describes the similarity between facing that mountain and the lion. "All obligations spent. Is this freedom?" Lyman asks. He is beginning to realize that freedom is not what he wanted after all. Complete freedom means no connections at all, which is awful. He ends the play alone, shaken and sobbing—with only the nurse's compassion to mitigate his isolation. We can find hope for his future in that he does seem closer in touch with the simple reality of the nurse and her family, and he seems to be groping his way slowly toward a better understanding.

Discussing *The Ride down Mt. Morgan* with theater scholar Jan Balakian, Miller explains: "Formally speaking it's very free flowing, a little bit like *Salesman* was. But this one spills in all directions; time is rather plastic. While the story is moving forward, it's also moving sideways and out." We cannot trust our eyes when watching a performance of this play because the line between reality and illusion is so carefully blurred and because the scenes flow together with no clear-cut beginnings or endings. The work is an example of the way in which Miller likes to play with the notions of both reality and time in his writing, both structurally and thematically.

In classic dream-play tradition, it becomes impossible to say for sure if any of *The Ride down Mt. Morgan*'s events exist outside Lyman's imagination as he lies in his hospital bed. Indeed, are Lyman's crash and hospitalization even real, or are they just the product of a guilty conscience? Opening the play with a man asleep is Miller's way of warning us that this whole play could turn out to be nothing more than one man's dream (or nightmare), with the patient waking, perhaps, only at the close with a strangled cry or perhaps never waking at all. We are kept deliberately unsure as to what exactly is real, and we must pass judgment without the nicety of certainty. In his dreams, at least, we see Lyman able to escape the human limitations of his casts and also, perhaps, the human limitations of his guilt, conscience, and sense of responsibility—all of which trouble him. This is no slice-of-life realism but an expressionistic evocation of one man's existential dilemma, much like *After the Fall*.

As in so many of Miller's plays, the names of central characters and the play's title have symbolic meaning. While in *Death of a Salesman* Willy Loman's name tends to evoke discussion of him as a "low-man" in terms of his abilities, character, or prospects, Lyman's name with its possibilities of outrageous deceit (lies), passion (to lie with), and, as critic June Schlueter suggests, the concept of one who is "lionized" clearly evokes a different sense of being. Meanwhile, Lyman's actual "ride" down what one critic refers to as "Mount More-Gain" is emphasized by the title, which can be taken as a metaphor for the dizzying experience of life toward the end of the millennium—comparable to hurtling down an ice-covered mountain. The last nine years for Lyman, since his encounter with the lion, have been a metaphorical ride down a steep slope, dangerous and out of control, hurtling toward an inevitable crash. Completing such a run without spinning off is a skill that we must learn to survive. Lyman is somewhat broken in the process of his ride, but he survives, which should draw our attention to the qualities that he possesses which allow for this.

FIRST PERFORMANCE

The Ride down Mt. Morgan ran at the Wyndham Theatre in London, GREAT BRITAIN, from October 23, 1991 to February 12, 1992, with the following cast:

Lyman Felt: Tom Conti
Nurse Logan: Marsha Hunt
The Father: Harry Landis
Theo Felt: Gemma Jones
Bessie: Deirdre Strath
Leah Felt Clare Higgins
Tom Wilson: Manning Redwood
Hospital Porter: Colin Stepney

Directed by MICHAEL BLAKEMORE
Set by Tanya McCallin
Music by Barrington Pheloung
Produced by Robert Fox

INITIAL REVIEWS

Miller premiered this play in Great Britain as he felt that Broadway was no longer welcoming serious drama. Critics welcomed a new Miller play but generally felt that this was not his best work; many disliked the play's ambiguity, faulted the plot, found the comedy disorienting, and had reservations about the casting. The play closed six weeks earlier than the planned run. The response of Michael Billington was fairly typical: The play had merit but was not "vintage Miller." Richard Christiansen described it as "an artistically unresolved play in a profoundly unsettled production," and Michael Coveney saw it as "stupefyingly banal" and filled with "self-indulgent ramblings."

William Henry, however, saw the play as "theatrically bold and intellectually subtle," showing Miller as an accomplished "poetic expressionist" at "the pinnacle of his talent"; John Peter insisted that "Miller is writing with all the vigour and agility of the commercial theatre at its most irresistible. This is the funniest play he has written. But it is an acid laughter, too, a laughter of bitter wisdom, and under the comic trimmings a serious moral and psychological argument is going on."

The American premiere at Williamstown in 1996 was relatively well received, with Ben Brantley praising Miller for his "constancy of vision" and "willingness to experiment," and suggesting that this might be Miller's first "bona fide comedy," even while it maintains a "moral earnestness" which Brantley links to *After the Fall.* Ed Siegel found the play "an accomplished, forceful piece of playwriting," and Robert Brustein even described the production as "engaging" and "an exhilarating journey." The subsequent New York productions, despite being sold out for their limited runs, did not fare so well from the critics, many of whom disliked Patrick Stewart in the lead role. Frances Conroy as Theo won critics' plaudits, however.

SCHOLARSHIP

Among published articles on the play to date are discussions by June Schlueter, Susan Abbotson, Bernhard Reitz, and STEVEN CENTOLA. Schlueter's essay sees the work as "a document of the moral narcissism of the Reagan years," which also illustrates "the elusiveness of the real." She offers an interesting reading of the play in which Lyman begins as the creative impulse behind the play but

loses control of his vision. In an essay published in *The Salesman Has a Birthday,* Abbotson shows the connection between Lyman Felt and his precursor, Willy Loman, while in *Student Companion to Arthur Miller,* she considers the mythological ramifications of the characters' names. Reitz examines the tragicomic structure of the play to highlight the complexity of its central protagonist, while Centola frames the play against the existentialist principles of JEAN-PAUL SARTRE to help clarify some of the "apparent inconsistencies within the play" in its uneasy mix of the comic and moral and thus illustrate the "depth and magnitude of Miller's artistic vision."

In *Arthur Miller's America,* Toby Zinman discusses the play's potential ABSURDISM, suggesting that Lyman is an alter ego for Miller; he also offers an interview with Patrick Stewart that helps highlight some of the changes that were made in the New York production, such as the deletion of the father figure. Terry Otten interestingly views Lyman as a pre-Fall Adam surrounded by seductive Eves and explores the play's tragic dimensions. Stephen Marino's exploration of Miller's language considers the play's network of metaphor and imagery. In *Arthur Miller: A Critical Study,* CHRISTOPHER BIGSBY sums up much of what he has thoughtfully said elsewhere about the way that the play is structured and about Lyman as "simultaneously a hypocrite and an honest man," comparing him at one point to Scott Fitzgerald's Jay Gatsby and SAUL BELLOW's Henderson. For Bigsby, the play is engaged in contemporary dilemmas, its contradictions being part of its message, and it offers an elucidative study of denial and hypocrisy. Basavaraj Naikar offers a close textual analysis of the theme of betrayal in the play, and Lenke Németh considers how it fits into the "family-play" tradition.

There are also several useful interviews in which Miller discusses this play, including ones by Peter Lewis, Christian Tyler, Janet Watts, and Jan Balakian. In Jeffrey Borak's 1996 interview, Miller admits that this is a difficult play, explains some of the changes that he made for the U.S. opening, and describes the play as "a story about the absurdities of the lives we lead and the value system behind those lives."

CHARACTERS

Father   In the initial version of the play, Lyman's father physically appears at the start to signify his importance and at several other junctures in the script. In the later version, he is not seen on stage, although his influence on Lyman remains. The father is a figure of hope and fear; inspiration and intimidation; his memory both encourages and restricts the son. Lyman's father died at 53, and Lyman worries about his life when he reaches the same age; this is the time he makes all these strange and daring changes in his life. His memory of his father is fraught with images of the restrictions that he placed on his son: He will not buy Lyman skates, restricting his movement (literally and symbolically); he warns him strongly about having anything to do with women, thereby restricting Lyman's future relationships and his ability to connect with women; he criticizes Lyman's looks and abilities, telling Lyman that he is "stupid" and a "great disappointment," which must restrict Lyman's intrinsic self-esteem. However, and it is this that makes us aware of Lyman's great spirit, Lyman has seemingly overcome these restrictions. In the world that he inhabits, he is a great success—a wealthy man with not one, but two attractive women to show off, and he has come a long way from his father's humble origins. However, he is to learn in the course of the play that he has really remained firmly within his father's restrictions because his success is false—he has not progressed spiritually, he has little connection with either of his women, and he still desperately seeks his father's approval.

Felt, Bessie   Bessie is Lyman's daughter by Theo and seems to act as a positive voice of conscience in the play. Refusing to compromise on the truth, Bessie forces her mother to listen to Leah's explanation that she is also Mrs. Felt rather than to dismiss Leah as crazy. On learning the truth of her father's activities, she soothes her mother and quietly chastises her father for his indulgences. She encourages her mother to leave Lyman and is anguished at the prospect that Theo may forgive him and allow him back. She alone of the women refuses to allow Lyman to set his responsibilities to others aside. She may be a small voice in the throng, but that should not make what she says any less important. "There are other people," she tells her father, and the balance that Lyman is seeking will involve those other people. Miller, by refusing to emphasize Bessie, allows us to risk missing the truth that she states, as indeed Lyman does until the close.

Felt, Leah   While Lyman's first wife, Theo, lives largely in the past, his second wife, Leah, 24 years younger than her husband, is a figure of the future. At the start of the play, Leah seems to be the more wily of the two, the one who is more capable of being the liar that her name phonetically suggests (and which she insists she be allowed to do to her husband in their wedding vows), and yet, ironically, she becomes the one who is more capable of accepting lies as much as truth. Lyman took her to Reno while he was supposedly divorcing Theo after Leah had had his son. When she asked to see the decree, he told her he had thrown it away, and she accepts this. When she meets Theo, she truly believes that Theo had been divorced and that she is Lyman's only wife, but she is not as completely thrown as Theo is by the news that she is not. Indeed, she later admits that she always had a feeling that he was not quite "on the level," but she chose to ignore it.

Leah is, throughout, fully aware that life is dangerous. With her greater verve, she is willing to make a scene, and she is not a fainter as is Theo. Though shocked to discover that her husband had not divorced his first wife as he had told her he had done, her instant response is to sue to ensure that she gets her share of his estate for herself and their son, Benjamin, and to get Lyman to sign a quitclaim on her house and her business, which he has evidently financed. Her union with Lyman has been an intensely sexual one, and she has been attracted to a hunger for life that she shares with Lyman. A strong businesswoman, Leah is the modern woman of ambition, a role that seems beyond the quieter Theo. Leah likes control and can be manipulative, despite her claims to the opposite. A clear example of this is the way that she manipulated Lyman about the baby and where she forced him into matrimony by playing on his jealousies, morality, and sense of guilt.

Felt, Lyman   The father's advice to Lyman regarding business and passion fully illustrates his son's inner conflict. Lyman is torn between the practical—the male world that his father invokes of cold cash and WASP principles—and the emotional—a female world of sex, recklessness and the Jewish lust for life. The two seem at odds; while his Father demands that the first take precedence, Lyman, rightly, needs a balance between them. Caught between his primal love for the Jewish Leah and the sexuality that she offers and the admiration he feels for the more reserved, WASPish Theo, he wants a combination of both, but that is hard to achieve.

Lyman is different with each of his women—the ultimate split personality—seeing himself as two warring identities: the Jew whom he associates with lawyers and judges against the Albanian whom he associates with bandits and anarchy. His two wives reflect this split: Theo, the conservative judgmental type who lives strictly according to rules, against Leah, the anarchist who will break those rules. He loves both in his way for each offers him something he needs. With Theo, he can be the strong provider and play it safe—a secure existence. With Leah, he can be the playboy with fast cars, planes, hunting—the apparent free spirit who can face fear with a casualness that belies his inner turmoil. As the play progresses, we see Theo and Leah gradually swap roles in his life, with Theo becoming the rebel and Leah the conservative.

Despite the wrong that he commits, it is hard not to like Lyman, and our attraction to Lyman is an integral aspect of his characterization, without which we are in danger of missing the point. Lyman is a truly American figure, multiethnic in background and sympathies. He has employed African Americans for years, and James Baldwin views him with brotherly affection. Also, he has had a Hispanic business partner, his sexual preferences are not race restricted, and he is half Jewish and half Albanian—the son of an immigrant. As a second-generation American, he epitomizes both the strengths and weaknesses of the U.S. vision. He has pursued and caught the traditional 20th-century American dream of success, having enough cash to keep two beautiful women in beautiful homes—though we are also shown the essential hollowness of that dream. Underneath it all, Lyman is not happy; he is constantly suffering, and it is this suffering with which he is finally left, once the rest is stripped away.

Despite our sympathy, however, we should not believe Lyman when he tells us that you can be true to yourself or to others but not to both. The first LAW of life is betrayal, Miller insists, largely because we are human and therefore fallible—but we can fight this! We need to recognize that the root of Lyman's problem is that he has not been honest to himself. Lyman does what he wants, but in the end, he is wracked with guilt and suffers for this selfishness. Lyman is a victim not only of social restrictions but also of his own excesses. So it would be best not to follow his example, but listen to the quiet voice of reason that Bessie offers: You have to be more socially responsible in life, whatever your desires, for your own good. Miller leaves it deliberately ambiguous as to whether Lyman truly learns this lesson, but he allows for the possibility.

Felt, Theo   Theo is Lyman first wife and the mother of Bessie. While Theo and Leah seem to offer Lyman two very different alternatives, on a closer look, their characters become more complex. There are similarities between them, symbolized by their identical fur coats, as well as a profound contrast. Theo's inflexible nature seems assured from the start as she is described as "stiff and ungainly." Theo is very practical and offers Lyman a sense of order, a sense that "everything ultimately fits together . . . and for the good." Lyman feeds off her naive optimism. She comes from a sheltered family background that has given her a limited outlook on life. She has idealized the U.S. concept of the small town, refusing to acknowledge its darker side, and looks back nostalgically to her past.

Theo seems to stand for a certain honesty, and Lyman is drawn to her strong sense of reality; yet with the shark episode, this becomes questionable. Theo may be as capable of lying and manipulation as is her husband. Apparently a homebody, she is conventional and accommodating, but she is controlling as well as controlled. She exhibits a need to control Lyman in the way that she likes to identify his quotes; it is for her a way of identifying and fixing him. Her association with truth, we learn, is based more on pretense than on reality.

As the play progresses, Theo changes, illustrated by her shedding her skirt along with many of her former inhibitions. She becomes more comfortable with herself and her position—even offering to share Lyman, although Bessie finally persuades her to go home alone. She recognizes the inadequacy of her earlier conformist views regarding socialism and Christianity, and she seems ready for compromise, although this horrifies the others.

Nurse Logan In comparison to most of the play's characters Nurse Logan lives a simple and undemanding life in which her biggest pleasure is being with her family fishing or buying shoes. Her compassionate response to Lyman helps lead the audience to find something redeeming in his character and leads Lyman to a better understanding of the mistakes that he has made. Maybe because she is Canadian, she is not as affected by the divisions that attend being in the United States. Perhaps, being black, she is more accustomed to living with conflict.

Wilson, Tom Lyman's lawyer and longtime friend, Tom Wilson, advises Lyman to lie and to be dishonest because the truth is often hurtful. Such moments allow us to question Tom's complicity, even though he finally takes a stand against his friend. Self-effacing, Tom has lived vicariously through Lyman, allowing him to take the risks. Tom is a kind of Everyman figure in the play because we are all prone to letting others live the sensational lives as we stand by and watch—becoming virtual "Uncle Tom" figures in our "yes man" complacency; through the ineffectual figure of Tom, Miller warns us against such complacency.

MOVIE AND TELEVISION ADAPTATIONS

Director Nicole Kassell has been working on a movie version of this play for some time, starring Michael Douglas, but it has not been released to date.

FURTHER READING

Abbotson, Susan C. W. "From Loman to Lyman: The Salesman Forty Years On." In *"The Salesman Has a Birthday": Essays Celebrating the Fiftieth Anniversary* of *Arthur Miller's Death of a Salesman,* edited by Steve Marino, 99–108. (Lanham, Md.: University Press of America, 2000).

———. "Alternate Perspective: A Mythic Reading." *Student Companion to Arthur Miller.* Westport, Conn.: Greenwood Press, 148–150.

Balakian, Jan. "A Conversation with Arthur Miller." *Michigan Quarterly Review* 29 (Spring 1990): 158–170.

Bigsby, Christopher. *"The Ride down Mount Morgan." Arthur Miller: A Critical Study.* New York: Cambridge University Press, 2005, 366–380.

Billington, Michael. *"The Ride down Mount Morgan." Guardian,* November 1, 1991. In *Theatre Record* 11, no. 22 (1991): 1,351.

Borak, Jeffrey. "Miller at 80 Fine-Tuning Play's American Performance." *Berkshire Eagle,* July 4, 1996: B1, 4.

Brantley, Ben. "Arthur Miller, Still Feeling the Pain After the Fall." *New York Times,* July 25, 1996, C13, 16.

Brustein, Robert. "The Ride Down Mount Rushmore." *New Republic,* September 16, 1996, 30–31.

Centola, Steven R. "'How to Contain the Impulse of Betrayal:' A Sartrean Reading of *The Ride down Mount Morgan." American Drama* 6, no. 1 (Fall 1996): 14–28.

Christiansen, Richard. "Arthur Miller Opens New Play in London for Good Reason." *Chicago Tribune,* November 13, 1991, sec. 1, p. 24.

Coveney, Michael. "Bloody Roman Theater." *Observer,* November 3, 1991, 64.

Henry, William A., III. "Arthur Miller, Old Hat at Home, Is a London Hit." *Time* November 11, 1991, 100–101.

Lewis, Peter. "Change of Scene for a Mellow Miller." *Sunday Times,* November 3, 1991, sec. 6, p. 6.

Marino, Stephen A. "Images of the 90s: *The Ride Down Mt. Morgan* and *Broken Glass." A Language Study of Arthur Miller's Plays: The Poetic in the Colloquial.* New York: Mellen, 2002, 135–156.

Naikar, Basavaraj. *"The Ride down Mt. Morgan: A Tragedy of Betrayal."* In *Arthur Miller: Twentieth Century Legend,* edited by Syed Mashkoor Ali, 372–389. (Jaipur, India: Surabhi, 2006).

Némth, Lenke. "Arthur Miller's *The Ride Down Mount Morgan* and the Family-Play Tradition." *Hungarian*

Journal of English and American Studies 11, no. 2 (Fall 2005): 77–88.

Otten, Terry. *"The Ride down Mount Morgan."* The *Temptation of Innocence in the Dramas of Arthur Miller.* Columbia: University of Missouri Press, 2002: 210–220.

Peter, John. "Review of *Ride down Mt. Morgan.*" *Sunday Times*, November 3, 1991, sec. 6, p. 7.

Reitz, Bernhard. "From Loman to Lyman: Arthur Miller's Comedy." *Contemporary Drama in English: New Forms of Comedy.* Trier: WVT Wissenschaftlicher Verlag Trier, 1994, 93–105.

Schlueter, June. "Scripting the Closing Scene: Arthur Miller's *Ride down Mount Morgan.*" In *The Achievement of Arthur Miller,* edited by Steven R. Centola, 143–150. (Dallas: Contemporary Research, 1995).

Siegel, Ed. "Miller Goes on *Ride* of Mirth, Morals." *Boston Globe*, July 23, 1996, D1.

Tyler, Christian. "Private View: The People's Playwright." *Financial Times*, November 2, 1991, 24.

"Vaudeville at the Edge of the Cliff." In *Arthur Miller's America,* edited by Enoch Brater, 164–173. (Ann Arbor: University of Michigan Press, 2005).

Watts, Janet. "The Ride down Mount Miller." *Observer,* November 3, 1991, 59.

Zinman, Toby. "Interview with Patrick Stewart." In *Arthur Miller's America,* edited by Enoch Brater, 174–179. (Ann Arbor: University of Michigan Press, 2005).

The Ryan Interview or How It Was Around Here (1995)

Directed by Curt Dempster and starring Mason Adams and Julie Lauren, *The Ryan Interview* was a short play that was produced in 1995 as part of the 18th annual festival of new one-act plays at the Ensemble Studio Theatre in New York. The title character is an affectionate tribute to Bob Tracy, one of Miller's ROXBURY, CONNECTICUT, neighbors, who only lived to age 80 but is given new life through Miller's portrait. Many of the tales that Tracy relates can be found in Miller's 1977 book *In the Country,* where he shares his recollections of Tracy. Ben Brantley praised the effortless accuracy of the play's

dialogue and its "engagingly easygoing pace." In 1996, the Actors Theater of Louisville mounted a production that was later filmed for television. With Eddie Bracken and Ashley Judd; it was the first of Kentucky ETV's dramas that were adapted from regional theaters for the PBS *American Shorts* series. This was aired in 2000. In 1998, when the *Michigan Quarterly Review* was publishing a special issue on Miller, it was given permission to reprint the script, and the editor, Laurence Goldstein, described the play as "a Chekhovian take on country life."

On his 100th birthday, Mr. Ryan is being interviewed by a young female reporter and is asked to recount what he sees as the changes that he has witnessed during his long life. He is able to provide her with a brief history of the area for the last century. Declaring that nothing much has changed in the last 50 years, Ryan takes us back to the 1930s to find a real contrast. Back then, his stories imply, people seemed more connected by their tolerance and humor, and Miller clearly sees this as now sadly lost. The people and community that Ryan recalls have vanished along with the farms in the area. In the 1990s, Ryan is a lonely man; he never married, he lives by himself in an isolated farmhouse in Connecticut (although he never farmed himself), and his repeated refrain of "I'm not due anywhere" reminds us that the majority of his former neighbors and friends are now dead. He is made all the lonelier by an external world in which people tend to keep to themselves. He sees them in their protective cars, speeding along so fast, and he wonders how they ever meet anyone anymore.

However, Miller's innate optimism seeps through, largely via the character of Ryan himself and the affable lightness of the short piece. Ryan may be lonely and at a loose end, but even at 100, he is still full of life. Staunchly antigovernment, he possesses no Social Security number and prefers to stay out of cities—he went to Hartford once but "couldn't find anywhere to sit down." His roguish humor and lifelong commitment to bucking the system warms any audience to him and turns him into an icon of resistance rather than despair.

FURTHER READING

Brantley, Ben. "Wilder and Miller in One-Act Festival." *New York Times*, May 6, 1995, sec. 1, p. 17.

Miller, Arthur. "The Ryan Interview." *Michigan Quarterly Review* 37, no. 4 (1998): 803–816.

———, and Inge Morath. *In the Country.* New York: Viking, 1977.

"Salesman at Fifty" (1999)

Written as a preface to an anniversary edition of the play to commemorate 50 years since the original BROADWAY production of *Death of a Salesman,* Miller discusses how theater audiences in the United States have changed since the 1940s when attending plays was deemed "an absolute necessity for a civilized life." This short essay was then reprinted in *Echoes Down the Corridor* (2000). For Miller, the ideal play is one that shows rather than tells its message, and he feels that *Death of a Salesman* fits this category as its continued popularity for 50 years attests. Masking its seriousness with honest emotions, it is a play, he asserts, that instructs but does so in an entertaining fashion, making it accessible to all from the most erudite to the common laborer. Insisting that he had no prior models from which to work, Miller views *Death of a Salesman* as a theatrical innovation in its depiction of "the way the mind . . . actually worked." He concludes by justifying the dramatic purpose behind some of his play's less than realistic dialogue and by asserting his opinion that the play is universal in its tale of human fallibility in a hostile society.

Salesman in Beijing (1984)

Written as a day-to-day journal of the eight weeks that Miller spent in China in 1983 rehearsing actors for the BEIJING PEOPLE'S ART THEATER's production of *Death of a Salesman, Salesman in Beijing* relates changes that Miller observes in China since his 1978 visit, along with his creative and personal journey in directing this landmark production of the play. Despite some advances, such as the proliferation of magazines, less overt censorship, and melodramatic but challenging plays becoming popular—plays that

are reminiscent of pre–World War I U.S. theater, such as one that he attends called *Warning Signals,* Miller still finds the populace in a state of recovery from the Cultural Revolution of Chairman Mao. China seems like a "country after a great war" in which goods and facilities are scarce and poverty is endemic. Certain street scenes remind him of his father, ISIDORE MILLER's, stories of life on the Lower East Side in turn-of-the-century New York. While efforts evidently are being made to rebuild, the way in which the older houses are being crowded out by new apartment blocks reminds Miller of his play's setting. The text is interspersed by a good number of rehearsal photographs taken by INGE MORATH, who accompanied her husband and their daughter REBECCA MILLER (who stayed with them for the first two weeks).

Miller begins by explaining how he came to be invited by Cao Yu and Ying Ruocheng (who would play Willy Loman). Although skeptical that the Chinese would be able to understand his play, he wanted to help Yu and Ruocheng in their desire to develop "new contemporary Chinese theatrical forms and acting styles." *Death of a Salesman* was chosen because of its experimental form: They wanted to consider possibilities beyond straight REALISM. Miller was invited to direct because they had felt insufficiently knowledgeable about Western theater to do the play justice. The play would be performed in Chinese in a literal translation written by Ruocheng, and Miller would direct through an interpreter. Miller openly admits to an initial naiveté when entering the project but felt that he was able to work through his misunderstandings and errors of judgment to produce a fascinating production that was well received by its Chinese audience.

Writing on March 21, Miller starts his journal while still suffering from jet lag, keen to offer up his first impressions on meeting the cast. Unable to guess if it is natural reticence or awe at a foreigner, Miller initially receives little response to his questions and wonders whether it would work better to set the production in China rather than in the United States. He asks the actors up front not to do their usual impersonation of Americans, a battle he will fight with them throughout rehearsals, as he

Scene from an all-Chinese production of *Death of a Salesman* at the Beijing People's Art Theatre in 1983 directed by Miller. *Photograph by Inge Morath: Magnum Photos.*

feels that it would be too stylized and would destroy the realistic aspects of the play. Despite impoverished resources, a set has been designed that is loosely based on JO MIELZINER's original, although altered enough to be off-putting, and Miller begins by asking for changes. He feels encouraged by the actors' apparent understanding of Willy's desire to make his sons successful, but he wonders if in their fierce nationalism the Chinese will find offensive his suggestion that a successful production of the play would "help to prove that there is one humanity," which is one of the central aims behind his direction.

Miller frequently explores differences between Chinese and U.S. behavior as revealed by the actors' reactions to what occurs in the play. They cannot understand why Charley is so kind to Willy, why the lascivious Happy is allowed to engender any sympathy, or why Biff longs to go out West, away from the city. The actress playing Linda, Zhu Lin, views Linda as a woman who never thinks of herself but only of Willy, rather than the "determined" woman that Miller wants to see. Miller also worries that the play is turning into a satire that presents Willy as foolish rather than noble. Miller leads them to find answers to these dilemmas in the play and from their own personal experience. He guides them not to admire Willy but to love him and to be inspired by his unshakable belief in the future. At the point where Miller convinces Ruocheng no longer to feel superior to Willy, he turns the actor's performance into something that equals that of Miller's favorite in the role, Lee J. Cobb. On several occasions, Miller recounts incidents from the U.S. premiere and from other productions of the play to elucidate his points, which usefully extends our background.

From the start, it is evident that Miller has strong doubts that his play can translate into Chinese culture, and he becomes increasingly excited by the growing evidence that it does—and on more than one level. He recounts a series of problems that he faces and how he deals with them. In the Chinese theatrical custom, actors speak their lines too slow, use too much gesture and emotion, and rely on sentimentality (what Miller refers to as "indicative acting"); in addition, they all want to wear white makeup and outlandish wigs as is usual when presenting "foreigners," and there are difficulties in getting props, lighting, and costumes just right. He holds back on correcting, not wanting to be too discouraging, but through repeated direction, badinage, and compromise, these difficulties are overcome or turned into strengths. Fate seems to be on Miller's side as the one actor about whom he felt doubtful suffers an illness that allows them to replace him with someone who is perfect for the role of Happy.

It surprises Miller how easily he follows Ruocheng's script even though he speaks no Chinese, as it maintains the same contours and flow of the original. He is also able to find a series of connections between the play and Chinese culture that allow the actors to create convincing performances. Central ones are his equating Willy's refusal to see the truth to China's general blindness to the true nature of the Cultural Revolution, and Biff's feelings for Willy being similar to the way the Chinese felt about Mao and his wife, Jiang Qing; they want to love them, but in their hearts, they knew that their ideology was faulty, and this caused angry frustration. It helps him to realize that he sees the United States differently from his actors, making him also recognize how similarly false is the U.S. view of the Chinese.

The education is not one-way, and Miller admiringly admits to the skill and perseverance of the actors. The way that the actress playing the Woman in Boston approaches her part leads Miller to realize that he had originally intended her scenes with Willy to seem like "hallucinatory surrealism," and so he sees the scene anew. Miller takes us through the good moments and the bad, the times that he feels he is really connecting and those when he dishearteningly sees himself as "the Foreign Expert who should never be contradicted in any serious way." In a more hopeful vein, he decides, "I

think that by some unplanned magic we may end up creating something not quite American *or* Chinese but a pure style springing from the heart of the play itself," and the audience's reaction on opening night seems to support this.

We hear that the U.S. embassy is worried the play will be used as anti-U.S. propaganda, and Miller is constantly nervous of government interference and suspicious of political control. Warned by literary people that the public will not be given the opportunity to attend and that the play may not be properly advertised, Miller begins to worry about the strangers who often watch rehearsal; could they be government spies? But the production manages to soar over the political tension caused by the United States giving a young Chinese tennis player asylum shortly before the opening. Various press conferences, Miller relates, show the interest within and outside China toward the production's progress and success. He also tells of a blunt discussion with *Foreign Theatre* magazine in which he asserts that all artists are by nature dissidents, and so China's attempts to demand complete support from its writers rather than allow for questioning kills art. He also complains about what he describes as a reductionist Chinese concentration on a play's "message" that leads to its other aspects being ignored.

Miller's running commentary offers the reader an excellent guide to the rehearsal process in any theater and conveys his understanding of the differences between Chinese and Western theater, as well as offering a picture of the rapid development of Chinese society after the end of the Cultural Revolution and its incapacitating effects. It is this speedy change that helps make the play's reference points less strange to the cast and the production a timely one. Uncertain that these actors can convey a sense of their characters' inner lives in their mechanical approach to acting, he leads them in Stanislavski's techniques to draw them into their roles. Miller's book offers not only an excellent guide to a specific production but also to Miller's view of the play and its characters in the explanations that he offers to the cast as he leads them toward a better understanding of his intent. *Death of a Salesman*, he insists, "is a love story between a man and his son, and in a crazy way between both of them and America."

On May 3, Rebecca calls her father from the United States to inform him that there has been a fire at his ROXBURY, CONNECTICUT, home. Ruocheng's wife points out that having all of your best books burned is a little like what happened to them in the Cultural Revolution. In the concluding section, Miller relates his own feelings and the audience reaction to the previews and opening night. The first preview is filled with workers who are unfamiliar with theater, who chat, change seats, and react unpredictably. Yet, the play still seems to work, which bolsters Miller for the subsequent performances. Prior to his departure shortly after the opening, Miller discusses with Ruocheng his comparative images for the play and how the translation worked. The premiere is a resounding success, Miller says his goodbyes, and he feels confident that his endeavor has made a difference to both sides of the Chinese–U.S. divide. Personally, he no longer sees the Chinese as mysterious because he now sees them on a human level, and he attributes this to the power of the theater that allowed them to bond as they worked toward a common goal. "The job of culture," he asserts, "is not to further fortify people against contamination by other cultures but to mediate between them from the heart's common ground."

Critical reaction to the volume was very positive, emphasizing the book's humor and honesty. Charles Hayford called it a "tough, sensitive exploration" and "a rewarding book," while Norris Houghton viewed it as a "remarkable document," as both a study of the "reactions of a superior stage craftsman" and a "highly sensitive and thoughtful" record of Miller's more general experiences in China. William B. Collins recommended the book "to everybody who has more than a superficial interest in the theater."

FURTHER READING

Collins, William B. "For the Chinese, *Salesman* Was a Cross-Cultural Journey." *Philadelphia Inquirer,* May 7, 1984, E4.

Hayford, Charles. "*Salesman in Beijing*." *Library Journal,* April 1, 1984, 730.

Houghton, Norris. "Understanding Willy." *New York Times Book Review,* June 24, 1984, 37.

"A Search for a Future" (1966)

The short story "A Search for a Future" first appeared in *Saturday Evening Post* in 1966 and was reprinted the next year in *The Best American Short Stories, 1967.* It was also included in Miller's story collections *I Don't Need You Any More* (1967) and *The Misfits and Other Stories* (1987). The story tells about a son who learns from his elderly father how to appreciate life by being fully involved and having definite goals rather than hiding behind a facade of acting and pretending that things do not matter. Significantly, Miller had just lost his own father about the time that he wrote this tale. The story also contains one of Miller's more overt references to the VIETNAM WAR outside of his nonfiction in the repeated image of the dresser's nephew who had his eyes shot out in Vietnam.

Written in the first person, Harry, a middle-aged Jewish actor, looks back on a life that is beginning to take on a pall of deadening repetition. He realizes that after 35 years of playing the same roles, he has lost interest and no longer feels the same joy when acting that he once felt. His father is elderly and in poor health and is currently in a nursing home, and Harry wonders if his own uneasiness has to do with his expectation that his father will soon die. As he prepares for his evening performance, a young man visits him backstage. In contrast to Harry, this young actor seems full of possibilities that Harry mocks but secretly envies. He has come to remind Harry of his promise to attend an anti-Vietnam peace rally. Harry has little commitment to the cause but agreed to appear to show up a rival. While he professes admiration for those with commitments, he has none of his own.

During his performance that night, Harry has an intriguing vision of everything in life being like it was a play in which everyone has an allotted role. The next day, he visits his father, who is in the home after a debilitating stroke and can no longer speak coherently. The home is sterile and cramped, and the rest of the residents appear to be torpid and waiting for death. In contrast, his father paces, moving around his room like a caged beast looking for an escape. Harry recalls the rally at which his attendance had been applauded and he was asked to speak. Uncertain how to respond, and not wanting to be labeled a rebel by the media, he cautiously muttered a few crowd pleasers about wanting the war to end and sat down. He was surprised by their effusive approbation, which made him feel good about himself, despite his vague support.

Speaking to his father, it is unclear if the man even recognizes his son, although he is pleased to have a visitor. Harry admits that he has always felt "deep currents" and a "force inside" his father that he admires. It is evident that his father has not given up and continues to hope for something better, but Harry convinces himself that "I am not built like him at all." Though his father is free to leave, Harry feels that he is better off in the home, more so because he does not want to take on responsibility for his father's care. Leaving the home, he visits his old haunts in Harlem to see if they can revivify his experience, but everything seems changed.

Back at his theater, putting on make-up, Harry realizes that his father may be the only person whom he knows who is not constantly playing a role, but someone who has authentic feelings and experiences on which he takes action instead of passively waiting on the sidelines. Later that night, the home calls him. After he left, his father walked out and has not returned. They have filed a missing person's report—the weather is inclement, and he has no warm clothing. Harry is elated at this sign of his father's spirit. A few hours later, he goes to look for him, taking a cab as it is still raining, but he has no luck. The police find his father the next morning and take him back to the home; he too had gone to Harlem and, like his son, had not recognized the place. Harry visits and finds his father injured from trying to avoid capture but unable to recall what he did. The father believes that he will be going home the next day, and this hope sustains him. Harry is impressed, feeling that it may be sufficient inspiration for him to become more engaged in life.

The root of Harry's problem is a lack of self-confidence; he tells himself that he cannot possibly make a difference, so why bother to try? Because of this belief, he has avoided commitment for his whole life, indicated by his never having married, a decision that he now regrets. Yet, Harry feels better about himself when he becomes involved by attending the rally, however reluctantly. His father has both a soul and a goal in life and instinctively refuses to accept his fate, something that Harry will need to discover if he is to have any future. On recognizing that his father has not given up on life and is still seeking a better future, Harry may find the inspiration to do the same himself. CHRISTOPHER BIGSBY calls the story a "minor masterpiece" in its understated tone and thorough depiction of a man who "is waiting for something to happen while everything he has done, or failed to do, ensures that this will seemingly never come about."

FURTHER READING

Bigsby, Christopher. "Fiction." *Arthur Miller: A Critical Study.* New York: Cambridge University Press, 2005, 444–472.

"The Shadows of the Gods" (1958)

Based on a talk that Miller had given to the New York Dramatists Committee at HAROLD CLURMAN's behest, which was intended to outline the various literary influences on his writing, the essay "The Shadows of the Gods" was first published in *Harper's* magazine in 1958. It has been reprinted several times since, including in *The American Playwrights on Drama* (1965) and *Theater Essays of Arthur Miller* (1978). While the essay mentions those writers whom Miller felt had an impact on his development, its emphasis is more on why Miller writes, the ground on which he stands, and his agenda for revitalizing a U.S. drama that he sees as beginning to languish. He starts with an assertion as to what he feels is wrong with much of contemporary drama and how he feels that this can be fixed.

Miller views drama as having come to "the end of a period," and the "limitations" of current plays need to be recognized and dealt with "if our theater is not to become absurd, repetitious, and decayed." Fearful of the implications of ABSURDISM, he asks for new standards in art. Viewing himself as an artist forged by the GREAT DEPRESSION, he outlines his Depression experiences (much as elsewhere) and describes the way in which the whole nation had felt that it had been set adrift. Connecting this feeling to the classical period, as if a punishment by the gods for the increasing greed of the 1920s, he suggests that it was this that gave himself and others a renewed sense of fate. It made Miller "fascinated by sheer process itself. How things connected," which are inquiries that inform his subsequent work. "The structure of a play," he states, "is always the story of how the birds came home to roost." This belief structures his drama.

Miller felt drawn to FYODOR DOSTOEVSKY because of his similar interest in "father and son conflict" and in the "hidden laws" that direct people's lives. HENRIK IBSEN attracted him "not because he wrote about problems, but because he was illuminating process." For Miller, Ibsen saw those connections that help reveal the buried laws of life. Through this, Miller formulated the idea of the writer as "the destroyer of chaos" in that by illuminating these hidden laws, he could help people better understand their lives. "I wrote," he explains, "not only to find a way into the world but to hold it away from me so that sheer, senseless events would not devour me." He saw the same interest in presenting "hidden forces" in the both the Greeks and German EXPRESSIONISM.

Moving on to discuss the impact of EUGENE O'NEILL, Miller describes himself as being ideologically different from his "reactionary" forerunner, but he finds a connection in their dramatic aims: Both are intrigued by fate and notions of power, albeit they see this power as coming from different sources. Eschewing O'Neill's religious belief, Miller looked to the impact of economics, politics, and history. His aim in writing a play is to ask, "What is its ultimate force? How can that force be released?" and "What is its ultimate relevancy to the survival of the race?" In his view, any play that does not

consider these dramatic and human concerns lacks balance. The best examples of playwrights who exhibit this balance, he suggests, are Shakespeare and ANTON CHEKHOV, who present not just individuals but also offer the social context in which they live. Suggesting that too many critics confused Chekhov "with the people he was writing about," Miller praises the writer's "psychological insight" and the way in which tradition informs his plays. He then suggests that among contemporary writers, TENNESSEE WILLIAMS comes closest to Chekhov in the way he uses Southern tradition in his drama. For Miller, "you cannot even create a truthfully drawn psychological entity on the stage until you understand his social relations and their power to make him what he is and to prevent him from being what he is not."

Complaining that many contemporary dramas are too introspective and are concerned only with youth rebelling against the old, Miller asserts that these playswrights need to expand to consider the "hidden, ulterior causation for this." He holds up two recent plays for consideration, Frances Goodrich and Albert Hackett's adaptation of *The Diary of Anne Frank* and Williams's *Cat on a Hot Tin Roof*. He objects to the sentimentality of the former, feeling that the play's view was too narrow, without any true connection to its society or its audience. Its concern to make "basically reassuring . . . what must have been the most harrowing kind of suffering in real life" puzzled him. To be relevant to the survival of the race, Miller suggests, it should have asserted "how we are brothers not only to these victims but to the Nazis" and so force its audience to confront their "own sadism" and their capacity to go along with power rather than make a stance for "humane principle." Such an inclusion would have raised the play, for Miller, to a higher level along the lines of Greek drama. Williams's play, by contrast, he sees as far more complex and satisfying.

Suggesting that it is not for a playwright to give answers but to open up possibilities, Miller sees in *Cat on a Hot Tin Roof* evidence of an artistic preoccupation that "extends beyond the surface realities of the relationships, and beyond the psychiatric connotations of homosexuality and impotence" to also include "the viewpoint . . . of the audience, the society, and the race." Williams conveys "an ulterior pantheon of forces" and "play of symbols" that point to a larger social question regarding "the right of society to renew itself when it is, in fact, unworthy." Although Miller dislikes the play's ending, he applauds Williams's ability to address issues of "tragic grandeur."

The essay's title refers to parents, whom Miller describes as "shadows of the gods," because for Miller, family relationships offer a microcosm of our wider society and our perception of the universe, and effective drama should allow for this wider picture to be glimpsed: "There is an organic aesthetic, a tracking of impulse and causation from the individual to the world and back again which must be reconstituted." Drama that does not "engage its relevancy for the race," Miller concludes, "will halt at pathos" and lack any worthwhile meaning.

"Should Ezra Pound Be Shot?" (1945)

Five writers were invited by *New Masses* to voice their opinions regarding the treason trial of poet EZRA POUND and to debate the title question. Miller's essay, the longest of the five, offers a compassionate view that finds Pound guilty of being a "Mussolini mouthpiece" and yet feels that blame should be shouldered by those writers and critics who allowed Pound to speak so irresponsibly. As an admirer of Pound's work, Miller is disappointed in the poet's evidently fascist viewpoint, "with all the ANTI-SEMITISM, anti-foreignism included." However, he concludes, "In a world where HUMANISM must conquer lest humanity be destroyed, literature must nurture the conscious of man." Being against capital punishment as an inhumane act, in Miller's view Pound should not be shot but should be guided better to understand the error of his narrow beliefs and should be guarded better against being allowed to spout any future racist opinions.

Situation Normal . . . (1944)

Dedicated to his brother Kermit, *Situation Normal . . .* is a book of reportage that Miller put together, based on army camp interviews that he had done when researching material for his work on *The Story of G. I Joe* screenplay. Although a difference of opinion with the producers led to Miller's withdrawal from the project, Miller was able, encouraged by his wife, MARY SLATTERY, and her editorial connections, to publish his first book. The ellipsis in the title refers to the military phrase often shorted to *snafu* (situation normal . . . all fucked up), neatly avoiding the expletive. It indicates both the pessimistic outlook of the enlisted men and the coarse sense of humor with which they coped. Those who reviewed the book responded positively, with corporal Maurice Basseches telling readers of *Saturday Review of Literature* that this was "one of the most important books about America and the war" that had been published. Marcus Duffield described it as a "provocative piece" of journalism, and Herbert Kupferberg declared, "Mr. Miller is an excellent reporter: He has an eye for the little things that give meaning to the big ones."

While he refuses to ignore the horrors of armed conflict, Miller strongly felt that the allied war against fascism was a moral necessity, but he wanted his readers to be better aware of the price that U.S. soldiers were paying through their engagement. Avoiding the jingoistic vision of the peppy, enthusiastic enlisted man, Miller relates the stories of several regular soldiers in the book with humor and blunt REALISM. His concern is less the soldier in combat but what happens to these men once they return home. Laurence Goldstein describes the subject of the book as "belief" and asserts that without such belief, Miller felt that "postwar America would sink into a different kind of warfare, a moral disorder inimical to the happiness and spiritual fulfillment of its citizens." As Miller states in the book, "I am beginning to feel the evidence of the existence of two kinds of men. Those who require a clear faith, and those who never pierce through to the need for any faith at all."

FURTHER READING

Basseches, Maurice. "'Tenshun!" *Saturday Review of Literature*, December 2, 1944: 64, 66.

Duffield, Marcus. "Whys and Wherefores." *Nation*, January 13, 1945: 50.

Goldstein, Laurence. "Introduction." *Michigan Quarterly Review* 37, no. 4 (Fall 1998): 585–589.

Kupferberg, Herbert. "Touring Training Camps." *New York Herald Tribune Weekly Book Review*, December 17, 1944, 3.

Some Kind of Love Story (1982)

Although initially rejected by U.S. critics on its 1982 premiere, the brief one-act play, *Some Kind of Love Story*, which accompanied *Elegy for a Lady* on the double-bill *Two-Way Mirror*, won better reviews in GREAT BRITAIN and with subsequent U.S. performances.

The background murder trial is based on real events. In 1973, Miller had learned about the case of PETER REILLY, who had been tried and convicted of brutally murdering his mother. His local community believed him to be innocent, and the indictment was suspicious. For the next five years, Miller assisted in uncovering the truth and freeing Peter, with the help of an ex-cop private investigator, James Conway, and lawyer, T. F. Gilroy Daly. They finally discovered a solid eyewitness affidavit that had been suppressed by the trial prosecutor, proving that Peter had been nowhere in the area when his mother was killed. Dismayed by the authorities' irresponsibility and inhumanity in pursuing and condemning a clearly innocent man, Miller tells us in *Timebends: A Life* that he felt that events "offered a vision of man so appallingly unredeemable as to dry up the pen." On later consideration, however, he realized that if he focused on those who insisted on proving Reilly's innocence, then it would offer proof of sufficient humanity that was alive to combat such authorities and allow his ink to flow. In 1990, Miller adapted the play into the movie *Everybody Wins*.

SYNOPSIS

Tom O'Toole, a private detective, arrives to talk with Angela, who is buried in her bed. She has been beaten by her husband, but she excuses him. She asked Tom to come as she has information about a man, Felix Epstein, who has been in jail for five years for the murder of his uncle, Abe Kaplan, and on whose case Tom is still working, but she seems reluctant to come to the point. The last time that she saw Tom, she sent him packing. He is married but has slept with Angela in the past. He tells her about his only true love whom he lost. She is worried that she has been blanking out—she is schizophrenic but cannot afford a psychiatrist—and is concerned that she may forget what she knows. He is angered by her delays and suggests that guilt is bothering her.

Felix's parents hired Tom to clear their son, but he wonders why Angela is so involved. The question forces her into another personality, Leontine, a tough whore who horrifies Tom as she gropes him and then fights him off. He calls a psychiatrist friend, Josh Levy, for advice. Tom believes that Angela has mob connections as a prostitute and thinks that she may be in danger, but his friend questions his objectivity. Angela returns to herself and explains that the police are following her, although Tom cannot see anyone outside. She warns him that he could be in danger; he suggests that if she talks, she will be in less danger. He reminds her of Cagney and other movie tough guys. She asks him to sleep with her, but he refuses; she asks him to reminisce about his years on the police force, and then they kiss. He is instantly regretful.

Tom admits that he has a grudge against the prosecutor, Callaghan, and needs to crack this case to save his reputation. As he pressures Angela for information, she becomes Emily, an abused child. He calls Josh again, who still seems skeptical; then Angela returns. Tom plans to leave, and in response to Angela's query, he tells her that he is researching someone for a company vice presidency, making sure that he is not homosexual, but that he is uncomfortable with such work. Angela tells him that she was dating Callaghan but that they broke up over the case. She explains that the probable murderer, Carl Linstrom, was a runner for

Kaplan who dealt drugs but that the police would not prosecute because they were on the take. She carried drugs for Kaplan, too. She has letters from Callaghan talking about the case, and the police have been leaning on her.

Tom asks to see the letters, but she does not want to hurt Callaghan. He is uncertain on whose side she is, and as he berates her, she changes into Renata Marshall, an upper-class lady. The phone rings as Angela resurfaces, and it is a client for whom she prepares. Tom calls Josh to tell him what Angela has said. Uncertain if he believes her, he looks outside again, and this time sees police. He pleads with her to go to a judge, but she asks for more time and suggests that she has other information. They arrange to meet the next day, and he takes her to her appointment.

CRITICAL COMMENTARY

The play's plot is simple: A detective interviews a witness who seems reluctant to give him the information that he needs. But through this conceit, Miller explores and challenges our conception of reality and how it is perceived. He strips away masks of illusion that individuals wear even while these might be necessary protection against realities that are too harsh to bear. Through dialogue between two characters, Miller exposes a wider society that makes various demands on both of them, and we watch as Tom and Angela struggle to recognize their own individual (and frequently opposed) motives against these demands. How these individuals struggle with the problem of a reality that needs to be simultaneously embraced and rejected for each to survive, and how they do survive, is the play's real subject.

Angela is caught in a web of moral choices: To save Felix, she must betray Callahan, and to protect Callahan is to condemn the innocent Felix. She asks Tom, with his apparent sense of moral righteousness, to guide her, but he is too wrapped up in his own obsessions to respond honestly to her moral dilemma. Within Angela's scattered personas lie fragments of a truth that we need to piece together. They contain a mixture of the real and the illusory, combining to create the mask behind which Angela survives in a hostile world. Her mul-

tiple-personality disorder is less a medical condition than a symbol of the modern condition by which it is hard for us all to maintain a sense of balance among divided loyalties and identities. We all must learn to accept the necessary balance between truth and illusion that will allow sanity, for to lose this balance is the way toward madness.

Though Angela's name suggests the "angelic," her presentation is ambiguous. Her intention to assist Felix seems altruistic, but she is also a potential liar and a possible whore. At the start of the play, she is physically hidden within the bed, an indistinct figure, and she will remain hard to see clearly throughout. From what we can piece together, Angela has led a troubled life: raped by her father, used as a prostitute by her "pimp" husband who is an abusive partner, and possibly involved in a variety of mob transactions and uncomfortable relationships. It is no wonder that so much of what she does is an act and that she variously tries to remold herself into a more worthless person who would deserve such a life or into a better person whom she can become.

Angela's alternate selves show us important facets of her personality: Leontine, an apparently hardened prostitute who shows no shame or remorse for her enthusiastic sexual antics; Emily, a timid, sexually abused child; and Renata Marshall, a higher-class lady whose self-assurance is in direct contrast to Angela's uncertainty. What Tom (and possibly Angela, too) needs to do is to make the connections between Angela's disparate personas and the information that each of them conveys to create a picture of what has really happened. In this way, at its heart, reality becomes a construction that is formed by a leap of creative imagination. Forging connections between the small things that we do know can provide a safety net against all that we do not (or even cannot) know.

Angela knows more than Tom because she has a wider perspective. She is not restricted to a single, limited self in the way that Tom is. Unfortunately, Angela is unable to use what she may or may not know efficiently because she is in constant danger of losing her balance. Tom, on the other hand, is initially unprepared to walk the tightrope between reality and illusion because he is striving too much to grasp, completely and solely, the real. He begins to learn the foolishness of such a goal through his experience with Angela. His name conjures up his options: Although *Tom* suggests that he is a "doubting Thomas" who has momentarily lost his faith, *Toole* evokes both his sexual vitality (even though relations with women have been strained) and potential usefulness. He and Angela had an affair in the past, but he now declares that he loves her only "in spirit." His family persuaded him to dump the only woman whom he "truly loved" because they had sex out of wedlock. Yet, he feels a sexual connection to Angela; his feelings may not be true love but are "some kind of love," just as Angela's love is for him.

Both Tom and Angela need to face responsibilities—to themselves, to each other, and to the wider community. Angela needs to uncover a stronger feeling of self-worth and to build a sense of security to survive the chaos that she sees around her. She needs to give Tom more than the information that will free Felix; she must also offer a sense of the fragmentary nature of reality that he must recognize to guard against his own threat of complacency. Angela, also, needs to reaffirm a sense of justice in her society as a whole. Tom, meanwhile, needs to discover a stronger sense of connection to others (he has always been squeamish of contact as his tale of his reluctance to use a public swimming pool attests). He also needs to give Angela not just human recognition and love but assistance in pursuing her goals of justice and in stabilizing her own character, and to reaffirm a sense of hope in his society as a whole, despite its current state. An honest connection between them will help both accomplish their needs, which is illustrated by how their moments of physical contact noticeably reassure them.

Tom has modeled himself after such movie heroes as James Cagney and Spencer Tracy—men who are strong, dependable, and determined. Yet, he is uncomfortable when Angela tells him about her tough past and is unable to offer any emotional support. He finds it hard to deal with people on a human, emotional level. He prefers to read and to recall his own life in episodes that smack more of the movies which he so admires than the messier, more complicated reality behind such lives. His

accounts of the "god-fearing cops" of old seem to be in direct contrast with the sinister contemporary police who may have framed Felix and are now, possibly, stalking Angela. The center of their difficulty may lie in the fact that Tom and Angela each create their own separate realities and what they have is not a shared truth. Unless they can forge a stronger connection, each will be unable to assist the other.

The honesty and the motives of Tom and Angela, intentionally, remain questionable. We are never really certain as to why Angela should be involved at all, especially when her involvement makes her so fearful. Tom is being paid by Felix's parents to clear their son, but his involvement assuredly goes further than this slight cash incentive. Is Tom merely out for personal revenge against Callaghan, to maintain contact with a woman who fascinates him, or because he really wants to right a wrong? Is Angela striving to avenge her wasted life, to maintain contact with a man she loves, or because she really wants to help Felix? Does she, in fact, know anything of importance? Tom thinks that she has crucial information, and maybe that belief is enough. Their motives, though mixed, do match—both are involved due to a complex combination of desire for revenge, for love, and for justice. It may be these mixed motives that, in the end, irrevocably connect and sustain them.

Whether or not Tom believes Angela becomes the central issue (irrelevant to whether or not she is telling the truth). Angela needs Tom to believe her to maintain her identity—his disbelief fragments her. It becomes an issue of trust and its necessity in human lives. Miller wants us to concentrate on Tom and Angela's relationship by emphasizing love in the title; the murder case is merely peripheral—the occasion rather than the subject of the piece. It does not matter whether or not Callaghan's letters exist so long as Tom will believe that they exist when Angela tells him they do.

Tom seems finally to recognize that he will never gain the whole truth that he has been seeking: "I mean I've got to stop looking for some red tag that says 'Real' on it." He realizes that he must allow feelings to conquer logic at times and to accept some things on faith to survive: "If it's real for me then that's the last question I can ask, right?" To continue his relationship with Angela, Tom can never allow the mystery to be realized fully, or it will mean an end. They manage to close without a full resolution, and so the game can continue for both. This seems to be, ultimately, what the play is about—how we sustain our lives through a complex mix of reality and fiction that allows us to forge connections and to accept responsibilities both tangible and intangible to assert our humanity and provide ourselves with those necessities for survival: a sense of security, a sense of morality, and a sense of life.

FIRST PERFORMANCE

Some Kind of Love Story previewed at the Long Wharf Theatre in Connecticut on October 26, 1982, with *Elegy for a Lady,* featuring the same actors, as part of a double bill titled *2 by A. M.* The title was changed to *Two-Way Mirror* for its 1989 British premiere. In the U.S. cast were:

Tom: Charles Cioffi
Angela: Christine Lahti

Directed by Arthur Miller
Set by Hugh Landwehr
Music by Stanley Silverman

INITIAL REVIEWS

The few reviewers who bothered to attend the U.S. premiere predominantly disliked it. Frank Rich complained that "the complicated murder story, though explained in tiresome, overpopulated detail, never comes into clear focus." Kevin Kelly called it an "entirely gratuitous exercise," and Alain Piette was equally disappointed in the play's irresolution and uncertainty. The 1989 British premiere, which was directed by DAVID THACKER and starred Helen Mirren and Bob Peck, was better received. Although some critics remained confused by the play, feeling that it was it too contrived, Michael Billington praised its "economy of language," David Nathan enthusiastically likened it to "a Raymond Chandler mystery," and Kenneth Hurren praised its fascinating mysteries and brilliant performances.

FURTHER READING

Bigsby, Christopher. Afterword. *Two-Way Mirror.* London: Methuen, 1984, 67–70.

Hurren, Kenneth. "*Two-Way Mirror.*" *Mail on Sunday,* January 29, 1989. In *London Theatre Record* 9, no. 1–2 (1989): 63.

Kelly, Kevin. "Arthur Miller's New Work a Double Disaster." *Boston Globe,* November 18, 1982.

Nathan, David. "*Two-Way Mirror.*" *Jewish Chronicle,* January 27, 1989. In *London Theatre Record* 9, no. 1–2 (1989): 62.

Peter, John. "Reflecting Our Split Lives." *Sunday Times,* December 2, 1990, sec. 7, p. 4.

Piette, Alain. "'Elegy for a Lady' and 'Some Kind of Love Story.'" *Theatre Journal* 35 (December 1983): 554.

Rich, Frank. "2 by Arthur Miller." *New York Times,* November 10, 1983: C21.

Speech to the Neighborhood Watch Committee (1988)

Reviewer Linda Winer described *Speech to Neighborhood Watch Committee* as a short monologue "about the destructive effects of material possessions." It was spoken as part of the revue, *Urban Blight,* which attempted through the contributions of 20 well-known writers to convey what made them laugh, cry, or become angry about the city, although some of the pieces ended up having no direct relationship to this assignment. The brainchild of director John Tillinger who codirected with lyricist Richard Maltby, Jr. (who along with composer David Shire, contributed several musical vignettes to the revue), *Urban Blight* played at the Manhattan Theater Club in summer 1988. Along with comedic pieces from Jules Feiffer, Shel Silverstein, and Christopher Durang, Miller's monologue offered a more sobering vision of urban life. Other contributing playwrights were David Mamet, Terrence McNally, A. R. Gurney, Wendy Wasserstein, Charles Fuller, and George C. Wolfe. Performers included Laurence Fishburne, Oliver Platt, John Rubenstein, Faith Prince, and Rex Robbins. Linda

Winer enjoyed the revue, and although she found it "uneven," she viewed Miller's piece as one of the show's more memorable pieces.

FURTHER READING

Winer, Linda. "Revue with Urban Bite." *Newsday,* June 20, 1988, sec. 2, p. 7.

The Story of Canine Joe (1944)

Another of Miller's wartime radio dramas, *The Story of Canine Joe* was aired on August 21, 1944, as part of the *Cavalcade of America* series. A dramatized account of the role that dogs played in the fighting abroad, the drama was little more than an advertisement for the sponsor Du Pont, who made sulpha drugs that could be used on both wounded soldiers and animals. CHRISTOPHER BIGSBY explains how Miller initially included a reference to dogs biting a salesman but had been pressured to change this to a mailman so as not to endanger sales. Unpublished, a typescript can be found at New York Public Library's Center for the Performing Arts.

FURTHER READING

Bigsby, Christopher. "The Radio Plays." *Arthur Miller: A Critical Study.* New York: Cambridge University Press, 2005, 40–53.

The Story of G. I. Joe (1943)

Based on his growing reputation as a radio dramatist, Miller was contracted to work on a film to be called *The Story of G. I. Joe,* which would celebrate the valor of the regular forces and the life of the war correspondent, Ernie Pyle, who had written so movingly about these ordinary soldiers. Wanting to help the war effort and sensing the possibility of writing something better than the usual Hollywood melodrama, Miller accepted the contract offer and began to visit army bases across the country to research the project. He was determined to

present the truth rather than a piece of cleansed and clichéd propaganda. His vision was to follow the experiences of a group of draftees who train together, are sent off to different units, and then meet again in the battle arena. He felt that the story required that most of them should be killed in action, a decision with which the movie executives were not happy. Dissatisfied with the scripts that he produced—finding them too uncomfortable—producer Lester Cowan eventually replaced Miller with other writers, and his name never appeared on the film's final credits. Miller published a book, based on the research that he had done called *Situation Normal . . .* (1944), and documents pertaining to his work on the screenplay can be found in the Lester Cowan Collection at the Academy of Motion Picture Arts and Sciences.

The Story of Gus (1947)

Published in 1947 in Joseph Liss's *Radio's Best Plays, The Story of Gus* had never been recorded. It was written years earlier for Liss, who had been editor of the OWI Domestic Radio Bureau, as one of a series celebrating the lives and contributions of merchant seamen, partly as a recruitment effort. The networks had refused to allow the bureau any airtime as the pieces did not conform to their usual format, being too character driven. To develop the character of Gus, Miller had interviewed men in East Coast and Gulf ports and had created a composite of the seamen whom he had met.

We are initially introduced to Gus through a fellow seaman, Mark Larson, a narrator who linked all the episodes together. Mark describes Gus as a simple Swede in his forties who is interested in taxidermy. He collects stuffed animals, and when we hear Mark, onboard ship, asking Gus about this hobby, we learn how Gus quit the sea for a time but felt impelled to return. Tired of travel near the onset of WORLD WAR II, he decided to settle with his girlfriend Theresa in St. Augustine, Florida, and fix up her bar and grill. They marry. He displays his stuffed animals and seems content giving brief lectures on these to their patrons. Gus learns that Theresa has an 18-year-old son, Maxie, who after being rejected by the army comes to live with them. Theresa is very happy that her husband and her son are both safe from the war, but Gus feels unsettled and unsure that he is setting a good example for his new stepson.

Theresa asks Gus not to mention his sea days in fear that it will incite Maxie to join the merchant marine. Maxie works as a taxi driver, but Gus is horrified when he learns that Maxie has been taking people to the beach to gape at wrecked ships, feeling that it lacks respect. He confesses to Maxie his relationship with the sea and concludes, "If I'm a seaman I oughta be on the sea." As expected, his stories captivate Maxie, who grows restless. When, one night, a ship is torpedoed within hearing, they both head to the beach to help, and Theresa realizes that neither plans to return. They feel a responsibility to help in the war effort, and none of Theresa's pleas will prevent them. Interspersed throughout the conversation between Mark and Gus onboard ship is the sound of a harmonica—Maxie is playing his harmonica in the engine room.

The play both overtly and subliminally persuades any potential seafaring listeners to enlist in the merchant marine, overtly by Gus's moral and patriotic claim, "It ain't the proper thing staying at home," and subliminally by Mark and Gus's homage to the sea's attraction which frames the play.

"Subsidized Theater"
(1947, 2000)

Back in 1947, less than five months after *All My Sons* had opened on BROADWAY, Miller wrote a controversial essay titled "Subsidized Theater" for *New York Times* that asked to put an end to the commercial demands and business standards that he saw as draining the life of the current theater. Miller argued that the only hope for the theater as a viable art form was to establish a subsidized theatrical network with funds drawn from public and private sources, much in the way that they do in Europe. Wary of censorship, Miller advised against including federal support but offered a call to all those who are professionally involved in the theater to be responsible for initiating these changes. Fifty-three years later, he wrote an essay with the same title as the conclusion to his collection *Echoes Down the Corridor* (2000). The chance of mounting a serious play on Broadway, he begins, has become even slimmer than in the past, and it is time to "consider alternatives" before serious professional theater in the United States is destroyed for good.

Unheeded on his first call to arms, Miller returns to this topic as one about which he feels passionately and one on which, this time perhaps, his better-known voice might be heard. The later essay reiterates many of the same points from the earlier essay regarding the overcommercialization of Broadway and theater throughout the country, the scant opportunities being offered to serious theatrical practitioners, from playwright and director to actors and stage designers, and the temerity of producers who seem no longer even to know how to assess a play. Admitting that financing plays was never easy in the United States, it has now become ludicrous. In Miller's eyes, the U.S. theater culture has become too greedy, pricing itself out of vibrancy to the point where little that is new receives a serious tryout: "It is a system which has almost literally eaten its own body alive."

Good drama, Miller insists—like that of HAROLD PINTER, Tom Stoppard, David Hare, or Michael Frayn, whose plays have all been subsidized in GREAT BRITAIN—is admittedly too chancy to "warrant investment-for-profit" but is also too important to lose. The United States has theaters and even playwrights, Miller opines, but "we don't have Theatre," as art has become incidental to commercial endeavor. Once again, Miller calls for subsidies, even government ones as he has witnessed in Sweden and China, to revive the system. "Theatre is not going to die," he concludes, but to keep it alive, we must "open the world of plays to students" because they will become the theater practitioners of the future and must be shown that theater can still have relevance in their lives.

That They May Win (1943)

Written for the New York-based, socially minded dramatic group Stage for Action, and first produced on December 21, 1943, in BROOKLYN for the Victory Committee of Welfare Center 67, *That They May Win* became one of the group's most popular plays. Openly intended as propaganda, the play exhorts women to fight for proper price controls on the home front, even to the point of informing on profiteers. Written in agitprop style that is reminiscent of CLIFFORD ODETS, with scripted interruptions from supposed audience members to draw everyone into the argument, it was published in Margaret Mayorga's *Best One Act Plays of 1944*.

While Danny Carroll has been in Italy fighting for his country and suffering a bayonet wound in the stomach, his wife Delia and their baby have been struggling to survive on his army allotment back home where prices have skyrocketed out of control. Danny is awarded a medal for killing 28 enemy soldiers but is shocked to find his wife in a slum apartment and the family struggling to feed itself. Delia tries to hide their poverty, but Danny overhears their friend Ina persuading Delia to accept a steak. Since Danny is unfit as yet for full-time work, Delia suggests that she take a full-time job while Danny cares for the baby because they cannot afford childcare if he works too.

Danny grows increasingly angry both at the situation and at his wife for accepting it. He insists that by politicizing the issue, changes can be made, but as he berates his wife for her complacency, a man from the audience tries to defend her and speaks of his sister being in the same position. While a second man tries to calm him so that the play can proceed, Man Who Knows speaks up and reiterates Danny's insistence that people do have the power to change things in a democracy but that they need to speak up if they want to be heard. Thus Miller moves the discussion into the public arena. Telling women to watch their storekeepers, report violations, and fight back, the Man Who Knows delivers Miller's central message: While their countrymen fight abroad, women must fight a war at home against greedy profiteers. Apologizing to Danny for interrupting, he is told that he has already explained the ending of the play.

The Theater Essays of Arthur Miller (1978, 1996)

In 1978, Robert A. Martin edited the first collection of essays that Miller had written on a variety of theatrical issues. It includes 26 pieces that were written between 1949 and 1972, most of which had been previously printed in newspapers and magazines. There are also reprints of some of Miller's introductions to play editions, an extract from *In Russia*, and an interview. The essays are grouped into different time periods, covering *Death of a Salesman* to *A View from the Bridge*, *The Collected Plays* to *The Misfits*, and *After the Fall* to Lincoln Center. There is a lengthy introduction from Martin that explains his choices, a brief foreword from Miller, and various useful appendices.

The book was mostly welcomed by critics: *Booklist* praised Miller's "serious and consistent assessment of the theatre's nature and aims," J. L. Styan found it "argumentative, stimulating, challenging," and Albert Johnston felt that the essays spoke "to the problems of the contemporary theatre and to the ills of our society." Others, however, felt it incomplete. While Michael Havener praised the collection for its "valuable insights," he also complained about "regrettable omissions," and June Schleuter claimed that the selection was largely unnoteworthy, reflecting a professional's view of the theater rather than that of a literary critic.

STEVEN CENTOLA's 1996 revision added 18 additional selections written between 1972 and 1994, and it updated the appendices. With several more interviews and essays on Miller's own work and that of others, the revised edition of *The Theater Essays of Arthur Miller* took the collection up to *Broken Glass*. While several essays in both editions address specific plays that Miller wrote and provide rationales, intentions, and explanations, many deal with more general theatrical concerns regarding the state of theater as a whole in the United States and elsewhere, offering analyses of form, technique, and impact.

FURTHER READING

Havener, Michael W. "*Theater Essays of Arthur Miller.*" *Library Journal*, March 1, 1978, 582.

Johnston, Albert. "*Theater Essays of Arthur Miller.*" *Publisher's Weekly*, January 2, 1978, 60.

Schleuter, June. "*Theater Essays of Arthur Miller.*" *Bestsellers* 37 (February 1978): 345.

Styan, J. L. "A View from the Crucible; or, the Compleat Playwright." *Michigan Quarterly Review* 18 (1979): 509–515.

"*Theater Essays of Arthur Miller.*" *Booklist*, February 15, 1978, 971.

They Too Arise (1937)

A revision of Miller's *No Villain*, his Hopward Award-winning first play, *They Too Arise* would be Miller's first play to reach production. It was performed three times in 1937 in Ann Arbor, Michigan, by a Jewish student theater group, the Hillel Players, and once more in Detroit through the auspices of the FEDERAL THEATER PROJECT. It also won Miller a $1,250 scholarship award from the THEATRE GUILD's Bureau of New Plays to study playwrighting with KENNETH ROWE, a professor at the UNIVERSITY OF MICHIGAN. Never published, the initial manuscript for this play is at the University of Michigan, and a later version that was written in 1938 can be found in the Billy Rose Theatre Collection in New York. This play would be further revised into *The Grass Still Grows* for an anticipated production in New York that never came to fruition.

Although it has the same plot as *No Villain*, which depicts the divisions within the Simon family as the father, Abe, struggles to keep his business afloat, *They Too Arise* makes several changes of emphasis. The moral vision of the play is taken from the older son Ben and placed in the younger brother Arnold's mouth. Arnold becomes more central and takes on the bigger speeches. It is made clearer that he is adamantly against his father's

business and sees his father as a pawn for the bigger businesses that are really in control. These bigger businesses are also brought more to the fore, and the battle now extends beyond the family as lines become drawn between small and large businesses. A new character, Liebowitz, is added to emphasize this aspect. He is a hard worker who has been defrauded by a major manufacturer; his hand is broken by gangsters for protesting. The Manufacturers' Association, which is dominated by big business, has become more prominent. It plans to hire strikebreakers to smash the hold of the unions and to gain greater control. Even Abe stands firm against what he sees as their dishonest way of conducting business and denounces their plan. Ben agrees with him, insisting that small businesses are more worker friendly.

Ben's potential marriage to the daughter of a fellow manufacturer, Helen, as a means of saving his own family's business is given greater consideration. It is again rejected, but this time because Helen's father steals an order that the Simons had needed, and it is Abe who sends him packing. The mother, Esther, is harsher with her husband as he struggles to keep afloat, but also, like *Death of a Salesman*'s Linda Loman, defends him against his sons' apathy. Like *All My Sons'* Joe Keller, Abe views the success of his business as a measure of his manhood. His sons can see beyond this, just as Chris Keller and Larry Keller try to show their father. In *They Too Arise*, Abe begins to see his sons' point and agrees that he will have to change, even to considering letting his company go. The question of responsibility to both self and others against tremendous forces that apparently are antagonistic to such humane values has become even stronger than in the earlier *No Villain*.

In the revised version of *They Too Arise*, Arnold becomes a confirmed communist rather than a character who simply flirts with Marxist ideals. Becoming even more central, he is also more doctrinaire as his speeches become less ideologically uncertain and as he refuses even to consider the dilemmas that are being faced by his father and brother: "I want the people to take the power that comes with ownership away from the little class of capitalists who have it now." The Manufacturers' Association now believes that communists are orchestrating the strike, and it is Ben who speaks the more firmly against them, offering threat for threat. His speeches make the conflict more physically violent than cerebral as it was before. Miller also adds more serious references to the plight of the Jews in Europe, a growing concern at that time.

In many ways, with its praise of the working class, incitements to rebellion, and critique of CAPITALISM, this later version is closer to the conventional proletarian-influenced agitprop of the period. It is more emphatic than the earlier draft and is less ambivalent regarding right and wrong responses; yet Miller still shows greater sympathy for the middle-class family than we see in a play such as CLIFFORD ODETS's *Waiting for Lefty*. Abe's declaration from the earlier version, in which he acknowledges his generation's need to change, is now given to his wife, Esther, but the fact remains that Miller refuses to write off anyone as beyond hope.

Thunder from the Hills (1942)

Broadcast on September 28, 1942, as part of the *Cavalcade of America* series, the radio play *Thunder from the Hills* tells the story of Benito Juárez, the liberator of Mexico, played by Orson Welles. A profoundly socialist vision, Miller depicts Juárez righteously fighting against the oppression of the dictators in control for the freedom of the common Mexican back in 1867. Juárez, with his "labor-toughened hand," is a man of the people. Miller pointedly makes a comparison between Juárez and Abraham Lincoln, just as Santa Ana and Emperor Maximilian echo the fascism of Hitler and Mussolini in their cruel endeavors to remain in control; thus, he makes the historical events seem closer to home and topical for an audience that is engaged in WORLD WAR II. Juárez finally captures Maximilian and argues persuasively for his execution, suggesting that to pardon him would make a mockery of DEMOCRACY. By this, Miller proffers his harsh vision of the would-be fate of all such tyrants.

Verse drama was fairly daring for prime-time mainstream radio of that era, and CHRISTOPHER BIGSBY considers it one of Miller's best radio plays. It was never published, and no extant typescript has so far come to light, but the Museum of Radio and Television holds a recording.

Timebends: A Life (1987)

Miller's autobiography takes us from childhood through to the late 1980s as Miller tends his ROXBURY, CONNECTICUT, property and ponders his development as a writer and a human being and his connection to his surrounding society. Reminiscent of LILLIAN HELLMAN's memoirs, Miller does not relate his life in a chronological progression but bends and curves time as he makes connections between different people, experiences, and events. As his story unfolds, Miller frequently returns to key periods in his life that have been most formative: the GREAT DEPRESSION, his growing understanding of the significance of the HOLOCAUST, his dealings with the HOUSE UN-AMERICAN ACTIVITIES COMMITTEE (HUAC) in the 1950s, his marriage to MARILYN MONROE, and his work with PEN, along with explanations of how he came to write many of his works (emphasis being on the plays). "Memory," he states, "keeps folding in upon itself like geologic layers of rock, the deeper strata sometimes appearing on top before they slope downward into the depths again." Miller tries to share some of his deeper strata here, acknowledging his doubts, mistakes, and desires as he tries to come to terms with who he is as a writer and what his legacy might be.

Divided into eight chapters, the book is 600 pages and includes 32 pages of photographs featuring Miller's family, friends, and acquaintances, as well as scenes from various productions of his plays. While the discussion is weighted toward his earlier years up to his marriage to Monroe, the final chapter swiftly covers the latter two decades of his life and sums up the effect of these previous experiences on his future outlook and work. Given Miller's reluctance to discuss his private life with biographers, this autobiography presents the most direct insight that we have as to the playwright's personal relationships, along with invaluable descriptions of his artistic process, the inspirations and intentions behind many of his creations, and commentary on his opinions and beliefs regarding the theater, politics, and life in general. "The desire to move on, to metamorphose," Miller suggests, "was given to me as life's inevitable and rightful condition. To keep becoming, always to stay involved in transition." It is a lesson that he learned early from his family and one that he has carried through life. We get the sense that even at age 72 (when he wrote this book), Miller would yet surprise us with something new.

Miller offers personal portraits of his family, friends, and the many theatrical and political figures with whom he has been involved. He describes the initial idealism and subsequent breakdown of his first two marriages, the first to MARY SLATTERY and the second to Monroe, and his later happiness with INGE MORATH, his third wife. We learn of his childhood explorations within BROOKLYN and his adult ones across the globe, his experiences working at CHADICK–DELAMETER AUTO-PARTS WAREHOUSE and at the BROOKLYN NAVY YARD. He relates beliefs that are closely informed by JUDAISM and his political and legal involvement in a variety of causes from the Soviet Union to local Connecticut to create a fairly complete picture of his life and its concerns. He also tells of his days at the UNIVERSITY OF MICHIGAN when he first began to write and briefly covers his time with the FEDERAL THEATER PROJECT and working with radio drama. Then each play from *The Man Who Had All the Luck* through to *Danger Memory!* is explicated in terms of its evolution, production, and critical reception. Although more time is spent on the better-known plays—recounting the Greek roots behind *All My Sons,* the rationale in creating *Death of a Salesman* and the relationship of Willy Loman to MANNY NEWMAN, and the decision to equate the House Un-American Activities Committee to the SALEM WITCH TRIALS in *The Crucible*—Miller shares insights about them all, as well as a few projects that never got off the ground, such as some abortive screenplay fantasies from the 1960s that envision the possibilities of world peace.

The book begins with a child's eye view of the playwright's mother, AUGUSTA MILLER, and pro-

ceeds to describe his family background, his relationship to his father ISIDORE MILLER, and his Jewish heritage. From the start, he occasionally leaps forward in time to offer a contrasting perspective. He lays out a family dynamic in which, early on, he is at odds with his older brother KERMIT MILLER and is siding with his mother who encourages his artistic endeavors. He openly admits that many of his characters share traits with people whom he has known, but he denies there are any strictly one-to-one portraits. He takes us through conflicts at home as his father's business goes under, his own flight to Michigan, and his subsequent return to New York, as well as how and why he became a playwright.

Miller admits to having a strong Jewish identity, having fully absorbed the culture if not the religion. It is this, he believes, that has given him his sense of "power and reassurance" and has defined his moral outlook. He recalls observing a Simchat Torah celebration at Temple with his great-grandfather, and he suggests a connection between JUDAISM and American Puritanism in terms of a shared idealism, devotion, "legalistic reductiveness," and longing "for the pure and intellectually elegant argument." Relating his youthful adventures in Harlem and his early experiences with blacks, Miller asserts his recognition that racism is irrational and immoral and must be fought. For Miller, racism and prejudice restrict the life of the self in that the perpetrators deny the humanity of others.

Miller tells us that, aside from his belief that playwrighting is the most effective means of literary communication, he was initially drawn to it as a form of "self-discovery." The autobiography offers a different picture of a playwright who has been described by others as a secure, self-certain moralizer, as Miller openly shares his doubts and insecurities, along with his sense that much of his work has been underappreciated and rejected. Although he may see himself as a prophet of sorts who has the unpopular task of enlightening the unenlightened masses about harsh realities, he has reluctantly shouldered this role, although felt it to be a necessary one. His motivation as a writer is to help people connect and mediate between opposing beliefs to find the common ground on which all can meet. He describes the roots of his dramatic interest as lying in the spiritual paradox of longing and rejection that people face as they seek to identify themselves. Life is a series of ups and downs, and he tries to reflect in his work what he sees as the inevitable contradictions of life.

For Miller, art is meaningful and can make a difference, and this validates the moral imperative that informs his work. He traces a growing recognition that there is a necessary balance to be found between illusion and reality, in which the binary tensions of life and the duality of existence can be reconciled. A philosophic outlook that welcomes the tension between opposites and the connective tissue of life is on display throughout the book. Miller's fierce belief in the potential of DEMOCRACY, his adoption of HUMANISM as the only feasible way forward, and his fears that the BROADWAY system might be destroying the potential of U.S. theater, are also made evident. He shares a belief that his condemnation by many in the United States comes from his refusal to ignore in his writing certain truths that people find too uncomfortable to face.

Miller's belief in the importance of the past, its continued influence, and how it helps to define the present runs through the book, which is itself a metaphor for how such a dynamic operates. "The past," Miller declares, "is a formality, merely a dimmer present, for everything we are is at every moment alive in us." The Depression is certainly the event that most impacted Miller in a personal sense, and the Holocaust is that which most informs his attitude toward society.

Miller also traces his evolving political beliefs from his early interest and rejection of COMMUNISM to his embrace of social humanism. He views both communism and fascism as extremes and as detrimental to human development. "Good art," he insists, "stands in contradiction to propaganda in the sense that a writer cannot make truth but only discover it." His trips abroad have helped him in his evolving definition of the United States as he measures nation against nation, drawing conclusions that find the United States both vibrant and lacking. While he admits to preferring European theater audiences for their greater openness and the less-commercial nature of their theaters, he

also finds time to praise the social experimentation of the United States in its innovation and its stature in his eyes as "liberty's home." Miller's political adventures, including his appearance at the Waldorf–Astoria Conference, the 1968 Democratic Convention, and dealings with HUAC and PEN are all recounted in informative detail, followed by Miller's opinions as to the lessons each conveyed.

Miller's opinions on the work of other playwrights, especially HENRIK IBSEN, EUGENE O'NEILL, CLIFFORD ODETS, and TENNESSEE WILLIAMS, are useful in placing him within the field of drama and assist in our growing understanding of how Miller uses language, symbol, and form in his own work. There are also scattered throughout the book interestingly subjective portraits of many theatrical people with whom Miller has worked, including directors (ELIA KAZAN, HAROLD CLURMAN, JED HARRIS), designers (JO MIELZINER, BORIS ARONSON, MORDECAI GORELIK), and actors (ARTHUR KENNEDY, LEE J. COBB, FREDRIC MARCH). It becomes clear that Miller has a greater faith in the creators of art than in its critics, although he also admits that writers need to go beyond politics if they are to produce anything of lasting importance. The task of the artist, in Miller's view, is to look at life fairly and to condemn any injustices that come to light.

The basis of Miller's continued optimism is displayed by his frequent references to his lifelong fight against nihilism and his refusal to give in to evil in the world while acknowledging its inevitable existence. Miller appears to have had a sense of renewal and a reduction of doubt in his life in the 1960s after marrying Morath and becoming a new father with the birth of REBECCA MILLER. His work with PEN also bolstered him and offered a new and firmer sense of direction, even as he worries about the impact of ABSURDISM, about the posthumanist impulse of the age, and about the difficulties of writing against a "culture of denial." His greatest hope is that U.S. theater can become more committed to art than to the bottom line. Miller equates his life as a writer to his work on his Roxbury estate where he plants seedlings in the hope that they will grow; the resulting trees are testament to the potential of that hope. The book concludes with an emotive image of the connections that he sees as existing between everything in his work: "The first truth, probably, is that we are all connected, watching one another. Even the trees."

Reviews of the book were mixed; though acknowledging its passion, many found it to be ponderous and poorly written and its rambling style disconcerting. Bruce Bawer caustically referred to it as a "remarkable document in self-celebration and political self-justification, as discursive, repetitive, and intellectually simplistic as many of his plays," and William A. Henry III called it "often muddled, even mawkish." *The Economist*, however, described it as "engrossing" as it is "complex and testing," Stephen Grecco felt it to be "searingly honest (and surprisingly witty)," and David Anderson found it a "fascinating . . . touching and straightforward" relation that was told "with a modesty that belies [Miller's] importance in American cultural life." Miller felt that, generally, GREAT BRITAIN received the book better than the United States.

FURTHER READING

Anderson, David E. "A Writer's Reflections on His Life." *Philadelphia Inquirer*, November 19, 1987, C5.

"Arthur Miller: Life of a Salesman." *Economist*, November 14, 1987, 104.

Bawer, Bruce. "A Salesman's Old Line." *American Scholar* (Winter 1989): 140–146.

Grecco, Stephen. "Autobiography." *World Literature Today* (Autumn 1988): 664.

Henry, William A., III. "Books: A Life of Fade-Outs and Fade-Ins." *Time*, November 23, 1987, 88.

Meyer, Kinereth. "A Jew Can Have a Jewish Face?: Arthur Miller, Autobiography, and the Holocaust." *Prooftexts* 18 (1998): 239–258.

Toward a Farther Star (1942)

Aired on November 2, 1942, this radio drama told the story of Amelia Earhart, played by Madeleine Carroll, and is an interesting early Miller depiction of a strong woman. Concerned with conveying both the expected patriotic message of the day and a feminist vision in which women are allowed to work alongside men without censure, Earhart's struggles against gender expectation, and her eventual triumph is meant to inspire both men and women. We are informed at the start about the number of women who currently pilot Civil Air Patrol planes and who are engaged in various kinds of necessary war work. Earhart counters men who refuse to employ her as a pilot because she is a woman, but she insists that the world is changing. In an impassioned speech, she points out that since women make up half of the population, to restrict their opportunities to become involved in society is tantamount to "flying with only one of its wings." At the close, Miller brings the play into the present and directs our attention again to what women were contributing to the war effort, with the underlying implication that war has forever changed the roles of women in modern society. Although unpublished, typescripts for this drama can be found at the HARRY RANSOM RESEARCH CENTER and at the New York Public Library.

"Tragedy and the Common Man" (1949)

Originally published in 1949 in the *New York Times* two weeks after the opening of *Death of a Salesman*, "Tragedy and the Common Man" is a defense of Miller's claims that *Death of a Salesman* was a TRAGEDY in the full dramatic sense. Miller's most controversial essay is a landmark statement that sparked decades of debate regarding modern dramatic theory, and it has been much anthologized since then. As Robert Martin, who included the essay in his 1978 edition of *The Theater Essays of Arthur Miller*, points out, Miller's "many theoretical statements on tragedy have in no small part contributed to the controversy surrounding" *Death of a Salesman*. As Martin explains, "This essay was primarily motivated by the initial critical response to the play, and represents Miller's first major statement on the tragic potential of modern drama."

"Tragedy and the Common Man" asserts that "the common man is as apt a subject for tragedy in its highest sense as kings were" to the Greeks. Miller goes on to argue that the average man can display the same "heart and spirit" as anyone who is nobly born and so should be as equally capable of heroism. In this sense then, we must surely view Willy Loman as a true tragic hero, although Miller does not refer to his own character or play once in the essay. Miller's aim in this piece is clearly to acknowledge the importance and significance of the lives of the ordinary people, the people about whom he wrote and would continue to write.

Miller begins the piece by pointing out that the modern world has become more skeptical and less inclined to believe in the possibility of heroes. This has led to an erroneous belief that tragedy is no longer appropriate or possible. Miller challenges this belief by asserting that anyone who is "ready to lay down his life" to secure his "sense of personal dignity" can be deemed a tragic hero, regardless of social status, and that such people exist in a modern world in which many of us fear displacement. Miller sees the heroes of Greek and Shakespearean tragedy as concerned with gaining their "rightful" position in their societies, a position that they either have lost or have yet to attain. The tragedy ensues from events that conspire to prevent this and includes the tragic hero's own flaw, which Miller condenses to mean "his inherent unwillingness to remain passive in the face of what he conceives to be a challenge to his dignity."

Miller explains, "In the tragic view the need of man to wholly realize himself is the only fixed star, and whatever it is that hedges his nature and lowers it is ripe for attack and examination." The terror and fear that tragedy is meant to invoke is born from the hero's refusal to accept the status quo, which necessarily insists that we reexamine all our lives. Through this reexamination, Miller insists, comes the learning that is also a necessary part of the tragic equation. Tragedy, to Miller, is "the consequence of a man's total compulsion to evaluate himself justly" in the pursuit of which he is destroyed. In evaluating this destruction, we can come to understand what is wrong with society that forces our hero to undergo such an experience, and

with this knowledge, we can set about improving that society. Thus, the hero's death has meaning and offers hope.

For Miller, tragedy is essentially optimistic as it celebrates humankind's "thrust for freedom," and "demonstrates the indestructible will of man to achieve his humanity." Although the hero will inevitably come to an unpleasant end, it is the "possibility of victory" that makes the battle tragic and ultimately optimistic. If the hero fights a battle that could not possibly be won, then Miller sees the hero's fate as merely pathetic and is so reduced to pessimism. Tragedy, he insists, contains a "nicer balance between what is possible and what is impossible" and allows us to continue to hope for the "perfectibility of man."

It is only when people try to view everything as a private individual dilemma with no connection to the wider society, Miller suggests, that tragedy truly becomes impossible, just as does seeing everything as society's fault with a faultless protagonist having no choice in his or her own destruction. Tragedy explores the relationship of the individual to society and must contain both elements to be effective.

Miller's authoritarian tone in the essay did as much to rankle academics as the challenges that his essay offered to many traditional assumptions regarding drama. At its publication, the essay received a mixed reception and continues to evoke extreme reactions, especially from those critics who wish to argue an Aristotelian view of tragedy, such as John Gassner or Joseph Wood Krutch. Although Gassner eventually came to see *Death of a Salesman* as a potential tragedy, he still felt a need to label it "low" tragedy as opposed to the "high" tragedies of the Greeks and Shakespeare. In 1949, many critics were still unconvinced that U.S. drama was even worthy of study, and so Miller's pronouncements in "Tragedy and the Common Man" were seen as provocative not only in their dismissal of previous definitions but also in their implication that U.S. drama was a formidable entity. Martin compares the effect of this essay on the critical establishment, albeit in a lesser degree, as similar to that of Darwin's *Origin of Species* on the complacent religious establishment of the 19th century.

FURTHER READING

Gassner, John. "The Possibilities and Perils of Modern Tragedy." *Tulane Drama Review* 1, no. 3 (June 1957): 3–14.

Martin, Robert A., editor. *The Theater Essays of Arthur Miller.* New York: Viking, 1978.

The Turpentine Still (2004)

Published in *Southwest Review* in 2004, the brief novella *The Turpentine Still* is one of Miller's final published works. Started two decades previously, the story is divided into three sections and begins in the 1950s during the height of the cold war. It tells the story of Mark Levin, once a committed leftist, who now has lost his passion for the cause and tries to convince himself that he is content with a less political life. His friend Jimmy, however, remains convinced that COMMUNISM can still work, and he persuades Levin and his wife Adele to take a trip to Haiti to witness what he sees as exciting artistic and political developments on the island. Needing to escape the limited outlook of a New York life that is bound by fears of communism, the couple find the prospect of Haiti with all of its mysterious violence an attractive change.

The Levins, we are told, are "serious people," being accomplished musicians who view life from a certain self-conscious and judgmental perspective. Levin is an admirer of Proust, who quit journalism to run his father's leather business. Sympathetic to liberal causes, they are not incapable of involvement but prefer to maintain a "discreet distance." They are detached from their own lives, and even their marriage has become something of a habit. Their Haitian experience has the potential to shake them up.

On their arrival they receive different perspectives of the island from the various influential guests of wealthy expatriate Pat O'Dwyer whom they visit. They feel uncertain about what to do for a nation that is so patently broken and in need of repair. Mrs. Pat began life as a Catholic, but, while involved in social work, recognized a pressing need for condoms. She began to manufacture them and

made a fortune. She has retired to Haiti and mostly donates her condoms to nonprofit organizations to help the populace but still remains somewhat apart from local life in her splendid house with its balconies and Klee and Leger paintings. Levin chats to Mrs. Pat's black Jamaican son-in-law, Vincent Breed, the second husband of her daughter, Lilly. Lilly comments that a friend has just seen the local commissioner, recently buried, walking along the street claiming to be a zombie. Although the white Episcopalian bishop declares it may be possible, as "some very strange things do happen," the local police chief, the only Haitian present, insists this is ridiculous and merely a case of mistaken identity. Thus he explodes the romanticized expectations of the foreigners.

Vincent is skeptical of all religions, being more concerned with helping the Haitians on a practical level. To this end, he keeps planting trees—although in the past they have been stolen before fully grown—to provide a useful resource. Vincent asks Levin why he is interested in Haiti, and Levin remains uncertain but jumps at the chance to see more of the island with this new friend the following day.

In part two of the story Adele decides not to join the men because the car looks too cramped. As they head up the mountain into the interior, Levin feels his attraction to his wife and wishes he made love to her more often. He resolves to work on their marriage upon his return. Levin observes the poverty of Haiti as he and Vincent travel and discuss the island's endemic unemployment, lack of proper education, corrupt political system, and paucity of reserves. They see a beautiful native woman and both feel an intense pity for the country.

Vincent tells Levin about Douglas. He is a man who quit an important company job in New York to cruise around the islands in an old naval boat, trying to make a living by showing films to the natives. Finding few with sufficient money to pay, he has now settled in Haiti with a plan to distill turpentine, a popular cure-all in Haiti. Vincent feels involved because he initially encouraged Douglas but is now uncertain the project is safe. The still Douglas has built is potentially dangerous, and Vincent feels that his friend knows too little about the process. Even the trees whose resin Douglas plans to use are not the ideal kind, and Vincent hopes to talk him out of continuing.

Arriving at Douglas's house, Vincent and Levin are welcomed by Denise, Douglas's beleaguered wife. There are also two children apparently going wild while their father obsesses over his project. The house is dank, with few possessions, and the family uses wooden boxes for tables and chairs. Denise has her arm, broken while trying to help unload a large metal drum for her husband, in a sling. She and Douglas are from upper-class background but live in Haiti in squalor, as he puts all they own into his business plans. Both are pleased to see Vincent, though for different reasons: Denise hopes Vincent can stop this crazy scheme and save her. Douglas hopes Vincent will give him the go-ahead. When Vincent voices his concerns over the safety of the equipment, which has been patched together from scraps but will need to be able to withstand high pressure, Douglas responds with an anguished determination to proceed. He sees it as his opportunity to create a new industry to aid a country he has grown to love. Levin finds his passion commendable but disconcerting. Vincent suggests that it springs from a desire "to create something" that can be viewed as wholly one's own and which would make one's entire life more meaningful.

They go to view the equipment, and Levin considers what he, personally, has created and realizes it is very little. He and his wife have not even had children. He wonders if Adele is content with their life and with him. The still is black and imposing. When Vincent asks Douglas to wait until they can have it inspected, he refuses, confessing he has cancer and needs to see the still working before he dies. Observing the couple, Levin decides that although she hates their life, Denise loves her husband deeply and will not abandon him. Vincent offers to expedite the inspection, and his apparent decision to get more involved allows Douglas to accept and embrace his friend. Levin is amazed at the "outbreak of hopefulness on all sides," not understanding its source. It seems to rest more in the camaraderie between these people as they work toward a common goal, rather than in the potential

success of the project. Levin considers how most people, including Proust, actually create their own reality.

On their return down the mountain, their car battery dies. A local truck stops, and the young driver offers them a spare battery. He refuses payment and trusts them to return the battery in a few days, without even ensuring they will know where to take it. They accept in amazement, realizing there is much about Haiti and Haitians that remains inexplicable—a little like life itself.

The third part of the story leaps forward 33 years. Adele has been dead for six years, and Levin is living a routine existence and feeling somewhat reduced by his loss. He has a friendship with a woman half his age but is uncertain if he should marry her. This seems connected to Miller's personal life at the time, as he mourned the loss of INGE MORATH and faced uncertainty as to where to take his new relationship with AGNES BARLEY. Going for a walk on the beach, always a transcendent experience for Miller's characters, Levin recalls Douglas. We learn that Vincent had died the year following their meeting, and that Jimmy has also died. Levin wonders if the turpentine still had ever been lit. He decides to return to Haiti and find out, planning to look up Vincent's stepson, Peter, who would now be in his forties (as was Levin on his first trip). His decision revivifies him, even while it is tinged by sadness because he must return without Adele.

Peter works for an export company and remembers Levin and Adele playing a piano duet for his family, but he has never heard of Douglas. Peter seems a tough character, living a narrow existence, but his curiosity is roused by Levin's description of Douglas. He offers to take Levin to see if they can find the still. As they travel, Levin notices the landscape has changed: most of the trees have been cut down and the road is badly eroded without their protection. Peter is intrigued by Levin's concern over the state of the country, having lost the habit, believing that nothing can be done about such things, even while he does seem to be positively involved—being part of a local business and helping various Haitians.

They pass a small impoverished village where locals have their junk set out for sale. Peter buys a small, worn spoon. He then asks Levin why he is so interested in Douglas, and Levin decides it must have something to do with Douglas's evident conviction. Levin wants to see if that conviction has held or if he just dreamed it. Peter gets drawn into this quest for meaning, evidently having lived with a vacuum of meaning in his own life. They stop by a broken down taxi, and Peter casually fixes it. He uses a rope he has been given by a passing horse rider who had refused payment, in another echo of Levin's earlier trip with Vincent. Peter fixes the taxi without thought of recompense but also without any enthusiasm or sentimentality, which bemuses Levin. He begins to see a likeness between himself and Peter; both tend to hide behind a facade of detachment.

Levin recognizes Douglas's driveway, and they find the house. The sparse furnishings remain, but the family is gone. They continue up the mountain to find the still, and Levin ponders if he might be doing this in an attempt to turn back the clock to a time he still had Adele. They ask some locals for guidance, and an elderly man, Octavus, admits he once worked for Douglas and can show them the equipment. Levin recalls Jimmy and his convictions, now buried along with the man. He wonders if something can possibly be left behind after such intense beliefs. Octavus takes them to the still, and both Peter and Levin are delighted to see it. They ask Octavus if it had ever been lit, and he explains how Douglas had briefly run the still. They had produced turpentine, but he had given most of it away until he had no money left to continue production and could find no one to buy the business to keep it going. We learn his wife abandoned him after all, returning to the United States with her children, and Octavus had kept an eye on Douglas during his final days. He bequeathed the still to Octavus, but Octavus had no money to pay anyone to run it, so it had remained unused.

On his deathbed, Douglas gave his helper a note of advice: "If the idea goes let it go, but if you can keep it, do so and it will surely lift you up one day." Octavus had never understood what this meant, but he feels happier at having passed the message along. Peter and Levin wonder as to its meaning. Levin senses it refers to the uplifting importance of hope. This is something Peter has evidently lost, having witnessed all the failures of his parents and grandparents' generations. Levin and Peter discuss the unfortunate state of Haiti as they return to town, and seem to see little that can be done. However, back at the hotel, Levin becomes infected by that very sense of hope Douglas displayed. He still cannot rationalize it, but he can appreciate it.

Douglas's passion and preparedness to sacrifice himself and his family to a crazy scheme to distill turpentine on the island has inspired Levin to reevaluate his own life. His discovery that the still *still* exists transforms him for he sees this existence as evidence of hope. Levin decides that passionate involvement, however apparently absurd, is its own reward and that a life without such passion is one that is hardly worth living. In his insightful commentary on the tale, CHRISTOPHER BIGSBY describes Levin's transformation in terms of a rediscovery of "his own passion in trying to account for someone else's" Finding the still, Bigsby suggest, has been Levin's act of invention to place him on a par with Douglas as a man who cares, regardless of the outcome.

FURTHER READING

Bigsby, Christopher. *Arthur Miller: A Critical Study.* New York: Cambridge University Press, 2005, 462–469.

Two-Way Mirror (1982)

Miller's one-acts *Elegy for a Lady* and *Some Kind of Love Story* previewed at the Long Wharf Theatre in 1982 as part of a double bill titled *2 by A. M.* However, the title was changed to *Two-Way Mirror* for its 1989 premiere in GREAT BRITAIN at the suggestion of CHRISTOPHER BIGSBY. While *2 by A.M.* conjures up a suggestion of those uncomfortable nightmares that one encounters at two in the morning—and it is certain that Miller intends for these plays to be anything but soothing—*Two Way Mirror* indicates more strongly the ambivalence of their visions. For Bigsby, such a title suggested a contemplation of "the deceptive nature of the world in which its characters exist. At times they suspect a hidden world of meaning and coherence but when they look they see nothing but their own anxieties and desires reflected back at them." In this way, Miller's characters are much like the figures in Plato's cave who see shadows and must take them for reality while they remained chained in the cave. In *Timebends: A Life,* Miller suggests: "In both plays the objective world grows dim and distant as reality seems to consist wholly or partly of what the characters' needs require it to be, leaving them with the anguish of having to make choices that they know are based on illusion and the power of desire."

The nature of a two-way mirror is that it only reflects on one side; the other side allows the viewer to see through it as if it were a pane of glass, to gaze on others and the wider world. The characters in these plays struggle to move beyond their own anxieties and desires, to go beyond themselves and their own reflections and to see from the other side of such a mirror. The man in *Elegy for a Lady* we know, is tired of his own reflection and wishes to go beyond it—but one cannot accomplish this without first accepting the truth of that initial reflection. When someone accepts this, then he or she will have the power to perceive further, beyond self and into the world beyond where others live. These acceptors will move to the alternate side of the mirror where they will not see their own reflection but will be able to gaze on the wider world beyond and hopefully make a connection.

The whole notion of the double vision suggested by the image of a two-way mirror supports Miller's concept of these two plays as explorations into the paradoxical nature of reality in a world where many of us settle for a balance between what is real and what is a necessary illusion. The two-way mirror metaphor also implies the double perspective that Miller feels we should each pursue. It allows us on one side to see ourselves (the individual) and from the other side to see others (society). The question becomes: Is each play double-sided, or does each one offer a view from only one side of the mirror? The ambivalent answer, Miller seems to offer, is that both options are possible.

Up from Paradise (1974)

Subtitled *A Theater Piece Spoken and Sung, Up from Paradise* is a musical version of Miller's 1972 play *The Creation of the World and other Business.* Composer Stanley Silverman asked Miller if he could use music that had been rejected from the earlier play in a concert at Whitney Museum with a possible play reading accompaniment (this finally took place in 1981 with Miller as the narrator, starring Austin Pendleton and Len Cariou). Back in 1974, Miller had welcomed the opportunity to develop the play into a lighter form than had appeared on BROADWAY. Although it follows the same essential storyline, there are quite a few differences, especially in terms of tone, and it is considerably shorter, with the first two acts of the earlier play being combined into a single act. Gone are most of the lengthy philosophical debates between God and Lucifer, and the ending is far more upbeat than before. This streamlining makes for a simpler but clearer message regarding the nature of people and their relationship to God, which was Miller's main intent. God is less ambivalent, clearly representing the agency of love against the ambition and hatred of Lucifer. The play's message remains the hope that humanity will find a way to embrace love to ensure the future of the race.

The musical begins with the angels lengthily praising God as he makes the finishing touches to Adam's design. Angels narrate the action throughout. Uriel, the Angel of Philosophy who proposes the intriguing possibility that "Man created God," has replaced Raphael. After God and Adam name things in a duet, Adam asks God for a companion rather than wait for God to suggest this as in the play. They celebrate Eve's creation until she unsettles everyone by asking a question. A song forbidding the apple follows this, but it is already clear that Eve will not be able to resist the chance for knowledge.

God's dialogue with Lucifer in which they debate whether or not humankind should be given knowledge is more direct than before, but it amounts to the same point: Why would God give people brains if He does not expect them to be curious? God has given people free will, so their praise of Him will mean more than that of the angels, but God hopes that they will choose to follow His rules. When Adam makes up some words without God, Eve is delighted, but Adam is nervous. This time, Lucifer tempts them both together, and Adam voluntarily bites the apple, grabbing it from Eve. They both sing about their new sense of clarity, but God is furious as before and casts them out of Eden and Lucifer to hell.

Lucifer is despondent at God's treatment, having expected to be rewarded, and when Eve trips over him, he offers to help her settle on earth. He sends Adam to build a house while he attempts to seduce Eve. As before, Eve resists his suggestion that she kill her growing baby, and God helps her deliver a boy, whom she calls Cain. The first act ends as God dances off with Eve and Lucifer is left staring at the new arrival, though this time without comment.

Act 2 begins with angels praising God, but Lucifer sends them packing. He caustically introduces the four humans, upset at their lack of interest in evil. God remains upset at their lack of interest in Him but does not send the Angel of Death who suggests that his appearance on earth may make the humans take more notice. God reminisces about the time before He invented humankind. Rivalry between Cain and Abel mounts, their parents confess that they were expelled from Eden, and Cain suggests that they build an altar. Instead of warning Abel, as in the play, Lucifer now talks to Cain, goading him to turn against his brother and God. As before, God prefers Abel's offering and upsets Cain. Lucifer offers to talk Cain out of killing Abel if God will let him rule beside Him, but God decides to trust in Cain's love. It is clearly love on which God bases all His hopes. Even though his parents try to talk him out of his bad mood, Cain swiftly takes out his anger on Abel, breaking his neck. This killing is depicted as far more deliberate than in the play. Lucifer sings, happy in this evidence that Cain has rejected God and His laws. God swiftly sends Cain away, and Lucifer is banished by Adam. Uriel narrates Adam and Eve's reaction to Abel's death and how life

continues as Eve is once more pregnant. Adam ends in a song of hope in recognition of God's love; which Eve and the full company joins as they decide to start anew.

Plans had been afoot to tour the musical in university theaters and possibly to open later in New York—the Michigan production was considered a work in progress—but these plans never evolved. Summarizing his view of the play as "God created man, who could choose, and man didn't choose Him," Henry Hewes had a few quibbles but mostly enjoyed the production and felt it a "definite improvement" on the earlier version, being simpler and more carefree. He felt the youth of the actors suited the material, especially Lucifer played as a "hip dude." The Jewish Rep mounted a brief New York production in 1983, directed by Ran Avni, which reviewer Edith Oliver enjoyed but felt that "the true wit and humor of the show" were in its "rich, melodic score" and the "performance of the singers and actors" rather than in the script. Frank Rich, too, felt that this was an improvement on the play version but still was amateurish, unremarkable, and apparently "a show very much in limbo."

FIRST PERFORMANCE

Staged at the Powell Center for the Performing Arts, UNIVERSITY OF MICHIGAN, Ann Arbor, April 23–28, 1974, with the following cast:

Narrator: Arthur Miller
God: Bob Bingham
Adam: Allan Nicholls
Eve: Kimberly Farr
Lucifer: Larry Marshall
Cain: Seth Allen
Abel: Dennis Cooley
Directed by Arthur Miller
Set designed by Alan Billings
Music by Stanley Silverman

FURTHER READING

Freedman, Samuel G. "Miller Tries a New Form for an Old Play." *New York Times,* October 23, 1983, H3, 5.

Gussow, Mel. "Arthur Miller Returns to Genesis for First Musical: Spontaneity Absent Work in Progress." *New York Times*, April 17, 1974, 37.

Hewes, Henry. "On Broadway and on Campus." *Saturday Review World* 1 (15 June 1974): 44–45.

Holland, Bernard. "Arthur Miller Play Set to Stanley Silverman Music Resurfaces." *New York Times*, October 2, 1981, C3.

Oliver, Edith. "Off Broadway." *New Yorker* November 7, 1983, 150–152.

Rich, Frank. "Miller's *Up From Paradise*." *New York Times*, October 26, 1983, C22.

A View from the Bridge [one-act] (1955)

While exploring corruption in the BROOKLYN docklands in the late 1940s, Miller was befriended by two men who were trying to fight against the corruption and unionize the workers. One of these was a lawyer, VINCENT LONGHI, who offered to show Miller around. It was Longhi who told Miller the story of a longshoreman who informed on two brothers who were related to him and living illegally in his house. He had told the immigration authorities to try to break the engagement of one of these men to his niece. His actions had disgraced him in his neighborhood, and he had had to leave; there were rumors that one of the brothers later had murdered him. Thus, the seed of the play *A View from a Bridge* was born, with Miller even keeping the figure of a lawyer as the person who tells the story. Initially written as a one-act play in a mixture of prose and free verse, Miller later developed this into a two-act all-prose drama.

The story that Longhi told Miller had lain dormant in Miller's mind for some months; it reemerged during a trip to Europe with Longhi during which they visited Italy and got a sense of the background from which such people as the Carbones would have come. The working title for the script was *An Italian Tragedy*. The Italian community in RED HOOK was a close-knit body; the LAW of the land did not concern them as much as their own codes of honor and respectability. This was a society in which blood was thicker than water, and to betray a family member was the ultimate sin. The idea for the play percolated, but the writing was not coming, so Miller turned to other projects.

In 1955, actor/director Martin Ritt, who was appearing in CLIFFORD ODETS's *The Flowering Peach*, asked Miller if he had a one-act play that he could give him to offer as a reading with his company one Sunday evening as an added draw. Miller offered him *A Memory of Two Mondays*. Miller's agent KAY BROWN felt that the play was too good for a single reading and suggested that Miller write another to accompany it to create an evening worthy of full production. Suddenly, the play he had striven to write earlier came together as a one-act play in the same vein as the Greek plays on which he now recognized it could be modeled. Miller quickly wrote *A View from the Bridge* as a curtain-raiser. In the meantime, *The Flowering Peach* closed, so Miller's double bill was produced for a full BROADWAY production.

Much of the speech in this version of the play is written as verse, and there is a heavy concentration on imagery that recalls the Italian ancestry of the characters, an ancestry that colors their behavior and responses. Although the plot is essentially the same in both play scripts, the focus of the one-act play was more heavily concentrated on Eddie, and the female characters were not as developed. Miller explains his objective in writing the one-act play in his essay "On Social Plays" that accompanied the play's publication. Stephen Marino argues convincingly for the poetic force of this earlier version of the play in his close study of the play's language that he feels "elevates Eddie's story to Greek-like mythic status by using both verse form and a series of images, metaphors, and symbols which connect Eddie to a universal destiny which all humans share."

FIRST PERFORMANCE

A View from the Bridge previewed at Fallmouth Playhouse and then opened at the Coronet Theatre in New York in a joint bill with *A Memory of Two Mondays* on September 29, 1955, with the following cast:

Louis: David Clarke
Mike: Tom Pedi
Alfieri: J. Carrol Naish
Eddie: Van Heflin
Catherine: Gloria Marlowe
Beatrice: Eileen Heckart
Marco: Jack Warden
Tony: Antony Vorno
Rodolpho: Richard Davalos
1st Immigration Officer: Curt Conway
2nd Immigration Officer: Ralph Bell
Mr. Lipari: Russell Collins
Mrs. Lipari: Anne Driscoll
Two "Submarines" Leo Penn, Milton Carney

Directed by Martin Ritt
Set designed by BORIS ARONSON
Produced by KERMIT BLOOMGARDEN and WHITEHEAD-STEVENS
It ran for 149 performances.

INITIAL REVIEWS

BROOKS ATKINSON felt that while the play contains "material for a forceful drama . . . Mr. Miller's blunt, spare characterizations . . . are not big enough for tragedy." But while Atkinson, along with the majority of reviewers, saw Eddie Carbone as dull and insufficiently sympathetic, some, such as Henry Hewes, felt that the character was "gripping,

Van Heflin, Eileen Heckart, and Gloria Marlowe in a scene from the premiere one-act version of *A View from the Bridge*, produced at the Coronet Theatre in 1955. *Courtesy Billy Rose Theatre Collection, The New York Public Library for the Performing Arts, Astor, Lenox, and Tilden Foundations.*

unflinchingly real as well as poetic." The *Theatre Arts* reviewer praised the play's "lean, taught narrative." The play actually won the New York Drama Critics Award for that year. Miller was more disappointed in this production than were the reviewers. He felt that the actors had failed to grasp the stylized mode of acting that he felt the play demanded and played it too naturalistically. He would prefer the way that the two-act version was produced in GREAT BRITAIN the following year.

FURTHER READING

Atkinson, Brooks. "Theatre: *A View from the Bridge.*" *New York Times,* September 30, 1955, 21.

Hewes, Henry. "Broadway Postscript: Death of a Longshoreman." *Saturday Review of Literature,* October 15, 1955, 25–26.

Marino, Stephen A. "Verse, Figurative Language, and Myth in *A View from the Bridge.*" *A Language Study of Arthur Miller's Plays: The Poetic in the Colloquial.* New York: Mellen, 2002, 81–106.

"A View from the Bridge." *Theatre Arts* 39 (December 1955): 18–19.

A View from a Bridge (1956)

Although Miller first wrote A *View from the Bridge* in 1955 as a one-act play, it is the two-act version that is almost exclusively produced and known. In the one-act script, Miller had written many speeches as free verse, but the two-act play was presented entirely as prose. However, in many cases, this switch from verse to prose only meant that Miller rewrote the original lines in prose format while keeping the same words; however, some of the verse speeches, especially those of Alfieri, were modified to sound more down-to-earth. His final speech, aside from its first line about settling for half, is entirely different. The longer version has essentially the same plot but leaves out a few details, such as Eddie having two children and some of the poetic imagery, including many of the Madonna references that are associated with Catherine. Instead, the two-act play put greater emphasis on Eddie's impotence with Beatrice and on the

Carbones' interaction with their friends and neighbors. Most critics see the difference between the versions being that the one-act strove to present a universal mythic tale, while the two-act wanted to convey a more realistic story with a stronger psychological and social underpinning. One notable change was that at the close of the one-act version, after being wounded by Marco, Eddie drags himself across the stage to die in Catherine's arms, and it is at this point that he kisses her rather than kissing her earlier; in the two-act version, Eddie dies in the arms of his wife.

Miller had been unhappy with the original New York production and was urged to expand the play into two acts by British director, Peter Brook. This more-polished version, in which Miller expanded the roles of the women and made Eddie more sympathetic, premiered in London, despite some difficulties with the licensing of the performance, to rave reviews. In 1956, it was still considered shocking to depict anything onstage associated with homosexual themes, and the Lord Chamberlain had refused a performance license. However, this obstacle was circumvented by having the audience become members of the New Watergate Club as part of their ticket price, which meant that the play could be treated as a private performance and shown without a license.

A View from the Bridge was also written at the height of the HOUSE UN-AMERICAN ACTIVITIES COMMITTEE (HUAC) hearings when the United States was seized in a fervor of anti-COMMUNISM and friends were being coerced to inform on friends. Miller had already tried to expose the injustice of the HUAC procedures in 1953 with *The Crucible,* but now he wanted to comment on those whom the committee persuaded to inform, such as Miller's close friend ELIA KAZAN. Many have seen the play as something of a response to Kazan's 1954 film *On the Waterfront* in which informing is portrayed as a virtuous act. When Miller was brought before the committee in 1956, he refused to give them any names. Using Eddie Carbone as his example, Miller shows that informing may have the LAW on its side, but for him it is morally indefensible and wrong. The play's central issue of a man fighting his infatuation with a younger woman also had strong resonance in Miller's private life. MARILYN MONROE moved to New York in 1955 and the two had become reacquainted. Unable to resist, Miller had begun a passionate affair that would lead to his first divorce; he fully understood the strength of an illicit attraction.

This two-act version of the play has enjoyed several major revivals on both sides of the Atlantic since its initial production. The most notable ones in GREAT BRITAIN would be the NATIONAL THEATRE's 1987 production with Michael Gambon as Eddie and DAVID THACKER's 1995 direction of Bernard Hill in the play. Of the leading U.S. productions, Miller particularly enjoyed the 1965 off-Broadway version with Robert Duvall and Jon Voight that had been directed by ULU GROSBARD and ran for 780 performances, as well as the award winning 1997 Roundabout Theater Company's production directed by Michael Mayer that starred Anthony LaPaglia.

The play also has been translated twice into an opera. It was first adapted in 1961 by Italian composer Renzo Rossellini and then again in 1999 by U.S. composer William Bolcom on a commission from the Lyric Opera of Chicago. Rossellini's version was titled *Uno Sguardo del Ponte* and came to the United States in 1967 to little acclaim, but Bolcom's version has received much praise with its effective chorus compiled of Eddie's neighbors and fellow workers. Miller cowrote the libretto with Arnold Weinstein, and it was based closely on the original one-act version of the play that seemed the better to lend itself to versification. An additional piece that Miller wrote especially for the opera was an aria for Marco titled *An Immigrant's Lament*.

SYNOPSIS

Act One

Mr. Alfieri, a local lawyer, comments on the action of the play as events unfold, and he begins the play by addressing the audience directly, introducing himself, the area in which he works, and the case of Eddie Carbone. The play is set in the RED HOOK section of BROOKLYN, New York, and the inhabitants are largely Italian immigrants. Eddie is seen pitching coins with his fellow workers and neighbors, showing that he is one of the group. As

he moves into his apartment, he meets his niece, Catherine, to whom he is clearly attracted, and she shows off her new outfit in a naively flirtatious manner. Catherine has lived with the Carbones ever since her mother, Beatrice's sister, died. Eddie is worried that Catherine's dress and actions might be making her too attractive and warns her about this and about men. She is upset by his disapproval but is also nervous as she tries to build courage to tell him that she has been offered a job even before finishing her secretarial training.

Meanwhile, Eddie tells his wife, Beatrice, that two of her Italian cousins have arrived. They are being smuggled past immigration that evening and will start work on the docks the next day. Beatrice is overjoyed and scrambles to make the place look nice. Eddie is more cautious with his hospitality, feeling his wife to be overgenerous but also accepting it as the honorable thing to do. On learning that Catherine has a job, he shows reservations, wanting her to stay close to home and not be exposed to a lot of new men. Beatrice takes Catherine's side and persuades Eddie to allow her to take the job, largely because Beatrice wants Catherine out of the way—Beatrice is unhappy with her husband's attachment to his niece. As Eddie accepts, the growing tension between Eddie and Beatrice is deflated, and they make plans for the arriving cousins. Eddie is most concerned that they keep the cousins' presence a secret from the Immigration Bureau. To let Catherine know what a serious issue this is, they tell her the tale of a nephew who informed on his uncle and was thrown out of their community for such a betrayal.

The cousins, Marco and Rodolpho, arrive that night. The family welcomes them, and they learn of the terrible poverty from which these men have come; Marco needs to make money to send to his wife and three children whom he could not afford to bring with him. Catherine and Rodolpho are attracted to each other, which upset Eddie and makes him defensive; this angers Beatrice. Most of this pent up emotion is conveyed in the stage directions rather than through what the characters say. Alfieri moves time along by commenting on Eddie's reaction to the growing relationship of Rodolpho and Catherine. During the next two weeks, Eddie becomes obsessed by jealousy, using every opportunity to criticize, trying to imply that Rodolpho is a homosexual and, therefore, no real threat to Catherine. Beatrice makes it clear that Eddie's attraction to Catherine has been affecting their marital relationship; they have not slept together for three months, and she is coming to the end of her patience. Eddie feels guilty but cannot stop himself.

Rodolpho's reputation among the longshoremen is as a joker, while Marco is known as a serious worker. Eddie tries to sour Catherine's relationship with Rodolpho by telling her that he is only after an American passport. Catherine almost believes him; Rodolpho does behave irresponsibly, spending his money on trivial things. Catherine wants to believe in Rodolpho's sincerity, but now she has doubts, and she is angry with Eddie for causing them. Beatrice tries to encourage her to stick with Rodolpho, as she wants Catherine to become more independent and realize the bad affect that her continual presence is having on Eddie. At this point, Eddie goes to Alfieri to see if he can legally prevent Rodolpho from marrying Catherine. The only way would be for him to inform on the brothers and have them deported. Alfieri warns Eddie that Eddie has "too much love" for his niece and that it would be best to let things take their course, but Eddie refuses to be consoled, just as he refuses to admit his real feelings for Catherine. Alfieri declares that he knew the outcome at this point but could do nothing to stop it.

Back at the Carbone household, there is constant tension between Eddie and the cousins. Beatrice tries to keep the peace, but Eddie takes every opportunity to insult Rodolpho and even tries to get Marco on his side. Marco stays neutral, and Catherine refuses to allow Rodolpho to be put down, so Eddie tricks Rodolpho into boxing with him to prove that he is the better man. It breaks up before Eddie can hurt Rodolfo, but Marco recognizes what Eddie is doing and warns him off by showing *his* strength: He picks up a chair by a single leg, something Eddie cannot do.

Act Two

By act two, some time has passed, and Catherine and Rodolpho are alone together in the house for the first time. Rodolpho has saved some money and

wants Catherine to marry him, but she is unsure because of the doubts that Eddie put in her mind. To test Rodolpho, she suggests that they go to Italy to live; he refuses and faces her suspicion without apology or explanation. It is hard to know whether Eddie is right or not about Rodolpho because his suggestions also arouse the audience's suspicions, but Rodolpho seems serious. Catherine is torn between her allegiance to Rodolpho and to Eddie; however, Rodolpho offers her a freedom that she will never have from Eddie for he promises not to run her life the way Eddie does; he wins her over, and they move into the bedroom together.

Eddie arrives home drunk in time to see Catherine and Rodolpho coming out of the bedroom. He demands that Rodolpho leave the house, and Catherine says that she will leave too. Having lost his inhibitions to alcohol, Eddie kisses Catherine on the mouth. Rodolpho defends his betrothed. The men fight, but Eddie easily holds Rodolpho and to embarrass him thoroughly before Catherine, kisses him on the mouth. Catherine attacks Eddie to make him let go, and Eddie does, mocking Rodolpho's weakness and warning Catherine not to go with him. With Beatrice's support, both Catherine and Rodolpho stay, and Eddie returns to Alfieri. Again, Alfieri insists there is no legal way for Eddie to bar the impending marriage. A phone booth that has been sitting to the side of the stage begins to glow to show the increasing temptation of Eddie's treacherous, last resort—to telephone the immigration authorities. Alfieri warns Eddie against this course of action, but Eddie cannot resist and makes the fatal phone call.

Meanwhile, Beatrice has moved Rodolpho and Marco to their neighbor's apartment to keep them away from Eddie. Beatrice is angry with Eddie for causing so much trouble, but he pretends innocence and suggests that it is Beatrice's fault. She knows that he is wrong and tells him that Catherine and Rodolpho plan to marry that week. She tries to persuade him to accept this, but Eddie, filled with guilt and shame at what he has done, asks Catherine to wait. The cousins will be rooming with two other illegal immigrants who are newly arrived. Eddie uses this information to try to save face. He suggests that the immigration authorities may have tracked these new men and that Marco and Rodolpho should immediately leave the house to be safe. His warning comes too late as the immigration officers arrive, and Beatrice and Catherine swiftly realize who has called them.

The authorities take all four immigrants into detention. Marco knows Eddie's part in this, and before they take him, he breaks away to face Eddie in front of all their neighbors, to spit in his face, and to accuse him of betraying them. Despite Eddie's protestations to the contrary, the neighbors believe Marco and turn their backs on Eddie. Alfieri offers to bail out the cousins until the hearing on the condition that Marco agrees not to hurt Eddie. Rodolpho and Catherine plan to marry immediately so that Rodolpho can stay, but Marco must return to Italy. Marco is outraged but agrees to Alfieri's conditions so that he can work a few extra weeks and attend his brother's wedding.

Eddie tells Beatrice that if she goes to the wedding, she cannot come home, and he demands an apology from Marco before he will let his family attend. Catherine denounces Eddie, but Beatrice goes to his defense, taking partial responsibility for his actions and agreeing to stay home. Rodolpho arrives to warn Eddie that Marco is coming, and the women try to keep them apart, but Eddie refuses to hide. Rodolpho tries to make amends, forgiving Eddie and apologizing for his treatment of Catherine, but Eddie does not listen—he is focused solely on Marco and regaining his lost reputation. As Eddie goes to meet Marco, Beatrice holds him, telling him that she loves him and trying, with the truth of his feelings for Catherine, to shock him into staying. But Eddie cannot face the truth and goes instead to meet Marco and his death. Although Eddie pulls the knife, Marco turns it on Eddie and kills him with his own weapon. Eddie dies in Beatrice's arms, acknowledging his love for her, while Alfieri concludes, stating his admiration for Eddie despite his actions.

CRITICAL COMMENTARY

What is important about this play's setting is the sense that Eddie Carbone is portrayed as an ordinary man who lives in a community of ordinary men. He lives in a small apartment that is part of a tenement building in which other hardworking longshoremen live. These men both work and play together, going bowling after a hard day's work on the docks. It is a close-knit community in which everyone seems to know one another's business, and they are happy to have it that way. What singles Eddie out is his guilty secret, so secret that he even keeps the truth from himself: He wants to sleep with his niece. He tells the Immigration Bureau about his wife's relatives so that they will returned the relatives to Italy and prevent Rodolpho from taking Catherine from him. Then, because he refuses to accept responsibility for his actions and hoping that his actions will be justified by his fears for Catherine, his guilt drives him toward self-destruction at the hands of Marco.

Eddie understands his responsibilities toward the immigrants, but he goes against them anyway in a misguided belief in what his responsibilities toward Catherine are. By going against all he had previously believed, Eddie loses his sense of self, shown by his demanding his name from Marco. It is this demand—to which Marco cannot in all conscience accede because he knows that Eddie is guilty as charged—that leads Eddie into the pointless conflict that will lead to his death. In a sense, Eddie causes his own death by refusing to accept responsibility for what he has done. In a third ending, written for the Paris production in response to suggestions that French audiences would not accept Eddie's refusal to accept and acknowledge his feelings for Catherine, Miller makes it clear that Eddie kills himself. This version was later used in the 1962 movie of the play that was filmed in France. In the published script, however, Eddie's death remains an ambiguous suicide, as it is Marco who uses the knife even though it is Eddie who draws it. Eddie knows that Marco is the stronger man and still insists on fighting. As he had commented earlier, "even a mouse" can break a hold if it really wants to; yet, he allows Marco to force his arm. How much he needs to die at this point to save his own innocence is left to debate.

Miller utilizes a typical Greek tragic format in the play that hinges on issues of fate. Eddie is fated to die, partly because of who he is and partly because of the world in which he lives. There is a sense, emphasized by Alfieri's commentary, that Eddie is inevitably rushing toward his doom and that there is little that can be done to save him: Given the same situation, Eddie would make the same mistakes and the result, therefore, is preordained. The Greeks believed in a world controlled by fates that were directed by the gods, but Miller prefers to believe that people's characters have the biggest influence in determining their fate. Eddie's problem is not dissimilar to that of John Proctor in *The Crucible*: His sexual desire has caused him to lose touch with his moral compass. Both try to reclaim their names, and through this a sense of moral rectitude, Proctor restores a selfhood which he then sacrifices to a greater truth, while Eddie cannot get Marco to back down and must die a traitor and liar.

Failure, in Miller's eyes, should not be blamed on an indefinable hostile fate or social system but on individuals who refuse to accept their responsibilities and connection to fellow human beings. While John Proctor nobly accepts his responsibility and connection to Rebecca Nurse and Martha Corey and dies rather than tarnish their reputations, Eddie chooses to act on his baser impulses, trying to keep Catherine away from other men and informing on his wife's cousins. An even deeper motivation is his lust for Catherine, an emotion that he does not choose but *could* choose to better control. On impulse, Eddie kisses both Catherine and Rodolpho, and Miller leaves the motivation for either kiss decidedly ambivalent because Eddie himself is not sure why he does it: Is he kissing Catherine to warn off Rodolpho or to fulfill his own lust? Is he kissing Rodolpho to embarrass him in front of Catherine or to fulfill a buried homosexual desire? The trouble with Eddie is that he has been lying to himself for so long about his feelings for Catherine that he can no longer recognize the truth, always a dangerous position.

As in any Greek TRAGEDY, *A View from the Bridge* contains a network of ironic references, symbols, and stage effects to foreshadow and underscore Eddie's fate, like Eddie's cautionary tales of stool pigeons or Beatrice declaring that he will "get a blessing" for taking in Rodolpho and Marco. It actually turns out to be Eddie who is the informer

(he even describes himself as a "pigeon" later in the play, although he intends it in a different context), and his "good favor" becomes his downfall. Also, the song which Rodolpho sings, "Paper Doll," sets the scene for future events as it sums up Eddie's attitude to Catherine: "It's tough to love a doll that's not your own." On other occasions, Eddie's eyes are described as being "like tunnels," to convey the sense of inevitability in his destructive behavior. The phone box from which Eddie rings the authorities "begins to glow" as Eddie feels the temptation to make the call, and it further contributes to this sense of fate. As Eddie approaches the phone, Alfieri disappears into darkness and the phone lights up to place Eddie in the ill-fated spotlight that kills him; it is a spotlight that he freely chooses to enter. The sense that Eddie is the author of his own fate is further underlined by the irony of his dying by his own treachery and on his own knife that has been drawn against a defenseless opponent.

An important theme that runs through the play is the issue of law. Alfieri represents the law, not justice, and Miller is careful not to mix these terms. As Alfieri tells us of many who were "justly shot by unjust men," we come to see that the law is a complex notion and that it has more than one side. On one hand, there is the law of the land that often is shown to be ineffective in Miller's plays, having no power to make the guilty pay for their crimes or to protect the ordinary individual. But on the other hand, Miller insists that there is a moral law that does operate successfully and that judges both our individual and our collective actions. Miller sees such a law as fundamental to the growth and development of U.S. culture and DEMOCRACY, for without this, we are protected insufficiently against chaos and evil. Thus, while the institutionalized law can do nothing to restrict or aid Eddie seriously, he pays a heavy price for breaking certain moral restrictions.

Eddie's case depicts the chasm between legality and morality because he does nothing illegal; indeed, legally, you should inform on illegal immigrants, even when their need to make money is as great as that of Marco. Worried about whether or not Rodolpho is taking advantage of his niece to get a passport, even though Eddie's motive may not be the purest, it is important to note that he finds no way to protect his niece legally. However, neither Eddie's lust for Catherine nor his betrayal of Rodolpho and Marco can be defended morally, and for these, he must pay, first, with the loss of his name, and because he will not accept this punishment, finally, with the loss of his life.

Eddie tries to maintain control by refusing to face the truth. The relationship between Eddie and Catherine lends itself to a psychoanalytical interpretation, as it offers an interesting twist on the classic oedipal complex. Although there is much evidence in the play that Catherine has stronger feelings for her uncle than may be proper, the focus is on Eddie and his feelings for his niece. The usual oedipal complex has the child desiring the parent or parent figure, and that figure neither reciprocates these feelings nor often even notices them. But in *A View from the Bridge*, it becomes clear that Eddie fiercely desires Catherine, and it is the failure to repress this desire fully that forces him to go so strongly against society's rules and betray the immigrant cousins. His unruly desire for his niece is the fatal flaw in his character that brings about his demise; just like the Greek hero Oedipus, he pays a heavy price for the disruption that his actions bring to his community.

From Eddie's first entrance, we are aware that there is something strained in his relationship with his niece. He is unusually shy and at times awkward with her—especially when she shows affection and behaves in an unwittingly seductive way before him. He is also overpossessive, not wanting her to draw the attention of other males. He rebukes her for the way she walks, the clothes she wears, even for a friendly wave to his friend Louis; he would like to keep her isolated from the rest of the world so that he might have her all to himself. Miller's stage directions help us to understand that something is wrong with Eddie's reactions, such as the way in which he becomes "strangely nervous" and "somehow sickened" on hearing of Catherine's intention to get a job and "strangely and quickly resentful" of his wife's efforts to make Catherine independent. Eddie does not want Catherine to grow up and escape his influence. Beatrice has noticed how Eddie treats her niece and is annoyed and jealous, but Eddie refuses to recognize any implications behind his treatment of Catherine, seeing it as paternal caution rather than sexual jealousy.

All through the play Eddie refuses to acknowledge how he feels for Catherine because he knows that such feelings are wrong. He calls her "Madonna" and through this designation keeps her pure and free from association with others, yet also unattainable even to him. But Eddie is so besotted with Catherine that has not been able to sleep with his own wife for the past three months. When Beatrice and Alfieri imply that his feelings for Catherine are too strong, he responds with angry denial. However, the night that he comes home drunk, his guard is down, and in the passionate kiss that he gives his niece, we should recognize his true feelings. He endlessly tries to justify his distrust of Rodolpho, by insisting that the boy is a homosexual and is only dating Catherine to get a passport, but his distrust is only created by Catherine's evident liking for Rodolpho. When Beatrice finally blurts out the truth, "You want somethin' else, Eddie, and you can never have her!" Eddie is shocked and horrified. It is shortly after this that he confronts Marco in his virtual act of suicide, as if death were now his only escape from the truth that he has tried so hard to avoid.

FIRST PERFORMANCE

A View from the Bridge premiered at the Comedy Theatre in London on October 11, 1956, with the following cast:

Louis: Richard Harris
Mike: Norman Mitchell
Alfieri: Michael Gwynn
Eddie: Anthony Quayle
Catherine: Mary Ure
Beatrice: Megs Jenkins
Marco Ian Bannen
Tony: Ralph Nossek
Rodolpho: Brian Bedford
1st Immigration Officer: John Stone
2nd Immigration Officer: Colin Rix
Mr. Lipari: Mervyn Blake
Mrs. Lipari: Catherine Willmer
A Submarine: Peter James

Directed and designed by Peter Brook
Produced by the New Watergate Club
It ran for 220 performances.

INITIAL REVIEWS

Although a couple of critics quibbled about the need for Alfieri as narrator, the reviews of the London production were predominantly positive. While Anthony Hartley contended that the play was powerful enough "to overcome its defects," Richard Findlater simply praised it as "a powerful and important play." Philip Hope–Wallace enjoyed the play's "relentless" quality, calling the acting and production "superb," and J. C. Trewin described it as "an economically-wrought play that drives straight at its point." Whereas it was generally felt that the longer version had a clearer story line and theme, Margaret Webster felt that the one-act version had been more effective and that the play had now lost its earlier "sense of a people of ancient lineage, reborn on the Brooklyn waterfront."

SCHOLARSHIP

In Robert Martin's *Arthur Miller: New Perspective*, J. L. Styan considers, as do Neil Carson, Dennis Welland, and CHRISTOPHER BIGSBY in their respective books on Miller, the play's expansion from one to two acts and how that affects its dynamic. Meanwhile Stephen Marino's chapter on the play in *A Language Study of Miller's Plays* offers a detailed examination of the "poetic elements" of both versions and shares close descriptions of the changes made to the original script. Marino also discusses the theme of "territoriality" in the play in an essay that he contributed to *Arthur Miller: Twentieth Century Legend* (2006).

Several articles argue the play's tragic status. Kailash Chander insists that the play is a "deep and disturbing tragedy," and Terry Otten treats it as a tragedy of the highest order, with Eddie becoming a prime example of his book's thesis regarding the destructive results of capitulating to the temptation of innocence. Steven Centola has pointed out both Beatrice and Catherine's partial complicity in Eddie's downfall, and Otten expands on Catherine's role. While Steven Centola portions the blame in his examination of the play's portrayal of the negative effects of compromise, Otten insists

that Eddie "dies believing in the innocence that ironically seals his tragic fate" rather than recognize his own wrong desires (much in the way of Willy Loman). Meanwhile, Albert Rothenberg, Eugene Shapiro, and John Edwards all feel that the play fails as a tragedy because its plot is too driven by sudden action rather than by psychological development, of which they feel there is not enough.

Sidestepping the tragedy issue are those who consider the play's mythic potential, such as Ronald Ambrosetti, Donald Costello, and Arthur Epstein. While Costello and Epstein balance their assessment against an awareness of the play's equally compelling claims to REALISM, Ambrosetti views it as "one of the oldest and most influential stories of the history of the world" with origins in Hellenistic Greece. Meanwhile, Myles Hurd explores the issue of homosexuality that first banned the play in London, wondering, as have others, if Eddie might be a closet homosexual. While recognizing that sexuality is a key issue in the play, critics remain as divided on what causes Eddie to kiss Rodolpho as they do on his equally ambivalent kissing of Catherine just prior. As Bigsby points out, "They are definitive actions that destroy the very thing he was so anxious to protect," that is to say, his ownership of Catherine and his domination over Rodolpho. Miller intends both kisses to be ambivalent.

Albert Wertheim's contribution to the *Cambridge Companion to Arthur Miller* offers a solid explication of the play and draws comparisons to Miller's earlier unproduced screenplay *The Hook*. He, like Brenda Murphy in *Congressional Theater*, considers the connection between Eddie and Elia Kazan as informers, and Wertheim concludes that Miller exhibits the "admirable ability to understand the mixed motives of his friends who named names. He can admire, condemn, and forgive them" and leads his audience to do the same for Eddie.

Bigsby suggests that the aspect of informing is only a side issue in the play and sees the central aspect as Miller's depiction of Eddie as a "victim of desire" who pays the ultimate price for his obsession. It is an obsession that "lifts him above the banality of routine and the safety that comes from compromising with passion" and that makes him interesting. This is, after all, why Alfieri has chosen to tell his story. Bigsby maps the growing tensions in the play, many of them nonverbal given the intellect of the participants, and shows how each action becomes "charged with meaning." "Eddie," he concludes, "dies to preserve his sense of himself and his vision of Catherine," and for all of Alfieri's talk about Eddie allowing "himself to be wholly known," it is those watching who are privy to this revelation rather than Eddie, who dies rather than face the awful truth.

CHARACTERS

Alfieri   Alfieri is an Italian-American lawyer who has set up office in the Red Hook area and lives a mundane life dealing with the petty legal squabbles of the neighborhood. It is he to whom Eddie goes for legal advice on getting rid of Rodolpho and he who deals with getting the brothers out on bail after they have been arrested. Born in Italy, he came to America when he was age 25, when gangsters like Al Capone still ruled the streets, but times have changed. Alfieri has seen violence in the area lessen over the years, but now in his fifties, he feels a little bored with the banality of his life. He tells us the story of Eddie as a kind of confession of his attraction to a darker, more dangerous kind of existence that he dare not live but can admire in another.

Acting as observer and commentator on the play's action, Alfieri directly addresses the audience as a kind of Chorus figure. He is only marginally involved in the events, and it is his "view" that we get as he stands on a metaphorical bridge between the characters and the audience. As a lawyer, he appears to represent the legal system in the play, which we realize has little influence on the events that unfold. As a man, in contrast to the neighbors, Alfieri shows sympathy for Eddie's downfall and offers a more balanced view of the action. It is Alfieri who invests Eddie's story with its mythic resonance, but one wonders how much he allows events to get out of hand as they do to experience some excitement; he gets Marco out of jail even while knowing that Marco was after Eddie's blood and does nothing to prevent their final confrontation.

Carbone, Beatrice   Beatrice is a good woman, and she has been very patient with her husband,

Eddie, trying to keep the peace, even when it makes her look bad. A compassionate woman, she takes in anyone who needs help without a thought, from her orphaned niece Catherine to her immigrant cousins. Upset at her husband's lack of sexual attention, she sees the cause and even confronts him with it: "You want somethin' else, Eddie, and you can never have her." She wants Eddie back, yet she will not throw Catherine out because she also wants to be fair to her niece. She talks to Catherine and tries to make her niece see the effect she is having on Eddie, warning her to think more carefully about how she acts. She even refuses to wholly blame Eddie for what happens, accepting partial responsibility herself, defending him against Catherine's scorn: "Whatever happened we all done it."

Beatrice is generous, but no fool—she is not a doormat and has her limits. She loves Eddie and will fight for him, warning Catherine off and encouraging her to rebel, trying to smooth things between Eddie and the cousins, and even agreeing not to attend Catherine's wedding to stay with Eddie. She demands her husband's attention and finally gets it in his dying moment as she holds him in her arms and takes full possession. Eddie sees his wife's love and acknowledges it before he dies, though he has bitterly complained along the way at her attempts to force him into being a better husband.

Carbone, Eddie   Eddie Carbone is a longshoreman in his forties who works on the Brooklyn docks. Married to Beatrice, he and his wife took in their niece after she was orphaned. The forces acting on Eddie seem to be entirely internal. He is totally inflexible; once he sets himself on his chosen course, his character cannot help but lead him to destruction. Eddie dies, still insisting that he has done nothing wrong, even though his desires for his niece and his betrayal of his wife's cousins to the immigration authority are apparent to all. Blinkered like a horse, he refuses to see things from any other perspective than that of his own innocence. Such a refusal is not enough to save him, though it does make him more sympathetic. He intends good but everything goes sadly wrong because he cannot handle his own emotions. When you betray all in which you believe, you betray yourself, which is what Eddie does. He knows that informing is wrong, and he knows that his love for Catherine is wrong, yet he cannot help himself. He tells Alfieri, when trying to imply that Rodolpho is not right, that even a mouse can break a hold if it really wants to, yet, at the close, he does not break the hold that Marco has on his knife arm. This suggests that Eddie wanted to die rather than face the consequences of his betrayals.

For a long time, Eddie has been overprotective of Catherine; because he can never have her, he wants to ensure that no one else has that chance. He would like her to remain a beautiful, innocent Madonna who is pure and untouched, but her emergence into womanhood is something that he cannot prevent. Reluctant to let her go out to work or wear high heels or short skirts, his every action is to keep her a child so that he can free himself of his sexual attraction. His shyness with Catherine turns into petulant resentment as his guilt grows, though he never consciously admits to his feelings for her, and we get no sense that he would ever act on them if he did. The only time that the truth comes close to emerging is when he is drunk and kisses her, although he justifies this to himself as a gesture of ownership to warn away Rodolpho rather than a lover's kiss.

Eddie casts doubts on Rodolpho's manhood, playing up the homosexual stereotype by mocking Rodolpho's singing, cooking, and dressmaking skills. All this is done to try to make himself feel more secure since he feels threatened by Rodolpho. As he tries to convince others, it seems more and more clear that he is really just trying to convince himself as all he has is very circumstantial evidence. His charge that Rodolpho is courting Catherine for a green card is potentially more convincing and even makes Catherine wonder, but it is just another excuse to avoid the real issue: his own attraction for the girl. He offers Catherine more freedom toward the end in the hopes that he can persuade her not to leave, but he has left it too late. His guilt at his own betrayal of the cousins and his failure to hold onto Catherine lead him to face Marco in what is a virtual act of suicide.

Catherine Catherine's mother was Beatrice's sister, and when she died, Beatrice and Eddie brought their niece to live with them. Catherine seems naive and initially responds to events very childishly. This is an aspect of her character that Eddie encourages as, in some ways, he would like to keep her a child and so more unobtainable both for himself and others. He likes to think of her as a Madonna, inviolate and untouchable. Yet, she tells Rodolpho that she knows more than they think. If this is true, then Beatrice is right to hold her partially to blame for having led Eddie on—talking to him while one of them was only partly dressed and acting the dependent baby when she was capable of being a grown woman.

Catherine's rebellion may be subconscious, but when she wears high heels and short skirts, she is asserting herself in the household in a way that Eddie is certain to find troubling. Catherine is ready to grow, but she is just too timid yet to assert herself too far. Catherine loves Eddie, and the extent and nature of her love is left uncertain, especially in her speech about what she would do if she were his wife, but she eventually listens to the warnings that others give her and gradually distances herself. On witnessing Eddie's violent and abusive reaction to her having slept with Rodolpho, she breaks away entirely, reacting with both fear and disgust. By the close, she is calling him a rat, but she still cares enough to try to prevent his conflict with Marco.

By nature, Catherine seems more submissive than her Aunt Beatrice and is manipulated by others easily; however, she grows during the play. She goes from being the eager child, forever craving approval, to recognizing the forces at work on her and facing them—she rejects Eddie and stands by Rodolpho in a show of mature courage. She and Rodolpho seem to be a good couple, and there is evidence that they could be in love or at least have enough in common that they might grow into a relationship. Furthermore, both are able to give the other what they want—Rodolpho can stay in the United States and Catherine can have greater freedom because Rodolpho does not wish to possess her as Eddie does but just to be her partner. She is as eager to marry as her Italian boyfriend.

Louis, Mike, and Tony   Eddie's friends and neighbors act as a barometer of local opinion. They work beside him at the docks and pitch coins or bowl with him in their leisure time. These men begin as close friends with Eddie, admiring him for helping his wife's relatives. Their lives being dominated by the macho bravado that defines their community, they even side with Eddie against Rodolpho as Eddie points out his effeminacy, although they have a growing respect for Marco. However, they turn completely against Eddie as soon as they learn of his betrayal, literally turning their backs as he tries to talk to them. In this community, you do not inform on fellow workers and relatives. Eddie knows this, and his fate can be no different from that of their old neighbor, teenage Vinny Bolzano, who was publicly beaten and spat on by his own family after calling in the Immigration Bureau on an uncle. In many Greek plays, the writer includes such a chorus—a group of minor characters who lead the audience by their reactions to events.

Marco   Marco is the older of the brothers and the more serious and cautious; Rodolpho is younger and is more eager and excitable. Marco's values are set in stone and the honor of himself and his family will come before anything else. Marco is politely formal and carefully observes; he dislikes imposing on others and is very concerned about appearing ungrateful in any way. Marco is in the United States to earn money for his wife and three children, fully intending to return to them in a few years. He looks after his brother and quietly takes charge of situations; when he instructs, Rodolpho obeys. There is a palpable force to Marco, and he is not a man to cross. Though quiet, Marco is no fool. Seeing how Eddie tries to belittle his brother, Marco calmly defends Rodolpho, warning Eddie off with the minimum of fuss. His ability to lift the chair when Eddie cannot should prepare us for who will win their final conflict. Marco's dignity and sense of honor are so evidently at stake here, and his condemnation of Eddie is incontestable.

Rodolpho   In contrast to his quiet, dark brother, Rodolpho is a voluble blond who loves to have fun. A chatterbox full of jokes, dreams, and stories,

he has come to the United States to experience everything that he can. He sings the latest songs and buys the latest shoes and the flashiest jacket. He wants to stay, as he has no responsibilities back in Italy, and is naively excited by the possibilities on offer in the United States. His conception of the American dream may be fairly shallow, but it is one in which he firmly believes. Catherine is instantly attracted to his lightness of spirit, emblematized in his hair color and friendly nature. But this lightness also allows even the audience to question his motives, along with Eddie, for courting Catherine. He raises the idea of marriage pretty quickly in their relationship—she may just be his meal ticket to a green card.

However, like Catherine, Rodolpho also grows in the course of the play, and we see a serious side to him that reminds us of his brother and suggests a possibility of growth. He faces Catherine's suspicions with a quiet dignity and maturely forgives Eddie, even accepting some blame for the way things turn out and quietly asking for pardon. Despite Eddie's accusations, we are given no proof from Rodolpho's behavior that any of them are true; indeed, alone with Catherine, he sounds most sincere.

Eddie's homophobic accusations that Rodolpho "ain't right" are testament to the homophobic responses of many who feel that masculinity is determined by such a narrow set of appearances and behaviors. Eddie's whole social milieu is defined by its rigid conception of masculinity, and so to accuse Rodolpho of homosexuality serves as the biggest insult that he can devise to deflate his rival. Eddie is apparently unaware of the inherent contradiction of the claim since, if Rodolpho truly is homosexual, then how could he be a rival for Catherine? Eddie's construction of Rodolpho as homosexual is based on Rodolpho's enjoyment of singing and interest in clothing and cooking. This is shattered on catching him sleeping with Catherine. Eddie's impulse is to kiss Rodolpho, as if to prove that he truly is a homosexual, but given Rodolpho's lack of response, the act only casts doubts on Eddie's sexual preference. Its aggression also incenses Catherine to leave him forever and to go *with* Rodolpho and so it is an assertion that backfires on every front.

MOVIE AND TELEVISION ADAPTATIONS

A film version was made in France, directed by Sidney Lumet under the title *Vu du Pont* with Raf Vallone, Carol Lawrence, Maureen Stapleton, and Morris Carnovsky. The screenplay was written by Miller's friend NORMAN ROSTEN who rearranged and cut several scenes as well as dispensing with Alfieri as narrator. It was released in 1962 to largely negative reviews that described Eddie as unappealing and the play a failed tragedy, despite moments of authenticity. Pauline Kael declared, "It's not so much a drama unfolding as a sentence that's been passed on the audience." Grosbard also produced his 1965 stage version of the play for television that same year. More recently, following his stage performance as Eddie in the 1997 Roundabout Theater production of the play, actor Anthony LaPaglia has been raising funds to produce a new film version, but the project has not been completed to date.

FURTHER READING

Ambrosetti, Ronald. "Next Door to the Earthly Paradise: Mythic Pattern in Italian-American Drama." *Journal of Popular Culture* 19, no. 3 (Winter 1985): 109–118.

Bigsby, Christopher. "*A View from the Bridge*." *Arthur Miller: A Critical Study*. New York: Cambridge University Press, 2005, 178–196.

Carson, Neil. *Arthur Miller*. New York: St. Martin's, 1982.

Centola, Steven R. "Compromise as Bad Faith: Arthur Miller's *A View from the Bridge* and William Inge's *Come Back, Little Sheba*." *Midwest Quarterly* 28, no. 1 (Autumn 1986): 100–113.

Chander, Kailash. "Neurosis, Guilt and Jealousy in *A View from the Bridge*." In *Perspectives on Arthur Miller*, edited by Atma Ram, 96–108. (New Delhi: Abhinav Publications, 1988).

Costello, Donald P. "Arthur Miller's Circles of Responsibility: *A View from the Bridge* and Beyond." *Modern Drama* 36 (1993): 443–453.

Edwards, John. "Arthur Miller: An Appraisal." *Time & Tide,* May 4, 1961, 740–741.

Epstein, Arthur D. "A Look at *A View from the Bridge*." *Texas Studies in Literature and Language* 7 (Spring 1965): 109–122.

Findlater, Richard. "No Time for Tragedy?" *Twentieth Century* 161 (January 1957): 56–62.

Hartley, Anthony. "Waterfront." *Spectator,* October 19, 1956: 538–540.

Hope-Wallace, Philip. "Theatre: *A View from the Bridge*." *Time & Tide* 37 (1956): 1267.

Hurd, Myles R. "Angels and Anxieties in Miller's *A View from the Bridge*." *Notes on Contemporary Literature* 13 (September 1983): 4–6.

Kael, Pauline. "*The Innocents* and What Passes for Experience." *Film Quarterly* 15 (Summer 1962): 27–29.

Marino, Stephen A. "Territoriality in Arthur Miller's *A View from the Bridge*." In *Arthur Miller: Twentieth Century Legend,* edited by Syed Mashkoor Ali, 203–215. (Jaipur, India: Surabhi, 2006).

———. "Verse, Figurative Language, and Myth in *A View from the Bridge*." *A Language Study of Arthur Miller's Plays: The Poetic in the Colloquial.* New York: Mellen, 2002, 81–106.

Murphy, Brenda. *Congressional Theatre: Dramatizing McCarthyism on Stage, Film, and Television.* New York: Cambridge University Press, 1999, 215–219.

Otten, Terry. "*A View from the Bridge*." *The Temptation of Innocence in the Dramas of Arthur Miller.* Columbia: University of Missouri Press, 2002, 76–88.

Rothenberg, Albert, and Eugene D. Shapiro. "The Defense of Psychoanalysis of Literature: *Long Day's Journey into Night* and *A View from the Bridge*." *Comparative Drama* 7, no. 1 (Spring 1973): 51–67.

Styan, J. L. "Why *A View from the Bridge* Went Down Well in London: The Story of a Revision." In *Arthur Miller: New Perspective,* edited by Robert A. Martin, 139–148. (Englewood Cliffs, N. J.: Prentice–Hall, 1982).

Trewin, J. C. "Quick Change." *Illustrated London News,* October 27, 1956: 720.

Webster, Margaret. "A Look at the London Season." *Theatre Arts* 41 (May 1957): 28–29.

Welland, Dennis. "Two New York Plays." *Miller the Playwright.* 2d ed. London: Methuen, 1983, 67–79.

Wertheim, Albert. "*A View from the Bridge*." In *Cambridge Companion to Arthur Miller,* edited by Christopher Bigsby, 101–114. (New York: Cambridge University Press, 1997).

"A Visit with Castro" (2003)

This essay is Miller's account of his trip in 2000 to Cuba to view the island, during which he was invited to meet FIDEL CASTRO. It was first printed as Miller's epilogue to *Cuba on the Verge: An Island in Transition* (2003), a collection of essays about the contemporary Cuban experience, edited by Terry McCoy. In January 2004, a shortened version was reprinted both sides of the Atlantic in *The Nation,* and *The Guardian,* the latter under the title "My Dinner with Castro."

Miller admits from the start that his feelings toward Cuba "have been mixed." He had welcomed Castro's overthrow of the corrupt Batista society and his rejection of U.S. CAPITALISM but frowned on his evident repression. He disapproves of the blockade by the United States, feeling that its motivation is suspect. He and INGE MORATH were invited as "cultural visitors" along with other artists and philanthropists, including William Styron, Patty Cisneros, and William Luers, and the group was invited to dinner with Castro. Miller describes Havana as having the "beauty of a ruin returning to the sand," with evident exploitation, prostitution, and endemic poverty, yet with an endearing sense of resilience and human solidarity. An acting class that he meets is enamored of the United States but does not want to hear that BROADWAY has been captured by musicals. A group of local writers question their presence, wrongly hoping that it may be an indication that the United States is planning to lift the embargo. Miller judges their insecure mood as similar to that of the United States in the 1950s under the threat of the HOUSE UN-AMERICAN ACTIVITIES COMMITTEE.

Arriving at the Palace of Revolution to meet Castro, Miller sees him akin to a movie star with a similar obsession with power and approbation. Although Morath's camera is initially confiscated, when Castro learns what a good photographer she is, it is returned. Castro keeps them talking well into the early hours, teasing them about an earlier visit to a dissident writer, mocking and berating the Soviet Union for its lack of current support, and parading his knowledge on a variety of topics.

The following day, Castro joins them for lunch. Although a notorious admirer of Ernest Hemingway, he pretends no knowledge of current U.S. culture, as if he wants to distance himself from contemporary U.S. reality. Miller suspects a similarly willful denial of his own nation's reality and likens Castro to an outmoded Don Quixote, vainly tilting at windmills that have been long collapsed into dust. Describing the Cuban leader as "a lonely old man hungry for some fresh human contact" and a "powerful vine" that both defends and chokes all growth in Cuba, Miller exhibits sympathy and frustration with a figure whose views on the necessity of revolution appear sound but whose enchantment with power has perverted his ambition. COMMUNISM, for Miller, seems the ideology of another age, grown dusty and useless like the "battered old Marxist–Leninist tracts" for sale outside his hotel. New policies and ideas are needed to save Cuba from "needless suffering," but the U.S. embargo stifles all chance of this happening by justifying Cuban defiance and giving Castro "an insurance policy against needed change."

"Waiting for the Teacher: On Israel's Fiftieth Birthday" (1998)

A fairly long poem written in 18 free-verse stanzas, "Waiting for the Teacher" was published in *Harper's* magazine in July 1998 and offers some insight into Miller's views on modern Israel. It begins by identifying with those who have died because of ANTI-SEMITISM over the years, but it also mourns the Arab dead. To Miller, all violence is self-defeating, and the way forward for Israel must be through nonviolence. The teacher who is wandering the desert and to whom Miller repeatedly refers remains unnamed but could be anyone who has preached pacifism from Gandhi to Jesus.

Miller recalls the beginnings of the modern state of Israel and how the Russians, despite their anti-Semitic history, recognized Israel from the start, and sees in this a ray of hope. The formation of a Jewish homeland is described as "Justice done!" after centuries of displacement, and having their own country has helped affirm the identity of all Jews. However, for 50 years, things have not improved as much as hoped, partly due to disagreements about Jerusalem and a series of assassinations. It is becoming hard to envision the future of Israel amid all the terrorist activity, and Miller blames all sides, describing them as stuck in a repetitive cycle of violence. He offers a vision of Israel being purer than human nature can plausibly create, given people's tribalism, but urges people to transcend such limitations. "Israel's power was moral first," but it is a power that is lost in the violence.

Miller criticizes the absolutism of orthodox branches of all religions and describes himself as an atheist, yet one who accepts and embraces his identity as a Jew. He closes with a final plea to listen to the voice of pacifism in the guise of a teacher waiting outside the city gates.

"What's Wrong with This Picture?" (1974)

Subtitled "Speculations on a homemade greeting card," the picture of which accompanies the text, this short essay first appeared in *Esquire* in July 1974 but was reprinted in *Echoes Down the Corridor*. Although their names are never mentioned in the text, the couple pictured on the card are VÁCLAV HAVEL and his wife, standing fully clothed in a lake with their dog between them, held afloat by a life preserver. It is a New Year's card that the couple sent to Miller, which arrived months late and caused him to consider Havel's plight in a country that is apparently hostile to its own artists. It is a call for the United States to take note of deteriorated conditions in Czechoslovakia since the Soviet Union's incursion six years previously and to also consider the many artists around the globe who are being unfairly censored and silenced.

Suggesting that the couple appear to be an ideal, law-abiding couple, he then points out how the man's writing has been censored and restricted, and he voices anger that the United States has not

become involved. He describes in detail what it is like to be a patriotic artist in a country in which all national cultural life is being eliminated and of the negative psychological effect this must have on writers like Havel. As a socialist, Havel even supports COMMUNISM, but cannot in all conscience capitulate to the absolutism of the current regime in his country. Miller points out the irony of his government suggesting that a man like Havel who refuses to emigrate must be unpatriotic. He suggests that the picture he has been sent mutely illustrates the absurdity and the unreality of Havel's life. Only being allowed to publish abroad in a foreign language can only disconnect writers from their work and damage a nation's cultural health. It is clear that Miller respects and admires Havel's strength but asks why such conditions should be forced upon any artist.

"White Puppies" (1978)

"White Puppies" was published in *Esquire* in 1978 and is an unusual short story, illustrating the difficulty that individuals face in honestly knowing and understanding another human being. It centers on the Gruhn family, who appear on the surface to be a perfect family: successful businessman, dutiful wife, five disciplined children, a dog, and a lovely country home. Buried beneath this veneer, Miller slowly reveals, is a desperately dissatisfied marriage and a son who will be driven to suicide. The white puppies of the title are three throwback boxers that were born to the family pet, and during the course of the tale, they are thrown into a lake to drown, thus illustrating both the carelessness toward life and possible fate of people like the Gruhns.

Karl and Caroline Gruhn's lives are marked by loss: They have few friends, have given up on their earlier radical politics, and exhibit no connection to their children. These are losses created by their own complacency and indifference. Caroline resents having wasted her education as a housewife, while Karl feels in competition with his mother, is dissatisfied with his wife and financial status, and regrets having given up his faith (he had been raised an Orthodox Jew). The story begins with their dog, Sally, giving birth to five puppies, three of which are the wrong color, and so to preserve the pedigree, they must be destroyed, even though they seem the most virile of the brood. It seems that at least one of the five Gruhn children is equally differentiated; the second eldest, Joseph, at age 12, has taken to collecting his urine in bottles all over his bedroom. The stench has driven his brother Charles to sleep in the attic, but no one is able to find out why Joseph does this. The parents consider various psychoanalytical possibilities, including marking his territory, asserting his sexuality, showing contempt for his parents, or displaying an Oedipal antagonism toward his father, but they never learn the cause and they dislike asking, assuming that Joseph will not tell them if they do.

Leaping forward, Miller informs us that in 10 years time, Joseph will commit suicide, significantly by drowning—the mode by which Caroline will get rid of the white puppies—his mystery still intact. Giving us character sketches of the parents, Caroline is described as calm and rational, while Karl is delicate, refined, and placid, and after 20 years of marriage, they are an outwardly handsome couple. Yet this picture is undercut by additional information that 11 years into the future, Karl will try to murder his wife with a jack handle. Both are heavy drinkers and despite the calm surface, internally, are raging torrents of largely negative emotion. Karl remains aloof from the problem of the puppies, insisting that his wife deal with it. He is more concerned over his relationship with his shrewd and overbearing mother, which initiates strange dreams of being attacked by an owl. The underlying violence of his nature is well buried but is there. Caroline senses it and tries to please him to keep it buried. She lies on top of him to lull him to sleep, and when he penetrates her in the dawn, she tries to reciprocate desire, although he satiates himself without paying attention.

When Caroline ties the white puppies together and takes them down to the lake the next morning to throw them in, we see most clearly an image of wasted life, violent aggression, and complacent disregard for other beings—all hallmarks of the Gruhns's mode of living. She returns and throws

away Joseph's urine collection, although she worries if this might not be a mistake. She then takes a rare daytime drink to relax, and when her mother-in-law phones, Caroline blames her for the death of the puppies. The connection seems to be that an unloving mother created an unloving husband and father, and as Caroline wonders if Sally even misses her puppies that were drowned, there is a suggestion that Caroline, too, is a part of this destructive cycle.

"Why Israel Must Choose Justice" (2003)

Miller's speech in June 2003 on receiving the Jerusalem Prize for achievement in the field of freedom of the individual in society was later published as an essay in *Nation*. Since the award cited his "activities in defense of civil rights" along with his writing, he chooses to talk in a political rather than literary vein and begins by talking about his work with PEN. True to fashion, Miller does not give a crowd-pleasing speech but one designed to provoke change. He offers an uncompromising call for the state of Israel to reconsider its settlement policy, which he sees as working against the spirit of its original charter and is destined to undercut Israel's future safety.

Miller optimistically asserts that "most people by far continue to believe in justice and wish it to prevail," and justice to Miller means justice for all; that includes the Palestinians who, he feels, also have a right to exist in a state of their own, though not at the cost of destroying Israel. Miller asks that Israelis choose HUMANISM over territorialism and that it reconnect with an age-old Jewish interest in justice as the only true stay against chaos and brute force. The creation of Israel, Miller asserts, was itself an act of justice and a repayment for the suffering of the HOLOCAUST. As such, it is hard to critique and has armed Israel in the past with a shield and a sense of right, but Israel's attempts to expand, the hard and uncompromising face it turns to the world, and its arrogant self-righteousness threaten to undo this sense, just as similar behavior on the part of the United States has lost it world support since 9/11. To renew Israel's original "visionary character," Miller concludes, new leadership is needed that will allow for "justice and equity for all" and thus restore Israel's "immortal light to the world" as a nation worthy of emulation rather than of disapproval.

William Ireland's Confession (1939)

The radio play *William Ireland's Confession* was broadcast in 1939 as part of the *Columbia Workshop* series and was subsequently published William Kozlenko's *One Hundred Non-Royalty Radio Plays* (1941). It tells the true story of an 18th-century forger, a tale that Miller had researched and found fascinating and that he spins to become a tale of defeated genius and a son who desperately seeks his father's approbation.

The play begins with the ghost of William Ireland offering us his biographical background, and complaining that he was unjustly treated. William's father, Samuel, is a dismissive figure, demeaning his son in public and deriding his attempts at literature. As a collector, his ambition is to discover some unknown paper of William Shakespeare's. In an effort to gain his father's attention, William finds an old prayer book that he suspects may have been Queen Elizabeth's but cannot authenticate. To make his find more persuasive, he forges a fake dedication page that utterly fools his father. This inspires him to try more forgeries.

William's problem is partly that of ego: He wants to be as famed and adulated as his namesake, William Shakespeare, and believes himself to be a great writer. To that end, he forges documents to give to his father as lost Shakespearean papers. He pretends he has a friend with a trunk full of such material. After his father has Francis Webb authenticate the document, William rewrites *King Lear* with a new ending. James Boswell and other scholars praise this find, saying that it is better than the known version. Suspicious these are forgeries, rival scholar Edmund Malone is more skepti-

cal. William's efforts to avoid detection become increasingly preposterous. Malone writes a pamphlet denouncing him as a fake, but William persuades the scholars to sign a certificate saying that his pieces are definitely Shakespeare's.

When William puts on his own tragedy, calling it a newly discovered piece by Shakespeare, Malone has people heckle from the audience, and it is closed. His father demands to see the mysterious friend to silence suspicion, and William admits that he wrote everything. Father and scholars are horrified and turn on him. Although he continued to write, William believes that his work was never given serious consideration, and as the play closes, Shakespeare joins his ghost to ask for advice on *Hamlet*.

Very like Miller's *The Pussycat and the Expert Plumber Who Was a Man*, his radio play of the following year, *William Ireland's Confession* derides the wisdom of the so-called intelligentsia, depicting such people as gullible and self-serving. Whether or not William is a good writer is debatable, but he is producing in a climate that is unwilling to consider the work of a young writer seriously, a concern with which Miller himself would have been in sympathy at that time. The plaintive call for recognition in William's final speech might well apply to either writer.

"With Respect for Her Agony—But with Love" (1964)

Following *Life* magazine's review of *After the Fall*, Miller was offered the opportunity to print this single-page essay in which he defends himself and his play against the critical onslaught that it elicited. Admitting that he knew that the play would attract controversy, Miller insists, "The character of Maggie . . . is not in fact MARILYN MONROE. Maggie," he continues, "is a character in a play about the human animal's unwillingness or inability to discover in himself the seeds of his own destruction." He also points out, in response to critics who had charged him with "cruelty toward the memory of Marilyn Monroe," that the character of Maggie is treated with "respect for her agony but with love," and people who commit suicide have troubled lives, so to present such a character as any less problematic than Maggie would be unrealistic.

Miller goes on to castigate the hypocrisy of those he sees leaping to Monroe's defense after death, whose treatment most enraged her when alive. "Find the Author," he suggests, is a game that anyone can play, but it is not very productive. Most writers use their own experiences in their work to ensure that it has a connection to reality, but what they produce from that, Miller insists, is art rather than biography and should be judged as such: All of the characters whom he creates for *After the Fall* are "drawn, not reported." Miller describes his play as "a dramatic statement of a hidden process which underlies the destructiveness hanging over this age."

Miller also faults critics who refer to the "exculpation of Quentin" in the play, insisting that "one of the play's major points" is that there cannot be any "divestment of guilt." Miller views Quentin as a character who recognizes his part in the evil that he sees and embraces responsibility for it. Just as critics misunderstood Hannah Arendt's *Eichmann in Jerusalem* as an apology for Eichmann's HOLOCAUST crimes, Miller feels that they have misunderstood his play deliberately, a play that similarly asks for individuals to recognize their own capacity for evil. He concludes, "It is, therefore, not that the play is personal which offends some people," but the fact that it does not allow its audience to hide from their complicity in the victimization of people like Maggie.

You're Next! (1946?)

Written sometime in the 1940s, *You're Next!* is an agitprop sketch that shows the evident influence on the young Miller of earlier playwright CLIFFORD ODETS. The piece illustrates the insidious power of the Rankin Committee (which would become HOUSE UN-AMERICAN ACTIVITIES COMMITTEE) over businesses and the general public during a

period of growing paranoia. Miller's aim is to point out the difficulty of doing business—be it running a barber shop or making a living as a playwright—in a climate where one could be branded a communist merely for being a liberal.

The play centers on Libertyville barber Jerry Marble, who supports liberal causes with collection cans and posters in his store. He is warned by a lawyer friend, Matty, that his activities may cause him to be viewed as a communist. While Jerry insists that being against fascism does not make him pro-communist, Matty warns him that people who are roused by unscrupulous political figures seeking reelection who are choosing to scare the public with anti-Red paranoia will not see the difference and will stop using his business. The United States no longer seems to be a nation where freedom of speech and principle is a reality, as local businesses remove their posters supporting the local reform candidate. Jerry takes his cans away and is unhappy. However, after hearing a headline that touts his town as a "Red Center" and being asked for support by a local butcher whom he despises—whose antilabor stance has led to him being boycott and who is suspected of informing on fellow businessmen as communists—Jerry announces his intention to remain an outward liberal, and damn the consequences. The play ends in a call to action as Jerry persuades the newsboy to shout an altered headline of "Beware, Rankin Threatens Liberty!"

When Miller was called before the HUAC committee in 1956 to be questioned about his political associations, this play was cited as potential evidence that Miller was sympathetic to COMMUNISM. They spoke of a production of the play being performed in 1947 for the benefit of the New York State Communist Party Building Congress, and an undated copy of the unpublished play in the John Gassner Collection at the HARRY RANSOM RESEARCH CENTER indicates that it was produced by Stage for Action in New York. In her study of McCarthyism on stage, scholar Brenda Murphy describes it as a play of "revolutionary realism," and points out that while it is certainly "a call for political action to resist HUAC," it is also "a call from the middle class to the middle class" rather than a piece of communist propaganda.

PART III

Related People, Places, and Topics

Absurdism Absurdism is a philosophy that states that the efforts of humanity to find meaning in the universe will ultimately fail because no such meaning exists. It has its roots in the 19th-century Danish philosopher, Søren Kierkegaard, and is an offshoot of both the avant-garde nonsense of Dadaism from the 1910s and developments in EXISTENTIALISM as seen in the writing of ALBERT CAMUS. The aftermath of WORLD WAR II provided the social environment that stimulated absurdist views and allowed for their popular development, especially in the devastated country of France. The Theatre of the Absurd was a movement that began among European playwrights of this period and denoted a particular style of presentation. Critic Martin Esslin coined the term and defined the concept for American audiences. Esslin cited Eugene Ionesco, SAMUEL BECKETT, Jean Genet, and Arthur Adamov as the leaders of a movement that gave artistic articulation to Camus's philosophy that life is inherently without meaning.

Absurdist drama tends to depart from realistic characters, situations, and all of the associated theatrical conventions. Time, place, and identity are ambiguous and fluid, and even basic causality frequently breaks down. Meaningless plots, repetitive or nonsensical dialogue, and dramatic non sequiturs are often used to create dreamlike or even nightmarelike moods. While Miller saw absurdity in life, he refused to take an absurdist response, seeing this as too defeatist.

Although absurd situations sometimes occur in Miller's work, be it the incongruities within pieces like "Elegy for a Lady" or *Mr. Peters' Connections*, or the borderline believable antics of *The Ride Down Mt. Morgan* or *Resurrection Blues*, Miller has never written a truly absurdist drama. In his essay "Ibsen and the Drama of Today," Miller critiques absurdism for its dismissal of the past as irrelevant, its obsessive concern with the immediate here and now, and its preference of situation over character. By contrast, his own plays are inseparable from their pasts and are anchored in character. Miller suspects that the horrors of the HOLOCAUST initiated people's belief in the absurd as a means of trying to deal with the untenable. But Miller never accepted the basic tenets of absurdism, insisting that positive action was always possible. He believed strongly in the force of life and a hidden order that structures that life in a meaningful way. He had drawn this idea from reading the novels of FYODOR DOSTOYEVSKY and strengthened it by applying the potential of a peculiarly U.S. brand of optimism as a bulwark against the forces of death and despair that were so prevalent in the latter half of the 20th century. For Miller, a viable value system by which to live is within the reach of every person if they so choose to embrace it. Those who embrace absurdism, in his opinion, have simply made a poor choice.

In his 1958 essay "The Shadows of the Gods," Miller describes drama as having come to "the end of a period," and insists that the "limitations" of the plays of that period needed to be recognized and dealt with if theater was "not to become absurd, repetitious, and decayed." Fearful of the implications of absurdism, the essay was partly a call for new standards in art. His 1968 drama *The Price* deliberately offers itself as an alternative to the negative rationale of absurdism and what he saw as a disturbing surge of self-involved avant-garde plays. As he explains in the essay "*The Price—The Power of the Past,*" "I was moved to write a play that might confront and confound both." When Gregory Solomon begins to laugh along with the record at the play's close, we can read it as a sign of his vivacity and spirit and not as an absurdist reaction to the pointlessness of life. Laughter for Miller has meaning, and it can be negative as in the father's hurtful laughter, but it can also be a curative against a culture that is too concerned with itself to appreciate the life on offer. While Miller can enjoy absurd humor and is certainly aware that life can often appear absurd, he found the determination of absurdist playwrights of the 1960s to find fault with traditional theater and their refusal to create character, structure, or plot in their works to be detrimental to good drama.

FURTHER READING

Esslin, Martin. *The Theatre of the Absurd.* Garden City: Doubleday, 1961.

Actors Studio   The Actors Studio was devised as a theatre workshop for professional actors, directors, and writers who would be admitted on the basis of talent and would use the opportunity to develop their craft and to experiment with new forms of theater freed from the pressures of production. Wanting to continue the pioneering work they had begun with the GROUP THEATER, the Actors Studio was founded in 1947 in New York by ELIA KAZAN, Cheryl Crawford, and Robert Lewis. Lewis resigned the following year, and LEE STRASBERG was invited to join in 1949, becoming artistic director in 1951 and continuing as such until his death in 1982.

A disciple of the acting techniques that were pioneered by Russian director Constantin Stanislavski with the Moscow Art Theatre, Strasberg would refine these to develop the style that was known as Method Acting, in which actors made their roles appear more real by tapping into personal experience so as to feel the role from the inside out. The Method would have a profound affect on U.S. stage and screen productions for years to come. In 1967, a West Coast branch would open in Hollywood. Both branches continue to operate, with many famous names going through their doors, including DUSTIN HOFFMAN, ELI WALLACH, Robert De Niro, and Al Pacino.

The Actors Studio's training helped to bring greater REALISM and intensity to U.S. theater, witnessed especially in Kazan's intense direction of several works of TENNESSEE WILLIAMS and Miller. Both *All My Sons* and *Death of a Salesman* benefited from casts that were trained largely in the Method. In 1953, Kazan introduced MARILYN MONROE to the Actors Studio, and she began to sit in on classes. Much praised by both Lee and PAULA STRASBERG, some accused them of sycophancy to Monroe's star power, but Monroe was very impressed by Lee Strasberg's theater credentials and, according to Miller, viewed him with respectful awe.

FURTHER READING

Hirsch, Foster. *A Method to Their Madness: The History of the Actors Studio.* Boulder, Colo.: Da Capo, 1986.

Albee, Edward (1928–)   Abandoned at two weeks old, Edward Franklin Albee III was soon after adopted by New York millionaires Reed and Frances Albee. A child prodigy, Albee began to write poetry at the age of six and at 12 wrote a three-act sex farce set on an ocean liner, *Aliqueen.* His father was stern and quiet, totally dominated by a wife who was considerably younger and taller than her husband; neither one showed much affection toward their son. Albee would satirize what he saw as their small-minded prejudices in many of his plays. After being expelled from Trinity College for not attending classes, he moved to Greenwich Village and concentrated on becoming a writer of short stories and plays but mainly poetry.

Approaching age 30, having achieved little, Albee wrote *The Zoo Story* (1959) as a last attempt to be noticed. It would become his breakthrough play and would be performed in Berlin, Germany, on a bill with SAMUEL BECKETT's *Krapp's Last Tape*, shocking audiences with its subversive nature and attack on the complacency of contemporary American life. The following year, it was performed off-Broadway by the Provincetown Players. Albee's early plays were seen as displaying an American mode of ABSURDISM, but like Miller, Albee is a playwright who has continually experimented with subject matter and form, and it would be wrong to categorize him so narrowly. Like Miller, Albee, too, has often been spurned by those refusing to accept his newer material.

Albee's *Who's Afraid of Virginia Woolf?* (1962) ran for two years on BROADWAY and won many awards but was denied the Pulitzer Prize as some felt that it was too offensive. *A Delicate Balance* (1966) won Albee his first Pulitzer Prize, but reviews were mixed. In 1975, he won a second Pulitzer Prize this time for *Seascape*, but the play had a short run. Although his output continued through the 1970s and 1980s, like Miller, Albee would not again win critical favor until the 1990s. In 1991, he was granted the WILLIAM INGE Award for distinguished achievement in the American theater (four years ahead of Miller). Then, in 1993, SIGNATURE THEATER's season featured Albee (four years before they featured Miller). In 1994, he won a third Pulitzer Prize; the play was *Three Tall Women* and Albee also was awarded an Obie for Sustained Achievement in the American Theatre. To date, he has written more than 30 plays.

Miller's commitment to serious drama and openness toward experimentation has influenced many younger American playwrights, and Albee can be counted among their number. Albee's plays display Miller's social concern and similarly play with theatrical convention. Behind much of his drama, as with Miller's, is an assertion of the need for the individual to acknowledge the nature of reality and the necessity for genuine human relationships. There is also a concern with what Albee saw as the collapse of American idealism. As social criticism that refuses to pull any punches, his plays attempt to combat the artificial values that he sees becoming too prominent in our society. The same can be said for any number of Miller's works.

In CHRISTOPHER BIGSBY's 1990 collection *Arthur Miller and Company*, in which various friends and colleagues pass comment on Miller in honor of his 75th birthday, Albee praises Miller as a writer who "understands that serious writing is a social act as well as an aesthetic one, that political involvement comes with the territory." Proud that he and Miller have often "been at the barricades together," he describes Miller's plays as "a cold burning force" and concludes, "I wish there were more like him." At the Memorial service held after Miller's death, Albee added, "Some writers matter and some do not. . . . Arthur Miller was a writer who mattered. A lot."

FURTHER READING

Roudané, Matthew C. "Arthur Miller and His Influence on Contemporary American Drama." *American Drama* 6.1 (Fall 1996): 1–13.

anti-Semitism   The term *anti-Semitism* refers to hostility toward or prejudice against Jews as a religious, ethnic, or racial group. This can range from individual hatred to institutionalized, violent persecution, the most extreme example of which was the HOLOCAUST during WORLD WAR II. But prior to the 19th century, most anti-Semitism was religious in nature, based on Christian or Islamic interactions with and interpretations of JUDAISM. Jews would become the targets of persecution for their refusal to change their religious convictions, and many Jews were chased from their homes around Europe throughout the Middle Ages or were forced to convert.

Racial anti-Semitism, with its origins in the early and popularly misunderstood evolutionary ideas of race that started during the Enlightenment, did not become the dominant form of anti-Semitism until the late 19th century. A hatred of Judaism as a religion was replaced with the idea that the Jews themselves, despite coming from a variety of nationalities, were a racially distinct group who were inferior by nature and were worthy of animosity due to their incorrigible badness. Fed by such pamphlets as the *Protocols of the Elders of Zion*, conspiracy theories about Jewish plots to dominate the world became a popular form of anti-Semitic expression, along with complaints that Jews were greedy, grasping, and exploitative. It was partly these theories that allowed Hitler to use the Jews as scapegoats in the 1930s and to unite his nation against them. Miller's play *Incident at Vichy* is partly an answer to those who were less than condemnatory toward the Holocaust; it highlights the indignity and the perversity of how Jews were rounded up for extermination. The Jews in the play range from a young boy to an old man, and none are grasping or plotting but simply terrified and concerned for their survival against a relentless dehumanizing institution.

Miller grew up in a predominantly Jewish neighborhood, and although he recalls feeling uneasy giving his father's evidently Jewish name so that he could obtain a library card, he did not experience anti-Semitism directly until he began to look for work after graduation from high school. Many jobs in the papers were restricted against Jewish applicants, just as were places at certain colleges or vacancies in certain resorts, hotels, and restaurants. His initial application to work at CHADICK–DELAMATER AUTO PARTS WAREHOUSE was first rejected because they did not usually employ Jews. However, a friend put in a good word, and the manager decided to give him an opportunity; although Miller initially felt that he was an outsider, he gradually became accepted to some extent. He also recalls another incident: In 1940, when collecting dialect speech for the folk division of the Library of Congress down South, he was chased off one man's property with a shotgun because he looked Jewish.

Although U.S. anti-Semitism was something that people preferred not to talk about, especially during the war years as news of the Holocaust trickled through, Miller was an early writer to address the topic openly in his controversial novel *Focus,* in which a man suffers professionally and socially because people begin to suspect that he is Jewish after he buys some new glasses. Although an anti-Semite himself, the book's protagonist Lawrence Newman is finally driven to recognize the humanity of the only real Jew on the block and so reassess his previously limited view. Given the massive diversity of humankind, to view anyone as part of a collective rather than as an individual is dangerously limiting and ripe for abuse, and so

Miller allows anti-Semitism to speak to the heart of all prejudice. The novel depicts anti-Semitism as backed by mainstream religion, fueled by ignorant, disgruntled people who are seeking scapegoats for their own frustration and permitted by the moral inertia of the masses who only want a quiet life.

Miller was not content simply to depict anti-Semitism, he was also concerned with reforming people's attitudes and responses. By exposing the ridiculous bases of anti-Semitism, he hoped to alter the way that it was perceived even by those who did not consider themselves to be prejudiced, but assumed that such things were unavoidable. For example, there has been a long history of anti-Semitism among the Polish, and even though they shared the Nazis as a common enemy during the war, they appeared to feel little compassion for the Jews who being slaughtered. But as Miller tries to show in *Playing for Time*, it is always wrong to judge individuals by a collective trait, be they Polish or Jewish. One of the play's characters, Elzvieta, may be Polish, but she is kindly toward Jews, despite the scorn of others, and through this, Miller is pointing out that prejudice is neither innate nor unstoppable.

As early as 1941, Miller spoke out publicly against international Jewish persecution in his article "Hitler's Quarry," and in his unpublished and unproduced 1942 play *Boro Hall Nocturne,* he first addressed the issue of U.S. anti-Semitism. It was evidently not a topic on which he was prepared to stay silent. Anti-Semitism was his biggest complaint against EZRA POUND in his 1945 article "Should Ezra Pound Be Shot?" and it would surface again in his assessment of Russian life in the 1969 *In Russia.* Another play that explores the affects of the issue is *Broken Glass*, in which Miller exposes U.S. complacency in the face of news of the Holocaust, with its implication that such complacency was rooted in an anti-Semitism that was so endemic to U.S. society that it had even damaged some American Jews such as Phillip Gellburg, turning them into self-hating individuals. Partly due to his recognition and fear of American anti-Semitism, Gellburg tries to sever his connections to other Jews and so deadens his own life for these are connections that he cannot avoid. We can also find references and resulting lessons regarding the unfounded bases of anti-Semitism in several other works, including *Homely Girl, a Life,* "Monte Sant' Angelo," and "The Performance."

Aronson, Boris (ca. 1900–1980)   A major force in stage design, Aronson came to America in the 1920s from the Soviet Union after a brief stay in Germany. Having been trained in the theatricalist tradition of the radical Russian director Vsevolod Meyerhold, deeply influenced by Modernist art, and stimulated by the visionary designs of Gordon Craig and Adolphe Appia, he found little to admire in the mundane REALISM that he saw on the American stage at that time. Openly scornful of the simplistic domestic dramas that he found dominating BROADWAY, his innovative and frequently metaphoric design concepts and his interpretative use of color were at odds with homegrown designers such as Lee Simonson, who viewed them as too exotic and foreign for American tastes. Aronson and Miller were friends, and in *Timebends, A Life,* Miller confesses that "Boris's Russian-Yiddish accent and his plastic attitude toward language were among my sources for Gregory Solomon," the old furniture dealer in *The Price.*

Aronson began to design constructivist settings for the Yiddish theater. His first Broadway credit is the 1932 revue *Walk a Little Faster,* and he had some success with George Abbott and John C. Holm's comedy *Three Men on a Horse* in 1935, a play that Miller would later adapt for the radio in 1946. This was followed by designs for several GROUP THEATER productions, including CLIFFORD ODETS's 1935 plays *Awake and Sing* and *Paradise Lost.* Working with directors HAROLD CLURMAN, ELIA KAZAN, and LEE STRASBERG on a variety of plays, his reputation grew. Married to Lisa Jalowetz, who worked as his assistant on many productions, his Tony award in 1951 for his work on Wolcott Gibbs's *Season in the Sun,* TENNESSEE WILLIAMS's *The Rose Tattoo,* and Odets's *The Country Girl* was the first of six, and he would design 25 Broadway productions in the 1950s alone, including Frances Goodrich and Albert Hackett's *The Diary of Anne Frank* (1955), WILLIAM INGE's *Bus Stop* (1955), Williams's *Orpheus Descending* (1957),

and Archibald MacLeish's *J. B.* (1958). These, and his work elsewhere, such as his grand design for Laurence Olivier's *Coriolanus* in 1959 at the Royal Shakespeare Theatre in Stratford, GREAT BRITAIN solidified his reputation.

It was in the 1950s that Aronson came to work on Miller's plays, first *The Crucible* and then the double bill of *A Memory of Two Mondays* and *A View from the Bridge;* he was nominated for a Tony Award for his design of the latter. Miller had admired Aronson's creations for Group Theater and was pleased to be able to work with him. His first design for *The Crucible* had been a modernist design, but the director JED HARRIS dismissed this in favor of a conventional one. Aronson would also design the sets for *Incident at Vichy, The Price,* and *The Creation of the World and Other Business.*

Aronson worked on a design with the playwright and the director for a long time, exhaustively researching every element of the play. When creating his design for *The Price,* another Tony nomination, he asked Miller to describe every piece of furniture that he imagined to be in the room. The set that he created was an amazing conglomeration of furniture that took on a life of its own, especially in the placement of the dead father's old chair, center stage.

In the 1960s, Aronson had also designed much lauded sets for *Fiddler on the Roof* (1964), and *Cabaret* (1966), and in the 1970s he began to collaborate on Stephen Sondheim's "concept" musicals that allowed him a more epic sweep and the chance to explore nonrealism on a large budget, producing award-winning designs for *Company* (1970), *Follies* (1971), and *Pacific Overtures* (1976). He did little further work on nonmusical drama. Aronson's range of theatrical expression was broad, and his designs were imaginative and challenging, often seeming to take on a life of their own, being of an organic rather than a decorative nature. He had a great impact on American designers who followed him, especially those working in regional and off-Broadway theaters, including his early apprentice Ming Cho Lee. Many of Aronson's sketches and models, including those for the Miller plays, can be found at the HARRY RANSOM RESEARCH CENTER.

FURTHER READING

Rich, Frank. *The Theatre Art of Boris Aronson*. New York: Knopf, 1988.

Arthur Miller Society   The Arthur Miller Society was founded on April 7, 1995, at the Second International Arthur Miller Conference at Millersville University in Pennsylvania. An international group of scholars and students decided to establish a society that would promote the study and production of Miller's plays. Since then, International Conferences have been organized by members of the society across the United States, from New York and New Jersey through Wisconsin to Las Vegas and California, many tied in to a new performance of a Miller play.

Founding president STEVEN CENTOLA also recommended that the society provide a forum for the exchange of information on Miller's lifetime of distinguished achievement in the theater through the publication of a society newsletter. In the ensuing years, up until 2005, the *Arthur Miller Society Newsletter* biannually published book and production reviews, feature articles on Miller's public appearances and interviews, and the proceedings of Arthur Miller conferences and special sessions at conferences sponsored by the American Literature Association and the Modern Language Association. In 2006, with funding from St. Francis College in BROOKLYN, the society was able to establish an academic journal to replace the newsletter, and the first issue of *The Arthur Miller Journal* was issued in June 2006 and continues to be published biannually. The society also maintains a website at <http://www.ibiblio.org/miller/> that contains information about Miller events and productions around the globe, a variety of bibliographic and background information, lesson plans, abstracts from past conference papers, and extracts from the newsletter.

Atkinson,   Brooks (1894–1984)   Born Justin Brooks Atkinson in Melrose, Massachusetts, his father a journalist, the famed theater critic was educated at Harvard and became the first president of the New York Drama Critics Circle in 1936. For 31 years, he was the most influential voice in American drama, and his reaction could make or break a play. He was respected and loved and was as popular with playwrights, directors, and actors as he was with his many readers. Requesting a leave of absence from drama criticism to cover war news, he was sent to China and Moscow. In 1947, he won a Pulitzer Prize for his postwar commentaries on the Soviet Union. In 1960, the Mansfield Theatre on BROADWAY was renamed the Brooks Atkinson Theatre; in 1972, he was one of the first named to the Theatre Hall of Fame and Museum; and in 1980, on his 86th birthday, Atkinson was presented with a medal by the Theatre Committee for EUGENE O'NEILL.

Atkinson began as a reporter for *Springfield Daily News*, but after a short spell teaching college English, he became assistant drama critic for *Boston Evening Transcript* for four years. From 1922, he worked for the *New York Times*, variously as a book-review editor, a drama critic, a foreign correspondent, and critic-at-large, until 1964 when he retired from full-time journalism to Alabama. In a posthumous profile for the *New York Times*, Richard Shepard described Atkinson as a figure who "exemplified the spirit of the Renaissance man with a mind that constantly inquired and fingers that always wrote." In the same article, his one-time managing editor Arthur Gelb called him "the conscience of the theater" and credited him with rediscovering off-Broadway in the 1950s when other critics could not be bothered. "His standards were high, but his criticism was tempered by compassion," Gelb insists. Then he concludes, "He had a compelling sense of courtesy toward the theater and an unfailing sense of optimism about its potential. He was the ideal theater critic for his time."

In *Timebends: A Life*, Miller credits Atkinson's two glowing reviews and his subsequent defense of *All My Sons* against those who saw it as unpatriotic as ensuring the play's lengthy run and facilitating Miller's "recognition as a playwright." Atkinson similarly lionized *Death of a Salesman*, calling it "superb" and "deeply moving," as well as Miller's adaptation of *An Enemy of the People*. Miller viewed him as one of the few critics in his corner, despite Atkinson's more hesitant reviews of *The Crucible*, *A Memory of Two Mondays* and *A View from the*

Bridge, and as a friend. Miller respected Atkinson's sense of responsibility toward the American theater and his belief in the need for serious drama to be produced in mainstream theaters to keep them socially relevant.

FURTHER READING

Atkinson, Brooks. *Broadway Scrapbook.* Westport, Conn.: Greenwood Press, 1970.

————, and Al Hirschfield. *The Lively Years: Reviews and Drawings of the Most Significant Plays Since 1920.* New York: Association Press, 1973.

Shepard, Richard F. "Brooks Atkinson, 89, Dead; Key Voice in Drama 31 Years" *New York Times,* January 15, 1984, sec. 1, p. 22.

Awards   Miller won an array of awards over seven decades of writing and activism, from his days as a student at UNIVERSITY OF MICHIGAN to international acknowledgements of his years of service to the theater and to the freedom of other writers. His first taste of success came with the two Avery Hopwood Awards that he won in the writing competitions that were held annually at his alma mater. As a sophomore, he won a minor award of $250 for *No Villain,* and the following year, as a junior, he was eligible for the major awards and won a $500 prize for *Honors at Dawn.* His senior entry, *The Great Disobedience,* placed second. In 1937, he also won a $1,250 scholarship award from the THEATRE GUILD's Bureau of New Plays to study playwrighting with KENNETH ROWE for his rewrite of *No Villain,* retitled *They Too Arise.*

Out in the theater world after college, it would take a few more years of development before he would begin to win further awards. His first BROADWAY outing, *The Man Who Had All the Luck,* may have closed after only six performances, but it did win the Theatre Guild National Award in 1944. Miller's following play, *All My Sons,* would win several professional awards, including both the Donaldson and the New York Drama Critics Circle Awards, beating out EUGENE O'NEILL's *The Iceman Cometh.* Miller also won a Tony Award as author and ELIA KAZAN one for direction. *Death of a Salesman* would be even more successful, winning among others the Pulitzer Prize, the New York Drama Crit-

ics' Circle Award, the Theater Club Award, and six Tony Awards for best play, author, director (Kazan again), producer, scenic design, and supporting actor for ARTHUR KENNEDY. Interestingly, LEE J. COBB was not even nominated for his creation of Willy Loman, and although GEORGE C. SCOTT gained a Tony nomination for his 1975 revival, he did not win. DUSTIN HOFFMAN won a Drama Desk Award for his turn as Willy, but it would be BRIAN DENNEHY's 1999 performance that would finally be awarded with a Tony (Miller received an additional Tony from this production for best play revival), and Dennehy also won an Olivier Award for his 2005 London interpretation.

The Pulitzer Prize for *Death of a Salesman* was Miller's only one; *The Crucible* only brought in Tony and Donaldson Awards for Best Play as well as an Obie in 1958 for its first major revival. Indeed, from this point on, awards for premieres of U.S. productions of his plays would grow sparse. Although several plays gained awards and nominations for featured actors, few were offered to the author or the plays. The 1955 one-act "A View from the Bridge" won the New York Drama Critics Award and a Tony for BORIS ARONSON's scenic design, but the Tony nominations for *The Price* and *The Ride down Mt. Morgan* failed to win. *The Ride down Mt. Morgan* was also nominated for a Drama Desk Award. *Broken Glass* had been nominated for a Tony but failed to win on its Broadway showing. Meanwhile, it was given the Olivier Award for Best New Play in GREAT BRITAIN, an indication of the difference with which his work was viewed on either side of the Atlantic. Indeed, in 1966, he had been given the Anglo–American Award, and in 1998 Britain voted him Playwright of the Century. He was, however, awarded a Drama Desk Lifetime Achievement Award in 1998 and a Special Lifetime Achievement Tony Award in 1999 in his home country. There were extensive tributes to Miller on his 80th and 85th birthdays in both Britain and the United States.

Several Broadway revivals of Miller's plays, including *The Price, A View from the Bridge, After the Fall, The Crucible, All My Sons, The Man Who Had All the Luck* and *Death of a Salesman,* have received various nominations and awards, some as best revival of their year. Miller has also been recognized for his television and film work. He won an Emmy for the 1966 version of *Death of a Salesman* and was nominated again in 1985 for the television version of Dustin Hoffman's performance as Willy Loman. Miller also won both an Emmy Award and a Peabody Award for 1980s *Playing for Time*. In 1997, he was nominated for BAFTA Film, Golden Satellite, and Academy Awards for his screenplay for *The Crucible*.

Among the various other awards with which he has been recognized, 1949's Father of the Year award was perhaps the one that most amused him. By 1954, academics had begun to recognize his importance as he received the National Association of Independent Schools Award, the Brandeis University Creative Arts Award in 1969, and in 1998, the Distinguished Inaugural Senior Fellow of the American Academy in Berlin. Becoming increasingly recognized globally, in 2002, Spain awarded him the Principe de Asturias Prize for Literature. He has been honored with several doctorates, including ones from University of Michigan, Oxford University, Harvard University, Brandeis University, and Carnegie–Mellon University.

In 1958, Miller was elected to the National Institute of Arts and Letters and was awarded their Gold Medal for Drama the following year, and in 1984, he received the John F. Kennedy Award for Lifetime Achievement. He was granted a Mellon Bank Award in 1991 for lifetime achievement in the humanities as well as the Algur Meadows Award, and in 1993, he was given the National Medal of the Arts by President Clinton. His lengthy essay "On Politics and the Art of Acting" was originally delivered as the Jefferson Lecture for 2001, an honor awarded to Miller by the National Endowment for the Humanities for distinguished intellectual achievement in the humanities.

Toward the close of the century, various award-giving foundations increasingly acknowledged Miller. Although he was sadly passed over for a Nobel Prize, in the final decade of his life, Miller's tremendous body of work was recognized by the William Inge Festival Award for distinguished achievement in American theater in 1995, the Edward Albee Last Frontier Playwright Award in 1996, the PEN/Laura Pels Foundation Award to a master American dramatist, the Lucille Lortel Award for Lifetime Achievement in 1998, the Dorothy and Lillian Gish Prize in 1999, as well as an NEH Fellowship, the National Book Medal for Distinguished Contribution to American Letters, Japan Art Association Praemium Imperiale International Arts Award, and the John H. Finley Award for Exemplary Service to New York City, all in 2001. He has also received acknowledgment for his activism beyond his drama with such awards as the 1997 Amnesty International USA Media Spotlight Award and the 1998 Hubert H. Humphrey First Amendment Freedoms Prize. In 2003, he was a controversial choice for the Jerusalem Prize for which he wrote the speech, "Why Israel Must Choose Justice."

B

Barley, Agnes (1970–) The daughter of an architect, Agnes Martin Barley was born in Jacksonville, Florida. Studying at the Parsons School of Design in New York and gaining her MFA from the Academy of Fine Arts in Vienna, Austria, Barley has exhibited widely in Europe as a minimalist abstract painter and had her solo debut in New York in 2004. Barley describes her work as "attempts to crystallize harmony, to distill form into careful constructs of line that reveal an internal structure and its absence" to create "constructions that whisper of a horizon with both movement and stillness." There is something of this that reminds one of some of Miller's more ambiguous later plays and gives some credibility to the couple's claim that they were soul mates.

Seven months after the death of his third wife, INGE MORATH, Miller met Barley at a dinner with mutual friends. Although uncertain because of their age difference—she was 55 years his junior—they began to see more of each other. As Miller would tell interviewer Deborah Solomon, "I like the company of women . . . Life is very boring without them. Women are livelier than men and more interested in people." Despite her family's and his childrens' reservations, the two were planning to marry shortly before his death. It was maybe of Barley that Miller was thinking when he has his elderly protagonist in the 2004 novella *The Turpentine Still* wonder about whether or not he should commit to a much younger girlfriend. A devoted companion during his final illness, Barley had her own art studio at Miller's ROXSBURY, CONNECTICUT, home and was at his bedside on the day he died.

Barnett, Louis (ca. 1860s–1943) Born and raised in Radomizl, the same Polish shetl as his daughter AUGUSTA MILLER's future father-in-law, Samuel Miller, Louis Barnett emigrated to the United States in the 1880s. Having done well as a clothing contractor, he was able to move his family from Broome Street on the Lower East Side of New York to the higher-class Harlem. His business prospered as so many others in the 1920s before he, too, lost everything and became dependent on his children. Despite this dependency, with his blunt Germanic manner, none of them ever dared to cross him. Although a devout Jew, he was also a die-hard Republican who believed that the United States would do better with a king. He reportedly threw an alarm clock across the room in anger on hearing the news that his grandson would be marrying MARY SLATTERY, a gentile.

Barnett always wore a yarmulke and a Vandyke beard, was vain of his appearance, and insisted that he be given funds to go to the barber every week even when the family was destitute during the GREAT DEPRESSION. After his wife Rose died of diabetes in 1928, he was shunted between his children, living for a time in BROOKLYN with Augusta and ISIDORE MILLER and sharing a room with the teenaged Miller, who found his stern grandfather to be a man so neat that he would fold his socks before putting them in the laundry and who rather disconcertingly liked to tease Miller about his looks. In *Timebends: A Life,* Miller asserts, "Not a word did I ever hear from him that might have some attachment to thought." His dislike of his grandfather's "narcissistic self-involvement" is exhibited in the self-concerned and ignorant grandfather depicted in *The American Clock.*

Beckett, Samuel (1906–1989) Samuel Barclay Beckett was born into an upper-middle-class Protestant family in Dublin, but after studying languages at college, he headed to France in 1928. In Paris, he met James Joyce and, becoming friendly, helped him to transcribe passages of *Finnegan's Wake* (1939). Both were fascinated with language, wanting to push linguistic boundaries. At the onset of WORLD WAR II, Beckett became active in the French resistance, working undercover as a farmer in Vichy France to avoid the Gestapo. After the war, he began to write novels in French and then translate them into English in an effort to pare down his style and to record only what was essential. His work of this period explored the idea of humanity in a state of existence without hope or meaning—a theme that he continued in his writing for the stage and a concept that connects him to ABSURDISM.

Waiting for Godot (1953) was his first attempt at a play, and it became a huge success. This and all his subsequent plays tend to offer a bleak and pessimistic vision of the world that Miller found troubling, even while he acknowledged Beckett's craftsmanship as a writer. Miller found Beckett a very negative playwright and was alarmed at the influence that his vision had on the contemporary theater, stripping it, in Miller's view, of any worthwhile meaning. Beckett was fascinated with humanity's dark side but grew so disillusioned that he finally even began to distrust language itself and toward the end of his life only wrote dramatic fragments, often with no visible character on stage. In 1969, he was awarded a Nobel Prize for literature.

In his essay "Notes on Realism," Miller describes Beckett's style of dramatic art as that of a "presentational thematic play" in which the language is stripped "clean as a bleached bone" to allow his theme its fullest potential. Up until the 1950s, Miller saw playwrights as transcending REALISM through elevated language, but under the influence of Beckett, Miller saw many doing it by emulating the "most common, undecorated speech." Yet, even as Beckett sheared away every metaphor or simile from his speech to create a new language, he did not make the mistake of leaving structure behind, which is why, for Miller, his plays work better than many of his imitators. Like Miller, Beckett was also strongly sympathetic toward beleaguered Czech writer VACLAV HAVEL, for whom Beckett wrote *Catastrophe* (1982).

Beijing People's Art Theater Beijing People's Art Theatre is the national theatre company of China. Four men established it in 1952: The dramatists Cao Yu; Jiao Juyin, the director; Ouyang Shanzun; and Zhao Qiyang. In its early years, the company mounted plays mostly by Chinese dramatists. Then in the early 1980s, it embarked upon the highly successful international tour of Cao Yu's play *Teahouse* to Germany, France, Switzerland, Japan, Canada, Singapore, and Hong Kong. This success encouraged them to pursue future collaborations with Western writers and directors in the spirit of international cultural and artistic exchange. While members of the People's Art Theatre have been invited to go abroad to lecture and direct plays in foreign countries, many writers, directors and actors, as diverse as U.S. actor Charlton Heston and the Russian actor/director Oleg Yevremov, have been encouraged to go to Beijing to take part in productions there.

Miller had met Cao Yu and Ying Ruocheng, who had directed many of the People's Art Theater productions, in 1978 during a visit to China. They had discussed the possibility and inherent difficulty in producing Western drama in China, which had been culturally isolated for so many years. One problem was that Chinese actors train in a very different style to those in the West. Performances had no pretense to REALISM, and Chinese acting would seem to Westerners overemphatic and melodramatic and would not work in a Western-style play. One of Cao Yu's aims in wanting to introduce Western drama to China was to see if this could help to influence new developments in Chinese theater and acting styles to keep them vital.

Both Yu and Ruocheng were able to visit the United States during the next two years to continue to explore their plan. Originally, they had discussed producing *All My Sons* but had changed their minds, now wanting to introduce *Death of a Salesman* to Chinese audiences, supposing that China's increasing Western contact would allow them to understand the play better. They were also excited by the innovation of the play's form and how that might impact a Chinese theater that had so far only experimented with realism and not yet witnessed the more complex subjective–realism of *Salesman*.

Uncertain if they could do full justice to this foreign play without aid, Miller was invited to come to China to direct it. Doubtful of the success of such a production, given that the play's exploration of capitalism would be antithetical to a Chinese culture in which 90 percent of its population were still peasants who had been raised with profoundly socialist values, Miller was reticent to agree. However intrigued by the challenge of directing a play in a foreign language that he did not even speak and by the chance to be the first foreign director to mount a new play in China with Chinese actors, he eventually agreed.

In 1983, Miller took INGE MORATH with him, staying in China for two months of rehearsal and leaving the day after the opening performance. He worked through an interpreter, directing an all-Chinese cast. He insisted that they did not try to look and act like Westerners because attempts to do that seemed too alien, and they explored together how the play could relate to an Eastern outlook. Cultural differences presented Miller with many obstacles, but he and the cast seemed to find a meeting place in the consistency with which they portrayed the characters, paying attention to their inner tensions and various motivations—characters whom they began to inhabit. The experience was one of both personal and creative discovery for Miller.

U.S. officials in China attended the opening with the Chinese, aware that this was a momentous chance to make cultural contact. The production was a great success, appearing to reach its audience who laughed at the same places as a U.S. audience and, like them, wept for Willy Loman. On his return to the United States, Miller published a day-to-day journal that he had written during rehearsals, titled *Salesman in Beijing*.

Bellow, Saul (1915–2005) Born the same year, raised during the years of the GREAT DEPRESSION, both Jewish intellectuals who had worked with the FEDERAL THEATER PROJECT and spent time together in Nevada seeking residency for divorces, Miller and Saul Bellow had a lot in common. Bellow is considered by many to be America's first important Jewish–American post-World War II novelist, but Malcolm Bradbury would offer that crown to Miller for his 1945 novel *Focus*, which followed Bellow's *The Dangling Man* (1944) by a year but is more concerned with the immigrant experience and Jewish identity in the New World than Bellow's debut wartime story in which the Jewish experience is not a central issue.

Solomon "Saul" Bellows was born in Quebec, Canada, to Russian-born parents but emigrated with his family to Chicago as a young child. Majoring in anthropology as an undergraduate, he went through to graduate school before serving in the marines in WORLD WAR II. In 1946, he accepted a teaching position at University of Minnesota, and he won a Pulitzer Prize in 1976 for *Humboldt's Gift* (1975). Bellow divided his life between teaching and writing, and by his death, the same year as Miller's, he had built a reputation as one of the most valuable contributors to U.S. literature through fiction that stretched over five decades.

Bellow had also been an active member of PEN, through which he had contact with Miller, but they had first met in 1956 and become friendly—despite Bellow's earlier dismissive review of *Focus* for *The New Republic* as too contrived—in Nevada, living in adjacent cottages while establishing the necessary six-week residency for divorce. They shared an editor at Viking Press who had arranged the accommodation, and Bellow stayed on as he was working on *Henderson the Rain King* (1959). He would later become one of Miller's ROXBURY, CONNECTICUT, circle of friends that would include JOHN STEINBECK, Philip Roth, and William Styron.

Bentley, Eric Russell (1916–) Born in GREAT BRITAIN, Eric Russell Bentley went on to become a notable drama scholar and critic and, in later years, a playwright. He was one of a cadre of theatrical commentators, including Joseph Wood Krutch and Robert Brustein, who continuously disdained the work of Miller. Bentley was early to find fault with Miller's poetic style, disliking *Death of a Salesman* intensely. He would go on to attack Miller more directly with *The Crucible,* claiming that Miller's naive liberalism and depiction of innocence reduced the play to melodrama.

After earning a degree from Oxford University, Bentley came to the United States in 1939 for his doctorate at Yale. Taking U.S. citizenship, he taught at several universities from Black Mountain College in North Carolina to State University of New York at Buffalo, with frequent trips to Europe as guest lecturer and invited director. His major body of work has been on European playwrights, especially Bertold Brecht and Luigi Pirandello, of whose work he has published many translations. Several of his studies on drama, including *The Playwright as Thinker: A Study of Drama in Modern Times* (1946) and *The Theatre of Commitment, and Other Essays on Drama in Our Society* (1967), created controversy in their general condemnation of modern theater for what Bentley viewed as its lack of concern for political affairs.

Bigsby, Christopher (1941–)   Born in Dundee, Scotland, Christopher William Edgar Bigsby is a leading scholar on drama and on Miller in particular, having published several works on Miller, edited volumes of his work, and liaised with the playwright concerning several of his later productions. After receiving his doctorate from University of Nottingham in 1966 and a brief stint teaching at University College of Wales, Bigsby came to lecture in American Studies at the UNIVERSITY OF EAST ANGLIA, Norwich, where in 1987 he became the director of the newly named Arthur Miller Centre for American Studies. Adviser and presenter for the BBC, Bigsby has contributed greatly to radio arts with discussion pieces, documentaries (including one on Miller), and plays (coauthored *The After-Dinner Game* and *Stones*) and has published several novels of his own, including *Hester* (1994), *Pearl* (1995; a prequel and sequel to Nathaniel Hawthorne's *The Scarlet Letter*),

Theater scholar Christopher Bigsby interviewing Miller at the 2004 International Arthur Miller Society Annual Conference held that year at St. Francis College in Miller's old stomping ground at Brooklyn. *Photograph by Stephen Marino.*

and *Beautiful Dreamer* (2002), aside from his great body of critical work. His *Modern American Drama: 1945–2000* (2000) and three-volume *Critical Introduction to Twentieth-Century Drama* (1998–2000, with Don Wilmeth) with their cogent and accessible writing style are landmark overviews of the field. Bigsby has published more than 40 books on British and U.S. culture and drama, including volumes on EDWARD ALBEE, Tom Stoppard, Joe Orton, David Mamet, Neil LaBute, several volumes on black literature, and his work on Miller.

Bigsby was responsible for pushing through the 1987 radio production of Miller's long-neglected *The Golden Years,* which Bigsby had come across while researching for his first publication specifically on Miller, his bibliographic *Miller on File* (1988). He also suggested to Miller the title of *Two-Way Mirror* for the 1989 premiere of those one-act plays in GREAT BRITAIN. This was followed by a collection of interviews with Miller and his contemporaries, *Arthur Miller and Company* (1990). Bigsby then updated HAROLD CLURMAN's original *The Portable Arthur Miller* (1995, revised 2003) for Penguin and edited *The Cambridge Companion to Arthur Miller* (1997). His *Arthur Miller: A Critical Study* (2005) is to date the most complete critical study of Miller. He was assisted by his close friendship with the playwright and access to many of his private papers and manuscripts. Shortly after Miller's death, Bigsby edited *Remembering Arthur Miller* (2005) as testament to his legacy, another collection of commentaries on the playwright by his contemporaries.

Blakemore, Michael (1928–) Born in Sydney, Australia, Michael Howell Blakemore began his career as an actor in GREAT BRITAIN's regional theaters but came to greater fame as a stage director, initially with Citizens' Theatre in Glasgow, Scotland, in 1966. Moving to London with his production of Peter Nichols's *A Day in the Death of Joe Egg,* he continued to direct a series of landmark plays, many at the NATIONAL THEATRE.

Blakemore's first foray into Miller was his 1981 London revival of *All My Sons,* and then, in 1990, he directed a controversial revival of *After the Fall* at the National Theatre with a black actress playing the part of Maggie. Impressed by his work, Miller asked him in 1991 to direct the world premiere of *The Ride down Mt. Morgan.* Blakemore would also be chosen to direct the British premiere of *Mr. Peters' Connections* in 2000.

Though best known as a stage director, Blakemore has also worked in film and television and has written a semiautobiographical novel, *Next Season,* which is loosely based on his early years as a member of the National Theatre Company. He wrote the screenplay for the film *Country Life,* based ANTON CHEKHOV's *Uncle Vanya,* relocating it to a sheep farm in rural Australia. It is perhaps Blakemore's ability to merge the serious with the comic that led Miller to choose him as a director of his later works. Blakemore had become friendly with Miller in 1981, and in *Remembering Arthur Miller* (2005), he asserted that Miller's work, like Miller himself, was always full of surprises and was "never quite what it was assumed to be." Testifying to Miller's comedic skills, he speaks of Miller's later plays as "particular and quirky" and defying categorization but continuously worthy of merit.

Bloomgarden, Kermit (1904–1976) Born in 1904 in BROOKLYN, New York, Kermit Bloomgarden's initial connection with the theater was as an accountant for producer Herman Shumlin, but by the 1930s, he had became a producer in his own right and would work with many preeminent playwrights and actors on BROADWAY. He was general manager or producer on many of LILLIAN HELLMAN's plays, as well as working on such hits as *The Corn Is Green* (1940; in which MILDRED DUNNOCK had come to fame), *The Diary of Anne Frank* (1956), *Look Homeward Angel* (1957), *The Music Man* (1957), and *Equus* (1974). He was the leading force on more than 40 Broadway productions. Attracted to serious and liberal-minded plays, he produced several of Miller's best known works. Recognizing Miller's talent and having had a chance to read the script, he had been keen to become involved with *Death of a Salesman;* since he had had some dealings with the GROUP THEATER and previously had worked with ELIA KAZAN (having reportedly hired Kazan as office boy at the Group Theater in its early days), he was given the opportunity to coproduce with Walter Fried (who had coproduced Miller's previous play, *All My Sons*). He would win a Tony Award for his involvement.

Bloomgarden had tried unsuccessfully to raise interest to have *The Hook* funded locally rather than in Hollywood, but he would go on to produce *The Crucible,* for which he won another Tony. At the insistence of Hellman, he suggested JED HARRIS as director. Bloomgarden asked ROBERT WHITEHEAD to help him produce the two one-act plays, *A View from the Bridge* and *A Memory of Two Mondays,* which he had enthusiastically persuaded Miller to run as a double bill on Broadway, even though Miller worried that this might be the wrong venue for such plays. As producer, Bloomgarden was instrumental in choosing many of the actors to play in these works and helped to shape each drama's presentation. He and his wife Virginia were friends with Miller for many years. In "Notes on Realism," Miller praises Bloomgarden and Robert Whitehead as his ideal producers, people "who longed for artistically ambitious and socially interesting plays and could put their money where their mouth was."

Broadway One of America's earliest large theaters was the 3,000-seat Bowery Theatre that opened in 1826 in New York City. It would play the popular revues of the time, revues that featured the music, dance, and comedy of that period. The first major playhouse for drama in the area arrived in 1893 when the American Theatre opened on West 42nd Street. During the years, New York rose to become the capital of U.S. theater and the place where most dramatists would like to see their names in lights. Even though the roadway named *Broadway* extends the length of the New York borough of Manhattan, since the 1880s the term has come to indicate the area in midtown Manhattan in which a majority of the city's primary theaters are located. EUGENE O'NEILL was the first American playwright to dominate the Broadway scene with serious drama, and many have made their names since with whole series of hit plays, but musicals have always had a firm hold in the area.

Oftentimes, a play would be given tryouts in a smaller regional theater to assess whether or not it would make it on the Broadway stage and allow directors and playwrights to make changes to increase the play's chances of success. Once it opened on Broadway, all of the major newspapers would review the production, and their responses would often make or break a show. Miller credits the enthusiastic reviews of *New York Times* theater critic BROOKS ATKINSON for going a long way to ensure the success of both *All My Sons* and *Death of a Salesman*. But the increasing dominance of the critics of the *New York Times* since the 1980s, as other papers have ceased publication, has created a dangerous monopoly of opinion that Miller felt prevented many new plays from getting a fair chance.

Although, since 1944's *The Man Who Had All the Luck,* Broadway has seen more than 30 Miller productions to date, both premieres and revivals (including three each of *Death of a Salesman* and *The Price* and four of *The Crucible*), Miller has often been outspoken about what he sees as the restrictive practices of these theaters and the difficulties of getting them to produce serious drama. Producers have grown increasingly resistant to taking chances since the 1950s when the theater began to lose much of its talent to films and television. Serious theater has continued to prosper in the United States but simply not so prevalently in Broadway theaters. Miller is not alone in his complaints, which have been addressed over the

years by the creation of alternative theatrical outlets, including off-Broadway and off-off-Broadway, and the growth of some very forceful and successful regional theaters.

Although all of Miller's plays up until the 1970s received Broadway openings, his ability to have a play produced in this area after this became more restricted; several have played only in regional theaters or off-Broadway. By the close of the 20th century, Broadway was once more dominated by musicals and the occasional comedy, with only rare space for serious drama. Miller's last two plays, *Resurrection Blues* and *Finishing the Picture* have not yet seen Broadway productions, and it is possible that they never will. His most recent Broadway show was the 2004 revival of *After the Fall* with Peter Krause, which did not fare well.

FURTHER READING

Atkinson, Brooks. *Broadway.* New York: Macmillan, 1970.

Brown, Gene. *Show Time: A Chronology of Broadway and the Theatre from Its Beginnings to the Present.* New York: Macmillan, 1997.

Frommer, Myrna Katz, and Harvey Frommer. *It Happened on Broadway: An Oral History of the Great White Way.* New York: Harcourt, 1998.

Brooklyn   Brooklyn has a profound resonance throughout Miller's work, and certain areas can almost be mapped out by the references that he makes in his writing. His family moved into this area in 1928; here, he would live with his first wife, MARY SLATTERY, and raise his first two children, JANE MILLER and ROBERT MILLER. Thus he had many of his defining experiences in this neighborhood. In his 1955 essay, "A Boy Grew in Brooklyn," he declares, "Brooklyn is the world" and describes many of the "characters and practical jokers" that he remembers from his teen years. In the 1940s and 1950s, he spent much time walking in certain areas, looking for inspiration and collecting his thoughts, often walking across Brooklyn Bridge into Manhattan. In *Timebends: A Life,* Miller explains how the bridge's structure encapsulated for him what he felt was the invigorating contradictory nature of life: "The beauty in the tension of opposites I saw everywhere—the pull of gravity actually strengthening the bridge's steel arches by compression." Miller set a number of his plays and fictional pieces in Brooklyn and has written extensively about his memories growing up in what he calls the "leafy borough."

Founded by Europeans in the 17th century on land that had been taken by treaty or bought from the American Indians, the Brooklyn area was originally just a collection of small villages. The town of Brooklyn, called Breukelen by the Dutch, was charted in 1646 by the Dutch West India Company but became part of British territory in 1664 when they captured Holland's New Amsterdam and renamed it New York. It would become the site for the Battle of Brooklyn in 1776, the first military conflict against the British of the Revolutionary War. Somewhat set apart from New York City, there was no regular ferry service between them until 1814. At this time, Brooklyn was still fairly rural with a third of the population of African descent; indeed, one of its earliest churches was built in 1818 for African Americans (although slavery was not abolished in New York State until 1827).

In 1816, the village of Brooklyn was incorporated within the Town of Brooklyn, which enlarged its borders further still as it became the City of Brooklyn in 1834. In the 1840s and 1850s, the first great wave of European immigration arrived, chiefly from Ireland and Germany, many of the latter being Jewish. Brooklyn's first synagogue, Union Temple, was founded in 1848. By 1860, Brooklyn had become the third-largest city in the United States with a population just less than 300,000. The area would receive another great wave of immigrants from the 1880s through to the early 20th century, mostly from eastern and southern Europe. In 1883, the landmark Brooklyn Bridge was opened, and in 1898 Brooklyn merged with New York City. By 2000, the population of Brooklyn had grown to just under two-and-one-half million.

In 1928, the Miller family relocated to Brooklyn from Harlem, first to one-half of a roomy Brooklyn duplex on Ocean Parkway and then to a small six-room house at 1350 East 3rd Street in the Midwood section of town, where Miller unhappily shared a bedroom with his grandfather LOUIS BARNETT. Brooklyn back then was less developed than it is

now. The Miller's home was on a dead-end street that led to a baseball field, a cemetery beyond, and close to the "el" train tracks that ran between Manhattan and Coney Island. The neighborhood still evokes the setting of the Loman house in *Death of a Salesman,* with close-set homes and nearby apartments overshadowing the area. But the Millers were not isolated here because across the street were the homes of their relatives, the Newmans and the Balsams, who had moved to Brooklyn after World War I almost 10 years earlier. To mark their new Brooklyn house, Miller planted in the backyard a pear tree that still exists today.

Although he left Brooklyn for the UNIVERSITY OF MICHIGAN, Miller would return there in 1940. Slattery would move into a shared apartment on

The house at which Miller lived with his family at 1350 East 3rd Street, Brooklyn, still stands. The pear tree Miller planted in 1928 is visible in the rear garden. *Copyright Jane K. Dominik.*

Pierrepont Street in Brooklyn Heights, where Miller would spend much of his time. After they married, they moved in together at 62 Montague Street. In 1941, Miller went to work on a night shift as a shipfitter's helper in the BROOKLYN NAVY YARD as part of the war effort. During WORLD WAR II, Brooklyn became a troop departure point for the European and North African theaters, bringing the war very close to home for the Millers. They also lived for a while at 18 Schermerhorn Street; then, in 1944, the couple moved to a duplex that was created out of an old brownstone at 102 Pierrepont Street, with Norman Mailer as their upstairs neighbor.

In 1948, with funds from *All My Sons*, Miller was able to buy 31 Grace Court, an elegant two-family terraced house in Brooklyn Heights, as the family's main residence, although he also bought his first ROXBURY, CONNECTICUT, farmhouse that same year to have as a getaway. Soon after this, he spent time in the RED HOOK area of Brooklyn, at the waterfront, researching material for his plays. Tired of being landlords, after a few years Miller and his family moved on to a single-family home at 151 Willow Street. Miller would live in the picturesque former coach house on Willow Street until he left his family for MARILYN MONROE in 1955. Although he would occasionally visit his old neighborhood after this, especially to visit his parents, he lived the rest of his life mostly between a permanent suite at the Chelsea Hotel and his Roxbury home.

Brooklyn Navy Yard   The New York Naval Shipyard, popularly but unofficially known as the Brooklyn Navy Yard, was established by the federal government in 1801 on Wallabout Bay and East River cove just north of the ferry landing. It bought the land from John Jackson and his brothers who had been running a modest shipbuilding business in the area since 1781. Under government ownership, it became the site for the construction of Robert Fulton's steam frigate, the *Fulton*, launched in 1815, as well as other historic vessels. It would produce several battleships that were used in both world wars, including the USS *Arizona* in 1915 and the battleship *Missouri* in 1944. A sign on the site once read "Builders of the World's Mightiest War Ships." During World War I, the workforce there

tripled to 18,000, and for WORLD WAR II, its size exploded with a workforce of 70,000, that included women as mechanics and technicians. Miller was one of these workers, volunteering his services for almost two years in 1941 and 1942 as a shipfitter's helper on the nightshift from 4 p.m. to 4 a.m. 13 out of 14 nights. His workmates were mostly Italian Americans, and Miller's story, "Fitter's Night" is informed by the people whom he met, the character of Tony Calabrese based on his boss Mike, and Baldu recalling his closest friend during that period, Sammy Casalino. The yard was decommissioned in 1966 and closed its doors, but the city of New York developed the site into an industrial park in 1971, which it remains to this day.

Brown, Katherine (Kay)   Miller's friend NORMAN ROSTEN had initially set Miller up with the Leland Hayward agency, but having sent them his script for *All My Sons* and not hearing back in some time, he grew frustrated. In 1946, he went to their offices to demand his script back, but the secretary suggested that he leave a copy of *All My Sons* for Kay Brown to read; Brown was an agent with Hayward's parent company MCA. She read it and telephoned Miller the following day to tell him how much she like it, asking to represent him. He accepted, and she became his agent for the next 40 years. She sent copies of *All My Sons* to people from the recently disbanded GROUP THEATER and the THEATRE GUILD. Both were interested, and Miller decided to go with the former, attracted by the idea of working with ELIA KAZAN and HAROLD CLURMAN.

Miller and Brown were also friends; he trusted her completely, and in 1956, she helped to arrange the quiet wedding ceremony between him and MARILYN MONROE. She would attend play openings with him, and keep him company while he nervously awaited the audience's response. It had been Brown who suggested that *A Memory of Two Mondays* was too good a play for the single reading that Martin Ritt initially intended and further suggested that Miller write another one-act play to accompany it to create a full evening that was worthy of production, thus persuading the playwright to pen the first version of *A View from the Bridge*.

Camus, Albert (1913–1960)   Born in Mondovi, Algeria, into a working-class family, Albert Camus's father was killed during World War I when his son was a year old. His mother, partially deaf and illiterate, allowed the young Camus and his brother to be raised by her mother. A bright student, he won scholarships to high school and college. Despite contracting tuberculosis as a teen, making him a target for depression, he graduated from the University of Algiers where he majored in classics and philosophy and then began a career in journalism. Like Miller, he considered COMMUNISM as a potential force for good but quickly became disillusioned and broke all ties. By 1942, he had moved to Paris and joined the French Resistance against German occupation. Working for a publishing house by day, he wrote for the underground newspaper *Combat* at night, where he became friendly with JEAN-PAUL SARTRE and other Parisian intellectuals. Leaving journalism after the war, he turned to fiction, essays, and drama. Awarded the Nobel Prize for Literature in 1957, his literary reputation was well established by his death at 46 in an automobile accident outside Paris.

Camus was the first major writer to emerge from modern North Africa and was best known for a trio of novels, *The Stranger* (1942), *The Plague* (1947), and *The Fall* (1956). Among his early plays were *Cross Purpose* (1944), *Caligula* (1944), *State of Siege* (1948), and *The Just Assassins* (1949), and he also adapted several other works for the stage including FYODOR DOSTOYEVSKY's *The Possessed* (1955) and William Faulkner's *Requiem for a Nun* (1956). Viewed by critics as an existentialist, Camus described himself as an "atheistic humanist." In the 1940s, values were being challenged as no longer relevant. With the atrocities and resulting feelings of hopelessness that were brought about by WORLD WAR II, many people concluded that human existence was pointless. While Camus perceived life's absurdity, he did not adopt this point of view; while he accepted the indifference of the universe, he saw it as benign and that humans, though innately wicked, were capable off improvement. It is most likely this view that drew Miller to his work. Several critics see Miller's roots in EXISTENTIALISM as coming from Camus.

Miller enjoyed Camus's democratic vision and was already familiar with his work when in about 1959 producer Walter Wanger asked Miller to write a screenplay for *The Fall*. In *Timebends, A Life*, Miller relates how he felt drawn to a story "about trouble with women" in which the main character is forced to question his own ability to judge, given the knowledge that he himself had erred, but Miller wanted to take this idea further and address questions that Camus does not face. "*The Fall*," he asserts, "ended too soon, before the worst of the pain began." In Camus's novel, the hero fails to help a suicidal girl and feels guilty. Miller wondered what would happen if the hero tried to help, but then he realized that this could achieve no good because such people could only help themselves. Miller also wished to explore reasons why the hero might offer help so as to assess whether or not this was selfishly motivated. Rather than write a screenplay, he wrote a play that was inspired by his own recent "trouble with women" and called it *After the Fall*.

CHRISTOPHER BIGSBY sees Miller's other play of 1964, *Incident at Vichy*, as also being influenced by Camus. Another of Camus's novels, *The Rebel* (1951), defines revolt as the "impulse that drives an individual to the defense of a dignity common to all men." The politically charged book sparked more controversy than any other writing by Camus due to its condemnation of Marxism and Stalin. It led to a much-publicized rift between Camus and Sartre but surely warmed him further to Miller's heart.

Capitalism   The term *capitalism* is commonly understood to mean an economic or socioeconomic system in which the means of production are predominantly privately owned and operated for profit. In such a system, money mediates the distribution and exchange of goods, services, and labor in largely free markets. Decisions regarding investment are made privately, and production and distribution are primarily controlled by companies that compete against each other, and all act in their own interest. It essentially creates the "dog-eat-dog" society that Chris Keller finds so disturbing in *All My Sons*.

Since his college days, as evidenced by his student plays, *No Villain, They Too Arise, The Grass Still Grows*, and *Honors at Dawn*, Miller had felt that the United States was being run by men of business who were solely concerned with private profit. While such men viewed those without wealth as pawns to be used, Miller wanted to show, through such characters as Abe Simon and his sons and Max Zibriski, that it was possible to resist. Yet money and finance, or at least the greed for more than was necessary, seemed to be behind many of the world conflicts. In *The American Clock*, Miller's alter ego, Lee Baum, is made to realize by his college friends that capitalism can lead to war, as Ralph and Joe point out the relationship between war and the country's economics. In *The Great Disobedience*, Miller uses prison as a metaphor for the wider society outside of the prison that is dominated by capitalism. The inherent danger in capitalism, Miller

suggests, is that it can cause freedom to become a mere illusion as people become trapped in a cycle of false need and hope.

Howard Wagner in *Death of a Salesman* is the epitome of the coldhearted businessman who, without a thought to the man's dignity, financial obligations, and years of service, callously takes away Willy Loman's job when he starts to lose business. Stanton Case, in *Broken Glass*, is similarly dismissive of Phillip Gellburg when he fails to get him a piece of property that he had wanted. Men like Wagner and Case are only concerned with the bottom line and are more interested in things than people; thus, Wagner is shown to be more interested in his tape recorder than in his employee, and Case is the same with his yacht. What fuels the hard-heartedness of such men is their desire for ever more acquisitions and wealth.

Miller sees the constant quest in the United States to be successful, especially in terms of wealth, as a potentially destructive and harmful one. Competition itself often creates negative values that may lead to success but at what Miller regards as too heavy a price. Successful people in Miller's plays are rarely happy in any other relationship than the one that they have with their own success, which makes them lonely individuals. Lyman Felt in *The Ride Down Mt. Morgan* is such a man; Walter Franz in *The Price* is another. While the best way to survive in a capitalist system is to become a better and more ruthless capitalist than your fellow workers, this system clearly privileges individuals over their society, and that is what Miller fears could lead to an eventual breakdown of that society. The ambitions of Thomas Putnam and his kind went a long way to cause the devastation of Salem village in *The Crucible*, and in *Resurrection Blues*, we see such breakdown as Felix Barriaux prepares to crucify a possible savior in the sole quest of big money.

Miller is not necessarily against capitalism as a system in and of itself, but he is wary that such a system can be readily abused. He views capitalism as a cultural creation, that is, humanmade, and so for Miller it is humanity's responsibility to make the system supportive rather than detrimental to the majority. Although *Death of a Salesman* has often been viewed as anticapitalist, this is not entirely

In 2000, Miller was part of a group of artists and philanthropists invited to Cuba as "cultural visitors." The group dined with Cuban leader Fidel Castro, and Miller's wife Inge Morath was later allowed to take this photograph. Castro is third from left, with his friend the Colombian writer Gabriel García Márquez to his left. Author William Styron is at the far left, and Miller is on the far right. *Photograph by Inge Morath: Magnum Photos.*

accurate, given the inclusion of such characters as Charley and Bernard. It is fine to make money, Miller tells us through this successful father and son, as long as one does not allow the moneymaking to become the raison d'etre of one's life and destroy one's humanity. It is greed that is frowned upon, and although such greed cannot always be given its comeuppance realistically as he allows the couple in the short story "It Takes a Thief," the cheating bakers in "Battle of the Ovens," or Joe Keller in *All My Sons,* Miller ensures that we recognize the intrinsic inhumanity of such people wherever they operate.

Castro, Fidel (1926–) An activist and fierce nationalist since his student days, Fidel Alejandro Castro Ruz became the leader of Cuba in 1959

when, leading the 26th of July Movement, he overthrew the regime of Fulgencio Batista y Zaldívar. In the years that followed, he oversaw the transformation of Cuba into the first Communist state in the Western Hemisphere. Since his accession to power, he has maintained a controversial profile, variously inciting condemnation, praise, or debate. Castro is a highly controversial leader who is viewed as a dictator by most, though some see him as a legitimate and popular leader.

After the failed U.S.-directed Bay of Pigs invasion of Cuba in 1961, Castro's leadership has been marked by tensions with the United States, a close partnership with the Soviet Union (resulting in the 1962 Cuban missile crisis) until its collapse in 1991, and foreign intervention in many countries of the Third World. As part of a group of artists that included William Styron, Miller was invited to Cuba in 2000 to experience the island. Styron was friendly with the writer Gabriel García Márquez who arranged for the group to dine with Castro. Castro enjoyed their company so much that he sought them out the following day for lunch. Miller recounted this visit in the 2003 essay "A Visit with Castro," in which he described the Cuban leader as "a lonely old man hungry for some fresh human contact." Miller exhibits sympathy and frustration with a figure whose views on the necessity of revolution appear sound but whose enchantment with power has perverted his ambition.

Centola, Steven (1952–) Born in Philadelphia, Pennsylvania, Steven Ronald Centola attended West Chester State University as an undergraduate and pursued graduate work at the University of Rhode Island, earning a doctorate in 1982 with a dissertation titled *Freedom and Responsibility After the Fall: A Sartrean Perspective of Arthur Miller's Existential Humanism*. Although they had corresponded while Centola was working on his dissertation, he was not able to meet Miller until 1982 when he was invited to the ROXBURY, CONNECTICUT, house and conducted the first of four lengthy interviews. One of these is recorded in Centola's 1993 volume *Arthur Miller in Conversation*, and the final one will be published in the winter 2007 issue of *Michigan Quarterly Review*. Centola began to publish critical essays on Miller in the mid-1980s, paying particular attention to the often-overlooked later plays. Now a leading U.S. scholar and authority on Miller, Centola became close friends with Miller in the playwright's later years. In 1992, Centola organized the first ever Arthur Miller International Conference to be held at Millersville University, where Centola is a professor of English, as the culmination of a yearlong slate of activities that had included Miller's visit to the campus the previous year. Centola edited a volume of essays, *The Achievement of Arthur Miller: New Essays* (1995), based on papers given at this conference, that helped to spark a reinterest in Miller's work both early and late.

At the second Arthur Miller International Conference that was held at Millersville in 1995, Centola led a group of scholars to form the ARTHUR MILLER SOCIETY to promote the continued study and production of Miller's plays; he was voted in as the society's first president. Centola edited an updated edition of *The Theater Essays of Arthur Miller* (1996) and Miller's later collection of essays, *Echoes Down the Corridor* (2000), on which he collaborated with Miller. His most recent publication is *The Critical Response to Arthur Miller* (2006): Coedited with Michelle Cirulli, this lengthy collection of previously published articles spans the entire career of Miller. Centola's reading of Miller's work as being grounded in EXISTENTIALISM and HUMANISM has become increasingly persuasive in critical circles. He has also published work on other writers, including WILLIAM INGE, E. M. Forster, James Joyce, JEAN-PAUL SARTRE, and Ann Beattie.

Chadick-Delamater Auto Parts Warehouse For a brief period in the early 1930s, Miller had worked driving a delivery truck for a school friend's father, Sam Shapse, an auto-parts retailer in Long Island City. However, this business went under in 1932, and Miller was laid off. Miller needed a job to raise the funds to attend the UNIVERSITY OF MICHIGAN and so applied for a position clerking at Chadick-Delamater Auto Parts Warehouse on Tenth Avenue in Manhattan, an area that would, ironically, become the site for the Lincoln Center for the Performing Arts and the home of the REPERTORY THEATER OF LINCOLN CENTER. The manager, Wesley Moulter, initially turned him down, but on the insistence of Shapse, who had been a good customer of the firm, Miller was offered the job and worked there until August 1934 when he had raised enough funds to go to college.

The problem had been that Chadick-Delamater did not usually employ Jews. On learning of this and being the only Jew in the building, Miller received his first real experience of U.S. ANTI-SEMITISM. He worked hard for his $15 a week, read on the subway to and from work, and after a few weeks was accepted by his fellow workers, but he never felt that he truly fit in. In 1955, he would write *A Memory of Two Mondays*, a strongly nostalgic piece that recalled his months working there. He also describes applying for his position and some of the people whom he met there in *Timebends: A Life*.

Chekhov, Anton (1860–1904) Born in Russia to a family that was freed from serfdom very shortly before emancipation, Anton Pavlovich Chekhov grew up accustomed to life's ups and downs, which are displayed sympathetically though unsentimentally throughout his work. His father, a tyrannical grocery-store owner, went bankrupt in 1875, and they lost the family house; nevertheless, Chekhov managed to complete his medical degree from the University of Moscow in 1884 and worked as a physician. He was, however, best known for his masterly short stories and plays. His initial urge to write had been prompted largely by the need to find additional financial support for his family, and his early comic stories earned him both pecuniary and popularity rewards.

The naturalistic and gently comic dramas of his later years, from his first produced play *Ivanov* (1887) through *The Seagull* (1896), *Uncle Vanya* (1899), and *The Cherry Orchard* (1900) to *The Three Sisters* (1901), had a profound affect on the development of modern theater. His ability to render psychologically complex characters, innovative use of understatement, anticlimax, and the flouting of stage convention with plotless dramas and offstage action and his refusal to pass judgment even on the most despicable characters combined to exert a great influence on subsequent dramatists. His objectivity made him a controversial writer in an age when villains were expected to meet their just rewards. Chekhov had his detractors, but his masterly use of subtext and verbal imagery won him critical acclaim and emulation, albeit not until some years after his death. He died in 1904 of tuberculosis, which had been affecting his health since the early 1880s, an illness he had contracted while tending the sick.

Miller had been introduced to Chekhov's plays at the UNIVERSITY OF MICHIGAN and responded to Chekhov's social call against indolence and to the necessity of seeking a purposeful life. The idea of freedom is central to all of Chekhov's work, especially freedom from lies. His goal was always the truth, and in this, we can see a clear connection to Miller. Feeling a kinship with a playwright who, like himself, was frequently pounded by the critics, several of Miller's plays have been described as hav-

ing a Chekhovian feel, including *A Memory of Two Mondays*, "The Ryan Interview," and *Mr. Peters' Connections*. Miller's use of subtext in many other plays, through his manipulation of time, verbal imagery, offstage action, and suggestive props, show a clear indebtedness to the dramas of Chekhov.

Clurman, Harold (1901–1980) One of the United States's foremost stage producers, directors, and critics, Harold Clurman was born in New York City. He attended Columbia University and studied at the Sorbonne before coming to the New York stage. He got his first break in 1924 with the Greenwich Village Playhouse and appeared on BROADWAY the following year in the THEATRE GUILD's revival of George Bernard Shaw's *Caesar and Cleopatra*. He would act, stage manage, and read plays for the Theatre Guild until 1929. In 1931, he helped found the GROUP THEATER, and his first outing as a director was with CLIFFORD ODETS's *Awake and Sing* in 1935. After that, he directed several more of Odets's plays, including *Paradise Lost* (1935), *Golden Boy* (1937), *Rocket to the Moon* (1938), and *Night Music* (1940). In *Timebends: A Life*, Miller relates his view of Clurman at this time as "a priest of a new kind of theater that would cry down injustice and heal the sick nation's spirit." When the Group Theater broke up, Clurman reluctantly headed to Hollywood and directed Odets's first screenplay, *The General Died at Dawn* (1946), but that would be his only movie credit. In 1943, he had married Stella Adler, and although they divorced in 1960, she would visit him at his deathbed.

Clurman's first love was the stage, and other than working with Odets, he directed several major Broadway successes including Carson McCullers's *The Member of the Wedding* (1950), WILLIAM INGE's *Bus Stop* (1955)—both produced by ROBERT WHITEHEAD—Jean Giraudoux's *Tiger at the Gates* (1955), EUGENE O'NEILL's *A Touch of the Poet* (1958), Marcel Achard's *A Shot in the Dark* (1961), and Rodgers's and Hammerstein's musical *Pipe Dream* (1955). He also directed LILLIAN HELLMAN's *The Autumn Garden* (1951) and TENNESSEE WILLIAMS's *Orpheus Descending* (1957) for the Broadway stage. In addition to these, from the 1940s through to his death, he wrote insightful reviews for several publications, including the *New York Times*, the *New Republic*, and the *Nation*. After BROOKS ATKINSON, Miller would view Clurman as the only other critic in his corner. When reviewer Albert Bermel publicly criticized Miller's work after the opening of *The Price*, it was Clurman who sprang to Miller's defense. His legacy as a director and a critic were marked shortly before his death by the naming of the Harold Clurman Theater in New York. In an address Miller made in honor of Clurman at the 1979 opening, he proclaimed his colleague to be "a man of honor" and "a greatly tolerant fellow."

Although Clurman had coproduced Miller's *All My Sons*, ELIA KAZAN was chosen to direct. He and Kazan stopped producing together soon after that, so Clurman was not involved with *Death of a Salesman*; Kazan brought KERMIT BLOOMGARDEN in to help produce. Whitehead later appointed Clurman as the executive consultant of the REPERTORY THEATER OF LINCOLN CENTER, 1964–65, so Clurman was the executive consultant for *After the Fall* and would finally direct a Miller play with *Incident at Vichy*. Clurman edited Penguin's first edition of *The Portable Arthur Miller* in 1971 and was set to direct *The Creation of the World and Other Business* in 1972; however, the production was problematic, and although he directed through to the previews, he was replaced by the opening. His final Broadway direction had been Inge's short-lived *Where's Daddy?* in 1966, although he continued to work in the theater up until his death. In *Salesman in Beijing*, Miller cites Clurman as the only director whom he has known "whose speeches seemed to energize and excite rather than confuse actors." Miller viewed Clurman and Kazan as having very different directing styles, with Clurman being a lot more amiable and less intense. He personally preferred Kazan as a director, feeling that Clurman, despite his more caring nature, sometimes fumbled.

Clurman's papers can be found at the Billy Rose Theatre Collection at the New York Public Library for the Performing Arts. These contain notebooks and journals, director's annotated scripts, manuscript drafts and annotated typescripts of Clurman's books, and photograph scrapbooks that document his career as a director, writer, and critic from 1935 to 1978.

FURTHER READING

Clurman, Harold. *The Fervent Years: The Story of the Group Theatre and the Thirties*. New York: Knopf, 1945.
———. *Lies Like Truth: Theatre Reviews and Essays*. New York: Macmillan, 1958.
———. *On Directing*. New York: Macmillan, 1972.

Cobb, Lee J. (1911–1976)   Born Leo Jacoby in New York City's Lower East Side, Lee J. Cobb was the son of a Jewish newspaper editor. A child prodigy in music, a broken wrist dashed his hopes of become a famous violinist. He first began to act in radio drama, and his first BROADWAY performance was in a short-lived 1935 dramatization of FYODOR DOSTOYEVSKY's *Crime and Punishment*. He joined the GROUP THEATER later that year and made a name for himself in CLIFFORD ODETS's dramas, including playing an elderly Mr. Bonaparte in the 1939 film version of *Golden Boy*. At the Group Theater, ELIA KAZAN would get to work with him, both as a fellow actor and director.

After a brief hiatus serving in the army during WORLD WAR II came his greatest stage success, as Willy Loman in the 1949 premiere production of *Death of a Salesman*. Although he won no awards, he became an iconic figure in the role and later would reprise it successfully in a 1966 television version. Miller has stated on several occasions that Cobb was his favorite Willy, even though he was not so certain at first. Kazan, who was directing, had brought Cobb in to play the part, having known him quite well from their days together at the Group Theater, and having worked with him more recently on the film *Boomerang!* (1947). In *Timebends: A Life*, Miller recalls how in rehearsal Cobb initially "seemed to move about in a buffalo's stupefied trance." Worried that this was how he would play the role, they were all relieved when nearly two weeks later Cobb suddenly came to life and stunned them all with a performance that fully conveyed "Willy's pain and protest," bringing many of them to tears. There were many elements in Cobb's character, both inner divisions and a capacity for badinage, that strongly reminded Miller of Willy. In *Salesman in Beijing*, he declares that Cobb "will always be the ultimate Willy to me" and talks admiringly of the way that Cobb invented a piece of stage business with a cigarette case which he takes from Bernard that encapsulated their whole relationship.

Although he appeared on Broadway a few times more, Cobb's biggest triumphs after Willy would be in films and on television, where he played a variety of roles until his death in 1976. In the 1950s, he was twice nominated for Best Supporting Actor Academy Awards, for his role in Kazan's *On the Waterfront* (1954) and as the father in Dostoyevsky's *The Brothers Karamazov* (1958). In 1953, he had been called before the HOUSE UN-AMERICAN ACTIVITIES COMMITTEE on charges that he was or had been a communist, and pressured to save his career and his wife's sanity, he had willingly named names. In *Timebends: A Life,* Miller wrote that Cobb was "more a pathetic victim than a villain, a big blundering actor who simply wanted to act, had never put in for heroism, and was one of the best proofs I knew of the Committee's pointless brutality toward artists." To show that he bore no grudge, Miller offered Cobb the role of Eddie Carbone in *A View from the Bridge,* but Cobb turned it down, uncomfortable appearing in a political play about informing.

Communism   In its purest manifestation, communism is a political ideology that seeks to establish a classless, stateless social organization that is based on common ownership of the means of production. It represents a branch of the broader socialist movement. In the late 19th century, the communist theories of Karl Marx motivated socialist parties across Europe. Marx insisted that the switch from CAPITALISM to communism could not be completed immediately but would require an interim stage which he described as a revolutionary dictatorship of the proletariat. After this, a communist society would emerge. While some would draw the line simply at reforming rather than at overthrowing capitalism, there have developed a number of political and economic regimes around the world under Communist Parties that have claimed to be a dictatorship of the proletariat; none, so far, appear to have made the final transformation.

A branch of the Russian Social Democratic Workers Party that was known as the Bolsheviks and was headed by Vladimir Lenin succeeded in taking control of the country after the toppling of the Provisional Government in the Russian Revolution of 1917 and changed their name to the Communist Party the following year. They came to define what the modern world perceives of as communism as opposed to other trends of socialism. While many socialist parties in other countries declared themselves to be communists, they did so with varying degrees of allegiance to the new Soviet Union. After WORLD WAR II, regimes calling themselves communist took power in Eastern Europe, and in 1949, the Communist Party of China led by Mao Zedong established the People's Republic of China. Among the other countries in the developing world that adopted a communist form of government at some point have been Cuba, North Korea, Vietnam, Laos, Angola, and Mozambique. By the early 1980s, almost one-third of the world's population lived in communist states.

A number of Americans in the 1930s became attracted to Marxism for a variety of reasons. The GREAT DEPRESSION had brought to the fore socialist concepts through which the general populace would be aided. Also, the horrors of the Spanish civil war had attracted the attention of many American intellectuals who supported the republican government in Spain against the fascist uprising led by Franco. This brought them into contact with the American Communist Party and in opposition to government policy, which was not supportive of the elected government in Spain. Some of these people had reached positions of influence during World War II, and by the late 1940s, the fear behind the investigations of the HOUSE UN-AMERICAN ACTIVITIES COMMITTEE (HUAC) was that they might now be working for foreign powers. HUAC investigated various so-called communist front organizations to determine if they effectively were under the control of the Communist Party and made public lists of those that they found to be suspicious.

As a youth, Miller recalls, in *Timebends: A Life* listening to a man spouting communist principles on a street corner and being intrigued. At the UNIVERSITY OF MICHIGAN, there were many students who were sympathetic to the principles of communism, as were both Miller and his new girlfriend

MARY SLATTERY. Both were socially committed and were concerned with the rights of the people, but they never became members of the Communist Party. Although he kept up with politics, Miller's main focus was on becoming a known playwright. After *All My Sons*, he became more politically active, being involved in several antifascist and pro-communist activities. His name appeared in an advertisement in the *Daily Worker* that protested the treatment of German antifascist refugees, and he auctioned off his manuscript of *All My Sons* to raise funds for the progressive Citizens of America. He once had flirted with the idea of joining the party, but after attending a few meetings, he realized that communism, as being practiced, was not for him. He rejected communism for the same reasons that he would reject Hollywood and remain in the theater—it was too restrictive of the artist. He viewed both communism and fascism as detrimental extremes to human development.

Despite this, he has often been accused of being a communist, even though HUAC could not prove it. After having the Federal Bureau of Investigation (FBI) follow him around, their best evidence was a possible application for membership from 1943 on which Miller would not comment. Miller recognized and was disheartened by the way the United States viewed communism in the cold-war years, not because he was a communist but because he was a humanist who believed in the freedom of speech. As early as 1937's *Honors at Dawn*, Miller was concerned about the unfairness of blacklisting communists, and in *You're Next*, he satirizes the way in which anyone liberal was being branded as a communist. In *The Crucible*, by equating McCarthyism to the way people acted in Salem, he illustrated how the 1950s U.S. vision of communism had become a moral issue that viewed communists as being in league with the devil. This was what he suspected made people hate communists so purely and allowed them to drop all of the usual civilities. Any opposition to HUAC was seen in terms of "diabolical malevolence" that allowed no sympathy, and any sign of fear or reticence would be taken as an admission of guilt. It seemed that any sign of social responsibility was being conflated wrongly with communism, and Miller, because he dared to find fault with U.S. society, must be in league with her enemies.

Several of Miller's works feature communist characters, and although they are not demonized, they are depicted as dogmatic as Sam Fink in *Homely Girl, A Life* or Arnold in *No Villain* and *They Too Arise*, as misguided as Bayard in *Incident at Vichy*, or as simply dreamers as Hélène in *Playing for Time*. In *The American Clock*, Edie is allowed to be right when she declares in communism's defense that "Everything's connected," but she is too idealistic to be entirely credible. She works as a cartoonist, drawing Superman. In the same way, her whole world is largely built on well-meaning fantasy. Marxism describes a capitalistic world in which relationships have come to be ruled by money. When that money is taken away, as in the Depression, the people must find something else to bind them together. Communism's answer unfortunately manifests itself in bloody revolution. Violence and war are unifying forces but are not ones of which Miller approves.

Communism in *The American Clock* proves itself to be a system that cannot sustain people, which is why Joe throws himself under a train in despair. At the Relief office, we meet Irene who preaches communism and sees it as a sane response to the times. Communism, she believes, will allow for the equality promised by the Constitution and the Bill of Rights (but denied in practice) to touch everyone, regardless of skin color. She is right that solidarity is the answer, but Miller shows us that people need not embrace communist dogma to find this, illustrated by a wonderful image of this solidarity as Irene persuades Grace to give the remains of her baby's bottle to feed the starving Matthew Bush. Apart from Irene, none of these people are communists. Moe Baum's dime, which is given to buy the man some more milk, is significantly not given as the 10 cents needed for dues to the Workers Alliance but more as a payment to be a member of a caring human community. This is Miller's true socialist vision. While Miller applauds social responsibility and connection, he also strongly believes that people need to be free as individuals, which is why he ultimately rejects communism in any form.

Miller's experiences in the Soviet Union and China, recorded in the books *In Russia* and *Chi-*

nese *Encounters,* offer a number of his opinions concerning communism and its negative affects on a society. He suggests that Chinese communism has evolved differently from that of the Soviet Union, despite its continued adherence to Stalinist thought, and appears less stringent, but without any codified LAW, it remains inherently unstable. In *Chinese Encounters,* Miller highlights what he sees as the central socialist problem: "how to sustain liberty and, at the same time, ample social and economic opportunity, rather than to justify the absence of one or the other." Communism, he feels, has not found a way to do this and has a tendency, given perverse human nature, to become another form of fascism. On his visit to Cuba in 2000, recollected in "A Visit with Castro," Miller, describes communism as the ideology of another age, grown dusty and useless like the "battered old Marxist–Leninist tracts" for sale outside his hotel.

FURTHER READING

Miller, Jeanne–Marie A. "Odets, Miller and Communism." *College Language Association Journal* 19 (June 1976): 484–493.

Copeland, Joan (1922–)   Miller's sister, Joan Maxine, was the third and final child born to AUGUSTA MILLER and ISIDORE MILLER. A favorite of her father, her childhood in the Miller household as the only girl was fairly privileged. Miller would use elements of his father's adoration of Joan to help form Eddie Carbone's attitude toward Catherine in *A View from the Bridge.* Due to her youth, the GREAT DEPRESSION did not have as big an impact on Joan as on her brothers because she could barely recall how things had once been in the Miller family before the WALL STREET CRASH and was quite satisfied with their BROOKLYN home. Joan would prove the studious type, more like KERMIT MILLER than like Arthur. She would also change her name to Joan Copeland and develop into an actress who was admired for her performances on stage and screen; in *Timebends: A Life,* Miller refers to her as a "gifted actress." In addition, she had a long and happy marriage to George J. Kupchik, and they had one son together, Eric.

Copeland debuted onstage in 1945 at the Brooklyn Academy of Music as Juliet in Shakespeare's *Romeo and Juliet;* she would play Desdemona in the Equity Library Theatre production of *Othello* in New York City the following year. Her first appearance on BROADWAY was in 1948 in the ACTORS STUDIO's shortlived production of *Sundown Beach* by Bessie Breuer, directed by ELIA KAZAN. Copeland greatly admired the Actors Studio's acting coach, LEE STRASBERG, from whom she felt that she learned a lot, and through the Actors Studio, she would become friendly with MARILYN MONROE in the 1950s. Indeed, Copeland's husband would serve on the board of Monroe's production company. Copeland had her first major hit in 1949 appearing in Sidney Kingsley's *Detective Story;* the drama ran for 18 months, and its set was designed by BORIS ARONSON.

Copeland has also appeared in her brother's plays. In 1953, Miller was invited to direct a production of *All My Sons* for the Robin Hood Theatre in Arden, Delaware, and his sister took the role of Ann Deever. While she was only the standby in 1968 for the character of Esther Franz in *The Price,* she played the role in several performances and, in 1981, was the lead actress in the American Jewish Theatre's production of the play. In 1970, she was the offstage voice of one of the character's wives in the film short *The Reason Why.* However, her most important role was as Rose Baum in Miller's 1980 drama *The American Clock.* Although the play only ran for 22 performances, she won a Drama Desk Award for her creation of a character that was largely based on her own mother, Augusta.

In addition to her stage work, Copeland has performed regularly on television since 1953, including in the 1960 televised film of EUGENE O'NEILL's *The Iceman Cometh.* This last led to roles in various films and television series through the rest of the century, including characters in several soap operas and in recent years a recurring role in NBC's *Law and Order* as Judge Rebecca Stein. Although she has been involved in several movie projects, none have been major hits, but she has proven herself to be a versatile actress, equally at home in dramas, comedies, and musicals—another Broadway triumph was as Vera Simpson in the

1976 revival of Rodgers and Hart's musical *Pal Joey*, for which she was nominated for a Drama Desk award. She successfully toured in 1964 as Eliza Doolittle in *My Fair Lady* and in 1983 in Neil Simon's *Brighton Beach Memoirs*. Her last Broadway role, in Simon's *45 Seconds from Broadway* (2001), saw her replaced during the previews; she has not appeared on Broadway since. Copeland was at her brother's side in ROXBURY, CONNECTICUT, when he died and has appeared at several memorials in his honor.

FURTHER READING

Schonberg, Harold C. "Joan Copeland Remembers Mama—And So Does Her Brother Arthur." *New York Times,* November 16, 1980, sec. 2, pp. 1, 5.

D

Democracy The term *democracy* comes from the Greek and literally means, "rule by the people." It is a type of government in which the members of the nation theoretically have approximately equal political power. Representative democracy has become the most common way of effecting this, so named because the people do not vote on most government decisions directly but select representatives to a governing body or assembly to vote in their interests. This form of government has become so increasingly popular during the 20th century that the majority of the world's population now lives under representative democratic regimes. Liberal democracy, of which the United States was the first proponent, is a type of representative democracy where the power of the government is limited by the rule of law and the separation of powers, while the people are guaranteed certain inviolable liberties and rights, such as freedom of speech. For Miller, this was the ideal government to have, and much of his work was aimed at preserving that ideal and pointing out what he saw as threats to its realization.

Miller sees the artist as a truth teller whose presence is necessary to preserve a meaningful moral life that is centered in human connection. His perception of the American identity and its relationship to democracy is crucial to his plan. The goal toward which Miller strives is a truly democratic society in which both the individual and the larger group may have a say and an importance. For American democracy to thrive, it is essential that Americans nurture their ability to make connections. As Miller once told Philip Gelb in an interview recorded in Matthew Roudané's *Conversations with Arthur Miller,* "The solution to a deficiency in democracy is—I think Lord Bryce said it—is more democracy. I think that struggle, the struggle to raise up men, is part of the given situation of man. It will never end." This is a belief that is clearly present in the works of Miller.

A play like *The American Clock* was intended as an encomium to American democracy, regardless of its possibly shaky future. In *Timebends: A Life,* Miller explains how at the play's end "we should feel, along with the textures of a massive social and human tragedy, a renewed awareness of the American's improvisational strength, his almost subliminal faith that things can and must be made to work out. In a word, the feel of the energy of democracy. But the question of ultimate survival must remain hanging in the air." We can witness this belief in the redemptive energy of democracy at work in many of Miller's other plays. Another example would be in *The Last Yankee,* where Leroy Hamilton's strong belief in the equality that lies at the heart of any true democracy, his evident tolerance and patience, all encourage us to see him as a near-perfect figure and guide. Quite possibly the Yankee of the title, he is a truly democratic man although, we are warned, perhaps the last of his kind. As Leroy suggests, it is self-serving types like John Frick who are promoting the growing insanity of contemporary existence as their false views and expectations are taking all of the true value out of

383

the Constitution and democracy. It was partly to expose such dangers that Miller wrote.

Miller has a strong faith in fundamental democratic American principles. What he felt was one of America's greatest strengths is the willingness of people like Leroy or Lee Baum in *The American Clock* or John Proctor in *The Crucible* to fight against restrictive ideologies and to embrace a more comprehensive vision. In *Timebends: A Life,* Miller recalls a moment of realization that he had while talking to a Russian writer: "The miraculous rationalism of the American Bill of Rights suddenly seemed incredible, coming as it did from man's mendacious mind. America moved me all over again—it was an amazing place, the idea of it astounding." While Miller was never blind to America's corruption, he refused to lose hope in her potential: "An America that might on bad days win the booby prize but withal was still liberty's home."

Dennehy, Brian (1938–) Born in Bridgeport, Connecticut, Dennehy began to study history at Columbia University on a football scholarship before transferring to Yale to study theater. He first appeared in various television series, which led to minor film roles in the late 1970s; by the 1980s, he was playing leads. These were mostly tough guys and killers, although he occasionally surprised audiences with a more sensitive figure, such as the cancer-ridden architect in Peter Greenaway's 1987 *Belly of an Architect,* for which he won acting awards. In the 1990s, he became more involved in writing, direction, and production.

Though best known as a television and movie actor, Dennehy's tour de force presentation of Willy Loman in the 50th anniversary BROADWAY production of *Death of a Salesman* won him new respect as a stage actor. He also won both Tony and Drama Desk Awards for his performance, which he recreated in the 2000 television version (for which he won a Golden Globe) and again on stage in GREAT BRITAIN in 2005 to continued acclaim and an Olivier Award. He won another Tony for his part in a 2003 revival of EUGENE O'NEILL's *Long Day's Journey Into Night* and has played in revivals of *A Touch of a Poet* and *The Iceman Cometh.*

An imposing, barrel-chested figure, he has a build that is similar to the original Willy, LEE J. COBB. His approach to the role was very naturalistic, and he emotively presented a Willy who was struggling with clinical depression. Ben Brantley's *New York Times* review of his performance best captures its essence: "The production plays hauntingly on the contrast between Mr. Dennehy's imposing frame and the sad, scared gestures of a sickly child. When Willy shields his face with his hands, palms outward, during an argument with his son Biff, the effect is devastating in a way it wouldn't be with a physically slighter actor. The image of a big man made small perfectly embodies the argument for *Salesman* as a bona fide tragedy."

FURTHER READING

Brantley, Ben. "Attention Must Be Paid, Again." *New York Times,* February 11, 1999, B1, 5.

Dostoyevsky, Fyodor (1821–1881) One of the foremost figures in Russian literature, Fyodor Mikhaylovitch Dostoyevsky influenced the development of both EXISTENTIALISM and EXPRESSIONISM through a series of powerful novels that feature passionate characters, explosive situations, and a philosophical quest for spiritual understanding. Some of his best-known works include *Notes from Underground* (1864), *Crime and Punishment* (1866), *The Idiot* (1868), and *The Brothers Karamazov* (1880). Born in St. Petersburg in 1821, Dostoyevsky had an unhappy childhood—both parents were dead by the time he was age 18. Politically involved, he was arrested and detained in 1849 for activities against Czar Nicholas I and was sentenced to five years of hard labor at a Siberian prison camp. On his release, he abandoned his radical sentiments, becoming deeply conservative and religious. Death and bad luck continued to haunt him: He ran a series of unsuccessful literary journals and lost both his wife and the brother with whom he was the closest. Financially crippled, he sank into a deep depression and began to gamble. Leaving Russia to escape his debts, Dostoyevsky's luck eventually changed; he remarried and began to see his writing better received, although he continued to be controversial up to his death in 1881 at age 60.

Dostoyevsky was one of the first major authors to whom the young Miller was exposed, and Miller would later declare Dostoyevsky and fellow Russian novelist, Leo Tolstoy, to be two of the greatest writers whose works he knew. While working at the CHADICK-DELAMETER AUTO PARTS WARE-HOUSE, Miller picked up *Crime and Punishment* to read on the way to work, having mistaken it for a detective story. Once begun, however, he was enthralled by the power of Dostoyevsky's writing, his concentration of detail, and his understanding of the complexity of human nature.

Always outspoken regarding censorship of both his own work and others', Miller was also interested in Dostoyevsky because he identified with Dostoyevsky's experience as a writer frequently unheeded in his native country and often suppressed. Although Miller did not face the same degree of political suppression that Dostoyevsky had faced, in the U.S. climate of the 1950s Miller was followed by the Federal Bureau of Investigation, which was trying to gather information to bring him before the HOUSE UN-AMERICAN ACTIVITIES COMMITTEE. Miller had seen his plays picketed and a potential film, *The Hook,* rejected because the studio did not like its political ramifications. His passport request to attend the Belgian premiere of *The Crucible* was denied.

In 1955, Miller's efforts to make a film about New York City youth gangs was blocked by pressure from the American Legion, the Catholic War Veterans, and the New York Police Department because of his suspected subversive associations. In 1956, Miller had just turned down an invitation to visit the Soviet Union, publicly objecting to what he saw as a lack of artistic freedom in the country. It was at this point that the *New York Times* asked him for a statement on the 75th anniversary of Dostoyevsky's death. His response was to describe the Soviet suppression of several of Dostoyevsky's works as an "indefensible act of cultural barbarism," while also pointing out that the survival of those works is a "testament to the futility of censorship."

Dunnock, Mildred (1901–1991) Born in Baltimore, Maryland, Mildred Dunnock received her education, first at Goucher College and then Johns Hopkins and Columbia University, after which she became a schoolteacher at Brearley School in New York. She did not turn to acting until her thirties but would go on to study with ACTORS STUDIO founders LEE STRASBERG, Robert Lewis, and ELIA KAZAN. Her first BROADWAY role was in Mary Macdougal Axelson's *Life Begins* (1932), which closed after only eight performances. Her first success was as a Welsh teacher in Emlyn Williams's *The Corn Is Green* (1940), for which KERMIT BLOOMGARDEN had been the general manager. The role of Miss Ronberry is the one for which she may be best remembered, aside from her 1949 creation of Linda Loman. Dunnock also appeared in the 1945 movie version of *The Corn is Green,* the first of many film and television appearances. During her film career, she received Oscar nominations for her supporting roles in the FREDRIC MARCH version of *Death of a Salesman* (1951) and TENNESSEE WILLIAMS's *Baby Doll* (1956).

Dunnock appeared in 23 Broadway plays into the 1970s, including LILLIAN HELLMAN's *Another Part of the Forest* (1946), which had been produced by Bloomgarden; and Williams's *Cat on A Hot Tin Roof* (1955) and *The Milk Train Doesn't Stop Here Anymore* (1963). Favored by both Kazan and Williams, she appeared in several other of their creations both on stage and film. Her only major theater award was a Drama Desk Award Outstanding Performance for her off-Broadway appearance in Marguerite Duras's *A Place Without Doors* (1971), but she was an incredibly versatile actress who could play farce through to Shakespeare. In her later years, she worked mostly for television.

When she first auditioned for *Death of a Salesman,* she was turned down, but she kept coming back until they gave her the part. For many years, her indelible performance as Linda Loman, opposite LEE J. COBB's Willy Loman, was the yardstick against which all others were measured. Linda became the firm center of the Loman family as a loving, supportive mother and wife. In *Timebends, A Life,* Miller approvingly describes Dunnock as a "capable" actress whose "Linda filled up with outrage and protest rather than self-pity and mere perplexity." She repeated this landmark performance not only in the 1951 film but again opposite Cobb in the 1966 television adaptation directed by Alex Segal, and for the Caedmon sound recording in the 1960s.

Existentialism Existentialism is a philosophical movement that is characterized by an emphasis on individualism, individual freedom, and subjectivity. It was inspired by the works of Søren Kierkegaard and the German philosophers Georg Wilhelm Friedrich Hegel, Edmund Husserl, and Martin Heidegger and became particularly popular around the close of WORLD WAR II in France. It was promoted there by such writer–philosophers as JEAN-PAUL SARTRE, Simone de Beauvoir, and ALBERT CAMUS. The movement's main tenets are set out in Sartre's *Existentialism Is a Humanism* (1946), where he posits "existence precedes essence" and asserts an individual's freedom and responsibility to choose to act to define his being. Sartre believed that people are not predetermined in any way but are free to do as they choose and so must be judged by their actions rather than by what they are because they are entirely what they do. The main problem for human beings becomes how to choose one's actions. Existentialism stresses the primacy of the thinking person and of concrete individual experience as the source of knowledge; it also emphasizes the anguish and solitude that are inherent in the making of choices. It is hardly surprising that Miller was attracted to Sartre's ideas from early on in his career, and critics STEVEN CENTOLA and CHRISTOPHER BIGSBY have both pointed toward the strong existential basis that underpins much of Miller's work.

In his article "The Fall and After: Arthur Miller's Confession," Bigsby applies Sartre's principle to Miller's belief that people should follow the "exis-tential cycle of transmuting guilt into redemptive action," for such behavior will free a person from alienation, imposing a moral coherence on a contingent world. Bigsby concludes that Miller insists that it is not beyond the human capacity to create values and to live up to them, even though such lives may be difficult. We see this idea illustrated in so many of Miller's plays, including the lessons in responsibility that Chris Keller tries to teach his father in *All My Sons* and the personal sacrifices of John Proctor in *The Crucible* or of Von Berg in *Incident at Vichy*. We also see it exemplified by characters such as Sigmund in *The Archbishop's Ceiling* who decides to remain in a country where he is constantly antagonized because that is where he will be of most use or in Sylvia Gellburg's decision in *Broken Glass* to stand up for herself.

Plays like *After the Fall* and *The Ride down Mt. Morgan* are more clearly existentialist in nature, depicting their central protagonists Quentin and Lyman Felt in the throes of existential debate as they try to discover their identities through an analysis of their past choices. But in an interview published in Matthew Roudané's *Conversations with Arthur Miller*, with Miller's agreement, Centola sums up the whole of Miller's work as deriving from a "vision of the human condition as a kind of existential humanism—a vision that emphasizes self-determinism and social responsibility and that is optimistic and affirms life by acknowledging man's possibilities in the face of his limitations and even sometimes in the dramatization of his failures." From *No Villain* to *Finishing the Picture*, Miller's work displays an inherent humanism that has been strongly influenced by existentialist principle, which insists that our creative will is sufficient to provide us with a sense of human values. It is to illustrate the necessity and importance of these values that Miller writes at all.

Expressionism Expressionism in its most general terminology is exhibited in many art forms, including painting, literature, film, architecture, and music. It refers to the tendency of an artist to distort reality for an emotional effect, and that emotion is rarely a cheerful one, being usually rooted in some kind of angst. In terms of theatre, a concentrated expressionist movement emerged in the early 20th-century plays of German playwrights, of whom Georg Kaiser and Ernst Toller were the most famous. Influenced by the late dream-vision plays and the confessional monologues of August Strindberg and the emblematic work of Frank Wedekind, early expressionists explored the use of highly stereotyped characters—often nameless or meant only to represent a single aspect of a personality—in single-focus works that were often rebellious in nature. Most tried to expose what they saw as the materialist values and hypocrisy of the bourgeois middle class.

In expressionist drama, the settings are often abstract or highly subjective (a major part of the dramatic force of a production), and techniques of distortion and incongruous juxtaposition are used to express the ideological position of the director, the dramatist, or the state of mind of the protagonist. Speech in these plays is rarely realistic and can range from expansively rhapsodic to clipped and telegraphic. Plotlines, meanwhile, are often episodic rather than having a smooth narrative flow and sometimes are little more than a string of startling images. Indeed, in many ways, one can see expressionism as the antithesis of REALISM. In the 1920s, expressionism became popular in the U.S. theatre through the plays of EUGENE O'NEILL (*The Hairy Ape, The Emperor Jones,* and *The Great God Brown*), Sophie Treadwell (*Machinal*), and Elmer Rice (*The Adding Machine*) but has tended to only appear sporadically since.

As 20th-century drama developed, expressionism became more of an occasional directorial approach than a playwright's creative choice. Miller often experimented with aspects of expressionism in a search for new and effective ways to present his plays. Although many see Miller as a strict realist, he quickly moved on from the more realistic dramas of his apprentice years and as CHRISTOPHER BIGSBY explains in *Modern American Drama,* "experimented with form, disassembled character, compressed and distended language." Miller dislikes definitions of his writing as realistic because he sees himself as one who is not attempting to create reality but rather to interpret it. Constantly trying out new techniques, Miller has created works whose artistic form is part of their message. Brenda Murphy rightly suggests in her essay "Arthur Miller: Revisioning Realism" that Miller's whole career since *Death of a Salesman* has been a continual experimentation with realistic and expressionistic forms to uncover an effective means of conveying the bifurcation of a human experience that he sees as split between a concern for the self and a concern for society as a whole. A play such as *The Ride down Mt. Morgan* is no slice-of-life realism but an expressionistic evocation of one person's existential dilemma, much like *After the Fall* had been. The audience's inability to distinguish between the real and the imaginary plays a major part in many of Miller's dramas, especially in his later years, and is both a reflection of a confusion inherent within the postmodern era and one of the keynotes of expressionistic drama.

F

Family Relationships Most of the conflict and the tension created in Miller's plays and in some of his fiction comes from the relationship and the interaction between various family members, be they dead or alive. Sometimes, the struggle is depicted between husband and wife, as with Eddie and Beatrice Carbone in *A View from the Bridge,* John and Elizabeth Proctor in *The Crucible,* Lawrence and Gertrude in *Focus,* or the two couples in *The Last Yankee.* Other times the conflict is between parent and child, as with Samuel and William Ireland in "William Ireland's Confession," Joe and Chris Keller in *All My Sons,* or Willy Loman and his sons in *Death of a Salesman.* Daughters are rare but do crop up on occasion, such as Clara in *Clara,* Janice Sessions in *Homely Girl: A Life,* or Rose Peters in *Mr. Peters' Connections.* We also see tension between siblings, as with David and Amos Beeves in *The Man Who Had All the Luck,* Victor and Walter Franz in *The Price,* Martin and Ben in "I Don't Need You Any More," Arnold and Ben in *No Villain, They Too Arise,* and *The Grass Still Grows,* or Harry and Max Zibriski in *Honors at Dawn.* Nearly every combination is explored in a variety of situations. For someone like Quentin in *After the Fall,* we witness everything: his unstable relationships with his parents, his wives, his children, and his brother.

In his essay, "The Family in Modern Drama," Miller begins by suggesting that family plays have traditionally been written in prose and have demanded REALISM in their presentation, while social dramas asked for a higher language and lent themselves to EXPRESSIONISM. He then asserts his intention to change all of that. He explains that his ultimate aim as a dramatist is the quest for a form that can successfully combine the best of both family plays and social dramas as a means to mend the increasing split "between the private life of man and his social life." In other words, he wants us to view his family plays as social drama.

Much of Miller's work is concerned with the question, "How may a man make of the outside world a home?" His word choice implies the connection of family to society, supported by his belief that it is within the family that humankind learns those values and elements that are necessary to survive in the wider world. He identifies these in "The Family in Modern Drama" as "safety, the surroundings of love, the soul, the sense of identity and honor." It is, however, the depiction of these values within a wider social context that gives them weight. He goes on to point out that if *Death of a Salesman* were only about family relationships, it would "diminish in importance," but "it extends itself out of the family circle into society," and its vision is expanded "out of the merely particular toward the fate of the generality of men."

Miller's families, from the Simons in his college plays to the Gellburgs in *Broken Glass,* act as microcosms for the larger society. Miller saw the typical family as facing many difficulties: members frequently work against each other rather than in unity, failing to take on sufficient responsibility or sometimes taking on too much, and not showing sufficient trust in, gratitude, compassion, or love for one another. Just as the family appears to be failing, so too is American society and for the same reasons. This is clearly illustrated in an early play like *All My Sons* in which we witness the families of both the Kellers and the Deevers who are torn apart by the actions of their members, culminating in the destruction of both fathers. On the larger social scale that Chris endeavors to get his father to comprehend, Joe Keller's irresponsible actions may have killed countless airmen and have wider social implications. This is brought home to Joe when he learns of his son Larry's suicide out of shame for his father and is brought to the realization that "all" of those airmen were "his sons."

Fathers and their sons, especially, have been highlighted as central characters in many of Miller's plays, and their relationship directs much of the action. HAROLD CLURMAN identifies in Miller's early work a "strong family feeling" by which Miller assigns the father the role of "prime authority and guide." He suggests a belief in Miller that fathers should stand for virtue and value and should offer their sons an example that they can be proud to emulate. However, Clurman explains, Miller's plays often depict a father whose "inability to enact the role of moral authority the son assigns to him and which the father willy-nilly assumes" becomes one of the central concerns. These fathers, such as Joe Keller in *All My Sons*, Willy Loman in *Death of a Salesman*, and Paterson Beeves in *A Man Who Had All the Luck*, at least for his older son, Amos, quite simply, cannot live up to the perfection demanded of them by their sons. Neither the sons nor the fathers can forgive such failure, and all carry a guilty burden of responsibility for each other, which is impossible to shirk.

However, this is not the only type of father whom Miller depicts, and his vision is not so narrow. There are also parents, like Mr. Franz in *The Price*, Samuel Ireland in "William Ireland's Confession," and Lyman Felt's father in *The Ride down Mt. Morgan*, who simply do not care to be examples of perfection. Their sons are there to be ridiculed or tricked into making sacrifices to help their parents. To balance this, there are also the caring fathers

who rise to the occasion and are able to offer their children positive examples of sensible living, such as Charley in *Death of a Salesman*, Moe Baum in *The American Clock*, and Leroy Hamilton in *The Last Yankee*. Daughters such as Janice Sessions, Clara Kroll, and Rose Peters also find that their fathers are admirable and display an uncomplicated affection; although Albert Kroll finds his daughter's adulation initially troubling, it also finally inspires him to become once again the man whom she had admired.

In *Timebends: A Life*, Miller describes the feeling that he had when he was growing up that he was the opposite of his brother, which makes it hard not to read the repeated tensions that we see between two brothers in his plays in an autobiographical light. KERMIT MILLER, he explains, was a well-behaved, good boy who took after their father, and Miller saw himself, with his ambitions and darker side, as being more like their mother. Miller always felt love and respect for his elder brother, but he viewed them both as being in competition well into adulthood. The brothers in the plays vary in presentation, but it is usually the elder who is the more self-sacrificing and caring toward the father, with the younger being the more conflicted. What the siblings offer most is a balance of differences, which together may make the complete man, for example, the Franz brothers in *The Price*: Neither is wholly at fault, and each performs a valuable service. Society needs both its surgeons and its policemen—those who take risks and those who play it safe; those who break rules and those who maintain strict order; those who are lionized by the public and those who perform a public service. Their fault is to blame the other for how they feel about this. Walter's guilt is his own and has nothing to do with Victor, just as Victor's choice to take the more secure but less rewarding path was his alone. We make choices and need to learn to live with them.

One choice that many of Miller's characters have made is that of marriage, and in terms of married couples, we again have variety. There are those like Elizabeth Proctor and Beatrice Carbone who suffer from a husband's actual or desired adultery; Linda Loman and Charlotte Peters love their husbands and never know about the infidelities. Then there are wives who are distraught by their husbands' failure, in their eyes, to provide adequately either psychological or financial support, wives such as Gertrude Newman (Hart) in *Focus*, Esther Franz in *The Price*, Patricia Hamilton in *The Last Yankee*, or Rose in *After the Fall*. Some wives seem to dominate and have the upper hand, like Kate Keller in *All My Sons*, but others are neglected and used, such as Karen Frick in *The Last Yankee* and Margarete Calabrese in "Fitter's Night." Caroline Gruhn's husband in "White Puppies" uses her for sex and later tries to murder her. While a few remain distant, a number of these couples do finally resolve their differences, leaving us with a concept of the necessary compromises that are needed in all relationships.

In terms of family connections, *After the Fall*'s Quentin pretty much covers the whole gamut. Here, the family truly does become the world, and Quentin is the everyman quester trying to find his place within. His relationships with women vary from being the neglectful husband (with Louise) to the neglected (with Maggie). Both women are demanding in their own ways, and both make him feel guilty and inadequate. Caught between his mother and his father, aided by a self-sacrificing brother, Dan, and troubled by his own relationship to his child, Quentin spends the entire play in a relational dilemma, but ends by forgiving himself and others for what has past, prepared to create a better future with Holga. It is through such discoveries on the family level that Miller hopes to teach us lessons about the world in general.

FURTHER READING

Abbotson, Susan C. W. "A Contextual Study of the Causes of Paternal Conflict in Arthur Miller's *All My Sons*." *Hungarian Journal of English and American Studies* 11, no. 2 (Fall 2005): 29–44.

August, Eugene. "*Death of a Salesman*: A Men's Studies Approach." *Western Ohio Journal* 7, no. 1 (1986): 53–71.

Bateman, Mary B. "*Death of a Salesman*: A Clinical Look at the Willy Loman Family." *International Journal of Family Therapy* 7 (Summer 1985): 116–121.

Burathoki, Dinkar. "Father–Son Relationship in Miller's Plays." In *Perspectives on Arthur Miller*, edited by Atma Ram, 75–85. (New Delhi: Abhinav, 1988).

Centola, Steven R. "Family Values in *Death of a Salesman*." *CLA Journal* 37 (September 1993): 29–41.

Clurman, Harold. "Arthur Miller's Later Plays." *Arthur Miller*, edited by Robert Corrigan, 143–168. (Englewood Cliffs, N.J.: Prentice–Hall, 1969).

Gross, Barry. "*All My Sons* and the Larger Context." *Modern Drama* 18, no. 1 (March 1975): 15–27.

Jacobson, Irving. "Family Dreams in *Death of a Salesman*." *American Literature* 47 (1975): 247–258.

Lyons, Donald. "*Salesman* Turns 50." *New York Post Online* (April 4, 1999). In *Arthur Miller's Life and Literature*, Stefani Koorey, 453–54. (Lanham, Maryland: Scarecrow, 2000).

Manocchio, Tony, and William Petitt. "The Loman Family." *Families under Stress: A Psychological Interpretation*. London: Routledge, 1975: 129–168.

Newman, William J. "Book Reviews: The Plays of Arthur Miller." *Twentieth Century* 164 (November 1958): 491–496.

Robinson, James A. "*All My Sons* and Paternal Authority." *Journal of American Drama and Theatre* 2, no. 1 (Autumn 1990): 38–54.

Scanlan, Tom. *Family, Drama, and American Dreams*. Westport, Conn.: Greenwood, 1978.

Stavney, Anne. "Reverence and Repugnance: Willy Loman's Sentiments toward His Son Biff." *Journal of American Drama and Theatre* 4, no. 2 (Spring 1992): 54–62.

Waterstradt, Jean Anne. "Making the World a Home: The Family Portrait in Drama." *Brigham Young University Studies* 19 (1979): 201–221.

Wooster, Gerald, and Mona Wilson. "Envy and Enviability Reflected in the American Dream: Two Plays by Arthur Miller." *British Journal of Psychotherapy* 14, no. 2 (1997): 182–188.

Federal Theater Project   The Federal Theater Project was designed to fund theater performances in the United States during the GREAT DEPRESSION. It was one of five Federal One projects sponsored by President Roosevelt's New Deal's Works Projects Administration (WPA) and is the only national theater effort that has ever been supported by the U.S. government. At its peak, the project employed more than 12,000 people in 158 theaters across the country. The Federal Theater's primary goal was employment of out-of-work theater artists, although the entertainment of poor families and the creation of relevant art were additional objectives. The program was established in September 1935 and ran until June 1939 when its funding was canceled, largely due to the controversial nature of so much of its work. Hallie Flanagan, a theater professor at Vassar, was chosen to lead the project and was given the daunting task of building a national theatre to employ thousands of unemployed artists in as little time as possible.

The theater's aim to be "free, adult, and uncensored" would cause problems from the start, with the U.S. Department of State objecting to a new play *Ethiopia* about Haile Selassie and his nation's struggles against Mussolini and invading Italians. The federal government soon mandated that the Federal Theater Project, a government agency, could not depict foreign heads of state on the stage for fear of diplomatic backlash. *Ethiopia* was a Living Newspaper production, a new kind of theater devised by Flanagan and her creative team in which performances were constructed around newspaper clippings of current events. The goal was to teach audiences about the subject and often to advocate for a progressive solution. The whole project was divided into different units across the country, and aside from the Living Newspaper, they also ran special units that concentrated on such aspects as children's theater, classical theater, Negro theater, and experimental theater.

Despite its brief existence, the Federal Theater was able to foster an extraordinary generation of theater artists, including Orson Welles, John Houseman, ELIA KAZAN, and Arthur Arent. Miller, too, would benefit in a lesser degree from their support. It would be through the auspices of the Federal Theater that Miller's *They Too Arise* would receive a Detroit production in 1937. Miller relates most of his dealings with the Federal Theater Project in *Timebends: A Life*. After graduating from the UNIVERSITY OF MICHIGAN, he followed the suggestion of his friend NORMAN ROSTEN to sign up as a writer for the project, and Professor KENNETH ROWE gave him letters of recommendation to friends who he knew were involved. Rosten had worked with the Federal Theater before taking the playwrighting seminar at Michigan where he had met Miller, and once Miller satisfied the WPA that he was a playwright who was unemployed and not living at home, the conditions under which artists were signed up, he and Rosten worked together on some projects. One play that they cowrote was *Listen My Children*, a one-act play that was never produced. Miller had hoped that the project might stage *The Grass Still Grows*, but the organization had been abolished before he had completed revisions. He had also begun *The Golden Years* with its more than two-dozen cast members with the project's resources in mind, but this had not been completed until 1941.

Fénelon, Fania   (1922–)   Born in Paris, with a Jewish father, Fania Fénelon studied under Germaine Martinelli and was becoming a fairly well-known musician and singer. During WORLD WAR II, when the Nazis took over France, she was arrested in 1943 as a member of the French Resistance and transported to Auschwitz–Birkenau. At Auschwitz, she became a significant member of the Women's Orchestra, and at Bergen–Belsen to where the orchestra was later moved, she slept in the same tent as Anne Frank. Although she nearly died of typhus, Fénelon survived the HOLOCAUST and was interviewed by the BBC on the day of liberation in 1945 when she performed "La Marseillaise" and "God Save the King."

Fénelon returned to her singing career after the war, moving to East Berlin for a time in the 1960s but later returning to France. In 1977, Marcelle Routier helped her write a novel–memoir of her time in the camps, *Playing for Time*. Some have taken issue with the accuracy of aspects of her tale, especially her presentation of Alma Rosé as a cruel disciplinarian and self-hating Jew who admired the Nazis and courted their favor. Although certainly egotistical, they view Rosé in a more heroic light, as someone who pushed her largely untalented orchestra to help them survive. There are errors in Fénelon's account, but her overall analysis of camp conditions is unsparing and effective. Fénelon's frank treatment of both prostitution and lesbianism in the camps was so controversial as to be abridged in the German and English translations of the book.

In 1979, Miller was asked by producer Linda Yellen to adapt Fénelon's memoir for a CBS television film *Playing for Time*, and six years later, he also wrote a version for the stage, adding in scenes that he had not been able to include in the film version. Fénelon was not happy with either Miller's screenplay, which she decried as false, or the decision to allow VANESSA REDGRAVE play her in the film, but she was blocked on both objections. Yellen insisted that not to use Redgrave because of her political beliefs would be tantamount to blacklisting.

Franks, Sidney   Sid Franks was Miller's closest friend when they were growing up. They lived on the same floor of the 110th Street apartment building where Miller was born, and Miller recalls them catching fireflies and playing together with the crystal radio sets that Franks liked to build. Miller always admired his scientific understanding. Franks's father was the president of a downtown bank and would head off to work each morning in a chauffeured car just as Isidore Miller would do. But when the bank's assets evaporated after the WALL STREET CRASH, Franks's father was ruined, his mother soon after died, and his sister committed suicide. Although he was able to complete his science degree at Columbia University, after his 1936 graduation, he went to work to support his father. He first sold vacuum cleaners door-to-door and did very well, but he grew tired of the lies and the manipulation that it took to make a sale and joined the police force instead, seeing better security in such a job. Although he would have liked to have pursued engineering, he realized that the GREAT DEPRESSION climate of 1938 would not support such a dream, and although he planned to stay with the police only until the economy picked up, he ended living his career on the force. Franks would provide the model for Victor Franz in *The Price*.

When Miller had to register for welfare in 1938 to be hired by the FEDERAL THEATER PROJECT, he had to pretend that he did not live at home. To allow his friend to fool the inspector, an episode to which Miller refers in *The American Clock*, Franks set up a cot for Miller in the rooming house into which he had moved with his father. Miller remained friendly with Franks into the 1940s as his friend was married and continued to serve in the police force, including a detail as airport security, but then Miller felt that they were growing apart. He saw him once more in 1955 with a group of off-duty policemen, but at this time, Miller was being denigrated in the press as supportive of COMMUNISM, and although they shook hands, Miller felt that his old friend was uncomfortable, having become one of the conservative masses.

Franz, Elizabeth (1941–)   Born in Akron, Ohio, Elizabeth Franz first appeared on BROADWAY in 1967, playing a variety of supporting roles in Tom Stoppard's *Rosencrantz and Guildenstern Are Dead*. Ten years later, she was seen in a revival of ANTON CHEKHOV's *The Cherry Orchard* and has since appeared in other Chekhov productions as well as several Neil Simon plays. In 1980, Franz won an Obie for her role in Christopher Durang's *Sister Mary Ignatius Explains It All for You*, but her biggest success thus far has been her much-lauded depiction of Linda Loman in the 50th anniversary version of *Death of a Salesman* in 1999. For this, she won a Tony Award and she recreated the part for television in 2000.

While critics praised the steely strength with which Franz portrayed Linda, this was not dissimilar to how MILDRED DUNNOCK had played the part. What Franz added, as theater scholar Brenda Murphy points out, is an element of sexuality, which took the part to a new emotional level. Miller told Peter Applebome of the *New York Times* that she "mounted a kind of wonderful outrage I've never quite seen before," and was pleased with how she played the role.

FURTHER READING

Applebome, Peter. "Present at the Birth of a Salesman." *New York Times*, January 29, 1999: B1, 27.

G

Gable, Clark (1901–1960) William Clark Gable was born in Ohio, his mother dying when he was an infant. Quitting high school at age 16, he worked in a tire factory but after seeing a play decided to act. Aside from touring stock companies, he also worked as a salesman and in the oil fields. Josephine Dillon, a theater manager who was 15 years his elder, married him and brought him to Hollywood in 1924, but they divorced in 1930. In the early 1930s, he began to gain some notoriety in roles in which he treated his female costars cavalierly, winning an Oscar in 1934 for his performance in Frank Capra's *It Happened One Night*. A series of hit movies, including *Mutiny on the Bounty* (1935) and *Gone with the Wind* (1939), made him a star, but when his third wife, Carole Lombard, whom he had married in 1939, died in a plane crash in 1942, grief-stricken, Gable joined the army air corps, leaving his movie career behind.

After his 1944 discharge, Gable returned to MGM and continued making movies on an average of two a year. However, few met with great success and in 1953 he decided not to renew his contract and worked independently thereafter. His fifth marriage, to a former sweetheart Kay, was more successful; he became stepfather to her two children and they were about to have one of their own, his first in wedlock. *The Misfits* was his final movie—he died of a heart attack two weeks after completing his role, and his son was born four months later. Some felt that the strenuous role of Gay Langland might have helped hasten the actor's demise. Miller admired Gable and felt that he was born for the role of Gay Langland. They were friendly on the set, with Miller feeling that Gable understood MARILYN MONROE and was sympathetic. Before leaving after the final shoot, Miller recalls Gable saying that he thought *The Misfits* was the best movie he had made in his life.

Gorelik, Mordecai (1899–1990) Born in Minsk, Russia, Mordecai Gorelik, known as Max to his friends, emigrated to America as a child in 1905. He studied set design under Robert Edmond Jones, Norman Bel Geddes, and others, beginning his theatrical career in 1920 as scene painter and technician with both the Neighborhood Playhouse and the Provincetown Players at their New York City venue. Gorelik enjoyed a long career working mainly as a set and costume designer for more than 50 BROADWAY shows during the 1930s through the 1950s but also becoming involved in production, direction, teaching, and playwriting. He worked in movies as well.

Gorelik's first Broadway credit was in 1932 for John Howard Lawson's *Success Story*, and he would work with its director, LEE STRASBERG, on several other productions. Connected to both the THEATRE GUILD and the GROUP THEATER, he also worked with HAROLD CLURMAN on several of CLIFFORD ODETS's plays, and with ELIA KAZAN on Robert Ardrey's *Casey Jones* in 1938 as well as several others before *All My Sons*. Miller had admired Gorelik's work for Group Theater and was pleased to have him as his set designer for *All My*

Sons. Gorelik created not only the set but also the lighting for the play, and his design included a small mound in the center of the Keller's backyard that concerned Miller, worried it might trip the actors. On asking Gorelik if it was really necessary, the designer, whom Miller describes in *Timebends, A Life* as "a beardless Abraham, a ramrod-straight fanatic with the self-certainty of a terrorist and the smile . . . of a blood-covered avenging angel," insisted it stay, telling Miller that the play takes "place in a cemetery where their son is buried, and he is also their buried conscience reaching up to them out of the earth." For Gorelik, the mound was essential, and Miller fearfully acceded.

Great Britain   In *Remembering Arthur Miller* (2005), director MICHAEL BLAKEMORE speaks of how "the regard with which he and his work were held in Britain saw him through periods of wounding neglect in his own country." Miller had been so disconsolate about getting a fair hearing in the United States that he even premiered his 1991 *The Ride down Mt. Morgan* in London. *Resurrection Blues* would also appear in the West End before any showing on BROADWAY. Most of Miller's plays have received important professional premieres and repeated revivals in Britain and have tended throughout to receive a far more positive critical response than in his homeland. Trying to explain why he felt that Miller was better received on British shores in CHRISTOPHER BIGSBY's *Arthur Miller and Company*, critic Michael Billington suggested that it was because Miller displayed a European dramatists' tendency "to ask daunting questions rather than provide [the] comforting answers" that U.S. audiences and critics seemed to prefer. Miller long favored Britain's subsidized theater, and wrote at length to encourage the same system in the United States, seeing it as the only real hope of more readily producing serious drama.

Respect for Miller has been demonstrated by the American Studies Center at the UNIVERSITY OF EAST ANGLIA being named in his honor in 1987, by his receiving a prestigious honorary doctorate from Oxford University in 1995, and by his being treated to elaborate celebrations to mark his 75th, 80th,

and 85th birthdays. In a poll taken by Britain's NATIONAL THEATRE to determine the best 100 plays of the 20th century, Miller's *Death of a Salesman* came in second to SAMUEL BECKETT's *Waiting for Godot,* and three other of Miller's plays were featured on the list: *The Crucible* at #6, *A View from the Bridge* at #45, and *All My Sons* at #66. All of these plays have long been staples on British grade-school syllabi from ninth grade and up.

British theater scholars have also been firm supporters of his work, from Dennis Welland to Bigsby. Working through Bigsby, who is the director of the Arthur Miller Center at the University of East Anglia, Miller was finally able to hear a production of his long-neglected play *The Golden Years,* which was aired on BBC radio in 1987. Miller has also worked closely with several British directors, most notably Peter Brook, Peter Wood, and DAVID THACKER. It was Brook who persuaded Miller to expand *A View from the Bridge* into a two-act play and Wood who helped Miller discover the best way to produce his sprawling 1980s play, *The American Clock.* Thacker, meanwhile, led the celebrations for Miller's 75th birthday in 1990, that included London revivals of *The Price* and *The Crucible.* He also directed the London premieres of *Two-Way Mirror, The Last Yankee,* and *Broken Glass* as well as a version of the last for BBC television, several other Miller revivals, and a four-part series on Arthur Miller called *Miller Shorts* for the BBC.

Great Depression   The Great Depression was an international economic downturn that began near the end of the 1920s. It was not just a U.S. experience: Cities around the world were hit hard, especially those whose economy was based on heavy industry. Construction virtually halted in many countries, and farmers and rural areas suffered as prices for crops fell by 40–60 percent. Conditions lasted through the 1930s, although recovery varied from nation to nation. The massive rearmament policies to counter the threat from Nazi Germany helped to stimulate the economies of many countries. The mobilization of manpower following the outbreak of WORLD WAR II in 1939 finally ended unemployment as people joined the armed forces or went to work in factories.

In the United States, the starting point of the period known as the Depression is generally considered to date from the WALL STREET CRASH of 1929, although as Miller has the character Arthur Robertson point out in *The American Clock,* a manufacturing slowdown had begun to affect businesses earlier than that date. This partly accounts for the fact that the Millers were forced to move into cheaper housing in 1928, a year prior to the crash, because ISIDORE MILLER's MILTEX COAT AND SUIT COMPANY was already suffering. However, with the crash, all of the elder Miller's cash reserves, which he had invested in stocks (as so many Americans had done), were wiped out. The head of the family destroyed financially and psychically by the Depression is a figure that features in several of Miller's plays, including *The American Clock, After the Fall,* and *The Price.*

Further deepened by drought conditions across the country that destroyed many crops, the Depression had a significant impact on the economy and the people of the United States at all levels of society. Both towns and rural areas were affected, as Miller depicts in *The American Clock.* At the time, the policies of President Herbert Hoover were widely blamed; against advice, he tried to keep wages and farm prices high, with public works going to ameliorate the distress—but it only made matters worse. He was defeated in 1932 by Franklin D. Roosevelt. Roosevelt launched a New Deal that was designed to provide emergency relief to upward of a third of the population to recover the economy to normal levels and to reform failed parts of the economic system. Unemployment lingered until the early 1940s, but during the 1930s, the Works Progress Administration (WPA) gave work to many, and Miller was able to avail himself of their services after college. It was through the WPA that he managed to enter the rolls of the FEDERAL THEATER PROJECT for the brief period before that organization was closed down.

To Miller, the Depression was a key event in U.S. history, one that changed the nature of people's outlook on the world and a time that personally taught him much about people and life. In his autobiography, *Timebends: A Life,* he describes the Depression as a "moral catastrophe" and only

"incidentally a matter of money," largely because it exposed many of the hypocrisies that had lain behind the prosperous facade of U.S. society. The old order had been proven to be both incompetent and inherently hollow. Having the rug pulled from under their feet for no real reason that they could ascertain, people lost many of the old certainties, becoming obsessively terrified of failure and yet feeling guilty when successful. Miller's father never fully recovered from the loss of a business that he had worked so hard to build, and his mother was often depressed or embittered by the family's reduced circumstances. However, both refused to give up hope for the future, an optimistic attitude that Miller carried with him throughout his career.

The Depression also carried elements of hope— when the corrupt structures had disintegrated, the ground had been left clear for new structures. The difficulty came in the uncertainty as to how to restructure U.S. society from the ground up. Miller saw neither socialism nor fascism as offering ideal social systems because each was too extreme and ultimately flawed. While the former privileged the community, the latter privileged the individual; what was really needed was a balance between the two. The 1930s struggled toward an understanding of this balance with the help of Roosevelt's New Deal, but Miller felt that the lessons that those people learned were lost over time. As the country approached the end of the millennium, Miller saw his nation needing to relearn the essential needs of both community and individual to combat a mounting spiritual malaise.

Roosevelt's restructuring of the economy in the 1930s had recognized the needs of all rather than the few. New Deal programs regulated the banks-and-securities industry, placed safeguards against cut-throat industry practices and monopolies, reformed the farming system, and encouraged unions in order to bargain for increased wages. More controversial measures were the labor codes, standards, and prices being set by the government and the massive increase in government spending that was necessitated by other reforms. By 1935, both Social Security and the national relief agency known as the WPA had been set up. Between 1933 and 1939, federal expenditure tripled, funded primarily by a growth in the national debt. Roosevelt's critics charged that he was turning the United States into a socialist state; by 1943, all of the relief programs would be abolished. However, spending on the New Deal would be far smaller than on the war effort.

In the United States, the massive war spending doubled the Gross National Product (GNP), helping to end the Depression. Businessmen ignored the mounting national debt and the heavy new taxes, redoubling their efforts for greater output as an expression of patriotism. Patriotism drove many to work overtime voluntarily and to give up leisure activities to make money after so many hard years. Patriotism also meant that people accepted rationing and price controls without any trouble. Cost-plus pricing in munitions contracts guaranteed that businesses would make a profit no matter how many mediocre workers they employed, no matter how inefficient the techniques they used. The demand was for a vast quantity of war supplies as soon as possible, regardless of cost. It is this aspect of the war business that Miller challenged in *All My Sons*, with its exposure of the dangers of war profiteering.

In an interview that was filmed by Albert Maysles to accompany the 1970 filmed version of *A Memory of Two Mondays*, Miller speaks of the romantic nostalgia people have for the Depression as being ridiculous; for him, it was a period in which life was frustrating and nothing less than "gruesome." Although the people whom we see in *A Memory of Two Mondays* are lucky enough to have jobs, their lives are mostly empty and dulled by the repetitiveness of those jobs, with the only refuge being booze and sex, both of which cause damage. Recognizing the tendency of many Americans to idealize the 1930s as a humanitarian era filled with human solidarity, when touching on this period in plays as he does in the *American Clock* and *Broken Glass*, Miller tries to show what he feels was the truer picture.

Although Miller references isolated moments of compassion and thoughtfulness during this period in *Boro Hall Nocturne* and *The American Clock*, he believes that the majority of people were selfishly out to survive personally and would tread on anyone who got in their way; this was suggested in the way that the characters Herman and Sam in

Homely Girl: A Life took advantage of the hardships of others by buying up their property and books so cheaply. In work that was set at later periods, the Depression is often referenced as a defining period for a character, such as John Frick in *The Last Yankee* who survived financially but has become obsessed with money or even Willy Loman who ironically survived the Depression but is left behind in the more prosperous 1940s.

Despite his recognition of the darker side of the Depression years, Miller also believed that people's optimism remained, being evidenced in the upbeat songs, musicals, and comedies of the period. The vaudevillian form of the final script of his main Depression-era play, *The American Clock*, conveys an authentic sense of the Depression, as vaudeville was an up-and-coming genre of the period, reflecting people's comic response to the pressures around them. It was, perhaps, rooted in the sense that things could not possibly get worse so they had to get better. "Underneath it all, you see," Miller told CHRISTOPHER BIGSBY when being interviewed for *Arthur Miller and Company*, "you were stripped of all your illusions and there's a certain perverse healthiness in that. . . . And I suppose that way in the back of your brain, you knew you were in America and that somehow it was going to work out." Miller, too, survived the Depression, but it is clearly an event that marked his outlook for life.

Grosbard, Ulu (1929–) Born in Antwerp, Belgium, Jewish writer and director Ulu Grosbard came to America with his parents in 1948; he studied at the University of Chicago and Yale School of Drama before beginning his career as a stage-and-screen director. He won both Drama Desk–Vernon Rice and Obie Awards for his powerful off-Broadway direction of *A View from the Bridge* in 1965, which he also produced for television. It was during this production that he suggested to an incredulous Miller that the young assistant stage manager, DUSTIN HOFFMAN, would make a good Willy Loman in a few years. In 1968, he guided *The Price* to the stage, but the actors grew argumentative over his direction. Shortly before opening, he left the production, leaving Miller to take over, and they did not work together again.

Aside from Miller's plays, his stage direction credits include such dramas as Frank D. Gilroy's Pulitzer Prize-winning *The Subject Was Roses* in 1964 and a new translation that he cowrote of Peter Weiss's *The Investigation* in 1966. After the moderate success of his 1971 film *Who Is Harry Kellerman and Why Is He Saying Those Terrible Things about Me?*, which he wrote, directed, and produced, Grosbard divided his time between stage and film. His movies include *Straight Time* (1978) with Dustin Hoffman, *True Confessions* (1981) with Robert Duvall (who had starred in his *A View from the Bridge*), *Falling in Love* (1984), *Georgia* (1995), and *The Deep End of the Ocean* (1999). Since *The Price*, he has also directed Broadway productions of David Mamet's *American Buffalo* (1977), Woody Allen's *The Floating Lightbulb* (1981), Beth Henley's *The Wake of Jamie Foster* (1982), and a revival of Paddy Chayefsky's *The Tenth Man* (1989).

The Group Theater The Group Theater was a collective formed in New York in 1931 by HAR- OLD CLURMAN, Cheryl Crawford, and LEE STRAS- BERG. The name *Group* came from the idea of the actors as a pure ensemble without any stars. It was intended as a base for the kind of theater in which they all believed—naturalistic, highly disciplined acting, and socially conscious drama—to create a better alternative than the light entertainment that they saw prevailing in the 1920s. From Paul Green's *The House of Connelly* (1931) to Irwin Shaw's *Retreat to Pleasure* (1940), they would offer BROADWAY audiences more serious theat- rical alternatives. They were pioneers of what would become known as method acting, which was derived from the teachings of Constantin Stanislavski. The technique bases a performance on inner emotional experience, which is explored through the medium of improvisation and various physical and psychological exercises. The com- pany included actors, directors, playwrights, and producers. In the 10 brief years of its existence, the group produced more than 20 original plays by contemporary U.S. playwrights, most nota- bly Green, Shaw, Sidney Kingsley, and CLIFFORD ODETS, whose *Golden Boy* (1937) proved to be their biggest hit.

Given the time period, many members of the company, including ELIA KAZAN (who joined in 1933), Kurt Weill, Stella and Luther Adler, John Garfield, Robert Lewis, and LEE J. COBB, held left- wing political views and wanted to produce plays that dealt with important social issues. In the 1950s, a large proportion of the group, by then defunct, would be investigated by the HOUSE UN-AMERI- CAN ACTIVITIES COMMITTEE. Despite the Group Theater's success, internal disagreements, financial problems, and the lure of Hollywood began to take their toll, and by late 1936, production was sus- pended. Many Group Theater members, including Harold Clurman, left for Hollywood; several did not return. In April 1937, Strasberg and Crawford resigned, but Lewis and Kazan restarted Group Theater workshops the following year. The Group Theatre Studio resumed with 50 actors who were chosen from 400 who auditioned. Lewis, Kazan, and Sanford Meisner were the principle teachers, and later that year, Clurman returned to direct Odets's *Golden Boy* to an acclaim that kept the group going a little longer. Although they folded in 1941, the Group Theater's influence on American theater remained strong, and many of their mem- bers became highly influential acting teachers and directors.

Miller had sent the Group Theater copies of both of his early plays, *The Grass Still Grows* and *The Golden Years,* but they had not selected either one for production. In his "Introduction" to *Arthur Miller's Collected Plays*, Miller speaks of his admira- tion for the pioneering work of the Group Theater in the way that they forged such strong connections between actor and audience. Although he disliked some of the plays that they produced, he found every performance that he attended inspiring. It would be to their leading lights, Clurman and Kazan, that he would have his agent KAY BROWN offer *All My Sons*, having been so impressed with the work that these two had done with the Group Theater.

FURTHER READING

Clurman, Harold. *The Fervent Years.* New York: Knopf, 1945.
Lewis, Robert. *Slings and Arrows.* New York: Stein and Day, 1984.

Guilt and Responsibility The issues of guilt and responsibility are inextricably linked within the work of Miller and are central to his entire canon. They are concerns that Miller addresses in nearly every play and piece of fiction that he has written and that he tries to explicate in a number of his essays. Fascinated with the idea of guilt and blame and with how to continue living with these in the world, Miller recognizes the importance of accepting responsibility for what one intended to do or even did by accident because someone has to be responsible. The issue of guilt, for Miller, goes back to the beginning of humankind, which he explores in *The Creation of the World and Other Business*. Through the action of this play, Miller suggests that humankind has a capacity for evil that cannot be ignored, and it must be recognized to be combated. Cain chooses to do evil, but he could have chosen just as easily not to kill his brother. People must learn to make the right choices, and that entails thinking about the implications of actions beyond themselves. It is only by accepting our responsibility for evil, as Quentin does in *After the Fall*, as Von Berg does in *Incident at Vichy*, and as Albert Kroll does in *Clara*, that we can break its hold over us and restore a sense of moral order to society.

There are those who just deny guilt, like Skip Cheeseboro in *Resurrection Blues*, but it is a decision that makes them appear to be less human. There are others who avoid guilt, as do the Franz brothers in *The Price*, a decision that ensures that the brothers remain estranged: They each blame the other rather than accept responsibility for their own choices. Then there are those like Lyman Felt, who after facing a lion, decides not to ever feel guilty again: By refusing to accept what he sees as the human limitations of his guilt, he becomes not godlike as he had hoped but less than human. It is this decision that leads to his downfall because guilt is the first step toward our connection to other people—it is guilt in a sense that binds us—and without it, Lyman ends in total isolation. Because he refuses to accept any guilt for his behavior, both wives, his old friend Tom, and his daughter Bessie all leave, and he is left with no one.

However, accepting guilt is only the first step. Simple guilt for the evil we choose to do is insuf-ficient for Miller; as he explains in his essay "Our Guilt for the World's Evil," guilt alone is never the answer because, as a passive reaction, guilt is destructive as opposed to the active reaction of accepting responsibility. Thus, John Proctor's simple feelings of guilt about Abigail in *The Crucible* or the self-hatred of *Broken Glass*'s Phillip Gellburg are crippling and ineffective, and Gus's guilt for neglecting his wife in *A Memory of Two Mondays* leads him to drink himself to death pointlessly in one final binge. Guilt alone is crippling and entirely negative. Kroll is so consumed by guilt that he cannot name the killer and becomes utterly ineffective; indeed, we even suspect for a time that he could be the killer. Unless he can transcend his personal guilt and hatred, he is in danger of becoming like Fine, who can only see negatives in the world. His final transformation comes with his acceptance of responsibility for the guilt he has concerning his daughter's death, which will allow a more enlightened future. In the same way, Lawrence Newman becomes much the better man in *Focus* by transforming his guilt for snubbing Finkelstein into responsibility as stands beside him in battle and reports the incident to the police station.

The key is first to accept the guilt but then to go beyond it; to accept guilt passively leads to complacency or even to paralysis, the latter quite literally in the case of *Broken Glass*'s Sylvia Gellburg (who symbolically represents all of U.S. society, which conceals collective guilt for blinding themselves to the plight of the Jews in Europe). But if we actively transform guilt into responsibility, Miller believes that we can transcend it, and it is this process that he illustrates time and again in his work, from Joe Keller in *All My Sons* to Henri Schultz in *Resurrection Blues*. Miller sincerely believes that no one is an island and that we are all responsible for one another if humanity is to survive, but we also have responsibilities toward ourselves as individuals, too, if we are to survive contentedly. It is this quest to discover this delicate balance between responsibility toward the self and toward others that preoccupies so many of his characters. From plays such as *They Too Arise*, *The Crucible* and *The American Clock* to the pointedly titled *Mr. Peters' Connections*, Miller repeatedly demonstrates the connections that he sees between individuals and society to point out people's responsibilities and to depict the disastrous results when these go unrecognized.

Miller's concept of guilt and responsibility has its roots in his Judaic upbringing (see the section on JUDAISM for more detail) and embraces both individual and social responsibilities because he views the two as inextricably linked. Miller asks us to choose to take responsibility for things that we cannot control as well as for things that we can control because a refusal of responsibility is ultimately a refusal of humanity. Ignoring responsibilities, either personal or social, will interfere with an individual's ability to connect. Through his plays, as Miller tells us in an interview recorded in Matthew Roudané's *Conversations with Arthur Miller,* he tries "to make human relations felt between individuals and the larger structure of the world." Recognizing the sense of connection that the individual characters had in Elizabethan drama, Miller sees such a sense as lacking in our contemporary world, but he tries to recreate it through his plays, and the key to this connection is responsibility.

Everyone needs to be responsible for what they create, and the consequences of their actions are as important as the actions themselves. An early Miller play such as *All My Sons* depicts the increasing strain of living under guilt and the harsh penalties accrued by those who for too long ignore their responsibilities. Chris finds his father guilty of social irresponsibility and demands that he be sent to jail to pay for his crime according to law. Keller's suicide can be read as either the desperate response of a man who is left with no way out or as an act of self-immolation in recognition of personal guilt. We can compare his suicide to the decision of Von Berg to give his pass to Leduc, or to Eddie Carbone's drive toward self-destruction at the hands of Marco in *A View from the Bridge,* as all are actions denoting responsibility to others.

Von Berg initially blinds himself to his complicity in events, feeling that it is enough just to passively disagree, but Leduc teaches him the error of this. Leduc counters that beneath it all, Von Berg simply is relieved that he is not Leduc. He seriously would not lift a finger to help Leduc, thus making Von Berg complicit with the crime. "Each man has

his Jew," Leduc declares, and it seems hardwired into human nature to hate the other—even Jews do this—and so Von Berg's friendship cannot matter while he allows such things to happen. Leduc points out that the cousin Von Berg had mentioned with affection was a notorious Nazi, and until Von Berg can see what that means through Leduc's eyes, he cannot see that his complacency makes him complicit and just as monstrous. Leduc asks not for guilt but for responsibility, and Von Berg begins to see the difference. In the end, he rises to Leduc's challenge to be responsible rather than guilty, which leads him to sacrifice his own safety by giving up his pass and allowing Leduc to escape.

Guilt is such a strong motivating force in Miller's plays that it often dictates the whole structure of the play, although Miller presents this in different ways. Whereas Keller's guilt in *All My Sons* is gradually revealed and the play builds to the climax when he atones for that guilt, in *Death of a Salesman,* Willy Loman's suicidal desire is indicated right from the start, and we know that this man must be harboring a burdensome guilt about something. The main question is what? Thus, Miller structures the whole play around Willy's growing desire to confess his guilty secret, and the memories that Willy selects to relive lead us there.

In *The Crucible,* Miller wanted to go beyond the discovery of guilt that had motivated his earlier plots and study of the results of such guilt. This is why he centers his study on John Proctor, a man who is caught between the way in which others see him and the way in which he sees himself. His private sense of guilt leads him into an ironically false confession of having committed a crime, although he later recants. What allows him to recant is the release of guilt that is given to him by his wife's confession of her coldness and her refusal to blame him for his adultery. Elizabeth insists that he is a good man, and this finally convinces him that he is.

It was to further explore the idea of guilt that led Miller to write *After the Fall.* He wanted to create a play in which he would complicate the straightforward guilt that the central protagonist of ALBERT CAMUS's *The Fall* had felt at not trying to save the girl, by having his hero Quentin both try to save the girl and fail, as well as recognize that he had a selfish motivation that guided his actions from the start. Quentin feels guilty for his whole life, and until he comes to terms with this, he cannot progress with Holga. He thinks that he needs to get free of his guilt somehow, but Holga leads him to understand that freeing yourself of guilt is unnecessary and that it is better to embrace it and to move on. He ends by accepting partial responsibility for all of the failures of family, marriage, and friendship in his past, also recognizing that he was not the only one at fault; this allows him a more hopeful perspective. A burden shared is a burden halved.

In *Playing for Time*, Miller faces the HOLO-CAUST, what he felt was the ultimate 20th-century example of people eschewing guilt and responsibility, and he counters it by showing the possibility of hope even there. Although only one among many, a character like Elzvieta displays both responsibility and guilt for what is happening to the Jews in the camp. She has fought with the Resistance, led a life free of ANTI-SEMITISM, and suffers along with the Jews in the camp; yet she still accepts a responsibility for what is happening and sees the human connection between all people, be they Gentile or Jew in the same way Lawrence Newman had done in *Focus*. She, as much as Fania—whose role as witness, caring for others, and embracing of her Jewish identity illustrate her acceptance of responsibility—offers a model of right behavior. Marianne, in contrast, has lost her sense of conscience, and so her behavior creates in her no feelings of guilt. She refuses to recognize any responsibilities in her drive merely to continue living, not even any responsibility to her own self and to her own dignity. She, in contrast, becomes a mere husk of a human being because this is Miller's belief: It is our guilt and responsibility that ultimately make us human.

H

Harris, Jed (1900–1979)   Jed Harris was a well-known BROADWAY producer and director. Born in Austria as Jacob Horowitz, he came to America at the age of three. In the late 1920s, he shot to fame after a series of Broadway successes that revolutionized the theater of that time. In 1928, he was chosen to appear on the cover of *Time* magazine.

After a shaky start with Lynn Starling's *Weak Sisters* in 1925, Harris produced a string of original hits beginning with Philip Dunning's *Broadway* in 1926, followed by George Abbot and Ann Preston's *Coquette*, George S. Kaufmann and Edna Ferber's *The Royal Family* in 1927, and Ben Hecht and Charles MacArthur's *The Front Page* in 1928. He then turned his hand to revivals, both producing and directing, and had moderate success with ANTON CHEKHOV's *Uncle Vanya* in 1930 and HENRIK IBSEN's *A Doll's House* in 1937, a production that Miller witnessed and found truly engrossing.

In terms of his direction, Harris made an indelible mark with his groundbreaking, award-winning premiere of Thornton Wilder's *Our Town* (1938) and several other plays. A man who liked to have total control, he would often intimidate or ridicule those around him, both writers and actors, to gain the upper hand. Miller recalls that Harris had reputedly "fought with practically everybody who was anybody in the Broadway theater." Despite Ruth and Augustus Goetz's *The Heiress* in 1947 with Wendy Hiller and Basil Rathbone, which he had directed to great success, by the 1950s, it was becoming hard for Harris to find work, and he

was virtually bankrupt. His last Broadway production had been a mediocre melodrama, *The Traitor* (1949) by Herman Wouk, and when Harris heard that Miller was looking for a new director for his latest play, he determined to put himself forward.

Harris was known for his affairs, once such being with the playwright LILLIAN HELLMAN. She had had a string of successful plays in the late 1940s and had gained political credibility by her refusal to testify before the HOUSE UN-AMERICAN ACTIVITIES COMMITTEE (HUAC). She was persuaded by her lover to lobby for him to direct *The Crucible* with Miller's producer, KERMIT BLOOMGARDEN, who had also produced many of her plays and took her recommendation seriously, despite being warned against Harris by friends. Harris managed to borrow a yacht to impress Miller and invited him to dine on board. Though wary, Miller was impressed by both Harris's theatrical knowledge and elegance and remembering that production of *A Doll's House*, agreed to have him direct. Their working relationship was strained from the start.

Miller had virtually written the part of John Proctor for actor ARTHUR KENNEDY who had appeared in two of his previous plays, but Harris hated Kennedy and wanted to cast the movie actor Richard Widmark in the role. Neither man turned out to be available, and so Harris left the role on hold as he cast the rest of the play. He also demanded a series of rewrites from Miller in an unsuccessful attempt to undermine the playwright's confidence in order to gain full control. He even tried to insist on a share of the royalties and a credit as coauthor, both of which were denied. When the play in which Kennedy had been appearing failed and he became free to play Proctor, Miller and Bloomgarden forced Harris to accept him. In umbrage, Harris repeatedly tried to humiliate and bully Kennedy during rehearsals. Kennedy stood firm, but other actors were uneasy with such a domineering and self-indulgent director—Cloris Leachman, for example, who had begun in the role of Abigail Williams, walked out and had to be replaced by Madeleine Sherwood.

Like ELIA KAZAN, who had directed Miller's previous successes *All My Sons* and *Death of a Salesman*, Harris was an intense director, but his style was very different, no doubt partly because his successes had come from an earlier period in U.S. theatrical history when direction of a serious play tended to emphasize formality over emotion. His direction of *The Crucible* was very static as he had characters make speeches to the audience rather than to each other, and he often kept them frozen in tableaux while speaking their lines. Miller describes Harris's vision of the production as a "'Dutch painting,' a classical play that had to be nobly performed," and this approach made the critics view it as cold, unemotional, and lacking in heart. Miller knew that Harris's production was misconceived and suspected that Harris knew it, too, but had worked on it for too long to want to pull the plug.

The dress rehearsal in Wilmington, Delaware, was a tense affair. Harris banned Bloomgarden from the theater, and Miller watched nervously from the back. When the enthusiastic audience called for the author to take a bow at the final curtain, Harris sprang forward and took credit as Miller watched in amazement; he later told the playwright that the actors (who everyone knew hated him) had pulled him onto the stage in gratitude. Once the play moved to New York and started to draw mixed reviews, Harris withdrew and allowed Miller to make changes without comment or interference. Miller reinstated a scene between Proctor and Abigail, redirected certain sections, and took away the heavy, realistic scenery to change the audience's expectations, but the damage of those early reviews had already been done, and the production closed shortly after.

Harris would only direct one more Broadway play, *Child of Fortune* by Guy Bolton in 1956. Based on novelist Henry James's *Wings of the Dove*, this was no doubt an attempt to recapture the glory of *The Heiress*, which had been an adaptation of James's *Washington Square*. It failed and closed after only 23 performances. Harris turned his attention to television and movies, but success continued to elude him to his death.

FURTHER READING

Gottfried, Martin. *Jed Harris, the Curse of Genius*. Boston: Little, Brown, 1984.
Harris, Jed. *A Dance on the High Wire*. New York: Crown, 1979.

Harry Ransom Research Center   The Harry Ransom Research Center was founded at the University of Texas at Austin in 1957 by Harry Huntt Ransom. Ransom had risen from English professor to president and chancellor of the University of Texas System and had long encouraged the library to expand its holdings. The university had been acquiring important private collections of books and manuscripts, such as those of John Henry Wrenn, George Atherton Aitken, and Miriam Lutcher Stark, since the turn of the century, and these would form the core of the center's initial holdings.

The creation of the research center ushered in a period of intense collecting, with a focus on rare books, manuscripts, and archival materials. Rather than compete with older established collections, the decision was made to concentrate on modern writers, and the center would soon become one of the U.S.'s foremost humanities research centers in 20th century literature with extensive collections of writers as varied as SAMUEL BECKETT, James Joyce, JOHN STEINBECK, George Bernard Shaw, Anne Sexton, John Osbourne, and Tom Stoppard. At present, the center collects first editions of 548 contemporary authors. Ransom also expanded the collection into materials relating to theater set design, architecture, and industrial design, thus initiating the center's distinguished Performing Arts Collection.

With a large endowment, the center is also able to offer more than 30 fellowships a year to scholars who come from around the globe to make use of the Ransom Center's collections that contain some 30 million leaves of manuscripts, more than one million rare books, five million photographs, 3,000 pieces of historical photographic equipment, and 100,000 works of art, in addition to major holdings in theater arts and film. Not all of their material is yet catalogued, and there are currently no online finding aids, but some inventories are available by request.

In 1961 and 1962, Miller first presented the center with a portion of his archives as tax relief against the financial ramifications of his divorce from MARILYN MONROE. After his death, the center was able to purchase the remainder of his papers. Works represented in the collection include *After the Fall, All My Sons, The Crucible, Death of a Salesman, Fame, From Under the Sea, The Golden Years, The Half-Bridge, The Hook, I Don't Need You Any More, A Memory of Two Mondays, The Misfits, They Too Arise,* and *A View from the Bridge.* Many of the typescripts contain the author's manuscript corrections, unpublished dialogue, notes on the writing of the plays, and comments about their production. For *Death of a Salesman* and *The Crucible,* there are notebooks containing the author's first notes on the stories, early sketches of dialogue, research findings, and outlines of plot and action. They also have the original draft, heavily revised, of Miller's novel *Focus,* along with the original manuscript of the unpublished novel *The Man Who Had All the Luck.* A printed list is available for four-fifths of the collection, and nearly all of the remainder is accessible via the Center's card catalog.

Havel, Václav (1936–)   Born in Prague, Czechoslovakia, Václav Havel has had an interesting career as both a playwright and a politician and has won countless awards for his service in both arenas. He began to write in his late teens and, in 1956 had his first outspoken public appearance with a highly critical address to a working party of new authors. After he completed his military service, unable to be accepted at Prague's Performing Arts Academy, he worked as a stagehand at ABC Theatre and later, from 1960, in the Theatre on the Balustrade. He became this theater's literary manager in 1963

and their resident playwright by 1968. Here, Havel's early plays, including *The Garden Party* (1963), *The Memorandum* (1965), and *The Increased Difficulty of Concentration* (1968), were produced to great acclaim for their inventive take on bureaucracy and their effects in creating a dehumanized society. Bordering on ABSURDISM, these plays are intensely funny political satires. After the Soviet invasion of 1968, however, Havel found his works banned and himself the target of government harassment and imprisonment for his outspokenness, even while his dramas were growing more popular abroad.

In 1977, as one of the three principal spokesmen for the Charter 77 manifesto that charged the Czech government with human and civil rights violations, Havel found himself imprisoned for dissent. During the next decade, he would find himself in and out of custody. Although Havel received many invitations to work in the West, he chose to remain in his homeland, afraid that if he left, he would not be allowed back in the country. Forbidden to work in the theater, he devoted much of his time to speaking out against government oppression. These experiences are reflected in many of Havel's later works, including the three "Vanek" plays and *Largo Desolato* (1984). Each depicts a dissident artist who is mired in hopeless conflict with an oppressive social order but nevertheless refuses to compromise his self-respect or sense of morality.

During Czechoslovakia's political upheaval in 1989, Havel, himself a socialist, emerged as the leader of the opposition to the communist government. In a unanimous vote by the country's parliament, he was chosen to serve as president, and when free elections were held the following year, Havel was reaffirmed as the country's leader. His speeches and essays during this period illustrate Havel's struggle with what he saw as the dichotomy of being both an intellectual and a politician. Noted for a humanistic administration that became a model for DEMOCRACY in the Eastern bloc, Havel would remain president until losing the 2003 election, after which he decided to retire from politics and to write his memoirs.

Havel had admired Miller's plays since the 1960s when they were first performed in Czechoslovakia. He first met Miller in 1969 in a friend's apartment in Prague, but he regretfully had to leave early to fetch his car. Miller did not recall that detail but does remember noticing police surveillance on the writers whom he was meeting. Miller was visiting Czechoslovakia as the president of PEN to show support for writers there, and Havel would later serve on the board of directors of PEN. He would not meet Miller again for 21 years, but in the interim, Miller did much to try to alleviate the censorship under which Havel was operating and to bring conditions in Czechoslovakia to the world's notice, such as by his 1974 article for *Esquire,* "What's Wrong with This Picture?" In 1982, Miller wrote a short satirical play in support of Havel, called "The Havel Deal," in which a communist proposes the arrest of Western writers, such as was occurring in Czechoslovakia at that time. The 1986 monologue *I Think About You a Great Deal* and a short untitled play in honor of Havel's receipt of the Erasmus Prize while he was still in jail showed Miller's continued support for this political figure.

Once Havel became president and had the freedom to leave the country, he was able to meet several times with Miller at various events. One such occasion was on a 1990 trip that Havel made to the United States to attend a preview of the Roundabout Theater's revival of *The Crucible* in the hopes of directing it himself in Prague. Havel's moral outlook and his dedication to his art and his country both served to make him heroic in Miller's view. He inspired the character of Sigmund in Miller's 1977 play *The Archbishop's Ceiling,* which depicts a group of writers who are trying to survive against various threats of suppression. Sigmund is the erstwhile writer who refuses to leave his homeland or to give in to the oppression of the current regime, a model of both Havel and, in many ways, Miller himself.

Despite being lionized in Europe and mocked for many years by U.S. critics, Miller continued to try and mount his plays in U.S. theater. Furthermore, despite risking further unpopularity, especially during the uncertain 1950s when he found it virtually impossible to publish criticisms of Senator McCarthy or the government, Miller continued to try and speak out against what he saw as bad politics. He was only grateful that he lived in a country,

unlike pre-1989 Czechoslovkia, that still allowed him to attempt this without being jailed (although his experiences with the HOUSE UN-AMERICAN ACTIVITIES COMMITTEE had made even that seem possible).

Hellman, Lillian (1906–1984) Born in New Orleans to a struggling shoe merchant and his upper-middle-class wife, Lillian Hellman had the advantages of a solid education and a well-traveled childhood before going to work as a manuscript reader for a big publishing firm and being drawn into the glamorous, bohemian life of New York. After her early marriage to press agent Arthur Kober split up, mystery novelist Dashiell Hammett, whom she had met in Hollywood, became her longtime lover and mentor. In between jobs working as a play reader in New York she had spent the first year of the 1930s in Hollywood as a scenario reader. Some critics believe that Hammett based his suave detectives Nick and Nora Charles on himself and Hellman, and Hammett certainly encouraged both her leftist political beliefs and her first provocative play, *The Children's Hour,* which was produced on BROADWAY in 1934. After this, she wrote a series of award-winning plays, which include *The Little Foxes* (1939), *Watch on the Rhine* (1941), *Another Part of the Forest* (1946), *The Autumn Garden* (1951), and *Toys in the Attic* (1960).

Although some critics found her work too melodramatic, it was nonetheless influential, and she became one of the U.S.'s leading playwrights with a career that stretched several decades. She also wrote screenplays, mostly based on her own dramas, and several controversial but award-winning memoirs, including *An Unfinished Woman* (1969), *Pentimento* (1973), and *Scoundrel Time* (1976), in which some critics questioned the veracity of her claims. What is interesting about these memoirs is their form that largely eschews the traditional chronological approach and, like Miller's *Timebends, A Life,* swings freely among her remembrances of places, times, and people.

Miller was initially surprised that Hellman was a socialist, having been unimpressed with what he saw as her middle-class dramas, although he admired the elegant dialogue and structure of her plays. For him, however, her theater lacked the fire of the GROUP THEATRE's efforts by younger contemporaries such as CLIFFORD ODETS. He admired her more for her political commitment, especially for her refusal to name names to the HOUSE UN-AMERICAN ACTIVITIES COMMITTEE, although he also found fault with her refusal to reject the Soviet Union long after evidence of its obvious corruption. Her loyalty bespoke an integrity that he could admire but ran hypocritically counter to her own impatience with deceit in others. It was Hellman who influenced KERMIT BLOOMGARDEN, who had worked with her on a number of plays, to hire JED HARRIS to direct *The Crucible.* Miller saw Hellman as domineering and competitive, resentful of his success, and although they met many times on the theater scene and over political issues, they never became close friends.

Hoffman, Dustin (1937–   ) Born into a Jewish family, after graduating from Los Angeles High School in 1955, Dustin Lee Hoffman briefly attended the Los Angeles Conservatory of Music, planning to become a concert pianist. However, he soon switched to Santa Monica City College to study medicine; he dropped out after a year due to bad grades. Although his parents had named him Dustin after actor Dustin Farnum, he initially chose acting for a profession because it seemed preferable to real work or joining the army. He trained at the Pasadena Playhouse for two years, where he met and became close friends with actor Gene Hackman.

Moving to New York in the late 1950s, he roomed with Hackman who had come to the city earlier. The pair greatly admired Marlon Brando as an actor, and Hoffman was trained in the Method with LEE STRASBERG. In *Timebends: A Life,* Miller recalls briefly meeting Hoffman in 1965 as assistant stage manager on ULU GROSBARD's 1965 production of *A View from the Bridge.* Despite Grosbard's suggestion that Miller should keep Hoffman in mind to play Willy Loman in a few years, with his looks and diction, Miller could not imagine "how the poor fellow imagined himself a candidate for any kind of acting career." Hoffman was finding it hard to convince others, too; he seemed not to be able to rise beyond stage manager or the occasional extra on BROADWAY, although he had done some television work and gained some reputation for his 1966 off-Broadway one-man show, *Eh!* It was this that made him noticed sufficiently to land the lead in the 1967 hit movie *The Graduate.* He cemented his reputation as a film actor by a series of challenging movie roles. Something of a perfectionist, Hoffman has a reputation for being difficult to work with, but he has been nominated for an Oscar seven times and has won twice, for *Kramer vs. Kramer* (1979) and *Rain Man* (1988). The American Film Institute gave him a Lifetime Achievement Award in 1999.

His fame as a film star turned out to be the ticket to get him on Broadway. In 1967, after the success of *The Graduate,* he was offered the lead in Murray Schisgal's *Jimmy Shine* (1968), which won him a Drama Desk Award. He would also have the opportunity to direct in 1974 with Schisgal's farce *All Over Town.* Living near Miller in ROXBURY, CONNECTICUT, after a friendly tennis match in summer 1983, the two agreed to coproduce a revival of *Death of a Salesman* that following year, bringing in ROBERT WHITEHEAD to assist. Hoffman had long revered Miller's work, even seeing him as something of an artistic father. Although the Chicago tryout was a little shaky, by the time they reached Washington, D.C., things were cohering. The Broadway opening was a big success, with sellout performances, and Hoffman won the Drama Desk Award for his turn as Willy Loman. Miller felt that Hoffman had captured much of his original concept of the role, especially as it had been written with the idea of a small man like Hoffman as Willy. Unfortunately, financial disagreements between Hoffman and Whitehead, forcing Miller to choose sides, led to a fallout between Miller and Whitehead for several years. In 1985, Hoffman reprised this role for television and won both an Emmy and a Golden Globe. In 1990, he produced Shakespeare's *The Merchant of Venice* on Broadway, in which he played Shylock to great acclaim, but he continues to spend most of his time working in films.

The Holocaust   Although we can learn about history from Holocaust dramas, literary critic Robert

Skloot believes that their greater significance "is that they search for meaning, or at least intelligibility, in an event which, from nearly every angle, shelters some kind of truth about us all." This is the very approach that Miller has chosen. The Holocaust is one of the most central events in Jewish history, and many schools use the Holocaust to instruct students in important social values that include tolerance, responsibility for self and others, respect for difference, and freedom from prejudice. The Holocaust is an extreme example of what can happen when the core values of a supposedly civilized society are overthrown. Skloot sees it as important that Holocaust playwrights should "struggle to make sense of the Holocaust experience and to draw from it some kind of truth which, whatever shape it takes, can inform our present and future lives. They know that within the Holocaust experience lie the most troubling questions we can raise about ourselves and others, about whole nations and peoples." As Miller declares in his *Theater Essays*, "the concentration camp is the final expression of human separateness and its ultimate consequence," and his Holocaust dramas try to teach audiences important lessons to combat such occurrences.

Miller has reacted strongly and sensitively to the Holocaust, an event that he felt reintroduced moral ambiguity into everyone's lives. For him, the death camps are a powerful symbol for contemporary life, with their accustomed violence, lack of communication and social responsibility, and dehumanization of feelings. He cites the Holocaust as the period when the world learned to turn away, and he feels that this is a problem that persists in society, whenever atrocities occur, from Bosnia to Africa. For Miller, the Holocaust is one of the most central events of the 20th century and one from which everyone can learn much about human nature. He insists that we combat the tendency to ignore what is unpleasant in life and involve ourselves before another Holocaust can occur. Humanity is "in a boiling soup," Miller has stated, "we change the flavor by what we add, and it changes all of us." It is not acceptable to refuse to act on the grounds that what a single person does cannot make a difference.

Although Miller observes what he sees as the lessons of the Holocaust in nearly all of his work,

there are a number of his plays that have a particularly close connection to the Holocaust, some actually reliving events from that period, including *Incident at Vichy, Playing for Time,* and *Broken Glass,* while others, like *After the Fall,* use the Holocaust as a key symbol.

It was not by accident that Miller made the dominating symbol of his stage set for *After the Fall* the "blasted stone tower of a German concentration camp." By this threatening tower, he tries to convey what he sees as the continuing, dark presence of the Holocaust in the minds of the cast and the audience. Throughout the play, Quentin relates various events of his life to the beliefs and attitudes that allowed the Holocaust to happen. Quentin's final discovery is that no one can be totally innocent, as we are all willing to betray others to save ourselves when placed in such a position. In this way, Quentin sees that blame for an event like the Holocaust needs to be accepted by everyone, however distant the event, for we are all capable of acting as the Nazis did.

Survivor guilt is central to *After the Fall,* and its direct connection to the Holocaust is inescapable. Only months prior to its writing, Miller and his wife, Inge Morath, visited Mauthausen concentration camp, after which they attended the Frankfurt war-crimes trials on which Miller wrote an essay for the *New York Herald Tribune.* Miller felt that he had witnessed at firsthand people's dangerous and irresponsible drive to forget or pretend innocence to deny guilt, and he objected to such a reaction, believing instead that we should each accept some responsibility for evil in the world. For Miller, *After the Fall* "was about how we—nations and individuals—destroy ourselves by denying that this is precisely what we are doing." After the Holocaust, Miller realizes that everyone is capable of evil and so demands that everyone be partly responsible for any evil that is performed in the world. Evil is represented in the play by the continual presence in the background of the death-camp watchtower. Miller wants us to know that remaining connected can bring suffering but that it is necessary to our remaining human. Quentin confesses his sins and conquers denial, reconnecting his life and forging a self-identity with which he can continue to live.

He learns what Miller sees as the lesson of the Holocaust.

Although the events of the Holocaust had become common knowledge by the end of World War II, and possibly earlier, it was not until the 1960s that literature attempted to approach the topic. While *After the Fall* utilizes the Holocaust as a symbolic icon, in other works, Miller depicts events more literally. *Incident at Vichy,* set in Vichy France of 1942 during a routine roundup of suspected Jews by Nazi troops, is an early dramatic example depicting what actually happened to Jews in Europe of that period. There has been controversy over the play because some critics see it as too reductive as well as historically inaccurate and therefore as such an insult to those who underwent such trials. Miller denies such charges, having based the central characters on real people, but he also insisted that dramatic license allows for some creativeness.

One troubling aspect in *Incident at Vichy* is Miller's depiction in the play of Jews as complicit in their own fate, through self-delusion, passive acceptance, or cowardice. This is a harsh possibility to accept but one that Miller sees as an important step to understanding how things happened so efficiently. Many Jews were impotent against the Nazis for the simple reason that what Hitler was attempting was so inconceivably evil they refused to believe that it was really happening. But Miller's focus in the play is not so much on the Jew as victim as on the role of the well-intentioned spectator; the question Miller wants to ask is what a person's moral responsibility is in the face of evil. This is the question Von Berg faces and passes with flying colors.

Broken Glass is set in New York of 1938 in the wake of Kristallnacht, and although it focuses on Sylvia Gellburg's mysterious illness and her failed marriage, the various characters' reactions to news of increasing Nazi hostility toward Jews in Europe are integral to the play. Miller sees Nazism as defined by its strong conformist pressure, chilling technological power, and erosion of autonomy—all of which led to people being stripped of their humanity. Miller resists such forces, just as he insists that the Nazi regime should have been

resisted. Believing strongly that an event like the Holocaust involves everyone, Miller insists that there can be no turning away without cost. The denial, resignation, or ignorance that we observe in *Broken Glass* is tantamount to complicity. Nonaction, Miller informs us, whatever its rationale, becomes destructive when it allows certain other actions to occur. Thus, the issue of potency versus impotency is central to the play.

Miller also takes us directly into the concentration camps of Auschwitz. Loosely based on the memoirs of real Holocaust survivor, Fania Fénelon, *Playing For Time,* follows the experiences of Fania from roundup to release. Miller explores the psychological impact of the Holocaust on those directly involved: Jews, Poles, and Nazis alike. Fania and others survive because they are useful to the Nazis as camp musicians, but they all survive at a cost, especially when they have to see so many others die. One of Fania's biggest incentives to stay alive is her self-chosen role as witness.

Miller depicts the evil dehumanizing effects of the Holocaust that threaten to engulf Fania against the humanizing and transcendent possibilities of her music with which she is able to stay connected in her role as a camp musician. Fania describes everyone's disorientation and feelings of dehumanization by the Nazis at the start of the play: "Like cattle. With the doors sealed up, nobody knew whether we were going north, south, east or west [. . .] never sure quite why." The important mood that this speech tries to convey is the sense of unawareness and disbelief that emphasizes the underlying pointlessness of the Nazi plan and the unfeeling cruelty of its execution.

The arrival at the camp is a study in dehumanization. Conditions in the boxcar on the way to the camp were bad enough, but Miller shows also how the Nazis attempt to take away everything from these people, from their few simple possessions to their dignity and identities. The contrast between the way the Kapos brutally strike without discrimination at the prisoners and the care with which they handle their belongings is indicative of the way in these camps that things become more valuable than people. But just because they treat these people as worthless does not mean that they are, and it is a definition that all the camp inmates must struggle against, incessantly, to maintain their spirits to survive.

Miller's aim is not just to educate his audience about the Holocaust but also to show us the results of such brutality whenever we allow it to occur. Miller explained to interviewer James Atlas that the situation that he describes in this play is "emblematic for Jews and for the human race; it revealed mankind at the abyss." In this light, we should not view the struggles of Fania and her friends to survive as viable human beings as merely a historical Jewish problem but as one which applies to all of humanity in the here and now. In Miller's eyes, the Holocaust is an event that affects us all, and as its living heirs, we each hold the responsibility that all survivors should accept—to try and ensure that such an event cannot occur again.

Miller has been criticized for his depiction of Nazis in *Playing for Time* as possessing human qualities, from a love of good music to Mandel's infatuation with, Ladislaus, the little blonde boy who came in on the transports and her evident deep distress when she is forced to let him go to the gas chamber. Mandel will at one moment take a woman's child and viciously beat her with a riding crop and the next will display a genuine concern for Fania's well-being, but such contradictions are essential to Miller's depiction. Many critics agree that Nazism is better depicted as terrifying for its very ordinariness rather than for any mythical demonic greatness.

Miller portrays his Nazi characters as flawed human beings rather than as absolute monsters; he recognizes that to imply that the Nazis are not human because of their inhumane agenda is to lessen the impact of the lesson of the Holocaust that he so keenly wishes to convey. The fact is that Nazis were human beings, and they could at times display humane reactions—they were not complete monsters even when they behaved monstrously. As Miller stresses in his article "Our Guilt For the World's Evil," as human beings, we all, sadly, have the same capacity within us for evil that the Nazis displayed, and this is something against which we need to be on constant guard. A drama like *Playing for Time* shows that while the Holocaust itself may be a unique event (at

no previous time had a nation so systematically attempted to destroy a people purely because of who they were), it is still an event that was created and executed by human beings and as such, contains universal lessons.

FURTHER READING

Atlas, James. "The Creative Journey of Arthur Miller Leads Back to Broadway and TV." *New York Times*, September 28, 1980, sec. 2: pp. 1, 32.

Bettleheim, Bruno. *The Informed Heart*. New York: Avon, 1960.

Des Pres, Terence. *The Survivor*. New York: Oxford University Press, 1976.

Isser, Edward. R. "Arthur Miller and the Holocaust." *Essays in Theatre* 10.2 (May 1992): 155–164.

Langer, Lawrence. *The Holocaust and the Literary Imagination*. New Haven, Conn.: Yale University Press, 1975.

Skloot, Robert. Introduction. In *The Theatre of the Holocaust*, edited by Skloot, 3–37. (Madison: University of Wisconsin Press, 1982).

Steiner, George. "Jewish Values in the Post-Holocaust Future: A Symposium." *Judaism* 16.3 (1967): 269–299.

House Un-American Activities Committee The House Un-American Activities Committee, popularly referred to as HUAC, existed as an investigative committee of the U.S. House of Representatives from 1938 to 1975 (although for its final six years, its name was changed to the Committee on Internal Security). When it was abolished in 1975, its functions were transferred to the House Judiciary Committee. It developed from the McCormack-Dickstein House Committee, which was named after its chairman and vice chairman, John W. McCormack and Samuel Dickstein. It was set up in 1934 to investigate propaganda, especially that of the Nazis: Its aim was to find out how subversive foreign propaganda was entering the country and the organizations that were responsible for its spread. It investigated and supported allegations of a fascist plot to seize the White House, known as the Business Plot. In May 1938, it was replaced by the Dies Committee, which swung to the other political extreme by investigating COMMUNISM.

Chaired by Martin Dies and cochaired by Samuel Dickstein, from 1938 to 1944 the attentions of the Dies Committee was supposedly aimed at German-American involvement in Nazi and Ku Klux Klan activity, but their investigation into the latter was minimal, especially under the influence of the openly racist committee member John Rankin (after whose name the committee was sometimes referred), who notoriously suggested that the Klan was above suspicion as "an old American institution." Rankin would be one of the targets of Miller's 1940s play *You're Next!* Instead of the Klan, HUAC decided to concentrate on investigating the possibility that the U.S. Communist Party had infiltrated the Works Progress Administration, including the FEDERAL THEATRE PROJECT. Their investigation led to the June 1939 shutdown of the project just months after Miller had managed to join.

HUAC would become a permanent committee in 1946 to investigate suspected threats of subversion or propaganda that attacked "the form of government guaranteed by our Constitution," but their ostensible target was anyone who exhibited communist sympathies or had at any time been affiliated with any potential communist organization. People were called before the committee often based on inconclusive or questionable evidence, and even if the committee's investigation came up empty, many of these people's lives were subsequently ruined, with their losing employment or being ostracized because of mere suspicion. It was this aspect that later characterized these investigations as "witch hunts" and led Miller to write *The Crucible* in an attempt to expose the hypocrisy of the increasingly ritualistic hearings.

Scant attention was paid while the committee investigated only government employees, but it came into the limelight after WORLD WAR II when they began to go after more prominent public figures in the entertainment industry. Artists, actors, and writers were subpoenaed to prove that they were not nor had they been active in the Communist Party. If they confessed to any communist activity, then they were expected to name the names of anyone else involved or they would be sent to jail for contempt of Congress. Involved in the business, Miller had many friends, such as

LOUIS UNTERMEYER, who would suffer from being put in the committee's sights.

The campaign against artists began with an initial nine days of hearings in 1947 into alleged communist propaganda in the Hollywood film industry. This led to the conviction on contempt of Congress charges of "The Hollywood Ten" for refusal to answer questions. Each had pled the Fifth Amendment, refusing to testify on the grounds that they might incriminate themselves. Even though none had confessed to any communist sympathies, the whole group was sent to jail for sentences ranging from six to 12 months, and they were subsequently "blacklisted." The example of their harsh treatment scared many into going along with whatever the committee asked rather than face such punishment themselves. ELIA KAZAN, CLIFFORD ODETS, and LEE J. COBB were all people who would agree to name names before the committee in the 1950s rather than face blacklisting, although Kazan and Odets would each declare more patriotic motives for their naming names. Others, including LILLIAN HELLMAN and Arthur Miller, when they were subpoenaed, refused to name names in a defense of the right to freedom of speech, regardless of the risks. In the film industry alone, more than 300 actors, writers, and directors were denied work in the United States through the informal Hollywood blacklist that evolved. Some, like Charlie Chaplin, left the country to find work, while others wrote under pseudonyms or the names of colleagues.

The anticommunist paranoia known as McCarthyism occurred in the 1950s, as suspicions increased and the government saw itself as actively countering alleged U.S. Communist Party subversion, its leadership, and others suspected of being communists or communist sympathizers. Sen. Joseph McCarthy's involvement with the phenomenon that would bear his name began with a speech that he made in 1950 to the Republican Women's Club of Wheeling, West Virginia. He produced a piece of paper that he claimed contained a list of known communists working for the State Department, which resulted in a flood of press attention.

Although McCarthy would serve on committees covering both government and military investigations into communist infiltration, he did not serve on HUAC, although his scaremongering helped to create the atmosphere that gave HUAC its credibility. After a 1954 documentary aired by newscaster/journalist Edward R. Murrow in which Murrow challenged many of McCarthy's statements, McCarthy began to lose public favor, but HUAC's investigations continued. In a 1983 essay, "The Night Ed Murrow Struck Back," Miller referred to Murrow's broadcast as offering a "voice of decency" that demonstrated "the persistence of scruple as a living principle" and claimed that the United States was "in Murrow's eternal debt."

By showing the connection of McCarthyism to the way people acted in Salem, Miller suggested in his play *The Crucible* that the 1950s U.S. vision of communism had become a moral issue that viewed communists as being in league with the devil. This was what made people hate communists so deeply and allowed them to drop all of the usual civilities. Any opposition to HUAC was seen in terms of "diabolical malevolence" that allowed no sympathy; any sign of fear or reticence would be taken as an admission of guilt. Miller was never actually blacklisted, partly because this punishment was less endemic within U.S. theater, but he did lose two potential film contracts, and there was some active campaigning by patriotic groups, such as the American Legion and the Catholic War Veterans, against his plays.

During this period, Miller spoke out publicly against HUAC's influence and for artistic freedom. For FREDRIC MARCH and his wife, Florence Eldridge, he would also adapt Henrik Ibsen's *An Enemy of the People*, a play in which the lead character significantly is accused by mob hysteria. The Marches felt that they had been losing work because a reporter had accused them of being communists, and they saw this play as a response to such scaremongering. Given the climate of the times, the production was not a success, closing after only 36 performances, and the press accused Miller, not for the first time, of creating anti-American propaganda. Miller was strongly suspected of holding communist sympathies and was being daily observed by the Federal Bureau of Investigation (FBI). Although not at the center of the situation, Miller was affected, and more importantly, he real-

ized just how far this growing atmosphere of distrust was affecting his country. The disconcerting experience of Miller and his friends during the years of HUAC's power lies behind much of the action in his play *After the Fall* and forms the background to Eddie Carbone informing on Marco and Rodolpho in *A View From the Bridge*. HUAC changed the lives of many Americans, robbing them of their livelihoods and security as a result of the committee's investigations.

Miller was not subpoenaed before HUAC until June 1956. He received his notification while in Reno, Nevada, establishing his residency requirement for a divorce from MARY SLATTERY so that he could marry MARILYN MONROE. It was quite likely his association with this currently popular movie star that brought him to the committee's attention. In *Timebends: A Life*, Miller relates how Francis E. Walter, the chairman of the committee, reportedly offered to go easy if Miller would allow Walter to be photographed shaking hands with Monroe. Miller rejected the offer. At his hearing on June 21st, Miller faced six congressmen, their counsel Richard Arens, and an audience of spectators that included ELI WALLACH. Miller had recently applied for a passport so that he could accompany Monroe to GREAT BRITAIN where she would be filming, and so that he could oversee the opening of his two-act play, *A View from the Bridge*. The hearing ostensibly was to determine whether or not Miller had denied under oath on a passport application that he had any ties to communism. The truer motive seemed to try to publicly prove that Miller had been an actual party member.

Backed by his lawyer, Joseph Rauh, Jr., Miller was quizzed about his contributions toward and support of potential communist organizations, his involvement at the Waldorf–Astoria Peace Conference, and his support of communist China and Spanish civil war refugees. Miller did not deny involvement in any of this, admitting that he had signed plenty of petitions in the 1930s and 1940s and contributed "a dollar or two" to what he had seen as worthy causes, but he had done nothing illegal. Arens then brought up *You're Next* and a play that Miller had written with NORMAN ROSTEN, *Listen, My Children*, from which he read the opening description as rather unconvincing evidence of Miller's communist agenda. When pressed about his current political stance, Miller began by stating, "I am still opposed to anyone being penalized for advocating anything" and concluded, "I am opposed to the laying down of any limits upon the freedom of literature." It would be such a belief that Miller would pursue in his later years working with PEN.

Miller was next questioned about his relationship with Kazan since Kazan had spoken to the committee, and Miller admitted that they had fallen out but that he had not been publicly critical of him. Tiring of the committe's questions, Miller asked for the point of the inquiry. Arens asked him directly if he had ever applied for membership to the Communist Party and went on to ask for the names of people whom he had seen at the meetings that he admitted he had attended. Pointing out they were asking about something that would have taken place 16 years previously, he asserted a lack of any clear recollection. "I want you to understand," Miller explained, "that I am not protecting the Communists . . I am trying to, and I will, protect myself. I could not use the name of another person and bring trouble on him. . . . I ask you not to ask that question." He refused to respond to any more such questions asserting, very much as John Proctor had done, "My conscience will not permit me to use the name of another person." He heroically stood by these convictions despite being threatened with a citation of contempt that might have led to a jail sentence.

Six days following this exchange, the committee gave him an ultimatum to name names or to be cited. He refused and arranged to defend the citation charge in court following his return from Great Britain, as he had been allowed his passport. On March 1, Miller entered a plea of not guilty, and the trial began on May 14, 1957. During the trial, Miller's lawyer insisted that HUAC was only after Miller to restore itself in the limelight because of his connection to Monroe, and he attacked the relevancy of the questions that Miller had been asked to answer. The government argued that the relevance went to Miller's credibility. Judge Charles F. McLaughlin found him guilty on a point of law but being sympathetic to his rationale, reduced the one-year sentence to a single suspended month and a $500 fine. Rather than accept a conviction that seemed to represent wrongdoing, Miller appealed. By August of the following year, the conviction was overturned by the U.S. Court of Appeals on the grounds that the questions that he had been asked to answer served no legislative purpose, but Miller still had to pay the $40,000 in costs. In 1999, the American Civil Liberties Union, who had refused to assist him in 1957, apologized and gave him a $5,000 award for protecting the right to privacy during the period of anticommunist hysteria.

Humanism The term *humanism* covers a broad category of ethical philosophies that affirm the dignity and worth of all people, based on the ability to determine right and wrong by appeal to universal human qualities. Humanism shows up in both religious and secular belief systems, but its emphasis is always on the concepts of rationality, self-determinism, everyone sharing a common history, and the value of experience. The core ideology of humanism, as its name implies, is centered on human beings rather than on any external power. It entails a commitment to the search for truth and morality through human means in support of human interests. Based on the commonality of human nature, humanists tend to espouse a universal morality system in which every individual across the globe shares a responsibility for the eventual outcome. His essay "Our Guilt for the World's Evil" firmly places Miller in the humanist camp, and his plays are equally replete with humanist philosophy.

As early as 1945, in his essay "Should Ezra Pound Be Shot?" Miller insisted that we live in a world "where humanism must conquer lest humanity be destroyed." He also asserted that literature's role is to "nurture the conscience of man." In an essay on Miller's first BROADWAY play, *The Man Who Had All the Luck,* theater scholar Brenda Murphy speaks of Miller's commitment to a "basic humanism" and asserts that he has been "examining and developing" what this means throughout his career. Miller intends to lead humanity, through his plays, to embrace more humanistic lives that will restore the sense of meaning that many people have lost. While toward the close of the 20th century Miller acknowledged the fragmented, dissolute state of our society, he also stressed the need for recuperation through the reassertion of values, continuity, and connectiveness. In short, Miller's plays strove to reassert our sense of belonging to a responsible community.

In *Modern American Drama,* CHRISTOPHER BIGSBY explains how Miller was distressed by the growing trend of theater in the 1980s to "prize and celebrate disconnectiveness for its own sake," feeling that, although disconnectiveness certainly existed, art should offer a fundamental "denial of the very chaos it observes and the artist is one who peoples desolation and inscribes the meaning he suspects may not exist." In the fragmented and suspicious world in which people seemed to be living, plays and performance could create an alternative world in which a lost sense of community would be momentarily restored among both actors and audience: It was toward this end that much of Miller's drama strove. Pretty much every Miller play from *No Villain* to *Finishing the Picture* espouses a humanism that views humankind and its development as the highest ethical goal. The balance between the individual and social interests and needs that these plays promote is achieved by asserting moral responsibility toward self and others.

With Miller's agreement, in Matthew Roudané's *Conversations with Arthur Miller,* STEVEN CENTOLA sums up Miller's work as deriving from a "vision of the human condition as a kind of existential humanism—a vision that emphasizes self-determinism and social responsibility and that is optimistic and affirms life by acknowledging man's possibilities in the face of his limitations and even sometimes in the dramatization of his failures." Miller's work displays an inherent humanism that insists that our creative will is sufficient to provide us with a sense of human values. He believes that we have the capability to define ourselves, the society we inhabit, and what we will stand for because we have free will. For Miller, morality is not innate but is a matter of reasoned choice, and so, though in one sense confining, moral responsibility is a matter of freedom so long as we believe in the existence of free will and in man as an essentially responsible and progressive being. Miller ensures that we do not fall into the trap of forgetting that we have the important and self-affirming capacity to choose; whatever the state of the world, we still have free will, and it is our responsibility to create the society in which we would live.

I

Ibsen, Henrik (1828–1906)   Born into a wealthy family in Skien, Norway, on March 20, 1828, Henrik Johan Ibsen would become known as the father of modern drama and would write an extensive selection of highly influential plays. When he was six, his father's business failed, so he grew up in poverty, being sent at age 15 to a small rural village called Grimstad to apprentice to an apothecary. He found the job and the surroundings dreary and oppressive. Three years later, he had an illegitimate child with a servant for whom he had to pay maintenance. In 1850, he gave up his job and went to Christiania (now Oslo) to become a student, but failing the entrance requirements, he tried his hand instead at writing poetry and drama. The first play that he wrote was *Catalina* (1850), under the pseudonym Brynjolf Bjarme. It was a historical verse TRAGEDY in the typical romantic vein of the period. Shortly after this, he signed up with the newly formed Bergen National Theatre as assistant stage manager.

He worked his way up in the theater to stage director and resident dramatist, was married, and began a family. In 1864, the group went bankrupt, so he moved to Rome. Not expecting to get them produced, he started to write more experimental plays such as *Brand* (1866) and *Peer Gynt* (1867). On publication, these visions of human vocation, idealism, and self-realization gained him a reputation in Scandinavia and a government pension, although they would not be produced on stage until 1885 and 1876, respectively. In 1875, he moved to Munich to explore what was happening in German theater and

began to write realistic prose that dealt with social issues. Early examples of these were *A Doll's House* (1879), which sparked great controversy over its portrayal of the double standards of marriage, and *Ghosts* (1881), about the damaging effects of syphilis.

The REALISM of Ibsen goes beyond mere set detail, although that is an important aspect of how he wished these plays to be produced. He wanted to create psychologically real people in commonplace social situations. Ahead of fellow playwrights August Strindberg and George Bernard Shaw, Ibsen would champion "discussion plays" over the moralistic "well-made plays" of the period. Well-made plays tended toward melodramatic plots and tidy denouements that left little for the audience to consider. Ibsen's plays continued to flout convention; *Enemy of the People* (1882), *The Wild Duck* (1884), and *Hedda Gabler* (1890) all explore Ibsen's concept of the "life-lie." In his book, *The Quintessence of Ibsenism* (1891), Shaw explained this principle and its relation to realism, helping to cement Ibsen's reputation as the forerunner of realistic drama. Ibsen and Shaw both believed that many people found reality so unpleasant that they tended to cover it with a mask of idealism to create an alternative, unreal "life" for themselves that was essentially a "lie." Both saw such self-deception as potentially dangerous, though on occasions necessary. In their plays, both playwrights tended to strip away the masks behind which their characters hide, forcing them to face the truth to reassess their lives.

The plays that Ibsen wrote toward the end of his career, after he had returned to Norway in 1891, include *The Master Builder* (1892), *Little Eyolf* (1894), and *When We Dead Awaken* (1899), and were more symbolic and mythic in nature. They were also highly autobiographical, reflecting many of the neuroses of his later life in their explorations of the conflict between art and life. In 1900, Ibsen's first stroke left him impaired; the following year, another one made him virtually helpless. He lingered for five years more, before dying at age 78.

Ibsen has long been a staple in theaters around the Western world; for example, during the 20th century, there would be 89 productions of his plays on Broadway alone, the most popular being *Hedda Gabler*, *Ghosts*, and *A Doll's House*. *An Enemy of the People* has so far appeared on Broadway in nine different productions, but only the one in 1950 was Miller's adaptation.

Miller was first introduced to the work of Ibsen in KENNETH ROWE's playwrighting seminars at the UNIVERSITY OF MICHIGAN. Rowe used Ibsen extensively to teach his students about how to write a play. As Miller explains in his essay "Ibsen and the Drama of Today," although he felt drawn to Ibsen's "indignation at the social lives of his time," it was the structure of his plays that most attracted him because it created "models of a stringent economy of means to create immense symphonic images of tragic proportion." Miller could see in Ibsen's work the playwright's craft, viewing Ibsen's plays as ones to emulate, in which everything fit and nothing was extraneous. It was this that inspired him to spend two years perfecting *All My Sons*, the play of his that shows the strongest influence from Ibsen. Also interesting to Miller was Ibsen's sense of the past and its influence on the present, which is from where he developed his sense of the chickens coming home to roost. For Miller, as he explained in "Introduction to *Arthur Miller's Collected Plays*," the "real" in Ibsen's realism is his "insistence upon valid causation," and he sees himself similarly striving as a playwright "to make understandable what is complex without distorting and oversimplifying what cannot be explained."

The concept of the delayed revelation, in which the audience is given discreet clues and symbols of something that is not apparent at the time but that later comes to light, was something that Ibsen pioneered. In *All My Sons*, we see this in subtle comments that gradually clue in the audience to Joe Keller's initial crime and and his son's subsequent suicide, as well as in the symbolism of the tree in their yard (which comes to stand for Larry, the son who committed suicide) and the repeated imagery of imprisonment (which surrounds Keller). Until he began *All My Sons*, Miller admits in his "Introduction to *Arthur Miller's Collected Plays*" that he had only once been "truly engrossed in a production—when Ruth Gordon played JED HARRIS's production of *A Doll's House*," and he was quick to acknowledge Ibsen as a chief dramatic influence, especially on his early work. He welcomed the opportunity in 1950 to create his own version of Ibsen's *An Enemy of the People* and has written several essays in which he defends Ibsen as a playwright still relevant to contemporary theater.

In "The Family in Modern Drama," Miller insists that while Ibsen's characters and situations may seem real, his subject matter is worked out on a symbolic level, which shows that realism is capable of greater complexity than some would allow. For Miller, Ibsen saw connections that help to reveal the hidden laws of life, and "Shadows of the Gods" includes an explanation of how, through Ibsen, Miller first formulated the idea of the writer as "the destroyer of chaos." By illuminating the hidden laws that Ibsen saw directing people's lives, the playwright could help people better understand their lives. In "Ibsen and the Drama of Today," Miller points out how in the 1930s, Ibsen had been a favorite of the Left for his "radical politics" but rarely was performed because his plays were perceived as dry and insufficiently entertaining. Critics wrongly thought, in Miller's eyes, that Ibsen lacked a "poetic spirit" and did not view him like Shaw, as a "visionary architect." Miller suggests that we partly miss Ibsen's lyricism as we only hear him in translation. His ideas, however, are sufficient to make his plays worthwhile and, Miller insists, not just the realistic social plays but also his mystical and metaphysical dramas.

Miller's sense of realism and the importance of the past come directly from Ibsen, as well as the idea of creating characters with whom an audience can identify, that they might recognize the relevance of the play's message to their own lives. In addition, Miller took from Ibsen an idea that remains central to much of his writing: the difficulty of finding true happiness in an essentially unpleasant and hostile world. But as Miller developed new techniques of his own, he left behind many of those that he had learned from Ibsen, although he never dropped the belief he shared with Ibsen that while plays should tell interesting stories, they must always be morally and socially responsible.

FURTHER READING

Barat, Urbashi. "Past and Present Reading *Death of a Salesman* in the Light of *The Wild Duck.*" In *Arthur Miller: Twentieth Century Legend*, edited by Syed Mashkoor Ali, 99–109. (Jaipur, India: Surabhi, 2006).

Dworkin, Martin S. "Miller and Ibsen." *Humanist* 3 (May/June 1951): 111–115.

Haugen, Einar. "Ibsen as Fellow Traveler: Arthur Miller's Adaptation of *Enemy of the People.*" *Scandinavian Studies* 51 (1979): 343–353.

Miller, Arthur. "Ibsen's Warning." *Index on Censorship* 18.6–7 (July–August 1989): 74–76.

Murphy, Brenda. "*The Man Who Had All the Luck:* Miller's Answer to *The Master Builder.*" *American Drama* 6.1 (Fall 1996): 29–41.

———. "The Tradition of Social Drama: Miller and His Forbears." In *Cambridge Companion to Arthur Miller*, edited by Christopher Bigsby 10–20. (Cambridge, London: Cambridge University Press, 1997).

Inge, William (1913–1973)   William Motter Inge grew up in Independence, Kansas, a small town in which he felt out of place, but trapped. He graduated from the University of Kansas in 1935 before moving to New York in 1940 where, ironically, he began to recognize more fully his Midwestern roots and claim his past through his writing. He fluctuated between the stage (both acting and writing) and a more lucrative career in teaching and journalism. His first play, *Come Back, Little Sheba*, was initially produced in 1949 by THEATRE GUILD in Connecticut before a 1950 BROADWAY success that established Inge in the world of drama. Other award-winning plays would follow, including the Pulitzer Prize-winning *Picnic* (1953), *Bus Stop* (1955), and *The Dark at the Top of the Stairs* (1957). He also won an Oscar for his 1961 film adaptation of *Splendor in the Grass.*

Often referred to as the playwright of the Midwest, Inge is best known for his perceptive psychological portraits and for his starkly realistic rendition of motivations and behaviors. The widespread recognition that *Picnic* received caused Inge to be favorably compared to TENNESSEE WILLIAMS and Miller, the first with whom he was friendly and received early support. His later works had troubled productions and met with less success. Disconsolate and feeling a failure, Inge committed suicide in 1973.

Inge had donated his manuscripts to his alma mater, Independence Community College, in 1969. After his death, the school named its theater for him and in 1982 launched an annual play festival in his memory, at which one playwright is given an award for Distinguished Achievement in the American Theater. The first recipient was Inge, but Miller received this honor in 1995.

J

Judaism Miller's status as a Jewish playwright has been overlooked by some, but it colors many aspects of his philosophy and work, not the least, his underlying morality. As Terry Otten suggests, Miller "alludes to his Jewishness and to biblical themes perhaps more than any other contemporary Jewish playwright, including Pinter and Mamet," and Louis Harap sees Miller's optimism and insistence that life has meaning and should be lived to the full as being firmly rooted in Judaism. Enoch Brater has pointed to Miller's Judaic influences, suggesting that they are most evidenced in Miller having his characters show us that: "Guilt is passive, responsibility active." Jewish theology does not espouse guilt, and it contains no real concept of sin. To do right is natural and sensible, for not to do right reduces the humanity of the individual. To passively accept guilt tends to lead to complacency.

The main message behind Miller's essay "Our Guilt for the World's Evil" is to insist that we should transform guilt actively into responsibility and that this will allow us to transcend it. It is only by accepting our responsibility for evil, Miller believes, that we can break its hold over us and restore a moral order to society. In a connected fashion, each year at Yom Kippur, every practicing Jew accepts responsibility for all evil done the previous year by themselves or others, atones for it to God, and promises to try to do better the next year. Although Miller did not attend High Holiday services past his youth, he seems to have internalized this essential message of Yom Kippur in the moral judgements he lays on his characters. A basic trait of Judaism is its recognition that all is not perfect. This is why observant Jews feel commanded to work for the improvement of this world and the enrichment of the lives of all its inhabitants. Such a motive seems to loom large in the work of Miller, even while he did not consider himself a practicing Jew.

Miller's interest in the past and its influence on the present also has strong Judaic roots. Since Judaism has no single institutional structure, scholar Nancy Haggard–Gilson suggests that Jews "must rely upon the recognition of a shared past and tradition which retain continuity and cohesiveness." The Jewish storyteller hopes to impart a lesson less through allegory "than through a historical narrative that makes the past part of the present." Miller is one such storyteller as his relationship to the past in nearly all of his work echoes such a dynamic. Another of the major 20th-century influences on Judaism is the way in which Jews have dealt with the HOLOCAUST, assigning it both a particular and universal importance in the world. CHRISTOPHER BIGSBY, who sees Miller's Jewish identity as being "crucial" to understanding much of his work, also suggests that Miller's sense of impending catastrophe, a feeling that lies in the background of much of his work, derives from his Jewishness. Bigsby goes on to suggest: "Whether practising Jew or not . . . [Miller] is of the Book, aware of the mythic potency of archetypes," and Bigsby points to Old

Testament resonances that sound through much of Miller's work, from the Joblike David Beeves to the countless (and in one case literal) evocations of Cain and Abel in his warring brothers.

Judaism and its beliefs heavily influenced Miller's upbringing and provided him with a strong moral and ethical center evident in his works and life, even while he saw himself as an atheist. His mother's father, LOUIS BARNETT, always wore a yarmulke and spoke mostly Yiddish; his great-grandfather was an observant Jew with a long beard. Miller attended Hebrew school after his regular school to learn the prayers and the readings expected of him at his bar mitzvah, which took place when he was age 13, shortly before the family moved to BROOKLYN. Miller admits to having a strong Jewish identity, having fully absorbed the culture if not the religion. It is this, he believes, that has given him his sense of "power and reassurance" and has defined his moral outlook. In a 1948 article, "Concerning Jews Who Write," Miller wrote, "To my mind the Hebrew religion is a matter of option to the Jewish writer as to all Jews, but Jewish culture is his to defend whether he is Jewish or not. For if he does not defend it he may die of its destruction."

Many critics have argued whether or not such characters as Willy Loman are Jewish and based their claims as to Miller's authenticity as a Jewish playwright on their findings. The characters in Miller's student plays were clearly Jewish, with speech full of Jewish idioms and outlooks redolent of Judaism. When *They Too Arise* was turned down for being "too Jewish,' wanting to be produced, Miller toned down this aspect of his writing for a time, although a close analysis even of his early dramas, including *All My Sons* and *Death of a Salesman*, can find remaining Jewish idioms and concepts. However, Miller has openly embraced his Jewish roots in both his plays and fiction with a broad selection of characters who are definitively Jewish. Miller explores issues of the Jewish identity and Jewish issues to a degree that makes any claim that he neglected his Jewish background seem ludicrous. These plays include *Boro Hall Nocturne, The Half-Bridge, Incident at Vichy, After the Fall, Playing for Time, The Ride down Mt. Morgan,* and *Broken Glass* and the novel *Focus,* the novella *Homely Girl, A Life,* and the short stories "Fame," "Monte Sant' Angelo," "I Don't Need You any More," and "The Performance."

FURTHER READING

Bigsby, Christopher. "Arthur Miller as a Jewish." *Arthur Miller: A Critical Study.* Cambridge: Cambridge University Press, 2005: 473–489.

———. "Arthur Miller: The Rememberer." In *Remembering and Imagining the Holocaust.* New York: Cambridge University Press, 176–218.

Brater, Enoch. "Ethnics and Ethnicity in the Plays of Arthur Miller." In *From Hester Street to Hollywood,* edited by Sarah Blacher Cohen, 123–136. (Bloomington: Indiana University Press, 1983).

Desafy–Grignard, Christiane. "Jewishness and Judaism Revisited in Two Short Stories by Arthur Miller: 'Monte Sant' Angelo' and 'I Don't Need You Anymore.'" *Journal of the Short Story in English* 43 (Autumn 2004): 87–106.

Haggard–Gilson, Nancy. "The Construction of Jewish American Identity in the Novels of the Second Generation." *Studies in American Jewish Literature* 11 (Spring 1992): 22–35.

Harap, Louis. *Dramatic Encounters: The Jewish Presence in Twentieth Century American Drama, Poetry, and Humor and the Black–Jewish Literary Relationship.* New York: Greenwood, 1987.

Mesher, David R. "Arthur Miller's *Focus:* The First American Novel of the Holocaust?" *Judaism* 29, no. 4 (1980): 469–479.

Otten, Terry. *The Temptation of Innocence in the Dramas of Arthur Miller.* Columbia: University of Missouri Press, 2002.

K

Kazan, Elia (1909–2003)   Born in what is now Istanbul, Turkey (then Constantinople), and named Elia Kazanjoglous, the famous director of stage and screen came with his parents to the United States as a young child as part of the great wave of immigrants prior to World War I. The family settled in New York City and changed their last name to Kazan. His father opened a business selling Oriental rugs and carpets, expecting his eldest son to follow him into the family concern. Kazan recorded these early experiences on film in 1963 with *America, America.* Schooled in New York and New Rochelle, Kazan graduated from Williams College in 1930 and, to his father's disappointment, decided to study acting at the Yale School of Drama before joining the GROUP THEATER after a short spell with the THEATRE GUILD as assistant stage manager.

KERMIT BLOOMGARDEN recalls initially hiring Kazan as an office boy, but Kazan apprenticed at the Group Theater under LEE STRASBERG and HAROLD CLURMAN and learned his craft well. It is little surprise that many of his later stage and film hits were filled with actors trained in the Method. In 1932, he met and married playwright Molly Day Thacher. Older then Kazan, he sought her astute advice on many projects, and although he had a number of extramarital affairs—including one with MARILYN MONROE in 1951 before he passed her on to Miller—he and Molly had four children and stayed together until her death in 1963 while he was rehearsing *After the Fall.* In 1967, he married Barbara Loden, who had played Maggie in that pro-

duction, until she too died in 1980. His third wife, Frances Rudge survived him.

Kazan started out as an actor and made his BROADWAY debut in 1932 in Rose Albert Porter's *Chrysalis.* He would appear in supporting roles in several Group Theater productions, including Sidney Kingsley's *Men in White* (1933), for which he was also stage manager, and a number of CLIFFORD ODETS's plays, including *Waiting for Lefty* (1935), *Till the Day I Die* (1935), *Paradise Lost* (1935), and *Golden Boy* (1937). Miller recalls seeing him in the latter, and Kazan would also appear in the British premiere of this the following year. His final stage role was in Lucille Prumbs's *Five Alarm Waltz* (1941) that closed after four performances.

Kazan's first professional stint as a stage director had been in conjunction with Alfred Saxe for a Theatre of Action production, *The Young Go First* in 1935, for which MORDECAI GORELIK designed the set. He would not direct again on Broadway until 1939 with Robert Ardrey's *Thunder Rock* (1939). After Hy S. Kraft's *Cafe Crown* (1942), Kazan only directed, but there followed a string of hits, including Thornton Wilder's *The Skin of Our Teeth* (1942), S. N. Behrman's *Jacobowsky and the Colonel* (1944), and Arnaud D'Usseau's *Deep Are the Roots* (1945). At this time, he also took to directing films, beginning with *A Tree Grows in Brooklyn* (1945).

Kazan's first Miller production was in 1947 with *All My Sons.* Miller's agent, KAY BROWN had sent the script to Clurman and Kazan, and they immediately came on board. Kazan was chosen to direct, and Gorelik would design the set. Kazan had taken Miller with him to watch him direct the film *Boomerang!* while they were deciding who to cast in *All My Sons*. After seeing their work on the movie, Miller asked for and got Ed Begley, Karl Malden, and ARTHUR KENNEDY for his play. As was his policy, Kazan worked closely with the playwright and the actors and won a Tony Award for his direction of *All My Sons*. He had also been working with Cheryl Crawford and Robert Lewis to found the ACTORS STUDIO, and toward the end of 1947, his landmark direction of TENNESSEE WILLIAMS's *A Streetcar Named Desire* opened. He invited Miller to a New Haven tryout and Miller was impressed, acknowledging in *Timebends: A Life* that this play partly inspired him to write his next play, *Death of a Salesman*, that Kazan would also direct.

Kazan would work closely with Williams on a number of his plays and films, including stage premieres of *Camino Real* (1953) with ELI WALLACH, *Cat on a Hot Tin Roof* (1955), and *Sweet Bird of Youth* (1959) and the films *A Streetcar Named Desire* (1951) and *Baby Doll* (1956), the latter also with Wallach. The film performances that he elicited from Marlon Brando in *A Streetcar Named Desire*, *Viva Zapata!* (1952), and *On the Waterfront* (1954) (for which Kazan won an Oscar) helped to make Brando a star. Other stage successes include Robert Anderson's *Tea and Sympathy* (1953), WILLIAM INGE's *The Dark at the Top of the Stairs* (1957), and Archibald MacLeish's *J. B.* (1958) and on film his Oscar-winning *Gentleman's Agreement* (1947), as well as *East of Eden* (1955) and *Splendor in the Grass* (1961). He also produced several of these works. His final film, outside of personal biography and some documentaries, would be a version of F. Scott Fitzgerald's *The Last Tycoon* (1976) starring Robert De Niro with a screenplay by HAROLD PINTER. Kazan was awarded an Oscar for lifetime achievement in 1999, an honor that was considered to be controversial.

The reason for the controversy was the occasion of Kazan having named names before the HOUSE UN-AMERICAN ACTIVITIES COMMITTEE (HUAC) in 1952. The Group Theatre had been a socially conscious company of actors whose political loyalties leaned firmly to the left. Kazan had joined the Communist Party while with the Group Theater but had resigned a few years later when they asked him to help take over the company. Like Miller, he had found the party too dogmatic and artistically limiting. Called before HUAC to testify, Kazan initially resisted, but when he was threatened with the loss of his film career, he identified eight people who had been, along with him, Communist Party members. Kazan felt that COMMUNISM was a real danger, so it was a patriotic necessity, even though painful, to cooperate with HUAC. He also saw no point in trying to defend a cause in which he no longer believed. In 1954, Kazan tried to present his case dramatically with the movie *On the Waterfront*, which presents informing as an honorable action, but many in the entertainment industry were unconvinced and refused to forgive what they saw as Kazan's betrayal. Although his testimony kept him from being blacklisted, it lost him many friends, including Miller and Bloomgarden.

Kazan and Miller had become close friends during and after *All My Sons*; as Kazan states in *Elia Kazan: A Life*, "Art was like a member of my family; I saw him almost daily and usually at my home." They had a lot in common in terms of background, and they shared everything. They planned Miller's next play together from the initial script, and Kazan admits: "Of all the plays I've directed, *Death of a Salesman* is my favorite." He wept when he first read it, feeling, as did so many others, that the Lomans were like his own family. In *Timebends, A Life*, Miller talks of Kazan's intensity as a director, saying he had "the devil's energy and knew how to pay attention to what the writer or his actors were trying to tell him." He could be manipulative, but he worked well with his leading actors to help them discover a part through their own experiences. He was not as voluble or even as likable as Clurman, but in Miller's opinion, his vision was firmer. LEE J. COBB had also been in *Boomerang!* (1947), and, even though Cobb's appearance was not what Miller had pictured for the role, Kazan suggested him for Willy Loman. The play, of course, was a huge success.

Heading to Hollywood to pitch *The Hook*, a film they had talked about doing since first meeting, Kazan turned down an offer to direct Williams's

The Rose Tattoo to work on Miller's screenplay. Sadly, they could not get the financing without major rewriting, and to Kazan's dismay, Miller chose to drop the project. While there, however, Kazan was able to introduce Miller to Monroe, and the three of them spent time together, Kazan encouraging Miller to loosen up. Miller fled back to New York to save his marriage, and Kazan stayed in Hollywood to film *A Streetcar Named Desire* and *Viva Zapata!*

Kazan phoned Miller beforehand about his decision to testify to HUAC. Although Miller understood Kazan's self-justification, he felt that Kazan's testimony "had disserved both himself and the cause of freedom," and their friendship was never the same. Miller went elsewhere for a director for *The Crucible* in 1953. Their correspondence tapered off,

and it was not until 1960 when Kazan was asked by ROBERT WHITEHEAD to help him get the REPERTORY THEATER OF LINCOLN CENTER off the ground that he and Miller would set their differences aside and work together again. In 1963, they met regularly to discuss *After the Fall* at Miller's suite in the Chelsea Hotel where Kazan advised Miller on his rewrites. It was Kazan who decided to have Barabara Loden play the role of Maggie in a blonde wig. Miller felt that Kazan's talent overweighed any scruples that he felt about working with him on the play, and although the play was heavily criticized, he felt that Kazan's direction of it was "one of the best things he had ever done."

Thomas Middleton and William Rowley's *The Changeling*, revived in 1964 as part of the Repertory Theater of Lincoln Center's first season to accom-

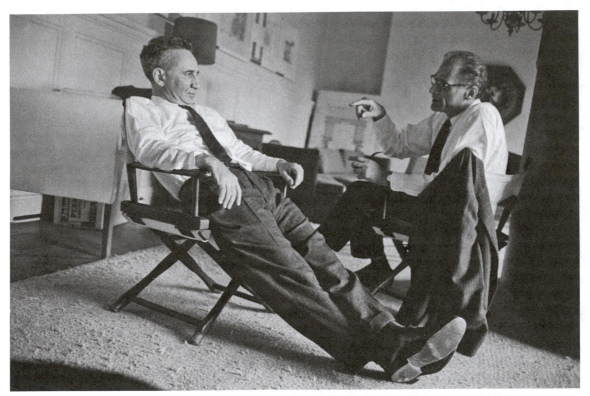

For a time, Elia Kazan and Miller were very close. Kazan directed both *All My Sons* and *Death of a Salesman*, but Kazan's cooperation with the HUAC caused a rift in their friendship. However, the two put their differences aside so that Kazan might direct Miller's *After the Fall*. Kazan and Miller are shown here in 1963, preparing for the production in Miller's suite at the Chelsea Hotel. *Photograph by Inge Morath: Magnum Photos.*

pany *After the Fall,* turned out to be the last play that Kazan would direct for the stage. Feeling that costs to present Broadway plays had become too high and no longer wanting to be involved with the Repertory Theater, he switched to movies and novels, the latter of which included *The Arrangement* (1966), *The Understudy* (1974), and *The Anatolian* (1982) and were fairly successful. Although he and Miller were never again as close as they had been in the late 1940s, when the controversy arose in 1999 regarding whether or not Kazan should be awarded his special Oscar, Miller sprang to his defense, insisting that Kazan deserved the honor.

FURTHER READING

Kazan, Elia. *Elia Kazan: A Life.* New York: Doubleday, 1988.

Miller, Arthur. "Kazan and the Bad Times." *Nation,* March 22, 1999: 6.

Murphy, Brenda. "Uneasy Collaboration: Miller, Kazan, and *After the Fall.*" *Arthur Miller Journal* 1, no. 1 (Spring 2006): 49–59.

Kennedy, Arthur (1914–1990)   John Arthur Kennedy was born in Worcester, Massachusetts, the son of a dentist, and died in Connecticut after a decades-long career as a versatile stage and screen actor. He attended Carnegie Institute of Technology and later became involved in local theatre groups. Active onstage from the age of 20, he married actress Mary Cheffrey in 1938 and moved to Los Angeles. Of their two children, Terence and Laurie, Laurie would carry on the family's acting tradition. Reportedly discovered by James Cagney while playing onstage in Los Angeles, Kennedy first came to movie screens playing Cagney's artistic kid brother in *City for Conquest* (1940). His film work during the years, mostly in supporting roles but covering more than 80 movies, earned him five Oscar nominations but no win. The 1960s until his retirement in 1979 saw Kennedy work increasingly on television and films both at home and abroad. He came out of retirement, while battling thyroid cancer, to perform one last role in the film, *Signs of Life* (1989), but he died shortly after its release.

Tall, weather beaten, and serious looking, he was often cast as surly individuals, cynical types,

and heels, but he was flexible enough for any role. However, the first few BROADWAY plays in which he appeared in the 1930s, including one with the FEDERAL THEATER PROJECT's Living Newspaper, all closed in under a month. His first major stage success was not until 1947 as Chris Keller in *All My Sons,* which he played for nine months. Miller had chosen him for the role after seeing him perform in *Boomerang!* (1947), directed by ELIA KAZAN. Kennedy won a Tony Award for his subsequent role as Biff Loman in *Death of a Salesman,* which he played for more than 18 months. Of his 11 Broadway outings, four were in Miller's plays and these were the most successful roles of his stage career. After his successes as Chris Keller and Biff Loman, Kennedy became an actor favored by Miller, who wrote the role of John Proctor in *The Crucible* with Kennedy in mind, then fought with the director, JED HARRIS, to have him hired. Seymour Peck's *New York Times* interview with Kennedy offers insight into the subsequently troubled relationship that Kennedy had with Harris during rehearsal and production. Kennedy would also be chosen to play Walter Franz in the premier of *The Price* where again he would have difficulty with the director, ULU GROSBARD. In *Timebends, A Life,* Miller describes Kennedy as a "very intelligent citizien. . . . capable of great lyricism."

FURTHER READING

Peck, Seymour. "Growth—and Growing Pains—of an Actor." *New York Times Magazine* February 15, 1953, 20, 34, 36.

Kushner, Tony (1956–)   Outspoken U.S. playwright Tony Kushner is best known for his seven-hour, two-part play *Angels in America* (1991–92), subtitled, *A Gay Fantasia on National Themes,* for which he was awarded nearly every possible prize, including a Pulitzer Prize. Although still a rarity on Broadway, he has written many other plays, including *A Bright Room Called Day* (1985), *Slavs!* (1995), *Henry Box Brown, or the Mirror of Slavery* (1998), *Homebody/Kabul* (2001), the musical *Caroline or Change* (2002), and several adaptations of other dramas. He also wrote screenplays for the 2003 television film of *Angels in America* and Stephen

Spielberg's *Munich* (2005). Much of Kushner's work is concerned with moral responsibility during politically repressive times, and it is little wonder that he feels drawn to Miller.

Born to Jewish parents in Manhattan, the family moved to Louisiana shortly after his birth. Kushner returned to New York in 1974 to attend Columbia University. He stayed in New York for graduate work while working as a switchboard operator at United Nations Plaza Hotel and writing plays. His first produced work was *The Age of Assassins* in 1982. In 1985, he became assistant director at St. Louis Repertory Theatre but returned to New York to be artistic director with the New York Theatre Workshop. Openly gay, in 2003 he and his long-time partner, editor Mark Harris, were married. At Miller's 2005 memorial, Kushner spoke movingly of Miller's dramatic mastery and praised him as "politically progressive" and "a great believer in democracy and self-reliance and in anything conducive to and supportive of individual human dignity and integrity." Kushner is the editor of the Library of America's *Arthur Miller: Collected Plays 1944–1961* (2006).

L

Law The law and lawyers, in many guises, inhabit Miller's plays, and it is clear that the gap between the law and morality is one that fascinates the playwright. Many of his characters would be found innocent of wrongdoing by the U.S. legal system, but there are certain moral laws that they cannot escape. Actual lawyers abound in Miller's work: George in *All My Sons,* Bernard in *Death of a Salesman,* Alfieri in *A View from the Bridge,* Quentin in *After the Fall,* Charlie Haggerty in *Everybody Wins,* Tom in *The Ride down Mt. Morgan.* There are also several judges; Bradley in *The American Clock,* Murdoch in *Everybody Wins,* as well as Danforth and Hathorne in *The Crucible.* It is interesting to note how Miller's lawyers are largely ineffectual in either helping or judging those who have committed moral or legal crimes, while his judges seem utterly self-serving and corrupt. These are indications of the separateness of morality and the law and, in some cases, the actual ineffectiveness of the former. In *A View from the Bridge,* Eddie Carbone brings on disaster by upholding a legal statute (against illegal immigration) rather than by violating one; it is a higher, moral order that he finds he cannot escape. The legal system cannot help him to protect his niece, for it is often seen as ineffectual and certainly limited; these are the main reasons why *After the Fall*'s Quentin gives up his law practice.

A character such as Alfieri represents the law, not justice, and Miller is careful not to mix these terms. As Alfieri tells us of many who were "justly shot by unjust men," we come to see that the law is a complex notion and has more than one side: On one hand, there is the law of the land that is often shown to be ineffective in Miller's plays, having no power to make the guilty pay for their crimes or to protect the ordinary individual, but on the other hand, Miller insists that there is a moral law that does successfully operate, and it judges both our individual and our collective actions. Miller sees such a law as fundamental to the growth and development of U.S. culture and DEMOCRACY, for without this we are insufficiently protected against chaos and evil. Thus, while the institutionalized law can do nothing to restrict or aid such men as Eddie Carbone or Joe Keller seriously, they pay a heavy price for breaking certain moral restrictions.

As Leonard Moss insists in his study of Miller, many of the playwright's plays incorporate the "accusation-defense rhythm of a trial" in their structure, despite the variety of their narrative schemes. Hidden guilt is hinted at and gradually brought to light as such plays progress toward judgment, with the protagonist on some occasions atoning but others paying a heavy price (often their own lives). A play such as *All My Sons,* in essence, is a courtroom drama, filled with trial metaphors. Although George is the only actual lawyer in the piece, all the characters seem to act as witnesses or to offer personal opinions regarding Joe Keller's level of guilt. The audience could be seen as the jury, while Joe's son Chris acts as prosecutor and judge—demanding a death sentence. In *Death of a Salesman,* Willy is similarly tried by his son, Biff.

In such a play as *The Crucible,* the main impetus is quite literally a trial, but we actually spend our time outside the courtroom to see more pointedly the unpleasant repercussions on a society that allows itself to be governed by laws that are clearly open to corruption in the pursuit of personal gain. In *Incident at Vichy,* when Leduc complains about Nazi racism, Monceau says that everyone is racist and that all people can do is to try to obey the law, even when it seems wrong. But Leduc sees this as blind indifference to reality—the law should not be obeyed when it is antagonistic toward basic human rights. Such incidents indicate Miller's belief in the ascendancy of moral laws over the laws of the land. Humanmade laws are too open to abuse, to destructive loopholes, and to personal agenda. Miller judges his characters by a higher moral standard.

Having said that, Miller also recognizes the importance of a legal system to maintain order. It is one of the things that worried him about China when he visited; China had yet to create a proper codified legal system, without which, Miller felt, any attempt to govern would remain inherently unstable. The problem is, as he explores in a screenplay such as *Everybody Wins,* how to keep the law honest and equitable, given humanity's evident capacity for evil. It is this willful disregard for obedience to basic laws that forced the ejection of Adam and Eve from Eden and had Cain sent away from his family after killing his brother—as Miller depicts in *The Creation of the World and Other Business.* The first law of life is betrayal, Miller insists here and in many other of his works, largely because we are human and therefore fallible—but we can fight this and should, and it is those who are engaged in this fight whom Miller holds up as heroic.

FURTHER READING

Engle, John D. "The Metaphor of Law in *After the Fall." Notes on Contemporary Literature* (1979): 11–12.

Longhi, Vincent   Vincenzo James Longhi was a man with many faces. To some he appeared to be a waterfront communist, a political operative with possible gangster connections, and a certified lawyer. But he also performed as the musician Jimmy Longhi, with artists including Pete Seeger, Leadbelly, Woody Guthrie, and Cisco Houston (the latter two with whom he joined the merchant marine in 1943), and he wrote stage plays as Vincent Longhi. Miller got to know him in 1947 when he received a telephone call from Longhi offering information about Pete Panto, a waterfront rebel whose disappearance had intrigued Miller, then in search for a good plot to follow *All My Sons.* Longhi and Mitch Berenson were continuing the work that Panto had begun, trying to organize opposition to what they saw as gangster Joe Ryan's domination of the longshoremen's union in the RED HOOK area. Much of what they told and showed Miller during the next six months about waterfront operations would feed his 1951 script *The Hook,* and it was Longhi who related to Miller the story of a longshoreman informing on two brothers to break an engagement between one of them and his niece; this would later evolve into *A View from the Bridge.*

Miller and Longhi became friends. Miller even helped persuade TENNESSEE WILLIAMS to make a $500 contribution to help Longhi in his 1948 congressional election hopes: He was running for the Republicans on an American Labor Party ticket. When Longhi declared his intention to tour Calabria and Sicily (in Italy) to drum up support among relatives in the United States, Miller decided to accompany him for the experience. They traveled together through France to Italy, visiting small Italian communities that would inspire both the short story "Mont Sant' Angelo" and the Sicilian characterizations that underpin *A View from the Bridge.* At one point, they met the mobster Lucky Luciano, who helped procure them transport in a tense situation that Miller recounts in *Timebends: A Life.*

M

March, Fredric (1897–1975) Born in Wisconsin, Ernest Frederick McIntyre Bickel, after a brief career in banking, would become better known as Fredric March, a stage and screen actor who would win two Oscars. When the Tony awards were established in 1947, March would win the first one for his role in Ruth Gordon's *Years Ago,* and another for his performance as James Tyrone in the premiere production of EUGENE O'NEILL's *Long Day's Journey Into Night* (1956). He would also become the first Willy Loman on film; although Miller disliked his interpretation of the role as a "psycho, all but completely out of control" in the 1951 movie of *Death of a Salesman.* March won a Golden Globe and was nominated for an Oscar for his performance. March had been one of Miller's first choices for the stage role, but he had turned it down.

March had begun to be cast as an extra in films in the 1920s and first came to BROADWAY in *Puppets,* a 1925 puppet play. Although he had a moderate run with Tom Cushing's comedy, *Devil in the Cheese,* it was not until the 1940s that he had a string of stage successes, beginning with Thornton Wilder's *The Skin of Our Teeth* in 1942 in which he and his second wife, Florence Eldridge, played the leads of Mr. and Mrs. Antrobus. Dividing his time between film and stage, he proved himself a truly versatile actor, but in 1949, he was proposed for possible blacklisting by the Californian branch of HOUSE UN-AMERICAN ACTIVITIES COMMITTEE for suspected communist sympathies. His response was to have Robert Lewis ask Miller to write a new translation of the HENRIK IBSEN's *An Enemy of the People,* all about unfair persecution and mob rule. March and Eldridge would play the Stockmanns on Broadway in 1950. Last seen on stage in 1961 in Paddy Chayefsky's *Gideon,* March's final performance was as Harry Hope in the 1973 film of O'Neill's *The Iceman Cometh.*

Michigan Daily The *Michigan Daily* has been the student newspaper of the UNIVERSITY OF MICHIGAN since 1890. Although housed on campus, it is financially and editorially independent of the school's administration and other student groups. Its archives can be accessed at 420 Maynard Street in Ann Arbor. Currently, the paper is published five days a week during semester and weekly during the summer; it has a circulation of more than 17,000 copies. During the years, it has made headlines with some of its more radical articles, and its radicalism in the 1930s certainly helped lead Miller toward more socialist sympathies.

Miller joined the staff as a reporter in May 1935 and earned his first byline for the paper on May 24, 1935, on the front page. Titled "Anti-Red Bill Sent to Senate," he reported on the passage in the House of the antiviolent-overthrow measure and was clearly in sympathy with the demonstrators against it. He signed the piece *Arthur A. Miller.* Miller's articles for the paper ranged from reports on national issues to information about campus events, interviews with professors, and reviews. His choice of topics, such as his sympathetic reports on the setbacks of the Works Progress Administration (WPA) ("Criticisms of Government Relief Are Offered by Social Workers" and "20 Per Cent Cut in Local Relief Seen by Wagg") indicate an interest in social issues. Others articles were purely informational, including his reports on a dictionary of Middle English words that was being compiled among several universities and institutions worldwide ("Educators of Four Countries Aid Middle English Dictionary") and a college pamphlet prepared by professors at the university ("New Pamphlet Lists 500 Books for College Men and Women"). He also wrote reviews of an on-campus talk given by an Irish poet ("Simplicity of Aran's Life and People Described by Stephens") and a foreign film that was screened by the Art Cinema League ("Schubert's Loves Are Displayed in Art Cinema's Latest Picture").

Miller also wrote about the work of various professors on campus, including reports on weight-loss experiments ("Fat Rolls Off for University Scientists in New Experiment"), the physiology department's experiments on dogs ("Scientists See and Hear What Dog's Brain Cells Are Doing" and "Oxygen, Usually One of Man's 'Best Friends,' Can Be Harmful"), and research being done in the humanities ("Griggs Locates Messages by Haiti Emperor"). Some professors he interviewed for their opinions on the state of the Michigan banking system ("Michigan Bank Failure Called Fault of Incompetent Officials") and the extinction of the Holding Company Act ("Holding Company Act Termed Too Severe by Prof. Waterman"). The period from October 1935 to March 1936 seems to have been his most prolific, for in fall 1936, he became a night editor and scaled back on the reporting.

Before this, Miller covered an even more controversial issue in March 1936 regarding the appropriateness of fostering the discussion of controversial subjects in the classroom ("Faculty Men Welcome Controversial Social Questions in Class Discussions"). Miller's covering of an on-campus symposium organized by the Michigan Student Alliance that same month strongly suggests his progressive alliance by this stage ("Sellars, Slosson, Shepard Speak on Fascism, Nazism and Hearst"). He also interviewed such people as retired marine general

Smedley D. Butler, who had come to speak on campus about the nefarious way that U.S. forces were being used to back campaigns that had predominantly economic motives. Always interested in politics, he was now becoming more politically aware and involved.

Miller wrote less inflammatory pieces, too, such as his exposure of the little-known Laboratory of Vertebrate Genetics on campus ("Tan, Blue, Brown Mice? Sure, the University Owns Hundreds"). Although there is no mention of it in the article, this was where he was paid to feed the mice. He was also given the opportunity to write editorials, such as a complaint against the university for refusing to let John Strackey come to campus to speak about his book, *The Coming Struggle for Power*. Another editorial from October 1936 responded to the positive references toward Hitler that were made at the Michigan Union by the vice chairman of the board of Chrysler Corporation; Miller sarcastically suggested that the Chrysler Corporation would prefer to run their factories like a concentration camp. His last publication in the *Daily* would appear on May 31, 1937, after he had already left the staff and it was a letter to the editor reporting on a local sit-down strike, showing sympathy toward the workers.

Mielziner, Jo (1901–1976) The much-lionized and influential scenic designer, Jo Mielziner was born in Paris, France, to American expatriates, attended primary school in GREAT BRITAIN, and then returned to the United States for high school. While studying art at Pennsylvania Academy of Fine Arts, Mielziner was recruited by his older brother Leo, better known in the 1920s and 1930s on stage and screen as actor Kenneth MacKenna, to come and stage manage with a summer-stock group in Michigan. Having become entranced by theater, Mielziner won traveling fellowships to study stage design in Paris, Vienna, and Berlin.

Mielziner's professional experience began by working with the THEATRE GUILD as a bit actor and assistant stage manager. His first BROADWAY role was in H. R. Le Normand's *The Failures* in 1923 before serving an apprenticeship with designer Robert Edmond Jones while Jones was working on

EUGENE O'NEILL's *Desire under the Elms* (1924). In 1924, Mielziner designed the set and lighting for the Theatre Guild's production of Ferenc Molnár's *The Guardsman*, (adapted by Miller into a radio play in 1945). After that, aside from a stint during WORLD WAR II working as a camouflage specialist with the U.S. Air Force, he designed nearly 300 major productions of plays, musical comedies, operas, and ballets and won countless awards for his artistic creations. In the 1930s alone, he designed 67 productions, for many of which he also designed the lighting.

Mielziner's work in scenic design was groundbreaking and influential, offering a whole new approach. Aside from the many musicals he designed, from *South Pacific* (1949), through *The King and I* (1952) to *Gypsy* (1959), Mielziner worked with numerous key dramatists in U.S. theater, including O'Neill, Maxwell Anderson, Elmer Rice, S. H. Behrman, LILLIAN HELLMAN, WILLIAM INGE, and TENNESSEE WILLIAMS, the latter for whom he designed, among others, *The Glass Menagerie* (1945), *A Streetcar Named Desire* (1947), *Summer and Smoke* (1949), and *Cat on a Hot Tin Roof* (1955). During his Broadway career, he received four Tony Awards for scenic design (and another one for lighting), the first of which was given for his imaginative set for *Death of a Salesman* in 1949, which also won a Donaldson Award. Theater scholar Harry Smith describes how this poetic set design became a "dominant icon" that significantly influenced the evolution of stage design in the United States. Reviewer Ward Morehouse described it at the time as a "triumph . . . in stagecraft." In *Salesman in Beijing*, Miller himself declares that "Jo was a genius and I believe this was his greatest set."

KERMIT BLOOMGARDEN first asked Mielziner to design the set for *Death of a Salesman*. Miller was uncertain of what he wanted, having originally conceived the play as taking place inside a giant expressionistic head but then feeling this might be too distracting. Mielziner centered his design on the Loman house, filled with abstract symbols to juxtapose its REALISM, and with scenes outside the home played on the forestage to keep the flow of the play going. Miller and ELIA KAZAN, the play's director who had worked before with Mielziner,

loved it so much that they agreed to delay the play's opening to adapt to the concept. Scholar Brenda Murphy views Mielziner's ideas as the "culmination of a style of design he had been developing in his productions of Tennessee Williams's plays" in his combination of translucent scenery, lighting, and sets changing from "drab realistic interiors to light, delicate frameworks" that only suggested surroundings. The Loman house was given a split-level look to incorporate all of its rooms simultaneously, with translucent backdrops to suggest trees and buildings beyond. Here, a subtle change of light could take the scene from a menacing red glow to the innocence of shimmering leaves. Mielziner used subtle lighting throughout the play to enhance its scenic expression and shifts of time. In *Timebends: A Life*, Miller describes Mielziner's set as reflecting "Willy's intense longing for the promises of the past."

Mielziner also designed the stage and lighting for *After the Fall* in 1964 and for the highly praised REPERTORY THEATER OF LINCOLN CENTER's 1972 revival of *The Crucible* with Robert Foxworth, directed by John Berry. Mielziner's aim was to create elliptical, even abstract stage pictures that would stimulate the spectator's imagination; he certainly did in his design for *After the Fall*—presenting the audience with a cascade of polymorphous steps on which the protagonist played out his memories as characters bled in and out of the surrounding darkness. His books, *Designing for the Theatre* (1965) and *The Shapes of Our Theatre* (1970), the latter with a preface by BROOKS ATKINSON, offer an overview of his legacy.

Mielziner also designed, codesigned, or was consultant designer for more than 15 new theatres, including the Repertory Theater of Lincoln Center and the interior of the ANTA–Washington Square Theatre. A pioneer in stage-lighting techniques, he was consultant on lighting to CBS during early days of television; he designed setting and lighting for the first meeting of the United Nations in San Francisco in 1945, and for the Michelangelo "Pieta" at the Vatican Pavilion in the New York World's Fair in 1964. Shows of Mielziner's stage designs have been held around the world. He was chair of the American Theatre Planning Board, a frequent lecturer at universities, and consultant to several firms. His final design for the Broadway stage was stage setting and lighting for Terence Rattigan's *In Praise of Love* (1974).

FURTHER READING

Henderson, Mary C. *Mielziner: Master of Modern Stage Design.* New York: Back Stage, 2001.

Mielziner, Jo. *Designing for the Theatre; A Memoir and a Portfolio.* New York: Atheneum, 1965.

———. *The Shapes of Our Theatre.* New York: Potter, 1970, with a preface by Brooks Atkinson.

Morehouse, Ward. "Triumph at the Morosco." *New York Sun,* February 11, 1949. In *New York Theatre Critics' Reviews* 10 (1949): 360.

Murphy, Brenda. *Miller: Death of a Salesman.* New York: Cambridge University Press, 1995.

Rowe, Kenneth. *A Theater in Your Head.* New York: Funk and Wagnalls, 1960.

Smith, Harry W. "An Air of the Dream: Jo Mielziner, Innovation, and Influence, 1935–1955." *Journal of American Drama and Theatre* 5 (Fall 1993): 42–54.

Miller, Augusta (Gittel) (1892–1961) Named Gittel by her parents, Rose and LOUIS BARNETT, Miller's mother much preferred to be called Augusta, Gus, or Gussie, and was best known by these appellations. First-generation American, her father's clothing business was successful enough for the family to be able to move from Broome Street on the Lower East Side of New York to the higher-class Harlem when she was a child. She had also been able to stay all the way through high school and was planning on a career as a teacher. However, her father and Samuel Miller teamed up to arrange her marriage to Miller's youngest son, ISIDORE MILLER, shortly after her graduation. They were wed on New Year's Eve 1911 and the following year had their first son, KERMIT MILLER. Three years later, Arthur would arrive, and seven years after that, a daughter, JOAN COPELAND, would be borne. They lived in a splendid apartment that overlooked Central Park, with summers at Rockaway Beach, until the GREAT DEPRESSION hit and destroyed her husband's prosperous MILTEX COAT AND SUIT COMPANY.

Augusta came from a large family and had four brothers, Moe, Hymie, Myron, and Harry, each

Miller at work in his studio on his property at Roxbury, Connecticut. Behind him, note the large picture of his parents, Augusta and Isidore Miller. *Photograph by Inge Morath: Magnum Photos.*

of whom would marry a woman of whom she did not approve, respectively, Celia, Stella, Minnie, and Betty. Betty had been a burlesque dancer, and Augusta felt that her disapproval was justified when Betty gave birth to Carl, who had Down syndrome. There were also three sisters, two of whom married salesmen who would eventually work for Isidore. These two couples, Esther and Lee Balsam and Annie and MANNY NEWMAN would also live on their same street after the family's move to BROOKLYN in 1928 as business began to suffer and her mother's death freed Augusta to leave Manhattan. Having lost his funds in the WALL STREET CRASH, Augusta's father would also come to live with them and share a small room with their teenage son, Arthur.

A vivacious, heavy-set woman, Augusta was proud of her husband's success in business, though she was very critical of his failings and illiteracy. The family's dictator of taste and provider of culture, she was an avid reader, listened to classical music, regularly attended shows, played the piano, and insisted on piano lessons for all three children. It would be Augusta who would first introduce Miller to the theater, taking him to matinees at the Shubert. In their more-affluent days, the family had a Knabe baby-grand piano, and Augusta would dress in fox furs and diamonds to show off her refinement, all of which would be subsequently sold or pawned to meet house payments after the family business collapsed. Miller saw her as highly resentful and slightly broken by the impact of the Depression on her life and family, although she never gave in and would go out to play high-stakes bridge to get some cash when needed.

Miller felt that he was his mother's favorite and that she would confide in him her discontents and joys, share family gossip, and vent her often cutting critiques of other family members. He saw her as an artist in the way that she could create alternate realities, and her ambivalent "nature to be blind and sighted at one and the same time" was something that made a strong impression on him. "My mother," he relates in *Timebends: A Life*, "was and was-not the woman who was tempting me sensually to capture her from my father, and was both culpable of disloyalty to him and, as herself, perfectly innocent." Miller begins his autobiography with an awed and appreciative child's-eye view of his mother, and she featured large in his life ever after. Often resentful of what she felt she had been forced to give up for marriage, there are many elements of *Broken Glass*'s Sylvia Gellburg in her outlook. She informs a number of other Miller characters, too, including the mothers in the short stories "I Don't Need You anymore," and "Bulldog" and those in the plays *All My Sons, After the Fall,* and *The American Clock.* Like Kate Keller, she tended to dominate her husband forcefully, and the vitriol but underlying regard that we see toward the husband after his business failure was in both Rose in *After the Fall* and Rose Baum in *The American Clock* and also strongly evident in the Miller household.

Delighted by her son's success as a playwright, excited by his marriage to someone as famous as MARILYN MONROE, in later life, she and Isidore moved into a smaller apartment, no longer needing the Brooklyn house. Her health began to fail in her late sixties due to the same diabetes from which her mother had suffered and due to the onset of breast cancer, but she had seemed in remission when tending to Isidore who was in hospital for a routine surgery. After he came through successfully, despite his heart briefly stopping during the procedure, she came home on March 7, 1961, and died peacefully in her own bed at the age of 70. Monroe, who had hoped but failed to have a closer relationship with her recently former mother-in-law, attended the funeral, as did Miller and the new love of his life, INGE MORATH.

Miller, Isidore (1885–1966)   Born and raised in the Polish shetl of Radomizl, Isidore's father Shmuel, an observant Jew, became Samuel Miller on his immigration to the United States. Coming ahead of the family as was the custom, Samuel sent money for his children to join him when he could. Being the youngest, Isidore was the last and had been left in Poland with an uncle who had soon after died; then he was shuttled from family to family like an orphan before being sent sufficient funds to make the trip. He arrived in the United States on the SS *Clearwater* at the age of six, to be met by his older brother Abe, 10 years old and an inveterate joker who teased his sibling about all the fine buildings that their father now supposedly owned. The family—the parents and their seven children—lived in a small apartment on Stanton Street on the Lower East Side of New York, and although he attended school briefly, at 12, Isidore began to work for his father, operating a sewing machine at S. Miller and Sons. A few years later, he would be selling dresses, even taking sales trips out alone to the Midwest in his teens. In 1911, his father arranged a marriage to AUGUSTA MILLER, the daughter of a fellow manufacturer, LOUIS BARNETT. She was seven years his junior, and they had three children together, KERMIT MILLER, Arthur, and JOAN COPELAND. Miller inherited his father's height but not his fair hair, complexion, and blue eyes.

Isidore broke away from his father to begin his own business shortly after World War I ended and built a successful women's clothing concern, MILTEX COAT AND SUIT COMPANY, that would finance the family's opulent lifestyle. He had been asked in 1915 by Bill Fox to invest in his movie studios and had been tempted, but Isidore refused, feeling that he did not trust Fox. He built up his own business instead, with a factory, an office, and showrooms, employing more than 800 workers. The Millers had a comfortable, upscale apartment overlooking Central Park, a fancy car and uniformed chauffeur, furs, diamonds and a baby-grand piano for his wife, and summers at Rockaway Beach. As they were laid off from other concerns, Isidore would generously take in his brothers-in-law Lee Balsam and MANNY NEWMAN and other relatives to work with him. All of this would be lost after the WALL STREET CRASH, which would strip him of the necessary funds to run a business that would gradually descend into bankruptcy. Both sons were brought in to assist, Kermit even quitting college to help full time, but by 1936, they finally had to close the business down.

At 51, Isidore was out of work for the first time since the age of 12, and dispirited, he would lie in bed, sit on the porch, and silently suffer his wife's scorn. Rallying a little, he would take a series of humiliating jobs, including delivering packages, to make ends meet. Miller recalls a momentous occasion in his youth when his father had to ask him for the carfare to get to work, a scene he recreates in *The American Clock*. Moe Baum is closely modeled after Miller's father as is Ike in *After the Fall*, the father in "I Don't Need You Any More," and that good-natured "peasant" Charley in *Death of a Salesman*. There are also elements of Isidore as the illiterate man who created a business out of nothing, is idolized by the local children, but is dominated by his strong wife, in *All My Sons*'s Joe Keller; the business-minded father figures of those early Michigan plays; and Mr. Franz from *The Price*, who was ruined by the crash and allowed his son to give up his education to help him out. Miller would even fetch the old family table from Isidore's youngest sister Blanche to use on the set for that play.

Although strong in business, Isidore had always been brow-beaten at home, initially by his mother, to whom he gave his paycheck in return for an allowance up until his marriage at 32, and thereafter by his wife. He appreciated the sacrifices that were made by his oldest son, Kermit, but his daughter Joan was a particular favorite, their relationship providing Miller with elements of the more innocent regard between Eddie Carbone and Catherine in *A View from the Bridge*. Miller felt both pity and anger at what happened to his father during the GREAT DEPRESSION and confesses in *Timebends: A Life*, "I admired his warm and gentle nature as much as I despaired of his illiterate mind." Alternatively describing him as a "peasant," "an albino buffalo" with "animal simplicity" yet "refreshingly unsentimental," and a man of innate refinement and good taste from whom "some undefinable authority emanated," Miller's feelings toward his father are a complex mix of admiration and disdain. He seems to have grown in stature in his son's eyes in retrospect as Miller came into an understanding that it was the system that failed rather than his father.

Isidore was fairly close to Miller's second wife, MARILYN MONROE, whose funeral he attended. He kept in his wallet a newspaper photograph taken of him and Monroe when she invited him to accompany her to Madison Square Garden in 1962 where she sang "Happy Birthday" to President Kennedy and introduced him to her ex-father-in-law. Although in hospital in 1961 when his wife died, he survived another five years, dying in 1966 in a Long Island nursing home, aged 81. That same day, Miller spoke at the New York PEN Congress. In *Timebends: A Life*, Miller tries to encapsulate the lesson that he feels he best learned from his father that informs much of his work: "His refusal to attribute naturally superior virtues to all Jews and ANTI-SEMITISM to all gentiles may have set up in me, if not a faith in, then an expectation of universal emotions ands ideas."

Miller, Jane (1944–   )   Jane Ellen Miller is Miller's first child, born on September 7, just two months before *The Man Who Had All the Luck* opened on BROADWAY. As a child, Jane attended the Little Red School House in Greenwich Village, a popular educational choice for local liberal artists with its curricular emphasis on creativity. One of her classmates there was Michael Meeropol, the son of Ethel and Julius Rosenberg. As a child, she summered with her parents in a rented bungalow near Port Jefferson, Long Island. While her younger brother, ROBERT MILLER, accepted his parents' divorce, the 12-year-old Jane took it badly, although she would visit with her father and his new wife, MARILYN MONROE, both in ROXBURY, CONNECTICUT, and in New York. Uninterested in college, she studied at the New School and became a weaver. When she was nearing 20 and Miller was about to become a father for the last time with REBECCA MILLER, Miller wrote and dedicated the children's book *Jane's Blanket* for his oldest daughter. This was possibly an attempt by Miller to let her know that she was still dear to him as he gained a new daughter. She married the Irish-Catholic sculptor Tom Doyle in 1966 and has led a quiet life since then, nearby her father's home in Roxbury. The half-sisters were friendly, and Rebecca would babysit for Jane's first child, although the baby sadly died from SIDS.

Miller, Kermit (1912–2003)   Miller's older brother, Kermit, was born three years earlier and as Miller writes in *Timebends: A Life,* "As the eldest son he had all the responsibility, and I had all the fun." Described by Miller as "pathologically honest," Kermit was the ideal son—handsome, hard working, responsible, good at sports, and keen to help out. When the brothers were teens, the family thought that Kermit might become the writer rather than his slacker younger brother who hated even to open a book. Kermit was the family pacifier, always trying to keep everyone happy. Fair and blue-eyed like their father, Miller saw himself and his brother in competition and at odds. Kermit did, however, take his younger brother to a prostitute for his 16th birthday. Miller greatly admired his older brother and felt some guilt at the opportunities which he had that his brother did not.

Kermit studied hard and graduated high school in 1930, going on to New York University. However, he quit in his sophomore year to help his father in the ailing family business. When Miller left for college, he recalls Kermit giving him his hat as he set off, clearly unresentful of his brother's ambitions. After the family concern went under,

Kermit began as a salesman in the carpet business of a friend's father and would help support Miller financially in his early days out of college. In 1942, soon after he married Frances, he signed up to fight in WORLD WAR II. Sent to Officer's Candidate School since he had attended some college, he was commissioned and sent to Europe.

Landing on a Normandy Beach, he led his infantry platoon toward the Ardennes Forest on the German-Belgian border. During the Battle of the Bulge, he was held down by enemy fire in a snowy foxhole. Despite frostbite in his feet, he carried a fellow soldier on his back to safety and the field hospital. Before being properly healed, he asked to be returned to his squadron, and when the request was denied, he got himself out of bed, dressed, and returned to the front anyway. In sincere admiration, Miller dedicated his book about soldiers, *Situation Normal . . .* to Kermit. Discharged in 1945 with a Purple Heart, Kermit suffered from shell shock and battle fatigue. He received a series of electric shock treatments as part of his rehabilitation treatment; these led to bouts of depression and forgetfulness for the rest of his life. He went back into carpet sales but moved from retail to wholesale, working directly for the mill.

Kermit is the inspiration behind many of Miller's sons and brothers, from the good brothers each named Ben in *No Villain, The Grass Still Grows,* and "I Don't Need You any More" to Victor Franz in *The Price,* the son who sacrificed and stayed behind and whose wife always hoped that he would do something more intellectual in life. We also see evidence of his influence on both Larry and Chris in *All My Sons* as caring soldiers, sportsmen, and helpmates; the good-hearted, gifted, and favored underachiever Amos in *The Man Who Had All the Luck;* and Dan in *After the Fall.* He is interestingly not depicted in *The American Clock*—Lee Baum has no siblings, but it was Kermit, not Miller, who cried as Lee does at the sight of his mother's bobbed hair.

Kermit was uncomfortable at the premiere of *After the Fall,* feeling that his family history was too painfully related, but he took pride in his brother's success as a playwright. Though perhaps not close, Miller did ask him to be his best man when he married MARILYN MONROE. Kermit had one son, Ross, who subsequently went on to become a university English professor and a friend of Philip Roth. Kermit died at the age of 91 on his brother's birthday in 2003.

Miller, Rebecca (1963–) The daughter of Miller and his third wife, INGE MORATH, born on September 15, Rebecca Augusta Miller was named after Miller's mother, AUGUSTA MILLER, who had died two years earlier. Reentering fatherhood in his 50s was an eye-opener for Miller, as he recounts in *Timebends: A Life*, "A child underfoot in middle age was a steady remonstrance against the prevailing pessimistic view of life in the warring sixties." In one sense, it was having Rebecca that steeled Miller against giving in to the nihilism of ABSURDISM.

Rebecca grew up in ROXBURY, CONNECTICUT, with occasional visits to the family's apartment at the Chelsea Hotel in New York. The famous photographer Henri Cartier–Bresson, a friend of her mother's, would read to her as a baby in French. Strong willed, she horrified her father when, as a teenager, she briefly converted to Catholicism. After graduating from Yale, she began a career as a painter and sculptor, but while on a fellowship in Germany in 1984, she had the revelation that she would rather be a filmmaker and have her pictures move. She returned to the United States and learned her new craft by acting in films under directors whom she admired, playing roles such as in Mike Nichols's *Regarding Henry* (1991) and Alan Pakula's *Consenting Adults* (1992). She also played the part of Edie in the television version of *The American Clock* (1993) and the painter Neysa McMein in *Mrs. Parker and the Vicious Circle* (1994). Once she had raised the money to direct her own movie, she quit acting for good. Rebecca's first outing as a writer and director was *Angela*, a film about a young girl who believes that the devil lives in her cellar. It won the Filmmaker's Trophy at the Sundance Film Festival in 1995. After this, she tried her hand at fiction, publishing a collection of short stories, many of them autobiographical, called *Personal Velocity* (2001). She would turn these into a film the following year. This popular art-house movie won the Grand Jury Prize at Sundance.

In 1995, while having dinner with Daniel Day-Lewis, Miller and Morath had offered him one of Rebecca's scripts for consideration. Although he perceived that it was well written, he did not feel able to take it on at that time and turned it down. Rebecca arranged for him to see *Angela*, and they met to discuss his reaction. Then in 1996, on the set of *The Crucible* where Rebecca was engaged to shoot production stills, she and Day-Lewis were able to spend more time together; they wed within months in a small ceremony in Vermont. Coming from a similar background, Day-Lewis had also grown up with a renowned writer for a father, in his case the poet Cecil Day-Lewis, and the couple had an instant rapport. They have two sons, Ronan and Cashel, and split their year between living in Ireland's Wicklow Mountains and in Roxbury and New York. It would not be until 2004 that Day-Lewis would finally perform in the script that he had originally turned down when his wife directed him in *The Ballad of Jack and Rose* (a story of a young girl trying to deal with a powerful and idealistic father). Rebecca also wrote the screenplay for the 2005 film of David Auburn's *Proof*, has completed a screenplay for *The Man Who Had All the Luck*, and has extensive footage shot for a documentary on her father that she plans to edit. At his side in Roxbury when he died, afterward, Rebecca became Miller's literary executor.

Miller, Robert (1947–) Robert Arthur Miller is Miller's second child, born May 31, four months after *All My Sons* opened on BROADWAY. As a child, Robert attended the Little Red School House in Greenwich Village, a popular educational choice for local liberal artists with its curricular emphasis on creativity. One of his classmates there was Robbie Meeropol, the son of Ethel and Julius Rosenberg. An easygoing boy, at nine years old Robert accepted his parents' divorce better than his older sister, JANE MILLER, and visited with his father and his new wife, MARILYN MONROE, both in ROXBURY, CONNECTICUT, and in New York.

Robert attended his father's alma mater, the UNIVERSITY OF MICHIGAN, but then became involved with Ken Kesey's drug circle, the Merry Pranksters, and thought about film producing or screenwriting. He began to grow apart from his father. Aside from some work as a production assistant, he was largely unsuccessful, so he turned for a while to directing television commercials. By the eighties, he was married with three children and working on the fringes of the film world in California. He had to push his father to allow him to help produce the 1996 film of *The Crucible*, but it proved to be a good bonding experience for the two. He would also coproduce the 2001 movie version of *Focus*.

Robert began to direct for the stage in 2002 when he took on Kenneth Ross's *Breaker Morant* for the Playhouse Repertory Company in Pittsburgh. He then served as a distinguished guest artist working with senior and graduate acting and directing students in Point Park University's College of Performing Arts. In 2004, he directed *A View from the Bridge* for The Rep, the professional theater company of Point Park. He has appeared and spoken at several of the memorials to Miller since his father's death and continues to reside in California.

Miltex Coat and Suit Company   Isidore Miller had broken away from his father to begin his own business shortly after World War I ended, and he built the successful women's clothing concern that he called Miltex Coat and Suit Company. It would amply finance his family's opulent lifestyle. Miltex boasted a factory, a showroom, and a front office. He employed more than 800 people at its height, including several of AUGUSTA MILLER's relatives such as Miller's uncles MANNY NEWMAN and Lee Balsam, who needed work after having been laid off from elsewhere. Business was already slowing before the WALL STREET CRASH, but after Isidore lost all his reserve funds in suddenly worthless stock, it was impossible to keep it running, despite the sacrifices made by his son KERMIT MILLER who quit college to help keep the company afloat.

Miller would also help during his summer vacations, carrying coats for his father's salesmen—an experience he draws upon for the short story "In Memoriam"—and doing general errands. In a 1998 essay, "Before Air Conditioning," Miller recalls the heat of the summer in his father's factory when a dozen men would be operating sewing machines to stitch together the thick woollen winter coats that they produced, and the cutters sweated profusely as they worked through the day to cut as much as they could as they were paid by the piece. He would not see workers so driven again until the 1980s when visiting a factory in China. By 1936, his father's business finally closed down for good.

Monroe, Marilyn (1926–1962)   Marilyn Monroe may be the most famous of Miller's three wives, but to put their marriage into perspective, we should note that although her four-year marriage to Miller was her most substantial out of three, it was only a quarter of the length of time that Miller was married to MARY SLATTERY and a 10th of the time that he spent with INGE MORATH. Miller's marriage to Monroe had a huge impact on his life and vision but should not overshadow the contributions that both of these other women made. Critics, however, have seen more characters who share characteristics with Monroe in Miller's work than his other wives, from the youthful temptresses Abigail Williams in *The Crucible* and Catherine in *A View from the Bridge* to the troubled sex icons Maggie in *After the Fall*, Cathy-May in *Mr. Peters' Connections*, and Kitty in *Finishing the Picture*. There are also echoes of her character in Angela in *Some Kind of Love Story*, and in *Everybody Wins*, in the unnamed wife in the story "Please Don't Kill Anything," in Roslyn in *The Misfits*, and in Florence in *Fame*. But these only convey aspects of her character, and none are wholly Monroe.

The truth of Monroe's life is hard to gauge, as there have been many imaginative biographies that were designed to embellish her popular image. However, the basic story begins in a charity ward of the Los Angeles County Hospital. Here Monroe began life as Norma Jeane Baker, born on June 1 to film-cutter Gladys Baker. Gladys's first husband had divorced her and taken her two children; a second husband had also left before Monroe was born; and it remains uncertain as to who Monroe's father was. Unwilling to raise the child herself, Gladys placed her in foster care, visiting every Saturday. When Monroe was seven, her mother bought a house and tried to raise her daughter but a few months later suffered a mental breakdown—there was apparently a history of insanity in the family—and Monroe as a ward of state was bounced from foster home to orphanage. At age 16, she married James Dougherty.

While Dougherty served in the merchant marines during WORLD WAR II, Monroe lived with her mother-in-law and worked in a factory, spraying airplane parts and inspecting parachutes. An army photographer, David Conover, working on an article about women contributing to the war effort saw her potential, advised her to become a model, and claims that the two had an affair. Monroe soon had a successful modeling career. By 1946, she had come to the attention of a talent scout for Twentieth Century-Fox, by whom she was hired, and that same year, she and Dougherty divorced. He would remarry the following year. On advice, "Norma Jeane" changed her name, the scout suggesting Marilyn, to which she added her mother's maiden name, Monroe. The studio taught her about hair, makeup, costumes, acting, and lighting and after six months began to give her minor roles; however after a year, the studio decided not to renew her contract, and she returned to modeling.

Meeting Johnny Hyde, one of Hollywood's top agents, turned things around. He arranged for her to be re-signed at Fox; supporting roles in *All About Eve* (1950) and *The Asphalt Jungle* (1950), the latter directed by John Huston, started to bring her notice. Her popularity grew despite the series of inconsequential roles she was given. She was also sleeping with Hyde. She turned down his offer of marriage but was upset when he died in 1951. ELIA KAZAN met her shortly after this while in Hollywood with Miller, looking for a producer for *The Hook*, and the two slept together. Kazan planned to escort Monroe to a Hollywood party but asked Miller to stand in for him so that he could take another actress whom he wanted to interview for a role. Miller and Monroe hit it off. Eleven years his junior, Monroe was attracted to his intellect and the respectful way he treated her, and he to her openness and evident charms. However, Miller was not yet ready to give up on his marriage, and shortly after, he returned to New York to his wife and children. He confessed his attraction to his wife, and she was as annoyed as the previous time he had done this.

Monroe and Miller remained friends and corresponded, but meanwhile she focused on her career and her new boyfriend, Joe DiMaggio, whom she met in 1952. This was also the year of her first starring role, as a deranged babysitter in *Don't Bother to Knock*. Although a minor movie, she had the lead, and her role in *Niagara* the following year gave her greater credibility as an actress, although her major hits would be in comedy. Sharing an apartment with actress Shelley Winters, the two would make lists of men they admired, and Miller was on Monroe's list, along with CLIFFORD ODETS and Albert Einstein. Around this time, nude photographs of Monroe began to surface, taken when she had been struggling for work. Instead of being embarrassed, she joked about it and endeared herself further to the public. Her roles in *Gentlemen Prefer Blondes* (1953) and *How To Marry A Millionaire* (1953) would cement Monroe's status as an A-list screen actress, and she quickly became a major movie star with her trademark platinum blonde hair and plunging-neckline dresses. She and DiMaggio married in San Francisco on January 14, 1954. On their honeymoon in Japan, she annoyed him by leaving to go and entertain troops in Korea. DiMaggio was not happy with his wife's sexual image, but the more he tried to control her, the more she rebelled. Reports of his being physically abusive began to surface, and she filed for divorce less then a year after the wedding.

Monroe was increasingly bothered being typecast as the dumb but good-hearted blonde. Tired of the studio roles that she was assigned, after completing *The Seven Year Itch* (1955), she broke her contract to head to New York to study acting and to put her recent divorce behind her. Arriving in the city, she met up with NORMAN ROSTEN and his wife Hedda, who would become her personal assistant, and began to attend classes at the ACTORS STUDIO with LEE STRASBERG. Here, she became friendly with ELI WALLACH and JOAN COPELAND. By this stage, Monroe had already become fairly dependent on drinking and barbiturates to get her through the night, but Strasberg was determined to help her as an actress, using the Method to get her to reach inside herself to develop a role. After five months in the city, she met Miller again at a party thrown by the Strasbergs. Miller called PAULA STRASBERG the following day to ask for Monroe's number, and the two began to see each other with increasing frequency.

Both the Rostens and the Strasbergs would host the couple's clandestine meetings, and the pair would go cycling together to Miller's old haunts. Tabloids got wind of the affair and began their reports. At the September opening of the one-act version of *A View from the Bridge,* despite being one of its investors, Slattery stayed home and sent the children with their grandparents. Miller's mother, AUGUSTA MILLER, reportedly introduced herself to Monroe who was sitting alone in the auditorium. The following month, Slattery asked Miller to leave, and he moved into the Chelsea Hotel before heading to Nevada to establish the necessary six-weeks residency for divorce.

Monroe saw her relationship with Miller initially as that of pupil to his teacher, and he would help her prepare lines for readings before the Actors Studio. The press had a field day with what they felt was an improbable coupling of beauty and brains, and both faced a fair amount of public ridicule. Monroe formed her own production company with Connecticut friend and photographer Milton Greene. Her contract at Fox was renegotiated, and she was given complete directorial approval as well as the option to act in other studios' projects. While Miller was in Nevada, she began to film her next role, which would be Cherie in *Bus Stop* (1956), based on WILLIAM INGE's play. Still playing a sex symbol, it was at least a better quality production, similar to her next project, *The Prince and the Showgirl* (1957), costarring and directed by Laurence Olivier and based on a Terrence Rattigan play.

It may have been his public relationship with Monroe that drew Miller into the spotlight of the HOUSE UN-AMERICAN ACTIVITIES COMMITTEE (HUAC) for when he applied for a passport to accompany Monroe to GREAT BRITAIN for the filming of *The Prince and the Showgirl,* he was subpoenaed to appear before them in June. He was granted a 10-day postponement to complete his Nevada residency. On his return from Nevada, he took Monroe to meet his parents and to announce his plans to marry, while Monroe promised them

that she intended to convert to JUDAISM. At his June 21 meeting with HUAC, Miller refused to name names and was ordered to speak or to face charges of contempt. In the meantime, on June 29, 1956, Miller and Monroe went through a civil ceremony at Westchester County Court House in White Plains, New York; Miller borrowed his mother's wedding band for the occasion. A small Jewish ceremony followed two days later, presided over by Rabbi Robert E. Goldberg, with Lee Strasberg giving away the bride and KERMIT MILLER as best man. Miller wrote to HUAC that he would not change his mind about naming people and was cited for contempt, but he was still granted a passport to accompany his new wife to England.

Filming for *The Prince and the Showgirl* was tortuous. Although Miller got on well with Olivier, Monroe found him patronizing and treated him rudely, often walking off set and leaving Miller to smooth things over. While her acting coach, Paula Strasberg, seemed to accept such behavior, others expected more professionalism, and thus began what for Miller felt like a tug-of-war over Monroe, a situation that he did not enjoy. However, he dealt with various crises, decisions, and tantrums as best he could and tried to offer his wife the constant support that she evidently needed. He viewed Monroe as a talented actress but too much the perfectionist, and he thought that her natural instincts would have served her better than the training that she was being given by the Strasbergs. During this period, he also oversaw the British premiere of the new two-act version of *A View from the Bridge* and worked on his "Introduction to *Arthur Miller's Collected Plays,*" which he would dedicate to "Marilyn."

Although Miller had been able to keep his ROXBURY, CONNECTICUT, farmhouse in the divorce from Slattery, Monroe had wanted to sell it and start afresh. They bounced around between several city apartments and a rented retreat on Long Island at Amagansett, where Miller was inspired by Monroe to write the story "Please Don't Kill Anything." Miller's contempt trial took place in 1957, with Monroe standing behind her husband's decision, despite threats of being blacklisted. That summer, she learned that she was pregnant, but it turned out to be ectopic, and she lost the child. There were rumors of depression and mood swings, with Miller having to prevent her jumping out of a 13th-floor window, as well as an overdose incident when he had had to call in an emergency medical team. To cheer his wife, Miller offered to write a screenplay for her based on his short story "The Misfits."

In 1958, the couple finally found a suitable property at 323 Tophet Road to make their permanent residence, close to the old Roxbury place. Monroe had wanted to rebuild and hired Frank Lloyd Wright to draw up plans, but Miller preferred simply to renovate the old farmhouse. He did, however, at Monroe's insistence, buy up much of the surrounding land to create a nicely secluded estate of 340 acres. Here, they set up home, with Monroe cooking and cleaning in between film work. In a 1958 piece for *Life* magazine, "My Wife Marilyn," Miller wrote of Monroe, "Her beauty shines because her spirit is forever showing itself." He also spoke of the "spontaneous joy she takes in anything a child does" and of her "quick sympathy and respect for old people . . . the child in her catches the fun and the promise, and the old person in her—the mortality." The drive in Monroe toward life and death seemed equally as strong. They had moments of marital bliss, but Monroe's drinking and dependency on drugs were not improving. After escorting Monroe to California to work on *Some Like It Hot*, Miller returned home to write. Again Monroe was having difficulties on the set and driving director Billy Wilder to distraction, so Miller went out to smooth things over and to help to wrap up the production. Soon after this, Monroe suffered another miscarriage. While waiting for the screenplay of *The Misfits* to be completed, she took on another studio project, *Let's Make Love*. Miller helped revise the script to improve her role, and when Gregory Peck dropped out, both he and Monroe recommended Yves Montand as a replacement; Miller had been impressed by his performance in *The Witches of Salem* (1957).

Taking another break from Monroe and leaving the director George Cukor to manage without his aid, Miller again left to work on his writing without distractions. During his absence, Monroe began an affair with Montand that soon hit the news columns. As Slattery had done, Miller chose to ignore these, but he and Monroe knew the marriage was not working. Deciding to film *The Misfits* before announcing their separation, they both flew to Nevada, but it was a long and exhausting shoot in the middle of the hot desert. Miller had been hoping that together in Nevada they might be able to save the marriage, but it was a vain hope. Monroe's tardiness became chronic, and the shoot was troublesome. Her hostility toward Miller was evident as he tried to keep the shoot going, during which she had to be hospitalized for 10 days for "exhaustion." He returned to these events in his final play, *Finishing the Picture*. After the movie was completed, Monroe announced their separation. She flew back to Los Angeles and he to New York, and by the November, their intent to divorce had been officially announced. Again, Miller was able to hold onto his Roxbury estate. Monroe took in President John F. Kennedy's inauguration en route to Mexico for divorce papers.

In interviews Monroe admitted that she had not been easy to live with but had hoped that Miller could take it; sadly he could not. She would attend his mother's funeral in March 1961 after another stay in the hospital for drug dependency, and a year later, she would take his father, ISIDORE MILLER, along to meet President Kennedy at Madison Square Garden, where she famously sang "Happy Birthday, Mr. President." She was still working on her final picture, *Something's Got to Give*, when she was found dead in her bed the morning of August 5, 1962, clutching a phone. Her death, officially ruled to be a probable suicide by drug overdose, has since become the subject of numerous conspiracy theories, and her status has become iconic as the archetypal sex symbol and film star. Miller would insist that it was this that most brought Monroe down—the media image that had been built up around her that she could not escape, even in death. In her will, she left Lee Strasberg control of 75 percent of her estate, expressing her desire that Strasberg, "distribute (her personal effects) among my friends, colleagues and those to whom I am devoted."

Miller did not attend her funeral, feeling that it would be something of a circus, but his father did.

Soon after, Miller wrote to a friend, "The earth shocks for a moment [but] her life–death will not enlighten many." It was perhaps enlightenment for which Miller strove in his 1964 play *After the Fall*, which evidently recalls many incidents between them and attempts to come to terms. Critics were largely uninterested and could only find fault with what they saw as an unflattering portrait of their icon. Monroe's death had sanctified her into a martyred goddess, and Miller would become one of the men blamed for her destruction. Always reluctant to discuss his time with Monroe, Miller would shut down in interviews when questions were too personal. His most complete discussion of his marriage in *Timebends: A Life* is compassionate and evidently loving, while cognizant of the self-destructive nature of his second wife. He describes her as having "a mind of immense capacity that had been assaulted by life, bludgeoned by a culture that asked only enticement of her," praises her "authenticity," and beside the photographs included of them as a couple wrote the simple caption "The best of times."

Morath, Inge (1923–2002)   Inge Morath, one of the leading photographers with the Magnum photographic agency and admired worldwide, was also Miller's wife for nearly 40 years, a woman whom he admired deeply both personally and professionally. Born Ingeborg Morath in Graz, Austria, on May 27, 1923, to independent-minded, Protestant parents—both scientists, her parents traveled with their family—Morath grew up in Hitler's Germany. Her two brothers served in the *Wermacht*—the regular German army—and one uncle reached the rank of general. After finishing school, she attended university in Berlin where she studied languages and journalism. Because she refused to join the Hitler Youth, the Nazis forced her to work assembling plane parts at Berlin's Tempelhof airport while it was being bombed daily. One day, a bomb blew away the gate, and Morath escaped and tried to make her way back to Austria through terrible conditions. In *Timebends: A Life,* Miller relates how at this point she considered jumping off a bridge and committing suicide but was persuaded by a wounded soldier not to give up. This man helped her get to Salzburg, where she struggled to find her bearings and finally found her mother still alive. Her experiences inform several elements of Holga's background in *After the Fall,* who is clearly connected to Morath.

After the war, Morath worked as translator and a journalist for various magazines. In the late forties, she interviewed and photographed the German chancellor Konrad Adenauer, and so impressed him, that he insisted that she become his chief secretary. She also wrote captions and text to accompany the photography of Ernst Haas and was invited to Paris in 1949 by Robert Capa, who had just founded the Magnum agency, to join the group as an editor. Morath began as a copywriter for the renowned photographer Henry Cartier-Bresson, with whom she became close friends. Almost by accident, after taking a series of photographs in Spain for a lark, she discovered that her true talent was photography rather than writing. She studied her new art form first in Paris and then moved to London in 1951 to study under Simon Guttmann. She would travel extensively throughout Europe, North Africa, and the Middle East during the following years, and her images would frequently appear on the pages of *Vogue, Life,* and *Paris Match.* As a photographer, Morath's greatest strength was the artistry of her portraits, and she was asked to take photographs of many contemporary celebrities.

Morath first visited the United States in 1951 on a brief assignment to Hollywood and was surprised at the hostile interrogation that she received from the immigration inspector. She was carrying in her suitcase a novel published by the Left Book Club of London and, given the tense social climate of the period, was suspected of having communist sympathies. She found it ironic that the inspectors were more interested in her potential connection to COMMUNISM rather than to the Nazis. Her first marriage in 1951 to journalist Lionel Birch lasted a mere three weeks. Having worked again with Cartier-Bresson as his researcher and producing her own professional work, Morath was invited to join the ranks of Magnum photographers in 1955. In 1956, she provided the photographs to accompany Mary McCarthy's *Venice Observed,* and since 1955, when *Guerre à la tristesse (War on sadness)* was first published, Morath produced a compelling series of books, including *De à la Perse l'Iran* (*From Persia to Iran*) (1958), *Bring Forth the Children* (1960), *Le Masque* (1967), *Portraits* (1986), and several other collections. Miller wrote some of the text for her 1999 collection, *Inge Morath: Portraits*. Her final book while living was the quirky *Saul Steinberg Masquerade Photographs* (2000), but the post-humously produced *The Road to Reno* (2006) went back to the time she first met Miller, being a collection of the photographs she took driving across the country to visit the set of *The Misfits*. In this book for the first time, her own writing accompanies her photographs, taken from the journal she kept while traveling, although the book also contains an aftterword by Miller.

In 1960, Cartier-Bresson had invited Morath to join the group of Magnum photographers covering the production of *The Misfits* in Nevada. She had photographed another John Huston shoot, *The Unforgiven*, just before, during which she had saved Audie Murphy from drowning; having spotted his inability to climb back into his capsized boat, Morath swam out to rescue Murphy. In Nevada, she met Miller for the first time, taking several photographs of both him and his wife, MARILYN MONROE. After the shoot was over, Morath returned to New York where she was temporarily staying between assignments. Monroe had announced her separation from Miller, and it was not long before Miller, asked a mutual friend for her number and called Morath. The two soon became friendly, and she was beside him at the funeral of his mother, AUGUSTA MILLER, in 1961. After Miller's divorce from Monroe came through, he and Morath were married. Dark and slender, stable and self-confidant, she was quite the opposite of Monroe, although like Monroe, she was several years his junior—in this case, eight. The ceremony took place on February 17, 1962, in New Milford, Connecticut, with 14 friends and relatives in attendance. Monroe was reportedly content that Miller had moved on, and she was not resentful of his new wife; she died six months later.

On September 15, 1962, the couple had their first child, Daniel Miller. It shortly became evident that he suffered from a severe case of Down syndrome, and like so many couples in that position in the 1960s, it was decided Daniel would be best cared for in a facility. They enrolled him at Southbury Training School, which would be close enough to visit. The couple always kept this personal catastrophe very private, and Daniel lived into his early forties. Miller's uncle Harry and his wife Betty had a Down-syndrome child in 1914, and the concern was that it might be genetic. However, they tried again and the following fall had REBECCA MILLER.

In 1962, the couple had toured the Rhineland together, and Morath had taken Miller to the Mauthausen concentration camp, an experience that would strongly influence the play on which he was working, *After the Fall*, providing its background imagery of the HOLOCAUST.

As a photographer, Morath often traveled as part of her job, and Miller, who previous to marrying her had only left the United States on rare occasions, now began to travel abroad quite frequently, taking Rebecca with them on most occasions. However, when at home, by 1963, the couple had made the ROXBURY, CONNECTICUT, house their main residence, although they also permanently rented suite 614 at the Chelsea Hotel so that Miller could more easily visit his older children. This arrangement also gave them both a place from

Miller with his third wife, Inge Morath, at the stage producer John Wharton's birthday party, July 29, 1969. *Courtesy Billy Rose Theatre Collection, The New York Public Library for the Performing Arts, Astor, Lenox, and Tilden Foundations.*

which they could work when in town. In February 1964, partly as an escape from the media backlash after the opening of *After the Fall*, the couple returned to Europe for Morath to visit family, and while there, Miller covered the war-crimes trial of a group of former Auschwitz guards in Frankfurt, Germany, for the *New York Herald Tribune*.

After the break up with the REPERTORY THEATER OF LINCOLN CENTER, Miller spent an increasing amount of time in Roxbury tending to his estate, while Morath decorated the home. He built a darkroom for his wife in the barn, and she would travel to New York twice a week to teach photography at Cooper Union. They worked together on several books that were based on their experiences both at home and abroad. The first described a trip that they made together to Russia in 1967 during which Miller had been trying to persuade Soviet Union writers to join PEN. The result, *In Russia*, was published in 1969; Miller wrote the text and Morath provided the photographs that made up nearly two-thirds of the book. They would repeat this in 1979 with *Chinese Encounters*, based on a trip the pair had made to China the previous fall. Miller admired the fact that Morath spoke several languages fluently, including English, French, Spanish, Italian, and Russian, and was fairly conversant in Mandarin, Greek, and Rumanian. She always liked to be able to converse with the people whom she was photographing in their own language, and

the couple found this a big help to them on their travels. Their 1977 collaboration, *In the Country*, had been closer to home, as they had turned their joint attention to their friends and neighbors in Roxbury. There, the text and the photographs are more intermingled rather than set apart as they had been in their other collaborations.

In Morath, Miller found his ideal wife, and in *Timebends*, he described their years together as "the best of my life." In 2001, Morath began to complain of backaches. She had been undergoing chemotherapy for lymphoma and had seemed to be rallying. They thought that it was under control; however, their optimism was premature—Morath died at age 78 on January 30, 2002. She was buried in a modest grave on the Roxbury property and a memorial service was held for her in the same barn that held her photo studio. Though clearly distraught at losing his wife of nearly 40 years, Miller hated being alone and would initiate a new relationship later that year with the painter, AGNES BARLEY.

Morath's photographs continue to be displayed in galleries and exhibits around the world. She received many awards and distinctions for her evocative photographs, such as an honorary doctorate from the University of Connecticut, the Medal of Honour in Gold from the city of Vienna, and the gold medal of the National Art Club. She also received the Austrian State Prize for Photography.

N

National Theatre In 1848, London publisher Effingham Wilson first proposed the need for GREAT BRITAIN to create a National Theatre such as that in Denmark, Sweden, Austria, and France to mount serious dramatic works from home and abroad to a high artistic standard. Support waxed and waned during the next century but would not gain real momentum until after WORLD WAR II when government subsidy for the project became a possibility with the creation of Britain's Arts Council. The London County Council assisted by offering a possible location on the South Bank of the Thames. Stalling for the next 10 years over financing difficulties, the project gained steam in 1961 when the London Council offered to provide the site rent free and to pay half the cost of construction. Councillor Hugh Jenkins moved a parliamentary resolution, carried unanimously, that the theater should be built without further delay.

Not wanting to wait until the new theater was built, a National Theatre Company was established with Laurence Olivier as artistic director, and a lease was taken on the Old Vic, an old London playhouse. The company's opening performance of *Hamlet* took place in 1963. After 10 successful years, Olivier was succeeded by Peter Hall, who in 1976 would finally lead the company into their new South Bank home with its three performance spaces as they were completed. Having produced more than 600 plays since its inauguration, the National Theatre has become a landmark British institution.

While Shakespeare has been the most-produced playwright by the company, with Bertold Brecht coming in second, Miller is, to date with 10 plays, the most-produced U.S. playwright by far with one more production even than his friend, the notable British playwright HAROLD PINTER. It is little wonder that Miller felt both respect and admiration for this repertory group. Laurence Olivier's 1965 direction of *The Crucible* was its first Miller production, followed by Michael Rudman's acclaimed direction of Warren Mitchell as Willy Loman in *Death of a Salesman* in 1979. Both these plays would be produced again, the first in 1980 and 1990 and the second in 1996.

The National Theatre has also acknowledged Miller's other work; when the premiere production of *The American Clock* failed to catch the spirit of the play, it was not until PETER WOOD's 1986 National Theatre production that the play really came together and caught the audience's imagination and approval. National productions would revive Miller's works in fresh ways, such as MICHAEL BLAKEMORE's decision to cast in the National's 1990 revival of *After the Fall*, black actress Josette Simon as Maggie to help reduce the distraction of the MARILYN MONROE connection. The British premiere of *Broken Glass*, directed by DAVID THACKER, opened the same April as the New York production and fared far better, including a transfer to the Duke of York Theater, an Olivier Award for Best New Play, and an extensive British tour. There were also notable productions of *A View from the Bridge* in 1987 and *All My Sons* in 2000. Miller also appeared at the National Theatre several times as part of their Platform series of interviews with playwrights. In *Timebends: A Life,* he describes subsidized theaters such as the National Theatre as being "alive with a spirit of artistic engagement and adventure refreshingly different from the tense semi-hysteria of New York's cash-blighted fear of every shadow."

Neaphus, Ralph (1914–1937) Ralph Neaphus grew up on a New Mexico ranch and had never been east of the Mississippi before attending the UNIVERSITY OF MICHIGAN, where he met Miller as they were washing dishes in the cafeteria together. In his autobiography, Miller describes him as "soft-spoken" with a "schoolteacherly look." After graduating, Neaphus offered to share the gas money and drove with Miller back from Michigan to New York in an old Model T Ford that Miller had bought for $22 out of the Hopwood award money that he had won for *No Villain.* Neaphus had decided to travel to New York to sign up with the Abraham Lincoln Brigade that was going to Spain to assist the communist troops who were fighting the fascists in the Spanish civil war. Politically sympathetic to any socialist cause, Miller was strongly tempted to join him, but his own uncertainty, his desire to write rather than fight, and his mother's disapproval kept Miller at home. Miller was thankful to hear that Neaphus had been captured by Franco's Moorish troops and so was safe from further combat, but then the news came through that all of the prisoners had been shot. The uncompromising and passionate idealist whose efforts achieve little tangible good is a character who would come to haunt much of Miller's work.

Newman, Manny (ca. 1880s–1947) A product of the turn of the century, Manny Newman was married to Annie, AUGUSTA MILLER's older sister, and lived the life of a salesman. When his father-in-law's business closed, he was taken on at the MILTEX COAT AND SUIT COMPANY by his brother-in-law, ISIDORE MILLER. He was living across the street from the Millers when they moved into BROOKLYN in 1928, and Miller recalls many incidents from his childhood of his uncle's enjoyment working with his hands, as well as escapades with his wild cousins. Newman had eloped with Annie against her father's wishes, and theirs was a close marriage. As well as two sons, Buddy and Abby, they also had two daughters, Isabel and Margie. With his small stature, loving marriage, underachieving but athletic and self-confident sons, and capacity for "fantastic inventions," Newman is an obvious model for Willy Loman. "Hope," Miller tells us in *Timebends: A Life,* was his uncle's "food and drink," and he was "lyrically in love with fame and fortune and their inevitable descent on his family." He is also behind the uncle in *Broken Glass* who has the shoebox collection of pornographic postcards.

Miller had always felt that Newman saw him as being in competition with his sons and determined that Buddy and Abby would be the bigger successes. Their early lives inform the characterizations of Biff and Happy Loman, with Buddy good at sports, Abby one for the ladies, and both convinced by their father that they would do well. Each would sadly die in their forties, having achieved very little. Miller informs us that "Manny had died with none of the ordinary reasons given," which made Miller suspect suicide. He had met his uncle shortly before this, after the 1946 Boston tryouts of *All My Sons,* coming out of a matinee. It was this meeting and the way that Newman treated him that Miller credits as having given him the idea for how to present *Death of a Salesman* as the subjective stream of consciousness of a central character who creates his own reality as he goes. Newman's "solution for any hard problem," Miller relates, "was always the same—change the facts." Yet, underneath his "unpredictable manipulations of fact," there was always "the river of his sadness." People despaired of Newman yet also admired him. Miller insists that it was "hard to remain unmoved by him" and that people would feel a certain respect for his "crazy courage in turning away from the ordinary rules."

Odets, Clifford (1906–1963) Born in Philadelphia, Clifford Odets was the son of a prosperous Jewish printer, rather than one of the working class so eloquently evoked in his early plays. His father was openly unfaithful. His mother died at an early age, and Odets's home life was not a happy one. A strong creative urge led him to acting; he left school at age 17 to work with local New York City theatre groups, where he played the occasional small role. By the late 1920s, he was playing juvenile roles in THEATRE GUILD productions. His first BROADWAY performance was in the Theatre Guild's *Midnight*, written by Claire Sifton and Paul Sifton, at the end of 1930. When the GROUP THEATER was formed, Odets immediately joined and continued to act, including a small role in Sidney Kingsley's *Men in White* (1933), directed by LEE STRASBERG. With larger roles eluding him, he turned his ambitions, instead, to writing. He wrote *910 Eden Street* and gave it to one of the Group Theater's founders, HAROLD CLURMAN, to read. Clurman found it was painfully subjective and unfit for production, but he would guide Odets in the writing of his next play, *Awake and Sing*, crafting many of the roles to fit specific Group Theater actors. However, the Group Theater could not afford to take the financial risk of mounting a production by an unknown writer. Undaunted, Odets wrote another play, *Waiting for Lefty*, for a New Theatre League play contest. It won and was soon being performed to great acclaim by the awarding organization on Sunday nights. In *The Fervent Years*, Clurman describes the drama as "the birth cry of the thirties. Our youth had found its voice. It was the call to join the good fight for a greater measure of life in a world free of economic fear, falsehood, and craven servitude to stupidity and greed."

Odets had proven himself, and the Group Theater now produced a long series of his works on Broadway. Within the same year—1935—Clurman directed *Awake and Sing* with staging by BORIS ARONSON (who would become one of Odets's close friends), Odets assisted Sanford Meisner in directing *Waiting for Lefty*, Cheryl Crawford directed *Till the Day I Die*, and Clurman directed *Paradise Lost*. From March to July, Odets had three dramas playing simultaneously on Broadway—enough to rival Eugene O'Neill, as a *Time* magazine article at the time suggested. Lured by such success to Hollywood, Odets worked on the screenplay for *The General Died at Dawn* (1936), but the film was not well received. His guilt at having left the Group Theater soon drove him back to New York, and he continued writing plays that Clurman would direct. The first, *Golden Boy* (1937), was a huge hit. The set was by MORDECAI GORELIK and ELIA KAZAN and LEE J. COBB were in the cast. Miller sat in the audience, amazed at the production's force. Clurman went on to direct *Rocket to the Moon* (1938) and *Night Music* (1940) before the Group Theater disbanded and Odets returned to Hollywood. Clurman briefly followed to direct Odets's screenplay, *Deadline at Dawn* (1946), but he swiftly returned to New York, hoping that Odets would follow.

Hollywood would never be as kind to the playwright as would the theater, and Odets would find, when he tried to return again to plays that his moment in the spotlight had passed. *The Big Knife* (1949) and *The Country Girl* (1950) were not without merit, but they failed to capture the critical acclaim of earlier works. Based on the story of Noah, *The Flowering Peach* (1954) was produced by ROBERT WHITEHEAD and became his final play. The critics were kind but not enthusiastic. Although many of his characters and certainly his language remain vibrant, the melodramatic plots and unclear ideologies in his plays have not worn well. All the rage in the 1930s, by the 1950s his plays had lost impact and felt outdated. Some felt him previously overpraised, but Miller considered him to be one of the most influential playwrights of U.S. theater.

In *Timebends: A Life,* Miller praises Odets as a "pure revolutionary" and a "bearer of light." When Miller was developing as a playwright in the 1930s, Odets, with plays like *Waiting For Lefty* and *Awake and Sing* stunning Broadway audiences, had seemed to him to be the playwright to emulate with his lyricism, revolutionary fervor, and commitment to socialism. Miller was attracted both to Odets's attempts at social protest in a theater that is often hostile to such attempts and to the poetic rhythms of his work. *Waiting For Lefty,* banned in seven cities, was a classic example of agitprop theater: a play that blatantly attempts to engage its audience with a call to arms. Although Miller developed a far more subtle and sophisticated form of agitprop, many of his plays retain something of this influence, as they call for some kind of responsive action from the audience to correct in themselves the type of destructive behavior displayed by the plays' characters. However, Miller saw Odets less as the "stormbird of the working class" than as "an American romantic" who is as keen for personal success as the next man. It was Odets's poetry more than his politics that impressed Miller.

Despite its melodramatic structure, the force of the dialogue in a play such as *Awake and Sing* was what Miller admired. It felt more real than anything before heard on the stage and inspired Miller to create a dialogue that could sound like realistic

speech, yet would contain many of the elements of poetry: rhythm, symbolism, and those resounding phrases that make much poetry so memorable. In his essay "Notes on Realism," Miller refers to Odets's stylized dialogue as "personal jazz" with "slashes of imagery" and acknowledges its poetic influence on him as a writer. Miller recalls meeting Odets in 1940 in a bookstore, but the playwright was uncommunicative when approached. Miller would not meet him again until 1949 when he chaired a panel at the Waldorf-Astoria Peace Conference on which Odets was speaking. By this time, Miller felt that Odets's relevance as a political figure had already passed. He found his speech faintly ridiculous and, in its diatribe against money, rather hypocritical because that seemed to be all Odets was trying to grasp out in Hollywood. Miller sensed that Odets felt a competitive resentment toward him, and the two never became friendly.

Odets's early sympathies toward COMMUNISM had benefited him in the 1930s, but by the 1950s, the social climate had changed. Although Odets had belonged to the party for an eight-month span in 1934, he soon left, claiming that it interfered with his freedom to write. He had joined a delegation that was traveling to Cuba in 1935 to investigate conditions there, but the Cuban government deported the group after the first day. Such activities had created a communist stigma around Odets that guaranteed that he would be called to testify to the HOUSE UN-AMERICAN ACTIVITIES COMMITTEE. He and Kazan, with whom Odets had been friendly since the group days, both agreed to name each other, and so Odets testified in 1952, losing further good will among those who saw the committee as evil. More screenplays would follow, and toward the end of his life, he wrote dramas for television, but he died sad and disillusioned, never again able to recreate the adulation that he had received nearly 30 years previously.

FURTHER READING

Clurman, Harold. *The Fervent Years: The Story of the Group Theatre and the Thirties.* New York: Knopf, 1945.

Odets, Clifford. *The Time Is Ripe.* New York: Grove, 1988.

O'Neill, Eugene (1888–1953)   Eugene Gladstone O'Neill was born in a New York hotel, a son of actor James O'Neill. His life was an unhappy one, and his family fared little better. His mother was addicted to morphine and lost his younger brother to illness as a child; his father was disappointed in an acting career that had trapped him in a single role; and his older brother Jamie was a derelict drunk. All of them would die in the early 1920s, leaving O'Neill alone. O'Neill's 1909 marriage did not go well. He tried escaping to sea and even attempted suicide in 1911, but by 1912 he was divorced and diagnosed with tuberculosis. During convalescence, he read voraciously and decided to become a playwright. Having grown up backstage watching his father perform, O'Neill understood how plays were constructed, but he was determined to write something better than the sentimental, melodramatic fare in which his father performed.

O'Neill earliest plays, begun in 1913, were mostly short, experimental pieces, reflecting his experience with life on the sea, including "Bound East for Cardiff," and "Thirst." In 1916, the Provincetown Players staged these two and went on to produce several others. In 1920, O'Neill conquered BROADWAY with his Pulitzer Prize-winning *Beyond the Horizon* and followed this with a series of plays that explored a variety of forms from the EXPRESSIONISM of *The Emperor Jones* to the REALISM of such historical costume dramas as *Marco Millions* (1928). O'Neill dominated drama in the United States from the 1920s, as 21 new plays of his were premiered in New York between 1920 and 1934, many staged by the THEATRE GUILD. Not all were critical and commercial successes, but he rarely repeated himself, and he won two more Pulitzers during his lifetime, for *Anna Christie* (1921) and for *Strange Interlude* (1928). In 1936, he became only the second American to win the Nobel Prize. In his acceptance speech, O'Neill acknowledged his award as a "symbol of the coming of age of the American theatre." His plays by this time, however, were receiving increasingly hostile receptions, and at his death, O'Neill felt sadly distant from the theater to which he had contributed so much. In 1946, Miller's *All My Sons* would beat out O'Neill's *The Iceman Cometh* for the New York Drama Critics Circle Award. O'Neill wired Miller congratulations, and Miller later invited O'Neill to the premiere of *Death of a Salesman,* but due to ill health, O'Neill was unable to attend.

To the young Miller, the generally accepted first, great American playwright, O'Neill, was admirable, but by the late 1930s (when Miller started to write) O'Neill had become too escapist and erudite. Miller argued with his professor KENNETH ROWE about the social relevance that he saw lacking in O'Neill's work. Where O'Neill was concerned with the relationship between man and God, Miller wanted to explore the relationship between man and man. He saw O'Neill's plays as too "cosmic" and other worldly, preferring dramas concerned with the here-and-now. Despite this, with its maritime connection and moments of lyricism, an indebtedness to O'Neill seems apparent in Miller's unproduced *The Half-Bridge,* which was written in the early 1940s. However, discussing the impact of O'Neill on his writing in his 1958 essay "The Shadows of the Gods," Miller describes himself as being ideologically different from his "reactionary" forerunner, although he finds a connection in their dramatic aims because both are intrigued by fate and notions of power, albeit they see this power coming from different sources. Miller's later essays "About Theater Language" and "Notes on Realism" both describe the impact of O'Neill on U.S. theater as a whole and his connection to realism.

Long Day's Journey into Night was written between 1939 and 1941 but was not produced until after his death for fear that the strongly autobiographical elements would be an embarrassment. Miller saw this play as O'Neill's most moving work and the culmination of his art. It won O'Neill a fourth Pulitzer Prize and once more elevated him to prominence, albeit posthumously. Miller viewed O'Neill's works of the late 1940s as very different and worthy of higher praise, allowing him to reassess his dramatic forerunner and to acknowledge better his uniqueness and visionary zeal. In *Timebends: A Life,* he describes O'Neill and CLIFFORD ODETS as being of equal importance, both being "prophetic spirits" and "playwrights of political consequence, not merely theatrical talents." For Miller, O'Neill was a more openly "aesthetic rebel," which made him an "isolated phenomenon" on Broadway. O'Neill's refusal to worry about commercial popularity freed him to experiment with "the unfamiliar world of spirit and metaphysic" that for Miller so marks his plays.

FURTHER READING

Evans, Lloyd Gareth. "American Connections—O'Neill, Miller, Williams and Albee." *The Language of Modern Drama*. Totowa, N.J.: Rowman and Littlefield, 1977: 177–204.

Herbert, Edward T. "Eugene O'Neill: An Evaluation by Fellow Playwrights." *Modern Drama* 6, no. 3 (December 1963): 239–240.

P

PEN The name *PEN* is an acronym for "poets, playwrights, editors, essayists, and novelists," although the organization now includes writers of any form of literature, as well as journalists and historians. Mrs. C. A. Dawson Scott and novelist and playwright John Galsworthy founded the first PEN Club in London in 1921; Galsworthy became International PEN's first president. Its first members included Joseph Conrad, George Bernard Shaw, and H. G. Wells. It quickly developed into an international organization of writers whose aims were to promote intellectual cooperation and understanding among writers, to create a world community of writers that would emphasize the central role of literature in the development of world culture, and to help to defend literature against the many threats posed by the modern world. The organization gives literary awards, sponsors translations, and also promotes freedom of expression by supporting and defending writers who are being harassed or persecuted by their governments. The organization's headquarters remain in London, and they have branches in about 60 nations. It is the world's oldest human-rights organization. Strictly nonpolitical, PEN is a nongovernmental organization that has formal consultative relations with UNESCO and Special Consultative Status with the Economic and Social Council of the United Nations.

In 1965, while visiting Paris, Miller was asked by David Carver, then the secretary general of the organization, to take on the presidency of PEN and was elected to office in 1965 for a four-year term.

His own dealings with the HOUSE UN-AMERICAN ACTIVITIES COMMITTEE and the censorship of his plays by the American Legion and the Catholic War Veterans gave Miller an understanding of how invasive censorship could be, and he accepted, glad to have an official excuse to make contact with Eastern European writers whose plight he found interesting. He was chosen for his known commitment to liberal politics and as a writer who had admirers and followers in both the East and the West. It was hoped that he could act as a potential connecting force. His first act as president was to attend a conference in Blad, Yugoslavia, and he would have the opportunity to visit many other European nations including Czechoslovakia, where he was able to briefly meet VÁCLAV HAVEL. As PEN president, Miller visited Moscow to persuade Soviet Union writers to join PEN, and he petitioned the Russian government to lift its ban on the works of Aleksandr Solzhenitsyn.

PEN gave Miller a new lease on life, suggesting that there were still concerned citizens who were willing to do something to make a difference. This also gave him hope that there remained an audience for his plays who were willing to accept his prompting that they should confront responsibility for the unpleasant way in which society was developing and would strive to affect change. Part of the PEN charter that all members must sign stipulates that members should "at all times use what influence they have in favor of good understanding and mutual respect among nations." Miller's books *In Russia, Chinese Encounters,* and *Salesman in Beijing* seem partly a response to this. Members also pledge "to do their utmost to dispel race, class, and national hatreds and to champion the ideal of one humanity living in peace in the world." The HUMANISM that underlies so much of Miller's work, both literary and sociopolitical, strongly reflects this ambition for universal tolerance and recognition of the human connection. After his presidency ended, Miller continued to work with the organization, making visits on its behalf, such as his trip to Turkey in 1985 with HAROLD PINTER.

Pinter, Harold (1930–) Born in a working-class district of London, Jewish writer Harold Pinter would develop into one of GREAT BRITAIN's foremost playwrights and be awarded the Nobel Prize for literature in 2005. A keen actor at school, he also wrote poetry and essays for the school magazine. Pinter took up professional acting on leaving school under the name David Baron and found work with several notable repertory theaters. He has acted in several of his own plays and since the 1970s, has done much directing, especially at the NATIONAL THEATRE where he became an associate director in 1973. He began to write plays in the late 1950s. His first full length play, *The Birthday Party* (1957), much like Miller's first BROADWAY outing, received mostly terrible reviews and closed within a week. But, like Miller again, his second major play, *The Caretaker* (1960), was an award winner that brought him to the public's attention. He has written dozens of plays since, including *The Homecoming* (1965), *Old Times* (1971), *No Man's Land* (1975), and *Betrayal* (1978), as well as several screenplays, radio dramas, and volumes of poetry.

Pinter's work, a unique blend of styles, has excited, intrigued, and frustrated audiences and scholars alike with its unconventional and illogical plots, unusual characters, inconclusive resolutions, and distinctive dialogue. Miller was impressed by Pinter's sense of structure, economy of language, and ear for speech. While some praise Pinter's work as original and innovative, others dismiss it as purposefully obscure, but his plays continue to be produced frequently around the globe. With a bow to REALISM in his psychological and linguis-

tic verisimilitude, the cerebral quality of his plays can at times remind us of the alienating epic theater. However, their surface humor but underlying menace are reminiscent of a particular brand of ABSURDISM.

Like Miller, Pinter is something of an existentialist who believes that the mode of a person's being determines his or her thinking. The two met when working with PEN, and they traveled together to make appeals to other countries to allow fuller freedom to their writers. The trip that they made to Turkey in 1985 is recounted in Miller's essay "Dinner with the Ambassador." Despite ill health, Pinter, in 2005 from a wheelchair, delivered his Nobel Prize acceptance speech in which he excoriated a "brutal, scornful and ruthless" United States over its involvement in Iraq, a speech that Miller would have strongly applauded. In CHRISTOPHER BIGSBY's *Remembering Arthur Miller* (2005), Pinter proclaims, "I admired Arthur tremendously. It was wonderful to be with him. I think he remains a tower of strength as a playwright. I have the utmost respect for his work," and he goes on to insist that he means the later plays as well as the earlier ones.

Pound, Ezra (1885–1972) Ezra Weston Loomis Pound was a driving force behind modernism and is best remembered for such poetic creations as "Hugh Selwyn Mauberley" (1920) and his controversial *Cantos* (1948–50). Born in Hailey, Idaho, and raised in Philadelphia, Pound was eager to travel to Europe. He graduated college in the United States where he associated with William Carlos Williams and H. D. (Hilda Doolittle), to whom he was engaged for a time, but by 1908, he was settled in London after a brief stay in Venice. He began to invent a new poetical diction, befriended and worked with W. B. Yeats and T. S. Eliot, and married the artist Dorothy Shakespear.

World War I shattered Pound's belief in modern Western civilization, and in 1920, he moved to Paris to experience artistic developments there and then back to Italy a few years later, where he became an enthusiastic supporter of Mussolini for whom he became a propagandist during WORLD WAR II. Speaking on Italian radio, he propounded his opposition to the war, his fascist beliefs, and his blatant ANTI-SEMITISM. After the war, Pound was brought back to the United States to face charges of treason. It was this that sparked Miller's response in the *New Masses* survey, "Should Ezra Pound Be Shot?" In *Timebends: A Life,* Miller recalls "the cold that had flowed into my heart" on catching Pound on a shortwave band radio speaking about the "necessity of killing Jewish people." Pound was found unfit to face trial because of insanity and was sent to St. Elizabeth's Hospital in Washington, D.C., where he remained for 12 years until campaigning by other poets such as Robert Frost won him a release. After this, he returned to Italy where he lived until his death.

R

Realism Realism in art and literature is the objective depiction of subjects as they appear in everyday life, without embellishment or interpretation. The intent of the realist is to render everyday characters, situations, dilemmas, and objects all in a "true-to-life" manner. In terms of theater, realists rejected the predominantly sentimental melodramatic plays of the 19th century, with their tidy plots and stock characters, in favor of depicting more commonplace people facing relevant social dilemmas. In keeping with reality, solutions became less trite and discussion plays, as opposed to the well-made plays of the past, were born. The discussion concerned that which would be elicited in the audience after watching the play, since not all of the issues that were raised objectively would have been tidily resolved. Basic maxims of realistic theater ask that the play must always be believable, that the "fourth wall" should be scrupulously maintained (with no asides, soliloquys, or monologues), and that the characters should address a societal problem in a linear plot with no subplots. The stage design would also mimic reality as closely as possible. Many credit Alexander Dumas fils with starting the realism movement when he wrote *La Dame aux Camellias* (*Camille*) in 1852, a play that aimed to provide an intentional contrast to the romanticism that had previously dominated dramatic modes. But it is HENRIK IBSEN who is viewed as the father of theatrical realism; though not the first to write a realistic drama, he was the most influential, assisted by George Bernard Shaw whose 1891 book, *The Quintessence of Ibsenism*, did much to bring Ibsen into popular attention.

The realism of an Ibsen play rests on his notion of the life-lie, a term he used to refer to the way in which people who find reality unpleasant or unbearable tend to create idealistic masks behind which to hide. Thus, they create an alternative unreal life that is essentially a lie. Ibsen saw this as dangerous because the further people live from reality, the more damage they do to themselves and others in their efforts to maintain that idealistic mask. As a realist, Ibsen strove to strip away the masks that his characters constructed and force the audience to see the true nature of such people. Thus, the realism of Ibsen's work went beyond mere set detail, even while that was also an important aspect of how he wished such plays to be produced. He tried to create psychologically real people in commonplace social situations. His evolving integration of symbolism in his earlier work does not negate the sense of reality that such works as *A Doll's House* (1879) or *Ghosts* (1881) generate. His later works would become more mythical and symbolic and more personal than socially concerned, but his designation as a realist had already been set. Some critics have made much the same mistake with Miller, labeling him a realist partly because of his open recognition of the influence of Ibsen on his work and because a few of his plays fit the parameters of realistic drama. However, the body of his work, including *Death of a Salesman*, does not.

Such plays as *All My Sons*, *The Crucible*, *The Price*, and *Broken Glass* are fairly realistic, although, like Ibsen's plays, they employ a fair amount of symbolism, but few others fit that description so neatly. As Miller once told Howard Kissel "All my plays are involved with high moral issues. The idea of simply replicating life is the farthest thing from my concerns." A play such as *After the Fall* is the very antithesis of realistic drama, being an entirely subjective presentation from the viewpoint of the central protagonist Quentin, and as such is pure EXPRESSIONISM. As CHRISTOPHER BIGSBY explains in *Modern American Drama*, Miller has "experimented with form, disassembled character, compressed and distended language." Miller dislikes definitions of his writing as realistic because he sees himself as one who is not attempting to create reality but rather to interpret it. Constantly trying out new techniques, Miller has created works whose artistic form is part of their message. Brenda Murphy rightly suggests in her essay "Arthur Miller: Revisioning Realism" that Miller's whole career since *Death of a Salesman* has been a continual experimentation with realistic and expressionistic forms. Miller's later works, especially, as commentaries on a confused contemporary society, reflect that in their style, a style that in works such as *Two-Way Mirror, The Ride down Mt. Morgan,* or *Mr. Peters' Connections,* is deliberately fragmentary and playful and without any notion of reality. While one could define this as a realism of a different hue, it is a long way from traditional interpretations of the term.

Death of a Salesman was a landmark play largely because it was not realistic. It introduced audiences to a new form, which carefully blended realistic and expressionistic devices to create the impression of what was actually going on inside the protagonist's head. While the play strives to create the actual reality of Willy Loman's house before the audience, it is also filled with symbols and effects that suggest something beyond the tangible world. As Murphy explains in *Miller: Death of a Salesman,* "Miller needed a dramatic form that would combine the subjectivity of expressionism with the illusion of objectivity afforded by realism." Miller was aided in the creation of this form by the play's original director, ELIA KAZAN, and its stage designer, JO MEILZINER. They both recently had worked with TENNESSEE WILLIAMS on the initial production of *A Streetcar Named Desire* (1947), which had similarly tried to blend nonrealistic and realistic elements to symbolize death, madness, and a degenerated South. Miller would continue to experiment with form for the rest of his career.

FURTHER READING

Kissel, Howard. "Standing at the Corner of Broadway and Miller." *Daily News,* February 7, 1999: n.p

Murphy, Brenda. "Arthur Miller: Revisioning Realism." In *Realism and the American Dramatic Tradition,* edited by William W. Demastes, 189–202. (Tuscaloosa: University of Alabama Press, 1996).

———. *Miller: Death of a Salesman.* Cambridge: Cambridge University Press, 1995.

Redgrave, Vanessa (1937–) Born in London into the distinguished Redgrave acting family, Vanessa Redgrave grew up knowing the trade. She attended the Central School of Speech and Drama and debuted in London, acting alongside her father Michael in N. C. Hunter's *A Touch of the Sun* (1958). She earned particular praise for her Rosalind with the Royal Shakespeare Company's 1961 *As You Like It* and as Nina in a 1964 revival of ANTON CHEKHOV's *The Seagull.* She was the first actress to embody the role of the fascistic Miss Brodie in Jay Allen's *The Prime of Miss Jean Brodie* (1966). Her first notable film appearance was as David Warner's wife in *Morgan!/Morgan—A Suitable Case for Treatment* (1966), which brought her first Best Actress Oscar nomination of six. She has been since then a regular on screen and stage (including several Broadway performances) with a variety of award-winning performances.

Redgrave has also developed a reputation as an outspoken and controversial activist. Heavily involved in her role as United Nations Children's Fund special representative for the arts, she has planned festivals in war-torn areas such as Kosovo. Also a member of the Workers' Revolutionary Party (standing for election to Parliament on four occasions) and a supporter of the Palestine Liberation Organization, her acceptance speech for her supporting performance in *Julia* at the 1978 Oscar ceremony (in which she referred to protesters as "Zionist hoodlums") led to an unfortunate backlash. She was accused of ANTI-SEMITISM, and Jewish groups, as well as FANIA FÉNELON, subsequently protested when Redgrave was invited to make her U.S. television debut in the lead of *Playing for Time* (1980). From the start, Miller supported Redgrave. Although he disapproved of her political beliefs, he refused to view her as anti-Semitic and felt determined that she should be allowed to play the role and be judged by her performance. Redgrave's sterling, Emmy-winning performance silenced most of the critics.

Red Hook The Dutch established the village of Red Hook (Roode Hoek) in 1636, making it one of the earliest areas in BROOKLYN to be settled. It was named for its red clay soil and the hook shape of the peninsular corner that projected into the East River. In the 1850s, the Atlantic Basin opened, and Red Hook became one of the busiest ports in the country.

Red Hook was always known as a tough section of Brooklyn. Long connected to gangsterism, this was where Al Capone started as a small time criminal. In 1950, at the peak of the era of longshoremen 21,000 people lived in the neighborhood, many of them in row houses that had been built in 1938 as one of the first and largest federal housing projects in the country. But as the 1950s progressed, Red Hook suffered a loss of jobs and population as shipping underwent dramatic changes, and the waterfront business moved to New Jersey. In recent years, there have been efforts to revive this area, but Miller remembers it best from the 1940s when he went there searching for information on the missing longshoreman Peter Panto and hung out with VINCENT LONGHI and Mitch Berenson. This neighborhood would give Miller material for both his unproduced screenplay *The Hook* and *A View from the Bridge*.

Reilly, Peter (1955–) In the fall 1973, Miller was sent a copy of a *New Times* magazine article by its author, journalist Joan Barthel. It told the story of the Connecticut state-police interrogation of 18-year-old Peter Reilly. After 24 hours without council and 10 hours of questioning, Reilly had confessed to brutally murdering his mother, Bar-

bara Gibbons, slitting her throat with a knife and sexually assaulting her with a bottle. He had been tried and convicted, but local neighbors had raised bail, unconvinced by the case and believing Reilly to be innocent. Barthel was trying to raise money for a new trial.

Reading extracts from the transcript, Miller felt that the interrogation had been fraudulent and that Reilly had been coerced psychologically into a false confession. He found the case compelling and stayed with it for the next five years, paying for a private investigator, James Conway, and assisting the lawyer whom he had persuaded to take the case, T. F. Gilroy Daly. They eventually proved that Reilly had been five miles from the crime scene and had a police alibi, a witness whose testimony had been suppressed by the prosecution. Reilly was fully exonerated and released. Miller used these events as background for his one-act play *Some Kind of Love Story*, which he later developed into the movie, *Everybody Wins*.

FURTHER READING

Connery, Donald S., editor *Convicting the Innocent.* Cembridge, Mass.: Brookline, 1996: 88–94.

Repertory Theater of Lincoln Center The Lincoln Center for the Performing Arts is a complex of buildings in Manhattan, New York, that serves as home for 12 arts companies, including the Lincoln Center Theater. In 1955, Lincoln Square was designated for urban renewal, and there was a groundbreaking ceremony in 1959. The first building to be completed was the Philharmonic Hall, and the 1,100 seat Vivian Beaumont Theater and 299 seat The Forum (renamed Mitzi E. Newhouse Theater in 1973) were completed in 1965. The Beaumont's first tenant was the Repertory Theater of Lincoln Center, that would remain active there, on and off, until 1973.

ROBERT WHITEHEAD had long held the dream of a repertory theater along the lines of the national theaters in Europe, and he welcomed the opportunity in 1960 when he was asked to head the new Repertory Theater of Lincoln Center. He brought in ELIA KAZAN as his artistic director and asked Arthur Miller for a new play to inaugurate the company.

Miller obliged with *After the Fall*. Whitehead and Kazan drew up plans for a 30-member acting company and appointed Robert Lewis as head of their actor's training program. The new theater space was scheduled for completion in 1963, but delays mounted, and the decision was made to begin production at a temporary site rather than wait. *After the Fall*, directed by Kazan, opened on January 23, 1964, at ANTA/ Washington Square Theater in repertory with a revival of EUGENE O'NEILL's *Marco Millions* and S. N. Behrman's *But For Whom Charlie*. Whitehead asked Miller for another play to put into the fall schedule and received *Incident at Vichy*, which ran in repertory with Thomas Middleton and William Rowley's *The Changeling* and Moliere's *Tartuffe*. But a repertory company was more costly than the board had expected.

Used to the way that commercial theaters were run, the board could not understand why the Repertory Theater was not more viable, not having taken into consideration the greater expense of running a permanent company. Whitehead was pressured to resign, and Kazan soon followed, with Miller angrily insisting that he would not offer them another play. When the Repertory Theater moved into the Beaumont, it gained new management, codirectors Herbert Blau and Jules Irving. Blau left after two years, but Irving stayed for six more seasons, presenting LEE J. COBB in *King Lear* and other star-name productions. By 1973, the Repertory Theater of Lincoln Center was defunct, but theater at Lincoln Center would survive.

Joseph Papp's New York Shakespeare Festival was in residence from 1973 to 1977, but after they left, until 1985, no permanent theater group took tenancy, and the theaters occasionally fell dark. In 1985, when Gregory Mosher became the artistic director of the not-for-profit Lincoln Center Theater, new life was brought to the site. Since then, a number of new and classic plays have been regularly staged at both the Beaumont and the Newhouse, including one more of Miller's, the 1987 double bill *Danger Memory!*, directed by Mosher himself.

Robards, Jason Jr. (1920–2000) Born in Chicago, the son of stage and film star Jason Robards Sr., Jason Robards Jr., eventually followed in his father's footsteps to even greater fame. He attended Hollywood High School in Beverly Hills and played on the football, baseball, basketball, and track teams, once entertaining the idea of becoming a professional athlete. After receiving the Navy Cross for his service in WORLD WAR II, he struggled as a small-part actor in local New York theatre, radio, and television (including a minor role in the 1959 television film of HENRIK IBSEN's *A Doll's House*) before being noticed in 1955 as Hickey in an Off-Broadway production of EUGENE O'NEILL's *The Iceman Cometh*. He then appeared on BROADWAY the following year as the alcoholic Jamie Tyrone in O'Neill's *Long Day's Journey Into Night*. He triumphantly created several other O'Neill roles on Broadway and was nominated a record-breaking eight times for Tony awards.

Robards received his first film break in George Tabori's *The Journey* (1959) and, despite his drinking problem, Robards rose rapidly to even greater fame as a film star, winning consecutive Oscars for Best Supporting Actor for *All the President's Men* (1976) and *Julia* (1977). He continued to divide his time between stage and screen, receiving a Kennedy Center Honors for lifetime contribution to arts and culture the year before his death in 2000. Robards preferred theater work and said once that he performed in films so that he could "grab the money and go back to Broadway as fast as I can."

Robards had been considered for Gay Langland in *The Misfits*, but CLARK GABLE had proved a more bankable star. He was then offered the role of Quentin in *After the Fall*. He and Miller did not get along. Robards found it awkward dealing with Miller and the director ELIA KAZAN, between whom he sensed tension, and asked for Miller to be kept out of rehearsals. Robards also began to drink again during production. Threatened with replacement with GEORGE C. SCOTT, he called their bluff and gave an opening-night performance that led to one of his Tony nominations. His final Broadway outing was in a 1994 revival of HAROLD PINTER's *No Man's Land*.

Rosten, Norman (1914–1995) Born in New York, Norman Rosten attended Brooklyn College and signed up with the FEDERAL THEATER PROJECT after graduation. Miller first met Rosten in his senior year at the UNIVERSITY OF MICHIGAN to which Rosten had come, having won one of the same scholarships as Miller, offered by the THEATRE GUILD to study playwriting with KENNETH ROWE. Rosten's poetry having been published in several respected journals impressed Miller, and sharing similar leftist political outlooks and an interest in drama soon made of them close friends.

Miller's girlfriend, MARY SLATTERY, brought along her roommate, Hedda Rowinski, to make up a foursome, and the following year, when he moved back to New York, Rosten married Hedda. Miller and Slattery would soon follow to New York, and the couples lived close by in BROOKLYN, with Rosten encouraging Miller to pursue radio drama as he was doing and to apply to the Federal Theater, to which Rosten had returned. He even helped Miller get an agent. So impressive was Rosten's radio work during the early 1940s that in 1945 he was honored with an American Academy of Arts and Letters Award for his "exploration of the Radio as a new medium for poetry." During their brief employment by the Federal Theater, Miller and Rosten collaborated on *Listen My Children*, which was brought up by the HOUSE UN-AMERICAN ACTIVITIES COMMITTEE when Miller was called in for questioning, although it had been Rosten who was more closely committed to COMMUNISM.

Rosten's *First Stop to Heaven* was produced off-Broadway in 1941 but closed after only five performances, an embarrassment that Miller would also face with his first BROADWAY production, *The Man Who Had All the Luck*. But Rosten's luck with stage drama never reversed, and although Miller helped him revise both *Mardi Gras* (1954) during its out-of-town tryouts and *Mister Johnson* (1956), based on the novel by Joyce Cary, neither won great support. As a favor, Miller let Rosten write the 1962 screenplay for *A View from the Bridge*, directed by Sidney Lumet, in France. Rosten had two more plays on Broadway in the 1960s but no breakthrough. Turning his back on theater, he wrote three novels that met better acclaim and continued writing poetry for which he was, perhaps, the better known. In 1978, he became the poet laureate of Brooklyn.

MARILYN MONROE reportedly befriended Rosten to get closer to Miller but ended up close friends with both him and his wife; Hedda later became Monroe's personal secretary, and Rosten would often escort her to museums and concerts. The couple helped Miller meet discreetly with Monroe, loaning them their summer rental. One columnist would describe Rosten as the "cupid" in the Monroe/Miller romance, and he would be one of the small group who attended their wedding. He also witnessed the couple's subsequent breakdown. Although close friends with Miller for many years, Rosten's outspokenness regarding Monroe in his 1973 book *Marilyn: An Untold Story* and his collaboration with Norman Mailer on *Marilyn* (1973) estranged him from the playwright. Miller felt exposed and betrayed, as this was a part of his life he preferred to keep private.

Rowe, Kenneth (1900–1988)   Kenneth Thorpe Rowe is the man whom Miller often credited with teaching him the dynamics of play construction. In *Timebends: A Life*, Miller describes him as "a combination of critical judge and confidant," and Rowe became Miller's mentor and friend until his death in 1988. They wrote to each other regularly, except for a brief hiatus for four years after *Death of a Salesman* when ELIA KAZAN took over as Miller's main confidant. After Kazan had named names to the HOUSE UN-AMERICAN ACTIVITIES COMMITTEE in 1953, he and Miller fell out, and Miller resumed correspondence with Rowe. On visits to his alma mater, Miller would visit his old professor, and one of the university's holdings is the Kenneth Thorpe Rowe, Student Play Collection, which contains numerous letters and manuscripts relating to Miller. A few years before his death, Rowe contributed a chapter to Robert Martin's *Arthur Miller: New Perspectives*, in which he shares his personal memories of Miller as a student who was keen to learn the craft of playwrighting, and he details Miller's student works. "I think of Arthur Miller," he concludes, "as a dramatist of respect," by which he underscores Miller's HUMANISM.

A professor of theater at the UNIVERSITY OF MICHIGAN since the 1930s, when Miller first arrived Rowe had been on sabbatical leave, working with the THEATRE GUILD in New York as a consultant on a playwrighting seminar for promising young dramatists. The seminar was so successful that the Theatre Guild arranged for subsequent sessions to be held at Michigan and offered grants to those whom they felt would benefit from attending. On the basis of *They Too Arise*, Miller was offered one of these scholarships and subsequently took playwriting seminars with Rowe in both his junior and senior years. NORMAN ROSTEN and TENNESSEE WILLIAMS would also be offered scholarships in 1937, although Williams declined his. Miller was attracted to Rowe's commonsense approach to drama and learned much about dramatic craft under Rowe's tutelage, including the necessary collaborative relationship between playwright and director, how to unify the conflict of a play, and the importance of pacing and rhythm.

Rowe's 1939 study *Write That Play!* uses detailed discussions of Lord Dunsany's *A Night at an Inn*, J. M. Synge's, *Riders to the Sea,* and HENRIK IBSEN's *A Doll's House* to illustrate his commentary on dramatic technique, history, and criticism. His classes offered similar lessons and led Miller to Ibsen, whose social commitment Miller found as inspiring as his craft and taught him the problem–complication–crisis formula of Greek TRAGEDY. Rowe was also keen to point out how Ibsen effectively used the past coming to life in the present as a means of creating drama. Rowe advised his students to look for plots in the lives of people whom they knew rather than use pure invention, although they were to do so imaginatively rather than mimetically. In Rowe's eyes, dramatic form that was supported by speakable dialogue which moves the plot forward was the key to a good playwright. His connections to drama went beyond the campus and his work with the Theatre Guild, for whom he headed the play department for a year in 1945—Rowe was also chairman of production of new plays for the American Educational Theatre Association, and his wife wrote radio drama. In 1960, he wrote a second volume on the history and criticism of drama called *A Theater in Your Head,* adding new commentary on theatrical production and direction; in this work, he also closely analyzed Kazan's production of *Death of a Salesman.*

FURTHER READING

Rowe, Kenneth T. "Shadows Cast Before." *Arthur Miller: New Perspectives*, edited by Robert A. Martin, 13–32. (Englewood Cliffs, New Jersey: Prentice–Hall, 1982).

———. *A Theater in Your Head.* New York: Funk & Wagnalls, 1960.

———. *Write That Play!* New York: Funk & Wagnalls, 1939.

Roxbury, Connecticut   The American Indian name of the town of Roxbury, located in Litchfield County, Connecticut, was *Shepaug*, which means "rocky water." Originally a part of Woodbury, the town was incorporated in October 1796 but had been settled since 1713. In the 18th century, nearby Mine Hill became known for its silver, Spathic iron, and granite mines, providing granite for the building of the Brooklyn Bridge and Grand Central Station. The town remained rural and secluded so that even by 2000, its population had only just topped 2,000 people.

After the success of *All My Sons*, Miller could afford a country getaway for the family. MARY SLATTERY had been working as an editorial assistant for Sidney Jaffe, the publisher of the magazine *Amerasia;* Jaffe who was looking for a buyer for his renovated farmhouse in Roxbury, so Miller bought it to use as a vacation home. He would write *Death of a Salesman* in a small studio that he had built himself on the property. In his 1956 divorce settlement with Slattery, he held on to the Roxbury property, but it was decided that he and MARILYN MONROE would sell and buy something in the same area that they could make their own. Two years later, the couple bought an old farmhouse from a local dairy farmer at 323 Tophet Road. Monroe had wanted to rebuild and hired Frank Lloyd Wright to draw up plans, but Miller preferred simply to renovate the place. He did, however, at Monroe's insistence, buy up much of the surrounding land to create a nicely secluded estate of 340 acres, and the couple lived there between Monroe's film work.

After his divorce from Monroe and marriage to INGE MORATH, the new couple made Roxbury their main residence. Getting involved in local politics, in

1968 Miller was elected by his Roxbury neighbors to be their delegate to the Democratic National Convention in Chicago. The title character of *The Ryan Interview* was based on a local Roxbury character, Bob Tracy, and many of the tales that he relates can be found in Miller's 1977 book *In the Country*, where he shares his recollections of Tracy and other Roxbury locals. By that time, Miller had lived there for more than 25 years, but he still felt that he was the outsider and was viewing the locals as having a culture from which he was excluded. But Roxbury was an area near which many new people were settling. Miller's oldest friends there were the sculptor Alexander "Sandy" Calder and his wife Louisa. Litchfield County's close proximity to New York drew in many other famous neighbors, including writers William Styron, JOHN STEINBECK, Philip Roth, SAUL BELLOW, the director Mike Nichols, and actors Richard Widmark and DUSTIN HOFFMAN, all of whom became part of Miller's circle of friends.

While in China in 1983, the Roxbury house was gutted by fire, and Miller lost many of his books; luckily, most of his manuscripts had been stored in a nearby barn and were unharmed. Rather than rebuild, Miller decided to restore the ruined building. Despite liking his privacy, Miller used his Roxbury homes as settings for some of his short stories and also allowed his estate to be used in two movies of his work, the film short *The Reason Why* in 1970 and scenes from the 2001 movie *Eden* based on his novella *Homely Girl, A Life*. Miller was so attached to the place that Roxbury was where Miller chose to die, requesting a special ambulance to take him there from his New York hospital. Shortly after his death, the town announced that May 7, 2005, would be the town's first official Arthur Miller Day. Family and neighbors attended a gathering at the local Town Hall where a bust of Miller created by Washington sculptor Philip Grausman was on display.

S

Salem Witch Trials Miller's interest in the 1692 Salem witch trials was partly prompted by reading Marion Starkey's *The Devil in Massachusetts*. He researched the period at the Historical Society in Salem, Massachusetts, and found the core of his plot in Charles W. Upton's 19th-century book, *Salem Witchcraft*. In terms of the play's historical accuracy, Miller admits that while it is predominantly accurate as regard to facts, he made some changes for "dramatic purposes." Aside from creating a relationship between Abigail and Proctor and its impact on events, he fused various original characters into a single representative, reduced the number of judges and girls "crying out," and increased Abigail's age. While he based characters on the originals, he asked for them to be considered properly as "creations of my own, drawn to the best of my ability in conformity with their known behavior."

In terms of what happened historically, the Reverend Samuel Parris was hired as the Salem Village minister in 1689. Three years later, in February 1692, his daughter Betty and several other village girls fell ill. One of the villagers, Mary Sibley, asked Parris's servant Tituba and her husband John Indian to bake a witch cake to help the girls recognize who was afflicting them. A few days later, Thomas and Edward Putnam, Joseph Hutchinson, and Thomas Preston swore complaints against Tituba, Sarah Good, and Sarah Osborne, who were arrested for suspicion of witchcraft. Salem Magistrates John Hathorne and Jonathan Corwin examined them. After Tituba confessed to witchcraft, all three were sent to a Boston prison, Osbourne dying there a few months later.

One week later, Martha Corey was summoned to appear before the magistrates to answer questions, after which a warrant was issued for her arrest. Rebecca Nurse was also accused of witchcraft by Abigail Williams, and thus began a series of accusations and arrests in the village. During the next few months, Elizabeth Proctor, Sarah Cloyce, Giles Corey, and others were examined and arrested. Elizabeth was John Proctor's third wife, but they had been married for 18 years. Proctor was a native of Ipswich, Massachusetts, and had moved to Salem in 1666. His inheritance from his father made him a wealthy landowner, with a tavern on Ipswich Road. He was sternly opposed to the witchcraft trials from the start. When he publicly supported and defended his wife, Proctor was sent to jail with Elizabeth, becoming the first male to be accused of witchcraft. Mary Warren was brought up on witchcraft charges and testified that Elizabeth had tried to make her sign the "Devil's Book." Abigail Williams identified Reverend George Burroughs as the "Black Minister," and a warrant was issued for his arrest, the sheriffs bringing him from his hometown in Maine to Salem for examination.

During May, matters escalated, and arrest warrants were issued for all three of the Proctors' children—Sarah, Benjamin, and William—along with several more villagers. Most were accused by spectral evidence, by which others claimed to have seen ghosts or visions. Governor Phips established a court to investigate allegations; Lieutenant Governor William Stoughton headed the nine-judge panel that included Samuel Sewall and John Hathorne. The first person tried, found guilty, and sentenced to hang was Bridget Bishop. Although 12 ministers of the colony advised the court not to rely on spectral evidence for convicting suspected witches, the court ignored their advice. The trials continued, and several more villagers, including Sarah Good and Rebecca Nurse, were hanged.

Fearing an unfair trial in Salem, John Proctor and other prisoners wrote to a group of ministers, including Increase Mather, to support their request for a change of venue. Their request was denied, and they were tried on August 5, along with Reverend Burroughs. Proctor was outspoken and hot-tempered, and these traits did not help him during his trial. Two weeks later, Burroughs, Proctor, and three others were hanged on Gallows Hill, but Elizabeth Proctor was given a stay of execution because she was pregnant. At his execution, Proctor pleaded for more time because he felt that he had not yet made peace with others and with God. Giles Corey refused to stand trial, so the court ordered the sheriff to pile rocks on him, and Corey was pressed to death. His wife was hanged soon after with seven others. However, in October, Increase Mather visited the Salem jail and found that several confessors wanted to renounce their earlier testimonies. The governor dissolved the court and a month later set up a new court to try the remaining people who had been accused of witchcraft. Several judges from the earlier court remained, including William Stoughton and Samuel Sewall, but there were new justices, including Thomas Danford, and spectral evidence was no longer considered. By May 1693, all of the remaining prisoners were pardoned, including Elizabeth. Although pardoned, she was still a convicted felon in the eyes of the law and so was barred from claiming any of her husband's property. Eighteen years later, she was paid 578 pounds and 12 shillings in restitution for Proctor's death.

Sartre, Jean-Paul (1905–1980)   Although he was born and died in Paris, France, Jean-Paul Charles Aymard Sartre traveled extensively both to study and to lecture, and his theories had a worldwide influence. He was a philosopher who also wrote novels, plays, screenplays, biographies, autobiography, literary and political criticism—and was extraordinarily prolific. Although he was the chief proponent of French EXISTENTIALISM, many critics believe that Sartre will be best remembered for his plays that include *The Flies* (1942), *No Exit* (1944), *The Respectful Prostitute* (1946), and *The Condemned of Altona* (1959). The existentialist philosophy that he developed infuses all of his writing and is based on his formula "Existence precedes essence," which posits an individual's freedom and responsibility to choose to act and thus to define his being, and he lived his own life accordingly. It is hardly surprising that Miller was attracted to his ideas in the 1940s, as he recounts in *Timebends: A Life*, where he praises Sartre's "politically usable democratic vision that was not bound to Moscow." On a 1948 trip to France, seeking inspiration for his next play, Miller recounts going to the Montana Bar that Sartre reputedly frequented, hoping to meet him. He was not there, but Miller saw him later on at a *réunion* of writers to which he had been invited.

During WORLD WAR II, after fighting with the French army, Sartre was imprisoned by the Germans for nine months. He then escaped to serve in the French resistance movement to the end of the war. It was these experiences that helped develop his dyspeptic view of humankind. Awarded the Nobel Prize for Literature in 1964, he refused to accept it, claiming that a writer "should refuse to allow himself to be transformed into an institution." Sartre was identified with various leftist causes—although he was never a party member and was vocally critical of Soviet and French COMMUNISM—and became increasingly confrontational in later years. He was also always staunchly opposed to Western capitalism, NATO, and the United States.

Like Miller, Sartre believed that people could change, but he also felt that they would prefer to remain in their errors and cling to what he termed "bad faith." This, for Sartre, was unacceptable: Because of the acceleration of violence and international competition, he felt it imperative that people be forced to change. His solution was that since the oppressive and privileged classes would not willingly give up their privileges, these must be wrested from them by violence and revolution. This would allow new relationships between human beings to evolve, based on reciprocity and openness instead of rivalry and secrecy. Miller's viewpoint, though hopeful, was less trusting. He decided that Sartre's views on socialism were too idealistic, and it was these that he felt tainted Sartre's vision of his play *The Crucible*, for which the philosopher wrote a screenplay in 1957, retitled *The Witches of Salem*. Miller disliked Sartre's adaptation, complaining that it "seemed to me to toss an arbitrary Marxist mesh over the story that led to a few absurdities," although he felt that the film had a "noble grandeur" and was not without merit.

Scott, George C. (1927–1999) Born in Virginia, George Campbell Scott lost his mother at the age of eight and was raised by his father. After a four year stint in the marines at the close of WORLD WAR II, he enrolled in journalism classes at the University of Missouri, but while there he decided to act and so moved to New York. Having won some awards off-Broadway in 1958, his subsequent successful BROADWAY and movie careers were marked by a series of acting nominations from 1959 on. He would appear in 17 Broadway productions and countless movies and television shows through the next four decades and was awarded a Drama Desk Honorary Award in 1996 for lifetime devotion to theater.

Although Scott did not appear in any of Miller's premiere productions, he was involved in a number of important revivals and television movies of Miller's work. His 1967 television performance as John Proctor in *The Crucible* brought that play a much wider audience, and in 1971 he would play Victor Franz in a television movie of *The Price*. Onstage, he also recreated Willy Loman in the 1975 Circle in the Square revival of *Death of a Salesman*, a performance that Clive Barnes found "exciting beyond words, and almost literally leaving criticism speechless." Scott had also directed it.

Walter Kerr suggested that Scott was introducing audiences to a new kind of Willy, not as a once successful man who was destroyed by the American dream but as a man who has "*always* had to compensate, to inflate his indeterminate place in the scheme of things." This he felt, made Scott's version a play about people rather than a social indictment of the "failed American myth." Others felt that this made Willy less empathetic and destroyed the play's universal nature. Despite Scott's strong performance, there was greater uncertainty about the production, both the staging and Scott's decision to cast Charley and Bernard with black actors. Miller had objected to the latter, suggesting that for the play's time period this would make Willy seem too much the social rebel, but he was ignored.

FURTHER READING

Barnes, Clive. "Scott Puts Acting Magic in *Salesman*." *New York Times*, June 27 1975: 26.
Kerr, Walter. "This *Salesman* Is More Man than Myth." *New York Times*, June 29, 1975, sec. 2: pp. 1, 5.

Slattery, Mary (1917–) Mary Grace Slattery was born and raised in Lakewood, Ohio, to a Catholic family. A tall, slender brunette, somewhat quiet, she had firm beliefs and a fierce idealism. Disowning her family's religion, she headed to nearby UNIVERSITY OF MICHIGAN a year behind Miller, to major in psychology and become a social worker. The two met at a party in 1936 and instantly hit it off, finding that they shared the same socialist political beliefs and view of the world. As Miller describes in *Timebends: A Life*, "We enjoyed a certain unity within ourselves by virtue of a higher consciousness bestowed by our expectation of a socialist evolution of the planet." He asked her for a date but had no money, so she treated him to the movies. Slattery would help Miller type his reports for the MICHIGAN DAILY and his various play manuscripts; they were soon inseparable. The following year, she introduced Miller's new friend NORMAN ROSTEN to her roommate, Hedda Rowinski, and the four would go out together, with Rosten later marrying Rowinski.

When Miller graduated, Slattery decided to drop out of college and go with him to New York. She went to work waiting tables until landing a job as a secretary with the publishing firm, Harcourt. She took an apartment on Pierrepont Street in BROOKLYN, where Miller spent most of his time, despite finally getting his own apartment on East 74th Street once his application to the WPA was approved. In October 1940, the couple headed to Ohio to marry. Miller's parents, but especially his grandfather LOUIS BARNETT, were disappointed that he was marrying a non-Jew, but both Miller and Slattery felt that religion had become obsolescent in the modern world. However, Slattery would insist on being married by a priest to keep her mother happy. A special dispensation was arranged while Miller got to meet her family, getting the plotlines for *The Man Who Had All the Luck* from the story of an aunt and uncle and for *All My Sons* from a piece of gossip that was relayed by Slattery's mother.

On their return to New York, they moved into an apartment building known locally as French Flats, at 62 Montague Street. Soon after their marriage, Miller departed on the SS *Copa Copa* on a fact-finding trip for a possible play about the merchant navy; funds were low so he went solo. This was indicative of how their marriage would proceed, with Slattery (and later their children) often being left behind as Miller put his work first; it would put an inevitable strain on their marriage. On his return, Miller signed up to work on a night shift as a shipfitter's helper in the BROOKLYN NAVY YARD as part of the war effort, while Slattery got a job with another publishing house, Harper and Brothers, as a private secretary to the head of the medical-books department.

By 1944 Miller and Slattery had moved into a duplex at 102 Pierrepont Street to gain a little more space as they began a family. After the birth of their first child, JANE MILLER, in September, Slattery tried freelance editorial work at home but found it difficult with the new baby. She returned to work at Harpers, this time as secretary to Frank Taylor who was the chief of the Reynal and Hitchcock division. While Miller was in Washington, D.C., researching material for the screenplay of *The Story of G.I. Joe*, he had met a woman whose husband was "Missing in Action" and felt strangely attracted to her. He admitted to himself that he would have tried to sleep with her if not already married. On explaining this experience to his wife, he was surprised at how angry she became. This episode would reappear

along with other scenes from their marriage in *After the Fall* where the characters of Quentin and Louise share a close affinity with Miller and Slattery. Regardless of her anger, Slattery recommended the book that Miller had written based on his interviews with soldiers to her new boss, Taylor, and he liked it enough to immediately authorize publication. *Situation Normal . . .* came out in December 1944, a month after the unfortunate failure of *The Man Who Had All the Luck* on BROADWAY and was far more kindly reviewed.

A second child, ROBERT MILLER, would be born to the Millers on May 31, 1947, four months after the success of *All My Sons*. After this, Slattery switched to work as a secretary for Sidney Jaffe, editor and publisher of *Amerasia*. In 1948, the family finally had sufficient funds to buy their own two-family house at 31 Grace Court, as well as Jaffe's farmhouse in ROXBURY, CONNECTICUT, for a vacation home. In *Timebends: A Life*, Miller recalls driving home with Slattery in 1949 after the successful opening of *Death of a Salesman* and feeling a increasing friction in their marriage. They did not talk as they drove together, and Miller explains, "I sensed in our silence some discomfort in my wife and friend over these struggling years. It never occurred to me that she might have felt anxious at being swamped by this rush of my fame, in need of reassurance. I had always thought her clearer and more resolved that I." It was during this period that their marriage seemed to really drift apart, although it would struggle along for a few years more.

The most intense pressure on their marriage would be Miller meeting and falling in love with MARILYN MONROE in 1951 while out in Hollywood with ELIA KAZAN trying to get funding for his screenplay, *The Hook*. Aware of his responsibilities, Miller returned to New York, determined to keep his marriage going, and again confessed his temptation to his wife, who was as angry as before. He went into analysis but found himself, as he explains in *Timebends: A Life*, swinging between "love and hope" and a feeling of being "endlessly judged, hopelessly condemned." Miller's dedication of *The Crucible* to Mary at this point with its theme of a failing marriage and guilt about adultery appears like an indirect attempt at expiation.

While it seems to confess openly a relationship outside of the marriage, it also suggests mutual guilt, as well as taking a strong and—considering the timing—dangerous stance against the political climate of the time about which Slattery would have been proud. Elizabeth Proctor's forgiveness of her husband might suggest the hope that the Millers too could start afresh. Selling Grace Court and moving into the single-family home at 151 Willow Street was the way that Miller tried to show his commitment to his family and to reinvigorate his marriage with a fresh start.

Miller worked on the new house, installing flooring and renovating the kitchen and, as he confesses in *Timebends: A Life,* "did fifty things a man does who believes in a future with his family, but the ease of mutual trust had flown from us like a bird, and the new cage was empty as the old where no bird sang." Monroe would send him letters, and they would occasionally speak on the phone. When Monroe moved to New York in 1955 after her divorce from Joe DiMaggio, the pressure increased. Slattery took yoga to try and change her lifestyle and personally invested some of her own money in the New York production of the single-act play *A View from the Bridge,* another tale about a man infatuated with someone far younger, but these would not pay off. Miller and Monroe began to meet with increasingly frequency, and there were numerous rumors in the newspapers. Slattery did not attend the September opening of *A View from the Bridge,* although Monroe noticeably did. A month later Slattery asked Miller to move out. He took a room in the Chelsea Hotel. His wife remained aloof from any scandal, insisting in a rare interview to the papers that Monroe was not the reason for their separation. Miller would go to Nevada soon after to get the required residency to apply for a divorce on the grounds of "extreme cruelty, entirely mental in nature." The couple reached a settlement whereby Slattery would receive the Willow Street house, child alimony, and a percentage of her ex-husband's future earnings until she remarried, which she never did.

Signature Theater Company   Since its founding in 1991 by actor/director James Houghton, Signature Theatre Company has championed season-long explorations of a single living playwright's body of work. It is the first not-for-profit theater company in the United States to structure its productions in this fashion. The company presents fully staged works by the chosen playwright at various theater spaces around New York. These include reexaminations of past writings as well as New York and world premieres. Each season engages a new playwright-in-residence in every aspect of the creative process, allowing tremendous insight into the scope, context, and substance of a playwright's work, legacy, and continuing achievements. Aside from Miller, past playwrights honored in this fashion have included EDWARD ALBEE, Lee Blessing, Horton Foote, Maria Irene Fornes, John Guare, Bill Irwin, Adrienne Kennedy, Romulus Linney, Sam Shepard, Lanford Wilson, and Paula Vogel. Miller was delighted to be chosen as the playwright-in-residence for the 1997–98 season, during which New York audiences witnessed reworked versions of the infrequently produced *The American Clock,* directed by Houghton; the one-act plays *I Can't Remember Anything* and *The Last Yankee;* and the world premiere of *Mr. Peters' Connections,* starring Peter Falk and directed by Garry Hynes. The season also featured Miller reading his children's story *Jane's Blanket* and a special performance of the 1940 radio play *The Pussycat and Expert Plumber Who Was a Man* at the New Victory Theater, featuring Matthew Broderick and Rebecca Schull. This was later broadcast on National Public Radio.

Steinbeck, John (1902–1968)   John Ernst Steinbeck was born in Salinas, California, where he worked as a hired hand on local ranches during his summers. He attended Stanford University but never graduated, trying instead, unsuccessfully, to make his mark as a New York writer. Returning to California, he continued to write to little acclaim until *Tortilla Flat* (1935), which marked a turning point in his career. In 1939, he would win a Pulitzer Prize for his epic of the GREAT DEPRESSION, *The Grapes of Wrath,* followed by several more successful publications. During WORLD WAR II, Steinbeck was a war correspondent for the *New York Herald Tribune.* In 1962, he was awarded the Nobel Prize for Literature, "for his realistic as well as imaginative writings, distinguished by a sympathetic humor and a keen social perception." A private person who shunned publicity, he and Miller met in the 1940s and later became friends.

Miller has described Steinbeck's writing as political, revolutionary, and quintessentially American. In *Timebends: A Life,* he describes being introduced to Steinbeck when he met columnist Ernie Pyle; Miller was developing the screenplay for *The Story of G. I. Joe* at the time. Awed by the writer's fame, Miller said little, observing Steinbeck's "basic sensitivity and sentiment covered by an aggressively cynical wit." Miller was surprised to realize that an "author of prose so definite and painterly" was "so personally unsure." In 1957, Steinbeck wrote an elegant defense of Miller's refusal to be bullied by the HOUSE UN-AMERICAN ACTIVITIES COMMITTEE in the June edition of *Esquire,* in which he described Miller as "one of our very best" writers, observing that "a man who is disloyal to his friends could not be expected to be loyal to his country" and complimenting Miller on his bravery in refusing to name names. Both men found themselves in the same circle of writers who lived between New York and Connecticut and later became friends until Steinbeck's demise. In *The American Clock,* a work that can be seen as Steinbeckian in its attempt to encapsulate the American experience, Miller includes a scene in tribute to Steinbeck's closing scene in *The Grapes of Wrath,* where the starving man drinks the mother's milk from Rose of Sharon's breast. Miller's version, no doubt made more respectable for stage performance, has a mother offer her baby's bottle to the starving Matthew Bush.

Strasberg, Lee (1901–1982)   Israel Lee Strasberg, born to an eastern European innkeeper, was brought to the United States as a child of seven. When the Moscow Art Theatre visited the United States, two of its company members defected and began to teach the theories of Russian director Constantin Stanislavski at the American Laboratory Theatre. It was there that Strasberg immersed himself in Stanislavski's "System," later adapting it to promote a mode of performance preparation that encouraged actors to live in their roles by drawing

on emotional experience and memory. For Strasberg, "Work for the actor lies in two areas: The ability to consistently create reality and the ability to express that reality." He attempted a brief acting career before helping to found the GROUP THEATER, for which he directed several plays and began to teach "The Method," as it became known. Strasberg's first wife had died in 1929, and at the Group Theater he met Paula Miller who would become his second wife and with whom he would have two children: John would go on to be an acting coach like his father at the ACTORS STUDIO; Susan would become an actress. His greatest influence was through the Actors Studio to which he was invited in 1949, becoming artistic director in 1951 until his death in 1982.

Although he never taught Marlon Brando, who had studied with Stella Adler, Strasberg influenced several generations of actors from James Dean to DUSTIN HOFFMAN. In *Timebends: A Life,* Miller describes Strasberg as the "heart and soul" of the Actors Studio, as well as its most public face. In *Elia Kazan: A Life,* ELIA KAZAN describes Strasberg at an acting session as a "tribal chief leading a movement that was to change the art of acting in our theatre." Both Miller and Kazan simultaneously admired Strasberg for the depth of his passion regarding the art of acting and the way he helped to open up the idea of the subtext of a play, but they also decried what they saw as his crippling desire for adulation, his lack of breadth, and the way he encouraged actors to be dependent totally on him. Each felt that Strasberg's techniques, while allowing actors new dignity, could also limit natural talent. Although Strasberg was revered by many actors, of whom Miller includes his sister JOAN COPELAND, Miller also mentions that Montgomery Clift, "a most astute analyst of acting and its problems," thought him a charlatan. Miller based the ambitiously pompous, self-involved character of Jerome Fassinger in *Finishing the Picture* on Strasberg.

Miller disapproved of the growing hold that both Strasberg and his wife Paula had over MARILYN MONROE, who had been taking classes from Strasberg since 1955. He felt that they abetted her deterioration by contributing to her confusion rather than helping her find herself as an actress. Monroe viewed Strasberg with what Miller describes as "a nearly religious dependency," but Miller saw him as akin to Willy Loman in the way that he would make up stories to make himself appear more important.

In the 1960s, upset not to have been asked to participate in the REPERTORY THEATER OF LINCOLN CENTER that Kazan and ROBERT WHITEHEAD were creating, Strasberg set the Actors Studio up as a rival. He used a revolving company that utilized big star names rather than the repertory format of the new Lincoln project. The Actors Studio mounted a series of successful BROADWAY hits, including revivals of EUGENE O'NEILL's *Strange Interlude* and ANTON CHEKHOV's *The Three Sisters*. However, the dismal film version of *The Three Sisters* followed by its disastrous London opening, for which Strasberg blamed the actors rather than take responsibility himself, led some to question his leadership. Many felt that Strasberg's growing involvement with well-known stars and the creation of vehicles to feature their talents ran counter to the Actors Studio's mission, whose emphasis had always been on development rather than the final performance. After this, encouraged by his ambitious third wife, Anna, whom he married after the death of Paula in 1966, Strasberg became totally commercialized, opening his Hollywood studio and concentrating on grooming stars.

On February 13, 1982, Strasberg made his last public appearance at the "Night of 100 Stars" benefit for the Actors Fund at Radio City Music Hall. Along with protégés Al Pacino and Robert De Niro, he danced in the chorus line with the Rockettes, but he died two days later. In her final will, Monroe had left Strasberg total control of 75 percent of her estate, including the licensing of her image as gratitude for his mentorship and kindness before and after she became a star. Although Monroe had asked that Strasberg distribute her effects "among my friends, colleagues and those to whom I am devoted," he never did, and after his death, Monroe's clothing and belongings went to Anna, who sold them in a Christie's auction in 1999 for $13.4 million.

Strasberg, Paula (1911–1966)   Born Paula Miller in New York City, her first of more than 20 Broadway acting credits was in 1927 when she was 16, in *The Cradle Song*, written by Gregorio and Maria Martinez Sierra. She appeared in several plays with the Civic Repertory Theatre between 1927 and 1930 and then joined the GROUP THEATER with which she appeared in, among others, Paul Green's *House of Connelly* (1931), Sidney Kingsley's *Men in White* (1935), and the role of Florrie in CLIFFORD ODETS's *Waiting for Lefty* (1935). She continued acting into the 1940s, but her final Broadway showing was in Gertrude Berg's 1948 comedy *Me and Molly*.

In 1934, she had married LEE STRASBERG, whom she had met within the Group Theater. Paula would assist her husband in teaching the techniques of The Method style of acting at the ACTORS STUDIO, which they both joined in 1949. In 1955, MARILYN MONROE became a favored pupil, many suspected for her star power rather than her acting potential, but Paula would become Monroe's personal on-the-set acting coach for the filming of several movies, including the tumultuous making of *The Misfits*, as well as the film version of WILLIAM INGE's *Bus Stop*. Paula herself did not have a screen career, possibly because ELIA KAZAN named her as a member of the Communist Party in 1952 in front of the HOUSE UN-AMERICAN ACTIVITIES COMMITTEE. She died in 1966 after a grueling battle with cancer.

In *Timebends: A Life*, Miller paints Paula as a vain and ambitious person, comparing her to a character out of Molière. Mocking her intense loyalty to the Actors Studio and her intense admiration of her husband, Miller felt Paula to be a clearly negative influence on Monroe in her final years. He describes her acting advice to Monroe as full of "half-digested, spitballed imagery and pseudo-Stanislavskian parallelisms" and "a spurious intellection that was thoroughly useless to her as an acting tool." He felt that the influence of both Strasbergs crippled Monroe as an actress rather than allowed her to use her natural talent. The ambitious, flamboyant character of Flora Fassinger in *Finishing the Picture* was based on Paula.

T

Thacker, David (1950–) British director David Thomas Thacker attended the University of York to major in English and pursued graduate studies specializing in Shakespeare. Starting as assistant stage manager at the York Theater Royal, he worked his way up to assistant director by 1975. After stints with various regional theaters in the North of England, including Chester Gateway and Duke's Playhouse in Lancaster, he moved to London in 1984 to become artistic director of the Young Vic, a position he held until 1993. He directed a radical, award-winning version of *Pericles* in 1990 for the Royal Shakespeare Company, and in 1993, he was invited to become a resident director for the company, where he stayed for two years and directed nine productions. About this period, he also directed two plays at the NATIONAL THEATER, both Miller's. Since 1992, he has worked increasingly in television and has produced a number of critically acclaimed films and series, including an adaptation of Thomas Hardy's *The Mayor of Casterbridge* and HENRIK IBSEN's *A Doll's House*. The television piece of which he is most proud is his BBC film of *Broken Glass*.

Thacker first became interested in the plays of Miller at the Young Vic, where he directed *The Crucible* and Miller's version of *An Enemy of the People*, and has been a staunch supporter of Miller since then, with the two becoming friendly and working together closely on several productions. Regarding why he felt drawn to Miller's work, Thacker explains, "They were bull's-eye plays that fitted perfectly with our policy of attracting young audiences. They moved and affected young people in ways that few other plays could achieve." Thacker has directed a number of Miller's plays, both revivals and premieres, and in honor of Miller's 75th birthday in 1990, he mounted a celebration that included London revivals of *The Price* and *The Crucible*.

In 1989, Thacker directed the British premiere of *Two-Way Mirror* with Helen Mirren and Bob Peck and functioned in the same capacity for the London premiere of the two-scene version of *The Last Yankee* in 1993. Another premiere in 1994, this time *Broken Glass* for the National Theatre, was repeated for television in 1996, as well as for radio and for an Israeli production in Hebrew. For the stage, he convinced Miller to add an additional scene between the three female characters near the play's close, and for the BBC he cowrote the screenplay with David Holman. He directed Bernard Hill in a 1995 revival of *A View from the Bridge* and worked closely with Miller on a 1996 revival of *Death of a Salesman* for the National Theatre with Alun Armstrong as Willy. The production featured a turntable stage that was scattered with artifacts from Willy's life, including his old car, a refrigerator, and beds from BROOKLYN and Boston. That same year, Thacker also filmed a television version of *Death of a Salesman* with Warren Mitchell, who had first played Willy in 1979. In addition to this, he has directed a four-part series on Arthur Miller called *Miller Shorts* for the BBC. In *Remembering*

Arthur Miller, Thacker affectionately recalls various rehearsals that Miller attended and the assistance that the playwright gave him during the years of their acquaintance.

Theatre Guild For almost 40 years, the Theatre Guild, with its initial mission to advance theater as an art rather than worry about box-office success, was one of the most influential producing organizations in the United States: Between 1919 and 1977, aside from other activities, they produced 228 Broadway productions. Lawrence Langner and Theresa Helburn, who had been key members of the experimental group, the Washington Square Players, were two of the Theater Guild's founders. Langner managed the finances, and Helburn the casting and script selection. Their premiere production in 1919—Jacinto Benavente's *The Bonds of Interest* (1907)—was a distinct failure. However, an interesting conflation of events by which most other theaters were closed due to union action guaranteed audiences for their second play, St. John Ervine's *John Ferguson.* Since the Theatre Guild was a cooperative in which everyone involved received a percentage of the box office, Actors Equity had not demanded that they join the strike. In 1920, Ervine's friend, George Bernard Shaw allowed them to premiere his *Heartbreak House,* and they would go on to produce several more of his plays.

Although initially criticized for exclusively producing European works, they turned to home-grown playwrights by 1923, producing works by Elmer Rice and Sidney Howard and from 1927 became EUGENE O'NEILL's exclusive producers. Initiating a subscription season, they were cushioned against the vagaries of the box office and made enough profit so that in 1925, they were able to open their own theater on 52nd Street in New York and to take their repertory company on the road to Chicago and Baltimore. Cheryl Crawford and HAROLD CLURMAN were Theatre Guild employees, but sensing a conservatism to which they objected, they left in 1931 to form their own GROUP THEATER with LEE STRASBERG, just as Robert Sherwood and Maxwell Anderson, displeased by their treatment within the Theatre Guild, would leave to form their own production company in

1938. While the Theatre Guild's activities reached their peak in the late 1940s, it lost credibility as a producer of serious theater, and with the deaths of Hellburn in 1959 and Langner in 1962, their productions severely dwindled under the leadership of Langner's son, Philip.

Some of the Theatre Guild's biggest successes had come during the years of WORLD WAR II, starting with Philip Barry's *The Philadelphia Story* (1939) and including the Rodgers and Hammerstein musicals *Oklahoma!* (1943) and *Carousel* (1945). These provided the Theatre Guild with sufficient funds to branch into radio drama with Theater Guild on the Air, for which Miller would provide a one-hour version of Jane Austen's *Pride and Prejudice* (1945). Miller's first connection with the Theatre Guild occurred in 1937 when his *They Too Arise* had won a $1,250 scholarship award from the Theatre Guild's Bureau of New Plays to study playwriting with KENNETH ROWE, a professor at MICHIGAN UNIVERSITY and an advisor to the Theatre Guild. When Miller tried to interest them in producing *The Golden Years,* they proved uninterested but viewed his Broadway flop *The Man Who Had All the Luck,* promising enough to receive the Theatre Guild National Award. However, when offered *All My Sons,* they were reluctant to commit and lost the chance to produce the play.

Tragedy In general usage, the term *tragedy* tends to refer to any event with a sad outcome, but in literature, especially drama, it has a more precise definition. The origins of tragedy go back to the Greeks, and the word loosely translates to mean "goat-song" for it was related to the animal sacrifices and the festivities surrounding the Festival of Dionysus. It was here that tragedies were first performed in competition as part of the festival. In *The Poetics,* Aristotle set out the precepts on which these tragedies were based. For the Greeks, tragedy was a form of drama that was characterized by seriousness and dignity, usually involving a conflict between a person of nobility and some higher power such as the law, the gods, fate, or society. The point of tragedy, according to Aristotle, is to produce a catharsis (emotional cleansing) in its audience through its instigation of fear and pity, which are brought on by the audience response to the suffering of characters in the play. Thus, it is imperative that characters suffer but are also sympathetic and can offer positive insights though their suffering.

While Aristotle described the tragic process as the tying of a knot and the unloosing of it, theater scholar Kenneth Burke divided the classic tragic structure into four stages, beginning with the setting of a problem. Once the problem is identified, purpose follows, which is the development in the tragic protagonist of the firm intent to solve the problem. Then the passion of the process takes over as protagonists put their all into finding the right solution. The last stage is perception, when the protagonist finally comes to terms with the deeper issues involved; this often entails a recognition that the tragic hero, him or herself, has been a part of the problem all along. This points us toward the concept of the tragic flaw, an aspect of the tragic protagonist that ensures that the protagonist not only suffers but also has brought that suffering upon him- or herself. In Greek times, that flaw, as with Oedipus, was often hubris, or pride—in Oedipus's case, the belief that he knew better than the gods. In Shakespeare's hands, this tragic format was extended in nuance by such complex characters as Hamlet, Othello, Macbeth, King Lear, or Romeo and Juliet, but the traditional view remained. His tragic heroes remained upper class or very intelligent, and they challenged, because of some personal flaw in their natures, the moral values of their societies. For daring such a challenge, these tragic heroes suffer, to prove to audiences that their society and its values are inviolable.

Given the classical definition, many critics felt that it was wrong to call a play such as *Death of a Salesman* a tragedy, but Miller disagreed. Through his insistence that the play was tragic in the full dramatic sense, Miller sparked one of the better-known debates among theatrical critics as he defended this concept in two articles for the New York newspapers, "Tragedy and the Common Man," and "The Nature of Tragedy," in which he insisted that "the common man is as apt a subject for tragedy in its highest sense as kings were." He does not mention his own plays in these essays, arguing his case in general terms, but he insists that the average person could display the same "heart and spirit"

as anyone who was nobly born and so should be equally capable of heroism. Tragedy, to Miller, is "the consequence of a man's total compulsion to evaluate himself justly" in the pursuit of which he or she is destroyed. In evaluating this destruction, we can come to understand what is wrong with society that our hero undergoes such an experience and, with this knowledge, set about improving that society. In this, the hero's death has meaning and offers hope. So for Miller, tragedy is essentially optimistic as it celebrates humanity's "thrust for freedom," and "demonstrates the indestructible will of man to achieve his humanity." Miller feels that literature that ignores the tragic dimension ultimately devalues humankind because it cannot allow for the celebration of human potential, which he sees as lying at the heart of tragedy.

Miller learned about Greek tragedy's problem–complication–crisis formula from Professor KENNETH ROWE at the UNIVERSITY OF MICHIGAN, and although Miller extends the parameters of the Greek formula, he does not change its essential format. Plays such as *All My Sons* and *A View from the Bridge,* with their networks of ironic references, symbols, and stage effects to foreshadow and underscore the central protagonists' fate, are clearly tragic in structure; Joe Keller and Eddie Carbone are tragic heroes with flawed natures that lead them astray but also with firm consciences that help bring them to justice. Willy Loman is certainly not a classic tragic hero, being lower-middle class and none too clever. The world that Loman inhabits is that of amoral, capitalistic big business rather than one with any clear moral value. However, for Miller, Willy Loman is a tragic hero, because in his view, tragic heroes are defined by their willingness to sacrifice everything to maintain their personal dignity—whatever their station in life. Loman may have a faulty vision of what makes a person successful, but regardless of the opposition and the ultimate cost to himself, he refuses to give up that vision, which makes him, in Miller's eyes, a tragic hero. Loman's death challenges the social mores of his time and is a call for change, which for Miller is the social imperative of all tragedy.

A tragic vein runs through much of Miller's work, which is unsurprising, given the connection he saw between tragedy and the kind of social drama that he strove to produce. *The Crucible*'s John Proctor is clearly tragic as he sacrifices himself to save his good name and to point out the injustice of the SALEM WITCH TRIALS; Phillip Gellburg from *Broken Glass* and Montezuma from *The Golden Years* are also tragic heroes who suffer trying to find their rightful place in a society that they are finding to be increasingly bewildering. Cases have even been made for the tragic status of such flawed individuals as *The Ride down Mt. Morgan*'s Lyman Felt and the Franz brothers in *The Price*. In *The American Clock*, it seems as though, in his ongoing interest in exploring new theatrical boundaries, Miller attempts to depict a whole society as tragic rather than just a single protagonist.

FURTHER READING

Adamczewski, Zygmunt. "The Tragic Loss—Loman the Salesman." *The Tragic Protest*. The Hague: Nijhoff, 1963, 172–192.

Bhatia, Santosh K. *Arthur Miller: Social Drama as Tragedy*. New York: Humanities, 1985.

Brashear, William R. "The Empty Bench: Morality, Tragedy, and Arthur Miller." *Michigan Quarterly Review* 5 (1966): 270–278.

Loughlin, Richard L. "Tradition and Tragedy in *All My Sons*." *English Record* 14 (February 1964): 23–27.

Mukerji, Nirmal. "John Proctor's Tragic Predicament." *Panjab University Research Bulletin: Arts* 4, no. 2 (April 1973): 75–79.

Otten, Terry. *The Temptation of Innocence in the Dramas of Arthur Miller*. Columbia: University of Missouri Press, 2002.

Prudoe, John. "Arthur Miller and the Tradition of Tragedy." *English Studies* 43 (1962): 430–439.

Steinberg, M. W. "Arthur Miller and the Idea of Modern Tragedy." *Dalhousie Review* 40 (1961): 329–340.

Trowbridge, Clinton W. "Arthur Miller: Between Pathos and Tragedy." *Modern Drama* 10 (1967): 221–232.

Wang Qun. "The Tragedy of Ethical Bewilderment." In *The Achievement of Arthur Miller: New Essays*, edited by Steven Centola, 95–100. (Dallas, Tex.: Contemporary Research, 1995).

U

University of East Anglia The University of East Anglia, GREAT BRITAIN, was founded in 1963 and was built on a site that is two miles outside of the city of Norwich that used to be a golf course. Its core buildings were designed by Denys Lasdun, the same architect who designed Britain's NATIONAL THEATRE. The choice of "Do Different" as the university's motto was a signal that it intended to consider new ways of providing university education. At the heart of its innovative thinking was the principle of interdisciplinarity where related subjects are studied in combination with each other. Its American Studies program, for example, has students study U.S. history, architecture, sociology, and literature side by side. The university has grown and currently offers 300 courses in 27 subject areas, accommodating more than 13,000 students a year.

In 1987, the university opened a center for American studies named the Arthur Miller Centre, under the direction of one of their professors, CHRISTOPHER BIGSBY. The center's purpose was to further interest in the study of the United States, to promote major new research projects, and to facilitate the movement of people between Britain and the United States. It was named after Miller in recognition of his personal integrity, his public commitment to U.S. values, and his close connection with the arts in Britain. Its activities include the annual Arthur Miller Centre International Literary Festival, which brings major writers from around the world to the center. It is also involved in book publication and has produced a highly praised CD-ROM on *The Crucible*. A founder member of the American Studies Network, it maintains a Europe-wide database of American Studies faculty and their research interests. Within the university, it sponsors undergraduate and graduate travel grants to the United States and awards the Arthur Miller Centre Prize.

University of Michigan The University of Michigan was founded in 1817 as one of the first public universities in the nation. It was first established on 1,920 acres of land that was ceded by the Chippewa, the Ottawa, and the Potawatomi people "for a college at Detroit." The school moved from Detroit to Ann Arbor in 1837 when the town of Ann Arbor was only 13 years old. In 1866, 25 years after the move, the University of Michigan became the largest university in the country, with 1,205 enrolled students and 33 faculty members. Today the university accommodates more than 51,000 students and 5,600 faculty at three campuses.

Miller had heard about the University of Michigan from a neighbor who had completed his freshman year there. The university's liberal reputation and relatively easy acceptance policies seemed attractive, with the $65 per semester tuition manageable together with relatively cheap accommodation. In the heart of the Middle West, it was also a comfortable distance from New York and his family. However, poor grades from high school led to a rejection of Miller's first two applications to Michigan. Miller started work at the auto-parts warehouse, CHADICK-DELAMATER, and tried to attend night school at City College of New York, which was free to those who could not afford to pay. After two weeks, he realized that he could not do both, so he quit night school. To try again for entrance to Michigan he wrote a plaintive letter to the dean, explaining how much more serious and motivated he had become and how keenly he wanted to attend. The dean offered him a probationary acceptance. Before he could attend, he would have to show a bank passbook with a balance of $500 to guarantee that he would be able to pay his way. Miller worked until he had that sum and then, in fall 1934, he set off for Michigan.

Living off-campus, Miller initially shared a room with fellow New Yorker Charlie Bleich but then moved into a single room at a rooming house run by the Doll family. He elected to major in journalism and by May had joined the staff of the *Michigan Daily*, the college newspaper, as a reporter. Not being as involved in sports as he had been at high school, Miller was well-prepared and found that he had more time for studies and by the end of the year, easily passed all of his courses. Miller enjoyed the range of people from all walks of life that he met at Michigan, which vastly expanded his social knowledge. It was a whole new way of life to him. For the *Daily*, he was able to write editorials and cover a variety of events, not just on campus, such as the sit-down strikes at General Motors in Flint, Michigan. He also interviewed such people as retired marine general Smedley D. Butler who had come to speak on campus about the nefarious way that U.S. forces were being used to back campaigns that had predominantly economic motives. Always interested in politics, he was now becoming more politically aware and involved.

In his sophomore year, Miller signed up for creative writing and, by the second semester, had met at a party MARY SLATTERY, who would subsequently become his first wife. Mary was then in her first year at Michigan, studying psychology, with plans to become a social worker. His bank balance having dwindled, Miller was washing dishes at a co-op cafeteria in exchange for free meals and existing on the $15 monthly pay that he received for tending the rats at a local genetics laboratory. He needed more funds to stay enrolled and saw the Avery Hopwood Awards—competitive writing awards that were administered each year by the university—as his main chance. He had spent his 1935 spring vacation week writing a play, which seemed to him the most tangible of the genres, and in 1936 won first prize for an undergraduate, a sum of $250 for his play *No Villain*. The following year, he would win again with *Honors at Dawn*, although in his final year, *The Great Disobedience* failed to please the judges.

After his victory with *No Villain*, Miller switched to English as his major and became a night editor at the *Daily*. Having rewritten *No Villain* into *They Too Arise*, Miller had submitted this to a student playwriting contest run by the THEATRE GUILD's Bureau of New Plays and won a $1,250 scholarship award to study with KENNETH ROWE, a professor at Michigan. Rowe had been on sabbatical during 1936, but Miller lost no time in signing up for his playwrighting seminar once he returned. Rowe would have a huge influence on Miller's early development as a dramatist in the two years that Miller had left at college. *They Too Arise* was even given a brief production by a campus theatrical group, The Hillel Players. Miller graduated in 1938 and moved back to New York to sign on with the FEDERAL THEATER PROJECT.

In 1953 Miller was asked to write a piece for *Holiday* magazine on how he felt that Michigan had changed since the 1930s. He wrote at that time that he found the university virtually unrecognizable and politically gutted by the COMMUNIST hunts of the period. However, he also acknowledged that the University of Michigan had been "the testing ground for all my prejudices, my beliefs and my ignorance, and it helped to lay out the boundaries of my life." His college years had been invaluable; they taught Miller how much he did not know, allowed him to make many new friends, and gave him a profound social and political experience. The university granted Miller an honorary Doctorate of Human Letters (L.H.D.) in 1956, and he was invited to revisit his alma mater on several occasions, often in support of liberal causes, including a teach-in to discuss the VIETNAM WAR in the mid-1960s. Enoch Brater, professor of English at the university, has held several events there devoted to Miller, celebrated Miller's later birthday milestones, held discussions of his works, and mounted productions and readings of his plays. First proposed in 1997, plans were created to build the Arthur Miller Theater on campus, the building of which actually began shortly after Miller's death, and was completed in 2007. The first play they presented was *Playing for Time.*

Untermeyer, Louis (1885–1977)   A liberal of no fixed political persuasion and most certainly holding no sympathies with COMMUNISM, Untermeyer was the author, editor or compiler, and translator of more than 100 books of stories and poetry for readers of all ages. He did much to fight the myth that poetry is a high brow art. Having developed a love of poetry when young, he published his own first volume, *First Love,* in 1911 with financial help from his father. He had dropped out of school in 1902 to go into his father's jewelry business, but in 1923, he resigned from this to give all of his attention to literary pursuits. Aside from a decades-long friendship with Miller, he was a regular correspondent of Robert Frost's for nearly 50 years and was close to EZRA POUND, William Carlos Williams, Edna S. Vincent Millay, and Marianne Moore.

In *Timebends: A Life,* Miller affectionately describes him as "a lovable master," full of jokes and puns, "who could easily spend an afternoon just talking and witticizing with kindred folk." In *Salesman in Beijing,* he calls Untermeyer "a good friend" and describes a trio of autobiographies that Untermeyer wrote at age 65, 77, and 88, "each more cheerful than the last," but Miller points out that "he died in the agony of his nineties uncertain of anything, let alone life's meaning and still less its success." What had most hurt Untermeyer was the blacklisting of the 1950s and losing his seat on the *What's My Line* game show panel because of an organized letter campaign against him by anticommunist groups; these were based on sentiments of social protest that he expressed in his 1914 volume of poetry, *Challenge,* 40 years earlier and his 1949 involvement in the Conference for World Peace at the Waldorf-Astoria Hotel. Miller reports what the producer told Untermeyer: "The problem is that we know you've never had any connection, so you have nothing to confess to, but they're not going to believe that. So it's going to seem that you're refusing to be a good American" Profoundly hurt by this experience, Untermeyer refused even to leave his apartment for the next 18 months. Like Miller, in his later years, Untermeyer developed a deep appreciation for country life, moving out from New York to spend most of his time in Connecticut.

V

Vietnam War The Vietnam War was a civil conflict in which North Vietnam (Democratic Republic of Vietnam) fought against South Vietnam (Republic of Vietnam). While the North found allies in the Soviet Union and the People's Republic of China, the South was supported by the United States and South Korea. U.S. forces were involved in the conflict from 1965 until their official withdrawal in 1973, but U.S. involvement had begun in 1955 when President Eisenhower had deployed the Military Assistance Advisory Group to train the South Vietnam army. The war ended on April 30, 1975, with the reunification of Vietnam.

Opposition to U.S. involvement began slowly and in small numbers in 1964 on various college campuses in the United States. By the time that U.S. troops were withdrawn, due to escalating U.S. casualties and a sense that the war was a hopeless conflict, the majority of the country's citizens were opposed. It is an oddly repeated fallacy that Miller paid little attention to events in Vietnam. How could a committed pacifist and someone so perennially concerned about his country's future have stayed silent? Miller spoke out against the war from the start of U.S. involvement, and although his drama does not confront the Vietnamese issue overtly, it is peppered by oblique references that make his stance clear.

Miller's first public statement against the Vietnam War was in the January 1965 essay "Our Guilt for the World's Evil," in which he criticizes U.S. passivity toward photographs of tortured Vietcong prisoners. In the essay, Miller suggests that all the people of the United States are complicit in such torture as they have armed the torturers and have condoned their actions implicitly. He attended a "teach-in" at the UNIVERSITY OF MICHIGAN in September to protest the war and to present a paper, but he declined an invitation from President Johnson to attend the signing of the Arts and Humanities Act because of his opposition to the president's policy on Vietnam. Miller would speak out at various antiwar demonstrations, even flying to Paris in an attempt to negotiate with the Viet Cong. In June 1966, he and the poet Robert Lowell paid tribute to a visiting Vietnamese monk at a town-hall event, and Miller denounced the U.S. presence in Vietnam. Two months later, he published the short story "A Search for the Future" that contains his most overt references to the conflict, outside of his nonfiction, beginning with the repeated image of the dresser's nephew who had his eyes shot out in Vietnam. The story's protagonist, Harry, attends an anti-Vietnam peace rally, at which he is asked to speak. Uncertain how to respond and not wanting to be labeled a rebel by the media, he cautiously mutters a few crowd pleasers about wanting the war to end and then sits down. He is subsequently surprised by his audience's effusive approbation, which makes him feel good about himself, despite his vague support.

In 1967, Miller worked on *The Price*, a play that he later insisted was written partly in reaction to Vietnam. In his essay, "*The Price*—The Power of the Past," Miller blames the United States for the unnecessary loss of U.S. and Vietnamese lives because of its "rigid anticommunist theology" that was born in the 1940s as well as the panicked division of Vietnam to prevent Ho Chi Minh taking full control. Miller explains how, in writing *The Price*, he had wanted to reconfirm "the power of the past" to try to make sense of such insanity by openly depicting the process of cause and effect. "If the play does not utter the word Vietnam," he insists, "it speaks to a spirit of unearthing the real that seemed to have nearly gone from our lives." That same year, he would take part in "Poets for Peace," a New York event at which he read a prose piece titled "Why Kill a Nation No One Hates?"

The *New York Times* reported Miller's resolution at a Democratic committee meeting in June 1968 that called for the immediate cessation of U.S. bombing of North Vietnam and asking for peace negotiations to begin. As a delegate to the 1968 Democratic National Convention in Chicago, he was one of a cadre of Democratic voices against the war. As he explains in his essay "The Battle of Chicago," although 80 percent of Democrats were against involvement in Vietnam, the delegates were largely restricted from any real debate for fear of fracturing the party. Those like Miller who supported Eugene McCarthy and refused to compromise on Vietnam were frowned upon as foolishly trying to rock the boat. Miller relates the inflammatory speech of one representative who mocked the concern of the nation's youth and turned the issue into a generational conflict. Miller and other delegates walked outside to the police lines to show their solidarity with the mostly youthful war protestors who were held there at bay. In 1969, Miller wrote an op-ed piece in the *New York Times* that was titled "Are We Interested in Stopping the Killing?" and that again questioned U.S. involvement in Vietnam; his short play *The Reason Why*, written that same

year, also symbolically references the Vietnam War in its commentary on the nature of killing and the pointlessness of war.

In the 1970s, Miller's opposition to the war would not slacken. His 1972 play *The Creation of the World and Other Business*, like *The Price*, was strongly influenced by Vietnam and the climate of the 1960s in its references to humanity's propensity toward murderous violence and the effects of idealistic disillusionment. The short 1976 play *The Poosidin's Resignation* is a more overt response with its opening scene in which young men are sent into the flames of a furnace to honor the god of war. Key buzzwords in his script stand out, such as *freedom* and *security*, and they are obviously contradicted by the actions taking place. When one man objects and asks why a nation is destroying her young in this way, he is unable to receive a clear answer, and his pleas are superseded by two lengthy speeches in which one president resigns and the new one takes office. They are hard to tell apart: Both pompously speak of their own greatness and the necessity of war to make themselves greater. Miller ends with a hypnotized mob, applauding to show how easily the people of the United States had been led by their smooth-talking presidents into a needless conflict.

There are also references to Vietnam in 1977's *The Archbishop's Ceiling*, in which the central character Adrian reconsiders his own lackluster resistance to the Vietnam War and how that has impacted his current position. Both *The American Clock* and *Mr. Peters' Connections* also contain references to Vietnam, the first in a sequence to highlight the pointless destruction of war and the second in references to the fate of a nightclub that went under during the Vietnam era. Miller intends the fact that the building fell into decline during the Vietnam War to suggest the cultural impact of this event on the U.S. psyche. For Miller, Vietnam had a profound affect on people's capacity to believe anything and, for a time, dangerously killed both optimism and pessimism in the United States.

FURTHER READING

Borders, William. "Democrats Begin Hartford Battle." *New York Times,* June 22, 1968, 19.

Cooke, Alistair. "Arthur Miller Tangles with LBJ." *Guardian,* September 28, 1965, 24.

"Crowd Here Hails Monk from Vietnam." *New York Times,* June 10, 1966, 9.

Miller, Arthur. "Are We Interested in Stopping the Killing?" *New York Times,* June 8, 1969, sec. 2, p. 21.

———. "Our Guilt for the World's Evil." *New York Times,* January 3, 1965, sec. 6, pp. 10–11, 48.

———. "The Past and Its Power: Why I Wrote *The Price.*" *New York Times,* November 14, 1999, sec. 2, p. 5.

W

Wallach, Eli (1915–   )   Eli Wallach was born in BROOKLYN to Jewish parents. He graduated from the University of Texas in Austin but gained his dramatic training at the Neighborhood Playhouse with Sanford Meisner and with the ACTORS STUDIO, where he learned the Method. He made his BROADWAY debut in 1945 and won a Tony Award in 1951 for portraying Alvaro in TENNESSEE WILLIAMS's *The Rose Tattoo*. Indeed, many of his early successes were in material written by Williams, including Kilroy in *Camino Real* (1953), and his screen debut, the highly controversial *Baby Doll* (1956), both of which were directed by ELIA KAZAN. Wallach split his time between Broadway and Hollywood for the next 50 years, with a string of hits in both fields, and has remained a much sought-after actor.

Wallach became friendly with MARILYN MONROE in 1955 when she was attending the Actors Studio. Although one reporter would accuse Wallach of taking Monroe around as a beard for Miller, Wallach states in his memoirs that he never met Miller at this time. In Washington, on tour with John Patrick's *Teahouse of the August Moon,* and during Miller's 1956 hearing with the HOUSE UN-AMERICAN ACTIVITIES COMMITTEE, Wallach attended witness proceedings; this was the first time Wallach saw Miller in person. He did not appear in a Miller production until 1960 when he was cast in *The Misfits,* in which Miller considered him "a pillar of the production."

In 1970, Wallach appeared in both the stage and the film versions of *The Reason Why*. The stage version was performed in a double bill with "Fame" in which Wallach appeared with his wife, Anne Jackson. Wallach also took a turn as Gregory Solomon in the 1992 Roundabout Theater revival of *The Price*, directed by John Tillinger, for which he was nominated for a Drama Desk Award. After this, he tried to convince Miller to write a play featuring Solomon and his daughter, but Miller refused. However, Wallach has continued to be connected to Miller's work. In 2002, he performed a reading of Miller's short story "Bulldog" for NPR's *The Connection* and has appeared at several of the memorials that were organized since Miller's death.

FURTHER READING

Wallach, Eli. *The Good, The Bad And Me: In My Anecdotage.* New York: Harcourt, 2005.

Wall Street crash   The Wall Street crash occurred in October 1929 when share prices on the New York Stock Exchange collapsed and would not regain pre-1929 levels again for 25 years. While the crash shares some blame for the GREAT DEPRESSION, it was not the sole element that ruined so many people's lives.

Business had been slack for ISIDORE MILLER'S MILTEX COAT AND SUIT COMPANY for sometime before, necessitating the family's move to cheaper accommodation in BROOKLYN in 1928. As the character Arthur Robertson in *The American Clock* observes, the economy had been slowing for some time before the crash, and a fall in stock prices was inevitable, but when people started to off-load shares in a panic, matters worsened. Stock prices had been fluctuating wildly throughout 1929, and the market was in a bubble with prices far too high, compared to the real economy. Attracted by rising stock prices, too many people had invested too heavily, often using borrowed money. Isidore Miller was one of these investors, and when the stock prices crashed, he was left with no money and huge debts.

The crash began on October 24, known as "Black Thursday," and the shockwaves continued through to the following "Black Tuesday," October 29, when nearly all the stock prices simply collapsed. People started to sell in a panic on Black Thursday, and by noon, there had been 11 suicides of fairly prominent investors. Miller depicts these events near the start of *The American Clock*, as we hear of the suicides of Diana's brother Randolph Morgan and later that of Jesse Livermore. William Durant joined with members of the Rockefeller family and other financial giants to buy large quantities of stocks to demonstrate to the public their confidence in the market, but their effort failed to stop the slide. Durant is depicted in *The American Clock* as a sensible man who faces financial ruin with courage rather than despair, and so survives. The banks that had lent heavily to fund share buying found themselves saddled with debt, causing many to fail. Only a teenager at the time, Miller counted himself lucky that he had withdrawn his savings to upgrade his bicycle a few days before the banks closed their doors. Sadly, the bicycle was stolen a few days later, another sign of the desperation of the times and is another scene that he depicts in *The American Clock*. With so many businesses going under, massive unemployment soon followed.

While the play that covers most closely the repercussions of the crash is *The American Clock*, recalling the anguish and fall of his own father, two other Miller characters are depicted as being similarly affected: the father in *After the Fall* and Mr. Franz in *The Price*. For Miller, this era was a period of great transformation, one that changed the U.S. character, creating a permanently new cynicism and distrust. In a way, for Miller, it marked the loss of American innocence.

Whitehead, Robert (1916–2002)   Born in Montreal, Canada, Robert Whitehead's father William owned textile mills, and his mother, Lena Mary LaBatt, was an opera singer who came from the family that owned the LaBatt brewery. After attending Montreal's Trinity College School, he moved to the States to become involved in U.S. theater. In the late 1930s, with Robert Stephens and two others, he formed the Producers Theatre that would present BROADWAY plays between 1939 and 1959, including the 1950 hit drama, Carson McCuller's *Member of the Wedding,* directed by HAROLD CLURMAN.

Whitehead was also managing director of the American National Theatre and Academy (ANTA) from 1952 to 1974, through which he presented several revivals and original plays. In 1960, he was asked to help to create the REPERTORY THEATER OF LINCOLN CENTER and brought in ELIA KAZAN to assist. Despite delays, they finally opened in 1964 with *After the Fall,* but after disagreements with the board, he and Kazan felt pressured to resign the following year. Miller was very indignant concerning the treatment of Whitehead and refused to offer the Repertory Theater any more plays. Whitehead and Stephens continued to produce plays together into the 1970s. Whitehead's final Broadway production was Terrence McNally's incredibly successful *Master Class* in 1995, which starred his second wife, Australian actress Zoe Caldwell, who won a Tony for her performance.

As one of the United States's leading theater producers, Whitehead presented plays by numerous important 20th-century playwrights and won five Tony Awards, including one for the 1984 revival of *Death of a Salesman* (for which he also won a Drama Desk Award). Receiving Tony nominations for his productions of *The Price* in 1968 and *Broken Glass* in 1994, Whitehead had produced nine Miller plays, the first being when KERMIT BLOOM-GARDEN asked him to help produce the two one-act plays, *A View from the Bridge* and *A Memory of Two Mondays* in 1955. In 1960 Whitehead asked Miller for a new play to inaugurate the opening of the Lincoln Center, and *After the Fall* finally premiered there when the center began producing in 1964. When Whitehead asked Miller for another play in

1964, following *After the Fall,* Miller wrote *Incident at Vichy.* Whitehead also produced *The Price* in 1968, *The Creation of the World and Other Business* in 1972—in which his wife played Eve—the Washington, D. C., premiere of *The Archbishop's Ceiling* in 1977, the 1984 revival of *Death of a Salesman* with DUSTIN HOFFMAN, and 1994's *Broken Glass.* Although friendly with Miller for many years, financial wrangling over Hoffman's cut for *Death of a Salesman* rather soured their friendship, and they were subsequently never as close.

Aside from Miller, Whitehead worked with such playwrights as CLIFFORD ODETS, TENNESSEE WILLIAMS, WILLIAM INGE, Thornton Wilder, Tom Stoppard, and HAROLD PINTER. Weeks before his death in 2002, he received a special Tony Award honoring his lifetime contributions to the theater. Although he had some film and television credits, he had worked almost exclusively in the theater for six decades. In *Timebends, A Life,* Miller describes Whitehead as "the most artistically ambitious producer on Broadway" and clearly admired Whitehead's desire for a permanent U.S. theater along the lines of GREAT BRITAIN's NATIONAL THEATRE, in which U.S. artists "could develop in a coherent way."

Williams, Tennessee (1911–1983)

The connection between Tennessee Williams and Arthur Miller is strong; they had a kinship and a mutual admiration. Together, they dominated U.S. drama in the late 1940s and through the 1950s, and although both suffered disfavor in later life, both nevertheless continued to write. While Miller lived long enough to see his work begin to come back into favor, Williams died before critics began to reevaluate his plays. During life, they were friends and were never jealous or competitive, each congratulating the other on their successes. In 1954, when the government refused to renew Miller's passport so that he could attend the Belgian opening of *The Crucible,* Williams wrote on his behalf to the State Department to complain, pointing out that "Mr. Miller and his work occupy the very highest critical and popular position in the esteem of Western Europe" and that to thus restrict him was to play into the rhetoric of COMMUNISM that depicted the United States as a fascist country. Both worked closely with director ELIA KAZAN; indeed, Kazan often had to choose between the two, turning down the offer to direct Williams's *The Rose Tatoo* to keep himself free to direct *The Hook,* which sadly never got funded. Although Miller acknowledged some indebtedness to Williams as a trailblazer, their work was in many ways very different, with Williams centering on the private life of his protagonists while Miller concentrated on their more public identity.

Born Thomas Lanier Williams in Columbus, Mississippi, the playwright's father relocated the family to St. Louis in 1918. They bought a gloomy house, in which his parents constantly argued, and Williams's possibly schizophrenic older sister, Rose, withdrew into her collection of glass animals. Frail and overly protected by his mother, Williams was a target for school bullies. His weakness and lack of physical prowess disappointed his father, who called him "Miss Nancy." Partly as escapism from a life that he hated, Williams began to write. An early story, "Isolated," was printed in his junior-high-school newspaper, and he won money from advertising and magazine contests. He was published professionally before he attended the University of Missouri in 1929 to study journalism, the same major that Miller would choose.

At college, Williams drank to cover his shyness and discovered the drama of ANTON CHEKHOV, August Strindberg, and HENRIK IBSEN, whose work, similar to Miller, inspired him to become a playwright. Being pulled out of college by his father to work in his company's warehouse, Williams was appalled by the job's monotony. By 1935, he suffered a nervous breakdown and went to recover with his grandparents in Memphis, where his first play, *Cairo, Shanghai, Bombay!,* cowritten with Doris Shapiro, was produced. Returning to St. Louis to complete his degree, he became involved with The Mummers, an amateur group that produced longer works, including, *Fugitive Kind* (1937), set in a flophouse during the GREAT DEPRESSION. The mental state of his sister Rose had worsened (she would later be institutionalized and be given a prefrontal lobotomy), and Williams, fond of his sister, could not face her deterioration. In 1937, he attended a playwriting course at the University of Iowa rather than take up the THEATER GUILD scholarship that he had been offered by which he would study with KENNETH ROWE at the UNIVERSITY OF MICHIGAN, the same seminar in which Miller was enrolled. One of the plays that he wrote at Iowa, *Not About Nightingales,* would, like Miller's *The Great Disobedience,* take place in a prison, although from a difference perspective.

After graduating in 1938, Williams traveled around the United States, gathering ideas and material, taking various jobs, and writing poetry and short fiction as well as plays. It was with the story "The Field of Blue Children," published in 1939, that he first called himself Tennessee Williams, and impressed by a collection of his early one-acts, the GROUP THEATER gave Williams a special $100 prize. In 1940, he was awarded a Rockefeller Fellowship, and the Theatre Guild produced his *Battle of Angels* in Boston with plans for New York. However, much the same as Miller's first major production, *The Man Who Had All the Luck,* Williams's play was panned and soon closed. Severely dejected, Williams returned to menial labor until his agent landed him a scriptwriting contract with MGM in 1943. Here, he developed one of his short stories, "Portrait of a Girl in Glass," into a screenplay, *The Gentleman Caller.* When the studio rejected this, he adapted it into *The Glass Menagerie* (1944), which would be the first in a string of BROADWAY stage and Hollywood screen successes.

The Glass Menagerie did much to enthuse other playwrights, including Miller and WILLIAM INGE, who were attracted to its poetic artistry. *A Streetcar Named Desire* (1947) would cement their adulation, exhibiting a similar eloquence of composition, and it won Williams his first Pulitzer Prize. Miller attended a New Haven tryout at the invitation of Kazan and was stunned at the way the play successfully blended realistic and nonrealistic elements. In *Timebends: A Life,* Miller acknowledges a great debt to *A Streetcar Named Desire,* which hit Broadway two years before *Death of a Salesman.* Miller was amazed by the play's sheer vitality, with its liberated and liberating use of words, and felt that it paved the way for the acceptance of a new form of drama which the United States could proudly

call its own. He saw Williams's use of language as a kind of poeticized REALISM that produced an everyday speech for his characters that had a lyrical quality. This, in Miller's view, allowed audiences to see more clearly the meaning of a play and its relevance to their own lives.

By this time, Williams had accepted the fact that he was homosexual and after indulging for a time in a promiscuous lifestyle, settled down with Frank Merlo. Pressures for the next hit were intense, and by the late 1950s Williams had become a psychological mess: Stressed out from work, suffering from alcoholism and constant hypochondria, he went into psychotherapy, but the death of Merlo in 1963 led to a relapse, after which his muse seemed to vanish and he had little success until his accidental death in 1983. He reportedly choked to death on the cap from a pill bottle. In recent years, critics have begun to reevaluate many of his later works.

In *Timebends: A Life,* Miller confesses to feeling an affinity to Williams because he sees himself as suffering from the same "sense of alienation" that Williams had felt. While Williams was alienated by his homosexuality, Miller felt alienated by a sense of morality that was clearly at odds with a commodified and materialistic society. Like Williams, Miller also believed in the possibility that theater could make a measurable difference in the wider society. Attracted to Williams's concept of the "plastic theater"—a theater that Williams saw as incorporating experimental use of lights, sets, music, and other nonverbal additions—Miller agreed that such experimentation could offer greater flexibility on the stage and could be highly instrumental in a play's effectiveness. Miller continued to experiment with these elements in his plays throughout his career.

In his 1958 essay, "The Shadows of the Gods," Miller approvingly insists, "Williams has a long reach and a genuinely dramatic imagination." After praising Anton Chekhov's "psychological insight" and the way in which tradition informs his plays, Miller suggests that among contemporary writers, Williams comes closest to Chekhov in the way that he uses Southern tradition in his drama. He also holds up two recent plays for consideration, Frances Goodrich and Albert Hackett's adaptation of

The Diary of Anne Frank and Williams's *Cat on a Hot Tin Roof*. He objects to the sentimentality of the former and suggest that Williams's play, by contrast, is far more complex and satisfying. Feeling that it is not for a playwright to give answers but to open up possibilities, Miller sees in *Cat on a Hot Tin Roof* evidence of an artistic preoccupation that "extends beyond the surface realities of the relationships, and beyond the psychiatric connotations of homosexuality and impotence" to also include "the viewpoint . . of the audience, the society, and the race." In Miller's view, Williams conveys "an ulterior pantheon of forces" and a "play of symbols" that points to a larger social question regarding "the right of society to renew itself when it is, in fact, unworthy." Although Miller disliked the play's ending, he applauds Williams's ability to address issues of "tragic grandeur."

In Miller's later essays "About Theater Language" and "Notes on Realism," he describes the impact of Williams on U.S. theater as a whole and his connection to realism. Just as he refutes any limiting description of CLIFFORD ODETS as a social realist, he makes similar claims regarding the contributions of Williams. Although a play like *The Glass Menagerie* has been termed realistic in psychological terms, Miller points out that it is also filled with symbolism and a "tragic vision" beyond conventional realistic plays.

FURTHER READING

Barclay, Dolores. "Literary, Arts Figures Mourn the Theater's Tremendous Loss." *Boston Globe*, February 26, 1983, 17.

Evans, Lloyd Gareth. "U.S. Connections—O'Neill, Miller, Williams and Albee." *The Language of Modern Drama*. Totowa, N.J.: Rowman and Littlefield, 1977, 177–204.

Hays, Peter L. "Arthur Miller and Tennessee Williams." *Essays in Literature* 4 (1977): 239–249.

Savran, David. *Communists, Cowboys, and Queers: The Politics of Masculinity in the Work of Arthur Miller and Tennessee Williams*. Minneapolis: University of Minneapolis Press, 1992.

Tynan, Kenneth. "American Blues: The Plays of Arthur Miller and Tennessee Williams." *Encounter*, 2, no. 5 (1954): 13–19.

Williamstown Theatre Festival   In 1955, Ralph Renzi, then news director of Williams College in Williamstown, Massachusetts, and the chairman of the drama program David Bryant, conceived of the idea of using the Adams Memorial Theatre for a resident summer-theatre company; thus, the Williamstown Theatre Foundation was formed. A 26-member company was assembled from New York professionals, Yale students, and Yale alumni, plus a few students from Williams. When Bryant left Williams the following year, Nikos Psacharopoulos became the artistic director (until his death in 1989), and the theatre's repertory became increasingly ambitious, with productions by such playwrights as George Bernard Shaw, TENNESSEE WILLIAMS, ANTON CHEKHOV, and Miller. A resident company of actors began to evolve with such talents as MILDRED DUNNOCK, E. G. Marshall, and Thornton Wilder joining, and by the 1970s, the Williamstown Theatre Festival had built a reputation for innovative versions of classics, as well as for premiering new plays.

The company's first Miller production was *The Crucible* in 1955, directed by Psacharopoulos, who would also direct *A View from the Bridge* in 1957 and in 1964 before returning to *The Crucible* in 1987. The company has thus far mounted 13 productions of Miller's works, several of them being key revivals of neglected plays. Director Austin Pendelton was invited to direct both a 1977 version of *After the Fall* and a rare production of *The American Clock* in 1988. In addition to these, in 1966, the company mounted *Incident at Vichy, The Price* in 1970 and 1999 (the latter production transferring to BROADWAY), another *After the Fall* in 1965, and *All My Sons* in 1996. They offered the American premiere of *The Ride down Mt. Morgan* in 1996. Miller had revised the play since its 1991 premiere in GREAT BRITAIN, and tired of the harsh reactions of New York critics to his work, he offered it to a theater where he felt that it would meet with a warmer and kinder reception. It was directed by Scott Elliott, with F. Murray Abraham in the lead role, and would later transfer to New York with Patrick Stewart taking over the lead.

Another Miller revival was Scott Ellis's 2001 production of *The Man Who Had All the Luck,* also

Miller, sitting with director Austin Pendleton and the company's artistic director, Nikos Psacharopoulos, discussing the Williamstown Theatre Festival's upcoming production of *The American Clock,* in 1988. *Williamstown Theatre Festival Archives.*

transferred to Broadway. While Michael Ritchie was artistic director between 1996 and 2004, nearly two dozen Williamstown Theatre productions transferred to Broadway, off-Broadway, and regional theatres throughout the country. In 2002, the Williamstown Theatre Festival received the 2002 Regional Theatre Tony Award, presented annually to a theatre company that has proven a continuous level of artistic achievement and contributed to the growth of theatre nationally. The current artistic director is British actor and director Roger Rees.

The Wooster Group   The Wooster Group is an ensemble of artists who collaborate on the development and production of theater and media pieces. Under the direction of Elizabeth LeCompte, they have, since 1975, conceived and constructed 16 works for the theatre, as well as several works for film, video, radio, and dance. Dedicated to cultivating new forms and techniques of theatrical expression that are reflective of and responsive to the evolving culture, Wooster Group theater pieces are constructed as assemblages of juxtaposed elements: radical staging of both modern and classic texts, found materials, films and videos, dance and movement, multitrack scoring, and an architectonic approach to theatre design.

One experiment, begun in 1981 with *Route 1 & 9,* was to present excerpts from a classic play, in

this case, Thornton Wilder's *Our Town,* in a wildly unfamiliar format, here against Pigmeat Markham comedy routines, with the actors playing in blackface. Such performances have been highly controversial. In 1984, the Wooster Group attempted to juxtapose sections of *The Crucible* against, among other things, a pastiche of speeches by 1960s drug guru Timothy Leary. The work was called, *L.S.D. (. . . Just the High Points . . .).* Miller caused a stir by bringing an injunction against the group to disallow them the use of any scenes from his play in this satirical piece, a request granted the following year. His objection, he told CHRISTOPHER BIGSBY, was on the grounds of theatrical standards, which he felt that the performance lacked, viewing it as a kind of graffiti "creating nothing excepting the excuse of not being bored." His refusal to allow his writing to be so used caused a bigger stir than the piece itself.

FURTHER READING

Aronson, Arnold. "The Wooster Group's *L.S.D.* (. . . *Just the High Points* . .)." *The Drama Review* 29, no. 2 (Summer 1985): 65–77.

Greene, Alexis. "Elizabeth LeCompte and the Wooster Group." In *Contemporary American Theatre,* edited by Bruce King, 117–134. (New York: St. Martin's, 1991).

World War II   World War II was a global military conflict that took place between 1939 and 1945. Even though Japan had been fighting in China since 1937, the conventional view is that the war began on September 1, 1939, when Nazi Germany invaded Poland. Within two days, Great Britain and France declared war on Germany, while the Soviet Union joined with Germany to conquer Poland and divide Eastern Europe. By 1940, France had surrendered to Germany, and shortly after this, Italy and Japan signed a mutual defense agreement with Germany. However, in 1941, Germany turned on its ally the Soviet Union, forcing it to join with Britain, although an earlier treaty prevented the U.S.S.R. from fighting Japan. After Japan attacked the United States in 1941, the United States also joined with Britain, as did China and most of the rest of the world. Battles raged on until 1945 when Germany, and later Japan, finally surrendered (Italy had given up in 1943). The war took a huge death toll of both military and civilians and ravaged much of Europe, not to mention unleashing the atomic bomb.

The United States had been reluctant to join what many saw as a European conflict, and Miller was a pacifist who had joined the peace movement at the UNIVERSITY OF MICHIGAN and signed the Oxford Pledge that declared that its signatories would not take part in any future war. However, these scruples apart, Miller clearly supported the necessity of this war. His 1941 essay "Hitler's Quarry" had shown him to be cognizant of the threat Hitler posed, just as *The Golden Years* offered a symbolic warning against the ruthlessness of fascism. Although Miller would be declared unfit for duty, he would perform war service by volunteering his services for almost two years, 1941–42, as a shipfitter's helper at the BROOKLYN NAVY YARD. On the night shift from 4 p.m. to 4 a.m. for 13 of every 14 nights, he revisits this experience in "Fitter's Night." He also used his skills as a dramatist for the cause, and his 1941 radio drama *Captain Paul* offered a commentary on the United States's inevitable entry into the war; to stay free, the United States would have to fight.

Aside from his episodes for the 1944 CBS radio series *The Doctor Fights*, Miller had already written a series of patriotic radio plays including *I Was Married in Bataan* that told of the trials of army nurses; *The Eagle's Nest* that relates Giuseppe Garibaldi's fight for a unified Italy to the contemporary conflict against fascism; *Listen for the Sound of Wings* about the trials and resistance of the anti-Nazi German pastor Martin Niemoeller; *The Story of Canine Joe* about the role that dogs played in helping to win the war; *The Story of Gus* about the compulsion of two men to serve their country by joining the merchant navy; The *Philippines Never Surrendered* about a brave school superintendent on the island of Mindanao; and *Bernadine, I Love You* that relates how a lonely soldier is helped by the Red Cross to contact his wife. Many of his other plays of this period were also given patriotic twists.

His patriotism was also seen in his stage work at this time, such as the agitprop *That They May Win*, which exhorted women to fight for proper price control on the home front, and the unproduced plays *Boro Hall Nocturne* and *The Half-Bridge*, both with their anti-Nazi themes and warnings against Nazi infiltration. Miller's short story "The Plaster Masks" showed his concern with the price of war, which was also where his attempts to write the screenplay for *The Story of G. I. Joe* took him. This lost him the contract, but he was able to turn the material into a sympathetic look at the lives of soldiers and veterans that he titled *Situation Normal . . . .*

Miller's brother KERMIT MILLER had signed up in 1942, was commissioned, and was sent to Europe where he was injured in the Battle of the Bulge. He was eventually discharged in 1945 with a Purple Heart and suffered from shell shock and battle fatigue. Miller had dedicated *Situation Normal . . .* to his brother and would include elements of his wartime experience into the character of Chris Keller in *All My Sons*. Although some considered *All My Sons* unpatriotic in its exposure of wartime manufacturing exploitation, it was a real problem that Miller had felt should be exposed for the country's good. The aspect of the war that would most inform his subsequent work, however, would be the HOLOCAUST.

PART IV

Appendices

SELECTED PRIMARY BIBLIOGRAPHY OF ARTHUR MILLER'S WORKS

After the Fall. New York: Viking, 1964.

After The Fall. [television adaptation] New York: Bantam, 1974.

All My Sons. New York: Reynal and Hitchcock, 1947.

The American Clock. London: Methuen, 1983.

The American Clock and *The Archbishop's Ceiling.* New York: Grove, 1989.

The Archbishop's Ceiling. London: Methuen, 1984.

Arthur Miller: Plays Five. London: Methuen, 1995.

Arthur Miller: Plays Four. London: Methuen, 1994.

Arthur Miller: Plays Three. London: Methuen, 1990.

Arthur Miller's Adaptation of "An Enemy of the People" by Henrik Ibsen. New York: Viking, 1951.

Arthur Miller's Collected Plays. New York: Viking, 1957.

Arthur Miller's Collected Plays. Vol 2. New York: Viking, 1981.

"The Bare Manuscript." *New Yorker,* December 16, 2002, 82–93.

"Beavers." *Harper's Magazine,* February 2005: 79–82.

"Bees." *Michigan Quarterly Review* 29, no. 2 (Spring 1990): 152–157.

"Bridge to a Savage World." *Esquire,* October 1958, 185–190.

Broken Glass. New York: Viking, 1994.

"Bulldog." *New Yorker* 77, no. 23 (August 13, 2001): 72–76.

Chinese Encounters [with Inge Morath]. New York: Farrar, 1979.

"Concerning Jews Who Write." *Jewish Life* 12, no. 5 (March 1948): 8–9.

The Creation of the World and Other Business. New York: Viking, 1973.

The Crucible. New York: Viking, 1953.

The Crucible: Screenplay. New York: Penguin, 1996.

Danger: Memory! [Contains "I Can't Remember Anything" and "Clara"] New York: Grove, 1986.

Death of a Salesman. New York: Viking, 1949.

"Ditchy." *Mayfair Magazine,* October 1944: 37+.

Echoes Down the Corridor, edited by Steven R. Centola. New York: Viking, 2000. [Includes "The Battle of Chicago: From the Delegates Side," "A Boy Grew in Brooklyn," "Clinton in Salem," "*The Crucible* in History," "Dinner with the Ambassador," "Get It Right: Privatize Executions," "Miracles," "A Modest Proposal for the Pacification of the Public Temper," "Notes on Realism," "*The Price,* The Power of the Past," "Rain in a Strange City," "*Salesman* at Fifty," "Subsidized Theatre," and "What's Wrong with This Picture?"]

Elegy for a Lady. New York: Dramatists Play Service, 1982.

Everybody Wins. New York: Grove Weidenfeld, 1990.

Focus. New York: Reynal and Hitchcock, 1945.

The Golden Years and *The Man Who Had All the Luck.* London: Methuen, 1989.

Grandpa and the Statue. Radio Drama in Action: Twenty-Five Plays of a Changing World, edited by Erik Barnouw, 267–281. (New York: Rinehart, 1945).

"Ham Sandwich." *Boston University Quarterly* 24, no. 2 (1976): 5–6.

"Hitler's Quarry" *Jewish Survey* 1, no. 1 (1941): 8+.

Homely Girl, A Life and Other Stories. New York: Viking, 1995. [Contains, *Homely Girl, A Life,* "Fame," and "Fitter's Night."]

I Don't Need You Anymore. New York: Viking, 1967. [Contains "I Don't Need You Anymore," "Monte Sant' Angelo," "Please Don't Kill Anything," "The Misfits," "Glimpse of a Jockey," "The Prophecy," "Fame," "Fitter's Night," and "A Search for a Future."]

An Immigrant's Lament. New York Times, August 4, 1999, P1.

Incident at Vichy. New York: Viking, 1965.

"In Memoriam." *New Yorker*, December 25, 1995, and January 1, 1996, 56–57.

In Russia [with Inge Morath] New York: 1969.

In the Country [with Inge Morath] New York: Viking, 1977.

I Think about You a Great Deal. Václav Havel: Living in Truth, edited by Jan Vladislav, 263–265, (London: Faber and Faber, 1986).

"It Takes a Thief." *Collier's*, February 8, 1947, 23, 75–76.

Jane's Blanket. New York: Crowell–Collier, 1963.

The Last Yankee [single scene]. New York: Dramatists Play Service, 1991.

The Last Yankee. New York: Penguin, 1994.

"Lines From California: Poem." *Harper's*, May 1969, 97.

"Lola's Lament." In *Unleashed: Poems by Writers' Dogs*, edited by Amy Hempel and Jim Shepard, 60–61. (New York: Crown, 1995).

The Misfits. [cinema novel] New York: Viking, 1961.

The Misfits. [screenplay] In *Film Scripts Three*, edited by George P. Garrett, O. B. Hardison Jr., and Jane R. Gelfman, 202–382. (New York: Irvington, 1989).

Mr. Peter's Connections. New York: Penguin, 1999.

"The Night Ed Murrow Struck Back." *Esquire*, December 1983, 460–462, 465, 467–468.

"The 1928 Buick." *Atlantic*, October 1978: 49–51, 54–56.

"On Broadway: Notes on the Past and Future of American Theater." *Harper's*, March 1999, 37–45.

On Politics and the Art of Acting. New York: Viking, 2001.

"Our Guilt For the World's Evil." *New York Times Magazine*, January 3, 1965, 10–11, 48.

"The Past and Its Power: Why I Wrote *The Price*." *New York Times*, November 14, 1999, sec. 2, p. 5.

"The Performance." *New Yorker*, April 22/29, 2002: 176–188.

"The Plaster Masks." *Encore: A Continuing Anthology* 9 (April 1946): 424–432.

Playing for Time. [teleplay]. New York: Bantam, 1981.

Playing for Time. Chicago: Dramatic Publishing Company, 1985.

The Poosidin's Resignation. Boston University Quarterly 24, no. 2 (1976): 7–13.

The Portable Arthur Miller, edited by Christopher Bigsby. New York: Penguin, 1995.

"The Presence." *Esquire*, July 2003: 108–109.

The Presence: Stories by Arthur Miller. New York: Viking, 2007.

The Price. New York: Viking, 1968.

The Pussycat and the Expert Plumber Who Was a Man. In *One Hundred Non-Royalty Radio Plays*, edited by William Kozlenko, 20–30. (New York: Greenberg, 1941).

Resurrection Blues. New York: Penguin, 2006.

The Ride Down Mt. Morgan. New York: Penguin, 1992.

The Ryan Interview. In *EST Marathon '95: The Complete One-Act Plays*, edited by Marisa Smith, 139–150. (Lyme, N.H.: Smith and Kraus, 1995).

Salesman in Beijing. New York: Viking, 1983.

"Should Ezra Pound Be Shot?" *New Masses*, December 25, 1945, 5–6.

Situation Normal. New York: Reynal and Hitchcock, 1944.

Some Kind of Love Story. New York: Dramatists Play Service, 1983.

The Story of Gus. In *Radio's Best Plays*, edited by Joseph Liss, 307–319. (New York: Greenberg, 1947).

"Subsidized Theater." *New York Times*, June 22, 1947, sec. 2, p. 1.

That They May Win. In *The Best One-Act Plays of 1944*, edited by Margaret Mayorga, 45–59. (New York: Dodd, Mead, 1945).

The Theatre Essays of Arthur Miller, edited by Robert A. Martin. New York: Viking, 1978. [Includes "The American Theater," "The Family in Modern Drama," "Introduction to Collected Plays," "The Nature of Tragedy," "1956 and All This," "On Social Plays," "The Shadows of the Gods," and "Tragedy and the Common Man."]

The Theatre Essays of Arthur Miller. Edited by Robert A. Martin and Steven R. Centola. Rev. ed. New York: Viking, 1995. [Includes "About Theater Language," "Arthur Miller on *The Crucible*," "Conditions of Freedom," "Ibsen and the Drama of Today."]

Timebends: A Life. New York: Grove, 1987.

The Turpentine Still. Southwest Review 89, no. 4 (2004): 479–520.

Two-Way Mirror: Some Kind of Love Story and *Elegy for a Lady.* London: Methuen, 1984.

Up From Paradise. New York: Samuel French, 1984.

A View from The Bridge. New York: Dramatists Play Service, 1957.

A View from The Bridge: Two One Act-Plays by Arthur Miller. New York: Viking, 1955. [Contains one-act version of *A View from The Bridge* and *A Memory of Two Mondays.*]

"A Visit with Castro." *The Nation* 278, January 12, 2004, 13–17.

"Waiting for the Teacher: On Israel's Fiftieth Anniversary." *Harper's,* July 1998, 56–57.

"White Puppies." *Esquire,* July 1978, 32–36.

"Why Israel Must Choose Justice." *The Nation* 277, August 4–11, 2003, 26–28.

William Ireland's Confession. In *One Hundred Non-Royalty Radio Plays,* edited by William Kozlenko, 512–521. (New York: Greenberg, 1941).

"With Respect to Her Agony—But with Love." *Life* 56, no. 6, February 1964, 66.

Interviews with Arthur Miller

Allen, Jennifer. "Miller's Tale." *New York* 16, January 24, 1983: 33–37.

Applebome, Peter. "Present at the Birth of a Salesman." *New York Times*, January 29, 1999, B1.

"Arthur Miller." *Vanity Fair*, March 1999: 280.

Atlas, James. "The Creative Journey of Arthur Miller Leads Back to Broadway and TV." *New York Times*, September 28, 1980, sec. 2, pp. 1, 32.

Balakian, Jan. "A Conversation with Arthur Miller." *Michigan Quarterly Review* 29 (Spring 1990): 158–170.

———. "An Interview with Arthur Miller." *Studies in American Drama 1945 to the Present* 6, no. 1 (1991): 28–47.

Barber, John. "Guilt Edged Miller." *Daily Telegraph*, September 10, 1979, 13.

Barthel, Joan. "Arthur Miller Ponders *The Price*." *New York Times*, January 28, 1968, sec. 2, pp. 1, 5.

Bigsby, Christopher. "Arthur Miller: The Art of the Theatre II, Part II." *Paris Review* 152 (Fall 1999): 208–224.

———, ed. *Arthur Miller and Company*. London: Methuen, 1990.

———. "Miller's Odyssey to a Brutal Decade." *Guardian*, August 4, 1986: 9.

———. ed. *Remembering Arthur Miller*. London: Methuen, 2005.

Breslauer, Jan. "The Arthur Miller Method." *Los Angeles Times*, June 19, 1994, Calendar: 8.

Carroll, James, and Helen Epstein. "Seeing Eye to Eye." *Boston Review* 14 (February 1989): 12–13.

Centola, Steven. *Arthur Miller in Conversation*. Dallas, Texas: Northouse & Northouse, 1993.

———. "The Last Yankee: An Interview with Arthur Miller." *American Drama* 5, no. 1 (Fall 1995): 78–98.

Century, Douglas. "Miller's Tale of 'Tribalism': The Playwright Returns to His Roots." *Forward*, April 22, 1994, 1, 10.

Cheever, Susan. "Arthur Miller: The One Thing That Keeps Us from Chaos." *New Choices for Retirement Living*, October 1994, 22–25.

Dunham, Mike. "Society, Art and Obligations: Conversation with Arthur Miller." *Anchorage Daily News*, September 1, 1996, 3H.

Edwards, Brian. "Arthur Miller: After the Canonization." In *In the Vernacular: Interviews at Yale with Sculptors of Culture*, edited by Melissa E. Biggs, 139–144. (Jefferson, North Carolina: McFarland, 1991).

"Every Play Has a Purpose." *Dramatists Guild Quarterly* 15 (Winter 1979): 13–20.

Fariello, Griffin. "Arthur Miller." *Red Scare: Memories of the American Inquisition*. New York: Norton, 1995, 340–345.

Feldman, Robert. "Arthur Miller on the Theme of Evil." *Resources for American Literary Study* 17 (Spring 1990): 87–93.

Funke, Lewis. "Interview with Arthur Miller." *Playwrights Talk about Writing*. Chicago: Dramatic, 1975, 175–195.

Gruen, John. "Arthur Miller." *Close-Up*. New York: Viking, 1968, 58–63.

Guernsey, Otis L. "Conversation with Arthur Miller." *Dramatists Guild Quarterly* 24, no. 2 (Summer 1987): 12–21.

Gussow, Mel. *Conversations with Arthur Miller*. New York: Applause, 2002.

Hattersley, Roy. "A View from the Barricades." *Guardian*, October 25, 1998, Features, 6.

Hayman, Ronald. "Arthur Miller." *Playback 2*. New York: Horizon, 1973, 7–22.

Hirschhorn, Clive. "Memories of a Salesman." *Plays and Players* (July 1986), 7–10.

Kaplan, James. "Miller's Crossing." *Vanity Fair*, November 1991, 218–221, 241–248.

Kullman, Colby H. "*Death of a Salesman* at Fifty: An Interview with Arthur Miller." *Michigan Quarterly Review* 37, no. 4 (Fall 1998): 624–635.

Lambert, Angela. "An Intellect at Ease." *Independent*, August 2, 1994, 17, 19.

"Learning from a Performer: A Conversation with Arthur Miller." *Gamut* 1 (1982), 9–23.

Meyer, Michael R. "A Playwright's Crusades." *Maclean's*, September 16, 1985, 6+.

Morley, Sheridan. "Miller on Miller." *Theatre World* 61 (March 1965): 4–8.

Ratcliffe, Michael. "Miller's Russian Tale." *Observer*, October 26, 1986, 23.

"Response to Audience Questions and Answer Session." *Michigan Quarterly Review* 37, no. 4 (Fall 1998): 817–827.

Roudané, Matthew C., editor. *Conversations with Arthur Miller*. Jackson: University Press of Mississippi, 1987.

Rudman, Michael. "Michael Rudman in Conversation with Arthur Miller." *Plays and Players*, October 1979: 20–21, 26–27.

Samachson, Dorothy and Joseph. *Let's Meet the Theatre*. New York: Abelard-Schuman, 1954: 15–20.

Scavullo, Francisco. "Arthur Miller, Playwright." *Scavullo on Men*. New York: Random House, 1977, 134–137.

Solomon, Deborah. "Goodbye (Again), Norma Jean." *New York Times*, September 19, 2004, sec. 6, p. 63.

Stevens, Virginia. "Seven Young Broadway Artists." *Theatre Arts* 31 (June 1947): 52–56.

Unger, Arthur. "Arthur Miller Talks of His Holocaust Drama." *Christian Science Monitor*, September 19, 1980: 19.

Wardle, Irving. "American Patron Saint of the English Stage: Arthur Miller." *Independent*, January 28, 1990: 36.

Wolfert, Ira. "Arthur Miller, Playwright in Search of His Identity." *New York Herald Tribune*, January 25, 1953, sec. 4, p. 3.

BIBLIOGRAPHY OF SECONDARY SOURCES

Abbotson, Susan C. W. *Student Companion to Arthur Miller.* Westport, Conn.: Greenwood Press, 2000.

Adam, Julie. *Versions of Heroism in Modern American Drama: Redefinitions by Miller, O'Neill, and Anderson.* New York: St. Martin's, 1991.

Ali, Syed Mashkoor, ed. *Arthur Miller: Twentieth Century Legend.* Jaipur, India: Surabhi, 2006.

Alter, Iska. "Betrayal and Blessedness: Explorations of Feminine Power in *The Crucible, A View from the Bridge,* and *After the Fall.*" In *Feminist Rereadings of Modern American Drama,* edited by June Schlueter, 116–145. (Rutherford, N.J.: Farleigh Dickinson University Press, 1989).

The Arthur Miller Journal (Spring 2006–   ).

Bentley, Eric. *Thirty Years of Treason.* New York: Viking, 1971.

Bhatia, Santosh K. *Arthur Miller: Social Drama as Tragedy.* New York: Humanities, 1985.

Bigsby, C. W. E. "Arthur Miller." In *A Critical Introduction to Twentieth-Century American Drama: Volume Two—Williams/Miller/Albee.* Cambridge, England: Cambridge University Press, 1984: 135–248.

———. *Arthur Miller: A Critical Study.* Cambridge: Cambridge University Press, 2005.

———. *Modern American Drama 1945–2000.* Cambridge, England: Cambridge University Press, 2000.

———, ed. *Arthur Miller and Company.* London: Methuen, 1990.

———, ed. *The Cambridge Companion to Arthur Miller.* Cambridge, England: Cambridge University Press, 1997.

———, ed. *Remembering Arthur Miller.* London: Methuen, 2005.

Bloom, Harold, editor. *Modern Critical Views: Arthur Miller.* New York: Chelsea House, 1987.

Brater, Enoch. *Arthur Miller: A Playwright's Life and Work.* New York: Thames and Hudson, 2005.

———. "Ethnics and Ethnicity in the Plays of Arthur Miller." In *From Hester Street to Hollywood,* edited by Sarah Blacher Cohen, 123–136. (Bloomington: Indiana University Press, 1983).

———, ed. *Arthur Miller's America: Theater and Culture in a Time of Change.* Ann Arbor: University of Michigan Press, 2005.

Carson, Neil. *Arthur Miller.* London: Macmillan, 1982.

Centola, Steven. "Arthur Miller and the Art of the Possible." *American Drama* (Winter 2005): 63–86.

———, ed. *The Achievement of Arthur Miller: New Essays.* Dallas, Tex.: Contemporary Research, 1995.

———, and Michelle Cirulli, editors. *The Critical Response to Arthur Miller.* Westport, Conn.: Greenwood, 2006.

Clurman, Harold. *Lies Like Truth.* New York: Grove, 1958.

Cohn, Ruby. *Dialogue in American Drama.* Bloomington: Indiana University Press, 1971.

Corrigan, Robert W. *The Theatre in Search of a Fix.* New York: Delacorte, 1973.

———, ed. *Arthur Miller: A Collection of Critical Essays.* Englewood Cliffs, N.J.: Prentice–Hall, 1969.

Driver, Tom. "Strength and Weakness in Arthur Miller." *Tulane Drama Review* 4 (May 1960): 45–52.

Dukore, Bernard F. *Death of a Salesman and The Crucible: Text and Performance.* Atlantic Highlands, N.J.: Humanities, 1989.

Freedman, Morris. *American Drama in Social Context.* Carbondale: Southern Illinois University Press, 1971.

Gassner, John. *Form and Idea in Modern Theatre.* New York: Dryden, 1956.

Gordon, Lois. "Arthur Miller." In *Contemporary American Dramatists,* edited by K. A. Berney, 407–414. (London: St. James, 1994).

Gottfried, Martin. *Arthur Miller: His Life and Work.* New York: Da Capo, 2003.

Griffin, Alice. *Understanding Arthur Miller.* Columbia: University of South Carolina Press, 1996.

Hayman, Ronald. *Arthur Miller.* New York: Ungar, 1972.

Hogan, Robert. *Arthur Miller.* Minneapolis: University of Minnesota Press, 1964.

Huftel, Sheila. *Arthur Miller: The Burning Glass.* New York: Citadel, 1965.

Koorey, Stefani. *Arthur Miller's Life and Literature.* Lanham, Maryland: Scarecrow, 2000.

Langteau, Paula, ed. *Miller in Middle America.* Washington D.C.: University Press of America, 2007.

Marino, Stephen. *A Language Study of Arthur Miller's Plays: The Poetic in the Colloquial.* New York: Mellen, 2002.

Martin, Robert A. "Arthur Miller: Public Issues, Private Tensions." *Studies in the Literary Imagination,* 21, no. 2 (1988): 97–106.

———, ed. *Arthur Miller: New Perspectives.* Englewood Cliffs, N.J.: Prentice–Hall, 1982.

Martine, James J., ed. *Critical Essays on Arthur Miller.* Boston: Hall, 1979.

Moss, Leonard. *Arthur Miller.* 2d. ed. New York: Twayne, 1980.

Murphy, Brenda. "Arthur Miller: Revisioning Realism." In *Realism and the American Dramatic Tradition,* edited by William W. Demastes, 189–202. (Tuscaloosa: University of Alabama Press, 1996).

———. *Congressional Theatre: Dramatizing McCarthyism on Stage, Film, and Television.* New York: Cambridge University Press, 1999.

Murray, Edward. *Arthur Miller, Dramatist.* New York: Ungar, 1967.

Nelson, Benjamin. *Arthur Miller: Portrait of a Playwright.* New York: McKay, 1970.

Otten, Terry. *The Temptation of Innocence in the Dramas of Arthur Miller.* Columbia: University of Missouri Press, 2002.

Overland, Orm. "The Action and its Significance: Arthur Miller's Struggle with Dramatic Form." *Modern Drama* 17 (1975): 1–14.

Parker, Dorothy, ed. *Essays on Modern American Drama: Williams, Miller, Albee and Shepard.* Toronto: University of Toronto Press, 1987.

Prudoe, John. "Arthur Miller and the Tradition of Tragedy." *English Studies* 43 (1962): 430–39.

Ram, Atma, ed. *Perspectives on Arthur Miller.* New Delhi: Abhinav, 1988.

Savran, David. *Communists, Cowboys, and Queers: The Politics of Masculinity in the Work of Arthur Miller and Tennessee Williams.* Minneapolis: University of Minneapolis Press, 1992.

Scanlan, Tom. *Family, Drama, and American Dreams.* Westport, Conn.: Greenwood, 1978.

Schlueter, June, and James K. Flanagan. *Arthur Miller.* New York: Ungar, 1987.

Schneider, Daniel E. *The Psychoanalyst and the Artist.* New York: Farrar, Straus, 1950.

Siebold, Thomas, ed. *Readings on Arthur Miller.* San Diego: Greenhaven, 1997.

Sievers, David W. *Freud on Broadway: A History of Psychoanalysis and the American Drama.* New York: Hermitage, 1955.

Steinberg, M. W. "Arthur Miller and the Idea of Modern Tragedy." *Dalhousie Review* 40 (1961): 329–340.

Trowbridge, Clinton W. "Arthur Miller: Between Pathos and Tragedy." *Modern Drama* 10 (1967): 221–232.

Vajda, Miklos. "Arthur Miller: Moralist as Playwright." *New Hungarian Quarterly* 16 (1975): 171–180.

Viswamohan, Aysha. *Arthur Miller: The Dramatist and His Universe.* Chennai, India: T. R. Publications, 2005.

Vogel, Dan. *The Three Masks of American Tragedy.* Baton Rouge: Louisiana State University Press, 1974.

Welland, Dennis. *Miller: The Playwright.* 3d ed. New York: Methuen, 1985.

Williams, Raymond. "The Realism of Arthur Miller." *Critical Quarterly* 1 (1959): 34–37.

Wilson, Robert N. *The Writer as Social Seer.* Chapel Hill: University of North Carolina, 1979.

Yim, Harksoon. "Arthur Miller's Theory of Tragedy and Its Practice in *All My Sons, Death of a Salesman,* and *The Crucible.*" *Publications of the Mississippi Philological Association* (1996): 57–63.

ARTHUR MILLER CHRONOLOGY

1915

Arthur Asher Miller is born on October 17 at 45 West 110th Street, Harlem, New York City, to ISIDORE MILLER and AUGUSTA MILLER. The second of three children, his brother KERMIT MILLER is older by three years.

1920–28

Attends Public School 24 in Harlem.

1921

Sister Joan is born (will become the actress JOAN COPELAND).

1923

Sees first play—a melodrama at the Schubert Theater.

1928

Bar-mitzvahed at the Avenue M temple. Father's business, MILTEX COAT AND SUIT COMPANY, is struggling and family move to BROOKLYN, first to duplex on Ocean Parkway, then to 1350 East 3rd Street where Miller shares a bedroom with his grandfather, LOUIS BARNETT. Plants a pear tree in the backyard. Attends James Madison High School with his brother.

1930

Kermit graduates, and Miller is reassigned to newly built Abraham Lincoln High School, which is nearer to home.

1931

Begins to work for father's business during summer vacations. Does an early morning bakery delivery before school. Uses savings to buy lumber to build a back porch on the house.

1932

With junior driver's license, drives a delivery truck for Sam Shapse, auto-parts retailer in Long Island City, until this business goes under. Brother Kermit quits college to work at family business full time. Miller graduates from Abraham Lincoln High School. Writes first short story, "In Memoriam," about an aging salesman, based on a man who worked for his father.

1933

Registers for night school at New York City College, but quits after two weeks. UNIVERSITY OF MICHIGAN has turned him down twice because of his poor academic record but finally offers him the possibility of probational acceptance. Considers various jobs to raise the money, including singing on a local radio station; then begins to clerk at CHADICK-DELAMATER AUTO PARTS WAREHOUSE.

1934

Attends University of Michigan in the Fall. Begins to study journalism. Reporter on student paper, the *Michigan Daily*. Student job tending rats in genetics laboratory, and washes dishes in a co-op cafeteria in exchange for meals.

1935

Meets fellow student MARY SLATTERY, and they begin to date. Writes *No Villain* in six days during spring vacation rather than face the expense of going home.

1936

Enters *No Villain* for a Hopwood Award and receives a minor award in drama. Transfers to English major. Becomes night editor of the *Michigan Daily*. Father's business finally goes under. Works to revise *No Villain*.

1937

Rewrite of *No Villain* titled *They Too Arise* receives a $1250 THEATRE GUILD award to study with KENNETH ROWE and is produced in Ann Arbor, directed by Frederic O. Crandall, and in Detroit through the FEDERAL THEATER PROJECT. Takes playwrighting seminar with Rowe. *Honors at Dawn* receives major Hopwood Award in Drama. Drives Ralph Neaphus east to join the Abraham Lincoln Brigade in Spain during their civil war, and considers accompanying him. Meets NORMAN ROSTEN.

1938

The Great Disobedience is entered but does not win a Hopwood prize; it is given a laboratory production at the university. *They Too Arise* is revised and retitled *The Grass Still Grows* for an anticipated production in New York that never materializes. Takes second playwrighting seminar with Rowe. Graduates with a B.A. in English, and moves in with parents, brother Kermit helping out with financial support. Joins the short-lived Federal Theater Project in New York City, having turned down a much better-paying offer to work as a scriptwriter for Twentieth Century-Fox in Hollywood. Writes play *Listen My Children* with Norman Rosten.

1939

Federal Theatre Project is abolished in June. Begins to write radio plays for *Columbia Workshop* (CBS) and for *Calvacade of America* (NBC), *William Ireland's Confession* airs on *Columbia Workshop*.

1940

Travels to North Carolina to collect dialect speech for the folk division of the Library of Congress. On August 5, marries Mary Slattery in Lakewood, Ohio. Move to Brooklyn Heights at 62 Montague Street. Travels on the merchant freighter SS *Copa Copa* to South America to research *Thunder from the Hills*. Completes *The Golden Years*. Meets CLIFFORD ODETS in a bookstore. Radio play *The Pussycat and the Expert Plumber Who Was a Man* aired on *Columbia Workshop* (CBS).

1941

Unable to sign up for the armed forces due to an old high-school-football injury; volunteeers as shipfitter's helper at BROOKLYN NAVY YARD. Turned down for a Rockefeller Fellowship. Radio plays *Joel Chandler Harris* and *Captain Paul* are produced. Publishes "Hitler's Quarry" (essay).

1942

Writes radio plays *The Battle of the Ovens, Thunder from the Mountains, I Was Married in Bataan, Toward a Farther Star, The Eagle's Nest,* and *The Four Freedoms.*

1943

Completes *The Half-Bridge*. One-act play *That They May Win* is produced in New York. Writes *Listen for the Sound of Wings* (radio play). Living at 18 Schermerhorn Street. Tours army camps to research *The Story of G.I. Joe.*

1944

Moves to larger apartment at 102 Pierrepont Street. Daughter, JANE MILLER, is born on September 7. In June, begins to work for CBS *The Doctor Fights* radio series for which he writes several episodes. Radio play *The Story of Canine Joe* is produced. Adapts Ferenc Molnar's *The Guardsman* for radio. Publishes first book, *Situation Normal. . . . The Man Who Had All The Luck* premieres on BROADWAY with Karl Swenson in the lead but closes after six performances (including two previews and a matinee), though receives the Theatre Guild National Award.

1945

Focus (novel) is published. Also article "Should Ezra Pound Be Shot?" in *New Masses*. Adapts Jane Austen's *Pride and Prejudice* for radio. Writes other radio plays *The Philippines Never Surrendered* and *Bernadine, I Love You. Grandpa and the Statue* airs on *Cavalcade of America.*

1946

Adapts George Abbott and John C. Holm's *Three Men on a Horse* for radio. Short story "The Plaster Masks" is published. Possible date of short play, *You're Next.*

1947

All My Sons premieres, directed by ELIA KAZAN with Ed Begley, Beth Merrill, and ARTHUR KENNEDY, and designed by MORDECAI GORELIK. It receives New York Drama Critics Circle and Donaldson Awards. Writes radio play *The Story of Gus.* Publishes short story "It Takes a Thief." Writes "Subsidized Theatre" for *New York Times* (essay). Son ROBERT MILLER is born on May 31. Briefly works in inner-city factory assembling beer boxes for minimum wage. Interviewed by John K. Hutchens for *New York Times.* Explores RED HOOK area, and tries to understand the world of longshoremen. Tries to find out what happened to Pete Panto, whose story will form the nucleus of his screenplay *The Hook.* Name appears in an advertisement in the *Daily Worker* protesting treatment of antifascist refugees.

1948

Buys 31 Grace Court in Brooklyn and a farmhouse in ROXBURY, CONNECTICUT. Builds small studio in which he writes *Death of a Salesman.* Trip to Europe with VINNY LONGHI to get a sense of Italian background that he will use for the Carbones and their relatives. Universal film production of *All My Sons* with Burt Lancaster and Edward G. Robinson released. First London production of *All My Sons,* at Lyric Theatre, Hammersmith, with Joseph Calleia, Margalo Gillmore, and Richard Leech.

1949

Death of a Salesman premieres with LEE J. COBB and MILDRED DUNNOCK, receiving the Pulitzer Prize, the New York Drama Critics Circle Award, the Antoinette Perry Award, the Don-

aldson Award, and the Theater Club Award. Directed by Kazan and staged by JO MIELZINER. It goes on lengthy tour with Thomas Mitchell in a separate production. *New York Times* publishes "Tragedy and the Common Man" and *New York Herald Tribune* "The Nature of Tragedy" (essays). Attends the Cultural and Scientific Conference for World Peace at the Waldorf–Astoria Hotel to chair an arts panel with Odets and Dmitri Shostakovich. First London production of *Death of a Salesman* at Phoenix Theatre with Paul Muni, Katherine Alexander, Kevin McCarthy, and Frank Maxwell.

1950

Adaptation of HENRIK IBSEN's *An Enemy of the People* premieres, directed by Robert Lewis with FREDRIC MARCH and Florence Eldridge. First sound recording of *Death of a Salesman* with Thomas Mitchell, Arthur Kennedy, and Mildred Dunnock.

1951

Meets MARILYN MONROE on a visit to Hollywood with Kazan. *The Hook* fails to reach production due to pressure from HOUSE UN-AMERICAN ACTIVITIES COMMITTEE (HUAC). Yiddish production of *Death of a Salesman,* translated by Joseph Buloff. First film production of *Death of a Salesman,* with March, for Columbia Pictures is released. Short story "Monte Saint Angelo" and Miller's version of *Enemy of the People* are published.

1952

Both Kazan and Odets testify before HUAC and name names. Miller visits the Historical Society "Witch Museum" in Salem to research SALEM WITCH TRIALS for *The Crucible.*

1953

The Crucible premieres directed by JED HARRIS with Arthur Kennedy, Beatrice Straight, and Madeleine Sherwood and receives the Antoinette Perry and Donaldson Awards. Miller directs a production of *All My Sons* for the Arden, Delaware, summer theatre with Joan Copeland playing Ann Deever. Miller family moves to 151 Willow Street.

1954

Unable to travel to attend the Belgian premiere of *The Crucible* as is denied a U.S. passport. First radio productions of *Death of a Salesman* on both CBC and NBC, adapted by Alan Savage and Robert Cenedella; both are severely cut and simplified. Helps Rosten rewrite musical *Mardi Gras*. Monroe divorces Joe DiMaggio. "A Modest Proposal for the Pacification of the Public Temper" (essay) published in *The Nation*. First British production of *The Crucible*, directed by Warren Jenkins, with Edgar Wereford, Rosemary Harris, and Pat Sandys. First meets Irish writer James Stern with whom will correspond on a regular basis.

1955

The one-act version of *A View From the Bridge*, directed by Martin Ritt, premieres with Van Heflin, J. Carrol Naish, Gloria Marlowe, and Jack Warden in a joint bill with *A Memory of Two Mondays*, using the same company. Essay "On Social Plays" is published to accompany these two plays. HUAC pressures city officials to withdraw permission for Miller to make a film that he had been planning about New York juvenile delinquency. Monroe moves to New York City, and she and Miller begin to see each other regularly. Essays "The American Theater" and "A Boy Grew in Brooklyn" are published.

1956

Miller lives in Nevada for six weeks, establishing residency requirement to divorce Slattery, and writes the short story "The Misfits." Essays published in *Atlantic Monthly* and *Colorado Quarterly*, respectively titled "The Family in Modern Drama" and "The Playwright and the Atomic World" [the latter will reappear in *Theater Essays* (1978) under the title "1956 and All This"]. Divorce from Slattery is uncontested, and Miller marries Monroe on June 29. She converts to JUDAISM for her new husband. Receives an honorary Doctorate of Human Letters (L.H.D.) from the University of

Michigan. Subpoenaed to appear before HUAC, and in testimony refuses to give names and is cited for contempt. Granted a temporary passport to go to Britain with Monroe and meets Laurence Olivier. Revises *A View From the Bridge* into two acts for Peter Brook to produce in London, with Anthony Quayle, Ian Bannen, Michael Gwynn, Megs Jenkins, and Mary Ure.

1957

Arthur Miller's Collected Plays published with a lengthy "Introduction." Indicted for contempt of Congress by federal court for refusing to name names to HUAC and is found guilty, fined, and given a suspended 30-day jail sentence. Appeals the verdict. "The Misfits" is published in *Esquire*. First television production of *Death of a Salesman* on ITA, England. French film production of *The Crucible*, retitled *The Witches of Salem*, with screenplay by JEAN–PAUL SARTRE, starring Yves Montand and Simone Signoret.

1958

United States Court of Appeals overturns Miller's contempt conviction. Elected to National Institute of Arts and Letters. *Esquire* publishes "Bridge to a Savage World." Symposium on *Death of a Salesman* published in *Tulane Drama Review*. "Shadows of the Gods" (essay) published. First British production of *A Memory of Two Mondays*, directed by Val May, with Terry Scully, Bryan Pringle, and James Cossins.

1959

Receives Gold Medal for Drama from National Institute of Arts and Letters. *Esquire* publishes short story "I Don't Need You Anymore." CBC television production of *The Crucible* with Leslie Nielsen and Diana Maddox. Granada television production of *The Crucible* with Sean Connery and Susannah York. Receives honorary degree from the Hebrew University of Jerusalem.

1960

The Misfits is filmed in Nevada. INGE MORATH documenting movie for Magnum. Short story "Please Don't Kill Anything" is published. Monroe announces that she and Miller are separated and that she will file for divorce. First London production of *The Man Who Had All the Luck*, directed by Charles Marowitz.

1961

Miller and Monroe divorce. *The Misfits* (film) premieres, directed by John Huston, with performances from Monroe, CLARK GABLE, Montgomery Clift, and ELI WALLACH, and the screenplay is published. *The Crucible: An Opera in Four Acts* by Robert Ward and Bernard Stambler is recorded with the New York City Opera. Sidney Lumet directs a movie version of *A View From a Bridge* for Paramount in France with Raf Vallone and Maureen Stapleton; the screenplay is by Rosten. Mother dies at the age of 70. Short story "The Prophecy" is published.

1962

Marries Morath on February 17. Visits the Mauthausen death camp while in Europe with Morath. Monroe dies August 4. NBC Television presentation of *Focus* with James Whitemore. August 7, son Daniel Miller is born. Short story "Glimpse at a Jockey" and essay "The Bored and the Violent" are published.

1963

Jane's Blanket (children's book) published. September 15, daughter REBECCA MILLER born.

1964

Covers the war-crimes trial of a group of former Auschwitz guards in Frankfurt, Germany, for the *New York Herald Tribune*. *After the Fall*, directed by Kazan with JASON ROBARDS, JR. and Barbara Loden, is offered as the opening production of the new REPERTORY THEATER OF LINCOLN CENTER in New York, and *Incident at Vichy*, directed by HAROLD CLURMAN with Joseph Wiseman, Hal Holbrook, and David Wayne, follows later that year at the same venue.

1965

Elected president of PEN, the international literary organization (a four-year term), and goes to Yugoslavian conference. First visits the Soviet Union. ULU GROSBARD's off-Broadway production of *A View from the Bridge*. Essay "Our Guilt For the World's Evil" appears in *New York Times Magazine*. Caedmon produces a vinyl-record version of *Death of a Salesman*. Major London revival of *The Crucible*, directed by Laurence Olivier.

1966

First sound recording of *A View From the Bridge* with Robert Duvall. CBS-TV airs *Death of a Salesman* with Lee J. Cobb and Mildred Dunnock to 17 million watchers. Sound recording of *Death of a Salesman* with Cobb and Dunnock released. Father dies on the day that Miller makes his opening speech at the New York PEN Congress. Short stories "Recognitions" (later revised as "Fame") and "A Search for a Future" are published. British premiere of *Incident at Vichy*, directed by Peter Wood with Alec Guiness and Anthony Quayle.

1967

I Don't Need You Anymore (short-story collection) published. Sound recording of *Incident at Vichy* with Joseph Wiseman, Hal Holbrook, and David Wayne. Television production of *The Crucible* on CBS with GEORGE C. SCOTT. Visit to the Soviet Union with Morath to gather material for their first book of reportage and to persuade Soviet writers to join PEN. British premiere of *After the Fall*, directed by Leonard Schach with Leon Gluckmann and Erica Rogers.

1968

The Price premieres at the Morosco Theater, New York, directed by Grosbard with Arthur Kennedy, Pat Hingle, Harold Gary, and Kate Reid. Attends the Democratic National Convention in Chicago as the Eugene McCarthy delegate, and relates his experiences in "The Battle of Chicago" (essay) for the *New York Times*. Petitions the Russian government to lift their ban on the works of Aleksandr Solzhenitsyn. Sound recording of *After the Fall* with Jason Robards, Jr., and Barbara Loden.

1969

In Russia published (reportage with photographs by Inge Morath). Visits Czechoslovakia to show support for writers there and briefly meets VÁCLAV HAVEL. Term ends as president of PEN, but stays involved. Refuses to allow his works to be published in Greece in protest of the government's oppression of writers. Publishes poem "Lines from California: Poem" in *Harper's*. Directs London premiere of *The Price* with Albert Salmi, Kate Reid, Harold Gary, and Shepperd Strudwick. Recieves Brandeis University Creative Arts Award.

1970

One-act plays *Fame* and *The Reason Why* performed in New York with Eli Wallach and Anne Jackson. Film short made of *The Reason Why* with Wallach and Robert Ryan. Miller's works banned in the Soviet Union as result of *In Russia*, and Miller's work to free dissident writers. Supports local Roxbury high-school teacher who refuses to say the Pledge of Allegiance in her classroom. Caedmon produce vinyl-record version of *An Enemy of the People*.

1971

Sound recording of *An Enemy of the People* directed by Jules Irving. Television productions of *A Memory of Two Mondays* on PBS with Kristoffer Tabori, Estelle Parsons, and Jack Warden, and *The Price* on NBC with George C. Scott. Helps release the Brazilian playwright Augusto Boal from prison. *The Portable Arthur Miller*, edited by Harold Clurman, is published. Elected to the American Academy of Arts and Letters.

1972

The Creation of the World and Other Business premieres in New York, directed by Gerald Freeman, with Bob Dishy, Stephen Elliott, Zoe Caldwell, and Mark Lamos. Attends Democratic National Convention in Miami as a delegate. First sound recording of *The Crucible* with Jerome Dempsey and Alexandria Stoddard. Essay "Arthur Miller on *The Crucible*" published. *Jane's Blanket* reprinted with new illustrations.

1973

Television production of *Incident at Vichy* on PBS with Richard Jordan. *Esquire* publishes the essay "Miracles." Hires private investigator to look into the PETER REILLY case.

1974

Up From Paradise (musical version of *The Creation of the World and Other Business*) premieres at the University of Michigan, narrated by Arthur Miller, with performances by Bob Bingham and Allan Nichols. Television production of *After the Fall* on NBC with Christopher Plummer and Faye Dunaway. Poem "Rain in a Strange City" published. British premiere of *The Creation of the World and Other Business* as part of the Edinburgh Fringe Theatre Festival. Essay "What's Wrong with This Picture?" published in *Esquire*.

1975

Appears on a panel before the Senate Permanent Subcommittee on Investigations to support the freedom of writers throughout the world.

1976

Boston University Quarterly publishes two short works: "Ham Sandwich," a brief story, and *The Poosidin's Resignation*, a play fragment.

1977

In the Country published (reportage with Inge Morath). Miller petitions the Czech government to halt arrests of dissident writers. *The Archbishop's Ceiling* premieres in Washington, D.C., at the Kennedy Center for a limited run, directed by Arvin Brown, with Tony Musante, John Cullum, Bibi Andersson, and Douglas Watson.

1978

Charges against Reilly are dropped as a result of newly uncovered evidence. *The Theater Essays of Arthur Miller*, edited by Robert A. Martin, published. *Fame* (film) appears on NBC *Hallmark Hall of Fame*, with Richard Benjamin and José Ferrer. Belgian National Theatre does 25th anniversary production of *The Crucible*, and this time Miller can attend. Short stories "White

Puppies" and "The 1928 Buick" published. Visits China with Morath in the fall.

1979

Chinese Encounters published (reportage with Inge Morath). Sound recording of *A Memory of Two Mondays* with Jack Warden and Estelle Parsons. Major revival of *Death of a Salesman* in London by the NATIONAL THEATRE, directed by Michael Rudman, with Warren Mitchell.

1980

Playing for Time (film) appears on CBS with VANESSA REDGRAVE and Jane Alexander and is later published. *The American Clock* previews, then premieres at the Spoleto Festival in South Carolina, and opens later in New York, directed by Vivian Matalon, with William Atherton, John Randolph, and Joan Copeland. TV film *Arthur Miller on Home Ground* shown on PBS.

1981

The second volume of *Arthur Miller's Collected Plays* published. Major London revival of *The Crucible*, directed by Bill Bryden.

1982

One-act plays *Elegy for a Lady* and *Some Kind of Love Story* are produced under the title *2 by A.M.* at the Long Wharf Theatre in Connecticut, directed by Miller, with Charles Cioffi and Christine Lahti in both plays.

1983

Directs *Death of a Salesman* at the PEOPLE'S ART THEATER IN BEIJING, the People's Republic of China. Fire causes extensive damage to the home in Roxbury, Connecticut. British premiere of *The American Clock*.

1984

Salesman in Beijing published. *Elegy for a Lady* and *Some Kind of Love Story* are published under the new title *Two-Way Mirror*. Miller receives Kennedy Center honors for distinguished lifetime achievement. The ceremony is held in the same room in which he had attended his HUAC hearings. Dispute with WOOSTER GROUP over unauthorized use of scenes from *The Crucible* in an experimental play, *L.S.D. (. . . Just the High Points . .)*. *The Archbishop's Ceiling* produced in original form in Cleveland, directed by Jonathan Bolt, with Morgan Lund, Lizbeth Mackay, John Buck, Jr., and Thomas S. Olenlacz. Major revival of *Death of a Salesman* in New York, directed by Michael Rudman, with DUSTIN HOFFMAN.

1985

New TV-movie version of *Death of a Salesman* with Hoffman, Kate Reid, and John Malkovitch airs on CBS to audience of 25 million. Miller goes to Turkey with HAROLD PINTER for International PEN. Goes as delegate to a meeting of Soviet and U.S. writers in Vilnius, Lithuania, where he tries to persuade the Soviets to stop persecuting writers. Provides voiceovers for Ken Burns's documentary *The Statue of Liberty*. Studio Theater production of *Playing for Time* in Washington, D.C. First British production of *The Archbishop's Ceiling*.

1986

I Think About You a Great Deal published in honor of Václav Havel. One of 15 writers and scientists invited to the Soviet Union to conference with Mikhail Gorbachov and to discuss Soviet policies. British production of *The Archbishop's Ceiling* at the Royal Shakespeare Company's Pit Theatre in the Barbican Center with a restored script, as well as an acclaimed production of *A View from the Bridge* and Peter Wood's production of *American Clock* (its first London production), both at the National Theatre.

1987

One-act plays *I Can't Remember Anything* and *Clara* are produced and published under the title *Danger: Memory!* Kenneth McMillan and James Tolkan appear in *Clara*, and Mason Adams and Geraldine Fitzgerald play in *I Can't Remember Anything*. Publishes *Timebends: A Life* (autobiography), which appears as a Book-of-the-Month-Club popular selection. UNIVERSITY OF EAST ANGLIA names the Arthur Miller Centre for

American studies, under the direction of CHRIS-TOPHER BIGSBY. *The Golden Years* is premiered on BBC Radio, with Ronald Pickup, Hannah Gordon, and John Shrapnel. Television production of *All My Sons* on PBS *American Playhouse,* with James Whitemore, Aidan Quinn, Joan Allen, and Michael Learned. Major London revival of *A View from the Bridge,* directed by Alan Ayckbourn, with Michael Gambon at the National Theatre.

1988

As part of musical review *Urban Blight,* contributes a monologue, *Speech to the Neighborhood Watch Committee.* London premiere of *Danger: Memory!*

1989

Essay "Conditions of Freedom" published to accompany a new edition of *The Archbishop's Ceiling* and *The American Clock.* Essay "Again They Drink from the Cup of Suspicion" appears in the *New York Times.* BBC radio broadcast of *The Price* with Richard Dreyfuss and Timothy West. London premiere of *Two Way Mirror.*

1990

Everybody Wins, a film based on *Some Kind of Love Story,* released with Nick Nolte and Debra Winger. Television production of Miller's version of *An Enemy of the People* on PBS *American Playhouse,* with John Glover. Short story "Bees" published. Tributes in Britain in honor of Miller's 75th birthday with London revivals of *The Price* and *The Crucible.*

1991

The single-scene one-act play *The Last Yankee* produced, with John Heard and Biff McGuire. *The Ride down Mt. Morgan* premieres in London, with Tom Conti, Gemma Jones, and Clare Higgins, directed by MICHAEL BLAKEMORE. Receives Mellon Bank Award for lifetime achievement in the humanities. Television production of *Clara,* with Darren McGavin and William Daniels, and an interview on A&E. *South Bank Show* television special on Miller, with Melvyn Bragg.

1992

Homely Girl, A Life (novella) published in a limited edition. First International Arthur Miller Conference is held at Millersville University in Pennsylvania.

1993

Expanded version of *The Last Yankee* premieres, with John Heard, Frances Conroy, and Tom Aldredge. Television production of *The American Clock* on TNT, with Mary McDonnell, Darren McGavin, David Strathairn, and Rebecca Miller. Awarded the National Medal of the Arts by President Clinton.

1994

Broken Glass premieres at Long Wharf, with Ron Rifkin, David Dukes, and Amy Irving, then moves to New York. *Broken Glass* premieres in London, directed by DAVID THACKER. Interviewed on *The Charley Rose Show,* PBS. Appointed to a one-year position as professor of Contemporary Theatre at Oxford University. Essay "Ibsen and the Drama of Today" appears in *The Cambridge Companion to Ibsen.* Sound recording of *The Crucible* with Michael York for L.A. Theatre Works. Essay "About Theater Language" is published to accompany new edition of *The Last Yankee.*

1995

Receives WILLIAM INGE Festival Award for distinguished achievement in U.S. theater, and an honorary doctorate from Oxford University, where he spends time working on a screenplay for *The Crucible.* Tributes to the playwright on the occasion of his 80th birthday are held in Britain and the United States. *Homely Girl, A Life and Other Stories* is published (novella and short stories). Poem "Lola's Lament" is published in the collection *Unleashed: Poems by Writers' Dogs.* Involved in appeals case of Richard Lapointe. Short story "In Memoriam" published in *New Yorker.* Involved in a public contretemps at restaurant with a reporter asking personal questions about Monroe. Second International Arthur Miller Conference held at Millersville University in Pennsylvania. ARTHUR MILLER SOCIETY founded. *The Ryan Interview* performed at the Ensemble Studio One-Act Play Marathon, with Mason Adams and Julie Lauren.

1996

Receives the Edward Albee Last Frontier Playwright Award. Revised and expanded book of *Theater Essays*, edited by STEVEN CENTOLA, published. Third International Arthur Miller Conference held at Utica College. Sound recording of *Broken Glass*, with David Dukes and Linda Purl, for L.A. Theatre Works. Revised version of *The Ride down Mt. Morgan* given its American Premiere in Williamstown, Massachusetts. Film version of *The Crucible* opens, with Daniel Day-Lewis, Joan Allen, Paul Scofield, and Winona Ryder, and the screenplay is published.

1997

BBC/*Mobil Masterpiece Theatre* television production of *Broken Glass*, directed by Thacker. Daughter Rebecca marries Daniel Day-Lewis. Undergoes eye surgery on the retina to correct vision. SIGNATURE THEATER announces that its new season will feature work of Miller.

1998

Mr. Peter's Connections premieres with Peter Falk. Major revival of *A View From the Bridge* with Anthony LaPaglia wins two Tony Awards. Revised version of *The Ride down Mt. Morgan* appears in New York, with Patrick Stewart. Named as the Distinguished Inaugural Senior Fellow of the American Academy in Berlin, receives the first PEN/Laura Pels Foundation Award to a master U.S. dramatist, named recipient of the Lucille Lortel Award for Lifetime Achievement, and given the Hubert H. Humphrey First Amendment Freedoms Prize. In Britain, he is voted "Playwright of the Century." Arthur Miller Symposium held at University of Evansville, Indiana. Fourth International Arthur Miller Conference held at Millersville University in Pennsylvania. Poem "Waiting for the Teacher: On Israel's Fiftieth Anniversary" and essay "Before Air Conditioning" are published.

1999

Death of a Salesman revived on Broadway for the play's 50th anniversary, with BRIAN DENNEHY and ELIZABETH FRANZ, winning Tony for Best Revival of a Play. Also, a revival of *The Price* transfers from Williamstown to New York. Essay "*Salesman* at Fifty" published as part of an anniversary edition of the play. Fifth International Arthur Miller Conference held at St. Francis College in Brooklyn. Special Symposium on Miller and the Holocaust held at Kean University, New Jersey. Sound recording of *All My Sons* with James Farentino and Julie Harris for L.A. Theatre Works. Essay "On Broadway: Notes on the Past and Future of American Theater" appears in *Harper's*. First issue of the biannual *Arthur Miller Society Newsletter*.

2000

The Ride down Mt. Morgan appears on Broadway with Patrick Stewart. There are major 85th-birthday celebrations for Miller held at University of Michigan and at the Arthur Miller Center at UEA, England. *Echoes Down the Corridor* (collected essays from 1944 through 2000) published. Goes to Cuba with William Styron on a visit, aiming to strengthen U.S. cultural links with the island nation and meets FIDEL CASTRO.

2001

Untitled, a previously unpublished one-act play that was written for Václav Havel appears in New York. Williamstown Theater Festival revives *The Man Who Had All the Luck*. *Focus*, a film based on the book, is released, starring William H. Macy. Miller awarded a NEH Fellowship and the John H. Finley Award for Exemplary Service to New York City. *On Politics and the Art of Acting* published (essay). Sixth International Arthur Miller Conference held at Felician College in Lodi, New Jersey.

2002

Broadway revivals of *The Man Who Had All the Luck*, with Chris O'Donnell, and *The Crucible*, with Liam Neeson. Inge Morath dies. Premiere of *Resurrection Blues* at the Guthrie Theater, Minneapolis. Two short stories "The Performance" and "The Bare Manuscript" published in *New Yorker*. Seventh International Arthur Miller Conference held at San Joaquin Delta College in Stockton, California.

2003

Awarded the Jerusalem Prize. Brother, Kermit, dies on October 17. Eighth International Arthur Miller Conference held at held at Nicolet College in Rhinelander, Wisconsin.

2004

Broadway revival of *After the Fall*. Premiere of *Finishing the Picture* at the Goodman Theater, Chicago. Ninth International Arthur Miller Conference held at St. Francis College in Brooklyn; Miller attends. *The Turpentine Still* published in *Southwest Review*.

2005

Short story "Beavers" published. Before impending nuptials to painter Agnes Barley, Miller dies at 89 of heart failure at his home in Roxbury on February 10. Final issue of the *Arthur Miller Society Newsletter*. Tenth International Arthur Miller Conference held at Saint Peter's College in Jersey City.

2006

First issue of the biannual *Arthur Miller Journal*. Premiere of *Resurrection Blues* in Britain, directed by Robert Altman. Royal Shakespeare Company revival of *The Crucible*. Eleventh International Arthur Miller Conference held at Community College of Southern Nevada in Las Vegas.

2007

Presence: Stories by published. Arthur Miller Theater opens in March with an inaugural production of *Playing for Time*.

INDEX

Boldface numbers indicate
major treatment of a topic.
Italic numbers indicate
illustrations.

A

Abbotson, Susan C. W. 48, 53,
72, 76, 90, 93, 140, 147, 195,
219, 222, 271, 273, 306, 309,
390, 488
Abbott, George 9, 361, 401
"About Theater Language" 20,
25, 477, 484, 497
Abraham, F. Murray 300, 477
absurdism 15, 199, 258, 278,
306, 316, 328, **357–358**,
359, 366, 405, 437, 447
    in "Ibsen and the Drama
    of Today" 199, 357
    in Miller's plays 282, 306,
    357
    in "*The Price*—The Power
    of the Past" 286
Actors Studio 166, **358**, 381,
385, 418, 461–462
    and Marilyn Monroe 13,
    358, 388, 434, 474
Adair, Jean 117
Adam, Julie 488
Adamczewski, Zygmunt 146,
466
Adamov, Arthur 357
Adams, Jane 291
Adams, Mason 194, 310, 496,
498
Adding Machine, The (Rice)
387
Aden, Estelle 208, 210
Adenauer, Konrad 437
Adhikari, Arvind Singh 174,
176
Adler, Luther 397
Adler, Stella 377, 397, 461

Adler, Thomas P. 90, 93
Aeschylus 161
After the Fall 15–16, 21, **25–
40**, 104, 162, 177, 204, 248,
306, 324, 352–353, 363, 374,
417, 424, 427, 431, 439, 483
    characters. *See also* Holga,
    Ike, Louise, Maggie,
    Quentin, Rose 16, 26,
    35–38, 165, 168, 459
    compared to *Death of a
    Salesman* 31, 141
    critical commentary **31–33**
    and existentialism 39,
    104, 305, 386, 387
    and expressionism 31,
    305, 387, 450
    and Holocaust 25, 28–29,
    31–32, 35–36, **406–407**,
    438
    initial reviews 16, **33–34**
    and Kazan 25–26, 33, 36,
    418, 420–421, 452, 494
    and Monroe 16, 25–26,
    33–34, 37–39, 437
    and Morath 16, 25–26,
    35, 437
    movies 38, 39, 495
    productions of 369–370,
    378, 440, 471, 474–475,
    477, 499
    scholarship 34–35, **38–40**,
    124
    and Slattery 16, 26, 36
    synopsis 16, **26–31**
"Again They Drank from the
Cup of Suspicion" 19, 125,
497
agitprop 9, 79, 324, 326, 353,
443
Albee, Edward 21, 147, **358–
359**, 368, 445, 460, 477
    on Miller 22, 359

Albert, Herb 89
Aldredge, Tom 218, 497
Alexander, Jane 270, 496
Alfieri (character) 284, 338–
344, **345**, 346, 348, 423
Ali, Syed Mashkoor 48, 53,
488
Allen, Jennifer 486
Allen, Joan 53, 124, 128, 497,
498
Allen, Seth 335
All My Sons 4, 13, **40–54**, 130,
170, 199, 211–212, 257, 323,
327, 358, 363, 367, 372, 380,
394, 395, 417, 424, 432, 444,
454, 459, 464, 483
    and capitalism 47, 51,
    374–375
    characters. *See also* Ann
    Deever, George Deever,
    Chris Keller, Joe Keller,
    Kate Keller, Larry Keller
    critical commentary
    45–47
    initial reviews 10, **48**,
    362, 370
    and Kazan 10, 40, 47–48,
    130, 139, 418–420, 492
    movies 10, 20, **53**, 492,
    497
    productions of 369, 378,
    381, 393–394, 402, 440,
    477, 492, 498
    and realism 40, 48–49,
    449
    scholarship 48–49, 53–54
    synopsis 9, **40–45**
    and tragedy 45, 48, 54,
    465
*Almost Everybody Wins. See
Everybody Wins*
Alpert, Hollis 243, 245
Alter, Iska 124, 488

Altman, Robert 291–292, 499
Ambrosetti, Ronald 344, 348
American Civil Liberties Union
411
American Clock, The 4, 18–19,
54–65, 76, 81, 100–101,
389, 392, 394, 423, 461, 466,
471, 473, 483
    characters. *See also* Lee
    Baum, Moe Baum,
    Rose Baum, Matthew
    Bush, William Durant,
    Edie, Irene, Joe, Jesse
    Livermore, Randolph
    Morgan, Ralph 3–4,
    55–60, **61–64**, 65, 356,
    496–497
    and communism 56–57,
    59, 61–63, **380**
    critical commentary
    57–59
    and democracy 18, 57,
    383
    and Great Depression
    55–59, 61–65, 101,
    395–396
    initial reviews **60**
    movies **64–65**, 497
    productions of 381, 440,
    460, 477–478, 496
    scholarship **60–61**, 65
    synopsis 18, **55–57**
American Legion 12, 129, 385,
410, 446
American Playhouse 20, 53,
155, 497
"American Theater, The" 13,
66, 484, 493
Amram, David 33
Anderson, David E. 329
Anderson, Maxwell 427, 464
Anderson, Robert 419
Andersson, Bibi 71, 495

Andorra (Frisch) 174, 177
Andre, Jacqueline 117
Andrews, Julie 224
Angela (character) 152–158,
    318–321, 433
Angell, Roger 243, 245
Another Part of the Forest
    (Hellman) 385, 404
Ansen, David 158
"Anti-Red Bill Sent to Senate"
    425
anti-Semitism 3, 26, 182, 349,
    359–361, 451
    in *Boro Hall Nocturne* 81,
        360
    in *Broken Glass* 86, 90,
        360
    in *Focus* 9, 170–176, 360
    in "Hitler's Quarry" 186,
        360
    in *Homely Girl, A Life*
        187–188, 361
    in *Incident at Vichy* 205–
        207, 360
    in *In Russia* 202, 360
    Miller's experience of 5, 7,
        360, 376, 430
    in "Monte Sant' Angelo"
        253, 361
    in "The Performance"
        264, 361
    in *Playing for Time* 269,
        271, 360, 400
    and Pound 317, 448
Antler, Joyce 90, 93
Appia, Adolphe 361
Applebome, Peter 392, 486
Archbishop's Ceiling, The
    17–19, 65, **66–76**, 100–101,
    208, 386, 404, 471, 475, 483,
    495–497
    characters. *See also*
        Sigmund 67–71, **72–76**
    critical commentary
        69–71
    initial reviews **71**
    scholarship **71–72**, 76
    synopsis **67–69**
archival material
    in Harry Ransom Research
        Center 7, 34, 81, 149,
        160, 179, 184–185, 191,
        198, 201, 214, 223, 265,
        329, 253, 403
    in Lester Cowan
        Collection 322
    in Library of Congress
        (rare books) 223

    in Lilly Library (Indiana
        University) 191
    in Museum of Radio and
        Television 223, 326
    in New York Public Library
        81, 95, 149, 198, 215,
        265, 322, 325, 329, 438
        images *9, 27, 41, 113,
        131, 140, 337*
    in University of Colorado
        at Boulder 79
    in University of Michigan
        184, 190, 256, 453
Ardolino, Frank 124, 141, 146
Ardrey, Robert 393, 418
Arendt, Hannah 31, 353
Arens, Richard 410–411
Arent, Arthur 391
"Are We Interested in Stopping
    the Killing?" 17, 471–472
Argo, Victor 99
Aristotle 464–465
Armstrong, Alun 146, 463
Arnold (character) 5, 184,
    256–257, 325, 380, 388
Aronson, Arnold 118, 124,
    478
Aronson, Boris 105, 107, 117,
    207, 234, 283, 328, 337,
    361–362, 363, 381, 442
Arthur Miller Centre for
    American Studies 19, 368,
    394, 467, 496–497, 498
Arthur Miller International
    Conferences 20, 362, 376,
    497–499
Arthur Miller Journal (journal)
    20, 361, 499
"Arthur Miller on *The
    Crucible*" **76–77**, 484, 495
"Arthur Miller on the Nature of
    Tragedy." *See* "The Nature
    of Tragedy"
Arthur Miller Society 20, 141,
    362, 376, 498
Arthur Miller Theater 469,
    499
Asphalt Jungle, The (Huston)
    434
Atherton, William 59, 496
Atkinson, Brooks 154–155,
    195, 213, 234, 236, 337–338,
    362–363, 370, 378, 425
    and *All My Sons* 10, 48, 53
    and *The Crucible* 117, 124
    and *Death of a Salesman*
        11, 140, 146
    in *Timebends: A Life* 362

Atlas, James 408, 486
Auberjonois, Rene 210
Auburn, David 432
August, Eugene 146, 390
Auschwitz 16, 18, 204, 266,
    274, 391, 407, 494
Austen, Jane 9, 464, 491
Austin, Gayle 141, 146
autobiographical elements 3,
    50, 74, 79–81, 94, 149, 152,
    165, 167–168, 196, 201, 214,
    224, 238, 246, 255, 389, 433
    in *After the Fall* 3, 16, 26,
        33–35, 162, 352–353,
        429–431, 437, 459, 473
    in *The American Clock*
        3–4, 54–55, 61–62, 65,
        429–430, 473
    in *The Crucible* 459
    in *Death of a Salesman* 4,
        130, 141–143, 430, 441
    in *A Memory of Two
        Mondays* 5, 231–233
    in *No Villain* 256–258, 431
    in *The Price* 3, 430, 431
    in *A View from the Bridge*
        338–339, 430, 460
Autumn Garden, The (Hellman)
    377, 404
Avni, Ron 335
Awake and Sing (Odets) 361,
    377, 442–443
awards 10–11, 363–364, 415
    for Miller 6, 8, 14, 18–19,
        21, 89, 139, 224, 415
    Avery Hopwood
        awards 5–6, 184,
        190, 256, 363, 441,
        468, 490
    Donaldson awards 40,
        48, 117, 363, 492
    Jerusalem Prize 21,
        351, 364, 499
    New York Drama
        Critics Circle
        awards 11, 40, 48,
        139, 338, 363, 492
    Pulitzer Prize 11, 139,
        363, 492
    Tony awards 11, 117,
        139, 363, 492
Axelson, Mary Macdougal 385

B

Babbin, Jacqueline 236
Babcock, Granger 146
Baby Doll (Williams) 385,
    419, 474

Bakey, Ed 210
Balakian, Janet N. 208, 210,
    305–306, 309, 486
Baldu, Looey (character)
    168–169, 372
Ballad of Jack and Rose, The
    (Miller) 432
Balsam, Lee 4, 130, 371, 428,
    430, 433
Bannen, Ian 343, 493
Barat, Urbashi 146, 415
Barber, John 486
Barclay, Dolores 477
"Bare Manuscript, The" 21,
    77–78, 483, 499
Barley, Agnes 22, 165, 167,
    332, **365**, 439, 499
Barnes, Clive 60, 65, 89, 93,
    105, 107, 250–251, 283,
    286, 458
Barnes, Howard 48, 53, 229,
    231
Barnett, Louis 3–4, 63, 81,
    365–366, 371, 417, 428–
    429, 459, 490
Barriaux, Felix (character) 21,
    177, 292–295, **296–297**, 374
Barry, Iris 174, 177
Barry, Philip 184, 464
Barthel, Joan 451, 486
Basseches, Maurice 317–318
Bateman, Mary B. 146, 390
"Battle of Chicago: From the
    Delegates' Side, The" 17,
    78–79, 471, 483, 494
Battle of the Ovens 8, **79**, 95,
    491
Baum, Lee (character) 3–4,
    55–59, **61**, 63–65, 374, 384,
    431
Baum, Moe (character) 3–4,
    55–59, **61–62**, 64–65, 380,
    389, 430
Baum, Rose (character) 3–4,
    55–57, 59–61, **62**, 63–65,
    381, 429
Bawer, Bruce 329
Baxandell, Lee 33, 38
Bayard (character) 204–207,
    208–209, 380
BBC 72, 368, 391
    radio 19, 179, 182, 394,
        497
    television 93, 146, 394,
        463, 498
Beattie, Ann 376
Beatty, John Lee 218
Beatty, Warren 155

Beaufort, John 60, 65
Beauvoir, Simone de 386
"Beavers" 22, **79–80**, 483, 499
Beck, Stanley 33, 207
Becker, Benjamin J. 146
Beckett, Samuel 15, 96, 208,
   215, 357, 359, **366**, 394, 402
   in "Notes on Realism" 25,
   258, 366
Bedford, Brian 343
"Bees" 79, **80**, 483, 497
Beeves, Amos (character)
   224–228, **229–230**, 388–
   389, 431
Beeves, David (character) 8,
   224–229, **230**, 231, 388
Beeves, Paterson (character) 3,
   224–229, **230**, 289
"Before Air Conditioning"
   433, 498
Begley, Ed 47, 419, 492
Behrman, S. N. 418, 426, 452
Beijing People's Art Theater
   19, 97, 140, 311–313, *312*,
   366–367, 496
Belasco, David 66
Bel Geddes, Norman 313
Bell, Ralph 234, 337
Bellow, Saul 34, 174, 177, 306,
   367, 455
Ben (character) 196–197,
   388, 431
Ben-Ami, Jacob 260
Benavente, Jacinto 464
Bendix, William 81
Benedek, Laslo 145
Benjamin, Richard 160, 495
Bennetts, Leslie 65
Bentley, Eric 117, 124, 141,
   367–368, 488
Berenson, Marisa 270
Berenson, Mitch 424, 450
Berg, Gertrude 462
Bergere, Lee 210
Bergeron, David M. 118, 124
Berghof, Herbert 229
Bergman, Herbert 118
Bermel, Albert 273, 378
Bernadine, I Love You 9, 81,
   479, 492
Bernard (character) 132, 134,
   137–140, **141**, 145, 375, 379,
   423, 458
Bernstein, Aline 154
Berry, John 427
Bert (character) 232–234,
   235, 236–237
Bettleheim, Bruno 408

Beyer, William 48, 53
Bhatia, Santosh K. 466, 488
Bi An (*Another Hope*) 97
Bigsby, Christopher vii, 225,
   368–369, 374, 386–387,
   412, 416–417, 450, 488
   and *Arthur Miller and
      Company* 20, 216, 266,
      359, 368, 394, 396
   and Arthur Miller Centre
      19, 467
   and fiction 159–160, 169,
      174, 177–178, 188, 190,
      196–197, 253, 276–277,
      289, 315, 333
   and interviews 55, 478,
      486
   and movies 244, 245, 271
   and plays 34, 38, 49, 60,
      65, 71, 76, 90, 92–93,
      105, 107, 141, 146, 150,
      152, 154–155, 165–166,
      168, 184, 208, 210, 219,
      222, 229, 231, 234–236,
      250–251, 283, 286, 296,
      299, 306, 309, 333–334,
      344, 348
   on radio 179, 183, 322,
      326, 497
   and *Remembering Arthur
      Miller* 369, 394, 447,
      463–464
Billings, Alan 335
Billington, Michael 20, 71, 76,
   89, 93, 152, 296, 299, 306,
   309, 394
Bingham, Bob 335, 495
Birch, Lionel 437
Bird, Norman 182
Blackwell, C. Thomas 207
Blake, Mervyn 343
Blake, Robert A. 124, 128
Blakemore, Michael 20, 26,
   246, 305, **369**, 394, 440,
   497
   on Miller 369
Blau, Herbert 452
Blessing, Lee 460
Bloom, Harold 49
Bloomberg, Michael 176
Bloomgarden, Kermit 11, 13,
   117, 139, 234, 337, **369**, 378,
   385, 401–402, 405, 418–419,
   427, 474
Boal, Augusto 18, 495
Bogart, Paul 155, 236
Boggs, W. Arthur 48, 53
Bohne, Bruce 296

Bolcom, William 21, 89, 199,
   339
Bolt, Robert 118
Bolton, Guy 402
Bonderie, Raymond 123
Bone, Larry Earl 195
Boomerang! (Kazan) 378, 419,
   421
Booth, David 124
Borak, Jeffrey 306, 309
Borders, William 472
"Bored and the Violent, The"
   15, 494
Boro Hall Nocturne 8, **81**, 183,
   396, 417, 479
   and anti-Semitism 81, 360
Bosco, Philip 155
Bourgeois, Louise 187
Bovard, Karen 124
Bower, Tom 210
"Boy Grew in Brooklyn, A" 13,
   81, 370, 483, 493
Bracken, Eddie 310
Bradbury, Malcolm 170, 174,
   177, 197, 239, 253, 289, 367
Bradshaw, Erica 249
Bramley, Raymond 117
Brandman, Michael 64
Brando, Marlon 261, 405,
   415, 461
Brantley, Ben 250–251, 306,
   309, 310, 384
Brashear, William R. 34, 38,
   466
Brater, Enoch 65, 76, 310,
   416–417, 469, 488
Brecht, Bertold 368, 440
Bredella, Lothar 124
Brer Rabbit 215, 260
Breslauer, Jan 486
Breuer, Bessie 381
"Bridge to a Savage World" 13,
   82, 483, 493
Brien, Alan 213
Brinckerhoff, Burt 100
Britain. *See* Great Britain
Broadway 25, 40, 349, 362,
   369–370, 474
   actors and 378–379, 381–
      382, 384, 385, 392, 418,
      421, 425, 451, 452–453,
      458, 474
   designers and 361, 393,
      426
   directors and 361, 377,
      397, 401, 418
   Miller's plays on 8, 20–22,
      48, 139, 162, 169, 228,

   232, 277, 286, 301, 311,
      336, 363, 370, 411, 432,
      447, 459, 477–478,
      491, 498
   other plays on 359, 370,
      404, 414, 415, 421,
      442–445, 462, 476
   restrictions of 6, 13, 184,
      258, 291, 300, 305,
      323, 394
Broadway Theatre Archive (film
   series) 146, 155, 210, 236
Broderick, Matthew 290, 460
Broken Glass 20, **82–94**, 229,
   324, 363, 394, 440–441, 463,
   474, 483, 497–498
   and anti-Semitism 86,
      90, **360**
   and capitalism 374
   characters. *See also*
      Stanton Case, Phillip
      Gellburg, Sylvia
      Gellburg **90–93**
   critical commentary
      86–89
   and Greek drama 87
   and guilt and responsibility
      398
   and Holocaust 20, 86–87,
      90, 93, 396, **406–407**,
      449
   initial reviews **89**
   movies 21, 83, **93**, 463,
      498
   scholarship **89–90**, 93–94
   synopsis 20, **83–86**
Bronson, David 155
Brook, Peter 14, 338, 344,
   394, 493
Brooklyn 176, 324, 362, 369,
   370–371, 372, 417, 453,
   463
   living in 3–4, 10–11, 327,
      365, 370, 371, 381,
      428–429, 441, 453, 458,
      473, 490
   as setting 55, 65, 81, 94,
      183, 191, 255–256,
      336, 339
Brooklyn Navy Yard 7, 168,
   372, 459, 479, 491
Brooks, Martin 154
Brothers Karamazov, The
   (Dostoyevsky) 5, 379, 384
Brown, Arvin 71, 495
Brown, Gene 370
Brown, John Mason 48, 53,
   117, 124

Brown, Katherine (Kay) 9, 40, 232, 336, **372–373**, 397, 418
Broyard, Anatole 201
Brustein, Robert 33, 38, 89, 93, 99–100, 194–195, 208, 210, 250–251, 283, 286, 306, 309, 368
Buckley, Tom 107
Buitenhuis, Peter 34, 38
"Bulldog" **94–95**, 429, 474, 483
Burathoki, Dinkar 390
Burg, Victor 204
Burgess, Grover 229
Burhans, Clinton S., Jr. 38
Burke, Kenneth 465
Burns, David 17, 277, 285
Burns, Margo 118, 124
Bush, George W. 259–260
Bush, Matthew (character) 56, 60–61, 63–64, 380, 401
Bus Stop (Inge) 361, 377, 415, 435, 462
Butler, Smedley D. 426, 468
Butterfield, Alfred 174, 177

C

Cagney, James 320, 421
Calabrese, Margarete (character) 168–169, 390
Calabrese, Tony (character) 168–169, 372
Calder, Alexander (Sandy) 79, 186, 192, 201, 455
Calder, Louisa 79, 192, 455
Caldwell, Zoe 105, 474, 475, 495
Cameron, Hope 47, 139
Camino Real (Williams) 419, 474
Campbell, Neve 291
Campbell, Rob 128
Camus, Albert 25–26, 34, 39, 208, 357, **373–374**, 386, 399
Canadian Broadcasting Corporation (CBC) 13, 105, 107, 124, 493
Canby, Vincent 158–159, 250–251
Canning, Charlotte 141, 146
Cannon J. D. 236
capitalism 6, 184–185, 198–199, 237, 249, 251, 262, 349, **374–375**
   in *All My Sons* 47, 51, 374–375
   in *The American Clock* 57, 61, 374
   in "Battle of the Ovens" 375

in *The Crucible* 374
in *Death of a Salesman* 137–138, 367, 374
in "It Takes a Thief" 375
in *The Price* 283, 374
in *Resurrection Blues* 295, 374
in *The Ride down Mt. Morgan* 374
in student plays 326, 374
Capra, Frank 393
Captain Paul 8, 79, **95**, 479, 491
Carbone, Beatrice (character) 337–344, **345**, 346, 388–389
Carbone, Eddie (character) 199, 213, 262, 336, 337–344, **345–346**, 347–348, 381, 388, 410, 425, 430
   as tragic hero 341–342, 344, 465
Cariou, Len 334
Carling, Victoria 182
Carnovsky, Morris 154, 348
Carr, Jay 124, 128, 176, 177
Carr, Kris 249
Carr, Susan *113*
Carroll, James 486
Carroll, Madeleine 198, 329
Carson, Neil 344, 348, 488
Carter, Rosanna 60
Cartier-Bresson, Henri 432, 437–438
Caruso, Cristina C. 118, 124
Carver, David 16, 466
Cary, Joyce 453
Caryn, James 159
Casalino, Sammy 372
Case, Stanton (character) 84–86, **90**, 374
Castellitto, George 72, 76
Castro, Fidel 21, 349, 375, **375–376**, 498
Casty, Alan 34, 38
Catastrophe (Beckett) 366
Catherine (character) 337–345, **346**, 347, 381, 430, 433
Catholic War Veterans 12, 129, 385, 410, 446
Cathy-May (character) 246–249, **250**, 251, 433
Cat on a Hot Tin Roof (Williams) 316–317, 385, 419, 427, 477
Cavalcade of America (radio series) 7–9, 79, 95, 149, 183, 196, 215, 223, 322, 326, 491

CBS
   radio 7, 9, 427, 479, 491–492
   television 16, 18, 20, 124, 146, 266, 270, 274, 391, 494, 496
Cenedella, Robert 13, 493
censorship 69, 79, 96–98, 203, 311, 313, 323, 350, 385
   of Miller's work 11–13, 74, 82, 129, 191, 385, 410, 446, 493, 495
   Miller's work against 17–19, 148–149, 197–198, 385, 404, 446–447, 495–496
Centola, Steve R. 38, 48–49, 53, 72, 76, 100, 105, 107, 146, 195, 306, 309, 344, 348, 362, **376**, 386, 488
   as editor 21, 149, 324, 376, 498
   and interviews 412, 390, 486
Century, Douglas 486
Chadick-Delamater Auto Parts Warehouse 5, 232, 327, **376**, 385, 468, 490
   and anti-Semitism 5, 360, 376
Chaikin, Milton 283, 286
Chalmers, Thomas 139
Chander, Kailash 344, 348
Chandler, David 60, 296
Chapman, John 34, 38, 117, 124, 154–155, 229, 231, 283, 286
Charley (character) 132–140, **141–142**, 145, 285, 312, 375, 389, 430, 458
Charyn, Jerome 195
Cheeseboro, Skip (character) 293–296, **297**, 398
Cheever, Susan 486
Chekhov, Anton 258, 316, 369, **377**, 392, 401, 451, 462, 475–477
   influence of 236, 250, 310, 377
Cherry Orchard, The (Chekhov) 377, 392
Children of the Sun. See Golden Years, The
Chinese Encounters 18, **95–98**, 149, 380–381, 439, 447, 483, 496
   and communism 96–97, 129, 381
Chinese opera 97

Christiansen, Richard 165, 168, 306, 309
Cioffi, Charles 152, 321, 496
Cirulli, Michelle 376, 488
Cismaru, Alfred 38
Cisneros, Patty 349
Citizens of America 10, 380
Clara 19, **98–100**, 129, 192, 194, 388, 398, 496
   characters. *See also* Fine, Albert Kroll, Clara Kroll 98–99, 298
   critical commentary **98–99**
   initial reviews **99–100**
   movies **100**, 497
   scholarship 100
   synopsis 19, **98**
Clark, Bob 64
Clarke, David 234, 337
Clarkson, Patricia 300
Clift, Montgomery 15, 243, 461, 494
Clinton, Bill 100, 126, 219, 259–261
"Clinton in Salem" 100, 483
Clothe, Barbara *140*
Clurman, Harold 277, 286, 315, 328, 361, **377–378**, 389–390, 393, 464, 474, 488
   and *All My Sons* 10, 40, 47, 378
   and *The Creation of the World* 101, 105, 107, 378
   and Group 372, 377, 397, 464
   and *Incident at Vichy* 204, 207–208, 210, 378, 494
   and Kazan 378, 418–419
   and Odets 377, 442
Cobb, Lee J. x, 328, 363, **378–379**, 397, 419, 442, 452
   and *Death of a Salesman* 11, 16, 66, 131, 139, 146, 312, 378–379, 384–385, 492, 494
   and HUAC 379, 409
   and *A View from the Bridge* 379
Cocktail Party, The (Eliot) 162
Coe, Richard L. 71, 76
Cohen, Nathan 34, 39
Cohn, Ruby 488
Coleman, Robert 117, 125, 140, 147, 155
Collins, Russell 234, 337
Collins, William B. 194–195, 314

Columbia Pictures 12, 145, 492

Columbia Workshop 7–8, 289, 352, 491

Combs, Robert 90, 93

Come Back, Little Sheba (Inge) 348, 415

Comeford, Ami Jo 147

communism 11, 13, 19, 28–30, 48, 72, 129, 152, 191–192, 237, 255, 262, 287, 327, 338, 372, **379–381**, 392, 410–411, 457
   in *The American Clock* 56–57, 59, 61–66, 380
   in China 96–97, 129, 379, 380–381
   in *The Crucible* 12, 77, 108–109, 125, 380
   in Cuba 349, 375–376, 379
   and Havel 350, 403
   in *Homely Girl, A Life* 187–188, 380
   and HUAC 252, 379, 380, 408
   in *Incident at Vichy* 205–206, 207, 208, 380
   and Kazan 419
   in *Playing for Time* 380
   in Soviet Union 202–203, 380–381
   in student plays 190, 256–257, 326, 380
   in *The Turpentine Still* 331
   at University of Michigan 379, 468
   in *You're Next!* 353, 380

Communist Party 5, 203, 353, 379, 380, 409, 411, 419, 462

"Concerning Jews Who Write" 10, 417, 483

"Conditions of Freedom" 19, 65, 76, **100–101**, 484, 497

Connection, The (NPR) 94, 474

Connelly, Mark 105

Connery, Donald S. 451

Connery, Sean 124, 493

Conroy, Frances 89, 218, 306, 497

Conti, Tom 305, 497

Conway, Curt 234, 337

Cook, Fiedler 285

Cook, Kimberley K. 271, 273

Cook, Larry W. 147

Cooke, Alistair 472

Cooke, Richard P. 283, 286

Cooley, Dennis 105, 335

Copeland, Joan Maxine 3, 22, 59–60, 65, 291, **381–382**, 428–430, 434, 461, 490, 492, 496

Corey, Giles (character) 108, 110, 112–117, **119**, 126, 127, 456–457

Corey, Martha (character) 108, 112, 114–117, **119**, 127–128, 342, 456–457

Corliss, Richard 219, 222

Corn Is Green, The (Williams) 369, 385

Corrigan, Robert W. 141, 390, 488

Costello, Donald P. 344, 348

Costello, Mariclare 33

Coughlin, Father 175

Country Girl, The (Odets) 361, 442

Coveney, Michael 60, 65, 306, 309

Cowan, Lester 322

Craig, Gordon 361

Crandell, George vii, 149, 186

Crawford, Cheryl 358, 397, 418, 442, 464

Creation of the World and Other Business, The 18, **101–108**, 334, 361, 471, 475, 483, 495
   characters **105–107**
   critical commentary **103–105**
   and guilt and responsibility 103, **398**
   initial reviews 18, **105**
   and law **424**
   scholarship 105, 107–108
   synopsis 18, **102–103**

Crime and Punishment (Dostoyevsky) 378, 384–385

"Criticisms of Government Relief Are Offered by Social Workers" 426

Crowther, Bosley 123, 125, 145, 147, 243, 246

Crucible, The ix, x, 12–13, 19, 21, **108–128**, 129, 212–213, 258, 338, 361, 385–386, 394, 420, 449, 459, 483
   characters. *See also* Giles Corey, Martha Corey, Danforth, Sarah Good, John Hale, Hathorne, Rebecca Nurse, Parris, Betty Parris, Elizabeth Proctor, John Proctor, Thomas Putnam,

Tituba, Abigail Williams 77, 108–118, **119–123**, 125–128, 342
   critical commentary **114–117**
   initial reviews **117–118**, 362, 368
   and law 109, **424**
   and McCarthyism 108–109, 115, 118, 126, 129
   movies 14, 17, 20, 77, **123–124, 126–128**, 432, 458, 493–494, 498
   productions of 361, 369–370, 394, 401, 404–405, 427, 440, 463, 467, 475, 477–478, 493–499
   and Salem witch trials 108–109, 327, 492
   scholarship **118–119**, 124–126, 128
   synopsis **109–114**
   and tragedy 109, 118

Crucible, The (Screenplay) 20, 124, **126–128**, 432, 433, 497–498

The Crucible: An Opera in 4 Acts 14–15, 109, 118–119, 125, 126, 494

"*Crucible* in History, The" **128–129**, 483

Cukor, George 436

Cullum, John 71, 495

Cultural Revolution 96, 97, 311, 313–314

Cunningham, Scott 33

Cushing, Tom 425

Cushing, Winnifred 139

Czimer, Joseph 283, 286

D

Dadaism 357

Daily Worker (newspaper) 10, 380, 492

Daly, T. F. Gilroy 318, 451

Daly, Timothy 155

Dan (character) 27, 30, 33, **35**, 37, 388, 390, 431

Danforth (character) 108, 112–115, 117, **119**, 120–121, 123, 126–128, 213, 423, 457

Danger: Memory! See also Clara, I Can't Remember Anything 19, 98, 129–130, 192, 195, 327, 452, 483, 496, 497

Dangling Man, The (Bellow) 367

Daniel, Yuri 203

Daniels, Marc 160

Daniels, William 100, 489

Dark at the Top of the Stairs, The (Inge) 415, 419

Davalle, Peter 182, 183

Davalos, Richard 234, 337

David, Thayer *113*

Davis, Harry 210

Davison, Bruce 128

Dawidziak, Mark 146, 147

Day-Lewis, Daniel 20–21, 124, 126, 128, 432, 498

Dead Souls (Gogol) 201

Death of a Salesman ix, x, 4, 11, 17, 19–22, 66–67, 115, 117, 129, **130–148**, 162, 199, 211–212, 248, 254, 311, 324, 327, 358, 363–364, 371, 385, 387, 392, 394, 399, 415, 417, 427, 441, 444, 450, 453–454, 459, 476, 483, 492, 496
   and capitalism 137–138, 367, **374**
   characters. *See also* Bernard, Charley, Ben Loman, Biff Loman, Happy Loman, Linda Loman, Willy Loman, Howard Wagner 11–12, 130–140, **141–145**, 285, 367
   in China 19, 97, 311–316, 367
   critical commentary **136–139**
   and family relationships 137, 138–139, 142–144, 161, 211, **388–390**
   initial reviews **139–140**, 362, 368, 370
   and Kazan 11, 130, 139–140, 419–420, 427, 450, 454, 492
   movies 14, 16, **145–146**, 364, 378, 385, 463, 493, 494
      with Dennehy **146**, 384
      with Hoffman 20, **146**, 496
      with March 12, **145–146**, 212, 385, 425, 492
   productions of 367, 369–370, 378, 384, 402, 405, 463, 474, 494, 496–498
   and *Ride down Mt. Morgan* 299–300, 305
   scholarship 140–141, 146–148
   synopsis **130–136**

Death of a Salesman (continued)
   and tragedy 48, 137, 140,
      146, 212, 262, 329–330,
      384, 465
Deedy, John 107
Deever, Ann (character) 10,
   41–45, 47, 49, **50**, 51–53,
   381, 389
Deever, George (character)
   42–44, 46–47, 49, **50**, 52–53,
   389, 423
DelFattore, Joan 118, 125
Demastes, William 72, 76,
   105, 107
democracy 74, 148–149,
   153–154, 190, 255, 259–260,
   262, 297, 326, 328, 342,
   383–384, 403, 423
      in *The American Clock* 18,
         57, 101, 383
      in *The Crucible* 384
      in *The Last Yankee* 383–384
Democrats 17, 78–79, 200,
   259, 327, 455, 471, 494, 495
Dempster, Curt 310
De Niro, Robert 358, 419, 462
Dennehy, Brian 21, 146, 363,
   384, 498
Dennis, Robert 60
Dent, Alan 243, 246
depression. *See* Great
   Depression
Dern, Laura 176
Desafy-Grignard, Christiane
   197, 253, 417
Designing in the Theatre
   (Mielziner) 427–428
Des Pres, Terence 408
Devil in Massachusetts, The
   (Starkey) 108, 126, 456
Dewhurst, Colleen 285
Diary of Anne Frank, The
   (Goodrich and Hackett)
   316, 361, 369, 477
Dies Committee. *See also* HUAC
Dillon, Josephine 393
DiMaggio, Joe 13, 240, 250,
   434, 460, 493
"Dinner with the Ambassador"
   148–149, 447, 483
Dishy, Bob 105, 495
"Ditchy" 8, **149**, 483
Ditsky, John M. 118, 125,
   235–236
Doctor Fights, The 9, 479, 491
Doll's House, A (Ibsen) 167,
   188, 401, 413, 414, 449, 452,
   454, 463
Doolittle, Hilda (H. D.) 447

Dostoyevsky, Fyodor 373,
   378–379, **384–385**
      influence of 5, 316, 357,
         385
      Miller on 202, 316, 385
Dougherty, James 434
Doughty, Louise 89, 93
Douglas, Michael 309
Doyle, Tom 16, 431
Dreifus, Claudia 65
Driscoll, Ann 139, 337
Driver, Tom 14, 488
Duffield, Marcus 317–318
Dukes, David 89, 497, 498
Dukore, Bernard F. 118, 125,
   141, 147, 488
Dumas, Alexander (Fils) 449
Dunaway, Faye 33, 38, 495
Dunham, Mike 486
Dunn, Ralph 154
Dunning, Philip 401
Dunnock, Mildred 11, 16, 66,
   131, 139, 146, 369, **385**, 392,
   477, 492, 494
Dunsany, Lord 454
Durang, Christopher 321, 392
Durant, William (character)
   55, 60, **62–63**, 473
Duras, Marguerite 385
D'Usseau, Arnaud 418
Duvall, Robert 339, 397, 494
Dworkin, Martin S. 155, 415

E

Eagle's Nest, The 8, 149, 479,
   491
Earhart, Amelia 8, 329
Eberson, Gustav (character)
   190, 224, 226–229, **230**
*Echoes Down the Corridors:
   Collected Essays 1944–2000*
   11, 21, 149–150, 376, 483,
   498
      essays in 78, 81, 100, 128,
         148, 237, 251, 258, 286,
         290, 311, 323, 350
Edelstein, Gordon 215
Eden (Gitai) 20, 189–190, 455
Edie (character) 57, 60–61,
   62, 64, 380, 432
"Educators of Four Countries
   Aid Middle English
   Dictionary" 426
Edwardes, Jane 71, 76
Edwards, Brian 486
Edwards, Christopher 60, 65,
   99, 100, 195
Edwards, John 344, 348
Efremov, Oleg 202

Egan, Jennie 117
Egerton, Kate 168, 296, 299
Eichmann in Jerusalem (Arendt)
   353
Eigsti, Karl 60
Einstein, Albert 434
Eisenhower, Dwight 260
Eldridge, Florence 11, 152,
   154, 410, 425, 492
Elegy for a Lady 19, **150–152**,
   218, 321, 333–334, 357,
   483–484, 496
      characters 150–151
      critical commentary
         150–151
      initial reviews 152
      scholarship 152
      synopsis 19, **150**
Eliot, T. S. 162, 175, 447
Elizabethan drama 98, 399
Elliott, Scott 477
Elliott, Stephen 105, 495
Ellis, Scott 225, 477
Elzvieta (character) 267–270,
   271, 272, 360, 400
Emperor Jones, The (O'Neill)
   387, 444
Enemy of the People, An (Ibsen)
   11, 152, 154–155, 198, 410,
   413–414, 425, 492
Enemy of the People, An (Miller)
   11–12, **152–155**, 410, 414,
   463, 483, 492, 495
      characters 152–154
      critical commentary
         153–154
      initial reviews **154–155**,
         362
      movies 20, **155**, 497
      scholarship 152, 155
      synopsis 11–12, **152–153**
Engel, Dorothea Daley 198
Engels, Frederick 256
Engle, John D. 39, 424
Epstein, Arthur D. 344, 348
Epstein, Leslie 208, 210
Epstein, Pierre 207
Equus (Shaffer) 34, 369
Erskine, Chester 10, 53
Ervine, St. John 464
Esbjornson, David 296
Escher, M. C. 129
Esping, Laura 296
Esslin, Martin 357–358
Ethiopia (Living Newspaper)
   391
Eulenspiegel, Till 260
Evans, Lloyd Gareth 141, 147,
   445, 477

Everybody Wins 19, 20, **155–
   159**, 318, 423–424, 451,
   483, 497
      critical commentary **158**
      initial reviews **158**
      production details **158**
      synopsis **156–157**
existentialism 104, 357, 376,
   384, **386–387**
      in *After the Fall* 39, 104,
         305, 386, 387
      and Camus 357, 373
      in *The Ride down Mt.
         Morgan* 305, 306, 386,
         387
      and Sartre 306, 457
Existentialism Is a Humanism
   (Sartre) 386
expressionism 11, 130, 146,
   161–162, 212, 223, 316, 384,
   387, 388, 444
      in *After the Fall* 31, 305,
         387, 450
      in *Death of a Salesman*
         11, 387
      in *The Ride down Mt.
         Morgan* 305, 306, 387

F

"Faculty Men Welcome
   Controversial Social
   Questions in Class
   Discussions" 426
Falk, Peter 246, 249, 251,
   460, 498
Fall, The (Camus) 25, 39,
   373, 399
Fallaci, Oriana 39
Fall of the City, The (MacLeish)
   179
Falls, Robert 162, 165
"Fame" 16, **159–160**, 186,
   195, 417, 483, 494
Fame (one-act) 17, 474, 495
Fame (Screenplay) 18, **160–
   161**, 195, 433, 495
"Family in Modern Drama,
   The" 14, **161–162**, 388,
   484, 493
      and Ibsen 161, 414
family relationships 214, 224,
   249, 306, 317, 327, **388–
   390**
      in *After the Fall* 28–29, 32,
         36, 388
      in *All My Sons* 40, 46–49,
         51, 388
      in *Broken Glass* 83–84,
         87–88

and Clurman 389
in *The Crucible* 115–116,
388
in *Death of a Salesman* 13,
137, 138–139, 142–144
in *The Price* 388–389
and realism 161–162, 388
in student plays 257
Fariello, Griffin 486
Farnum, Dustin 405
Farr, Kimberly 335
Fascism 6, 8–10, 129, 149,
199, 205, 229, 266, 317, 327,
379–381, 441, 447, 475, 479
Fassinger, Flora (character)
163–165, **166**, 462
Fassinger, Jerome (character)
163–165, **166**, 461
"Fat Rolls Off for University
Scientists in New
Experiment" 426
Faulkner, William 373
FBI 12, 40, 252, 380, 385, 410
Federal Theater Project 6–7,
11, 179, 194, 223, 325, 327,
367, 390, 392, 395, 421,
452–453, 465, 491
and communism 7, 409
Fefu and Her Friends (Fornes)
90, 94
Feiffer, Jules 321
Feingold, Michael 219, 222,
250–251
Feldman, Joe 63
Feldman, Robert 271, 273, 486
Felt, Bessie (character) 301–
305, **307**, 308–309, 398
Felt, Leah (character) 301–
305, **307**, 308
Felt, Lyman (character) 20,
296, 301–307, **308**, 309–310,
374, 386, 398, 466
and Willy Loman 299–
300, 305, 306
Felt, Theo (character) 301–
307, **308–309**
Fences (Wilson) 141, 147, 148
Fénelon, Fania 18, 266, 270–
271, 391–392, 407, 451
Fénelon, Fania (character)
266–270, **271–272**, 273–
274, 400, 407, 451
Ferran, Peter W. 60, 65
Ferres, John H. 118, 125
Fervent Years, The (Clurman)
378, 397, 442, 443
Fichandler, Zelda 147
Fields, Joseph 8, 224, 229
Findlater, Richard 344, 348

Fine (character) 98–99, 398
Finishing the Picture 15, 21–22,
162–168, 240, 370, 387,
412, 436, 499
characters. *See also* Flora
Fassinger, Jerome
Fassinger, Kitty **166–
168**
critical commentary
164–165
initial reviews **165–166**,
168
scholarship **166, 168**
synopsis 21–22, **162–164**
Fink, Sam (character) 187–
189, 380, 396
Finkelstein (character) 170–
173, **174**, 176, 398
Finlay, Fiona 93
Fishburne, Laurence 321
Fisher, Frances 165
Fishler, Moe 224, 255
"Fitter's Night." *See also* Looey
Baldu, Margarete Calabrese,
Tony Calabrese **168–169**,
186, 195, 372, 390, 429, 483
Fitzgerald, F. Scott 306, 419
Fitzgerald, Geraldine 194, 496
Flanagan, Hallie 391
Flanagan, James K. 105, 107,
489
Fletcher, Lawrence 229
Flowering Peach, The (Odets)
231, 232, 336, 442
Focus 9, **169–177**, 367, 388,
390, 415, 483
and anti-Semitism 9,
170–176, 360
characters. *See also*
Finkelstein, Gertrude
Lawrence, Lawrence
Newman **174–176**
critical commentary
173–174
and guilt and responsibility
398, 400
initial reviews **174**
movies 9, 15, 21, **176**,
433, 484, 498
scholarship 176–177
synopsis **170–173**
Foote, Horton 460
Ford, Constance 139
Fornes, Maria Irene 90, 94,
460
Foulkes, Peter A. 118, 125
Four Freedoms, The 7, 491
Fox, Frederick 229
Fox, James 291

Fox, Robert 305
Foxworth, Robert 427
Franco, Francisco 379, 441
Frankfurt trials 16, 204, 406,
439, 494
Franklin, Nancy 225
Franks, Sidney 4, 6, 277, **392**
Franz, Elizabeth 21, 146, **392**,
498
Franz, Esther (character) 278–
282, **283–284**, 285, 381
Franz, Mr. (character) 3, 17,
278–282, **284**, 285, 389,
430, 473
Franz, Victor (character) 17,
278–283, **284**, 285, 388–389,
392, 398, 431, 458, 466
Franz, Walter (character) 17,
277–283, **284–285**, 374,
388–389, 398, 421
Frayn, Michael 323
Freedman, Gerald 105, 495
Freedman, Morris 488
Freedman, Samuel G. 335
French, Warren 244, 246
Freud, Sigmund 212
Frick, John (character) 20,
215–218, **219–220**, 303, 396
Frick, Karen (character) 20,
165, 216–219, **220**, 221–222,
390
Fried, Walter 10, 11, 47, 139,
369
Frommer, Harvey 370
Frommer, Myrna Katz 370
Frost, Robert 448, 469
Fu, Du 96
Fuller, Charles 321
Fulton, Julie 41
Funke, Lewis 291, 486
Furtseva, Ekaterina 203

G
Gable, Clark 15, 240, 243,
393, 452, 494
Gabriello, Varró 283, 286
Galsworthy, John 446
Gambon, Michael 339, 497
Ganz, Arthur 34, 39
Garden Party, The (Havel) 403
Gardner, Elysa 296, 299
Gardner, R. H. 71, 76
Garfield, John 397
Garibaldi, Giuseppe 8, 149,
479
Gary, Harold 17, 277, 283,
494, 495
Gassner, John 33, 39, 48, 54,
109, 125, 330–331, 489

Gehlawat, Ajay 244, 246
Gelb, Arthur 362
Gelb, Philip 383
Gellburg, Phillip (character)
83–89, **90–91**, 92–93, 360,
388, 398, 466
Gellburg, Sylvia (character)
83–89, **91–92**, 93, 386, 388,
398, 407, 429
Gellburgs, The. See Broken Glass
General Died at Dawn, The
(Odets) 377, 442
Genet, Jean 357
Gentleman's Agreement
(Hobson) 170, 419
Gerard, Jeremy 89, 94
Gersten, Bernard 99, 194
"Get It Right. Privatize
Executions" 20, **177**, 483
Ghosts (Ibsen) 413, 414, 449
Gianakaris, C. J. 34, 39
Gibbs, Wolcott 125, 361
Giglio, Gino 291
Gilbert, Lou 105, 154
Gill, Brendan 105, 107
Gilliatt, Penelope 283, 286
Gilroy, Frank D. 397
Giraudoux, Jean 377
Gitai, Amos 190
Given, Pamela *113*
Glaspell, Susan 190
Glass Menagerie, The (Williams)
34, 39, 258, 427, 476–477
Gleiberman, Owen 126, 128
Glenn, Scott 165
"Glimpse at a Jockey" 15,
177–178, 195, 483, 494
Glotfelty, Cheryll 244, 246
Glover, John 155, 497
Glover, William 71
Goetz, Augustus 401
Goetz, Ruth 401
Gogol, Nikolai (Nikolay) 201
Gold, Jack 130
Golden, John 66
Golden Boy (Odets) 377, 378,
397, 418, 442
Golden Years, The 7, 19, **179–
183**, 224, 368, 391, 394, 464,
466, 479, 483, 491, 497
critical commentary
181–182
initial reviews **182–183**
synopsis **179–181**
Goldstein, Laurence 310,
317–318
Good, Sarah (character) 108,
111, 113, 117, **122–123**,
127, 456–457

Goode, James 243, 246
Goodman, Henry 93
Goodman, Walter 65
Goodrich, Frances 316, 361, 476
Gorbachev, Mikhail 19
Gordimer, Nadine 94
Gordinier, Jeff 128
Gordon, Hannah 182, 497
Gordon, Lois 489
Gordon, Ruth 414, 425
Gore, Al 259–260
Gorelik, Mordecai 47, 54, 328, **393–394**, 418–419, 442, 492
Gottfried, Martin 34, 39, 105, 107, 125, 223, 283, 286, 402, 489
Gould, Jack 124, 125, 146, 147
Grandpa and the Statue 9, **183**, 483, 492
Grant, Sydney 229
Grapes of Wrath, The (Steinbeck) 460–461
Grass Still Grows, The. See also Abe Simon, Arnold Simon, Ben Simon 6, **183–184**, 256, 325, 388, 391, 397, 491
Graubard, Mark 118, 125
Grausman, Philip 22, 455
Graves, Karron 99
Great Britain 7, 14, 18–21, 26, 54, 67, 71, 124, 136, 151–152, 179, 182, 186–187, 213, 216, 224, 229, 249, 270, 274, 291, 305, 318, 323, 329, 333, 338–339, 361, 363, 367, 369, 384, **394**, 410–411, 435, 440, 447, 467, 475, 477, 493–497, 499
Great Depression 3, 6, 46–47, 81, 136–137, 175, 219, 224, 237, 255, 315, 326–327, 365, 367, 379–381, 390, 392, **394–396**, 428–430, 460, 473, 475
    in *After the Fall* 28, 395
    in *The American Clock* 55, 56–59, 61–65, 101, 380, 395–396
    in *A Memory of Two Mondays* 232, 396
    in *The Price* 277–278, 281, 284, 395–396
    in *Timebends* 395
Great Disobedience, The 6, **184–185**, 363, 468, 491, 476
Grecco, Stephen 329

Greek drama 40, 45, 48, 87, 199, 261–262, 316, 330, 336, 341–343, 347, 454, 464–465
Green, Blake 222
Green, Paul 397, 462
Greenaway, Peter 384
Greene, Alexis 118, 125, 478
Greene, James 33, 207
Greene, Milton 435
Gregorio, Rose 218
Griffin, Alice 72, 76, 90, 91, 94, 489
"Griggs Locates Messages by Haiti Emperor" 426
Grizzard, George 105, 155, 236
Grosbard, Ulu 16, 17, 277, 283, 339, 348, 396–397, 405, 421, 494
Gross, Barry 49, 390
Gross, Klaus-Dieter 119, 125
Group Theater, The 9, 40, 179, 211, 358, 372, 378, 393, **397**, 405, 461–462, 476
    and Aronson 361, 397
    and Clurman 377, 397, 464
    and Kazan 369, 372, 397, 418–419
Gruen, John 486
Gruhn, Caroline (character) 350–351, 390
Guang, Su 96
Guardsman, The (Molnár) 9, 427, 491
Guare, John 460
Guernsey, Otis L. 486
guilt and responsibility 17, 151, 320, **398–400**
    in *After the Fall* 25, 30–32, 34–35, 398–400
    in *All My Sons* 9, 46, 48–51, 53, 399
    in *Broken Glass* 398
    in *Creation of the World* 103, 398
    in *The Crucible* 115, 122, 212–213, 398–399
    in *Focus* 398
    in *Incident at Vichy* 17, 208, 398–399
    and Judaism 399
    in "Our Guilt for the World's Evil" 398
    in *Playing for Time* 271–273, 400
    in *The Price* 398
    in *The Ride down Mt. Morgan* 302–305, 307–308, 398

Gurney, A. R. 321
Gus (character) 232–234, **235**, 236, 398
Gussow, Mel 162, 168, 336, 486
Guthmann, Edward 124, 125, 128
Guthrie, Woody 424
Guttmann, Simon 437
Gwynn, Michael 343, 493

H

Haas, Ernst 437
Hackett, Albert 316, 361, 476
Hackman, Gene 405
Haggard-Gilson, Nancy 416–417
Hale, John (character) 109–117, **120**, 121, 126, 128
Half-Bridge, The 7–8, 81, 183, **185–186**, 417, 444, 479, 491
Hall, Peter 440
Hamilton, Alexander, 215–217, 221
Hamilton, Dan 236
Hamilton, Leroy (character) 20, 25, 215–219, **220–221**, 222, 383–384, 389
Hamilton, Patricia (character) 20, 25, 165, 216–219, 220, **221–222**, 390
Hamilton, William 243, 246
Hamlet (Shakespeare) 181, 440, 465
Hamm, Nick 67
Hammen, Scott 244, 246
Hammerstein, Oscar 377, 464
Hammett, Dashiell 404
Hampden, Walter 117
Hampton, Gregory 147
"Ham Sandwich" **186**, 276, 483, 495
Harap, Louis 416–417
Hard Times (Terkel) 55, 65
Harris, Ed 156
Harris, Herbert H. 8, 224, 229
Harris, Jed 13, 117, 328, 361, 369, **401–402**, 405, 414, 421, 492
Harris, Leonard 105, 107
Harris, Michael 187
Harris, Richard 343
Harry (character) 314–315, 470
Harry Ransom Research Center **402–403**
Harshburger, Karl 140, 147
Hart, Lorenz 382
Hartley, Anthony 346, 348

Hathorne (character) 108, 112–115, 117, **120**, 121, 423, 456–457
Hattersley, Roy 486
Haugen, Einar 155, 415
Havel, Václav 17, 19, 101, 366, **403–404**, 446, 495, 498
    in *I Think About You a Great Deal* 19, 197–198, 404, 496
    and Sigmund 17, 74, 404
    in "What's Wrong with This Picture?" 18, 350, 404
Havel Deal, The 19, 404
Havener, Michael W. 324–325
Hawkins, William 234, 236
Hawthorne, Nathaniel 118, 124, 128, 368
Hayford, Charles 314
Hayman, Ronald 486, 489
Hays, Peter L. 147, 477
Heard, John 215, 218, 497
Hecht, Ben 401
Heckart, Eileen 234, 337
Hedda Gabler (Ibsen) 413, 414
Heflin, Van 234, 337, 493
Heiress, The (Goetz) 401, 402
Helburn, Theresa 464
Hèlène (character) 267, 270, 380
Hellman, Lillian 33, 39, 40, 326, 401, 404–405, 377, 385, 427
    and Bloomgarden 369, 405
    and HUAC 401, 405, 409
Hemingway, Ernest 186, 276, 349
Henderson, David W. 186, 187
Henderson, Mary C. 428
Hendrickson, Gary P. 125
Henley, Beth 397
Henry, William A., III 99, 100, 306, 309, 329
Herbert, Edward 445
Herrera, Emil 296
Hersholt, Jean 71
Herzog (Bellow) 34
Heston, Charlton 366
Heuvel, Wendy vanden 296
Hewes, Henry 335–336, 337–338
Hewitt, Alan 139
Hewlett, Brian 182
Higgins, Clare 305, 497
Hiley, Jim 152
Hill, Bernard 339, 463
Hillel Players 6, 325, 468

Hiller, Wendy 401
Hingle, Pat 277, 283, 494
Hirsch, Foster 358
Hirschhorn, Clive 487
Hitler, Adolf 28, 34, 35, 39, 55, 63; 181, 186, 187, 205, 223, 260, 263–264, 326, 360, 407, 426, 437, 479
"Hitler's Quarry" 7, **186**, 360, 479, 483, 491
Hobson, Laura Z. 170
Hoffman, Dustin 19, 140, 146, 358, 363–364, 396–397, **405–406**, 455, 461, 475, 496
Hoffman, Jane 117
Hogan, Robert 489
Holbrook, Hal 33, 207, 494
Holden, Stephen 176, 177
"Holding Company Act Termed Too Severe by Prof. Waterman" 426
Holga (character) 16, 26–29, 31–33, 35–36, 37–38, 390, 437
Holland, Bernard 336
Hollis, John 182
Hollywood 8, 10, 12–13, 129, 164, 166–167, 171, 175, 191, 243–244, 322, 358, 369, 377, 380, 393, 397, 404, 419–420, 434, 437, 442–443, 452, 459, 462, 474, 476, 491–492
Hollywood Ten, The 409
Holm, John C. 9, 361, 492
Holman, David 93, 463
Holocaust 12, 20, 99, 174, 177, 199, 208, 237, 252, 264, 351, 353, 357, 359, 391, **405–408**, 416, 479,
   in *After the Fall* 25, 28–29, 31–32, 35–36, 406–407, 438
   in *Broken Glass* 86–87, 90, 93, 406–407
   in *Incident at Vichy* 204, 208, 210, 263, 269, 360, 406–407
   in *Playing for Time* 18, 266–274, 400, 406–407
Homely Girl, A Life (*Plain Girl*) 20, 90, 93, 187–190, 455, 497
   and anti-Semitism 187–188, 361
   and communism 187–188, 380
   critical commentary **188–190**

movies 190
   synopsis **187–188**
Homely Girl, A Life (Collection) 159, 168, 186–187, 483
homosexuality 30, 98–99, 168, 316, 391, 476–477
   in *The Half-Bridge* 185
   in *A View from the Bridge* 262, 338, 340, 342–343, 344, 346, 468, 491
Honors at Dawn 6, **190–191**, 363, 388
   and communism 190, 380
Hook, The 10–12, **191–192**, 344, 369, 385, 424, 434, 450, 475, 492
   compared to *On the Waterfront* 192
   and Elia Kazan 11, 191–192, 419–420, 459
Hoover, Herbert 55, 63, 65, 395
Hope-Wallace, Philip 344, 348
Hopkinson, Amanda 94
Horton, Everett 7
Houghton, James 460
Houghton, Norris 314
Houseman, John 391
House of Connelly (Green) 397, 462
House of Un-American Activities Committee 11, 12–14, 50, 82, 154, 202, 223, 252, 338, 349, 379, 397, 401, 405, **408–411**, 425
   in *After the Fall* 26, 28–29, 36, 410
   in *The Crucible* 108–109, 117, 118, 212, 409–410
   and Kazan 11, 36, 117, 409, 411, 419–420, 443, 453, 462, 492
   and Miller 12–14, 129, 154, 326–327, 385, 404, 409–411, 435, 446, 461, 474, 492–493, 495
   and *You're Next* 353, 409, 410
Howard, Sidney 464
How to Marry a Millionaire (Negulesco) 434
HUAC. *See* House of Un-American Activities Committee
Huftel, Sheila 49, 489
Hughie (O'Neill) 177
humanism 186, 262, 317, 327, 351, 373, 376, 380, 386–387, **411–412**, 447, 453

Hunt, Linda 160
Hunt, Marsha 305
Hunter, N. C. 451
Hurd, Myles R. 344, 348
Hurrell, John 141
Hurren, Kenneth 99, 100, 321
Huston, Daniel 190
Huston, John 15, 166, 239, 240, 243, 246, 434, 438, 494
Hutchens, John K. 10, 54, 492
Hynes, Garry 249, 460
Hytner, Nicholas 124, 126, 128

I

Ibsen, Henrik 141, 198, 229, 258, 295, 328, 475, **413–415**, 449
   and *All My Sons* 40, 48, 49, 199, 414
   in "The Family in Modern Drama" 161, 414
   influence of 316, 414–415, 454
   in "Introduction to *Arthur Miller's Collected Plays*" 198, 211–212, 414
   in "Shadows of the Gods" 316, 414
"Ibsen and the Drama of Today" **198–199**, 414, 484, 497
"Ibsen's Warning" 415
I Can't Remember Anything 19, 98, 129, **192–195**, 299, 460, 496
   characters 192–194
   critical commentary **193–194**
   initial reviews 99–100, **194**
   synopsis 19, **192–193**
Iceman Cometh, The (O'Neill) 48, 141, 362, 381, 384, 425, 444, 452
"I Don't Need You Anymore." *See also* Martin 14, 94, **195–197**, 253, 388, 417, 429–430, 483, 493
I Don't Need You Anymore (Collection) 17, 159, 160, 169, 177, 186, **195**, 237, 252, 275, 287, 314, 483, 494
Ike (character) 3, 27–31, 33, 35, 37–38, 388, 390, 430, 473
Immigrant's Lament, An 21, 199, 339, 484
Incident at Vichy 16–18, 33, 76, **204–211**, 262–263, 361,

374, 396, 417, 424, 452, 475, 477, 484, 493
   characters. *See also* Bayard, Leduc, Von Berg **208–210**, 204–207
   and communism 205–208, 380
   critical commentary **206–207**
   and guilt and responsibility 398–399
   and Holocaust 406–407
   initial reviews 16, **208**
   movies **210**, 495
   scholarship 76, **208**, 210–211
   synopsis 16, **204–206**
Inge, William 348, 361, 376, 377–378, **415**, 419, 427, 435, 462, 475–476
   festival award 21, 359, 364, 415, 497
Inge Morath: Portraits (Morath) 438
"In Memoriam" 5, 147, **201**, 433, 484, 490
In Russia 17, 149, **201–204**, 324, 380, 439, 447, 484, 495, 497
   and anti-Semitism 202, 360
   and communism 202–203, 381
   initial reviews 204
Inside of His Head, The. See Death of a Salesman
In the Country 18, 149, **200–201**, 310–311, 439, 455, 484, 495
   initial reviews 201
"Introduction to *Collected Plays*" 198, 211–213, 397, 414, 435, 484, 493
Ionesco, Eugene 357
Ireland, Samuel (character) 352, 388–389
Ireland, William (character) 352, 388
Irene (character) 56, **60**, 63, 380
Irving, Amy 85, 89, 94, 497
Irving, Jules 453, 495
Isser, Edward R. 271, 273, 408
Italian Tragedy, An. See A View from the Bridge
I Think About You a Great Deal 19, **197–198**, 404, 484, 496
"It Takes a Thief" 10, 213–214, 375, 484, 492

Ivey, Judith 158
I Was Married in Bataan 8, **198**, 479, 491

J

Jackson, Anne 160, 249, 474, 495
Jackson Penitentiary 6, 184
Jacobson, Irving 34, 39, 197, 253, 390
Jaffe, Sidney 454, 459
James, Henry 402
James, Peter 343
Jane, Tom Elliot 190
Jane's Blanket 16, **214–215**, 431, 460, 484, 494, 495
Jaques, Damien 165, 168
Jayasree, A. 141, 147
J.B. (MacLeish) 361, 419
Jenkins, David 71
Jenkins, Martin 182
Jenkins, Megs 343, 493
Jens, Salome 33
Joe (character) 55–57, 60–62, **63**, 64, 374, 380
Joe, the Motorman 7
Joel Chandler Harris 8, **215**, 491
John Ferguson (Ervine) 464
Johnsey, Jeanne 271, 275
Johnson, Claudia Durst 118, 125
Johnson, Vernon E. 125
Johnston, Albert 201, 324–325
Jones, Chris 168
Jones, Christine 296
Jones, Dan 152
Jones, Gemma 305, 497
Jones, Norman 182
Jones, Robert Edmond 393, 476
Jordan, Richard 210, 495
Joyce, James 366, 376, 402
Juárez, Benito 8, 326
Judaism. *See also* religious references 14, 90, 197, 205, 253, 283, 359, 416–417
   and Holocaust 359, 416
   Miller's background 3, 327, 399, 435, 493
Judd, Ashley 310
Julia (Zinneman) 451, 456
juvenile delinquency 13, 82, 149
Juyin, Jiao 366

K

Kael, Pauline 158–159, 348
Kafka, Franz 208

Kaiser, Georg 387
Kakhtangov, Yevgeny 202
Kalem, T. E. 105, 107
Kane, Joseph vii, 296, 299
Kang, Taekyeong 147
Kang-Hu, Kiang 96
Kaplan, James 487
Kassell, Nicole 309
Kataria, Gulshan Rai 147
Kauffmann, Stanley 123, 125–126, 128, 158–159, 243, 246
Kaufman, George S. 401
Kaye, Virginia 33
Kazan, Elia 11–12, 15, 170, 328, 344, 358, 361, 363, 369, 378–379, 381, 385, 390, 393, **418–421**, 420, 442, 451–453, 461–462, 474
   and *After the Fall* 25, 33, 36, 418, 420–421, 452
   and *All My Sons* 10, 40, 47–48, 130, 139, 372, 378, 402, 418–420, 492
   and *Death of a Salesman* 11, 130, 139–140, 402, 419–420, 427, 450, 454, 492
   and Group 369, 372, 397, 418–419
   and *The Hook* 11–12, 419–420, 459, 492
   and HUAC 11, 36, 117, 338, 409, 411, 419–420, 443, 453, 462, 492
   and Monroe 12–13, 358, 418, 420, 434
   and Williams 358, 419–420, 475–476
"Kazan and the Bad Times" 421
Keach, Stacy 165, 210
Keefer, Don 139
Keitel, Harvey 236
Keller, Chris (character) 8, 10, 42–47, 49, **50–51**, 52–53, 257, 325, 374, 386, 388–389, 399, 421, 431, 479
Keller, Joe (character) 8, 40–47, 49–50, **51**, 52–53, 81, 212, 257, 325, 375, 386, 388–389, 398–399, 414, 423, 430, 465
Keller, Kate (character) 10, 41–45, 47–50, **51–52**, 53, 390, 429
Keller, Larry (character) 4, 8, 40–47, 49–51, **52–53**, 257, 325, 389, 414, 431

Kelly, Kevin 100, 152, 274, 321
Kennedy, Arthur 47, 117, *131*, 139, 283, 328, 363, 401–402, 419, **421**, 492, 494
Kennedy, John 163, 165, 430, 436
Kennedy, Leo 174, 177
Kerr, Walter 33, 39, 60, 65, 117, 125, 458
Kesey, Ken 432
Kierkegaard, Søren 357, 386
Kimbrough, Clint 33, 207
King, Robert L. 296, 299
King Lear (Shakespeare) 34, 48, 53, 141, 147, 452, 465
Kingsley, Sidney 352, 381, 397, 418, 442, 462
Kirchway, Freda 125
Kirkpatrick, Melanie 219, 222
Kissel, Howard 60, 65, 219, 222, 450
Kitty (character) 162–166, **167**, 168, 433
Klein, Laura 89
Knight, Shirley 270
Koon, Helen Wickam 141, 147
Koorey, Stefani vii, 489
Koppenhaver, Allen J. 39
Kouvaros, George 243, 246
Koven, Stanley 195
Kraft, Hy S. 418
Krause, Peter 26
Kristallnacht 83, 84, 87, 88–89, 91, 407
Kroll, Albert (character) 98–99, 298, 389, 398
Kroll, Clara (character) 98–99, 388–389
Kroll, Jack 60, 65, 270, 274
Kronenberger, Louis 48, 54, 229, 231
Krutch, Joseph Wood 48, 54, 330, 368
Kuchwara, Michael 165, 168
Kuder, Edward 265
Kullman, Colby H. 487
Kupferberg, Herbert 317–318
Kushner, Tony 22, **421–22**

L

LaBute, Neil 368
Ladislaus, Lob 174, 177
Lahr, John 88, 89, 91, 94, 201
Lahti, Christine 152, 321, 496
"La Marseillaise" (song) 268, 270, 391
Lambert, Angela 487
Lambert, J. W. 208, 210
Lamos, Mark 105, 495

Lampert, Zohra 33
Lancaster, Burt 10, 53, 492
Landis, Harry 305
Landwehr, Hugh 152, 321
Lang, Stephen 165
Langella, Frank 26, *27*
Langer, Lawrence 208, 210, 408
Langland, Gay (character) 237–243, **244–245**, 393, 452
Langner, Lawrence 464
Langteau, Paula 168, 489
LaPaglia, Anthony 21, 339, 348, 498
Lapoint, Richard 21
Lardner, John 48, 54
Lascelles, Kendrew 176
Lask, Thomas 274
Last Yankee, The (1 act) 20, **215**, 460, 484, 497
   first performance 20, **215**
Last Yankee, The 20, 25, 165, **215–222**, 383–384, 388–390, 394, 463, 484, 497
   characters. See also John Frick, Karen Frick, Leroy Hamilton, Patricia Hamilton 215–218, **219–222**
   critical commentary 25, **217–218**
   initial reviews **219**
   scholarship **219**
   synopsis 20, **216–217**
Laughton, Charles 9, 183
Lauren, Julie 310, 498
Lavin, Linda 165
Law 19, 29, 39, 58, 156, 199, 212, 214, 308, 316, 381, **423–424**
   in *All My Sons* 40, 42, 46, 50, 423
   in China 96, 424
   in *Creation of the World* 424
   in *The Crucible* 109, 424
   in *Incident at Vichy* 206, 424
   in *A View from the Bridge* 336, 338, 342–343, 345, 423
Law, John Philip 33
Lawrence, Carol 348
Lawson, John Howard 393
Lazarus, Emma 183
Leachman, Cloris 402
Leaf, Paul 291
Learned, Michael 53, 300, 497
LeCompte, Elizabeth 125, 478

lectures
    at Harvard University
      128, 161
    for Jerusalem Prize
      351–352
    for NEH (Jefferson) 21,
      259, 304
    to New York Dramatists
      Committee 315
Leduc (character) 204–208,
    209, 263, 399, 423
Lee, Ming Cho 361
Lee, Will 207
Leicester, Margot 93
Lenin, Vladimir 349, 379, 381
Le Normand, H. R. 426
Lerner, Max 54
Let's Make Love (Cukor) 15,
    436
Lewis, Allan 34, 39
Lewis, Anthony 270, 274
Lewis, Ira 207
Lewis, Peter 306, 309
Lewis, Robert 12, 152, 154,
    358, 385, 397, 418, 425,
    452, 492
Lida, David 99, 100
Liguri, Alberto 149
Lima, Robert 118, 125
Lin, Zhu 312
Lincoln, Abraham 255, 259,
    326, 441
Lindberg, Charles 186
Lindholdt, Paul 155
"Lines from California: Poem"
    17, **222–223**, 484, 495
Listen for the Sound of Wings 8,
    223, 479, 491
Listen My Children 7, **223**, 391,
    453, 491
    and HUAC 223, 410, 453
Lithgow, John 234
Liu, Wu-chi 96
Livermore, Jesse (character)
    55, 60, **62–63**, 64, 473
Living Newspaper 258, 391,
    421
Lloyd, John Bedford 296
LoBianco, Tony 207, 236
Loden, Barbara 26, 33, 418,
    420, 494
"Lola's Lament" **223–224**,
    484
Loman, Ben (character) 132–
    139, 141, **142**, 144–145, 147
Loman, Biff (character) 4,
    130–139, 141, **142–143**,
    144–145, 212, 312–313, 384,
    390, 421, 423, 441

Loman, Happy (character) 4,
    130–139, 141–142, **143–144**
Loman, Linda (character) 66,
    130–139, 141–143, **144**,
    145–146, 312, 325, 385,
Loman, Willy (character) 3–4,
    11–12, 31, 61, 66, 115, 130–
    143, **144–145**, 146, 178,
    201, 212, 219, 311–312, 327,
    363, 367, 384, 388–390, 392,
    396, 399, 405, 417, 423, 427,
    440, 441, 450, 458, 462
    and Cobb 378–379, 384,
      385, 419
    and Lyman Felt 299–300,
      305, 306
    as tragic hero 137, 262,
      330, 344, 465
Long, Huey 260
*Long Day's Journey into Night,
    A* (O'Neill) 348, 384, 425,
    444, 452
Longhi, Vincent 10, 12, 252,
    336, **424**, 450, 492
Loquasto, Santo 89
Loughlin, Richard L. 454
Louise (character) 16, 27–29,
    31–33, **36**, 37, 388, 390, 459
Lowell, Robert 470
Lowenthal, Lawrence D. 208,
    210
Loyal Hearts (Shuyang) 97
Loynd, Ray 65, 100
L.S.D. (Wooster) 118, 124,
    478, 496
Lubimov, Yuri 206
Luers, William 349
Lukas, Paul 223
Lumet, Sidney 348, 453, 494
Lynch, Thomas 165
Lyons, Donald 390

M

MacArthur, Charles 401
Macbeth (Shakespeare) 123
MacDonald, James 229
Machinal (Treadwell) 387
MacKenna, Kenneth 426
MacLeish, Archibald 179,
    361, 419
Macy, William H. 21, 176, 498
Madame Butterfly (Puccini)
    266, 269
Maddox, Diana 124, 493
Maggie (character) 16, 26–35,
    36–37, 38–39, 352, 369,
    388, 390, 418, 433, 440
Mahaffey, Valerie 155
Maier, Charlotte 218

Mailer, Norman 8, 372, 453
Malden, Karl 47, 419
Malkovitch, John 496
Maltby, Richard, Jr. 321
Mamet, David 141, 321, 368,
    397, 416
Mandel (character) 267–271,
    408
Man for All Seasons, A (Bolt)
    118, 126
*Man in Black, The. See Broken
    Glass*
Mann, Daniel 270
Mann, Judy 266, 274
Mann, Paul 33, 207
Manocchio, Tony 147, 390
*Man Who Had All the Luck,
    The* 8–9, 21, 40, 90, 169,
    190, 211–212, **224–231**,
    327, 363, 368–369, 370, 411,
    415, 430, 453, 459, 477,
    483, 498
    characters. *See also* Amos
      Beeves, David Beeves,
      Paterson Beeves, Gustav
      Eberson 190, 224–228,
      229–31
    critical commentary
      228–229
    initial reviews 8, **229**
    movies 22, 225, 432
    scholarship **229**, 231
    synopsis 8, **225–228**
March, Fredric 11–12, 145,
    152, 154, 155, 212, 328, 385,
    410, **425–426**, 496
Marco (character) 199, 337–
    346, **347**, 410
Marco Millions (O'Neill) 444,
    452
Mardi Gras (Rosten) 453, 493
Marianne (character) 266–
    271, **272–273**, 274, 400
Marino, Stephen A. vii, 48, 54,
    72, 76, 90, 94, 118, 125, 141,
    147, 208, 210, 306, 309, 336,
    338, 344, 348, 489
Marlow, Stuart 125
Marlowe, Gloria 234, *337*, 493
Márquez, Gabriel Garcia 349,
    375, 376
Marshall, E. G. 117, 477
Marshall, Larry 335
Martin (character) 94, 196–
    197, 388
Martin, George N. 89
Martin, Robert A. 34, 39, 125,
    147, 213, 324, 329, 331, 344,
    348, 453, 489, 495

Martine, James J. 109, 118,
    125, 141, 147, 489
Marx, Karl 56, 61, 129, 379,
    381
Marxism 63, 77, 123,
    167, 279, 325, 349, 374,
    379–380
Mason, Jeffrey D. 296, 299
Massa, Ann 283, 286
Master Builder, The (Ibsen)
    229, 231, 414–415
Master Class (McNally) 474
Matalon, Vivian 54, 60, 496
materialism 47, 53, 137–138,
    237–238, 295, 296, 298
Matthaei, Konrad 71
Mauthausen 15, 25, 406, 438,
    494
Max, D. T. 128
Mayer, Michael 339
Mayorga, Margaret 324
Mayron, Melanie 270
Maysles, Albert 252, 396
McCabe, Bruce 93, 94
McCallin, Tanya 305
McCarten, John 33, 39, 145,
    147, 208, 210
McCarthy, Eugene 17, 78,
    471, 494
McCarthy, Joseph 12–13, 200,
    404, 409–410
McCarthy, Kevin 243, 492
McCarthy, Mary 437
McCarthyism 13, 108–109,
    115, 118, 126, 129, 154, 155,
    210, 212, 348, 353, 380,
    409–410
McCormick, Frank 147
McCoy, Terry 349
McCullers, Carson 377, 474
McCully, Emily A. 214
McDonell, Mary 64, 497
McGavin, Darren 64, 100,
    497
McGill, William J., Jr. 125
McGovern, John 47
McGuire, Biff 215, 234, 497
McIntyre, Alice T. 243, 246
McLaughlin, Charles F. 411
McLean, Robert A. 270,
    274
McMillan, Kenneth 99, 496
McNally, Terence 321, 474
McQueen, Steve 155
McVeigh, Timothy 291
Meeker, Ralph 33
Meisner, Sanford 397, 442
Melton, Robert W. 250–251
Member of the Wedding, The
    (McCullers) 377, 474

Memory of Two Mondays, A 3, 13, 213, **231–237**, 261–262, 336, 361, 369, 372, 376, 377, 396, 398, 474, 485, 493–494, 496
  characters. See also Bert, Gus 235–236
  critical commentary **233–234**
  and Great Depression 232
  initial reviews **234**, 362
  movies **236**
  scholarship **234–235**, 236–237
  synopsis **232–233**
Mengele, Dr. 264, 266–269, 273
Men in White (Kingsley) 418, 442, 462
Meredith, Peggy 47
Merrill, Beth 47, 492
Merritt, Michael 99, 194
Mesher, David R. 174, 177, 417
Method acting 166, 358, 405, 418, 434, 461–462
Meyer, Kinereth 208, 210, 329
Meyer, Michael R. 487
Meyer, Nancy 39
Meyer, Richard 39
Meyerhold, Vsevolod 202, 361
"Michigan Bank Failure Called Fault of Incompetent Officials" 426
Michigan Daily, The (newspaper) 5, 190, **425–426**, 490–491, 458, 468
Mielziner, Jo 11, 33, 130, *131*, 139–140, 147, 312, 328, **426–428**, 456, 492
Miller, Augusta (Gittel) 3–5, 7, 15, 201, 327, 365, 381, 389, **428–429**, 432–433, 435, 441, 490
  as character 4, 37, 62, 196, 256
  death of 15, 429, 436, 438, 494
Miller, Daniel 15, 438, 494
Miller, Isidore 3–5, 7, 15–16, 81, 141, 201, 311, 327, 365, 381, 389, 395, 428, **429–430**, 436, 441, 473, 490
  as character 3, 35, 61, 81, 256
  death of 16, 277, 314, 430, 494
Miller, Jane Ellen 8, 12, 16, 36, 214, 320, **430–431**, 432, 459, 491

Miller, Jeanne-Marie A. 118, 125, 381
Miller, Kermit 3–5, 233, 317, 327, 381, 389, 428–430, **431–432**, 433, 435, 490
  as character 35, 50, 389
  death of 22, 432, 499
  in war 8, 431, 479
Miller, Paula. *See* Paula Strasberg
Miller, Rebecca Augusta 16, 21, 22, 64, 124, 126, 200, 214, 225, 311, 313, 327, 431, **432**, 438, 494, 497–498
Miller, Robert Arthur 10, 12, 20, 36, 80, 124, 126, 128, 176, 370, 431, **432–433**, 459, 492
Miller, Samuel 265, 428, 429
Miller, Timothy 118, 125
Miller Shorts (Thacker) 394, 463
Miltex Coat and Suit Company 3–5, 98, 201, 327, 395, 428, 430, **433**, 441, 473, 490
Minot, Anna 154
"Miracles" **237**, 483, 495
Mirren, Helen 152, 463
"Misfits, The" 13, 15, 195, **237–239**, 436, 483, 493
Misfits, The (screenplay) 15, 162, 166–167, 195, 237, **239–246**, 324, 393, 436, 438, 462, 474, 484, 493
  characters. See also Gay Langland, Roslyn Taber 240–243, **244–245**, 452
  critical commentary **242–243**
  initial reviews 243
  scholarship 243–244, 245–246
  synopsis **240–242**
Mitchell, Cameron *131*, 139
Mitchell, Norman 343
Mitchell, Warren 146, 440, 463, 496
"Modest Proposal" 177, **251–252**, 483, 493
Modine, Matthew 165, 291
Molière 452
Molnár, Ferenc 9, 427, 491
Monroe, Marilyn 12, 160, 156, 167, *239*, 246, 250, 275, 429–432, **433–437**, 453, 474
  and *After the Fall* 16, 25, 33–34, 37–38, 352–353, 440
  death of 15, 25–26, 34, 430, 436–437

and Kazan 13, 358, 418, 420, 434
and Miller 10, 12–16, 116, 239, 275, 287, 326–327, 339, 372, 410–411, 431, 433–437, 438, 454, 459, 460, 492–494
and *The Misfits* 162, 237, 239–240, 243–244, 246, 393
and Strasbergs 13, 166, 358, 461–462
Montand, Yves 15, 123, 240, 436, 493
"Monte Sant' Angelo" 12, 195, 197, 252–253, 417, 424, 483, 492
Montezuma. See The Golden Years
Montgomery, Robert 9
Moore, Marianne 469
Moraga, Cherríe 141, 148
Morath, Ingeborg 25, 204, 349, 432, **437–439**, *438*
  as co-creator 17–18, 96, 200, 201, 311, 439, 495–496
  death of 22, 162, 167, 332, 365, 439, 499
  and Miller 15–17, 327–328, 367, 406, 429, 433, 454, 494, 496
  photographs by *189, 239, 312, 375, 420, 428*
Morehouse, Ward 48, 54, 229, 231, 427–428
Morgan, Edmund Sears 128
Morgan, Marie 128
Morgan, Randolph (character) 55, **62**, 64, 473
Morley, Sheridan 100, 194–195, 219, 222, 487
Morrison, Blake 194–195
Morrison, Toni 100
Morton, Samantha *189*, 190
Moscow Arts Theatre 358, 461
Moscowitz, Sid 6, 184
Mosher, Gregory 99, 129, 194, 452
Moss, Leonard 39, 49, 244, 246, 423, 489
Mozes, Alan 249
Mr. Peter's Connections 21, **246–251**, 357, 369, 377, 388, 398, 450, 460, 471, 484, 498
  characters. *See also* Cathy-May, Charlotte Peters, Harry Peters,

Rose Peters 246–249, **250–251**
  critical commentary **248–249**
  initial reviews **250**
  scholarship **250**, 251
  synopsis 21, **246–248**
Mukerji, Nirmal 118, 125, 466
Muni, Paul 149, 492
Murder in the Cathedral (Eliot) 162
Murphy, Audie 438
Murphy, Brenda vii, 34, 39, 48, 54, 136, 140, 147, 192, 208, 210, 229, 231, 344, 348, 353, 387, 392, 411, 415, 421, 427–428, 450, 489
Murray, Edward 34, 39, 49, 489
Murrow, Edward R. 410
Musante, Tony 71, 234, 495
Mussolini, Benito 149, 317, 326, 391, 447
"My Dinner with Castro." *See* "A Visit with Castro"
"My Wife Marilyn" 436

N

Nadel, Norman 33, 39, 208, 211
Naikar, Basavaraj 306, 309
Naish, J. Carrol 234, 337, 493
Naked and the Dead, The (Mailer) 8
Nanda, Bijaaya Kumar 126
Nathan, David 60, 65, 89, 94, 152, 321
National Theatre (London) 18, 26, 54, 89, 101, **440–441**, 463
  and Miller 146, 339, 369, 394, 447, 467, 475, 495–497
Native Boy (Wright) 7
"Nature of Tragedy, The" 11, **253–254**, 465, 484, 492
Navasky, Victor 128
Nazis 260, 391, 399, 437
  and anti-Semitism 83, 91, 186, 206, 209, 424
  fight against 149, 223, 478, 479
  and the Holocaust 32, 35, 208, 252, 266, 406–408
  in *Incident at Vichy* 204–210, 263
  oppression of 7, 8, 72, 81, 88, 92, 185, 204, 360, 394

in *Playing for Time* 266–274, 369
universal lessons of 32, 89, 210, 316
NBC
    radio 7, 491, 493
    television 13, 39, 139, 236, 285, 494, 495
Neaphus, Ralph 6, **441**, 491
Neeson, Liam 21, 499
Neill, Heather 219, 221, 222
Nelson, Benjamin 234–236, 489
Nemeth, Lemke 306, 309
Newman, Abby 4, 130, 142, 371, 441
Newman, Buddy 4, 130, 142, 371, 441
Newman, Gertrude (Hart) (character) 170–173, **175**, 176, 388, 390
Newman, Lawrence (character) 170–174, **175–176**, 360, 388, 398, 400
Newman, Manny 4, 130, 327, 371, 428, 430, 433, **441**
Newman, William J. 390
New Masses (magazine) 9, 317, 448
"New Pamphlet Lists 500 Books for College Men and Women" 426
New Theater Workshop 17, 160, 296
New Watergate Club 338, 344
New York City College 5, 490
New York City Youth Board 82
Nicholls, Alan 335, 495
Nichols, Mike 369, 432, 455
Nielsen, Leslie 124, 493
Niemoeller, Martin 8, 223, 479
"Night Ed Murrow Struck Back" 410, 484
Nightingale, Benedict 89, 94
Night Music (Odets) 377, 442
"1956 and All This" 14, **254–255**, 484, 493
"1928 Buick, The" 224, **255–256**, 484, 496
Nixon, Richard 163, 165, 237
Nobel Prize 21, 364, 366, 373, 444, 447, 457, 460
Nolan, Paul T. 34, 39
Nolte, Nick 20, 158, 497
Nordenson, Lars 152, 154
North, Alex 139, 140, 243
Nossek, Ralph 343

"Notes on Realism" 25, 258–259, 366, 369, 477, 483
Novick, Julius 147, 236, 286
No Villain. See also Abe Simon, Arnold Simon, Ben Simon 3, 5–6, 183, 190, **256–257**, 258, 325, 363, 387–388, 490–491, 412, 441, 468
    and communism 256–257, 380
NPR 290, 460, 474
Nurse, Rebecca (character) 108, 110, 112, 114–115, 117, 119, **120**, 122, 127–128, 342, 456–457

O

O'Brien, Jack 53, 155
O'Casey, Sean 25, 258
O'Connor, Francis 244
O'Connor, John J. 38–39, 53–54, 155, 210–211, 234, 236, 270, 274
Odets, Clifford 7, 11, 118, 184, 231, 336, 361, 378, 381, 393, 397, 405, 418, 434, 442–443, 462, 475, 477, 492
    and Clurman 377, 442
    and HUAC 11, 409, 443, 492
    influence on Miller 190, 258, 324, 353, 443
    in "Notes on Realism" 25, 258, 443
    in *Timebends: A Life* 326, 328, 443
O'Donnell, Chris 21, 224, 225, 498
Oedipus 46, 48, 53, 212, 343, 468
off-Broadway 13, 16, 20, 222, 278, 336, 339, 359, 361, 385, 396, 370, 405, 452, 458, 478, 494
off-off-Broadway 278, 370
Oliver, Edith 219, 222, 335–336
Olivier, Laurence 14, 361, 435, 440, 493–494
Olson, Ray 150
"On Broadway" 484, 498
O'Neill, Eugene ix, 48, 141, 147, 161, 177, 185, 328, 362–363, 370, 442, **444–445**, 447
    in "About Theater Language" 25, 444
    in "Notes on Realism" 258, 444

productions of 377, 384, 387, 425, 427, 452, 462, 464
    in "The Shadows of the Gods" 316, 444
On Politics and the Art of Acting 21, **259–261**, 364, 484, 493
"On Screenwriting and Language" 158
"On Social Plays" 13, **261–262**, 336, 484, 493
On the Waterfront (Kazan) 192, 338, 419
Oreskes, Daniel 249
Orpheus Descending (Williams) 361, 377
Orr, Forrest 229
Osbourne, John 34, 39, 402
Othello (Shakespeare) 381, 465
Otness, Harold 201
Otten, Terry 26, 34, 39, 48, 54, 60–61, 65, 72, 76, 90, 94, 105, 107, 118, 126, 141, 147, 208, 211, 219, 222, 235, 305, 310, 344, 348
"Our Guilt For the World's Evil" 17, 237, **262–263**, 398, 408, 411, 416, 470, 472, 484, 489, 494
Our Town (Wilder) 118, 162, 401, 478
Överland, Orm 49, 489
OWI Domestic Radio Bureau 10, 322
Oxford Pledge 5, 479
"Oxygen, Usually One of Man's 'Best Friends,' Can Be Harmful" 426
Ozieblo, Barbara 90, 94

P

Pacino, Al 358, 462
Pakula, Alan 432
Palmer, R. Barton 243, 246
Panto, Pete 10, 191, 424, 450, 492
Papatola, Dominic P. 251
Papp, Joseph 452
Paradise Lost (Odets) 361, 377, 418, 442
Parker, Al 214
Parker, Dorothy 489
Parris (character) 109–115, 117, **120–121**, 122–123, 126–128, 456
Parris, Betty (character) 109–110, 113, **119**, 120–121, 123, 127, 456
Parsons, Estelle 236, 495, 496

Partridge, C. J. 118, 126, 147
Pasternak, Boris 201
Patrick, John 474
Patten, Dick Van 236
Patton, Will 158
PBS 20, 53, 93, 155, 210, 310, 495–497
Pearson, Michelle 126
Peck, Bob 152, 463
Peck, Seymour 421
Pedi, Tom 139, 234, 331
PEN (Poets, Essayists and Novelists) 16–17, 19, 129, 148, 326–328, 351, 411, 417, 439, **446–447**, 496
    Miller as president 17, 404, 430, 446, 494–495
Pendleton, Austin 334, 477, 478
Penn, Leo 234, 337
"Performance, The" 21, 263–265, 417, 484, 499
    and anti-Semitism 264, 361
Peter, John 71, 76, 89, 94, 152, 219, 222, 321
Peters, Charlotte (character) 247–249, **251**, 389
Peters, Harry (character) 21, 246–250, **251**
Peters, Kelly Jean 113
Peters, Rose (character) 246–249, **251**, 388–389
Petitt, William 147, 390
Pheloung, Barrington 305
Philippines Never Surrendered 9, **265**, 479, 492
Phillips, Michael 89, 94, 115, 168
Picker, David 124, 128
Pickup, Ronald 182, 497
Piette, Alan 152, 321
Pinter, Harold 19, 21, 90, 93, 152, 416, 440, **447**, 452, 475, 496
    in "Dinner with the Ambassador" 148–149, 447
    Miller's opinion of 21, 447
    on Miller
Pirandello, Luigi 368
Pittas, Christos 182
Plain Jane. See Eden
Plakkoottam, J. L. 126
"Plaster Masks, The" 9, **265–266**, 479, 484, 492
Playing for Time (Fénelon) 391

Playing for Time (teleplay) 18, 264, **266–274**, 364, 392, 417, 451, 484, 496
  and anti-Semitism 269, 271, 360
  characters. *See also* Elzvieta, Fania Fénelon, Hélène, Mandel, Marianne, Mengele, Alma Rose **271–273**
  and communism 380
  critical commentary **268–270**
  and guilt and responsibility 271–273, 400
  and the Holocaust 18, 266–274, 406–408
  initial reviews **270–271**
  scholarship **271**, 273–274
  synopsis 266–268
Playing for Time 18, 266, **274**, 392, 467, 484, 496, 499
"Playwright and the Atomic World, The." *See* "1956 and All This"
"Please Don't Kill Anything" 14, 195, 239, **275–276**, 433, 435, 483, 493
Plummer, Christopher 38, 495
Pollock, Arthur 155
Poosidin's Resignation, The 186, **276**, 471, 484, 495
Popkin, Henry 34, 39, 208, 210, 244, 246
Porter, Rose Albert 418
"Portrait of a Girl in Glass" (Williams) 476
Pound, Ezra 9, 96, **447–48**, 469
  and anti-Semitism 36, 317, 448
  in "Should Ezra Pound be Shot?" 9, 317, 360
  in *Timebends: A Life* 448
Prasad, Amar Nath 48, 54
"Presence, The" 21, **276–277**, 484
Presence, The (collection) 22, 77, 79, 94, 263, 276, 331, 484, 499
Press, David 244, 246
Preston, Ann 401
Preston, Rohan 250–251, 296, 299
Prete, Heather 165
Price, Jonathan 33, 39
Price, The 3, 17, 19, 21, 48, **277–286**, 361, 363, 276, 331, 484, 499

and absurdism 278, 286, 358
and capitalism 374
characters. *See also* Esther Franz, Mr. Franz, Victor Pranz, Walter Franz, Gregory Solomon 277–282, **283–285**, 361
critical commentary **281–282**
and family relationships 388–390
and Great Depression 277–278, 281, 284
and guilt and responsibility 398
initial reviews **283**
movies 18, **285–286**, 458, 495
productions of 370, 381, 394, 396–397, 463, 474–475, 477, 494, 497, 498
scholarship **283**, 286
synopsis 17, **278–281**
and Vietnam War 278, 286, 471
"*Price*, The Power of the Past, The" 286–287, 471, 472, 483–484
and absurdism 286, 358
Pride and Prejudice (Austen) 9, 464, 491
Prideaux, Tom 33, 39
Primus, Barry 33, 105
Prince and the Showgirl, The (Olivier) 14, 435
Proctor, Elizabeth (character) 77, 108–117, 120, **121**, 122–123, 126–128, 388–389, 398, 456–457, 459
Proctor, John (character) 77, 108–120, **121–122**, 126–128, 129, 213, 342, 384, 386, 388, 398–399, 401–402, 411, 421, 456–457, 458
  as tragic hero 118, 122, 466
Proof (Auburn) 432
"Prophecy, The" 14, 195, **287–289**, 483, 494
Provincetown Players 359, 393, 444
Prudoe, John 466, 489
Prumb, Lucille 418
Psacharopoulos, Nikos 477, 478
Pullman, Bill *41*
Puritanism 327

in *The Crucible* 108, 114–116, 119, 120, 122, 128
Pushkin, Alexander 201
Pussycat and the Expert Plumber Who Was a Man, The 8, **289–290**, 352, 460, 484, 491
Putnam, Thomas (character) 108–109, 113, 115, 117, 120–121, **122**, 127, 374, 456
Pyle, Ernie 8, 322, 461

Q

Qing, Jiang 96, 97, 313
Qiyang, Zhao 366
Quayle, Antony 343, 493, 494
Quentin (character) 16, 25–36, **37–38**, 165, 168, 353, 386, 388, 390, 398–400, 406–407, 423, 452, 459
Quigly, Isabel 124, 126, 243, 246
Quinn, Aidan 53, 497
Quintessence of Ibsenism, The (Shaw) 413, 449
Quixote, Don 349

R

Rabe, David 21
Rabkin, Gerald 126
Rahv, Philip 208, 211
Raines, Mary B. 283, 286
"Rain in Strange City" **290**, 483, 495
Ralph (character) 56, 60–61, 64, 374
Ram, Atma 489
Randolph, John 59, 496
Rankin, John 409
Rankin Committee. *See also* HUAC 409
Rascoe, Burton 229, 231
Ratcliffe, Michael 487
Rathbone, Basil 401
Rathod, Baldev C. 34, 39
Rattigan, Terence 428, 435
Rauh, Joseph, Jr. 410
Rawls, Eugenia 229
Reagan, Ronald 141, 259–261, 303, 306
realism 11, 25, 33, 97, 161–162, 187, 211, 258, 261, 317, 358, 361, 366, 387–388, 427, 444, 447, **449–450**, 476–477
  in Chinese drama 311, 366
  and Ibsen 40, 161, 198, 212, 258, 413–414, 449
  in Miller's plays 9, 11, 40, 48–49, 93, 115, 130,

136, 179, 213, 258–259, 344, 381, 387, 449–450
  and Russian drama 203
Reason Why, The 17–18, 160, **291**, 455, 471, 474, 495
"Recognitions." *See* "Fame"
Redgrave, Vanessa 18, 266, 270, 392, **450–451**, 496
Red Hook 10, 191, 336, 339, 345, 372, 424, **450**, 492
Redwood, Manning 305
Rees, Roger 478
Reeve, F. D. 204
Reid, Kate 155, 283, 494, 495, 496
Reilly, Peter 18, 318, **451**, 495
Reis, Irving 53
Reisz, Karel 156, 158
Reitz, Bernhard 306, 310
religious references. *See also* The Creation of the World, The Crucible, Up from Paradise 31–32, 35, 47, 54, 56, 69, 158, 180–182, 208, 263, 281, 306, 309, 319–320, 358
  Christ imagery 27–28, 30, 32, 34, 37, 39, 47, 49, 127–128, 292–299, 349
  God 30–31, 58, 71, 273
  Jewish identity 48, 89, 90, 252–253, 268–269, 271, 327, 350, 367, 400
    Bar mitzvah 3, 490
    Shabbat 106, 253
    Simchat Torah 196, 327
    Yom Kippur 196–197, 416
  Madonna 338, 343, 346
Reno, 1960 240
Repertory Theater of Lincoln Center 5, 25, 33, 39, 204, 376, 378, 420, 427, 439, **451–452**, 462, 474, 494
Republicans 63, 188, 259, 365, 424
Resurrection Blues 18, 20–22, 177, **291–299**, 357, 370, 394, 398, 484, 499
  and capitalism 295, 374
  characters. *See also* Felix Barriaux, Skip Cheesboro, Henri Schultz 292–295, **296–299**
  critical commentary **294–295**
  initial reviews **296**

scholarship **296**, 299
synopsis **292–294**
Retreat to Pleasure (Shaw) 397
Revolutionary War 8, 79, 95, 371
Ribkoff, Fred 147
Rice, Elmer 387, 427, 464
Rich, Frank 60, 65, 152, 321, 335–336, 362
Richardson, David 71
Richenthal, David 165
Ride Down Mt. Morgan, The 20–21, 94, **299–310**, 415, 484, 497
  and capitalism 374
  characters. *See also* Bessie Felt, Leah Felt, Lyman Felt, Theo Felt, Tom Wilson 296, 301, 306, **307–309**
  critical commentary **303–305**
  and *Death of a Salesman* 299–300, 305, 357, 363, 389, 450
  and existentialism 305, 306, 386, 387
  and expressionism 305–306, 387
  and guilt and responsibility 302–305, 307–308
  initial reviews **305–306**
  movies 22, **309**
  productions of 369, 394, 477, 498
  scholarship 94, **306, 309–310**
  synopsis 20, **301–303**
Riders to the Sea (Synge) 454
Ridley, Clifford A. 250–251
Rifkin, Ron 85, 89, 497
Ritchie, Michael 478
Ritt, Martin 231, 234, 336–337, 372, 493
Ritter, Thelma 243
Rix, Colin 343
Rizzo, Sergio 128
Road to Reno, The (Morath) 438
Robards, Jason Jr. 33, 34, **452, 494**
Roberts, Stanley 145
Robertson, Ralph 154
Robins, Laila 296
Robinson, Edward G. 10, 53, 265, 492
Robinson, James A. 48, 54, 283, 286, 390
Robotham, J. 204

Rocket to the Moon (Odets) 377, 442
Rodgers, Richard 377, 382, 464
Roe, Patricia 33
Romeo and Juliet (Shakespeare) 381, 464
Roosevelt, Franklin D. 6, 57, 59, 259, 261, 390, 395–396
Rose (character) 27–33, 35, **37**, 38, 388, 390, 427
Rosé, Alma (character) 266–270, 272, **273**, 391
Rose, Charlie 83, 94, 290, 497
Rosefeldt, Paul 49, 54
Rosenberg, Ethel 109, 431, 432
Rosenberg, Julius 109, 431, 432
Rose Tattoo, The (Williams) 361, 420, 474, 475
Ross, Kenneth 433
Rossellini, Renzo 331
Rosten, Norman 6, 223, 372, 410, **452–453**, 491, 493
  and Federal Theater 6–7, 223, 391, 452–53
  and Mailer 453
  and Monroe 13, 434–435, 453
  and University of Michigan 6, 453, 454, 458
  and *A View from the Bridge* 14, 348, 453, 494
Roth, Philip 367, 432, 455
Rothenberg, Albert 344, 348
Rothstein, Mervyn 299
Roudané, Matthew C. 61, 140, 141, 148, 359, 383, 386, 399, 412, 487
Roush, Matt 65, 93, 94
Route 1 & 9 (Wooster) 478
Rowe, Kenneth 6, 325, 363, 391, 414, 428, **453–454**, 464, 476
  as Miller's mentor 6, 184, 391, 444, 453–454, 465, 468, 471
Rowley, William, 420, 452
Roxbury, Connecticut 10–11, 14–18, 20, 22, 79–80, 130, 189, 200, 326, 328, 428, 431–432, 435–436, 438, **454–455**, 459
  death at 365, 382, 499
  filming at 189–190, 291
  fire at 19, 313, 450, 496
  neighbors 367, 376, 405, 439, 455, 469

Royal, Derek Parker 34, 39
Royal Hunt of the Sun, The (Shaffer) 182
Royal Shakespeare Company 361, 451, 463
  and Miller 67, 71, 496, 499
Rudge, Frances 418
Rudman, Michael 440, 487, 496
Rudolph, Sarah J. 296, 299
Rudy Vallee Show 7
Ruocheng, Ying 311–314, 366–367
Ryan, Robert 18, 291, 495
Ryan Interview, The 21, 200, **310–311**, 377, 455, 484, 498
Ryder, Winona 124, 128, 498

S

Sadler, Dudley 47, 229
Salem Witchcraft (Upton) 108, 456
Salem witch trials 12, 100, 108–109, 118, 124–125, 128–129, 213, 327, **456–457**, 466, 492
"*Salesman* at Fifty" **311**, 483, 498
Salesman in Beijing 19, 142, 149, **311–314**, 367, 378, 427, 447, 469, 484, 496
  initial reviews 314
Samachson, Dorothy 487
Samachson, Joseph 487
Samson, John 182
Sankowich, Lee D. 140
Sartre, Jean-Paul 100, 208, 210, 306, 309, 373–374, 376, 386, **457–458**
  and *The Witches of Salem* 77, 123, 493
Sauvage, Leo 60, 65
Savage, Alan 13, 493
Savran, David 34, 39, 477, 489
Saxe, Alfred 418
Sayre, Nora 150
Scanlan, Tom 390, 489
Scheck, Frank 89, 94
Schell, Maximillian 292
Schiff, Ellen 208, 211, 286
Schissel, Wendy 118, 126
Schlöndorff, Volker 146
Schlueter, June 49, 71, 76, 105, 107, 124, 305–306, 310, 324–325, 489
Schneider, Daniel E. 489
Schonberg, Harold C. 65, 382

"Schubert's Loves Are Displayed in Art Cinema's Latest Picture" 426
Schulberg, Budd 192
Schull, Rebecca 290, 460
Schultz, Henri (character) 292–296, **297**, 398
"Scientists See and Hear What Dog's Brain Cells Are Doing" 426
Scofield, Paul 128, 498
Scott, George C. 17, 124, 140, 285, 363, 452, **458**, 494, 495
Scott, Harold 33, 207
Seagull, The (Chekhov) 377, 451
"Search for a Future, A" 17, 195, **314–315**, 470, 483, 494
Segal, Alex 124, 146, 385
Seiler, Andy 128
"Sellars, Slosson, Shepard Speak on Fascism, Nazism and Hearst" 426
Sessions, Janice (character) 187–189, 388–389
Seymour, Gene 128
Shadow of a Man (Moraga) 141
"Shadows of the Gods, The" **315–317**, 484, 493
  and absurdism 357–358
  and Ibsen 414, 316
  and Williams 316–317, 476–477
Shaffer, Peter 34, 39, 182
Shakespeare, William 34, 48, 259, 316, 352, 381, 440, 463
Shalet, Diane 33
Shanzun, Ouyang 366
Shape-Up, The. See The Hook
Shapiro, Eugene D. 344, 348
Shapse, Sam 5, 376, 490
Sharpe, Robert B. 229, 231
Shatzky, Joel 141
Shaw, George Bernard x, 198, 377, 402, 413, 414, 446, 449, 464, 477
Shaw, Irwin 397
Shea Stadium 177
Sheehan, Jack 229
Sheffer, Isaiah 195
Shepard, Richard 362–363
Shepard, Sam 283, 286, 460
Sherwood, Madeleine 117, 392, 402
Sherwood, Robert 464
Shockley, John S. 141
Sholokhov, Mikhail 203
"Should Ezra Pound Be Shot?" **317**, 360, 411, 484, 491

Shrapnel, John 182, 497
Shuyang, Su 97
Siebold, Thomas 141, 489
Siegel, Ed 53, 54, 306, 310
Sievers, David W. 489
Sigmund (character) 17, 67–73, 74–75, 76, 108, 386, 404
Signature Theater 21, 60, 215, 246, 249, 290, 359, **460**, 498
Sign of the Archer, The. See All My Sons
Signor, Tari 249
Signoret, Simone 123, 493
Silverman, Stanley 105, 152, 321, 334–336
Silverstein, Shel 321
Simon, Abe (character) 5, 256–257, 325–326, 374, 388
Simon, Ben (character) 5–6, 184, 256–257, 325–326, 388, 431
Simon, John 33, 39, 48, 54, 89, 94, 283, 286
Simon, Josette 26, 440
Simon, Neil 165, 382, 392
Simonov, Konstantin 201, 203
Simonson, Lee 361
Simonson, Robert 94, 222
"Simplicity of Aran's Life and People Described by Stephens" 426
Singh, Amrendra Narayan 141, 148
Sinha, Prashant K. 126
Sinyavsky, Andrei 203
Situation Normal . . . 8, 149, 317–318, 322, 431, 459, 479, 484, 491
Skin of Our Teeth, The (Wilder) 418, 425
Skloot, Robert 406–407, 408
Slattery, Mary Grace 8, 26, 36, 78, 80, 116, 224, 237, 317, 370, 410, 435–436, 453–454, **458–460**
    at college 5–6, 458, 461, 490
    marriage to 7, 10, 12–13, 116, 327, 365, 372, 433, 485–486, 491
Slavin, Neal 176
Smiley, Jane 170, 177
Smith, Art 154
Smith, Harry 427–428
Smith, Howard 139
Sofer, Andrew 72–76
Solomon, Deborah 168, 365, 487

Solomon, Gregory (character) 17, 277–284, **285**, 286, 358, 361, 474
Solzhenitsyn, Aleksandr 17, 446, 494
Some Kind of Love Story. See also Angela 18–19, 150–151, **318–321**, 333, 451, 484–485, 496, 497
    critical commentary **319–321**
    and Everybody Wins 20, 156
    initial reviews **321**
    synopsis 19, **318–19**
Some Shall Not Sleep. See Focus
Sommer, Josef 71
Sondheim, Stephen 361
Sontag, Susan 34, 39
Spanish civil war 6, 379, 410, 441, 481
Speech to the Neighborhood Watch Committee 19, **321–322**, 497
Spielberg, Stephen 421–422
Splendor in the Grass (Kazan) 415, 419
Srivastava, Ramesh K. 54
SS Copa Copa 7, 185, 459
Stage for Action 8, 324
Stalin, Josef 96, 107–108, 202, 260, 374
Stanislavski, Constantin 259, 313, 358, 397, 461–462
Stanton, Barbara *113*, 117
Stanton, Stephen S. 39
Stapleton, Maureen 348, 494
Starkey, Marion 108, 126, 129, 456
Starling, Lynn 401
Stavney, Anne 148, 390
Stearns, David Patrick 146, 219, 222
Steinbeck. John 367, 402, 455, **460–461**
    defense of Miller 461
Steinberg, M. W. 466, 489
Steinberg, Sybil S. 186, 187
Steiner, George 408
Stepney, Colin 305
Stevens, Robert L. 71, 89, 234, 337, 474
Stevens, Virginia 487
Stewart, David J. 33, 207
Stewart, Fred 117
Stewart, Patrick 21, 301, 306, 310, 477, 498
Stiller, Jerry 236

Stinson, John J. 34, 39
Stone, John 343
Stoppard, Tom 323, 368, 392, 402, 475
Story of Canine Joe, The 8, **322**, 479, 491
Story of G. I. Joe, The 8, 265, 317, 322, 459, 461, 479, 491
Story of Gus, The 10, 322–323, 479, 484, 492
Strackey, John 426
Straight, Beatrice 117, 492
Strange Interlude (O'Neill) 54, 444, 462
Strasberg, Lee 166, 184, 358, 361, 385, 393, 397, 405, 418, 442, **461–462**, 464
    and Monroe 13, 166, 358, 434–435, 461–462
Strasberg, Paula 13, 15, 166, 461, **462**
    and Monroe 166, 240, 358, 435, 461–462
Strath, Deirdre 305
Strathairn, David 64, 497
Streep, Meryl 234
Streetcar Named Desire, A (Williams) 419–420, 427, 450, 476
Strickland, Carol 94
Strindberg, August 199, 258, 387, 413, 475
Strong, Michael 33, 154, 207
Strout, Cushing 118, 126
Studio Theatre 274
Styan, J. L. 213, 324–325, 344, 348
Styron, William 21, 349, 367, 375, 376, 455, 498
"Subsidized Theater" 10, **323**, 483, 484, 492
Sullivan, Barry 285
Sullivan, Dan 54, 59
Sundaram, Subbulakshmi 235, 237
Susskind, David 285
Sweeney, Joseph 117
Sweet Bird of Youth (Williams) 419
Swenson, Karl 215, 224, 229, 491
Swift, Jonathan 177, 251
Synge, J. M. 25, 258, 454

T

Taber, Roslyn (character) 15, 237–244, **245**, 433
Tabori, George 452

Tabori, Kristoffer 236, 495
Tairov, Alexander 202
Tallack, Douglas 118
"Tan, Blue, Brown Mice? Sure, the University Owns Hundreds" 426
Taubman, Howard 34, 39, 208, 211
Taylor, Frank 243, 459
Teachout, Terry 165, 168
Teahouse (Yu) 366
Teahouse of the August Moon (Patrick) 474
Terkel, Studs 55, 65
Testament of Dr. Mabuse, The (Lang) 144
Thacher, Molly Day 418
Thacker, David 19, 83, 89, 93, 146, 152, 216, 219, 339, 394, 440, **463–464**, 497–498
That They May Win 8, 79, **324**, 479, 484, 491
Theater Essays of Arthur Miller, The 11, 21, 149, 484, **324–325**, 376, 406
    essays in 25, 66, 76, 100, 161, 198, 213, 253, 254, 261, 315, 329, 331, 493
Theater in Your Head, A (Rowe) 428, 454
Theatre Guild 6, 8–9, 40, 179, 224, 325, 363, 372, 377, 393, 415, 418, 426–427, 442, 444, 453–454, **464**, 468, 476, 491
    of the air 9, 464
They Too Arise. See also Abe Simon, Arnold Simon, Ben Simon 6, 183, 256, **325–326**, 363, 380, 388, 391, 398, 417, 454, 464, 468, 491
"Thirst" (O'Neill) 444
Thoemke, Peter 296
Thomas, Jeremy 156, 158
Thompson, Alan 155
Thompson, Terry W. 142, 148
Three Men on a Horse (Abbott and Holm) 9, 361, 492
Three Sisters, The (Chekhov) 9, 361, 492
Thunder from the Hills 8, **326**, 491
Tillinger, John 89, 219, 222, 321, 474
Till the Day I Die (Odets) 418, 442
Timebends: A Life 3, 13, 20, 50, 57, 65, 76, 81, 89, 118, 128, 150, 188, 192, 196, 255, 318,

326–329, 334, 370–371, 376–379, 381, 383, 385, 389, 391, 394–395, 404–405, 410, 419, 421, 424, 427, 428, 430–432, 437, 439–441, 443–444, 448, 453, 457–462, 469, 475–476, 484, 496
  initial reviews 20
Tituba (character) 108–110, 113, 115, 117, 119, 121, **122–123**, 126–127, 456
Tolkan, James 99, 496
Toller, Ernst 387
Tolstoy, Leo 203, 385
Touch of the Poet, A (O'Neill) 377, 384
Toward a Farther Star 8, **329**, 491
Tracy, Bob 200, 310, 455
tragedy 10, 45, 48, 254, 258, 262, 317, 413, **464–466**, 477
  and *Death of a Salesman* 48, 137, 140, 146, 212, 262, 329–330, 384, 465
    in Greece 45, 48, 454, 464–465
    in "The Nature of Tragedy" 219, 220, 222, 253–254
    in other Miller's plays 25, 38, 54, 57, 90, 93, 109, 306, 341–342, 344
    in Shakespeare 330, 465
    in "Tragedy and the Common Man" 11, 329–330, 465
"Tragedy and the Common Man" 11, 253, **329–331**, 465, 484, 492
Traitor, The (Wouk) 401
Trask, Richard 154
Trauber, Shepard 234, 237
Treadwell, Sophie 387
Trewin, J. C. 344, 348
Trowbridge, Clinton W. 466, 489
True West (Shepard) 283, 286
Turpentine Still, The 21, 80, 331–333, 376, 484, 499
Turpin, George 210
Tuttle, Jon 100
Twentieth Century-Fox 6, 124, 126, 430, 434–435, 491
"20 Per Cent Cut in Local Relief Seen by Wagg" 426
2 by A. M. See Two-Way Mirror

Two-Way Mirror 19, 150, 152, 318, 321, 333–334, 368, 394, 450, 463, 484, 496–497
Tyler, Christian 306, 310
Tynan, Kenneth 229, 231, 477

U
Uncle Vanya (Chekhov) 369, 377, 401
Unforgiven, The (Huston) 438
Unger, Arthur 270, 274, 487
University of East Anglia 19, 368, 394, **467**, 496, 498
University of Michigan 6, 14, 17–18, 63, 184, 186, 190, 232, 255–256, 325, 327, 335, 371, 376, 377, 379, 391, 425, 432, 440, 453, **467–469**, 470, 476, 478–479, 493, 495
  application to 5, 468–489, 490
  awards from 5–6, 184, 190, 256, 363
  teachers at 414, 453–454, 464–465, 468, 491
Untermeyer, Louis 36, 409, **469**
Unwin, Paul 67
Up from Paradise 18, 101, 105, **334–336**, 484, 495
  initial reviews 18
Upton, Charles W. 108, 456
Urban Blight (revue) 19, 321, 497
Ure, Mary 343, 493

V
Vajda, Miklos 489
Valente, Joseph 126
Vallone, Raf 348, 494
"Vanek" plays (Havel) 403
Vietnam War 78, 293, 469, **470–472**
  Miller on 17–18, 78, 100, 263, 286–287, 470–471
  in Miller's work 57, 68, 75, 101, 249, 276, 278, 283, 286–287, 291, 293, 314–315,
View from the Bridge, A (1 act) 10, 13, 213, 232, 234, 261–262, **336–338**, 361–363, 372, 434, 460, 485, 493
  initial reviews 337–338
View from the Bridge, A 14, 16, 18–19, 21, 192, 203, 213, 324, **338–348**, 363, 379,

388, 394, 484, 493, 416, 424, 435, 450
  characters. *See also* Alfieri, Beatrice Carbone, Eddie Carbone, Catherine, Marco 284, 338–344, **345–348**
  critical commentary **341–343**
  and homosexuality 262, 338, 340, 342–344, 346–347
  initial reviews **344**
  and law 336, 338, 342–343, 345, 423
  movies 14, 22, 341, **348**, 396–397, 453, 494
  productions of 361, 369, 396, 405, 433, 440, 463, 474, 494, 496–498
  opera 21, 199, 339
  scholarship 124, **344–345**, 348
  synopsis **339–341**
  as tragedy 341–342, 344, 465
"Visit with Castro, A" 21, **349**, 376, 381, 485
Viswamohan, Aysha 489
Viva Zapata! (Kazan) 419–420
Vogel, Dan 141, 148, 489
Vogel, Paula 466
Voight, Jon 339
Von Berg (character) 204–209, **210**, 263, 386, 398–399, 407
Vorno, Antony 234, 337
Voznesensky, Andrei 201, 203
Vu du Pont (A View from the Bridge) 14, 341, 348, 453, 494
Vyas, Manish A. 105, 108

W
Wade, David 183
Wagner, Howard (character) 133–134, 136–139, 141, **145**, 374
Wagrowski, Gregory *41*
Waiting for Godot (Beckett) 316, 394
Waiting for Lefty (Odets) 326, 418, 442–443, 462
"Waiting for the Teacher: On Israel's Fiftieth Anniversary" **349–350**, 485, 498
Wakeman, John 195
Waldorf-Astoria Peace Conference 11, 328, 410, 443, 469, 492

Wall, Kim 182
Wallach, Eli 15, 18, 94, 160, 243, 291, 358, 410, 419, 434, **473–474**, 494, 495
Wall Street crash 4, 81, 136, 381, 392, 395, 428, 430, 433, **473**
  in *After the Fall* 28, 35
  in *The American Clock* 55, 58, 62, 64
  in *The Price* 278, 280–281, 284–285, 287
Walter, Francis E. 13, 410
Walton, David 186, 187
Walton, James E. 148
Waltzer, Jack 33, 207
Wandor, Michelene 76
Wanger, Walter 25, 373
Wang Qun 48, 54, 466
War and Peace (Tolstoy) 23, 233
Ward, Richard *140*
Ward, Robert 15, 109, 126, 494
Warden, Jack 158, 234, 236, 277, 337, 493, 495, 496
Wardle, Irving 219, 222, 487
Warner, David 451
Warning Signals (Xingjian) 311
Waterstradt, Jean Anne 390
Watson, Douglas 71, 495
Watt, Douglas 208, 211
Watts, Janet 306, 310
Watts, Richard, Jr. 34, 40, 140, 148
Wayne, David 33, 207, 494
Weales, Gerald 60, 65, 71, 76, 118, 126, 141, 148
Weber, Bruce 283, 286, 296, 299
Webster, Margaret 344, 348
Wedekind, Frank 387
Weill, Kurt 397
Weinstein, Arnold 339
Weiss, Jeff 249, 296
Welland, Dennis 34, 40, 49, 60, 65, 71, 105, 108, 229, 231, 270, 274, 344, 348, 394, 489
Welles, Orson 8, 326, 391
Wells, Arvin 49
Wertheim, Albert vii, 40, 48, 54, 192, 198, 223, 344, 348
Westgate, Chris 126
"What's Wrong with this Picture?" 18, **350**, 404, 483, 495
Wheeler, Lois 47

Whitehead, Robert 13, 15–16, 25, 33, 71, 89, 105, 204, 234, 277, 283, 337, 369, 377–378, 405, 420, 442, **474–475**
and Repertory Theater of Lincoln Center 451–452, 474
Whitemore, James 15, 53, 176, 494
"White Puppies" **350–351**, 390, 485, 495–497
White Snake, The (opera) 97
"Why Israel Must Choose Justice" 21, **351–352**, 364, 485
"Why I Wrote The Crucible" 125
"Why Kill a Nation No-One Hates?" 471
Widmark, Richard 401, 455
Wiest, Dianne 27
Wild, Duck, The (Ibsen) 141, 146, 413, 415
Wilde, Billy 434
Wilder, Thornton 118, 162, 310, 401, 418, 425, 475, 477–478
Wiley, Catherine 148
Willet, Ralph W. 286
William Ireland's Confession 7, 352, 388–389, 485, 491
Williams, Abigail (character) 77, 108–114, 116–117, 119, 121–122, **123**, 125–128, 213, 398, 402, 433, 456
Williams, Emlyn 385

Williams, Raymond 236–237, 489
Williams, Tennessee ix, 34, 39, 90, 93, 141, 147, 229, 231, 234, 328, 361, 415, 424, 445, 454, **475–477**
in "About Theater Language" 25, 477
defense of Miller 475
influence on Miller 258, 476
and Elia Kazan 358, 419–420, 475–476
in "Notes on Realism" 258, 477
plays by 377, 385, 419–420, 427, 450, 474, 477
and plastic theater 476
in "The Shadows of the Gods" 316–317, 476–477
Williamstown Theatre Festival 20, 224, 225, 291, 300, 306, **477–478**, 498
Willmer, Catherine 343
Wilmeth, Don 368
Wilson, August 141
Wilson, Edwin 89, 94
Wilson, Mona 90, 94, 229, 231, 390
Wilson, Robert N. 489
Wilson, Tom (character) 301–305, **309**, 398, 423
Winegarten, Renee 283, 286
Winer, Linda 165, 168, 250–251, 321–322

Winger, Debra 20, 158, 497
Wiseman, Joseph 207, 494
Witches of Salem, The (Les Sorcières de Salem) (Sartre) 14, 77, 123, 126, 436, 458, 493
"With Respect to Her Agony— But with Love" 16, 33, 39, **352–353**, 485
Wolfe, George C. 321
Wolfert, Ira 487
Woliver, C. Patrick 118, 126
Wood, Peter 18, 54, 60, 101, 394, 440, 494, 496
Wooster, Gerald 90, 94, 229, 231, 390
Wooster Group 125, **478**, 496
and LSD 118, 124, 478, 496
Works Progress Administration (WPA) 56, 61, 390–391, 395, 409, 426, 459
World War One 4, 16, 61, 171, 175, 311, 372–373, 418, 430, 433, 447
World War Two 4, 28, 40, 129, 173, 182, 277, 326, 367, 372, 373, 378, 409, 427, 440, 460, 464, **478–479**
effects of 57, 137, 255, 357, 379, 394, 407, 457
in Miller's plays 8, 28, 35, 46–47, 61, 72, 81, 168, 185, 204, 251, 322
outbreak of 95, 366, 391
veterans of 9, 47, 183, 265, 317, 431, 452, 458

Wouk, Herman 401
Wright, Frank Lloyd 14, 436, 454
Wright, Richard 7

Y

Yates, Peter 156
Yellen, Linda 156, 266, 270, 392
Yevremov, Oleg 366
Yevtushenko, Yevgeny 201
Yim, Harksoon 489
Yoon, So-young 148
York, Susannah 124, 493
Yost, Agnes Scott 229
Young, B. A. 183
You're Next! 9, 223, **353**, 409, 492
and communism 380
and HUAC 353, 410
Yu, Cao 97, 311, 366–367
Yu, Han 96
Yu, Qiao 97
Yuan, Ma Qih 96
Yulin, Harris 165, 210

Z

Zedong, Mao 96, 311, 313, 379
Zibriski, Harry (character) 6, 190–191, 388
Zibriski, Max (character) 6, 190–191, 374, 388
Zimmerman, Paul 195
Zinman, Toby 306, 310